BIBLE HANDBOOK

AND

A-Z BIBLE ENCYCLOPEDIA

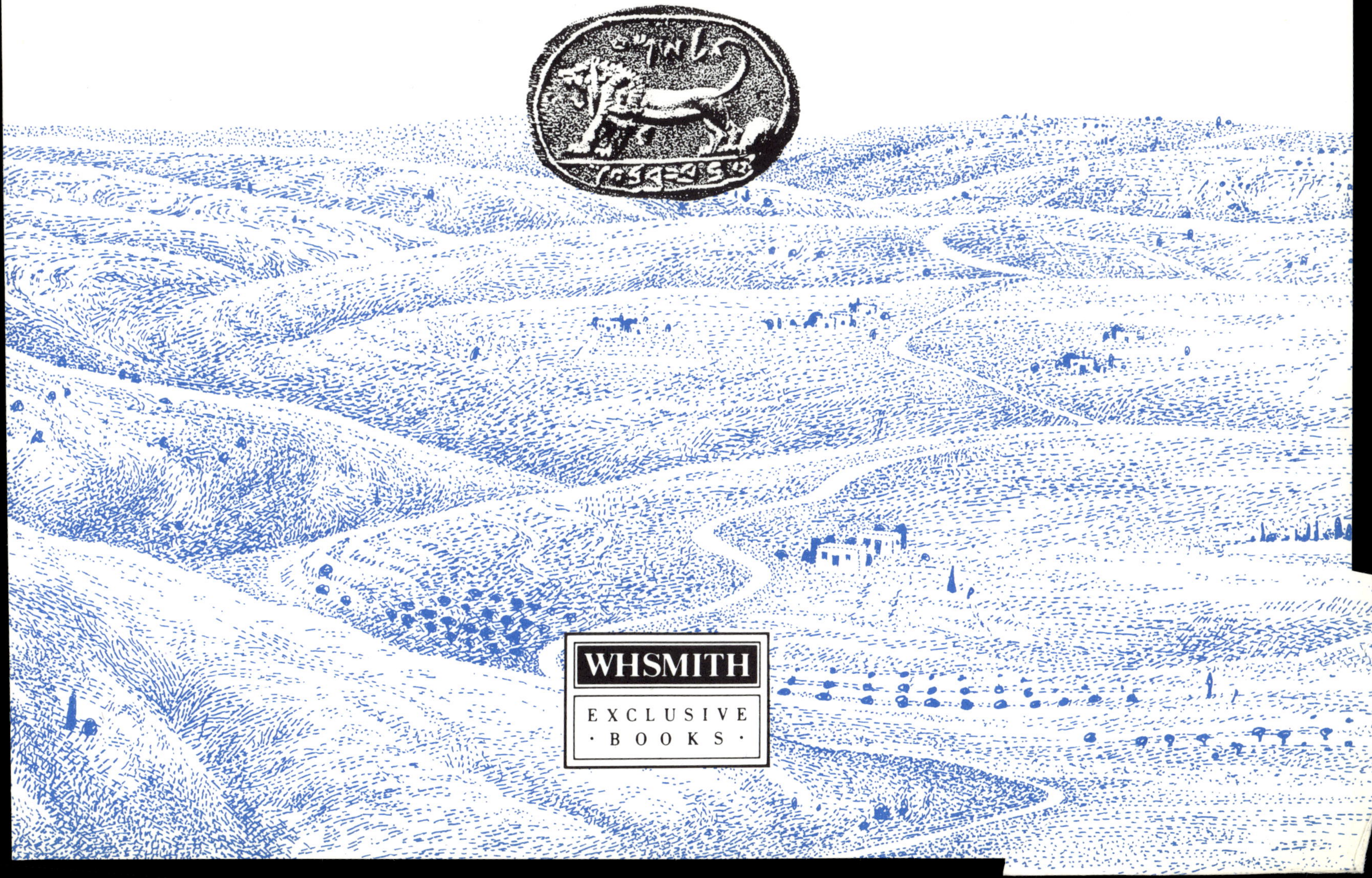

WHSMITH

EXCLUSIVE
· BOOKS ·

PARTS 1, 2 AND 3
Editors David and Pat Alexander

Consulting Editors

David Field, Vice-Principal, Oak Hill Theological College, London

Donald Guthrie, formerly Vice-Principal, London Bible College

Canon Pastor Gerald Hughes

I. Howard Marshall, Professor of New Testament Exegesis, Aberdeen University

Alan Millard, Rankin Reader in Hebrew and Ancient Semitic Languages, Liverpool University

OUTLINE-GUIDE (Parts 2 and 3) by Pat Alexander

Contributors

The Rev. Dr Phillip J. Budd, Lecturer, Westminster College, Oxford and Ripon College, Cuddesdon *(The Sacrificial System, Feasts and Festivals)*

Sir Frederick Catherwood, Member of European Parliament and Chairman of Committee on External Economic Relations *(The Bible and Society)*

David J.A. Clines, Professor of Biblical Studies, Sheffield Univeristy *(The Apocrypha)*

The Rev. Arthur E. Cundall, Principal, Bible College of Victoria, Australia *(Unravelling the Chronology of the Kings)*

The Rev. David Field, Vice-Principal, Oak Hill Theological College, London *(The Bible and Christian Living, The Kingdom of God and the Kingdom of Heaven)*

Dr Richard T. France, Principal, Wycliffe College, Oxford *(Jesus Christ and the Bible, The Religious Background of the New Testament)*

Canon Michael Green, Lecturer in Evangelism, Regent College, Vancouver *(Early Christian Preaching)*

The Rev. Geoffrey W. Grogan, Principal, Bible Training Institute, Glasgow *(Holy Spirit in Acts)*

Dr Donald Guthrie, formerly Vice-Principal, London Bible College *(The Letters: Introduction)*

The late Dr Colin J. Hemer, formerly Research Fellow, Tyndale Library for Biblical Research *The Historical and Political Background of the New Testament)*

Kenneth G. Howkins, Senior Lecturer in Religious Studies, Hertfordshire College of Higher Education *(Meeting Objections)*

The Rev. F. Derek Kidner, formerly Warden, Tyndale House and Library for Biblical Research, Cambridge *(Poetry and Wisdom Literature: Introduction)*

I. Howard Marshall, Professor of New Testament Exegesis, Aberdeen University, *(The Gospels and Jesus Christ, The New Testament Miracles)*

Alan R. Millard,Rankin Reader in Hebrew and Ancient Semitic Languages, Liverpool University *(Other Creation Accounts, Flood Stories, The Old Testament and the Ancient Near East, The Cities of the Conquest, The Temples, The Threat of Assyria, Exile to Babylon)*

Dr Leon Morris, formerly Principal, Ridley College, Melbourne University, Australia *(The Gospels and Modern Criticism)*

The Rev. Alec Motyer, Vicar of Christ Church, Westbourne, Bournemouth *(The Names of God, The Tabernacle, The Meaning of Blood Sacrifice, The Prophets: Introduction)*

Dr Harold Rowdon, Senior Lecturer, London Bible College *(Pilate)*

The Venerable John A. Simpson, Archdeacon of Canterbury *(The Virgin Birth)*

The Rt. Rev. John B. Taylor, Bishop of St Albans *(The Five Books: Introduction, The Historical Books: Introduction)*

Dr Gordon Wenham, Senior Lecturer in Religious Studies, The College of St Paul and St Mary, Cheltenham *(Literary Criticism and the Old Testament, Covenants and Near Eastern Treaties)*

The Rev. John Wenham, formerly Principal of Tyndale Hall, Bristol and Warden of Latimer House, Oxford *(The Large Numbers of the Old Testament)*

The Rev. Canon David Wheaton, Vicar of Christ Church, Ware *(The Accounts of the Resurrection)*

Illustrators

Mark Astle, Simon Bull, Pauline O'Boyle, Angela Pluess, Dorothy Tucker
Stanley Willcocks; maps by Roy Lawrance and Lesley Passey

PART 4
Organizing Editor Pat Alexander

Consulting Editors

Dr John W. Drane, Lecturer in Religious Studies, Stirling University

The Rev. David Field, Vice-Principal, Oak Hill Theological College, London

Alan Millard, Rankin Reader in Hebrew and Ancient Semitic Languages, Liverpool University

Contributors and Authors of Major Articles

David Clines, Professor of Biblical Studies, Sheffield University *(Feasts and festivals, Jesus' teaching, Law, Prophets, Religion of Israel, Temple)*

E. W. Crabb, Former Headmaster, Stanburn School, Stanmore, Middx.

Margaret Embry, Lecturer at Trinity College, Bristol *(Building, Clothes-making, Education, Farming, Medicine, Mining, Pottery, Trade and commerce, War)*

The Rev. David Gillett, Director of Extension Studies, St John's College, Nottingham

Ralph Gower, formerly Staff Inspector for Religious Education, ILEA, London *(Daily life, Family life, Food, Towns, Villages)*

The late Colin Hemer, formerly Research Fellow, Tyndale Library for Biblical Research *(Greeks, Greek and Roman religion, Rome)*

Dr Kenneth Kitchen, Reader in Egyptian and Coptic, School of Archaeology and Oriental Studies, Liverpool University *(Egyptians, Egyptian religion)*

Alan Millard, Rankin Reader in Hebrew and Ancient Semitic Languages, Liverpool University *(Archaeology, Assyria, Assyrian and Babylonian religion, Babylonians, Canaanites, Canaanite religion, Dead Sea scrolls, Writing)*

Margaret Moore *(Exile, Exodus, Flood)*

The Rev. Stephen Parish *(Travel and transport)*

Professor John Paterson, Emeritus Professor of Geography, Leicester University *(Geography of Israel)*

The late Canon R. W. F. Wootton, formerly Leicester Diocesan Chaplain for Community Relations, Leicester *(Bible translation, Bible: modern English versions)*

Illustrators

Mark Astle, Simon Bull, Pauline O'Boyle, Stanley Wilcocks

Text first published in
The Lion Handbook to the Bible copyright © 1973 Lion Publishing and
The Lion Encyclopedia to the Bible copyright © 1978 Lion Publishing and
The Lion Concise Bible Encyclopedia copyright © 1980 Lion Publishing

Produced exclusively for WHSmith

Published by
Lion Publishing plc
Sandy Lane West, Oxford, England
ISBN 07459 2018 7

British Library Cataloguing in Publication Data
Bible handbook and A-Z Bible encyclopedia.
1. Bible
220
ISBN 0-7459-2018-7

Printed in Italy

PREFACE

The Bible is one of the world's most influential books. Yet many people understand little of it or of the background in which it was written. This book combines two major reference tools in one to provide that information: a handbook to the Bible, in three sections, and an A-Z encyclopedia. The contents has been distilled from two bestselling works, *The Lion Handbook to the Bible,* of which there are now 1,500,000 copies in print worldwide, and *The Lion Encyclopedia of the Bible,* which has enjoyed worldwide acceptance since its publication in 1978.

Part One introduces the Bible and sets it in its context. The second and third parts, on the Old and New Testaments respectively, go through the Bible book by book, section by section. A heading or brief description gives the main theme. Notes on difficulties aid understanding. Drawings, maps and charts help build up a vivid and accurate picture of the setting of the passage. Brief articles by experts allow special interests to be followed up in more detail.

The emphasis of the book is on sheer information presented in a simple, helpful and visually interesting way. Many of the contributors have previously written at a technical level on subjects which they summarize here for a wide readership. Throughout, the aim is to shed light on the content and meaning of the Bible.

Part Four complements this aim in a different way. It provides an A-Z reference tool for readers who want to know more about a particular theme. It gives considerable attention to the historical, geographical and cultural setting of the Bible, as well as to matters of belief.

The resulting volume is a rich mine of information that is fascinating in itself and that will make the meaning and the message of the Bible itself clear.

CONTENTS

PART ONE

Introducing the Bible

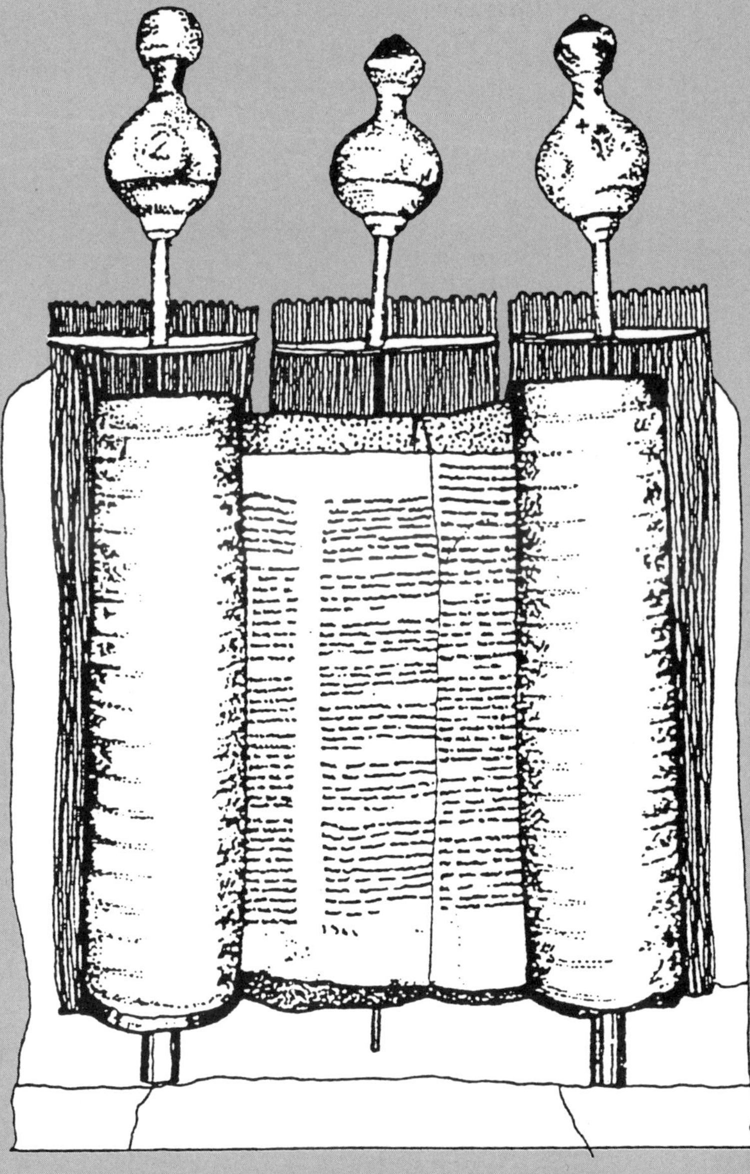

JESUS CHRIST AND THE BIBLE

Richard France

As a Christian I want to follow Jesus Christ. I want to do what he said, go where he leads, follow his example, enter into the life he offers.

To do so I must read the eye-witness accounts of those who knew him. I discover that he claimed to be the revelation of God himself, the One who shows us what God is like. And I discover too that he is the culmination of centuries of God's revelation recorded in documents going back hundreds of years before his time.

So I seek the authority of Jesus; and I am led on by him to see the authority of the Bible.

Read the beginning of John's first letter.

We cannot have one without the other. Certainly Jesus revealed God to man in a way the written Old Testament alone could never have done. Ordinary people saw him, heard him, touched him, lived with him. But we were not there ourselves. Nor can we know what Jesus was like, what he said and did, by consulting the secular historians of the time. They will only tell us that a Jewish prophet called Jesus lived, preached, fell foul of the authorities and was executed. One or two may also suggest some knowledge of his resurrection. But that is as far as it goes. If we are to know the revelation Jesus gave, we must turn to the New Testament to find it.

The fact that a book is necessary to know Jesus is not something to be regretted. It is in fact what Jesus intended. One of his top priorities was the selection and training of his apostles – that inner circle of his disciples who were to preserve and pass on his teaching. The church was founded on the apostles' teaching. The New Testament is the record of what they taught. It is a collection of those books which the early church accepted as written by the apostles themselves, or by their close associates, and which therefore set out the true apostolic faith.

THE BIBLE OF JESUS

If we are to know Jesus and his teaching, then, we must turn to the New Testament, to the testimony of those he himself chose and trusted to pass on his teaching. To do so he himself sent the Holy Spirit to 'guide them into all the truth'.

See John 14:26; 15:26; 16:13-15

If we accept the authority of Jesus we may well accept the New Testament as the source of all our knowledge of him and of his teaching. But we are also bound to accept the Old Testament. For Jesus himself, the incarnate Son of God, accepted it as God's own word to man. If he is our authority, we can do no less.

Teaching about the Old Testament

Jesus said some strong things about the Old Testament:

Matthew 5:17-18

'Think not that I have come to abolish the law and the prophets; I have come not to abolish them but to fulfil them. For truly, I say to you, till heaven and earth pass away, not an iota, not a dot, will pass from the law until all is accomplished.'

John 10:35

'Scripture cannot be broken.'

Luke 24:44

'Everything written about me in the law of Moses and the prophets and the psalms must be fulfilled.'

Mark 7:1-13

Some of his harshest condemnations were reserved for those who tried to evade the plain commands of God (set out in the Old Testament law) by means of merely human traditions, however venerable.

Appeal to the Old Testament

Examples: Matthew 12:3-4, 5, 7; 21:16; 22:32, 44

Matthew 4:4, 7, 10

Mark 15:34; Luke 23:46 quoting Psalms 22:1; 31:5

Much more impressive than occasional pronouncements of Jesus about the Old Testament is his constant appeal to it in a wide variety of different situations. In controversy with his opponents, he regularly uses a quotation from the Old Testament to settle the argument. And this was not simply in order to meet men on their own grounds. He relies no less on the authority of the Old Testament in his confrontation with the devil! Even in the final agony on the cross, it is words from the Old Testament which are on his lips.

Quotations from the Old Testament

Matthew 24; Mark 13; Luke 21

Matthew 24:29-31: from Isaiah 13:10; 34:4; Daniel 7:13; Zechariah 12:12; Isaiah 27:13; Deuteronomy 30:4; Zechariah 2:6

It is in Jesus' teaching to his disciples, however, that he refers most frequently to the Old Testament, both by explicit quotations and by innumerable verbal echoes, so that some passages seem like a patch-work of Old Testament words and ideas. For instance, Jesus' prediction of the destruction of Jerusalem and of his own second coming is full of Old Testament language. The words of only three verses draw on no less than seven Old Testament passages.

Fulfilment of the Old Testament

Matthew 19:18-19; 22:37-40 – see Deuteronomy 6:5; Leviticus 19:18

Matthew 5:21-22, 27-28, etc.

But it is not just a matter of language. The actual content of Jesus' teaching relies heavily on the Old Testament. His central ethical rules are drawn from the law of Moses. And if he differed from his contemporaries in ethical matters, it was only because he accused them of taking the Old Testament commands too lightly and superficially.

Luke 24:27

Above all, his teaching about his own role in the purposes of God depends entirely on the conviction that he must fulfil the Old Testament. His teaching after the resurrection, when 'beginning with Moses and all the prophets, he interpreted to them in all the scriptures the things concerning himself', was the climax of what he had been teaching them through the years of his ministry.

Luke 4:21; Mark 9:12-13; Luke 18:31; Mark 14:21, 27; Luke 22:37; Matthew 26:54; Luke 24:44-47

In a number of passages there are emphatic statements that he had come to fulfil the scriptures. But these are only the outcrops of a conviction which underlies all his teaching about his own mission. He had come 'to fulfil', and there was a divine compulsion about what was written. It *must* be fulfilled.

So the Christian is a follower of one for whom the Old Testament was the unquestionably authoritative word of God. Jesus believed its statements, endorsed its teaching, obeyed its commands, and set himself to fulfil the pattern of redemption which it laid down. It is clearly inconsistent for one who calls Jesus 'Lord' to think lightly of those scriptures which were to him the supreme revelation of God.

THE NEW TESTAMENT ENDORSES THE OLD

The rest of the New Testament, needless to say, fully

endorses Jesus' view of the Old Testament. Constant Old Testament quotations and allusions show the same reliance on the Old Testament teaching for the disclosure of God's character and purposes. It was God who spoke through the prophets, declares the writer of Hebrews. Indeed, says Paul to Timothy, 'All scripture is inspired by God.' The Old Testament is the message of God.

Hebrews 1:1; see too 2 Peter 1:21; 2 Timothy 3:16

Romans 3:2

It is interesting that the New Testament makes no distinction between what 'Scripture' says and what God says. Old Testament quotations are given as what God said, even though God was not the speaker in the Old Testament context. Conversely, words spoken by God in the Old Testament narrative are ascribed to 'Scripture'. Where Jesus led the way in his acceptance of the Old Testament as the word of God, the New Testament was content to follow. If we Christians set our own judgement or our inherited traditions above the Old and New Testament scriptures we part company with the Lord and the apostles, and cut ourselves off from our one source of knowledge of God.

Matthew 19:4-5; Acts 4:24-25; Hebrews 1:6-12

Romans 9:17; Galatians 3:8

DEALING WITH PROBLEMS

This is not to eliminate all problems in advance. The interpretation and application of the Bible's teaching poses many problems, and Christians may legitimately differ in their interpretation at some points. But where such differences occur, our aim must always be to discover, by the most careful and rigorous study of which we are capable, what the relevant passages really mean, whether this turns out to agree with our own previous ideas or not. Then, having discovered the true meaning, we must accept it as the word of God. It will not always be easy; it may sometimes be impossible; but that is the ideal.

We may be convinced in our minds of the Bible's authority: we will be even more convinced when we allow it to have its authority in our lives. We will know for ourselves the experience of God speaking through his written revelation to us. The Bible is God's word, what God has said. He still speaks to us through it today.

THE BIBLE AND CHRISTIAN LIVING

David Field

The Bible can be read as great literature, or as a history of Israel, or as a source-book of theological information. It is all of these things. But none of them does full justice to the purpose of Scripture as set out by the Bible writers themselves, or to the cumulative experience of Bible users through the centuries.

When Ezra the scribe read from the law of Moses to the returned exiles in Jerusalem, the people, we are told, not only 'understood the reading' but alternately 'wept when they heard the words of the law' and made 'great rejoicing'. And they came back the next day to build shelters for the Feast of Tabernacles, in obedience to the law's commands. The act of hearing and understanding the scriptures had aroused their emotions and stirred them to action.

Nehemiah 8

Centuries after Ezra, J. B. Phillips describes his similar experience in translating the New Testament. 'Although I did my utmost to preserve an emotional detachment', he writes, 'I found again and again that the material under my hands was strangely alive; it spoke to my condition in the most uncanny way.'

These reactions accurately reflect the vivid metaphors we find in the Bible, used by its writers to describe the impact God's word made in their own experience. It is a fire to warm and a hammer to break, water to cleanse, milk to nourish, meat to invigorate, light to guide, a sword for the fight, and a mirror to reveal. It is 'at work in you believers', 'able to build you up', 'living and active ... piercing ... discerning'.

Jeremiah 23:29; 1 Peter 2:2; Hebrews 5:13-14; Psalm 119:105; Ephesians 6:17; James 1:23-25; 1 Thessalonians 2:13; Acts 20:32; Hebrews 4:12

THE BIBLE IS RELEVANT

All this means that the reader who approaches the Bible in a purely detached way is in danger of failing to appreciate its primary purpose, which is a practical, dynamic one. Its aim is to *do something* in the life of the person who reads it, as well as to capture his aesthetic interest and supply him with historical and theological information. The huge cultural gaps which separate Bible times from our own make such a purpose all the more remarkable, but the Bible can justify its claim to contemporary relevance in two ways.

In the first place, it deals with those elements in *human nature* which are timeless. The men and women we read about in the Bible have aspirations and failings with which we easily identify, and even the heroes of Scripture are displayed in the cold light of truth. As Augustine put it, 'The sacred record, like a faithful mirror, has no flattery in its portraits.'

Then, secondly, the truths of the Bible are ever-relevant because *God himself* does not change, either in his nature or in his dealings with men. Through reading the Bible we discover fundamental truths about God, and see them demonstrated by events in the lives of his people which illuminate his character and illustrate his will for all men at all times. So it is that even events from the distant past 'were written down for *our* instruction' in order that in the present and for the future 'by the encouragement of the scriptures we might have hope'.

1 Corinthians 10:11; Romans 15:4

THE BIBLE IS PRACTICAL

The Bible, then, retains its contemporary bite. What are the practical purposes it aims to achieve?

It points people to Jesus

The purpose of John's Gospel is clearly set out: 'Now Jesus did many other signs in the presence of the disciples, which are not written in this book; but these are written that you may believe that Jesus is the Christ, the Son of God, and that believing you may have life in his name.'

John 20:30-31

In writing with this frankly propagandist aim – to focus on Jesus Christ – the disciple was being faithful to the remarkable way in which his Master summed up the purpose of *all* Scripture. 'You search the scriptures', Jesus once replied to his critics, 'because you think that in them you have eternal life; and it is they that bear witness to *me*. If you believed Moses, you would believe me, for he wrote of *me*.'

John 5:39, 46

Not surprisingly, the listening disciples were slow to grasp the full meaning of these words. After the resurrection Jesus had to rebuke them for their dullness before showing them once again – and this time more explicitly – how, like the spokes of a wheel, the whole message of the Bible converged on himself. 'Beginning with Moses and all the prophets, he interpreted to them in all the scriptures the things concerning himself.' And Luke goes on to tell us that Jesus drew special attention to those passages from the Old Testament which spoke of his death and resurrection, as a stimulus to repentance and the basis for forgiveness of sins.

Luke 24:27

Jesus clearly believed that the main aim of the (Old Testament) scriptures was to point people to himself; which meant in practice (if we add Luke's evidence to John's), that through repentance and faith men and women should find the forgiveness and life which he had died and risen to make possible for them.

By their preaching and writing, the apostles showed that they had finally grasped Jesus' point that the Bible's main practical purpose is to draw people to himself as their Saviour. 'To him', preached Peter, 'all the prophets bear witness, that every one who believes in him receives forgiveness of sins through his name.' James pleaded with his readers to 'receive with meekness the implanted word, which is able to save your souls'. Paul reminded Timothy 'how from childhood you have been acquainted with the sacred writings which are able to instruct you for salvation through faith in Christ Jesus'.

Acts 10:43; James 1:21; 2 Timothy 3:15

It builds a relationship with God

In Martin Luther's words, just as a mother goes to the cradle only to find the baby, we go to the Bible only to find Christ. It is the Bible's primary purpose to bring men to their Saviour by arousing the beginnings of faith. But this is not the only practical function it aims to fulfil. Peter and the author of the letter to the Hebrews use the analogy of birth and growth to illustrate a further purpose of Scripture. Those who have put their trust in Jesus as Saviour 'have been born anew ... through the living and abiding word of God'; but, like all new-born babes, they must 'long for the pure spiritual milk' of the word if they are to survive and grow; and once beyond babyhood they need solid food – which is the 'meat' of God's word.

1 Peter 1:23; 1 Peter 2:2; Hebrews 5:12-14

This growth process is, above all, a growing up in relationship with God. It is the Bible's function to feed the personal knowledge of the Father which the Christian 'child' enjoys. And 'enjoy' is exactly the right word, because as the believer learns more about God his delight becomes more intense. That is why Bible study should never be dull for a Christian. 'Thy words', cries out Jeremiah, 'became to me a joy and the delight of my heart; for I am called by thy name, O Lord, God of hosts.' Any personal relationship is fostered by words, and through the pages of his Bible the Christian hears God speaking to him; an experience, says the Psalmist, that is 'sweeter than honey'.

Jeremiah 15:16; Psalm 19:10

If this sounds like love-letter language we should not be surprised, because the relationship into which God invites believers is a love-relationship. His, however, is a love which makes exacting demands. The information about God and his will which the Christian receives through reading the Bible calls for a tough response that is anything but sentimental. 'If a man loves me', Jesus taught, 'he will *keep* my word, and my Father will love him, and we will come to him and make our home with him ... and the word which you hear is not mine but the Father's who sent me.'

John 14:23-24

It equips for battle

Such a stern demand is appropriate because once a man becomes a Christian he finds himself enlisted on God's side in a lifelong battle. He is called upon both to defend his faith against stiff opposition and to spread it among his friends. For both operations, offensive and defensive, his chief weapon is the Bible. It is the 'sword of the Spirit', declares Paul, with which he can combat hostile ideas and cut a straight path for God's truth into the innermost strongholds of the human will.

Ephesians 6:17; Hebrews 4:12

Jesus himself set the pattern for this very practical use of the Bible in his own ministry. Honest enquirers, like the lawyer who asked him about the greatest commandment, were impressed and attracted by his Bible-based teaching (though, as with the rich young ruler, they did not all respond to it positively). On the other hand Jesus fought off false teaching, whether the arguments of men like the Sadducees or the insidious suggestions of the arch-enemy in the desert, with the words of his Bible. Bible words do not have magical powers in themselves, but because all words express ideas, and ideas lie behind action, the word of God is a mighty weapon to influence men's convictions and conduct. Jesus fought his battles with his own words and with the words of his Bible, and he sent his disciples out to preach both.

Mark 12:28-34; Matthew 19:16-22; Matthew 22:23-33; Matthew 4:1-11

This gives the Christian all the incentive he needs to fill his mind with Bible doctrine. Without (for example) a grasp of what the Bible teaches about human nature he will soon be speechless before the claims of twentieth-century humanity. If he is vague about the meaning of Christ's death and resurrection, he cannot hope to introduce others to Jesus as their Saviour. Hence the insistence of the later books of the New Testament that anyone who aims to serve Christ faithfully must make it his aim to know and conserve God's truth. 'Guard the truth that has been entrusted to you by the Holy Spirit', writes Paul to Timothy, 'and what you have heard from me before many witnesses entrust to

2 Timothy 1:14; 2:2

faithful men who will be able to teach others also.'

It guides conduct

In his earlier letter to Timothy, Paul had already drawn attention to the importance of maintaining right standards of conduct alongside right beliefs. To 'wage the good warfare' involves 'holding faith *and a good conscience'.* The one cannot be made a substitute for the other; indeed, any failure in right conduct inevitably brings about a downfall in right beliefs. 'By rejecting conscience, certain persons have made shipwreck of their faith'. This is a major Bible theme. In the Old Testament, farmer Amos, with rustic bluntness, flays those who attempt to keep up a religious façade without matching conduct; and James, his outspoken New Testament counterpart, exposes those who are 'hearers of the word' but not 'doers' of it. Jesus makes the same point in his parable of the two builders.

1 Timothy 1:18-19

James 1:22

Matthew 7:24-27

The same pressures which threaten to muddle his faith can seduce the Christian into moral laxity; but the Bible, which provides his main line of defence against false teaching, is also an effective weapon against moral temptations. It sets out, by example as well as by direct command, the differences between right and wrong, so that the man who measures his conduct by Bible standards gains from it both 'reproof' when he is in the wrong and 'correction' to set him back on a right course. The Bible becomes his bastion against moral powerlessness, too, by reminding him constantly of the divine power that is available to overcome his weakness ('for God is at work in you, both to *will* and to *work* for his good pleasure'). The man who knows and claims the Bible's promises is empowered to live a kind of life which would otherwise be completely beyond his grasp.

2 Timothy 3:16

Philippians 2:13

The moral commands of the Bible are presented more as main guiding principles and ideals than as a set of meticulously detailed regulations for daily living. They reach behind right actions to right motives, and their application may differ from person to person according to circumstances. Goodness is defined as that which pleases God, so the Christian with a clear conscience is the one who is totally absorbed with pleasing him. And, as we have already seen, it is the Bible's function to feed and foster such a relationship.

See Romans 14

Hebrews 13:21

THE BIBLE IS FOR ORDINARY PEOPLE

The Bible is not written in a secret spiritual code which must be cracked if its message is to be understood. Provided it is read sensibly (see the section 'Understanding the Bible'), it is clear enough for the simplest Christian to live by, as well as being profound enough to exercise the mind of the brightest scholar for a lifetime. The decisive qualifications for profitable Bible study are spiritual rather than intellectual.

Among the qualities which the Bible itself suggests, the following are particularly prominent:

A will to obey

John 7:17

'Whoever has the will to do the will of God', said Jesus, 'shall know whether my teaching comes from him.' This is a fundamental requirement, if the teaching of the Bible is going to make its full impact on any reader's life. It has been well said that 'the Bible is never mastered by the reader who refuses its mastery of him'.

Concentration

Words calling for sustained effort ('search', 'meditate', 'examine') are used in the Bible to describe the way the scriptures must be read for maximum benefit. *'Concentrate* on winning God's approval, on being a *workman* with nothing to be ashamed of, and who knows how to use the word of truth to the best advantage.'

2 Timothy 2:15, Phillips

Patience

Hebrews 6:12

It is 'through faith and patience' that the Bible's promises are to be obtained. Patient conviction that God's word is to be trusted will bring the believer through times of perplexity.

See Hebrews 11:17-19

Persistence

Luke 8:18

Jesus' promise and warning, 'To him who has will more be given, and from him who has not, even what he thinks that he has will be taken away', was made in the context of hearing the word of God. To the persistent seeker the Bible yields more and more of its riches.

Submission to the Holy Spirit

When Jesus met his disciples after the resurrection 'he opened their minds to understand the scriptures', by relating what they read in their Bibles to what was happening around them. It is through the prompting of the Holy Spirit that the Bible reader gains the mind of Christ, which enables him to apply teaching given centuries ago to contemporary life.

Luke 24:45

See 1 Corinthians 2:9-16

It would be impossible to better Paul's summary of the practical and devotional potential of the Bible: 'Your mind has been familiar with the holy scriptures, which can open the mind to the salvation which comes through believing on Christ Jesus. All scripture is inspired by God and is useful for teaching the faith and correcting error, for re-setting the direction of a man's life and training him in good living. The scriptures are the comprehensive equipment of the man of God, and fit him fully for all branches of his work.'

2 Timothy 3:15-17, Phillips

UNDERSTANDING THE BIBLE

Often the meaning of a Bible passage is plain and obvious. When it is not, the following points may help in its understanding and application today.

Stage One
1
UNDERSTAND
What does the passage actually say?

Setting
When and where was the book or passage written?

Purpose
Why was it written?

Form
How, or in what form, was it written?

Context
What is the book as a whole about?

Words
What is the meaning of individual words?

History/Biography
Old Testament historical books, Gospels and Acts in the New Testament
- What was the historical background to the passage? (See historical charts and maps.) eg Ezra 1:1; Luke 2:1-2; 3:1-2
- What actually happened? Who were the people involved? eg Nehemiah 1
- Where did it happen? eg Isaiah 36
- Often material was selected to make a point: is there one stated or implied? eg Judges 6:1,7,8

Law
Exodus, Leviticus, Deuteronomy, Numbers
- Is the passage:
moral law, matters of behaviour? eg Exodus 20
social, state law? eg Leviticus 25:13f
domestic law, matters of hygiene? eg Leviticus 12
religious law, worship, sacrifice? eg Leviticus 1-7
blessings and curses? (See article on Covenants in Part Two.) eg Deuteronomy 28
- What was the main aim of the law at the time? eg Leviticus 20:22-26
- Was it superseded in the New Testament? If so, what was the principle involved? eg Hebrews 9

Poetry
Job, Psalms, Song of Solomon, prophets, etc.
- Is it a drama with characters, as in a play? eg Job
- Or poetry, expressing one person's feelings which we can share? eg Psalms 29, 42, 68
- Is it highly symbolical? Is the language from the worship or history of Israel? If so, what is referred to? eg Psalms 77, 78, 79
- Is there a historical setting which will help us understand the poem? Or was it written for use in Israel's worship? eg Judges 4-5; Psalms 134, 136
- Is there repetition or contrast for poetic effect? (See Introduction to Poetry and Wisdom Literature, Part Two.) eg Psalm 67; Proverbs 10:11

'Wise sayings'
Proverbs, Ecclesiastes
- Is it a proverb or saying which stands alone, or is there a common theme? eg Proverbs 8; 23:13-14
- Is it a witty comment on life? Or a statement of what happens as a general rule? Or expressing the situation of man without God? eg Proverbs 10:1-4; 25:25 Ecclesiastes 1:2-11

Prophecy
Old Testament prophets, Revelation
- What was the historical background? (See historical charts, and notes on each book.) eg Daniel 1:1
- Is it written in poetic form? (See on Poetry above.) eg Isaiah 36:22-29
- Is the language highly symbolical? If so, what is the imagery taken from? (See notes in Parts Two and Three.) eg Daniel 7; Revelation 6
- What was the original purpose of the prophecy in its time?
- What is the universal principle involved? eg Isaiah 30:1-5
- Are there specific claims to its fulfilment in the New Testament? eg Isaiah 53; Acts 8

Parable
Gospels, Old Testament historical and prophetic books
- Was the parable told to answer a question or illustrate a point? eg Luke 10:25-37 2 Samuel 12:1-5
- What was the main point? eg Luke 10:36-37
- Are the details given meaning in the passage itself? Or are they just part of the story-telling? eg Mark 4:1-20; Luke 14:15-24

Letter
New Testament letters
- What was the purpose of the letter? Who wrote it? To whom? (See notes on letters in Part Three.) eg 1 John 4:13 1 Corinthians 1:1-2
- What is the argument or theme of the book as a whole? How does the passage fit into this? eg Galatians 1:6

Stage Two
2
EXPLAIN
What does the passage mean?

- What did the passage mean to its original readers?
- What is the main point or teaching of the passage?
- How does it compare with other, perhaps clearer, Bible passages?
- If it was written to meet particular needs at the time, what is the general principle?

Stage Three
3
APPLY
What does the passage mean today?

- What is an equivalent situation today to that of the original readers?
- Does the passage have some specific teaching about God, man, the world, the church . . . ?
- Is there an example to follow, or a warning, or a promise?
- Is there any action to be taken in the light of the passage?
- Does it lead to prayer or praise? Can we make the writer's words or expression of feeling our own?

THE BIBLE AND SOCIETY

Sir Frederick Catherwood

God created the universe. He sustains it. He cares for the whole of mankind and has given us in the Bible a guide-book by which to live.

The Bible tells us how to conduct ourselves in relation to God and to our fellow men. And since God is timeless, the wisdom of the Bible is timeless too.

The Bible is not only relevant to individuals, it is relevant to society. Christianity is not just for private behaviour and public worship. It is a world system which competes with other world systems. It argues on more than equal terms with Marxism, Existentialism, Nationalism, Capitalism. Each of these systems is based on its own particular view of human behaviour, and all have their own standards of morals. The Christian believes that since the Christian teaching is true, it will be more useful and more relevant than that of any other system. The Bible offers to twentieth-century man the very things he cries out for.

THE BIBLE ANSWERS FUNDAMENTAL HUMAN NEEDS

If there is no God, there can be no divine law. If there is no divine law men must try to agree among themselves what is right and what is wrong. But if they disagree, who is to have the last word? So classes and nations fight it out, and conflict escalates as external authority is removed.

Deuteronomy 6:24

The Bible declares that there is an external morality given by God for the good of all mankind. Rulers and ruled alike are answerable to him. His standards are binding on all men.

A basis for science

Other philosophies are said to depend on science. But science itself is based on Christian teaching. It was belief in a God of order, a God of reason, a God of unchanging decrees, which led to the development of the scientific method in the 17th century. When science forsakes this basis it loses its way. Some people have made a god of it. Many are now rejecting it altogether. Its hope lies in a return to its Christian basis.

A realistic view of man

Genesis 3; Jeremiah 17:9; Matthew 15:18-19

Evil is all too apparent in our world. Education does not eradicate it, nor does an improved environment. Revolution and change of government all too often mean simply exchanging one set of evils for another. The Bible explains why. Evil is not simply external, it is deep inside man himself. The initial disobedience to the Creator has left human nature with a permanent, in-born bias to evil. Neither reason nor force will change this. The Bible also teaches that God provides all men with certain common benefits – conscience, the recognition of right and wrong, and certain institutions (family, state, church) which encourage good and discourage evil.

Humanity restored

Genesis 1:26-31; Psalm 8:3-8

The all-pervasive rationalism of our own century, infiltrating our whole culture and philosophy, has reduced man to an animal, condemned to a meaningless existence terminated by death. But men cry out against this. They feel there is something outside the box of time and space in which they find themselves. And they grope instinctively after the Christian truth that man is not just body, he is soul and spirit too. He is not just a passing atom of an overwhelming universe, but is of eternal significance.

THE BIBLE AND THE SOCIAL ORDER

The Bible's relevance is not confined to broad generalities. It enables us to understand and evaluate ourselves and the world we live in. It provides us with a world-view – a philosophy to live by. But it speaks also to practical situations, to the way we run our lives and order our society.

Much of the Bible's teaching goes back to the way we are made; it goes back to creation itself. The same basic principles were backed up in Old Testament law and, in the New Testament, reinforced by Jesus himself.

Hebrews 9

The Old Testament ceremonial law came to an end at the crucifixion, its purpose fulfilled. The civil law applied directly only to Israel as a nation and cannot be lifted out of its context, though many of the principles it embodies are still highly relevant to modern society. But the moral law of the Old Testament retains eternal validity. Men may be forced to change their laws but God does not change his. This moral law includes the ten commandments. Christ came to fulfil the moral law, not to destroy it. He pointed out its full implications in the Sermon on the Mount and elsewhere. Not only was the act of adultery wrong, but even a lustful look. The moral law had been covered with casuistry and hypocrisy. Christ ripped away the cover and put men's obligations to their fellow men on full view.

Exodus 20 Matthew 5:17-48

Not only is the Christian moral law valid for all time, it applies to all men. Though they may find the standards high, most people believe in right and wrong, truth and falsehood. The Christian law has wide support – and for good reason.

A law that protects the weak

The large mass of the world's population is open to exploitation of one kind or another. The Christian moral law is a bulwark against this, whenever men can be taught to respect it. It protects the weak against the strong, the poor against the rich, the women and children, fatherless and widows against those who would neglect and exploit them.

The intention of the Old Testament law on usury, for example, was to make a man use his good fortune to help tide his less fortunate neighbour over a bad patch until he could again become self-sufficient. The law protected farmers living near subsistence level who needed something to carry them over from one harvest to the next, especially if the harvest had been bad. Without some such law the rich could hold the poor to ransom. They could charge such a rate of interest that the poor farmer would have to sell his land to pay it. It was certainly not a prohibition on lending money at a rate of interest which can be earned by the recipient. Lending of unused savings is vital to economic development.

Deuteronomy 23:19-20

Most people agree that the moral law protects the weak. The trades unionist suspects that in competitive capitalism the weak go to the wall. The working man takes naturally to a creed which aims to help the weak.

Leviticus 25

Similarly, the principle of the Law of Jubilee was that the rich should not be allowed to accumulate all property rights. Every fifty years there was a redistribution of land back to the original owners.

The concept of law and order

Romans 13:1-7

The Christian law protects society against chaos. The civil power, Paul tells the Romans, is ordained by God to uphold good and suppress evil.

Exodus 21-22

When it comes to crime and punishment, the penalties laid down in the Old Testament for offences against the person are more severe than for offences against property. People matter more than things – an ideal we are often in danger of forgetting today.

Crime demands just punishment. But the criminal must be treated with compassion. So the Christian stands between the 'hard' line on punishment and the 'soft'. The Old Testament laws endeavoured to ensure that punishment was no greater than the offence, and in any case was less than private retribution. Christ himself said to the woman caught in adultery – for which the punishment was death – 'Go, and do not sin again.'

John 8:11

At the other extreme, the Christian is not at liberty to base his view of crime and punishment on the pre-supposition that all crime is just another kind of sickness, and just as capable of cure. The Bible sees crime as a moral act for which the criminal is responsible, which sickness is not. The Christian's concern for the reform of the criminal should never make him either deny the offence or fail to protect society against the offender. But once the sentence has been paid, the criminal is entitled to society's help to become a good citizen.

One danger of treating all crime as sickness is that it makes the criminal a second-class citizen. A judge's sentence is normally limited by the nature of the offence, but a doctor can detain until he decides a patient is cured. And if an objective moral standard is thrown over, what is to stop the majority in society – or even a minority in power – from putting away in a mental institution those who do not see eye to eye with them until they are 'cured'? It has been done.

Support for the family

The Christian law protects the basic institution of society – the family. The Bible has a great deal to say about the concept of the family, and the Christian ideal differs markedly from some current concepts.

Matthew 19:5-6

The idea of permanence is basic to Christian marriage. This gives security to both partners and children. Relationships can be far freer within a secure framework than when partners or children have to take into account the possible collapse of the whole basic structure. The strains arising from insecurity can often precipitate collapse. Whole new areas of jealousy and friction arise.

The Bible nowhere allows divorce on the grounds of incompatibility. There are some incompatibilities in every marriage. But the Bible sets marriage in a wider context. It is not just a romantic attachment between two individuals to the exclusion of the world at large. The wider family on both sides is involved. So too is society. The wider family protects husband and wife, as well as children, from the stresses and strains of today's tiny nuclear family, where all contact with uncles, aunts, cousins and even grandparents is limited to a weekly long-distance phone-call.

Ephesians 5:21-33

The Christian ideal is marriage between one man and one woman – a factor which has greatly raised the status of women in the world. Anyone inclined to question the advisability of monogamy should read of the troubles of Jacob, David and others who took more than one wife. The husband is to cherish his wife. He has no absolute rights over her. But he is, none the less, the head of the family, the final arbiter.

Genesis 2:24; 1 Corinthians 6:16

Strictly speaking, the Bible regards pre-marital sex as a contradiction in terms. Living together in physical union *is* marriage. The two partners become one flesh. But it cannot stop there. Marriage is social as well as physical. It involves leaving parents. It involves other people – society generally. The marriage ceremony gives recognition to this. The one ground of divorce seemingly allowed by Christ is the adultery of one or other partner with a third person.

Matthew 19:1-9

Sex, as seen in the Bible, is part and parcel of a wider relationship. It should be the expression of a lasting respect and self-sacrificing love. Within that relationship it increases the love and respect. Outside it, it seems to have the opposite effect. And the woman, because of her greater dependence, is usually the loser.

2 Samuel 13

Promiscuity has always been with us. No one knows what society would be like if everyone acted on the advice of those who openly advocate it. Even so, the majority of mankind do not find this view practicable or desirable. The Christian view of marriage on the other hand is both practical and a good deal happier than any alternative.

THE OFFER OF NEW LIFE

These are simply illustrations of the Bible's relevance to present-day society, to modern man. They are based primarily on creation and a law which is true to man and society as they really are.

But the Bible does not limit itself to God's law for humanity. It recognizes that man is unable either to keep these laws, or to make reparation for his offences against a holy God. So the law is intended not simply to regulate conduct in an imperfect world, but to show up our imperfections and so lead us to Christ.

Romans 3:9-26

For Christ, by his death, has served sentence for our sin, and offers forgiveness and a new life to all men. To Christians of all generations for two thousand years and of all nations and races, this is the supreme reality. They know forgiveness. They know fellowship with God through prayer and worship. They know the presence of the Holy Spirit who changes their lives. They know that God's laws are good and true. For them the Bible is not just a realistic book about human nature. They have put it to the test and found it true.

MODERN ENGLISH TRANSLATIONS OF THE BIBLE

The **Authorized,** or **King James' Version** of the Bible was translated over 350 years ago. The **Revised Version** in the last century kept the same language but made revisions in the light of increased knowledge of the original Hebrew and Greek texts. In the 20th century there have been a number of new translations concerned not only to reflect an accurate text but also current English usage. Their main differences are:

1. Some are revisions (e.g. **The Revised Standard Version**), some wholly new translations from the original languages (e.g. **New English Bible, Jerusalem Bible, Good News Bible**).
2. Some use 'literary' language, including formal or academic words (e.g. **New English Bible, Jerusalem Bible**). Others use colloquial English (e.g. **The Living Bible**), or 'common' English (**Good News Bible**), the language common to both written and spoken English.
3. Some translations are concerned to keep the idiom and general force and meaning of the original; others to keep as closely as possible to the original words and sentence structure.
4. Some keep the literary forms of the original when possible, e.g. by printing poetry as such.
5. Some translations are produced by one man, others by a group.
6. Some translations are made to conserve particular theological or linguistic traditions.

The main 20th-century English translations

1903
R.T. Weymouth, *The New Testament in Modern Speech*
A classical scholar's translation of the New Testament into dignified modern English.

1913 and 1924
James Moffatt, *A New Translation of the Bible*
A free, vigorous, idiomatic translation which takes some liberties with the text.

1927
E.J. Goodspeed, *The Complete Bible: an American Translation*
A very readable version appreciated both in the United States and elsewhere.

1944 and 1949
Ronald Knox, *The Holy Bible*
A Roman Catholic translation based on the Latin Vulgate.

1946 and 1952
The Revised Standard Version (The Common Bible)
Revision of the American Standard Version of 1901, which was in turn a revision of the Authorized/King James' Version. Translated by a committee of 32 scholars, with the aim of producing a version which would retain the good qualities of the Authorized/King James' Version but take full account of modern scholarship.

1950 and 1960
The New World Translation
Produced by the Jehovah's Witnesses, emphasizing their interpretation of particular texts.

1955
H.J. Schonfield, *The Authentic New Testament*
A translation by a distinguished Jewish scholar, emphasizing the Jewish background of the New Testament.

1958
The Amplified Bible
A version giving alternative words to suggest different possible meanings; produced by 12 editors in California.

1958
J.B. Phillips, *The New Testament in Modern English*
A fresh, vigorous, free translation of the New Testament; revised 1972.

1959
The Holy Bible: The Berkeley Version in Modern English
The New Testament is the work of a single scholar, the Old Testament the work of a team of 20, in the USA: a conservative revision concerned for accuracy.

1961 and 1970
The New English Bible
A completely new translation by panels of scholars taking into account the most accurate and up-to-date linguistic, textual and historical findings; sponsored by the main British churches and Bible Societies.

1966
The Jerusalem Bible
Based on the textual studies of the Roman Catholic School of Biblical Studies, Jerusalem, this is a clear, accurate, scholarly translation.

1966 and 1976
Good News Bible
A completely new, fresh, straightforward translation in 'common' or non-academic English; produced by the American Bible Society.

1971
Kenneth Taylor, *The Living Bible*
A colloquial, conservative American paraphrase designed for family reading and to help ordinary people understand the Bible.

1974 and 1979
New International Version
A new translation by an international, interdenominational team of evangelical scholars.

FIRST ENGLISH TRANSLATIONS

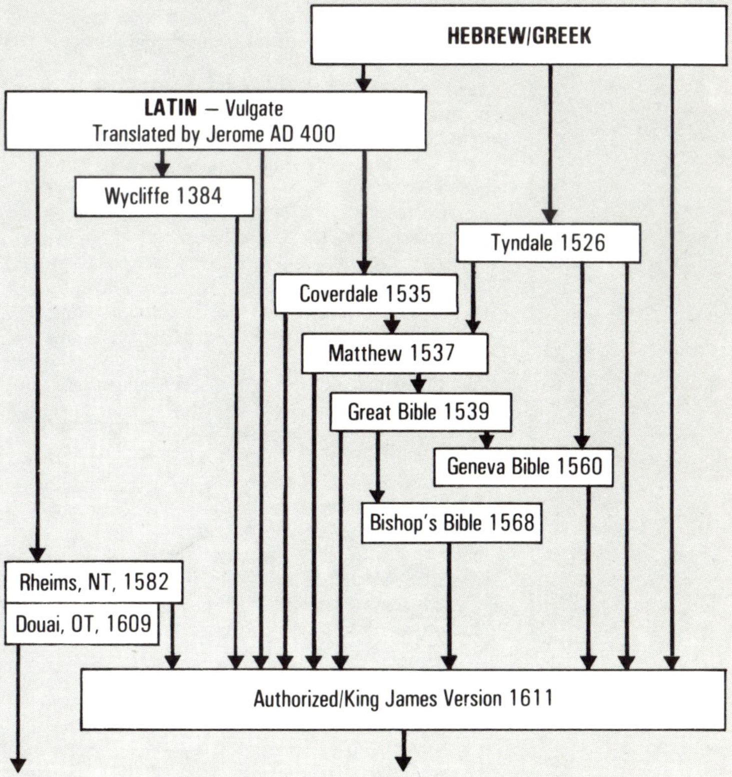

MEETING OBJECTIONS

Kenneth Howkins

Much of the Bible is in the form of history. It is not however *mere* history. If that is all we see, we miss the point. It is history from one point of view, history with an aim. Stories are recorded not simply because they happened, but because they reveal something of God and his activity in the world. So it is sometimes called a 'history of salvation'.

HISTORY WITH A DIFFERENCE

This alters the perspective. The secular historian may be amazed that an ancient Hebrew nomad, Abraham, occupies more than thirteen chapters, while a powerful despot, Omri, is dealt with summarily in less than a dozen verses. Archaeological records do not even mention Abraham, though his story fits well into what is known of his times; but Omri was known far and wide to later generations. In the Bible, Abraham was the founder of Israel, a man chosen by God, a man of faith, the recipient of God's promises, and a man of profound significance to both Jew and Christian; but Omri founded the city of Samaria and was an evil man. Thus he is dismissed from the story. As God's revelation of himself unfolded, and as his work of salvation continued, men and events in history assumed different proportions.

Discrepancies

It is easy to find historical problems in the Bible. But patient research has gradually solved many of them. Apparent discrepancies between different parts of the Bible are sometimes due simply to the lack of detail given, and we should not too hastily pounce on contradictions. For example, in both Acts and Galatians there are references to Paul's visits to Jerusalem. It is difficult to fit the two together, and to know which visits in the two books correspond. But Acts is clearly not intended to give a complete account of Paul's activities, and he may well have visited Jerusalem on other occasions which are not recorded.

Again, there may be apparent discrepancies between the biblical version of a story and the version in other ancient records. It is strange that those who wish to discredit the reliability of the Bible sometimes seem to have such strong faith in the reliability of other ancient records! So first we need to be sure that the other record is in fact reliable and, second, we need to remember how little total evidence we have from the ancient past. The debate on the book of Daniel illustrates this. It is no longer possible just to dismiss Darius as 'unhistorical'. There are problems: but there are also possible solutions.

Problems with numbers

A difficulty arises on various occasions in connection with numbers in the Bible. Here we find that the manuscripts themselves may vary in the figures they give. It must be remembered that letters of the alphabet in both Hebrew (at least after the exile) and Greek served also as numerals. Because of the similarities of certain letters, errors in copying could easily creep in. Also different methods of reckoning were employed. A year may be reckoned by the sun, or by the reign of a king. Inclusive reckoning was also used. For example, midday on Sunday until midday on the following Sunday could be called eight days, rather than seven, as eight days were involved, even though the first and the last were incomplete. Again, there are problems, but some progress can be made with them.

Myth

An objection frequently heard today is that it is being unduly literalistic to discuss whether or not the Bible history is true. We are told that what matters is not whether a certain event happened, but what it means. This is the opposite extreme to the views that it is *mere* history; the claim is that the stories are not history but 'myth' – a term used in varying ways, and notoriously hard to define exactly. It does not imply that the story is completely untrue, but that it is not literally true. The term is brought in whenever there is anything supernatural or different from the ordinary course of nature.

Now the first question to consider is whether the biblical writers intended their words to be taken as history or as myth. It is clear that the accounts of miracles in the Bible are written just as factually as the accounts of other events. The second question, therefore, is whether we can accept them as history, or whether we must treat them as myth and 'demythologize' them, that is, assume that the miracle did not actually occur as a miraculous event, but that some spiritual truth is enshrined in the story in symbolic form.

The basis for this line of argument is that the Bible was written in an unscientific age, when people thought of 'a three-decker universe', with a God who kept on interfering; but that now, in our enlightened scientific age, we know that their view of the world was quite wrong. Miracles are supposed to fit in with the unscientific views of the ancients, but not with our own scientific views. It is claimed that we now know that the world operates in accordance with laws, and so we do not need to bring God in to explain things.

Now this view of science is already out of date. Science, or rather scientists, no longer hold such a rigid view of the laws of nature. The laws are descriptions of what is observed to happen normally. If a law does not account for all that happens, then it has to be modified. Science, as such, does not rule out miracles, though some scientists may reject them.

We have been considering the subject of history. The question of whether miracles happened or not is a question of history and not of science. History deals with what happened, and then tries to find explanations. Science takes the knowledge of what happened and tries to systematize that knowledge.

THE QUESTION OF MIRACLES

The biggest miracle in the Bible is the resurrection of Jesus from the dead. Some would say that the universe is such that a resurrection could not take place, and they would base this assertion on 'science'. But in view of the historical evidence for the resurrection, it would be more scientific to ask what light is thrown on the nature of the universe by the occurrence of such a resurrection. In other words, science does not disprove the resurrection: the resurrection is one of the facts which science must take into account. And what is said of the resurrection may be said of other miracles.

Of course there are objections here which must be faced. If miracles were always taking place, there would be no order in the universe, and without the regularity of nature we should not know where we were. Moreover, if God were always intervening to get us out of difficulties or dangers, we should never learn to become responsible people. But the Bible does not give us a miracle on every page. It covers about two thousand years of history, but most of the miracles are clustered round a few persons and events:

Moses and the beginning of the nation of Israel;

Elijah and Elisha and the emergence of a line of prophets who called the nation back to their covenant-agreement with God;

Jesus and the final revelation of God and his salvation, followed by the apostles and the founding of the Christian church.

Thus most of the miracles occur in these three separate periods. They must be seen in perspective.

Complementary accounts

In science it is not always possible to find one theory which accounts for and describes every aspect of an event. It is sometimes necessary to have two or more theories, not as alternatives, but held together. Light can be described in terms both of waves and of particles. Neither description alone is sufficient; both are needed. There can be a number of different levels of explanation.

Now when a scientist investigates a 'miracle', he may, or may not, be able to offer a 'natural' explanation. This is the function of science. The account of the crossing of the Red Sea in the Bible refers to a strong wind. That is the natural explanation. But the same account also ascribes the event to God. There are two levels of description. Both are true. One answers the question of *how*, the other the question of *why*. To say that God did it is to give the ultimate cause and to give meaning to it. The description given by science (where one is possible) explains *how* God did it.

In the Bible miracles are not as sharply divided from other events as they tend to be in our thinking. The ordinary events of nature, as well as the extraordinary, are ascribed to God. God is seen as active in all nature, and not only in miracles; they are simply his unusual ways of working.

Religious and historical truth

On the philosophical level another objection is raised against taking the miracle stories as historically true. We are told that there are two categories which must be kept absolutely apart. Thus the objectors would want to say that it is a 'religiously' true statement that God raised Jesus from the dead, and this has a spiritual meaning; but that on the level of history, Jesus died and remained dead and buried. We are told that to say the body of Jesus actually lived again is 'to confuse the categories'. But what are those categories, and where do they come from? They exist solely in the mind of the man who invented them. They can be neither proved nor disproved. But there is something more important still. If we start off by accepting these categories, then we start off by saying that Jesus did not rise from the dead, in the ordinary sense of those words. No matter how strong the historical evidence for the resurrection, we shall never accept it. We shall simply look for some other explanation.

This philosophical objection is really the same as the so-called scientific objection that miracles just do not occur in this world or universe. In both cases the objection is simply assumed to be valid, without proof, and before the evidence has even been considered. Indeed, all 'evidence' is automatically discounted. This is a fine example of question-begging: it assumes the answer before it starts. To such objectors we simply put the question: what sort of evidence would you require to be convinced that miracles did occur?

Creation stories

A similar problem arises at the very beginning of the Bible, in the creation stories. Some dismiss these as myth in the sense of old wives' tales. Others call them myth, meaning to say that they contain truth, even though they are not literally and historically true. If this is the case, in what sense are they true? What is the real point of the stories?

Objections to the creation stories are made in the name of science. So it may be surprising to find how little there is which impinges on the realm of science. It is boldly shown that God is the Creator of all – the universe, man, and everything else. But it is not shown how God did it. If God made man from the dust of the earth, that tells us something about the nature of man, the creature, as compared with God, the Creator. We are mere dust, and live only because God has made us live. Therefore, apart from God, our lives have no meaning. But how did God make man from dust? That is a scientific question, and so we turn to science, not the Bible, for an answer, or a suggested answer. We shall not be satisfied with a theory which does less than justice to the biblical view of the nature of man, but at the same time we need to be sure that we really have grasped the biblical view, and not just read our own ideas into it.

THE VALIDITY OF THE OLD TESTAMENT

Some people reject the Old Testament, partly or wholly, as being non-Christian, or sub-Christian. This is no new idea. In the first place, the Christian's view of the Old Testament must be Christ's view of it. It is quite clear that he accepted its authority and its validity. The question is whether Christ and Christianity have presented a new and truer view of God which invalidates the Old Testament picture.

In certain respects the Old Testament *is* now invalidated. Sacrifices are no longer necessary, as Christ himself has offered the final sacrifice, once for all. The rest of the Jewish ceremonial law is similarly superseded. But that does not mean that those Old Testament rituals should now be completely ignored. They reveal something permanently true about the nature of God and man's relationship with him. The teaching is the same, but the practical outworking is different, because of Christ. God is still holy.

The parts of the Old Testament which cause greatest offence are those which depict God as a God of anger, who orders his servants to act in judgement for him. This, it is said, is a primitive view of God, and quite different from the New Testament picture, which proclaims that God is love. But there is no fundamental opposition between the Old and New Testaments. There is much about the love and forgiveness of God in the Old Testament, and much about his righteous anger and judgement in the New. Indeed some of the strongest words are found on the lips of Jesus himself. Those who reject the Old Testament picture are compelled to reject also parts of the New. The whole idea of God's righteousness, anger against evil, and judgement is not pleasant, especially in a permissive age. But this does not make it any less true. (See Parts Two and Three for notes on particular moral difficulties.)

MEN OR MACHINES?

A final objection to a Christian view of the Bible is that it bypasses human thought, and makes men into machines. It is said that on this view the writers mechanically wrote what God said, and the readers do not need to think, because every bit of truth is presented on a plate. But this objection reveals a radical misunderstanding. Although the Bible's claim for itself is that God did directly speak through men, and that he so controlled them that they said what he wanted them to say, it is clear also that the men concerned used their own minds in the process. Their own personalities come through in the different styles of writing and their different approaches.

Clearly also the Christian must use his own mind to receive the word of God. He must read carefully, compare one passage with another and use all the aids he can. Besides this he needs to seek the help of the Holy Spirit, through whom Scripture was written, to illuminate its meaning. As with the writers of Scripture, so with its readers, the mind and whole being needs to be dedicated to God. It is one of the remarkable features of the Bible that it contains enough to occupy the greatest intellects for a lifetime, and yet the simplest soul can read and understand, and in reading with an obedient heart find God himself.

PART TWO

The Old Testament

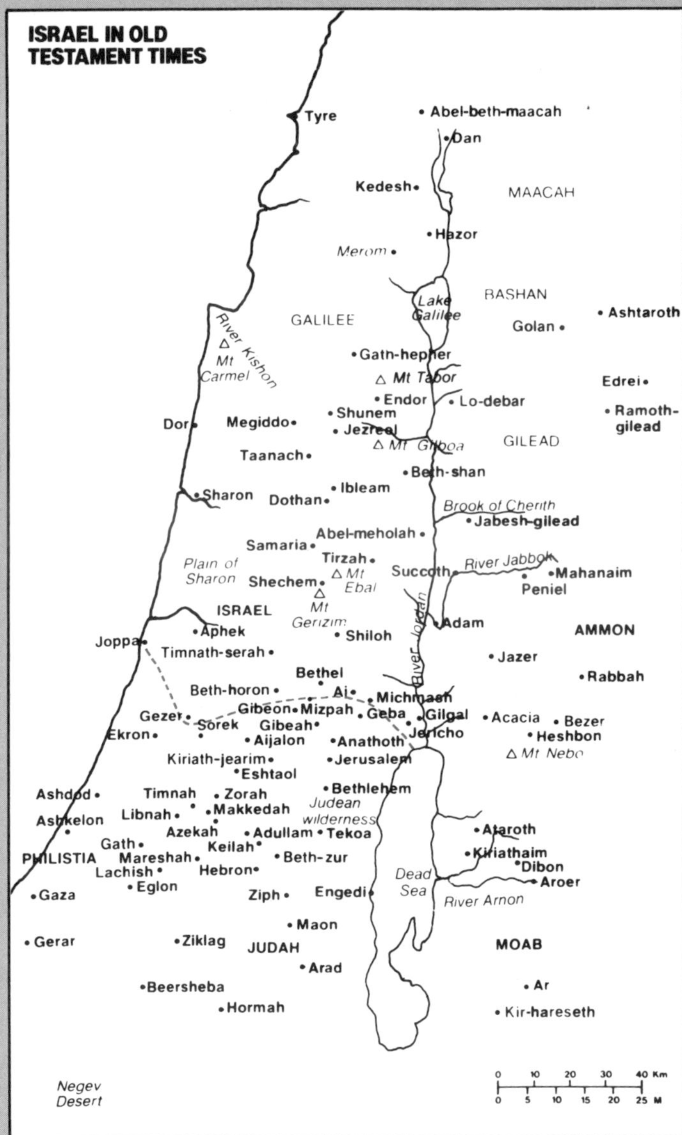

OLD TESTAMENT HISTORY AT A GLANCE

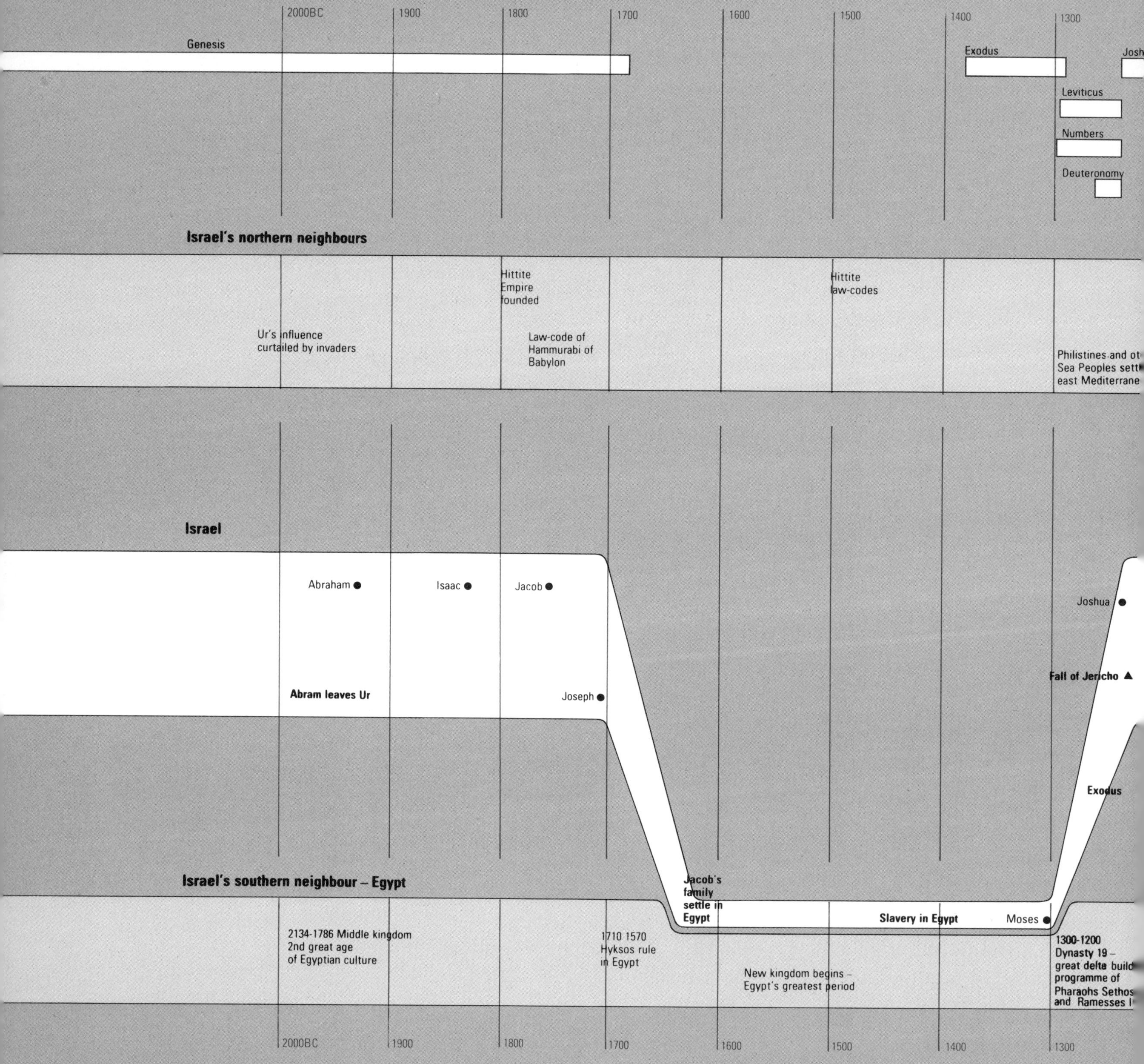

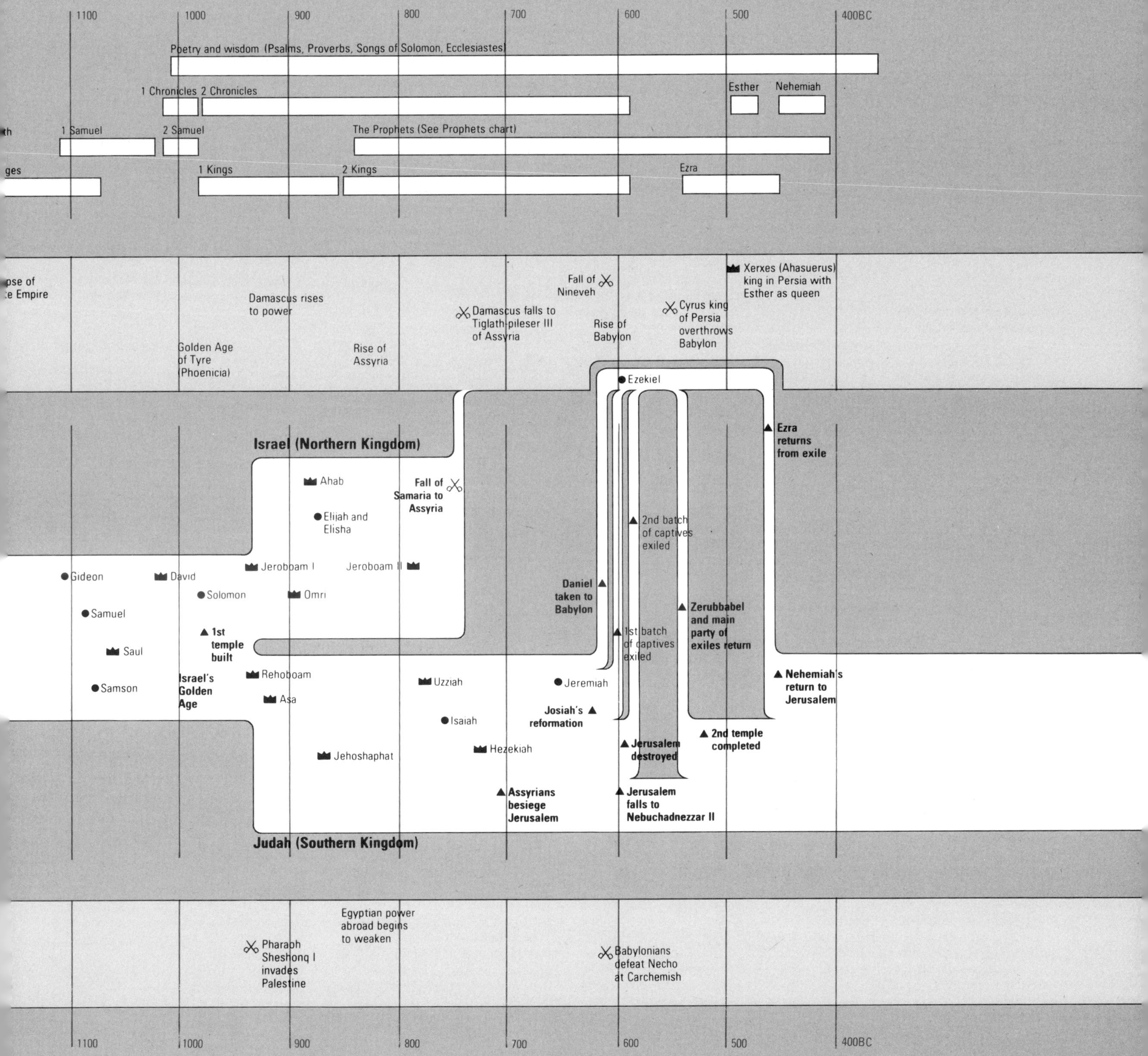

1100
1000
900
800
700
600
500
400BC
Poetry and wisdom (Psalms, Proverbs, Songs of Solomon, Ecclesiastes)
1 Chronicles
2 Chronicles
Esther
Nehemiah
th
1 Samuel
2 Samuel
The Prophets (See Prophets chart)
ges
1 Kings
2 Kings
Ezra
pse of
e Empire
Damascus rises to power
Golden Age of Tyre (Phoenicia)
Rise of Assyria
Damascus falls to Tiglath-pileser III of Assyria
Fall of Nineveh
Rise of Babylon
Cyrus king of Persia overthrows Babylon
Xerxes (Ahasuerus) king in Persia with Esther as queen
Ezekiel
Israel (Northern Kingdom)
Ahab
Elijah and Elisha
Fall of Samaria to Assyria
2nd batch of captives exiled
Ezra returns from exile
Gideon
David
Jeroboam I
Jeroboam II
Solomon
Omri
Samuel
Daniel taken to Babylon
Zerubbabel and main party of exiles return
Saul
1st temple built
1st batch of captives exiled
Samson
Israel's Golden Age
Rehoboam
Uzziah
Jeremiah
Nehemiah's return to Jerusalem
Asa
Josiah's reformation
Isaiah
2nd temple completed
Jerusalem destroyed
Hezekiah
Jehoshaphat
Assyrians besiege Jerusalem
Jerusalem falls to Nebuchadnezzar II
Judah (Southern Kingdom)
Egyptian power abroad begins to weaken
Pharaoh Sheshonq I invades Palestine
Babylonians defeat Necho at Carchemish
1100
1000
900
800
700
600
500
400BC

Old Testament section 1

THE 'FIVE BOOKS'

Introduction/John Taylor

The name 'Pentateuch' is given to the first five books of the Bible. It comes from two Greek words meaning 'five scrolls'. But it is better to think of the Pentateuch as one book divided into five sections, rather than as five books rolled into one. In this way justice is done not only to its Hebrew origin, where it was called the 'Torah' (Law) or the 'Five fifths of Moses', but also to its own inherent unity.

That does not mean to say that the Pentateuch consists of an extended piece of narrative writing in strict chronological order. It is immediately obvious to the reader that it contains a wide variety of literary material – narratives, laws, ritual instructions, sermons, genealogies, poetry – which have been drawn together from different sources. It does mean, however, that the material has been carefully constructed within a narrative framework, with a clear purpose in mind and with recognizable objectives on the part of the author or editor.

THE FRAMEWORK

The framework of the Pentateuch consists of the story of God's people from the call of Abraham to the death of Moses. It spans a period of over 600 years, i.e. from about 1900 BC to about 1250 BC, though it is notoriously difficult to be sure of dates at this early stage of Israel's history. The story is in two sections. The first is dominated by the four generations of the patriarchs – Abraham, Isaac, Jacob and Joseph (Genesis 12-50); the second by the majestic figure of Moses (Exodus-Deuteronomy). It is preceded by a prologue (Genesis 1-11), consisting of ancient records and traditions, which serve not only to introduce the main themes of the narrative but also to relate them to God's purposes in the world of fallen men, of divided nations and of a created order which was originally good. It is best to look first at the main themes of the books as a whole, and then examine the significance of these introductory chapters.

FOUR IMPORTANT THEMES

Election

The Old Testament was written for the people of Israel – the people who looked back to Jacob (=Israel) as their common ancestor and to Abraham as the founder of their nation. Christians, too, look to Abraham as the father of all those who depend in faith on God rather than on anything they can do for themselves (see Romans 4:16). We therefore read the story of Abraham's call by God to become the ancestor of God's chosen people, not simply as an event in the distant past, but as something of present-day significance to us.

The idea of 'election' – God's special choosing of individuals – carries with it two subsidiary features: promise and responsibility. Genesis 12-22 is interspersed with words of promise spoken by God to Abraham. Abraham is promised descendants as countless as the stars of heaven. He is given the land of Canaan as his children's inheritance. He is promised a great name in days to come. And the Lord's special favour was to be shown not only to Abraham and his family but to all men through him.

So God's promises to Abraham were not just for the selfish enjoyment of a chosen few. They were to be used responsibly so that others might share in the benefits. Right at the heart of God's choice of Israel it is made plain that God has a missionary purpose. Israel's history must be read as the long story of her attempts to fulfil her responsibilities – with some successes, but with many conspicuous failures.

Covenant

To the modern mind a 'covenant' is simply a matter of legal documents and sealing-wax. But to the Hebrew mind it covered all human relationships. It was the bond which united people in mutual obligations, whether through a marriage contract, a commercial enterprise or a verbal undertaking. It was natural that man's relationship to God should have been expressed in covenant terms.

These covenant terms are used to describe three separate occasions in the Pentateuch:

— God's promises to Noah that he would never again send a flood upon the earth (Genesis 9:9).
— God's promises to Abraham (Genesis 15:18; 17:4).
— The Sinai covenant established with Moses and summarized in the 'book of the covenant' (Exodus 24:7).

Though covenants were made between equals, the religious use of the term always referred to a relationship between a greater and a lesser partner. The form of the covenant between God and Israel in Exodus and Deuteronomy has been helpfully illuminated by recent discoveries of Hittite suzerainty-treaties made between a king and his vassal. They consisted of a historical introduction, a list of stipulations, curses and blessings invoked on the parties, a solemn oath and a religious ceremony to ratify the covenant. Most of these features can be found in the Old Testament pattern of covenants. (See article 'Covenants and Near Eastern Treaties'.)

More important than the form of the covenant, however, was its theological significance.

It was based on the initiative of God. He acted in mercy and with sovereignty. He made an unconditional promise never to judge mankind with another flood (Genesis 9:11). He chose Abraham and his descendants to be the channels of his mercy to a fallen world. He cemented this election by committing himself to the Israelite nation with the words, 'I will take you for my people, and I will be your God' (Exodus 6:7).

It implied a new revelation of God. He appeared to Abraham as his shield (Genesis 15:1) and as God Almighty ('El Shaddai', Genesis 17:1). He appeared to Moses as 'Yahweh' ('I am who I am', Exodus 3:14), and later on as 'Yahweh your God, who brought you out of the land of Egypt' (Exodus 20:2). (See article 'The Names of God'.)

It made moral and ritual demands upon the people. The stipulations of the covenant included both these features. Ritual was represented by the rite of circumcision given to Abraham (Genesis 17:10), by the keeping of the sabbath, the day of rest (Exodus 20:8ff.) and by all the detailed requirements relating to worship and sacrifice found in the Pentateuch. At the same time the ethical requirements were spelt out in the Ten Commandments and other laws. Though at first sight these two demands seem strangely unrelated, they do in fact meet in the idea of God's holiness. A holy God requires his people to reflect his character both in worship and in behaviour.

Law

The idea of law is central to the Pentateuch and, as we have seen, it gave its name to the book as a whole. At its simplest, it covered the Ten Commandments (Exodus 20; Deuteronomy 5) but associated with these were various collections of laws which have been classified as:

— the book of the covenant (Exodus 21-23);
— the holiness code (Leviticus 17-26);
— the law of Deuteronomy (Deuteronomy 12-26).

Comparisons have been made with other ancient Near Eastern law-codes, especially the Code of Hammurabi, and many similarities noted. This illustrates the fact that Israel was a part of Eastern Mediterranean culture and shared in the ideas and experience of her neighbours. But what is so significant is not so much the similarities as the differences which made Israel's laws distinctive. These may be summarized as:

— their uncompromising monotheism (everything is related to the one God);
— their remarkable concern for the under-privileged: slaves, strangers, women, orphans;
— their community spirit, based on the convenant relationship shared by all Israel with the Lord.

It has also been pointed out that the laws in the Old Testament may be classified as either 'apodictic' in form ('thou shalt ...' or 'thou shalt not ...') or 'casuistic' ('when a man ..., he shall ...'). As most ancient law-codes consisted of the casuistic type, it may be that the apodictic was a peculiarly Israelite form, in which case the Decalogue (the Ten Commandments) was unique to Israel.

Some Christians have mistakenly seen Jesus' teaching in the Sermon on the Mount as a rejection of the

Jewish law in favour of his new law of love. But Jesus' criticisms were in fact directed not at the laws, but at the way the rabbis had interpreted them. ('You have heard that it was said' was the traditional rabbinic formula for introducing their interpretation.) He was uncovering the inner motivation behind the commandments, which interpreters had failed to appreciate.

Some too have criticized the Ten Commandments for being negative. But they follow a positive assertion: 'I am the Lord your God ...' Those who have experienced deliverance by the hand of God, and who live under his sovereignty, must show it by distinctive behaviour. The Ten Commandments therefore began as God's charter for his liberated people. They consisted not of generalities but of specific commands for specific situations: worship, work, home life, marriage, respect for life and property, elementary justice and the personal realm of the will. To all these areas of human experience God had a word that was explicit and inescapable. Christ did not destroy it: he fulfilled and enlarged it.

The same cannot be said of the ceremonial and ritual laws which occupy much of Leviticus and other parts of the Pentateuch. The purpose of these laws was not only to provide guidance for the day-to-day running of the Israelite community, but to teach how a holy God was to be worshipped by a holy people. So, in addition to regulations for worship (festivals, sacrifices, etc.), detailed guidance was given for the preservation of ritual purity. The Israelite people had to be kept free of contamination from outside sources, especially the corrupting influence of Canaanite religion. They must approach God with a due sense of his moral and ritual distinctiveness.

These regulations no longer apply to the Christian church, though the underlying principles still have much to teach. And the elaborate sacrificial system has found its fulfilment in the one sacrifice of Christ – the perfect Lamb of God – through whom sins are forgiven and atonement is made for all men for ever (see Hebrews 10:1-18).

Exodus

The fourth major theme found in the Pentateuch, and recurring throughout the Bible, is the exodus from Egypt, described in Exodus 1-12. To the Jew this was the great saving act of God to which all later generations looked back with thankfulness. It was a miraculous intervention by God in response to the cries of his enslaved people (Exodus 3:7). It was essentially God's act – 'with mighty hand and outstretched arm'. It was a great victory over the gods of Egypt which demonstrated his total supremacy. It was a moment in history recalled every year in the Feast of the Passover. Later generations were frequently reminded that they were once members of a slave community whom the Lord had mercifully redeemed from bondage. They were encouraged to remember the past and warned of the danger of forgetting what God had done for them (e.g. Deuteronomy 6:12).

As a historical event the exodus was definitive. The fact that God had done it once meant that he could do it again. When Israel was in exile in Babylon the nation looked for a second exodus (Isaiah 51:9-11). And when Christ came, his work of deliverance was described in the language of the exodus (e.g. Luke 9:31).

These, then, are the four themes which are never far below the surface of the Pentateuch. They are the constant preoccupation of these five books. The only other theme – which recurs with depressing regularity – is the persistent sinfulness of the people of Israel. They were slow to accept Moses as their deliverer. They grumbled about the hardships of the journey. They even hankered after the old life in Egypt (suitably glamorized, Numbers 11:5). They were daunted by the prospect of moving into the land of Canaan. And they wandered for 40 years in the wilderness of indecision. Not even Moses was immune, and he was punished by not being allowed to lead the people into their promised land. But sin was no new problem. To discover why, we must turn to the introductory chapters of Genesis.

THE PROLOGUE

The early chapters of Genesis were once regarded by some Christians as an embarrassment. But the old science-versus-faith controversies are increasingly a thing of the past. In fact, these chapters are now reckoned to be among the foremost theological statements the Bible contains. Once men were released from trying to defend them as scientific documents they were able to listen to what the text was actually saying.

The form of this message has often been described as 'myth'. But this is a misleading term, even when 'myth' is understood in the technical sense of a 'religious text designed to account for a custom, institution or other phenomenon'. It is also misleading because it is thought to be unhistorical and untrue. But in fact these early chapters of Genesis *are* historical, in that they bear witness to events which actually took place. The world was created; man and woman were made in God's image; the fall did take place in time. The problem is the degree of symbolism used in describing these events. On this, opinions will continue to vary considerably.

It is to these chapters that we turn for biblical guidance on the fundamental questions concerning God, man and the world. At every stage God is present. He is not simply presupposed; he is constantly and actively at work. This world is his world. Human history is the outworking of his plan. He is totally responsible for the world and all that is in it. All men are his creation, made 'in his image' – with spiritual capacities for goodness, worship and fellowship with him. There is no place whatsoever for other gods. Genesis 1 is all-embracing: sun, moon and stars are his handiwork, with duties to perform in his ordered universe; even the sea-monsters (the *tanninim* of ancient mythology) were created by him (Genesis 1:21).

Man is the climax of creation, superior to all else but subordinate to his Creator. Only when man aspires above his station and wants to be like God does he fall to a lowlier position in which all his relationships are soured. Sex, from being a good, companionable, shame-free relationship, becomes secretive, lustful, anomalous. Child-bearing is painful and hazardous. The noble art of husbandry becomes a drudgery. Even the ground is affected, and instead of producing food plentifully it has to be coaxed and sweated over. There is nothing that sin has not blighted. Its taint reaches out to family life, where religion turns to rivalry, brotherly love becomes murder, and justice degenerates into blood-lust (Genesis 4).

God's response to sin is, consistently, a blend of judgement and mercy. From the provision of skins for Adam and Eve, and the guarding of the way to the tree of life, to the confusion of tongues at Babel, God tempers justice with salvation. Beyond the immediate punishment of casting Adam out from the garden of Eden or Cain from human society, beyond the destruction of the flood and the scattering of the nations, there was always God's ultimate intention for man's well-being and blessing. Thus in a world of disorder and corruption, it was totally in keeping with God's nature that he should call out one man, Abraham, and through him his descendants the Jews, to be the channel of grace and revelation to all mankind.

It is this story which the Pentateuch tells.

Old Testament 1.1

GENESIS

The book of Genesis is an epic, a drama on a grand scale. It begins at the very beginning. God made the world, a world that was good. He made man, the apex of all creation.

The 'prologue' (chapters 1-11) provides us with a general history of man over some thousands of years. We see God's good creation progressively soured as a result of man's sin in overreaching himself in trying to become like God. Then everything is swept away in the great flood. A new beginning is made – only to end in the folly of Babel and the division and dispersion of the nations.

In chapter 12 the emphasis shifts. From the history of man in general we focus down to the story of a single individual, Abraham, and his descendants. God will not destroy his creation. Instead he begins to work, through one man of his choice, and one nation of his choice, for the renewing of the world. Genesis takes the story on through Isaac and Jacob to the death of Joseph in Egypt. And still the story of God's great purpose for mankind is scarcely begun. It continues on through the pages of Scripture to the very last words of the book of Revelation.

1 - 2:4 CREATION

The great drama of the beginning of all things starts with God. The language is simple but vivid. It evokes the wonder and richness of creation from formlessness to teeming life.

But it is more than poetic. It tells us what we need to know in order to understand ourselves and the world around us:

- The origin of the world and of life was no accident. There is a Creator: God.
- God made everything there is.
- All that God made was good.
- The high point of all God's creative acts was the making of man.
- Mankind is distinguished from all other creatures in two respects: he alone is made in God's own likeness; and he is given charge over all the rest.
- God's six 'days' of creative activity followed by a 'day' of rest, sets the pattern for man's working life.

Creation is described as taking place in six days. There are eight acts of creation, each introduced by the words 'and God said ...'

DAY 1
Light and darkness/day and night
DAY 2
Earth's atmosphere (the firmament)
DAY 3
Dry land and seas separated
Plants and trees
DAY 4
Sun, moon and stars: seasons, days, years
DAY 5
Sea creatures and birds
DAY 6
Land animals
Man
DAY 7
Creation completed, God rests

The events are described from the standpoint of an observer seeing the development of creation around him. The order is not necessarily chronological (a modern idea!). Light and darkness, for example, are described before the sun, moon and stars. The account is one which we can all understand – from the simplest peasant to scientifically educated 20th-century man.

This is not a treatise on geology, biology, or any other science. We are not told *when* creation took place. Nor are we given details as to *how* God brought the earth and life into being – nor how long it all took. The 'days' are taken by some to be periods of time. Others think that this pattern of seven days is simply the most vivid means of expressing the creative energy and satisfaction of God, the orderliness and simple majesty of the way he created all things.

The 'image' or 'likeness' of God (1:27): of all creation, only man (including both man and woman) is described as being made in God's likeness. However it is understood, the phrase sets man apart from the animals. It establishes him in a special relationship with God. God gives man control over the newly-made world and all its creatures. The 'likeness' is so basic to man's structure that the Fall did not destroy it. Sin has certainly spoiled and blurred it, but man remains a reasoning, moral, creative creature. He is still intended to be in control of his environment. To make him no more than animal is to make him less than man in God's likeness.

2:5 - 3:24 MAN: TESTING AND DOWNFALL

2:5-25 Focus on man

This second description of creation is not simply a duplicate of the first. It is written from a different point of view – this time focussing on man. It also uses a different name for God. In the first account it was *Elohim*, God the Creator, the great and lofty One who inhabits eternity. Now it is *Yahweh* (Jehovah) *Elohim*, God in relation to his people (see article 'The Names of God'). The two accounts may represent two different traditions or sources. But that is no reason for trying to make them contradict each other. Nor should this be an excuse to try to carve up Genesis to fit a theory – about the evolution of religion or anything else.

A 7th-century BC clay tablet inscribed with a part of the Babylonian account of the creation.

OTHER CREATION ACCOUNTS

Alan Millard

Creation stories belonging to other ancient peoples have given currency to the view that Genesis contains merely another version, adapted to suit Hebrew beliefs. Genesis 1 and 2 consist of a general account of the creation of the heavens and the earth, followed by a more detailed description of the making of man. Stories of cosmic and of human creation, either separately or as unities, are numerous, and many have several points in common: pre-existent deity; creation by divine command; man the ultimate creature; man formed from the earth as a pot is made; man in some way a reflection of deity. Almost all polytheistic faiths possess family-trees of their gods which can figure in creation stories. A primal pair or even a single self-created and self-propagating god heads the divine family, all of whose members represent or control natural elements and forces.

For some peoples, the physical universe or a basic element such as water or earth always existed, and the gods arose from it. For others it was the handiwork of a god or gods. These are simple concepts based on observation and elementary logic. For example, man as 'dust' is easily deduced from the cycle of death and decay.

However, common ideas need not share a common origin; it is misleading to reduce differing stories from all over the world to their common factors in order to claim that they do. A single source for all, or large numbers, of different stories is improbable.

Ancient Near Eastern stories

Nevertheless, it is quite in order to set Genesis beside other accounts from the world of the Old Testament. When we do so, we find that few of the ancient creation stories share more than one or two basic concepts – such as the separation of heaven and earth, and the creation of man from clay. The Babylonian literature, however, affords some striking resemblances. In the century since one was first translated into English, the Babylonian accounts have been cited as the ultimate source of the Hebrew's beliefs. Recently, the recovery of more texts and the re-assessment of those long known have shown that many of the accepted similarities are in fact illusory.

The famous *Babylonian Genesis,* usually linked with the Hebrew creation story, is one of several, and was neither the oldest nor the most popular. Written late in the 2nd millennium BC to honour Marduk, god of Babylon, who is its hero, it begins with a watery mother-figure, Tiamat, from whom the gods are born. (The name is related to the Hebrew word for 'the deep' through the pre-historic linguistic connections between Babylonian and Hebrew.) She is killed by Marduk in a battle with her children whose noise had angered her, and her corpse is formed into the world. Man is made to relieve the gods of the toil of keeping the earth in order.

There are clear indications that this story was made up from older ones, and earlier compositions have been found which contain some of these features. Only one theme recurs often, the relief of the gods from their labour by the making of man with a divine ingredient. The battle of the gods in the Babylonian Genesis has no Old Testament equivalent, despite attempts by many scholars to discover underlying references to it in the text of Genesis 1:2 and other passages which speak of God's power over the waters.

An epic of early man

One Babylonian poem, the *Atrakhasis Epic,* bears further comparison with Genesis. This is concerned with the infancy of man and the beginning of society, and hints at the order of the world without describing its creation. It starts with the minor gods working to irrigate the land, then rebelling at their lot, from which they are relieved by the creation of man who is to do the work instead. Man is a satisfactory substitute until his noise causes disturbance and leads to his destruction in the flood (see Flood Stories).

In outline, *Atrakhasis* (known from copies made about 1600 BC) has some similarity to parts of Genesis 2-8. Man is made from clay and a divine part ('breath' in Genesis, the flesh and blood of a god in *Atrakhasis*): man's task is to keep the earth in order (arduous labour in *Atrakhasis,* control of a paradise in Genesis); man is eventually destroyed by flood, all except one family. On the other hand, *Atrakhasis* has man toiling from the first, has no single 'Adam', no separate making of woman, no Eden, and no Fall – in fact no moral teaching at all. The sense is rather that this is how man's lot came to be, and he should accept it.

A Sumerian version names five important cities in the time before the flood, and they link with separately preserved lists of pre-flood kings whose ages far exceeded those of the patriarchs in Genesis 5. Babylonian writers looked upon the flood as a major interruption in their country's history. In their over-all coverage, therefore Genesis and the tradition represented by *Atrakhasis* look back to the same events. Some of the themes in the Babylonian story – in particular, man's place as a substitute worker – can be traced in a Sumerian poem, *Enki and Ninmakh,* written before 2,000 BC. These factual similarities only serve to emphasize the wide difference in moral and spiritual outlook between the Hebrew Genesis and its closest counterparts. There is no need to argue that Genesis was derived from the others, as critics of the Bible have hastened to do. The differences of standpoint and content are in fact so marked that they serve to highlight the divine inspiration of Genesis rather than undermine it.

God creates man. (The Hebrew word translated 'Adam' means 'man'.) He plants a garden in Eden in the east, where man is to live. But man is not made for a solitary, self-sufficient existence. Neither birds nor animals provide the kind of companionship he needs. So God creates woman, a new being, yet sharing man's own essential nature.

The pattern of chapter 1 shows the principle of one day's rest in seven. The account of chapter 2 sets the pattern for human marriage.

The two trees: the phrase 'good and evil' may well be a Hebrew idiom standing for the full range of moral knowledge represented by the two extremes. To eat of the tree of the knowledge of good and evil will therefore make man like God. The tree of life, inaccessible to man once he had sinned, appears again in the last book of the Bible. It stands beside the river in the city of the new Jerusalem, where God and his people once more live together – and its leaves are for 'the healing of the nations' (Revelation 22:2). True life is ultimately dependent on the presence of God.

3 Man disobeys God

The serpent questions what God has said, then calls God a liar. The woman has to set the enticing fruit, the desire to have knowledge like God himself, against God's plain command. The decision is deliberate, and fatal. Man has disobeyed God, rejected his authority, chosen to go his own way and become a 'god' himself.

The result is inevitable. A holy God cannot live with sin. The serpent is sentenced first (verse 14 does not mean that he had legs before). The woman is to experience suffering – in childbirth, the most fundamental human process. She is to know what it means for her husband to 'rule' over her. From now on Adam's work is to be sweat and toil.

Because of sin, access to the tree of life is now denied them. They are to leave the garden, and there is no return. Spiritual death, being cut off from God, is immediate. Physical death follows in the course of time. God's warning was true. Yet he continues to care for them, and clothes them before they go.

4 THE FIRST FAMILY – AND THE FIRST MURDER

Adam and Eve, after their expulsion from the garden, have two sons: Cain, the farmer, and Abel, the shepherd. In due course each brings his offering to God. Abel's is accepted, but not Cain's. It was not *what* Abel offered, but his faith, which made his gift acceptable (Hebrews 11:4). Cain's bitter resentment shows a very different spirit.

Cain kills Abel – it is a short step from rebellion to bloodshed – and God condemns him to a nomadic life, but provides protection against death. Verses 17-24 list some of Cain's descendants, and show the beginnings of civilized life. Enoch builds the first city. His successors learn to play and enjoy music – also to forge iron and bronze. If good things flourish, so do evil. Lamech takes two wives, and boasts to them of the murder he has committed, outdoing Cain.

The last two verses give a glimmer of hope. Seth is born to Adam and Eve, and men begin 'to call upon the name of the Lord'.

Cain's wife: verse 17 and verses 14-15 give the impression of an earth already, to some extent, populated. The simplest way of accounting for this is to assume other, unnamed children of Adam and Eve. Others would argue from the fact that the word *adam* = man, or mankind, that a race was created, not a single pair. But however we resolve the problem we must never cut across the basic teaching of other scriptures, that one man's disobedience plunged the whole human race into sin, subjecting us all to death (see for example Romans 5:12ff.).

5 FROM ADAM TO NOAH

Family-trees (genealogies) similar to this one are often given in the Bible attesting a line of descent. Many of them are selective, sometimes in order to give a pattern of a certain number of names (e.g. Matthew 1). So we cannot work out the length of the whole period simply by adding up all the figures given.

The life-span of these men is remarkable. It ranges from 777 years for Lamech to Methuselah's 969 years (apart from Enoch, whom God 'took' at 365). Many races have traditions of exceptionally long life amongst their early forebears. But none of the various attempted explanations has so far proved satisfactory.

FLOOD STORIES

Alan Millard

Memories of a great flood or floods are worldwide. As one would expect, they have such common features as escape by boat, animals taken aboard, and grounding on a high peak. Only Babylonia has given us a story so close to Genesis that the question of borrowing or of direct influence is seriously considered.

For a century this story has been known from the *Epic of Gilgamesh*, Tablet 11. Its theme is that man cannot hope for immortality, the only one who gained it being the Babylonian Noah. It was taken into the Gilgamesh series from an older work the *Atrakhasis Epic* (see 'Other Creation Accounts'). Here it forms part of a longer account of man's history from his creation, as in Genesis.

Babylonian account

After the first men were made, it relates, the noise of their many children was so great that the god of the earth could not sleep. His schemes for reducing man's noise were thwarted when the pious Atrakhasis won the help of the god whose creature man was. Finally, the gods decided upon a catastrophic flood, all swearing to keep the plan secret. Again, Atrakhasis was warned, the god instructing him in a dream to build a boat, take on board his family and animals, and explain his action to his fellow men as a punishment inflicted upon him which would bring benefit to them. When all were aboard, the storm broke, and all mankind was swept away.

The gods themselves were also affected. With man destroyed, they lost the food and drink supplied in sacrificial offerings, and sat miserably in heaven until the seven days tempest had ended. Then Atrakhasis sent out birds to learn whether the land was habitable again (an episode preserved only in the *Gilgamesh* version), and offered sacrifice on the mountain where his boat had come to rest. Eagerly, the gods gathered 'like flies', smelling the savour of the offering, swearing not to cause such destruction again. The mother-goddess swore by a necklace of blue stones. But the god whose sleep had been disturbed was not yet appeased, and after the unfairness of indiscriminate punishment had been discussed, a system was set up in which some women avoided childbirth by entering religious orders, while others lost infants through disease, thus limiting the population. (The terms used make it clear that this was an explanation of the social system of the author's time.)

A question of theology

The flood story in Babylonia is also known from a Sumerian text telling virtually the same tale, though more briefly, and many Sumerian compositions refer to the distant days of the flood or before.

The Genesis flood story has a recognizable background in Mesopotamia, and the numerous similarities suggest it is a record of the same event as the Babylonian. But its moral and theological content are obviously very different. God's revelation consists not only in the telling of the facts but also in their interpretation.

Each of the ten records follows the same formula:

When A had lived x years he became the father of B. He lived after the birth of B y years and had other sons and daughters. Thus all his days were z years, and he died.

The sombre note of the final phrase 'and he died' is varied only in the case of Enoch, the man who 'walked with God'. For him God had other plans. Noah, the last of the ten, in his turn also 'walked with God' (6:9). And in his case, too, God intervened to save him from death.

6 - 9 THE GREAT FLOOD

6 - 9:17 The rescue, and God's promise to Noah

Flood-stories have been handed down in many languages from most parts of the world. The Babylonian (Sumerian, and particularly Akkadian) accounts have considerable similarity with the story recorded here. This is not surprising, if both reflect memories of an actual event in the same general area. There is no need to assume the writer of Genesis must have drawn on the Babylonian stories for his information. Indeed, the crudeness of these (with their many bickering, capricious gods) makes this unlikely.

Extent and date of the flood: if we take the terms used in Genesis 7:19ff. in their modern sense, the flood must have been universal. But biblical writers use similar phrases in contexts where it is clear they are not speaking of the whole world as we understand it (Genesis 41:56-57; Acts 2:5). Taking the description at the very least, the flood covered a vast area, the 'whole world' of man's early history as recounted in Genesis 2ff.

Its universality as far as human life is concerned depends on when it actually happened, and we can do no more than guess at the date. The list of nations descended from Noah's sons (Genesis 10) makes it clear that the flood must have occurred very early indeed. It was certainly long before the various South Mesopotamian floods of which traces have been found in the course of excavation.

The ark: the Hebrew word means 'box' or 'chest'. It is used elsewhere only for the watertight 'basket' in which the baby Moses floated on the Nile – an interesting parallel.

The ark is vast, designed to float, not sail – and there were no launching problems! An 18-inch cubit gives the measurements as 450 x 76 x 45 feet or 137 x 23 x 14 metres.

The covenant (6-18): an important and recurring theme in Scripture. God establishes his covenant (agreement) successively with Noah, with Abraham, with the nation of Israel (through Moses), and with David. Each covenant grows progressively richer in promise, until the coming of Christ ushers in the 'new covenant'.

In every instance God takes the initiative – this is no agreement between equal parties. God draws up the terms. He makes them known. And he alone guarantees their keeping. Men enjoy the blessings of the covenant in so far as they obey God's commands.

See article 'Covenants and Near Eastern Treaties'.

9:18-29 Noah's drunkenness

Even a completely fresh start does not change man – as this shameful little story makes plain. Ham dishonours his drunken father, and Noah curses him through his descendants. The Canaanites – descended from Ham through Canaan – did indeed become subject to Shem's descendants, the Israelites.

10 - 11 FROM NOAH TO THE CALL OF ABRA(HA)M

10 The families of Noah's three sons

The genealogy is arranged in the following pattern:

Heading (1)
Japheth's descendants (2-4)
Extra detail on Javan (5a)
Summary (5b)

Ham's descendants (6-7, 13-18a)
Extra detail on Nimrod (8-12)
and Canaan (18b-19)
Summary (20)

Shem's descendants (22-29a)
Extra detail on Shem (21)
and Joktan (29b-30)
Summary (31)
Summary to the whole list (32)

Shem's family comes last, as these are the nations around which the next stage of the narrative develops.

11:1-9 Babel

In Shinar, kingdom of Nimrod the hunter (10:10), men get together on a great building project – a city and a tower with its top in the heavens.

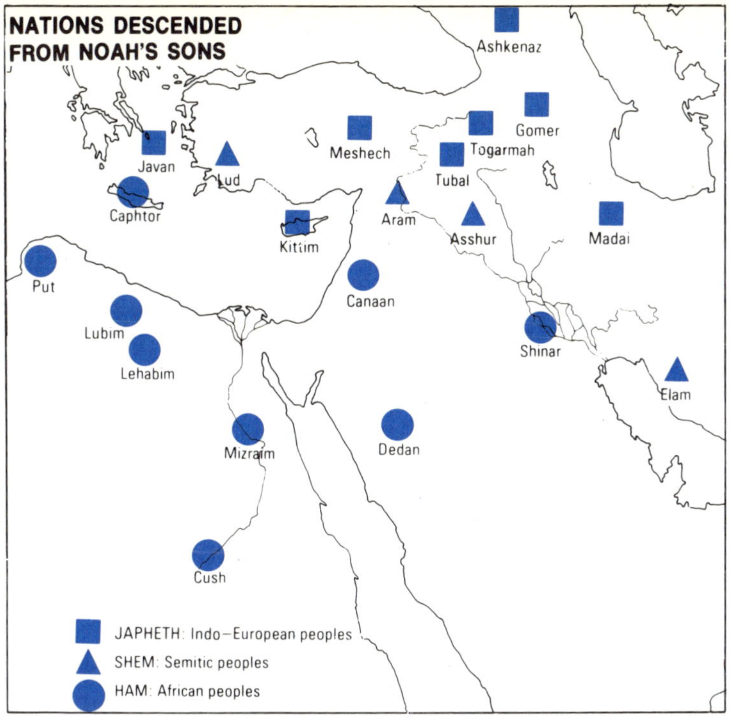

God looks down at this co-operative effort of man trying to make himself god-like, and sees it as the beginning of worse rebellion against him. So he divides men by language barriers, and scatters them abroad – the very thing they were trying to insure against. And the great tower remains unfinished.

The tower of Babel was in all likelihood a multi-storeyed temple-tower, or ziggurat, similar to those developed in Babylonia in the early 3rd millennium BC.

11:10-32 Shem to Abraham

Here again the list of names is selective, probably abbreviating the total length of time involved. Noah's ancestors were considerably longer-lived than Terah's, and the age of parenthood is now much younger.

The partially reconstructed ziggurat or temple-tower at Ur shows how the Tower of Babel may have been built, with stairways leading from one level to the next.

When Terah's name is reached the list becomes more detailed. This is the family we are to concentrate on. Terah's three sons are named, and their home-town given as Ur of the Chaldeans. After the death of Haran, Terah sets out for Canaan, with his grandson Lot and his son Abram and childless daughter-in-law Sarai. En route, however, they settle at Haran. Terah dies, and the stage is set for the story of Abraham (the new name records God's promise to make this man the father of many nations, 17:5).

12 - 25:18 ABRAHAM: A NEW START

12:1-9 God's call, and the journey to Canaan

12:1 records God's call and promise

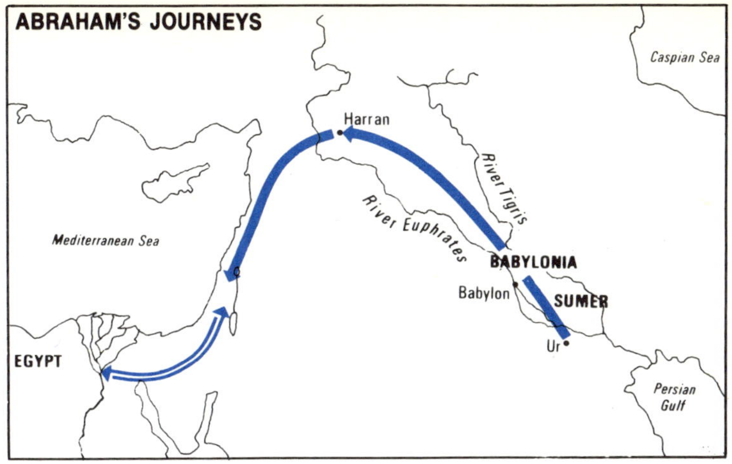

to one man, Abram, and his obedient response. Yet the consequences of this simple beginning were to spread like ripples on a pond. As a direct result a new nation is born. And in course of time the whole world reaps the benefits.

'So Abram went ... ' He had already left Ur, a prosperous city with security and a high standard of living. Now he sets out on the second stage of the journey, with Sarai, his childless wife, and his nephew Lot.

At Shechem, in the midst of Canaanite country, God speaks again. 'This land' is to be the heritage of Abram's descendants. Yet the journey continues, down towards the Negev, a dry region of some 4,500 sq. miles, stretching south from Beersheba to the Sinai highlands. Here there is pasturage for nomadic flocks and herds.

12:10-20 Famine

Hunger drives Abram into Egypt. Under stress of fear and insecurity he adopts a pretence which puts God's whole plan at risk. God intervenes with plagues, and Abram is ignominiously deported.

Sarai's age: it seems surprising to find Sarai, at 65, described as 'very beautiful' (12:14). Presumably, since it is said that she lived to 127, her sixties would be equivalent to our thirties or forties.

13 The parting with Lot

Increasing flocks and herds precipitate the last break in family ties. Lot, generously given the choice by his uncle, selects the fertile pasturage of the Jordan Valley.

14 War of the kings, and the meeting with Melchizedek

In Abram's day, although a semi-nomadic existence was common, there was also settled life in villages and walled 'cities'. These were ruled over by local 'sheiks', who in turn were often vassals of more powerful kings.

Chedorlaomer of Elam (1): the overlords of the Dead Sea towns came from distant Elam and Babylonia. Trade-routes made for easy travel and communications between the land of Abram's birth and Canaan. The Elamites had considerable power in Babylonia. Ur was amongst the cities they conquered and sacked at this time.

Amorites (7): Abram's allies belonged to a tribe sharing the land with the Canaanites. They had good reason to support Abram, since their own people had been victims of the attack. Speed of pursuit and a surprise attack gave Abram victory.

Melchizedek (18): this is the only appearance of the rather mysterious king/priest of Salem (probably Jerusalem). Melchizedek's authority (the 'tithe' was God's portion, so by giving Melchizedek a tenth of everything Abram recognized him as God's representative), his lack of any named ancestors and descendants (extremely important for any man claiming kingship or priesthood), and his dual role as priest and king, led later writers to see in him a fore-shadowing of the Messiah (see Psalm 110:4; Hebrews 7:1-10).

15 The covenant confirmed

Archaeology has shown that customs recorded here and in later chapters reflect the known social and cultural patterns of north Mesopotamia in the 2nd millennium BC.

The heir: it was not uncommon practice at the time for childless couples to adopt an heir, sometimes, as here, a slave. The adoption contract might contain a proviso that if a natural son was born he would take precedence as the legal heir.

Verse 6: 'And he believed the Lord; and he reckoned it to him as righteousness.' One of the most significant verses of Scripture, and in the circumstances a response of remarkable faith. Galatians 3:6ff. teaches that, as in Abram's case, our standing before God is entirely dependent on faith. We cannot win a place in heaven by good deeds – neither did he.

The covenant ritual: a typical procedure for the confirmation of a treaty (see Jeremiah 34:18). By killing and dividing the animals the parties to the treaty made it clear that the penalty for breaking the agreement was death. Here, significantly, it is only God who puts himself on oath by passing between the pieces. Darkness, smoke and fire mark the presence of God, as at Sinai (see Exodus 19:18; Hebrews 12:18).

Four hundred years (15:13) ... the fourth generation (15:16): the word 'generation' may also mean 'lifetime', and the lifetime of Abram was well over a century.

Verse 16b: New English Bible 'for the Amorites will not be ripe for punishment till then.' This helps us understand the orders to destroy the Canaanite nations at the conquest. It was a matter of justice. God gave them more than four centuries to show a change of heart. By Joshua's time they had reached the point of no return. As with Sodom and Gomorrah, judgement could no longer be delayed.

16 A son by a slave-girl

The childless Sarai falls back on custom in giving her slave-girl to Abram. This provision could be written into the marriage contract. The resulting child would become the wife's. But human emotions in such a situation are complex, and the unhappy sequel is not surprising.

17 New names and a covenant sign

God's fifth affirmation of his covenant with Abram is marked by the giving of new names – Abram becomes 'Abraham'; Sarai becomes 'Sarah' – and the physical sign of circumcision. Twenty-four years after the departure from Harran the time of the promised son's arrival is announced.

Circumcision: this was no new rite. In the nations around it marked admission to adult status in the tribe. But for Israel it was the outward sign of a relationship: God was to be their God; they were to be his people. It was a mark of ownership, and a reminder of the covenant 'between me and you and your descendants after you' (17:7). Some stress the medical grounds for the practice and the choice of the eighth day, despite the dangers.

18 Three visitors, and Abraham's prayer for Sodom

Abraham welcomed a stranger and, all unknowingly, took the Lord himself into his home. The lavish welcome and provision (despite the inconvenience of the visitors' arrival during the midday siesta) are typical of hospitality amongst nomadic desert people even today. The 'morsel of bread' offered to the guests turns out to be a meal of fresh cakes, curds and milk, and the best veal. The words 'Is anything too hard for the Lord?' reveal the visitor's true identity, and Sarah's incredulous laughter changes to fear.

Abraham's prayer gives an insight into the quality of his relationship with God. No wonder 2 Chronicles 20:7 describes him as God's 'friend' In the event, Sodom could not produce even ten good men, but we have seen something of the lengths to which God's mercy goes.

19 The destruction of Sodom and Gomorrah: Lot's rescue

The New English Bible makes the meaning of verse 5 plain. The 'knowledge' desired is through homosexual relations. Every man in the city is implicated – not one supports Lot's protest against the infringement of the most sacred laws of hospitality (not to say humanity).

The destruction: it is known from archaeology that the area was emptied of settled occupation after about 1900 BC. This catastrophe – probably caused by an earthquake and explosion of gases – may be the reason. The shallow southern waters of the Dead Sea now cover the cities. Nothing could save the cities from God's judgement, yet for Lot's sake he spares Zoar and delays the cataclysm till Lot is safe. 'I can do nothing until you are there' (19:22). Even so Lot's wife drags behind, stopping to look, and dies. Local tradition calls salty crags by the Dead Sea after her still.

Moab and Ammon (37-38): both tribes were to prove a constant snare to Israel (see Numbers 25, and the frequent denunciations of the prophets).

20 Abraham and King Abimelech

A repetition of the same sin under similarly testing circumstances does not make this a duplicate of 12:10-20. Abraham is not the only man to be put to shame twice before those he considered to have 'no fear of God' to guide their actions. (On Abimelech, see 26:1.)

21:1-21 Isaac is born: Hagar and Ishmael leave

Twenty-five years have elapsed between the promise and its fulfilment. Isaac's elderly parents have reason to be overjoyed at his birth. Sarah's demand that Hagar and Ishmael should be sent away ran counter to custom. Abraham needs a word from God before he is willing to agree. Galatians 4:22ff. shows why the rift was inevitable.

The child (14): Ishmael was by now in fact about 16. Isaac would have been two or three years old by the time he was weaned.

21:22-34 A dispute over wells

Wells were precious to the herdsmen in the dry climate of southern Palestine, and disputes about ownership not infrequent (see 26:17ff.). Monthly rainfall in the area drops from 4 inches/100mm in January to nothing at all in the four summer months.

22 The supreme test

Abraham's previous experience of God would certainly not have led him to suppose child-sacrifice would please him. Nor was this general practice in Abraham's time. In addition, God had specifically promised descendants through Isaac, and he was not yet married. It can only be, as Hebrews 11:19 says, that such was Abraham's faith in God's word, he believed him able to raise the boy to life again. This is implied in Abraham's 'we will come back to you' (verse 5). The parallel between Abraham's sacrifice and the greater sacrifice of God's own Son is striking – yet the lesson Hebrews draws from this chapter is one of faith.

The land of Moriah (2): Abraham's offering took place on one of the hills on which Jerusalem now stands (possibly the temple hill itself – see 2 Chronicles 3:1). The journey of about 50 miles took him three days.

23 The death and burial of Sarah

These Hittites may have been early migrants from the Hittite Empire in

This statue of a ram standing upright beside a tree comes from Ur, 2500 BC.

Turkey (founded about 1800 BC). The whole transaction conforms in detail to known Hittite law (the mention of the trees, the weighing of the silver by current standards, and the proclamation in the presence of witnesses at the city gate). Family-tombs, often caves or cut from rock, were also customary. The traditional site of the burial-cave at Hebron is today covered by a mosque.

24 A wife for Isaac

This is one of the loveliest and most beautifully told stories in the Old Testament. It reflects the traditional Eastern arranged marriage. The steward's gifts in verse 53 seal the betrothal. It is a fitting conclusion that God, who has so clearly guided at every stage, should set his seal on the marriage in the deep love of Isaac for Rebekah.

25:1-11 Abraham's last days

Keturah's sons became the ancestors of a number of north Arabian peoples. Isaac remained his father's sole heir, and on Abraham's death the blessing of God became his.

25:12-18 Ishmael's descendants

'Havilah to Shur' – the tribes occupied Sinai and north-west Arabia.

25:19 - 26:35 ISAAC'S UNHAPPY HOUSEHOLD

Once again the line is continued by the direct action of God. After 20 years' waiting Esau and Jacob are born.

The birthright (25:31): as firstborn son Esau would succeed Isaac as head of the family, and inherit a double share of the estate. When he sells his birthright he forfeits all title to the blessing which goes with it.

There is no commendation of Jacob's cool calculation – but Scripture openly censures Esau's attitude. He was 'worldly minded' (Hebrews 12:16-17) – 'he sold his birthright for a single meal'. 'Thus Esau showed how little he valued his birthright' (25:34, New English Bible).

Abimelech, the Philistine king (26:1): the name is probably a family or throne-name. this is therefore likely to have been a later king than the one Abraham encountered (20-21). The Philistines (one of the trading Sea Peoples, many of whom settled the east Mediterranean coastlands), who gave their name to Palestine, invaded the area in force in the 12th century BC. The group met by the patriarchs would have been amongst earlier settlements of Aegean traders.

27 - 35 DECEIT AND SHARP PRACTICE: JACOB'S EXILE AND RETURN

27 The blessing

Not one of the family comes out well in this story. Isaac's plan goes against what God revealed before the boys were born (25:23). Esau, in agreeing to the plan, is breaking his oath (25:33). Jacob and Rebekah, although in the right, make no reference to God, but cheat and lie to achieve their ends.

Isaac relies completely on his senses, each of which lets him down – even the sense of taste on which he prided himself. When his ears tell him the truth, he will not listen. The blessing is Jacob's, as God always intended – but at a heavy price. Esau is ready to do murder. The relationship between Isaac and Rebekah is spoilt. And Rebekah will never again see her favourite son. Jacob, the home-lover, goes into exile.

28 The fugitive

Isaac's parting blessing recognizes Jacob as heir to God's promise.

Paddan-aram, or Aram-naharaim, 'land of the two rivers' (**2**): Rebekah's homeland, Paddan-aram, lay between the upper Euphrates and Habur rivers. The Aramaeans later penetrated south and east, settling in Syria and Mesopotamia.

Bethel, 'house of God' (**19**): Jacob reaches Bethel, 60 miles north of Beersheba, as darkness falls. In this desolate spot, at a moment of unutterable loneliness, God stands beside Jacob. He repeats to this unpromising man the promise made to Abraham and Isaac. And he adds his personal guarantee of company and protection, with the assurance of eventual safe return.

The 'ladder' is in fact a stairway (perhaps like that of the ziggurat), since angels are going up and down it (compare Jesus' words to Nathanael in John 1:51).

The 'pillar' – not very large – consecrated by the oil is set up to commemorate the vision.

29 - 31 The years with Laban: Jacob meets his match

These three chapters cover the 20 years of Jacob's exile: 14 years' service for his two wives, 6 for flocks of his own. The years hold little joy for Jacob, who meets a crooked dealer after his own kind in his uncle Laban. The deceit over Leah leads to an intolerable home life. The unloved wife hopes with each new son to win her husband's affection. Rachel, lovely and loved, is embittered by continuing childlessness. And Jacob finds himself traded between the two. Small wonder the law later forbade a man to marry his wife's sister during the wife's lifetime.

29:14: 'Surely you are my bone and my flesh!' The implication may be that Laban is adopting Jacob as his son – particularly as no son of his own is mentioned at this time. Marriage to a sister by adoption was quite customary.

29:18: Jacob offers service in place of the usual marriage gift. Laban is not slow to exploit the generosity of the offer. The gift of a slave-girl to his daughter (verse 24) may have been part of the dowry.

29:26: the custom Laban refers to is not otherwise known.

29:28: after the week's festivities Rachel was given to Jacob, on condition he served another seven years for her.

30:3: this reflects the same custom as Sarah observed (16:1-2).

30:14: mandrakes were thought to induce fertility – which makes Leah's subsequent pregnancy ironic.

30:37ff.: Jacob thought the sight of the rods during gestation would affect the unborn lambs. In fact he owed his flocks to the overruling of God, and to the practice of selective breeding which the dream revealed.

31:14: Leah and Rachel were entitled to part of the wealth their marriage-gifts brought Laban.

31:19: Rachel acted, so she thought, in Jacob's interest. The possession of household gods would support the legality of his claim to an inheritance.

31:44: the non-aggression pact made by Laban and Jacob has many contemporary parallels. The covenant meal seals it.

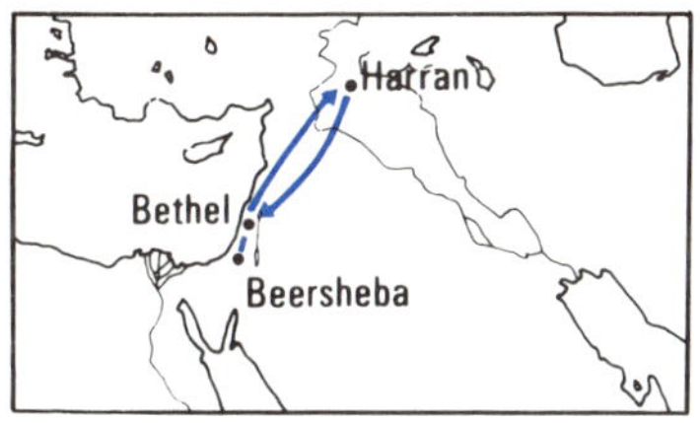

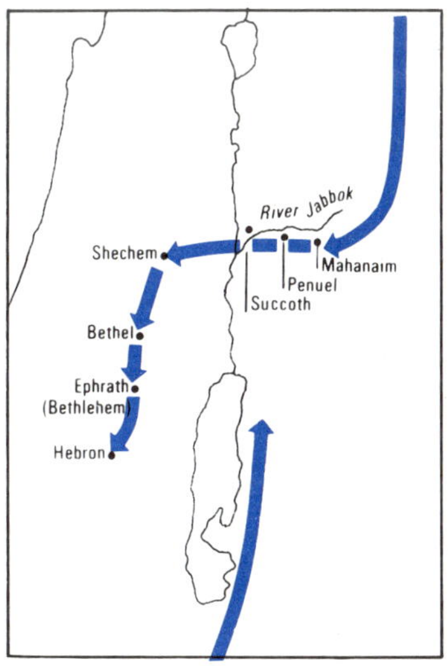

JACOB'S JOURNEY AND RETURN

32 God meets Jacob

Although Esau has settled in Seir in the far south, the meeting between the two brothers is inevitable. The news that Esau is coming at speed, and with a force, strikes terror into Jacob. This time, though, he plans *and* prays.

Alone, and sleepless, Jacob's lifetime struggle against God culminates in this strange wrestling-bout. At the end of it, Jacob is crippled, but a new man. The next altar he erects will be, not to the God of his fathers, but to 'God, the God of Israel' ('El Elohe Israel', 33:20).

33 Jacob meets Esau

Esau's welcome to the brother who had wronged him is so amazingly generous that Jesus may have had him in mind when he told the story of the prodigal son (see Luke 15:20). Jacob's gift, and Esau's acceptance of it, seal the reconciliation.

Verse 14: Jacob has no intention of going to Seir, as the next stage of the journey shows. Even now he cannot be straight-forward about it.

34 Dinah and Shechem: rape and massacre

The city of Shechem has a long and important history. Jacob's stay there cost him dear – and the treacherous vengeance of Simeon and Levi was not forgotten (see 49:5ff.).

35 The return to Bethel: Benjamin is born: Rachel and Isaac die

This chapter rounds off the section of Genesis centring on Jacob. Foreign gods are put aside. God reaffirms his covenant with Israel. Rachel dies near Bethlehem (Ephrath) giving birth to the last of Jacob's 12 sons. Esau and Jacob come face to face again at the death of the aged Isaac.

36 ESAU AND HIS DESCENDANTS

Once again, before starting a new stage in the story, we catch up on the other branch of the family.

Seir/Edom (8): the valley between the Dead Sea and the Red Sea (Gulf of Aqaba) and the mountainous area on either side. The king's highway, an important trade route, ran down the eastern plateau. In later days there was little love lost between Edom and Israel.

37 - 50 JOSEPH, THE FAMINE AND THE MIGRATION TO EGYPT

37 Joseph sold into Egypt

The final section of Genesis, centring on Joseph, now begins.

Joseph's special robe (3): Joseph's brothers saw this as a sign that Isaac intended to pass them by and make Joseph his heir (see 48:21-22 and 49:22ff.).
Verse 24: the pit, here mercifully dry, was intended for water storage.
Ishmaelite and Midianite merchants (28): both these groups of desert-dwellers were descended from Abraham. The names are interchangeable (compare verses 28 and 36; Judges 8:24). The use of alternative names is a characteristic feature of Near Eastern writing. The 'balm' of Gilead (an area roughly east of the Jordan and north of the Jabbok) was famous, and the spice-trade an important one from earliest times. Spices had many uses – in food preparation and the manufacture of incense and cosmetics. The trade-route from Damascus to the coast ran past Dothan.
Verse 28: despite the way the verse reads, and the New English Bible's interpretation, verse 27 and 45:4 make it far more likely that Joseph was sold by his brothers. Reuben's absence is not improbable – there were flocks to be seen to. Neither this, nor the matter of Ishmaelite and Midianite merchants, makes it necessary to see the story as a combination of two different traditions.
Officer (36): the word is usually translated 'eunuch', as in the New English Bible, but it may also have the more general meaning of 'court official', which is more likely here in view of Potiphar's marriage.

38 Judah's sons

This none-too-creditable story is probably included because it forms part of the family-tree of the (later) royal house, from which the Messiah himself was descended (Matthew 1:3; Luke 3:33).
Verses 8-10: if a man died childless, his brother was duty bound to raise heirs to him by his widow (set out as the Levirate law, Deuteronomy 25:5).

39 Joseph accused and imprisoned

The account of Joseph's life in Egypt given in chapters 39-50 fits perfectly into the background of Egypt under the Semitic Hyksos pharaohs. They ruled from about 1710-1570 BC, from a capital (Avaris) in the eastern part of the Nile delta. Goshen was also somewhere in this region.

The Egyptian *Tale of Two Brothers* narrates similar incidents to those in this chapter – underlining the unfortunate fact that such things do happen.

40 The dreams of the butler and baker

The story brings out the significance of dreams and their interpretation at this time. Egyptian sages had dream-manuals to help them make their interpretation. Joseph, by contrast, depends completely on God to make the meaning clear.
The butler (1): Pharaoh's cup-bearer, an important official (compare Nehemiah 2:1).

41 Pharaoh's dream and Joseph's promotion

Two years later Pharaoh himself has a dream which defeats his magicians and wise men, despite all their training and a whole library of reference books. When the cup-bearer at last remembers Joseph, he not only proves able to explain God's message, but comes up with a clear-cut plan of action.
Verse 14: Egyptian custom dictates that Joseph must be shaven and dressed in linen for an appearance at court.
Verses 40-43: Joseph's investiture follows Egyptian tradition – the ring (his badge of authority), fine linen (court dress) and a gold chain or collar in reward for his services. Horses and chariots had helped the Hyksos pharaohs to gain ascendancy in Egypt. After 13 years as a slave, Joseph becomes Pharaoh's vizier.
Verse 45: On (Heliopolis, 10 miles north-east of Cairo) was the centre of Egyptian sun-worship.
Verse 54: severe famine was not unknown in Egypt. But it was rare for famine to hit Egypt and Palestine simultaneously.

Statuette of an Egyptian high official from the time of Joseph.

42 - 45 Famine, and family reunion

These chapters give a moving account of Joseph's meeting, testing and eventual reunion with his brothers. Behind his apparent harshness lies complete and generous forgiveness of the wrong done him, and a deep understanding of the way God controls human destiny (45:5ff.). Under each new stress the brothers show a genuine change of attitude from the old days. Twenty years have not obliterated their sense of guilt (42:21-22). They will not behave towards the new favourite (Benjamin) as they did towards the old.
43:32: the Egyptians probably considered that the presence of foreigners at the table defiled their food. For the same reason, later, Jews would not eat with Gentiles.
44:2, 5: Joseph may have used his silver cup for divination (interpreting events by the movement of drops of oil on water). Or the steward may be implying the impossibility of escaping detection by his wise and powerful master.
45:10: in times of famine nomads from Palestine are known to have been allowed pasturage in the eastern delta.

46 - 47 Israel settles in Egypt

Jacob's household numbers 70 on entry to Egypt (the 66 of 46:26 excludes Jacob, and Joseph and his two sons were there already). With all the wives and servants the company would be much larger.
46:34: the Egyptian dislike of the nomadic shepherds is probably no different from the feelings of most settled people towards wandering gypsies. Here the dislike serves a useful purpose in keeping the family as an isolated unit. Otherwise the group's identity might quickly have been lost.
47:16-19: Under Joseph's economic policy Pharaoh gains ownership of the land, and the people become his tenants. Only the priests keep their estate.

48 - 49 Jacob's blessing

The blessing of Joseph's sons was an act of faith (Hebrews 11:21). How simply Jacob's hands cross over to convey God's blessing to the younger son. What a contrast to the story in chapter 27. Joseph enjoys a double inheritance through Ephraim and Manasseh.

Jacob's dying blessing focusses on the distant future, when the descendants of these twelve will occupy the promised land.
Verse 4: the outrage recorded in 35:22 costs Reuben his birthright as first-born son.
Verses 5-7: Jacob's judgement of Simeon's and Levi's conduct at Shechem (34:13ff.) is clear. Both tribes were to be scattered, but Levi's as the nation's priesthood.
Verse 10: from Judah came the royal line of Israel, from which the Messiah would eventually be born.
Verse 13: although near enough to acquire wealth from maritime trade, Zebulun's territory did not stretch to the sea.
Verse 19: such raids are recorded on the 9th-century Moabite Stone.

Measuring grain for taxation purposes; from the Tomb of Menna, west Thebes, about 1400 BC.

50 The death of Jacob to the death of Joseph – the end of the beginning

Jacob joins Leah in the family tomb at Hebron – the last member of the family to be buried in Canaan for more than 400 years. The huge canvas of Genesis, begun with the great strokes of creation and pulsating life in Eden, continued through destruction, promise, and the birth of a new nation in Canaan, is finished with the death of Joseph in Egypt.
Verses 2-3: it was normal to employ professional embalmers – but perhaps Joseph wanted to avoid religious entanglements. Two centuries later the normal embalming period was 70 days. The mourning observed for Jacob was only two days shorter than that for a pharaoh.
Verse 22: Joseph's life-span of 110 years was the Egyptian ideal, a token of God's blessing. His dying request sums up the faith of a lifetime.
Verse 26: the coffin would be of wood, with a painted head.

Old Testament 1.2

EXODUS

The book of Exodus is the story of the birth of Israel as a nation. It is an epic dominated by the central figure of Moses. It was he who led the people out from Egypt, the 'exodus' which gives the book its name. Through him God gave the law. The book falls into two main parts:

1. Israel's escape from slavery in Egypt (chapters 1-19).
2. The giving of the law and construction of the tabernacle at Sinai (chapters 20-40).

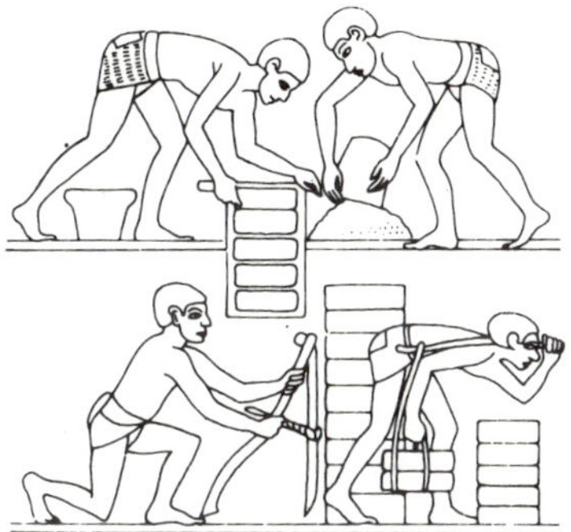

An ancient Egyptian tomb-painting shows the process of making bricks and building.

1 - 12:36 ISRAEL IN EGYPT; MOSES, GOD'S LIBERATOR

1 The scene is set

Nearly 300 years have elapsed since the death of Joseph, and the end of Genesis. Jacob's people have been in Egypt some 370 years. Their old privileged status is gone. Now they are a slave nation under a new pharaoh, of a dynasty which has long forgotten Egypt's debt to Joseph (see Genesis 41).

Things have changed in Egypt. The power of the Hyksos pharaohs has been broken and the Upper and Lower kingdoms once again united. The nation is at the height of her military power, ruled from Thebes and Memphis by a new dynasty of pharaohs. But with the accession of Sethos I (probably the 'new king' of 1:8) attention once again focusses on the fertile delta region. A great building programme is begun, including a new residence for Pharaoh. It is named after Sethos' successor, Rameses II (who was mainly responsible for building it), 'the House of Ramesses', 'Raamses' (1:11). And there is a large, ready-made, economic labour-force resident in the area – the Israelites.

The existence of such a large (see 12:37) alien group in his borderlands has for some time made Pharaoh uneasy. Here is his chance to ensure they keep out of mischief. The people are organized into gangs, under taskmasters, to dig out mud and make the bricks for building the new cities.

But no matter how hard they are worked the population explosion continues. Pharaoh decides to tackle the problem in more direct ways (15-22), only to be defeated by the midwives' faith.

2 Moses, prince and refugee

So now all Hebrew boy-babies are to be cast into the Nile. That is Pharaoh's decree. But the water which drowns can also be used to float a watertight basket (the same Hebrew word as Noah's 'ark') – and Moses' life is saved by his mother's resourceful action.

Moses was 40 when he tried to strike his first blow for freedom (2:11-12), which ended in disaster. A further 40 years passed before the events of chapter 3 (Acts 7:23 and Exodus 7:7).

Pharaoh's daughter would probably be a daughter by one of his concubines, not a princess of blood-royal. She would have taken Moses back to the harem where he would be brought up with others, learning to read and write the Egyptian hieroglyphic and 'cursive' scripts and gaining expertise in various skills and sports (see Acts 7:22). It was not unknown for foreigners to be brought up in this way, and trained for responsible posts in the army, priesthood or civil service.

Midian (15): the Midianites were descendants of Abraham through his second wife, Keturah. They were desert-dwellers, so Moses could scarcely have had better preparation for the wilderness journeys with Israel than these years of nomadic life.

3 - 4 The burning bush: God calls and equips his man

Moses is actually at Sinai (Horeb), the very place where he will later receive the law, when God's call comes. God has a stupendous commission for Moses – he is to be God's messenger to Pharaoh, and lead his people to freedom – but the missionary is most reluctant. He raises one objection after another, and each is countered by God:

— **3:11:** 'I am not up to the job.' But 'I will be with you', says God.
— **3:13:** 'How am I to explain to people who you are?' God reveals himself as the God of their ancestors, and God of the present: 'I am.'
— **4:1:** 'The people won't believe me.' God gives him three signs with which to convince them.
— **4:10:** 'I am no speaker.' God made him; he will enable him to speak.
— **4:13:** 'Please send someone else.' This God will not do, but he will allow him Aaron as spokesman.

Mt Horeb (3:1): the precise location is uncertain, but long tradition identifies it with Jebel Musa (7,363 feet) at the southern tip of the Sinai peninsula.

The spoil from Egypt (3:21f.): see 11:2-3; 12:35-36. It was from this that the tabernacle was furnished (35:20ff.).

4:19: Pharaoh's death was recorded in 2:23.

Aaron (4:14): three years older than Moses (7:7), presumably born before Pharaoh's edict. Miriam would have been older than both.

Circumcision (4:24-26): Moses failed to circumcise his son – and God cannot overlook disobedience, even in one he has chosen. Zipporah puts the matter right and Moses' life is spared.

5 - 6:13 The first round goes to Pharaoh

The first request to Pharaoh merely aggravates the situation. The people turn against their 'deliverer'. Moses in his frustration turns once again to God.

The request (5:1): this seems less than the whole truth; but it is in the nature of a test-case. Israel had to leave Egypt in order to sacrifice because the nature of their sacrifice was offensive to the Egyptians (8:26). Pharaoh's reaction reveals his implacable hostility, already predicted by God (3:19).

Access to Pharaoh: Ramesses II is known to have made himself available even to ordinary petitioners (compare 5:15ff.). Moses, brought up in the harem, had a special claim to Pharaoh's attention.

A man of uncircumcised lips (6:12): New English Bible 'a halting speaker'.

6:14-27 The family-tree of Moses and Aaron

As so often in Scripture, the list is selective. Moses and Aaron are shown to have descended from Jacob through the line of Levi. The list covers the period of Israel's stay in Egypt.

6:28 - 10:29 The contest with Pharaoh: the nine plagues

Pharaoh has heard and rejected Moses' request. He has shown the sort of man he is: 'Who is the Lord ...? I do not know the Lord, and moreover I will not let Israel go' (5:2).

Now God begins a series of judgements to teach Pharaoh and his people who the Lord is, and to show them the extent of his power over all creation (7:5, 17; 8:10, 22; 9:14). Nine times God acts, and Pharaoh, his magicians and all the gods of Egypt are powerless to reverse his judgements. The magicians may counterfeit, but they cannot countermand.

1. The Nile – heart of the nation's economy and worship – turns to blood, its polluted waters killing the fish (7:14-24).

2. Seven days later, frogs, driven from the river banks by the rotting fish, seek shelter in the houses (7:25 - 8:15).

3 and 4. First gnats and then flies, breeding amongst the carcases of fish and frogs, plague the land (8:16-32).

5 and 6. Disease strikes the cattle,

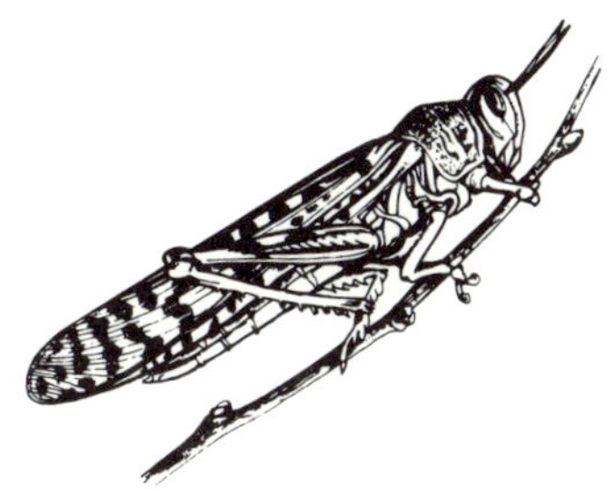

The eighth plague was a swarm of locusts.

THE NAMES OF GOD

J. A. Motyer

THE WORDS AND THE NAME

Two Hebrew words are translated 'God':

El 'The Deity', God in the power and distinctiveness of his divine nature.

Elohim Plural in form signifying not 'gods' but the One who completely possesses all the divine attributes.

There is also a third word used for God:

Adon Describes God as 'Sovereign' or 'Lord', pointing to his divine authority and executive rule.

In distinction from these nouns, there is also the personal name Yahweh. To avoid using this divine name itself (out of supposed reverence) a word meaning 'Lord' was substituted in public reading. English Bibles unfortunately perpetuate the same scruple, representing Yahweh by 'Lord', or, when it is used in connection with Adonai (a form of Adon), as 'Lord God'. Much is lost in Bible reading if we forget to look beyond the substitute word to the personal, intimate name of God himself.

By telling his people his name, God intended to reveal to them his inmost character. As a word, Yahweh is related to the Hebrew verb 'to be'. This verb goes beyond 'to exist'; it means rather 'to be actively present'. Yahweh (Exodus 3:13-16) is the God actively present with his people – but the moment he chose to make this known was when they, as doomed slaves, needed to be redeemed.

In other words, the idea of 'active presence' tells us that God is with us but not what sort of God he is. In choosing the time of the exodus to reveal the meaning of his name, he identifies himself as the God who saves his people and overthrows his adversaries.

The holiness of God lies at the root of his self-revelation as Yahweh (Exodus 3:5). This works out in the holy redemption and holy wrath of the Passover (Exodus 12).

The Old Testament's understanding of the character which the name reveals is well seen in passages such as Exodus 34:6ff.; Psalms 103; 111; 146; Micah 7:18-19.

THE PROGRESS OF REVELATION

The name Yahweh appears in the Bible from the earliest times (Genesis 4:1) and in such ways as to imply that men both knew and used it (e.g. Genesis 4:26; 14:22). How then can God say to Moses (Exodus 6:2-3) that 'by my name the Lord I did not make myself known to them' (i.e. to Abraham, etc.)?

Specialist Old Testament study has long answered this question by saying that we have differing traditions of the early history of the people of God: one tradition in which the divine name was known from the earliest times, and another – contradictory – tradition that it was first revealed to Moses.

Influential as this theory has proved, it is neither inescapable nor necessary. 'To know' in the Old Testament goes beyond the mere possession of information, to the active enjoyment of fellowship with the person known. For instance, the sons of Eli certainly knew the name as a divine 'label' but they 'had no regard for (literally, 'did not know') the Lord' (1 Samuel 2:12; compare 3:7; Exodus 33:12-13). So Exodus 6:2-3 is telling us that what had hitherto possessed only the significance of a 'label', a way of addressing God, now became significant as a statement of the character possessed by the God who was so named – that he is the holy Redeemer and Judge, ever present with his people.

This view of the meaning of Exodus 6:2-3 is borne out by the evidence of Genesis. If Abraham had been asked 'Who is Yahweh?' he would undoubtedly have replied 'God Almighty' or one of the other titles of God used by the patriarchs:

El Shadday: Shadday probably means 'mountain', used symbolically of changelessness and enduring strength, contrasted to the helplessness of man. See for instance Genesis 17:1f.; 28:3f.; 35:11; 43:14; 48:3; 49:25.

El Elyon: 'God Most High', Genesis 14:18.

El Roi: 'God of Seeing', Genesis 16:13.

El Olam: 'The Everlasting God', Genesis 21:33.

El Bethel: 'God of Bethel', Genesis 31:13.

El Elohe Yisrael: 'God, the God of Israel', Genesis 33:20.

So when Yahweh is said to be 'the God of your fathers' in Exodus 3 (verses 6, 13, 15, 16), all this richness of meaning is added to the revelation of the holy Redeemer.

'WHO IS A GOD LIKE THEE?'

God in himself

Some attributes of God so express the heart of his divine nature that they are used as titles:

The Holy One: The most centrally important title of all: see Joshua 24:19; Isaiah 5:16; 10:17; Habakkuk 1:12.

The Holy One of Israel: A variation used especially by Isaiah, e.g. Isaiah 1:4.

The God 'whose name is jealous': shows his passionate love for his people: see Exodus 34:14.

The Lord of Hosts: is often repeated and points to the 'hosts' of potentialities and powers in the divine nature, conveying something very much like 'omnipotent'. See, for instance, Jeremiah 32:18b-23.

Furthermore, he is the *true, living* (Jeremiah 10:10) *high* (Micah 6:6) and *rewarding* (Jeremiah 51:56) God.

God of all the world

Such a God cannot be confined to one people. He is:

Creator: Isaiah 40:28.
Judge: Genesis 18:25.
King: Jeremiah 10:7.
God of all flesh: Numbers 16:22; Jeremiah 32:27.

The God of Israel

He is the God who specially reveals himself to one people:

The Angel of the Lord: Without diminishing his deity, he accommodates himself to speak to man: Genesis 16:7f.; Judges 13:16f., etc.

The God of the Hebrews: Exodus 5:3.

The God of Israel: Joshua 24:2.

He is also, as if to stress the grace and condescension involved, **the God of Jacob:** (Psalm 81:4), in holiness (Isaiah 1:4) and power (Psalm 132:2).

The God of the individual

Within his chosen people, he is the God of the individual: 'my beloved' (Isaiah 5:1), 'the God of my salvation' (Psalm 18:46). The richness of personal awareness of God in the Old Testament is hardly better seen than through the wealth of metaphors for the God who was known and loved in daily life:

Rock: A title stemming from Exodus 17:1-7. See especially Deuteronomy 32.
Shepherd: Psalm 23:1.
Shield, stronghold: Psalm 18:2.
Light: Psalm 27:1.
Strength: Psalm 28:7.
Refuge: Psalm 37:39.
Sun: Psalm 84:11.
Father: Psalm 89:26; Isaiah 63:16.
Mother-bird: Psalm 91:4; compare Isaiah 31:5.
Help: Psalm 115:9.
Shade: Psalm 121:5.
Portion: Psalm 142:5.
Song: Isaiah 12:2.
Redeemer: Isaiah 41:14.
Warrior: Isaiah 42:13.
Potter: Isaiah 45:9.
Husband: Isaiah 54:5.
Fountain: Jeremiah 2:13.
Dew: Hosea 14:5.
Lion, leopard, bear: Hosea 13:7-8.

and skin infection breaks out on man and beast, carried by the frogs and insects (9:1-12).
7. Hail and thunderstorms ruin the flax and barley crops – but not wheat and spelt, which have not yet grown. And those Egyptians who take note of God's warning remain safe (9:13-35).
8. The wind blows in a plague of locusts from Ethiopia which strip the country bare of greenstuff (10:1-20).
9. For three days the light of the sun is blotted out by 'thick darkness' (probably a khamsin duststorm) (10:21-29).

The plagues probably occurred over a period of about a year. In each case God chose to use natural disorders to confound Pharaoh and the gods of Egypt (12:12). He caused the 'Nile-god' to bring ruin, not prosperity; the frogs to bring disease instead of fruitfulness; and the power of Re, the sun-god, was blotted out. The whole sequence of events follows a logical pattern which could have started with unusually high flooding of the Nile, bringing down red earth and microcosms which polluted the water. But however it happened, this was no mere 'chance' – God was demonstrating his absolute control. He distinguished between his people and the Egyptians. He controlled the extent and the areas affected by each plague. He announced the timing of each, and could call a halt at any time in answer to prayer.
The hardness of Pharaoh's heart: several times in these chapters God is said to have hardened Pharaoh's heart and made him obstinate (4:21; 10:1, 20, 27). But this was not done against Pharaoh's will. Rather, where God *could* have softened Pharaoh's heart (as he did Paul's) he simply let him be. God gave him up (see Romans 1; 9:17) – let him be what he himself wanted, let him have his own way – so that in the end God's power would be plain for all to see.

Pharaoh Ramesses II.

11 - 12:36 The death of the firstborn, and the Passover

Preliminaries are over: God's warning of 4:22-23 is about to be realized. This is the end of the road for Pharaoh and his people. But for Israel it is the beginning. This is a day to remember down the ages: when God dealt death to the first-born of Egypt, but spared and freed his own people. A new feast is instituted, and a new (religious) year begun. The Passover lamb or kid speaks of God's protection and provision for his people – Israel is his firstborn. The bitter herbs remind them of all their suffering in Egypt. The flat unleavened bread recalls the haste of their departure (no time to use yeast and wait for the bread to rise). Even so, they do not go empty-handed. The years of slavery are in some measure paid for by the clothes and jewellery heaped upon them by the Egyptians, now only too anxious to see them go.

12:37 - 19:25 OUT OF EGYPT: ON TO SINAI

12:37 - 13:21 The journey begins; instructions about the Passover, Unleavened Bread and the firstborn

Just as God foretold (Genesis 15:13-14), after four centuries in a foreign land (from the 18th century BC to about 1300 or 1290 BC) Israel is free. The journey to the border begins. But first there are further instructions about how the Passover is to be celebrated, who may join in, and where it is to take place. The events are to be further commemorated in two ways:

— For a seven-day period after Passover the people are to eat unleavened bread as a reminder of the hasty departure from Egypt.
— As Israel's freedom has been purchased by the death of the firstborn of Egypt, the nation's firstborn belong in a special sense to God and are to be 'bought back' from him.

600,000 men (12:37): counting the women and children this would amount to a total of some two million people – a high (though not necessarily impossible) figure which presents some problems. Subsequent chapters make it plain that their number was certainly too great for the wilderness to support – hence God's special provision of manna. They were also at times short of water, although they no doubt learnt to manage on very little, and their encampments would have been spread out to take advantage of several watercourses at each halt in the journey.
Joseph's bones (13:19): see Genesis 50:24-25.

14 Pursuit and disaster

Hemmed in between sea and mountains, with water before them and Pharaoh's forces at their backs, the people of Israel meet their first big test of faith – and they panic. As God drives back the waters so that they can cross in safety, and as he sends the wall of water rushing down upon Pharaoh's forces, Israel learns the truth of Moses' words: 'The Lord will fight for you, and you have only to be still' (14:14).

15:1-21 Moses' triumph-song

If ever a victory deserves to be recorded for posterity this one does. Moses leads the people in a great paean of triumph: God has saved Israel; he has destroyed their enemy. Miriam and all the women take up the refrain, and dance for joy. The song is a fine example of ancient Semitic poetry (see 'Poetry and Wisdom Literature', introduction).

15:22 - 17:7 The grumbling begins, but God provides

It is not long before the complaints start. There were plenty of fish to eat in Egypt, and fruit and vegetables – and no shortage of water. But in the desert the people are soon thirsty and hungry – and mutinous. God's method of provision is designed to teach them obedience, and daily dependence upon him.
Quails (16:13): twice a year the common quail's migration route takes it across the region where the Israelites were at this time. Exhausted by the journey, the birds were easy to catch.
Omer (16:16): a bowl holding about 4 pints/$2\frac{1}{4}$ litres.
Manna (16:31): various natural phenomena have been identified with the description given here, but none fits exactly. This substance was Israel's staple food for 40 years, ceasing abruptly when they entered Canaan.
Water from the rock (17:6): Sinai limestone is known to retain moisture. This incident, and the names Massah and Meribah, became a byword for rebelliousness (see Hebrews 3:7ff.).

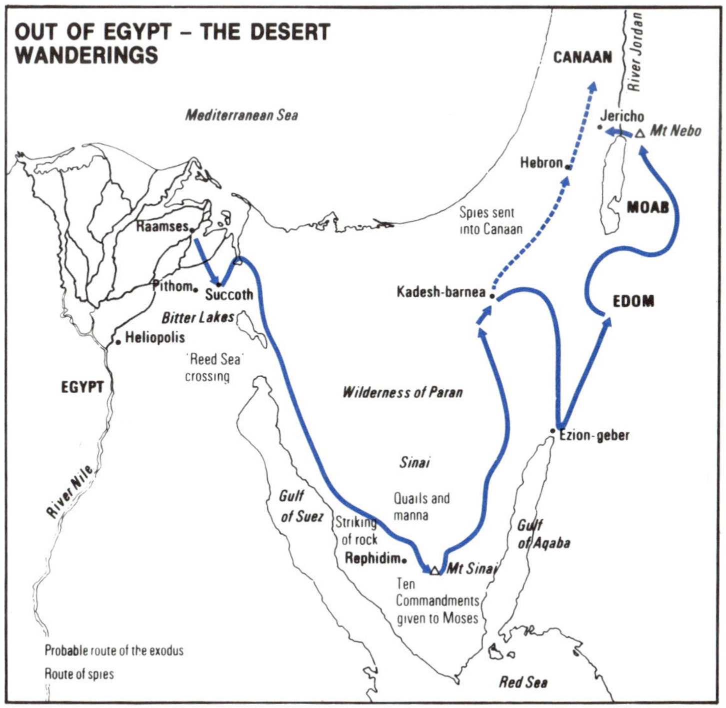

OUT OF EGYPT – THE DESERT WANDERINGS

This imposing mountain, Jebel Musa, is generally held to be Mount Sinai, where God gave the Law to his people.

The route of the exodus. This is not absolutely certain. They did not take the direct coastal route (13:17) because they were unready to encounter the Philistine forces. Instead they journeyed south to Succoth, turned north before crossing the sea, and then south again down the west of the Sinai peninsula. The 'Red Sea', or 'sea of reeds', can refer to the Bitter Lakes region or to the Gulf of Suez. The actual crossing probably took place somewhere between Qantara (30 miles south of Port Said) and just north of Suez – over the papyrus marshes.

17:8-16 Battle with the Amalekites

Joshua (Moses' successor) leads a picked force against this nomadic tribe descended from Esau. But it is God who gives the victory, through Moses' intercession.

18 Jethro's advice

The burden of leadership is heavy, and Jethro's practical suggestion for reorganization and delegation is a sound one. Jethro, although a non-Israelite, is reckoned a godly man. He is welcomed and his advice taken. In religious matters, however, he learns from Moses (8-11), not vice-versa as some suggest. It is not clear when Zipporah returned home – perhaps soon after the incident recorded in 4:24-26.

19 The camp at Sinai

As God promised (3:12), Moses brings God's people to him at Mt Sinai, where he will establish his covenant with the nation. Thunder, fire, earthquake and lightning herald God's presence and demonstrate his power (20:20 explains why; compare Elijah's experience in the same place - 1 Kings 19:8ff. - and the contrast drawn in Hebrews 12:18-25). The Lord God, holy, awesome, unapproachable, speaks.

20 - 40 GOD'S LAW FOR ISRAEL; THE SETTING UP OF THE TABERNACLE

20:1-21 The Ten Commandments

This summary and climax of God's covenant-agreement with his people sets out a basic ethical norm applicable to all men in all ages (since they are in fact the 'Maker's instructions'). The first four commands concern men's relationship to God, the remaining six their relationship to one another. Hence Jesus' two-clause summary of the law in Matthew 22:37-40.

The commandments show God's concern for the whole of life. He sets out standards governing family relationships, regard for human life, sex, property, speech and thought. God made us: he alone can show us how we are designed to behave.

Written on stone tablets, preserved in the ark of the covenant, the ten 'words' were the basis of Israel's law. In form they follow the standard pattern of Near Eastern treaties current in the 13th century BC, particularly those between vassals and their overlords (see 'Covenants and Near Eastern Treaties'):

— Title: identifying the author of the covenant (2a).
— Historical prologue: describing past relations of the two parties (2b).
— Obligations imposed on the vassal (3-17), accompanied by 'blessings' (e.g. 6,12b) and 'cursings' (5,7b).

20:22 - 23:33 God's law-code for Israel

This section, known as 'the book of the covenant', is the oldest record we have of Jewish law. It consists of 'judgements' - i.e. case-laws - and 'statues', straight-forward commands. Although similar in form to other ancient law-codes of Western Asia, the Jewish code has several distinctive features:

— The whole code rests on the authority of God, not of a king.
— There is no division between civil and religious law. Most oriental codes deal with legal matters only: morals and religion belong elsewhere. In the Bible legal, moral and religious laws are inseparable, showing God's concern for life as a whole.
— There is one law for all, whatever a man's status. Regulations protecting the weak and helpless (slaves, orphans, widows, foreigners) are particularly striking.
— A high view of human life is demonstrated by fixed, limited penalties – one crime, one punishment.

The legislation looks forward to the settled agricultural life of Canaan – Israel's rebelliousness had not yet condemned her to 40 years in the Sinai peninsula. The section may be summarized as follows:

— General instructions about worship (20:22-26)
— Civil laws (21:1 - 23:13) the rights of slaves (21:1-11) manslaughter and injury to human life (21:12-32) injury, theft and damage to property (21:33 - 22:15) social and religious obligations (22:16-31) justice and human rights (23:1-13)
— Laws for the three main feasts – Unleavened Bread, Firstfruits and Harvest (23:14-19)
— God's undertakings for his obedient people (23:20-33)

These regulations fill out in detail the summary of 20:1-17.

A reconstruction of the tabernacle at the Bible Museum, Amsterdam.

24 The covenant is ratified

The people's assent to the covenant is formally sealed by a special sacrifice, and by the covenant meal eaten by their representatives in the presence of God. The blood sprinkled on the people and on the altar unites the two parties to the agreement. In effect, each is swearing to keep it on pain of death.

Nadab and Abihu (1): two of Aaron's sons who later died after committing sacrilege (Leviticus 10:1-2).

They saw the God of Israel (9-11): having a meal with someone is the essence of fellowship in the Near East. Here the writer gropes for words to describe the indescribable communion which followed the sacrifice and fulfilled the covenant.

Hur (14): obviously a man of standing in Israel. He and Aaron held up Moses' hands in prayer during the battle with Amalek (17:12).

Forty days and nights (18): certain numbers have special significance in the Bible. The round number '40' occurs at almost every new stage in Israel's history: e.g. at the flood, the time of the spies in Canaan, Elijah's journey to Horeb, Jesus' time in the wilderness, and the time between his resurrection and ascension.

25 - 27 Instructions for making and furnishing the tabernacle

God has brought the nation out of Egypt. He has set out the terms of his covenant and they have been agreed. Now, as a visible sign that these are his people with whom he will always be present, he gives Moses instructions to build a special tent for him. He is to have a home

THE TABERNACLE

J.A. Motyer

The people of God were encamped at Mt Sinai. Every day they gazed with trembling at the cloud covering the mountain (Exodus 19:16-20), for it signified God's coming down to speak with them. But during their stay, at Moses' instruction, they provided materials for the construction of the very complex tent which has come to be called the tabernacle. On the day when it was finally completed and erected, as they watched, 'the cloud covered the tent of meeting, and the glory of the Lord filled the tabernacle' (Exodus 40:34). The Lord in his glory had actually come to dwell amongst his people. This is the supreme significance of the tabernacle.

Sinai

The law had been given at Mt Sinai. But there was more to it than that. The ceremony described in Exodus 24 places the law-giving in its correct context. It included the following elements:

— The altar with its twelve pillars (verse 4) stands for the bringing of the whole people of God into his presence (for there were twelve tribes of Israel). This truth is represented in stone: the relationship is a permanent one.

— Dashing half the blood of sacrifice (verse 6) against the altar signifies that it is by means of shed blood that the people can come into the presence of God. Sin inevitably means death, being cut off from God. But when the death penalty has been satisfied, the people can be brought to God and established permanently in his presence.

— Next, Moses goes through the law of God, the pattern of obedience which God requires from his blood-bought people (verse 7).

— The people commit themselves to a life of obedience, and Moses sprinkles the remainder of the blood over them (verse 8) – identifying them with the sacrifice made on their behalf both initially and for the failures and sins of everyday life.

So Mt Sinai stands for the fulfilment of one half of the covenant promise of Exodus 6:7: 'I will take you for my people'. God has brought them to himself, and in the shed blood has provided a way for them to live and walk with him.

The indwelling God

But what about the other half of the covenant promise? God had also said 'and I will be your God' (Exodus 6:7). By taking up residence amongst them, pitching his tent in the midst of their tents, the Lord makes this second sort of identification with his people. He is indeed their God. The tabernacle represents the completion and climax of God's redemption of his people. Everything he had done was for this final purpose, 'that I might dwell among them' (Exodus 29:43-46).

There is great emphasis on this fact of God's indwelling throughout the tabernacle narrative. It is stressed in two specific ways. First there is a whole series of verses with this as their topic (e.g. 25:8, 22; 29:42ff.; 40:34-38). It was God's intention that his people should always carry with them the values learnt at Mt Sinai. There God dwelt among them and they saw the visible manifestation of his presence. But God was not just providing a memory to cling to. He is determined to live amongst his people, to travel with them. The tabernacle represents something even more intense than the experience at Sinai (compare 24:18 with 40:35). They are not left with the diminishing glow of a receding experience. Instead, by living among them, God will himself guarantee the unabated reality of his personal presence.

The story of the tabernacle is interrupted and marred by the incident of the golden calf (Exodus 32-34). On the one side of this act of rebellion lie the details of the plan for the tabernacle (Exodus 25-31), and on the other side the details of the execution of that plan, point by point (Exodus 35-40). Why are we taken through the process of construction in such detail? Why is the summary statement of 40:16ff. not sufficient? Why must each separate moment of the work be dwelt upon? It is surely to emphasize this great truth: that not even the most audacious acts of human wilfulness and rebellion can deflect the Lord from his chosen purpose to dwell among his people. He has set his hand to it along lines dictated by his own will, and nothing can deter him. Man may impatiently rebel, but God will patiently continue.

God-centred religion

The general truth expressed by the tabernacle, then, is that the Lord determined to live among his people and the will of God – what he wants – equally governs the whole plan of the great tent and its construction. From 25:10 onwards the description moves from the inside to the outside: first the furnishings, the ark, table and lampstand (25:10-40), then the tent-covering (26:1-37), then beyond it to the altar and the court (27:1-19). It is an ordered story, but on reflection the order is striking and unexpected. One might reasonably have expected that the 'building' would come first and then the things it housed. But this would have been to start from the visible, and the whole tabernacle exists as the necessary 'wrapping' for the invisible God when he comes down to be with his people. God and his nature determines all, not man and his needs.

In this way the tabernacle sums up a basic biblical truth about religion: it must conform to the will and nature of God. Much in the Bible exists to expose man's tendency to make religion suit his own pleasure, or (as might be said) match what he finds 'helpful'. But if religion does not match the will of God it is ultimately futile (see, for example, Isaiah 29:13).

The ark of the covenant

At the very centre of this whole divinely-dictated religion was the ark. Everything pointed to it. Three matching entrances (26:31, 32, 36, 37; 27:16, 17) led to it – for the purpose of entering the court of the tabernacle was to enter the presence of God himself. Along the path leading to the ark lay the altar of burnt-offering (27:1-8), the altar of incense (30:1-6), and the mercy-seat where the blood of sacrifice was finally sprinkled (25:17ff.; Leviticus 16:14) – showing that it was only by sacrifice, prayer and the effectiveness of the shed blood that man could come to God.

Inside the ark were the tablets of the law – the supreme verbal statement of God's holiness (25:16); at one and the same time the reason why God dwelt alone (for none can match his holiness), and why by means of blood a sinner might enter his presence (for the blood speaks of life laid down in payment for sin).

The whole structure of the tabernacle, therefore, speaks clear and splendid truths. It provides a visible summary of the central affirmations of the Bible: that God indwells his people (see 1 Corinthians 3:16; Ephesians 2:19-22); that he intends his people to worship him according to his will and not their own whim (see Mark 7:6-13); and that only by means of sacrifice and shed blood can sinners ever come to live with the Holy One (see Ephesians 2:11-18; Hebrews 10:19-25).

amongst them like their own homes. He will guide and accompany them wherever they go – and they will know that he is no local deity whose power is limited to Sinai. Portable, prefabricated tent-shrines similar to the tabernacle were constructed in Egypt even earlier than this. Here, although the description is detailed, some practical points are missing – it is not a complete workman's blueprint. The roof of the tent, for example, may have been flat or raised with a ridge-pole. The framework of the actual tent was hung with linked curtains of linen, over which was a layer of goatskin, topped by two weather-proof coverings (of rams' skins dyed red, and of sealskin or porpoiseskin).

Many of the materials used were brought by the Israelites from Egypt (11:2-3) and willingly given, so that God's tent might be as worthy of him as they could make it. Before the days of banks it was practical to convert wealth into jewellery, which could be worn and carried round easily. Wood is scarce in the Sinai desert, but the acacia is one of the few trees which grow there. Their own herds provided skins, and the sealskins came from the Red Sea.

The peoples of the ancient Near East were skilled in spinning, weaving and using natural dyes (scarlet from the cochineal insect; purple, for the wealthy, from the murex shellfish). Fine embroidery was also produced. Precious and semi-precious stones were rounded, polished and engraved (as those for Aaron). Gold and silver were beaten and worked into elaborate designs. All these skills God called into play for the construction of his tabernacle.

28 - 30 The priests and their duties

If God's tent is to be a place of beauty and splendour, his priest must also be fittingly robed. His garments, as the New English Bible puts it, are intended 'to give him dignity and honour' (28:2) – not on his own account, but as befits the One he serves and represents. The precious stones engraved with the names of the twelve tribes point to his other function, as representative of his people, making atonement for their sin.

Urim and Thummim (28:30): two objects which stood for 'yes' and 'no'. Just how they were used to discover God's will is not known.

A model of the high priest shows the blue robe fringed with bells and pomegranates; the shorter tunic (ephod) tied with a girdle; and the breastplate with its 12 precious stones, 1 for each of the 12 tribes. He holds an almond branch.

The bells on the hem of Aaron's robe (28:33-34): perhaps to ensure he does not enter God's presence unannounced.

The consecration: everything about this elaborate ceremonial points to the 'otherness' of God. He will be with his people, but there can be no familiarity. He is to be approached only in the ways he lays down. Sin disqualifies all men from entering God's presence. The priests and every item of equipment must be specially set apart for his service. So Aaron and his sons must be cleansed, robed and their sins expiated by sacrifice before they may take office. The living God is no impotent image to be worshipped as man thinks fit. He lays down the only terms on which it is possible for him to take up residence with his people.

31:1-11 God chooses his craftsmen

When God selects individuals for a particular job he also equips them to do it. Verse 3 is one of the earliest references to the work of the Holy Spirit.

31:12-18 Sabbath law

The way the sabbath is kept is an index of the nation's spiritual health. Obedience in this is a test of their obedience to God in other ways too.

32 The worship of the golden calf, and its aftermath

Only six weeks after making their solemn covenant-pledge with God the people are clamouring for a replica of the old gods of Egypt. And God's high priest not only makes the bull-calf, but identifies it with God. Death is the penalty for those who break covenant – but Moses' selfless intercession prevents Israel's extermination. The broken tablets dramatically proclaim the broken covenant. Such sin cannot go unpunished: Moses' own tribe, the Levites, mete out God's judgement.

Aaron's gold bull was modelled on one of the old Egyptian gods. This apis bull, in bronze, was found at Ashkelon in Israel.

33 Moses prays again, and sees God's glory

God will not go back on his promise, but Israel has forfeited his presence. And without that, the promised land is nothing. Again Moses pleads for the people at a time of crisis. God's answer encourages him to press a personal plea for a revelation of God in all his splendour.

34 The covenant is renewed

The tablets are engraved afresh in token of God's renewal of the covenant. This particular selection of laws is influenced by Israel's recent idol-worship, also by the coming temptations of Canaanite religion. Israel's firstborn belong to God, but are 'bought back' from him – there is to be no child-sacrifice as in Canaan. They must not forget sabbath law in the coming busy seasons of sowing and harvest. The firstfruits are to be brought to God, since it is he who makes the land fruitful. Israel is not to resort to the Canaanite practice of boiling a kid in its mother's milk to increase fertility.

Moses' long communion with God shows in his face when he returns to the people: he begins to reflect something of God's own glory (see 2 Corinthians 3:18).

35 - 40 The setting up of the tabernacle

These chapters record how the instructions given in chapters 25-31 are carried out to the letter. The craftsmen set to work, the people pour in their gifts, and the tabernacle, its fittings and the priests' robes are all completed exactly as God has laid down. When the work is finished, God gives Moses his instructions for setting up and arranging the tabernacle, and for its consecration. Aaron and his sons are anointed for service. When all is done, God signifies his satisfaction. The cloud, the visible token of his presence, rests on the tabernacle, and the place is filled with his glory. For 300 years, until it is replaced by the temple in Solomon's day, the tabernacle will remain the focal centre of the nation's worship.

Old Testament 1.3

LEVITICUS

Leviticus is essentially a rule-book – the book of laws given by God to his people through Moses at Sinai. The laws cover ritual and worship and many aspects of life – but all seen in relation to him. The book takes its name from the fact that it was the Levitical priests (Aaron and his sons and descendants, helped in the practical work of the tabernacle by the rest of the Levites) who administered the laws. But the book is not for the priests alone. God intended all his people to know and keep his law. Again and again Moses is told to 'speak to the people of Israel'.

To many modern readers it may seem a strange book, perhaps even a repulsive one with all its blood-sacrifices. Some see it as reflecting only an odd set of ancient taboos. Yet take it away and whole areas of Scripture become inexplicable. Without the message of Leviticus the key event of all time, the death of Jesus Christ, is an enigma. The ritual and the rules were never simply an end in themselves. As the sacrifices were performed day after day, year after year, as the Day of Atonement came and went, Israel was constantly reminded of the sin which cut them off from God's presence. They had broken covenant with God by disobeying his laws and were under sentence of death. But God in his mercy showed them that he would accept a substitute – the death of an animal, perfect and blameless, instead of the offender. God was holy – a moral holiness unknown in the gods of the nations around. He demanded holiness in his people. The laws on ritual purity hammered this home in practical everyday experience.

Yet the book has value apart from its vital role in God's message of salvation. The laws in Leviticus show God working in harmony with his own natural laws for the good of his people. Although Israel had to obey the laws in blind trust (when they chose to do so at all), we can see how those laws were actually working for the nation's health and well-being. Because we know more today about the sources of infection and pollution, about quarantine and isolation, hygiene and preventive medicine, we can watch Israel's obedience actually fulfilling God's promise to take away their sickness (Exodus 23:25). And this not by magic, but by the natural working of principles we now, at least in part, can understand.

Many of the laws which seem strangest to us fall into place, too, when we look at them in relation to the contemporary religions of Egypt and Canaan. Against this dark backcloth the morality and religion of Israel shines like a star. Only God himself can account for it.

1 - 7 THE SACRIFICES

Priests and people are given instructions about five different offerings:

1. The burnt-offering (chapter 1 and 6:8-13): the only one in which the whole animal was burnt; a token of dedication.

2. The cereal- or meal-offering (chapter 2 and 6:14-18); often an accompaniment to burnt- and peace-offerings.

3. The peace-offering (chapter 3 and 7:11-36): re-establishing fellowship between the offerer and God; or it could be a thank-offering.

4. The sin-offering (4:1 - 5:13 and 6:24-30): made in order to obtain forgiveness. The relationship between this and the guilt-offering is not clear. Generally speaking the sin-offering seems to have referred to offences against God, and the guilt-offering to social offences. (But even sin against others is seen as sin against God, as 6:2 plainly states.)

5. The guilt- or trespass-offering (5:14-6:7 and 7:1-10). There was a standard pattern of ritual. The worshipper brought his offering (a physically perfect animal from his herd or flock, or, in the case of a poor man, doves or pigeons) to the forecourt of the tabernacle. He laid his hand on it, implying that it represented him, and slaughtered it. (If it was a public offering the priest did this.) The priest took the basin of blood and spattered it against the altar. He burnt a specified part with certain portions of fat (or the entire animal in the case of the burnt-offering). The remainder was then eaten by the priests, or by the priests and their families, or (in the case of the peace-offering) by priests and worshippers together.

Sacrifice of some sort was almost universal practice amongst ancient peoples, and Israel's sacrifices have some similarities with those of her neighbours. Nonetheless, certain features are unique:

- Israel's absolute monotheism – belief in the one true God – and the ritual as a direct revelation from him.
- The emphasis on ethics and morality, stemming from God's own absolute moral holiness; sin as a bar to communion; the need for repentance and atonement; the insistence on obedience to God's law (moral as well as ceremonial).
- The complete absence (and prohibition) of associated practices in other religions; no magic or sorcery.
- The high tone of the sacrificial system: no frenzy, or prostitution, orgies, fertility rites, human sacrifice, etc.

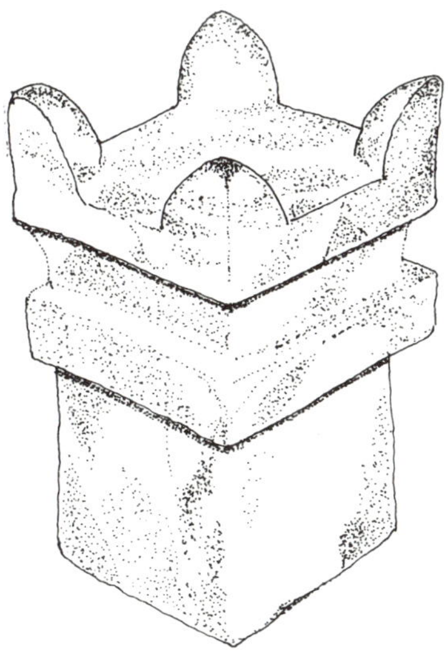

This small stone incense altar with four 'horns' was found at Megiddo in Israel.

THE SACRIFICIAL SYSTEM

Philip Budd

The offering of sacrifice was a regular feature in ancient Near Eastern religion. Israel appears to have shared many of the techniques and conceptions of sacrifice of her neighbours, but her own observances were set firmly in the framework of God's revelation at Sinai. The procedures set out in Leviticus presuppose a sanctuary, an altar, and an officiating priesthood, though the historical use and development of these rituals remains obscure.

Burnt-offering (Leviticus 1)

The distinctive feature was the burning of the whole animal. The Hebrew name for the sacrifice conveys the idea of 'going up', and the phrase a 'pleasing odour to the Lord' is common. These points taken together suggest that the burnt-offering symbolized the worshipper's homage and total dedication to God. In laying his hand on the animal he identified himself completely with the sacrifice. The offering had to cost him something – one of his herd of cattle or flock of sheep and goats (a bird was permitted for the poor), and it had to be of the best – a male without blemish.

Peace-offering (Leviticus 3)

The outstanding feature is the sharing of the sacrifice. Part was burnt in acknowledgement of God, part belonged to the priests and part was eaten by the offerer and his family. The Hebrew name indicates 'peace' or 'well-being', and these sacrifices are sometimes seen as communion or fellowship rites. On the whole they are best regarded as expressing a desire to maintain and demonstrate right relations between God, man and his neighbour. This harmony might be expressed as an offering which accompanied a vow of some kind (Leviticus 22:21), or as a thank-offering (Leviticus 22:29) or free-will offering (Leviticus 22:21). The offerings expressed the individual's gratitude to God for his goodness, or were simply spontaneous expressions of devotion.

Cereal-offering (Leviticus 2)
The Hebrew word has the sense of 'gift' or 'tribute'. No distinct meaning is evident; the offering probably expressed homage and thankfulness.

Sin and guilt-offerings (Leviticus 4 - 6:7)
The procedure is similar for both these sacrifices, and it is difficult to pin-point a difference of meaning. It may be that the sin-offering deals with infringements of God's laws, whereas the guilt-offering, since it raises the question of compensation, deals with situations where human injury is involved. Both offerings demonstrate the need for sin to be dealt with objectively, and give prominence to the use of the blood. Both sacrifices deal with unwitting or unavoidable breaches of law. Hence 'sin' in these contexts often has a purely ritual meaning – as with the sin-offering after childbirth (Leviticus 12:6). In this case the sacrifice brings the offerer back to full membership of the holy community.

In various parts of the Bible all these offerings are said to 'alone' – to cover sin – indicating that any act of worship was set squarely in the context of God's forgiving grace.

The sacrificial system was clearly open to abuse, and on more than one occasion was criticized by the prophets (e.g. Amos 5:25; Isaiah 1:11-12; Jeremiah 7:22) probably in the light of contemporary attitudes. And a number of other texts stress the fact that obedience counts for more than sacrifice (e.g. 1 Samuel 15:22-23; Psalm 40:6-8). It was only too easy to assume God's acceptance of the offering and neglect the moral obligation to obey him. By making sin a purely external thing its seriousness was minimized.

On the other hand the sacrificial system did demand a right inward attitude. The sin-offering had to be accompanied by confession, and, where possible, a genuine attempt to put things right (Leviticus 5:5; Numbers 5:7). On the Day of Atonement the high priest confessed the sins of the whole community before the scapegoat was released (Leviticus 16:21). Furthermore the law provides no sacrifice for sin 'with a high hand', i.e. wilful and deliberate sin (Numbers 15:27-31).

Each sacrifice, upheld by God's promise and power, had real effect and potency, but this was not a power that could be manipulated by man. On the contrary, it was recognized that the system was divinely appointed from beginning to end. It was a God-given area of contact between God and man, bringing man into fellowship with God. Viewed in this light, a meticulous observance of these laws could inspire confidence in God. In any case, human activity was not the only factor in the observances. The priests, as God's representatives, were required to declare God's acceptance or rejection of the worshipper and his offering.

The letter to the Hebrews makes it clear that the Old Testament sacrifice was at best an incomplete answer to the problem of sin. The sacrifices themselves have disappeared, but they go far to help us understand the meaning of the cross, the sacrifice of Jesus Christ.

See too 'The Meaning of Blood Sacrifice' and 'Feasts and Festivals'.

A pleasing odour to the Lord (1:9): a human way of expressing God's satisfaction with the offering. The people knew God did not need to be fed by them – *he* was feeding *them* with manna.

No leaven nor any honey ... you shall offer salt (2:11ff.): leaven (yeast) or honey caused fermentation. Perhaps the part played by wine in the excesses of Canaanite religion lay behind this ruling. Salt, on the other hand, is a preservative and a reminder of the solemn covenant meal.

You shall eat no blood whatever (7:26): the reason is given in 17:10-14; and see article 'The Meaning of Blood Sacrifice'.

8 - 10 THE CONSECRATION OF AARON AND HIS SONS

8 The investiture

Now that the priest's sacrificial duties have been listed, Moses implements the instructions given in Exodus 29. In an elaborate and impressive ritual Aaron and his sons are instituted to the priesthood. Moses performs the priestly duties on their behalf. The blood on Aaron's ear, hand and toe indicate the dedication of the whole man to God's service.

9 Aaron and his sons take office

The order of their first sacrifices is significant:

1. A sin-offering: obtaining cleansing and forgiveness.

2. A burnt-offering of dedication to God.

3. A peace-offering: fellowship and communion with God is restored and enjoyed.

10 Sacrilege

The rejoicing is short-lived. In no time Aaron's sons are deciding to do things *their* way: and God reduces the priesthood to three. Perhaps they were under the influence of drink (10:9). Whatever the reason, God's terrifying holiness cannot allow disobedience in those dedicated to his highest service. His commands are absolute; no man may tailor them to suit his fancy.

Verse 6: mourning is forbidden.

Verse 9: God's priests are to avoid the excesses of Canaan, where wine featured prominently.

Verse 16: the people's sin-offering should have been eaten by the priests in the holy place as a sign that God accepted the offering – Aaron's excuse is not clear, but Moses accepts it.

11 - 15 LAWS FOR DAILY LIFE: PURITY AND IMPURITY

Today we are more able to understand and appreciate the sound principles of diet, hygiene and medicine which these laws express. God works in and through the processes he has built into the natural world.

11 Food-laws: clean and unclean creatures

Israel may eat:
— Animals which chew the cud *and* have cloven hoofs.
— Sea creatures with both fins and scales.
— Birds not listed as forbidden.
— Insects belonging to four classes of the locust family.

Amongst those banned are:
— Carnivorous animals – which readily transmitted infection in a warm climate where flesh decayed rapidly.
— Pork – specially dangerous in this respect, as the old British saying about eating it only when there is an 'r' in the month (i.e. the cold months) bears out. Pigs are also hosts to various parasites.
— Vermin and predatory birds – likely disease-carriers.
— Shellfish – even today these often cause food-poisoning and enteritis.

Verses 32-40 set out measures to prevent contamination of food and water supplies. The same principles govern present-day public health regulations.

12 Purification after childbirth

In Canaan, prostitution and fertility rites were all mixed up with worship. In Israel, by sharp contrast, anything suggesting the sexual or sensual is strictly banned from the worship of God – as this chapter and chapter 15 make plain. The intention is not to write off this side of life as 'dirty', as is plain elsewhere in Scripture. The purpose is to ensure its separation from the worship of God. The rule of strict cleanliness in all sexual matters was also a positive safeguard to health.

13 - 14 Uncleanness due to skin diseases

Although the word 'leprosy' is used throughout, true leprosy as we would define it is only one of the diseases mentioned here. Chapter 13 is written in technical jargon – a professional textbook on diagnosis for the priest-physician, enabling him to distinguish between 'acute' and 'chronic' forms of the various diseases. This is the earliest formulation of quarantine

THE MEANING OF BLOOD SACRIFICE

J.A.Motyer

The practice of sacrifice, the shedding of the blood of animals, goes back to the very beginning of God's dealings with sinful man (see Genesis 4:4). It pervades the whole of the Bible. In the New Testament it provides the terms in which the death of Jesus Christ is explained (see for instance Hebrews 9:11ff.).

The key verse, Leviticus 17:11, says that sacrifice is something that God has given to man: it is his provision for human need. It is a contradiction of this to say (as many Old Testament specialists do) that the basic meaning of sacrifice is an offering or gift to God. The word translated 'offering' certainly means gift. So, it is said, the person bringing the offering gains possession of the life, the blood, of the sacrificed animal, and can give it to God. By this means he injects new life into his relationship with God. Or else he is able to interpose a living screen between himself as a sinner and God the holy One. But how can that which God gives to man be interpreted as something man gives to God?

Leviticus 17:11 gives us two great clues to the meaning of blood and sacrifice. First: the purpose of the blood is to make atonement. Whenever the word translated 'atonement' was used it meant paying a price – a ransom price. So it is not sufficient to say that the blood 'screens' the offender. One must say that it does so by providing a price sufficient to pay off a debt of sin before God.

So here, as always in the Bible, 'the wages of sin is death'. No sin, no sinner, can come into the presence of an utterly holy God. To be cut off from God is death. Only if this price can be paid, the penalty taken, the sentence borne, can sinful man hope to be forgiven and come again into God's presence. This, says Leviticus 17:11, is precisely what the blood does.

We are told, second, that the blood can do this 'by reason of the life'. 'By reason of' translates a Hebrew preposition regularly used to express price or expenditure (e.g. 1 Kings 2:23; Proverbs 7:23; Lamentations 5:9). It is found in a basic legal passage on the necessity for exact justice, in the phrase 'life for life' (Deuteronomy 19:21), i.e. 'life in payment for life'. So in Leviticus 17:11, just as 'to make atonement' means 'to pay the atonement/ransom price', so 'by reason of the life' means 'by reason of the payment of life'.

In other words 'blood' means death – the termination of life – just as it does in ordinary metaphorical usage (see, for instance, Genesis 9:5, 37:26; etc.). In the sacrifice, life was terminated. The flowing blood was the symbol and proof that life had been taken in payment for the sins of the guilty and as a substitute for his own guilt-stained life.

Animal sacrifice expressed the principle. The full reality took place in the death of the Lord Jesus Christ. In the Old Testament the people had a God-given preview of the shed blood of Jesus, his substitutionary death on our behalf, for our sins, the just for the unjust, once and for all.

regulations and preventive medicine relating to these diseases so far recovered from the ancient Near East.

As far as clothing and buildings are concerned, the 'leprosy' is a mould, or fungus.

14:34ff.: we have a similar system of house inspection and treatment for dry rot today.

Cedarwood (14:49): contains a substance used in medicine for skin diseases.

Hyssop (14:49): a herb, possibly marjoram, containing a mild antiseptic.

15 Uncleanness due to bodily discharge

See under chapter 12. Regulations are given for both normal (seminal and menstrual) and abnormal, possibly malignant, discharges. Washing is prescribed both to prevent and sterilize infection.

16 THE DAY OF ATONEMENT

The 10th day of the 7th month (Tishri – September/October) was to be the annual Day of Atonement ('at-one-ment') for the nation. Only on this occasion was Aaron allowed into the innermost part of the tabernacle, where the ark of the covenant was housed. He must first obtain forgiveness and cleansing for his own sin. Only then might he cleanse the tabernacle and offer on behalf of the people's sins. For a New Testament look at the Day of Atonement, see Hebrews 9 and 10.

Azazel (8,10): a place in the wilderness to which the scapegoat was sent, symbolically carrying away the sins of Israel. The meaning is uncertain, but it cannot refer to an offering to a demon, as some suggest, for this was strictly forbidden (see, e.g., 17:7).

Outside the camp (27): neither offering might be eaten, since no one was to eat any of his own sin-offering, and Aaron identifies himself with the people in their sin-offering.

17 FURTHER REGULATIONS ABOUT SACRIFICE

As a safeguard against apostasy (17:7), sacrifice might be offered only in the proper place, and to the proper Person. On 17:10ff. see 'The Meaning of Blood Sacrifice'.

18 - 20 ETHICAL AND MORAL LAWS

18:3 provides a key to these chapters. From what we know of Canaanite and Egyptian religions it is clear that many of these laws are directed against the specific practices of Israel's neighbours.

18 Sexual offences

6-18: marriage between those closely related by blood or by marriage is forbidden in Israel. In Egypt, which had no marriage-laws, such marriages were common.

19-30: adultery, child-sacrifice, homosexuality, bestiality (perhaps a hangover from animal cults) were all part of the indescribably debased religions of Canaan. Israel is to shun behaviour which is bringing God's judgement on the land (compare Genesis 15:16).

19 Various laws

19:2 stands at the heart of the moral law for Jew and Christian alike (see 1 Peter 1:15-16). God's holiness, the holiness we are to reflect, shows itself in concern for the under-privileged (9-10, 14, 20), in honesty, fair dealing and impartial justice (11, 13, 15) and in respect for life and reputation (16-18).

Verses 23-25: the likelihood of heavy cropping is greatly increased by this practice.

Verses 26b-31: these are all heathen practices.

20 Serious offences and crimes punishable by death

Verses 6-21 list the penalties for disobedience to laws in chapters 18 and 19 (compare, e.g., 6 with 19:31; 9 with 19:3; 10 with 18:20). That such a wide range of offences should be punishable by death seems incredibly harsh to the modern reader. It is worth noting, however, that the offences listed are either in deliberate defiance of God's holy law, or offences against people – not property.

Molech (2-5): an Ammonite god. Amongst the Phoenicians live infants were placed in the arms of an idol, and died in the flames burning inside it. Some equally horrible practice is in mind here.

21 - 22 RULES FOR THE PRIESTS

Because of their position and duties the priests are subject to particularly stringent regulations on ritual purity. Any defilement disqualified them from contact with the holy things. The rules for the high priest (21:10-15) are even stricter (compare 11 with 1-2; 13-14 with 7). No one with any physical defect may serve as priest, though he may share in eating the

FEASTS AND FESTIVALS

Philip Budd

From very early times the Jewish year was punctuated by the great festivals – the 'feasts of the Lord'. Some were timed to coincide with the changing seasons, reminding the people of God's constant provision for them, and providing an opportunity to return to God some token of all that he had given. Others commemorated the great events of Israel's history, the occasions when in an unmistakable way God had stepped in to deliver his people. All were occasions of whole-hearted delight and enjoyment of God's good gifts, and at the same time sober gatherings to seek his forgiveness and cleansing.

They were never intended to be observed out of mere formality and empty ritual. The prophets had sharp words for those who reduced them to this level. The purpose of the festivals was spiritual: a great and glorious meeting of God and his people.

There were probably many local festivals (Judges 21:21), but on three occasions in the year all the men were required to attend great national celebrations:

1. Passover and the Feast of Unleavened Bread (Exodus 12:1-20; 23:15). These two feasts, combining pastoral and agricultural elements, were observed together to commemorate Israel's departure from Egypt (see on Exodus 11-12). The observance began on the fourteenth day of the first month and lasted for a week.

2. The Feast of Weeks (Harvest) (Exodus 23:16; Leviticus 23:15-21). Later known as Pentecost, it was celebrated 50 days after the beginning of Passover. It was essentially an agricultural celebration at which the first-fruits of the harvest were offered to God.

3. The Feast of Ingathering (Tabernacles) (Exodus 23:16; Leviticus 23:33-43). An autumn festival at the end of the fruit-harvest. The people lived for seven days in shelters made of branches – essentially as an agricultural thanksgiving, but also as a reminder of their tent-dwelling days in the wilderness (Leviticus 23:43).

All of these festivals were regarded as 'holy', occasions when all ordinary work stopped. There were also other celebrations (all in some way connected with the number seven).

4. Sabbath. On the seventh day all work was forbidden and the daily sacrifices were doubled. This observance was connected with the completion of God's work of creation (Exodus 20:11), the deliverance from Egypt (Deuteronomy 5:15), and man's simple need for rest and refreshment (Exodus 23:12). After the exile the sabbath rules were strictly enforced (Nehemiah 13:15-22), and their observance became one of the outstanding features of Judaism.

5. New moon. This is often mentioned along with the sabbath (e.g. Isaiah 1:13). Special sacrifices (Numbers 28:11-15), and the blowing of trumpets (Numbers 10:10) were distinctive features of the new moon festival. There were also special meals and family sacrifices in early times (1 Samuel 20:5, 24), and sometimes prophets were consulted (2 Kings 4:23). On the new moon of the seventh month there was a special **Feast of Trumpets.** (Numbers 29:1).

6. Sabbatical year. By law, every seventh year the land lay fallow (Leviticus 25:1-7), and every fiftieth year was a **Jubilee Year** (Leviticus 25:8-34) when mortgaged property was returned to its owners and Hebrew slaves were freed.

7. Day of Atonement (Leviticus 16). On the tenth day of the seventh month there was a special annual ceremony of confession and atonement for sin.

There were other feasts not mentioned in the biblical laws. One was the **Feast of Purim** (Esther 9) to commemorate the Jewish deliverance from Haman, and later the **Feast of Dedication** (John 10:22) celebrating the purification of the temple after its desecration by Antiochus Epiphanes in 168 BC.

Israel's religious festivals marked the high points in the farmer's year. The diagram shows the months of the Jewish calendar and how they relate to the calendar we use today.

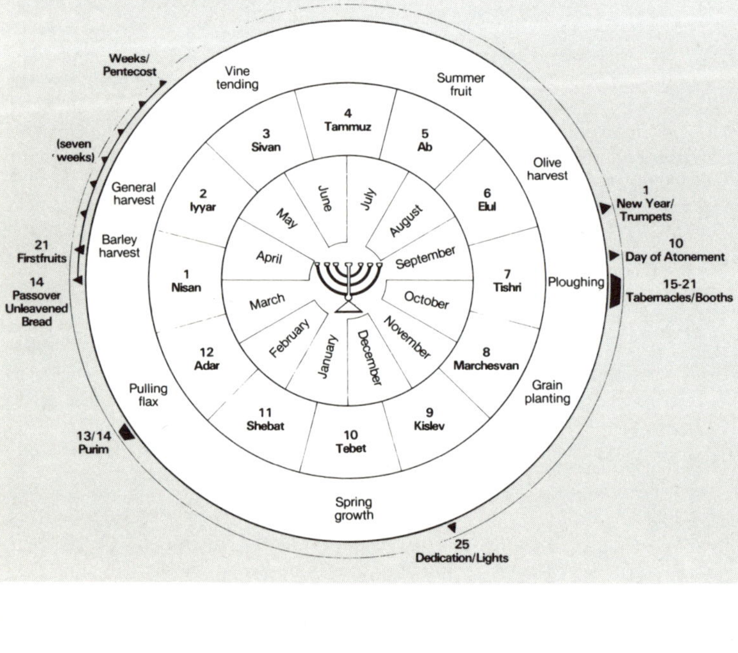

offerings. Only the best man can give – whether in the priesthood or sacrificial offerings – is in any measure worthy of God.

23 THE SET FEASTS

Israel's special festivals, like the weekly sabbath, reflect a pattern of sevens – pointing back to God's hallowing of the seventh day at the creation.

1. The sabbath: one day of rest in seven.

2. Passover, followed by the seven-day Feast of Unleavened Bread (March/April).

3. Firstfruits (April), followed seven weeks later by

4. The Feast of Weeks (Pentecost): the harvest festival (June).

5. The Feast of Trumpets: first of three festivals in the seventh month (September/ October); the others being

6. The Day of Atonement; and

7. The Feast of Tabernacles (Booths): a perpetual reminder of the nation's tent-dwelling days following the deliverance from Egypt.

24 THE LAMP, SHEWBREAD, AND THE SIN OF BLASPHEMY

Chapter 24 turns from special festivals to two regular duties: the lamp which must be kept burning, and the weekly offering of 12 loaves. The loaves remind the tribes of their complete dependence on God's provision. They are not put there for God to eat (as in pagan religions). Aaron and the priests are openly instructed to eat the bread themselves.

Verses 10-23 record the ruling about a breach of the third commandment. The emphasis is on one law for Israelite and resident foreigner alike. **The law of retaliation (lex talionis, verses 15ff.):** the principle this law expresses is of exact public justice, as opposed to individual revenge. In the event, compensation for injury often took the form of a fine (as the exception made in the case of murder implies – Numbers 35:31ff.). The fact that literal retaliation by bodily mutilation was legally allowed does not necessarily mean it was practised. It was a strict, legal statement against such practices as family feuds (the evils of which are shown, for instance, in Greek drama).

25 THE SEVENTH AND FIFTIETH YEARS: SABBATH AND JUBILEE

The pattern of sevens reflected in the festivals (chapter 23) is now extended to the land. One year in seven it is to lie fallow: a year in which the people, freed from much of their ordinary work, are to be taught and trained in God's law (Deuteronomy 31:10ff.). The fifieth year, following the seventh seven, is an extra fallow year for the land, which reverts to its original owner. It is a time when those who have fallen on bad times have their freedom and property restored. Jubilee serves a dual purpose. It reminds the people that the land belongs to God; and it prevents the wealthy from amassing land.

26 PROMISE AND WARNING: BLESSING AND CURSING

The reward of obedience is pictured as an idyll of peace and plenty. Best of all, God will walk amongst his people, as he walked in the garden with the first man. This is Eden restored. Disobedience, on the other hand, will bring calamity on the nation: fatal disease, famine, wild beasts ravaging the land, and war leading to exile. The cursings are more detailed than the blessings: human nature being what it is, fear brings a readier response than love. Yet even after all the disobedience, God still promises to respond to the call of genuine repentance.

27 VOWS AND TITHES

Firstborn sons, the firstlings of flocks and herds, and firstfruits of the field are God's by right (he accepts part for the whole). One-tenth of all cattle and produce are also his due. Over and above this, men might vow individuals or possessions to God as a dedication or thank-offering. Normally these would be redeemed for their set valuation, plus one-fifth.

Devoted to the Lord (28): deliberately set apart for God and therefore no longer available to man. Verse 29 presumably refers to someone 'set apart' under a death sentence.

Verse 34 brings us back to the source of authority for these and all the laws in Leviticus. The commands are God's, given through Moses, at Sinai.

LITERARY CRITICISM AND THE OLD TESTAMENT

Gordon Wenham

'Criticism' is an indispensable aid to interpreting the Old Testament. In everyday speech it is a decidedly negative word. But in the specialized sense it covers a range of disciplines which apply to most types of literature, and it has made a very positive contribution to the understanding of the Bible.

The six main branches of biblical criticism are textual, source, tradition, redaction, form and historical criticism. The first five are basically concerned with the structures of literature and the various ways in which an author expresses himself. The last, historical criticism, is more concerned with the meaning and truth of the author's statements.

Textual criticism

Textual criticism is concerned with recovering the original text of a document. Mistakes are liable to creep into every document copied by hand, and it is the task of the textual critic to spot these errors and – wherever possible – correct them. By studying numerous manuscripts, textual critics have been able to work out a set of principles which can be applied to many different sorts of document.

For the most part the scribes who copied the Pentateuch were very careful, and it would seem that very few errors crept into the Hebrew text. In the case of other Old Testament books – notably Samuel and Jeremiah – there are passages where it is more difficult to re-establish the original text.

The discovery of the Dead Sea Scrolls was therefore very important, since they give us a Hebrew text of much of the Old Testament about a thousand years older than anything we had before.

Source criticism

Source criticism is the attempt to discover and define the written material on which the different biblical writers drew. It has important bearings on the reliability of the Bible books. Some Old Testament books describe events that occurred many years before they were written. The book of Kings for instance must have been written after the last event it mentions – the release of King Jehoiachin from prison in 562 BC – yet it also relates the accession of Solomon, some 400 years earlier, as well as numerous events in between. Stories simply handed down by word of mouth over that length of time are likely to be less accurate than those written down from the beginning. But source critics, prompted by the recurring refrain 'And the rest of the deeds of King X, are they not written in the Book of the Chronicles of the Kings of Judah/Israel?', have concluded that much of the early material in the book has in fact been taken from royal annals and other trustworthy contemporary records.

It is extremely difficult to distinguish different literary sources within a document unless some of those sources have actually survived. In that case the source material may be subtracted from the document in question to leave the author's own contribution or material taken from another source. In the Bible we rarely possess two or more parallel documents where we can see how one writer used another as his source. The Synoptic Gospels (Matthew, Mark, Luke) in the New Testament and the Old Testament book of Kings with its parallel in Chronicles are the exceptions.

Elsewhere, though it is a reasonable assumption that the biblical writers used sources, there is little or no objective evidence that this is so. More subjective, less dependable criteria, such as variation in style or vocabulary, have to be used to distinguish the sources. Using such criteria it has become customary to distinguish at least four sources in the Pentateuch (commonly designated J,E,D and P). More recently, however, it has been argued that the differences in Hebrew style which are used to define the pentateuchal sources have no significance in the light of ancient literary conventions, and that a fresh approach to this aspect of the criticism of the Pentateuch is required.

Tradition criticism

Tradition criticism attempts to trace the development of a biblical story or tradition from the time it was first told to the time it was written down. For instance, the stories of Abraham were probably passed on by word of mouth for several generations before being incorporated in a written source later used by the author of Genesis. A historian concerned to reconstruct the life of Abraham as exactly as possible wants to know what changes the story of Abraham went through in the process of retelling. Tradition criticism tries to pin-point and explain such changes. However, except where the precise means and circumstances in which a story was transmitted are known, the results of tradition criticism are open to question and must be treated with caution.

Redaction criticism

The task of redaction criticism is to determine how the editor (redactor) of a biblical book utilized his sources, what he omitted and what he added and what his particular bias was. Only when the critic has access to all the sources which were at the disposal of the editor can his findings be absolutely certain. And in the Old Testament the critic has, at best, only some of the sources (e.g. the book of Kings used by the author of Chronicles). Elsewhere the sources are precariously reconstructed out of the edited work itself. Then redaction criticism is of limited value, but its methods can help to bring out the special interests of the editor and so lead to a fuller appreciation of the theology expressed in his work.

Form criticism

Form criticism is concerned with the study of literary form in the

Bible. Different writings have different forms. An essay differs in form from a poem. The form of a law differs from that of a psalm. Often the form of a piece of literature may throw light on the nature of the piece and its background, or 'life-setting'. The basic method of form criticism is to compare like with like, to determine the characteristic features of a particular type of literature, and then to suggest reasons for these features.

Form criticism has been most profitably used in the psalms and has revolutionized our understanding of them. The psalms fall into different categories, such as hymns, thanksgivings, laments, royal psalms, pilgrimage songs, etc. It used to be held that most of the psalms were personal poems of pious Jews after the exile. Now, thanks to form criticism, it is recognized that most of the psalms were sung in the public worship of the temple prior to its destruction in 587 BC.

Historical criticism

Historical criticism is a very broad discipline covering all aspects of history writing. There are two aspects of it which are of particular concern to biblical studies.

First, historical criticism has determined the techniques used for dating a document. How do we know when it was written, and the date of the copy we possess? Unless we have the original, the date of composition will of course always be earlier than a copy. The latter is relatively easy to determine with modern methods in palaeography and archaeology. However, our earliest manuscript of Exodus dates from about 250 BC, and all agree that it is not an original and that Exodus must have been composed much earlier. To discover that date is a much more involved process. If its author were named in the text, this would help. But a forgery could always claim to be written by Moses in the same terms as an authentic Mosaic document. A second clue to the date of a book lies in the events it records. Obviously its date of composition must be later than the last event mentioned – in the case of Exodus, the erection of the tabernacle. But this only tells us the earliest date at which the book could have been written, not the latest date, which is of more interest.

If there are no explicit statements in the text itself about its date of composition, we have to rely on indirect evidence, such as the assumptions of the writer. The author of the book of Judges shows when he was writing by remarking several times, 'In those days there was no king in Israel; every man did what was right in his own eyes.' The obvious implication is that the writer had experienced the order a just king could create, and was writing after the establishment of the monarchy.

The second important task of historical criticism is to verify information found in the biblical sources. When a document says something, how do we know it is telling the truth? This basic question may be broken down into a number of smaller ones. How close is the document to the events it describes? Are its statements backed up by other sources, biblical or non-biblical, or by archaeology? Could the events have occurred just as they are described? In trying to answer these questions the historian will be able to build up a fuller and richer picture of what happened. Discovering the author of a source may greatly illuminate the meaning of a narrative; and non-biblical sources can often fill in the background to the biblical account.

In these various ways biblical criticism has been of use in interpreting the Old Testament and defending its integrity against those who question its truth. Only too often Old Testament criticism, especially historical criticism, has been marred by the introduction of unjustified rationalistic assumptions (e.g. that miracles do not happen). But on the whole, the value of criticism has been proved by its generally positive conclusions. Certainly all who believe in the value of the Old Testament must take criticism seriously, as they will be the first to want to establish an accurate text and be sure of its meaning.

Old Testament 1.4

NUMBERS

Numbers covers 38 years in the history of Israel: the period of desert wandering in the Sinai peninsula. It begins two years after the escape from Egypt. It ends on the eve of entry into Canaan. The title comes from the 'numbering' (census) of Israel in the early chapters and chapter 26. The book might have been called 'The grumblings of a nation'. It is one long sad story of complaining and discontent. As a result, of the entire generation that had seen the marvels of God's deliverance from Egypt, only three men – Moses, Joshua and Caleb – survive to the end of the book. And only two – Joshua and Caleb – were to enjoy the promised land.

1 - 10:10 ISRAEL IN THE WILDERNESS OF SINAI

1 The general census

The purpose of the census is to list all men over 20 fit for military service. The Levites, by virtue of their other duties, were exempt. Moses and Aaron, the civic and religious heads, are in charge of the count, assisted by one representative from each tribe. In the second census (chapter 26), taken 38 years later, after Aaron's death, his son Eleazar takes his place. The later total, 601,730, is slightly less than the figure here, 603,550. In Egypt Israel's population rose rapidly, but now the tough desert conditions and the judgements their disobedience brings upon them keep the figures static.

The problem of high numbers: a military force of over 600,000 would mean a total population of some 2-3 million. The Bible account makes it plain that the numbers involved were considerable. Israel could not have survived in the desert without God's miraculous provision. Even so, 2-3 million would equal the entire population of Canaan. And other passages imply that the Canaanites were more numerous than the Israelites (Deuteronomy 7:7, 17, 22). For this reason, various attempts have been made to reduce the numbers. Some believe, for example, that the word translated 'thousands' should be 'captains'; others that it should be 'families'. It is also possible that the numbers are used as symbols of power and importance, rather than a literal count of heads. See further 'Large Numbers of the Old Testament'.

2 The encampment

When the nation moved, the three eastern tribes, headed by Judah, led the way. 10:17 gives a slightly different order for the middle section – Gershonites and Merarites carrying the tabernacle, then Reuben, Simeon and Gad, followed by the Kohathites with the sanctuary. The northern tribes, Dan, Asher and Naphtali bring up the rear. The tribal leaders are the same as those who helped in the census. Ramesses II of Egypt (Moses' contemporary) used this same hollow rectangular formation in his Syrian campaign, so it looks as if Moses was making good use of his earlier Egyptian military training.

The standards (2:2): according to Jewish tradition, a lion for Judah, a human head for Reuben, an ox for Ephraim and an eagle for Dan.

3 God chooses the Levites for special service

God's claim to the firstborn goes back to the night of the Passover (Exodus 12). Now God accepts the Levites instead of the firstborn of all Israel. The first census pairs them off man for man, leaving a surplus of 273 who are redeemed by money.

Shekel of the sanctuary (3:47): a weight of about 10gms, not a coin.

4 The Levitical families are assigned their jobs

The second census of Levites lists those between 30 and 50, eligible for the service of the tabernacle. (The age-limits varied at different times: see 8:24; 1 Chronicles 23:24.)

Verses 1-20: the **Kohathites** are responsible for carrying the sacred objects of the sanctuary after the priests have dismantled and covered them.

Verses 21-28: the **Gershonites** are in charge of transporting the curtains and coverings of the tabernacle and forecourt under Ithamar's supervision.

Verses 29-33: the **Merarites** are to look after and transport the framework – pillars, pegs, cords – also under Ithamar's supervision. Wagons drawn by a yoke of oxen are provided for the Gershonites and Merarites (7:7-8).

5 Various laws; the jealousy ordeal

Verses 11-31 describe the trial by ordeal for suspected infidelity. Trials of this kind were not uncommon in ancient times, and they are also well known from Africa and India. This one is mild by some standards – and also less heavily weighted than many towards a verdict of guilty. It is not clear whether the water contained some herb which would induce miscarriage if the woman were guilty and pregnant, or whether it worked simply by psychological suggestion.

6:1-21 The Nazirite

A special vow gives the Nazirite his (or her) spiritual status. The outward marks of consecration to God are:

- abstinence from wine and strong drink;
- uncut hair;
- special care to avoid defilement through contact with a dead body (see on chapter 19).

The vow was usually for a limited time, but Samson (a somewhat unorthodox Nazirite) had a lifelong vow (Judges 13-16). Samuel may also have been a Nazirite. It is not known how or when these practices originated.

6:22-27 Aaron's benediction

7 The tribes bring their offerings

The dedication of the altar preceded the events of Numbers 1 by a month. On successive days the leader of each tribe brings a silver plate and silver basin filled with a cereal offering, a golden dish of incense, and animals for burnt-offering, sin-offering and peace-offering (see on Leviticus 1-7).

8 Consecration of the Levites

Those who serve God must be clean through and through. Washing and shaving ensure outward cleanliness. The blood of sacrifice cleans man of the inward stain of sin.

9:1-14 Rulings about the Passover

No one may opt out of celebrating the Passover (see Exodus 12). But the absentee and anyone ritually unclean at the time may observe the feast one month later.

9:15-23 The cloud and the fire

God's guidance in the wilderness was a clear and visible reality. Cloud by day and fire by night marked his presence at the tabernacle, which was quite literally in their midst. When the cloud lifted they moved on. Where it settled again, they encamped: no movement of the cloud, no movement of the people.

10:1-10 The silver trumpets

These sounded the alarm, summoned the assembly, and announced the feasts and new months. Long trumpets like these were common in Egypt about 1400-1300 BC. Some were buried with the Pharaoh Tutankhamun (about 1350 BC).

10:11 - 12:16 FROM SINAI TO KADESH

10:11-36 The journey begins

About three weeks after the census they strike camp and leave Mt Sinai. (See on chapter 2 for the marching order.) Moses' brother-in-law goes with them as guide. The direction and company of the Lord is a very real thing (33-36).

11 Complaints about the monotonous diet

The first delicious taste of manna (see Exodus 16) was like wafers made with honey. Now sheer monotony makes it stick in the gullet like sawdust. Mouth-watering thoughts of all the fish and vegetables that abounded in the Egyptian delta soon produce an irresistible craving. God gives them what they want – till they are sick of it! And with it comes judgement for the attitude which lay behind the outcry.

Verse 29: a remarkable attitude in a leader – power without a streak of corruption (see 12:3).

A flock of quails, on their migration flight, satisfied the Israelites' craving for meat.

Quails (31): as in the previous year (Exodus 16), this was a migratory flight returning in spring to Europe.

Homer (32): 'a donkey load'; 10 homers is the measure of their gluttony.

12 Miriam and Aaron challenge Moses' leadership

The real bone of contention is not Moses' marriage, but his position. As Miriam is the one to be punished, presumably she was the instigator. Moses is silent, but God's answer is a remarkable tribute to the man (6-8).

Cushite (1): this is usually taken to mean 'Ethiopian'.

13 - 20:21 IN THE KADESH AREA

Details are few, but it seems that the best part of 38 years – a whole generation – was spent around here.

13 - 14 The twelve spies and their reports; mutiny

From Deuteronomy 1:19-25 it seems plain that Moses intended to go straight on into the promised land at this point; it was the people's suggestion that they should send spies ahead. No doubt Moses afterwards wished he had not listened. The two men of faith put the true interpretation on the facts (Numbers 13:30), but the people listened to the ten prophets of doom, with their tales of giants and grasshoppers. God, and the good land, was forgotten. Within sight of the goal, a whole generation cut itself off from all that was promised. Moses' prayer at this point is staggering. Only God's intervention has saved him from death by stoning. Yet here he is, pleading for the life of the stubborn nation that caused him nothing but trouble! Time and time again he stands between Israel and utter destruction (Exodus 32:7-14; Numbers 11:1-2; 16:41-48; 21:5-9). Now his plea involves him in sharing their sentence with them.

The Anakim ... the Nephilim: see Genesis 6:4. Nothing is known of them outside the Bible, but they were evidently a race of Goliaths.

Caleb never lost his whole-hearted trust in God. Forty-five years later, at the age of 85, he chooses Anakim territory to conquer as his possession (Joshua 14:6-15).

15 Various laws

Verses 1-31: offerings to be made after the conquest of Canaan.

Verses 32-36: the seriousness of sabbath-breaking.

Verses 37-41: the border of tassels to remind forgetful Israel of God and his commands.

16 The rebellion of Korah, Dathan and Abiram

This unholy alliance has a two-pronged attack. Korah the Levite's grievance is Aaron's monopoly of the priesthood (10b). Dathan and Abiram challenge Moses on the grounds of high-handedness and his failure to bring them into the promised land (13-14). But at root the attack is on God (11), and it is God who puts the rebellion down.

Put out the eyes (14): New English Bible 'hoodwink' gives the sense. Our equivalent of the Hebrew idiom is 'to pull wool over the eyes'.

The earth opened its mouth (32): God makes use of natural forces to execute judgement (as in the nine plagues of Egypt). The phenomenon here may be the breaking up (perhaps by storm) of the hard crusty surface which forms over deep lakes of liquid mud in the Arabah rift valley where this incident occurred.

17 Aaron's rod produces the fruit

Like all biblical miracles, this one has a very practical point. Everyone can see where God's choice falls, and there is no more room for dispute.

18 - 19 Duties and dues of the priests and Levites; the purification ritual

Neither priests nor Levites share in the inheritance of the land. Instead, God gives the priests the remainder of all the sacrificial offerings, first-fruits and firstlings. The Levites are given the nation's tithes (one tenth of all the flocks and herds and produce), of which they in turn give one tenth to the priests.

The ritual with the red heifer (19:1-10) is the remedy for defilement by contact with a dead body, described in verses 11-22. To minimize the risk of accidental defilement, tombs were later painted white (see Matthew 23:27).

20:1-13 Miriam's death; water from the rock

Miriam, Aaron (20:25ff; 33:38f.) and Moses (Deuteronomy 34:5-8) all died in the same year – on the brink of entry into Canaan. The best part of 38 years has passed since 13:1.

Verses 2-13: Moses' sin seems to be his failure to give God credit for the water-supply. It cost him the land he had so longed to enter. Even the greatest of God's servants, after a long lifetime of trust and obedience, can fall. Nothing seems to cure the people's grumbles. They were moaning when they first left Egypt. They are moaning still, after all the years of God's providing.

Water out of the rock: Sinai limestone is known to retain water (see on Exodus 17:6).

20:14-21 Edom refuses a safe-conduct

Your brother Israel (14): not just a manner of speaking, the Edomites were descendants of Esau, Jacob's brother.

King's Highway (17): Edom's refusal to let Israel pass along this main road involves them in a long detour south and round.

20:22 - 21:35 DETOUR TO AVOID EDOM

20:22-29 The death of Aaron

Mt Hor may be Jebel Madeira, north-east of Kadesh, on the north-west border of Edom.

21 Victories over Arad and Sihon; the incident of the poisonous snakes

Complaints begin again on the trek south to the Gulf of Aqaba (the 'Red Sea' here) to clear Edom's territory. Jesus used the incident of the bronze serpent to explain his own death in his discussion with Nicodemus (John 3:14). In the wilderness the people had only to look, and they lived.

The well (16): water lies close to the surface in some parts of the Sinai peninsula and southern Transjordan. The Israelities often had only to dig shallow pits to find it.

22 - 36 ISRAEL IN THE PLAINS OF MOAB

22 - 24 Balak and Balaam: the blessing of Israel

With the Israelites encamped on his doorstep, the king of Moab sends to Pethor (probably Pitru, near Carchemish) on the Euphrates for Balaam the diviner to come and curse his enemies. It was a routine business arrangement for the prophet, in a day when everyone believed in the power of words (especially formal 'blessings' and 'cursings') to influence events. What is surprising is the disclosure that the source of Balaam's knowledge is God himself. And neither bribe nor threat will budge him from the truth as God reveals it to him.

Three times they go through the same ritual (22:41 - 23:10; 23:13-24; 23:27 - 24:9). Three times Balaam blesses Israel, to the increasing anger of Balak. The fourth oracle tops all (24:15-24) – a remarkable prediction of Israel's future.

The incident of the ass: God's purpose seems to be so to impress Balaam, that no matter how hard Balak works on him, the prophet will stick to the truth.

The origin of these oracles: it is not known how these oracles came to be included in Numbers. But linguistic and other factors indicate that the oracles were written down by the 12th century BC.

25 Idolatry at Peor

It was on Balaam's advice (31:16, Revised Standard Version) that the Midianite women brought Israel low at Peor. And he paid for it with his life (31:8).

Play the harlot (1): they did so literally and also as far as religion was concerned. By joining in pagan worship, Israel broke faith with God.

Baal of Peor (3): the local deity of the place. 'Baal' (meaning 'master') gradually became a proper name for the great fertility god of the Canaanites. The events described here already show a blend of sexual and religious practices.

Moabite ... Midianite: the interchange of terms sounds confused, but from late patriarchal times on, there was in fact a good deal of overlap in the use of the terms 'Midianite', 'Ishmaelite', 'Medanite', 'Moabite'.

26 The second census

See on chapter 1.

27:1-11 The right of daughters to inherit

Women could not normally inherit in other ancient Near Eastern countries, but in Israel the ruling is given that brotherless daughters may inherit. However, to safeguard the tribal inheritance, they must marry within their own tribe (see chapter 36).

27:12-23 Joshua appointed as Moses' successor

Moses' life is almost over. Joshua, his right-hand man (Exodus 17:9ff.; 24:13; 33:11; Numbers 11:28) and one of the two faithful spies (14:6ff.), is now invested with authority to lead the nation in his place.

Mt Abarim (12): the name of the mountain range. Mt Nebo, overlooking Jericho, was the actual summit from which Moses viewed the land.

You rebelled against my word (14): see on 20:2-13.

28 - 30 Rules for public worship and vows

28: 1-8, daily offerings; 9, 10, sabbath offerings; 11-15, offerings for each new month; 16-25, offerings for Passover and Unleavened Bread; 26-31, the Feast of Weeks (Firstfruits).

Chapter 29: the feasts of the seventh month. Verses 1-6, offerings for the Feast of Trumpets; 7-11, for the Day of Atonement; 12-38, for the Feast of Booths.

For feasts, see Leviticus 23, and article. For offerings see on Leviticus 1-7, and article.

Chapter 30: vows. Men in Israel are unconditionally bound by vows of any kind (1, 2). Verses 3-15: the terms under which vows made by women are binding.

31 Vengeance on the Midianites; dealing with the spoil

The Midianites are punished for their sin in inducing Israel to worship false gods (see chapter 25 and notes). Army and nation divide the spoil fifty-fifty. One five-hundredth of the army's share goes to the priests; one fiftieth of the nation's share to the Levites. Verses 48-54 record the army's special offering given in gratitude for their safe return.

32 Reuben, Gad and half Manasseh settle east of the Jordan

See map. This is permitted only on condition that they help in the conquest of Canaan before returning to a settled life.

33 A list of the stages of the journey from Egypt to the plains of Moab

Figured stones ... high places (52): i.e. stone carvings, and hilltops or artificial 'high places' where shrines were built. The intention is to wipe out everything associated with idolatrous religions.

34 The ideal boundaries of Israel

See also Joshua 13-19.

35 Cities and pasture for the Levites: the six cities of refuge for those who cause death by accident

See also Joshua 20-21.

36 Safeguards in the case of daughters' inheritance

See on 27:1-11

THE LARGE NUMBERS OF THE OLD TESTAMENT

John Wenham

The Old Testament at various places records numbers which seem impossibly large. It has often been assumed that these figures were simply invented, and are evidence that the Bible is historically unreliable. But who would make up figures which are patently absurd? Would any man in his senses invent a story of a bus crash in which 16,000 passengers were killed? It is much more likely that these Old Testament numbers were faithfully copied out, despite the fact that they did not seem to make sense. Invention does not satisfactorily account for them. The explanation must lie elsewhere. And in fact patient research has gone a long way towards resolving this knotty problem.

The corruption of numbers

There is evidence that the Old Testament text is on the whole marvellously well preserved. There is also evidence from the parallel passages in Samuel, Kings and Chronicles and (especially) in Ezra 2 and Nehemiah 7 that numbers were peculiarly difficult to transmit accurately. We have instances of extra noughts being added to a number: 2 Samuel 10:18 reads '700 chariots', 1 Chronicles 19:18 reads '7,000'. A digit can drop out: 2 Kings 24:8 gives the age of Jehoiachin on accession as 18, whereas 2 Chronicles 36:9 gives it as 8. An entire numeral can drop out: 1 Samuel 13:1 says 'Saul was years old'. In Ezra 2 and Nehemiah 7 the digits often vary by one unit.

And there are other errors of copying, many of which are easily explained.

The confusion of words

In the modern Hebrew Bible all numbers are written out in full, but for a long time the text was written without vowels. The absence of vowels made it possible to confuse two words which are crucial to this problem: *'eleph* and *'alluph*. Without vowel points these words look identical: *'lp*. *'eleph* is the ordinary word for 'thousand', but it can also be used in a variety of other senses: e.g. 'family' (Judges 6:15, Revised Version) or 'clan' (Zechariah 9:7; 12:5, 6, Revised Standard Version) or perhaps a military unit. *'alluph* is used for the 'chieftains' of Edom (Genesis 36:15-43); probably for a commander of a military 'thousand'; and almost certainly for the professional, fully-armed soldier.

Military statistics

At certain periods warfare was conducted by two sharply distinguished types of fighting men – the Goliaths and the Davids – the professional soldiers who were fully armed, and the folk army, whose only weapons were those of the peasant shepherd. It seems clear that in a number of places the word for professional soldier has been misunderstood as meaning 'thousand'. Take, for example, the attack on the little town of Gibeah in Judges 20. Verse 2 says that 400,000 footmen 'that drew the sword' assembled. If these were in fact 400 fully armed foot-soldiers, the subsequent narrative makes excellent sense. The Benjamite forces (verse 15) consist of 26 soldiers armed with swords, together with 700 men armed only with slings. At the first attack (verse 21) the Israelites lose 22 of their crack soldiers, the next day (verse 25) they lose a further 18; on the third day (verses 29,34) an ambush is set, consisting of, or led by, 10 of them. (Could 10,000 men take up their positions undetected?) The losses begin again (verse 31) 'as at other times' – and in this case the scale of loss has been clearly preserved, for about 30 Israelites (not apparently sword-armed soldiers). 25 Benjamite soldiers and 100 others are killed. Eighteen of them were killed in the first stage of the pursuit, 5 were later 'cut down in the highways' and 2 more at Gidom. The remaining 600 slingers took refuge in the rock of Rimmon. Similarly, in the assault on Ai (Joshua 7-8) the true proportions of the narrative become clear when we realize that the disastrous loss of 36 men is matched by the setting of an ambush, not of 30,000 men of valour, but of 30.

David's feast in Hebron in 1 Chronicles 12 appears to be attended by enormous numbers, not of ordinary men, but of distinguished leaders – some 340,800 of them. In this case it looks as though in fact there were 'captains of thousands' and 'captains of hundreds', and that by metonymy or by abbreviation 'thousand' has been used for 'captains of thousands' and 'hundreds' for 'captains of hundreds'. 'Thousand' and 'hundred' have been treated as numerals and added together. When these figures are unscrambled, we get a total of roughly 2,000 'famous men', which seems eminently reasonable.

Along these lines most of the numerical problems of the later history fall into place. In 1 Kings 20:27-30, the little Israelite army killed 100 (not 100,000) foot-soldiers, and the wall of Aphek killed 27 (not 27,000) more. The Ethiopian invasion had a thousand, not a million, warriors (2 Chronicles 14:9). 10 (not 10,000) were cast down from the top of the rock (2 Chronicles 25:12).

The size of the Israelite nation

The most interesting, most difficult and (from the historian's point of view) the most important question is the size of the Israelite population at the different stages of its history. The present texts indicate that the 70 souls of Joseph's day had risen to two or three million at the time of the Exodus (Numbers 1) and to at least five million in the time of David (2 Samuel 24:9; 1 Chronicles 21:5). With regard to the latter, R. de Vaux rightly says: '(2 Samuel) lists 800,000 men liable for military service in Israel, and 500,000 in Judah ... The lower total, in 2 Samuel, is still far too high: 1,300,000 men of military age would imply at least five million inhabitants, which, for Palestine, would mean nearly twice as many people to the square mile as in the most thickly populated countries of modern Europe.'

The solution of the problem of the Exodus numbers is a long story. Suffice it to say that there is good reason to believe that the original censuses in Numbers 1 and 26 set out the numbers of each tribe, somewhat in this form:

Simeon:
57 armed men; 23 'hundreds' (military units).
This came to be written:
57 *'lp*; 2 *'lp* 3 'hundreds'.

Not realising that *'lp* in one case meant 'armed man' and in the other 'thousand', this was tidied up to read 59,300. When these figures are carefully decoded, a remarkably clear picture of the whole military organization emerges. The total fighting force is some 18,000, which would probably mean a figure of about 72,000 for the whole migration.

The figures of the Levites seem consistently to have collected an extra nought. The mystery of Plato's Atlantis has been solved by recognition of this same numerical confusion. Plato obtained *from Egyptian priests* what now turns out to be a detailed account of the Minoan civilization and its sudden end. But as all the figures were multiplied by a factor of ten, the area was too great to be enclosed in the Mediterranean, so he placed it in the Atlantic; and the date was put back into remote antiquity, thousands of years too early. This same tenfold multiplication factor is found in the figures of the Levites in the book of Numbers. When it is eliminated Levi fits into the pattern as a standard-size tribe of about 2,200 males. These figures agree remarkably well with the other indications of population in the period of the conquest and the judges.

David's census

The discrepancy between the two sets of figures for David's census can be accounted for by recognizing at different stages in transmission, first, the addition of noughts, and then, a misunderstanding of *'lp*. If we postulate original figures: Israel: 80,000 plus 30 *'lp*; Judah: 40,000 plus 70 *'lp*, the present text of both Samuel and Chronicles can be accounted for thus:

Chronicles
Stage 1
Israel: 80,000 plus 30 *'lp*
Judah: 40,000 plus 70 *'lp*

Stage 2
Israel: 800,000 plus 300 *'lp*
Judah: 400,000 plus 70 *'lp*

Stage 3
Israel: 1,100,000
Judah: 470,000

Samuel
Stage 1
Israel: 80,000 plus 30 *'lp*
Judah: 40,000 plus 70 *'lp*

Stage 2
Israel: 800,000 plus 30 *'lp*
Judah: 470,000

At this stage it would seem that the copyist was perplexed by the floating '30 *'lp*', which he took to be 30,000. He wrongly combined it with the Judah figure, so producing:

Stage 3
Israel: 800,000
Judah: 500,000

If the original figures totalled 120,000 men of military age, together with 100 professional soldiers, the entire population would have been nearly half a million, which again tallies well with other indications in the text.

By the use of these methods a very large proportion of the numerical difficulties can be resolved.

Old Testament 1.5

DEUTERONOMY

Deuteronomy is the record of Moses' farewell addresses to Israel, given about 1260 BC on the plains of Moab, on the eve of entry to the promised land. The title, which comes from the Greek translation, implies a second law-giving, but in fact the book contains a restatement and reaffirmation of the Sinai covenant. It follows a specific treaty-pattern (see article 'Covenants and Near Eastern Treaties'):

1 *Introduction* 1:1-5
2 *Historical prologue* 1:6 - 4:49
3 *Stipulations* 5:1 - 26:19
4 *Curses and blessings* 27:1 - 30:20
5 *Succession arrangements and public reading* 31:1 - 34:5

The laws recorded in Exodus, Leviticus and Numbers are brought together and applied specifically to the settled life of Canaan which is about to begin.

1:1-5 INTRODUCTION

Time and place are carefully specified. Forty years after the exodus, at the end of the wilderness wanderings, in the plains beyond Jordan, Moses gives God's message to Israel.

Eleven days' journey from Horeb ... (2): the journey from Jebel Musa (traditional site of Mt Sinai/Horeb) to Dahab on the east coast of Sinai, up the coast and across to Kadesh (the Ain Qudeirat area) has recently been shown to take just this time.

1:6 - 4:49 HISTORICAL PROLOGUE: MOSES LOOKS BACK

1:6-46 Sinai to Kadesh; the spies and the revolt

Verses 9-18: Moses recalls how he found relief from the solitary burden of leadership in delegating responsibility. The wise advice to do so came from his father-in-law, Jethro (see Exodus 18:13-26).

Verses 19-46: see on Numbers 13-14.

That great and terrible wilderness (19): 'wilderness' simply means uninhabited land. North of Sinai the land is barren and desolate, with rugged peaks and the earth covered with stones and flints. But there are oases, with a surprising amount of vegetation after the winter rains.

Amorites (44): Numbers 14:43 uses the wider term 'Canaanites'.

2 Edom, Moab, Ammon; war against the Amorites

Verses 1-8: see Numbers 20:14-21. Although the Edomites refused Israel passage along the King's Highway, it seems that some were willing to sell them food. The friendliness shown to Edom (Esau's descendants), Moab and Ammon (Lot's descendants, see Genesis 19:36-38) on grounds of kinship is characteristic of patriarchal and Mosaic times. God keeps his word down the ages, and he expects his people to keep theirs.

Verses 26-37: see Numbers 21:21-35.

Seir (8): the mountains of 'Seir', i.e. Edom, rise to the south and east of the Dead Sea.

Made his heart obstinate (30): the Old Testament sees no conflict between God's sovereignty and man's freedom. God is never described as 'hardening the heart' of a good man. See also on Exodus 6-10.

3 War against King Og; settlement of the two and a half tribes

See Numbers 21:33-35, and chapter 32. Og's land was part of the Amorite kingdom. Bashan, famed for its cattle, with the area around was an attractive proposition to the stockmen of Reuben, Gad, and Manasseh.

His bedstead (11): probably a coffin. The 'common cubit' was about 18 inches or 450 mm.

The Arabah (17): the rift valley which runs from the Sea of Galilee south to the Gulf of Aqaba. 'Chinnereth' is Galilee: the word comes from the harp shape of the lake. The 'Salt Sea' is the Dead Sea.

Verses 23-26: the price of disobedience was a heavy one. What Moses longed for above all was to lead his people into the promised land. 'On your account' is not merely an attempt to shift the blame. It was the people's provocation which stung him to anger.

4:1-40 Moses' warning and call to obedience

Moses has recounted the history of God's dealings with Israel over the past 40 years. Now he reminds them of God's character as shown in his acts, and warns of the inevitable consequences of disobedience to him. 'The Lord is God in heaven above and on earth below; there is no other ... Keep his statutes ... then all will be well with you.'

Baal-peor (3): see Numbers 25.

Statutes (8): permanent rules of conduct;

ordinances/judgements: case-laws, judicial decisions.

4:41-43 Three cities of refuge for Transjordan

4:44-49 Historical and geographical setting of the covenant restated

5 - 11 BASIC COMMANDMENTS

5 The Ten commandments and the law-giving at Sinai

See also Exodus 19:16 - 20:21 (and the notes on Exodus 20 above). Moses does not hesitate to modify the application, so that it relates more closely to a settled life (14-16,21).

6 The great commandment; instruction to teach future generations

Jesus said that the whole law could be summed up in the words of verse 5 and Leviticus 19:18 (see Matthew 22:37-40).

An orthodox Jew wears his phylactery (passages from the law, in a small box) bound to his forehead in literal obedience to Deuteronomy 6:8.

You shall write them (9): ordinary people possessed no copy of the law, so it was to be taught by word of mouth, and important parts written down where they could not fail to see

COVENANTS AND NEAR EASTERN TREATIES

Gordon Wenham

Hebrew uses the same word for an international treaty and a covenant between God and his people. Recent study has shown that similarities between ancient Near Eastern treaties and Old Testament covenants extend much further than this, and considerable light has been shed on the characteristics of Old Testament covenants, and our understanding of the Old Testament generally, by comparing them with treaties.

Most of the ancient treaties discovered this century date from about 1500 to 600 BC, a period in which much of the Old Testament was composed. It therefore seems likely that the writers would have been familiar with the way in which treaties were drafted. Furthermore their use of treaty terms and ideas shows that they found the relationship between treaty-partners an apt picture of that between God and his people.

The earliest covenant recorded in Scripture was made with Noah (Genesis 9). Covenants were also made with Abraham (Genesis 15, 17). But by far the most important covenant in the Old Testament is the covenant of Sinai (Exodus 19ff.). Though Sinai is commonly thought of as the occasion when God's law was made known to Israel, in fact the law-giving was only one part of a much larger event, the call of Israel to be a holy nation owing exclusive allegiance to the Lord. The new relationship was termed a covenant. The covenant made at Sinai was the decisive step in the creation of Israel as a nation; all subsequent covenants looked back to Sinai as their model, and in a sense were regarded as renewals of it.

Covenants resemble treaties in three principal respects: in language, form and ideology.

Language

The purpose of a treaty is to secure the entire allegiance of a vassal-king or state to the other partner in the treaty, whether it be a king or an empire. To this end florid and rhetor ical language is used in the treaties to stir the emotions of the vassal and impress on him the importance of obedience. Rhetorical style has long been regarded as characteristic of Deuteronomy, a work that in other respects bears a close resemblance to a vassal treaty. Certain terms are used in treaties to describe an obedient vassal's behaviour. A good vassal should 'go after', 'fear', 'love', 'hearken to the voice of his lord'. A rebellious vassal 'sins'. This phraseology is often echoed in the Old Testament.

Form

The most striking similarity between treaties and Old Testament covenants is in their form, in their basic outline structure. The classical Near Eastern treaty used by the Hittites had six parts:

1. A preamble naming the author of the treaty.

2. A historical prologue setting out the relations between the parties prior to signing the treaty.

3. Stipulations explaining the mutual responsibilities of the partners.

4. A document clause describing the treaty document and arranging for the vassal to read it at regular intervals.

5. A list of gods witnessing the treaty.

6. Curses and blessings threatening the vassal with illness, death, deportation, etc. if he breaks the treaty, but promising him prosperity and blessing if he remains faithful.

Old Testament covenants have a similar though not identical structure. For instance, believing in one God, they omitted the list of gods as witnesses. Deuteronomy contains most elements of the treaty form:

1-3 Historical prologue
4-26 Stipulations
27 Document clause
28 Blessings and curses.

Exodus 19-24, Joshua 24, and 1 Samuel 12 are other shorter examples of the treaty form in the Old Testament.

Ideology

Treaties and covenants both begin with history and both insist on the grace and mercy of the author of the covenant. The Hittite king can remind his vassal of his kindness in allowing him to continue as king of the vassal state in spite of his recent rebellion. God in similar tones reminds Israel of his mercy, 'I am the Lord your God, who brought you out of the land of Egypt' (Exodus 20:2).

In both treaties and covenants, the basis of the stipulations is the undeserved favour of the overlord. Stipulations or laws come after the vassal has been reminded of what the treaty-lord has done for him. He is expected to obey the stipulations out of gratitude. Similarly in the Old Testament, law follows grace. Because of the way God has saved them, Israel is encouraged to obey.

Blessing and prosperity are promised if the vassal remains obedient, but curses are invoked on him if he rebels. Drafters of treaties and the authors of the Old Testament, well knowing the human heart, tend to dwell much more on the curses than the blessings. Appalling pictures are drawn of the sufferings the people will endure if they disregard the demands of the covenant (see Deuteronomy 28:15-68). Prophetic threats of coming judgement often echo these covenant curses. The prophets remind the people that the covenant relationship involves responsibility as well as privilege (e.g. Amos 3:2).

The Dead Sea Scrolls show that covenant ideas continued to be important in Jewish theology up to the New Testament era. Jesus himself clearly assumed that his disciples were familiar with covenant thinking, when he referred to his death as inaugurating the new covenant (Mark 14:24).

it. The whole law was also engraved on plastered stones and set up in public places (see 27:1-10; Joshua 8:32).

Cisterns (11): pits for storing water collected from rainfall or from a spring. The inside was coated with waterproof mortar. The pits narrowed at the top to reduce evaporation.

Massah (16): see Exodus 17:6-7.

7 - 11 Moses calls the nation to faith and obedience

Moses turns from the past to the present and future. Israel will soon be right in amongst the pagan nations. They will taste the heady glory of victory (chapter 7). Prosperity will bring an unprecedented rise in the standard of living. There will be much to enjoy (chapter 8). And all these things bring dangers: the danger of losing their identity as God's people; the danger of false pride (chapter 9), of patting themselves on the back for all they have achieved; the danger of leaving God out of account.

But if they will let it, the past can keep them on the right lines for the future. So Moses urges them: 'Remember'; 'Do not forget.' Remember Egypt (7:18). Remember the wilderness (8:2). Remember what you were really like (9:7). Remember God's love, his power, his provision, his law, his judgements. And let that memory keep you humble, faithful, obedient (chapters 10-11).

Not like the land of Egypt (11:10): there the vegetable crops depended on irrigation, using water from the Nile.

Blessing and curse: Gerizim ... Ebal (11:26ff.): see on chapter 27.

12 - 26 DETAILED LAWS

12 - 13 Idols to be destroyed; the place for offerings; dealing with offenders

12:1-14: all the places where the Canaanites practised their depraved rites are to be wiped out. Israel is not to use them. When the nation is settled God will select a specific place for the sacrifices.

12:15-32: meat was not a staple food for the ordinary Israelite, but all enjoyed it at feasts and sacrifices. On the matter of the blood, see Leviticus 17:10ff. and article 'The Meaning of Blood Sacrifice'.

13:1-18: the danger of being enticed away to false religions was very real. Anyone encouraging this must be summarily dealt with. It was a case of drastic action to prevent contagion.

14 Clean and unclean animals; tithes

Verses 3-21: see on Leviticus 11.

Verses 22-29: see also Leviticus 27 and Numbers 18. All man's wealth is God's gift. To remind him of this, a proportion is regularly set aside. Jewish writers generally see the tithe (one tenth) here as a 'second tithe', the first being given to the Levites. It provides an occasion for enjoyment, for entering into the result of one's labour, and for generous sharing with others.

15 The seventh year

Every seventh year is a year of release for Hebrew slaves, and cancellation of debts contracted by fellow-Israelites. See on Leviticus 25.

Verses 19-23: see on Leviticus 27.

16 The three main feasts

See the full list, Leviticus 23, and article 'Feasts and Festivals'. Three times each year – Passover, Weeks (Pentecost), Booths (Tabernacles) – all Jewish men were required to present themselves at the chosen place of assembly.

Asherah ... pillar (21-22): wooden images, and symbols of pagan deities.

17 The death-penalty for idolatry (1-7); legal problem-cases (8-13); the future king (14-20)

Verses 14-20: God permits the monarchy, but does not set it up. The dangers foreseen here – military aggression, and sensuality leading to idolatry – became an uncomfortable reality in Solomon's reign, 300 years later.

18 Revenue for priests and Levites (1-8); witchcraft (9-14); the future prophet (15-22)

Verses 1-8: see also Numbers 18.

Verses 9-14: compare Leviticus 18:3, 24-30; 20:1-6.

A prophet like me (15): God raised up many prophets in succeeding centuries. But the New Testament seems to see in this a reference to the prophet *par excellence*, Jesus himself (John 5:46; Acts 3:22-26).

19 Cities of refuge (1-3); provisions covering accidental death and murder (4-13); prohibition of acquiring property by fraud (14); witnesses (15-21)

Three cities of refuge in Canaan are added to the three in Transjordan (4:41-43). Joshua 20 lists them as: Kedesh, Shechem, Kiriath-arba (Hebron), Bezer, Ramoth and Golan.

Avenger of blood (6): the dead man's next of kin, whose duty it was to avenge his death. The regulations here are designed to prevent the development of a blood-feud.
Landmark (14): a stone inscribed with the boundaries of the property.
The law of retaliation (21): see on Leviticus 24.

20 Rules for war

Those who have built a new house or planted a new vineyard, the newly married, and the fainthearted are excused military service. Verses 10-18 make a distinction between the treatment of Canaanite nations and those further afield.
You shall utterly destroy ... (17): in contrast to the compassion and humanitarianism of verses 1-11 and the concern for conservation in verses 19-20 this ruling seems incredibly harsh. But there is nothing arbitrary about it. The evil and corrupt religious practices of the Canaanite nations – child sacrifice, prostitution and much else – were highly contagious and therefore highly dangerous to the new nation of Israel. And God, in his patience, had given these nations long centuries in which to change their ways (Genesis 15:16).

21 Murder by an unknown hand (1-9); women captives (10-14); the right of the firstborn (15-17); sons beyond parental control (18-21); execution by hanging (22-23)

God sets a basic value and dignity on every human life – even of the individual society sets least store by.
Shave her head (12): either a sign of purification from heathenism, or a mourning.
Right of the firstborn (17): already ancient custom. The trouble in Jacob's family stemmed from this kind of favouritism.
The stubborn and rebellious son (18) was casting off the authority not only of his parents but of God himself.
Accursed by God (23): see Galatians 3:13-14.

The Law-Code of King Hammurabi of Babylon (about 1750 BC) is inscribed on this dark stone obelisk.

22 Lost animals and lost property (1-4); keeping the sexes distinct (5) birds-nesting (6-7); building, farming, clothing (8-12); sexual relations (13-30)

These are rules which encourage attitudes of mutual help and care, and a concern for purity.
Verse 5: a rule intended as a protection against perversion and immorality.
Verses 9-11: man should not obliterate the clear distinctions God has made in nature.
Tassels (12): see on Numbers 15:37-41.
Tokens of virginity (14): a blood-stained cloth from the wedding-night is still displayed as proof of the bride's chastity in some places in the Near East.

23 Membership of the congregation (1-8); social rules (9-25)

The Lord's community is both inclusive (7-8) and exclusive (1-6). It is marked by purity and holiness (10-14, 17-18) and practical humanity (15-16, 19-20).
Verses 1 and 17-18: a protest and safeguard against Canaanite cultic practices. 'Dog' (18) refers to a male prostitute.
Verse 2: a condemnation, not of the individual concerned, but of the illicit sexual relationship in which he was conceived.
Balaam (4): see Numbers 22-24.
Verse 15: Paul's letter to Philemon provides an interesting New Testament comment.

24 Divorce (1-4) humanitarian laws (5-22)

Verses 1-4: Moses is not instituting divorce, but regulating ancient practice, first by insisting on a definite grievance, and second by issuing a formal document.

Verses 5-22: even in exercising their rights, God's people are to be thoughtful of others. To take away one millstone, for example, left the other useless for grinding flour to make the day's bread.
Leprosy (8): the term includes various skin diseases. See on Leviticus 13 - 14.
Miriam (9): see Numbers 12.

25 Corporal punishment (1-3); compassion for working animals (4), the Levirate marriage law (5-10), fights (11-12), fair weights (13-16), punishment of the Amalekites (17-19)

Verses 1-3: the lash is to punish guilt, not extract confession. It must never take away human dignity or self-respect. The 'forty stripes' later became 39, for fear of inadvertently overstepping the limit (see 2 Corinthians 11:24).

Verses 5-10: the Levirate ('husband's brother') law was intended to prevent the calamity of the family name dying out. See Ruth (and for the sandal custom, Ruth 4:7).
Muzzling the ox (4): the New Testament extends this principle – see 1 Corinthians 9:3-14.

26 Firstfruits and tithes (1-15); concluding plea (16-19)

See on 14:22-29. The firstfruits ceremony includes the recital of a lovely prayer of remembrance and praise summarizing Israel's career.

Verses 16-19: blessing comes through obedience.
A wandering Aramaean (5): after leaving Ur, Abraham stayed in Aram-naharaim, where part of his family settled (becoming Aramaeans) while he journeyed on to Canaan.

27 - 30 CURSES AND BLESSINGS

The curses and blessings are an integral part of the ancient Near Eastern covenant. See 'Covenants and Near Eastern Treaties'.

27 1-10 The law is recorded

See on 6:9.

27 11-26 The curses

Gerizim and Ebal are the two most prominent hills in the natural centre of Palestine. With six tribes on either side, the Levites are to pronounce a curse on twelve infringements of the law, and the people to add their assent. See Joshua 8:30-35.

28 1-14 Blessings

Obedience will bring the benefits of victory, peace, fruitfulness, prosperity.

28 15-68 Solemn curses

Disobedience will result in disease, famine, defeat, subservience, and ultimately exile, loss of homeland and all the joys of life. This is no idle threat, as events later proved, even to the horrors of siege (see 2 Kings 6:24-30; Lamentations 2).
Powder and dust (24): sandstorms and duststorms in place of rain.

27 - 30 Moses calls the nation to a new commitment

Moses' life is fast drawing to a close. He puts his whole heart into this final appeal. He pleads (29:2-15). He warns (16-28). He encourages (30:1-14). He confronts them with the

choice: life or death, blessing or curse (15-20).
Moist and dry alike (29:19): New English Bible, 'this will bring everything to ruin' catches the spirit of the proverb.
Sodom and Gomorrah, Admah and Zeboiim (29:23): cities at the southern end of the Dead Sea engulfed in the catastrophe of Genesis 19:24ff.
Secret things (29:29): certain matters of eternal significance are known only to God (see also Acts 1:7).
30:11-14: Moses speaks of the accessibility of God's word. Paul (Romans 10:5-8) takes the thought and applies it to Christ, the Word made flesh.

31 THE COVENANT PLACED IN SAFE-KEEPING: THE SUCCESSION ASSURED

The law is safely deposited with the Levites, and provision made for regular public reading. Throughout their subsequent history, Israel prospered in so far as they listened to God's word and obeyed it. Joshua is formally appointed as Moses' successor (see Numbers 27:12-23).
Go out and come in (2): New English Bible 'move freely' gives the sense. The phrase is used of citizens who 'go in and out' of a city, etc.

32:1-47 MOSES' SONG

God is the best of teachers. He instructs Moses to warn his people of their future treacherous disloyalty in song, to make it unforgettable (31:19).
Apple of his eye (10): the pupil, on which sight depends.
Jeshurun (15): a poetic name for Israel.

32:48 - 34:12 MOSES' BLESSING AND DEATH

32:48-52 Moses receives his last orders

33 Moses blesses the tribes

After all the warnings, this last blessing looks forward to a great and glorious future for Israel. Simeon is omitted from the tribes: his people were later absorbed by Judah. (Compare Jacob's blessing in Genesis 49.)
Verses 2-5: the law-giving at Sinai is pictured as an eastern sunrise.
Let Reuben live (6): the tribe's numbers were reduced through the rebellion of Dathan and Abiram (Numbers 16).
Thummim and Urim (8): two objects kept in the high priest's breastplate by which he ascertained God's will (see Exodus 28:30).
Massah, Meribah: see Exodus 17 and Numbers 20.
Makes his dwelling between his shoulders (12): either a picture of God as Shepherd, carrying his lamb, or a reference to God's house at Jerusalem, which would be built on Benjamite territory.
Choicest fruits (14): the valleys of Ephraim and Manasseh were laden with fruit, year by year.
Your going out ... in your tents (18): Zebulun's success was in commerce, Issachar's in agriculture and domestic life.
The lake and the south (23): the fertile land south and west of the Sea of Galilee.
Oil (24): Asher's territory was famous for its olives.

34:1-8 The death of Moses

At last Moses sees the land he has for 40 years longed to enter. Israel sees him no more. But we meet him once again in Scripture – on a mountain, talking to the Lord (Mark 9:2-4)

34:9-12 Conclusion

The action now passes to Joshua – but the book closes with a simple and moving tribute to the greatest of all Israel's leaders. There would be no prophet to match him until Elijah; no one to surpass him but Christ himself.

Old Testament section 2

THE HISTORICAL BOOKS

Introduction/John Taylor

In the Hebrew Bible the account of Israel's history was in two separate sections:
The Prophets included Joshua, Judges, 1 and 2 Samuel, 1 and 2 Kings;
The Writings included 1 and 2 Chronicles, Ezra and Nehemiah.

PROPHETIC HISTORY

The historical narrative from Joshua to 2 Kings was in fact given the title 'The Former Prophets' in Hebrew. This was to distinguish the books from the Latter Prophets – Isaiah, Jeremiah, Ezekiel and the twelve minor prophets. What is interesting is that it was called prophecy at all.

There are two possible reasons for this. Either it was because the main aim of the books was to teach; or else because they are the history not so much of the nation as of the way God's message was fulfilled in the nation's life.

This group of six books (not counting Ruth, which belongs to 'The Writings' in the Hebrew Bible) has been regarded by many scholars as one complete historical work. Some call it the 'Deuteronomic history', because the theological viewpoint expressed is similar to that of Deuteronomy.

If the books are treated as a basic unity in this way, the earliest date that could be given to the entire work would be shortly after the last event in 2 Kings – the release of King Jehoiachin from prison in 561 BC. However, this would apply only to the latest editorial work. Most of the material is much earlier and contemporary sources were often used.

Sources quoted in the text include the Book of Jashar (perhaps an ancient national song-book of Israel), the Book of the Acts of Solomon and the Chronicles of the Kings of Judah and Israel (unconnected with the Books of Chronicles in our Bibles). These were court archives, or popular histories based on them. They illustrate two things: the amount of historical writing that had gone on in Israel during the monarchy; and the number of written sources which were available to the biblical authors. It is fair to assume that the sources quoted were not the only ones used, and that other writings – such as a Court-history of David and a collection of Elijah-Elisha stories – were also freely drawn upon.

The period covered by these books extends from Joshua's entry into the land of Canaan until the middle of the exile. Most scholars prefer the late 13th century date for the conquest to an earlier one (1400 BC has been suggested on the basis of 1 Kings 6:1) and would see the events of Joshua and Judges as taking place between 1240 and 1050 BC.

Joshua covers the life-span of Moses' successor and describes the conquest of Canaan from the crossing of the River Jordan to the covenant-renewal ceremony at Shechem which established the tribes in a united allegiance to the Lord. Space is also given to a detailed description of the apportionment of Canaan among the twelve tribes (Joshua 13-21).

Judges begins with a reminder that the conquest under Joshua was by no means complete and that almost every tribal allotment still contained pockets of enemy resistance. In fact, this was the setting for the whole book, for throughout the period of the Judges individual tribes suffered from the incursions of hostile neighbours (or former residents!) and the judges, or 'liberators', were raised up to lead the tribes against them in open battle or guerilla warfare.

Chief among these were *Deborah and Barak*, who led the combined forces of Zebulun and Naphtali against the Canaanites under Sisera; *Gideon* of Manasseh who defeated the Midianites and Amalekites; *Jephthah* the Gileadite who subdued the Ammonites; and *Samson* the Danite who successfully baited the Philistines. The book ends with two bizarre episodes. The first describes the establishment of a new sanctuary for the tribe of Dan (Judges 17-18). The second deals with the punishment of Benjamin for an outrage committed by the people of Gibeah (Judges 19-21).

So far the historical element in the writings has been relatively small: the style has been episodic, occasionally moralistic, and owing a good deal to the art of story-telling. With **1 and 2 Samuel** (the division between them is artificial and probably due only to the length of a scroll) we begin to have a more chronological record of events, and this is particularly true of the story of David. *Samuel* is an important figure at the start, being judge and prophet combined, but the interest is really focussed on the question of kingship, and Samuel fades into the background as first *Saul* and then *David* dominate the scene. Saul probably reigned from shortly after the defeat at Aphek in 1050 BC, when the ark was captured by the Philistines, until about 1011 BC. David reigned from then until 971 (from Hebron for the first seven years and then from Jerusalem).

1 and 2 Kings continue the record, from the accession of *Solomon* to his father's throne, through the break-up of the kingdom 40 years later, and the continuing rivalry between the northern and southern kingdoms of Israel and Judah. This lasted until Israel became absorbed in the Assyrian Empire after the fall of Samaria in 722 BC. After that, Judah survived precariously for over a century, experiencing a miraculous deliverance from an Assyrian siege in the reign of *Hezekiah* and enjoying the extensive reforms of *Josiah's* reign (640-609). Then came collapse before the combined weight of God's displeasure and Nebuchadnezzar's armies, and exile in Babylon. The gloom of defeat is alleviated only by the concluding words of 2 Kings which tell of the release of King *Jehoiachin* from his Babylonian prison-cell. The hope of a survivor from David's line had not been totally extinguished.

As we have seen, one of the main points of interest in this prophetic or 'deuteronomic' history is **kingship**, and in particular King David's dynasty. In Judges 9 there was the abortive attempt of Gideon's son, Abimelech, to establish himself as hereditary monarch in Shechem. In Judges 17-21, the evils of the day were attributed to the fact that 'there was no king in Israel; every man did what was right in his own eyes'. In 1 Samuel, five chapters (8-12) are devoted to the setting up of a monarchy. It appears to have been rather grudgingly accepted by the historian, since Israel was a theocracy, and the Lord her only rightful King. But with the rise of David all such hesitations disappear, even though his personal morality often left much to be desired. The high point of his reign was God's promise of a lasting succession (2 Samuel 7). The fulfilment of this word can be traced in the lives of the subsequent kings of Judah.

A second main interest was prophets and **the word of the Lord**. The writer's treatment of Deborah and Samuel, Nathan and Gad, Ahijah and Micaiah, Elijah and Elisha, bears witness to the importance he accorded to the office of prophet. These men could make and break kings. They acted as court advisers and political watchdogs. They were the men of power because they in turn were controlled by the word of God. And, in the view of the writer, it was the word of God which controlled history. A word once spoken – the curse on the house of Ahab, for instance – inexorably worked its way to fulfilment.

A third interest of the writer was the **temple** at Jerusalem. From the beginning of 1 Samuel we can trace a special concern about the welfare of the ark of the Lord as it moved from Shiloh to Philistia, back to Kiriath-jearim and eventually was brought to Jerusalem. It was David's desire to build it a more permanent home that provided the occasion for Nathan's prophecy of the hereditary kingship. And in Solomon's time the temple was finally erected.

Finally, there was the fixed standard against which all kings were assessed. This was primarily a matter of **worship**. Was the Lord worshipped at Jerusalem in purity, or were foreign, idolatrous influences allowed in? Were high places (the old, pagan shrines) stamped out or allowed to continue? By the nature of the evaluation, all the kings of Israel came short because they perpetuated worship at the Bethel and Dan sanctuaries which Jeroboam had set up. Kings of Judah also were found wanting when for political reasons they incorporated the religious practices of a foreign overlord as a mark of submission to him. Only Hezekiah and Josiah receive unqualified commendation. So it is reasonable to conclude that the historian's own theological standpoint was influenced by their reforms.

THE CHRONICLER

The second part of the account of the history of Israel, included in 'The Writings' in the Hebrew Bible, was originally one book. The author or compiler is often called the Chronicler. The period before the exile was covered by 1 and 2 Chronicles, and the first hundred years after the exile by Ezra and Nehemiah. At first only the second section was incorporated into the Hebrew Bible, probably because of the overlap between Chronicles and Samuel-Kings, but subsequently 1 and 2 Chronicles were admitted. That is why in the Hebrew Bible Ezra-Nehemiah precedes Chronicles. In order to make their original unity apparent, the opening verses of Ezra were tacked on to the end of 2 Chronicles.

A summary of contents clearly shows the Chronicler's particular interests and the ground covered.

1 Chronicles 1-9: genealogies from Adam to Saul.
1 Chronicles 10-29: reign of David.
2 Chronicles 1-9: reign of Solomon.
2 Chronicles 10-36: the history of Judah from Rehoboam to the exile.
Ezra 1-6: the rebuilding of the temple after the exile.
Ezra 7-10: Ezra's arrival in Jerusalem and reforms.
Nehemiah 1-7: Nehemiah's rebuilding of the walls of Jerusalem.
Nehemiah 8-13: Ezra's reading of the law and Nehemiah's reforms.

From this it can be seen that the northern kingdom, Israel, is ignored, and that most space is given to David and Solomon and matters to do with the Jerusalem temple. To this extent the author was following in the same steps as the deuteronomic historian. He was a strong advocate of David's dynasty and did not regard the northern kingdom after its secession from Judah as belonging any more to the true people of God. Similarly, when the rebuilding operations were in progress on both the temple and the city walls, he was careful to note that the Samaritans – descendants of the mixed Israelite population – were debarred from participating in the work, or were actively hostile to it.

The Chronicler was also a devotee of David as the chief architect of the temple, its worship and its organization. Even though Solomon was the builder, the ideas were all from David's mind. This resulted in what some have called an idealized picture of David, very different from the fallible guerilla-leader-turned-monarch of the Samuel-Kings version. But it is not fair to accuse the Chronicler of deliberately whitewashing David. He was not writing a political history of Israel. He ignored events and records which had no bearing on the temple. His prime concern was to trace the temple and its worship back to its earliest origins and to tell as much of David's and Solomon's contributions as would enhance its glory.

Unlike the author of Samuel-Kings, however, the Chronicler was fascinated by the part played by priests and Levites, and their importance was frequently emphasized. So too was the uniqueness of their position as cultic officials.

The evaluation of the individual kings of Judah tallies with that of 1 and 2 Kings. But the Chronicler was keen to give reasons for unusual features where a strict law of retribution did not appear to work out – for instance in the tragic death of a good king such as Josiah, or the long reign of a bad king such as Manasseh. Again, there is no evidence to show that he twisted or invented the facts to make his point, but he clearly used his material selectively because he was writing as an ecclesiastical, not a political, historian.

His interest in things priestly did not cut him off from the world of prophecy. For in addition to his extensive use of the annals – e.g. 'the book of the kings of Israel and Judah' and many similar records – he also made use of many collections of the sayings of prophets, such as Samuel, Nathan, Gad and Iddo. This encourages us to respect the painstaking care with which he assembled and selected his material.

In the Ezra-Nehemiah period he was able to use memoirs of both these men (notice the use of the first person singular in Ezra 7:27-9:15 and Nehemiah 1:1-7:5; 13:6-31). Indeed Jewish tradition has held that Ezra was himself the Chronicler, and this is by no means impossible. Otherwise we can say at least that the Chronicler was almost certainly on the temple staff, that he was a man of deep piety and that he wrote in the late 5th or early 4th century BC.

Old Testament 2.1

JOSHUA

The book of Joshua takes the story of Israel's history on from the death of Moses, through the conquest of Canaan, to the death of Joshua. Chapters 1 - 12 cover the first five or six years after Moses' death. The events recounted in the last two chapters probably took place about 20 years later. The conquest probably began somewhere about 1240 BC, according to recent archaeological and other evidence. It seems likely that this account was written down in the early days of the monarchy (1045 BC), during Samuel's lifetime, and before David captured Jerusalem (see Joshua 15:63).

Joshua himself was born in Egypt. He became Moses' right-hand man during the exodus and desert wanderings. He was a fine military commander (Exodus 17:8ff.). In the law-giving at Sinai he was Moses' companion (Exodus 24:13). Joshua was one of the 12 spies sent by Moses to reconnoitre the land. He and Caleb alone had the faith and courage to recommend advance (Numbers 14:6ff.) – and in consequence were the only ones to survive the 40 years of wandering. When Moses died, Joshua was an obvious choice to succeed him in leading the nation (Deuteronomy 34:9).

1 - 4 ISRAEL ENTERS THE PROMISED LAND

1 Joshua takes over as leader

This account of Joshua's accession is one of the great chapters of the Bible. Moses is dead: but God's purpose for the nation continues. The keynote of this prelude to the conquest is the repeated call to be strong and take courage (6, 7, 9, 18).

This book of the law (8): see Deuteronomy 31:24-26. Joshua was with Moses when the law was given at Sinai.

Within three days (11): either the events of chapter 2 have already taken place, or the meaning is simply 'soon'.

Remember the word ... (13): see Numbers 32.

2 Rahab and the spies

Jericho, the 'city of palm trees', lies just west of the River Jordan. Joshua's intention was to make his first thrust into the centre of Palestine, driving a wedge between north and south. Jericho stood directly in his path, an obvious first target. See article 'The Cities of the Conquest'.

Rahab's action in harbouring the spies stemmed not from fear, but from belief that Israel's God is the *true* God (see Hebrews 11:31, which commends her faith, not her immorality). Rahab's house was built on or into the city walls, with a flat roof on which produce could be spread out to dry – in this case flax, from which she would spin linen thread. Her house was somewhere the spies might go with no questions asked; and no doubt a good place to pick up information. The Israelites kept their promise to her (6:22ff.). Rahab was naturalized, married Salmon, and through her son Boaz (see Ruth 2-4) became an ancestress of David, and of Jesus himself (Matthew 1:5).

3 The Israelites cross the Jordan

It was spring, and the river swollen with melted snows, when God took his people across Jordan. As the priests stepped into the flood-water, a blockage at Adam, 16 miles up river, dammed the stream, leaving 20 or 30 miles of river-bed dry. (In 1927 earth tremors caused a collapse of the high clay river-banks at the same spot, and the Jordan was dammed up for over 21 hours.)

The ark of the covenant (3): containing the tablets inscribed with the law. It was a visible symbol of God's presence with his people – and of his leading and guidance.

Sanctify yourselves (5): i.e. 'prepare yourselves before God', by ritual purification and moral self-scrutiny.

4 The memorial stones

Two piles were made. One where the priests had stood in the eastern edge of the river, the other at Gilgal, their base-camp on the west. Both were to serve as a perpetual reminder of the greatness of God. (This is the same stretch of Jordan where John the Baptist's ministry and Jesus' baptism took place.)

For you ... for us (23): not many of those who had crossed the Red Sea now remained. Of the over-20s at the time the spies were sent out, only Joshua and Caleb still lived.

5:1-12 GILGAL: ISRAEL CIRCUMCISED

The rite of circumcision had not been practised because the convenant itself was, so to speak, in suspension for 40 years as a result of the people's disbelief and disobedience (Numbers 14). Now the circumcision of the new generation marks the renewal of the old relationship between God and his people.

Flint knives (2): bronze tools had superseded stone by this time, but the traditional tools are used for the religious rite.

The manna ceased (12): see Exodus 16:13ff. This special provision of God had never failed through all the years in the wilderness. Now it was no longer needed.

5:13 - 6:27 THE FALL OF JERICHO

The conquest of Canaan was a holy war. God was at the head of the army. No one knew this better than Joshua, after his experience of 5:13ff. Israel knew it, as the ark of God's presence led the forces. And Israel's enemies knew it, and quaked (2:10-11; 5:1). It was a war of nerves for the men of Jericho; day after day the encircling troops, the trumpet-blasts, the silent army, building up to the great climax of the seventh day.

Things devoted to destruction (18): the city and all its contents are dedicated utterly to God. It becomes sacrilege then, for anyone to take anything for himself.

Outside the camp (23): until such time as they were 'cleansed' by a period of purification.

Cursed ... be the man (26): the mound lay in ruins for 400 years, until Ahab's reign. Then Hiel rebuilt Jericho – and fell heir to the curse (see 1 Kings 16:34).

7 ACHAN'S DEFIANCE

Because of Achan's sin (see on 6:18) 36 men died at Ai, and the whole nation was shamed before their Canaanite enemies. God requires absolute obedience; and the disobedience of one individual affects the whole people of God.

THE CITIES OF THE CONQUEST

Alan Millard

The Bible's accounts of Israel's entry into Canaan record the actual destruction of only a few cities. Throughout, they emphasize that Israel drove out the former inhabitants and took over (inherited) their property. A desolate land with its towns in ruins would be of little benefit to the Israelites, just emerging from 40 years of semi-nomadic life. What *had* to be destroyed were the pagan shrines of the Canaanites with their cultic paraphernalia.

Jericho was a special case. The city was an offering to God, a 'first-fruit' of the conquest. Ai and Hazor were also sacked. But again they were exceptional cases, perhaps as focal points of opposition. If the biblical record is to be believed, then, we shall not expect to find much physical evidence of the Israelite conquest. The change of ownership probably left few recognizable marks except in the religious sphere. More cities may have been sacked at that time than Joshua and Judges indicate, but the Hebrew accounts do not demand it.

So it is misleading to try to link all signs of destruction in Canaanite cities of the Late Bronze Age with the Israelite invasion. Excavations at the sites of Bethel, Beth-shemesh, Debir? (Tell Beit Mirsim), Hazor and Lachish have all revealed signs of violent destruction during the 13th century BC, but the dates are only approximate and the cities may not all have been destroyed at the same time. After their destruction the cities were deserted, or else reoccupied on a less elaborate scale.

Smaller towns and villages, with mud-brick houses, would have offered little resistance to Joshua's army. The village pictured here is in Syria.

It is important to realize that Israel was only one of the Canaanites' enemies, although ultimately the worst. The history of the 13th century BC includes major military actions, invasions, and a general decline in cultural standards. Egypt's pharaoh was lord of Canaan, and of Lebanon and Damascus. His governors and officials resided in major cities (e.g Gaza, Megiddo), and other places served as garrison towns. There were periodic rebellions which were quelled by loyal neighbours or by Egyptian forces. Following a period of Egyptian weakness, Pharaoh Seti I campaigned in Canaan and east of the Jordan about 1300 BC. Archaeologists often identify his invasion with destruction levels in ruined cities, as at Hazor. Shortly afterwards, his son, Ramesses II, had to curb a revolt following an unsuccessful battle with the Hittites in Syria. He penetrated as far as Moab at this time (about 1285 BC).

Perhaps as a result of these firm measures, once Ramesses had made peace with the Hittite king (in about 1270 BC), there was no further invasion from Egypt for over half a century. Trouble came again in the reign of Merneptah, Ramesses' son. Little is known beyond the fact of Egyptian intervention in Canaan, and indirect evidence of continuing Egyptian control there. One record supplies the oldest non-biblical reference to Israel, as one of a number of defeated foes. Merneptah had halted a wave of invaders from the north-west, the 'Peoples of the Sea'. Egypt was safe until another wave repeated the threat, marching through Syria and Canaan as well as coming against Egypt by sea.

This wave was stemmed by Ramesses III who destroyed the fleet and stopped the advance before it reached the frontier, re-establishing his control of Canaan for a while. But many of the invaders remained, some seizing certain cities. The Philistines, for example, took over Ashdod, Ashkelon, Ekron, Gath, and Gaza; and another group took control of Dor. All these events, and others unknown to us, brought pillage and destruction to the towns of Canaan around the time of the conquest. Neighbouring princes could create as much devastation as an invading force.

Nevertheless, we are told that three cities – Jericho, Ai and Hazor – were set on fire by Israel. At Hazor in Galilee, there is evidence that the last city of the Late Bronze Age was violently destroyed at some time in the 13th century BC. The ruins of the last Canaanite city were not well preserved, partly because of exposure to the elements and damage by ploughing. But enough remained to show a city of importance, even if past its zenith. Other towns of the same date are closely similar. All were well fortified, although the city walls often incorporated (or were renovations of) earlier defences. Cities on the main roads – Megiddo, for example – tended to be far wealthier. On the other hand the relative poverty of such sites as Tell Beit Mirsim (Debir?) concentrated the excavators' attention on details of pottery styles, on which Palestinian archaeology depends for its comparative chronology.

At Jericho, the site where the clearest evidence of Israel's attack might have been expected, nothing has been found to show the existence of a city there in the middle of the 13th century BC. Severe erosion of the mudbrick ruins has left little trace of some earlier periods in the city's life. For this reason, the possibility of a fortified city standing there later in the century cannot be discounted. Its ruins would have disappeared during the long desertion of the site from Joshua's time to Ahab's (about 400 years; see 1 Kings 16:34). The city walls, thought at one time to be evidence of Joshua's attack, in fact date from a much earlier period; the excavations show a city which had already been frequently destroyed and rebuilt before the time of Joshua.

Ai also presents a problem. Excavations have revealed that the city was derelict from about 2500 BC until after 1200 BC, although it was important in the earlier period. The name Ai means 'ruin', and many see the Joshua story simply as an attempt to explain the very impressive ruins. But even accepting the archaeological evidence, it is still possible that a group of Canaanites made use of the old fortifications of this strategic stronghold in their fight against the Israelites. Such a brief occupation would have left little or no trace.

In short, we need not expect to find widespread and unmistakable signs of a specifically Israelite conquest in the ruins of Canaan. Israel's mission was in any case not totally destructive. And there were other causes of destruction. Towns may have lain deserted as a result of general turmoil, or have been only partially inhabited, until the Israelites were established in the land and able to exploit it. This they could not do fully while they were menaced by the Philistines and enemies from across the Jordan. The poor remains in several post-Canaanite (early Iron Age) sites attest this situation.

Many scholars have explained Israel's possession of the promised land in terms of a gradual infiltration by nomadic herdsmen. Or they see it as a combination of infiltration and a movement of a few tribal groups from Egypt, perhaps on more than one occasion and over several generations. Or they even envisage a general revolt of the people of the land. These widely varying opinions are all connected with theories involving the documentary analysis of the Pentateuch. These assign stories to a number of different sources, so proposing separate origins for them, and fostering views of unrelated tribal histories. Closely linked with this is a theory that the concept of Israel as a nation was formed long after the 'conquest', and read back into early times by later Israelite historians.

The idea of a gradual process is supported by analogy with other invasions and movements with peoples. It is emphasized that the occupation was limited. (Judges 1 for example lists the main Canaanite cities on the major roads as unconquered, or only occupied jointly with the native citizens.) The stories in Joshua are attributed to tribal or cultic sources. They are thought to describe what were really small, local events, or to relate folk-tales woven around the origin of ruined cities whose real history was forgotten.

It always pays to be cautious in arguing from analogies and this is certainly so in the case of the 'conquest'. The analogies of nomadic infiltration are used in order to fit Israel into a known pattern. But all her records claim that Israel was different. At best such approaches should be regarded as experimental, not factual. To rule out the account actually given in the Bible on the grounds that it is unusual is prejudiced and unscientific.

Ai (2): 'The Ruin'. See article 'The Cities of the Conquest'.
Sanctify yourselves (13): see on 3:5.
Which the Lord takes (14): the guilty man was discovered by means of the sacred lot, the two stones kept in the high priest's breastplate. It is not now known exactly how this was done.
Stoned him ... burned them (25): i.e. the stolen goods, unless his family were also in the know and therefore to blame (see Deuteronomy 24:16).

8 AI CONQUERED

The evidence of the mound at Et-Tell is difficult to accord with the biblical record here – which suggests that this may not in fact be the correct site of Ai. But see 'The Cities of the Conquest'. Joshua's flight and ambush strategy makes capital out of Israel's previous defeat.

From Ai, Joshua moves north to establish himself at Shechem, in the valley between Mts Ebal and Gerizim. In God's name he takes possession of the land. And the covenant is sworn as Moses had commanded (Deuteronomy 27).

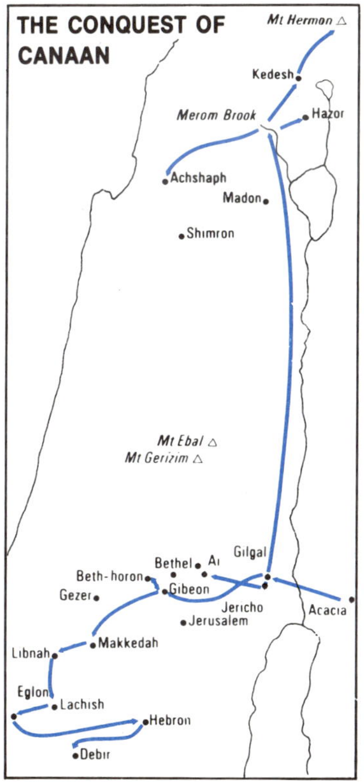

THE CONQUEST OF CANAAN

30,000 (3): This may refer to the total force, unless there were two ambushes (12). But high numbers in the Old Testament present a real problem. See on Numbers 1, and 'The Large Numbers of the Old Testament'.
Bethel (9): the place where Jacob had his vision. A well-fortified and prosperous city during Israel's early days in Egypt; somewhat declined by Joshua's day. Either on this campaign (Bethel and Ai were only 1½ miles apart) or later, the king of Bethel was defeated (12:16).

9 - 10 THE CAMPAIGN IN THE SOUTH

9 Gibeon tricks Israel into a treaty

Gibeon was an important city about six miles north of Jerusalem. The treaty obtained by such cunning (even to the pretence that news of the recent victories at Jericho and Ai had not reached them, 9-10) also included three other cities (17). Israel could not draw back from a treaty sealed in friendship (the meal eaten together, 14). It still held good in David's day. The worst they could do was reduce the Gibeonites to slave status (21).

10 Alliance of the five Amorite kings; the 'long day'

The treaty with the Gibeonites promptly involves Israel in war. All five Amorite kings are killed at Makkedah and their city-states (all except Jerusalem) destroyed in the campaign following the rout at Beth-horon. All the strategic cities of the south fall before Joshua's army. Israel now controls the land from Kadesh-barnea in the south to Gaza on the west, and as far north as Gibeon.
The long day (12-14): usually taken as an extension of daylight (not necessarily by a literal standing still of the sun). But it may be a prolongation of *darkness*. Recently it has been suggested that there may have been an eclipse of the sun. Joshua's surprise attack was at dawn (as the positions of sun and moon in verse 12 also indicate) and the hailstorm increased the gloom and consequent confusion. 'Go down' (13) may simply mean 'come' or 'go'.
Book of Jashar (13): a book of songs praising national heroes.
Put your feet upon the necks (24): customary gesture of total subjection.
Goshen (41): a town south of Hebron, not Goshen in Egypt.

11 THE NORTHERN CAMPAIGN

The powerful king of Hazor, commanding his vassals, assembles an even more formidable alliance than that of the south. But with no more success. Although the strategic cities were in Israel's hands within a short time of their entry into Canaan, mopping-up operations took a great deal longer (18).
Hazor (1): a vast metropolis of 40,000 people, many times the size of Jerusalem in David's day. The lower city which Joshua destroyed was never rebuilt. See 'The Cities of the Conquest'.
As far as Great Sidon (8): Tyre had evidently not yet risen to prominence.
The Anakim (21): the colossal race who struck fear into the hearts of the spies (Numbers 13:33).
Gaza, Gath, Ashdod (22): all Philistine strongholds. Gigantic Goliath came from Gath (1 Samuel 17:4).

12 LIST OF THE DEFEATED CANAANITE KINGS

Thirty-one kings are listed, including those defeated under Moses. The list rounds off the section on the conquest.

13 - 21 DIVISION OF THE LAND

Not all the land allocated had been completely subdued – and not every

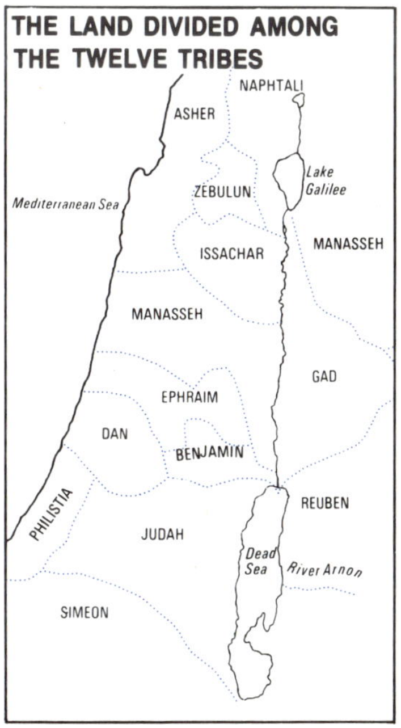

THE LAND DIVIDED AMONG THE TWELVE TRIBES

tribe realized its ideal by conquering all its allotted territory. In several places the writer comments on the situation in his own day (e.g. 15:63).

13:1-7 Land still unconquered

13:8-14 The land east of Jordan

13:15-23 The tribe of Reuben

13:24-28 The tribe of Gad

13:29-33 The half-tribe of Manasseh

14:1-5 The land west of Jordan

The inheritance of each tribe is decided by lot, by the high priest.

14:6-15 Caleb claims Hebron

Forty-five years after the spy episode (Numbers 13-14) Caleb remains a man of unwavering faith. Despite 10:21ff. there are still Anakim survivors to deal with (15:14; Judges 1:10-15, 20). Hebron became Levite property (21:11-13), but Caleb retained the surrounding land and villages.

15 The tribe of Judah

Judah's inheritance included Caleb's lands – and also Jerusalem, or part of it (18:28). But the city remained unconquered when Joshua was written (63).

16 - 17 Joseph's sons: the tribes of Ephraim and Manasseh

They were to have extended their territory by clearance and conquest. But the horses and chariots of the Canaanites holding the plains deterred them.

18:1-10 The move to Shiloh; the land survey; the inheritance of the seven remaining tribes

18:11-28 The tribe of Benjamin

Jerusalem seems to have been partly on Judah's land, partly on Benjamin's (15:63; Judges 1:8,21).

19:1-9 The tribe of Simeon

Simeon's people, whose land was part of Judah's territory, became absorbed into the larger tribe.

19:10-16 The tribe of Zebulun

19:17-23 The tribe of Issachar

19:24-31 The tribe of Asher

19:32-39 The tribe of Naphtali

19:40-48 The tribe of Dan

19:49-51 Joshua's city

20 The cities of refuge

See Numbers 35:6-34; Deuteronomy 19:1-13. The cities were a safeguard against vengeance and blood-feud, protecting those who caused accidental death.

21 The cities of the Levites

The Levites receive no tribal inheritance: God is their inheritance. But they are given 48 cities, with pasturage, by the other tribes. This ensures that the leaders of the nation's faith and worship are dispersed amongst the tribes.

22 THE TRIBES SETTLED ON THE EAST OF THE JORDAN RETURN HOME; THE ALTAR OF WITNESS

Reuben, Gad and Manasseh have fulfilled their obligations to help in the conquest. Now they return home, with Joshua's blessing, and a share of the spoil. Fear that, once across Jordan, Israel may at some future time disown them prompts the building of the altar which caused such misunderstanding. This was neither a sign of idolatry, nor a second sanctuary. It was a token of solidarity with the rest of Israel to whom they were bound by faith and worship of the one God.

The sin at Peor (17): when Israel worshipped Baal (Numbers 25).

Achan (20): for his sin 36 men died (chapter 7).

The Mighty One, God, the Lord (22): a solemn oath, twice repeated, and using all three names of God: El, Elohim, Yahweh. (See article 'The Names of God'.)

23 - 24 JOSHUA'S LAST DAYS

23 Joshua counsels the leaders

Some years have elapsed since the division of the land. Joshua has reached the end of a long life, and is appointing no single successor. It is therefore vital to ensure that the leaders keep the law and remain faithful to God – the God who keeps his promises (23:14; see 21:45).

24 Joshua and the nation renew the covenant

Here, as in Deuteronomy, the covenant pattern follows that of contemporary treaties (see article, 'Covenants and Near Eastern Treaties'). The King's title (2a) is followed by a rehearsal of his past favours (2b-13). The stipulations are made in 14-15, with warnings on the consequences of disobedience (19-20). Joshua's own readiness to commit himself wholly to God remains unwavering at the end of a long life. The eagerness of the people to follow him in renewing the covenant is in itself sufficient tribute to his leadership. Verse 31 is an indication of the strength of this man's influence for good.

Balak ... Balaam (9): see Numbers 22-24.

I sent the hornet (12): a vivid image of the panic and confusion into which God threw Israel's enemies.

Old Testament 2.2

JUDGES

Judges covers the period in Israel's history between Joshua's death and the rise of Samuel – roughly 1220 to 1050 BC. It was a time of transition, when the scattered tribes were held together only by their common faith. Loyalty to God meant a strong united nation. Turning to the gods around brought weakness and division.

The writer looks back, probably from the days of Israel's first kings – Saul or David – to the time when the nation had no king. He wrote after the destruction of the sanctuary at Shiloh (18:31), but before David captured Jerusalem (1:21). He weaves together the stories of the nation's heroes; and Deborah's song, written just after the battle, he quotes verbatim. Six of the 12 judges mentioned are described in some detail: Othniel, Ehud, Deborah/Barak, Gideon, Jephthah, Samson. These 'judges' of Israel were not simply legal advisers. They were men of action who delivered tribe or nation from subjection to the nations around and became local or national rulers.

The human scene in Judges is a depressing one. The nation's fortunes follow a monotonous, repetitive cycle. Israel deserts God for the heathen gods. In consequence God allows them to suffer at the hands of the Canaanites. Israel cries to God for help. God sends a deliverer. All is well until his death: then the old pattern of infidelity reasserts itself. Nowhere in Scripture is man's essential bias to sin more graphically portrayed – a bias which shows itself even in those who know God.

The wonder is God's constant love and concern in the face of all this. Despite their past unfaithfulness, and what he knows will happen again, as soon as Israel turns to him he answers. And he uses the most unpromising people: Jael, who breaks all the sacred laws of hospitality; Ehud, who stoops to assassination; Samson, who leads a life of sexual promiscuity; a nation that gloats over acts of cruel revenge against the enemy. *And the Bible nowhere commends these things* or whitewashes the individuals who committed them. God took and used them because of their faith (Hebrews 11:32ff.), and despite their morals. So, because God is a God like this, there is hope for sinful man.

Chronology. Eastern writers do not show the same preoccupation with precise time-order as modern western historians. Added together, the figures in Judges total 390 years. Yet, with the most probable date for the conquest at about 1240, the period covered must be under 200 years. One of the reasons for this seeming discrepancy is the overlap between the periods of the different judges. We know, for example, from 10:7 that the Ammonite oppression in the east and the Philistine oppression in the west occurred at the same time. It is likely there is considerable overlap elsewhere. A further factor is the frequent use of 'forty years' as a round figure for 'a generation' rather than a precise length of time.

A. E. Cundall suggests the following approximate chronology:

1200 Othniel
1170 Ehud
1150 Shamgar
1125 Deborah and Barak
1100 Gideon
1070 Jephthah
1070 Samson

1 - 2:5 EXTENT AND LIMITS OF THE CONQUEST FOLLOWING JOSHUA'S DEATH

1:1-21 Campaigns in southern Canaan

Verses 10-15: see Joshua 15:13-19.

City of palms (16): Jericho.

Chariots of iron (19): this was the beginning of the Iron Age. The Philistines introduced and controlled the iron industry in Palestine and guarded it jealously (see 1 Samuel 13:19-22). Until the days of David, Israel were at a disadvantage against the superior iron weapons and chariots of their enemies.

1:22-26 Capture of Bethel
1:27-36 Unconquered cities
2:1-5 God's judgement on disobedience

The angel of the Lord (1): mentioned a number of times in Judges (here and in the stories of Gideon and Samson) as well as in other Bible passages. He always comes as God's representative, with a special message from God. He speaks in God's name, and is virtually identified with God by those to whom he appears (see e.g. 13:22). Sometimes he shows himself as an ordinary man, sometimes as an awesome heavenly being (see chapter 13). But none who see him are left in any doubt of his authority.

2:6 - 16:31 ISRAEL UNDER THE JUDGES

2:6 - 3:6 Introduction

Verses 11-23 set out the repeated pattern of events which began once the conquest generation had died out (10). As a result of disobedience the surrounding nations are not driven out. They remain to test Israel and keep her a fighting nation (2:20 - 3:6).

Baals and the Ashtaroth (2:13): local male and female fertility/vegetation gods.

Five lords of the Philistines (3:3): rulers of the city-states of Ashdod, Ashkelon, Ekron, Gaza, Gath (see the Samson story, chapters 13 -16, and 1 Samuel 17:1-54). Judah did not hold her three cities for long (1:18).

3:7-11 Othniel

If Cushan-rishathaim was indeed king of 'Mesopotamia' (8: i.e. modern east Syria, north Iraq) the attack must have come from the north – which makes his defeat at the hands of a southern champion surprising. But some would emend the name to 'Cushan chief of Teman' (in Edom).

The Spirit of the Lord came upon him (10): the same phrase is used of Gideon, Jephthah and Samson. The might of these champions was a special gift from God.

3:12-30 Ehud

Eglon of Moab headed an eastern alliance which included Ammonites and Amalekites. They not only overran the land east of Jordan, but crossed the river to set up an outpost at Jericho.

Like Ehud, many of the Benjaminites were left-handed or ambidextrous – the tribe's left-handed slingers had a high reputation (see 20:16; 1 Chronicles 12:2). On this occasion

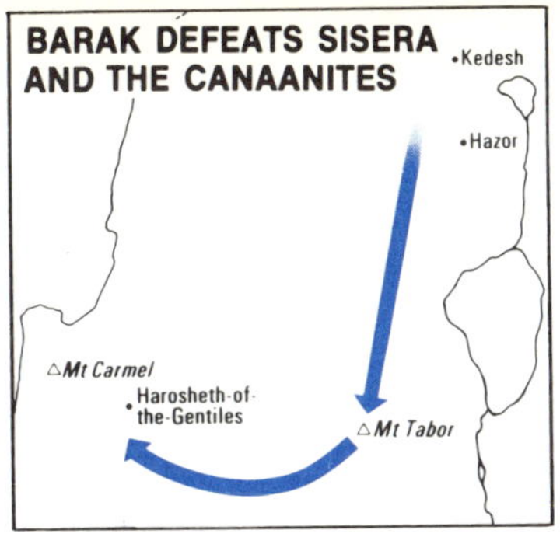

it meant that the movement aroused no suspicion.

3:31 Shamgar

This isolated action did not restrain the Philistines long. See chapters 13-16.

4 - 5 Deborah and Barak

Deborah is the judge in the judicial sense, Barak the military leader. Deborah's song – one of the most ancient pieces of writing in the Old Testament – provides the clue to the victory. A cloudburst changed the Kishon to a raging torrent (5:21). Many of the chariots were swept away, the rest completely bogged down in the mud.

Hazor (4:2): Joshua defeated an earlier Jabin, and destroyed the city. The lower part was never rebuilt, but the mound (tell) was re-fortified by the Canaanites, and later by Solomon.

6 - 8:28 Gideon

Bedouin from the east, the Midianites, swept through southern Israel as far as the Philistine city of Gaza. The terror spread by these fierce camel-riders is vividly pictured in 6:11. Gideon is forced to thresh his meagre grain harvest secretly, in the confines of the wine press. The faith of this man, for all his initial caution, is seen in his preparedness to face the Midianite hordes with a force of only 300 men. Gideon used his wits in the surprise attack, but the victory in the ensuing rout is God's.

The Asherah (6:25): a wooden image of the Canaanite mother-goddess.

An ephod (8:27): probably an image of God, which the law forbade. The place then became a rival to Israel's official sanctuary.

8:29-35 Gideon's later years

9 The rise and fall of the usurper Abimelech

Gideon, with some claim to kingship, firmly rejected it. Abimelech, his brutal and ambitious son, shows no such scruples.

The scene of Gideon's surprise attack on the Midianites.

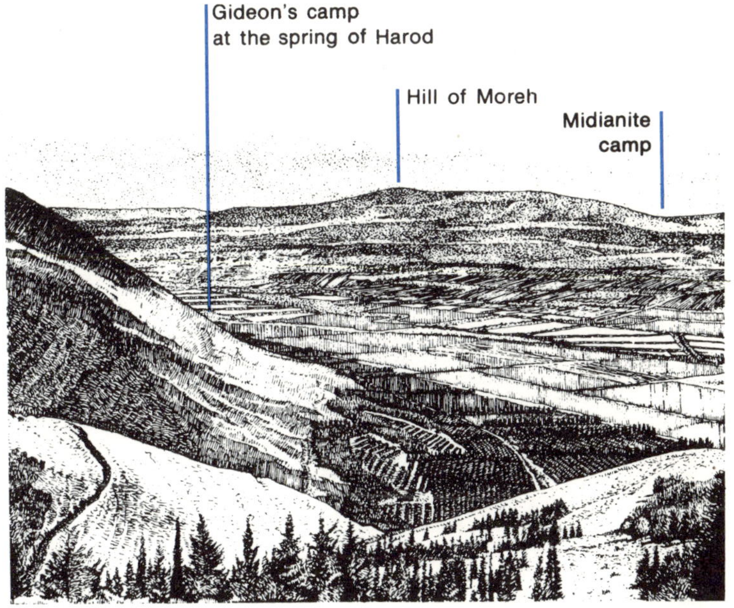

Shechem (1): in the heart of Palestine; see map. Shechem was the central sanctuary of Israel in Joshua's day. But now it had a temple to Baal (for 'house', verses 4 and 46, read 'temple' with New English Bible). The city's history goes back to Jacob's day and earlier.

Sowed it with salt (45): symbolically consigning the city to permanent desolation. It was in fact rebuilt 150 years later in the time of Jeroboam 1.

Upper millstone (53): grain was ground between two heavy circular stone slabs about 18 inches across.

10:1-2 Tola

10:3-5 Jair

10:6 - 11:40 Jephthah

Southern Israel is now caught in a vice between the Philistines on the west and the Ammonites on the east. Against Ammon, the new champion is the brigand-chief, Jephthah. Numbers 20-21 describes the events referred to in the parley of 11:12-28. Moab in fact had the better claim to the land, as part of it had been theirs until Sihon dispossessed them.

Three hundred years (11:26): i.e. it was now the third century since the events described (in fact about 160 years).

Jephthah's vow, and other moral problems in Judges: the vow is an indication of how little the Israelites understood God at this time. Human sacrifice might please the heathen gods, but never the God of Israel. Yet, though ignorant and mistaken, the vow was made in good faith, and kept, though it cost Jephthah his only child. And the New Testament writer of Hebrews commends this man's faith – as he commends the faith of Samson, Gideon and Barak (Hebrews 11:32). This instance of child-sacrifice, Jael's hideous murder of Sisera, Ehud's assassination of Eglon, Samson's selfish, sensual and irresponsible behaviour (see Introduction) are a real source of embarrassment to many Christians. How can people like these be commended for their faith? How could God use them? There can be no completely satisfactory answer to questions like these. The 'heroes' of Judges are people of their age – an age which the Bible plainly shows was one of religious decline, falling far short of the standards of the Old Testament law, let alone those which Christ sets. The fact is – the wonder is – that God did and still does use men whose lives are far from blameless, who may even be acting from completely wrong motives. We are not meant to imitate their shortcomings. Their immorality is neither condoned nor glossed over in Scripture. Only their

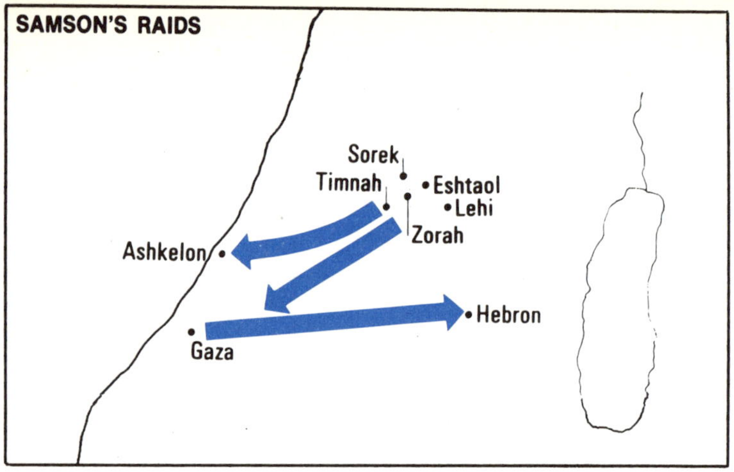

faith and courage are commended. God does not permit his ultimate purposes to be thwarted even in an age of seemingly hopeless decadence. The dark ages of a period like that of Judges may be followed by a time of real spiritual advance.

12:1-7 Ephraimite jealousy
Where Gideon used soft words to placate these touchy tribesmen (8:1-3), Jephthah takes up the sword. At the fords the men's dialect pronunciation of 'Shibboleth' gives them away.

12:8-10 Ibzan
12:11-12 Elon
12:13-15 Abdon
13:1 - 16:31 Samson
The champion against the enemy in the west (see 10:7) is set apart for the task from the moment of his conception. For Samson the Nazirite vow (see Numbers 6) was lifelong. Yet he treats it with a casualness amounting to contempt, eventually allowing Delilah to shave off the long hair which was the sign of his dedication to God. Moral weakness robs the strong man of both spiritual stature and physical prowess – since his strength is God-given for an explicit purpose.

Samson's marriage: not the usual Jewish type, although formally arranged by the parents. Instead of the bride returning to Samson's home she stayed with her family and her husband visited her, bringing gifts. Because of the deceit over the riddle there was no consummation at the end of the seven-day feast. A hasty second marriage to the best man was an attempt to lessen the bride's disgrace.

Three hundred foxes (15:4) more probably jackals, who hunt in packs and would therefore be easier to catch in large numbers than the solitary fox.

17 - 21 APPENDICES
This closing section differs from the rest of Judges. The writer turns from Israel's heroes to two incidents which illustrate the low state of religion and morality in the days when Israel had no central government and everyone 'did what was right in his own eyes'.

17 - 18 Micah, the Levite and the Danite migration
This story relates to the time when Philistine pressure on their southern territory led to the mass migration of the Danites to the far north of Israel. The image set up by Micah was strictly forbidden by the law the Levites were supposed to administer. 'Ephod and teraphim' were used as means of divination – equally strictly prohibited.

19 - 21 Rape of the concubine at Gibeah; punishment of the Benjaminites
When the Benjaminites refuse to hand over the men of Gibeah – their fellow tribesmen who committed the outrage – civil war results. The outcome is the near-extinction of Benjamin, and great national grief. Chapter 21 relates the lengths to which the tribes go to circumvent the rash oath made at Mizpah (21:1).

The writer has no need to point a moral. The simple statement of verse 25 is sufficient. The whole book makes plain the disastrous consequences of breakdown of authority, when men become a law unto themselves, setting their own standards of permissiveness.

Old Testament 2.3
RUTH

This quiet tale of ordinary life stands in strong contrast to the war and strife of Judges, which relates to the same general period. No doubt many people lived just such a normal peaceful life during this age. And although religion generally was at a low ebb, the book of Ruth makes it clear that the personal faith of many in Israel remained strong. The most striking feature of this simple and beautiful story is the sense of God's intimate concern in humble affairs. He is the One who orders all the circumstances of daily life, even for the most unimportant people. And so the new-found faith of a Moabite girl, and her sacrificial love for her mother-in-law are woven into the great tapestry of God's plan of salvation. For descended from Ruth is King David, and from the line of David comes the Messiah himself.

1:1-5 Elimelech takes his family to Moab
The journey was about 50 miles, to the far side of the Dead Sea.

1:6-22 The widowed Naomi returns to Bethlehem with Ruth, her daughter-in-law
The famine is over: God has again shown his care for his people. Orpah, sorrowfully, returns home to the hope of a second marriage. But Ruth will not leave Naomi to a lonely old age. Her choice is Naomi's people, and, significantly, Naomi's God. The two reach Bethlehem in April.

2 Ruth goes gleaning and wins Boaz' protection
There were not many ways for widows to earn a living, and Ruth and Naomi were poor. But the law (Leviticus 19:9-10) laid down that the gleanings of the harvest must be left for the poor. By 'chance' in the common open field, Ruth gleans in the part belonging to Boaz, Elimelech's kinsman. His kindness goes far beyond the law's demands (9, 14-16).

Parched grain (14): fresh ears of barley roasted in a pan.

An ephah of barley (17): the ephah was a large container holding about 22 litres. Ruth had gleaned about ½ cwt of barley by her own hard work and Boaz' generosity.

3 The threshing-floor; appeal to Boaz as next of kin
Under the Levirate law (referred to by Naomi in 1:11-13), when a man died childless his brother was bound to raise an heir to him by the widow. This law extended to the next of kin, hence Naomi's plan. Ruth, by her action in verse 7, was claiming this right. The issue is complicated by the fact that Boaz is not in fact Elimelech's closest kinsman, but he promises to take up her case.

4:1-12 The transaction between the kinsmen
The city gate was the place for important assembly. It was also the place where legal business could be publicly transacted, as here. The elders acted as witnesses. In addition to his obligation to raise an heir to carry on the dead man's name, the next of kin also had to buy his land, to keep it in the family. Boaz discusses the land first, then the widow. The kinsman would have bought the land to add to his own inheritance. But when he hears it will in fact go to Ruth and her son, and that he will have Ruth to provide for, he declares himself unable to purchase.

Perez (12): ancestor of Boaz; son of Tamar by her father-in-law, Judah, because of his refusal to honour the custom later formalized as the Levirate law.

4:13-22 Ruth marries and becomes the great-grandmother of King David
So Boaz fulfils his own prayer of 2:12. God rewards Ruth with the gift of a husband and a son. And Naomi finds solace for her grief in this grandson. When God steps in, the ordinary events of life take on extraordinary significance. The child Obed became grandfather to the founder of the royal line of Israel from which Christ himself took human flesh, in another birth at Bethlehem.

THE OLD TESTAMENT AND THE ANCIENT NEAR EAST

Alan Millard

The Bible is an ancient text, a historical record. As such it is very helpful to study it in the light of our knowledge of the world in which it was written.

There is nothing un-Christian in doing this. The Christian faith depends on historical events, things which actually happened. The events recorded and explained in the Bible can be set alongside other events known from other historical sources. The Bible itself consists of documents as ancient and as historically verifiable as any others.

Checking the accuracy of the Bible

Its accuracy can also be tested and checked against other known historical sources. However, this is not always as simple as it may seem. Documents are often damaged or incomplete. Archaeological evidence is in many cases open to more than one interpretation. We possess very few ancient writings which describe the same events the Bible describes, and in any case two observers will rarely describe the same event from an identical standpoint.

The Hebrews were a relatively insignificant people. Their career made little impact on the major powers whose records we possess. Hardly any of the biblical characters appear in other writings, apart from some of the later kings of Israel and Judah. None the less, where we are able to make comparisons, the accuracy of the biblical writers is impressive. Although we seldom find parallel accounts of the same events, we often find examples of customs and occurrences very like those described in the Old Testament, even though they are in no way connected. A superficial similarity can of course be misleading, so we have to be cautious. And a knowledge of the ancient Near East can help, even when it provides neither direct nor circumstantial evidence of the Bible's historical accuracy: the study of Israel's neighbours – customs, culture, literature, history – gives us an idea of what to expect in the case of the Hebrew nation.

These three types of evidence – direct evidence, circumstantial evidence and the evidence of analogy – must be taken in turn to show how they shed light on the Bible.

Direct evidence

As we have seen, direct references to Israel are rare, and almost solely limited to royal names. Amongst those we do have is the record of an invasion by Shishak who was king of Egypt – he ruled about 945-924 BC (1 Kings 14:25f.). His inscription at Thebes, badly preserved, lists many towns conquered in Palestine – evidence of his campaign there. Tiglath-pileser III (about 745-727 BC) re-established Assyrian rule over Syria and Palestine following some decades of weakness, when Jeroboam had made Israel prosperous and Uzziah had built up Judah. The Assyrian records the tribute paid by Menahem of Samaria and claims to have been responsible for replacing Pekah by Hosea (2 Kings 15:19-20, 30). In 2 Kings 15:19 (see also 1 Chronicles 5:26) Tiglath-pileser is called Pul and he was known by that name to Babylonian chroniclers of the 6th century BC, when it is believed 1 and 2 Kings were finally compiled. Subsequently Assyrian rule in Samaria involved Judah as a vassal, but her kings preferred to struggle for independence, seeking Egypt's aid. So Hezekiah rebelled, and Sennacherib brought his forces to overwhelm Judah and lay siege to Jerusalem. The Assyrian tells of this in many inscriptions. He relates how Hezekiah sent tribute to him in Nineveh (the amounts seem to differ slightly from 2 Kings 18:14ff.), yet lays no claim to the capture of Jerusalem, nor, naturally enough, does he mention his army's fate.

In the account of Solomon's building projects, 1 Kings 9:15 names three major cities besides Jerusalem – Hazor, Megiddo and Gezer. Excavations at each one have uncovered city walls of the 10th century BC, all of the same pattern. Each city wall is pierced by a massive gateway, and all are identical in plan and in measurement, to within a few inches. Here is a material record demonstrating the truth of the biblical text. Here, also are physical signs of an overall planning authority, a central power. Indeed, Solomon's glory, fabulous though it may appear, becomes more and more credible when set in its ancient context.

Circumstantial evidence

Most of the discoveries which feature in books on archaeology and the Bible fall into the class of circumstantial evidence – matters which make no direct reference to biblical events, but supply examples of practices or incidents apparently comparable with passages in the Bible. In this way we learn that Abraham's marriage to the slave-girl Hagar because of Sarah's childlessness, and his later refusal – until reassured by God – to send her from his household, agree with requirements in the contemporary Laws of Hammurabi of Babylon. The names of the patriarchs of Israel also accord with names generally used in the 2nd millennium BC, now known from thousands of contemporary documents.

Another of Solomon's glories gains evidence from Egyptian sources. According to 1 Kings 9:16, he married the pharaoh's daughter. Yet two or three centuries earlier, in Egypt's heyday, the princesses of Egypt did not leave the court, and when an important foreign king requested one as his bride he was refused. In the 10th century BC however, under the less glorious 21st dynasty and its successor, this rule was broken. So it was that Solomon received his bride.

A little before Solomon's time, the hero Gideon called on a boy to write down the names of trading men in Succoth – apparently just a boy who happened to be available (Judges 8:14). That names could be easily written and recognized then is shown by copper arrowheads, found near Bethlehem, and in other places, inscribed with their owners' names and dated to the 12th and 11th centuries BC.

The evidence of analogy

The fact that we have virtually no written record of ancient Hebrew life, thought and history apart from the Old Testament means that many aspects of life can hardly be known at all. Normal processes of decay have destroyed any documents on leather or papyrus buried in the cities of Palestine along with furniture and clothing. Where such items are preserved in neighbouring cultures, it is possible sometimes to attribute similar usages to ancient Israel. Each case needs thorough testing to ensure that the circumstances really are parallel, but some are sufficiently clear to help us evaluate the Old Testament.

No literature has survived from Israelite towns, but there is no doubt it existed. The Old Testament itself is witness to that, although scholars debate just how old its written form is. In Egypt and Babylonia the complicated writing-systems gave the scribes a monopoly. In Israel (and adjacent states) the simple 22-letter alphabet was learnt easily by any who wanted, so writing was more widespread amongst the population, although professional scribes still had an important role. Evidence from various minor written documents demonstrates this fact for ancient Israel. If writing was used for daily affairs, this implies it could be used for works of literature, too. The written word was treated with respect. Valuable old books were copied with great care. They could be revised or edited, but the way this has been done is seldom detectable unless the older copies survive for comparison.

Egypt, Assyria and Babylonia, the Hittites and Canaanites all had elaborately-arranged religious rites, sacrifices, and priestly orders. Their temples were finely built and lavishly furnished, especially by successful kings. If Israel had been different in this they would have been the odd ones out, but in fact they were not. These analogies show that the tabernacle, Solomon's temple, and the Levitical regulations were Israel's counterparts. As in neighbouring nations, moreover, the mass of the people toiled and suffered to provide for the magnificence demanded by the king.

We would expect Israel, as a nation among nations of related stock, to share similar modes of thought and expression. When Babylonian or Egyptian literature shows features strange to modern thought, we take great pains to understand them – to account for inconsistencies, paradoxes, and apparent contradictions without impugning the accuracy of the texts which are our only sources of information (unless there are firmly-founded objective reasons for doing so). Israel's literature may be expected to contain similar quirks, and they too should be treated with respect. Some are clear, for instance the narration of events out of chronological order, or the collecting of items without evident relation to the context.

Similarities and differences

These examples are sufficient to show the value of gathering, studying and applying whatever the ancient Near East affords by way of background to the Bible. The direct and indirect evidence agrees so strikingly with the Old Testament that it makes attempts to discredit its picture of Israel's culture and career very dubious indeed. No discovery has been proved to contradict the Hebrew records. There may be discrepancies, uncertainties, unanswered questions. The incomplete nature of all our evidence makes this inevitable. New discoveries solve old problems, frequently revealing false premises in modern theories. At the same time they may raise fresh questions and stimulate deeper study, new approaches, and better understanding.

If the similarities between Israel and her neighbours form the bulk of the contribution made by biblical archaeology, the differences merit attention as well. The Old Testament proclaims an unbridgeable gap between Israel and her neighbours. Whereas her language and culture shared so much, her faith stood apart. To find material traces of Israel's monotheistic faith, imageless worship, centralized cult, is difficult. Her neighbours reckoned her God as no more than a national god like their own (Chemosh of Moab, or Milcom of Ammon), unaware of his unique place. To make things more complicated, Israel never remained entirely faithful, so pagan religious objects can be found in the ruins of her cities.

It is in comparing biblical teaching with contemporary texts that the distinctions are best seen. The absolute demands of the Ten Commandments, the exclusive devotion to Israel's electing God, the equality of individuals balancing their corporate responsibility, the altruism of the prophets – all these, and many others, find no true echo in the world of the Old Testament.

Some may find them incredible, yet we possess actually preserved manuscripts which guarantee them an antiquity of over 2,000 years.

Some may find them unacceptable, but although so old they still speak sense to modern man.

If the historical and cultural aspects harmonize with our knowledge of ancient times, as in fact is the case, the ethical and religious distinctions need explanation. The Old Testament gives one: God spoke.

Old Testament 2.4 and 5

1 AND 2 SAMUEL

These two books were originally one volume in the Hebrew Bible. They provide a history of Israel from the end of the Judges period to the last years of David, the nation's second and greatest king – roughly 100 years (about 1075-975 BC). This is essentially religious history: the story of God and the nation – particularly, God and the nation's leaders. Samuel gives his name to the books, not as author, but as the dominating figure of the early chapters, and Israel's 'kingmaker' under God's direction. It was he who anointed first Saul and then David as king.

The historian may well have drawn his material from Samuel's own writings (1 Samuel 10:25) and those of the prophets who followed him (1 Chronicles 29:29). He certainly knew some of David's poems (which he quotes in 2 Samuel 1:19-27; 22:2-51; 23:1-7). And he was himself a born storyteller and master of suspense. He must have written some time after the division of the kingdom. (He several times refers to the separate kingdom of Judah, but the nation was not yet in exile: see, e.g. 1 Samuel 27:6.) 900 BC is therefore the earliest likely date for the books as we know them. Critics have argued for several authors, largely because of the 'duplicate' accounts of various events (e.g. the two sparings of Saul's life; the two occasions when Samuel announced God's rejection of Saul). On closer inspection, however, most of the so-called duplicates emerge quite clearly as two separate if similar events, recounted by the author in order to emphasize certain points. Repetition is a feature of his literary technique.

1 - 3 SAMUEL'S BIRTH AND EARLY YEARS

1 God answers Hannah's prayer for a child

In the Old Testament, when God has a special purpose for a man there is often something special about his birth. Like Hannah, Sarah and Rebekah in the Old Testament and Elizabeth in the New experienced the bitterness of being childless. Like Samuel, Isaac and Jacob and John the Baptist were the God-given answers to many years of prayer. Each had a special role to play in the great plan of God. When God gave Hannah the son she longed for he also gave Israel the last and greatest of the judges, and the first (after Moses) of the great prophets – the man who was to usher in the kings.

To sacrifice ... at Shiloh (3): the centre of worship in the Judges period; the place where Joshua had set up the tabernacle (Joshua 18:1). (The 'temple' proper – verse 9 – was not built till Solomon's day.)

I will give him to the Lord ... (11): the child is dedicated to God for life under a Nazirite vow (see Numbers 6, and compare the vow made by Samson's parents in Judges 13).

Only her lips moved (13): it was usual to pray aloud. Eli is quick to jump to the wrong conclusion. Religious life must have been at a low ebb if worshippers came drunk to the tabernacle. Compare the conduct of Eli's own sons, 2:12ff.

When she had weaned him (24): Samuel would have been two or three years old.

2:1-10 Hannah's song of thanksgiving

Hannah's song is echoed by Mary in the New Testament (Luke 1:46-55). In the small mirror of her own experience Hannah sees reflected all the wonder of God's character. God has reversed her fortunes (1). Peninnah's taunts have been silenced (3, 5). Emptiness, misery, shame are gone – in their place, life, joy, honour. And what God can do for one, he can and will do for all his people.

Sheol (6): the shadowy land of the dead.

His King (10): this is either inspired prophecy on Hannah's part, or verses 2-10 are part of a psalm added by the narrator, as being singularly appropriate to her experience.

2:11-36 Eli the priest and his no-good sons

The priests were entitled to a share in the sacrificial offerings (see Numbers 18:8-20; Deuteronomy 18:1-5). But what is going on here is a travesty of the law. Eli's sons seize the best bits before the offering has even been given to God (15). What is more, they are bringing prostitution into the worship of God, in the worst traditions of Canaanite religion (22). On his death these two will be the nation's 'archbishops' – and all Eli can do is reason with them!

Verses 27-36: the man of God's prediction is fulfilled in the death of Eli's sons in battle at Aphek (4:11). The priesthood passed from Eli's family to the line of Zadok in David's day (2 Samuel 8:17).

A linen ephod (18): a tunic worn by the priests (see verse 28).

It was the will of the Lord to slay them (25): the writer puts it this way because God is sovereign in every circumstance. It is equally true that their death is a direct outcome of their own free choice to disobey God. The Bible sees no conflict between God's sovereignty and man's free will. See on Exodus 6:28 - 10:29.

3 Samuel hears God's call

In the early hours (before the oil for the lamp ran out, as it would at dawn), when he is on duty near the ark, inside the tabernacle, Samuel hears God speak to him for the first time – a message of judgement for Eli. From this time on, Samuel is God's messenger, and the whole nation knows it, from Dan in the far north to Beersheba on the edge of the southern desert.

4:1 - 7:1 THE PHILISTINES AND THE ARK OF GOD

4:1-11 The Philistines defeat Israel and capture the ark

The ark (see Exodus 25 - 27) was Israel's most precious possession, the focal point of the tabernacle. A copy of the law was kept inside it. Its lid was the mercy seat, symbol of the presence of God.

But now the nation wants to use it as a talisman, the ultimate protection against the Philistines. The result is total disaster: the army defeated, the ark in enemy hands.

Philistines (1): one of a group known as the Sea Peoples, who migrated into the Near East from the Aegean area in the 14th-13th centuries BC.

This plaster-cast of the head of a Philistine soldier is from Thebes in Egypt, 12th century BC.

They were defeated by the Egyptians and settled the southern coastal area of Palestine.

4:12-22 Death of Eli

The ark never returned to Shiloh. Although there is no mention of it here, the Philistines probably followed up their victory by destroying this city (see Jeremiah 26:6). These verses record the fulfilment of God's judgement on Eli's family (2:27-36; 3:11-14).

He had judged Israel forty years (18): most of Israel's judges were warrior-leaders (see Judges). But the last two, Eli and Samuel, were religious leaders and administrators of justice.

5 The ark in Philistine hands

To the Philistines' way of thinking, Dagon, their god, has given them victory. So they place the ark as a war-trophy at his feet. But Dagon is not in the same class as the God of Israel. God is no man-made idol. He treats the figure of Dagon as they might have treated a captive king (see Judges 1:6-7). As a further demonstration of his power there is an outbreak of plague (bubonic plague, carried by the rat-flea; see verse 6 and 6:4, New English Bible). Moving the ark simply spreads the disease.

6 - 7:1 Return of the ark

After seven months of this, the Philistines have had enough. The religious leaders advise the ark's return – but in a way which will show, once for all, whether or not Israel's God is responsible for the disasters. The cows, not trained for the yoke, are unlikely to pull together. In the nature of things they would also be expected to stay near their calves. Yet they respond to the yoke like a team of oxen, and head straight for the border.

Verse 19 (Revised Standard Version) sounds a sombre note in all the rejoicing. Even Israel must learn not to overstep the mark. It is not safe to treat God as an object of idle curiosity.

7:2-17 NATIONAL REVIVAL: SAMUEL AS JUDGE

Twenty years pass, and there is a genuine turning to God (verse 2, New English Bible). The old idols – Baal and Ashtoreth, the Canaanite fertility gods – are destroyed. And Samuel, judge and religious leader in Eli's place (see 15-17), leads the nation in an act of repentance and cleansing. Immediately the test comes. The Philistines are advancing, and God uses the occasion to show Israel just what he will do for a people who keep faith with him. Israel is needed only for the mopping-up operation. The name of the place of a former defeat (4:1) is chosen to mark the present victory (12). It is God's help which makes such a dramatic reversal possible.

All the days of Samuel (13): this includes most of Saul's reign. War continued, but Saul and David kept the Philistines at bay until the great battle of Gilboa when Saul and Jonathan lost their lives.

From Ekron to Gath (14): the two inland Philistine city-states. Israel won back their border towns.

Bethel, Gilgal, Mizpah, Ramah (16-17): Samuel did an annual circuit of the four sanctuary towns.

8 - 12 SAUL BECOMES ISRAEL'S FIRST KING

8 The people ask for a king; Samuel's warning

History repeats itself in the case of Samuel's sons. They turn out little better than Eli's (2:12). This provides the people with a ready-made excuse to ask for a king, like the nations around. Samuel warns of the cost. They have only to look at their neighbour states to see that having a king means conscription, forced labour, taxation, and loss of personal liberty. But even this does not deter them.

9 - 10:16 Saul becomes king: the private anointing

A search for lost donkeys, of all things, brings Israel's future king from Gibeah to Ramah, and the meeting with Samuel. All Israel knows the prophet, but not, apparently, this young provincial.

The oil (10:1) sets Saul apart for his high office. The detailed fulfilment of Samuel's predictions assures Saul of the prophet's authority. Saul goes home a new man (10:9).

The high place (9:12): the shrine; the phrase has not yet acquired the idolatrous associations of later times.

A bed ... upon the roof (9:25): a pleasantly cool place in the summer heat.

Down ... to Gilgal (10:8): the instruction seems to relate to mustering for battle. When this took place (chapter 13) Saul disobeyed.

When they came to Gibeah ...(10:10): Saul's ecstatic experience took place in his own home town.

10:17-27 The public proclamation

God chooses Israel's king; it is not left to the people.

11 Saul's first victory melts the opposition

God moves Saul to make his appeal (6) and the people to respond (7). For perhaps the first time since Joshua the nation is united: a good beginning to the new king's reign.

12 Samuel cautions the people at Gilgal

Samuel has always been alert to the dangers of monarchy (8; 10:17ff.). Politically the move to choose a king was no doubt wise. Religiously, it was a step in the wrong direction, a step away from the ideal of God alone as Israel's King. And if God ceases to be King for his people, both nation and monarchy will be swept away (25).

Verse 9: *Sisera* defeated by Deborah and Barak (Judges 4 - 5); *the king of Moab* – Eglon, assassinated by Ehud (Judges 3:12-30).

Verse 11: *Jerubbaal* – i.e. Gideon (Judges 6 - 8); *Jephthah* – Judges 11 - 12; *Samuel* – this seems odd coming from his own lips. Perhaps we should read 'Samson' (New English Bible; Judges 13 - 16).

13 - 15 SAUL DISOBEYS AND IS REJECTED

13 - 14 War with the Philistines: Saul's disobedience and stupidity

Saul musters his troops and waits seven days, during which time the army steadily dwindles. But he fails to see the seventh day out. And his disobedience and arrogance in taking over the function of the prophet costs him his dynasty.

Chapter 14: Jonathan and his armour-bearer seem to have been taken for deserters, so they were able to catch the Philistines on the hop.

Earth tremors add to the panic and confusion. And Israelite deserters change sides to help Saul to victory. Jonathan is seen as a man of outstanding faith and courage. By contrast, the narrative begins to bring out those flaws in Saul's make-up which later developed into serious mental disorder.

13:1: the text is incomplete. Acts 13:21 puts Saul's reign in round figures at 40 years. Possibly a tens-unit has dropped out here and the text should read 32 years (but see article 'Unravelling the Chronology of the Kings'). We know from 9:2 that Saul was a young man when he came to the throne. By this time he must be in his thirties since he has a son old enough to fight. When he died, a younger son, Ishbosheth, was himself 40 (2 Samuel 2:10).

Thirty thousand (13:5): more probably 3,000 – see article 'The Large Numbers of the Old Testament'.

The people hid themselves (13:6): the atmosphere is much the same as it was in Gideon's day, when the people went in fear of the Midianites (Judges 6:2).

Bring hither the ark (14:18): perhaps in view of Saul's command to the priest in verse 19, New English Bible translates 'ephod' rather than 'ark'. This was the tunic with the breastpiece containing the Urim and Thummim (41), the lots which were cast to discover God's will.

Sinning ... by eating with the blood (14:33): forbidden in Leviticus 17:10ff.

Ishvi (14:49): short form of Ishbosheth.

Abner (14:50): he later set up Ishbosheth as king in opposition to David (2 Samuel 2:8 - 3:39).

15 God orders the destruction of the Amalekites; Saul again disobeys

This time the disobedience is deliberate (9). Saul is personally rejected by God as king, and Samuel pays him no more official visits. The prophet had foreseen trouble. He might well have relished Saul's downfall. Instead he went home grieving.

Amalek (2): the Amalekites were old enemies whose punishment had long been forecast (Exodus 17:8-16; Deuteronomy 25:17-19). Even so, we find it hard to swallow the order to destroy them completely – notwithstanding the unparalleled atrocities of our own century. In the more realistic, less individualistic world of Saul's day the whole community was held responsible for the misdeeds of its members, and suffered the consequences. Saul's disobedience (for the lowest of motives) left his people open to continued harassment from the Amalekites.

Kenites (6): a nomadic Midianite tribe into which Moses had married. The Kenites acted as Israel's guides in the desert (Numbers 10:29-33).

To obey is better than sacrifice (22-23): Samuel's declaration became a major theme of later prophets.

16 - 31 SAUL AND DAVID

16:1-13 Samuel anoints David king

With the anointing, as in Saul's case, comes spiritual power (13). Again God chooses his man and prepares him long before he becomes a national figure.

16:14-23 David finds a place at court

When the Spirit of God leaves Saul, evil forces take charge. Saul is at the mercy of his own ungovernable temperament. His disordered mind plunges him into black depression and violence. But music can push back the shadows, and so Saul's need becomes David's opportunity.

David's harp was a 'kinnor', the first musical instrument mentioned in the Bible. This reconstruction is from the Haifa Music Museum.

An evil spirit from God (15): to the observer, Saul is 'possessed' by a spirit sent by God in punishment.

17 David and Goliath

The Philistine champion is ten feet tall, fully armed and mailed. But David's time in the hills alone with the sheep has taught him faith – and deadly accuracy with the sling. The giant doesn't stand a chance.

Verses 55-58: this is difficult to tie in with 16:18ff. The events of chapter 17 may have taken place while David was still attending court only occasionally, when Saul's black moods came on him. 16:21-22 then refer to a later time. Or possibly the enquiry is a purely formal one concerning David's family background. The victor had, after all, been promised the king's daughter in marriage (17:25).

18 The friendship with Jonathan; Saul grows jealous

David was to look back on his friendship with Jonathan as one of the best things in his life (2 Samuel 1:26). Nothing could shake the amazing bond between the king's son and the man who, humanly speaking, was to rob him of the throne.

As David's prestige grows, Saul's jealous suspicion increases, and he plots David's death. David's poverty gives Saul the chance to suggest a bride-price which is likely to cost him his life. Such a toll could be exacted only from the Philistines, Israel's number one enemy; the other nations practised circumcision. David doubles Saul's demand and returns unharmed, to claim his royal bride.

19 - 20 Attempts on his life force David to leave Saul's court

Jonathan's first attempt at reconciliation succeeds (1-7). But one of Saul's black moods follows and only Michal's deception saves David's life (8-17). For a time he joins Samuel and his school of prophets at Ramah (18-24). Jonathan tries to secure David's safe return, but his father only turns on him (20:30-33). And the two friends are forced to part (35-42).

Is Saul also among the prophets? (19-24): compare 10:10-13. So irresistible is the power of the Spirit of God that not only is Saul's evil plan frustrated, but the king himself becomes 'infected'. Like his messengers, he too – for the time at least – turns prophet.

Tomorrow is the new moon (20:5): the first day of each new month was a feast day.

21 Ahimelech helps David to escape

The priest pays dearly for David's deception (22:11-19). But David is fed and armed, and makes good his escape to the Philistine city of Gath. In danger of recognition he feigns madness and plays the part so effectively that Achish is completely convinced (see also 27:5-12).

Nob (1): Israel's central shrine at that time.

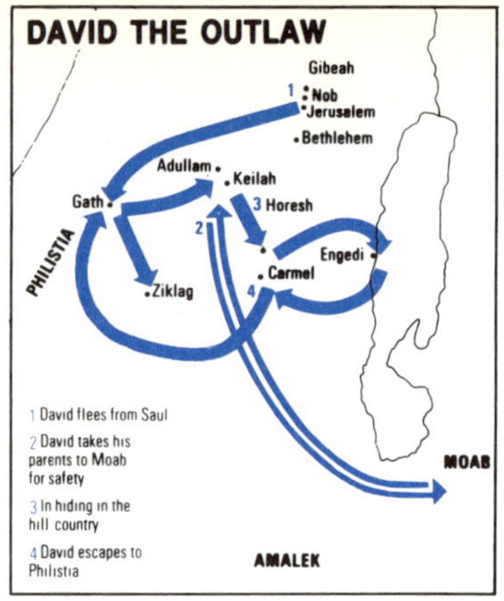

Holy bread (4): each sabbath twelve fresh loaves were placed on the altar and the twelve stale ones removed. Only the priests were entitled to eat them.

Vessels (5): i.e. 'bodies' (New English Bible). Israelite soldiers abstained from sexual intercourse during campaigns. If Uriah had not steadfastly stuck to the rules, David would have had no occasion to resort to murder (2 Samuel 11:11).

22 David the outlaw; Saul's revenge on Ahimelech

He left them with the king of Moab (4): for safety. David had Moabite blood in his veins (see Ruth).

Doeg (9ff.): the title of Psalm 52 relates it to this episode.

23 The hunt is on: Keilah, Ziph, Maon

David welds his band of outlaws into an effective military force. But Saul's relentless pursuit keeps them continually on the move.

The ephod (6): see on 14:18.

24 David spares Saul's life in the cave at Engedi

Saul is completely at David's mercy. His refusal to take a short-cut to the throne brings the king to his senses. But Saul's word cannot be relied on.

25 The death of Samuel; David and Abigail

Not until Elijah will there be another religious leader to equal Samuel. The old prophet had anointed Israel's greatest king, but did not live to see him reign.

David's request to Nabal is not unreasonable. He is not demanding protection money, but asking some return on past services (15-16). After all, the man was rich and it was sheep-shearing, a feast time. Abigail's quick action saves the lives of her husband and household (22). She evidently made a good impression on David (see verse 39). God attends to Nabal's punishment. He dies of a double stroke.

26 David again spares Saul's life

The pro-Saul Ziphites again lay information against David. And once again it is Saul who finds himself at David's mercy and is shamed into repentance. No doubt Macbeth would have seen this as a heaven-sent opportunity for advancement. David knew God could and would put him on the throne without any assistance from him.

Abishai the son of Zeruiah (6): Abishai, Joab, and Asahel, David's military leaders, were all sons of his step-sister. Though brave, they caused him a great deal of trouble when he was king (2 Samuel 3:39; 18:14; 20:10).

27 Back in Philistine country

Achish is once again completely taken in (see 21:10-15). While pretending to raid Israel and her allies (10), David in fact wipes out enemy cities (8), leaving no one alive to tell the tale (11).

28 Saul consults a medium

Saul can get no reply from God (6). Witchcraft had always been forbidden in Israel (Leviticus 19:31). But in desperation he sets out at night and in disguise on a dangerous journey, close to the enemy camp at Shunem, to consult the medium at Endor. However, he finds Samuel no more reassuring in death than he had been in life.

29 David is not trusted

The other Philistine overlords are less gullible than Achish, so David is spared the awkward predicament of facing his fellow countrymen in battle. This chapter refers to earlier events than chapter 28. The Philistines muster at Aphek. They have not yet moved north to Shunem.

30 The Amalekite raid on Ziklag; David's successful reprisal

David's return is well-timed, and the slave's information more than a stroke of luck. All is recovered. And Judah and the Calebites, also victims of the raid (14), share in the spoil.

31 The battle of Gilboa; death of Saul and Jonathan

The writer of Chronicles (1 Chronicles 10) found this account of Saul's death more credible than the Amalekite's story (2 Samuel 1:4-10). The latter may well have adjusted the facts to suit his own ends. Fittingly, it is the men of Jabesh who rescue the bodies. They have not forgotten what they owe to Saul's first great victory (chapter 11).

2 SAMUEL 1 - 4 THE EARLY YEARS OF DAVID'S REIGN

(The reign of David is also recorded in 1 Chronicles 11 – 29.9)

1 News of Saul's death; David's lament

The Amalekite's story differs from the account of Saul's death in 1 Samuel 31. If he twisted the facts in hope of a reward, he did not know David. After the Amalekite raid on Ziklag (1 Samuel 30) David had no cause to love this race. But it was his strong conviction that the king's life was sacred (14; and see 1 Samuel 24 and 26), not racial discrimination, that led to the death sentence.

The lament for Saul and Jonathan is one of the most moving and beautiful of all David's poems. His regret for the king seems wholly sincere; his distress at the loss of Jonathan, deep and genuine.

On the third day (2): it was 100 miles from Gilboa to Ziklag.

The book of Jashar (18): a lost anthology (see Joshua 10:13).

The shield ... anointed with oil (21): the shield was leather; oil prevented it drying and cracking.

2 Civil war; Abner kills Asahel

Only Judah (by this time probably including Simeon) acclaims David as king. The other ten tribes follow the lead of Abner, Saul's army commander, and give allegiance to Ishbosheth, Saul's son. For two years the nation is divided.

An attempt to settle the issue by representative single combat (14, see New English Bible) at Gibeon is inconclusive, and full-scale civil war follows.

Sons of Zeruiah (18): see on 1 Samuel 26:6.

The butt of his spear (23): Abner did not intend to kill Asahel. But the butt was sharp so that it would stick in the ground, and the blow proved fatal.

The Arabah (29): the long rift valley from Galilee to the Dead Sea and beyond; here, the Jordan Valley.

3 Abner makes terms; Joab avenges his brother

Ishbosheth is not the man his father was. Abner is the real power. If he transfers his support to David, he carries the nation with him. But he reckons without the implacable hatred of Joab. David leads the nation's mourning for Abner. Despite a public declaration of innocence, the taint of the murder remains with him all his life (1 Kings 2:5).

Saul had a concubine (7): a king's harem normally passed to his heir, which makes Abner's action tantamount to a claim to the throne. Compare Absalom's action, 16:20ff. Rizpah appears again in chapter 21.

A dog's head of Judah (8): i.e. 'one of David's contemptible supporters'.

Dan to Beersheba (10): the whole country, north to south (in Britain one would say, from John o' Groat's to Land's End).

My wife Michal ... (14): see I Samuel 18:20-27. Saul had given David's wife to another man.

One who has a discharge ... (29): who is defiled and therefore disqualified from religious service; *holds a spindle*: fit only for women's work.

4 The assassination of Ishbosheth

A second incident (compare 1:1-16) which shows the complete failure of David's supporters to understand his attitude to Saul and the royal family. Ishbosheth is given honourable burial, the two murderers are publicly disgraced.

5 - 12 DAVID'S KINGDOM ESTABLISHED

5 David, king of all Israel; the new capital at Jerusalem

The writer makes it clear that David is no usurper. God has given him his title to the throne: a fact recognized by Saul (1 Samuel 24:18-20), by Abner (3:9-10) and finally by the whole nation (5:2).

Although part of Jerusalem fell to Judah at the conquest (Judges 1:8), the fortress itself had never been taken (Joshua 15:63; Judges 1:21). The Jebusites had some ground for their boast that a garrison of blind men and cripples could hold it (6). But they underestimated David. Jerusalem was held by Judah until Nebuchadnezzar destroyed it 400 years later. It was a first-rate choice of capital.

The Millo (9): part of the fortifications.

Hiram, king of Tyre (11): contemporary with David and Solomon (1 Kings 5). Hiram reigned about 979-945 BC. The sea-port of Tyre was capital of the Phoenician kingdom. Hiram's reign was a golden age of political expansion and commercial prosperity, when arts and crafts flourished. His craftsmen helped to build the temple.

6 The ark is brought to Jerusalem

See also 1 Chronicles 13, 15-16. After the Philistines returned the ark (1 Samuel 4 - 6), it remained at Kiriath-jearim (Baalah in Judah; see 1 Chronicles 13:6). Now David brings it to his new capital. The occasion is marked with all the exuberance of Jewish worship. Even the king dances for joy. Only Michal stands aloof and outside it all, cold and

Part of the modern city of Jerusalem.

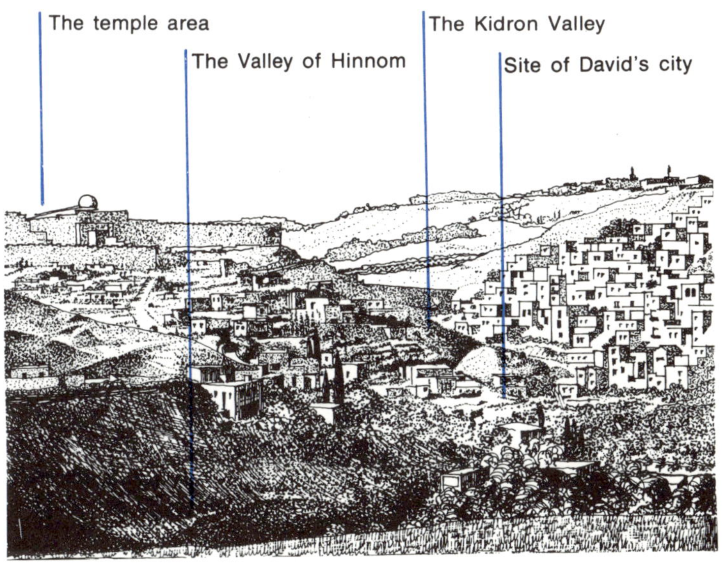

unmoved by the presence of God.
Uzzah put out his hand to the ark (6): which not even the Levites might touch. David blames himself for not following the instructions Moses laid down (1 Chronicles 15:2-15). At the next attempt the Levites carried the ark on poles.

7 The house of God and the throne of David

David is not the man to build God's temple – that is for his son, a man of peace, not a warrior (1 Chronicles 22:7ff.). But God compensates for the disappointment by promising a 'house' for David, a dynasty which will be 'for ever' (16). On this promise rests a hope which runs right through the Old Testament, the hope of a Messiah. And when he came, the promise was fulfilled. Christ was born in David's birthplace, Bethlehem, and 'of the house and lineage of David' (Luke 2:4). The angel tells Mary: 'The Lord God will give to him the throne of his father David, and he will reign over the house of Jacob for ever; and of his kingdom there will be no end' (Luke 1:32-33).
Your son ... shall build (12-13): Solomon did build (1 Kings 5-7). But David contributed a great deal: he drew up the plans and provided materials (1 Chronicles 28:11ff.; 22:2ff.).

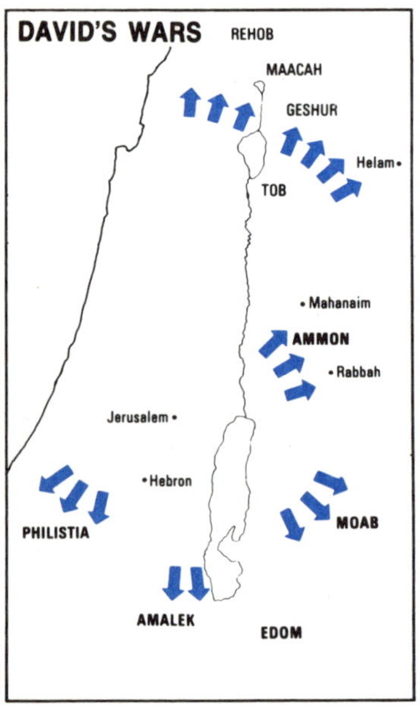

8 David's victories

This chapter predates the events of chapter 7 (see 7:1).
Moab (2): previously David was on good terms with them (1 Samuel 22:3-4).
Valley of Salt (13): probably in the barren section of the great rift valley south of the Dead Sea.
Cherethites ... Pelethites (18): Philistine mercenaries.
David's sons were priests (18): although not from a priestly family, David was himself something of a priest-king (see chapter 6), like Melchizedek, a much earlier king of Jerusalem (Genesis 14:18).

9 David and Mephibosheth, Jonathan's son

The events of chapter 21 may predate this chapter. If so, no doubt the king's summons terrified Mephibosheth. But David's motives are wholly good, 'for Jonathan's sake' (see 1 Samuel 20:42). He restores the family estates (7) and treats the young man as his own son (11).
Lo-debar (4): in north Gilead, not far from Jabesh.
Verse 10: this sounds contradictory, but being at court would mean an increase in general expenses, even if meals were provided.

10 Defeat of the Ammonite/Syrian alliance

See also 1 Chronicles 19. Hanun provoked the war by his outrageous treatment of the ambassadors. But no doubt neighbouring nations were suspicious and afraid of Israel's powerful king.

The campaign in verses 16-18 may be the one mentioned in 8:3ff.

11 David's adultery with Bathsheba

His army is fighting the Ammonites, but this spring the king is not with them. He is taking an after-siesta stroll in the cool, on the palace roof. And from his vantage-point he can see down into the open inner courtyard of a nearby house, where Bathsheba is going through the purification ritual. The events that follow – adultery and murder – are the watershed in David's life. From this point on he reaps the bitter harvest of his sin.
Rabbah (1): present-day Amman, capital of Jordan.
Uriah the Hittite (3): to make matters worse, Uriah was one of David's special guard (23:39), away on the king's war.
Verse 11: the army is on campaign, under canvas, and the rule is that the men abstain from sexual intercourse. Had Uriah been a man of less principle he would have gone home to his wife. The child could then have passed as his and he would not have been killed. But maybe he already suspected the truth.
Jerubbesheth (21): i.e. Jerubbaal/Gideon (Judges 9). 'Baal' being a pagan name, the scribes later substituted the word 'bosheth'/'besheth', 'shame'. So Jerubbaal became Jerubbesheth; Eshbaal became Ishbosheth; Meribbaal, Mephibosheth, and so on.

12 Nathan's visit; death of the child

Uriah is dead; the wedding over; the child born. It all seems to have blown over very nicely – until Nathan arrives. And then the whole sordid episode is exposed. David is made to see himself as God sees him: a humbling experience for a king (see Psalm 51). God forgives him, but he is punished, and the child dies.
Restore ... fourfold (6): see Exodus 22:1.
Verses 10-11: the prophecy was fulfilled. Three of David's sons were murdered, two by their own brothers. And in the rebellion Absalom took over his father's harem (16:22).
Sent a message ... (25): presumably to reassure David that this child would not die.
A talent of gold (30): about 66lb/30kg.

13 - 20 DAVID AND HIS ELDEST SONS: ABSALOM'S REBELLION

13 Amnon and Tamar; Absalom's revenge

Faced with the appalling rape of his daughter by her half-brother, David does nothing at all. The strong king is a fatally weak father (see 1 Kings 1:6). Had David taken action he might have prevented both the murder and the later rebellion.
Speak to the king (13): Tamar does not think marriage out of the question (though in view of Leviticus 18:11 they would have needed a special dispensation). The 'impossibility' of verse 2 lies in her careful seclusion – Amnon only wanted to satisfy his lust, he had no thought of marriage.

14 The woman from Tekoa; Absalom forgiven

Joab pierces the king's defences much as Nathan had done (chapter 12), but with a fake law-suit. This time the appeal is to waive the next-of-kin's obligation to avenge his murdered relative. The application to David is obvious. He is willing to overrule in the case of one of his subjects: why not for his heir?

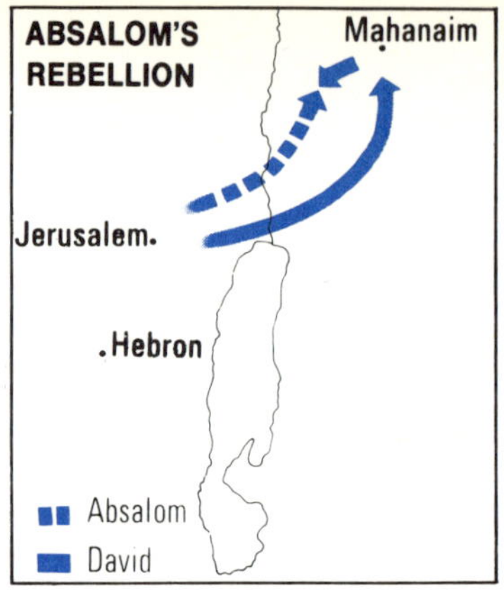

Joab wins his point, and Absalom returns from exile. But two long years pass before he is admitted to his father's presence.
Verse 26: it was Absalom's hair which eventually brought about his death (18:9). The weight is $3\frac{1}{2}$-4lb.

15 Absalom's rebellion; David leaves Jerusalem

With Amnon out of the way, and Abigail's son dead, Absalom is next in line to the throne. But Solomon is David's chosen heir. For four years Absalom lays his plans (1-6), gradually winning the people over. When he does come into the open (7-12) the challenge to David is extremely serious.

The king is caught unprepared. To save the city, and gain time, he leaves Jerusalem. But he organizes a spy-ring. And Hushai is sent back to outwit Ahithophel, whose far-sighted council is otherwise likely to win the day for Absalom.
The gate (2): where the city's business and legal transactions took place (see Ruth 4:1ff.).
Hebron (7): David's former capital, in Judah.
The Mount of Olives (30): the place where Jesus spent the night of his betrayal.
Ahithophel (31): Bathsheba's grandfather; wisest of all David's advisers.

16 Ziba and Shimei; Hushai and Ahithophel

Ziba (1-4) clearly has an eye to the main chance. Mephibosheth later denies the charges made against him (19:24-30). Shimei (5-14) takes a vindictive pleasure in the downfall of the man who robbed his family of the throne (5-8).

In Jerusalem (15-19) Hushai succeeds in convincing Absalom of his loyalty. Verses 20-23 provide an example of Ahithophel's political strategy. By taking over David's harem, Absalom will convince his followers that reconciliation with his father is impossible. No king could forgive such a public insult.

17 Absalom rejects Ahithophel's plan

Ahithophel's advice is to strike quickly, and only against the person of the king – so avoiding civil war. But Hushai gains time for David by a scheme which appeals to Absalom's vanity (11ff.). Ahithophel has the foresight to realize the probable consequences – hence his suicide (24). Meantime Jonathan and Ahimaaz, on their way to David with the information, narrowly escape discovery by hiding in a dry cistern – one of many hollowed out for storing rain-water (17-20).

18 - 19:8 Defeat and death of Absalom; David's grief

Joab is shrewd enough to see that only the death of the pretender – or the king – can settle the issue. But David still loved his son, and he did not forgive Joab for ignoring orders (see 19:13). It was ironic that Absalom's beautiful hair (14:26) should tangle in the oak and leave him a helpless prey to Joab.

18:33 - 19:8: grief and remorse (see 12:10) blind the king to the effect of his conduct on the people. Joab's harsh words bring him to his senses and save him from political disaster.

Great heap of stones (18:17): a cairn marked the grave of a criminal.

I have no son (18:18): presumably those mentioned in 14:27 died young.

Ahimaaz and the Cushite (18:19-32): Joab chooses the dark-skinned Sudanese to take the bad news. The king would naturally have assumed (as he does in 27) that the priest's son brought good news. Joab may also have been thinking of the fate of earlier messengers (1:11-16; 4:9-12). But the direct hill-route proved slower than the route Ahimaaz took along the Jordan Valley (23).

19:9-43 The aftermath of rebellion

Judah had backed Absalom. David's attempt to win them back, and his appointment of Amasa (Absalom's army commander, and his own nephew) in Joab's place lead to further trouble (41-43 and chapter 20). David is in effect punishing loyalty and rewarding rebellion. Now that the king is back in power, there are some who are anxious to get back into favour (Shimei, 16-22, see 16:5-14; Mephibosheth, 24-30, see 16:1-4; on Shimei and Barzillai, see also 1 Kings 2).

20 Sheba's revolt; Joab kills Amasa

Despite the statement in verse 2, those who actively supported Sheba, when it came to it, were few (14ff.). Joab is as quick to kill Amasa (a member of his own family) as he was to kill Abner, when his own position was threatened before. In both cases his treachery is despicable. The kiss and the sword thrust bring to mind Judas' betrayal of Jesus. David did not forget, or forgive (see 1 Kings 2:5-6).

Your lord's servants (6): the men of David's special guard (7 and 23:18ff.), led by Abishai.

It fell out (8): into Joab's hand.

Adoram (24): in a post not likely to win friends! He was stoned to death in the reign of Solomon's son.

21 - 24 RECORDS OF EVENTS IN DAVID'S REIGN

With Sheba's death, the nation is once more united and at peace. The writer now brings together events and information belonging to various periods of David's reign.

The old titles to the Psalms link many of David's psalms to events in his life.

Escape from the palace: 1 Samuel 19:11ff.: Psalm 59

David feigns madness:
1 Samuel 21: Psalm 34 (though the difference in names may indicate a further occasion not recorded in Samuel)

David in hiding in the cave:
1 Samuel 22:1ff.: 24:3ff.: Psalms 57, 142

Doeg's betrayal of the priests at Nob: 1 Samuel 22: Psalm 52

The Ziphite informers: 1 Samuel 23:19ff.: Psalm 54

David in the Judean desert:
1 Samuel 24:1-2,22; and again in 2 Samuel 15ff.: Psalm 63

Defeat of the Edomites: 2 Samuel 8:13: Psalm 60

David's sin over Bathsheba:
2 Samuel 11-12: Psalm 51 (and probably 32)

Absalom's rebellion: 2 Samuel 15:13ff.: Psalm 3

David's song of deliverance:
2 Samuel 22: the same poem as Psalm 18

21 The appeasement of Gibeon; defeat of the Philistine giants

Verses 1-14 probably precede Mephibosheth's welcome at court (chapter 9). The story of Israel's pact with Gibeon is told in Joshua 9:3-27. Saul had broken the treaty, despite close family connections with the city (1 Chronicles 8:29ff.).

That you may bless ... (3): and so remove the curse that brought the famine.

Hang (6): the Hebrew does not specify the manner of death.

Merab (8): the daughter who had been promised to David as wife.

Took sackcloth and spread it ... (10): to form a tent. Rizpah may have been there as long as six months. The coming of rain brought an end to the famine, and to the curse, leaving David free to act.

Elhanan ... slew Goliath (19): this seems to conflict with 1 Samuel 17. The text here may be confused. R. K. Harrison suggests it should read, 'Elhanan, the son of Jairi the Bethlehemite, slew the brother of Goliath', which ties in with 1 Chronicles 20:5. Another possibility is that a new champion took the name of the one killed by David.

22 David's victory song

This is virtually identical with Psalm 18, and can be compared with Moses' song in Deuteronomy 32. It belongs to the period of David's great early victories. Verses 21-25 contrast with the deeper self-knowledge which followed the Bathsheba/Uriah episode, expressed in Psalm 51.

23:1-7 David's 'last words'

These may be the last words he set down in poetry (see 1 Kings 2 for his final charge to Solomon). His thoughts centre on what makes a good ruler, on his own standing before God, and on the promised dynasty – a fitting close to the life of the king who was 'a man after God's own heart'.

23:8-39 Annals of the men of David's special guard

The exploits of 'The Three' against the Philistines (8-12) are followed by an incident from the campaign described in 5:17-25 (13-17; Bethlehem was David's home town). Then come the exploits of two leaders (Abishai, leader of 'The Thirty', and Benaiah, leader of the Philistine mercenaries), followed by a list of the special guard. The group was probably formed at Ziklag, and helped to put David on the throne (1 Chronicles 12:1; 11:10). More than thirty are listed – those killed (e.g. Asahel, Uriah) were replaced by others.

Ariel (20): 'lion of God'; either lions of exceptional size, or a metaphor for great warriors.

24 The census and the plague

It is not clear why it was wrong to take the census. Perhaps it indicated reliance on numbers, instead of on God. Satan does the inciting in 1 Chronicles 21:1. Here it is God, since all is ultimately under his control.

Verses 8-25: the first readers did not need to be told the tremendous significance of David's purchase, explicitly mentioned in 1 Chronicles 21:18 - 22:1. On this threshing-floor the temple was built, close to the place where Abraham offered up Isaac (2 Chronicles 3:1; Genesis 22:2).

Old Testament 2.6 and 7

1 AND 2 KINGS

Four centuries of Israel's history are covered by the books of Kings. We move from the close of David's reign, through the golden age of Solomon and the rift between Israel and Judah, to the fall of Samaria in 722 BC and the destruction of Jerusalem in 587 BC. The account begins with a stable, united kingdom under a strong king and ends with total collapse and mass deportation to Babylon. It is a sombre story, and one in which the writer sees a clear moral. God is the Lord of history, actively involved in the affairs of men. When the nation and its leaders look to him and obey his laws, peace and prosperity follow. Political and economic disaster overtake Israel and Judah as a direct consequence of the weakening of the nation's moral and religious fibre.

The writer is unknown; probably a prophet in Babylon during the exile, about 550 BC. He mentions a number of his sources (e.g. 1 Kings 11:41; 15:31): court and official records and cycles of stories about the prophets. He wrote his account as one volume, to be read through from beginning to end. Much of the material is paralleled in Chronicles.

1 - 2 DAVID'S LAST DAYS: SOLOMON'S ACCESSION

1 Adonijah and Solomon; rivals for the throne

King David is now an old man. Thoughts turn to his successor. With his three elder brothers dead, Adonijah is heir apparent. He has the backing of Joab, the army commander, and Abiathar, one of the two chief priests. But the throne has been promised to Solomon (1:13, and see 1 Chronicles 22:9). And thanks to some quick thinking by the prophet Nathan, and even quicker action by the old king, Adonijah is outmanoeuvred. Solomon is made king, co-regent with David.

Abishag the Shunammite (3): from Shunem near Nazareth. Although Abishag is sometimes identified with the heroine of the Song of Solomon, there are no real grounds for this.

Knew her not (4): did not have sexual intercourse with her. The verb 'know' often has this sense in the Old Testament (Genesis 4:1).

Verses 7-8: Zadok and Abiathar, see 2 Samuel 15:24ff.; Benaiah, 2 Samuel 23:20-23; Nathan, 2 Samuel 12. The mighty men: David's special guard, 2 Samuel 23:8-39.

Gihon (33): a spring just outside the eastern wall of Jerusalem, in the Kidron Valley.

Cherethites and Pelethites (38): foreign (Philistine) mercenaries.

The tent (39): in which the ark was kept.

Horns of the altar (50): curved pieces at the four corners.

2:1-12 Last instructions to Solomon; David's death

High-toned advice (1-4) is abruptly followed by worldly wisdom of doubtful morality (5-9).

Joab (5): see 2 Samuel 3:26-30; 20:8-10.

Barzillai (7): see 2 Samuel 17:27-29; 19:31-40.

Shimei (8): David did not regard his pledge to Shimei as binding on Solomon. See 2 Samuel 16:5-14 and 19:16-23.

The basins on wheeled stands used in the temple courtyard may have resembled this bronze stand, from 1200 – 1100 BC.

2:13-46 Solomon secures his position

This time Adonijah pays dearly for what may have been an unthinking request. Solomon interprets it as a claim to the throne, since possession of his predecessor's harem was part of the eastern king's title to the throne (compare Absalom's action, 2 Samuel 16). Abiathar and Joab are dealt with at the same time. And Shimei, another potential trouble-maker, is put on parole in Jerusalem to keep him away from fellow-Benjaminites. When he breaks parole, even though for an innocent reason, Solomon has him killed.

The word ... concerning the house of Eli (27): see 1 Samuel 2:27-36.

3 - 11 THE REIGN OF SOLOMON

3:1-15 Solomon's dream; the gift of wisdom

Solomon is at Gibeon, the town six miles from Jerusalem where the tabernacle and altar are kept, when God appears to him. His reign is outstanding for wise judgement, economic prosperity and fame – the very things God promised.

Verse 1: 'the city', i.e. the citadel on Mt Zion.

High places (2): the old Canaanite shrines (often, but not always, on hill-tops) which the Israelites took over. It was not long before the worship of God in these places became mixed with crude pagan practices. The later prophets condemned them.

Burnt offerings (4): for sacrifice generally, see on Leviticus 1 - 7.

3:16-28 Solomon the wise judge

We are given one example to illustrate Solomon's God-given gift. Where it is a case of one woman's word against another, special insight into human nature is needed to uncover the true facts. The incident shows the king's accessibility to ordinary folk, even two prostitutes.

4 State officials: arrangements for provisioning the court

Solomon's harem alone was enormous (11:3). His court – which included not only the royal family, but ministers, civil servants and domestics – must have numbered several thousand. No wonder elaborate arrangements are necessary for their maintenance (7-28).

The king outshone his greatest contemporaries in wisdom, which he expressed, as they did, in proverbs and songs and sayings based on natural and animal life (see, for example, Psalms 72 and 127, both of whose titles ascribe them to Solomon, and Proverbs 10:1 - 22:16).

Verses 1-6: Azariah was head of inland revenue, in charge of those who collected taxes (in kind). 'King's friend', i.e. king's councillor.

Every man under his vine ... (25): a proverbial phrase indicating idyllic conditions of peace and plenty.

5 The trade-pact with Hiram; work on the temple begun

Friendship with Tyre (see on 2 Samuel 5:11) is further cemented by the agreement that Hiram should supply raw materials for the temple in return for foodstuffs.

Cedars of Lebanon (6): the finest timber available. Few of these great trees remain today, but Lebanon was once densely forested.

Cor (11): a measurement of capacity. A cor of wheat: a donkey-load. A cor of oil: 48 gallons.

6 The building of the temple

In size the temple was a chapel rather than a cathedral. It was intended as a house for God, not a building to hold vast gatherings of people. It measured about 90ft long x 30ft wide x 45ft high, divided into two sections, with part of the inner section curtained off to form the sanctuary. In front was a 15ft entrance porch, and along the sides were store-rooms.

480th year (1): the exodus probably took place something over 300 years before Solomon built the temple. The figure here (12 x 40) may indicate twelve generations rather than a precise number of years.

Neither hammer nor axe was heard (7): even at this stage the place was regarded as holy. The stone was quarried close to the site, but so deep underground that no sound would carry.

7 Other building projects; cast bronze furnishings for the temple

Verses 1-12: Solomon builds the House of the Forest of Lebanon (possibly an armoury, see 10:17; Isaiah 22:8), the Hall of Pillars, Hall of Judgement, and palaces for himself and for pharaoh's daughter (his queen; it may also have housed the rest of the harem).

Verses 13-51: Hiram, the craftsman from Tyre, supervises the casting in bronze of two decorative pillars for the entrance to the temple (15-22); a huge bowl able to hold nearly 10,000 gallons of water (23-26); ten wheeled

THE TEMPLES

Alan Millard

In the journey through the wilderness, when the nation was living in tents, Israel had a 'tent' shrine, the tabernacle. The basic idea of a portable pavilion is attested in Egypt from before 2,000 BC. Surviving examples have a framework of wooden beams and rods, plated with precious metal and made with joints and sockets for easy erection. Ancient pictures show how they were once hung with curtains.

Israelite craftsmen trained in Egypt would have known how to make such a structure, and all the materials used were obtainable in Sinai, or already in their possession (the gold and silver, for example).

The tabernacle was built to a simple plan. A courtyard contained the two-roomed holy place, the altar for burnt offerings and the basin for ritual washings. The two rooms were about 15 feet wide. The inner one, the 'holiest place', was square; the outer about 30 feet long. After the conquest of Canaan, the tabernacle was moved from one place to another until Solomon laid it up in the temple.

It was David's great ambition to build a temple, though this was only realized by his son. It was natural for a powerful king to honour his God in this way, and the existing tabernacle provided the pattern for a simple central sanctuary. The hill-top David bought is the site now covered by the 'Maram es-Sherif', the Mosque of Omar, in Jerusalem. The central rocky crust was perhaps the site of the altar of burnt-offering.

The detailed descriptions in 1 Kings 6 - 7, and 2 Chronicles 3 - 4, give a fairly complete picture of the temple. This is supplemented by evidence from archaeological discovery. The tabernacle plan was extended by an entry porch, the resulting three rooms forming a scheme similar to some Canaanite temples (e.g. at Hazor and Ras Shamra). This may have been the work of the Phoenician builders whose skill Solomon utilized. A series of storage chambers three storeys high ran round the outside of the holiest place and the middle room (the 'holy place'). The doorway was flanked by two giant free-standing pillars whose function is uncertain.

Comparison with Ezekiel's temple suggests that the whole building stood on a platform above the level of the courtyard. An officiating priest would have crossed the courtyard, passing the great bronze altar for the sacrifices (about 33 feet square, 10 feet high) and the enormous bronze basin for water supported by twelve bronze bulls, before climbing the steps to the shrine. Apparently the porch had no doors; gates may have closed the passage, but he would have faced a pair of folding doors at the entrance to the 'holy place'. These were made of cypress wood, carved with flowers, palm-trees, and cherubim, and plated all over with gold, as was all the woodwork. In this room he would see the golden incense altar, the table for showbread, and five pairs of lampstands. Additional light came from a row of windows high in the wall. Beneath his feet was a golden floor. And if he could see into the 'holiest place' the whole room would have shone a dim gold in the light admitted through the doorway. But these doors were opened rarely, perhaps only for the annual Atonement ceremony. The decorative motifs are well known from Phoenician ivory-carvings and bronze-work of the centuries around Solomon's time. And Egyptian and Babylonian kings boast of ornamenting their temples with golden pavements, doors and furnishings.

Solomon's temple was destroyed by Nebuchadnezzar in 587 BC. Much of its glory had already been torn away and paid as tribute when foreign conquerors menaced Judah. The disconsolate exiles in Babylonia were heartened by Ezekiel's vision of a new temple (Ezekiel 40 - 43), described with minute attention, and including facts about the courtyard which hardly occur in the account of Solomon's work. This sanctuary was never built, but the exiles who returned about 537 BC, after some delay, completed the rebuilding of the old one in 515 BC. The little we know about it shows it followed the old design closely, however inferior its appearance. Nothing has survived from the first temple. But a length of stone walling above the Kidron Valley, on the east of the site, may be a part of the platform on which this second temple was erected, and which Herod incorporated into his walls.

The cosmopolitan nature of Jerusalem after the exile caused trouble to Nehemiah by bringing non-Jews into the sacred precinct (Nehemiah 13:4-9). It probably resulted in dividing off an outer courtyard from an inner one which only Jews could enter. This was certainly true of Herod's temple. Two stone blocks have been found inscribed with a warning to non-Jews that they passed in at their own risk (see also Acts 21:17ff.).

Herod's temple was the Idumaean king's attempt to curry favour with his Jewish subjects. Most of it was built between 19 and 9 BC, although work continued until AD 64. The Romans destroyed it in AD 70. Parts of its massive substructure are still visible on the west (the 'Wailing Wall') and east sides, and some blocks from the parapets have been recovered in excavations.

Descriptions by the Jewish historian Josephus, and notes in rabbinic writings, supply us with information about this splendid building. The great courtyard was surrounded by a portico where schools were held, and business transacted (John 10:23; Luke 19:47; John 2:14-16). Beyond the barrier mentioned was the Women's Court where the money-boxes stood (Mark 12:41-44), then the Court of Israel, and finally the Priests' Court in which the altar and the temple proper stood. This last was a larger version of Solomon's design.

The 'holiest place', however, was empty, as in the second temple. The ark holding the terms of the covenant, upon whose covering lid (the 'mercy-seat') God had appeared, was no longer in existence. Significantly, the temple, too, disappeared with the establishment of the new covenant and the new Israel.

Stevens' reconstruction of King Solomon's temple.

stands to support more bowls (27-39), and numerous smaller items of equipment (40).

8 Dedication of the temple; Solomon's prayer

Work complete, the ark is brought from the citadel and installed in the inner sanctuary. And the whole building is filled with the glory of God's presence – the cloud that once rested on the tabernacle in the desert (Exodus 40:34-38).

Solomon's prayer, for the royal house (23-26) and for the nation (27-53), echoes the language of Moses. He asks that God will hear the prayers and forgive the sin of his people when they focus on the temple – even though no building on earth could ever contain the God of heaven.

Prayer is followed by blessing (54-61); blessing by sacrifice (62-64); sacrifice by feasting throughout the land (65; see on 2 Chronicles 7).

That my name might be there (16): God himself is present in a special sense in the temple, as he was in the tabernacle. But in contrast to the heathen temple, Israel's contained no statue to represent their God.

An oath (31): in which he solemnly swears his innocence.

9:1-9 God once again speaks to Solomon

He speaks in promise (3-5) and in warning (6-9).

As ... at Gibeon (2): when Solomon was given the gift of wisdom:3:3-14.

9:10-28 Trade and commerce; building and public works

For all his wealth, Solomon has his balance of trade problems. On this occasion (10-14) he makes 20 cities over to Hiram of Tyre as security against a loan.

Verses 15-22: the vast labour force needed for new building and defence works is raised from two sources. Native Canaanites provide permanent slave-labour. And the Israelites are pressed into short-term forced labour.

Verses 26-28: Solomon is the first of Israel's kings to create a merchant navy. His ships traded with Arabia and beyond.

Ophir (28): suggestions include South Arabia, East Africa, and even India.

10:1-13 The visit of the Queen of Sheba

Intriguing reports of Solomon's wisdom and splendour bring the queen from the Yemen to Jerusalem. Unlike the people of Christ's day (Matthew 12:42) this woman was prepared to undertake a long journey to find out for herself the truth of what she had heard.

Almug wood (11): possibly the red sandal-wood of Ceylon and India.

10:14-29 Solomon's wealth and power

Solomon's revenue through trade and taxed (including a lucrative tourist trade, 24-25) is enormous. But consumer spending more than keeps pace. The country's position made him a convenient middle-man for chariots from Egypt and horses from Turkey (Kue=Cilicia).

Talent (14): about 66lb/30kg. The purchasing-power of the bullion is not known.

Shekel (16): $\frac{1}{2}$oz/11.4gm.

Mina (17): $1\frac{1}{4}$lb/500gm.

Ships of Tarshish (21-22): large deep-sea cargo vessels.

11 Solomon's folly, and his enemies

Verses 1-13: Solomon's political marriage-alliances no doubt contribute to the country's peace and security. But foreign wives bring with them foreign gods. And Solomon in his old age turns from God to worship idols – a sin which costs his son the greater part of his kingdom and divides the nation.

Solomon's reign is not wholly trouble-free. In the south there is trouble from Hadad of Edom (14-22; a story reminiscent of Joseph's); in the north from Rezon of Damascus (23-25); and within his own nation there is Jeroboam (26-40), the man destined by God to rule over the ten break-away tribes after the king's death.

Ashtoreth, Milcom, Chemosh, Molech (5, 7): worship of these gods involved perverted and gruesome practices – child sacrifice, fertility rites, prostitution, sexual deviations.

One tribe (13): the southern state of Judah also included the much smaller tribe of Benjamin (12:21). The other ten tribes broke away to form the northern kingdom of Israel.

House of Joseph (28): the tribes of Ephraim and Manasseh.

Shilonite (29): from Shiloh, sanctuary-city of Israel in Eli's day.

Book of the acts of Solomon (41): otherwise unknown.

Verses 41-43: this formula, with slight variations, is repeated throughout Kings at the end of each reign.

12 - 14 THE KINGDOM SPLITS IN TWO

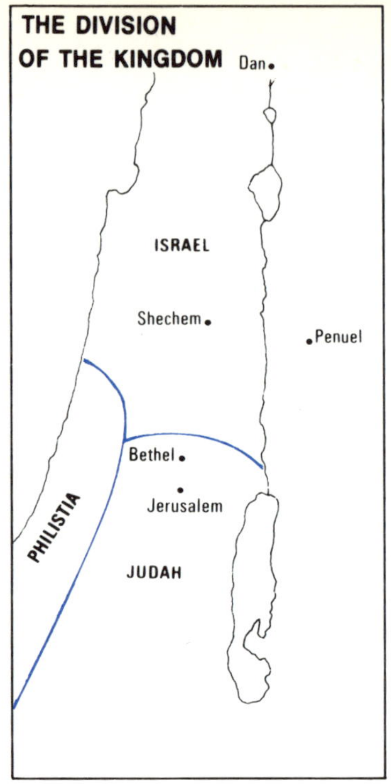

It was never easy to hold the twelve tribes together. Ephraim, in particular, envied Judah's power. A split had threatened in David's day (2 Samuel 20). The secret of national unity and strength always lay in the bond of common worship of the one God. The monarchy in itself was no substitute. Without the religious tie, king and people would go down together, as Samuel so clearly foresaw at Saul's coronation. 'If both you and the king ... will follow the Lord your God, it will be well; but if you ... rebel against the commandment of the Lord, then the hand of the Lord will be against you and your king' (1 Samuel 12:14-15). The nation's history as recounted in Kings fully bears this out. The division is a direct consequence of Solomon's idolatry. And as Israel strays further and further from the law and worship of God, things go from bad to worse. Internal strife weakens both kingdoms. The nation becomes prey to stronger neighbours, and is eventually devoured by the great powers.

12:1-24 Rehoboam succeeds Solomon; the revolt

The northern tribes find a leader and spokesman in Jeroboam. But negotiations break down in face of Rehoboam's strong-arm tactics. The rebel tribes declare independence and set up the rival kingdom of Israel, but this kingdom never enjoyed the stability of a single dynasty as did Judah.

The division is permanent, with a constant state of hot or cold war between the kingdoms. Only in the reigns of Ahab-Ahaziah-Joram in Israel and Jehoshaphat-Joram-Ahaziah in Judah was the breach temporarily healed through a marriage alliance. And that resulted in the near-extinction of the royal house of Judah at the hands of Queen Athaliah.

Scorpions (11): barbed whips used on slaves.

Adoram (18): the Adoniram of 4:6; 5:14.

A hundred and eighty thousand (21): the figure seems too high. See article 'The Large Numbers of the Old Testament'.

12:25-33 Jeroboam king in Israel; a new capital and new religious centres

Jerusalem had been the religious centre of the united kingdom. Jeroboam now creates two new sanctuaries for the northern kingdom to counter its draw and prevent the people from going to Jerusalem and coming under the influence of the king of Judah. But his action encouraged idolatry, and as time went by Israelite worship became more and more degenerate.

13 The man of God and the prophet

The man of God is wrong to accept the prophet's word when it contradicts God's own word to him. His death is a sign to Jeroboam and Israel of the severity with which God deals with disobedience. But there are none so blind as those who will not see (33).

Josiah (2): the king who initiated the most thoroughgoing reform in Judah. See 2 Kings 23.

Dried up (4): paralysed.

A lion (24): lions roamed Palestine, particularly the Jordan Valley, until the Middle Ages. Here the strange sight of the lion standing by its prey but leaving both the body and the ass untouched marks the event as having special significance. It is a 'sign' to Israel.

14:1-20 Ahijah's prophecy against Jeroboam

Ahijah had predicted Jeroboam's rise (11:29ff.). Now he announces his downfall.

He only ... shall come to the grave (13): meaning that all the rest will die violently.

Scatter them beyond the Euphrates (15): Israel was taken into exile by Assyria after the fall of Samaria (2 Kings 17).

Tirzah (17): capital of Israel in Baasha's day (15:33).

Book of the Chronicles ... (19): not the same as Chronicles in the Bible.

14:21-31 Rehoboam's reign in Judah

The southern kingdom also turns back to pagan gods. The weakened state loses the temple treasures to the invading Egyptian pharaoh. See 2 Chronicles 12:1-12.

Shishak (25): Sheshonq, Libyan founder of the Egyptian 22nd dynasty. He left a record of his campaign carved on a temple in Karnak, Egypt.

This bracelet could well have been made from gold plundered from the temple. It belonged to Nemoreth, son of the Pharaoh Shishak who defeated Rehoboam and stripped the temple of gold.

15 - 16:28 KINGS OF ISRAEL AND JUDAH

The dates for the kings of Judah in this section include a number of periods of co-regency between one king and his predecessor. Almost all the dates given can only be approximate. See articel 'Unravelling the Chronology of the Kings'.

15:1-24 Abijam and Asa of Judah

The writer of Kings defines a good king as one who promotes the worship of God; a bad king as one who strays into idolatrous practices. On this definition, Abijam's three-year reign (about 913-911) was a bad one (see 2 Chronicles 13). Asa, by contrast, was a good king. He ruled for 41 years, about 911-870. The war with Israel continued but he made an alliance with Syria. See 2 Chronicles 15-16.

The matter of Uriah the Hittite (5): see 2 Samuel 11.

Maacah (10, 13): Asa's grandmother.

Ramah (17): Only a few miles north of Jerusalem.

15:25 - 16:28 Kings of Israel

All Israel's kings were automatically bad by the writer's definition, though some were worse than others. After ruling for two years (910-909) Nadab (15:25-32) was murdered by Baasha.

15:33 – 16:7 Baasha introduces a new dynasty and rules Israel for 24 years, about 909-886.

16:8-14: his successor, Elah, rules for two years (886-885) before his assassination by Zimri.

16:15-20: Zimri introduces a short-lived new dynasty (885) and commits suicide when under siege by Omri.

16:21-28: although only briefly mentioned here, Omri was one of Israel's most powerful kings politically. He introduces a new dynasty and rules for 12 years, about 885-874, fortifying Samaria as his new capital. For 150 years from this time, Assyria refers to Israel as 'the land of Omri'.

According to the word of the Lord (15:29): see 14:6-16.

Jehu (16:1): a prophet, not the later king.

16:29 - 2 KINGS 1, KING AHAB AND THE PROPHET ELIJAH

Religious life in Israel reached an all-time low in Ahab's 22-year reign. He and his thoroughly evil wife, Jezebel of Tyre, introduced the corrupt worship of the Phoenician god Melqart (the 'Baal' of these chapters). Into this crisis situation God sent Elijah, the greatest of all the prophets (see Matthew 17:3 and 10-13).

One of the famous ivory carvings from Samaria. This winged creature is typical of decoration from the period of King Ahab.

16:29-34 Ahab of Israel 874-853

Verse 34: see Joshua 6:26.

17 Elijah predicts drought; the widow of Zarephath

Baal was worshipped as a weather-god. God therefore stages a demonstration to show that he alone has power over sun and rain. And he provides for Elijah in Baal's own country, at Zarephath near Sidon!

Verse 21: Elijah may have used the 'kiss of life'; but the cure was the result of his prayer, not just a particular method of resuscitation.

The contest with the prophets of Baal on Carmel challenged them on their own ground: Baal as a weather-god is shown here holding axe and thunderbolt; 8th century BC, from Syria.

18 The contest with the prophets of Baal on Mt Carmel

After three years, in which Jezebel has done her best to eliminate the worship of God in Israel (4), Elijah returns with a challenge. Baal should have been able to produce fire as readily as rain. But the result of the contest provides tangible evidence that God is God, and Baal is impotent. Even so, there was no deep and lasting religious reform.

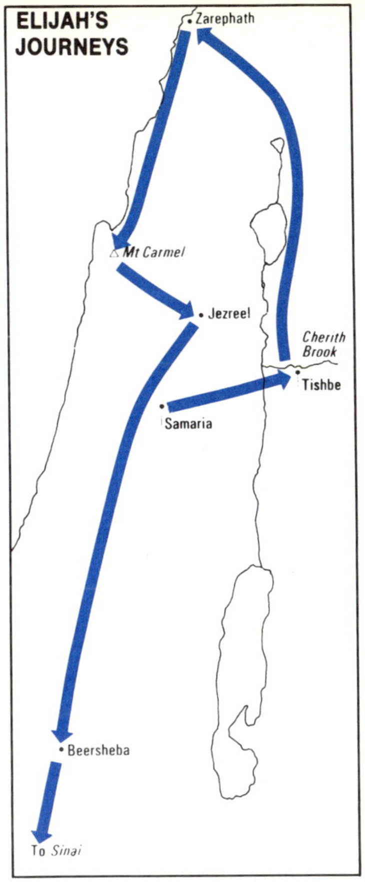

He ... ran before Ahab (46): 17 miles to the summer palace at Jezreel.

19 The escape to Sinai; Elisha's call

Elation passes. Spiritual and physical strain leave Elijah in the grip of depression, fear, disappointment. Jezebel still holds the whip hand. Elijah escapes south to the desert and Sinai (Mt Horeb). In the place where God made himself known to Moses, he speaks to Elijah, out of the stillness. Self-pity is dealt with, a sense of proportion restored, and the path ahead mapped out. Elijah had felt himself intolerably alone, his work finished. He is given a companion and successor, Elisha. God's work goes on.

Anoint Hazael ... and Jehu ... and Elisha (15-16): Elisha is 'anointed', called to become a prophet, by Elijah's symbolic action in throwing his cloak around him. But Elijah leaves the anointing of Hazael and Jehu to Elisha (2 Kings 8-9).

20 War between Israel and Syria

Benhadad of Syria and the allied kings of 32 city-states attack Samaria. The diplomatic exchange (2-9) is difficult to follow. But Benhadad has to eat his words in face of Israel's double victory. Ahab spares his life, but in doing so stores up trouble for Israel. (Israel and Syria fought as allies against Shalmaneser III of Assyria at Qarqar in 853, but later fell out – see 22:1-2.)

All ... Israel, seven thousand (15): presumably representatives of all Israel.

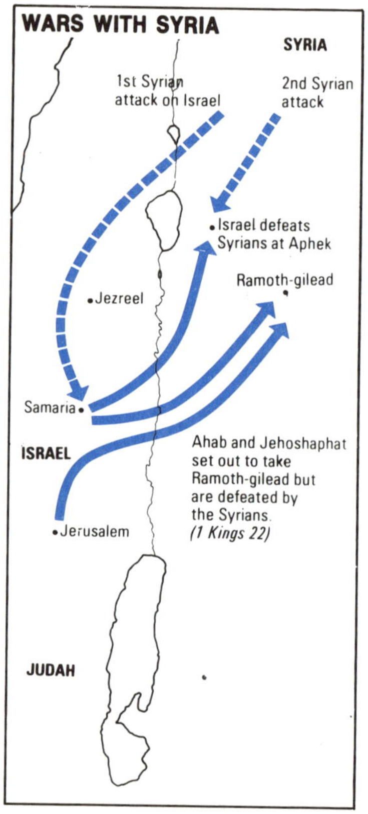

100,000 ... 27,000 (29-30): the figures seem exaggeratedly high. See article 'The Large Numbers of the Old Testament'.

My father ... your father (34): meaning ancestor, not actual father.

21 Ahab takes Naboth's vineyard; Elijah pronounces judgement

Seizure or compulsory purchase of land was illegal in Israel. A man's heritage had to be handed on to the next generation. But other people's rights do not bother Jezebel. While her husband sulks like a spoilt child, she quietly arranges for Naboth's liquidation. She has only to contrive a blasphemy charge – backed of course by the statutory number of witnesses – and the 'criminal's' lands are forfeit. Elijah, the old prophet of doom, is the only fly in the ointment. But Elijah speaks true (see 22:37; 2 Kings 9:30-37).

22:1-40 The alliance with Judah; Micaiah's prophecy; Ahab's death

See also 2 Chronicles 18. Jehoshaphat's son Jehoram has married Ahab's daughter Athaliah. Israel and Judah are, temporarily, allies against Syria. It is Jehoshaphat's request which brings Micaiah to the king with his fateful prophecy. The warning is ignored, and Ahab meets his death in battle at Ramoth-gilead, east of the Jordan. (For true and false prophets, see on 2 Chronicles 18.)

22:41-50 Jehoshaphat of Judah 873-848

See 2 Chronicles 17-20. Jehoshaphat was a 'good' king. He reigned 25 years.

Verse 48: see on chapters 9 and 10. The strong north winds may have blown the fleet on to the rocks.

22:51 - 2 Kings 1, Ahaziah of Israel 853-852

Ahaziah reigned two years during which time Moab seized independence. Ahaziah consults the Philistine god after a fall and Elijah pronounces God's judgement on his idolatry. It takes three military posses to bring Elijah to the king. But nothing can alter the sentence.

Baalzebub (3): 'Lord of the flies', a derogatory pun on the god's real name, Baalzebul.

2 - 8:15 STORIES OF ELISHA

2 Elijah's dramatic exit

Elijah seems to want to face this last experience alone. But Elisha stays with him right through the journey. The final scene – the whirlwind which catches up the prophet, and Elisha's vision of a fiery chariot and horses – is played out east of the Jordan, close to the place where Moses died. It is a remarkable end to a remarkable life. Elijah's reappearance at the transfiguration of Jesus (Matthew 17) underlines the unique position of this man amongst all the prophets of God. Elisha, left alone, takes up his task straight away.

Sons of the prophets (3): groups possessing ecstatic gifts; not always men of high spiritual calibre.

UNRAVELLING THE CHRONOLOGY OF THE KINGS

Arthur Cundall

At first glance there seems to be quite enough data on the kings of Israel and Judah to construct an accurate time-chart.

The reign of each king is clearly given (except for Saul: 1 Samuel 13:1 is uncertain); and during the period after the split between Israel and Judah, the accession of each king is related to the reign of the king in the other kingdom.

There are also 'check-points', where one event simultaneously affected both kingdoms, such as Jehu's slaying of Joram of Israel and Ahaziah of Judah on the same day (2 Kings 9:21-28). The historian has carefully integrated the chronologies of the two kingdoms. He keeps both histories parallel by dealing with the whole reign of one king from his accession until his death, and then returning to deal with the kings of the other kingdom whose reigns *began* during this period. The only exception is in 2 Kings 8-9 where Jehu's murder of Joram and Ahaziah made it necessary for the historian to mention Jehoram and Ahaziah of Judah (2 Kings 8:16-29), who would not normally have been dealt with until after the death of Joram of Israel.

Problems

However, serious problems arise on closer inspection. For instance, in Judah, the total from Rehoboam to Ahaziah's death is 95 years, whereas the identical period of Israel, from Jeroboam to Joram's death, totals 98 years.

A greater discrepancy appears in the period from Jehu's coup to the fall of Samaria. There the combined total for Judah's kings is 165 years and that for Israel is only 144 years. A further minor problem is that although we are told Queen Athaliah the usurper reigned for six years (2 Kings 11:3), she was not included in the normal chronological scheme.

We have another headache in the apparently conflicting dates for the accession of Jehoram of Israel (2 Kings 1:17 and 3:1). It is reasonably certain that Solomon's death cannot have been earlier than 930 BC, which makes the period between this event and the fall of Jerusalem in 587 BC about 343 years. But the lowest total we can set to the biblical figures supplied for this period is about 372 years.

Clues

Three factors, however, greatly increase our understanding of the apparent problems of the chronology of the period and go a long way towards resolving them completely.

Two different methods of reckoning the reigns of the kings were used in the ancient Near East. One was the 'non-accession-year' method, the other the 'accession-year' method.

In the non-accession-year (or ante-dating) system the death of a king meant that a year was counted twice, since the portion of the year falling to the king who died was counted as a full year to him, whilst the remainder of the year was counted as a full year to his successor. To reduce this system to an accurate chronological reckoning, one year must be deducted for each king who reigned.

The accession-year (or post-dating) system did not count any *portion* of a year in the total years of a king's reign. The portion of the year falling to a king *before* his first, full calendar-year, was regarded as his accession year. This system allowed for an accurate chronological reckoning.

It is clear that, in the early period of the divided monarchy Israel used the first method and Judah the second. The discrepancy in totals between the two kingdoms corresponds to the greater number of Israelite kings in this period. A possible further complication is evidence suggesting that the year in Judah (in the earlier part of the period at any rate) began in the month of Tishri (September/October), whilst the year in Israel began in the month Nisan (March/April).

Some reigns overlap because of the practice of co-regencies. The precedent for this is found in the case of David and Solomon, which effectively prevented Adonijah seizing power (1 Kings 1). Another clear instance is the case of Jotham, who acted as co-regent when his father Uzziah was smitten with leprosy (2 Chronicles 26:21). No doubt this practice, which appears to have been confined to Judah, lent stability to David's dynasty.

Most scholars accept co-regencies between Asa and Jehoshaphat, Jehoshaphat and Jehoram, Amaziah and Uzziah, Jotham and Ahaz, Ahaz and Hezekiah, and Hezekiah and Manasseh. In certain cases the younger man (for example, Hezekiah) outshone his father (Ahaz) and this led to events being dated by reference to the co-regent rather than to the actual king (e.g. 2 Kings 18:9-10).

An awareness of this custom means a reduction of the over-all total of the reigns of Judean kings, and also helps us to understand the significance of the biblical figures. For example, Manasseh of Judah reigned from 687 to 642 BC. 2 Kings 21:1 says he reigned for 55 years, which leads us to assume a co-regency from 697 to 687, made the more plausible by Hezekiah's severe illness (2 Kings 20:1).

Some reigns may have taken place at the same time as each other. This is probably what happened in the northern kingdom of Israel during the last turbulent decades after the death of Jeroboam II. The combined reigns of the six kings of this period is 41 years 7 months, whereas historically the period cannot have been more than 31 years; indeed, most scholars hold that it was only about 24 years. The probability is that, in a period of near-anarchy, there were occasions when rival kings were 'ruling' over different parts of the kingdom at the same time.

External checks

By a careful application of these factors, the chronologies of Judah and Israel can be integrated. But the process of relating the resultant chronology to the events of the surrounding world, to obtain an absolute rather than a relative chronology, has been made possible largely by archaeological discovery. The most significant finds are as follows:

The Assyrian Limmu or Eponym lists. In Assyria an official holding annual office gave his name to that particular year. Remarkably complete lists of these officials have survived covering the period 892-648 BC, and significant events during their period of office were noted down. An eclipse of the sun is mentioned in the month Simanu when Bur-Sagale was *Limmu,* which astronomers have fixed as occurring on 15 June 763 BC. This provides a reliable basis for determining all other dates in the *Limmu* lists. Since biblical and Assyrian histories converge at various points, biblical events can also be dated accurately.

The Khorsabad king list. This, and duplicate copies, gives a complete list of Assyrian kings until 745 BC, often including the length of their reigns. This list agrees with the *Limmu* list.

The Canon of Ptolemy. Although this work dates from the 2nd century AD, its accuracy has been demonstrated beyond any reasonable doubt. It preserves the names and lengths of reign of the Babylonian kings from the accession of Nabonassar in 747 BC.

The Babylonian Chronicle. These tablets, some only recently published, deal with Babylonian history during the period from Hezekiah to the fall of Jerusalem. They are of special interest to biblical scholars for the period when Judah was subject to Babylon, i.e. after 605 BC. Many facts which before were not clear have now been resolved. For instance, it was not known what encouraged the Judean king, Jehoiakim, to rebel against the Babylonians in 601/600 BC, or why the revolt was not put down until 598/597 BC. The Babylonian Chronicle tells us that in November/December 601 BC there was a fierce encounter between Babylonia and Egypt on the borders of Egypt. Although the battle was indecisive, Babylonian losses were great and meant a withdrawal from the area and a regrouping of the army. It was this apparent weakness which led Jehoiakim to rebel. The Chronicle gives the only exact date for an event in Old Testament history, the capture of Jerusalem on 15-16 March 597 BC.

One minor problem remains. It is not certain whether the Hebrew civil year uniformly followed the Babylonian pattern. This makes for an uncertainty of one year in dates during the reign of Zedekiah, the last king of Judah. The fall of Jerusalem, for example, is given as either 587 or 586 BC. The two modes of reckoning appear in Jeremiah 52:12 and 29, where, on first sight, the prisoners were taken from Jerusalem a year before it was captured!

A bronze cast of the original Seal of Shema, which is inscribed: '(belonging) to Shema, Servant of Jeroboam'.

Numerous contemporary inscriptions also relate to particular events: such as the battle of Qarqar in 853 BC, fought between Assyria and a coalition of small states including Israel under King Ahab; or Jehu's payment of tribute to the Assyrian king, Shalmaneser III in 841 BC; or the fall of Samaria to the Assyrians in 722/721 BC. These records supply reliable pegs on which to hang the biblical information.

By carefully applying the principles underlying the biblical chronologies, and correlating them with the fixed chronology made possible by contacts between Judah and Israel and contemporary world-powers, we can establish an absolute chronology, including all the biblical data, which is accurate to within a year for the greater part of the period of the kings. The reign of Saul remains an exception. The 40 years given in Acts 13:21 is probably a round figure, and seems to be too high. Since '2' is the only figure remaining in the Hebrew text, most scholars accept that a tens-unit has dropped out and suggest a reign of 12, 22 or 32 years. Twenty-two is probably the most acceptable since it fits in best with the other chronological data, such as the period of the Judges.

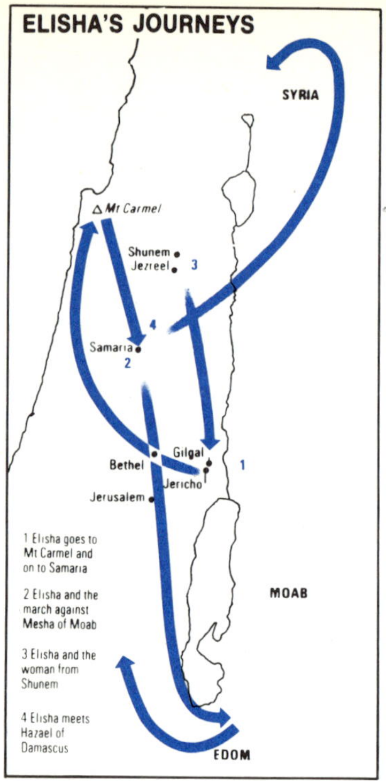

A double share (9): i.e. the portion which fell to the heir, the eldest son, who inherited twice as much as anyone else. So Elisha asks, not for twice Elijah's spiritual power, but for the share which would mark him out as the prophet's spiritual heir.
Chariots of Israel ... (12): meaning that Elijah was of more value to the nation than its armed forces.
Some small boys (23): young men – local louts, yelling abuse at the prophet and his God, telling him to 'Go up' like Elijah.

3 Jehoram of Israel, 852-841, and the Moabites

Jehoram reigned 12 years. A punitive expedition against Moab by the allied forces of Israel, Judah and Edom is made hazardous by drought. Elisha, his faculties stimulated by music (a common prophetic custom), promises an end to the drought, and victory.
Who poured water (11): i.e. who served Elijah.
There came great wrath (27): the sacrifice of the king's son so heartened the Moabites, or so terrified the Israelites, that the advance was halted.

4 Four of Elisha's miracles

Elisha's miracles, like the Lord's, show God's care for ordinary people and their needs. Verses 1-7: the widow whose children were to become slaves to discharge her debts; 8-37 the childless woman of Shunem who gave Elisha generous hospitality; 38-41 and 42-44 the feeding of the hungry. These are not necessarily recounted in chronological order.
Oh, my head ... (19): the child had sun-stroke.
Neither new moon nor sabbath (23): special times of religious observance when it would be natural to visit a holy man. The woman did not tell her husband the child was dead.
Wild gourds (39): in the famine one man gathered colocynths, a powerful laxative, bitter and poisonous in large quantities.
Bread of the firstfruits (42): the offering normally made to the priests at the beginning of the harvest.

5 The healing of Naaman the leper

God's concern is not limited to Israel (see Luke 4:27; Syria was often at war with Israel, and Naaman was the army commander). A young Israelite slave-girl, captured in a border raid, tells her Syrian master of Elisha's power. A visit is arranged through diplomatic channels. The prophet's instructions are not what Naaman expected. But his staff persuade him to try, and he is healed. Deeply impressed by the cure and Elisha's refusal of payment, the army chief of Syria becomes a follower of the God of Israel. Gehazi's greed might have undone it all, and could not go unpunished.
Talents, shekels (5): there were no coins as yet; these were weights: see on 1 Kings 10.
Two mules' burden of earth (17): he took soil from the land of Israel's God so that he could worship him in his own land, not realizing his character as God of the whole world.

6:1-23 Elisha and the Syrian army

Verses 1-7: the floating axe-head. The thick woods of the Jordan Valley provide a ready source of timber for the new community building needed by the prophets. Elisha's miracle was simply an act of disinterested kindness.

Verses 8-23: God's people are under his protection, and this is a very real thing. Elisha seemed at the mercy of the Syrian army. In fact he has them in the palm of his hand – and shows *them* mercy.
Dothan (13): ten miles north of Samaria.

6:24 - 7:20 The siege of Samaria

The peace secured by Elisha (23) did not last for ever. Samaria is besieged by the Syrians and reduced to starvation and cannibalism. The king blames Elisha for telling him to hold out and promising deliverance (33). The lepers, who depended on gifts of food, are worse off than most. Their desperate hunger makes them the first to discover the truth of Elisha's prediction. The Syrian army fled at the approach, so they thought, of a relief force.
6:25: the ass was an 'unclean' animal, forbidden food; dove's dung, some kind of weed. In the famine, both fetched astronomical prices.

8:1-15 Elisha and Hazael of Damascus

Verses 1-6 belong in time after 4:8-37 and before Gehazi's leprosy, 5:25-27.

Verses 7-15: Elisha fulfils God's commission to Elijah (1 Kings 19:15). Hazael, like Macbeth, resorts to murder to turn prediction into fact and seize the throne.

8:16 - 17:41 KINGS OF ISRAEL AND JUDAH TO THE FALL OF SAMARIA

The writer returns to the history of the kings which has been interrupted by the stories of Elisha.

8:16-24 Jehoram of Judah 853-841

Jehoram was a 'bad' king, influenced by his wife Athaliah, daughter of Ahab and Jezebel. He reigned eight years plus a co-regency, during which time successful revolts by Edom (to the south-east) and Libnah (on the Philistine border, south-west) crippled Judah. See 2 Chronicles 21.

8:25-29 Ahaziah of Judah 841

Ahaziah was another king who turned from God and went his own way. He reigned only one year. See 2 Chronicles 22.

9 Jehu anointed king of Israel (841-814); death of King Joram and Jezebel, the queen mother

Elisha carries out the last of Elijah's commissions (1 Kings 19:16) while the armies of Israel and Judah are defending Ramoth-gilead against Syria. With the king conveniently recovering from his wounds at Jezreel, 35 miles away, the time is ripe for Jehu's coup.
This mad fellow (11): the man's ecstatic state enables the army officers to recognize him as a prophet.
The property of Naboth (21): the vineyard seized by Ahab, 1 Kings 21.
Verse 26: see 1 Kings 21:19.
She painted her eyes (30): women's make-up, even in those days, was sophisticated: black kohl to outline the eyes; blue eye-shadow from lapis lazuli; crushed cochineal to serve as lipstick; and scarlet henna to paint finger- and toe-nails. There were also powders, and an array of perfumes and ointments.
You Zimri ... (31): King Elah's assassin, 1 Kings 16:8-10.
The word of the Lord ... by ... Elijah (36): 1 Kings 21:23.

10 Jehu's purge

Jehu's reign opens with a blood-bath in which all Ahab's family (1-11), many of the royal house of Judah (12-14), and the prophets, priests and worshippers of Baal (18-27) lose their lives. Objects connected with Baal-worship are destroyed. But Jeroboam's shrines at Bethel and Dan are left and God's law neglected. Jehu reigned 28 years, starting a new dynasty. During his reign, territory east of Jordan was lost to Syria.

11:1-20 Queen Athaliah of Judah 841-835

Athaliah reigned six years. See 2 Chronicles 22:10 - 23:21. These are some of the darkest days in the nation's history. The royal line of David is all but wiped out; only the

THE BLACK OBELISK

Shalmaneser III erected an obelisk in honour of his own victories. It includes a panel which reads:

The tribute of Jehu, son of Omri. Silver, gold, a golden bowl, a golden vase, golden cups, golden buckets, tin, a staff for the royal hand (?), puruhati-fruits.

The scene from the Black Obelisk which specifically mentioned Jehu. The king is shown bowing before Shalmaneser.

baby Joash survives. The priest Jehoiada (husband of princess Jehosheba, who rescued Joash) leads the well-planned and virtually bloodless coup which puts Joash on the throne. The constitutional monarchy is restored, and loyalty to God reaffirmed in the swearing of a new covenant-pact.

11:21 - 12:21 Joash of Judah 835-796; the temple repaired

Joash was one of Judah's best kings, ruling for 40 years. See 2 Chronicles 24. Under Jehoiada's guidance Joash rules well. But for some years money intended for temple repairs gets no further than the priests. A new method of collection is devised and the work put in hand. Funds come from tax (2 Chronicles 24:6; Exodus 30:11-16) and freewill offerings. Joash's later years see a decline in political (17ff.), moral and religious spheres (2 Chronicles 24:17ff.). Syria makes inroads into Judah and threatens Jerusalem. The king dies at the hands of his servants.

13:1-9 Jehoahaz of Israel 814-798

Jehoahaz reigned 17 years during which time Israel fell under Syrian domination.

A saviour (5): various suggestions have been made: Adad-nirari of Assyria, who took tribute from Damascus and from Jehoash of Israel; Jeroboam II; Elisha.

Verse 7: contrast Ahab's 2,000 chariots.

13:10-25 Jehoash of Israel 798-782

Jehoash reigned 16 years. There was war with Judah. Elisha's last prediction of victory over Syria is realized. The prophet dies.

Chariots of Israel (14): see on 2:12.

14:1-22 Amaziah of Judah 796-767

Amaziah was a 'good' king who reigned 29 years. See 2 Chronicles 25. Victory over Edom goes to his head. The disastrous challenge to Jehoash brings the forces of Israel right into Jerusalem, looting the temple and other treasures. The people make Azariah co-regent. A further conspiracy against Amaziah ends in his death at Lachish.

In the book of the law (6): Deuteronomy 24:16.

Valley of Salt (7): the area south of the Dead Sea.

A thistle on Lebanon (9): Joash replies in sneering parable to Amaziah's fool-hardy challenge to battle.

Elath (22): Ezion-geber on the Gulf of Aqabah, naval base of Solomon's Red Sea fleet. The port fell into the hands of the Edomites but was recovered by Amaziah's victory.

14:23-29 Jeroboam II of Israel 793-753

Jeroboam II ruled for 41 years, including a time as co-regent. He was politically strong, dominating the land from north of Lebanon (Hamath) to the Dead Sea (Sea of Arabah). He defeated a weakened Syria. Jeroboam's reign is Israel's Indian summer. After his death the nation falls apart. Amos (2:6ff.) and Hosea reveal the corruption within Israel: extremes of wealth and poverty: the grinding down of the poor and the weak.

How he ... are they not written (28): the meaning of the text is not clear.

15:1-7 Azariah (Uzziah) of Judah 791-740

Azariah, a 'good' king, reigned 52 years, including a time as co-regent. See 2 Chronicles 26. Azariah was a strong king who defeated the Philistines and Arabs and reduced Ammon to a vassal state. But pride brought him to an unpleasant end (5; 2 Chronicles 26:16ff.).

15:8-31 The succession in Israel 753-732

Verses 8-12: Zechariah son of Jeroboam rules six months and is assassinated by Shallum, 753-752.

Verses 13-16: Shallum rules only one month before his assassination by Menahem.

Verses 17-22: Menahem introduces another new dynasty, rules 10 years (752-742) and becomes vassal to the powerful Tiglath-pileser III (Pul) of Assyria.

Verses 23-26: Pekahiah son of Menahem rules two years and is overthrown by an army coup led by Pekah, 740.

Verses 27-31: Pekah introduces a new dynasty and rules 20 years, dating his reign from Menahem's accession, 752-732. His anti-Assyrian policy leads to mass deportation of the people by Tiglath-pileser. He is assassinated by Hoshea.

15:32-38 Jotham of Judah 750-732

Jotham was a godly king. During his 16-year reign (and co-regency) he encountered opposition from Syria and Israel.

16 Ahaz of Judah 735-716

Ahaz was one of Judah's worst kings. See 2 Chronicles 28; Isaiah 7. During his 16-year reign and co-regency Judah was under attack from all quarters: Syria and Israel to the

King Tiglath-pileser III, depicted on the palace walls at Nimrud.

north; Edom and Philistia to the south. The temple was stripped of silver and gold to pay the heavy tribute demanded by Assyria in return for help. Some of Isaiah's prophecies date from this time.

17 Hoshea, last king of Israel, 732-723; Samaria falls to Assyria

Hoshea reigned nine years as Assyria's vassal. An attempt to win Egyptian support proved fatal. Samaria fell after a three-year siege, and the whole remaining population was deported. Israel's fate is seen as the direct consequence of long-standing idolatry, of pursuing heathen practices, disobeying the law, and ignoring the prophets (7-18).

Assyria repopulated the land with other conquered peoples, each with its own religion. But troubles are attributed to their failure to placate the local god, and an Israelite priest is sent back as a missionary. From this strange hotch-potch of religions a purer form of worship emerged amongst their descendants, the Samaritans.

Verse 6: the people were deported to north and east Mesopotamia (Halah, Gozan, Media): i.e. north-east Syria/Turkey and Iran.

18 - 25 KINGS OF JUDAH TO THE FALL OF JERUSALEM

18:1-12 Hezekiah's reign begins

Hezekiah was one of Judah's finest kings, and ruled for 29 years plus a co-regency, 729-687. See 2 Chronicles 29-32.

The bronze serpent (4): see Numbers 21:4-9. This goes to show how easily an object which is innocent in itself can be misused once it has served its purpose.

18:13-37 Sennacherib attacks Jerusalem

Eight years after the fall of Samaria, the Assyrians turn their attention to rebel Judah. Lachish, in the lowlands 30 miles south-west of Jerusalem, is besieged, and messengers sent to Hezekiah. The three Assyrians (the 'Tartan', commander-in-chief of the army; 'Rabsaris', high military official; 'Rabshakeh', probably high civil dignitary) are masters of psychological warfare. They refuse private talks with Hezekiah's cabinet, and insist on a public harangue. And they play on the people's fears by speaking Hebrew – not the diplomatic language, Aramaic – so that everyone understands. But their boast that God cannot save Judah from Assyria seals their fate.

An Assyrian soldier, from the palace of Sargon II. He wears a curled beard, and carries a quiver and bow, sword and heavy club.

19 Hezekiah consults Isaiah; death in the Assyrian camp

See Isaiah 36-39; 2 Chronicles 32:9-23. Crisis brings out the best in the king. God answers his prayer and vindicates his trust. Isaiah's prophecy is fulfilled. Jerusalem is saved.

Isaiah (2): one of the great prophets

SENNACHERIB'S PRISM
Sennacherib's own views about the siege of Jerusalem may be read on this hexagonal clay prism, inscribed with the details of his eight campaigns. It is also known as the 'Taylor Prism', and stands 15in/375mm high.

But as for Hezekiah, the Jew, who did not bow in submission to my yoke, forty-six of his strong walled towns and innumerable smaller villages in their neighbourhood I besieged and conquered by stamping down earth-ramps and then by bringing up battering rams, by the assault of foot-soldiers, by breaches, tunnelling and sapper operations. I made to come out from them 200,150 people, young and old, male and female, innumerable horses, mules, donkeys, camels, large and small cattle, and counted them as the spoils of war. He himself I shut up like a caged bird within Jerusalem, his royal city. I put watch-posts strictly around it and turned back to his disaster any who went out of its city gate. His towns which I had despoiled I cut off from his land, giving them to Mitinti, king of Ashdod, Padi, king of Ekron, and Sillibel, king of Gaza, and so reduced his land. Moreover, I fixed upon him an increase in the amount to be given as katre-presents for my lordship, in addition to the former tribute, to be given annually. As for Hezekiah, the awful splendour of my lordship overwhelmed him, and the irregular and regular troops which he had brought in to strengthen Jerusalem, his royal city, and had obtained for his protection, together with 30 talents of gold, 300 talents of silver, precious stones, antimony, large blocks of red stone, ivory (inlaid) couches, ivory arm-chairs, elephant hide, elephant tusks, ebony-wood, box-wood, all kinds of valuable treasures, as well as his daughters, concubines, male and female musicians he sent me later to Nineveh, my lordly city. He sent a personal messenger to deliver the tribute and make a slavish obeisance.

of Judah. According to Isaiah 1:1 he prophesied during the reigns of Uzziah, Jotham, Ahaz and Hezekiah. His home was in Jerusalem. See further under the book of Isaiah.
Libnah (8): ten miles north of Lachish.
Tirhakah (9): Pharaoh Taharqa, of Ethiopian descent; in charge of the army, but not yet on the throne.
Gozan (12): in north-east Syria; *Eden:* the Aramaean city-state of Bit-Adini on the Euphrates.
My hook (28): God will lead them meekly captive as a man leads a bull or a horse. The Assyrians drove rings through the noses of captive kings.
The angel of the Lord went forth (35): it is not clear what happened, possibly an outbreak of bubonic plague. See 2 Chronicles 32:21; Isaiah 37:36.

20 Hezekiah's illness; the embassy from Babylon

Verses 1-11: to men of the Old Testament hope of life after death was vague. The prospect of death fills Hezekiah with distress (see also his poem, recorded in Isaiah 38:9-20).

Verses 12-21: Babylon at this time was a small state south of Assyria, looking for allies. Isaiah predicts its future power, and the fate of Judah.
A cake of figs (7): a fig poultice was routine treatment for ulcers and boils.
Verse 11: 'made the shadow go back ten steps on the steps of Ahaz' (Jerusalem Bible; similarly New English Bible) – a staircase used as a form of sundial.

21:1-18 Manasseh 696-642

Manasseh was Judah's Ahab. He reigned 55 years, part of the time as co-regent, and brought Judah to the point of no return; a degradation worse than that of the Canaanite nations the Israelites had destroyed. The prophets declare God's inevitable judgement. Jerusalem will share the fate of Samaria. See also 2 Chronicles 33, which records a complete change of heart before the end of Manasseh's life (33:10-13).

21:19-26 Amon 642-640

Amon was another evil king. After ruling two years he was assassinated by his own house servants. See 2 Chronicles 33:21-25.

22 Josiah 640-609; Hilkiah discovers the book of the law

Josiah reigned 31 years. He was the best of Judah's kings, carrying out thorough-going religious reform. See 2 Chronicles 34-35. A book of the law (probably a copy of Deuteronomy) is found in the course of repairing the temple. Reading it shows just how far short of the standards Judah has fallen – and the penalty.

23:1-30 Josiah's reformation

Public reading of God's law is followed by renewal of the covenant-pact with God (1-3). Then comes a purge of public places, ridding the land of objects associated with pagan worship (4-14). The clean-up extends beyond Judah to former Israelite territory (15-20). The neglected Feast of Passover is celebrated once more (21-23; see 2 Chronicles 35), and private malpractices dealt with (24-25). God's judgement is delayed but not reversed: the nation's heart is not changed by an official reformation. Josiah dies in futile conflict with Pharaoh Necho, who was marching to join forces with Assyria, after the Assyrian capital (Nineveh) had fallen to the Babylonians.

23:31-35 Jehoahaz 609

Jehoahaz was on the throne for an evil reign of three months. Then he was deported to Egypt by Necho. See 2 Chronicles 36:1-4.

23:36 - 24:7 Jehoiakim 609-597

Josiah's son Eliakim, renamed Jehoiakim as a sign of his subjection, was put on the throne by Pharaoh Necho. He ruled for 11 years. At first subject to Egypt, Jehoiakim became Babylon's subject after Egypt was defeated at Carchemish in 605. Judah remained a vassal of Nebuchadnezzar for three years, then defected to Egypt again. This brought more attacks from the Babylonians, and repeated warnings from the prophet Jeremiah. See also 2 Chronicles 36:5-8.

24:8-17 Jehoiachin 597

Jehoiakim's son, Jehoiachin, was removed from the throne after three months by Nebuchadnezzar. He was taken to Babylon with the treasures of Jerusalem and all the leading men of Judah.

24:18 - 25:30 Zedekiah 597-587; the destruction of Jerusalem

See also 2 Chronicles 36:11-21; Jeremiah 37-39. The new puppet king also rebels. Jerusalem suffers a terrible 18-month siege. Zedekiah attempts to escape south but is caught and taken to Babylon. The city falls to the Babylonian army, is looted and utterly destroyed. All but the poorest people, left under the governor, Gedaliah, are taken into exile. But Gedaliah is murdered and the people escape to Egypt to avoid the inevitable wrath of Babylon. 25:27-30 conveys a glimmer of hope. Under a new king in Babylon 35 years later, Jehoiachin, the deposed king of Judah, is released from prison and kindly treated.

BABYLONIAN ACCOUNT OF THE FALL OF JERUSALEM
The capture of Jerusalem is described on a Babylonian tablet as follows:

In the seventh year, in the month of Kislev, the Babylonian king mustered his troops, and, having marched to the land of Hatti, besieged the city of Judah, and on the second day of the month of Adar took the city and captured the king. He appointed therein a king of his own choice, received its heavy tribute and sent (them) to Babylon.

KINGS OF ISRAEL AND JUDAH

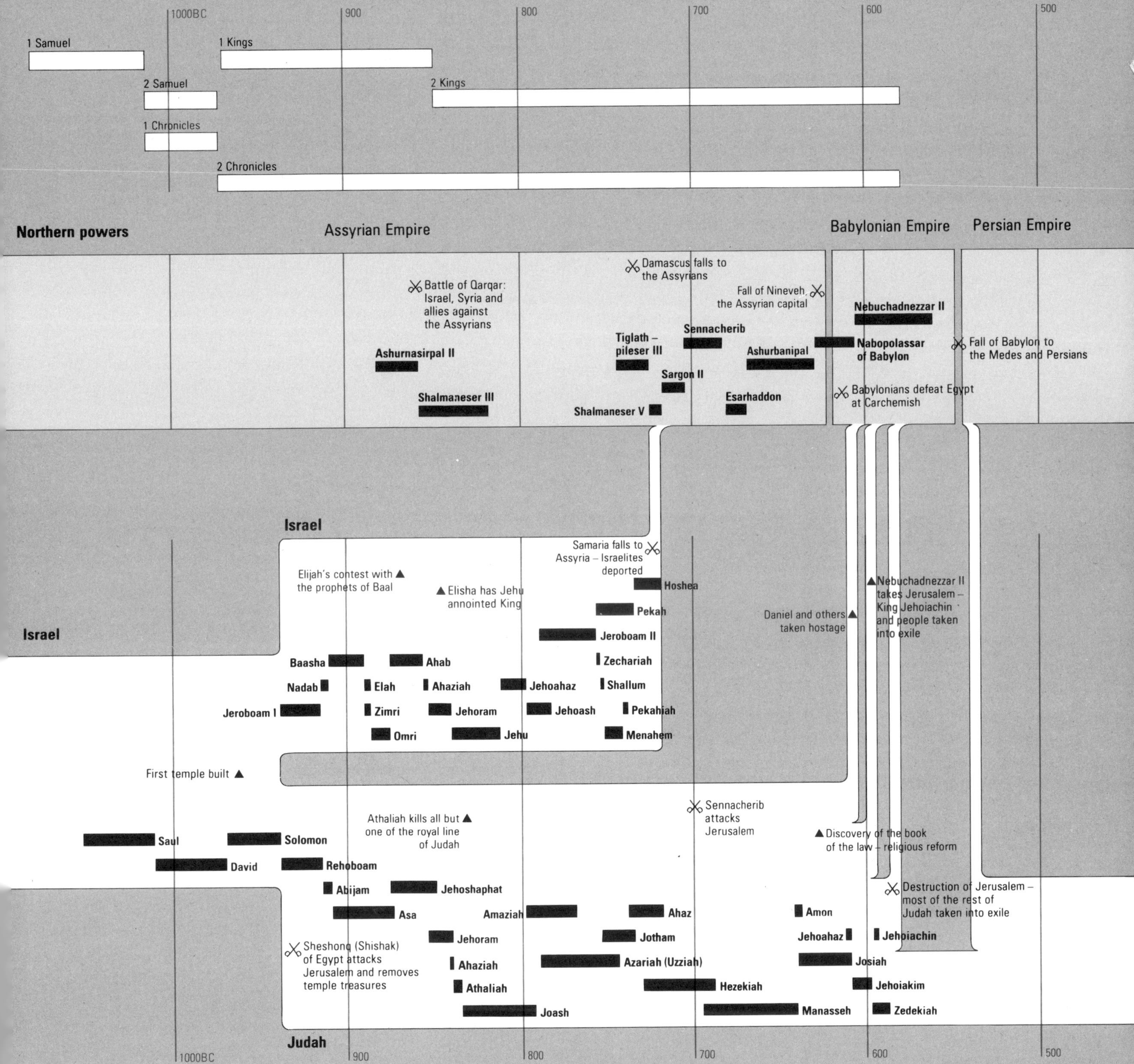

Old Testament 2. 8 and 9

1 AND 2 CHRONICLES

On the face of it, Chronicles seems to repeat in duller and more moralistic fashion what we already have in 2 Samuel and Kings. In fact, the Chronicler was writing for those who knew the earlier books. He had no need to repeat, except in so far as it suited him. He was free to follow particular themes within a roughly chronological historical framework. And he was specially interested in two themes – true worship and true kingship in Israel – so he selected his historical material accordingly. (After the division of the kingdom, for example, he follows the fortunes of the kings of David's line only, ignoring the northern kingdom. And even in the introduction – the family-trees of chapters 1-9 – he concentrates on the southern tribes, Judah and Benjamin, and the tribe of Levi, which gave Israel her priests and ministers.) This is not to say, as some have done, that the Chronicler twists the facts of history to suit himself. A book does not have to be a history text-book to be historically reliable.

The Chronicler chose these particular themes with his original readers in mind – the men who had returned from exile to rebuild Jerusalem under Ezra and Nehemiah. (He may have written about 400 BC; and his books form part of the longer series, Chronicles-Ezra-Nehemiah.) The new community needed to be linked with the past. They needed to know the right lines on which to re-establish patterns of worship. And, if history was not to repeat itself, they needed most of all to be reminded of the greatest lesson their history had to teach: that prosperity and well-being depend absolutely on faithfulness to God. Idolatry and neglect of God's law always has and always will result in judgement and disaster.

To assert the essential historical reliability of Chronicles is not to deny that there are problems. The Chronicler does not mind 'modernizing' – describing events in terms the people of his own day would understand. His high statistics are also a difficulty to modern (though not ancient) man. See article 'The Large Numbers of the Old Testament'. And names are often spelt differently in Chronicles from the earlier books, though changes made by those who copied the text must account for some at least of these. (It does no harm to remind ourselves of the wide variety in English spelling before Johnson compiled his dictionary – witness the various ways of spelling 'Shakespeare'.)

1 - 9 SKELETON FAMILY-TREE OF ISRAEL: ADAM TO THE EXILE AND AFTER

The lists are not intended to be complete. In line with his purpose the Chronicler gives most attention to the family of David, and the tribes of Judah, Benjamin and Levi (see introduction above). The family-trees provide a lead-in to the history which begins at chapter 10 and a link with those for whom the book was first written.

1:1 - 2:2 Adam to Israel and his family

1:1-27: Adam to Abram; Noah's descendants through Japheth, Ham and Shem. The list is drawn from Genesis, though the spelling of many names is slightly different here.

1:28-54: Abraham, Isaac, Israel (Jacob); descendants of Ishmael and Esau. Attention narrows down to the father of the nation.

2:1-2: the twelve sons of Israel.

2:3 - 3:24 The royal line

2:3-55: the descendants of Judah: David's ancestors.

3:1-16: David's dynasty to the exile.

3:17-24: the royal line from the exile on.

Achar (2:7): Achan. See Joshua 7.
Chelubai (2:9): Caleb. Not necessarily Joshua's contemporary, who was not an Israelite, although he was adopted into the tribe of Judah.
Father of Kiriath-jearim (2:50): i.e. founder of the town.
Bathshua (3:5): Bathsheba.
Elishama (3:6): Elishua.
Johanan (3:15): not a king of Judah.
Zerubbabel (3:19): a leader in the return from exile. See Ezra.

4 - 7 The tribes of Israel

4:1-23 Judah; 4:24-43 Simeon; 5:1-10 Reuben; 5:11-22 Gad; 5:23-26 the half-tribe of Manasseh.

6 Levi. Verses 2-15: the line of the high priests; 16-30 the families of Gershom, Kohath and Merari; 31-48 families of the singers; 49-53 descendants of Aaron; 54-81 list of Levitical cities.

7:1-5 Issachar; 7:6-12 Benjamin (this does not tie in with chapter 8; it has been suggested that 6-11 is Zebulun and 12 is the end of an otherwise lost list of Dan); 7:13 Naphtali; 7:14-19 Manasseh; 7:20-29 Ephraim; 7:30-40 Asher.

Reuben (5:1): the reference is to Genesis 35:22.
Tilgath-pilneser (5:5): Tiglath-pileser.
5:26: Pul and Tiglath-pileser are one and the same.
6:27: 'Samuel his son' should be inserted after Elkanah. The reference is to the prophet Samuel.

8 The line of Benjamin; Saul's family 9:1-34 Those who returned from exile to live in Jerusalem 9:35-44 Saul's family-tree

10 - 29 THE REIGN OF DAVID

10 The death of Saul

See on 1 Samuel 31 and 2 Samuel 1. The story of Saul's rise and fall is told in 1 Samuel 9ff. For the Chronicler the history of the monarchy begins with David – 10:13-14 is sufficient comment on Israel's first king.

11 - 12 David made king

11:4-9: the capture of Jerusalem. Verses 10-47: David's special guard – see on 2 Samuel 23. 12:1-22: David's supporters at Ziklag. Saul's own kinsmen went over to David, and the warriors from Gad were so eager to join him that they crossed the River Jordan when it was in spate. Verses 23-40: the troops who made David king at Hebron.

Ariel (11:22): probably means great warrior, or hero.
12:21: see 1 Samuel 30.

13 The first attempt to bring the ark to Jerusalem

See on 2 Samuel 6. In line with his purpose of outlining the *religious* history of the nation, the Chronicler assigns this event first place in the record of David's reign. In actual point of time it came somewhat later.

14 Foreign affairs

See 2 Samuel 5. David was well able to handle the nations around. His family life was his weak point, as the other records make plain (2 Samuel 13ff; 1 Kings 1:6).

15 - 16:16 The Levites bring in the ark

See also 2 Samuel 6. After three months, David brings the ark to Jerusalem and installs it in the tent he has had made. The original tent (the tabernacle) and altar remain at Gibeon. The Chronicler details the role of the levites in the ceremony. Proper worship is characterized by both orderliness and joy. From earliest times music has held a special place in worship.

16:7-43 A call to praise; regular offerings reinstituted

Extracts from various psalms are brought together in verses 8-36. These may be typical of what Asaph's choir sang before the ark, rather than the actual words. At Jerusalem and at Gibeon provision is made for daily sacrifices and praise to God in words and music.

17 David's request to build the temple

See on 2 Samuel 7. It seems wrong to David that he should have a palace to live in while the ark of God is still housed in a tent. And his attitude is right (contrast Haggai 1:4). God refuses the request, none the less. But he expresses his love and approval of David in the promise of a dynasty which will never die out, and in allowing Solomon to build the temple. David does not let disappointment shadow his glad acceptance of God's answer.

18 David's victories; expansion of the kingdom

Verse 4: the numbers are large. This problem is not unique to the Old Testament. Other contemporary documents give similarly large numbers of soldiers and chariots. Statistics given by the opposing sides in a war rarely tally – even today! See further 'The Large Numbers of the Old Testament'.
Chief officials (17): the writer of Samuel calls them 'priests', but by the Chronicler's time the word priest had acquired a technical meaning, hence the change.

19 - 20 Wars with the Ammonites, Syrians and Philistines

Chapter 19: see on 2 Samuel 10. The Bathsheba and Uriah episode took place between 20:1 and 20:2. This is not an attempt to whitewash David; the Chronicler regularly omits details

of private life, in line with his purpose. In any case, these incidents were already known from the earlier records.
19:18: 2 Samuel 10:18 says 700 chariots, a more likely figure. But the word chariot here can mean simply 'mounted men'. The foot-soldiers here are the 'horsemen' of Samuel, since at this time in the ancient Near East horsemen dismounted to fight.

21 - 22:1 Census and plague: the purchase of the temple site

See on 2 Samuel 24. For the Chronicler the census and plague are significant simply as the lead-in to David's decision (22:1) to build the temple on the site of Ornan's threshing-floor, a fact not even mentioned in Samuel.
Satan (21:1): 'God' in 2 Samuel. Satan has power only within the limits set by God (see Job 1-2). His existence in God's world, and God's use of him, remain a mystery.
Guilt upon Israel (3): national solidarity is a fact. When the king as leader sins the people suffer.
Verse 5: these numbers differ from 2 Samuel 24:9. The Chronicler may have taken his figures from a different source.
Verse 18: the threshing-floor was a flat open space where the sheaves could be spread out. Oxen pulling studded sleds loosened the grain, which was then winnowed by tossing it into the wind. 'Ornan' is the 'Araunah' of Samuel. Difficulty may have arisen because it was a foreign name.
Hid (20): perhaps in the cave beneath the rocky floor, which now lies under the Dome of the Rock mosque, erected on the temple site.
Verse 25: 2 Samuel records the price paid for the threshing-floor, this verse apparently the price paid for the whole site.

22:2-19 Preparations for the temple

This section has no parallel in Samuel. It follows naturally from the mention of the temple in verse 1. In point of time it probably belongs to the period of Solomon's co-regency with his father (23:1; 1 Kings 1), which may have lasted some years. David never stopped longing to build God a house fit for him. He accepted the set-back of God's refusal and turned all his energy and enthusiasm to the things he *could* do: selecting the site; amassing materials; deciding the plan.
Aliens (2): the Canaanites who remained in the land were pressed into a permanent slave-force of navvies.
You have shed much blood (8): this does not imply that Solomon was morally better than David, or that David's wars were not justified (God is often stated to have been with him in his campaigns). These very wars bought Solomon's reign of peace in a strong kingdom, and with it the freedom for king and nation to concentrate at last on the great task of building God's temple.
Verse 14: taken literally, this would make David far richer than Solomon. The meaning is clear: David had laid up colossal supplies: a fortune in gold; fantastic wealth of silver; a vast mass of bronze and iron.

23 The duties of the Levites

Chapters 23-27 record David's organization of the nation's religious and civil administration.

From the earliest days of desert-wandering, the job of the Levites had been the care and transport of the tabernacle. They had also served the priests – in later times at the many shrines scattered throughout the land. Now the ark was to have a permanent home, and worship was to be centralized in the temple at Jerusalem. So David allocates new duties to the Levites: the care-taking and maintenance of the temple; appointments as magistrates, janitors, musicians and choristers; and general assistance of the priests.
Verses 3, 27: the age at which a Levite qualified to serve had been 30. David ordered that once the temple was completed it should be 20.
Verse 13: the sons of Amram were descendants of Aaron and Moses.

24 Divisions of priests

Twenty-four groups of priests were to be in charge of the temple sacrifices, each serving for two weeks a year. The order was decided by lot.
Nadab, Abihu (1): see Leviticus 10.
Verse 4: the fact that Eli's family was descended from Ithamar partly accounts for the reduced numbers. Because of the sins of Eli's sons, many of their descendants met a violent death (see 1 Samuel 2:30ff.).

25 The musicians

Music, both instrumental and vocal, was important in Jewish worship, as it was in social life generally. The temple musicians were 'leaders in inspired prophecy' (25:1, 3, New English Bible). Asaph, Heman and Jeduthun were amongst the famous: they are named in the Psalms. But

Musicians from Carchemish, 8th century BC.

status does not come into the temple service. Teacher and pupil alike share an equal place (8). David, himself a skilled musician (1 Samuel 16:15ff.; 2 Samuel 23:1), must have taken special delight in this part of the arrangements, over which he exercised personal supervision (2,6).

26:1-19 The janitors

These were to take turns on guard outside the temple and store-house.
Verse 18: the meaning of 'parbar' is not known; New English Bible gives 'colonnade'.

26:20-32 Temple treasurers, clerks and magistrates

The temple treasuries – gifts and taxes from the people, and the spoils of war – were vast.

27 Army commanders, tribal leaders, civil service and government officials

All twelve army chiefs seem to have come from David's special guard of 'mighty men' (see chapter 11). Verses 26-31 list those in charge of the royal estates, each specializing in a particular branch of agriculture.
Below twenty (23): under-twenties were not eligible for military service and were never counted in the census.
Verse 32: Jonathan and Jehiel were tutors to the king's sons.
Verse 33: Ahithophel and Hushai both appear in the story of Absalom's rebellion, 2 Samuel 15:31ff. 'King's friend' is an official title.

28 - 29 The government passes to Solomon; plans and instructions for the temple

A formal public assembly marks Solomon's official coronation, after the hasty affair of 1 Kings 1 (see 29:22). David presents his son to the people (1-8) and gives him a solemn charge (9, 10) before committing the plans for the temple to his care (11-19). The design is God-given, closely following the pattern given to Moses for the construction of the tabernacle. At the same time, David hands over the lists of temple duties (21; see chapters 23-36).

Chapter 29: in addition to all he has put by over the years, David makes a last lavish personal gift for the temple building fund (1-5). His example and appeal (5) calls forth a willing, joyful response from the people, and the gifts pour in (6-9). Deeply moved, David thanks God from his heart that such giving is possible from men who apart from God's goodness have nothing. His prayer is one of the greatest in the whole of the Old Testament. It shows, as perhaps no other passage does, just why this man could be described as 'a man after God's own heart'.
Verse 4: see on 22:14.
Darics (7): a Persian gold coin; anachronistic for David's day, but a clue to the date at which the Chronicler wrote.
All the sons of King David (24): ear-

lier, Adonijah had attempted to wrest the throne from Solomon (1 Kings 1); later, Solomon put him to death. But for the present there was concord.

2 CHRONICLES 1 - 9 THE REIGN OF SOLOMON

1 Solomon established on the throne

See on 1 Kings 3 and 10.
Shephelah (15): the low hills between Judea and the Philistine coastal plain.

2 Trade arrangements with Huram over building materials for the temple

See on 1 Kings 5.
Huram (3): the 'Hiram' of Kings. See also on 2 Samuel 5.
Huramabi (13): elsewhere shortened to Huram or Hiram.

3 The construction of the temple

See on 1 Kings 6 - 7, and illustrations.
Mt Moriah (1): it was on a mountain in the land of Moriah that Abraham was told to offer up Isaac (Genesis 22:2).
Parvaim (6): not known; possibly in Arabia.
The veil (14): the sanctuary in which the ark was kept was divided off from the main part of the building by this curtain.

4 - 5:1 The temple furnishings

See on 1 Kings 7.
3,000 baths (5): i.e. about 14,500 gallons, on the usual reckoning of 4 gallons 6¾ pints/22 litres to one bath. 1 Kings 7:26 gives 2,000 baths (10,000 gallons).

5:2 - 6:11 The dedication of the temple

See on 1 Kings 8. The ark is installed with joyful music and singing and great thanksgiving. The glory of God's presence fills the temple (2-14). Solomon speaks to the people (6:3-11).
The Levitical singers ... (12): see on 1 Chronicles 25.
Verse 2: in the desert days, when they themselves lived in tents, the people made a tent for God (the tabernacle). Now that they are settled in houses, the temple is built as a house for God. It was not a cathedral in which they met for worship. Assemblies took place in the open, in front of the temple, where the altar and great basin stood.

6:12-42 Solomon's prayer

See on 1 Kings 8. The ground for this prayer, and all prayer, is the fact that God and his promises are utterly dependable. The requests are based on other vital facts about God: his love for his people; his absolute moral standards; his readiness to hear and forgive those who genuinely turn away from sin.
Verses 41-42: a free quotation of Psalm 132:8-10.

7 The dedication feast; God's answer to Solomon

See on 1 Kings 8 - 9. Flame burns up the sacrifices in token of God's presence and approval. The seven days of festivity run on into the week-long Feast of Tabernacles, with a final day of solemn meeting before they all disperse (this clarifies 1 Kings 8:65-66).

Verses 11-22: God agrees to all Solomon's requests. But in return he expects loyal obedience.

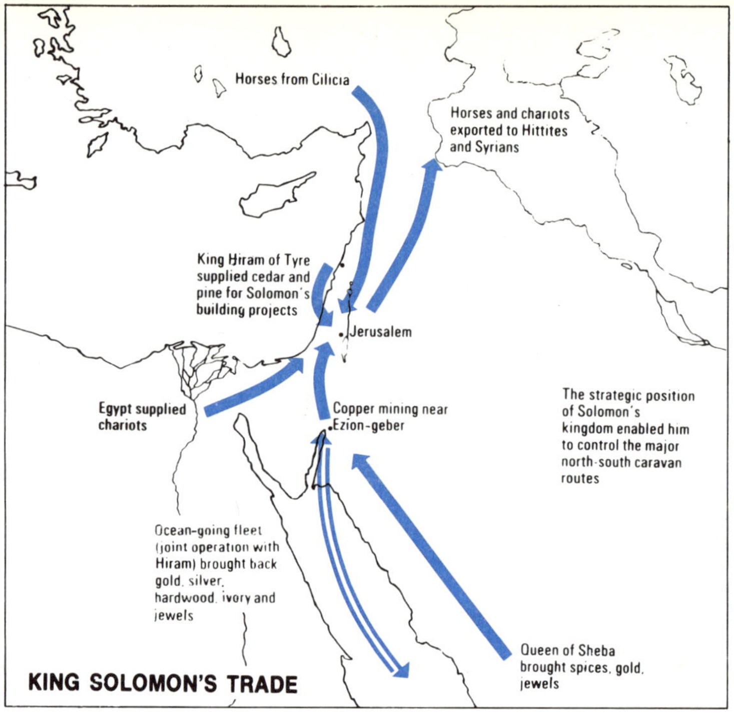

KING SOLOMON'S TRADE

Model of a merchant ship from King Solomon's fleet, from the Maritime Museum, Haifa, Israel.

8 Solomon's building and trading operations

See on 1 Kings 9:10ff.
Verse 2: the cities of 1 Kings 9:10-14, redeemed from Hiram by Solomon.
Verse 10: the 250 officers plus 3,600 overseers (2:18) add up to the same total as the 550 plus 3,300 of 1 Kings 9:23; 5:16.
Law of Moses (13): for the set feasts see Leviticus 23; the sacrifices, Leviticus 1-7.
Verse 14: David's instructions are given in 1 Chronicles 23-26.

9:1-12 The visit of the Queen of Sheba

See on 1 Kings 10. The Chronicler includes the visit as an illustration of Solomon's widespread fame and reputation.
Algum (10): a foreign word, the 'almug' of 1 Kings.

9:13-31 Solomon's wealth and glory

See on 1 Kings 10:14-29.
Verse 21: a voyage from Elath, round Africa, to Tarshish (Tartessus) in Spain is highly unlikely. In Kings the phrase 'ships of Tarshish' describes the type of vessel – deep-sea cargo ships.
Prophecy of Ahijah (29): this source is now lost, but two of Ahijah's prophecies are recorded in 1 Kings 11 and 14.

10 - 36 THE KINGS OF JUDAH

The dates and length of reign of each king are given in the parallel sections of 1 and 2 Kings. Many of them include a period of co-regency with a predecessor, so there is often some overlap. See article 'Unravelling the Chronology of the Kings'.

The Chronicler does not recognize the kings of Israel. Only David's descendants are the nation's true kings. From the time of the split he therefore largely ignores the northern kingdom, and frequently refers to Judah as 'Israel'. Even so, the ten tribes are still considered part of the Israelite nation, and contain elements which continue loyal to God and to the rightful king.

10 King Rehoboam and the split between Israel and Judah

See also 1 Kings 12. Rehoboam

inherited from Solomon a wealthy kingdom beginning to show signs of weakness. By the time of his death only a fraction of that land and income remained to be handed down to his successor.
In Egypt (2): see 1 Kings 11:26ff.
The word spoken by Ahijah (15): 1 Kings 11:30-39.
Hadoram (18): the Adoram (Adoniram) of Kings.

11 Rehoboam strengthens Judah's defences

A timely word from Shemaiah averts civil war (1-4). Instead, Rehoboam concentrates on fortifying his tiny kingdom against attack from her larger and stronger neighbours, particularly Israel and Egypt. Refugee priests flock to Judah from Israel following Jeroboam's measures to break the religious ties with Jerusalem (see 1 Kings 12:26-33).
Satyrs (15): the goat-like desert-demons of the old nature worship.
Abijah (20): the Abijam of Kings.
Daughter of Absalom (20): the Old Testament often uses 'son of', 'daughter of', in the wider sense of 'descendant'. Maacah was Absalom's granddaughter (see 13:2).

12 Rehoboam turns unfaithful; Shishak's invasion

Invasion, here and later, is seen as a direct consequence of disloyalty to God. National repentance limits its effects, but Judah remains under Egyptian domination for some years. See also 1 Kings 14.
All Israel (1): the Chronicler means the true Israel, i.e. Judah.
Shishak (2): Sheshonq 1, Libyan founder of the 22nd dynasty of Egypt.

13 King Abijah; full-scale war with Israel

See also 1 Kings 15:1-8. The fuller account here enlarges on what constitutes 'proper' worship, and on the reason for Judah's victory.
Micaiah (2): Maacah (11:20; 1 Kings 15:2).
Covenant of salt (5): salt had a ceremonial use in the ratification of treaties. It stood for faith, loyalty and long-lastingness (particularly in 'pacts' made with God).
500,000 (17): best taken as meaning simply 'a large number'.

14 Peace under King Asa; Zerah's invasion

See also 1 Kings 15:9-24.
Zerah (9): Ethiopia/Cush is modern Sudan. Zerah was probably an Egyptian or Arabian chieftain (the earlier identification with Pharaoh Osorkon has now been abandoned).
A million (9): best taken to mean simply 'an enormous number'.

15 Azariah's message from God encourages religious reform

Ephraim, Manasseh and Simeon (9): loyal men from the two northern tribes migrated to Judah. But Simeon's territory had always been in the south, and the tribe had been assimilated long ago by Judah.
Maacah (16): Asa's grandmother. See on 11:20.
Verse 17: on the face of it, a contradiction of 14:3. But Asa probably destroyed the shrines where foreign gods were worshipped and left the others.

16 The alliance with Syria against Israel

Asa's faith weakens under test in his later years. He calls in foreign aid. And he turns to medicine-men whose cures were effected by magic. Nonetheless, in death, his people honour him.
Fire (14): not a cremation, but the burning of spices (see Jeremiah 34:5).

17 Jehoshaphat: a king to be reckoned with

See also 1 Kings 15:24; 22:1-50.

Jehoshaphat builds up a strong army and defences. He arranges for the people to be taught the law. And he is much respected by the surrounding nations.
The Arabs (11): former nomads settling in Edom and Moab.
Verse 14: as they stand, the figures for the muster are over-high. It is possible that the term 'thousand' is a group term rather than a numeral. See article 'The Large Numbers of the Old Testament'.

18 Military and marriage alliance with Ahab; battle at Ramoth-gilead

A repetition of the story in 1 Kings 22.
The marriage alliance (1): Jehoshaphat's son Jehoram married Athaliah, Ahab's daughter. Far from reuniting the kingdom, this link brought near-disaster to Judah in later years (22:10).
True and false prophets (4ff.): it was never easy to distinguish between the two. Here Jehoshaphat senses from the shallow optimism of their message that these prophets are merely telling Ahab what he wants to hear. The false and the true can only be distinguished by their life and message, not by methods or manner (see Deuteronomy 18:17-22). No true prophet made a prediction which failed to happen; practised or encouraged immorality; or led people away from God and his law.

19 Reform of the legal system

After Ramoth-gilead, Jehoshaphat concentrates on home affairs. He appoints civil judges, sets up local law-courts and a mixed court of appeal in Jerusalem.
Jehu (2): probably grandson of the Jehu in 1 Kings 16:1. It was not unknown for names to alternate like this within families.
Law of the Lord (8): cases covered by the law of Moses; the other lawsuits ('disputed cases', Revised Standard Version) are civil matters.
Brethren (10): fellow judges, not kinsmen as in New English Bible.

20 War with the allied forces of Ammon, Moab and Edom

Judah's trust in God is amply vindicated. The invaders quarrel among themselves and leave the spoil to Judah. Only the alliance with Israel spoils the good record of Jehoshaphat's reign.
Meunites (1): from a district of Edom near Mt Seir.
The Sea (2): the Dead Sea.
Verse 33: this agrees with 1 Kings 22:43; but contradicts 17:6. (See on 15:17.) The high places (often but not always on hills) were simply platforms on which cult objects stood. As the places themselves were regarded as holy, nothing short of the desecration carried out by Josiah could stop people using them.
Tarshish (36): see on 9:21.

21 King Jehoram

See also 2 Kings 8:16-24. The evil influence of Jehoram's wife (Athaliah was the daughter of Ahab and Jezebel) proved stronger than his father's good example. Jehoram lost control over Edom and Libnah (on the Philistine border), and led the nation into idolatry. No one regretted his death (20): a terrible epitaph.
Elijah's letter (12): it would appear from 2 Kings 3:11 (in Jehoshaphat's reign) that Elijah was no longer alive, though we cannot be certain. Possibly, foreseeing how things would go, the prophet left a written message which was delivered by a successor.
Jehoahaz (17): an alternative way of writing Ahaziah (22:1). Both are a compound of 'Ahaz', meaning 'he has hold', or 'possession' and the name of God (written Jeho- or Jo- as a prefix; -iahu or -iah as a suffix). The whole name thus means 'God has possession'. Most of Judah's kings have names compounded in this way.

22:1-9 King Ahaziah

See also 2 Kings 8:25-29. Ahaziah learnt nothing from his father's horrible end. Friendship with Israel led directly to his death in Jehu's purge.
Verse 2: 42 should be 22, as 2 Kings 8:26.
Verse 9: this seems to be at variance with 2 Kings 9 and 10, where Ahaziah dies at Megiddo, and before his nephews' deaths. It is possible that 'Samaria' is used here of the kingdom rather than the city itself.

22:10 - 23:21 Athaliah seizes the throne; the rising in favour of Joash

See also 2 Kings 11. Ahaziah's infant son Joash is the rightful heir. But so many of the royal family have been wiped out (21:17; 22:8) that the queen mother is able to make her bid unchallenged. After six years the usurper is overthrown. The Chronicler lays his stress on the role of the priests and Levites in restoring the rightful monarch to the throne.

24 King Joash; the repair of the temple

See also 2 Kings 11:21 - 12:21. Under Jehoiada's influence, Joash began well. After the priest's death the king came under less healthy influences, till he sank to the murder of Jehoiada's son for his outspoken criticism. In consequence his own life ends in ignominious defeat and assassination.
The tax (6): see Exodus 30:12ff.

25 King Amaziah

See also 2 Kings 14. Amaziah's cruel victory over Edom leads to his downfall. He brings home the foreign gods. And in his bumptious pride he throws down the gauntlet to powerful Israel. Defeat turns the people against him. It seems that Uzziah, the 'Azariah' of 2 Kings, was made co-regent. And an eventual conspiracy succeeded in ending Amaziah's life.
Verse 4: Deuteronomy 24:16.
100,000 (6): a round figure indicating a large number.
Israel ... Ephraimites (7): the Chronicler makes it clear that in this instance he means the northern kingdom.

26 King Uzziah

See also 2 Kings 15:1-7. A strong king, Uzziah begins well, seeking God and extending his sovereignty as far south as the Red Sea. He loves the land and protects the cattle from desert raiders (10). He sees that his army is well-equipped and armed with the latest in guided missiles (14-15). But as with many a good man before and since, power and success are his undoing. In his pride he takes on the role of priest. God strikes him with leprosy, a visible token of that unseen defilement of sin which made him unfit for God's presence.

27 King Jotham

See also 2 Kings 15:32-38. Jotham proves a good king. He maintains and increases his father's power, adding Ammon to his tributary-states. But the religion of the people remains mixed.

28 King Ahaz

See also 2 Kings 16; Isaiah 7. The terrible apostasy of Ahaz brings Judah near to destruction. God even uses the idolatrous northern kingdom to punish his people – and to show them up by almost unheard-of clemency to the prisoners-of-war. There were still some 'Good Samaritans' in Israel. Crisis brings some people to deeper faith, but not Ahaz.

Valley of the son of Hinnom (3): the Valley of Gehenna, south of Jerusalem.

King of Syria (5): Rezin, see 2 Kings 16.

Tilgath-pilneser (20): Tiglath-pileser. This is not an invasion, but the imposition of crushing tribute.

Altars (24): to pagan gods.

29 King Hezekiah

See also 2 Kings 18-20. Hezekiah's first concern is to restore the temple to its proper use. The detailed account of the cleansing and rededication of the desecrated temple is characteristic of the Chronicler. When the building has been made ready, king, priests and people are themselves made clean from sin by the offering of sacrifices.

Verse 25: see 1 Chronicles 25. Gad and Nathan were both prophets of David's day.

The song to the Lord (27): many of the psalms were written for use in the temple on various occasions.

30 The great Passover celebration

(For the origin and meaning of Passover see on Exodus 11-13.) Samaria had fallen to Assyria in the reign of Ahaz (when Hezekiah was co-regent) – see 2 Kings 17. Most of the northern Israelites had been taken captive and their land re-settled. Hezekiah's appeal is to the few remaining Israelites to join with Judah for the feast (9). Despite the poor response, there had been no Passover to equal this since Solomon's day. And such was the general rejoicing that they extended the feast an extra week.

Verse 3: the normal date was the 14th of the first month, but Numbers 9 also allows the later date.

Verse 15: many priests and Levites were slow to return to the reformed worship (29:34).

Verse 19: the Chronicler, who set great store by proper forms of worship, makes it clear that it is the attitude of heart that matters most.

31 The priests resume their functions; tithes and offerings brought in

The old laws governing worship and the support of the priests are reintroduced. The sheer volume of produce raised by the tithe takes everyone by surprise. Special care is taken to see that it is properly distributed.

Verse 7: people began to give in May/June at the grain harvest and continued to the end of the fruit and vine harvests in September/October.

32 Sennacherib's invasion

See also 2 Kings 18-19. Having wiped out the northern kingdom, the Assyrians make inroads into Judah, who have shown signs of independence. But Sennacherib fails to take Jerusalem. The reason, says the Chronicler, is that in the crisis Judah's king put his trust wholly in God.

Verse 12: the Assyrian emissary misunderstood Hezekiah's reforms.

Verse 18: they used Hebrew. The people would not have understood Aramaic, the diplomatic language.

Verse 31: see 2 Kings 20:12ff. 'Left to himself' Hezekiah exhibits his treasures with foolish pride.

33:1-20 Manasseh's evil reign

See also 2 Kings 21:1-18. For almost all of his long reign Manasseh was one of Judah's worst kings, responsible for desecrating the temple and practising human sacrifice. But the Chronicler relates a change of heart not mentioned in Kings. Possibly Manasseh was caught up in the revolt of Ashurbanipal's brother, vassal-king of Babylon, and was called to account there after Ashurbanipal was victorious. God answered the king's desperate prayer, and his release and return changed him, but not the people.

Verse 6: the Valley of Gehenna.

Hooks (11): kings conquered by the Assyrians had hooks or rings driven through their noses.

HEZEKIAH'S CONDUIT

To secure his water-supply from the invaders, Hezekiah channelled the water from the Spring of Gihon to the Pool of Siloam. The tunnel is over 1,700ft/620m long, and winds to follow the lie of the rock.

In 1880 a boy who had been bathing in the Pool of Siloam found an inscription which tells its own story:

... And this is the story of the piercing through. While (the stone-cutters were swinging their) axes, each towards his fellow, and while there were yet three cubits to be pierced through, (there was heard) the voice of a man calling to his fellow, for there was a crevice (?) on the right ... And on the day of the piercing through, the stone-cutters struck through each to meet his fellow, axe against axe. Then ran the water from the Spring to the Pool for twelve hundred cubits, and a hundred cubits was the height of the rock above the head of the stone-cutters.

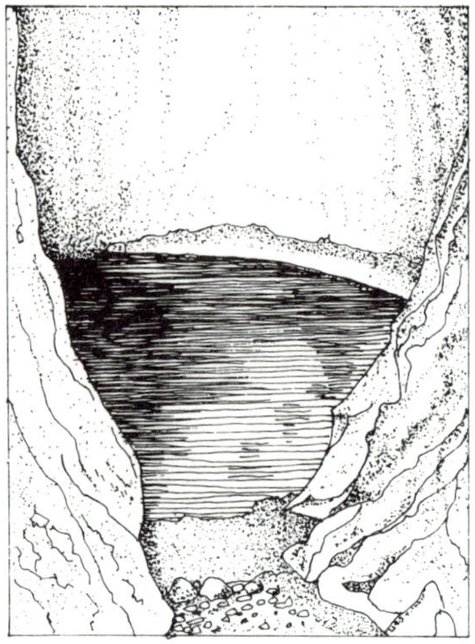

The Spring of Gihon, from which Hezekiah's conduit was channelled.

The inscription carved by workmen on the tunnel wall.

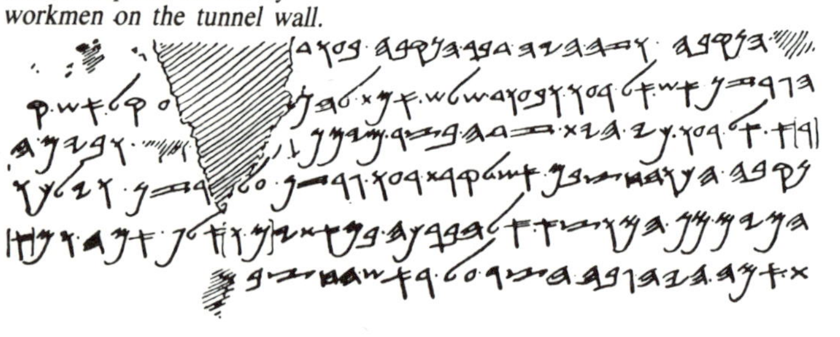

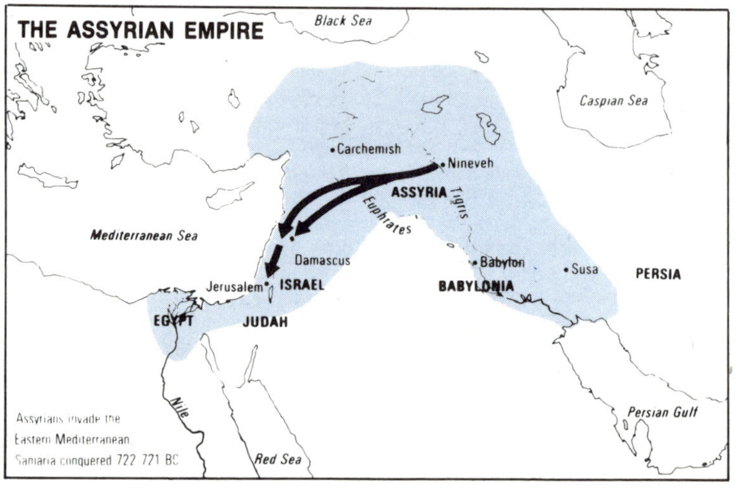

33:21-25 Amon
See also 2 Kings 21:19-26. Amon reigned two years, 642-640. He followed Manasseh's evil example and was murdered by his servants.

34 Josiah: Judah's last and greatest reformer
See also 2 Kings 22-23. Josiah desecrates and demolishes places and objects of pagan worship, and repairs the temple. During his reign the book of the law is discovered, and a measure of true repentance follows. But, despite the king's lead, the people's response is too little and too late to avert judgement. There are some differences between the accounts in Kings and Chronicles, mainly in the order of events, but neither writer is primarily concerned with chronology. The real significance of the events lies in what they teach.

Verse 3: Assyrian power was declining, and Scythian hordes attacking her in the north, so Josiah became gradually freer to take the politically dangerous step of ridding his land of the Assyrian gods.

35 Josiah's Passover; the tragic end to his reign
See 2 Kings 23:21-30. Passover had been neglected during the monarchy. Now the celebration forms the climax to the reforms. The nation remember their deliverance from slavery in Egypt – within a few short years of a second slavery, to Babylon.

Verse 20: Necho was marching north in 609 to help Assyria fight off Babylon. On his way home he deposed and deported Josiah's successor, Jehoahaz. But in 605 he was defeated by Nebuchadnezzar of Babylon at Carchemish.

Jeremiah (25): the prophet's lament has not been preserved.

36:1-4 Jehoahaz
See also 2 Kings 23:31-35 See on 35:20.

36:5-8 Jehoiakim
See also 2 Kings 23:36 - 24:7. Jehoiakim began as a puppet of Egypt, and ended as a captive in Babylon.

36:9-10 Jehoiachin
See also 2 Kings 24:8-16. After only three months Jehoiachin was deposed and taken captive to Babylon. (He was 18 when he became king, not 8; and Zedekiah was his uncle.)

36:11-21 Zedekiah; the destruction of Jerusalem
See also 2 Kings 24:18 - 25:30. God gave Zedekiah and the nation many warnings through Jeremiah and the other prophets, but they were all ignored. The judgement that came spelt death or exile for the whole nation. The exile lasted until the Persians took over the Babylonian Empire.

Sabbath (21): the Chronicler implies that these sabbaths were not kept under the kings. See Leviticus 25:1-7; 26:34-35.

36:22-23 New hope
When the book of Ezra was detached from Chronicles, these verses were retained at the end of Chronicles and repeated at the beginning of Ezra. Chronicles could not end at verse 21. God had not utterly abandoned his people. Jeremiah had spoken scalding words of God's judgement and condemnation. But he had also spoken of God's continuing love for his exiled people, and of their eventual return (Jeremiah 24:4-7).

THE BABYLONIAN EMPIRE

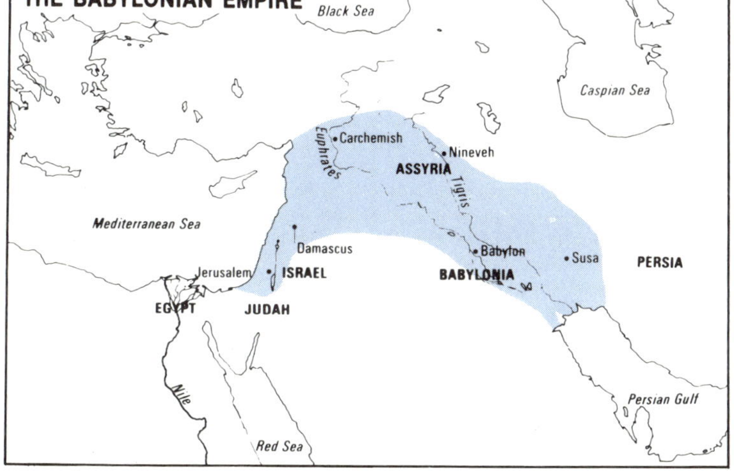

Old Testament 2.10

EZRA

Ezra, Nehemiah and Esther cover the last century of Old Testament Jewish history, roughly 538-433 BC. Ezra follows on from Chronicles (2 Chronicles 36: 22-23 and Ezra 1:1-3 are identical), which ended with the destruction of Jerusalem and the people being taken into exile in Babylon by Nebuchadnezzar (587). Ezra and Nehemiah describe the three-stage return: the main party, who returned with Zerubbabel in 538/7; the party that returned with Ezra 80 years later, in 458 (on the traditional dating – but this does raise some major problems, and debate on the subject continues); and Nehemiah's party in 445. Esther's story belongs to the time between the rebuilding of the temple at Jerusalem and Ezra's return (Ezra 7:1).

On the wider plane, the Jewish events belong to the time following the overthrow of the Babylonian Empire by Cyrus, king of Persia, in 539. Ezra and Nehemiah span the reigns of five Persian kings.

The writer. It is not clear who wrote what, or when. The compiler may have been the Chronicler. But it seems plain that the personal memoirs of Ezra and Nehemiah make up the bulk of the books named after them.

Cyrus 559-530
The return from exile. Ezra 1
End of Daniel's life (1:21; 10:1)

Cambyses 530-522
Not mentioned

Darius I 522-486
The temple rebuilt. Ezra 4:5, 24;5
Haggai and Zechariah

Xerxes I 486-465 (Ahasuerus)
Ezra 4:6. The king who made Esther his queen and Mordecai his grand vizier

Artaxerxes I 464-423
Ezra 4:7-23; 7:1ff.; Nehemiah 2:1.
The king who sponsored the return of Ezra and of Nehemiah.
Jerusalem rewalled. Reforms.
Malachi

1 - 2 THE EXILED JEWS RETURN TO JERUSALEM

1 Cyrus' proclamation
The policy of the Babylonian kings had been to deport the peoples they conquered. But Babylon has now fallen to Persia (as the prophets predicted). And one of Cyrus' first actions is to repatriate the exiled peoples, and allow them to reinstate their national gods. Among those who benefit from the change of policy are the Jews. (See Isaiah's remarkable prophecy, Isaiah 44:26-28; 45:1-13.)

Verse 1: see on 2 Chronicles 36:22-23.

Verse 6: God saw to it that the exiles did not return empty-handed, as he had done at the exodus (Exodus 12:35-36).

2 The list of those who returned
See also Nehemiah 7.

Jeshua (2): the Joshua of Haggai 1:1.

Nehemiah (2): not the same individual as the later governor.

Verse 59: family-trees were reckoned of great importance. Those unable to prove their ancestry were barred from the priesthood.

Barzillai (61): 2 Samuel 17:27; 19:31ff.

Verse 64: the figures given do not add up to this total. There may have been mistakes in copying or interpreting the numbers.

3 - 6 REBUILDING THE TEMPLE

3 The foundation is laid
The first thing to be rebuilt is the altar, so that worship and sacrifice may begin again, on the pattern laid down by Moses (Leviticus 1 - 7). Lebanon again provides choice cedarwood for the building (see 2 Chronicles 2). But the work makes little progress beyond the foundations.

Verses 10-11: see 1 Chronicles 25. There are two choirs (or choir and soloist) singing alternately.

Verse 12: the older men wept for the glories of the temple that had been destroyed.

4 Work is halted

Verses 1-5,24: the opposition succeeds in bringing the work to a standstill for 15 years, until Darius is king. Verses 6-23 interrupt the chronological sequence to carry the account of the opposition through to the time of Ezra and Nehemiah. Here the bone of contention is the rebuilding of the city walls (12).

Judah and Benjamin (1): it was mainly exiles from the southern kingdom who returned. Their 'adversaries' are the mixed people Esarhaddon settled in the land, later known as Samaritans. They worshipped God, but alongside other 'deities' (2 Kings 17:24-41).

Verse 7: Aramaic was the international diplomatic language of the Persian Empire.

Osnappar (10): An Aramaic version of Ashurbanipal. 'Beyond the River'/ 'Beyond Euphrates': title of the fifth 'satrapy' or province, which included all Palestine and Syria.

Eat the salt (14): i.e. they were maintained by the king; his paid officials.

Verse 23: this is the situation recounted in Nehemiah 1:3.

5 - 6 The temple completed

Urged on by the prophets Haggai and Zechariah, the people again start building. This time an attempt to get the new king, Darius, to stop it has the opposite effect. In four years the temple is finished and the people are able to celebrate Passover. For a nation recently delivered from a second 'bondage', this must have had special meaning.

6:11: a common form of execution in Persia; in effect crucifixion.

King of Assyria (22): i.e. king of what was once Assyrian territory.

7 - 10 EZRA'S RETURN TO JERUSALEM

Nearly 60 years separate 7:1 from 6:22, during which time Esther is able to avert a complete massacre of the Jewish people and, indirectly, to save the lives of Ezra and Nehemiah. Artaxerxes is favourably disposed towards the Jews, and Ezra the scholar and teacher (direct descendant of the high priests) is given official sanction to teach the law and appoint magistrates in his homeland, to offer sacrifices and beautify the temple. (Ezra's own memoirs, written in Hebrew, begin at verse 27.)

Verse 9: the 900-mile journey took four months.

8 The men who accompanied Ezra

Ezra's party of over 1700 includes priests, people and, somewhat reluctantly, Levites. With them they take gifts valuing more than £1,000,000. Ezra is faced with a long and dangerous journey at a time of great unrest. And having boasted his confidence in God, he can hardly now apply to the king for an escort! His prayer is heartfelt, and his faith rewarded by God's own safe-conduct.

Satraps (36): very powerful governors; usually only one to each 'satrapy' or province, with several subordinates.

9 - 10 The problem of mixed marriages

Since their return, priests and Levites, rulers and people alike have intermarried with the heathen peoples around, a thing forbidden by God (Deuteronomy 7:1-5), not out of racial prejudice but because it led to idolatry. This very practice had been a major factor in the nation's downfall under the kings. Yet even the horrors of defeat and exile have not taught the people their lesson. Small wonder Ezra's bitter distress at the disclosure. His close identification with the offenders and the deep grief of his prayer move the nation to prompt action, despite the time of year (heavy December rains, 10:9). His lead saves the whole nation from extinction. The blame for all the unhappiness of broken marriages rests not on Ezra, but on those listed in 10:18-44 – the men who contracted those marriages in defiance of God's law. And some of them (as Malachi 2:10-16 makes clear) had even broken former marriages to Jewish wives in order to marry pagans. See also under Nehemiah 13.

Old Testament 2.11

NEHEMIAH

See introduction to Ezra.

1 - 2 NEHEMIAH RETURNS TO JERUSALEM

1 Bad news; Nehemiah's prayer

In December 446, Nehemiah's brother Hanani (see 7:2) brings sad news of the colony in Jerusalem (see Ezra 4:23). Nehemiah holds the trusted position of king's cup-bearer at the Persian court, at that time resident in the winter capital of Susa. It is his job to taste the king's wine, in case it is poisoned. Although far from his homeland, he is so concerned for his people that for four months he continues to grieve and pray over the situation. And, characteristically, when the opportunity comes he has a practical plan to put to the king.

Remember the word (8): e.g. Deuteronomy 30:1-5.

This man (11): the Persian king.

2 The king consents; Nehemiah's tour of inspection

The sorry state of Jerusalem is a direct consequence of Artaxerxes' decree that building should cease (Ezra 4:7-23). Nehemiah therefore takes his life in his hands in championing a city which has been represented to the king as a hot-bed of rebellion. Even by letting his grief show in the king's presence he places himself in grave danger. But Nehemiah's concern for his people outweighs self-interest. God answers his prayer, and Artaxerxes grants his request.

On arrival in Jerusalem he mentions his plans to no one until he has made a secret personal inspection of the city.

Verse 6: Nehemiah returned after 12 years as governor (5:14), but the term agreed on here was probably shorter.

Sanballat, Tobiah (19): see also 4:1-9; 6:1-18; 13:4-9. *Geshem* (Gashmu, 6:6): tribal chief of Kedar in north Arabia.

JERUSALEM IN NEHEMIAH'S TIME

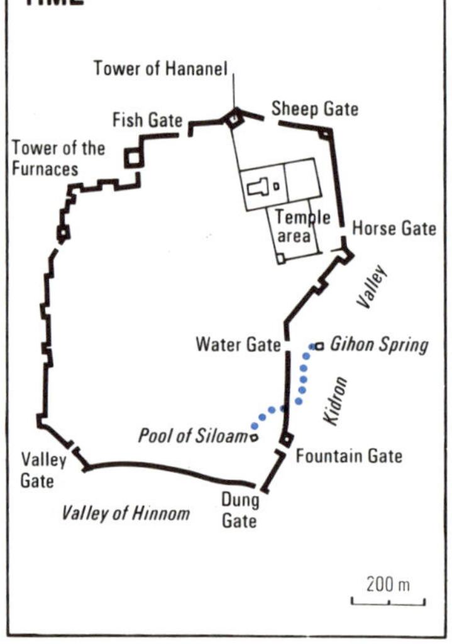

3 - 6 THE BUILDING OF THE WALLS

3 A list of the builders

People of all sorts join together in the work of rebuilding. The list mentions priests and perfumers, goldsmiths and merchants, rulers, even women. Some undertook a double section. Nehemiah, astute as always, sets the people to work on sections near their own homes, for which they naturally have a special concern. The leaders named are citizens of long standing; neither Ezra nor the men of his party are mentioned.

4 Enemy opposition

The people have a will to work, and a dynamic leader. Nonetheless they have to face first ridicule, then terrorism from powerful opponents. Nehemiah's reply is prayer and faith, plus practical action: 'we prayed ... and set a guard' (9); 'Remember the Lord ... and fight' (14).

Verse 2: the walls had been burned, and fire made the local limestone disintegrate.

Verses 4-5: Old Testament prayers like this one fall short of Christ's standards. But the motive behind them is not personal vengeance, but concern for God's honour which is at stake when his people are under attack.

5 Internal troubles

While Nehemiah has been buying back Hebrew slaves and loaning money and food to the poor (even providing his own support as governor), rich Jews have been exacting interest from their fellow countrymen, contrary to the law (Exodus 22:25) and selling them as slaves to foreigners. Nehemiah takes firm action to set this right.

6 The wall is finished

The opposition realize that their only chance of stopping the work is to get rid of Nehemiah. Their first move is to try and persuade him to leave Jerusalem for talks (2). When that fails they try blackmail (5-7) and intimidation (10). Nehemiah's replies (3, 8, 11) are superb. He will allow nothing to deflect him from his God-given task. And in under two months the walls are finished – such a fantastic achievement that even Israel's enemies are forced to acknowledge God's hand in it.

7:1-73a LIST OF THOSE WHO RETURNED WITH ZERUBBABEL

Verses 6-73: see also the practically identical list in Ezra 2. It refers to the first, and main, party of Jews to return home in 538 following Cyrus' decree.

7:73b - 8:18 EZRA READS THE LAW TO THE PEOPLE

The request comes from the people (8:1). Ezra reads and the Levites explain, possibly also translating for some who knew no Hebrew. When they learn the full measure of God's standards the people are overwhelmed with grief at the extent of their failures (just as King Josiah had been, long before; 2 Kings 22).

In the course of study, they rediscover the original instructions for the Feast of Tabernacles. And for the first time since Joshua's day they make leafy shelters to live in, as a reminder of the time of desert-wandering.

9:1-37 THE PEOPLE'S CONFESSION AND EZRA'S PRAYER

The nation's repentance is genuine. Wrongs are righted and the people turn to God in confession and worship. Ezra's prayer – the prelude to renewal of the covenant – recalls God's loving and faithful dealings with his rebellious people from the time of Abraham to his own day.

9:38 - 10:39 THE COVENANT IS RENEWED

Nehemiah the governor, priests, Levites and leaders sign the renewed covenant-agreement on behalf of the nation. It is ratified with a curse (on those who break it) and an oath (of loyalty to God). The people pledge specifically to keep the law's requirements on marriage, the sabbath, and taxes, tithes and offerings for the upkeep of the temple services, priests and Levites.

11 - 12:26 LISTS OF RESIDENTS

11:3-19: probably a list of those already living in Jerusalem (it is substantially the same as 1 Chronicles 9:2-17). The number was increased by a 10 per cent levy on the villages around.

Verses 25-36: a list of occupied villages.

12:1-9: the priests and Levites who returned with Zerubbabel.

11:23: see 1 Chronicles 25.

12:9: there were two choirs who sang or chanted in reply to one another.

12:27-47 THE DEDICATION OF THE WALLS

Two processions, each led by a choir, make their way in opposite directions along the broad top of the wall, meeting in the temple area for the concluding thanksgiving and sacrifices. It is an occasion of tumultuous joy.

13 ABUSES AND REFORMS

Verses 1-3 seem more closely linked with 4-9 than with 12:44. In 433 Nehemiah went back to the court of King Artaxerxes. On his return he finds that various abuses have arisen in his absence. The high priest, of all people, has given Nehemiah's old enemy, Tobiah (who is not even an Israelite) quarters in rooms attached to the temple. The income for the Levites has not been forthcoming. Sabbath laws are being flagrantly broken. And yet again (see Ezra 9-10) the Israelites have contracted marriages with foreign women, Nehemiah adopts strong measures to deal with the abuses, and the offenders.

The achievements of Ezra and Nehemiah in the crucial years following the return of their decimated nation from exile are notable. Without the teaching of the law, without the invincible faith and fearless action of these two leaders, it is doubtful if a distinctive Jewish religion and community – with all that means for the world through the birth and death of Christ – could have survived. To this end their strong line on mixed marriage was essential. The objection to foreign women was not on the grounds of race, but because of their debased religions. (The Old Testament does not condemn inter-racial marriage if both partners worship the God of Israel.) History had taught them that the admixture of paganism, with its easy standards and its appeal to the lowest in human nature, could quickly bring the Jewish faith to the brink of extinction.

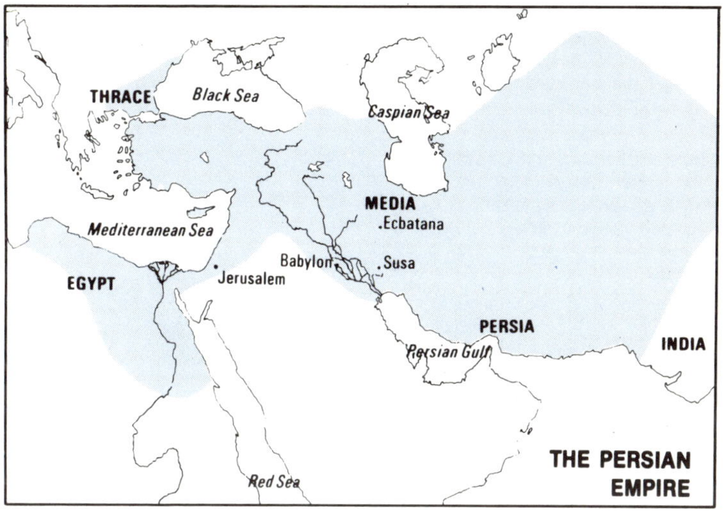

Old Testament 2.12

ESTHER

Esther tells the story of a plot to exterminate the entire Jewish nation in the days of the Persian king, Ahasuerus (Xerxes), and how it was thwarted. It also explains the origin of the Jewish Feast of Purim. Estimates of the book vary – largely on account of the seeming improbability of the events. Some regard it as pure fiction. Others see it as a historical novel. Others again think that the knowledge we have of Persian affairs in the 5th century BC gives good grounds for treating Esther as history.

The writer is unknown, but his nationalism and accurate knowledge of Persian ways make it likely that he was a Jew who lived in Persia before the empire fell to Greece.

Although the book does not mention God by name, it speaks plainly of his over-ruling in the affairs of men, and his unfailing care for his people. Had Haman's plot succeeded there would have been no Nehemiah and, far more important, no Christ.

1 Ahasuerus dethrones his queen

Ahasuerus reigned over an empire stretching from the Indus to northern Sudan (see map). His winter capital (unbearably hot in summer) was Susa, a city in Elam, 150 miles east of Babylon. The Greek historian Herodotus describes him as a cruel, capricious, sensual man – which fits well with his character in this book. In 483 he gives a huge feast, the climax to a six-month display of his wealth and power. But his queen (we are not told why) refuses to play along with his wish to make her part of the exhibition. And on the advice of his astrologers the king deposes her.

Queen Vashti (9): Herodotus says Amestris was Ahasuerus' queen. It may be she succeeded both Vashti and Esther. The king may have had more than one wife, but there would have been only one queen.

He sent letters (22): Darius had set up an excellent fast-courier postal service which operated throughout the empire.

2 Esther becomes queen; Mordecai saves the king's life

The years of the disastrous Greek war – the battles of Thermopylae and Salamis – intervene between chapters 1 and 2. Four years pass before the king is able to get round to choosing a new queen. Among the beautiful

A Persian guard, in multi-coloured glazed brick, from the palace walls at Susa.

girls rounded up to be taken to the capital for twelve months' beauty treatment, sampled by the king, and then for the most part forgotten, is a young Jewish girl, Esther, Mordecai's cousin. When her turn comes, she delights the king and he makes her his queen.

Verses 5-6: Mordecai would have been nearly 120 if he personally had been taken captive in 597. It probably means that his family was among the captives.

Hadassah/Esther (7): some make much of the fact that the names 'Esther' and 'Mordecai' are similar to those of the Babylonian gods 'Ishtar' and 'Marduk'. But this is not surprising if both were names given to them in captivity, as this verse says Esther's was.

Tebeth (16): December/January 479.

Verse 23: this record in the court diary later proves important (6:1-2).

3 Haman's promotion and plot against the Jews

We are not told why Mordecai refused to make obeisance. He must have considered that Haman's demand went beyond court courtesy. To have complied would have involved idolatry. In his unreasoning fury Haman plans the destruction of an entire race. Superstition insists he must choose a 'lucky day'. And fortunately for the Jews it was eleven months off. The king's assent is easily won by accusing the Jews of rebellion and promising a £3,000,000 rake-off. (Haman plans to raise the money by plundering Jewish goods and confiscating their lands.)

A Persian gold armlet, decorated with griffins, from the Treasure of the Oxus, Persia.

4 Esther hears the news

Esther is the only one of her people with access to the king, and she has not been summoned to him for a month. The only way open is the dangerous step of going to him unbidden. Anxiously she agrees to take the risk.

Verses 14-16: although God is not mentioned, Mordecai's faith is plain. The fast would involve prayer.

5 Esther gives a dinner-party

The king permits an audience. But Esther proceeds cannily. She invites the king and his favourite to dinner. In the mellow after-dinner atmosphere she gives a second invitation. Haman – suspecting nothing, knowing nothing of Esther's relationship to Mordecai – is greatly flattered. He goes home and builds a gallows topping the city wall, on which he intends to hang his enemy.

6 The king honours Mordecai

A sleepless night and the reading of the court diary give events a new twist. To his mortification Haman finds himself heaping on his enemy honours he had thought were intended for himself. His superstitious advisers see in this the beginning of his downfall.

7 Haman's villainy unmasked

After dinner on the second evening Esther makes her request. Haman is dumb-founded. And his action in throwing himself at Esther's feet as she reclines on her couch only succeeds in adding attempted rape to the charges against him. In the supreme irony of things, he ends his life on the gallows he himself had made.

They covered Haman's face (8): i.e. in token of the death sentence.

8 Mordecai becomes grand vizier; a new edict

There still remains the problem of Haman's edict. Since it was issued in the king's name and under his seal it cannot be revoked (8). But in answer to Esther's further plea the king authorizes a second decree permitting the Jews to defend themselves against attack.

Verse 11: the Jews were allowed to treat their enemies exactly as they were to have been treated themselves (see 3:13).

9 Jewish vengeance; the Feast of Purim

When the appointed day arrives, the Jews rid themselves of their enemies, including Haman's ten sons; but they take no plunder. There can be no excuse for Esther's vindictive request. She shows herself to be a child of her age. The bodies of Haman's sons are hanged to make their fate public knowledge.

In commemoration of the nation's deliverance, the 14th and 15th Adar become annual feast days, preceded by a fast on the 13th. To this day the Jews celebrate Purim, reading the book of Esther aloud, and remembering many more recent miracles of deliverance.

10 Conclusion

The author closes with a final historical note, attesting the good use Mordecai made of his power.

Old Testament section 3

POETRY AND WISDOM LITERATURE

Introduction/Derek Kidner

POETRY

The word 'poetry' may suggest to us a highly specialized branch of literary art, produced by the few for the few. But this would be a misleading term for any part of the Old Testament. A closer modern equivalent would be the measured oratory of, for instance, a Winston Churchill –

We shall fight on the beaches,
We shall fight on the landing-
grounds,
We shall fight in the fields and in the
streets

– in which reiteration (or other devices) and rhythm join to make a passage doubly memorable and impressive.

Reiteration was a favourite Canaanite technique, and is also a mark of some of the earliest biblical poetry:

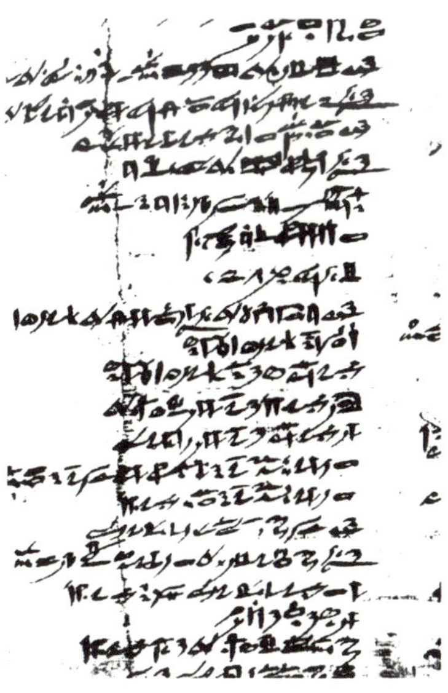

Proverbs is paralleled in contemporary cultures by other collections of wisdom. ***The Wisdom of Amenemope,*** *on this papyrus from Thebes, Egypt, dates from about 1000 BC.*

Spoil of dyed stuffs for Sisera,
Spoil of dyed stuffs embroidered,
Two pieces of dyed work
embroidered for my neck as spoil
(Judges 5:30).

The rhythm, though tighter than this in the original, is a flexible matter of stresses, or beats, not of fixed numbers of syllables. Most often there will be three stresses to a line, matched by another three in the following line which pairs with it to form a couplet. But this pattern may be varied by an occasional longer or shorter couplet, or by a triplet, in the same passage; or again the predominating rhythm may be of couplets in which a three-beat line is answered by another of two beats:

How are the mighty fallen
in the midst of the battle!

This last rhythm, with its touch of fading or drooping, is often used for taunts or laments (as in the book of Lamentations), and this has suggested the name *Qinah* (lament) for it, although its use is not confined to such themes.

What is almost the hallmark of biblical poetry, in contrast to our own, is parallelism: the echoing of the thought of one line of verse in a second line which is its partner:

Has he said, and will he not do it?
Or has he spoken, and will he not
fulfil it? (Numbers 23:19)

There are many varieties of this, from virtual repetition to amplification or antithesis. It has a dignity and spaciousness which allows time for the thought to make its effect on the hearer, and often also the opportunity to present more than one facet of a matter:

For my thoughts are not your
thoughts,
neither are your ways my ways, says
the Lord (Isaiah 55:8).

Bishop Lowth, whose lectures on Hebrew poetry in 1741 first introduced the name 'parallelism' for this poetic style, pointed out that this structure, based as it is on meaning, survives translation into the prose of any language with remarkably little loss, unlike the poetry that relies on complex metre or a special vocabulary. There are, of course, such points of style in Old Testament verse, and occasionally such devices as assonance, rhyme, refrains, word-plays and acrostics; but they are secondary. The essence of this poetry is that it has great matters to convey forcibly to people of all kinds. It is therefore unselfconscious, and remarkably free from artificialities of language.

For this reason, poetry is not segregated into a few poetical books, but breaks out in various contexts at moments of special importance. The examples quoted above are drawn from books we might call histories (but the Jews called them the 'Former Prophets') and from prophecy. In fact nearly all prophetic utterances are in this form, and are rightly set out as lines of poetry in recent translations of the Bible.

Three books of the Old Testament, however, were given a more elaborate system of accents than the rest by the Jewish grammarians, to mark them out as distinctively poetic. These were Job, Psalms and Proverbs. To our ears, a better candidate than Proverbs would have been the Song of Solomon; its pure lyric poetry a third example of Hebrew poetry to stand beside the rich eloquence of Job and the singable verse of the Psalms. On Job, more will be said under the heading of Wisdom, below; but purely as poetry it has been hailed as one of the masterpieces of world literature, for the wealth and energy of its language and the power of its thought. In the Psalms, poetry is put to work, to be 'the way to heaven's door' in worship or in teaching, furnishing inspired words for public festivals and royal occasions, and for the individual who might come to confess his sins, or plead for healing, or rejoice over some deliverance or revelation. The Song of Solomon, by contrast, scarcely gives the name of God a mention, but responds rapturously to his creation and to its crowning glory, the gift of love between man and woman. Its presence in the Bible is the most graceful of tokens that God's world is not properly divisible into secular and sacred, and that holiness cannot be indifferent to beauty.

WISDOM LITERATURE

Wisdom, in the Old Testament, is the voice of reflection and experience, rather than of bare command or preaching. We are persuaded, even teased, into seeing the connection between God's order in the world and his orders to men, and the absurdity of going against the grain of his creation.

It takes many forms. A vivid comparison, perhaps expanded into a parable or an allegory, is a favourite device; the Hebrew word for it, *mashal*, does duty for any of these, and equally for a proverb or a taunt. A riddle or an enigmatic saying is another means of pricking a person into thought. At a deeper level there will be searching reflection on the way God governs the world, and on the ends for which men live.

Like poetry, Wisdom is not confined to the books which we group under this name (in the Old Testament, Proverbs, Job, Ecclesiastes), for proverbs and pointed sayings are part of every culture, and Israel's was no exception. In the narratives we have, for instance, Jotham's fable of the trees, Samson's riddle, and various proverbs; while in the Psalms and prophetic oracles the teaching style of the Wise makes itself clearly heard from time to time (e.g. Psalm 1; Isaiah 28:23ff.; Jeremiah 17:5ff.; Hosea 14:9). We are confirmed in identifying this as a distinct ingredient in Scripture by the fact that Israel itself heard it as a third voice alongside Law and Prophecy. There was even a proverb to this effect: 'The law shall not perish from the priest, nor counsel from the wise, nor the word from the prophet' (Jeremiah 18:18).

Of all reputations for wisdom, Solomon's is pre-eminent; and it rests not only on his own brilliance but on his patronage of learning and the arts. The Queen of Sheba was but one of a stream of visitors who poured into Israel to hear him and put him to the test. The names and places of 1 Kings 4:30-33 give a glimpse of an intellectual world that briefly found its capital in Jerusalem; and this openness to foreign enquirers finds some reflection in the authorship of Proverbs 30 and 31:1-9, which are apparently the work of non-Israelite converts.

Israel's Wisdom literature, then, never professed to have developed in an intellectual vacuum. Just how rich was the surrounding culture is becoming clear as the wisdom of Egypt and Mesopotamia comes increasingly to light. Some of their fables, popular sayings and precepts have been preserved, and they are largely concerned with the common stuff of life that occupies the biblical proverbs: teachability, sobriety, wise speech, kindness, trust in divine help, magnanimity, friendship. There is a certain amount of mere worldly wisdom here, but much, too, that is sound and high-principled, although the biblical material moves at a consistently higher level of informed faith. Another class of literature from these countries wrestles with the problems of suffering and the meaning of existence, arguing the points at considerable length in skilfully constructed poetic monologues and dialogues.

The fact that questions of this depth were being debated in writing, not only in the time of Solomon but for a thousand years before him, and that the Israel of his day was anything but a cultural back-water, should dispose of the idea (still current in some circles) that Israel's stock of wisdom consisted at this time of short popular sayings, which supposedly developed by degrees into longer and more religious units, and only in the latest period into the connected discourses of Proverbs 1-9 or the probings of Job and Ecclesiastes. The dating of these calls for better criteria than a scheme of religious evolution.

But while it is illuminating to see how high a level of discussion existed from these early times, the Old Testament treatment of these themes remains distinctive. In the book of Job, God is recognizably the faithful, righteous Lord whose ways, while they are past finding out, are to be trusted to the end. Job does not have to conclude, like one of the Babylonian sufferers, that what is evil on earth may be counted good in heaven; nor is there any question of placating God with gifts; still less of throwing in one's hand and renouncing him. And in Ecclesiastes the apparent pessimism of the book has only a surface resemblance to the deep-dyed cynicism of the Babylonian Dialogue between Master and Servant, where nothing has meaning or value, and only caprice remains. Ecclesiastes does indeed reduce everything the world offers to a mere breath, but this is done precisely because man was made for something bigger than time and space: the fear of God, whose assessment of every deed and 'every secret thing' as good or evil invests the whole of life with meaning (Ecclesiastes 12:13-14).

That expression, the fear of God, to which Ecclesiastes moves as its conclusion, is the starting-point of Proverbs (1:7) and the pivot of all the Wisdom literature (see Job 28:28; Psalm 111:10; Proverbs 9:10). Secular philosophy tends to measure everything by man, and comes to doubt whether wisdom is to be found at all. But the Old Testament with this motto turns the world the right way up, with God at its head, his wisdom the creative and ordering principle that runs through every part; and man, disciplined and taught by that wisdom, finding life and fulfilment in his perfect will.

Old Testament 3.1

JOB

The book of Job stands alone amongst the books of the Old Testament. It forms a part of the 'Wisdom' material (Proverbs, Ecclesiastes; see 'Poetry and Wisdom Literature', Introduction), but in form and theme it is unique. No one knows who wrote it, or just when it was written, but the story is set in the days of the patriarchs. Job is a wealthy and influential sheikh – wealthy in terms of flocks and herds rather than cash. Part of the year he is a man of the city; for the rest, on the move with his cattle. He belongs to the days before the priesthood and organized religion or to a region where these things were not needed. He reminds us very much of Abraham: a man of the east.

A prose prologue introduces the great debate between Job and his friends which the author records in magnificent poetry. The subject is as old as the hills and as modern as the space-age. If God is just and good, why does he let innocent people suffer? (Why the casual victims of war and terrorism? Why the child dying of cancer?) As a man Job is *really* good: about the best any man could ever hope to be. Yet calamity overwhelms him. Loss of possessions and family is followed by grim, prolonged physical suffering that shakes his faith to the depths.

As they tussle with the problem, both Job and his friends are hampered by ignorance of the larger issue, the challenge of Satan related in the prologue. They have no assurance of a future life. For them death is the end. So justice must be seen to be done in this life. According to orthodox theology – the position championed by the three friends – prosperity was God's reward for good living, calamity his judgement on the sin of the individual. Generally speaking this held good. But the friends reduced a general truth to a rigid, invariable rule. If Job suffers, then he must be a wicked man. But Job knows this is untrue. So the argument goes back and forth, neither side shifting position, until they reach complete impasse, at which point God himself intervenes. He does not answer Job's questions. But, seeing God, Job is satisfied. If his friends' theology had been too narrow, his own concept of God had been too small.

The book leaves much unsettled. It is only in the New Testament that we approach an answer to the problem. As we look at Christ on the cross we see the suffering of the only really innocent Man. And we see a God who cares so much for us he is prepared to shoulder the whole burden of human sin and suffering. Yet the book of Job is not out-dated. Even today, suffering men and women find that this book speaks to their need as no other book in the Bible.

1 - 2 PROLOGUE

1:1-5: Job is introduced (see introduction).

1:6-12: in the court of heaven Satan accuses Job of serving God for what he can get out of it. God allows him to test this out – a measure of his confidence in Job – but Job himself is to be spared.

1:13-22: in the space of a single day Job loses everything –

Transition from wealth to poverty can be swift for any nomadic people. But Job's misfortunes were out of the ordinary.

possessions, servants, family – but his confidence in God remains unshaken (compare verse 21 with Paul's words in Philippians 4:11-12).

2:1-6: Satan has lost the first round. Now he says Job is only really concerned for his own skin. So God allows a further test, stopping short only at Job's life.

2:7-13: Job's body breaks out in running sores. The great man becomes an outcast. His wife fails him. The three friends who remain loyal sit in silence, appalled at what has happened. But still Job holds fast to God.

Uz (1:1): a town to the east of Palestine – in Edomite territory, or possibly in the Hauran, south of Damascus.

Sons of God (1:6): angels of God's court in heaven. Satan is among them, under God's authority.

Sabeans (1:15): nomads of south-west Arabia; *Chaldeans* (17): nomads from south Mesopotamia, Abraham's homeland.

Job's friends (2:11): wise men from towns in Arab and Edomite territory, a region renowned for its sages.

3 - 14 THE FIRST ROUND IN THE DEBATE

3 Job's first speech: the bitterness of life

Job's suffering makes him wish he had never been born. He longs to find peace and release in death.

Verse 8: Job refers to magicians who can make a day 'unlucky'. Leviathan may be the monster supposed to have been imprisoned by God at creation. In chapter 41 Leviathan is the crocodile.

Verse 24: sighs and groans are his daily diet.

4 - 5 Eliphaz' first speech

Job has often helped others in trouble; now he should be prepared to swallow his own medicine. God destroys the guilty, not the innocent (4:7). No one is blameless before him (17). Trouble is an inevitable part of life (5:7). The best course is to turn to God (8), accept his reproof (17), and wait to be restored to favour.

There is much in what Eliphaz says, but his diagnosis happens to be wrong in Job's case.

5:4: cases were tried and contracts made at the town gate; it was the hub of public life.

6 - 7 Job's reply

It is nauseating advice (6:6-7) to tell a man at the end of his tether to be patient (11-12). Job wants only to cease to be. His friends have failed to show sympathy when he needed it most (14ff.). He has done nothing to deserve suffering (30). Life is a succession of pain-filled days and sleepless nights (7:3-6).

7:11-21: Job turns to God and pours out his heart to him – his fear, his longing for death. Why won't God leave him alone? If sin is the trouble, why won't he forgive?

6:18-19: the caravans of traders crossing the desert come looking for water, and not finding it move on to die of thirst.

7:5: Job's sores breed maggots.

8 Bildad's first speech

Eliphaz had begun gently. Bildad takes a firmer line as Job's words grow wilder. God is just. He rewards the good and punishes the wicked. Bildad's words are salt to an open wound (4).

Papyrus (11): the reed which grew in the Egyptian marshes and from which paper was made.

9 - 10 Job's reply

Job believes as Bildad does in the justice of God. But his own case will not square with his belief. God has condemned an innocent man. How can anyone call him to account? Good, bad – it is all one (9:22). Disaster strikes both. Why (10:2)? The Creator has turned Destroyer (8). Will he allow no respite before life is over (20-22)?

Rahab (9:13): the legendary monster of chaos.

God as an unjust judge. Like many a man before and since, Job's basic problem was to get a hearing at all (19), and even if he got as far as the court he could not be sure of a fair hearing and impartial administration of the law.

11 Zophar's first speech

Zophar's words are harshest of all. Does Job think himself innocent? God is letting him down lightly (6). Job must put away his sin (13-14); then God will restore him.

12 - 14 Job's reply

Job is stung to sarcasm. His friends are not the only ones who can work things out. God is all-wise, all-powerful. If he turns the norms of wisdom and justice upside-down, what can anyone do about it (12:7-22)? Job's experience gives the lie to the arguments of his friends (13:1-4). He will put his case to God direct, and God will acquit him (18). What are the charges against him (23)? Life is short and there is no waking a man from the sleep of death (14:1-12). Job cries to God to hide him away in the land of the dead until his anger is past, and then to restore him (13-17). But despair floods back – what hope is there (19)?

15 - 21 THE SECOND ROUND

15 Eliphaz' second speech

The debate grows more heated. Job has needled his friends, and they make no allowances for the stress he is under. It never crosses their minds he may really be innocent. They go on doggedly defending their position and trying to bludgeon Job into submission.

Job is a self-opinionated old windbag (2)! All he has said – his wild accusations against God; his attempts to justify himself – merely serve to prove his guilt (6). Job is wrong in saying that the wicked get off scot-free. Their fate is a terrible one (17-35).

16 - 17 Job's reply

It is cold comfort his friends have to give. How easy for them to talk, when it is Job who bears the pain. (Like many since, their silent sympathy, 2:13, helped more than their well-meaning words.) God has worn him out with suffering and the cruelty of his fellow men. The pictures Job paints (16:9, 12-14) convey his intense, unbearable agony – a tortured body and a mind tormented at the thought that God could do all this to him. Even now he cannot believe God is unjust: there must be one who will plead his cause in heaven (19; see 1 John 2:1). If his case rests till he is dead, what hope is there (17:13-16)?

17:3: Job speaks to God.

18 Bildad's second speech

Bildad bitterly resents Job's angry rejection of their advice. He replies by painting a terrible picture of the fate of the wicked, meant to put Job in his place. But Job is innocent, and Bildad's tirade irrelevant.

19 Job's reply

Job's friends have become his tormentors, levelling false accusations and offering no answer to his desperate questions. He is shut in on himself (8), despairing (10), utterly alone (13-16). He has become an object of loathing to those he loves most (17). Even pity is denied him (21-22).

Yet even in his darkest moments, faith and hope still well up inside him. He is certain of vindication. One day God himself will take up his case and clear him – and he will be there to see it (25-27). Then those who have maligned him will find themselves answerable to God.

20 Zophar's second (and last) speech

Zophar takes up Bildad's theme: the fate of the wicked. Their prosperity is short-lived, their punishment certain. We hear no more from him after this: either he has nothing further to add, or a section of the third round of speeches has been lost. It is possible that 27:7-23, which sounds so strange coming from Job, belongs in fact to Zophar.

21 Job's reply

Zophar's theology is all very well, but it flies in the face of experience The condition of Job, the good man, is pitiful (5). Yet more often than not, evil men flourish, live happily and die peacefully (7-18). The friends will argue that God's vengeance falls on their children (19). But what kind of justice is that? Their so-called comfort is nothing but a pack of empty lies.

22 - 31 THE THIRD ROUND

22 Eliphaz speaks for the third and last time

It is still the same stubborn line of argument. Job is in the wrong – Eliphaz even lists out his sins (5-9)! Job had thought he could hide the fact from God (14). Let him return to God, put away his sin, and all will be well again.

Ophir (24): so famous for the export of gold (see 2 Chronicles 8:18) that 'Ophir' and 'fine gold' became synonymous. The location is unknown.

23 - 24 Job's reply

If only he could find God and put his case to him. But God is not to be found, and his ways are inexplicable.

'Mines where copper is smelted': in the mountains near the port of Eilat the ancient mines are being worked again today.

Chapter 24: look what goes on in the world. Life is neither fair nor just. God delays judgement, and those who trample the helpless underfoot seem to get away with it.
Remove landmarks (24:2): i.e. seize lands. The landmark was a stone sometimes inscribed with the land-owner's title-deeds and boundaries.
Take in pledge (24:3, 9): take as security for credit, or seize in payment of debt.

25 Bildad speaks for the third and last time

If the speech is complete as it stands, Job's friends have exhausted their argument. They have nothing more to say. Bildad merely reiterates the obvious truth that no man is 100 per cent perfect in God's sight. This does not help Job. What point is there in godly living if God's punishment falls equally on good and bad?

26 - 31 Job's last reply

Chapter 26: in the created universe we catch a glimpse of God's dynamic power. But who can think to comprehend that power in all its fullness?

Chapter 27: his friends want him to deny his integrity, but Job will not perjure himself. Verses 7-23 sound strange coming from Job. This has previously been the argument his friends have put forward. Either Job's thinking has changed, or this passage really belongs to one of the others (perhaps Zophar's missing third speech).

Chapter 28: Job's mind turns again (see 26:14) to the question of wisdom. This is the heart of his problem: how to understand the inscrutable ways of God. But no miner can uncover a vein of wisdom; all the wealth in the world will not buy it. Only God knows where to find it. And man becomes wise through reverence for God and by rejecting evil.

Chapter 29: Job looks back on the golden days of God's favour – past enjoyment of home, of success in business, of universal respect.

Chapter 30: 'But now': he returns to the bitter present, which has made him the butt of all, an outcast, incessantly gnawed by pain.

Chapter 31: all this has befallen a man who has avoided immorality, even in his thinking (1); who has played fair with his employees (13); been generous in relieving need (16); never become obsessed with money (24) or turned idolater (26-27); turned no one from his door (32); harboured no secret sins (33); never kept quiet for fear of what others might think or how they might react (34). Job is prepared to swear to all this before God. How many of us could honestly do the same?
Abaddon (26:6; 28:22): another word for 'Sheol', the shadowy land of the dead.
Rahab (26:12): see on 9:13.
Ophir (28:16): see on 22:24.

32-37 ELIHU'S TIRADE

Chapter 32: Elihu is the original angry young man. His elders are lost for words, but he is simply bursting with indignation at Job's attitude, dying to have his say.

Chapter 33: Job has declared himself the innocent victim of God (9-11); but God will not answer his charge (13). Elihu says God speaks to man through warning dreams (15) and through suffering (19) – in order to save, not destroy him (30).

Chapter 34: Job has said God is in the wrong (5-6), and there is nothing to be gained by making him our delight (9). But God is the judge of all men: supreme, just, impartial (10-30). Job has added to his other sins resentment and rebellion against God (36-37).

Chapter 35: Elihu (wrongly; see 2 Samuel 11:27; 12:13) sees good and bad conduct as a matter between men (8): God remains high above, untouched by either. People cry out to him in their need (9). But they are concerned for their own skins, not for him (10-12). This is why he does not answer (13).

Chapter 36: God is almighty, all-wise (5). He is a Teacher who uses suffering to open men's ears to listen and learn where they have gone wrong (8-10). Job should not be longing for death (20), but learning his lesson (22).

Chapter 37: God is great. He commands the thunder and lightning, rain and snow. He spreads out the clouds and the shining skies. Man is as nothing beside God's awesome splendour, his unassailable holiness. Men are right to fear him (24). He pays no attention to people (like Job!) who grow too big for their boots.

38 - 42:6 JOB FINDS SATISFACTION IN GOD'S ANSWER

God breaks in just when Elihu has finished his list of excellent reasons why Job cannot expect an answer! God *is* almighty, far and away above humanity. But he is also near. He hears, and he cares. Job had imagined himself putting his case to God, asking his questions. But imagination is not reality. It is God, not Job, who asks the questions now. And through the succession of searching questions Job finds his opinion of himself shrinking, his concept of God expanding. His mental image of God had been altogether too small. The God who confronts him is God on a different scale altogether.

Chapters 38 and 39: where was Job when God made the world, light and darkness, wind and rain, the constellations in their courses? What does Job know about the creatures of the wild – the lion, the goat, the wild ass and ox, the ostrich, the horse, the eagle? Did he make them? Can he feed them, tame them – *as God can?*

Chapters 40 and 41: is Job God's equal, that he calls him to book, and questions his justice? (Job's wild words had brought him dangerously near the sin of the first man.) Look at just two of my creatures, says God – Behemoth (the hippopotamus) and Leviathan (the crocodile). Look at their strength (40:16; 41:27); their sheer untameability (40:24; 41:1-2). Man is utterly powerless to control them. What folly then to claim equality with God who made them!

42:1-6 contains Job's reaction, the climax of the book. Job now realizes he had been dabbling in things beyond his understanding, totally out of his depth. Before, he had gone by hearsay; now he has seen God for himself, as he longed to do. There is now no question of putting his case; seeing God is enough. His questions remain unanswered, but he is satisfied. It is unthinkable that this God could ever let him down or act inconsistently. He can trust, where he does not understand. Now he can accept what comes. Self-righteousness melts away. Job regrets the bitter things he has said. As he looks at God and worships, he sees himself and his problem in perspective.

42:7-17 EPILOGUE

Verses 1-6 are the high point in the story. This final passage in prose merely rounds things off. Job has been vindicated, and this must be visibly demonstrated. (There is no promise of a fairy-tale ending to every case of suffering.)

God has taken Job to task for his reaction to suffering, but his integrity is beyond question. Job's good name is as clear as his conscience. It is the three friends who have been wrong. Job's was an honest search for truth. They would not allow for truth being bigger than their understanding of it – and so they were guilty of misrepresenting God. They must obtain Job's forgiveness before God will forgive them.

Significantly, it is at the point when Job has accepted his suffering and forgiven his friends, that God reverses his fortunes. Friends, prosperity, family are all restored to him, with a long life in which to enjoy them.

Old Testament 3.2

PSALMS

The psalms express the whole range of human feeling and experience, from dark depression to exuberant joy. They are rooted in particular circumstances, yet they are timeless, and so among the best-loved, most-read, parts of the Bible. In our modern age we are stirred by the same emotions, puzzled over the same fundamental problems of life, cry out in need, or worship, to the same God, as the psalmists of old. We find it easy to identify with them. And we find their sheer, dogged faith, the depth of their love for God, both a tonic and a rebuke.

Psalms, the Old Testament hymnal, is a collection of five books: 1 - 41, 42 - 72, 73 - 89, 90 - 106, 107 - 150. At the end of each section (e.g. 41:13) the break is marked by a 'doxology' (a formal ascription of praise to God), Psalm 150 forming a doxology to the whole collection. Within the five books the psalms are often grouped, according to common themes, a common purpose, or a common author/collector. Most of the psalms are prefaced by a title or heading (these are omitted in the New English Bible and the Jerusalem Bible) which is later than the psalm itself but preserves very ancient Jewish tradition. Some name the author or collector, and relate to specific events in history (those linked with David's life-story have already been listed). Seventy-three psalms bear David's name – some, no doubt, dedicated to him as king; some collected by him; and a good many, surely, the work of his own pen. (1 Samuel 16:17-23 and 1 Chronicles 25:1-8 are not the only indications that the king was a gifted poet and musician.) Many other titles concern the musicians, instruments, musical settings, or indicate the type of psalm ('Maskil', 'Miktam'), although the meaning of many of the terms used can now only be guessed at.

There have been many attempts to classify the psalms, and they can be grouped in a number of ways, for example by theme. There are psalms which plead with God and psalms which praise him; appeals for forgiveness, or the destruction of enemies; prayers for the king, or for the nation; 'wisdom' psalms and psalms which probe life's problem-areas; and psalms (such as 119) which celebrate the greatness of God's law. Many psalms are a blend of several of these common themes. All are part of the religious life of Israel.

Perhaps one of the most helpful ways of grouping the psalms is by the main literary types:

— Hymns, in praise of God's character and deeds (e.g. Psalms 8; 19; 29).
— Community laments, arising out of some national disaster (44; 74).
— Royal psalms, orginating in some special occasion in the life of the reigning king (2; 18; 20; 45).
— Individual laments (3; 7; 13; 25; 51).
— Individual thanksgivings (30; 32; 34).

It is very difficult to date individual psalms, or to discover just how and when they were collected and compiled, though the process began with David, if not before, and continued into the days after the exile. Manuscripts found at Qumran have shown that the whole collection as we have it must have been finalized some time before the Maccabean period (2nd century BC).

The words of C.S. Lewis underline one further important point:

'The psalms are poems, and poems intended to be sung: not doctrinal treatises, nor even sermons ... They must be read as poems if they are to be understood ... Otherwise we shall miss what is in them and think we see what is not.'

Before turning to the psalms themselves, read the introduction to the Poetry and Wisdom section, which explains the conventions of Hebrew poetry.

BOOK 1

Psalm 1 The blessing which results from the study and practice of God's law

Verses 1-3 depict the happy man, who resolutely turns his back on evil and sets his heart and mind on God's law. 4-6, in terrible contrast, picture the present life and future fate of the wicked.

Verse 3: compare the picture here with Jeremiah 17:7-8.

Psalm 2 Rebel man – sovereign God

Verses 1-3: the world-rulers enter into a futile conspiracy. 4-6 depict the power of God and his chosen man (primarily the king, ultimately the Christ, see note on Christ in the Psalms). 7-9: God delegates authority. 10-12: the psalm ends on a note of solemn warning.

Zion (6): the citadel of Jerusalem.

Psalm 3 A cry to God in time of danger

The title refers the psalm to the specific time of Absalom's rebellion against his father, King David, 2 Samuel 15.)

Verses 1-2 outline the situation. 3-6: in God, the God who answers, is security and freedom from fear. 7-8: the psalmist calls on God to save him.

Psalm 4 A prayer for the night

Trust in God sets mind and body at rest.

Verse 1: past answers to prayer give grounds for present confidence. 2-5: a reprimand is followed by command. 6-8 describe the joy and peace which nothing can shake.

Psalm 5 A prayer in the morning

Beset by men who lie and flatter

CHRIST IN THE PSALMS

The primary meaning of the psalms is always to be sought first of all in their immediate, historical context. But this does not exhaust their significance. No one can read the psalms without becoming aware that certain psalms and individual verses have a deeper, future significance beyond the simple meaning of the words. The Messiah is not mentioned by name, but his figure is foreshadowed, as later generations of Jews came to realize. And the New Testament writers are quick to apply these verses to Jesus as the prophesied Messiah.

Some psalms, particularly the 'royal psalms' (of which 2, 72, 110 are the most striking) picture an ideal divine king/priest/judge never fully realized in any actual king of Israel. Only the Messiah combines these roles in the endless, universal reign of peace and justice envisaged by the psalmists.

Other psalms depict human suffering in terms which seem far-fetched in relation to ordinary experience, but which proved an extraordinarily accurate description of the actual sufferings of Christ. Under God's inspiration, the psalmists chose words and pictures which were to take on a significance they can hardly have dreamed of. Psalm 22, the psalm Jesus quoted as he hung on the cross (verse 1, Matthew 27:46), is the most amazing example. Compare verse 16 with John 20:25; verse 18 with Mark 15:24. (See also Psalm 69:21 and Matthew 27:34, 48).

There are also many other verses in the psalms which New Testament writers apply to Jesus as the Christ:

Psalm 2:7, 'You are my son': Acts 13:33
Psalm 8:6, 'all things under his feet': Hebrews 2:6-10
Psalm 16:10, 'not give me up to Sheol ...': Acts 2:27; 13:35
Psalm 22:8, 'let him deliver him': Matthew 27:43
Psalm 40:7-8, 'I delight to do thy will': Hebrews 10:7
Psalm 41:9, 'my bosom friend ... has lifted his heel against me': John 13:18
Psalm 45:6, 'your divine throne endures for ever': Hebrews 1:8
Psalm 69:9, 'zeal for thy house has consumed me': John 2:17
Psalm 110:4, 'a priest for ever after the order of Melchizedek': Hebrews 7:17
Psalm 118:22, 'the stone which the builders rejected ...': Matthew 21:42
Psalm 118:26, 'blessed be he who enters in the name of the Lord': Matthew 21:9

while they plot his downfall (6, 8-10), the psalmist appeals to the God who loathes every semblance of evil (1-5), the Defence and Rewarder of the good (11-12). This is the God he will worship and serve (7).

Psalm 6 A cry of anguish

Sick at heart (disturbed in mind, ill in body), the psalmist pleads with God for his life (1-7), and is assured of God's answer (8-10).

Sheol (5): the shadowy world of the dead. Although the psalmists thought in terms of some kind of continued existence beyond the grave it was largely negative. Death cut a man off from all he could experience of God during his life. His tongue was still; he could no longer sing God's praises.

Psalm 7 A prayer for protection and the just judgement of God

The psalmist casts himself on God, knowing his cause is just (1-5). He calls on God to clear his name, to support the right and break the wicked (6-11). He describes the terrible fate awaiting those who refuse to repent (12-16) and closes on a note of thanksgiving.

Psalm 8 God – and man

Verses 2-4: as he contemplates the great expanse of the universe the psalmist is overwhelmed by a sense of man's littleness. He marvels that God not only bothers about man, but has set him over all other creatures (5-8). The psalm ends, as it began, with a refrain of praise to God (1,9)

Verses 4-6: see also Hebrews 2:6-9 and Genesis 1:28.

Psalm 9 A song of praise

One of a number of 'acrostic' psalms, in which the first letter of each verse follows the order of the 22-letter Hebrew alphabet. Only the first 11 letters (with one omission) are used here, and the acrostic seems to continue (imperfectly) in Psalm 10.

Verses 3-8 give the reason for the outburst of praise. God has executed justice and upheld the right. He is an unassailable fortress (9-10). Praise him (11)! Trouble is by no means over (13), but past experience gives ground for fresh hope (15-20). 'Thy kingdom come'!

Psalm 10 A prayer to God to defend the helpless

Verses 1-11: times are bad. Evil men defy God and disregard his laws and get away with it. The poor are their helpless victims. 12-18: the psalmist calls on God to act, confident that he will break oppression and defend those who have no one but himself to turn to.

Psalm 11 A declaration of faith

No matter what the danger, the man who trusts in God has no need to panic (1-3). He knows God is still sovereign: the champion of justice, the Judge of evil (4-7).

Psalm 12 A prayer for God's help

Surrounded by men whose word cannot be trusted (1-4), the psalmist puts his faith in the utterly dependable promises of God.

Psalm 13 From despair to hope

In his misery it seems to the psalmist that God has forgotten him. How much longer must he bear it? Will only death bring an end to it (1-4)? No! All his past experience assures him he will again have cause to thank God for his goodness (5-6).

Psalm 14 The folly of godless man

Society is corrupt: the bias to sin universal (1-3). In wilful blindness men pit themselves against a God who not only exists but punishes and avenges every aggressive act against his people (4-7).

Verses 1-3: Paul uses these verses to support his case that no human being is sinless when measured by God's standards (Romans 3).

Jacob ... Israel (7): the psalmist calls the nation by the two names of its founder. The wily Jacob was given the new name 'Israel' after his momentous encounter with God at Peniel (Genesis 32:28).

Psalm 15 Testimonial of the man of God

What does God require of the individual who seeks his company? He expects right conduct, right speaking (2-3a), right relationships with others (3b-4), and a right use of wealth (5). See also Psalm 24.

Who swears ... (4): i.e. who keeps his word whatever the cost.

Verse 5: one of the Jewish laws, see Leviticus 25:36-37. It was not a total ban on lending at interest, but applied to fellow Israelites.

Psalm 16 The way of faith

The man who sets his heart on God and puts his life in God's hands (1-6) finds joy and security for the present and need not worry about what lies ahead (7-11).

The lines (6): used to measure out the plot of land a man inherited.

Verse 10: the psalmist is probably thinking of premature or sudden death. Paul, applying the words to Christ, sees their deeper significance (Acts 13:35-37).

Psalm 17 Appeal to God from a clear conscience

This psalm raises two problems which occur in a number of other psalms: self-justification and vengeance. See note below.

Apple (8): the pupil; the part of the eye a man instinctively protects.

Psalm 18 Praise to God for deliverance

This is a revised version of David's victory song (2 Samuel 22). The outburst of love and praise (1-3), and the cataclysmic terms in which he describes God's rescue (7-19), give some idea of his previous desperation. He owes his life, his triumphs, his throne, everything to God (28-50).

Sheol (5): see on Psalm 6.

Verses 20-24: for the problem of self-justification see special article.

Psalm 19 God's wonderful creation; his perfect law

God's universe describes his glory in speech without words (1-4). The psalmist's thought leaps straight from the sun, with its all-pervading, searching rays, to the law of God – pure and clean, bringing joy and wisdom, instruction and enlightenment to man's heart (4b-11); and to his own need of protection and cleansing from sin (12-14).

Psalm 20 Prayer for victory for the king

A national prayer; the king himself speaks in verse 6.

Psalm 21 Thanksgiving for the king

Verses 1-7 rejoice in all God's goodness. Verses 8-12 look to the future. With God's help the king will put down all his enemies. King and people join to praise him (13).

Psalm 22 Suffering and salvation

It was the opening words of this psalm that Jesus used to express his anguish on the cross (Matthew 27:46). And the terms the psalmist chose to describe his own agony of mind and body became an extraordinarily precise description of the last hours of the Messiah. The psalmist only *felt* himself deserted by God (confidence returns, verse 22), but the separation Jesus experienced was real – the crushing, suffocating weight of human sin which shut him out from the Father's sight.

The shepherd leads his sheep to fresh pasture.

Despair at God's silence (1-2) and his own situation (6-8, 12-18) alternates with hope – hope that springs out of every recollection of God's past dealings with him (3-5, 9-11). The final prayer (19-21) brings new inward assurance, expressed in open praise (22-31). If, at the deepest level, the early verses of Psalm 22 speak of Christ's suffering, surely the closing verses speak of the worldwide deliverance he made possible.

Bulls of Bashan (12): Bashan, north of Gilead on the east of the Jordan, was famous cattle country.

Psalm 23 Sheep and Shepherd

This best-known, best-loved of all psalms pictures God, the Good Shepherd (see also John 10). He provides all that his people need. He leads them through life. He secures them from all harm (1-4). Verse 5 introduces a second picture: God, the perfect host, feasting his people with good things.

His name's sake (3): i.e. because this is his nature. God's love and care are wholly in keeping with his character.

Psalm 24 Worship

This psalm is a processional hymn, possibly written for that great occasion in David's life when the ark was first carried into Jerusalem (2 Samuel 6:12-15).

The whole world and everything in it is God's. Who then is worthy to stand in his presence (1-3)? The answer (4, and see Psalm 15) would lead to despair if God were not 'the God of Jacob' (6) – the twisted character God took up and made the founder of Israel. Verses 7-10: the ark is at the gates of the city: open the doors for God himself to enter!

Psalm 25 Prayer of a troubled man

An acrostic psalm (see on Psalm 9). The psalmist is harassed by the incessant attack of his enemies, and disquieted in his own conscience (1-3, 16-21). Deeply aware of his need, he turns to God for his help and leading, asking to experience again his love and forgiveness (4-15). What more reassuring verse for any of God's children than verse 10?

Psalm 26 Prayer of a good man

The psalmist is not claiming perfection but a consistent life of trust and obedience to God. Compare this self-portrait with the first part of Psalm 1.

Psalm 27 Trust and commitment to God

The man whose priorities are right (4,8) has nothing to fear (1-3, 5-6). He knows where to turn in trouble (7-12) and his hope is well founded (13-14).

Psalm 28 Prayer – and its answer

Danger leads to a cry for help, and a plea for the punishment of those evil men who are the source of the trouble (1-5). Prayer turns to praise at the assurance that God has heard and answered (6-9).

Psalm 29 The thunder of God

In the torrent of rain, the ear-splitting thunderclaps, the blaze of lightning, the roaring wind that sets the great forests in motion, the psalmist hears God's voice. For God made and orders them all (3-10). Let the hosts of heaven sing his glory (1-2) – and may he bless his people on earth (11).

The style of this psalm is very similar to ancient Canaanite poetry.

Sirion (6): 9,000 ft Mt Hermon, on the Israel/Lebanon border.

Kadesh (8): a place in the desert south of Beersheba.

Psalm 30 Thanksgiving for a new lease of life

(The events in 1 Chronicles 21 may possibly provide the background to this psalm.) The dark days when life was in danger are past (2-3, 6-10). Easy times bred self-reliance (6). But this experience has put life into perspective (5) and shown the psalmist his own helplessness (7-10). Now that the danger is behind him, he gladly and openly acknowledges his debt of gratitude to God (11-12).

A blind harpist, from Egypt. The psalms were part of the temple music. Many of their titles refer to musicians and instruments.

Psalm 31 Trial and trust

Verses 1-8: the psalmist turns to God for refuge (1-5); trust deepens as he recalls God's past dealings with him (6-8). 9-13: his mind returns to the painful present. 14-24: from his own trouble he turns to God again, with such renewed trust in his goodness and love that he is able to give encouragement to others (23-24).

Verse 5: with his dying breath Jesus echoed these words (Luke 23:46).

Psalm 32 Confession and the joy of God's forgiveness

Guilt suppressed becomes an intolerable burden (3-4). Confession and forgiveness bring a joyous lightness of heart (1-2, 5). Out of his own experience the psalmist encourages others to pray to God with confidence. (In verses 8-9 God himself speaks.)

Psalm 33 Everybody sing!

Tune up the instruments. Sing aloud in praise of God's character (4-5) and his great power (6-7). Stand in awe of him (8-9). Praise his sovereign rule in the affairs of men – his unfailing care for all who honour him (10-19). Sing a song of trust in him (21-22).

A new song (3): to surpass the best of the old. Every fresh experience of God calls forth new praise. John, in his vision, heard a new song in heaven (Revelation 5:9-10; 14:3).

Psalm 34 God's care for his people

An acrostic poem (see on Psalm 9). The title seems to refer to the incident in 1 Samuel 21:10 - 22:1, although the king's name there is Achish.

A man with such a story to tell of God's faithfulness cannot help sharing it. He owes it to God and his fellow believers (1-10). In the psalmist's experience, the man who honours God finds life (11-14). His misfortunes may be many, but God brings him through them all (19-22).

Psalm 35 A prayer to God to uphold the right

(For the ethical problems raised by the psalm see note on Self-justification, below.) Confident that right is on his side (he states his case in 7, 11-16, 19-25), the psalmist calls on God to pay back his enemies in their own coin (1-6, 17, 26) and clear his good name. Then he will praise God and tell others of his righteousness (9-10, 18, 28).

Psalm 36 The unfailing love of God

Verses 1-4 portray a man dedicated to his own evil ways. 5-10 contrast the character of God – loving, faithful, good; the source of life and light and all the good that man enjoys. 11-12: a personal prayer.

Psalm 37 Good and evil

An acrostic poem (see on Psalm 9) full of the proverbial sayings that the wisdom writers loved (see 'Poetry and Wisdom Literature', Introduction).

Wherever one looks, people are flagrantly disobeying God's law, and getting away with it. Don't be tempted to envy them, says the psalmist. Things are not what they seem (1-2, 7b-9). The wicked are in a far from enviable position. Their time will soon be up, but blessing and security await God's people (the message drummed home by the proverbial sayings of 10-40, which paint the contrast between the wicked and the good). Go on doing good; be patient; and trust God to act (3-7a).

Psalm 38 In great distress: a prayer for forgiveness

Sin has resulted in physical sickness (3, 5, 7), as well as mental anguish (2, 4, 6, 8). Friends and family stand aloof (11), and the opposition have the chance they have been waiting for (12, 16). The psalmist admits his sin, with bitter regret, and cries to God for help (21-22).

Psalm 39 Man's 'little life'

The psalmist struggles to contain his thoughts, for fear of dishonouring God, but they burst out (1-3). He feels death at his shoulder; life as insubstantial as a puff of wind (5-6). And he cries out to God to reassure (4) and forgive him (8), and to remove his troubles (10-13).

Psalm 40 Praise and prayer from a full heart

The psalmist has openly declared God's marvellous dealings with him (9-10). He looks back with deep thankfulness (1-3), and spells out for others the things he has learnt about God (4-8). But his troubles are not yet over (11-17). He is still conscious of his need. And he appeals afresh to God for his help. (Verses 13-17 are repeated in Psalm 70.)

Psalm 41 'Prayer of a sick and lonely man'

Verses 1-3 state a general truth. Happy the man who helps those in need; when trouble hits *him* he finds that God is at hand to help. 4-12 outline the psalmist's own case: his illness, his isolation, his reliance on God. Verse 13 is a formal stanza of praise to God, added to mark the end of the first book of psalms.

BOOK 2

Psalms 42 and 43 Longing for God

These two psalms share the same theme and the same refrain (42:5, 11; 43:5), and probably began as a single poem.

The psalmist is in exile in the north (42:6), surrounded by godless men who mock his faith (42:3, 10; 43:1-2). Deeply dispirited, he contrasts past joys (when he led the pilgrim throng to the sanctuary, 42:4) with the unhappy present. He is filled with longing for God's presence (42:2; 43:3-4). And, black as things are, faith and hope still break through (42:5, 11; 43:5).

Verse 6: the River Jordan rises near the foot of Mt Hermon on Israel's northern border. 'Mount Mizar' remains unidentified.

Psalm 44 National lament

This psalm is prompted by a disastrous defeat. Israel is bewildered. After all the stories of God's amazing actions in their early history (1-3), and their complete reliance on him (4-8, 17-18), now this defeat! God has deserted them (9-12). They are disgraced (13-16), and cannot understand why (17-22). Verses 23-26 are a real cry from the heart for God's help.

The switch to 'me' and 'my' in 4, 6, 15 may indicate a single voice (that of the king or high priest) leading the public prayer.

Verse 19: 'the place where jackals live', i.e. the desert.

Verse 22: Paul quotes these words, describing the experience of Christians (Romans 8:36).

Psalm 45 A royal wedding song

The actual occasion may have been the wedding of King Ahab of Israel to Jezebel, princess of Tyre (12, and see on 8 below). If so, the king's reign soon changed for the worse (1 Kings 16:29-33).

Verses 1-9: the poet's eloquent praise of the king's majesty and godly rule. 10-15: a word to the bride in all her finery. Verses 16 and 17 are addressed to the king.

Ivory palaces (8): a further possible link with Ahab. Archaeologists have discovered beautiful carved ivories in his palace at Samaria.

Ophir (9): see on 1 Kings 9:28.

Tyre (12): important sea-port and city-state; modern Sour in Lebanon.

Psalm 46 'A mighty fortress is our God'

This psalm – the one on which Luther based his famous hymn – may have been written following Sennacherib's attack on Jerusalem (2 Chronicles 32), some natural disaster, or in anticipation of the events heralding Messiah's coming. Verses 4-5 have a parallel in Revelation 22:1-5, where the ideal is perfectly realized. The psalmist glories in God's presence with his people (1, 4-5, 7, 11), and his real and unassailable protection.

Psalm 47 Shout and sing!

A psalm acclaiming God as Israel's King and Lord of the world. Let everyone rejoice and sing his praises.

Psalm 48 Zion, glorious city of God

An outburst of relief and joy at the city's reprieve from invasion (perhaps Sennacherib's, see 2 Chronicles 32).

The far north (2): Mt Zion in Jerusalem is in the south of Israel. The psalmist may have used this phrase because the north was the traditional seat of the gods.

Verse 7: New English Bible, 'like the ships of Tarshish when an east wind wrecks them'. For 'ships of Tarshish', see on 1 Kings 10:22.

Psalm 49 Meditation on life and death

A typical piece of 'wisdom' on life's inequalities. At the end of the line death waits for the materialist – not even he can buy himself off. The 'moral' is similar to that of Jesus' parable of the rich man (Luke 12:16-21).

Generally speaking the psalmists have no clear concept of life after death, and verse 15 is therefore often taken as a reference to premature death. But this undermines the reasoning, which requires an ironing out of this life's inequalities beyond the grave.

Psalm 50 God calls man to account

In verses 1-4 the summons comes. 7-15: God speaks in warning to his loyal people. It is not enough to go through the ritual motions. It is the thankful heart, not just the token thank-offering, that counts. 16-21: there are serious charges against those who mouth God's commands, yet disobey them; who take up with crooks but are prepared to ruin a member of their own family, leaving God out of account.

Psalm 51 Plea for forgiveness

The title links this psalm with Nathan's confrontation with David following his adultery with Bathsheba and the death of Uriah (2 Samuel 12). But verses 18-19 seem to be later, belonging to the time after Jerusalem fell to the Babylonians.

The psalm itself is profoundly moving. It lets us see right into the soul of a man who has loved God yet fallen into grievous sin. He has been made to see himself through God's eyes, and he is heart-broken. He makes no excuse, simply accepts God's judgement and admits his guilt. All he can do now – knowing God's love and mercy – is ask forgiveness and the chance of a fresh start.

Verse 5: the meaning is not that conception or childbirth are sinful in themselves, but that sin is ingrained from the very first moment of existence.

Hyssop (7): the herb used in the purification ritual described in Numbers 19.

Bloodguiltiness (14): this certainly fits David's case. He arranged for Uriah's death in order to cover up his own sin (2 Samuel 11).

Psalm 52 The doom of the wicked

Verses 1-4 describe man's guilt; verse 5 God's certain reprisal. 8 and 9 are a personal expression of trust and thanksgiving. The occasion of the psalm, according to the title, is Doeg's betrayal of David (1 Samuel 22).

Psalm 53

A revised version of Psalm 14, see above.

Psalm 54 Cry for help

According to the title, this is David's appeal to God after the Ziphites betrayed his position to Saul (1 Samuel 23:19ff.).

Psalm 55 Prayer of a man in trouble

The title attributes the psalm to David. The content fits in well with the time of Absalom's rebellion (2 Samuel 15-17), when Ahithophel, David's most trusted adviser, defaulted.

On top of all his other trouble (1-4, 9-11), a friend and fellow believer's treachery is the last straw (12-14, 20-21). The psalmist is full of conflicting emotions: fear and longing to opt out of the whole situation (4-8); and the desire to see his enemies worsted (9, 15). But trust eventually wins (16-18, 22) – for friends may be faithless, but not God.

Psalm 56 'In God I put my trust'

The psalmist has plenty to worry him and shake his nerve (1-2, 5-6). But he knows the answer to fear (3-4, 10-11). And he can safely and thankfully (12-13) leave God to deal with his enemies (7-9).

The title refers to the incident described in 1 Samuel 21:10-15.

Psalm 57 Prayer from among ferocious enemies

Circumstances may be black (4, 6), but the man who fills his mind with God can sing his praise, come what may (1-3, 5, 7-11). Traditionally the prayer belongs to the time when David was in hiding from Saul (1 Samuel 22:1; 24), but Paul and Silas also knew the truth of it (Acts 16:19-25).

Psalm 58 'There is a God who judges'

The psalmist calls down God's terrible judgement on corrupt and evil men in power. See note on cursing and vengeance in the Psalms.

Gods (1): a sarcastic reference to the rulers and judges.

Adder (4): 'deaf' because it does not respond to the snake-charmer.

Verse 8a: in popular belief, slugs and snails left slimy trails because they melted as they moved.

Psalm 59 Prayer for protection and punishment

The title links the psalm to the incident in 1 Samuel 19:11-17, echoed in the refrain 'Each evening they come back ...' (6, 14). The psalmist addresses his very personal prayer (1-4, 9-10, 16-17) to the Lord of all the nations (5,8,13).

Jacob (13): i.e. the nation of Israel.

Psalm 60 The nation in defeat

The title associates the psalm with the campaign recorded in 2 Samuel 8, when the faith of verse 12 and God's word in verse 8 were realized in eventual victory.

Verses 6-8: God's power over Israel – Shechem, in the heart of the country, between Mts Ebal and Gerizim; Succoth, a city east of the Jordan; Gilead, Israelite land east of the Jordan; Manasseh, Ephraim, Judah, the 'big three' of the twelve tribes – and over Israel's traditional enemies – the Moabites, east of the Dead Sea; Edomites, to the south-east; and Philistines, on the Mediterranean coast.

Psalm 61 Prayer of a burdened king

Precarious on his throne (2, 6-7), the king craves the safety and security only God can give (1-4).

Psalm 62 A psalm of longing and trust

Humbly, trustingly, the psalmist commits his cause to God. Man is bent on destruction (3-4), but what *is* he (9-10)? Power belongs to God, who wields it with love and justice (11-12).

Psalm 63 The thirsting heart

Having tasted the full joy and satisfaction of God's presence (2-8), who can bear to lose it (1)?

Verses 9-10: in sharp contrast to the

The people of Israel looked to God as all-powerful against the forces of evil. This relief illustrates the fears of the nations around. The Assyrian god Ninurta, armed with a thunderbolt, drives a demon from his temple.

SELF-JUSTIFICATION, CURSING AND VENGEANCE IN THE PSALMS

Christians reading the psalms are bound to come across two special problem areas. One is the self-justification of the psalmists. The other is their tendency to call down and spell out the most terrible vengeance. We cannot simply discard the offending passages. They are part of God's word, alongside passages no one would question. Nor will it do to excuse the psalmists on the grounds that they did not possess the teaching of Christ. Because they did possess the law. They knew as well as we do that no man is perfect by God's standards; and they were taught to behave in a loving way to others (Leviticus 19:17-18), even their enemies (Exodus 23:4-5). The law did not license retaliation, it set limits to it (an eye for an eye, *and no more*).

Self-justification. Two comments may help. First, the psalmist is claiming comparative, not absolute righteousness (i.e. in comparison with other people, not measured by God's standards). 'A good man may sin and yet be a good man.' There is all the difference in the world between those who endeavour to do right and those who deliberately set aside the common laws of God and society. David, in particular, was well aware of his shortcomings before God (see Psalms 51 and 19:11-13). Deep repentance features alongside self-justification in the psalms.

Second, the psalmist is very often picturing himself as 'the indignant plaintiff' putting his case before God the Judge. And, however much we dislike his self-righteous tone, from this point of view he is unquestionably 'in the right'.

Cursing and vengeance. Before we rush to condemn these passages as utterly 'unchristian', there are a few points worth bearing in mind.

The first concerns God's holiness. In emphasizing God's love we tend today to be over-sentimental about rank evil. But the psalmists knew God as One 'whose eyes are too pure to look upon evil', who cannot countenance wrongdoing. And this is what motivates their call for vengeance on the wicked. God's own character – his good name – demands it.

Second, the psalmists are realistic in recognizing that right *cannot* triumph without the actual overthrow of evil and punishment of wrong. We pray 'Thy kingdom come'. But we are often horrified when the psalmists spell out what this means – perhaps because we are less in love with good, less opposed to evil than they were; or because many of us have never known real persecution for our faith; or because we value life more than right.

However, if the psalmists are guilty of actually gloating over the fate of the wicked, if personal vindictiveness creeps in under the cloak of concern for God's good name, we are right to condemn it – and beware. We can ourselves so easily be guilty of the same thing. But in the psalmist's case the wrong thinking (if wrong thinking there is) never carries over into wrong action. There is no question of him taking the law into his own hands; no Inquisition. Vengeance is always seen as God's province, and his alone.

rest of the psalm. See note on vengeance.

Psalm 64 Prayer for protection

In verses 1-6 the psalmist pictures his trouble. In 7-9 he expresses his certainty that God will punish all who plot and scheme and slander. The punishment will fit the offence exactly (compare verse 7 with verses 3-4).

Psalm 65 Hymn of thanksgiving

All praise to God who hears and forgives (1-3), who blesses, satisfies and saves (4-5). Praise to God the Creator and Controller of the natural world (6-8). Praise to God who gives the harvest and makes the whole earth ring with joy (9-13).

Psalm 66 Praise and worship: national and individual

Praise God for national deliverance, from the earliest days (5-7) until now (8-12). And thank him for his love and care for every individual (13-20).

Psalm 67 Harvest

At the sight of God's blessing poured out on Israel every nation will sing his praise.

Psalm 68 Israel's song of triumph

A battle-march cum processional hymn, sung as the ark was carried into Jerusalem (2 Samuel 6), or at the ceremony commemorating that event (see the allusions in verses 1, 7, 17-18, 24-25). The psalm paints a series of vivid pictures of God's victorious power.

Verses 1-6, a tribute to God; 7-10 God leads the nation through the desert; 11-14, the conquest of the land; 15-18, God chooses Mt Zion in Jerusalem to be his home; 19-23, salvation to Israel – death to the enemy; 24-27, the procession; 28-31, may God make a show of his strength to subdue the nations; 32-35, let everyone sing the power and majesty of Israel's God!

Verses 14-15, 22: 'Bashan' is the Golan Heights area, north-east of the Sea of Galilee. In the wide sense the region stretched as far as Mt Hermon, which may be the mountain referred to here. 'Zalmon' is probably another of the mountains in this region.

Psalm 69 Prayer of a man overwhelmed by suffering

A psalm often quoted in the New Testament (John 2:17; 15:25; Romans 15:3). The psalmist's picture in verses 2, 14-15 could be taken for an actual description of Jeremiah's case (Jeremiah 38:6). Verse 35 seems to pinpoint a time following the wholesale destruction of Judean cities, but before the fall of Jerusalem itself.

The psalmist is in desperate trouble, through no fault of his own. His suffering is borne for God's sake (1-12). He prays that God, in his love, will rescue him (13-18). The guilt of his tormentors is clear (19-21): may they be punished for all they have done (22-28). May God set him free to praise him; let the whole earth ring with praise at the restoration of God's people (29-36).

Psalm 70 An urgent call for help

These verses also appear at the end of Psalm 40.

Psalm 71 A prayer in old age

At the end of a long and troubled life (9, 20) there is still no let-up (4, 10-11). But trouble has schooled the psalmist in trust (6-7). Nothing can make him despair. As long as God is with him (9, 12, 18), the future is full of hope (14-16, 19-24).

Psalm 72 Prayer for the king

This last psalm in Book 2 is a fitting one for Solomon's reign (see title) – Israel's golden age of peace, prosperity and power. But it also looks beyond it to the perfect ideal: an endless reign (5) over the entire world (8, 11); a rule of God-like justice and righteousness (7, 12-14); a time of unequalled fruitfulness (16).

The River (8): Euphrates.

Tarshish, Sheba (10): meaning 'the remotest outposts of empire'. Sheba may be a region in Arabia. Tarshish is probably Tartessus in Spain.

Like Lebanon (16): for a small country Lebanon produces an amazing abundance and variety of fruit and vegetables.

BOOK 3

Psalm 73 This unjust world

How is it that those who flout God's laws prosper, and trouble falls on those who least deserve it (3b-14)? It is enough to make a good man envious and bitter (3, 21), and tempt him to say things better left unsaid (15). Only as he turns to God does he learn to see beyond appearances (16, 17). In reality, God's people have

The psalmists cry out for judgement. God's people suffered cruel atrocities at the hands of enemies like this Assyrian soldier who holds a decapitated head.

everything that matters (1, 23-26, 28). The wicked – for all their wealth – are destined for destruction (17-20, 27).

Psalm 74 Lament for the destruction of the temple

God has turned against his people (1-2). The temple has been desecrated and destroyed (3-8). How long will the anti-God enemy remain master (9-11)? The psalmist thinks of the power of his God (12-17) and pleads with him to keep his promise to Israel (19-20) and sweep the blasphemous enemy away (18, 22-23).

Verses 13-15: a description of the deliverance from Egypt, pictured first as a dragon, then as Leviathan, the crocodile of the Nile.

Psalm 75 God is Judge

Israel rejoices in God's sovereign justice. He alone has power to judge all men.

Verses 2-5: God is speaking.

Verse 5: a picture of arrogant power.

Psalm 76 A song of deliverance

Israel marvels at the terrible glory of the God who overthrows all the might of the enemy.

Salem, Zion (2): Jerusalem.

Psalm 77 Past and present

The psalmist calls to mind all God's great deeds on behalf of his people (11-20). But now he seems no longer to care for them (5-10), and there is no comfort in the present troubles (1-4).

Verses 2-6: the trouble which sets the psalmist thinking may be a personal, or a national, crisis.

Psalm 78 Lessons from Israel's history

For a long time Ephraim was the most powerful of the twelve tribes. Joshua was an Ephraimite, and the tribe had great prestige under the judges (Judges 8:2; 12). But with David's accession Judah took the lead. The psalmist thinks over the reasons for Ephraim's rejection, and finds them in Israel's history.

God gave Israel the law to remind them of him (5-8). But Ephraim disobeyed (9-11). They forgot what had happened in Egypt and the desert – the miracles (13-16, 23-29, 44-53), the rebellions and the punishments (17-22, 30-43). They forgot the pattern that repeated itself after the conquest of the land (54-66). And God chose Judah instead – a city of Judah (Jerusalem) as capital and a man of Judah (David) to be king (67-72).

Verse 9: this seems to be a reference to the defeat of Saul and Israel on Mt Gilboa (1 Samuel 31:1).

Zoan (12): an ancient capital of Egypt.

Verses 13-16: see Exodus 14 and 17.

Verses 24-31: see Exodus 16; Numbers 11.

Verses 44-51: see Exodus 7-12.

Ham (51): one of Noah's three sons, ancestor of the Egyptian people.

Shiloh (60): for a long time the principal sanctuary in Israel – presumably destroyed when the ark was captured by the Philistines (1 Samuel 4).

Psalm 79 Jerusalem in ruins

A lament for the destruction and bloodshed of the fall of Jerusalem (1-4; the city fell to Babylon in 587 BC, see 2 Kings 25:8ff.). The people call on God to forgive and help them (5, 8-10a, 11), and to destroy the pagan enemy (6-7, 10b, 12).

Psalm 80 A prayer for the restoration of Israel

The time may be after the exile of the northern kingdom of Israel (2 Kings 17) but before the fall of Jerusalem (2 Kings 25). (The psalmist mentions two northern tribes, and Benjamin, but not Judah in the south.)

Israel is pictured as a great vine planted by God (8-16), stretching out to the mountains and cedars of Lebanon in the north (10), west to the Mediterranean and east to the River Euphrates (11).

Walls (12): i.e. the walls enclosing and protecting the vineyard.

Verse 17: the name 'Benjamin' means 'son of the right hand'.

Psalm 81 God's message at harvest

Verses 1-5: the people are summoned to celebrate the Feast of Tabernacles. God reminds his people of all he has done for them (6-7) and all he longs to give (10, 14-16). Yet in obstinate disobedience they refuse him and choose trouble (8-9, 11-13).

A voice I had not known (5): a puzzling statement, unless it refers back to the time before Moses' day (see Exodus 6:3).

Verse 6: a description of Israel's slave-labour in Egypt.

Meribah (7): see Exodus 17:1-7.

Psalm 82 The justice of God

There is corruption and injustice in the law-courts: God calls the judges to account.

The gods (1): probably meaning those men who exercise God's right of judgement over others.

Psalm 83 Prayer for help

The nation is in grave danger from an alliance of all the old enemies, plus powerful Assyria (2-8). The people call on God's aid, remembering past victories (9-18).

Children of Lot (8): Lot fathered Moab and Ammon (see Genesis 19:36-38).

Verses 9-12: see Judges 4 and 5. Oreb and Zeeb, Zebah and Zalmunna, were Midianite princes put to death by Gideon (Judges 7 and 8).

Psalm 84 A pilgrim's song

He comes with a heart singing for joy at the prospect of worshipping God in his temple. The happiest people in the world – it seems to him – are those who can be there always (4, 10).

Baca (6): possibly an actual valley the pilgrim passes on his way to Jerusalem. But New English Bible 'the thirsty valley' gives the sense.

Psalm 85 Thanksgiving and a prayer

Praise for God's forgiveness in the past (1-3) and prayer for restoration in the present (4-7). All he knows and has experienced of God's love and faithfulness fills the psalmist with optimism (8-13). What God has yet to give will far exceed his past goodness.

Psalm 86 Prayer of a man in trouble

Because he knows God – and all his love and goodness (5, 7, 13, 15) and power (8-10) – he can be confident in putting his case (1-4, 6-7, 14), and trust God for the answer.

Poor and needy (1): a 'bankrupt', not financially, but before God.

Psalm 87 Zion; city of God, mother of nations

A prophecy of the holy city's glorious future: a capital whose citizenship includes even former enemies (4). The Old Testament sees this largely in material and geographical terms, the New in spiritual (Revelation 21:1 - 22:5).

Rahab (4): a poetic synonym for Egypt.

Psalm 88 Cry of a desperate man

This is the darkest of all the psalms. Here is a man who feels life ebbing away (3-9a), and he has no hope beyond death (10-12). There is no one to turn to but God, who is crushing him with trouble (7-8, 13-18). He is in the grip of the blackest depression. Yet faith lives on – how else can one account for his persistent cry to God?

Sheol, the Pit, Abaddon (3, 4, 11): all meaning the shadow-land of the dead.

Psalm 89 A hymn and prayer

The psalmist sings the story of God's faithful love to Israel; his covenant and promise to the line of David (1-37). But now, in a very different present, God is angry with his people; the covenant is broken. Where is his 'steadfast love of old' (38-51)?

Rahab (10): see on Psalm 87.

Tabor and Hermon (12): Tabor, the rounded hump of mountain near Nazareth from which Deborah and Barak swept down to victory (Judges 4 - 5); Hermon, the 9,000 ft peak on the border with Lebanon.

Verse 52: the 'doxology' (see Introduction) added to mark the end of Book 3.

BOOK 4

Psalm 90 A short life and a hard one

The title links this psalm with Moses, who must often have felt like this in the long years of desert wandering. Ecclesiastes also shares the psalmist's mood.

The everlasting God (1-4) – and man, as transient as a blade of grass (5-6). His span of life is short, yet even this must be worked out under God's judgement (7-10). The psalmist appeals to God's pity as he begs for the return of joy and gladness (13-17).

Psalm 91 Trust God and rest secure

In this psalm the voice of encouragement (1-13) and the voice of God (14-16) speak to the man of faith. Under God's protection nothing can touch him – neither man nor beast, by day or by night; not war, nor disease. (This is not to say his life will be all roses, or verse 15 would have no meaning.)

Verses 11-12: the devil quoted these verses to tempt Jesus (Luke 4:9-12). But Christ had no need to test the truth of God's word, neither had he come into the world to take the soft option.

Psalm 92 'A song for the sabbath'

A joyous thanksgiving in music and song for all that God has done (5-9); his goodness to each individual, and to all his people (10-15).

Psalm 93 'The Lord reigns'

– eternal, almighty; his laws and his holiness unchanging.

Psalm 94 God's justice

The starting-point is the wicked – how fully they deserve God's judgement; their stupid lack of understanding (1-11). But as he thinks of God, though the thought of vengeance is never far away, the psalmist moves on to all the help and love and blessing God pours out upon his afflicted people (12-22).

Psalms 95-100 are a group of psalms written in exultant praise of the God who reigns over all his creation.

Psalm 95

Let us praise and worship God our Maker (1-7a), remembering that he expects obedience (7b-11).
Verse 8: see Exodus 17:1-7.

Psalm 96

A song of God's salvation, of his greatness and his glory. A song of universal joy at his coming in judgement.

Psalm 97

In praise of God – supreme, triumphant; the Saviour and delight of all who hate evil.

Psalm 98

A song to God the Victor. He comes to rule his kingdom. Let the whole world go wild with joy.

Psalm 99

God the King, the Holy One, is on his throne; God who forgives and disciplines his people, from the least to the greatest.

Psalm 100

'The Lord is God; 'the Lord is good'. Let the whole earth sing and be glad.
His gates, his courts (4): i.e. the temple.

Psalm 101 The king's manifesto

The king pledges himself to root out evil from private and public life and to reward integrity.
House (2): household and court.
Verse 8: most probably a reference to his daily administration of justice in Jerusalem.

Psalm 102 The cry of man on the rack

Verses 1-11 describe his suffering: ill in body, sick at heart, taunted by enemies, cast off by God. His life is slipping away (11), but God is not subject to time (24, 27). He is Sovereign for ever (12). Surely he will pity his city and free his people (13-22). Surely he will answer the psalmist's prayer (23-28).

Psalm 103 The love and mercy of God

A psalm of humble, heartfelt gratitude to God for all his goodness, but above all for his mercy and his unchanging, unchangeable love. What he has done for one (1-5), he does for all (6-18): so let everyone, everywhere praise him.

Psalm 104 To God the great Creator

The psalmist marvels at the grandeur and the detail, the perfection and completeness of God's work in creation (1-24 – verse 24 sums it all up). Earth and sea (25-26), with everything in them, are his work, and depend entirely upon him (27-30). The train of thought leads into a song of praise (31-35).
Badgers (18): probably the Syrian rock hyrax, a shy little animal about the size of a rabbit, which lives among the rocks.
Leviathan (26): usually the crocodile (see Job 41), but here used more generally of large sea-creatures.

Psalm 105 Praise to God for his covenant with Israel

The call to praise (1-11) is followed by a history of how God chose Israel and gave them the land (12-45): the patriarchs (12-15); Joseph's story (16-23; Genesis 37-46); the deliverance from Egypt (23-38; Exodus 1-12); God's provision in the desert (39-42; Exodus 16-17) and the possession of Canaan (43-45).

Psalm 106 Israel's disobedience

The psalm begins with praise (1-5), but from verse 6 on becomes a confession of the nation's sin, from the very beginning to the psalmist's own day.
Verse 7: the first instance of rebellion, see Exodus 14:10ff.
Wanton craving (14): for the good food of Egypt. God gave them meat but punished them with a plague (Numbers 11).
Verses 16-18: see Numbers 16.
A calf in Horeb (19): Horeb=Mt Sinai. While Moses was in the mountain receiving God's instructions, the people made a golden calf to worship after Egyptian custom (Exodus 32).
Land of Ham (22): see on Psalm 78.
Baal of Peor (28): the people turned to idol worship and laid themselves open to God's judgement (Numbers 25).
Meribah (32): see Numbers 20:2-13.
Did not destroy ... but mingled (34-35): Judges 1 and 2 summarize this part of Israel's history. From that time on (40-46) the story became a repetitive pattern of rebellion against God, followed by enemy occupation, followed by repentance, followed by freedom, followed by further rejection of God.
Verse 48: the 'doxology' which closes the fourth book of psalms.

BOOK 5

Psalm 107 In praise of God the Redeemer

A single theme (man is beset by troubles of his own choosing or making, but God rescues him from them all) is spelt out in four word-pictures (the traveller, 4-9; the captive, 10-16; the sick man, 17-22; the sailor, 23-32). Circumstances differ for each individual, but all share the same experience: as they cry out to God in their need, he hears and answers. All have equal cause to praise him. Verses 33-43 describe God's unchanging love in dealing with his people.

Psalm 108 A hymn to God

The psalm combines extracts from Psalm 57:7-11, and Psalm 60:5-12.
Verses 7-13: see on Psalm 60.

Psalm 109 A cry for vengeance; a call for help

People the psalmist has loved and treated well have returned evil for good. They have no excuse for the attack which has reduced him to a shadow (1-4; 22-25). His bitterness is understandable, but the tirade of 6-20 seems to overstep the mark. See note on cursing and vengeance in the Psalms.

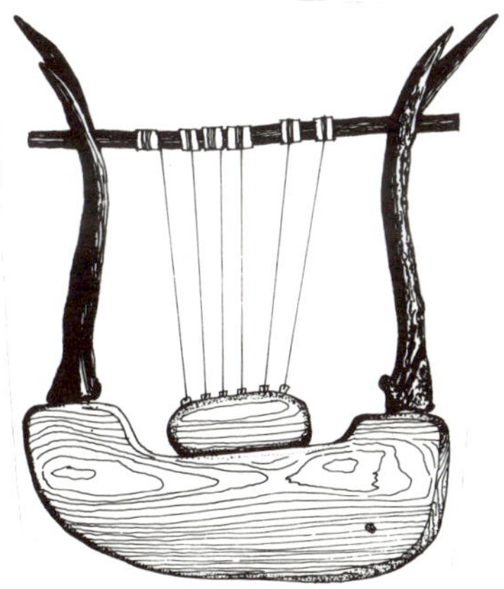

An ancient harp, the 'nevel', reconstructed here in the Music Museum at Haifa, Israel.

Psalm 110 'King and priest for ever'

This psalm speaks of the ideal, fully realized only in Christ, as the New Testament writers make plain (Matthew 22:41-46; Luke 22:69; Hebrews 5:8-10; 10:12-13). See 'Christ in the Psalms'.
Melchizedek (4): the mysterious priest-king to whom Abraham gave a tenth of his possessions (see Genesis 14:17-20).

Psalm 111 In praise of God

This psalm is identical in form with Psalm 112. Both consist of 22 phrases each beginning with a successive letter of the Hebrew alphabet.

The psalmist rejoices in God's greatness; his faithfulness and justice; his integrity and trustworthiness; his provision and his redemption. Respect for God is the true starting-point of all human wisdom.

Psalm 112 Happy the man who respects and obeys God

For the form, see on Psalm 111 above.

The man who obeys God and cares for his fellow men is sure of reward. He can withstand life's knocks, secure and unafraid.
Verses 2-3: the psalmist describes the reward in material terms because in his day there was no clear concept of the afterlife. What he says is *generally* (but not invariably) true. God's people have their full share of trouble, but are given resources to meet it (7-8).

Psalms 113-118 are a group of psalms linked traditionally with the Jewish feasts of Tabernacles (Harvest) and Passover. In Jewish homes Psalms 113 and 114 are sung before the Passover meal; Psalms 115-118 after it (see Matthew 26:30).

Psalm 113 Our incomparable God

He is above and beyond his creation, yet closely concerned for the humblest of his people.
Ash heap/dunghill (7): the rubbish dump, the place for outcasts (see Job 2:8).

Psalm 114 Passover hymn: God present with his people

The nation recalls God's marvels on their behalf at the time of the exodus.
Verses 3,5: the reference is to the crossing of the Red Sea (see on Exodus 14) and the later crossing of Jordan (Joshua 3).
Verse 8: see Exodus 17:1-6.

Psalm 115 The living God: lifeless idols

A psalm which gives an indication of the way many psalms must have been sung – with a single voice leading and the congregation joining in the response (9-11, etc.).
House of Aaron (12): i.e. the priests.
Verse 17: meaning that praise is for

the living: death stills all tongues.

Psalm 116 Hymn of thanks

A psalm for the individual as he comes to make his thank-offering in the temple. God has heard his prayer and brought him through dark days. Now he pours out his heart in gratitude.

Cup of salvation (13): this is vivid picture-language. God gave him back his life; now he offers it up to God in thanks.

Psalm 117 Call to praise

Psalm 118 A hymn for the Feast of Tabernacles

The hymn was sung in procession by king, priests and people. As they approach the temple, the king recalls God's victory for his people (1-18).

Verses 19-27: the procession, carrying branches, moves from the gateway to the altar.

Verse 22: the despised nation of Israel has become the great power. By Jesus' day Israel, in turn, had forfeited her privileged position (Matthew 21:42-43).

Psalm 119 In praise of the word of God

This is the longest psalm of all – and the most formal and elaborate in concept. There are 22 eight-verse sections. Each section begins with a successive letter of the Hebrew alphabet, and each verse within the section begins with the same letter. Within this stylized pattern the psalmist makes a series of individual, though not isolated or disconnected, statements about the 'law' (God's teaching) and the individual – interspersed with frequent prayers. He uses ten different words to describe it: God's law, his testimonies (instruction), precepts, statutes, commandments, ordinances (decrees), word, ways (paths), promises and judgements (rulings). And one or other of these descriptions occurs in all but a very few verses. He seems to have taken the same delight in the discipline set by this complex poetic form, as he did in the study of the law itself. In the psalm we see how eagerly and persistently he applies himself to the task of understanding the law. He learns it by heart. He longs for more. Nothing is allowed to deflect him from it. God's word rules his life and conduct, gives him hope and peace, leads him into life. His confidence in it is unbounded, and to see it broken genuinely distresses him. We possess far more of God's word than the psalmist did. But his love and regard for it often puts us to shame.

Psalms 120-134 (the 'Songs of Ascents') are a collection of songs thought to have been sung by pilgrims on their way to Jerusalem to celebrate the three great annual feasts. In many of them the thought and imagery focusses on the holy city.

Psalm 120 The whiplash of wagging tongues

The psalms are full of references to the sins of the tongue – lies, scandal, slander, hypocrisy. The man of God may suffer as much from what people say as from what they do.

Verse 5: a poetic way of saying he is living among barbarians!

Psalm 121 God, the Guardian

The man who trusts God knows where to turn in trouble. With God to guard him he can come to no harm.

The hills (1): perhaps those on which Jerusalem stands.

Psalm 122 Jerusalem, city of God

The pilgrim prays for the peace of the city, the centre of worship and seat of government for the whole nation.

Psalm 123 Plea for mercy Psalm 124 God, the Rescuer

Without God's help the nation could not have survived the onslaught of their enemies. The credit is his alone. (How many times this has been true in Israel's history!)

Psalm 125 Secure in God

Those who trust in God enjoy complete security. But let the wicked be warned.

Psalm 126 Laughter and tears

A psalm often associated with the return from exile and the hardships that followed. Verses 1-3 express the people's exuberant joy at God's blessing; verses 4-6 the need to experience this yet again (or a prayer for the restoration of the nation as a whole).

Verse 4: for most of the year the riverbeds in the southern desert (Negev) are dry, but when the rain comes the water rushes down them in torrents.

Psalm 127 The futility of human effort without God

Verse 5: disputes and business deals were settled at the city gate. Here the grown-up sons support their father in maintaining the family's interests.

Psalm 128 Blessings of the man who respects and obeys God

The psalmist's picture describes everything the man of his own day asked of life. But see also on Psalm 112:2-3.

Verse 3: the vine and the olive are symbols of peace and plenty – the fullness of God's blessing.

Psalm 129 A prayer for the downfall of all who have crushed God's people

Verses 5-8: see note on cursing and vengeance in the Psalms.

Psalm 130 Praying, waiting, hoping for God's redemption

Psalm 131 A psalm of simple trust

Psalm 132 In commemoration of the day the ark was brought to Jerusalem

Verses 1-10: see 2 Samuel 6:12-15; 11-12: God's promise of a royal dynasty (see 2 Samuel 7:11-16); 13-18: Jerusalem is chosen as the religious centre of Israel.

Ephrathah (6): Bethlehem, David's birth-place.

Jaar (6): an abbreviation for Kiriath-jearim, where the ark was kept for 20 years following its return by the Philistines.

Psalm 133 The family-unity of God's people

Verse 2: at the high point in his consecration ceremony the high priest was anointed with oil (Exodus 29:7).

Verse 3: the dew is seen as a symbol of blessing. Mt Hermon has an exceptionally heavy dewfall, which meant greater fertility there than elsewhere in the days before piped water and mechanical sprinklers.

Psalm 134 A psalm for those on night-watch in the temple

Psalm 135 Hymn of praise for public worship

This psalm echoes many earlier ones. God is to be praised for choosing Israel (1-4), for his greatness (5-7, 15-18) and his mighty works (8-14). Let priests and people sing his praise (19-21).

Sihon ... Og (11): see Numbers 21.

Psalm 136 The 'Great Praise' (Hallel)

The description of God's great works in creation (4-9) and history (10-24) alternate with the people's refrain to God's unchanging, timeless love.

Verse 13: see Exodus 14.

Verses 19-20: see Numbers 21.

Psalm 137 Lament of the exiles in Babylon

The old joyful songs stick in the exiles' throats at the memory of the terrible destruction of their city and temple. Instead they cry out for the punishment of the barbarian invaders.

Edomites (7): descendants of Esau and therefore closely related to Israel, but centuries-old hostility divided the two. The Edomites gloated at the news of Jerusalem's ruin (Obadiah 8-14).

Verse 9: see the note on cursing and vengeance in the Psalms. The Israelites had no doubt witnessed just such atrocities committed in Jerusalem by the Babylonian army (8).

Psalm 138 A song of thanks

God has answered prayer. Once again he has shown his faithful love. He is great and high, yet he cares for insignificant men and women. The psalmist has a continuing story to tell of God's protective care for individuals.

Psalm 139 The God who is there

The psalm is concerned with God's all-knowingness and 'everywhere-presentness', not in an abstract, but

These Egyptian musicians wear disks of perfume which melt and 'drip' down their cheeks; from the Tomb of Nebamun, Thebes, about 1400 BC.

in a highly personal way. God is all-knowing: he knows *me* through and through, even my thoughts. He has known me from before the day I was born (1-6, 13-16). God is present everywhere: wherever *I* go, he is there. He is always with me (7-12, 18b). I will align myself with him in the fight against evil. Let him search out and deal with all that is wrong in me (19-24)

Psalm 140 Prayer for help

The psalmist is in real trouble from the plotting of violent men, and from their venomous tongues. He prays that God will guard him (1-8) and punish them (9-11), in the confident knowledge that God is for the right and implacably opposed to evil (12-13).

Verses 9-11: see the note on cursing and vengeance in the Psalms.

Psalm 141 A prayer for right reactions

The pull of evil is a force to be reckoned with. The psalmist asks that God will keep him from the very things he condemns in others, in thought and word and action.

Psalm 142 Prayer of a man alone and in trouble

The title links this psalm with the time when David was on the run and in hiding from Saul (1 Samuel 23:19ff.). He cries to the One who knows all about him: the Lord, his refuge.

Psalm 143 Prayer for God's help

The psalmist has reached the end of the line: no more reserve or resources (3-4). But in a desperate situation one refuge remains: God himself (5-12). 'O Lord ... teach me ... deliver me ... lead me ... bring me out of trouble.'

Psalm 144 A song for the God of victory

What is man that the great God should spare him so much as a passing thought (1-4)? Yet time and again God comes to the rescue (5-11). The song closes with a prayer for peace and prosperity for the future generation (12-15).

Psalms 145-150 are a group of psalms in praise of God, probably intended for public worship. They are used by Jews today in daily prayer. Psalms 146-150 each begin and end with an Alleluia – 'O praise the Lord'!

Psalm 145 'Great is the Lord'

An acrostic (see on Psalm 9). One letter, missing from the Hebrew text, has been taken into the English versions from the Greek Septuagint as 13b.

Praise is poured out to God for his greatness and power (1-7, 10-13a), and for his character: loving, forgiving, good and faithful, just and kind, satisfying the needs of his creation (8-9, 13b-21).

Psalm 146 Praise from the individual

The focus is on God, the hope and help of his people, utterly dependable, caring for all in need.

Psalm 147 Praise from the nation

God commands the universe (4), the seasons (8), the nations (14), the elements (16-18), with a power that puts him utterly above and beyond mankind. Yet his heart goes out to individuals; all who are hurt and unhappy (2-3). He takes pleasure in those who love and respect him (11). And he gives his people his word to live by (19). Praise the Lord!

Psalm 148 Universal praise

Everything that is owes praise to the Creator: the angels in heaven; sun, moon and stars; nature; the deep; every creature on earth and all mankind.

Waters above the heavens (4): i.e. the rain.

Horn (14): symbol of power. New English Bible 'he has exalted his people in the pride of power' gives the sense.

Psalm 149 The song of God's faithful people

His people rejoice in the victory God has given, and exult at the judgement of the opposing nations.

A new song (1): see on Psalm 33.

Two-edged swords (6): in the New Testament the two-edged sword is a metaphor for the word of God (Hebrews 4:12; Revelation 1:16).

Vengeance (6b-9): see note above. Victory for the downtrodden *must* entail defeat for the forces of oppression.

Psalm 150 Choral symphony of praise

This is the grand climax and finale to the whole collection of Psalms. Every instrument in the orchestra, everything with life and breath in the whole creation, joins in a mighty crashing paean of praise to God.

Old Testament 3.3

PROVERBS

Proverbs is a book of wise sayings: not simply an anthology, but an oriental textbook, schooling young men in wise and right living by the repetition of wise thoughts. It is wisdom distilled into short, sharp phrases, dramatic contrasts, and unforgettable scenes from life. It sets out what is right and what is wrong (not just a slick formula for success), because 'wisdom' in Proverbs is based on reverence for God and obedience to his laws. The 'fear of the Lord' is the essence of all true human wisdom. This is the starting-point. Proverbs applies the principles of God's teaching to the whole of life, to relationships, home, work, justice, decisions, attitudes, reactions, everything man does and says, and even thinks. God has taught what is best for man. Experience proves it.

The book divides into eight main sections: a general introduction on wisdom (chapters 1 - 9); six collections of sayings (10:1 - 31:9); and an acrostic poem on the perfect wife (31:10-31). For details see below.

It is now fairly generally agreed that in content the proverbs belong to the days of Israel's first kings, although editing continued for some centuries. King Hezekiah, who organized some of the editorial work (25:1), reigned 250 years after Solomon. The book as we have it was finalized, at the latest, by Ben Sira's time (180 BC).

The precise part Solomon played in all this is not known. His name appears in the title, and he is the author/compiler of the two longest collections (10:1 - 22:16 and chapters 25 - 29). Solomon was a man of outstanding wisdom (see 1 Kings 3; 4:29-34) and his court became an international centre for the exchange of learning. 1 Kings 4:32-34 tells us that Solomon 'uttered three thousand proverbs; and his songs were a thousand and five. He spoke of trees ... he spoke also of beasts, and of birds, and of reptiles, and of fish. And men came from all peoples to hear the wisdom of Solomon, and from all the kings of the earth, who had heard of his wisdom'. Through marriage with pharaoh's daughter, Solomon had close links with Egypt, and perhaps knew the *Teaching of Amenemope* which is so closely paralleled in Proverbs 22:17 - 23:14, as well as other collections of wise sayings. He and his wise men culled the wisdom of the east, but they incorporated nothing that was not in line with God's standards. See 'Poetry and Wisdom Literature', introduction.

From chapter 10 on, Proverbs is best digested a few sayings at a time. It may also be a help to study them under themes. This way we can weigh one saying against another, and get an idea of the general teaching on a particular topic. It is important to bear in mind that proverbs are by nature *generalizations*. They state what is *generally*, not *invariably*, true. The writers do not deny that there are exceptions. But exceptions are not within the scope of proverbial sayings. For instance, Proverbs states that those who live by God's standards will prosper in the world. This is generally the truth. But it is not an unqualified 'promise'. Job, and above all the life of Jesus, show the other side of the coin.

1:1-7 INTRODUCTION

Proverbs opens with a statement of its purpose (2-6) and basis (7). It is aimed especially at the young and uninstructed – but no one is too old or too wise to learn.

Verse 1: best taken as the title to the whole book, not just the first section. Solomon's own proverbs begin at 10:1.

Fear of the Lord (7): an important recurring phrase in Proverbs (see themes, below). It describes a wholesome awe and respect for God which expresses itself in obedience, reliance on God and deliberate avoidance of evil (3:7).

1:8 - 9:18 LESSONS ON WISDOM

The teacher addresses his pupils as a wise father would his son. The young man has a vital choice to make: between the right course and the wrong one; between wisdom and folly; between going God's way through life and going his own. The teacher describes the two alternatives, and shows where each leads. The theme of every lesson is the same: 'Get wisdom'. Repetition is still a good teaching method!

Chapter 1

Resist the blandishments of violent men (10-19). Listen instead to the voice of wisdom (20-33). All who disregard her call will live to regret it.
Verse 12: the Pit of death, 'Sheol' – the place of the dead.
Wisdom (20): the teacher pictures wisdom as a great lady. She competes for Everyman's attention with another woman – Folly – who is no lady at all (see chapter 9). See note on Wisdom under themes.

Chapter 2

Wisdom is to be found through knowing God. It is hard-won, but worth every effort (1-10). It is a safeguard against wrong company, both male (12-15) and female (16-19). It sets men's feet on the right path (20).

Chapter 3

Take wise teaching to heart; stay humble; trust God (1-12). Wisdom offers the things that money can't buy: peace, happiness, security (13-26). Wisdom was at work in creation. It continues to be worked out in the do's and don'ts of everyday life and relationships (27-35).

The 'woman at the window' seen in this ivory carving was a popular subject with Near Eastern craftsmen. Proverbs warns young men against the shameless seduction practised by some married women.

Chapter 4

The teacher passes on his own father's instruction. Wisdom is the thing to go for: it leads to life. Steer clear of wrong-doing and the company of wrongdoers.

Chapter 5

Be wise when it comes to women. Don't fall for a cheap line, especially from a married woman. She is a *femme fatale* in more than name. Find your pleasure in your own wife: see that you stay in love with her.

Chapter 6

This chapter gives some timely warnings. Beware of accepting unlimited liability for anyone (1-5). Beware of idleness (6-11). Beware the fate of a 'bad lot' (12-19). Keep God's commands. They will save you from the schemes of seductive women.
Six things ... seven (16): see on 30:15.
Eyelashes (25): this seems a surprisingly modern touch! But long before Solomon's time women wore the equivalent of mascara, if not of false lashes.
Verse 27: the Jerusalem Bible translates 'can a man hug fire to his breast ...?'

Chapter 7

The teacher describes a young man falling for a married woman's shameless seduction. To judge by the number of warnings in Proverbs this was common enough. Even Solomon, with all his wisdom, was as weak as any at this point – and in the end his foreign wives led him into idolatry (1 Kings 11:1-13).

Chapter 8

In marked contrast to the sly woman of chapter 7, slipping out at dusk to catch her man, Wisdom makes an open appeal to all men as they go about their daily business. She is straight and true, the value of her instruction beyond any earthly fortune (6-21). She stands at the head of God's creation, the very first of all created things (22-31).

Chapter 9

All the teacher's previous lessons are crystallized in this vivid picture of Wisdom (1-6) and Folly (13-18). Each invites man – empty-headed, wayward man – to a feast. Wisdom sets life before him. On Folly's menu there is only death.

10 - 22:16 PROVERBS OF SOLOMON

The young man has been faced with the choice and urged to choose wisdom. Now the instruction begins; practical instruction that ranges over every aspect of life. In this first collection, the sayings get their punch from contrast. The second line, or half, of each saying is the antithesis of the first. Each proverb is complete in itself, though some are linked by words or themes into series. They reveal sound psychology and accurate observation of life. They demonstrate the out-working of wisdom and folly in the practical business of living. For the teaching in 10:1 - 31:9, see under themes.
15:11: even the realms of the dead (Sheol and Abaddon) are open to God.
17:8: the man is confident his bribe will work, but the practice is wrong (see verse 23).
18:18: in Old Testament times it was common practice to discover God's will by casting lots.
20:10: Leviticus 19:35 condemns the giving of short weight, and the prophets also denounce all such cheating in business.

22:17 - 24:34 TWO COLLECTIONS OF SAYINGS OF WISE MEN

It seems likely that in this section Proverbs makes creative use of material from abroad (see introduction, and 'Poetry and Wisdom Literature'), in addition to material from Israel's own 'wise men'. The sayings in this section are more connected than in the previous one. They begin with 'things to avoid' (22:22-29). Then come the hazards of social climbing (23:1-8); father and son – discipline and advice (23:12-28); a portrait of a drunkard (23:29-35); teaching on wisdom and folly (24:1-14), and right living (24:15-22). The group of additional sayings (24:23-34) focusses on justice and hard work, with a sketch of the lazy man in verses 30-34. See also under themes.
Thirty sayings (22:20): the Hebrew has several possible meanings, but it seems to imply a book of sayings which consists of (roughly) 30 paragraphs or chapters.
Ancient landmark (22:28): stones set up to mark out boundaries.
Narrow well (23:27): i.e. one it would be difficult to get out of.

25 - 29 MORE OF SOLOMON'S PROVERBS (HEZEKIAH'S COLLECTION)

Under King Hezekiah Israel returned to the old neglected patterns of worship. He repaired the temple and resumed the sacrifices, restoring the temple music along the lines laid down by David (2 Chronicles 29). What is more likely than that he should then have turned his attention to the classic wisdom of Solomon? At any rate, it was his men who published this collection of Solomon's proverbs. There is more grouping here than in 10:1 - 22:16, and the proverbs rely more on comparison than contrast for effect. For the teaching, see under themes.
25:6-7: Jesus uses the same theme in Luke 14:7-10, but he broadens it to cover a whole attitude to life.
26:4-5: these two verses are probably meant to be complementary, not contradictory. It is usually pointless to argue with a fool, but there are times when his false reason must be shown up for what it is.
26:8: what could be more nonsensical than fixing a stone to a sling so that it can't come out?

The ideal wife, amongst many other virtues, spins her own thread and weaves her own cloth.

30 SAYINGS OF AGUR

Both Agur and Lemuel (31:1) are non-Israelites. 'Massa' was an Arab tribe descended from Abraham's son Ishmael. The east was famous for its wisdom, right down to Christ's own day (see Matthew 2:1). Agur is a man whose close observation of life and nature have taught him humility.
Three ... four (15): a device indicating that the list is not exhaustive. See also 18, 21, 29 and 6:16.
Verse 19: he finds four sources of wonder: how the eagle can soar; how the serpent can move without legs;

how the ship can ride the waves; and the mysterious attraction which draws a man to a woman.

31:1-9 SAYINGS OF KING LEMUEL

See under chapter 30 above. Lemuel outlines his mother's teaching. We seem to catch a tone of mild reproach in verse 2.

Son of my vows (2): the vows made when she prayed for a son.

31:10-31 THE PERFECT WIFE

Proverbs paints a remarkable picture of the power of woman, for good and for ill. It closes with this lovely acrostic poem (see on Psalm 9) about the ideal wife: responsible, capable, hardworking and completely trusted. Not only do her husband, family and household depend on her provision and foresight for their physical needs; they owe her their well-being at a much deeper level (11, 12, 26). Her influence extends beyond this immediate circle to society at large (20). And she finds ample scope for all her gifts in the wider spheres of buying and selling and business transactions (16, 18, 24). Where does her secret lie? In that same 'fear of the Lord' in which all true wisdom has its roots.

IMPORTANT THEMES IN PROVERBS 10-31

Wisdom and folly – the wise man and the fool

This is the main strand of the whole book, the subject of the first nine chapters. The sayings point the contrast between wisdom – living by God's standards, keeping to what is right, and folly – man wilfully going his own way. Wisdom leads to life and all that is good; folly is a mere half-life that ends in death. The verses listed below detail the wise course of action in many different circumstances. They outline the wise man's character, in contrast to the life and character of the 'fool', who shuts his mind to God and reason.
10:8, 13-14, 23; 12:1, 15-16, 23; 13:14-16, 20; 14:1, 3, 7-8, 15-18, 24, 33; 15:5, 7, 14, 20-21; 16:16, 21-23; 17:10, 12, 16, 24, 28; 18:2, 6-7, 15; 19:25, 29; 21:22; 22:3; 23:9; 24:3-7, 13-14; 26:1, 3-12; 27:12, 22; 28:26; 29:8-9, 11.

The righteous and the wicked

The individual's response to life's alternatives determines which of these two groups he joins. The wise man, on Proverbs' definition of wisdom, will be righteous. The gullible fool is always teetering on the edge of wrongdoing. It is more than likely he will end up among the wicked. The proverbs below describe the righteous life – the life of integrity – and the blessing it brings to the individual and the community. God loves and protects the righteous. The wicked are subject to his wrath. If they flourish, it is only for a short time. They are heading straight for death and destruction.
10:3, 6-7, 11, 20-21, 24-25, 27-32; 11:3-11, 17-21, 23, 28, 30-31; 12:2-3, 5-7, 10, 12-13, 21, 26, 28; 13:5-6, 9, 21-22, 25; 14:9, 11, 14, 19, 32; 15:6, 8-9, 26, 28-29; 16:8, 12-13; 17:13, 15; 18:5; 20:7; 21:3, 7-8, 10, 12, 18, 26-27; 24:15-16; 25:26; 28:1, 12, 28; 29:2, 6-7, 16, 27.

Words and the tongue

Proverbs places tremendous stress on the power of words and speech, for good and for ill. What we say, and how we react to what others say – advice, or rebuke, or gossip, or tempting suggestions – betrays what we are (see Matthew 12:34-37). The tongue is an incalculable force: it takes a wise man to master it (see also James 3). The proverbs below are full of sound advice and timely warning.
10:18-21, 31-32; 11:9, 11-14; 12:6, 14, 17-19, 22; 13:2-3; 14:5, 25; 15:1-2, 4, 23; 16:1, 23-24, 27-28; 17:4, 7, 27; 18:4, 6, 13, 20-21; 19:5, 9; 20:19; 21:6, 23; 22:10; 25:11, 15, 23, 27; 26:20-28; 27:2; 28:23; 29:20.

The family

Fads and fashions change, but the basic structure of family life, its joys and sorrows, remain constant. There are still unfaithful husbands, and wives who bicker and nag their husbands out of existence. There are still children from good homes who go off the rails. Proverbs' wise advice on the things that make for a happy and stable home-life, and the things that undermine it, is as sound today as ever.
Parents and children: 10:1; 13:1, 24; 17:21, 25; 19:13, 18, 27; 20:11; 22:6, 15; 23:13-16, 19-28; 28:7, 24; 29:15, 17; 30:11, 17.
Wives: 12:4; 18:22; 19:13-14; 21:9, 19; 25:24; 31:10-31. (The main advice to husbands comes in the earlier section, e.g. chapter 5.)

Laziness and hard work

Proverbs contains a good many sketches of the lazy man, too idle to begin a job, too slack to see it through, yawning his way through life until it is too late, and poverty and hunger are on him. There is nothing to commend slackness, but 'in all toil there is profit'.
10:4-5, 26; 12:11, 24, 27; 13:4; 14:23; 15:19; 18:9; 19:15, 24; 20:4, 13; 21:25; 22:13; 24:30-34; 26:13-16; 28:19.

SOME SECONDARY THEMES

Rich and poor; poverty and wealth:
10:15; 11:4, 24-25; 13:7-8, 11; 14:20-21, 31; 18:11, 23; 19:4, 7, 17; 21:13, 17; 22:1-2, 7, 16, 22-23; 23:4-5; 28:3, 6, 11, 20, 22; 30:8-9.

The world of business and affairs; plans and decisions:
11:1, 15, 26; 15:22; 16:3, 9-11, 33; 17:8, 18, 23; 18:16; 19:21; 20:10, 14, 16, 18, 23; 21:14; 22:26-27; 27:23-27; 28:8.

The proud and the humble:
11:2; 12:9; 15:25; 16:18-19; 18:12; 21:4, 24; 22:4; 29:23.

Friends:
17:9, 17; 18:24; 19:4, 6; 27:6, 10;
and neighbours: 25:8-10, 17-18; 26:18-19; 27:10, 14; 29:5.

Masters and servants:
11:29; 14:35; 17:2; 29:19-21; 30:10, 22-23.

Kings and rulers:
16:13-15; 19:12; 20:2; 23:1-3; 24:21; 25:1-7; 28:15-16; 29:12, 14; 31:4-5.

Hopes and fears; joys and sorrows:
12:25; 13:12-19; 14:10, 13; 15:13, 30; 17:22; 18:14; 25:20; 27:9.

Anger:
14:17, 29-30; 15:18; 16:14, 32; 19:11-12, 19; 20:2; 22:24-25; 29:22.

The 'fear of the Lord'
(although the phrase does not occur all that often, this is no secondary theme; as the basis of all wisdom, it is absolutely fundamental to the whole book): 10:27; 14:26-27; 15:16-33; 16:6; 19:23; 22:4; 23:17; 24:21. See also in the earlier section, e.g. 1:7; 3:7.

Old Testament 3.4

ECCLESIASTES

Ecclesiastes is a piece of 'wisdom literature' (see 'Poetry and Wisdom Literature', Introduction), a popular form of writing in Near Eastern countries in Old Testament times. It is not a familiar form today, and can seem disjointed to us, with its apparently disconnected thoughts and sayings and observations on life. But the theme of Ecclesiastes is singularly 'modern': it is shared by any number of 20th-century novels and plays.

The book simply observes life around and draws the logical conclusions. This is life 'under the sun', life as man sees it. The author imposes no preconceptions. Life as man lives it, without God, is futile, meaningless, purposeless, empty. It is a bleak picture. Nature and history go round in circles: there is nothing new. Add up the profit and loss of human life and you are better off dead. Life is unfair; work is pointless; pleasure fails to satisfy; good living and wise thinking are rendered futile by death. 'Be realistic', says the book. 'If life without God is the whole story, see it for what it is. Don't pretend. Don't bury your head in the sand. This is the truth about life.'

But this is not – like so many modern writings – just cynicism and despair. God never intended man to leave him out of the picture. God can inject joy into every aspect of living: from food and work to home and marriage (2:24-26; 3:10-15; 5:18-20; 9:7-10). He intended man to find ultimate satisfaction not in life but in him. The wise man dies like the fool, it is true, but wisdom is still good and right (2:13). And God will judge the just and the wicked (3:17). Enjoy life, not as an Epicurean ('eat, drink, for tomorrow we die'), but as a man of God, because you depend on him for life and for enjoyment (3:13; 5:19). An empty, futile existence is not inevitable: remember God while you are still young (12:1); fear him and keep his commandments (12:13).

'Ecclesiastes' is the Greek translation of 'Qoheleth' (Revised Standard Version 'the Preacher'; New English Bible 'the Speaker'), a word which seems to indicate the author's official title rather than his name. It could be a pseudonym for Solomon, who was 'son of David, king in Jerusalem' (1:1, 12) and the embodiment of wisdom. What man was better qualified to pronounce on life, having tasted it to the full – power, fame, riches, women, all that any man could wish for – and tested out what life was like both under God and without him?

'What do we gain from our work?' asks the Philosopher. This Assyrian workman, carrying a rope, is depicted on the walls of King Sennacherib's palace.

Chapter 1

The author states his theme: the emptiness and futility of life. Men come and go. The cycles of nature and history are constantly repeating themselves. There is nothing new. Even the search for wisdom – man's highest goal – is futile, for 'the more a man knows, the more he has to suffer'.

Verses 1, 12: see introduction.

Under the sun (3, 9, 14): a recurring phrase in Ecclesiastes. It indicates 'the world, seen simply from a human stand-point'.

Chapter 2

What is man to do with his days (3)? If he lives for pleasure – all that wealth and status can afford – life is still empty (10-11). Wisdom is far better than folly, but in the end death makes fools of us all. The things we work for must be left behind for others to enjoy. This is the futility of life 'under the sun'. For there is no joy or satisfaction in life apart from God (24-26).

Chapter 3

There is a time for everything in life (1-9). God has made it so. Man understands time, but he cannot comprehend the whole of God's work (11). So he learns to stand in awe of God. There is injustice and corruption in life (16ff.), but God has set a time for just judgement, although all men must die.

Chapter 4

Such are the oppressions in life that man is better dead; better still never to have been born (1-3). Men wear themselves out with work, trying to outdo one another, never stopping to ask what it's all for (4-8).

From this point in the book the thoughts and observations are more frequently interspersed with advice and teaching, in the proverbial manner adopted by the 'wise'. Wisdom may look foolish in the world's eyes (1:17, 18; 2:14-17) but 'Qoheleth' clearly still believes in it and intends men to live by it (see 12:9-11).

A threefold cord (12): three are even better than two. A rope made of three strands is hard to break.

Chapter 5

Sound advice on promises made to God (1-7) and attitudes to money (10-12). Another of life's evils (13-17) is the business crash. The way to live is to enjoy work, and to enjoy prosperity if it comes, for these are God's gifts. Enjoyment is the antidote to gloom about the passing of the years (20).

Verses 8-9: the meaning is not clear. New English Bible translates verse 9, 'The best thing for a country is a king whose own lands are well tilled.'

Chapter 6

What value is long life to a man, without the chance to enjoy all he has worked for (1-6)? Better be stillborn or miscarried (3). The man who is ruled by his appetite and desires will never be satisfied (7-9).

Chapter 7

The wise man takes account of death as well as life (2). His outlook on life is serious (1-6). He knows how to enjoy good times and learn from bad ones (14). 'Qoheleth' observes another of life's anomalies (15). There are good men who die young, and wicked men who grow old in their wickedness. Everything is brought to the test of wisdom (23), but life will not add up. Man as God made him was all right; his troubles are all of his own making (29).

Verse 18: the advice is to avoid extremes. Verses 16-17 sound like the cynical tones of worldly wisdom. God would never say we were overdoing real goodness, or advise a little wickedness!

Verse 28: he has found only one man in a thousand worth the name, and not one woman!

Chapter 8

Faith cannot resolve the problem of evil: good men getting what the bad deserve; wicked men admired and having a cushy time. The man of God can only assert what he knows is true, though all the evidence is against it (12). Enjoyment is the best thing in life, says 'Qoheleth' (15). Yet he applies his own energy to wisdom, even though God has concealed from man the answer to life's mysteries (16-17).

Chapter 9

One fate – death – comes to all men, good and bad alike (with this one difference, that the good are in God's hands, 1). There is no knowing how long any man has (11-12). So work hard and enjoy life while it lasts, for death cuts men off from all the world has to offer (7-10). Wisdom may not pay, yet it is still worth more than power (13-18).

Chapter 10
A collection of proverbs on wisdom and folly, wise sayings and practical advice, continued in chapter 11.

Chapters 11 and 12
Practical advice leads straight in to the author's conclusions. If life is long, rejoice in it. Rejoice in the light before the dark night of death begins. Let the young rejoice in their youth, always mindful of God who calls all men to account. Don't wait till old age. Don't wait till life has become futile and empty and there is nothing ahead but death. Fear God – hold him in awe – and obey him.

12:2-6: verse 2 depicts life drawing to an end, the darkness of death closing in. Verses 3-5 are a series of pictures of old age, when strength fails, teeth are few, sight grows dim. Moffatt translates verse 5: 'When old age fears a height, and even a walk has its terrors, when his hair is almond white, and he drags his limbs along, as the spirit flags and fades.' The 'silver cord ...' (6): metaphors of death.

Verses 9-14: the author's (or editor's) postscript. He has spoken the truth about life, shown it up for what it is without God. His constructive advice is scattered through the book. Now he pinpoints the one thing on which man's life turns: his attitude to God. There is a judgement, when good and evil will be sorted out. Man must live in the light of it. The 'fear of the Lord' (as Proverbs makes so plain) is where true wisdom – and real life – begins.

Old Testament 3.5

THE SONG OF SOLOMON

This 'song of songs' is a series of lyric poems on the theme of love between man and woman. The setting is pastoral: the poems are full of images from the countryside. The time, appropriately, is spring. They are full of the passion and delight of human love.

The poems defy complete analysis and, partly for this reason, have been subject to all kinds of interpretation. Jews and Christians alike have seen them as allegories – of God's love for Israel; of Christ's love for his bride the Church. But the poems themselves give no direct warrant for this. Some see the poems as a drama with two characters: bride and royal bridegroom; some say three: Solomon, the girl, and her shepherd lover. There is, however, no evidence apart from the Song that this kind of literature existed in Israel. Others regard the poems as a series of songs sung during the week-long wedding-feast, as in Syria today, with the bride and groom crowned king and queen.

Whatever the form, the poems as they stand celebrate the beauty and wonder of human love. There is a frank and open delight in physical attraction, which underlines the fact that God intends man to enjoy physical love within the laws he has given.

The notes below provide only a general outline of the Song. Both the New English Bible and the Jerusalem Bible give a detailed analysis.

Chapter 1
The Song begins (2-8) with a dialogue between the bride, a country girl, and the women of Jerusalem (probably the court or harem). The bride and bridegroom then converse (9-17).

Song of Songs, which is Solomon's (1): the title may imply that Solomon wrote it, or that it was written for, or about, him. He was as renowned in the field of love (1 Kings 11:1-3) as he was in the field of wisdom. But he can hardly be taken as the ideal of single-minded devotion! Nor does the country-shepherd image suit him, unless the language is pure literary-pastoral convention. Hence the appeal of the three-character interpretation of the Song, in which Solomon attempts to win the heart of the girl, who remains true to her shepherd lover.

The king and his bride: The Egyptian King Tutankhamun and his queen are pictured on the backrest to the throne found in his tomb.

Kedar (5): a nomadic Arab tribe. Bedouin tents are made of black goatskin.

My own ... (6): she is talking about her complexion, burnt brown by the sun.

Pharaoh's chariots (9): Solomon ran a thriving import-export trade in the horses and chariots for which Egypt was famous (1 Kings 10:26-29).

Verses 12-13: 'nard': spikenard, a perfumed ointment. Those women who could afford such luxuries wore sachets of fragrant myrrh, suspended from the neck, beneath their dresses; or on their cheeks.

Verse 14: a red cosmetic dye was made from henna. 'Engedi': a beautiful freshwater 'oasis' close to the barren shores of the Dead Sea.

Chapter 2
The bride's thoughts are filled with the sweetness and longing of love. The bridegroom calls to her in the idyllic beauty of springtime (10ff.). It

is all in a country setting. Only verse 7 contains any hint of the court.
Verse 7: see also 3:5; 8:4. The significance of this refrain seems to be that love must be allowed to grow naturally, in its own time. It is not to be forced or given an artificial stimulus.
The foxes (15): jackals. If they damage the blossom there will be no fruit.

Chapter 3

In a dream sequence the bride describes the desolate feelings separation brings, and the joy of reunion. Verses 6-11 describe the grand procession of King Solomon.
Wood of Lebanon (9): the famous cedar, imported for building the temple and palaces.

Chapter 4

The bridegroom glories in the beauty of his bride. The imagery is oriental, but love the world over shares the same delighted appreciation of the human form.
A flock of goats (1): their silky black coats gleam in the sun as they ripple over the hillside.
Verses 2-4: her teeth are white and even; her cheeks full and rosy; her neck like a tower hung with trophies.
Senir, Hermon (8): the 9,000 ft mountain on the Israel-Lebanon border.
Verse 16: the voice of the bride inviting the bridegroom to enjoy his 'garden' – herself.

Chapter 5

The bride dreams again (2-8). This time the bridegroom comes and she is too slow in letting him in. And again joy turns to desolation. In reply to the women (9) she describes what he looks like. He is as 'altogether desirable' to her as she is to him.
Myrrh ... (5): she is perfumed as a bride on her wedding night.

Chapter 6

The women question; the bride replies – and the bridegroom again describes the beauty of his one and only love. Not all the queens and concubines can rival her.
Tirzah (4): a beautiful city, the early capital of the northern kingdom of Israel.
Verse 12: New English Bible translates, 'I did not know myself; she made me feel more than a prince reigning over the myriads of his people.'
Shulammite (13): if 'Shulam' is a place, its location is not known. There are no grounds for linking the girl here with Abishag the Shunammite (1 Kings 1:3-4), as some have done.

Chapter 7

Again the bridegroom marvels at the physical beauty of his bride. He cannot tear his eyes away. Every detail is perfection. The bride loves him utterly, without reserve (10-13), in all the glory of the springtime.
Carmel (5): the mountain of Elijah's contest with the prophets of Baal, which today makes an impressive backcloth to the port of Haifa.
Mandrakes (13): a plant considered from very early days to have aphrodisiac powers.

Chapter 8

The bride longs to display her affection openly. At verse 5 the scene changes, and the two are together at last. There is *nothing* that can destroy true love.
Verses 8-9: the girl's brothers debate how to preserve her honour. This she declares she has kept (10).
Verses 11-12: the 'vineyard' is probably a poetic allusion to Solomon's harem and all its attendants. Let him keep it! The bride's love and person is her own to give: it is not for sale.

Old Testament section 4

THE PROPHETS

Introduction/Alec Motyer

The people of Israel had become a nation. They had been redeemed from slavery in Egypt. They had been given the law. They were committed to a life of obedience to God, and a religion which constantly reminded them of their dependence on God's forgiveness and mercy.

But they were constantly falling down on their calling and their promises. With idol-worship, civil war, immorality, complacency, the nation needed to be recalled again and again to the whole point of their existence.

The call to obedience

The prophets were men raised up by God to do just this – to call the people back to God and his way. Slackness had grown into forgetfulness. God's holy law for life had ceased to be an effective force moulding men and society.

Sometimes the fault was more a reversal of right priorities. The sacrifices were intended to make provision for lapses into disobedience. But there were periods in Old Testament history when they were seen as substitutes for the life of obedience – ritual techniques for keeping God happy.

When the nation's religion was corrupted into this sort of non-moral ritualism, the prophets raised their protest. This explains a whole series of verses in which the prophets at first sight seem to deny the divine authority behind the sacrifices (Isaiah 1:11ff.; Jeremiah 7:21ff.; Hosea 6:6; Amos 5:25; Micah 6:6-8). Their intention is rather to recall the people from false priorities; to insist on God's primary requirement that his people should obey his commands and live out his standards.

Distinguishing false from true

Our world today is full of conflicting voices, all claiming to be authoritative pronouncements. Religious opinion varies so widely that quite often there is headlong collision between different views, all of which are put forward in the name of God. How can we tell where the truth lies?

What the prophets said in a similar situation was that what accords with Scripture can be taken as God's truth. In Deuteronomy 13 the false prophet is one who calls people away after 'other gods' and speaks 'rebellion against the Lord your God, who brought you out of the land of Egypt ... to make you leave the way in which the Lord your God commanded you to walk'.

In other words, the truth about God spoken by Moses stands as a test of the truth of people's opinions. This passage specifically mentions the commandments of the Lord: does a prophet subscribe to the old morality of Mt Sinai, or is he preaching a new morality?

We can see this test at work in Jeremiah 23:9-22. Both in his personal life (verses 9-15) and in his public ministry (verses 16-22). the false prophet subscribes to another morality and encourages his hearers to do likewise. Consequently, Jeremiah infers, this man cannot have 'stood in the council of the Lord' (verses 18, 22).

The prophet's call

The true prophet claimed the privilege of being in the Lord's 'council', a word which conveys the idea both of consultation (see 1 Kings 22:19-22) and of close companionship with God.

It is this experience of being brought into close fellowship with God and learning his mind 'in council' that lies behind the three words describing the prophet. All three appear in 1 Chronicles 29:29.

The word translated 'prophet' signifies 'called (by God)', with the consequent task of proclaiming the message of God to men. God's call is not an invitation but an appointment. For instance, the Lord 'took' Amos (7:15) in order to make him a prophet 'to my people'.

The two other Hebrew words are both translated 'seer', meaning 'one who sees'. These words point to the fact that by God's inspiration the prophets have an altogether unique ability to 'see': both into the affairs of men and into the mind of God.

The three words are used synonymously throughout the Old Testament (though 1 Samuel 9:9 points back to a time when some distinction was observed in usage). Taken together, they show the two sides of the prophetic experience. 'Seer' refers to the change God makes in the man he 'takes' for this task (see 2 Peter 1:21). 'Prophet' indicates God's revelation of his mind and will to and through that man (see 2 Timothy 3:16).

'Thus says the Lord'

The prophets, then, were essentially men whom God chose to bring close to himself. The prophet's calling was not hereditary, like the priest's. And God chose his men from many different walks of life. Some, like Jeremiah and Jonah, were very reluctant recruits, especially when they learnt what God wanted them to do.

But out of their fellowship with God (see 1 Kings 17:1) the prophets came with his message for their contemporaries, and for us too (see Acts 7:38). Sometimes they emphasized their message by means of dramatic action (e.g. Jeremiah 19; Ezekiel 4; see 2 Kings 13:14-19). But mostly their messages were presented in carefully constructed spoken discourses which bear all the marks of premeditation and preparation.

The prophets are very reticent about how they received these messages. We are often told no more than that 'the word of the Lord came' (e.g. Jeremiah 47:1; Ezekiel 17:1; Zechariah 8:1). 'Came' translates the Hebrew verb 'to be', meaning that 'the word of the Lord became a living, present reality', which tells us the content but not the nature of the experience.

However, there is no doubt that the prophets intended their claim to be taken seriously. 'Thus says the Lord' meant precisely what it said. They received from the Lord the very 'words' (note the plural, Jeremiah 1:9; Ezekiel 2:7; 3:4) which they spoke.

We can offer no logical description of their experience. We must simply observe the facts. On the one hand they themselves claimed to speak words which God gave to them; on the other hand they were clearly not impersonal 'tape recorders' of an external 'message'. On the contrary, they were great and colourful personalities.

From the far more remarkable personality of the Lord Jesus – Son of God, Son of man – we can only conclude that when man is wholly at one with God then true humanity, full individual personality comes to perfection. So, in the case of the prophets, God brought them into such close intimacy of fellowship with himself, such harmony of mind and will, such consecration of life (and all by means of the characteristic experiences of salvation) that they both grew to full maturity themselves and by his unique inspiration became the mouthpieces of God (see Exodus 4:15-16; 6:28 - 7:1).

The present and the future

A glance at the accompanying chart will show that these remarkable men were rooted in history. They were deliberately placed by God at crisis-points.

Amos spoke at a time when financial affluence and religious formalism combined to produce a high-tide of social decadence and permissiveness (see Amos 3:15 - 4:1; 4:4-5; 2:6-8).

Hosea addressed an era in which established social forms were dissolving before men's eyes.

Isaiah, according to God's estimate of the situation, preached to a people who by rejecting his message would have passed the point of no-return and condemned themselves out of hand (Isaiah 6:9ff.).

Jeremiah belongs in the thick of the final agonies of Jerusalem, and Ezekiel in the first traumatic experiences of exile.

They spoke in the name of the God who is neither an observer nor an occasional visitor but always the active Ruler of human history. Inevitably, therefore, the prophets not only explained the past (Amos 4:6ff.) and exposed the tendency of the present (Isaiah 5:11-13) but declared above all what God was about to do.

To predict what was about to happen was to them an essential consequence of their fellowship with the Lord of history (e.g. Amos 3:7). When in his presence they felt obliged to ask the vital question 'How long?' (Isaiah 6:11) and to wait to hear the answer. But when they proclaimed that answer it was not in order to satisfy men's curiosity about the future; it was to use their certainty about what was to come as a lever to bring people to repentance here and now.

The characteristic prophetic use of prediction is seen in the words of John the Baptist, the last and most privileged of the prophets. He did not say, 'Repent, in order that the kingdom of God may come,' but, 'Repent, for the kingdom of heaven is at hand' (Matthew 3:2). The sure facts of the future call for a present moral re-alignment, a getting right with God (see Isaiah 2:5, 10, 22; 3:1ff.; 31:6-7; etc.).

The message of the prophets

God rules in history, he calls men and women to repentance. These are two of the prophets' themes. With three others they constitute the core of their teaching.

The Lord as Ruler of all history. The prophets took this so seriously that they were prepared to risk depicting the mighty empires of their day as 'tools' in the hand of God (Isaiah 10:5-15). This constitutes a problem for Habakkuk (1:5-11, 12-17): how could the holy God use unholy, corrupt instruments? The only answer the Bible offers is to re-affirm God's sovereign control of the world, a control so intricately exercised that sinners act responsibly according to the dictates and pressures of their own natures, but over all the just and holy Ruler presides, governs and guides (see 2 Kings 19:25, 28; Ezekiel 38:3-4, 10-11, 16; 39:2-3).

The primary need to be right with God. Since it is God who determines the outcome of every situation, the important thing is not to have the best and strongest human allies (see Isaiah 30:1-2; Hosea 5:13) but to side with God, to get right with him (see Isaiah 30:15). God is always at work to bring his people back to himself (Amos 4:6-11); and the prophet summons men and women to personal readiness to meet with God (Amos 4:12).

The moral foundation of religion and society. We have already mentioned Jeremiah's rejection of a religion without morality (Jeremiah 7:1-15). The prophets as a whole insist that to be right with God men and women must live in obedience to his standards and commands, and that this produces a sound society. Once people are alienated from God they cannot maintain right relationships with each other (compare Amos 2:7-8 with 9-12).

A blend of judgement and hope. Time and again, as we hear the prophets analyse the situation in which they live, we see that God's judgement is inevitable. The whole landscape is filled with threatening clouds of gathering wrath, and yet, suddenly, surprisingly, a bright shaft of hope pierces through (Isaiah 6:13; 28:5; 29:5; 31:5; Amos 9:11ff.; etc.). This blending of darkness and light, judgement and hope is more than a fact of the prophetic message: it is a necessity, for they spoke in the name of Yahweh, the Lord, the God who-saves-his-people-and-judges-his-enemies, the God of the exodus (see the article 'Names of God').

The messianic kingdom. We use this heading as a general description of the bright future state God has in store for his people. It is seen as the setting up of the perfect covenant relationship (Isaiah 54:10; Jeremiah 31:31-34; Ezekiel 37:26-27), and in many other ways also. But it is chiefly described as centring upon some great coming Person. He is:

The new 'David': Ezekiel 37:24
The 'branch' of David's line (or, to stress his divine ancestry) the 'branch of the Lord': Isaiah 11:1; Jeremiah 23:5-6; 33:14-16; Zechariah 3:8; 6:12; Isaiah 4:2
Immanuel, 'God with us': Isaiah 7:14
The 'mighty God' occupying David's throne: Isaiah 9:6-7
The servant, dying for his people's sins: Isaiah 53
The anointed Conqueror of his people's foes: Isaiah 63:1-6
The Lord himself coming in the wake of the appointed forerunner: Malachi 3:1
Born in Bethlehem, born of a virgin: Micah 5:2; Isaiah 7:14

It is the crowning glory of the Old Testament prophets that God permitted and enabled them to see this radiance afar off. It sets the seal on their prophecies as God's word to men, that all was so perfectly fulfilled in the Lord Jesus. And what greater incentive could we have to get to know the writings of these men than Jesus' own statement that without them we cannot understand him, but that with them we can both know him (Luke 24:27, 32) and preach him to the world (Luke 24:44-48)?

THE PROPHETS IN THEIR SETTING

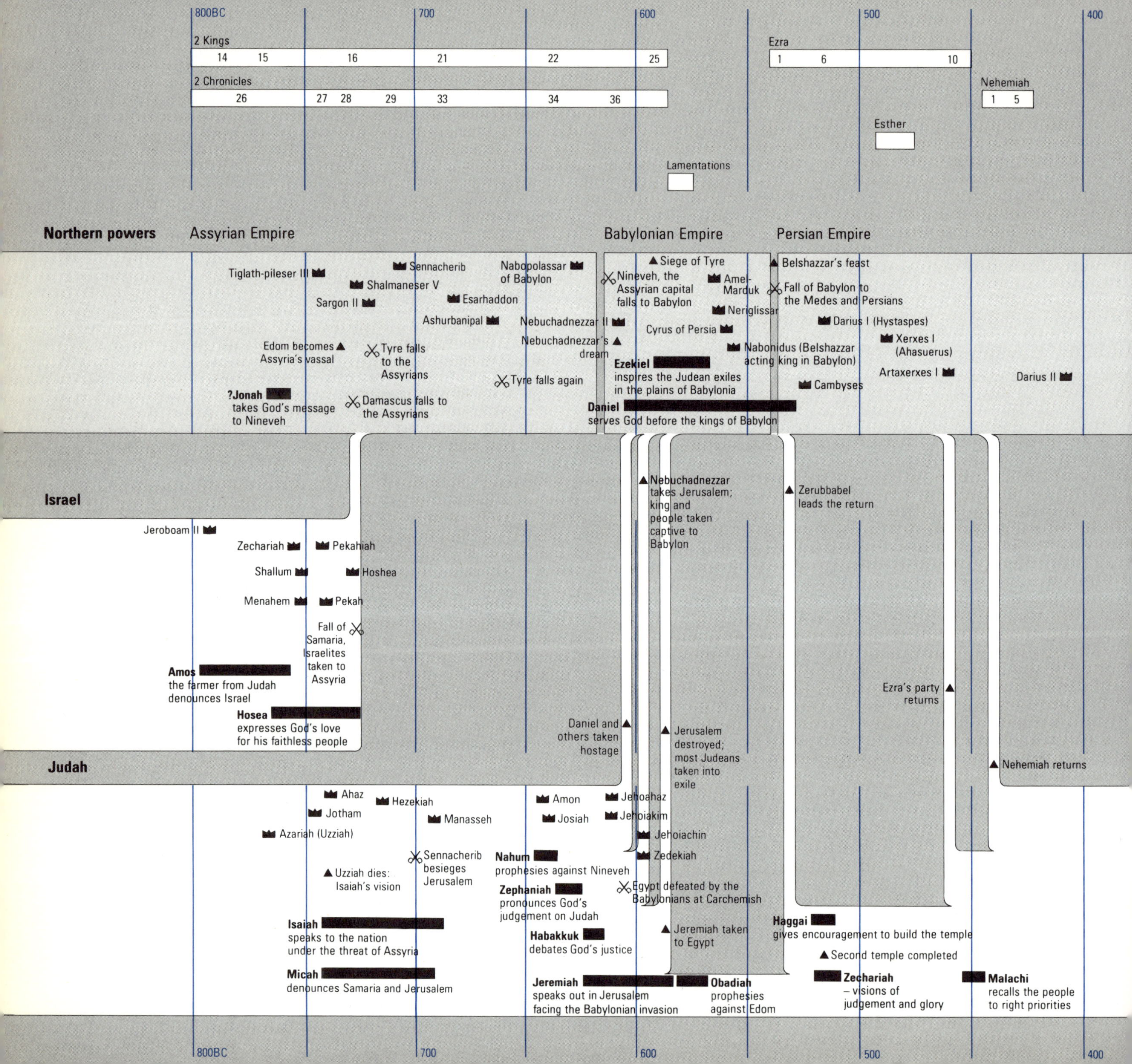

Old Testament 4.1

ISAIAH

The prophets. Isaiah stands at the head of 'The Prophets', the third great section of the Old Testament. Sixteen prophets are named, and we have 17 books of their visions and prophecies (the odd one out being Lamentations: known in the Greek versions as the 'Lamentations of Jeremiah'). The four 'major' prophets are Isaiah, Jeremiah, Ezekiel and Daniel; the twelve 'minor' prophets, Hosea, Joel, Amos, Obadiah, Jonah, Micah, Nahum, Habakkuk, Zephaniah, Haggai, Zechariah, Malachi.

The books of the prophets belong to the time of the nation's decline, the exile and the return to their homeland. They span, altogether, a period of 250-300 years. Most of them address their messages primarily to the southern kingdom of Judah – Isaiah, Joel and Micah before Jerusalem fell to Babylon in 587 BC; Jeremiah, Habakkuk and Zephaniah at the time of the fall and during the exile; Haggai, Zechariah and Malachi at the time of the return, 538 BC and after. Of the others, Hosea and Amos had a special mission to Israel (the northern kingdom which fell to Assyria in 722 BC); Jonah and Nahum to the Assyrian capital, Nineveh; Daniel in Babylon; Ezekiel to the Jewish exiles in Babylon; and Obadiah to Edom, Israel's long-standing enemy.

God sent these prophets on a daunting and sometimes dangerous mission. They were for the most part despatched at the eleventh hour, to try to halt the people's headlong rush to destruction; to warn them of judgement; to call them back to God in repentance – and after the great crash came, to comfort the survivors with the assurance of God's continuing love and purpose for them. To a man, the prophets went out in the burning conviction that they had a message from God. Some braved death to make it known.

The book of Isaiah. Isaiah's place at the head of the prophetic books is well deserved. There is nothing to equal his tremendous vision of God and the glory in store for God's people until we reach John's book of Revelation, at the end of the New Testament. Other prophets came before him historically, but there was none greater.

Isaiah lived in Jerusalem in the 8th century BC. (For the historical background see article 'The Threat of Assyria'). In chapter 6 he describes his call from God in the year of King Uzziah's death (about 740 BC). He prophesied for over 40 years, through the reigns of Jotham (a godly man like his father), Ahaz (one of Judah's worst kings) and Hezekiah. He may have lived on into the dark days of the evil King Manasseh. He knew from the outset that his words would fall on deaf ears, but he did have one great triumph. When Sennacherib's Assyrian army was hammering at the gates of Jerusalem in Hezekiah's reign (701 BC) the king took Isaiah's advice and the city was saved (chapters 36 - 37).

The initial vision of God in all his glory in the temple (chapter 6) coloured Isaiah's whole mission. He had seen God as the 'Holy One of Israel' and he never forgot it. He had seen human sin for the appalling thing it is, and he never forgot that either. And he had been forgiven and taken into God's service. Throughout his life, he preached God's righteousness, warned of the judgement on sin, and comforted his people with the knowledge of God's love, his longing to forgive, and all the glories in store for those who remained faithful to him.

In the book of Isaiah we have a collection of visions and prophecies belonging to various periods of the prophet's life. It is not always easy to follow – partly because we are unfamiliar with the language and ways of prophets and visionaries; partly because we do not know the principles which determined the present arrangement of material. In places there is clearly a time-sequence. Other parts seem to be

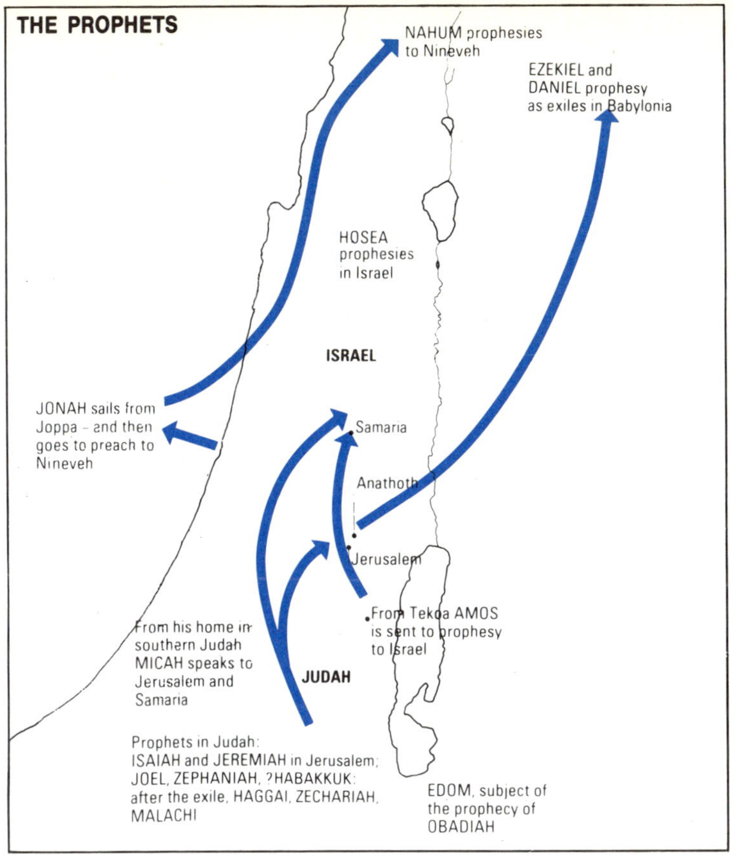

arranged according to subject. Also, because Isaiah was a visionary, his thoughts range freely over the whole scale of time. One minute he is describing God's judgement on the Jerusalem he knows (the Assyrians about to pounce); the next it is God's universal judgement on evil – the end of the world as we know it; the beginning of a reign of perfect peace and justice. What he sees happening in his own time is the outworking of principles which are eternal and universal. And he moves in a flash from the particular to the universal and back again.

We do not know how the book was eventually put together. No doubt Isaiah himself wrote down at least some of his prophecies (see 30:8, and the use of the first person in chapters 6 and 8). Over the past century there has been a great deal of discussion over the differences between chapters 1 - 39 and 40 - 66. These have led many scholars to argue for more than one author – even allowing for the fact that the book was always written on a single scroll, and that the New Testament (which quotes Isaiah more than any other Old Testament book) assumes a single author. Some of the theories on authorship, in the past at least, have been open to criticism on the grounds that they have grown out of a basic presupposition that prediction in the prophets can simply be discounted. On this view, the 8th-century Isaiah could not have predicted with such accuracy events which took place long after his death (notably the fall of Babylon to Cyrus the Persian, 44:28ff.). But this runs counter to one of the main themes of Isaiah 40 - 48: that God demonstrates that he and he alone is God by announcing in advance the events which he as Lord of history will bring about. However, this by no means accounts for all the arguments about authorship. The debate continues.

1 - 5 GOD'S MESSAGE FOR JUDAH AND JERUSALEM

1 The sordid corruption of Judah

Although Jerusalem was not finally destroyed until 587 BC, by Isaiah's time the nation has already virtually reached the point of no return. They have rejected God. And God is sickened by their moral degradation, social injustice and religious hypocrisy. Yet he still offers forgiveness (18). Swift and terrible judgement will fall on all who persist in refusing.

The vision (1): Isaiah describes what God enables him to see in his mind's eye. 'Amoz' is not the same as the prophet Amos.

Holy One of Israel (4): Isaiah's special title for God. It is used only twice in other parts of the Bible.

Verses 7-9: the Assyrians have overrun Judah. The northern kingdom of Israel has already fallen. Only Jerusalem (the 'daughter of Zion') remains. Genesis 19 describes the destruction of Sodom and Gomorrah, two utterly corrupt cities at the southern end of the Dead Sea.

New moon and sabbath (13): the first day of each new month and the weekly sabbath were holy days.

Scarlet ... crimson (18): both fast colours; only God could 'wash' these out.

Oaks (29): the sacred groves where Canaanite rites took place; symbols of the nations' idolatry.

2 - 4 God's coming day: peace and judgement

In these chapters Isaiah looks far ahead to the time when Jerusalem will become the city of God for people of all nations (2:1-5). But before that God will execute fierce judgement on all the wickedness and pride which pollute his people (2:6 - 4:1). For evil has no place in the renewed city; only the few who are faithful to God will survive to enjoy it (4:2-6). The theme is developed in chapters 11 - 12.

Mountain (2:2): Mt Zion, i.e. Jerusalem.

2:6: the practice of magic (forbidden in Leviticus 19:31) and foreign alliances both led to idolatry.

2:13-16: symbols of pride. Solomon used the famous Lebanese cedarwood for his temple. The ships of Tarshish were great ocean-going vessels, the pride of the fleet.

The vineyard (3:14): symbol of the nation, see chapter 5.

Baldness (3:24): heads were shaved as a sign of mourning or degradation.

4:1: so many men have been killed in battle that the women offer to provide their own keep (unheard of in those days), if only the man will marry them.

The branch (4:2): new growth shooting from the old roots (see 11:1); the community is to be reborn.

4:5: cloud and fire – the symbols of God's presence when they journeyed through the desert (Exodus 13:21).

5 The song of the vineyard

The Jewish nation is the vineyard of God. He has done everything necessary to ensure a heavy yield. But the vintage is bitter; so God will abandon the vineyard (but not for ever, see chapter 27). Jesus uses the same picture in Matthew 21:33-41.

In the land of Judah the vast estates built up at the expense of the poor (8) will become waste land. Ten acres of vines will yield only 22 litres; the harvest will be only a tenth of the seed sown (10). Again the prophet denounces pride, luxury, drunkenness, injustice. God will give the signal for the enemy invasion (26ff.) – Assyria first and then Babylon – to destroy them.

Sheol (14): the shadowy world of the dead.

6 ISAIAH'S VISION OF GOD AND CALL TO SERVICE

For the effect this had on his mission, see introduction to the book. Isaiah had many visions, some so terrible, some so wonderful, he could hardly put them into words: but none to equal this. The knowledge that he had seen God with his own eyes, experienced his forgiveness and been sent out in his service would sustain him all his life. And he would need it: for God sent him to a nation deaf and blind to his entreaties (9-10); a nation that would be destroyed and taken captive (11-12). Yet there was hope: the germ of a new nation would survive (13).

Verses 9-10: we trip up here, as elsewhere, over the Hebrew idiom which expresses result as if it were purpose. God did not intend to stop people repenting. He sent Isaiah out with the express purpose of saving people from judgement. But when they heard him they shut their ears and refused to act.

7 - 12 PRESENT AND FUTURE

7 The threat from the north: God warns King Ahaz

The date is about 735 BC. The new king, Ahaz, defied God (2 Kings 16), and in consequence his kingdom came under attack from all quarters. When he refused to join the Israel/Syria alliance against Assyria, they attacked Judah. It is at this point that Isaiah goes to him with God's message (3-9). In the crisis, Ahaz turned to Assyria, not God, for help. But Assyria would soon become a razor (20) in God's hand, to shave his rebel people of their pride and strength.

House of David (2): the royal household.

Syria and Ephraim (2 and 5ff.): Syria (strictly speaking at this date, Aram) was ruled from Damascus. As predicted, the kingdom was crushed by Assyria in 732. 'Ephraim' is the northern kingdom of Israel, which also fell to Assyria. 734-722 BC.

Shearjashub (3): the name means 'a remnant shall return'. The names of both Isaiah's sons stood as a constant reminder of his teaching – see chapter 8 and on 10:20.

Fuller's Field (3): the fuller needed to be near water for his job of cleaning and whitening cloth.

Verses 14-16: the sign seems to have both present and future significance. 1. In the few years it takes for a child conceived now to reach an age when he can choose for himself, Israel and Damascus will cease to be a threat. 2. There will one day be born a child who will truly be 'Immanuel', 'God with us' (see Matthew 1:23).

Curds and honey (15, 22): these symbols of natural plenty, here stand for a waste land where cattle and bees afford the only remaining food supply.

8 Isaiah's own family becomes a sign

God has any number of ways of getting his message across. This time, the fact that Damascus and Samaria are riding for a fall is embodied in the name of Isaiah's baby son. (Maher-shalal-hashbaz means 'Speed spoil, hasten plunder'.) When Assyria has dealt with the rebels she will sweep on into Judah, till Jerusalem itself is surrounded (see chapters 36 - 37).

The prophetess (3): Isaiah's wife.

Shiloah (6): probably an aqueduct outside Jerusalem. Hezekiah's Siloam tunnel had not yet been constructed.

The River (7): Euphrates.

9:1-7 The prince of peace

Isaiah sweeps his listeners far into the future with this glorious vision. Zebulun and Naphtali in Galilee were the first of the tribes to be crushed by Assyria. They will be first to see the light, to taste the joy, to be set free by the prince of peace. Nazareth, in Galilee, was the home of Jesus; Cana in Galilee the place where his public ministry began with the very first miracle.

The way of the sea (1): the main highway between Egypt and Syria passed through Galilee.

Day of Midian (4): the day of Gideon's great victory against the Midianites, Judges 7.

9:8 - 10:4 God warns Israel of what is coming

Isaiah switches abruptly to the present. Israel (the breakaway northern kingdom) stands condemned for her arrogance and rebellion, injustice and oppression. She has already had a taste of judgement, but learnt nothing from it. Therefore God will not spare her.

(The Assyrians took many Israelites captive in 734, but Samaria held out till 722. Israel had turned a deaf ear to the warnings of Amos and the appeals of Hosea (Isaiah's contemporary), the two prophets God had specially sent them.)

The prophecy is written in four stanzas, each ending with the same refrain (12, 17, 21, 10:4).

10:5-34 God sends Assyria against his people

God makes use of a proud and cruel nation to punish his people. But Assyria's excessive ferocity is not excused: it will be punished. Even at the height of judgement God never loses sight of his purpose to save. A remnant – pathetically few – of his people will survive to trust and serve him.

Verse 9: a list of cities and city-states conquered by Assyria – all Syrian except for Samaria.

There was none ... (14): a vivid way of expressing the total absence of any resistance.

The remnant (20): this is one of the key themes in Isaiah. It goes back to the day God called him into service (6:13), and runs as a thread of hope through the darkest messages of judgement. This same faithful remnant is to realize all the glorious promises for the future.

Verse 26: see Judges 7 and Exodus 14.

Verses 28ff.: Gibeah, just north of Jerusalem was Saul's capital; Anathoth, a few miles east, the home of Jeremiah. Isaiah pictures an attack on Jerusalem from the north, the usual route of invading armies from countries to the north or east.

Sennacherib actually approached from Lachish, to the south-west.

11 - 12 The perfect king: the perfect kingdom

The theme of earlier passages (2:2-4; 4:2-6; 9:1-7) is developed more fully here. The coming king will be from David's family ('Jesse', 1, was David's father). He will possess the Spirit of God himself: just, righteous, faithful, like God. His will be an international kingdom, free of enmity and evil, utterly transformed. There will be a great gathering in of all God's people, and the song of God's salvation will be on everyone's lips. Isaiah pictures it all in physical terms. But what he sees is a radical change. This is a new, God-centred earth (see 65:17ff. and Revelation 21).

13 - 23 GOD WARNS THE NATIONS OF JUDGEMENT

A collection of prophecies against foreign nations given at various times. God's concern is not limited to Israel. The world was his then; it is his now, and his people should realize that.

13 - 14:23 Babylon

See also chapters 46 - 47. In Isaiah's day Babylon was struggling for independence from Assyria. Here he steps forward 100 years to see Babylon at the height of her power – and to look beyond, to the day when Babylon in turn would be brought down. In 539 Babylon fell to the Medes and Persians led by Cyrus. Xerxes destroyed the city in 478, and it was finally abandoned in the 4th century BC. In the New Testament, Babylon is universalized, as the city of rebel man, implacably opposed to God (Revelation 17; it also serves as a cover-word for Rome).

Ophir (13:12): see on 1 Kings 9:28.

13:21-22: a list of repulsive creatures. The 'satyrs' are demons of desert places.

King of Babylon (14:4): the taunt-song is addressed, not to a particular king, but to the dynasty, representing the whole kingdom.

14:13: the very same thoughts which brought God's judgement on Babylon's predecessor, Babel (Genesis 11:1-9).

14:24-27 Assyria

Assyria's fate is also sealed (see on 10:5-34). Ultimately Babylon will break the power of Assyria. But before that there will be a signal defeat in God's own land (25; see chapters 36 - 37).

14:28-32 Philistia

The date is probably 716 BC. Assyria is in trouble, and the Philistines (old enemies of Israel, occupying the coastal plain) try to persuade Judah to join them in rebellion. But the Assyrians are far from finished (29, 31); and the Philistines are doomed. God's people must learn to trust in him.

15 - 16 Moab

The Moabites were descendants of Abraham's nephew, Lot. They occupied the plateau land east of the Dead Sea. It was from Moab that Ruth came. At times the Moabites were on good terms with the Israelites, but they had no share in Israel's faith. Isaiah is stirred to sympathy at the spectacle of Moab's suffering (15:5), now only three short years away (16:14). Moab sends to Jerusalem for help, and God urges his people to take the fugitives in (16:1-5).

The cities of Moab fell to Assyria in successive campaigns. They were to fall again to Nebuchadnezzar of Babylon.

15:1-9: these are all towns in Moab. 'Nebo' is the mountain from which Moses viewed the promised land; 'Zoar' a town at the southern end of the Dead Sea, spared in the overthrow of Sodom. The 'Brook of the willows' is probably the boundary between Moab and Edom to the south.

Baldness (15:2): see on 3:24.

Sela (16:1): 'the rock', the fortress in Jordan where Petra now stands.

16:3-5: these verses may be Moab's plea to Judah or God's word to his people.

Vine of Sibmah (16:8ff.): a region famous for its wine – here a symbol of national prosperity.

Years of a hireling (14): the hired man works no more than the time contracted for; so, 'three years, and barely that'.

17 Damascus

A prophecy from Isaiah's early days – see on chapter 7. In response to King Ahaz' appeal for help against the Syria/Israel alliance, the Assyrians launched a series of raids in which Damascus was plundered and King Rezin met his death. This prophecy also attacks Israel for siding with Syria against their own brother-nation of Judah.

Asherim ... (8): Canaanite cult-images and altars.

Hivites, Amorites (9): tribes destroyed by the Israelites in the conquest of Canaan.

18 Ethiopia/Cush

This is modern Sudan. In Isaiah's day Egypt was ruled by an 'Ethiopian' dynasty. The Assyrian threat brings envoys from afar. But God will deal with the invader on the very eve of victory (5 - 6 – see 37:36ff.). And the far-off nation will send gifts in grateful homage to God (7; see 2 Chronicles 32:23).

19 Egypt

Isaiah foretells the disintegration of Egypt: internal strife, followed by conquest, a ruined economy and breakdown of leadership (1-15). Egypt was defeated by Assyria when Sennacherib's army besieged Jerusalem (701 BC). Further defeats culminated in the sack of Thebes in 663 BC when the Assyrians pillaged centuries of temple treasures. But God uses the sword for surgery, not anarchy. Verses 16-24 reveal his ultimate purpose, the conversion of Egypt. 'That day' (i.e. the day of God's judgement – both temporal and final – a frequent phrase throughout Isaiah) is the day of God's final intervention in judgement and salvation on a worldwide scale. That day, the New Testament tells us, is the day of Christ's return.

After Jerusalem fell in 587 there were numerous influential colonies of Jews in Egypt and in Assyria. A copy of the Jewish temple was even constructed at Leontopolis in Egypt about 170 BC. But all that was only a pale shadow of what Isaiah envisages here.

Zoan (11) ... Memphis (13): respectively the current and ancient capitals of Egypt. Zoan (Tanis) was in the delta region; Memphis just south of it on the Nile.

City of the sun (18): Heliopolis = On; centre of Egyptian sun-worship

20 Egypt and Ethiopia

'The year' (1) is 711 BC, when the Assyrians crushed the Philistine rebellion at Ashdod. The support expected from Egypt had not materialized. God instructs Isaiah to play the role of a slave (2) to illustrate the coming captivity of Egypt and warn his people to place no reliance on help from that quarter. In 701 BC (see on chapter 19 above) Egypt was defeated by Assyria.

Naked (2): i.e. wearing only a loin-cloth.

21 Babylon; Dumah (Edom); Arabia

The 'wilderness of the sea' (1) is Babylon (9). See on chapters 13 - 14. The downfall of Babylon will be good news to the captives from Israel (10). Even so, Isaiah is appalled by what he foresees. There is temporary respite for Edom (Dumah, 11-12) – but judgement was to follow (see 34:5). Not even the remote tribes of Arabia (13-16) will escape the long arm of Assyria. This prophecy became reality when Sargon attacked Arabia in 715 BC.

Verse 16: 'Kedar', a powerful Bedouin tribe; 'years of a hireling', see on 16:14.

22 Jerusalem, the 'valley of vision'

Jerusalem was Isaiah's base, the place where he had his visions. The city is surrounded by valleys and mountains, and he may have had a particular spot in mind. Despite the reprieve in Hezekiah's day (chapters 36 - 37), Isaiah foresees the future destruction of Jerusalem. (Nebuchadnezzar II of Babylon eventually took the city after a terrible siege in 587 BC. The walls were broken down and the temple destroyed.) The people's reaction in the face of disaster is a mixture of frenzied activity and sheer escapism (8-13). Verses 15ff. relate to Isaiah's own day. Shebna, a high official in Hezekiah's court (36:3) is to be demoted, and Eliakim promoted. But he will find himself unable to cope with his hangers-on, and his authority will be short-lived.

Elam ... Kir (6): outposts of the Assyrian Empire which no doubt supplied conscripts to the army.

House of the forest (8): an arsenal, see 1 Kings 7:2; 10:17.

Verses 9, 11: it was vital to any city to ensure its water supply in the event of siege. See 2 Chronicles 32 for the Siloam tunnel, Hezekiah's solution to the problem.

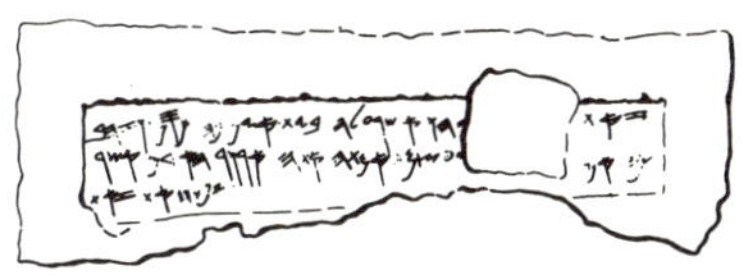

The lintel of a tomb, found at Siloam in Jerusalem, with the name of a royal steward, possibly Shebna. The inscription is one of the longest in ancient Hebrew so far discovered.

23 Tyre

For centuries Tyre (modern Sour in Lebanon) dominated the sea-trade in the eastern Mediterranean. Her colonies, of which Cyprus was the

nearest, were widespread. And her merchantmen ventured as far afield as the Indian Ocean and the English Channel. A major tradeline was Egyptian grain (3). Tyre was a city corrupted by her own wealth and success, and Isaiah warns of the approaching end. He spoke truly. In 722 the city fell to Sargon of Assyria. In 701 the ruler of Tyre fled to Cyprus as Sennacherib approached. As Assyria declined, Tyre regained her power, only to lose it again to the Babylonians.
Tarshish (6): probably 'Tartessus' in Spain.
Chaldeans (13): Chaldea was part of south Babylonia, but when Chaldean kings came to power in Babylon the term was used of the Babylonian kingdom as a whole.
Seventy years (15): probably a round figure, meaning a lifetime.

24 - 27 GOD'S FINAL JUDGEMENT AND VICTORY

From the particular – God's judgement on specific nations – we move to the universal – his judgement on the whole world and everyone in it. Life will not go on for ever just as it is. There will come a point when God will step in and end the world as we know it; when the earth will rock on its foundations. Isaiah was in no doubt about it. Neither was Jesus (see Matthew 24). But God's purpose is not just to condemn. One chapter (24) on judgement is followed by three (25-27) on his glorious salvation.

A song of joy in God, who makes the weak and helpless his concern (25:1-5), leads into a description of the joys awaiting God's people on the far side of judgement (25:6-12). Chapter 26 breaks into song again. Its theme is trust. In life there is waiting (8ff.), suffering and failure (16-18). But God holds fast his own, even through death (19). The song of the vineyard in 27:2-13 contrasts with chapter 5. The day will come when God's purpose for his people will be fulfilled. The present punishment is intended as a corrective. The exile will end. In the final harvest all God's people will be brought home.
That day (24:21, etc.): see on chapter 19 above.
Moab (25:10): the current enemy of God's people stands for all such enemies.
Thy dew (26:19): a picture of God's power to revive the dead.
Leviathan ... (27:1): the dragon/serpent figure from pagan mythology. God's judgement extends to the superhuman realm (see 24:21). The same figure is used in Revelation 12:9 to depict Satan.
Asherim (27:9): see on 17:8 above.
27:10-11: refers to the oppressors, whose suffering will be far greater than that of God's people.

28 - 31 MORE WARNINGS TO GOD'S REBELLIOUS PEOPLE

28 Woe to Samaria and Judah's leaders

Attention is turned once again to the sins of Isaiah's own day. Verses 1-6, addressed to Israel, belong to the time before Samaria fell. The pleasure-loving, luxury-loving city is ripe for the plucking – and Assyria's hand is outstretched to take it. Yet a remnant (see on 10:20 above) will remain.

The leaders come under special attack (7ff.). Religious leaders and rulers alike have not led but misled the people. They are so cocksure, they think they can dictate terms to death itself. They will discover how wrong they are (18). Real security rests with God.
Verses 9-13: J. B. Phillips translates 10, 13: 'The-law-is-the-law-is-the-law, The-rule-is-the-rule-is-the-rule.' Isaiah's hearers are deliberately making nonsense of God's message; 9-10 may be their sneering reply to the prophet. To those who treat God's words as gibberish, Isaiah says that God will deliver his next message in Assyrian!
Verse 21: refers to David's victories; see 1 Chronicles 14:8-17.
Verses 23-29: a parable, meaning there is method in the 'madness' of God's present actions, just as the farmer has good reason for the way he works.

29 Woe to Jerusalem

'Ariel' stands for Mt Zion/Jerusalem (8). The city will be besieged (3) and then reprieved (5ff. and see 37:36). God's word to his people has become a closed book, because they pay him only lip-service (11-16). But the day is coming (17ff.) when those who are deaf and blind to his message will hear and see, when God's people will once again fear and obey him.
Verse 17: a picture of things suddenly reversed: the forests become fields and fields forests. The same thought continues in the verses that follow.
The meek ... the poor (19): people loyal to God, not simply the victims of social injustice (see Matthew 5:3, 5).

30 - 31 Woe to the rebels who rely on Egypt

Judah is in league with Egypt and thinks herself secure against Assyria (28:15), despite all Isaiah's earlier warnings. But when it comes to the crunch Egypt will sit tight (7) while the Assyrians invade Judah (chapters 36 - 37). It is God – the One they would not trust (9-12) – who will save them in the end (27-33; 31:5-9; 37:36). He calls on them yet again to turn to him (31:6).
Zoan (30:4): see on 19:11.
30:6: the gifts are carried through the Negev desert to Egypt.
Rahab (30:7): a poetic synonym for Egypt.
30:33: the oppressor will be utterly destroyed. 'Topheth' ('a burning place') is in the valley of Hinnom, just outside Jerusalem, where in Israel's darkest days children were sacrificed to the pagan god Molech. The valley later supplied the name for hell, 'Gehenna'.

32 - 35 THE GLORIOUS FUTURE – AND THE DARK DAYS PRECEDING IT

32 The future king; peace by a hard road

Isaiah sees far into the future (1-8), returns to his own day at verse 9, and at verse 15 looks forward again to a time of lasting peace, justice and righteousness brought about by the working of God's Holy Spirit in his people. But before the king comes, present evil must be swept away, and people shaken out of their complacency. They will lose all that they now enjoy – until God steps in once again (15).
Verse 9: the cossetted women of Jerusalem typify the society of Isaiah's day.

Assyrian soldiers return from a victory.

Verse 19: the meaning is not clear; 'forest' and 'city' may refer to enemies.

33 When God intervenes

This is a chapter with many changes of speaker and mood. Isaiah does not name the destroyer (1). His description (7-9) can apply to many times beside his own. Only those who live by their faith in God remain unshaken in circumstances like these (2-6; 15-16). God never deserts his own; the city defended by him is unassailable (17-24). His presence guarantees stability, prosperity, security (20-21).

34 Judgement on the nations

God will one day avenge the wrong done to his people (8; see also chapter 24). Edom – the enemy par excellence – is singled out as an example. The destruction is total: the whole land rendered uninhabitable for man.
Bozrah (6): at various times Edom's capital city.

35 Salvation for God's people

This chapter stands in striking contrast to the horror of 34. Destruction gives way to re-creation. God is coming to bring his people home by a safe highway. At the sight of him everything is changed. The dry and lifeless desert, bursting for joy, becomes a paradise of flowing streams, great trees and the glowing colours of flowers.

36 - 39 CONTEMPORARY EVENTS: CRISES IN HEZEKIAH'S REIGN

See on 2 Kings 18 - 20, an almost identical account apart from Hezekiah's poem (38:9-20). See also 2 Chronicles 32. Hezekiah's illness and the embassy from Babylon probably preceded the siege (about 705-702 BC). The events may have been reversed here to provide a lead-in to the following chapters, which are focussed on Babylon as the world power she later became. 'Peace in my time' was Hezekiah's reaction to the terrible prediction of conquest and captivity (39:5-8). Isaiah could draw no comfort from the thought.

40 - 48 ON THE BRINK OF FREEDOM

Up to this point Isaiah has been largely taken up with the threat from Assyria. Now that particular crisis is behind him. He is given a new vision for a new situation. Jerusalem has been saved from Assyria, but the city *will* fall to Babylon and the captive people will be taken into exile. This will not be the end of the nation, though it will seem like it. In due course Babylon itself will be overthrown by Cyrus the Persian, and he will return the exiles to their homeland. All this God reveals to the prophet, so that he may comfort and encourage the people, reassuring them for the bitter times ahead. So clear is all this in Isaiah's mind that from now on he leaves current events behind. In 40 - 48 he stands with the captives in Babylon at the end of their long exile.

40 A message of comfort: God's forgiveness and his infinite power

There is comfort for God's people: he is coming as he promised (1-11; see chapter 35). Israel's God is God the Creator: incomparable, eternal. He never stops caring for his people (12-31).

Double (2): not twice as much, but an equal measure.

Verses 3-5: these verses sum up the mission of John the Baptist, see Luke 3:1-6.

Verse 11: Jesus took up this picture, describing himself as the good shepherd, see John 10:11.

41 'Fear not ... I will help you'

God's tone is stern as he brings the nations to book (1). But with his own people he is infinitely loving and tender (8ff.). He is at hand to help. They have nothing to fear.

One from the east (2) ... one from the north (25): 44:28 names the new conqueror, Cyrus the Persian (from Israel the route was north, then east).

Verses 21-24: the pagan gods – who are no gods – cannot predict things to come. Only God, the one true God, can do that.

42 A light for the nations

A new theme begins to unfold, alongside the forecast of Babylon's downfall: God's plan to open the eyes of the whole world and bring salvation to all mankind. This was, from the very beginning, the intended role of Israel (Genesis 22:18). So, to begin with the servant of God in Isaiah's series of 'songs' is the nation (or faithful remnant) of Israel. But Israel failed to be God's true servant in the way he intended (19-25). And so, in the series of portraits which follow (49:1-13; 50:4-9; 52:13-53:12; 61:1-4), the realization gradually dawns that God's purpose will ultimately be fulfilled not through the nation but through one who will be his true servant. The New Testament writers are in no doubt that the servant Isaiah foresaw – who would save men by suffering on their behalf – was Jesus Christ (Matthew 12:15-21). They have Christ's own authority for saying so (Luke 4:16-21).

43 God's unfailing love and care

By their constant disobedience, God's people have forfeited all right to his care (22-24) – yet he forgives (25). In all their sufferings he is beside them (2). He will set them free again, simply because he loves them (4ff.).

Verses 16-17: this refers to the exodus from Egypt.

44 - 45 No God but God; the forecast of Israel's return

These chapters continue the themes that run through the whole section: Israel as God's servant, the object of his love (44:1-5); God as Lord of history, the only Person able to draw back the veil on the future (44:6ff.); the lifeless no-gods that men worship; God's promise that he will set his people free. 44:26 - 45:13 take us a stage further. The general promise becomes specific. In the reign of Cyrus, Jerusalem and its temple will be rebuilt (see on Ezra 1:1-4ff.).

Cyrus (44:28): many find it hard to believe Isaiah could actually have named the king so far in advance. God can reveal what no man could possibly predict (41:21-24, 26-27; 42:9; 43:12-13; 44:6-8; 45:18-21).

45:22-25: God's love reaches beyond Israel to the world. The New Testament applies verse 23 directly to Christ; see Philippians 2:10-11.

The superstition and fear involved in idol-worship is expressed by this colossal statue, which stands about 15ft/5m high.

46 - 47 The downfall of Babylon

See also chapters 13 - 14 above. The indictment of pagan gods reaches its climax in the passive submission of the Babylonian gods Bel and Nebo. These dumb idols burden the backs of their worshippers. The real God is One who carries his people's burdens, who has power not only to speak but to act. Chapter 47 (like 14:4-21) is a taunt-song. Babylon will be shown as little mercy as she has shown others.

47:1: 'Virgin daughter', the city of Babylon; 'Chaldeans', see on 23:13.

48 God's patient love for faithless Israel

The history of Israel is one long tale of hypocrisy, rebellion, scepticism, idolatry. She has fully deserved all she has suffered. God always purposed peace for his people (18), but there could be 'no peace for the wicked'. Now the moment of liberation has come: he says 'Go forth'.

Verse 16: there is a change of speaker here; the voice may be the prophet's or that of the servant/Messiah, as in 49:1, etc.

49 - 55 THE SERVANT OF GOD AND THE REDEMPTION OF HIS PEOPLE

These chapters give us a series of portraits of God's servant and his mission (see on chapter 42 above) in the course of God's message to his people. The context generally indicates when the term 'servant' refers to Israel, and when it refers to that individual representative of the true Israel who was yet to come

49 - 50 A word to put new heart into Israel

God's servant has a mission to Israel – and beyond Israel to the world (49:6). Comfort, compassion and restoration are the keynotes of 49:14 - 50:3. 50:4ff. returns to God's servant, and for the first time we glimpse his suffering and rejection (see chapter 53). But nothing can deflect him from his purpose.

50:1: God did not divorce his unfaithful 'wife', Israel; he brought her lovingly home (see Hosea 3:1; Hosea was declaring his message to Israel at the same time as Isaiah proclaimed God's word in Judah.)

51 - 52:12 Israel released and restored

God urges his people to draw comfort from past history, and to look forward to a greater exodus yet. It is time to shake off grief and lethargy. There is good news. God is about to escort his people home.

Rahab (51:9): see on 30:7.

52:13 - 53:12 God's servant suffers for his people

The scene shifts from the joyous home-coming to the lonely figure who paid the price of it. He bore the whole burden of sin which estranged humanity from God, and it cost him his life. Isaiah, eight centuries before Christ, clearly foresaw him. He knew why he must come and what he would do. He saw the Saviour giving his life for mankind. He saw God raise him high in exaltation. (Compare 53:5-9 with Matthew 27:11-13, 26-31, 41-43, 57-60. Compare 53:4-6, 10-12 with Romans 5:6-9, 18-19; 1 Peter 2:21-24; Philippians 2:5-11.)

54 - 55 The expanding kingdom; salvation for all nations

God pledges himself in tender, unswerving, enduring love to his people. In peace and security the foundations of a new and dazzling city are laid (54:11ff.; and compare Revelation 21:18ff.). The gates stand wide in welcome to men of every nation who respond to God's invitation (55:1-7).

The vision in the later chapters of Isaiah (as earlier, at 2:2-4; 4:2-6; 9:2-7; 11 - 12; 25; 35) goes far beyond the events of the actual return from exile. The restoration of Israel which took place then, merges into a vision of the final glorious day when sin and sorrow will be no more, and the whole Israel of God (see Romans 9 - 11; Galatians 3) will be for ever at home with the Lord (Revelation 21).

56 - 66 ISRAEL'S SHAME AND ISRAEL'S GLORY

Isaiah turns back from Babylon and the exile to the land of Israel. In these final chapters scenes of sin and failure mingle with scenes of future glory.

56:1-8 Welcome for the outcasts

There is nothing exclusive about the love of God. There is a place among his people for all who will follow and obey him (1-8), even the most despised.

56:9 - 59:21 God's accusations against Israel

59:1-2 gets right to the heart of the matter: sin cuts men off from God. Israel has been guilty of many sins – the charges are quite specific. Spiritual and secular leaders alike have gone soft and failed in their jobs (56:9-12). The nation has gone running after pagan gods, joining in sexual rites and child-sacrifice (57:4-13; see 2 Chronicles 33:1-9). Their religious observance is a hollow mockery: the people love neither God nor their fellow men (58). Society is rotten to the core, riddled with lies, dishonesty, injustice, malice and violence (59:1-13). It has no time for truth and justice, or for the individual who upholds them (59:14-15). All these things stand in stark contrast to all that God, in his amazing love, wants for his people (57:14-19; 58:6-14; 59:20-21).

Beds (57:2): i.e. their graves.

57:5-8: the pagan rites involved prostitution. Idolatrous Israel unfaithful to God, is pictured as a prostitute.

Molech (57:9): see on 30:33.

Public squares (59:14): the 'lawcourt' of the day, where cases were heard and justice was dispensed.

59:21: compare this with the new covenant described in Jeremiah 31:31-34.

60 - 62 The nation's glory

In the unbridgeable gap between the shame of Israel and her glory stands the figure of God the Avenger and Redeemer (59:16-21). Chapter 60 pictures the incredible transformation. Isaiah sees the return to God's favour in very 'earthly' terms: fabulous wealth, power, influence. But it is very different from the earth we know (17-22); and the New Testament translates Isaiah's concept into spiritual and universal terms (see on chapters 54 - 55 above).

Although unnamed, the voice in 61:1-4 is that of the servant (see Luke 4:16-21). In 61:5-9 God's people become the nation of priests he always intended them to be (Exodus 19:6; and see 1 Peter 2:9), breaking into a song of praise (10-11). The day is coming (62) when God will be able to rejoice and delight in his people: a day to long for, pray for, prepare for.

60:6-7: 'Ephah', a Midianite tribe; 'Kedar' and 'Nebaioth', Arabian tribes. Their wealth lay in their camels, sheep and goats.

Double portion (61:7): here Isaiah has in mind the share of the firstborn son.

63:1-6 A vision of the Avenger

See also 59:16ff. Edom (which means red) and its capital, Bozrah, represents all the enemies of God's people. This is an appalling picture; but until the enemy is defeated, God's people cannot be set free (see Revelation 19:11-16).

63:7 - 64:12 Prayer for God's people

The recollection of all God's past goodness and faithfulness (63:7-14) leads into an impassioned appeal for his response to the crying need of his people.

65 - 66 God's answer: new heavens and a new earth

God will answer the prayer for his people in a way which exceeds their wildest dreams. But the answer will be two-edged: for those who align themselves against him, total destruction, the sweeping away of every vestige of evil; for his faithful ones, life, joy, peace beyond imagining, in a heaven and earth made new. So the final prophecies of Isaiah highlight the contrasting destinies of men, in a sharp play of light and darkness. God cannot overlook evil. Those who go their own sinful way (65:1-7, 11-14), who refuse to listen to God (66:3-4), will be punished. But God has a place reserved in his new world for men of humble faith: not only for faithful Israel, but for people of all nations (66:18-23).

65:8: the bunch is poor, but it contains some good grapes which are not to be wasted.

Fortune, Destiny (65:11): pagan gods of fate, Gad and Meni, to whom sacrificial offerings were made.

65:25: see 11:6-9.

66:19: Isaiah pictures men streaming in from distant lands – from Spain (Tarshish) in the far west, from Africa (Put, Lud) to the south, from the far north, Anatolia (Tubal) and across from Greece (Javan).

THE THREAT OF ASSYRIA

Alan Millard

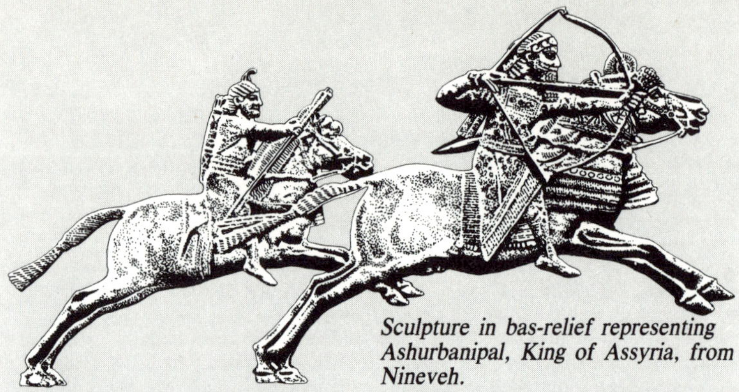

Sculpture in bas-relief representing Ashurbanipal, King of Assyria, from Nineveh.

For 200 years, from about 850 to 650 BC, the kingdoms of Syria and Palestine were over-shadowed by Assyria. Her kings had reached the Mediterranean in the days of Israel's Judges, but pressure from Aramaean tribes then establishing themselves in Syria stopped them keeping control so far afield.

In 853 BC Shalmaneser III led Assyria against a coalition including Ben-hadad of Syria and Ahab of Israel, although he gained no clear victory until 841 BC. Ahab brought Israel into direct conflict with Assyria, who now looked upon her as a tributary state. Jehu's embassy is shown on Shalmaneser's Black Obelisk, bringing valuable gifts.

Assyrian activity gave Israel some relief from oppression by Damascus. Although the usurper Hasael briefly reimposed this yoke (see 2 Kings 8:12; 12:17ff.), it was broken by an Assyrian campaign about 800 BC when Jehoash paid tribute; and Israel rapidly expanded. Jeroboam II and then Uzziah of Judah seem to have become the principal monarchs of southern Syria and Palestine while Assyria's fortunes varied.

However, in 745 BC Tiglath-pileser III began to restore Assyria's imperial state. Menahem of Israel paid tribute, but anti-Assyrian elements replaced his son by their nominee Pekah, only to see him displaced in due course by the Assyrian-approved Hoshea. It was Hoshea's defection that resulted in the Assyrian capture of Samaria in 722 BC and the deportation of its people.

The policy of exile had always been employed by powerful kings, and was an ever-present threat to smaller nations. Assyrian kings did not apply it indiscriminately; it was a final weapon against obstinately rebellious states. Where a vassal and people were loyal they lived undisturbed, even helped by Assyria when enemies attacked. It is in this light that Assyria's relations with Israel and Judah should be seen.

Pekah's anti-Assyrian stance pushed Ahaz of Judah into Assyria's arms for protection, and so Hezekiah's independent policies brought harsh retribution from Sennacherib (701 BC). Thereafter, Manasseh remained loyal to Assyria, following an enforced visit to Babylon (2 Chronicles 33:11), and enjoyed a long reign (about 687-642 BC). Josiah profited from Assyrian complacency to strengthen Judah, but he lost his life trying to hinder Egyptian troops going to help the last Assyrian king (609 BC; 2 Kings 23:29). It was to these situations that the prophets Amos, Hosea, Micah and Isaiah spoke. They showed that God's people could not escape the consequences of faithlessness in human affairs, any more than the other nations they quoted as examples. They showed, too, that God's people could not escape the consequences of disloyalty to their alliance with God. He could use other nations to chasten them in furthering his purpose.

Old Testament 4.2

JEREMIAH

Jeremiah appears on the scene about 100 years after Isaiah. He was born into a priestly family at Anathoth (Anata), a few miles north of Jerusalem, about 640 BC, and was called to be God's prophet in 627. 2 Kings 22 - 25 and 2 Chronicles 34 - 36 provide the historical background to Jeremiah's prophecies.

The power of Assyria was already crumbling when he began to declare God's message to Judah. For 40 years – through the reigns of Judah's last five kings – Jeremiah warned of coming disaster and appealed in vain to the nation to turn back to God. With the death of godly King Josiah in 609 religious and political affairs worsened. Judah was caught in the crossfire between the contending world powers: Babylon to the north, and a resurgent Egypt to the south. Babylon emerged supreme, to become the instrument of God's

JUDAH'S LAST KINGS

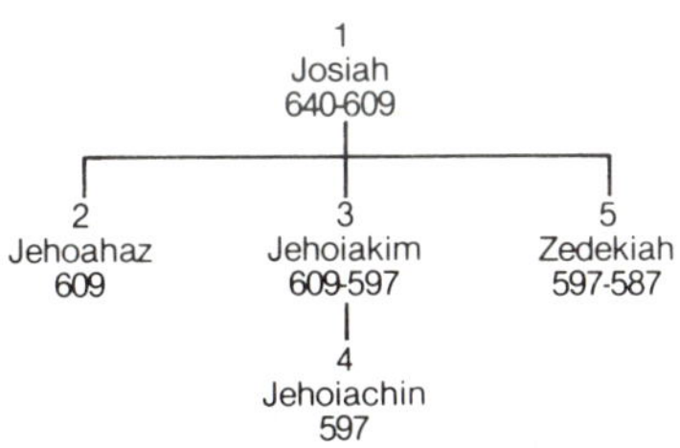

judgement on his godless people. In 587 the army of Nebuchadnezzar of Babylon broke into Jerusalem, destroyed the city and took the people captive into exile. Jeremiah was offered a comfortable life at court, but chose instead to remain in Judah. When Gedaliah (the governor appointed by Nebuchadnezzar) was murdered, the people fled to Egypt, taking Jeremiah with them. As far as we know he ended his days there, still declaring God's words to men who refused to listen.

Jeremiah was not the only prophet of his day. Among his contemporaries were Habakkuk and Zephaniah; Daniel, at the Babylonian court; and Ezekiel, among the exiles in Babylon. But he stands out, a lonely figure: isolated by a message from God which made him increasingly unpopular; branded a traitor for advocating submission to Babylon. He was imprisoned and often in danger of his life. Yet this sensitive, unselfconfident man never once compromised his message from God. He could not help but declare the terrible fate he saw in store for his nation. And he grieved over their stubborn refusal to take notice. The times were dark; his message sombre; yet to write him off as a born pessimist does him injustice. There is a strong streak of hope running through his prophecies. After the judgement, after the exile, God will restore the joy and prosperity of his people in their homeland.

Jeremiah's book (which grew from the scroll dictated to Baruch, chapter 36) is a glorious mixture of literary forms: prose and poetry, taunt and lament, acted parable, biography and history. He added bits to it at various times, and not all of them are dated. The material is not arranged in historical order, which makes some of it difficult to set against the right background. The key events of Jeremiah's lifetime are listed, and dates are indicated in the text wherever possible.

MAJOR EVENTS OF JEREMIAH'S LIFETIME

627 Jeremiah called to be God's prophet. Death of Ashurbanipal, last great king of Assyria.

621 Discovery of the book of the law. King Josiah's great reformation begins.

612 Nineveh, capital of Assyria, falls to Babylon.

609 The Egyptian army marches north to bolster collapsing Assyria. Josiah intercepts it at Megiddo and is killed. On his return from Assyria, Pharaoh Necho deposes the new king, Jehoahaz, placing Jehoiakim on the throne.

605 Egyptian forces routed at Carchemish by Nebuchadnezzar of Babylon.

604 Nebuchadnezzar subdues Syria, Judah and Philistine cities.

598 Alliance with Egypt brings the Babylonian forces down on Judah again.

597 King Jehoiakim dies. Jerusalem falls to Babylon after a two-month siege. The new king, Jehoiachin, is deported with others to Babylon. His uncle, Zedekiah, is put on the throne.

588 Under pressure from the pro-Egypt party, Zedekiah breaks faith with Babylon. Jerusalem under siege for 18 months.

587 The Babylonian army breaks into Jerusalem. The people are deported; the city plundered and burned. Three months later, governor Gedaliah is murdered. Jeremiah is taken to Egypt.

1 - 25 GOD SPEAKS TO JUDAH AND JERUSALEM

1 Jeremiah's call to be God's prophet

The date is 627 BC. Jeremiah is a young man, probably in his early twenties, and as reluctant to become God's spokesman as Moses before him (Exodus 3:10 - 4:17). But about one thing he had no doubt. His message was a word from God himself. 'The word of the Lord came to me' runs as a refrain right through the book, from first to last. In this lay his certainty, and his compulsion.

Verses 1-3: see introduction.
Almond ... watching (11-12): there is a play on words in the Hebrew. The almond is the first tree to blossom in spring. God's actions follow his words equally swiftly.
Verse 13: the forces of Babylon are like a cauldron about to pour its scalding contents on Judah. In this period of Jewish history trouble always came from the north: the powerful armies of Assyria first; then, in Jeremiah's day, the Babylonians.

2 - 3:10 God charges his people with unfaithfulness

The heathen nations are at least loyal to idols (10-11). Not so the people of the living God. Their offence is set before them in a series of vivid pictures. They prefer their own polluted water to God's fresh spring (13). They would sooner turn to Egypt and Assyria for help than to God (18). The vine of Israel has gone wild (21). Like a wife turned common prostitute, the nation has run after foreign gods (20, 23-25, 33; 3:1-10).
Baal (2:8): the Canaanite god
Cyprus ... Kedar (2:10): from west to east (Kedar is in Arabia): the whole pagan world.
2:13: compare Jesus' words: John 4:13-15; 7:37.
Memphis ... Tahpanhes (2:16): cities of Egypt – Memphis near Cairo; Tah-

A pagan altar at Byblos, Lebanon.

panhes a frontier town in the eastern Nile delta, on the route to Palestine.
Strangers (2:25): pagan gods.
3:1 such a thing was unlawful; see Deuteronomy 24:1-4.
3:6-10: 'Israel' here refers to the northern kingdom whose people had been carried into exile a century before, in 722 BC (verse 8). King Josiah's religious reforms (beginning in 621 BC), far-reaching though they were, did not change the heart of the nation.

3:11 - 4:4 'Return, O Israel, says the Lord'

Even now God will save his people if they repent. He will bring them back from exile a united nation (18) whose worship is a living reality, not a mere ritual (16; 4:4; and compare 31:31-34).
The ark (16): in which the law was kept in the inner sanctuary of the temple. It is no longer needed when God's law is written on every heart.
The shameful thing (24): a euphemism for 'Baal'.
4:4: all Jewish boy babies were circumcised when they were eight days old, as a sign that they had entered into covenant relationship with God (Genesis 17:1-14). But no external mark can make a man God's child without an accompanying 'circumcision' of heart, mind and will.

4:5-31 Approaching disaster

Destruction and devastation are about to fall on Judah. Jeremiah is given a preview of the nation's collapse before the Babylonian army which fills him with unspeakable horror (19-31).
Verse 11: the scorching desert wind is a symbol of destruction.
Dan (15): the northernmost town in the land; first in the path of the invader.
Verse 23: God is unmaking the earth; see Genesis 1:2.
Verse 30: a picture of Jerusalem (the 'daughter of Zion'), unrepentant still; still seeking foreign aid.

5 National corruption

God searches in vain for a vestige of truth and justice among his people. The nation is steeped in idolatry; happy with a rotten society; untroubled by conscience. God and his prophets alike are disregarded. It is false prophecy the people want to hear. God has no option but to punish.

6 Declaration of war

All God's warnings have fallen on deaf ears. His call to men to walk 'the good way' (16) has met with flat refusal. So God has rejected his people (30) and turned them over to the invading armies. Even Jerusalem will be besieged.
Tekoa, Beth-hac-cherem (1): two hills south of Jerusalem.
Shepherds (3): a picture of the enemy encampments.
Noon (4): it was not usual to attack in the heat of the day.
Sheba (20): in Arabia; famous for the incense it exported.
Assayer (27): testing the nation, as precious metals are tested.

7 - 8:3 In the temple

The people had a superstitious faith in the temple. They thought Jerusalem could not fall because of the temple; but they were wrong. God knows the difference between religious ritual and real religion (10). He sees all that goes on (9). Jerusalem is no more sacrosanct than Shiloh, the sanctuary the Philistines destroyed (see on 1 Samuel 4). Security and well-being rest on obedience to God (23).
Verse 11: Jesus quoted these words of the temple in his day (Matthew 21:13).
Ephraim (15): the leading tribe of the breakaway northern kingdom.
Queen of heaven (18): the fertility goddess Ashtoreth/Astarte/Ishtar, whose worship involved sexual immorality.
Verse 22: Jeremiah is not denying that the system of sacrifices was instituted at God's command (see Leviticus 1 - 7). But the people were substituting sacrifice for obedience. Jeremiah is urging them to get their priorities right. As Samuel said long before, 'to obey is better than sacrifice' (1 Samuel 15:22).
Topheth (31): see on Isaiah 30:33.

8:4-17 A false sense of security

The people refuse to repent, and the men of religion aid and abet them with their smooth words. The scribes (professional interpreters of God's law), the wise men who applied God's laws to the practical matters of life, prophets and priests, are all alike motivated by self-interest.

8:18 - 9:26 Lament for the coming destruction

Jeremiah shares God's own deep grief at his people's sin and its tragic consequences. Society is sick (9:3-6, 8): sick as a direct result of the nation abandoning God and his laws and going their own way (12-14). So inevitable has judgement become (15-16) that the professional mourners can already be called in (17).
Balm (8:22): Gilead was famous for its healing ointment from very early times (Genesis 37:25).
Wormwood (9:15): a bitter-tasting plant, and so a symbol for sorrow.
9:25-26: despite the outward mark of his covenant (see on 4:4), God's people have made themselves like the pagan nations around. And like them they will be punished. See chapters 46 - 51.

10 The living God - and idols made by men

The idols man creates - no matter how elaborate - are lifeless, powerless, motionless, speechless. Not so the God of Israel. This was one of Isaiah's great themes: Isaiah 40:18-20; 44:9-20.
Tarshish ... Uphaz (9): Tarshish, Tartessus in far-away Spain; Uphaz may be Ophir (as New English Bible), famous for its gold.
Gather up your bundle (17): get ready to flee.
Shepherds (21): leaders.
Verses 23-25: Jeremiah's prayer on his people's behalf.

11:1-17 The broken covenant

The terms of God's covenant-agreement with his people, made at Sinai after the exodus (see Deuteronomy 5ff.), are still in force. By persistent disobedience to God's law, and by idol-worship, Judah has broken that agreement and come under the curse (see Deuteronomy 11:26-28; 27).

This chapter seems to belong to the period of reaction following Josiah's reforms (2 Kings 23).

11:18 - 12:17 The plot against Jeremiah's life

Jeremiah's message aroused such intense anger that the men of Anathoth, his hometown, were prepared to kill him (18-23). The discovery leads Jeremiah to question God about the way evil men get on in the world (12:1-4). He is neither the first, nor the last, to puzzle over this (see Psalm 73; Habakkuk 1:12-13). In answer, God tells him there is worse to come (5-6)! Nonetheless, he *will* punish (7-13), and afterwards restore (14-17).
Jungle of Jordan (12:5): the Jordan runs below sea-level from the Sea of Galilee to the Dead Sea; and in Old Testament times the river was bordered by dense, steamy thickets which were the haunt of wild animals.
House, heritage (7), vineyard (10): metaphors for the nation.

13 The loin-cloth: a dramatic parable

God makes use of every teaching method in the book to get his message across. The prophets often act out their message (see chapters 18, 19, 32). Actions often speak louder than words, and stick in the mind. Jeremiah got no joy from announcing God's vengeance (17), though he had earlier cried out for it (11:20).
Verse 4: the Euphrates represents the captivity and exile of the nation. It is some 350 miles from Jerusalem.
King and queen mother (18): almost certainly Jehoiachin and Nehushta (see 2 Kings 24:8-16).

14 - 15 The drought; Jeremiah's prayer

There is severe and prolonged drought (14:1-6). The people once again appeal to God (7-9), but God

Looking south from the walls of the present city of old Jerusalem, with the Kidron Valley.

will not listen (10-12). Neither will he listen to Jeremiah's pleas that they have been duped by the lies of false prophets (13ff.). Yet Jeremiah goes on praying for them (13-22) though God is deaf and the people reward him with hatred (15:10). His self-pity (15:15-18) is understandable. Its cure lies in turning away from himself to God, in renewed confidence.

Sword, famine, pestilence (14:12): all regarded, from earliest times, as punishments from God. The three together imply full-scale judgement (see also 16:4; 24:10; Ezekiel 14:21; Revelation 6:8; 18:8).

Thy glorious throne (21): the temple.

Moses and Samuel (15:1): both interceded successfully for the nation (Exodus 32; 1 Samuel 12:19-25).

15:4: under Manasseh the nation reached an all-time low; see 2 Kings 21; 2 Chronicles 33.

16 Jeremiah forbidden to marry

By remaining single, in a society where this was almost unheard of, Jeremiah becomes a living symbol of God's message. Very soon there will be the most terrible famine and slaughter in Jerusalem. This is no time, no place, to raise a family. As God removes his peace and his love from them (5) the people will at last know him as the Almighty (21). Yet he still has a future for them (14-15).

Verses 6-7: customs connected with mourning, some of them pagan (see Leviticus 19:27-28).

17 God and the human heart; the sabbath

Judah's sin is indelible (1). Yet God still sets the alternatives before them (5-8; see Psalm 1). If only the people will listen (24) judgement can be averted.

Disregard for the day of rest which God instituted (19-27; see Exodus 20:8-11) is symptomatic of the nation's general disobedience.

Verse 1: an iron stylus was used to incise inscriptions on rock or stone. The nation's sin is just as permanently engraved on her hard heart.

Asherim (2): see on Isaiah 17:8.

Verses 14-18: this is Jeremiah's prayer.

18 The potter and the clay; more plots against the prophet

Another dramatic parable (see on chapter 13). Like the human potter, God has the unquestionable right to remould the spoilt nation. We can never simply assume that things will always be the way they are (7-10).

In verses 18-23 Jeremiah is so

A potter works his wheel.

touched on the raw by those who spurn his God-given message that he comes out with a really vengeful prayer (very different from his reaction in 13:17).

Sirion (14): Mt Hermon, usually capped with snow all year round.

East wind (17): see on 4:11.

19:1-13 The shattered jug

Again, an acted parable: God will break the city and people as surely and as irreparably as the jug the prophet shatters before their eyes.

Ben-hinnom (2), Topheth (11): see on Isaiah 30:33.

19:14 - 20:18 Jeremiah in the stocks

Jeremiah goes straight from the Hinnom Valley to the temple; and there his message lands him in trouble. With hands and feet made fast in the wooden stocks he pours out his heart to God. Jeremiah was not a thick-skinned man; it hurt to be hated and ridiculed (20:7-8). Yet he was continually driven by an inner compulsion to make God's word known (9). His role as prophet put him under tremendous pressure. And his mood fluctuates between confident faith (11, 13) and utter misery (14-18).

21 King Zedekiah's enquiry

The date is about 589, when Judah was involved in her final struggle with Babylon. Zedekiah turns to the prophet, hoping for a word of comfort. But none is forthcoming. The only hope lies in surrender.

22 A warning for King Jehoiakim

This prophecy is earlier than chapter 21. Jehoiakim reigned from 609 to 597 – the year Jerusalem first surrendered to Babylon, and 18-year-old Jehoiachin (Coniah, 24) was taken into exile with the first batch of captives. Verses 13ff. contrast Jehoiakim – who sees his kingship in terms of cedarwood palaces – with his godly father, Josiah.

Him who is dead (10): probably King Josiah, killed at Megiddo.

Him who goes away (10), Shallum (11): King Jehoahaz, taken to Egypt by Pharaoh Necho on his return from Assyria in 609.

Lebanon, Bashan, Abarim (20): mountain ranges to the north, north-east and east of Judah.

23 Against the leaders and false prophets

The government (1-8) and religious leaders (9ff.) alike receive a stinging rebuke. Misrule, and the lies pronounced in God's name, will not go unpunished. God will set on the throne a king of his own choice (5-8). With such a message against the men of religion (9-40), it is not surprising that Jeremiah encountered bitter hatred from the priests and prophets – as Jesus himself did (26:11; compare Matthew 21:45-46; 26:66).

Branch (5): see on Isaiah 4:2; 11:1.

Adulterers (10): those who played God false by turning to pagan gods whose worship involved sexual rites and prostitution.

Burden of the Lord (33): i.e. a message from God.

24 The two baskets of figs

The date is some time after 597 (verse 1; 'Jeconiah' is Jehoiachin). The exiles are the pick of the bunch of God's people. (Ezekiel was among these first captives, and Daniel had been taken to Babylon earlier still.) And God is shaping a future for them. For those who remain in Judah there is no future but destruction. Yet through Jeremiah God still perseveres with his 'bad figs'.

25 Prediction of Nebuchadnezzar's invasion and the exile

The year is 605 (1), when Nebuchadnezzar routed the Egyptians at Carchemish. For 23 years Jeremiah has been repeating God's message, and still the people remain unmoved. Now he tells them that the city will fall and they will serve the Babylonians for 70 years in exile. The judgement of God will also fall on the pagan nations who so richly deserve it, and on Babylon itself (12-38).

Verse 13: for Jeremiah's prophecies against the pagan nations, see chapters 46 - 51.

26 - 45 JEREMIAH'S LIFE AND TIMES

26 Jehoiakim's reign: Jeremiah's life in danger

The date is 609 or after; the situation has links with chapter 7. It was one of those times when it is dangerous to declare the plain truth of God (15), and Jeremiah's straight speaking almost cost him his life. The priests and prophets wanted him dead (11), but the name of God still counted for something among the rulers and people (16). Uriah (20ff.; known only from this passage) was less fortunate.

Shiloh (6): see on chapter 7.

Verse 18: see Micah 3:12. The prophet's words are remembered a century later (Micah was Isaiah's contemporary).

27 - 28 Zedekiah's reign: the yoke of Babylon; Hananiah's false prophecy

It is 597: the Babylonians have taken the first captives from Jerusalem and placed Zedekiah on the throne. But already there is subversion. Jeremiah walks the streets of the city wearing a wooden yoke in token of submission to Babylon. Only by servitude can Judah (27:12-15) and the nations (27:3-11) escape destruction. It was not a popular message, and provoked a head-on clash with the false prophets. Hananiah flatly contradicted Jeremiah; broke the yoke (28:1-5, 10), and told the people what they wanted to hear. But time proved the truth of Jeremiah's words (28:15-17; and compare 27:19-22 with 52:17-23).

29 Jeremiah's letter to the exiles

The exiles to whom Jeremiah wrote were the captives deported with King Jehoiachin, among them Ezekiel. The false prophets predicted a swift return. Jeremiah advises the exiles to settle down and live a normal life: the exile will last 70 years. Then they will return. But even from Babylon his enemies stir up trouble for him (24ff.).

30 - 31 The promise of a new covenant

The message of hope comes at the nation's darkest hour. When it looked like total extinction, God promised his people a future. They would be saved (30:10ff.) and restored (18ff.). The exiles would return rejoicing to their homeland (31:7ff.). And a new covenant would replace the old one made at Sinai, which they had broken. This time God will remake them from within, giving them the power to do his will (31:31-34; and compare Romans 8:1-4; 2 Corinthians 5:17). Like Isaiah before him, Jeremiah here telescopes future events. He is talking, in the short-term, of the actual return from exile; in the long-term he looks forward to the new covenant brought in by Christ himself (see Hebrews 8ff.).

Ramah, Rachel (31:15): Rachel, mother of Joseph and Benjamin, died at Ramah near Bethlehem. Jeremiah pictures her weeping for her exiled sons. Matthew 2:18 sees this as a prophecy of the grief caused by Herod's slaughter of the young children.

32 Jeremiah buys land

It was 588/7, when Jerusalem was under siege, and Jeremiah's home town, Anathoth, under enemy occupation. Hanamel must have been an opportunist to try to sell land then! But Jeremiah's purchase spoke louder than words: 'God has a future for Judah.' And everyone in the city must have heard about it. Jeremiah acted under orders from God; only afterwards does he admit his puzzlement (25). In answer God outlines his immediate, and his ultimate purpose for the nation.

Verse 8: land was a family heritage; it never came up for sale on the open market. See Leviticus 25:25.

Baruch (12): Jeremiah's secretary; see 36:4ff.

Verse 35: see on Isaiah 30:33.

33 God's unbreakable promise

The theme is still future restoration. Where God has destroyed, he will rebuild (6ff.). Joy and prosperity will return (10-11), and an ideal king will rule (14-16). It will happen as surely as night follows day (20).

Verse 21: see 2 Samuel 7 and Numbers 25.

Two families (24): judging by verse 26, this means the family of Jacob (the nation) and the family of David (the kings).

34 The Jewish slaves

The date is still 588/7. After receiving God's message (1-7), King Zedekiah issues an order to free all slaves, hoping that this will win God's favour (see Deuteronomy 15:12ff.). But their owners quickly go back on it. And God condemns them as law-breakers.

Verses 4-5: see 39:7. There is no record of Zedekiah's death.

Verses 18-19: the ceremony invoked a similar fate on whoever broke the covenant. See Genesis 15.

Withdrawn (21): there was a temporary let-up while Nebuchadnezzar dealt with pharaoh's army (37:5).

35 The Rechabites

Chapters 35 - 36 take us back ten years to the earlier siege of Jerusalem. The Rechabites were bedouin descendants of Jehonadab, who took God's part against the Baal-worshippers in 2 Kings 10:15-23. Fear of the invading army brings them to the city (11), where their obedience to a pledge made 200 years before puts the people of God to shame.

36 King Jehoiakim burns Jeremiah's scroll

This is one of the most vivid and dramatic chapters in the whole Bible. The year is 605/4. Jeremiah is banned from the temple (5; no doubt to prevent him repeating what he said earlier, chapter 26). But the word of God cannot be stifled. The message is written; the prophet bides his time; and then within a single day it is read aloud in the hearing of the people, the rulers, and the king himself. Jehoiakim may burn the scroll, but not even he has power to destroy the message, or prevent its fulfilment. Patiently, Jeremiah and Baruch write the words again.

Beneath Jerusalem, even today, are ancient cisterns designed to conserve every drop of water. In Jeremiah's time they were mostly round, carved out of rock. This one is below the Ecce Homo Convent in Jerusalem.

Verse 30: within three months of Jehoiakim's death his son was deported to Babylon.

37 - 38 Jeremiah's imprisonment

Zedekiah is king; the year, 588 (5). Jeremiah's counsel to surrender (38:2) lands him in his deepest trouble yet. He is flung into prison as a subversive influence and a traitor. Only through the prompt action of a good friend, and the intervention of the king, is his life saved (37:20-21; 38:7-13). Zedekiah is anxious to know God's word (37:3, 17; 38:14), but lacks faith and courage to act on it. So Jeremiah's terrible vision (38:22-23) becomes reality (39:6-8). But even in the midst of judgement, God does not lose sight of individuals. Ebed-melech's life is saved (39:15-18).

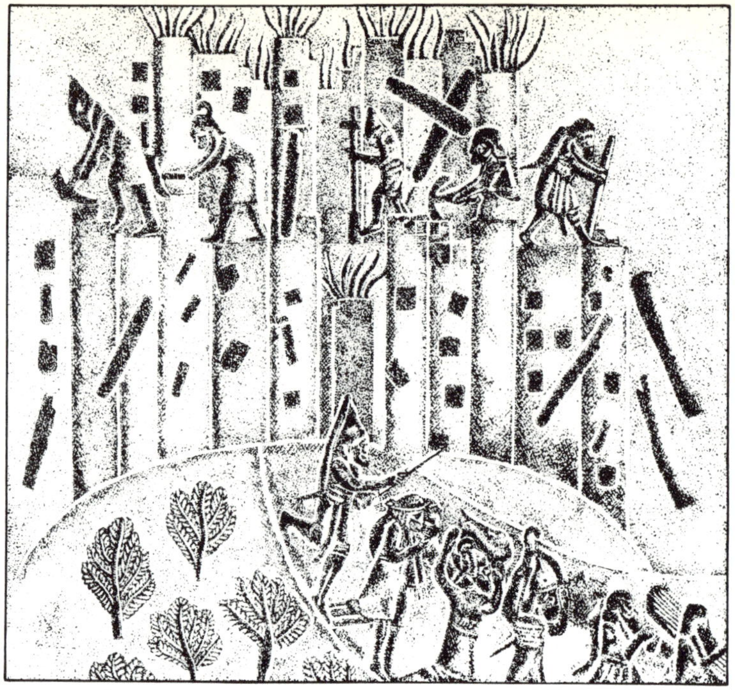

Assyrians besiege a city; relief from the palace of Ashurbanipal at Nineveh.

39 - 40:6 Jerusalem falls; Jeremiah's choice

See also chapter 52; 2 Kings 25; 2 Chronicles 36. God's warnings finally give way to judgement (39:1-10) and Jeremiah is the only man to have any say in his own future (39:12; 40:1-5). Offered a place of honour at the Babylonian court, he chooses instead to throw in his lot with the have-nots, left behind in the land of Judah.

Riblah (39:5): Nebuchadnezzar's base was a town to the south of Hama in Syria.

Gedaliah (39:14): son of the man who earlier saved Jeremiah's life (26:24).

Because you sinned (40:3): the nation, not Jeremiah.

Mizpah (40:6): a town a few miles north of Jerusalem; a place of national assembly from Samuel's time.

40:7 - 41:18 Assassination of the governor, Gedaliah

Gedaliah made a good start as governor. Those who had fled before the army returned and they gathered in a good harvest, after the hungry days of occupation. But after three months he was murdered, and the people, fearing reprisals, made ready to escape to Egypt.

41:9: see 1 Kings 15:16ff.

42 - 43:7 Escape to Egypt

For all their declared willingness to obey God's word, when the message came telling them to stay put, they disobeyed. Egypt seemed safer. They took Jeremiah and Baruch with them. And as God had predicted (15-18) in due course the long arm of Nebuchadnezzar, king of Babylon, reached down into Egypt (568 BC). According to Josephus, there were Jews among the captives he took back with him.

43:3: Baruch had obviously already warned them against going to Egypt.

Tahpanhes (43:7): see on 2:16.

43:8 - 44:30 In Egypt: Jeremiah's last appeal

Jeremiah enacts his last recorded parable (43:8ff.). But despite all that has happened, the people still refuse to listen. They will go back to worship-

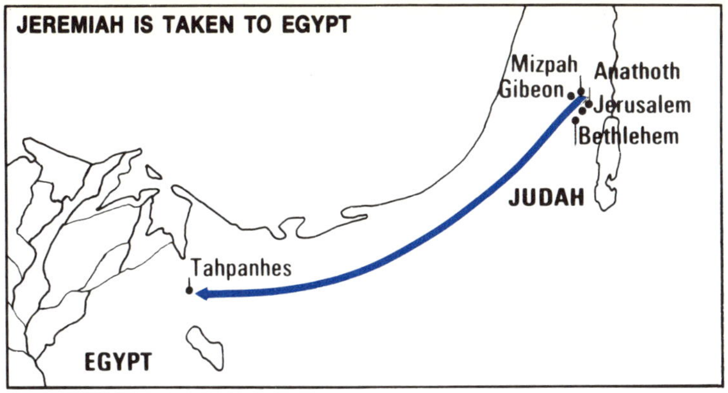

ping the 'queen of heaven' (see on 7:18), and all will be well again! We hear no more of Jeremiah after this. Tradition has it he was stoned to death in Egypt.

The pavement (43:9): archaeologists have uncovered a large area of brick paving on the site.

Heliopolis (43:13): see on Isaiah 19:18.

45 Baruch

This short chapter relates to the writing of the scroll in 605 (chapter 36). Baruch shared something of the prophet's distress. God promises him life in the coming slaughter (as he promised Ebed-melech, 39:15-18). That is enough.

46 - 51 PROPHECIES AGAINST THE NATIONS

See 25:13. Jeremiah, like Isaiah before him, sees God controlling the history of the world, not just one corner of it. God deals with evil wherever it occurs. These chapters contain some of the most magnificent poetry in the book.

46:1-26 Egypt

Verses 1-12 describe the defeat at Carchemish in 605. Verses 13-26 forecast Nebuchadnezzar's invasion of Egypt (which took place in 568). Isaiah and Ezekiel also prophesied against Egypt: Isaiah 19-20; Ezekiel 29-32.

Verse 9: these are the mercenaries: from Sudan (Ethiopia) and Libya (Put).

Balm (11): see on 8:22.

Apis (15): the Egyptian sacred bull. God has overthrown the gods of Egypt.

Amon (25): god of Thebes.

46:27-28 Comfort for Israel

47 Philistia

See also Isaiah 14:28-32. Pharaoh Necho controlled Gaza at the time of his march north in 609, but the city often changed hands. Calamity is predicted from the Babylonians in the north. Nebuchadnezzar must have overrun the Philistine cities when he quelled Judah in 587. Other prophecies: Ezekiel 25:15ff.; Amos 1:6-8; Zephaniah 2:4-7; Zechariah 9:5-7.

Gaza, Ashkelon (1, 5): Philistine cities.

Caphtor (4): Crete, the island from which the Philistines originally came.

Anakim (5): people of giant height who had some connection with the Philistines (Joshua 11:22). But this may not be the right word here.

48 Moab

See on Isaiah 15-16. Moab, Ammon and Edom seem to have joined forces with Judah in rebelling against Nebuchadnezzar (27:1-3). Presumably he dealt with them when he dealt with Judah. Other prophecies: Ezekiel 25:8-11; Amos 2:1-3; Zephaniah 2:8-11.

Nebo (1): the city, not the mountain.

Chemosh (7, 13): chief Moabite god. Bethel was the sanctuary set up in the northern kingdom of Israel to rival Jerusalem.

Arnon (20): the river which was once Moab's northern boundary.

Dibon (22): the capital.

Horn (25): an image of power, strength, might.

Kir-heres (31): original capital of Moab; present-day Kerak in Jordan.

Verse 37: a picture of mourning.

49:1-6 Ammon

See on Moab above; also Ezekiel 25:1-7. Ammon is condemned for seizing Israelite land, but will later be restored.

Milcom (1): the Ammonite god.

Rabbah (2): the capital; modern Amman, capital of Jordan.

49:7-22 Edom

Other prophecies: Isaiah 21:11-12;

EXILE TO BABYLON

Alan Millard

At about the time Jeremiah began to prophesy, the Assyrian Empire crumbled. Nabopolassar, Chaldean governor of southern Babylonia, took control of Babylon (626 BC) and gradually ousted the Assyrian garrisons from other towns. Then, allied to an army of Medes and Scythians from the Persian hills, he attacked Assyria, finally sacking Nineveh in 612 BC (see Nahum). The last vestige of Assyrian power was destroyed two years later, and the forces of the Egyptian Pharaoh Necho routed at Carchemish in 605 BC (see Jeremiah 25).

Thus the Chaldeans became masters of the 'Fertile Crescent', although the northern provinces of the Assyrian Empire fell under Median rule. The famous Nebuchadnezzar became king in 605 BC. His first 20 years saw much fighting as he subdued rebellious provinces, Judah among them.

After Carchemish, he retained Jehoiakim (the Egyptian nominee) as king in Jerusalem, exacting an oath of loyalty, and taking hostages (Daniel 1:1). The Judean disregarded his oath and linked his country to Egypt again. In righteous fury, Nebuchadnezzar brought his forces to besiege Jerusalem, whose king refused to surrender, despite Jeremiah's pleas.

The king died. His son, Jehoiachin, reigned a month or two until the city fell and he was taken into exile in Babylon (597 BC). There, according to ration-lists found in the ruins, he and his family were supplied from the royal stores. The throne of Judah was given to Zedekiah, yet he failed to learn the lesson, falling prey to Egypt's lures as his predecessors had done.

Judah's fate was inevitable. Babylonian forces attacked again, took Jerusalem and sacked it (587/6 BC). Large numbers of surviving citizens were settled in Babylonia, and the territory of Judah was placed under a governor.

The exiles seem to have been moved to Babylonia itself, living in various towns and villages as well as in the capital city. They were free to establish themselves as part of the community, so far as can be discovered, to maintain their own traditions and to practise their own religion as they wanted. No doubt the new surroundings and the refurbished splendour of ancient Babylon (justifying Nebuchadnezzar's boast, 'Is not this great Babylon, which I have built'; Daniel 4:30) awed the men of Judah. Some may have felt that Marduk of Babylon and his host of attendant gods was superior to the God of Israel. Others certainly found a profitable way of life in their new surroundings. Others longed to return to the promised land

The impress of Babylonian culture can be seen in the figures of Ezekiel's visions and in the stories of Daniel. It was an amalgam of native concepts and foreign. In the streets and workshops of the city, exiles and visitors from Egypt, Syria and Palestine rubbed shoulders with others from Cilicia and Caria and Ionia, all speaking a common language, Aramaic.

Yet the empire of the Chaldean kings was not to last. As Isaiah, Jeremiah and Daniel foresaw, the hill-men of the east and north would overcome it. The picture, vague in Isaiah and Jeremiah, is clear in Daniel. Media grew ever more powerful after ridding herself of Scythian rule. By 585 BC the Median yoke extended half-way across Anatolia. And Media was clearly a rival to Babylon when, in 550 BC, her vassal, Cyrus the Persian, seized the throne.

In Babylon, Belshazzar governed while his father Nabonidus lived in northern Arabia. The king returned only to see his realm fall to Cyrus in 539 BC. The new king's policies were generally peaceable, and he liberally allowed Jews to return and restore Jerusalem's temple as he restored many other shrines.

A line of prisoners. The Babylonians (like the Assyrians pictured here) removed whole nations from their homelands, taking them into exile.

Obadiah (who seems to have borrowed some passages from Jeremiah). Edom's judgement will be total: see on Isaiah 34.
Verse 18: see Genesis 19.
Jungle of the Jordan (19): see on 12:5.

49:23-27 Damascus
See also Isaiah 17.
Hamath, Arpad (23): Hama, in Syria; and a town just north of Aleppo.
Ben-hadad (27): the name or title of a number of Syrian kings.

49:28-33 Kedar
As predicted, Nebuchadnezzar routed these nomadic tribes in 599.
Hazor/Hazer (30): probably nomad settlements; not the city in northern Galilee.

49:34-39 Elam
Jeremiah spoke in 597. Within a year Elam, east of Babylon, was attacked by Nebuchadnezzar.

50 - 51 Babylon
See on Isaiah 13 - 14 and 46 - 47. Jeremiah's impressive prophecy was sent with the delegation that went to Babylon in the fourth year of Zedekiah's reign, six years before the fall of Jerusalem. It was given a public reading, then sunk in the Euphrates, as Babylon itself would sink before its conqueror (51:59-64). The Medes (51:11) would pour in on Babylon from the north like the sea. God's people are warned in advance to be out of harm's way when it happens. Cyrus, at the head of an army of Medes and Persians, took Babylon in 539. Babylon was God's instrument to punish his people (as the Assyrians had been earlier), but God could not overlook her sinful pride. He cannot ignore evil; judgement must always come.
Bel, Merodach (Marduk) (50:2): the Babylonian gods.
50:21: there is a play on the names Merathaim and Pekod, two Babylonian tribes.
Vengeance for his temple (50:28; 51:11): Jeremiah wrote this prophecy before the temple was destroyed: this note was probably added after the destruction in 587.
51:27: Ararat in eastern Turkey; Minni in north-west Iran; Ashkenaz, the Scythians, in the same area. All were subject to the Medes.
Her sea (51:36): Babylon's prosperity and security depended on her elaborate system of canals and lakes.
Seraiah (51:59): Baruch's brother (32:12).
Thus far ... (64): taking the reading of the Revised Standard Version margin, this note seems to belong to the end of verse 58, making 59-64 and chapter 52 additions.

52 HISTORICAL APPENDIX
See on 2 Kings 24 - 25, which are almost identical with this chapter; and Jeremiah 39.
Verses 28-30: the captives were deported in 597, 587 and 581.
Verse 31: with the accession of Nebuchadnezzar's son (562-560), things improved for Jehoiachin, a token of new hope for the nation.

Old Testament 4.3
LAMENTATIONS

We do not know who wrote these laments – although the Greek versions name Jeremiah. They are anonymous in the Hebrew text. And they differ in style and content from Jeremiah's prophecies. But the author must at least have been a contemporary of the prophet. The first four poems were obviously written by an eye-witness to the destruction of Jerusalem by Nebuchadnezzar's Babylonian army in 587 BC.

To the people of Judah, the fall of the city meant more than the loss of their beautiful and almost unassailable capital. It was more than just the destruction of a nation's capital city: because Jerusalem was in a very special sense God's city. His temple was there. This was where he chose to live with his people. And when Jerusalem was burned, the temple destroyed, the people deported, they knew that God had given them up to the enemy. It could not have happened otherwise. So these laments express the poet's grief, not simply over the suffering and humiliation of his people, but over something deeper and far worse, that God had rejected his people because of their sin.

The first four poems have the rhythm of the dirge, and they are written as acrostics. In 1, 2 and 4, each of the 22 verses begins with a new letter of the Hebrew alphabet. In 3, there are three verses to each letter. The fifth poem (chapter 5) also has 22 verses, but is neither a dirge nor an acrostic.

The poems are still read aloud in Jewish synagogues in mid-July to mark the anniversary of the destruction of the temple in 587, and remembering the later destruction in AD 70.

Chapter 1 The first lament
Jerusalem is alone, deserted, mourning; the people gone; the temple defiled and destroyed. God has judged and punished her for the enormity of her sin. Now, at last, she cries out to him.

Chapter 2 The second lament
The poet sees again the outpouring of God's anger: the starving children; the slaughter; the ruin of city and sanctuary. He hears again the taunts of old enemies, gloating over the fate of Jerusalem. Let her call out to God to look, and pity.

Chapter 3 The third lament
We see the agony of the nation focussed in the experience of a single individual. In the darkness, crushed and battered to the point where all hope dies (18), faith still rekindles at the thought of God in all his love and mercy (19-33). When he is all but lost, there comes the knowledge that God is near (54ff.) But he cannot forgive the bitter provocation of his enemies (59-66).

Chapter 4 The fourth lament
The city's former glory – and the horrors of siege. The cries of starving children; wizened faces; shrivelled bodies; never to be forgotten. The sins of the people, the prophets and the priests, have brought the city low. And Edom – the old arch-enemy – gloats, not knowing that her punishment is yet to come (21-22).

Chapter 5 The fifth lament – a prayer
The poet vividly depicts defeat: the loss of freedom, loss of land, loss of respect; rape and cruelty; forced labour; near-starvation. And all because of sin. He prays to God for restoration.

Old Testament 4.4

EZEKIEL

In 597 BC King Jehoiachin surrendered Jerusalem to the Babylonian army, and was taken into exile. With him went 10,000 men – statesmen, soldiers, craftsmen (2 Kings 24:14). And among them was Jeremiah's younger contemporary, Ezekiel, then in his mid-twenties. Ezekiel was in training as a priest, looking forward to service in the temple like his father before him. Exile in the plains of Babylonia, far from Jerusalem, meant the end of all his hopes.

But five years later, when he was 30 (the age at which he would probably have taken up his duties as a priest – Numbers 4:3; and see on 1:1), God called him into service as a prophet. The call was accompanied by a vision of God which coloured his entire ministry (just as Isaiah's had done nearly 150 years earlier). He saw God in all his awesome majesty, above and beyond the world of men, all-seeing, all-knowing. It was a vision of fire and glory. And against this dazzling brilliance Ezekiel saw his people's sin in all its blackness. He saw the inevitability of judgement. And for six years this was his message. Only after the city and temple of Jerusalem were destroyed in 587 did he really begin to stress God's intention to 'resurrect' (chapter 37) and restore Israel, and to look forward to the time when the ideal would be realized: to the new temple in which God's people would offer him perfect worship (chapters 40ff.).

As he declared God's message to the exiles, a great weight of responsibility rested on Ezekiel. He saw himself as a 'look-out', who must give warning of danger or be held accountable. One of his most characteristic themes is that of individual responsibility before God. Ezekiel was an extraordinary man, a visionary, imaginative, by training a man who appreciated and understood ritual and symbol. He was passionate, dedicated, utterly obedient to God. The most hardened onlooker could not fail to be impressed as Ezekiel acted out his sobering messages.

The book – written entirely in the first person, apart from the note in 1:2-3 – is in keeping with the man. The prophecies are meticulously ordered and dated, even to the day of the month. Message and language are consistent (often repetitive) throughout the book. Characteristic themes and phrases run right through. And although some scholars have questioned the authorship and background of Ezekiel, the various arguments tend to cancel one another out. Ezekiel's message is very close to that of Jeremiah (another prophet given to acted parables), whom he may have heard as a young man in Jerusalem. But although he writes for the most part in 'cold' prose, Ezekiel is more flamboyantly visual than the other prophets. With him, prophecy merges into 'apocalyptic' (see Revelation). The Bible book closest in spirit to Ezekiel is Revelation, which borrows many of his images.

For many Christians Ezekiel is a closed book, apart from a few familiar passages (the watchman; the valley of dry bones; the vision of the temple). It is easy to give up at the first chapter – the vision of flashing lights and peculiar creatures and wheels with eyes. But this is our loss. Because in our materialistic, man-centred world, we need Ezekiel's vision of the almighty God. We need to see sin as God sees it. We need to be reminded of our own accountability. We need to know that God is God – before we learn it the hard way, as Israel did, through judgement. Reading the Old Testament also helps us to understand the New. We need to be acquainted with Ezekiel in order to understand Revelation.

1 - 3 EZEKIEL'S CALL AND VISION OF GOD

Ezekiel is a book of visions and symbolic actions – beginning with this great vision of God. As Ezekiel gazed out over the plain, he saw what looked like an approaching storm: thunder, lightning, black clouds. Then he made out the figures of four cherubim (see 10:15), angelic creatures, standing wing-tip to wing-tip, forming a hollow square. At the centre, fire glowed; and above, under the blue vault of the heavens, was the Lord of glory in human form, seated on a throne, encircled by a dazzling rainbow. Beside each four-faced cherub was a terrifying, whirling wheel, moving like a castor and full of eyes. Who could look on this and live?

The Almighty, the God of Israel was present in all his power in the far-flung lands of Babylon. He came to make Ezekiel his messenger to the exiles, the watchman sent to warn the remnant of God's rebel people (2:1-7; 3:16-21). And the words of God, though they were hard, were satisfying (2:8 - 3:3). It became Ezekiel's life-mission to let God's people know that he is the Lord. They would learn it first through the terrors of judgement (7:4). Afterwards they would see his power to restore and renew (36:8-11).

Thirtieth year (1:1): most probably Ezekiel's own age. If, as seems likely, this was the age at which a priest took up his duties, it would have been a year of special significance for the prophet. But to become eligible at last for his life's work as a priest, when in exile, hundreds of miles away from Jerusalem and its temple, must have been a bitter experience.

Chebar (1:1): usually identified as the great canal which ran from the Euphrates north of Babylon, close to the city of Nippur.

Verses 2-3: a note added to explain Ezekiel's opening sentence. The date was 593 BC (see introduction).

Living creatures (5): cherubim (10:15), the figures which spread their wings over the mercy-seat above the ark of the covenant (Exodus 25:18ff.). As the son of a priest, Ezekiel may have been familiar with the figures of cherubim which decorated Solomon's temple. Similar winged, sphinx-like creatures frequently appear in Babylonian art.

Verse 26: although it was normally reckoned that no one could see God and live, there were some who shared Ezekiel's privilege and described what they saw – see Exodus 24:9-11; Isaiah 6; Daniel 7; Revelation 4.

Son of man/man (2:1): Ezekiel is addressed in this way throughout the book. It simply means 'human being'. This is the term Jesus most often used to describe himself.

Briers and thorns ... scorpions (2:6): a vivid picture of the hostile reception.

2:10: normally a scroll had writing on only one side; perhaps the implication is that there was no room left for Ezekiel to add anything of his own.

3:7: the call of Isaiah, and of Jeremiah, was equally daunting: see Isaiah 6:9-12; Jeremiah 1:17-19.

3:25-27: the meaning seems to be that Ezekiel would be dumb except on the occasions when God had a message for him to give. But some take this as a self-imposed, ritual dumbness, rather than an actual loss of speech. Either way, it gave added force to the utterances he did make. The dumbness lasted until news reached him of the fall of Jerusalem (24:27).

4 - 24 ISRAEL'S SIN: GOD'S JUDGEMENT

4 - 5 Ezekiel enacts the siege and destruction of Jerusalem

The 'props' for the drama were ready to hand: a large sun-dried brick on

Winged creatures carved in ivory to decorate a piece of furniture.

which Ezekiel drew an outline of the city; and the metal plate on which they baked their flat loaves of bread. The people watched, and got the message. They watched with growing horror as Ezekiel weighed out his meagre measure of mixed grain and eked out his water ration. They saw the prophet wasting away, as the population of Jerusalem would do under siege. They watched him shave his head, sharing Jerusalem's disgrace. They saw him burn the hair and toss it away, till only a tiny handful – representing the exiles themselves – remained. It was a telling lesson.

4:5-6: the Greek version has 190 days; from the fall of Samaria in 722 BC to the return of the exiles in 538 is 184 years. From the fall of Jerusalem in 587 to 538 is 49 years. 40 may represent a generation, rather than being an exact figure.

4:9: under siege no one is fussy about the ingredients they use to make bread.

Twenty shekels (10): about 8 ozs/220 gms.

Sixth part of a hin (11): about a pint/ 0.6 litre.

Unclean (13ff.): using dung for fuel defiled the food, according to Jewish regulations. It was hard for Ezekiel, a man trained to maintain ritual cleanness, to do as God instructed. Compare Peter's reaction in Acts 10:9-16.

6 - 7 Against the land of Israel: the end has come

The acted message is reinforced by the spoken word. The people's flagrant idolatry is about to bring destruction upon them – judgement from which there is no escape. Then they will know that the Lord is God indeed. Terrible, total calamity is befalling the land.

From the wilderness to Riblah (6:14): from south to north. Riblah, on the River Orontes, is near Israel's northern boundary.

The seller mourn (7:12): because he has been forced to sell the land which was his heritage.

7:18: shaven heads were a sign of disgrace as well as of mourning.

Cast their silver (7:19): their money is useless.

8 - 11 Ezekiel's vision of Jerusalem – its guilt and its punishment

September 592. Ezekiel is transported in vision (or, as John would have said, 'In the Spirit') to Jerusalem, and set down beside the temple (8:1-4). What he sees may be actual practices, or the description may be symbolic. Either way the meaning is plain. There has been a total departure from the true religion of Israel. In the temple of God an image of the Canaanite goddess Asherah/Astarte (the 'image of jealousy', 3) has been set up, as in the days of King Manasseh. The nation's leaders are secretly practising animal worship (8:7-13). The women are mourning the Sumerian god Tammuz, who was supposed to die with the old year and rise again with the spring. Men turn their backs on God to worship the sun (8:16-18).

Contrary to popular belief (8:12), God both sees and judges (9:9-10). Only those who grieve for the loss of the true faith will be spared (9:4-6).

Chapter 10: following the terrible slaughter which made Ezekiel cry aloud for his people (9:8), he sees again the vision of the cherubim, the glory, the whirling wheels, that he first saw on the plains of Babylon (chapter 1). What greater contrast imaginable than this sight of God in all his glory – and the loathsome scenes of idolatry in his temple (chapter 8). Because of all this the glory of God will finally depart from Jerusalem.

But first Ezekiel sees two men he recognizes, rulers who are advocating resistance to Babylon, despite the insistence of God's prophets that this would prove fatal (11:1-4). Ezekiel pronounces God's judgement, and as he speaks, to his alarm, Pelatiah falls dead (11:5-13) in confirmation of God's word. But God is not making a 'full end' (13). The future lies with the exiles. And on this note, and with this message (25), the vision ends.

Jaazaniah (8:11): his father was King Josiah's secretary of state; his brother Ahikam, Jeremiah's friend. Not the same man as in 11:1.

The branch ... (8:17): possibly a reference to some pagan practice.

A mark (9:4): Jeremiah, Baruch and the foreigner, Ebed-melech, were among those 'marked' to be spared (Jeremiah 40:4; 45; 39:15ff.). In Revelation God's men are marked (14:1), and so are those who sell out to the forces of evil (13:16). The 'mark' here is the last letter of the Hebrew alphabet, *taw* written as a cross in the oldest script.

11:3: a difficult verse, most likely meaning that this was not the moment for peace-time building. The cauldron protects the meat from the flames.

A new spirit (11:19): compare Jeremiah 31:33-34; Ezekiel 36:26.

12 Ezekiel plays the part of an exile

Although most people refuse to listen, the prophet continues to make God's word known (1-3). As he put together the bare necessities, ready for flight, and as he broke through the mud-brick wall at night, Ezekiel was playing the part, not just of any exile, but of King Zedekiah ('the prince', 10). Compare 12-13 with Jeremiah 52:7-11. Ezekiel's prophecy proved accurate to the last detail. It was as God said it would be, and within a very short space of time (21-28).

The exiles provided useful slave labour. Here timber is hauled for building King Sargon's new capital at Khorsabad, Assyria.

13 False prophets

The work of Jeremiah and Ezekiel was constantly undermined by false prophets, who told people what they wanted to hear, and claimed God's authority for their message of false hope. They were like plaster, concealing the crumbling structure of the nation, but unable to stop it falling (10-16); for what God says will happen, always happens. Among them were prophetesses, practising magic and holding helpless individuals in thrall (17ff.).

Souls (18): the whole person; the idea of disembodied spirits was completely alien to Jewish thinking.

14 Idolatry and its consequences

God claims a unique place in the hearts of his people. Those who deny him his rightful place, worshipping other 'gods' alongside, are destined for destruction. The majority regard the few godly men among them as an insurance against disaster. But at this point in time not even a Noah or a Job could save anyone but himself.

Daniel/Danel (14): probably an otherwise unknown Jewish patriarch, and not Ezekiel's contemporary in exile. The name of the biblical Daniel is spelt differently. There is also a hero of this name in an ancient Canaanite epic.

Verse 21: these judgements represent the worst fears of ancient peoples (see on Jeremiah 14:12).

15 The parable of the vine

The vine was a popular symbol for Israel. There is by this time no question of it bearing fruit, and as wood the vine is useless. Israel is already partially destroyed (4): there is nothing for it now but total destruction (6-8).

16 The unfaithful wife: an allegory

God took Israel up when she was nothing – an abandoned waif – and lavished his love on her, making her into a great and glorious nation. She owed him everything. But prosperity turned her head and, like a wife turned prostitute, she played fast and loose with foreign nations. She 'courted' them and worshipped their gods, with all the hideous practices that involved (20-29). God was forgotten; the covenant (like the marriage-vow) broken. He must punish Israel (35-43): but he will also restore (53,60).

Amorite ... Hittite (3): the reference is to moral, not literal, parentage. Israel had become as decadent as the nations she destroyed at the conquest of Canaan.

Verse 4: these were the midwife's duties.

Spread my skirt (8): with this symbolic gesture he claimed her in marriage. See Ruth 3:9. God sealed the contract with the Sinai covenant.

Verse 38: adultery was punishable by death.

Verse 46: 'Samaria': capital of the northern kingdom; destroyed in 722. 'Sodom': the city at the southern end of the Dead Sea, wiped out for its gross immorality (Genesis 19).

17 The eagles and the vine

The first eagle is Nebuchadnezzar of Babylon, who took King Jehoiachin captive (3,4; see introduction). The seed he plants (5, 13) is Zedekiah. But Zedekiah soon turned to Egypt (the second eagle) for help (7,15), bringing the Babylonians back to destroy Jerusalem. In 587, within three or four years, the prediction of 17-21 came true (see Jeremiah 52). But God will take a 'cutting' from the line of Israel's kings (the cedar) which will take root (22-24).

Verse 8: it seems best to take this as stressing the fact that Zedekiah was well off under Nebuchadnezzar (as in 5).

18 Each individual accountable to God

Contrary to popular belief (2), God is not so unjust as to punish one generation for the sins of another (20). He holds every man answerable for his own sins. It gives God no pleasure to sign the death warrant for any man (23). His concern, always, is that men should turn away from evil and live (30-32). And he makes his standards plain (5-9; 14-17).

Soul (4): see on 13:18 above.

Verse 20: Ezekiel is redressing the balance, not denying the basic principle that in life children do suffer the consequences of their parents' wrongdoing (Exodus 20:5).

19 A lament for Israel's rulers

The poem is written in the familiar dirge-rhythm. The lioness is Judah; the kings her cubs. The first (3) is Jehoahaz, carried off to Egypt by Pharaoh Necho in 609. The second (5) is Jehoiachin (see introduction). Now, thanks to Zedekiah's rebellion, both the nation and its line of kings will be destroyed (10-14).

20:1-44 A history of the nation's rebellion

July/August 591. Ezekiel turns from allegory to historical fact. From the time in Egypt and the wilderness right down to his own day, Israel's history has been a weary repetition of idolatry and rebellion against God. All along, God held back from making an end of the nation. But now he will cut off the rebels (38). His own, he will restore (40-44).

I gave them ... (25-26): these difficult verses seem best understood in the light of Romans 1:24, etc. God 'gave them up' to the evil things they wanted.

Bamah (29): high place. There is a play on words in this verse.

Verse 37: Jerusalem Bible translates: 'I mean to make you pass under my crook and I will bring a few of you back.'

20:45 - 21:32 Fire and sword

God's judgement will sweep across the land from south to north like a forest fire (20:45-48). The sword of God is drawn against Israel. It is in the hands of the king of Babylon (21:19), who will destroy the capital cities of both Ammon and Judah (21:20). (Five years after Jerusalem fell, Nebuchadnezzar attacked Ammon.)

Negeb (20:46): today this region is arid desert, but Palestine as a whole was more wooded in Old Testament times.

Rabbah (21:20): Amman, present capital of Jordan.

Until he comes ... (21:27): see Genesis 49:10. There is one coming to whom the kingship rightly belongs.

22 The charges against Jerusalem

God's people are guilty – guilty of bloodshed, oppression, extortion, bribery, and sexual sin; they have made a mockery of their religion (6-12). When God tests them by fire, no trace of genuine metal will be found (17-22). Every section of society shares the guilt: rulers, priests, prophets and common people alike (23-31).

Unclean and clean (26): see on Leviticus 11.

Verse 28: see 13:8-16.

23 Parable of the two sisters, Oholah and Oholibah

Oholah is Samaria, capital of the northern kingdom of Israel. Oholibah is Jerusalem. Both sisters have behaved like common whores. Their appetite for their lovers (the pagan gods) is insatiable; their behaviour utterly disgusting. They have run, in turn, after Egypt and Assyria. Now Judah, outdoing her sister, is running after Babylon. Jerusalem will share Samaria's fate – shame and destruction at the hands of her latest lover. Her punishment is fully deserved (45).

Verse 10: the Assyrians destroyed Samaria in 722 BC.

Verse 23: Pekod, Shoa and Koa were probably tribes on the eastern borders of the Babylonian Empire. The Babylonians and Chaldeans were not separate peoples.

24 Jerusalem besieged; Ezekiel's wife dies

The date is the same as in 2 Kings 25:1; Jeremiah 52:4 – usually thought to be 15 January 588 BC. Jerusalem is like a rusty cooking-pot, set on the fire to burn. The behaviour of the people has polluted the city. The very same day that the siege is laid, Ezekiel's much-loved wife is suddenly taken from him. But God forbids him the customary forms of mourning. Ezekiel's personal loss is part of a grief beyond expression. Men will eat their hearts out for the fate of Jerusalem, though they go about dry-eyed, like the prophet. And when news of the city's fall reaches them, Ezekiel will at last be able to speak freely (27; see 3:26-27); the judgement will be over.

Verse 17: the mourning customs of the day: noisy lamentation; bared head sprinkled with dust and ashes; bared feet; veiled face; and the funeral meal provided for the mourners.

25 - 32 PROPHECIES AGAINST FOREIGN NATIONS

Although the prophets concentrated mainly on Israel/Judah, all of them were very conscious that God was Lord of the whole world. There is no nation beyond the reach of his judgement; and what he condemns and punishes in his own people, he condemns and punishes in other nations too. This collection of prophecies effectively marks the break in Ezekiel's ministry before, and his ministry after, the fall of Jerusalem in 587 BC.

25 Ammon, Moab, Edom, Philistia

For other prophecies, see on Jeremiah 47 - 49. These four nations were Israel's closest neighbours, and her oldest enemies. All took a vengeful delight in Israel's downfall, for which God will punish them. Shortly after this, Ammon, Moab and Edom were overrun by Nabataean tribesmen. The Philistines disappeared from history after Maccabean times.

26 - 28:19 Tyre

See on Isaiah 23. The date of Ezekiel's prophecy is probably the end of the 11th year – February 586 – assuming that Ezekiel learnt of the fall of Jerusalem that year, rather than the following one (see on 33:21). The forecast of chapter 26 proved all too true. Tyre did not laugh long over Jerusalem's fate. Within a few months Nebuchadnezzar's army was at her own gates, and for 13 years she was under seige.

Tyre was a tempting prey. The city lay at the foot of the Lebanese mountains and possessed the finest natural harbour in the eastern Mediterranean. It was in fact a double harbour, as the main city was built on an offshore island (26:5). As a centre of trade and commerce Tyre was fabulously wealthy, and her own glassware and purple dye were world famous. Ezekiel fittingly pictures the city as a great trading vessel (chapter 27) laden with the choicest of cargoes, and commanding human skills and resources from far and wide. News of her wreck will put the world into mourning. Chapter 28 is a lament for the king of Tyre, whose pride has proved his downfall.

Senir (27:5): Mt Hermon.

Gebal (27:9): Byblos, now Jubail, in Lebanon.

Daniel (28:3): see on 14:14.

28:12ff.: much of the imagery is drawn from Genesis 2-3.

28:20-26 Sidon

Another famous Old Testament seaport, Sidon is in Lebanon, 20 miles north of Tyre. Today both Tyre (Sour) and Sidon are small fishing-ports. The charge against Sidon is, again, contempt for God's people (24). Sidon, like Tyre, fell to Nebuchadnezzar. Verses 25-26 are a message of hope for Israel.

29 - 32 Egypt

A collection of seven prophecies, all (except the one beginning at 30:1) carefully dated.

29:1-16, January 587. By his insufferable pride in placing himself among the gods, Pharaoh has exposed his whole land to God's anger. But he will learn who is God!

29:17-21, New Year's day, 571 (the latest prophecy in the book). The long and costly siege of Tyre ended about 574. Ezekiel declares that Egypt will be Babylon's next prey.

30:1-19, undated. Ezekiel depicts the judgement Nebuchadnezzar will execute on Egypt and her allies. God will put an end to Egypt's wealth (10-12) and her 'gods' (13ff.).

30:20-26, April 587. Pharaoh Hophra's army had made a half-hearted attempt to relieve besieged Jerusalem, but had been defeated. His power will be yet further broken.

31:1-18, June 587. Egypt is likened to a great cedar tree (2-9). Because of its over-bearing pride the tree will be felled (10-14). Egypt will be removed to the place of the dead (15ff.).

32:1-16, March 585 (after the news of Jerusalem's fall had reached the exiles). A lament for Pharaoh.

32:17-32 (? March) 585. Egypt will join the other fallen nations: Assyria, Elam, Meshech, Tubal, Edom, Sidon. They are consigned to a great burial-chamber full of graves.

Pharaoh (29:2): the particular pharaoh is Hophra. All the pharaohs were worshipped as gods. So also was the Nile crocodile ('dragon', 3).

Migdol to Syene (29:10): i.e. from north to south – the whole land. Migdol was a city on the Nile delta; Syene is modern Aswan.

Pathros (29:14): upper Egypt.

30:5: Egypt's allies.

31:3: although the Authorized Version, Revised Version and New English Bible name Assyria

here, the Revised Standard Version and Jerusalem Bible translations make better sense.
32:22-30: 'Assyria', the great power in Isaiah's day, overthrown by Babylon. 'Elam', a nation east of Babylon. 'Meshech and Tubal', little-known nations on Assyria's northern frontier. 'Princes of the north', presumably city-states north of Palestine.

33 - 48 ISRAEL RESTORED

33:1-20 The watchman

These verses reiterate the teaching of two earlier passages, 3:17-21; 18:5-29.

33:21-33 The exiles hear that Jerusalem has fallen

The news did not take Ezekiel by surprise. God had already given him back his speech, as promised (24:27), by the time the messenger arrived. Some texts have 'eleventh year' for 'twelfth' in verse 21, in which case the news takes the more likely time of six months to reach them. Those left behind in Judah, far from repenting, were busy annexing other people's property. And in Babylonia the exiles who seemed to lap up Ezekiel's words came simply for entertainment. They neither believed them nor acted on them: a depressing state of affairs after all that had happened!

34 God denounces the leaders and people of Israel

Both 'shepherds' (1-10) and 'sheep' (17-22) come in for condemnation.

Phoenician figure of a shepherd.

They have greedily, cruelly, selfishly exploited those committed to their care. But God will be a true shepherd, bringing his scattered flock back to good pasture in their homeland (11-16; and see Luke 15:4-7). He will appoint a good shepherd - a new David - to care for them (23-24; and see John 10:11), and the flock will dwell secure.

35 Prophecy against Edom

Edom is marked out for destruction, because of her callous reaction to Israel's downfall. She not only gloated, but planned to make capital out of it by seizing the land (10; the two nations are Israel and Judah). See 25:12-14 above. Other prophecies against Edom: Isaiah 21:34; Jeremiah 49:7-22; Obadiah.

36 The return to the homeland

God tells the desolate land it will soon be inhabited. His people are coming home. Israel's defeat has made men despise the God of Israel as powerless. Their return will vindicate his honour. The nations will know, and God's people will know, that he is the Lord. Those who returned from exile were truly and permanently cured of idolatry (25). But the total transformation of a 'new heart' is realized only 'in Christ' (2 Corinthians 5:17). Ezekiel was thinking of something far more complex than a heart transplant: the heart, in Jewish thought, stood for the whole personality, the essential man.

37 The vision in the valley of dry bones

After ten years in exile, and with Jerusalem destroyed, the people have given up hope. Not all Ezekiel's promises of restoration can raise a spark in his hearers. The nation is dead. But God can take even skeletons and make them into a living army. Ezekiel plays his part by making God's word known, but it is the Spirit of God who gives life. Israel will be re-made and live again. The two warring kingdoms will become one nation under one king - a new David. And here (21-28) the promise to the exiles merges into the full blessing of the future golden age. The return is only a foretaste of all God has in store for his people.
Into one (17): Ezekiel holds the two ends together in his clenched fist, making the two sticks look like one.
David (24): the ideal, messianic king, who will rule for ever in peace and righteousness.

38 - 39 The prophecy against Gog

Magog, Meshech, Tubal (2) and Gomer (6) were all sons of Japheth (Noah's son). They gave their names to Indo-European peoples living in the Black Sea/Caucasus region, on the northern fringe of the then-known world. Ezekiel pictures an invasion of these barbaric hordes from the north, led by the unidentified Gog, who may personify the cosmic forces of evil. Allied with armies from far and near (Persia, Sudan and north Africa, 5) he will wage war on the Lord's people. And God will demonstrate his power in the sight of all by taking on all the forces of evil single-handed, and destroying them once and for all. 'Gog' is responsible for the plan, but the Lord's hand is always in control.

Chapter 39 repeats and enlarges on 38. So vast is Gog's army that the weapons provide Israel with seven years' fuel supply. And the carnage is so great it takes seven months to clean up the land. (For the Jews, the number seven symbolized perfection and completeness.) The judgement of God is a terrible thing, and Ezekiel conjures it up in horrifying pictures. The fact that these chapters immediately precede Ezekiel's vision of the new temple in which God dwells among his people, gives added point to John's choice of Gog and Magog to represent all who oppose God in the last great battle instigated by Satan at the end of time (Revelation 20:8).

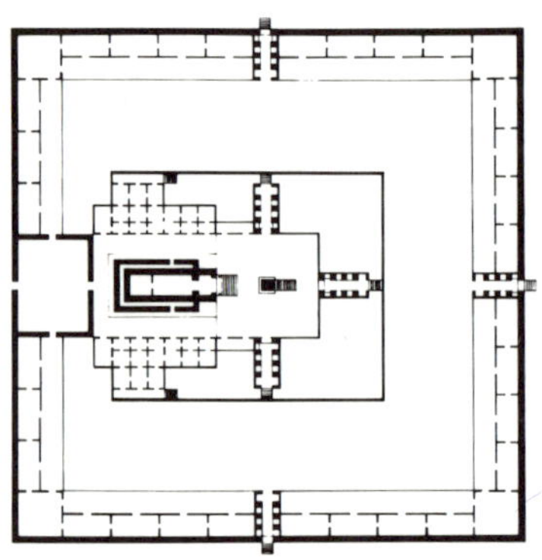

Ezekiel's vision of the temple was a detailed reconstruction of the temple area in Jerusalem. But through it flowed the 'river of life'.

40 - 48 The vision of the temple

These chapters were written some years after the rest (except for 29:17-21), in 573 BC. Although, for the most part, they make rather dull reading, they are in a very real sense, the climax to the whole book. Ezekiel began with a vision of God in the plains of Babylon. It ends with a vision of God returning in glory to a new temple - God in the midst of his people once again, never to depart.

For all the detail, Ezekiel's description is no mere blueprint for the second temple. It was not the old Jerusalem, but a structure *like* a city that he saw (40:2). It is true that the new temple follows much the same layout as Solomon's temple, and is all set out for the sacrifices (40:38ff.). But when God returns in all his glory it is to live for ever in a temple and among a priesthood and people cleansed from evil (chapter 43). Everything is perfect. This is the ideal. Yet it is not as far-reaching as the vision in Revelation. It is still envisaged in earthly terms: there is still a temple and sacrifices; the people of God are synonymous with Israel (44:6ff.); the laws continue, so does death, so does the need for a sin-offering (44:15-27). Again there is the subtle blending and telescoping of near and distant future which is characteristic of the prophets. The laws, the offerings, the feasts of Exodus and Leviticus are reinstated (chapters 45 and 46). Yet suddenly, in chapter 47, we are given something gloriously new. Out of God's temple flows a great life-giving river bordered by trees whose fruit is for food and whose leaves are for healing (see Revelation 22:1-2). The new tribal boundaries with which the book concludes (47:13ff.) are stylized, rather than geographically feasible. And at the very end the city is named. It is not now Jerusalem, but 'The Lord is there' (compare Revelation 21:22ff.).
Long cubit (40:5): about 20.4in/520mm.
Sons of Zadok (40:46): Zadok, who replaced Abiathar (1 Kings 2:26-27, 35), was the first high priest to officiate in the temple.
43:3: see chapter 10 and chapter 1.
47:9-10: the salt water of the Dead Sea is made fresh. The 'Great Sea' is the Mediterranean.

Old Testament 4-5

DANIEL

Daniel was a Judean exile at the court of Babylon. He was taken there as a boy a few years earlier than Ezekiel and the first main batch of exiles. He belonged to a noble (possibly royal) family and was exceptionally able and intelligent. Strictly speaking, Daniel was a statesman rather than a prophet, but his book rightly belongs among the prophetic writings. The first six chapters relate to historical events in Babylon over a period of 70 years. The remaining chapters, written in the first person, record a series of visions of future events. Two languages are used: 2:4 - 7:28 is in Aramaic, the international language; the rest in Hebrew. Right at the beginning of Israel's history God had his man – Joseph – at the Egyptian court. Now again, at this great crisis-point, God placed Daniel in a position of influence at the political centre of the Babylonian Empire, for the whole period of the exile.

To help explain a number of historical difficulties in Daniel (see in the text below), many think that the book as we have it was written in the 2nd century BC by an unknown author who used Daniel's name to give his work added authority. But the book of Daniel was widely accepted as Scripture in that same century, and the Jewish authorities were scrupulously careful about examining writings before they were given official approval. So either they had no objection to the real author adopting the name of the 6th-century prophet; or they were themselves taken in by one of their own contemporaries. There is the added problem that although these men lived only 400 years after the events recorded in Daniel, they failed to spot (or at least failed to challenge) the book's historical inaccuracies. At the heart of the issue is the question of prediction, since Daniel alludes to events long after his own day. If the possibility of genuine prediction in prophecy is allowed, the book can be taken as it stands, as the record of the life and visions of Daniel himself. Only if it is denied is one bound to conclude that the book cannot be earlier that the 2nd century BC.

An artist's impression of 'great Babylon', based on archaeological excavation.

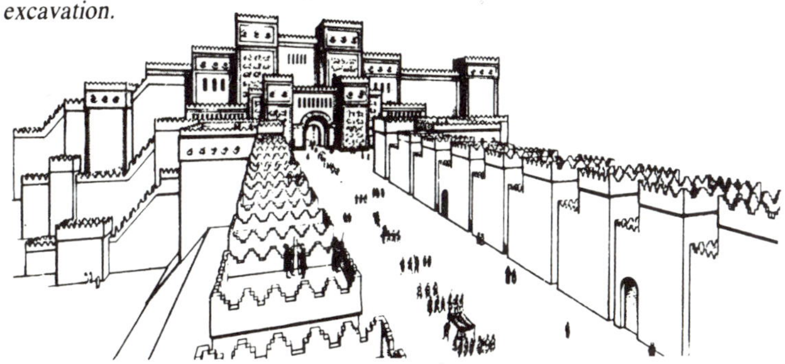

1 - 6 DANIEL AT THE BABYLONIAN COURT

1 Daniel and his friends win a place at Nebuchadnezzar's court

Daniel arrived in Babylon in 605 (see below). Good looks and natural ability ensured a place for him and his friends among those selected for special training. But the Babylonians did not observe Jewish rules on clean and unclean food (Leviticus 11), nor did they drain away the blood when they slaughtered animals (Leviticus 17:10ff.). Young as they were, Daniel and his friends were determined not to compromise their religion. So their only course was to restrict themselves to a vegetarian diet – and they thrived on it. What is more, they graduated from the king's school with honours!

The third year ... (1): the date is 605. After defeating Egypt at Carchemish, Nebuchadnezzar attacked Jerusalem. Daniel and others were taken hostage for the good behaviour of King Jehoiakim, who had been placed on the throne by the Egyptian pharaoh. Daniel uses the Babylonian reckoning for Jehoiakim's reign, beginning the year following the accession year. So 'the third year' here is the same as the fourth year (Jeremiah 25:1; 46:2) in Palestinian reckoning.

Shinar (2): the old name for Babylonia.

Verse 7: the endings of the Hebrew names (-el, -iah) link them with the name of Israel's God. At least one of the new names (Belteshazzar) is linked to that of a Babylonian god (see 4:8).

First year of King Cyrus (21): mentioned not because it was the year of Daniel's death (see 10:1), but because it was the year of the decree repatriating the exiles (Ezra 1:1-4).

2 Nebuchadnezzar's dream

Daniel had only just graduated when he was faced with this test. Nebuchadnezzar had either genuinely forgotten his dream, or he was deliberately making things difficult. It is clear from this chapter that Daniel's faith went much deeper than mere observance of the law. With his own life and the lives of many others at stake, he turns in complete trust to God. Astrology and divination, at which the Babylonians excelled, are not for him.

The image stands for four world empires: Babylonian (with Nebuchadnezzar as head), Medo-Persian, Greek and Roman. In the days of the Roman Empire, God would begin to carve out a new, everlasting, kingdom which would become universal. See further in chapters 7ff. (Those who think in terms of a 2nd-century writer looking back on events cannot include the Roman Empire, and are forced to make separate Median and Persian Empires. In point of historical fact, although there were Median kings, there was never a dominant Median Empire.)

Chaldeans (2): in its general sense the term simply means 'Babylonian'; later it was used in a restricted sense of a class of wise men. Daniel uses the word in both ways.

Verse 4: the Aramaic section starts here, and ends at 7:28. We do not know if the original used both languages.

3 The golden image and the fiery furnace

The years pass and Nebuchadnezzar, forgetting he once acknowledged Daniel's God as supreme, sets up his 90 ft idol, demanding that all his people worship it. But Daniel's companions will not compromise. They know God is *able* to deliver them from a terrible death; they do not know if he *will* (17). But come what may, they will not deny him (18). In the event, the flames killed those who flung them in, and burned through their own bonds; but they came out with not so much as a smell of burning about them. And a godlike figure walked through the fire with them. Again the king is compelled to worship.

Satrap (2): one of a number of Old Persian words which occur in Daniel. There is no reason why Daniel should not have used them; they were known before his day, and he lived on into the period of Persian supremacy. Or it may be that this Aramaic section (see on 2:4) is a later, or updated, translation.

Lyre, trigon, harp (5, Revised Standard Version): these are all Greek words. The instruments themselves are Mesopotamian, but Greek cultural influences had spread across this part of the world before Nebuchadnezzar's time. Greek colonies were widespread, and Greek mercenaries served in many armies.

Assyrian musicians.

Furnace (6): a kiln (probably for baking bricks) with an open top and an open door at the side through which the king could see the men.

4 The king's madness

Nebuchadnezzar himself authenticates this extraordinary story (1-18, 34-37). Perhaps sensing that this dream is against himself, he does not turn to Daniel straight away (6-8). It is clear from Daniel's dismay that he does not wish the king ill. But the king's pride in his achievements (and archaeology shows they really *were* something to be proud of) overrides Daniel's wise advice. He is stricken with a rare mania, believing himself to be an animal. (Other cases are known, where patients have exhibited precisely the same symptoms: roaming out of doors, and living on a diet of grass and water.) Yet God is at work in the depths of his now humble mind, and as he worships the one true God his reason returns.

One would hardly expect to find open reference to such a seemingly shameful illness in contemporary official records. But events of the later years of Nebuchadnezzar are not known from ancient texts.

Verses 3 and 34-35: the echoes from Psalms and Isaiah may reflect Daniel's influence on the king.

Seven times (16): the length of time here as elsewhere in Daniel is unspecified. It was a definite, limited period of time fixed by God.

5 Belshazzar's feast

Strictly speaking, Nabonidus (556-539 BC) was the last king of Babylon. But he retired to Arabia early in his reign, leaving his son Belshazzar acting king in Babylon (hence the fact that Daniel could be made only 'third ruler', 16).

The date is 539, 23 years after Nebuchadnezzar's death. The great feast at the palace is going with a swing, when a mysterious hand begins to write on the wall. Three words are written. They are weights, or units of money: 'a mina, a mina, a shekel and a half-shekel'. Daniel, now an old man, is summoned to interpret; and he goes to the root meanings of the words: 'number', 'weigh', 'divide'. The king's days were indeed numbered. That very night Cyrus the Persian took the impregnable city of Babylon, so the ancient historians tell us, by diverting the course of the River Euphrates and entering along the dry river-bed, while the Babylonians were at a feast of their gods.

Gold drinking vessel of the time; Persian, from the Oxus Treasure.

Father (2): i.e. ancestor, predecessor. The word often has this sense in the Old Testament.

The queen (10): as Belshazzar's wives were there already, this may have been Nebuchadnezzar's widow.

Darius the Mede (31): no other historical record so far found mentions anyone of this name, or places any ruler between Nabonidus/ Belshazzar and Cyrus. Darius has been variously identified, but none of the suggestions is completely satisfactory. This does not mean we can write Darius off as a fictional character. Since Cyrus was so well known the author could hardly have hoped to get away with such an invention.

6 Daniel in the lion's den

All his life Daniel has been a man of God. He is now in his eighties, and his enemies still cannot fault him. They can only attack him through his religion (4-5). Daniel could have stopped praying for a month, or he could have prayed in secret. But he is no more ready to compromise now than he was as a boy. So his enemies have him. The king's hands are tied by his own decree, but God's hand is not. Daniel was as safe from harm in the lion-pit as his friends had been in the furnace.

Verses 8, 15: see Esther 1:19; 8:8.

The den (16): most probably an enclosure with an open top around which was a spectator's gallery. There was also a small entrance at the side, which Darius sealed up (17).

7 - 12 THE RECORD OF DANIEL'S VISIONS

7 The four beasts

Like chapter 2 this is a pictorial representation of history. Again there are four successive empires, and then the kingdom of God is established. The winged lion is Babylon; and verse 4 has Nebuchadnezzar particularly in mind. Verse 6 depicts the Greek Empire of Alexander the Great, on his death divided among his four generals. Seleucus founded a dynasty in Syria. Ptolemy founded a dynasty in Egypt. The other two kingdoms were Greece and Asia Minor. The 'ten horns' (7, 24) equate with the toes of the image in chapter 2, though the precise identification has been much debated. Verses 9-12 picture God's judgement of the world empires. In 13-14 God gives total dominion to 'one like a son of man', Jesus' favourite title for himself. The kingdom inaugurated at Christ's first coming will be finally realized when he returns (see Matthew 26:64). Opposing God's people in different guises throughout history is the 'little horn' (8, 20-21), until God finally removes its power. It is from this chapter that Revelation 13 draws its imagery.

A time, two times, and half a time (25): often taken to mean $3\frac{1}{2}$ years; but see on 4:16. Evil is given its head, but for a strictly limited time.

8 The ram and the he-goat

The vision focusses on the second and third empires. The two-horned ram which symbolizes Medo-Persia will be superseded by the swift-footed goat – Alexander's Greek Empire. Alexander himself is the 'great horn'. The 'four horns' are the kingdoms into which his empire was divided (see on chapter 7). The little horn, in this chapter, refers to Antiochus IV, who ruled Syria 175-164 BC. Verses 9-14 vividly depict the atrocities of his reign (see on chapter 11), which resulted in the Maccabean revolt. 1 Maccabees 1 - 6 (in the Apocrypha) recounts this period of Jewish history.

Susa (2): east of Babylon; one of the four capitals of Persia.

Prince (11, 25): God himself. In attempting to wipe out the Jewish religion Antiochus was directly challenging the God of Israel.

Verse 14: i.e. 2,300 days (see Genesis 1). Antiochus first meddled in Jewish affairs in 171; he died in 164.

Gabriel (16): this is the first time God's messenger-angel is named. It was Gabriel who appeared to Zacharias, father of John the Baptist, and again to Mary before the birth of Jesus.

The end (17): this usually refers to the winding-up of history, and God's final judgement. But verse 26 relates the vision to the distant future, and 19 to the period when the suffering will be over. The Bible writers often seem to step clear of time, and view contemporary and future events as one aspect of the total, final events of 'the end'.

9 The seventy weeks; Daniel's prayer

The date is 538. Babylon has virtually ruled Judah since the Battle of Carchemish in 605. The 70 years' captivity spoken of by Jeremiah is almost up. Daniel pleads with God for the return of his people to their homeland. He is completely one with his people, sharing the blame for sin (5ff.), and his request rests solely on God's mercy (18). He saw the answer to his prayer that same year, but Israel's troubles were not over. God now shows Daniel something of what lies ahead.

Verses 24-27 are very difficult, and numerous interpretations have been suggested. God has ordained a period of 70 x 7 ('seventy weeks of years') in which the salvation of his people will be completed (24). For the Jews, the number seven itself symbolized completeness, perfection. And it may be best to take the numbers symbolically. But the period of time between the decree to rebuild and restore Jerusalem and the beginning of Jesus' ministry (25) comes very close to the 7+62 weeks=483 days, standing for the same number of years – the total reached if we take the figures literally (though there is more than one possible starting-point, and even the end-date is not absolutely fixed). Verse 26 seems to point to the death and rejection of Christ and the destruction of the temple which followed in AD 70 – with a wider reference at the end. But the subject of verse 27 is not at all clear. 'He' is taken by some to be the Messiah, by others to be the destroying prince of the previous verse.

10 - 11:1 Vision and conflict

After a long fast, Daniel receives an awe-inspiring vision of a glorious figure: very like John's vision of Christ in Revelation 1:12-16. He is given insight into the continual battle raging in the spiritual realm between those protecting God's people and those bent on their destruction (see Ephesians 6:12). Michael is the special guardian angel of the Jewish people (12:1). The 'princes' in this chapter are patron angels of the various nations.

11:2-45 The struggle for power

This chapter claims to set out the course of future history in detail. And from our vantage-point in time we can look back on its amazingly accurate fulfilment in the history of the Greek Empire. There are to be three more Persian kings (2; Cambyses, Gaumata and Darius I), followed by a fourth (Xerxes). Xerxes invaded Greece but was defeated at Salamis in 480 BC. The power then passed to Greece (3-4; see on chapter 7). Verse 5 refers to Egypt (the 'king of the south') and to Ptolemy's one-time general, Seleucus, who became 'king of the north' – the powerful kingdom of Syria and the east. Fifty years later (6) the daughter of Ptolemy II married Antiochus II of Syria. But she was divorced and murdered, and her brother avenged her by attacking Syria (7). Verses 9-13 reflect the struggles between the two powers at the end of the 3rd century BC. The Jews then joined forces with Antiochus III of Syria to defeat Egypt (14-15). They gained their freedom from Egypt (16), and Antiochus made a marriage alliance with Ptolemy V (17). Antiochus invaded Asia Minor and Greece but was defeated by the Romans at Magnesia in 190 BC (18-19).

The 'exactor of tribute' (20) was his son Seleucus IV, who was shortly succeeded by his brother Antiochus IV, the persecutor of the Jews. Verses 21-24 aptly portray his character and policies. Through the treachery of Ptolemy's own men, Antiochus briefly gained control of Egypt in 173. On his return he attacked Jerusalem and slaughtered 80,000 Jews (25-28). The next time he attacked Egypt he was thwarted by the Roman fleet (29-30). He turned on Jerusalem again and desecrated the temple (31). He was aided and abetted by some Jews, but others refused to compromise their faith, though they died for it (32-33). Judas Maccabaeus instigated a successful revolt, so helping the faithful (34).

Verses 36-45 do not describe actual events at the end of Antiochus' life. They may refer to the end of Syrian domination, at the hands of Rome, the new king from the north. Or they may anticipate events at the end of time (see on 8:17), which the sufferings of God's people under Antiochus foreshadow. This then leads in to chapter 12.

12 Deliverance

Daniel is the first Old Testament book to speak explicitly of resurrection, though he is thinking only of the Jewish nation ('your people'). When that day comes, and all the terrible troubles are past, those who have shown themselves wise by their faithful obedience to God will rise to shine like stars for ever. All evil will be done away. But as for times, those are in God's hand. Not even Daniel understands this (6-8) – so a cautious approach to these matters may still be the wisest course!

Old Testament 4.6

HOSEA

Hosea was one of Isaiah's contemporaries, a prophet of God in the 8th century BC. But Hosea, unlike Isaiah, was a northerner. His message was for Israel, the northern kingdom, although he occasionally refers to Judah. And Israel in his day was in a mess. Hosea became a prophet at the end of the reign of the nation's last powerful king, Jeroboam II. He prophesied for the next 40 years, until just before Samaria fell to Assyria in 722 BC. And during that time the country went rapidly down hill. Rejection of God and the wholesale adoption of pagan religious practices brought about a moral and political landslide. 2 Kings 14:23 - 17:41 gives the history of the period. But the fact that after Jeroboam's death Israel had six kings in just over 20 years, and four of them assassinated their predecessors, gives some idea of the state of the country.

What Israel's idolatry meant to God – how he continued to love and long for his people's return to him – Hosea learnt through bitter personal experience, as his own wife betrayed and deserted him. His message comes straight from the heart. And this is what makes the book unique.

1 - 2:1 Hosea's wife and children

God instructs Hosea to marry Gomer, a woman God knows will prove unfaithful. (This seems to be the only tenable interpretation of verse 2.) Three children are born, and each is given a name which speaks God's message to Israel (compare Isaiah 8). Through the prophet, God is giving his people a last opportunity to repent before judgement breaks on the land (2 Kings 17:13-14). Yet even though they refuse, his loving purpose is not thwarted (1:10 - 2:1).

Jezreel (4): the site of many bloody battles; here the reference is to the slaughter recounted in 2 Kings 10.

2:2-23 Unfaithful Israel; God's steadfast love

Hosea's voice, pleading with his unfaithful wife through his children, becomes one with the voice of God addressing Israel. The people are worshipping Baal, the Canaanite fertility god, thinking he is the one who gives good crops and plentiful harvests; when all the time it is God. Israel will be taught by punishment, and afterwards become God's dearly loved bride again (19-20).

Achor (15): near Jericho; the place where Achan sinned and was punished (Joshua 7).

My Baal (16): a substitute word must be used because 'baal', which was the everyday word for 'lord/master/husband' was also the name of the Canaanite god.

Jezreel (22): the word means 'God sows'.

3 Probation

Gomer, now seemingly the slave of another man, is bought back and put on probation. Again Hosea's action, and his continuing love, provide an object-lesson. For a while, Israel too will be deprived of the things she

The background to Hosea is one of idolatry. This tile from Assyria shows a worshipper standing before a statue of his god.

counted on – her king and her religious emblems – but in time she will turn back to God.

Cakes of raisins (1): offered to pagan gods.

Verse 4: sacrifice and ephod (part of the priest's regalia) belonged to the legitimate religion; pillar and teraphim (household gods) were part of the pagan admixture.

4 Idolatry in Israel

From now on there is no further mention of Hosea's family. But the experience is there – and it colours the rest of the book. Real faith in God issues in obedience to his standards. The prostitution of Israel's religion led to literal prostitution (11-14). Paganism brought in its wake sexual degradation (13-14) and the breakdown of law and order in society (1-2). It still does. The priests – who failed to make God's laws known, and feathered their own nests into the bargain (4-10) – and the men of Israel (14) are responsible for what has happened. And God holds them accountable.

Beth-aven (15): a derisory name for Bethel, one of the religious centres in the northern kingdom.

Ephraim (17): Israel. Ephraim was the leading tribe.

5:1-14 Judgement

A generation has grown up to whom God is a stranger (7). The alarm is sounded on Judah's borders, for Judah shares the sin to which Israel has become addicted (8-12). Not even the great king of Assyria (13; Tiglath-pileser III – see 2 Kings 16:5ff.) can save them from God's judgement.

Mizpah, Tabor, Shittim (1-2): places where there were shrines for Baal worship.

5:15 - 6:6 A change of heart

Suffering turns the people to God again. But there is no deep change. Their 'love' evaporates as quickly as dew in the hot sun. It is lasting love and real knowledge of him that God looks for.

6:7 - 7:16 Catalogue of evil

Priests have turned butcher. At the heart of the nation's religion, at Shechem, there is intrigue and murder (6:7-10). At court it is the same. Kings fall at the hands of hot-heads and conspirators (7:6-7; see introduction). Israel turns to foreign peoples (8-9), foreign powers (11), foreign gods (16): but never to the Lord.

Oven (4-7): they baked their flat loaves on saucer-shaped 'hot-plates' placed upside down over the embers. The 'cake' (8) must be turned over to cook both sides.

8 God is forgotten

Israel will be caught up in the whirlwind of God's judgement. They have made gods, made up laws, set up kings to suit themselves: as if God and his laws did not exist. But neither idols nor allies will avail when the God they have forgotten strikes.

Calf (5): Israel's first king set up two images at shrines in his own land to rival Jerusalem as religious centres (1 Kings 12:28). The calf had a long association with pagan cults in Egypt and in Canaan.

9 A terrible destiny for Israel

It was probably at the height of the festival to mark the grape-harvest that Hosea spoke out (1-5). The people may call him a fool, but he knows he is God's watchman, and he will not hold his tongue (7-8). Israel will become a slave-nation to Assyria, as she once was to Egypt (3, 6). Sin has become habitual, ingrained, to the point where God finally withdraws his love (12, 15).

Gibeah (9): see Judges 19.

Baal-peor (10): see Numbers 25.

Gilgal (15): the place where Saul was acclaimed king (1 Samuel 11:14-15). The people's eagerness to have a king had in it the seeds of danger. Some of the later kings would usurp God's place as the true Leader of his people.

10 Under the yoke

Outwardly, affluent Israel made a great show of religion (1), but inwardly the people moved further and further away from God. The calf-image at Bethel had become the nation's only 'king' (3-5), a king marked for destruction (6-8). Now they are reaping what they have long sown (13). Yet they could still sow an altogether different crop (12).

Shalman (14): probably a reference to the recent invasion of Gilead by Salamanu of Moab.

11 The Father's love

This chapter lets us see right into the infinitely loving heart of God. All down the long years of history, from Egypt on, and despite all he has done for them, Israel has rejected God's love (1-4). The nation deserves no mercy (5-7). Yet God still shrinks from destroying them (8-9). He is torn between love and justice, neither of which can be denied. This is the pain he took to himself in the cross of Christ.

Admah and Zeboiim (8): two cities to the south of the Dead Sea, presumably destroyed with Sodom and Gomorrah (Genesis 19).

12 Lessons from history

This is not an easy chapter to follow. Israel needs to be reminded of scheming Jacob (3-6, 12), and how he learnt to lean on God – and forget her proud independence and reliance on foreign powers. The people deride the prophets of their own day. They need the reminder that it was through a prophet (Moses, 13) that God brought the nation into being.

Verses 3-4, 12: incidents recounted in Genesis 25:21-26; 32:22-32; and 29.

13 The east wind of God's judgement

Israel may turn to Baal and other idols, but there is in fact no God but God (what was true then is still true now). Men may forget him, or discount him, but he exists: and he has power to carry out all that he has warned of.

East wind (15): the scorching wind from the desert which dries and shrivels everything in its path.

14 'Return, O Israel'

After the fierce tones of chapter 13, this last chapter is full of love and pleading. The way is open. There is no need to pass through the fire of judgement. Men have only to give God their loyalty (2-3) to find his love and forgiveness, and embark on a new, transformed life (4-7). This is the truly wise course (9).

Hosea makes the way so plain. It is more than sad to realize that his contemporaries ignored it all – until the Assyrians swept down and destroyed their splendid capital, Samaria; took the remaining Israelites into exile; and repeopled their land with foreigners. When God gives warning of judgement, he is not playing with words. How many of the practices he condemned in Israel do we see all around us in our own society? How long do we expect his patience to last?

Old Testament 4.7

JOEL

We know nothing at all about this prophet, apart from his father's name (1:1). And the prophecy contains few clues to the date when it was written. Joel is obviously familiar with themes which also occur in Isaiah, Amos and Ezekiel – particularly the 'day of the Lord', when God will finally judge the world and his own people. We may guess at dates – and guesses range from the 8th century BC to the 4th century BC and later – but the book itself is timeless.

1 The disastrous plague of locusts

Even in our own century Jerusalem has been stripped of all vegetation by a plague of locusts like the one Joel describes so vividly. The swarm of several million insects is carried into Palestine by the desert wind from Arabia. The locust grows rapidly from larva to winged adult (4), and at every stage its appetite is insatiable. It is worse than an invading army: when it moves on there is no green or growing thing left (6-12). There is nothing to offer to God (9,13), or so little that the people are using all they have to ward off starvation. For Joel, the locust swarm is an object-lesson, a warning of the terror of God's approaching judgement day (15). He calls for a national day of prayer (14).

2:1-27 The coming day of the Lord; repentance and restoration

The locust-army becomes a picture of the invading army of God on the day of his judgement: the sky black with insects (2); the 'scorched earth' in their wake (3); their inexorable, totally irresistible, onward march (4-9). This is what God's judgement will be like. Who can bear it (11)? But no one need endure God's judgement. He is still calling all men to repent (12). Joel calls the whole nation to turn to God and plead for mercy (13-17). And in response God promises to restore in profusion all that the locusts have robbed them of. He will rid the land of his great army (25), which is now identified with all his enemies ('the northerner', 20: see on Ezekiel 38 - 39; it is very unlikely that the locusts actually came from the north).

2:28 - 3:21 The outpouring of God's Spirit: judgement on the nations

Joel foresaw a day when God's Spirit would be poured out, not just on priests and prophets, but on ordinary people, regardless of sex, age, or class. He little dreamt that God spoke not just of Israel, but of all nations (Acts 2). Equally, God's judgement awaits men of all nations who refuse his call, including Israel (32). But all who call out to him, and whom he calls, will escape.

The nations will be punished for all they have inflicted on God's people (3:2-8). Multitudes will be gathered to God's judgement. There He will decide their destiny (14). All evil will be done away on that momentous, earth-shaking day. God will make his home in a city and among a people at last made holy; and the whole land will share in this abundant blessing (16-18).

Tyre, Sidon, Philistia (3:4): see on Ezekiel 25 - 28. Artaxerxes III sold the Sidonians as slaves in 345 BC, and in 332 Alexander the Great sold the people of Tyre and the Philistine city of Gaza into slavery.

Sabaeans (8): famous Arabian traders.

3:10: Joel reverses Isaiah's famous words (Isaiah 2:4).

Valley of Jehoshaphat (12): probably a symbolic name; it means 'the Lord judges'.

Old Testament 4.8

AMOS

Amos was a layman, a shepherd and dresser of fig-trees. His home was in Tekoa, about 12 miles south of Jerusalem, on the edge of the Judean desert. But God sent him as his prophet to the northern kingdom of Israel. His base was the religious centre of Bethel, where Jeroboam I had set up a calf-image when the nation had first split into two rival kingdoms. Amos lived in the reign of Jeroboam II (793-753), Israel's Indian summer of prosperity and influence. But beneath the affluence the nation was rotten. Amos was sent to denounce the social and religious corruption, and warn of God's impending judgement. But the people turned a deaf ear, as they did to his contemporary, Hosea. And the king's chaplain told him to get back to Judah (7:10ff.)! Thirty years after Jeroboam's death the Assyrians destroyed Samaria and took the people into exile. Israel ceased to exist. But the prophet has a word for any nation in Israel's condition. Put his descriptions in 20th-century dress and they still strike home.

1 - 2:5 The indictment of Israel's neighbours

Syria, Philistia, Tyre, Edom, Ammon, Moab and Judah are each condemned in turn. Their offences are many (the formula 'For three ... for four' indicates an indefinite number). They stand condemned for their crimes against humanity. Only Judah is judged against the full standard of God's law. The Syrians are guilty of wanton cruelty (running studded threshing-sledges over the bodies of their captives, 3); the Philistines of selling their fellow men. Tyre and Edom have transgressed the laws of kinship. Ammon's atrocities have been committed simply to gain more land. By desecrating a corpse Moab has violated one of the most universal of all ancient unwritten laws. God will punish each and every one.

Hazael, Ben-hadad (1:4): kings of Syria. Hazael seized the throne in Elisha's time and founded a dynasty.

Kir (5): the place the Syrians originally came from.

Gaza, Ashdod, Ashkelon, Ekron (6-8): four of the five Philistine cities.

His brother (11): Edom and Israel were descendants of two brothers, Esau and Jacob.

Rabbah (14): the Ammonite capital; modern Amman, capital of Jordan.

2:6-16 Israel's crimes

The other prophets make it plain that Israel's basic sin was in turning away from God to worship idols. But Amos emphasizes the moral and social decline which resulted. They have grown hard and callous in their dealings with others; young and old make use of temple prostitutes; and they have gagged God's spokesmen. None will escape God's punishment.

Verse 8: the law humanely ordered that garments taken in pledge be returned by nightfall (Exodus 22:26-27).

Amorite (9): here an umbrella term for the original inhabitants of Canaan.

Nazirites (11): men consecrated to God by a special vow which involved renouncing wine.

Cart/wagon (13): more likely the threshing-sledge (as in the Jerusalem Bible).

3 Punishment

Israel has broken the covenant-agreement with God and must suffer punishment. It is simple cause and effect (like the other instances given in verses 3-6). God has spoken; he will act. Of beautiful Samaria, with its great stone houses and exquisite ivory panels, only a trace will be left; just enough to show that the city once existed. And God will demolish the trappings of debased religion at Bethel (verse 14).

4 God's warnings

The luxury-loving women of Samaria ('cows of Bashan'), living it up at the expense of the poor, will be led away with hooks. (The Assyrians actually did this to their captives.) While they crushed their fellow men, the people still kept up the religious facade (4-5). But 'insurance policy' religion is a mockery of the real thing (see James 1:26-27). By famine and drought, blight and disease God warned them where they were heading – all to no avail.

Amos protested against the 'houses of ivory' being built by the rich while the poor were oppressed. Many ivories of the period have been found. This one is from a palace in Assyria.

5 'Seek me and live'

The lament (1-3) is quickly followed by an appeal. God calls on his people to save their lives by seeking him. And this means, not yet more sacrifices at the nation's corrupt sanctuaries (5, 21-23, 25-26), but reformed living – a return to God's standards of justice and right conduct in public as well as private life. Otherwise the 'day of the Lord' (18ff.), the day on which they expect to enter into God's blessing and see their enemies destroyed, will be a terrible day of condemnation for God's people.

The gate (10): the city gate was the place for business transactions and the administration of justice.

Joseph (15): Ephraim and Manasseh (descended from Joseph's two sons) were leading tribes in the northern kingdom.

Verse 25: the meaning seems to be 'Was it *only* sacrifice and offerings you brought to me...? Was it not also right living and obedience?'

Sakkuth, Kaiwan (26): Assyrian gods associated with the planet Saturn.

6 Exile

Affluence and comfortable living (then as now) insulate men from the real issues, and breed false security. Self-sufficiency and pride have been man's downfall from first to last (e.g. Genesis 11:1-9; Ezekiel 28).

Calneh, Hamath (2): two towns in Syria; Hamath is modern Hama.

Lo-debar, Karnaim (13): towns east of the Jordan, which Israel took from the Syrians.

Arabah (14): the dry valley running south from the Dead Sea to the Gulf of Aqaba.

7 The plumb-line

Twice Amos prevails on God to stay his hand; but judgement cannot be delayed for ever. Israel does not begin to measure up against the straight line of God's standards.

God's man and 'official religion' meet head-on in the confrontation between Amos and Amaziah. (10-17). The prophet has God's authority for his message and will not be silenced. Amaziah will die in exile. The invading army will abuse his wife, kill his children and seize his land.

The Lord repented (3, 6): i.e. he mercifully changed his mind (this does not imply that his original intention was wrong).

Sycamore (14): a kind of fig-tree; not the tree we call sycamore.

8 Israel ripe for ruin

Men like to think their 'little' sins too small for God to notice. But he sees everything: greed and sharp practice; short weight and sub-standard goods. And the poor, who always come off worst, are his special concern.

Ephah ... shekel (5): this was a double cheat; the trader reduced the size of the measure for the grain (ephah) *and* increased the weight of the silver paid for it (shekel).

Ashimah (14): a Syrian goddess worshipped in Israel. Dan, in the far north, was the town where Jeroboam I erected his second calf-image.

9 Evil destroyed; the faithful remnant restored

For the nation as a whole judgement will be inescapable. God will deal with them like any foreign nation (7a). But for the faithful few the future holds unimagined blessing (11-15).

Caphtor (7): Crete, where the Philistines originally came from.

Old Testament 4.9

OBADIAH

A prophecy of Edom's downfall (for other prophecies against Edom, see Isaiah 34:5-15; Jeremiah 49:7-22; Ezekiel 25:12-14; 35:1-15; Amos 1:11-12). Edom occupied the mountainous region south-east of the Dead Sea. The capital, Sela (now Petra), was perched high on a plateau above a sheer rock cliff approached by a narrow gorge. It was virtually impregnable. From mountain strongholds like this the Edomites launched their raids on Palestine. As Esau's descendants they were in fact kin to Israel, but there was never any love lost between the two. The final outrage – and the occasion of Obadiah's prophecy – was their invasion of Judah while Jerusalem was being sacked by the Babylonians in 587 BC.

Obadiah denounces Edom's pride. The Edomites thought their strongholds invincible, but they would be utterly destroyed. In the 5th century BC Arabs took Edom, and in the 3rd century the region was overrun by the Nabataeans (who built the rock-city of Petra in present-day Jordan). Some Edomites settled in southern Judah. Herod the Great, ruler of the Jews at the time of Jesus' birth, was one of their descendants. After AD 70 the Edomites entirely disappeared from history. In contrast to dispossessed Edom, Obadiah foretells the return of Israel to possess a greatly extended land including former Edomite territory.

Teman (9): an important town in Edom, home of Job's friend Eliphaz; Mt Esau is Mt Seir.

Verse 19: 'Negeb', the southern desert; 'Shephelah', the hill-country behind the western coastal plain; 'Ephraim and Samaria', the northern kingdom of Israel; 'Gilead', east of the Jordan.

Verse 20: 'Halah', in Mesopotamia; 'Zarephath', modern Sarafand in Lebanon.

Old Testament 4.10

JONAH

2 Kings 14:25 is the only other mention of this prophet, and that would place him in the mid-8th century BC. Nineveh, capital of powerful Assyria (Israel's enemy) and subject of this book, was destroyed by the Babylonians in 612 BC. If Jonah did not write the story himself, it was probably written after this date (see 3:3). Whether we take the book as 'history with a moral' or as parable (and the Bible contains many parables, though none as long as this), there is no doubt about the main message. God's concern extends beyond Israel to the whole world. Jesus focussed attention on two further points: the parallel with the three days between his own death and resurrection; and the ready repentance of the Ninevites in contrast to his hearers (Matthew 12:40; Luke 11:32).

1 Jonah runs away

4:2 tells us why. Jonah was not afraid to go to Nineveh (verse 12 shows plenty of courage!). But he knew God: he knew that if the Ninevites changed their ways God would forgive them. And Jonah wanted this cruel threatening enemy nation destroyed. So in deliberate disobedience he sets out in the opposite direction. By trying to save his life, the heathen sailors display more humanity than the man of God (13).

A great fish (17): although sperm whales and large sharks capable of swallowing a man are not unknown in the eastern Mediterranean, this incident is clearly intended to be seen as a miracle. It is one of the many things God 'appoints' in the story (see 1:4; 4:6-8). Argument over this must not be allowed to blind us to the whole point of the story.

2 Jonah's prayer

This psalm records Jonah's cry to God when he was at death's door ('the belly of Sheol', 2). At last he comes to his senses, remembering his 'true loyalty' (8). And God, who has already saved him from death, gives him a 'second life'.

3 Nineveh's response

Given a second chance, Jonah leaps to obey. And his message produces a remarkable effect. The whole city, from the greatest to the least, repents. And God spares them.

Three days' journey (3): this applies to the district of Nineveh as distinct from the city: 'Greater London', so to speak.

God repented (10): see on Amos 7:3.

4 A hard lesson for Jonah

Jonah wanted God to confine his love and mercy to Israel. Let the heathen get their deserts. Far from being delighted that his message provoked such a fantastic response, he was furious. And it wasn't simply that he didn't want to look a fool. There was no spark of compassion for the people of Nineveh in Jonah's heart. And so God used a plant (the shady castor-oil plant) to make him feel something of his own pity for men and women: 'Should I not pity Nineveh?'

Verse 11: the city could well have housed this number of people. The inner wall formed a circuit of 7¾ miles. Not knowing their 'right hand from their left' expresses their utter ignorance of God and his laws.

Old Testament 4-11

MICAH

Micah was one of the 8th-century BC prophets, contemporary with Amos and Hosea (in the northern kingdom of Israel) and Isaiah (in Jerusalem). He was a countryman, from a town in south-west Judah, on the Philistine border. His message is for Samaria and Jerusalem, capital cities of the two kingdoms. And from a comparison with Amos it is clear that Judah had become infected with the same sins that beset Israel. So Micah, too, denounces rulers, priests and prophets; deplores the money-grubbing exploitation of the helpless; dishonesty in business; sham religion. God's judgement will fall on Samaria and Jerusalem; only after that will there be restoration. But Micah also sees a glorious future, when Jerusalem will become the religious centre of the world, and Bethlehem give birth to a greater David who will rule over all God's people.

1 The two cities

God is pictured coming down from heaven, treading upon the mountains, to destroy Samaria for her persistent idolatry. The gangrene has spread into Judah, and God's judgement is at the gates of Jerusalem. Micah pictures the approach of the invading army, coming from the coastal plain through the hills of Judah to Jerusalem (10ff., where the place-names frequently conceal a play on words). The parents in Judah will mourn for their exiled children. In 722 BC the Assyrians destroyed Samaria. In 701 they besieged Jerusalem, and the city escaped by a miracle (see 2 Kings 18:9 - 19:37). Micah most probably lived through both.

Verse 1: Jotham (750-732) and Hezekiah (729) were good kings; Ahaz (735-716) was one of the worst, introducing terrible heathen practices, including child-sacrifice. (Overlapping dates indicate periods of co-regency.)

2 - 3 Exploitation; misrule; a perverted priesthood

The men with power and influence are all of them on the make, and they are not fussy about the means. So property is seized and families made destitute; and the preacher is told this is none of his business. (2:12-13 moves abruptly to the future, picturing God at the head of the remnant of his people.) The ordinary people are just so many animals to the rulers (3:1-3). Every man has his price: judge and priest and prophet alike (3:11).

4 Future greatness

Micah is full of contrasts. Verses 1-8 sweep us on to a new Jerusalem, from which God's word goes out to all men, and to which the nations flock, in an era of peace and plenty. Verses 9-10 return us to the condemned city, to a nation in exile, to God's judgement: not on his people alone, but on all nations around (11-13).

Verses 1-3: almost identical with Isaiah 2:2-4.

Babylon (10): the enemy in Micah's day was Assyria, but like Isaiah he looks 100 years ahead to the power which would destroy Jerusalem.

5 The king from Bethlehem

In the midst of the Assyrian siege, Micah speaks of a deliverer – *the* ultimate deliverer – who would come, like David of old, from Bethlehem (see Matthew 2:1-6). Historical perspectives blur, as so often in the prophets, and current events melt into those of the near and far distant future. In the messianic peace, even the Assyrian will be overcome. But Judah too will be purified 'in that day' (10ff.). All that she has relied on in place of God will be destroyed: armies, defences, witch-craft and false gods.

Ephrathah (2): the district around Bethlehem.

Seven ... eight (5): idiomatic, for 'an indefinite number': no matter how many leaders are needed they will be forth-coming.

Nimrod (6): Assyria (see Genesis 10:8-12).

6 What God requires of his people

Verse 8 gives us the essence of true

worship. God accepts no substitute. Though men may try to buy him off with all kinds of impressive gifts, he sees and will punish their sharp practice, their violence and deceit.
Verse 5: see Numbers 22 - 24.
Shittim to Gilgal (5): i.e at the crossing of the Jordan (Joshua 3 - 4).
My first-born ... (7): the sacrifice of the firstborn crept into Israel with other pagan practices in the dark days of the nation's last kings.
Verse 11: see on Amos 8:5.
Omri ... Ahab (16): two kings of Israel notorious for introducing Baal-worship.

King Sennacherib recorded his victory over the fortress city of Lachish in Judah in a series of scenes carved in stone which lined his palace walls at Nineveh.

7 Darkness and light

Micah watches the breakdown of society in his country. The rot which began at government level has permeated the whole nation. And now all human relationships are crumbling. Friendship and family count for nothing. The human scene is black. But with God there is still light. He may still be relied on. His promise will not fail. He will build again. He will deliver again. In his compassionate love he will forgive again.
Watchmen (4): the prophets were posted as watchmen to warn of coming judgement (see Ezekiel 3:17-21).

Old Testament 4.12

NAHUM

The subject of Nahum, like that of the earlier book of Jonah, is Nineveh, the great capital city of Assyria. But whereas Jonah records the city's reprieve, Nahum predicts its destruction. The date is somewhere between the fall of Thebes to the Assyrians in 663 BC (3:8-10), and the fall of Nineveh to the Babylonians and Medes in 612 BC. Nahum seems to have been a Judean, but apart from this we know nothing about him, except that he was capable of writing the most graphic poetry in the whole of the Old Testament.

1 Vengeance on God's enemies; comfort for his people

Nahum starts, not with Nineveh, but with God: his power, his anger, his goodness. The days of Assyria, whose armies had destroyed Israel and threatened Jerusalem itself less than a century before, are now numbered.
An overflowing flood (8): impregnable Nineveh eventually fell when floodwaters breached her walls, making way for the attacking army.
One (11): perhaps Sennacherib, the Assyrian king who took Lachish and then laid siege to Jerusalem in 701 BC (see Isaiah 36 - 37).

2 The assault on Nineveh

Once, God had used the armies of Assyria to punish his people. Now the forces attacking Nineveh are his instruments. Blood and thunder; plunder and desolation; the den of the Assyrian lion is no more. Nahum pictures the final assault in all its horror.
Mantelet (5): a siege-engine armed with battering-ram.
Verse 6: see on 1:8.
Its mistress (7): this may be Ishtar, the Assyrian goddess of love and war.

A siege-engine with battering-ram is shown being used by the Assyrians in this relief at Nimrud.

3 Destruction

Nahum pictures the city as a prostitute, enticing the nations into submission. Now she will receive a prostitute's punishment (5-6). She will share the terrible fate she inflicted on the Egyptian city of Thebes (No-Amon). (At Thebes, city of Amun, state-god of Egypt, the treasures of centuries had been accumulated. The Assyrians took the city with fire and slaughter and plundered all its wealth.) Though the nation is as great as a swarm of locusts they will vanish like a swarm that has flown. For all its might, Nineveh fell quickly into ruin, leaving no trace but a mound which is known today as Tell Kuyunjik, 'the mound of many sheep'.
Ethiopia (9): present-day Sudan, which supplied a dynasty of Egyptian kings. 'Put' may be Libya or possibly Somalia.

Old Testament 4.13

HABAKKUK

The prophet Habakkuk is battling with much the same problem as Job and the writer of Psalm 73: the fact that while God's people suffer, the wicked go free. Current events faced him with this problem in a particularly acute form. God had announced that he would use the Babylonians – a far more wicked nation – to punish his own people. So Habakkuk, the man of faith, questions God.

The book belongs to the latter part of the 7th century BC, when Jeremiah was prophesying in Jerusalem. Some would place it before, some just after, the fall of the Assyrian Empire (Nineveh was taken by the Babylonians in 612 BC) and the defeat of Egypt at Carchemish in 605. Babylon is on the march, but so far Judah has escaped. In 597 BC, not long after this, Jerusalem fell into enemy hands, and the city was destroyed in 587.

1 The prophet's dilemma

In response to Habakkuk's first question (2-4), God presents him with an even greater stumbling-block (5-11). How can God, who is just and good, who hates evil, send against his people a nation that he openly admits makes a god of its own might? Will he let Babylon ('the Chaldeans', 6) fish the sea of humanity forever (17)?

'I will climb my watch-tower,' says Habakkuk. From towers like this a constant watch was kept over the vineyards as the fruit ripened.

2 God's answer

The answer is no. When the final scores are added up, only the man who trusts God and remains loyal to him will live. God will punish all man's arrogant pride. Woe betide those who greedily grab what belongs to others; who for selfish ends justify the cruellest means; who climb to power on the backs of others; who destroy and dehumanize; who give their worship to man-made idols. The lives of all such men are forfeit whatever their nationality.

3 The triumph of faith – Habakkuk's prayer

The musical form of this prayer has led some to believe that Habakkuk was a Levite, attached to the temple. Its focus is on God himself; God approaching from the mountains of the southern desert (Teman is in Edom; Paran part of Sinai); God wrapped about with thunder and lightning in the storm of his wrath; God setting the world trembling with a glance. Habakkuk sees the inevitability, the fury of judgement. Yet though it means the loss of every good thing in life, God is still to be trusted. The prophet will wait for the day when God deals with the invader (16). He will rejoice in God, though life is stripped of all that gives natural joy and satisfaction.

Old Testament 4.14

ZEPHANIAH

Zephaniah prophesied in King Josiah's reign (640-609 BC), about the time Jeremiah's ministry began. From his stern words, it seems he spoke before Josiah launched his great programme of reform in 621, following the discovery of the law-book in the temple. The two previous kings, Manasseh and Amon had brought the religion and morality of the nation to an all-time low. Zephaniah himself seems to have been of royal blood, tracing his ancestry back to Hezekiah, who was king in Isaiah's day, 70 years or so before.

1 The great and terrible day of judgement

In popular thinking the 'day of the Lord' would bring untold blessing to all God's people, and destruction to their enemies. Amos, years before this, had warned that on that day all evil would be punished, making it a black day for many in Israel. Zephaniah spells out the same message, in detail, to Judah. The day is close at hand when all who are guilty of idolatry (4-6), violence, fraud (9), all who sit by in idle indifference (12), will be set apart for destruction (this is the meaning of verse 7). And their cry will be heard in every quarter of the city of Jerusalem (10-11).

Baal (4): the Canaanite god of fertility whose worship involved sexual licence and prostitution.

Milcom (5): the national god of the Ammonites.

The hills ... the Mortar (10-11): districts of Jerusalem.

Thickening upon their lees (12): a picture drawn from wine-making; one of the secrets in making wine is not to let it settle.

2 Judgement on the nations

The only hope for God's people is to seek him, and begin living by his standards. If they do not, they will share the fate of the nations around: Philistia (4-7) to the west; Moab and Ammon (8-11) to the east; Ethiopia (12) to the south; Assyria (13-15) to the north.

Gaza, Ashkelon, Ashdod, Ekron (4): the four remaining Philistine city-states.

Cherethites (5): the Philistines, who originally came from Crete.

Sodom, Gomorrah (9): cities at the southern end of the Dead Sea, destroyed by God for their wickedness (Genesis 19).

Ethiopians (12): from modern Sudan; at this time the ruling dynasty in Egypt.

Nineveh (13): capital of Assyria; see on Nahum, particularly chapter 3.

3 Jerusalem condemned; a remnant saved

The city (1-7) is not named, but it is clearly Jerusalem. Beginning with rebellion against God, and the corruption of religion, the rot spreads into every sector of society. In the end, God has no alternative but to wipe the city out – but not completely. Zephaniah has already spoken of 'a remnant' (2:7, 9). Now he enlarges on God's purpose for the humble, faithful few who will survive when all human pride and self-sufficiency is done away. There is cause for great rejoicing. God is in the midst of his people: he will pour out his love on them. He will change and make them into those who are 'pure of heart' (9, 13). With exultant song they will be brought home and restored to favour. All the nations of the world have their share in this (9).

Old Testament 4.15

HAGGAI

The last three books of the Old Testament take us on past the exile to the time when the Jews were repatriated, the time of Ezra and Nehemiah. Haggai delivered his 'word from the Lord' in 520 BC, Zechariah in 520-518. When the first party of exiles returned to their homeland under the leadership of Zerubbabel (grandson of King Jehoiachin) in 538, they made an enthusiastic start on rebuilding the temple which had been destroyed by the Babylonians in 587. But opposition and apathy very soon brought the work to a standstill (Ezra 4:4-5). For years nothing was done, until Haggai and Zechariah began to stir things up (Ezra 5:12). Thanks to them, by 516 the temple was completed. Haggai's little book is one of the gems of the Old Testament. It has permanent relevance, because its basic concern is not with the rebuilding of the temple but with priorities.

Four times Haggai comes to the people with a message from God (1:2-15; 2:1-9; 2:10-19; 2:20-23). 1:2-15: life is hard, with food and clothing in short supply, and prices soaring. Why? Because the people have their priorities wrong. Every man is wrapped up in his own selfish concerns. God is neglected. And so the very things man works for evade him. For all the good things of life are God's to give or withhold. Haggai's words strike home to the nation's conscience. Within three weeks, work on the temple is resumed.

2:1-9: Solomon's fabulous temple had been demolished 70 years before. Few of those now building would have seen it – but all had heard of it. And the glory had lost nothing in the telling. The new temple seems a feeble thing in comparison. But let the builders take heart. The present building is just a foretaste of the splendour and glory of the end-time, the era of peace and prosperity to which the prophets all looked forward.

2:10-19: work on the temple has been resumed, but this in itself will not make the workmen 'holy' (right with God). It is rottenness, not soundness that is contagious (Haggai makes his point from the ritual law). Their previous neglect of God brought all kinds of unpleasant consequences. But from the day they begin to put first things first, God will bless every aspect of life.

2:20-23: a word for Zerubbabel. It is to Zerubbabel the heir to David's throne, rather than to Zerubbabel the individual, that these messianic promises are made. He stands in the line from David to Christ.

Old Testament 4.16

ZECHARIAH

Zechariah came from a family of priests, and with Haggai was closely involved in the rebuilding of the temple following the return from exile (see on Haggai, and Ezra 5 - 6 for the historical background). Like Daniel and Ezekiel he was a visionary. And his book at one and the same time distils the wisdom of many of the earlier prophets, and brings the events of the far future into sharp focus. It contains detailed references to the Messiah which are clearly fulfilled in the life of Christ. There is a marked break (some would say a change of author – someone writing much later) between the visions of the first eight chapters and the spoken messages of chapters 9 - 14.

1:1-17; The four riders

In point of time, verses 1-6 slot in between Haggai 2:9 and 10; the vision of verses 7-17, two months after Haggai's last recorded message. Zechariah is probably a young man (his grandfather, Iddo, returned with the exiles less than 20 years before: Nehemiah 12:4). Verses 2-6 retell past history, warning the present generation not to behave as their fathers had done. Zechariah's first vision (7-17) is of four horsemen patrolling the world on God's behalf, like the mounted patrols which 'policed' the Persian Empire. (The significance of the colours, if any, is now lost.) The message is one of comfort and encouragement for God's people. Jerusalem will be rebuilt; prosperity will return.

1:18-21 The four horns

The second vision is a vivid picture of the destruction of the hostile powers which had ground the nation down. ('Four' indicates completeness – the four quarters of the earth.)

2 The measuring-line

The man may be Zechariah's projection of his own image, measuring up the city for rebuilding. The walls had been destroyed in 587. They were not rebuilt until Nehemiah's day (445, 75 years after this prophecy). But God pledges himself to protect Jerusalem. He calls to the remaining exiles to return.

The land of the north (6): Babylon; in point of fact, east, but the invading armies of Assyria and Babylon all entered Palestine from the north.

3 The investiture of the high priest

The taints of exile, when strict observance of dietary and other laws was impossible, are removed. And Joshua – high priest and partner with the ruler Zerubbabel in the exiles' return – is fittingly robed for office. God promises to send the long foretold Messiah, the Branch (8, and see Isaiah 11) from the family of David; the all-seeing, all-knowing 'stone' (the seven facets are literally seven eyes). He will usher in a day of universal peace and prosperity (this is the meaning of the vine and fig-tree idiom, 10).

4 The lamp and the olive-trees

Both these images are taken up in Revelation (1:12, 20; 11). The seven-branched lampstand stood in the tabernacle and temple. Here it may represent God's people or their worship, supported and 'fed' by the royal and priestly leaders, Zerubbabel and Joshua (the two olive-trees). From small beginnings (the start already made on the temple) great things will be accomplished, through the power of God's Spirit. Zerubbabel will lay the last stone in the temple building, as he had laid the first.

5 Sin removed

In ancient thinking a curse possessed destructive power. This is the concept behind the picture of the scroll. The woman in the great measure, or barrel, is sin personified; perhaps particularly the sin of idolatry, since she is removed to Babylon (Shinar is the old name) where a temple is built for her.

6 The four chariots

This last vision is like the first (1:7-17). God is keeping watch over the whole world. He is actively in control. His 'patrol' has power to execute judgement (this time there are chariots, not just reporting horsemen). In verses 9-14 the crowning of

Joshua prefigures the dual role of the Messiah, as priest and king.

7 The question of fasts

The fast in the fifth month (July/August) commemorated the fall of Jerusalem in 587. The fast in the seventh month was in memory of the murdered governor, Gedaliah (2 Kings 25:25). Now that the temple was being rebuilt, need the fasts continue? In reply, God questions *them* about the spirit in which the fasts were kept, and reminds them of the standards they refused to keep before the exile (8-14). They still apply.

8 Hope burns bright

God promises a glorious future for his people and for Jerusalem. His purpose is wholly good. Judgement is past. God will return to make his home in the city. His people will enjoy peace and plenty. Right will prevail. And men and women of every nation will flock to Jerusalem seeking God. At the time of the prophecy only a few had returned from exile; the building was scarcely begun. But it was a foretaste of the wonderful days to come.

Verse 19: the two additional fasts were probably to mark the beginning of Nebuchadnezzar's siege of Jerusalem (the tenth month) and the breaching of the walls 18 months later (the fourth month). In answer to the question in 7:3, Zechariah replies that God wants all these fasts to be turned into feasts. The future for God's people is one of rejoicing.

9 - 11 Israel and the nations

For the break at this point, see introduction. Chapter 9 pictures the joyous arrival of the Messiah, riding an ass (not a war-horse), inaugurating a rule of peace (9-10; see Matthew 21:5). Before him Israel's old enemies will fall (1-8). There will be no more oppression. The Philistines (5-7) will be absorbed into Israel, as the Jebusites (from whom David captured the city of Jerusalem) had been long before. The Jewish captives will be released, and Israel's military power will equal even that of rising Greece. God is his people's protection and salvation.

Chapter 10 condemns the careless leaders of God's people. He is full of pity for the straying flock. Every one will be brought home.

In chapter 11 the prophet becomes shepherd to God's flock – but the people prefer exploitation to genuine care. They get what they want (15-16). The covenant with God is broken and the nation divided.

9:1-7: many relate this to Alexander's advance after defeating the Persians in 333 BC.

10:2: in the absence of any real spiritual lead, the people are dabbling in magic. The old household gods (teraphim) were used in divination.

11:1-3: the 'clearance' in preparation for the returning Israelites. In Old Testament times the thickets fringing the Jordan were the haunt of lions.

Thirty shekels (11:12): the prophet sarcastically calls it a 'lordly price' – this was the price of a slave (Exodus 21:32; and see Matthew 26:15; 27:3-5).

12 - 14 Israel's future

Chapter 12 pictures God strengthening his people for a great battle against the nations (1-9). But in the midst of triumph there is national mourning – the people weep as the pagans wept for their dying vegetation-god (11). The phrase 'him whom they have pierced' inevitably makes us think of Christ. But if Zephaniah is speaking of the Messiah, this national Jewish remorse for the One they crucified is yet to come.

13:1 takes our thoughts to Christ again. Verses 2-9 describe the 'refining' of God's people; the removal of everything that offends God. 'The prophets' are false prophets; the 'wounds' are self-inflicted – part of the religious frenzy of the old prophets of Baal (1 Kings 18:28).

Chapter 14 pictures the last battle and the age to come. God himself will appear, ushering in perpetual day. The idea of life-giving water flowing from Jerusalem echoes Ezekiel 47. The whole earth will become God's kingdom. Those who set themselves against God will be destroyed. All who survive will worship him. Everything will be sacred. But the world is still not perfect. The possibility of disobedience and punishment remains. It is not yet the new Jerusalem of Revelation.

Old Testament 4.16

MALACHI

The name means 'My messenger', which may have been the prophet's actual name or a pseudonym. From the conditions reflected in the book it is usually dated around 460-430 BC – either just before Nehemiah became governor of Jerusalem, or during his absence later on. This is about 80 years after Haggai and Zechariah spurred the people on to rebuild the temple. And since then disillusionment had set in. Times were hard, and the promised prosperity had not been realized. The people tended to feel that the prophets had been shooting them a line; that God was a bit of a let-down. This showed in an increasingly casual attitude to worship and the standards God had set. Malachi's message about God's claims on his people was needed. It still is.

1 The very best for God

Malachi's starting-point is God's love. His people, struggling with economic hardship and persistent sniping from the opposition (see e.g. Nehemiah 1:3; 4), cannot see much evidence of it. In answer they are told to look at their brother-nation, Edom – overrun like themselves by Babylon, but not restored (see on Obadiah). Israel enjoys a unique Father-son relationship with God. He is in a special sense their Lord. But their attitude over the sacrificial offerings shows their contempt for him. The left-overs are good enough for God, although they know the rules (Leviticus 22; Deuteronomy 15, 17). They dishonour and belittle his greatness. It would be better to close the temple and stop the sacrifices altogether (10).

Love ... hate (2-3): the Hebrew idiom is over-strong in English. It means, not literal love/hate, but the special choice of one and not the other.

Verse 11: God is receiving more acceptable worship from the Gentiles – a statement intended to shock Malachi's Jewish hearers.

2:1-9 God's charges against the priests

The task God committed to his ministers, the Levites, was to teach the truth, and by their own lives to set an example (6). But instead of turning people away from wrong, they have actively misled them.

2:10-16 Marriage and divorce

See on Ezra 9-10 and Nehemiah 13. When God and his laws are respected, so are our fellow men. Indifference towards God is soon reflected in callousness towards one another. The Jews were marrying pagan women (11), which was forbidden (on religious, not racial, grounds). What is more, the older men were cruelly discarding their ageing wives for these attractive young foreigners – a situation not without parallel! And family life, as always, suffered. God cares about these things. He requires faithfulness from his people: faithfulness to himself and faithfulness in human relationships.

2:17 - 3:18 Justice; and giving

God's people can always look around and see godless men and women flourishing. It seems unfair (2:17; 3:13-15). But in the final winding-up of things there will be absolute justice (3:1-5). The Lord is coming, first to purify, and then to judge. And a messenger will be sent on ahead to prepare the way (see on 4:5).

God does not change; nor do his people (6, New English Bible). They have been fickle from first to last. God gives them all they have, yet they rob him even of his legal dues. (The tithe was a sort of income tax to provide for the upkeep of the temple and the 'salaries' of the ministers.) Anything we give to God is only a small return on all we owe him. When we hold back from giving, through self-interest, we deprive ourselves of all the good things God would otherwise give us.

Verses 16-18 warm the heart. There are still some who encourage one another in the love of the Lord; and he knows and honours them.

4 The Day of the Lord

The day is coming when God will even things out once and for all. For some (the wicked) the fierce brilliance of that day will burn like fire. But those who honour God will rejoice in its healing rays.

Verses 4-5 serve as postscript, not just to Malachi but to the Old Testament as a whole. They look back to the laws given at Sinai (Horeb), and these must always be kept in mind. They look forward to a new age, to the reconciling work of Christ and the end of all things. With Malachi the voice of Old Testament prophecy falls silent. Four hundred years later, God sent one last prophet, John the Baptist (the promised 'Elijah'), to herald the coming Messiah (Matthew 17:10-13).

Sun (2): Malachi draws his picture (but not his theology) from the winged disk which represented the sungod in Persian and Egyptian art.

THE APOCRYPHA

David Clines

To most people the word 'apocrypha' means, quite simply, a work of fiction. An apocryphal story about a historic personage is a fabricated, and often a far-fetched, tale. However, that is not the meaning of the term when applied to the ancient writings which we know as the 'Apocrypha' of the Old Testament.

The word means in Greek 'the hidden', that is, 'the hidden books', and its use for these writings goes back to the great biblical scholar Jerome (died AD 420). He held that these books, which were to be found in Greek and Latin Bibles but not in the contemporary Hebrew Bible, should not be regarded as equally authoritative with the canonical books, though they might be read in church for edification. In using the term 'apocryphal', he was probably alluding to a distinction made in 2 Esdras 4:14ff., one of the apocryphal books, between the 24 canonical books of the Old Testament (39 by our reckoning), and others containing esoteric knowledge and mysteries suitable only for the wise and therefore to be 'hidden' from the general public.

The church's attitude

Jerome's view was a minority one, though a number of scholars both before his time and since have made the same distinction between the books of the Hebrew canon and the apocryphal books. However, from the 1st century AD the churches used some at least of the apocryphal books as if they were Scripture, and continued to do so until the Reformation.

Luther, in his Bible of 1534, extracted the apocryphal books from their accustomed places among the biblical books, and grouped them together at the end of the Old Testament under the heading:

'Apocrypha: these are books which are not held equal to the Sacred Scriptures and yet are useful and good for reading.'

The Anglican statement was very similar: Article VI of the Thirty-Nine Articles, after listing the canonical books of the Old Testament, says:

'And the other Books (as Hierome [Jerome] saith) the Church doth read for example of life and instruction of manners; but yet doth it not apply them to establish any doctrine.'

This statement in the Westminster Confession of Faith (AD 1647) is typical of the lower status given to the Apocrypha in the Reformed churches:

'The Books commonly called Apocrypha, not being of divine inspiration, are not part of the canon of Scripture; and are therefore of no authority in the Church of God, nor to be any otherwise approved, or made use of, than other human writings.'

The Roman Catholic Church, on the other hand, partly as a reaction against the Reformers' affirmations, and partly to perpetuate what had long been customary in the church, declared at the Council of Trent (AD 1546) that the Old Testament contained 45 books, i.e., in addition to the 39 books universally recognized, most of those known as the Apocrypha. Catholics refer to the disputed books as the 'deutero-canonical' books, and reserve the term 'Apocrypha' for the books Protestants call the 'Pseudepigrapha' – works of similar character and date to the Apocrypha which were never considered canonical.

The books of the Apocrypha

The Apocrypha, which is about a quarter the length of the Old Testament, contains 15 books:

First Esdras (otherwise **Third Esdras**)
Second Esdras (otherwise **Fourth Esdras**)
Tobit (Tobias)
Judith
The rest of the **Book of Esther**
The Wisdom of Solomon (The Book of Wisdom)
Ecclesiasticus (The Wisdom of Jesus the Son of Sirach)
Baruch the Prophet
The Letter of Jeremiah

The Song of the Three (Holy) Children
The Story of Susanna (Daniel and Susanna)
Of Bel and the Dragon (New English Bible, Daniel, Bel, and the Snake)
The Prayer of Manasseh (Manasses)
The First Book of Maccabees
The Second Book of Maccabees

The Letter of Jeremiah is missing from the list in the Thirty-Nine Articles since it is there counted as the sixth chapter of Baruch. Catholic Bibles do not contain First or Second Esdras or the Prayer of Manasseh; the additions to Esther are included in Esther and the Letter of Jeremiah in Baruch; and the Song of the Three Children, Susanna, and Bel and the Dragon form part of Daniel.

The books of the Apocrypha form a very varied collection of Jewish literature from the period between about 300 BC and AD 100. The majority of the books were written in Hebrew, but in many cases the original Hebrew has disappeared since the Jews themselves eventually refused to recognize these writings as inspired. Most of the books have survived only through their use in Greek and other versions by the early Christian church.

Historical books

1 Esdras (the Greek form of the name Ezra) is largely identical with our canonical Ezra, though it begins the story with the events of 2 Chronicles 35 (Josiah's Passover celebrations) and ends with the story of Ezra's reading of the law (Nehemiah 8). Its major addition to the biblical account is the 'debate of the three young men' (1 Esdras 3-4) which purports to explain how Zerubbabel gained permission from the Persian king to rebuild the temple.

1 Maccabees is a much more valuable book, since it is our chief source for the history of the Maccabean revolt against foreign and Jewish purveyors of Greek culture. Apart from his obvious desire to eulogize the family of the Maccabees, the author has no axe to grind, and provides us with an essentially reliable as well as graphic history of the years between 175 and 134 BC.

2 Maccabees covers much the same ground as 1 Maccabees, but is less reliable. It is written from a distinctly Pharisaic point of view, and tends to lay greater weight upon moralizing and doctrinal observations than upon historical accuracy.

'Religious fiction'

Tobit is a charming tale of domestic piety. It was so popular among early Christians that it was translated from Hebrew into Greek, Latin, Armenian, Syriac and Ethiopic. The story tells how Tobias, a righteous but afflicted Jew, is healed of his blindness and his son Tobit is saved from an unpleasant death. It has many folk-tale motifs, and is plainly not a historical work.

Judith contains the tale of an altogether more daunting heroine, who used her charm to lure the invading Assyrian general Holofernes to his death by decapitation. This rather horrific story not without its lighter moments contains some gross historical blunders, but these would not have detracted from its purpose of stiffening the resolve of Jewish freedom fighters in Maccabean times.

The additions to **Esther** are popular expansions of the biblical story, partly designed to introduce some religion into that apparently secular book, which does not even mention the name of God.

The additions to **Daniel** are partly legends about Daniel the sage and Godfearer (**Susanna, Bel and the Dragon**), and partly liturgical texts: **The Song of the Three Children** contains a historical prayer attributed to Daniel's companion Azariah, and a doxology (the *Benedicite* of Christian worship) attributed to the three in the fiery furnace.

'Wisdom'

'Wisdom' literature is represented in the Apocrypha principally by Ecclesiasticus and the Wisdom of Solomon. **Ecclesiasticus,** composed by Joshua (or Jesus) ben Sira (Sirach) about 180 BC, offers advice on practical and godly living in the spirit of the Proverbs. Chapter 44 contains the memorable lines beginning, 'Let us now praise famous men.' A great favourite in the early Christian centuries (James 1:19, for example, probably alludes to Ecclesiasticus 5:11), the book, earlier known as the Wisdom of Jesus ben Sira, became entitled the 'church-book' (Ecclesiasticus).

The Wisdom of Solomon, a 1st-century BC composition, more indebted to Greek ethics and rhetoric than any other Jewish wisdom book, pays homage in its title to the traditional founder of wisdom literature without seriously claiming to be written by Solomon.

Baruch, likewise ascribed in honorific manner to an Old Testament notable, contains a prayer of confession, a poem in praise of wisdom, and songs of comfort. Its appendage, the **Letter of Jeremiah,** is an attack on idolatry cast in the form of a letter to the exiles (compare Jeremiah 29); and the **Prayer of Manasseh** is a free composition based on 2 Chronicles 33:13, 19.

Apocalyptic

Only one example of this fourth category is included in the Apocrypha:

2 Esdras. Written probably in the 1st century AD, 2 Esdras comprises some Christian chapters 'predicting' the rejection of the Jews in favour of the church, and a Jewish book of visions of the future ascribed to Ezra.

The Apocrypha today

What is the Christian today to make of the Apocrypha? The theological problem of its authority remains. Here we must acknowledge the fact that Christians have never been in complete agreement over the precise limits of the Old Testament, though they are at one in affirming its authority and inspiration. There is some evidence that the Bible which Jesus and the apostles held as authoritative was the Hebrew Bible of 39 books, which did not include the apocryphal books. Even those who regard the Apocrypha as Scripture would admit that its authority is secondary to, and derived from (or dependent on), that of the 39 books.

But even though the Christian may not give the Apocrypha the same standing as the books of the Hebrew Old Testament, he will find within it passages of deep piety and thoughtful spirituality.

In *Grace Abounding*, John Bunyan recounts how, searching for the verse, 'Look at the generations of old, and see, did ever any trust in God and were confounded', he was at first daunted to find it came from the Apocrypha (Ecclesiasticus 2:10). But he came to realize that 'as this sentence was the sum and substance of many of the promises, it was my duty to take the comfort of it, and I bless God for that word, for it was of God to me'. The person who reads the Apocrypha devotionally will know how to handle it, for he will discriminate, as he does when he reads any religious literature, between what conforms and what does not conform to the essentials of his faith.

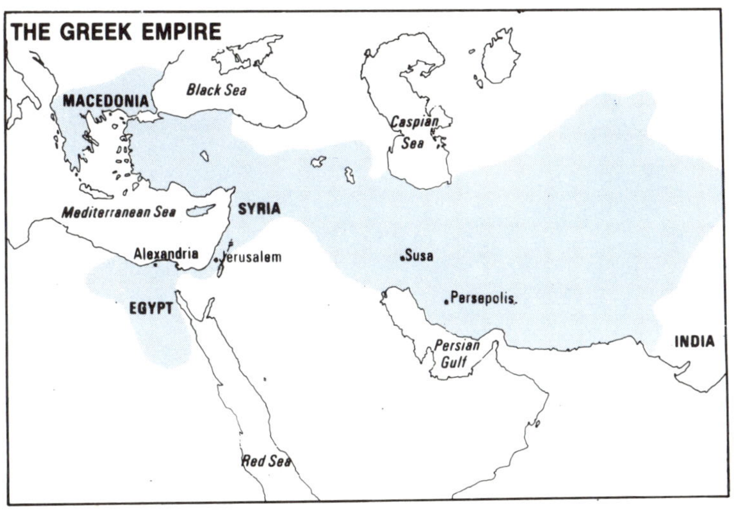

THE GREEK EMPIRE

PART THREE

The New Testament

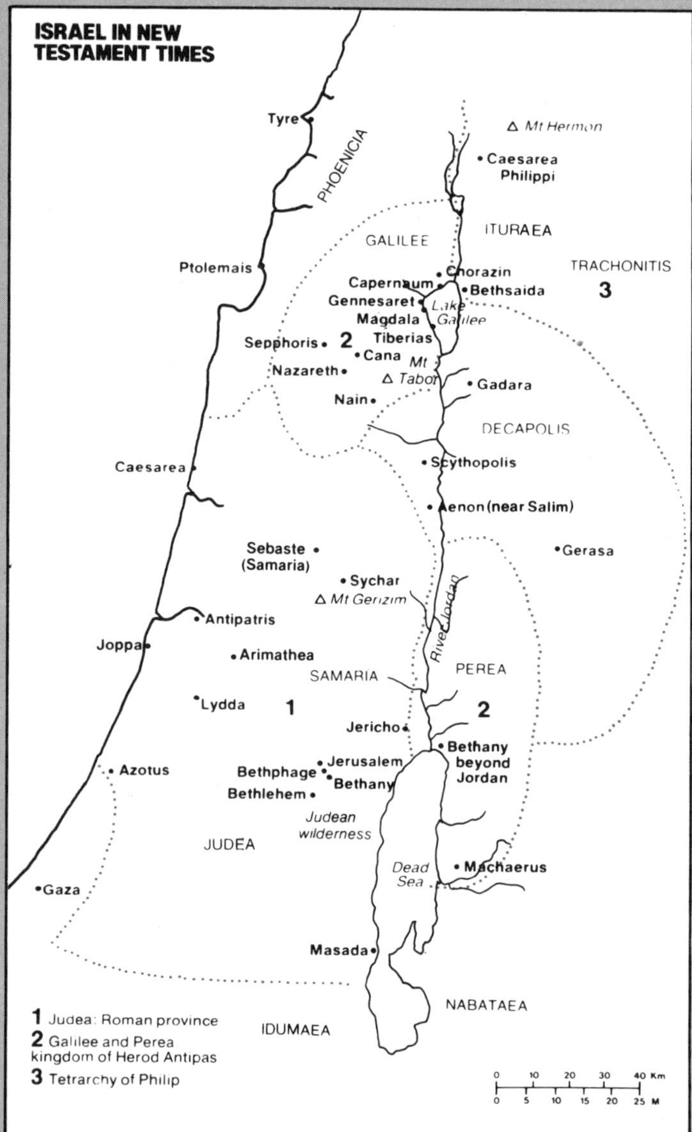

NEW TESTAMENT HISTORY AT A GLANCE

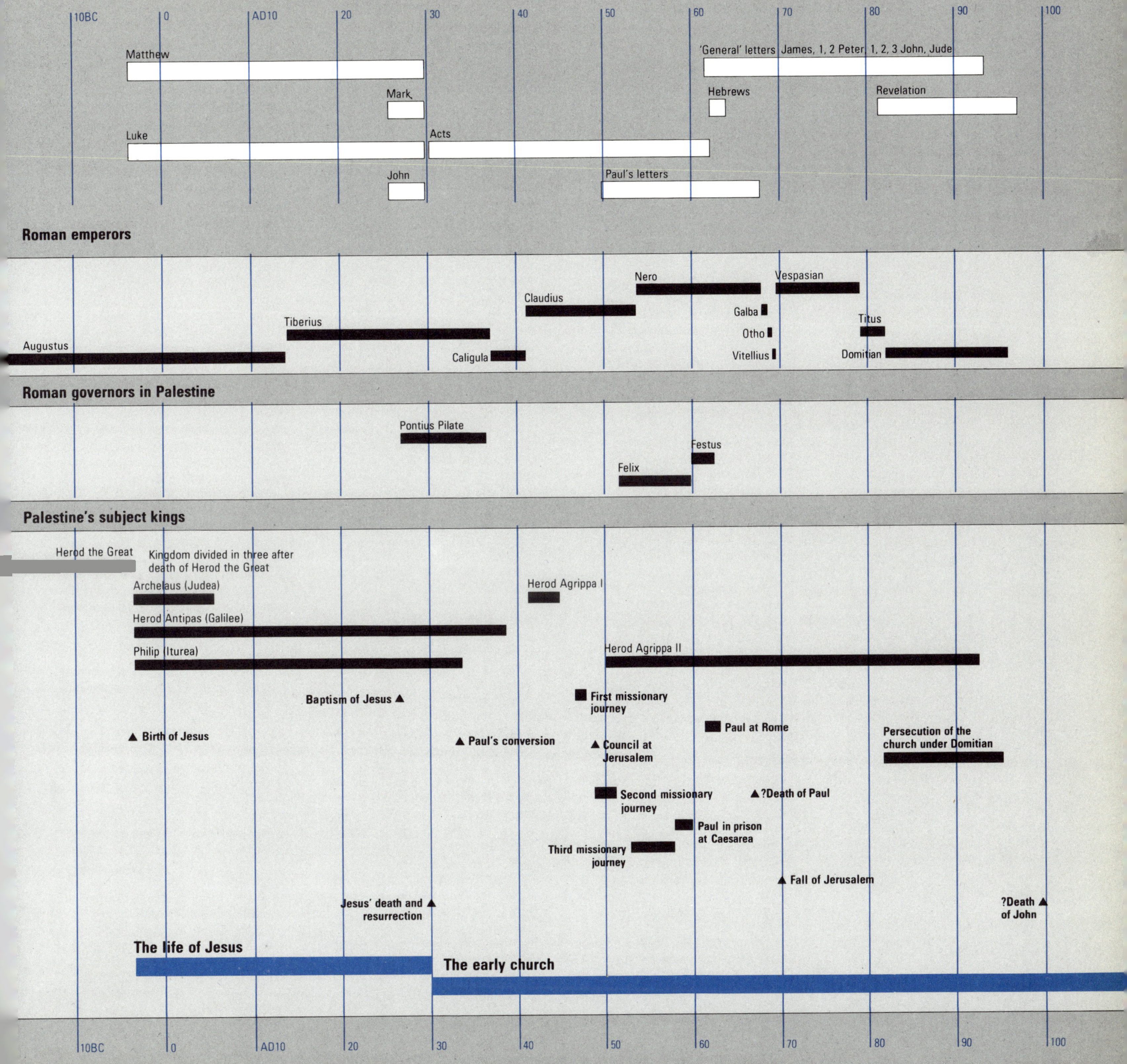

New Testament section 1

THE GOSPELS AND ACTS

The Gospels and Jesus Christ/Howard Marshall

Virtually all we know about the earthly life of Jesus is to be found in the four Gospels contained in the New Testament. The life of a travelling preacher in an obscure corner of the Roman Empire was not likely to find its way into the writings of Roman historians, who had (as they thought) more important things to occupy their attention. Tacitus refers very briefly to Jesus, and then only by way of explanation of the name of the 'Christians' who were put to death by Nero.

Even Jewish historians offer us little more. The standard history of the Jews was written by Josephus towards the end of the 1st century, and he does refer to Jesus at one point in his narrative as a miracle-worker who was the Messiah; he was put to death by Pilate but later reappeared to his disciples. The passage may have been tampered with by later Christian scribes (for would Josephus have called Jesus the Messiah?), but is probably genuine in essentials.

Other Jewish traditions about Jesus have been preserved in the writings of the rabbis. They tell us that he practised magic, beguiled the people, and said that he had not come to destroy the law or add to it. He was hanged on the eve of Passover for heresy and misleading the people, and had five disciples who healed the sick. This gives some idea of how Jesus would have been regarded by people who shared the outlook of the Sanhedrin, the Jewish council that condemned him to death.

More recent discoveries do not alter the picture. The Dead Sea Scrolls, the library of a Jewish sect living just before and during the time of Jesus, shed light on the thought-world of ancient Palestine, but they make not the slightest reference to Jesus. What is recorded of the members of the sect and their enemies in no way affects the historicity of Jesus.

A more promising source of information lies in various 'gospels' which were not included in the New Testament. Such works have long been known, but in recent years interest has been rekindled by the discovery of the 'Gospel of Thomas' at Nag-Hammadi in Egypt. This work contains a set of sayings ascribed to Jesus. They have obviously been worked over by radical Christians, but it is possible that here and there in this and other similar documents fragments of genuine tradition about Jesus may be preserved. However, the fact that the early church excluded them all from the canon of Scripture is some indication that the hunt is not likely to be very successful.

This means that for all practical purposes our knowledge of Jesus must come from the New Testament alone. Within the New Testament itself the field narrows down to the Gospels. The letters of Paul and the other apostolic writers make very little reference to the life of Jesus as such – though this is not because they did not attach great importance to his ministry as a historical fact, or were not strongly influenced by what he had taught.

The Gospel records

It is, then, to the Gospels that we must turn for the written record of the life and teaching of Jesus. The Gospels were not composed until at least 30 years after the death of Jesus. During this period the material for them was preserved and handed down both by word of mouth and by written records that no longer survive.

The tradition would have been handed down carefully. The Jewish rabbis were extremely careful to hand down oral material accurately, and we may presume that the Christians did the same. The Gospel material was originally taught in Aramaic, the language spoken by Jesus, and in a poetic form which was easy to memorize.

People remember what they want to remember. This does not mean that Jesus' hearers conveniently forgot what they found disturbing and unpalatable. On the contrary, there is much in the Gospels that must have been challenging and difficult, and yet it has been faithfully preserved. The story of Jesus was remembered and retold because it was relevant to the life of the church. For example, the first Christians had to argue with the Jews, so it was essential to remember how Jesus had debated with them. Faced with decisions on ethical issues such as marriage and divorce, they needed his teaching as their authority on such matters. So it is good, when we read a passage in the Gospels, to ask what significance it had for the early church. The story of Jesus was not preserved out of an academic interest in history for its own sake, but because of its practical relevance for the first Christians. It was not 'pure' but 'applied' history.

People also tend to remember and pass on stories and teaching in a certain pattern. Stories of healing miracles, for example, describe in turn the condition of the sufferer, the way in which the cure was effected, and the results it produced. Many stories about Jesus describe a situation in which he was placed, or a question which was put to him, and culminate in the essential point; an authoritative saying of Jesus on the topic at issue.

The article on 'The Gospels and Modern Criticism', shows how these factors have been used to try to explain the actual composition of the Gospels. The clearest example is John's Gospel. For the author has to some extent interpreted the story of Jesus to show its significance for his readers. He has offered a kind of commentary on the ministry of Jesus in which it is hard to distinguish between the original 'text' and its 'interpretation'.

The important point, however, is that there really is a 'text' which he is explaining for us; he is not commenting on something that never existed. Behind the Gospel stands the figure of John the apostle, just as apostolic testimony is the basis of the other Gospels. It is also being increasingly recognized by scholars that it is one and the same Jesus who is described in all four Gospels. Whereas the critics of a former era argued that the Gospel of John had little or no basis in history, it is now seen that all four Gospels build on historical tradition, each preserving different aspects of it.

The purpose of the Gospel writers

John's Gospel raises the question of the relation of the Gospels to history. Did what is described in the Gospels really happen? We have already indicated that the Gospels rest on reliable tradition, handed down with care in the church. At the same time we must bear in mind that the Gospels are concerned to present the Christian significance of Jesus. Their basic purpose is to preach the gospel in order to convert the unbeliever and to build up the believer in his faith.

This means that they are not simply historical reports, as for example the biography of some famous soldier might be. The writers were not biographers, giving a detailed historical account of Jesus' life with everything in proper chronological order. We have only to compare the order of events in Mark 4 - 5 with Matthew 13; 8; 9 to see this fact plainly.

Or again, the Gospels record very little of some aspects of Jesus' life: scarcely anything is mentioned before he reached the age of 30; and even the account of his ministry is incomplete. There is by no means enough incident to fill the whole time it lasted. We have no right to blame the Gospel writers for not doing something they never intended.

But this does not mean they were unconcerned about history. The Gospels are not invention. In the preface to his Gospel (Luke 1:1-4), Luke lays particular stress on the fact that he was making use of authentic eyewitness testimony. History certainly mattered for him, and there is no reason to think that the other writers thought differently.

What, then, were they trying to do? They were preaching the gospel, the good news. They were presenting Jesus as the Christ, the Son of God (Mark 1:1). They wrote in order that their readers might believe in him and so have eternal life (John 20:31). They therefore portrayed Jesus as his followers saw him. To them he was no ordinary man, not even a unique prophet. He was the Lord whom God had raised from the dead and who was now alive and active in heaven. They knew no other Jesus than this. They might have thought differently about him before the resurrection (see Luke 24:19-24), and even the resurrection did not compel everybody who heard about it to believe. But they had come to believe in Jesus as a result of the total impact which he had made upon them, and so they could not present him in any other way.

So the history in the Gospels is history as seen by Christians. A non-Christian would see it differently; he would claim, for instance, that the resurrection could not have happened. It might be interesting to have an account of Jesus written from that point of view, but none has come down to us. What we have are the Gospels, written by Christian believers, written to persuade men to believe, but none the less historical for that.

Four portraits of Jesus

Each of the Gospel writers presents Jesus to us in his own characteristic way. The greatness of this person could not have been captured in one picture. So we have four portraits, each bringing out its own distinctive facets of the character of Jesus.

Matthew concentrates on the relationship of Jesus to the Jewish faith. He shows how Jesus came to fulfil the Old Testament, but at the same time to judge the Jews for their unfaithfulness to their religion. No other Gospel denounces so forcibly the hypocritical outlook of the Pharisees. The Jews are called to see Jesus as the promised Messiah, the Son of David; and judgement is pronounced upon them for their failure to respond to him. Matthew portrays Jesus very much as a teacher. He has given us systematic accounts of Jesus' teaching for the church's inner life and evangelistic mission.

Mark emphasizes action rather than teaching. He stresses how Jesus taught his disciples that the Son of man must suffer and be rejected, and that they must be prepared to tread the same path. Those who tried to understand Jesus other than as a crucified Saviour would misunderstand him. The Jews expected a Messiah who would be a political leader and a figure of glory. They found it hard to recognize Jesus as the Messiah because he chose the path of humble service and suffering. Only at his second coming would he appear as the King in his glory.

The Gospel of Luke stresses the blessings of salvation brought by Jesus. It emphasizes the signs of the coming of the Messiah, prophesied in the Old Testament, and seen in Jesus' healing of the sick and preaching of the gospel to the poor and needy. Luke especially brings out the grace of God revealed in Jesus and bestowed upon those who seemed least worthy of it, sinful women and rapacious tax-collectors; for this is precisely what grace means, that men and women can do nothing to deserve it.

Finally, the Gospel of John reveals Jesus as the One sent by God the Father into the world to be its Saviour. As the Son, he has his Father's authority, living in close communion with him. John goes deepest into the things God has revealed and brings out the eternal significance of the 'God-become-man'.

An outline of the life of Jesus

Behind these four accounts stands a figure who is recognizably the same in all of them. Jesus was the son of the virgin Mary, born at Bethlehem shortly before the death of Herod the Great (4 BC). He spent his early life in Nazareth where he worked as the village carpenter. When John the Baptist began to preach beside the River Jordan (about AD 27), Jesus came and was baptized by him. He immediately received the gift of the Spirit, commissioning him for his work. In the strength of the Spirit he withstood Satan's inducements to divert him from his calling. He then commenced a ministry of preaching and healing, mainly in Galilee. This was preceded by a period in Judea (John 1 - 3) and included visits to Jerusalem. It concluded with a journey to Jerusalem which culminated in his arrest and death at Passover time (about AD 30).

Jesus' message was concerned with the good news of the rule (or kingdom) of God. In the Old Testament the prophets looked forward to a future era when God would act in power and set up his rule over Israel. This hope was associated with the coming of a king (or Messiah; Greek, 'Christ') who would belong to the kingly line of David. In the time of Jesus, the people had come to expect a warrior-king to deliver them from their Roman over-lords.

Jesus taught that this hoped-for era was already dawning. He looked forward to the future consummation of God's rule, with himself as King. But the coming of God's rule was to be seen not in military victories but in Jesus' mighty works of healing and his preaching of salvation. God was already acting in the ministry of Jesus.

This good news demanded a response from men. Jesus called them to repent of their sin; he offered forgiveness to the penitent; and he summoned men to become his disciples. To accept the good news of the rule of God meant accepting Jesus as Master. Out of the many who responded, Jesus appointed twelve men to be the leaders of the new people of God who were to replace the old Israel which rejected the message of God, and to be associated with his missionary work.

Jesus taught his disciples a new way of life. It is summed up in the Sermon on the Mount (Matthew 5 - 7). Jesus took over the Old Testament commandments to love God and one's neighbour and filled them with new life and vigour.

Jesus taught with such self-confident authority that men asked who he thought he was. Some people dismissed him as mad. Others were prepared to see him as Messiah, but when he showed no inclination to lead them to war against Rome they turned away from him. This was probably why Jesus did not claim the title of Messiah openly. He preferred to speak of himself cryptically as the 'Son of man', a phrase which he took from Daniel 7:13 and filled with new content. For him it meant a figure who would one day be invested with power and glory by God (Mark 14:62), but who was for the time being humble and unknown (Matthew 8:20) and destined for suffering and death (Mark 8:31).

After his disciples had realized who he was, he began to teach them that he must die, although they were slow to take it in. Jesus saw himself fulfilling the role of the Servant of the Lord who suffers humiliation and death (Isaiah 52:13 - 53:12). He laid down his life as a ransom for men to save them from death (Mark 10:45; John 10:11). Only to his closest disciples did he reveal that he was the Son of God in a unique, intimate manner. And he shared with them his privilege of addressing God in prayer by the name of 'Abba', 'Father' (Matthew 6:9; 11:25-27; Mark 14:36).

Throughout his ministry Jesus was involved in conflict with the religious authorities, mainly because of his scorching criticisms of their man-made traditions which diverted men from the real purposes of God's law. He attacked the hypocrisy which substituted tradition for the law of Moses. His messianic claims spurred the Jewish leaders on to arrest him. They feared he might be the centre of a popular uprising against Rome which would lead to grim reprisals and the loss of their own positions (John 11:47-53). So when Jesus came to Jerusalem and flung down the gauntlet by his attitude to the temple, they took steps to arrest him with the connivance of one of his followers.

Meanwhile Jesus held a last meal with his disciples. He filled a familiar table ritual with new content by using the bread and wine as symbols: his body was about to be broken in death on their behalf, and his blood about to be shed sacrificially, to ratify God's new covenant with men and to bring in his kingdom. After the meal, he went out to pray – and to meet his enemies. He was put through a trial which appears to have broken the appropriate legal rules. When the witnesses failed to produce sufficient evidence to condemn him, he was forced to make what his judges regarded as the blasphemous statement (to Christians it was the simple truth) that he was the Messiah. He was condemned to death. The Jews handed him over to the Roman governor as a political rebel against Rome, and although the governor was privately convinced of his innocence he allowed him to be put to death by the Roman punishment of crucifixion.

From the third day after his death, however, many of his disciples claimed that his tomb was empty and that he had himself appeared to them. God had raised him from the dead. The appearances took place over a period of 40 days, at the end of which time Jesus gave his final command to his disciples to be his witnesses throughout the world, and ascended from their presence as a symbol of his return to be with God and as a promise of his second coming to them at the end of the world.

That is the gospel story in brief. There is no other Jesus. The attempts of sceptical scholars to peel off the Christian interpretation and leave behind an ordinary, human person as the real 'historical' Jesus have proved fruitless.

It leaves with us the picture of a person about whom men must make up their minds. Throughout the Gospels Jesus appears as more than a man. His message, his deeds, and his person force the reader to decision.

New Testament 1.1

MATTHEW

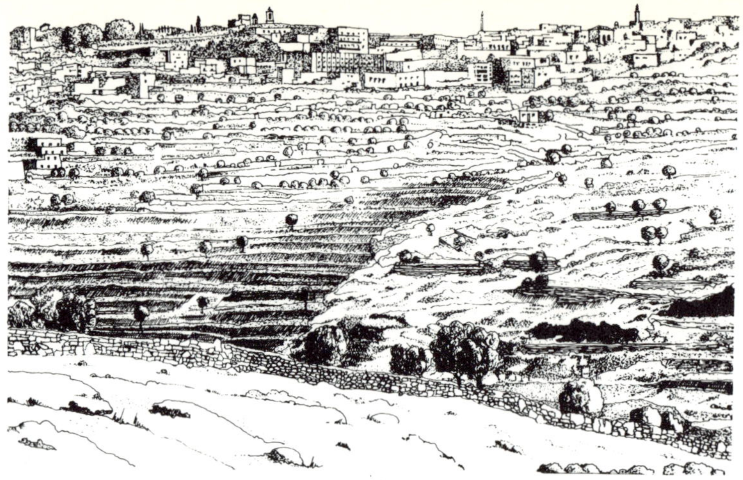

Modern Bethlehem, the small hill-town where Jesus was born.

Each of the four Gospels has its own special emphasis. Matthew, writing for his fellow Jews, concentrates on Jesus as the long-awaited Messiah – the Christ predicted in the Old Testament (see article 'The Religious Background of the New Testament'). Many Jews were expecting a political leader who would free them from Roman domination. So Matthew is careful to record what Jesus said about his kingdom – the kingdom of heaven. He gives us a great deal of Jesus' teaching, which he collects together into five main sections. These alternate with sections of narrative in the Gospel, and include the famous 'Sermon on the Mount'. Matthew's Gospel, more than any other, is the link between the Old Testament and the New, the old Israel and the new world-wide church of God's people.

The writer. The Gospel does not name its author, but from earliest times it has been attributed to Matthew, the apostle and one-time tax collector. Little is known of him. And beyond the fact that it belongs to the period between AD 50 and AD 100 no one knows for certain when or where the Gospel was written. Much of Matthew's material is almost identical with Mark's – and Mark's source of information was Peter. Scholars today mostly believe that Matthew drew on Mark – not vice-versa; see article 'The Gospels and Modern Criticism'.

STORIES AND EVENTS FOUND ONLY IN MATTHEW

Parables
The tares
Hidden treasure
The pearl
The drag-net
The hard-hearted servant
The workers in the vineyard
The two sons
The marriage of the king's son
The ten 'bridesmaids'
The talents

Miracles
The two blind men
The dumb man who was possessed
The coin in the fish's mouth

Incidents
Joseph's dream
The visit of the wise men
The escape to Egypt
Herod's massacre
Pilate's wife's dream
The death of Judas (also in Acts)
The 'saints' resurrected in Jerusalem
The bribing of the guard
The great commission

Some of Jesus' **teaching** is found only in Matthew, including his wonderful invitation to 'Come unto me'.

1 - 2 JESUS, THE MESSIAH, IS BORN

1:1-17 Christ's family line

See also Luke 3:23-38. The two lists are in reverse order and give a different set of names from David onwards (only Zerubbabel and Shealtiel appear in both). Matthew is showing Jesus as Messiah, descended from the royal line of David. He may be listing the heirs to the throne, while Luke lists Joseph's particular line. Matthew's list is stylized and abbreviated to fit his pattern: 14 names from Abraham to David; 14 from David to Jechoniah; 14 from Jechoniah to Jesus. This pattern of '14s' may have been suggested by the fact that the Hebrew letters in the name 'David' add up to that number. (The letters of the alphabet also served as numbers.)

Son of David (1): King David was promised an unfailing succession. But Israel ceased to be a monarchy at the time of the exile. And the promise came to be understood as referring to the Messiah.

Verses 3-6: it was unusual to list women. And if God's love and purposes had been limited to decent people of a particular race none of these would have been included. *Tamar* had children by her father-in-law, Judah (Genesis 38); *Rahab* was a Jericho prostitute (Joshua 2); *Ruth* a foreign Moabite woman (Ruth 1 - 4); and *Uriah's wife* was Bathsheba, with whom David committed adultery (2 Samuel 11).

Verse 11: 'father', like 'son' (verse 1), can be used in a wider sense. Josiah was Jechoniah's grandfather.

1:18-25 Mary and Joseph

Luke's fuller account of the birth focusses on Mary; Matthew's on Joseph. It takes little imagination to appreciate the very human dilemma. But Mary's pregnancy had a supernatural beginning. Matthew recalls Isaiah's words, giving them a significance the prophet could not have dreamt of. 'Jesus' means 'the saviour'; 'Emmanuel', God with us, in the world of men. (See also article 'The Virgin Birth'.)

Betrothed (18): betrothal, unlike modern engagement, was legally binding and could be broken only by divorce.

Verse 25: the implication is that after the birth Mary and Joseph lived a normal married life (see also 13:55-56).

2 The arrival of the wise men; the massacre; escape to Egypt

The wisdom of these men lay in the stars and their meanings. They were astrologers. And they had no doubt what the new star meant – the birth of the promised king in Judah. Tradition, not the Gospels, says there were three kings and that the presents they gave the baby had special significance – gold for a king; incense for God; myrrh for mortal man.

The news was not so welcome at the palace. Herod was king of the Jews (this is Herod the Great, who reigned 40-4 BC). He wanted no rivals. The massacre is in keeping with other cruelties mentioned in the historical records. The little family escape to Egypt, as Jacob's family had done long before when famine struck.

Verse 6: Matthew part-quotes, part-interprets Micah's words.

The house (11): some time has passed; the cave where the animals were stabled was only temporary shelter.

Rachel (18): mother-figure of Israel; Jacob's much-loved wife who died in child-birth at Ramah on the way to Bethlehem.

Archelaus (22): inherited one third of Herod's kingdom, but his repressive measures soon led the Romans to depose him and take control of Judea.

3 - 4 JESUS' BAPTISM AND TEMPTATION

3 The preaching of John the Baptist; Jesus' baptism

See also Mark 1:2-11; Luke 3:2-22. Luke 1 tells the story of John's birth. John's compelling preaching – calling men to make ready for the Messiah – draws the crowds out to the desert to hear him. Peter's brother, Andrew, was one of those baptized by John, following genuine repentance for past wrong-doing. The 'washing' of baptism symbolized a radical cleaning up of a man's life – wiping the slate clean of all previous wrong – in preparation for the coming rule of God. This was not necessary in Jesus' case. He was baptized, not in order to be forgiven, but to identify himself completely with men. When he stepped into the Jordan, it was as if he was asking to take on the responsibility for human sin. He was accepting his destiny with all that that involved. God's words (17), combining Psalm 2:7 and Isaiah 42:1, proclaim Jesus as his Son, the Messiah, and the Servant who would suffer for his people.

Verse 4: see note under Mark 1:1-8.

Pharisees and Sadducees (7): see article 'The Religious Background of the New Testament'.

4 The temptation; the call of the first disciples; Jesus begins to teach

See also Mark 1:12-13; Luke 4:1-13. In the temptations that follow his 40-day fast, Jesus faces up to all he will have to go through in his ministry. He now has power – power to feed the hungry, heal the sick, raise the dead. How will he use it? To satisfy his own needs? To try God out? To compel a following? When it comes to it, will he use his power to save himself, or will he trust himself entirely to God and tread the path to the cross? Jesus replies to Satan's test questions in words from Deuteronomy (8:3; 6:16; 6:13) – key passages from Israel's 40 years in the desert, when God tested their obedience to him (Deuteronomy 8:2).

After John's arrest, Jesus travels north, making the lakeside town of Capernaum his base. Here he calls his first disciples and begins his public ministry.

Decapolis (25): ten free Greek cities south-east of Galilee.

Many of Jesus' healings and much of his teaching took place in the area around Lake Galilee. The view here is the north-eastern corner of the lake, from Tiberias.

5 - 7 THE SERMON ON THE MOUNT: STANDARDS OF DISCIPLESHIP

See also Luke 6:20-49. The 'sermon' is the first and longest of the five sections in which Matthew gathers together the Lord's teaching. Jesus shows his followers how man ought to live – not simply according to a set of rules but by an inner revolution of attitude and outlook. The glorious thing is that having set a seemingly impossible standard, he went on to give men the power to live up to it.

5:1-16 Where true happiness lies

Jesus turns ordinary human ideas about happiness upside down. Contrary to general opinion, it is not the go-getters, the tough ones, those who bend the rules, who are the real successes. The truly happy ones are those who recognize the spiritual poverty (verse 3) of self-reliance and learn to depend wholly on God. Everything else follows from this. The people who can be certain of a future are the humble, the forgiving, the pure, those who set their hearts on what is right, who try to heal the rifts. And here and now, these are the ones who put the seasoning into life, who stop the rot, who light up the way. By what they do and say and how they react, they show men something of what God himself is like.

5:17-48 The old law and the new

Nothing can ever supersede or do away with the law God gave through Moses. But the law is a minimum standard. It can only deal with actions, not with the thoughts that give rise to them. Jesus takes five examples to show what the principles expressed in the law involve at the personal level. Sin begins in the mind and will. That is where it must be rooted out. The standards of the new society – God's kingdom – are way above the standards of the law-courts.

The five case-studies: murder (21-26; Exodus 20:13); adultery (27-32; Exodus 20:14); oaths (33-37; Numbers 30:2 – and see Matthew 23:16-22); retaliation (38-42; Exodus 21:24); loving others (43-48; Leviticus 19:18; see also Luke 10:29-37).

The law and the prophets (17): i.e. all the Old Testament precepts. There were three divisions in the Jewish Bible – the Law (Genesis to Deuteronomy); the Prophets (Former: Joshua, Judges, Samuel, Kings; and Latter: all the prophets except Daniel); and the Writings (the rest of our Old Testament).

Verse 22: the progression is difficult to understand, unless 'fool' should be 'apostate' – meaning that any man who calls another an outcast of God is in danger of being cast out himself.

Verse 23: a sacrifice offered by an individual was of no value if he had not put right an offence committed against a fellow man.

Verses 31-32: in Moses' day a wife could be dismissed at whim. His law gave her some security. Jesus goes back to the fundamental meaning and purpose of marriage. The bond made when the two become 'one flesh' is indissoluble. Divorce is unthinkable, except where one of the partners has broken the bond already. See 19:3-9.

6:1-18 Warnings against a mere parade of religion

Motives, thoughts, intentions, what goes on deep inside, are what matter in religion, too. God gives no prizes for an outward show of piety. So Jesus tells us to give and pray and fast without drawing attention to ourselves – and God will reward us. Our prayer is to be simple, trusting. We are to come as children to our Father, eager to please, conscious of our failings. (Luke 11:2-4 also records the Lord's Prayer.)

6:19-34 Singlemindedness

Men can choose what to set their hearts on. They can go all out for money and material things, or for God and spiritual things. But not for both. Everyone must decide his own priorities. Those who put God first can rest assured he knows all their needs and will not fail to supply them. They can be free from worry.

Verses 22-23: the eyes were thought of as windows, letting light into the body.

7 Instructions and warnings

Do not be harshly critical (1-5); do be discriminating (6). Never give up praying (7-11). Always treat others as you would like them to treat you (12). Make sure you are on the right road to eternal life (13-14), there are plenty of people out to mislead (15-20). And many more are self-deceived (21-23). Words are not enough, the only safe course is to act on what we hear Christ say (24-27).

At the end of the teaching, it is the note of authority that most impresses the listeners. They have heard no one before like this man.

8 - 9:34 HEALING AND TEACHING

8:1-17 Miracles of healing

Verses 1-4: the leper. To the Jew lepers were unclean, untouchable. Jesus could have healed the man with a look, or a word – instead he reached out and touched him. (For the leprosy regulations, see Leviticus 13-14: the term 'leprosy' in the Bible covers a number of skin diseases.)

Verses 5-13: the centurion's boy. Jesus' mission is to Israel, but nowhere among his own people has he found faith to equal that of the Roman officer who recognized authority when he saw it.

Verses 14-17: Jesus cures physical, spiritual and psychological ills at Capernaum.

8:18-27 Storm and calm

Son of man (20): a phrase Jesus often uses to describe himself. It emphasizes his humanity (Psalm 8:4), yet points beyond it (Daniel 7:13-14).

Verses 21-22: the disciple wants to wait till after his father's funeral before joining Jesus. This need not mean that his father is dead. 'I must first bury my father' is a colloquial way of saying, 'I will follow you sometime – when my father is dead and I am free to go'. Jesus' reply stresses the urgency of his work. It calls for a response now, not sometime in the future.

Verses 23-27: see also Mark 4:36-41, with some differences of detail.

8:28 - 9:8 Further healings

Verses 28-34: two men possessed by demons. In their accounts, Mark and Luke focus on just one of the men, 'Legion' (Mark 5:1-17; Luke 8:26-37). Here Matthew tells how Jesus restored both men to sanity. But the residents of Gadara – a town six miles from the lake – would rather turn Jesus away than run the risk of losing more pigs.

9:1-8: the man with paralysis. Jesus uses the physical healing as proof that the spiritual cure, the man's forgiveness, is equally real.

His own city (9:1): Capernaum – see 4:13.

9:9-17 Matthew's call; questions about fasting

In Mark (2:13-17) and Luke (5:27-32) the tax collector is called Levi, and they make it clear that the feast is held at his house. 'Matthew' may have been Levi's 'Christian' name, as 'Peter' was Simon's. Jesus' presence in such company scandalizes the religious Pharisees. John's followers are also puzzled. Why does Jesus feast whereas John fasted? Luke (5:36-37) gives Jesus' answer most clearly. His radically new teaching cannot be squeezed into the mould of the old legalism. It must find new forms of expression – or else the old will be destroyed and the new spoilt. Luke 5:39 is a perceptive comment on human nature – the conservatism which mistrusts anything new.

9:18-34 More healings

Verses 18-26: Jairus' daughter; the woman with a haemorrhage (see on Mark 5: 21-43; Luke 8:40-56).

Verses 27-31: two blind men. The reason for secrecy (30) is not explained. Presumably Jesus is anxious to avoid his miracles giving people the wrong ideas about his mission.

Verses 32-34: the dumb man who was possessed.

Flute players (23): musicians were often hired to play dirges at a house where someone had died.

9:35 - 10:42 JESUS' CHARGE TO THE TWELVE

The second teaching section. See also Mark 6:7-13; Luke 9:1-6, and other parallel passages. The choice and training of the Twelve was a vital part of Jesus' mission. The task of spreading the good news about eternal life would rest with them after his death. Now he sends them out for the first time, with power to heal. He gives them their instructions (some only temporary – see Luke 22:35-36) and warns them of the kind of reception they are likely to get, both now and in the future. They are to expect hardship; trust in God's care; and fear no one.

The tax collector (10:3): it seems Matthew could never forget he was once a social outcast.

Verse 23: Jesus said that even he did not know when his second coming would be. The reference here may be to his triumphant return from death at the resurrection.

Beelzebul (25): see 12:22-24.

The housetop (27): a favourite place for gossip and discussion.

Verse 28: only God, not Satan, has this power.

Verses 34-35: the division is a *result* of Jesus' teaching. The Bible often expresses consequences as if they were deliberate intention.

Verse 39: 'he who finds' – i.e. the man who denies his faith to save his skin.

11 - 12 THE CLAIMS OF JESUS

This is one of Matthew's narrative sections – but it contains a good deal of teaching.

11:1-19 Messengers from John the Baptist

John – imprisoned by Antipas, younger son of Herod the Great, and ruler of Galilee and Perea – is puzzled by reports of Jesus. He expected the Messiah to come in judgement. Jesus' reply reminds him of the other aspect of Messiah's work (predicted in Isaiah 35:5-6; 61:1), which he is fulfilling. John is the last and greatest of the Old Testament prophets – the latter-day Elijah predicted by Malachi (4:5). Jesus thinks no less of him for his doubts. But the humblest Christian enjoys far greater privileges (11).

Verse 12: it is difficult in retrospect to see exactly what Jesus meant. He may be referring to Zealot militants, from whom he disassociated himself; or to the fact that the kingdom opens its gates to those who are desperate, not just drifters (see Luke 16:16).

Verses 16-17: like sulky children, Jesus' contemporaries refuse to 'play weddings' with him, or to 'play funerals' with John. They will listen neither to good news – nor to warnings.

11:20-30 'Come to me'

Most of Jesus' miracles took place in the small area at the north of the sea of Galilee – around Capernaum, Chorazin and Bethsaida. They evoked so little response from the people that God's judgement on their stubborn disbelief was inevitable. Tyre and Sidon – the prosperous, godless sea-ports denounced by the prophets (e.g. Isaiah 23) – even Sodom, that byword for evil (Genesis 19), could not have seen what they had seen and remained unmoved.

It was the ordinary folk who received Jesus – and he was glad. To all who are worn down by burdens he offers relief. Those who enter his service will find him no crushing task-master.

12:1-14 The Lord of the sabbath

See on Mark 2:23 - 3:6.

12:15-37 Hope of the nations? Or devil's emissary?

The Pharisees see Jesus as the devil's agent (24), despite the transparent goodness of his work (22-23). If they were right, Satan would be set on a suicide course (25-29) – as are all who, like the Pharisees, call good evil. They are stubbornly denying the Holy Spirit's work, and making their own forgiveness impossible (31-32).

12:38-50 'Give us a sign'

After all Jesus' miracles of healing, the lawyers and Pharisees have the effrontery to demand a spectacular sign. Only one such sign will be given – Jesus' resurrection from the dead – the incontrovertible proof that he is who he claims to be.

Verses 43-45: the story is a warning to those who have repented as a result of what they have seen and heard. Unless they take the further step of whole-hearted commitment, they are in grave danger.

Verse 40: by Jewish reckoning any part of the 24 hours which make up day and night could count as the whole. So Friday afternoon to Sun-

THE KINGDOM OF GOD AND THE KINGDOM OF HEAVEN

David Field

The two expressions 'kingdom of God' and 'kingdom of heaven' represent exactly the same idea. To a devout Jew the word 'God' was far too sacred to be used lightly or frequently. Matthew, writing primarily for Jewish readers, therefore normally speaks about the 'kingdom of heaven', whereas Mark and Luke prefer the alternative 'kingdom of God', as an easier expression for non-Jews to understand.

It is surprising to find that neither expression is used at all in the Old Testament. And even in the New Testament the phrases seldom occur after the first three Gospels. This highlights the important part the theme of the kingdom played in the teaching of Jesus himself. We are told that it was right at the heart of his gospel message (Mark 1:15), and when the disciples were sent out on their first missions it was the message of 'the kingdom' that they were to proclaim (Luke 9:2; 10:9-11).

The meaning of 'kingdom'

Jesus never defined exactly what he meant by the kingdom of God. But in answering the charge of rebellion before Pontius Pilate he was careful to disown all claims to temporal, territorial dominion. 'My kingdom', he said, 'is not of this world' (John 18:36). Some modern versions translate 'kingdom' in this verse as 'kingship' or 'kingly authority'. The kingdom of God, in the Bible, normally means God's active reign in the world. Sometimes Jesus could talk about 'entering' the kingdom (e.g. Mark 10:23), much as we might speak of entering a country, but the idea behind the word he used is far more often that of 'rule' than of 'realm'. Perhaps the Lord's Prayer comes closest to an exact definition when it equates the coming of God's kingdom with the doing of his will. Where God's will is done with perfect submission, there, according to the New Testament, is his kingdom revealed.

Although the Old Testament authors did not write about the 'kingdom of God' as such, they eagerly anticipated the great Day when he would display his glory (Isaiah 24:23) in such a dramatic way that all men would acknowledge his rule (Zechariah 14:9). This keen sense of anticipation, both a cosmic hope and a longing for the liberation of the land, persisted well into Jesus' time. (Joseph of Arimathaea, Mark tells us, was one man who was 'looking for the kingdom of God'.) So when John the Baptist announced 'the kingdom of heaven is at hand' (Matthew 3:2), he was immediately surrounded by crowds of excited people who had come to witness the long-expected display of God's ruling power in history.

God's kingdom – present and future

Jesus' first preaching was apparently couched in very similar terms to John's, but according to Mark he prefaced his announcement of the kingdom's imminence with the words 'The time is fulfilled' (Mark 1:15). This declaration of fulfilment strikes a note which sounds right through the Gospels, that in Jesus the kingdom of God has become a living reality. His miracles, and especially his exorcisms, testify to the fact that God's sovereign rule is breaking in upon man (Matthew 12:28). His preaching, with its unique note of authority, is evidence of the kingdom's arrival (Mark 1:27; Matthew 11:5). Because 'the kingdom of God is in the midst of you', he tells his disciples (Luke 17:21), the kingdom's blessings – forgiveness, salvation and eternal life – are theirs to enjoy, not only for the future but in the present. For centuries the prophets had forecast a time when God's kingly power would be displayed on earth; now, in the person and ministry of Jesus, that time had come.

If Jesus taught that the kingdom had actually arrived in his own person, it is equally clear that he looked to the future for a final demonstration of God's ruling power. His disciples must *pray* 'Thy kingdom come' and watch alertly to see 'the kingdom of God come with power' (Mark 9:1; Matthew 25:1). The miracles they saw him perform – and performed themselves, in his strength – were a mighty token of the kingdom's presence, but the battle with Satan still raged and the result, though not in doubt, awaited the final show-down (Matthew 25:41). Forecasts of a great future consummation intertwine, therefore, with clear evidence of the kingdom's present arrival, and it is obvious from the 'parables of the kingdom' in Matthew 13 that Jesus intended his disciples to grasp both truths. The seed is sown and grows before the climax of harvest is reached.

The demands of the kingdom

Whether present or future, God's kingly rule demands man's obedient submission. Men are not called upon to build or establish the kingdom for themselves, but only to seek for it and enter it (Matthew 6:33; Mark 9:47). Its ethical standards are exacting – far above those of the scribes and Pharisees (Matthew 5:20) – and they call not only for theoretical knowledge but for practical expression (Mark 12:34). In short, entry into the kingdom requires the unquestioning obedience of a child (Mark 10:15) and makes absolute demands on the disciple's loyalty and devotion. Yet submission to God's rule is in man's very best interests, because his kingdom, like hidden treasure or a pearl of great price, is the one thing of supreme value in life, for which any sacrifice is worth while (Matthew 13:44-46).

day morning is spoken of as three days and nights.
Verse 42: the Queen of Sheba (1 Kings 10:1-10).
Verse 49: presumably younger children of Mary and Joseph (see on 1:25). It is usually thought that Joseph was dead by this time.

13:1-52 PARABLES ABOUT GOD'S KINGDOM

The third teaching section. Jesus made many of his points by means of parables – stories that could be taken at two levels, the superficial or the more perceptive. They were a means of sorting out his followers; discovering who had come just because of the miracles, and who really wanted to understand his teaching. The former were happy to listen to stories; the latter were prepared to look for the deeper meaning and ask him to explain. There was so much misunderstanding – even among the disciples – about the nature of his kingdom that he needed to straighten them out one point at a time.

Verses 1-9: the seed and the soils (explained in 18-23) pictures the varied response his message will bring.

Verses 24-30: the wheat and the weeds (explained in 36-43) is concerned with the mixture of good and bad in this life, to be sorted out at the judgement.

Verses 31-33: the mustard-seed, and the yeast. From small beginnings, quietly and unnoticed, the kingdom will make great growth.

Verses 44-45: the treasure, and the pearl. So valuable is the kingdom, it is worth giving all we have to make sure of it.

Verses 47-50: the fisherman's net. This describes the sorting out of good and bad at the end of time.
Verse 52: New English Bible, 'When, therefore, a teacher of the law has become a learner in the kingdom of Heaven ...'

13:53 - 14:12 NAZARETH REJECTS JESUS; THE DEATH OF JOHN THE BAPTIST

See on Mark 6:1-6 and 14-29.

14:13 - 17:27 TEACHING AND MIRACLES IN GALILEE AND THE NORTH

14:13-36 5,000 people fed; Jesus walks on the water

See on Mark 6:30-56. See also Luke 9:10b-17; John 6:1-21.

15:1-20 The Pharisees and the question of tradition

See also Mark 7:1-23. From the first, Jesus' teaching on religion (6:1-18) brought him into conflict with the Pharisees. For them 'tradition' (the oral teaching of the rabbis which supplemented and interpreted Scripture) was binding. But Jesus never hesitated to denounce tradition wherever it watered down or undermined scriptural principles. Their ruling on vows is a case in point. Exemption from his duty to maintain his parents was allowed a man if he dedicated the money to God. That way he could still enjoy the proceeds himself. It is not clean hands (2) but a clean heart (18) that matters.

15:21-39 The Canaanite woman; further healings; 4,000 fed

Tyre and Sidon (21) lay outside Jewish territory. Jesus could not refuse a request made with such tenacious faith.

Verses 29-39: the differences of detail between this passage and 14:13-21, and the fact that Mark also records both miracles, make it unlikely that this is a second account of the same event, despite the basic similarity.
The dogs (26): an abusive term for Gentiles. Jesus is testing the woman out, leading her to faith.
Magadan (39): the location is not known.

16:1-12 Jesus warns against the teaching of the Pharisees and Sadducees

See also Mark 8:11-21. The Pharisees had demanded a sign once before (12:38ff.). Now the Sadducees, the rationalists, join them. Jesus' answer is still the same.

16:13-28 Peter's great declaration: Jesus predicts his death

Simon speaks for all the apostles in asserting his belief that Jesus is the Messiah. And Jesus sees in him the man of rock (Peter) he will become after the shattering experience of denial and forgiveness (26:69-75). It is Peter the natural spokesman who will be responsible, more than any other, for the formation of the church at Pentecost (Acts 2 - 5).

Verses 21-28: Jesus begins to prepare his disciples for the suffering that lies ahead. But the recent promise has gone to Peter's head. The rock becomes an obstacle. God's spokesman turns devil's advocate.

Verse 19: the authority given to Peter is given equally to the others (see 18:18). The idea of the keys echoes Isaiah 22: 22. God is not bound by whatever Peter may say. But anything done by the disciple in accordance with Christ's will is to have permanent validity.
Verse 28: see on 10:23.

17 The transfiguration and what follows

See on Mark 9:2-32; Luke 9:28-45.
Verses 24-27: as Son of God, the one on whose behalf the tax is levied, Jesus is exempt. But as Man, identified with men, he pays it.

18 LIFE IN GOD'S COMMUNITY

This is Matthew's fourth teaching section. God's kingdom operates by totally different standards from the world's. Status-seeking is out (1-4). So is the policy of 'the weakest to the wall'. On the contrary, the spiritually weak are the special responsibility of the strong (5-14). In the new community wrongdoing matters; every effort must be made to set the defaulter right (15-20). Unlimited forgiveness is expected from those whom God has forgiven (21-35).
Verses 8-9: see on Mark 9:44-45.
Verses 24, 28: 'millions' and 'a few pounds' (New English Bible): the point being the immeasurable extent of our 'debt' to God, compared to anything we may have to forgive our fellow men.

Those who led 'little ones' astray, Jesus said, were fit only to have a millstone tied round their necks and be cast into the sea. These millstones are in the Agricultural Museum, Jerusalem.

19 - 20 THE JOURNEY TO JERUSALEM

19:1-15 Marriage and divorce

See also 5:31-32; Mark 10:2-12; Luke 16:18. The rabbis disagreed about divorce. Some allowed it for anything that displeased the husband; others only for unfaithfulness. Jesus goes back to God's purpose for man and woman at the very beginning. That is the ideal. Moses, dealing with a situation that fell far short of the ideal, placed a restriction on divorce. Jesus says that unfaithfulness is the only legitimate reason for it.
Verses 10-12: see New English Bible or Good News Bible.

19:16 - 20:16 Eternal life; the disadvantage of wealth; rewards

9:16-30: see also Mark 10:17-31; Luke 18:18-30. Jesus' first answer is the one any Jewish teacher would have given. And the man – a ruler in the synagogue – could claim he had kept the commandments. But Jesus pinpoints the root of this man's trouble. His commandment-keeping is not wholehearted. His possessions mean too much to him. Because of them he is failing to love God and his neighbour without reserve. So Jesus tells him to sell up. It is better to possess nothing than to love things more than God.

20:1-16: this story, illustrating Jesus' words in 19:30, comes only in Matthew. He is not talking about pay structures, or saying that all will be equal in heaven. The point is that many who expect to be made much of will be in for a rude shock in God's kingdom. God will honour some very unexpected people. Eternal life is for all who will receive it: 'good' and 'bad', young and old. The remarkable thing is the landowner's (God's) generosity – not his unfairness.
19:24: there have been various 'explanations' of the 'Needle's Eye'. But it seems that Jesus is being deliberately humorous in suggesting the impossible – a camel going through the eye of a literal needle.
19:25: they were surprised because they thought riches were a reward for goodness – an index of a person's spiritual state.
19:28: the apostles have a special place in the new kingdom. Only Matthew records these words.
19:29: those who follow Christ will be repaid many times over, here and now – but 'with persecutions' (see Mark).
20:2: New English Bible gives the meaning, 'the usual day's wage'. The denarius was a Roman silver coin.
20:3-6: the times are 9 a.m. (the third hour), 12 noon, 3 p.m. and 5 p.m. – an hour before sunset, which was when the men were paid for the day's work.

20:17-34 Jesus again predicts his death; status in God's kingdom; two blind men healed

See also Mark 10:32-52; Luke 18:31-43. Jesus' patience is amazing. Over and over again he explains that the kingdom is for the humble. There is to be no lording it. Yet even when he speaks of his death the disciples are taken up with their own status. The place at the top is reserved for the disciple who – like his master – is prepared to live for others and if need be to die for them.
Sons of Zebedee (20): i.e. James and John.
The cup (22): i.e. the cup of suffering. James was the first of the loyal apostles to meet a violent death (Acts 12:2).
Verses 29-34: Mark and Luke mention only one blind man – perhaps because Peter knew one of them personally (Bartimaeus – see Mark).

21 - 25 JESUS IN JERUSALEM

It was spring, and people from far and near were crowding into Jerusalem for Passover, the great feast commemorating the nation's liberation from Egypt. Not all could find lodgings in the city itself. Jesus and his friends stayed at nearby Bethany, where Martha, Mary and Lazarus had their home. Each day they walked the two miles into Jerusalem, over the shoulder of the Mount of Olives and down through the thick groves of trees.

21:1-11 His triumphant arrival

See on Luke 19:28-44. See also Mark 11:1-10. Characteristically, Matthew quotes the prophecy from Zechariah 9:9.

21:12-17 The purging of the temple

See also on John 2:13-25. The dealers operated in the outer court of the temple, the Court of the Gentiles. Jews from abroad were not allowed to use their own currency to pay the annual temple dues. And the moneychangers fixed a high rate of exchange. (The annual revenue from the temple tax is estimated at £75,000: the moneychangers' annual profit at £9,000.) Poor people, who could only afford the cheapest sacrifice (two pigeons), were charged extortionate prices. The priests turned a blind eye to all this. Yet their indignation knows no bounds at the 'irreverence' of Jesus. He actually healed people in the temple courts and let the children chant the earlier tributes of the crowds!

21:18-22 The fig-tree

See also Mark 11:12-14, 20-24. A healthy fig-tree bears fruit for ten months of the year. Since the tree was in leaf, there should have been green figs. Mark makes it clear that it was the following day when the disciples found the tree withered. Jesus uses the incident as an object lesson: faith can move insurmountable obstacles. It also indicates the fate of the spiritually barren nation of Israel.

21:23-46 The priests question Jesus' authority

The question is natural, in the light of

Jerusalem in New Testament times

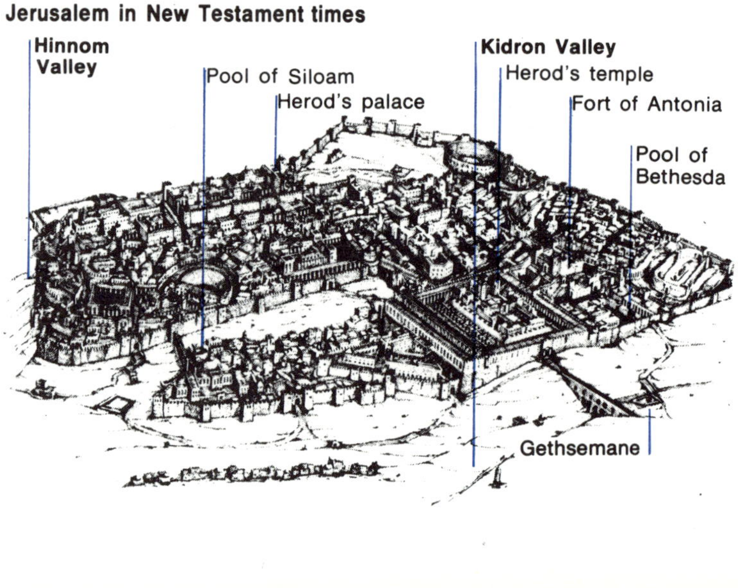

what has happened (12-17). Jesus makes no direct answer, but it is clear that he and John derive their authority from the same source. In the three parables that follow his critics find themselves under fire.

Verses 28-32: the two sons. The first represents the religious leaders, with their mock obedience; the second the social outcasts, who have made a genuine response to John and to Jesus.

Verses 33-41: the vineyard (the nation of Israel whose owner is God – Isaiah 5:1-7). The men to whom God has entrusted spiritual leadership have abused the prophets and are about to kill his Son.

Verses 42-43: see Psalm 118:22-23. Jesus transfers the picture from Israel to himself – cast aside, crucified, by the nation, but reinstated by God.

22:1-14 The parable of the wedding-guests

Jesus illustrates what he has just said (21:43). The day will come when God no longer invites those who repeatedly refuse him. The invitation will go to others. Verses 11-13 are a warning to the new-comers. Those who come must come on God's terms.

22:15-46 Test questions; the Pharisees plot against Jesus' life

See on Mark 12:13-44.

23 Jesus denounces the lawyers and Pharisees

Chapters 23 - 25 contain the fifth and last teaching section. The subject is judgement. Jesus launches into a scathing attack on Israel's legalistic, but much-respected religious leaders. The man who cared so deeply and had such patience with ordinary people – even the wicked, the weak-willed and the stupid – could not stomach the religious sham, the self-righteous pride, the hair-splitting pedantry of the Pharisees and scribes. Proud and selfish hearts still lurk beneath such 'proper' exteriors. How he must hate to see Pharisaic hypocrisy in his own followers.

Verse 2: in the synagogue they stood to read the law, but sat to expound it.

Verse 10: New English Bible 'teacher' gives the sense. The same Greek word is used today of a 'professor'.

Verse 15: New English Bible 'twice as fit for hell' gives the sense. New converts are often more fervent than those brought up in the faith.

Mint, dill, cummin (23): common garden herbs.

Verse 27: tombs were specially white-washed for Passover to prevent people inadvertently touching them and becoming ceremonially defiled.

Verse 35: this may be Zechariah son of Jehoiada, as there is no record of the prophet Zechariah being murdered. Genesis 4:8; 2 Chronicles 24:20-21.

Verses 38-39: Jesus may be predicting the destruction of the city. Verse 39 refers to his return in glory and judgement.

24 - 25 The fall of Jerusalem and Jesus' return in judgement

24:1-44: questions and answers. See also Mark 13; Luke 21 and 17:23ff. Jesus is answering questions about when the temple will be destroyed and what indications there will be that the age is coming to an end. Jerusalem and the temple were actually to be destroyed by the Romans in AD 70. The disciples seem to think of the end closely following. And Jesus does not clearly separate them – both are part of the total judgement of God (although more than 1900 years already separate the two events). The disciples are not to be misled – there will be many wars and natural disasters, persecutions and false Messiahs (4-13, 23-27). These are not signs of the end. There will be time for world-wide preaching of the gospel (14). And when the end does come, it will be totally unexpected (36-44). But there will be clear warning signs of the destruction of Jerusalem (15-22, 32-35).

24:45 - 25:46: parables of judgement. Jesus uses stories to drive home the points of the previous chapter.

24:45-51: the good and bad servants. Because his return will be unexpected, Jesus' followers must always be ready.

25:1-12: the wise and foolish girls. The same lesson, but stressing that one day time will run out, and preparedness is an individual thing. It cannot be borrowed from someone else.

25:14-30: the 'talents'. The talent was a large amount of money – not a coin. Each man is entrusted with a capital sum in line with his business ability, and he is expected to trade with it. Our future depends on how we use what we have been given in this life.

25:31-46: the sheep and the goats. At the judgement God takes account of how we have treated others in this life. In the parable, the 'goats' are punished for failing to do what they should have done.

Verse 15: Daniel 11:31. An alternative rendering, in line with Luke's paraphrase is 'so when you see the abominable sign spoken of by the prophet Daniel (let the reader understand)'. This could be a reference to the emperor's image on the ensign carried by the Roman soldiers.

Verse 21: over 1,000,000 people lost their lives in the fall of Jerusalem, and Herod's magnificent cream stone and gold temple was razed to the ground.

Verse 28: the picture seems to be of the 'eagles' of the Roman army converging on the 'corpse' of the city.

Verses 29-31: symbolic language used of Christ's return. In the light of verse 36, 'immediately' cannot be taken literally. Jesus is again telescoping the two 'comings in judgement'.

Verse 34: a reference to the destruction of the temple within the lifetime of his hearers. It took place about 40 years after Jesus' prediction.

Jesus' words about the destruction of Jerusalem were dramatically fulfilled in AD 70. The Romans destroyed the city and plundered the temple. The scene is pictured on the triumphal arch of Titus in Rome. The seven-branched candlestick was taken from the temple.

THE PASSOVER AND THE LAST SUPPER

The Passover meal followed a fairly standard pattern in every Jewish household. First comes the opening prayer – the blessing of the cup (the first of four cups of wine passed round during the ceremony). Then each person takes herbs and dips them in salt water (see Matthew 26:23). The head of the family takes one of the three flat cakes of unleavened bread, breaks it and puts some aside. Then, in response to a question from the youngest member of the family, the story of the first Passover is recounted and Psalms 113, 114 sung. The second cup (see Luke 22:17) is filled and passed round.

Before the meal itself, all wash their hands (probably the point at which Jesus washed the disciples' feet, John 13:4-12), grace is said and bread broken. Bitter herb dipped in sauce is distributed (this was when Jesus gave the sop to Judas, John 13:26). The climax of the ritual is the festive meal of roast lamb.

It was after this that Jesus instituted the Lord's Supper, breaking the bread laid aside earlier and passing round the third cup of wine, the 'cup of blessing'. (The words 'this is ...' (Matthew 26: 26, 28) must mean 'this represents ...' since he was himself there, giving the disciples the bread and wine.) The ritual concludes with the singing of the remaining 'Hallel' (or Hallelujah) psalms (115 - 118) and the 'Great Hallel', Psalm 136. These psalms are probably the 'hymn' Matthew mentions (26:30). Then the final cup of wine is drunk.

The setting of the Lord's Supper at the heart of the Passover meal explains its meaning. Jesus is thinking of himself as the Passover lamb, offered up for the deliverance of his people. The wine speaks of his death, and of the new covenant it ratifies, reconciling God and man. Until he comes again, we are to remember the significance of what he has done for us.

26 - 27 THE FINAL CLASH: JESUS' TRIAL AND CRUCIFIXION

26:1-5 Jesus forewarns his disciples; the Jewish leaders plot his death

26:6-13 A woman anoints Jesus

See on Mark 14:3-9.

26:14-29 Judas turns traitor; the Last Supper

See also Mark 14:12-25; Luke 22:7-38; John 13 - 14.

On the first evening of the festival, Jesus and his close friends meet as a family to eat the Passover meal together. At the exodus each Jewish household sacrificed a lamb or kid and daubed the blood over the door to ensure their safety as death struck the firstborn of every Egyptian family. Now the Lamb of God (John 1:29) is about to offer himself, to secure life for the whole world. The old Passover is transformed into the Lord's Supper. At the exodus, the nation of Israel was born. By Christ's sacrifice, the church is born, a people drawn from all the nations. The Passover looked back. The Lord's Supper is also a reminder for us today of a past event. It looks forward, too, to the joyous day when Christ will come and make his home with his people, in a new world which has no place for sin or death or pain.

26:30-56 The garden of Gethsemane; Jesus is arrested

See also Mark 14:26-52; Luke 22:39-53. It is Luke who depicts most vividly the agony of Christ's prayer in the garden. So intense was Jesus' last plea that – God willing – he might be spared the terrible suffering about to begin, that his sweat fell like great drops of blood. What was it he shrank from? Surely not simply physical suffering. We can never know just what he faced during that lonely hour. But the prospect which filled him with such horror was God's judgement on *our* sin – the penalty which would have been ours had Christ not paid it for us (1 Peter 2:24).

The moment passes, and as the mob comes out to arrest him he is once more utterly in command. He expresses only love for the traitor. When Peter draws his sword (John 18:10), Jesus heals the injured man (see Luke). No man can ever have been so completely in control of such a situation. He had come to fulfil the scriptures. He knew it must be so – even when everyone deserted him.

26:57-68 Trial before the high priest

See on Mark 14:53-65.

26:69-75 Peter denies all knowledge of Jesus

See on Luke 22:54-65.

27:1-26 Judas commits suicide; Jesus before Pilate

Only Matthew records Judas' remorse. He flings back the money – but a clear conscience is not so easily bought. (Acts 1:16-20 has a slightly different version of the story.) For the trial before Pilate, see on Luke 23:1-25.

27:27-56 Mockery and crucifixion

See on Mark 15:16-41.

27:57-66 Jesus' burial; a guard is set

See on Mark 15:42-47. Matthew is the only one to mention the guard; see also 28:11ff.

28 THE RESURRECTION

See on Luke 24 and 'The Accounts of the Resurrection'.

Verses 1-10: the women hear the news and see the Lord. Verses 11-15: the guards are bribed to lie. The penalty for falling asleep on duty was death. But perhaps Pilate could also be squared with a bribe. Verses 16-20: Jesus' last command. This most Jewish of all the Gospels closes with a word from the Lord that throws the kingdom open to men of every nation.

THE RELIGIOUS BACKGROUND OF THE NEW TESTAMENT

Richard France

Jesus was a Jew. The Christian church began its life in Palestine, and its first members were Jews. So the most important element in the religious background to the New Testament is the Jewish religion itself.

JEWISH RELIGION

The last of the Old Testament prophets lived 400 years or more before John the Baptist appeared. Since that time the Jewish religion had not stood still. The classical religion of the Old Testament had evolved (some might say, degenerated) into Judaism.

Some important institutions in Judaism

The temple. The simple temple built by the Jews who returned to Jerusalem after the exile had been replaced by a magnificent structure commissioned by Herod the Great (40-4 BC). It was begun in 19 BC; it was still not complete in the time of Jesus (John 2:20), and was not finished until AD 64 – six years before it was destroyed by the Romans! It was this imposing complex of buildings in huge cream-coloured stones, marble and gold, which evoked the admiration of Jesus' disciples (Mark 13:1). Here the age-old ritual of sacrifice and worship continued, with its elaborate establishment of priests and temple servants, though all under the watchful eye of the Roman garrison in the fortress of Antonia, which overlooked its courts (Acts 21:31ff.). Here too, in the Court of the Gentiles (beyond which no Gentile dare venture, on pain of death – Acts 21:28-29; Ephesians 2:14), was the thriving market in sacrificial animals and sacred money for the temple offerings which was the object of Jesus' anger. And here in the shaded porticos men would gather to listen to any teacher who cared to set up his stand.

The synagogue. There was only one temple, but each community had its synagogue. Here there was no sacrificial ritual. It was the local centre for worship and study of the law. On the sabbath day the community would meet, men and women seated apart, to listen to the reading and exposition of the set passages from the Law and the Prophets (Luke 4:16ff.), and to join in the set liturgical prayers. But the synagogue was more than a place of worship. It was the local school, the community centre, and the centre of local government. Its elders were the civil authorities of the community, the magistrates and guardians of public morals.

The law and the traditions. Israel had always had a law, since the days of Moses. But from the time of Ezra (5th century BC; following the exile in Babylon which the prophets saw as a direct result of the nation's disobedience to the law) greater emphasis had been placed on the study of the law, until the Jews had become 'the people of the book'. This intensive study had resulted in an increasing body of 'traditions', which came to be regarded as no less binding than the law itself. *Scribes*, professional students and exponents of the law and traditions, were needed to prescribe exact regulations for every occasion. There were, for example, 39 types of action prohibited on the sabbath: reaping and threshing were forbidden – this included plucking ears of corn and rubbing the grain out in the hands (Luke 6:1-2); a 'sabbath day's journey' (Acts 1:12; about two-thirds of a mile) was the maximum travel permitted. Sadly, in their meticulous care over details of tradition the scribes sometimes forgot the more fundamental concerns of the law itself (Mark 7:1-13; 3:4-5; Matthew 23:23).

Parties, sects, and movements in Judaism

The Pharisees. These were the religious purists – a party which grew from the 2nd century 'Hasidim' (God's loyal ones) and concentrated on control of religious, rather than political, affairs. Their supreme concern and delight was to keep the law (including, of course, the traditions) in every exact detail. (Most scribes belonged to the Pharisee party.) Judged by this standard, they were model Jews (Philippians 3:5-6). To this end, they kept themselves as far as possible apart from other men: they could not eat with a non-Pharisee in case the food had not been tithed (i.e. one tenth given to God).

Inevitably, perhaps, this policy of separation led to disdain for all lesser mortals, a 'holier-than-thou' attitude which has made their name a term of reproach today. This arrogance, combined with a dry legalism which put exact ritual observance before love and mercy, led them into conflict with Jesus. He did not dispute their orthodoxy, but the proud and unloving way in which they upheld it. The influence of the Pharisees was out of all proportion to their numbers, which were seldom large. It was the Pharisees who laid down the lines along which Judaism developed after the destruction of Jerusalem in AD 70. They ensured a continued emphasis on individual piety and strict ethical standards, as well as their better-known rigid legalism. They were respected, if not loved, by other Jews.

The Sadducees. The Sadducees were the other main party at the time of Jesus, though they were already declining in influence. They were drawn largely from the rich landowning class who in earlier days, by shrewd manipulation of political advantage, had secured a dominant position. They still controlled a roughly equal proportion of the seats in the Sanhedrin (the Jewish supreme council) with the Pharisees (Acts 23:6-10). Many of the chief priests were Sadducees, or worked closely with them. Their religious position was conservative, to the extent of refusing to accept any revelation beyond the Five Books of Moses (Genesis to Deuteronomy). They thus rejected more recent religious ideas, such as the belief in immortality, resurrection, angels and demons, which were fostered by the Pharisees (Mark 12:18; Acts 23:8). As an aristocratic minority, they enjoyed little popular support.

The Essenes. This rather shadowy 'party' has come dramatically to light with the discovery of the Dead Sea Scrolls since 1947. These scrolls are from the library of the *Qumran Community*, a monastic sect living in isolation in the barren desert near the shores of the Dead Sea. Although this sect cannot firmly be identified as Essenes, it was certainly very similar. The sect was founded by the otherwise unknown 'Teacher of Righteousness', probably about 165 BC, and survived until AD 68, when it was destroyed in the Jewish revolt. They regarded themselves as the true people of God, and all others, including the Jewish leaders at Jerusalem, as his enemies. They were the 'Sons of light', and they lived for the day when in the final battle against the 'Sons of Darkness' they would be given the victory and dominion which was their due.

Meanwhile they kept themselves to themselves, occupied in the diligent study of the scriptures, bound by a strict monastic discipline, loving one another and hating all those outside. They produced elaborate biblical commentaries, applying every phrase of the Old Testament passages to their own situation and expectations. They looked forward to the coming of two Messiahs, of Aaron (priestly) and of Israel (royal) – or possibly one Messiah combining both roles. The importance of the Qumran documents is not so much for the sect in itself, but that they give evidence of an ascetic, apocalyptic strain in Judaism, far removed from the Jerusalem establishment, which may well have been much more widespread than this single isolated group. If before 1947 we were tempted to think of Pharisees and Sadducees as constituting 'the Jews', we must now recognize that the situation was not so simple.

The Zealots. While Pharisees and Sadducees tried to make the best of Roman rule, and the men of Qumran dreamed of the mighty intervention of God to deliver them, many Jews sought salvation more actively. The Zealots, as they later came to be called, were the freedom fighters, the revolutionaries of the Jewish people. It was they who eventually sparked off the great rebellion which led to the Roman destruction of Jerusalem in AD 70. By the time of Jesus abortive revolts had already occurred (Acts 5:36-37; and possibly Barabbas), and the people were ripe for revolutionary propaganda. Intensely patriotic, the Zealots founded their appeal on the belief that subjection to Rome was treason to God, the true King of Israel. At least one of the apostles was a former Zealot.

The apocalyptic movement. In this atmosphere the type of literature known as the 'apocalypse' (revelation) flourished. Many apocalypses were written in Palestine from the 2nd century BC onwards. They are marked by a strong dualism: good and evil, God and Satan, light and darkness, are irreconcilably opposed and on a collision course. The present world-order is under the control of the forces of evil, but the final battle is about to be fought, and then the tables will be turned. God will crush all opposition, destroy all evil for ever, and create a new blessed order, in which his faithful people will be released from their oppression and reign in glory.

This message is conveyed in often extraordinary visions, with symbolic numbers, and a careful calculation of dates and times, usually in cryptic form. It is a message of hope for a people near despair, a triumphant appeal to the sovereignty of the one true God, the God of Israel. The New Testament book of Revelation is in many ways a typical apocalypse (though written from a Christian standpoint), except that its author uses his own name, whereas Jewish apocalyptists attributed their visions to such famous Old Testament figures as Enoch, Moses, Elijah, or Ezra. Another important difference is that Jewish apocalyptists wrote past history as if it were prophecy, whereas Revelation concentrates on the future.

Messianic hopes. The extravagant visions of the apocalypses were only one among the many hopes currently cherished by the Jews. Many messianic figures from the Old Testament had taken firm root in popular expectation: the prophet like Moses (Deuteronomy 18:15-19); the returning Elijah (Malachi 4:5-6); but above all the Son of David, a great king and warrior, whose mission it would be to bring victory, peace, and glory to Israel. Some saw a place for the Gentiles in this hope, others were exclusively nationalistic. Some thought of spiritual restoration, most of victory over the Romans. To utter the word 'Messiah' (Greek, 'Christ') would inevitably stir up hopes of political independence, so it is no wonder that Jesus was cautious in letting others call him 'Christ'. He came to a people who, if they were not agreed quite *what* they were hoping for, were united in eagerly 'looking for the consolation of Israel' (Luke 2:25). But none expected it to come by way of a cross.

'The Dispersion'. So far we have thought only of the Jews in Palestine. But the Christian church soon spread outside Palestine, and there, too, its first contacts were with Jews. At least since the exile in the 6th century BC Jews had begun to scatter around the world of the Middle East and the eastern Mediterranean, so that by the 1st century AD there were a million Jews in Egypt alone. In Alexandria Jews made up a considerable part of the population, and in most of the main cities a Jewish colony, with its own synagogue (or at least a place for prayer, Acts 16:13), was to be found. These are the Jews of the Dispersion (Greek, *Diaspora*), sometimes referred to, a little inaccurately, as the Hellenistic Jews.

'Hellenism', the wave of Greek culture and ideas which had rolled over the Mediterranean world and far beyond with the conquests of Alexander the Great, was still the dominant strand in the culture of the Roman Empire, and these dispersed Jews, away from the more conservative atmosphere of Palestine, adapted more readily to the Greek way of life. Not that they abandoned their distinctive religion and culture, and ceased to be Jews; but they were more willing to learn from and enter into dialogue with Greek ideas. Many of the later Jewish writings, particularly those from Alexandria (e.g. the Wisdom of Solomon, or the writings of Philo) are deeply influenced by Greek philosophy. Apollos, the learned Jew from Alexandria (Acts 18:24), no doubt belonged to this school, before his gradual conversion to Christ.

Proselytes. The Jews are often unjustly charged with a rigid exclusivism. In fact, particularly among the Dispersion, they recognized their mission to the Gentiles, and there was a sincere attempt to win converts. To accept the Jewish religion was no light matter for a Gentile. He must accept circumcision and baptism, and agree to keep the whole law of Moses, including such ritual prescriptions as the sabbath and the laws about unclean food. He must in fact renounce his own nationality. There were a considerable number who took this drastic step, and it is to them that the term 'proselyte' applies.

Many more were attracted by the monotheistic faith and the strict morality of Judaism in contrast with the decadent polytheism of Rome. They were prepared to identify themselves with the faith and ideals of the Jews, but stopped short of the proselyte's full commitment. These fellow-travellers, many of them rich and influential officials, are known in the New Testament as 'those who fear God' or 'the devout' (Acts 13:26, 43, 50; 17:4).

The Samaritans. The Samaritans were descendants of the surviving Israelites of the northern kingdom who intermarried with the newly imported alien population after the fall of Samaria in 722 BC. They never effectively made common cause with Judah, and in the time of Nehemiah the rift was clearly irreparable. The building of the Samaritan temple on Mt Gerizim, overlooking Shechem (John 4:20), set the seal on the Jewish rejection of this heretical sect. It was the Jewish king Hyrcanus who destroyed the Samaritan temple in 128 BC. Yet the Samaritans worshipped God, as the Jews did. Their authority was the Five Books of Moses (Genesis to Deuteronomy; but not the rest of the Old Testament), hardly altered from the Jewish version. Like many of the Jews, they awaited the coming of a prophet like Moses. Jewish hatred and disdain for the Samaritans sprang more from historical and racial considerations than from any fundamental difference of religion.

GREEK AND ROMAN RELIGION

The old classical religion of the Greeks, with its pantheon of gods and goddesses who loved, quarrelled and fought like men and women, had become effectively fused with the similar polytheism of Rome. It was preserved and officially fostered as part of Greek and Roman culture. Most Greeks and Romans would still give a formal assent to the old beliefs, and take part in the rituals, but the heart had gone out of them.

Further east in the Empire these gods were associated with local deities, sometimes producing absurd results, such as the identification of the earthy fertility-goddess of Ephesus with the severely chaste Artemis of the Greeks (Roman Diana; Acts 19:24ff.). The Lycaonian worship of Zeus and Hermes (Roman Jupiter and Mercury; Acts 14:11ff.) was probably a similar dignifying of a local cult with the classical Greek names.

It was from the East that new religious ideas came. One such was the worship of the emperor. This was not officially encouraged by the Roman emperors until Domitian (AD 81-96) insisted on being addressed as 'Lord and God'. But it was freely practised in the East by their grateful (or flattering) subjects throughout the New Testament period. Even before the birth of Christ, Herod the Great had renamed the city of Samaria 'Sebaste', in honour of Augustus (Greek, *Sebastos*, 'The one to be worshipped'), and built in it a temple of Augustus.

Those who wanted a more personal and emotional faith gravitated to the mystery religions. The Greek mysteries – those of Eleusis, or the Orphic cult – had long been known in the West, but the spread of the Empire brought to light similar cults from Egypt (Isis and Osiris/Serapis), Persia (Mithras), and elsewhere in the East. Although these religions differed in detail, they shared the element of personal commitment by initiation into what amounted to a secret society, whose rites were never divulged to an outsider. The rites often centred on a mythology of the death and resurrection of the god (Persephone, Orpheus, Osiris, and the rest), which was re-enacted in a drama in which all participated. They inspired a spirit of warm, personal devotion, far removed from the cold intellectualism of the official state religion.

Also from the East came the fascination of astrology (still very much with us today), divination, magic, demon-worship, and other occult practices, all trying to bring a reality and a practical efficacy into religion.

About the time the New Testament letters were being written there began to develop a number of sects which later (in the 2nd century) came under the general heading of 'Gnosticism'. They varied considerably in detail, but shared the basic belief that 'matter' was evil and spirit was good. It followed that God could not have created the world out of matter, nor could his Son have become incarnate in it. So they envisaged a whole range of subordinate beings between God and the world. Men share in the evil of the material world, but they also (or some of them) contain a divine spark which can be set free and thus redeemed. In order to be redeemed men need to have knowledge (Greek *gnosis*) of their heavenly origin. These views were expressed in fantastic myths and made known to initiates in sects like those of the mystery religions.

The world was, as Paul put it, '*very* religious' (Acts 17:22). Men wanted a faith worth following, not an empty mythology. It was a world searching for God, eagerly trying every avenue which might lead to a real, practical, satisfying religion.

HEROD'S TEMPLE

An artist's drawing, from a reconstruction at the Bible Museum, Amsterdam; style and decoration are guessed.

1 Porticos
2 Court of the Gentiles
3 'Wall of Partition' (no non-Jew might go beyond this point)
4 Beautiful Gate
5 Court of the women
6 Court of Israel
7 Court of the priests
8 Altar
9 Bronze laver
10 The Holy Place (and Holy of Holies)

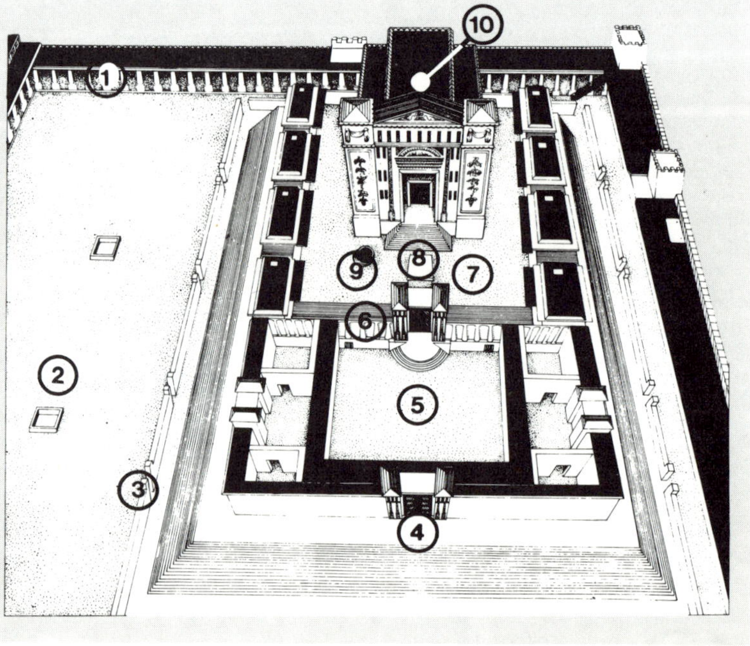

New Testament 1.2

MARK

Matthew is formal and stately. Mark is bustling with life; full of action. Matthew collects Jesus' sayings. Mark concentrates on the marvellous things Jesus did, and the places he went to.

This is the shortest of the Gospels, and probably the first to be written (AD 65-70 or even earlier). There is a strong early tradition that John Mark wrote it in Rome, setting down Jesus' story as he had heard it direct from the apostle Peter. This would certainly account for the Gospel's extraordinary vividness. And Mark often explains Jewish customs, so he obviously had non-Jewish readers in mind.

He tells the story roughly in the order things happened – moving swiftly through from Jesus' baptism to the critical events of the cross and resurrection. Within this framework the material tends to be grouped by subject. Only four paragraphs in these 16 chapters are unique to Mark. All the rest appears again in either Matthew or Luke, or both. Yet to lose Mark would be to lose something beyond price. In Mark we see Jesus in action. And as we watch, the things he does convince us that he is the Son of God himself.

The writer. The name 'John Mark' occurs often in Acts and the epistles ('John' the Jewish name, 'Mark' the Latin). His mother had a house in Jerusalem where the early church met (Acts 12:12). And he was cousin to Paul's companion, Barnabas. Mark blotted his copybook with Paul by going home half-way through the first missionary tour. But Barnabas gave him a second chance, and he later won the love and respect of Paul and of Peter. He was a real comfort to Paul in prison (Colossians 4). And Peter, whose companion he became, loved him as his own son (1 Peter 5:13).

1:1-13 THE GOOD NEWS OF JESUS

1:1-8 John the Baptist

See also Matthew 3:1-12; Luke 3:2-22, and map. Mark passes over Jesus' birth. For him the good news begins with John, the voice Isaiah had predicted, crying out from the desert, urging the nation to make ready for God's coming. The rest of his account will show that Jesus is the Messiah – the one whose coming John announced – and Son of God.

Verses 2-3: Mark, like Matthew, combines Old Testament references: Exodus 23:20; Malachi 3:1; Isaiah 40:3.

Verse 8: water is a symbol. It can only clean the outside. The Holy Spirit can clean heart and mind and will.

The prophet from the desert: the 'wilderness' or desert-country around Jericho and south of Jerusalem is rough and uninviting. Scarcely anything grows: it is empty of human habitation, occupied only by wild animals. No doubt the very loneliness of the place, and the freedom from distraction, made it the ideal training-ground for John. Paul, too, was prepared for his mission during a time in the desert. There seems to be something in the stark simplicity of desert life which puts men – some men at least – in close touch with God. In the harsh sunlight there is only black or white, no shades of grey. It afforded John no other luxuries – only the simplest of food and rough clothing. His camel-hair tunic and leather belt may have been worn in conscious imitation of Elijah (see 2 Kings 1:8 and the prophecy in Malachi 4:5). He was certainly recognized instantly as a prophet. He not only looked the part, he possessed the prophet's cast-iron assurance that he had a God-given message to proclaim. The people flocked from far and wide to hear him, probably gathering beside the Jordan near Jericho, close to the place where Joshua had crossed into the promised land so many centuries before.

1:9-13 Jesus' baptism and temptation

See on Matthew 3 - 4; Luke 3:21;4:1-13. Mark gives only a brief résumé.

1:14 - 9:50 JESUS IN GALILEE

Galilee. The Roman province, under Herod's jurisdiction, lay to the west of the Sea of Galilee. We tend to think of it as a remote country district. But in Christ's day the region was prosperous and densely populated, criss-crossed by Roman military roads and ancient trade routes – north, south, east and west. The fresh-water Sea of Galilee – 13 miles long, 7 miles wide, sunk in the deep trough of the Jordan rift valley over 600 feet below sea-level – is the focal point in Jesus' travels. It divided Herod's territory from that of his half-brother Philip, to the east. Most of the apostles came from the towns around the lake-shore which enjoyed a sub-tropical climate. Capernaum was Jesus' base. Tiberias, 10 miles away, was a spa town famous for its hot baths. Many of the sick people Jesus healed must have come to the area for the mineral waters at Tiberias. On the hill behind the town was Herod's splendid summer palace. The lake is ringed round with hills – brown and barren on the east; in those days green, fertile, wooded on the west. Over the tops, and funnelling down through them, races the wind that can whip the lake into a sudden fury of storm. North, the snow-capped summit of Mt Hermon dominates the skyline – the mount of the transfiguration. In Jesus' day palms, olives, figs and vines grew on the hillsides round the lake. And the little towns and villages on its western shore were thriving centres of industry – fish pickled for export; boat-building; dyeworks; potteries. John the Baptist lived an ascetic life in the desert. By contrast, Jesus chose to be in the thick of things, in Galilee, one of the busiest, most cosmopolitan regions of Palestine.

At Capernaum the local Roman centurion contributed to the building of the synagogue. The ruins of the Capernaum synagogue shown here probably date from the next century, but they show a combination of Roman and Jewish symbols.

1:14-20 Jesus calls his first disciples

John's voice is silenced. Jesus travels north again, and begins his own public proclamation of God's good news. By the Sea of Galilee he calls his first disciples – all of them fishermen. (John 1:35-42 fills in the background.)

Peter and Andrew probably used a cast net rather like this one. They also fished from their boats, using drag nets.

1:21-45 Jesus begins to teach and heal

From now on Capernaum is Jesus' headquarters. His teaching in the synagogue and his handling of the possessed man both convey an extraordinary *authority.*

Again and again, as in the case of the leper here, Mark stresses Jesus' insistence on *secrecy.* The people were expecting the Messiah to be a political leader. News of Jesus' amazing powers, which marked him out as the Messiah, could easily have sparked off a rising against the Roman occupation. It was imperative the miracles should be accompanied by teaching to explain the kind of 'kingdom' Jesus had come to inaugurate, and the Messiah's real mission.

Verse 32: at sunset the sabbath was

over, and restrictions on movement no longer applied.

Verse 44: see Leviticus 14:1-32. In the Bible, the term 'leprosy' covers a variety of skin diseases.

2:1-12 The paralytic walks

It is easy enough simply to tell a man his sins are forgiven. But by healing him Jesus visibly demonstrates his power in both physical and spiritual realms. When he says the word, something really happens.

Verse 4: the house would have an outside staircase leading to a flat roof, giving extra living-space. The roof would be made of tiles or lath and plaster – not difficult to break through.

Verse 11: ordinary people slept on the floor on a mat or bedding which could be rolled up in the daytime.

2:13-22 Levi (Matthew) becomes a disciple; the question of fasting

See on Matthew 9:9-17; Luke 5:27-39.

Scribes, Pharisees (16): see article 'The Religious Background of the New Testament'.

2:23 - 3:6 The purpose of the sabbath; opposition

See also Matthew 12:1-14; Luke 6:1-11. Jewish interpretation of the fourth commandment (Exodus 20:8-11; 34:21) had hedged it about with so many petty rules and restrictions that its primary purpose was lost. The day of rest was intended for man's physical and spiritual good, not to deny him food and help. It is a day for doing good – and not only in an emergency.

Verses 25-26: see 1 Samuel 21:1-6. The loaves David took were those the priests placed each week on the altar.

Herodians (6): supporters of Herod Antipas. They collaborated with the Romans, and were therefore normally abhorrent to the scrupulous Pharisees.

3:7-19 The Twelve

Crowds flock to Jesus from the south (Judea, Jerusalem, Idumaea); from the east across the Jordan; and from Tyre and Sidon, the coastal towns in the north-west.

Jesus chose an inner circle of 12 disciples who became founder-members of the new kingdom – the counterparts of Jacob's 12 sons, who gave their names to the tribes of Israel. Three – Peter, James and John – were specially close to him. Four of the Twelve, all from Galilee, were partners in a fishing business (Peter and his brother Andrew; James and his brother John). One (Matthew/Levi, who may have been the brother of James son of Alphaeus) was a tax collector, serving the Romans. Simon, at the other end of the scale, belonged to an extremist guerilla group (the Zealots) working to overthrow the occupation. We know little of the others. The full list also appears in Matthew 10:2-4 and Luke 6:12-16. The 'Thaddaeus' of Matthew and Mark seems to be the same as 'Judas son of James' (Luke, Acts 1:13). Bartholomew is often identified with the Nathanael of John 1. They were certainly a very mixed bunch of men.

Verse 12: see on 1:21-45.

3:20-35 Suspicion and accusation

See on Matthew 12:15-37 and 49.

4:1-34 Jesus teaches in parables

See on Matthew 13:1-52.

Verses 1-25: the seed and the soils.

Verses 26-29: the wheat and the weeds.

Verses 30-32: the mustard-seed.

Verse 12: in Jewish idiom, result is often expressed as if it were intention. This verse refers to the *consequence* not the *purpose* of Christ's teaching. It is clear from verses 22-23 that the reason for wrapping up the meaning is to encourage the listener to search it out for himself.

4:35-41 Jesus calms the great storm

Sudden storms sometimes whip the Sea of Galilee into fury. Jesus has power to control the elements.

5:1-20 Across the lake; the man possessed by demons

See also Matthew 8:28-34; Luke 8:26-39. The man is a pitiful sight – a fragmented personality at the mercy of a hundred conflicting impulses; totally incapable of a normal life. Is any greater contrast imaginable than the description of 2-5 and verse 15? Jesus had power not only over nature but also over human nature; and not only over human nature but over the spiritual forces of evil.

Country of the Gerasenes (1): the general area south-east of the lake. At only one point on the eastern bank is there a steep slope (13).

Decapolis (20): ten free Greek cities – see map.

5:21-43 Jairus' daughter restored to life; the woman with the haemorrhage

See also Matthew 9:18-26; Luke 8:40-56.

The woman tries not to advertise her presence, because the haemorrhage makes her polluted and untouchable to her fellow Jews. There is no magic about Jesus' clothes. He knows the difference between the casual contact of the crowd and someone reaching out in need. The incident must have encouraged Jairus. The fact that he came to Jesus shows that not all religious leaders were against him.

Verse 39: this was not just a coma – the child really was dead. Everyone knew it (40). Jesus' words describe death as God sees it – a sleep from which we wake to a new day.

6:1-13 In and around Nazareth; the Twelve sent out

Verses 1-6: in Jesus' home town it is not a case of 'local boy makes good' but 'who does this jumped-up carpenter think he is?' It was not in line with Jesus' purpose to make a display of his powers in order to convince sceptics (see Matthew 4:6-7).

Verses 7-13: see on Matthew 9:35 10:42.

Verse 3: see on Matthew 12:49. James later became the leader of the church in Jerusalem (Acts 15:13). Judas wrote the Epistle of Jude.

6:14-29 Herod and John the Baptist

Guilt and superstition make Herod think Jesus is John come to life again. Herod had divorced his own wife to marry Herodias, wife of his half-brother Philip. John had denounced this as incest (Leviticus 18:16; 20:21), and been imprisoned for his pains. According to Josephus his prison was the fortress of Machaerus in the far south, east of the Dead Sea. But Herodias wanted to still the preacher's tongue permanently.

Five loaves and two small fish, given to Jesus, fed 5,000 people. These fish from Lake Galilee are known as St Peter's fish, as their large mouths, in which they carry their eggs, could hold a coin (see Matthew 17:27).

6:30-44 5,000 miraculously fed

See also Matthew 14:13-21; Luke 9:10b-17; John 6:5-14. John's death casts a shadow. Jesus is desperately tired and hard-pressed. Yet instead of being annoyed or irritable with the pursuing crowds, his heart goes out to them.

Verse 37: needless to say they did not have this kind of money: the denarius was a working man's wage for the day – this would be over six months' wages.

6:45-56 Jesus walks on the lake

It was some time between 3 a.m. and 6 a.m. Again it is the disciples' need that calls out Jesus' love. And again he demonstrates his supreme power over creation: he is Lord of wind and water.

Fringe (56): the blue-tasselled border of his cloak.

7:1-23 The Pharisees and their traditions

See on Matthew 15:1-20. Mark adds an explanatory note for non-Jewish readers (3-4). The Pharisees were concerned not with hygiene but with religious 'cleanness.' Man's real problem is not dirty hands but a polluted heart, which no amount of washing can clean. Jesus exposes their wrong thinking.

7:24-37 The Greek woman's daughter; the deaf mute

Verses 24-30: see on Matthew 15:21-28.

Verses 31-37: the man's speech defect, as so often, was the result of his deafness. Saliva was popularly thought to have healing power.

8:1-21 4,000 fed; the demand for a sign; the 'yeast' of the Pharisees

Verses 1-9; see on Matthew 15:29-39. Dalmanutha is not known.

Verses 11-21: see on Matthew 16:1-12. The disciples lack spiritual discernment. They are so taken up with the bread-supply that they cannot see that Jesus is warning them against the ever-present danger of religious hypocrisy (see Luke 12:1) and materialism (the prime concern of the pro-Herod faction).

8:22-26 A blind man regains his sight

Jesus once again guards against publicity – see on 1:21-45.

8:27 - 9:1 'Who do men say I am?'; Jesus predicts his death

See on Matthew 16:13-28. Here and elsewhere Mark records in full incidents which show Peter's failings, but plays down the credit side – understandable if the information came from Peter himself. This episode is a pivotal point in the story. From now on, Jesus stresses the suffering which lies ahead.

Caesarea Philippi (27): 25 miles north of the Sea of Galilee.

9:1: see on Matthew 10:23.

JESUS IN GALILEE AND THE NORTH

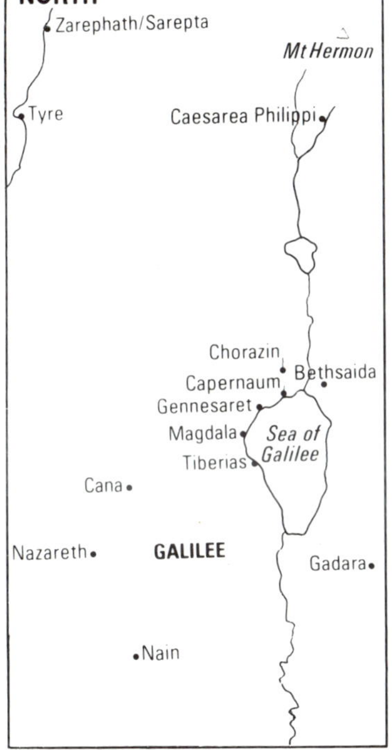

9:2-13 The disciples see Jesus transfigured

See also Matthew 17:1-13; Luke 9:28-36. The apostles are sure now that Jesus is the Messiah. This special glimpse of his glory, given to the inner three, must have been tremendously reassuring through all that lay ahead. Moses (Israel's great law-giver) and Elijah (the first great prophet) converse with Jesus about his coming death (Luke 9:31).

Verse 2: the mountain is believed to be 9,000 foot Mt Hermon as it is only 12 miles north-east of Caesarea Philippi. The tradition that it was Mt Tabor does not fit the geography so well. Peter wants to prolong the present moment. Perhaps Moses and Elijah will stay if they make shelters for them, like the tent (tabernacle) where God was present in the old days, before the temple was built. The glory of all he saw that day imprinted itself indelibly on Peter's memory (2 Peter 1:16-18).

Verse 13: 'Elijah', i.e. John the Baptist (see Matthew 17:13). Malachi (4:5) had predicted a reappearance of Elijah to announce the day of God's coming.

9:14-29 The epileptic boy

See also Matthew 17:14-19; Luke 9:37-42. The disciples fail because of their lack of faith (see Matthew 17:19-20). Yet Jesus will accept even a grain of faith in him (24). He does not wait to heal the child until the father's faith is greater.

9:30-50 Status and Christian responsibility

See on Matthew 18. No one who is preoccupied with selfish ambition can become a 'great' Christian. It has to be other people first, self last. Today we lay great stress on self-fulfilment and the full development of personality. Jesus puts this in perspective. It is better deliberately to limit that fulfilment, to handicap ourselves in this life (44-45) than miss God's kingdom altogether.

Verses 43-48: Jesus draws his terrible picture of hell from Jerusalem's permanently smouldering refuse-tip in the valley of Hinnom (Gehenna), and the dead bodies gradually eaten away by worms.

Verse 49: 'Salted with fire' – i.e. purified in the 'refinery' of suffering.

10 ON THE WAY TO JERUSALEM

10:1-12 Divorce

See on Matthew 19:1-15.

10:13-16 Jesus blesses the children

To enter God's kingdom we must all become, not childish, but childlike – receiving him with humble, loving trust (15).

10:17-31 The positive disadvantage of wealth

See on Matthew 19:16-30; Luke 18:18-30. This incident does not imply that all Christ's followers must become penniless. He is speaking to one man, not to all, and in this case the man's possessions kept him from becoming a disciple. Anything that takes first place – God's place – in our lives must go. So Jesus tells him, 'Go, sell' *and* 'Come, follow me'.

10:32-45 Jesus again predicts his death; the disciples bicker over their future status

See on Matthew 20:17-34.

10:46-52 Blind Bartimaeus

See also Matthew 20:29-34 (where there are two men); Luke 18:35-43. Only Mark tells us the beggar's name. As he afterwards joined the company of Jesus' followers, Peter presumably came to know him.

11 - 13 JESUS IN JERUSALEM

11:1-11 The triumphant entry

See introduction to Matthew 21; and see on Luke 19:28-44.

11:12-26 The fig-tree; the purging of the temple

See on Matthew 21:18-22 and 12-17.

11:27 - 12:12 The religious leaders question Jesus' authority; the parable of the vineyard

See on Matthew 21:23-46.

12:13-44 Test question; Jesus in the temple

See also Matthew 22:15-46; Luke 20:19 - 21:4. Luke 20:19-20 gives the background to these questions.

Verses 13-17: there was little love lost between the strictly religious Pharisees and the opportunist Herodians. But they join forces to try to trap Jesus into a treasonable statement.

Verses 18-27: the materialist Sadducees try to ridicule the idea of resurrection with an absurd case of Levirate marriage (see Ruth). But the laugh is on them, because there *is* a resurrection – to a life where there is no sexual union or procreation because there is no death.

Verses 28-34: the third question is a genuine one. With 613 commandments to choose from, Jesus replies in the words of Israel's creed (the Shema; Deuteronomy 6:4-5) and Leviticus 19:18. If the Pharisees hoped for an unorthodox reply (Matthew 22:34-35) they were disappointed. The astonishing wisdom of Jesus silences his opponents – but *he* has not finished with *them* (35-40).

In strong contrast to the self-advertisement of the men of religion comes the little incident in verses 41-44. What counts with God is not the size of the cheque, but the amount of love and self-sacrifice it represents.

13 Judgement on Jerusalem: Jesus speaks about his return

See on Matthew 24. See also Luke 21 and 17:22ff.

14 - 16 JESUS' DEATH AND RESURRECTION

14:1-11 The plot against his life; the costly flask of perfume; betrayal

See also Matthew 26:6-13; John 12:1-8. Jesus' public ministry is at an end. As the Passover festival approaches (see on Matthew 26) events move swiftly to a climax. Against a dark backcloth of hatred and treachery shines the story of one woman's love for the Lord (3-9). Perhaps intuitively sensing the tragedy ahead, Mary (see John 12:3) pours out the precious perfumed oil in a lavish, extravagant gesture of affection. (A working man earned one denarius a day. This luxury import was worth nearly a year's wages.) John (12:1-8) places the event some days earlier and tells us the unpleasant truth about Judas' embezzlement of the funds. In Luke 7:36-50 the occasion is similar, but the woman concerned different.

14:12-25 The Last Supper

See on Matthew 26:14-29.

14:26-52 Gethsemane; Jesus is arrested

See on Matthew 26:30-56. There seems little point in the mention of the young man (51-62) unless this is Mark himself.

14:53 - 15:15 The Jewish trial; Peter denies Jesus; the Roman trial

See on Luke 22:54-71.

The trials

The Jewish court which tried Jesus was the Sanhedrin, the supreme court at Jerusalem. Its 71 councillors came from influential families – elders, lawyers, Pharisees and Sadducees. The high priest for the year presided. The Sanhedrin had wide powers in civil and religious matters in Judea, but under Roman rule was not empowered to carry out the death sentence. So Jesus had also to appear before the Roman governor on a charge which would merit the death sentence under Roman law. Blasphemy was sufficient for the Jews. To be sure Pilate would ratify the sentence, the safest charge was treason. The Jewish trial was far from regular. It was held at night. There were no defence witnesses. The witnesses for the prosecution could not agree. And the death sentence, which should not have been pronounced till the day following the trial (the Jewish day ran from sunset to sunset), was immediate.

The sequence of events

1. The audience with Annas, father-

PILATE

Harold Rowdon

In 1961 a stone slab was discovered at Caesarea bearing the name Pontius Pilatus. This is one of the few pieces of evidence outside the Bible for the life and work of this unhappy man. Tacitus, the Roman writer, does refer to the execution of Jesus by Pilate, and two Jewish writers, Josephus and Philo, relate several incidents. Apart from this, we have only the biblical evidence. In addition to the accounts given by the writers of the Gospels, there are brief references to him in Acts 3:13; 4:27; 13:28; 1 Timothy 6:13.

Pilate was evidently a middle-class Roman with military and administrative experience who in AD 26 was appointed to the office of procurator of Judea. As procurator (or governor) he possessed very wide powers, especially in military and financial matters. He appointed the high priest and controlled the temple funds.

Philo describes Pilate as a harsh, spiteful and brutal man. According to Josephus, in one of his historical works, Pilate antagonized the Jews almost as soon as he was appointed. He allowed the Roman troops to bring their regimental standards into Jerusalem. These contained representations of the emperor, and the Jews were furious because they felt that the holy city had been desecrated by these idolatrous symbols. Pilate bowed to the storm and ordered the removal of the standards.

On another occasion, according to Philo, the Jews took violent objection to some golden shields which Pilate had dedicated in his residence in Jerusalem. This time Pilate refused to remove them, but the Jews appealed to the Emperor Tiberius, who ordered them to be removed to Caesarea, Pilate's headquarters.

Josephus records an incident arising from Pilate's plan to use money from the temple treasury to finance the building of an aqueduct to bring water from a spring 25 miles away into Jerusalem. Mass protests were met by force, and many Jews died. This may be the incident referred to in Luke 13:1.

Each of the Gospels records the trial of Jesus before Pilate (Matthew 27:1-26; Mark 15:1-15; Luke 23:1-25; John 18:28 - 19:16). Mark records the basic story. Luke adds the sending of Jesus to Herod (23:6-12) and Pilate's triple assertion that Jesus was innocent (23:4, 14, 22). Matthews relates the dream and message of Pilate's wife (27:19), how Pilate disclaimed responsibility for Jesus' death (27:24f.), and his setting a guard on the tomb (27:62-66). John, who had been present at the trial, supplies even fuller details.

Pilate's final blunder was to seize a number of Samaritans who had assembled on Mt Gerizim as a result of a rumour that sacred vessels from the tabernacle were hidden there. Some of the ringleaders were executed. In response to a Samaritan protest, Vitellius, governor of Syria and Pilate's superior, ordered the ham-fisted procurator to answer to the emperor for his handling of the affair. The reigning emperor, Tiberius, died before Pilate reached Rome. We do not know the outcome of the affair, but Eusebius, the 4th-century Christian historian, recorded a report that Pilate had committed suicide.

Several unreliable traditions regarding Pilate's body are in existence. A number of *Acts of Pilate*, alleged records of Pilate's rule, appeared during the early Christian centuries. They are forgeries, intended to discredit Christianity.

in-law of high priest Caiaphas (John 18:12-14).
2. The late-night session at Caiaphas' house before the Sanhedrin (Matthew 26:57-68; Mark 15:53-65; Luke 22:54-65; John 18:24).
3. The early morning ratification of the sentence by the Sanhedrin (Matthew 27:1; Mark 15:1; Luke 22:66-71).
4. Jesus before Pilate (Matthew 27:2, 11-14; Mark 15:2-5; Luke 23:1-5; John 18:28-38).
5. Since Jesus is a Galilean, Pilate refers him to Herod (Luke 23:6-12).
6. Jesus before Pilate again. He is scourged, sentenced and handed over to the soldiers (Matthew 27:15-26; Mark 15:6-15; Luke 23:13-25; John 18:29 - 19:16).

15:16-41 Mockery and crucifixion

Jesus is now utterly alone. The Gospel writers play down the physical horror of the six hours (9 a.m.-3 p.m.) on the cross when Jesus touched a depth of suffering in body, mind and spirit beyond the stretch of our imagination. But the whole New Testament declares that his suffering was 'for us'. By his death he paid in full the penalty for our sin. He saved us from the death sentence, making possible the free gift of eternal life.

Seven times in those six hours (the last three in darkness) those who watched heard him speak.

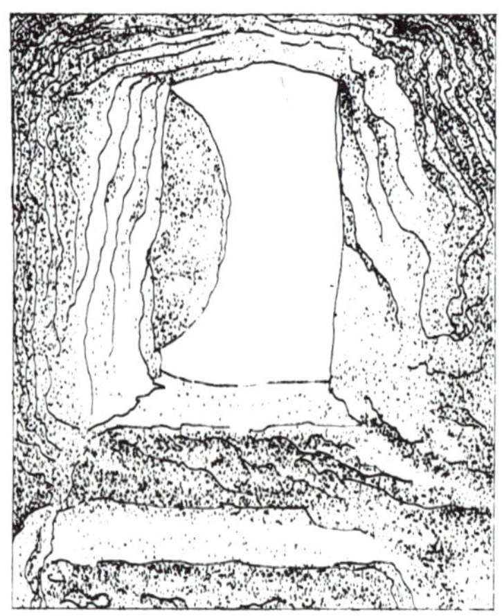

A first-century rock-cut tomb at Nazareth, seen from the inside, with the entrance stone rolled partway back.

The words from the cross

1. *'Father, forgive them; for they know not what they do'* (Luke 23:24) – a prayer for the Jewish people and the Roman soldiers.

2. *'Truly, I say to you, today you will be with me in Paradise'* (Luke 23:43) – his word to the repentant thief, crucified beside him.

3. *'Woman, behold your son!' 'Behold your mother!'* (John 19:26-27) – commending his mother to John's care.

4. *'My God, my God, why hast thou forsaken me?'* (Matthew 27:46; Mark 15:34) – expressing in the words of Psalm 22:1 the agony of separation from God as the full weight of human sin pressed upon him.

5. *'I thirst'* (John 19:28).

6. *'It is finished'* (John 19:30).

7. *'Father, into thy hands I commit my spirit!'* (Luke 23:46).

Verse 21: Cyrene in north Africa had a strong Jewish colony. Alexander and Rufus evidently became Christians. This may be the same Rufus as the one mentioned in Romans 16:13.
Salome (40): Zebedee's wife; mother of James and John (Matthew 27:56).

15:42-47 Burial

Death by crucifixion was long drawn out. It often took two days or more. But Jesus was dead in six hours. Joseph saves him from the final indignity of a mass grave.
Day of preparation (42): i.e. the day before the sabbath, which began at 6 p.m.

16 The resurrection

See on Luke 24. For some unknown reason – most probably damage to very early copies of the Gospel – the best manuscripts we have of Mark end abruptly at 16:8. Verses 9-20 represent early attempts to round the Gospel off more satisfactorily.

New Testament 1.3

LUKE

Luke gives us the fullest life-story of Jesus we possess. The Gospel is part one of a two-part history of Christian beginnings – Luke/Acts. Both parts are dedicated to the same man, the Roman Theophilus, and both are written with the same purpose. The Gospel is carefully compiled from reliable, first-hand sources. Luke is not simply a biographer. His overriding concern is to get at the truth of what happened in Palestine in the critical years of Jesus' life-time. His Gospel shows Jesus as the Saviour of all men; his coming, a world-event. He lets us see Jesus the Man. And his selection of stories reflects his own warm interest in people, especially the sick and helpless, the poor, women, children, the social outcasts.

The writer. The Gospel does not mention the author's name, but all the evidence points to Luke the doctor, Paul's companion on his missionary journeys (see introduction to Acts). The precise way diseases are described in the Gospel fits in well with this. From the Gospel itself it is clear the writer is an educated man, with a wide vocabulary, and capable of marshalling and selecting material. He is an artist with words. And he is at home with both Greek and Jewish backgrounds – although he writes for non-Jews, using Greek titles and quoting from the Greek version of the Old Testament. Archaeology has proved him an accurate historian. Luke worked with Mark and knew him well (Colossians 4:10, 14; Philemon 24), and the Gospel Mark wrote is one of his main sources.

1:1-4 PREFACE

The church very soon realized the need to get down in writing the stories of Jesus and his teaching which were circulating by word of mouth. Luke – perhaps having time on his hands, and opportunity to check on the facts during Paul's imprisonment at Caesarea – sets himself the task of compiling an accurate record.

Theophilus (3): an otherwise unknown Roman, who had at least some interest in Christianity. 'Most excellent' may be his title as a high-ranking official.

1:5 - 2:52 THE BIRTH AND CHILDHOOD OF JOHN AND JESUS

Only Matthew and Luke take their accounts as far back as Jesus' birth. The two accounts supplement one another. Luke's is fuller. Much of his information must surely have come from Mary herself.

1:5-25 The angel's message to Zechariah

God was in the events which led up to the birth of Christ. John's conception is in itself inexplicable on a purely human level (as with Isaac, Jacob, Samuel, Samson). Zechariah was in Jerusalem for his annual two-week spell of duty as a priest. This year came the honour of a lifetime. He was chosen to offer the incense alone in the temple. And at that moment God sends to tell him that the long years of prayer for a son are over. He will remove the stigma of childlessness – but more than that. As he answers the deep inner longing of this couple God at the same time fulfils far wider purposes – for the nation, and for the world. John will be the link between the Old Testament and the New. He will be the new Elijah (17; Malachi 4:5), herald of the long-promised, long-awaited Messiah.

Verse 15: compare Samson's dedication to God, Judges 13:4-5; and the Nazirite rules, Numbers 6.

1:26-38 The angel's message to Mary

Six months later the Messiah's birth is announced – this time to the young woman chosen to be his mother, and without the agency of a human father. Mary's quiet acceptance of a situation bound to cause scandal, and possibly the breaking of her marriage contract, shows something of the kind of woman through whom God chose to fulfil his purposes.

1:39-56 Mary visits Elizabeth

Having heard the news, Mary sets straight out on the four- or five-day journey south. It is a meeting of special joy and significance for the two women who have much to share. Their thoughts and feelings are crystallized in Elizabeth's benediction and Mary's hymn of praise. The hymn is full of the Old Testament phrases which Mary must have known and loved from childhood (see especially Hannah's song, 1 Samuel 2:1-10). Matthew 1:18-25 tells us what happened after Mary went home.

1:57-80 The birth of John

The child's strange name, Zechariah's sudden recovery of speech and the outburst of prophecy as his pent-up thoughts find voice, make a deep impression on the people around. They expect great things of John.

In the desert (80): other people at the time also withdrew, world-weary, from ordinary life and people. For instance the Essene community at Qumran flourished in John's day in the same area. John, by contrast, had a message for his nation. See also the note under Mark 1:1-8.

2:1-20 The birth of Jesus

Bethlehem – 6 miles south of Jerusalem, 70 south of Nazareth – had a long history. It was the home of Ruth and Boaz, birthplace of King David. But for Jesus there was no room; just an outhouse, a cradle shared with the animals. And the only ones to be told that the King of glory has come are some humble shepherds. 'He became poor' – Paul's phrase was the literal truth.

Verse 2: we know Quirinius governed Syria-Cilicia AD 6-9, but Luke's census is at least nine years earlier. It may be that Quirinius served an earlier term as governor; or possibly the name should read Saturninus. Luke has been proved such a reliable historian elsewhere that it is difficult to think he would make such a factual blunder.

Verse 7: the 'inn' (Revised Standard Version) may equally well be the guest-room of a house (see New English Bible and Matthew 2:11). The animals were probably stabled in a cave beneath the house.

Verse 14: 'his peace for men on whom his favour rests'. God's peace does not come to men because they deserve it.

2:21-40 The presentation of Jesus in the temple; Simeon and Anna

Leviticus 12 gives the Jewish background. Forty days after Jesus' birth his parents present him to the priest in the temple. They are poor people who cannot afford to sacrifice a lamb. It is all routine procedure – until Simeon and Anna see the child, and recognize their Messiah.

Verse 39: Matthew 2 supplies the other events which took place before the family settled in Nazareth.

2:41-52 Jesus astonishes the teachers in the temple

When he was 12, a Jewish boy underwent preparation for adult status in the religious community. This visit to Jerusalem is therefore a special one

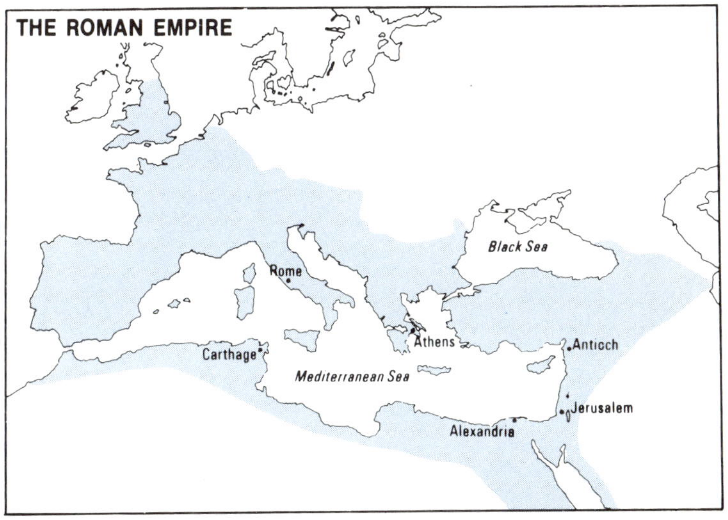

THE VIRGIN BIRTH

John Simpson

Both Matthew (1:18-25) and Luke (1:30-35) state that Jesus Christ was conceived by an action of the Holy Spirit without the intervention of a human father, and thus born of a virgin, Mary. We call this event the virgin birth - or, more accurately, the virginal conception - of Jesus.

In both Matthew and Luke the emphasis lies on the power and activity of the Holy Spirit in the birth of Jesus. It is this, not the absence of a human father, nor even the co-operation of the virgin mother, which is the important point. From his mother, Jesus was born as a man, but by the creative act of the Spirit his is a new humanity, the starting-point of a new race.

It is arguable that this would have been possible apart from a virgin birth, but the biblical evidence points to this miracle as the means which God employed in order to bring his Son into the world. We are not told anything about the physiology of the incarnation, but simply that it was through the activity of the Spirit that Mary became pregnant.

That is indeed all that can be said, since we are concerned here with the entry of the infinite God into his own creation, and this is something that cannot be described, any more than the act of creation itself can be described. Nor can the virgin birth be rejected simply because it is a miracle. The supreme miracle is the incarnation itself, and if we can accept that miracle, there should be no difficulty about accepting the means by which God chose to effect it.

The virgin birth is seldom mentioned elsewhere in the New Testament. That is a warning to us not to get it out of proportion. The fact is stated, but Scripture nowhere makes the deity of Christ, nor his incarnation, nor his sinlessness stand or fall by the method of his birth. The prophecy of Isaiah 7:14 that a 'young woman' should conceive and bear a son called 'Immanuel' ('God with us') was seen to have a deeper meaning after the birth of Jesus (see Matthew 1:22-23). In Mark 6:3 the people of Nazareth call Jesus 'son of Mary', a phrase that may well have been an insult based on the rumour that Joseph was not his father. John 8:41 contains a similar slander. Some have found further references to the virgin birth in Galatians 4:4 where Paul says that God 'sent forth his Son, born of woman', and again when he spoke of Jesus as the 'second Adam', the first of the new race (1 Corinthians 15:45-47).

for Jesus. Visitors flocked into Jerusalem for Passover travelling in large parties for safety. Jesus' parents had no reason to suspect he was missing till the evening halt. Next day they retraced their steps, and on the following morning found him in the temple. This is the first indication we have that Jesus realized his special relationship with God. The next 18 years are passed over in total silence.

3 - 4:13 JOHN THE BAPTIST AND JESUS

3:1-20 The preaching of John

See also on Matthew 3; Mark 1:2-8. Luke's historical detail makes it possible to date John's ministry (and the beginning of Jesus' ministry a few months later) somewhere between AD 26 and 29. Verses 10-14 occur only in Luke. Genuine repentance shows itself in daily life – in kindness, generosity, honesty. The soldiers are told, 'No bullying; no blackmail; make do with your pay!' (New English Bible).

Verses 19-20: see on Mark 6:14-29.

3:21-22 Jesus' baptism

See on Matthew 3.

3:23-38 Jesus' family line

See on Matthew 1:1-17. Luke traces the line beyond Abraham to Adam, emphasizing Jesus' work for all mankind, as well as establishing his claim to be the Messiah descended from David.

4:1-13 The temptation

See on Matthew 4; Mark 1:9-13. Luke reverses the order of the second and third temptations. The real target of attack is Jesus' relationship as Son to his Father. Satan's attempts to undermine it and sow doubts are not so different from his methods in Genesis 3 – 'Did God say? ...' But this time he does not succeed.

4:14 - 9:50 TEACHING AND HEALING IN GALILEE

See note on Galilee, under Mark 1-9.

4:14-30 In Nazareth

Luke chooses to start here, although this was not the first event in Jesus' ministry. Astonishment at Jesus' teaching quickly changes to hostility. And at the implication that because of their disbelief the gospel will be offered to non-Jews, the people are all set to lynch him. See also Matthew 13:53-58; Mark 6:1-6.

The synagogue (16-17): anyone might be invited to take part in the service of prayers, readings and sermon. The leader stood to pray and read from the scrolls, sat down to teach (20).

Verses 26-27: see 1 Kings 17:8-16; 2 Kings 5:1-14.

4:31-44 Capernaum

See on Mark 1:21-45.

Judea (44): the term is used here of Palestine generally, not the south in particular. Jesus went there later.

5:1-11 The catch of fish; Peter and his partners follow Jesus

Luke fills in detail omitted in Matthew (4:18-22) and Mark (1:16-20). The decision to follow Christ was based on more than casual contact.

Gennesaret (1): another name for Galilee.

5:12-16 Jesus heals a leper

See on Matthew 8:1-4.

5:17-26 The paralytic walks

See on Mark 2:1-12.

Pharisees (17): see 'The Religious Background of the New Testament'.

5:27-39 Levi (Matthew) becomes a disciple; questions about fasting

See on Matthew 9:9-17.

6:1-11 Controversy over the sabbath

See on Mark 2:23 - 3:6.

6:12-16 Jesus chooses the Twelve

See on Mark 3:7-19. Only Luke tells us of Jesus' night of prayer. He tells us more about Jesus as a man of prayer than any other Gospel writer.

6:17-49 Jesus teaches his disciples

This is most probably a shorter version of the sermon recorded in Matthew 5 - 7. Jesus must have taught these truths on many different occasions. Having chosen the Twelve, Jesus comes some distance down the mountainside to a level area. Here he sits down to teach, with the apostles, disciples and crowd gathered round him. His words are for his followers – those who realize their poverty in God's sight, who have an appetite for spiritual truth, who grieve at the evil they find in their own hearts. This is not a question of material poverty or riches.

Verses 20-23: a description of Jesus' disciples – men who seem pitiable now, but who have a great future.

Verses 24-26: the dreadful predicament of those who enjoy all life offers now, and fail to look beyond it. See on Matthew 5:1-16.

Verses 27-36: the command to treat others as God treats us – even in the face of injustice; even those who do us down. See on Matthew 5:17-48.

THE NEW TESTAMENT MIRACLES

Howard Marshall

The Gospels contain stories of about 35 different occasions when Jesus performed various kinds of deeds that seemed miraculous to those who saw them. In addition there are several passages where we are told in quite general terms that Jesus performed miracles.

More than half of these stories about Jesus tell how he healed the sick of various diseases including fever, leprosy (probably not the modern disease of that name), dropsy, paralysis, blindness, deafness, and dumbness.

In other cases he cast demons out of people who were suffering from physical or mental disorders.

Three times we hear that he raised people from the dead.

The remaining stories show his power over things – to feed a large multitude with very little food, to walk on the water and still a storm, to curse a fig-tree so that it withered away, to change water into wine, and to catch enormous quantities of fish.

Modern objections to miracles

These stories testify to the tremendous impression which the work of Jesus made on those who saw it. Even if the stories were legendary (which they are not), we should still want to know what it was about Jesus that made people tell such stories about him. One thing is certain at the outset, that we cannot dismiss the miracles to try to have a non-miraculous Jesus. They are an integral and central part of the story. Why, then, do people try to dismiss them?

First, it is argued that science rules out the possibility of miracles. In fact, however, this argument is nothing more than the statement of a presupposition, namely that in a purely material universe nothing can happen that cannot be accounted for in terms of natural causes. But that is purely an assumption about the nature of the universe which cannot be proved to be true. At most it could be argued from it that normally miracles do not occur; but it is illegitimate to claim that therefore miracles can never occur. We ought at least to have open minds on the point.

Second, it is argued that we have no reliable historical evidence for miracles. We must have good evidence that the alleged miracle happened, and that it cannot be explained in a non-miraculous manner. Since we are dealing with something as unusual as a miracle, the evidence needs to be extremely strong, since (it is argued) it is more likely that the witnesses got it wrong than that a miracle actually happened.

The resurrection

If, however, only one miracle could be claimed as historical, this would be sufficient both to demonstrate that miracles are possible and to make further ones probable. Such an event is the resurrection. The evidence that reliable witnesses claimed to have seen Jesus alive after his death (1 Corinthians 15:3-8) is incontrovertible. The only explanation that makes sense of the evidence is that he was miraculously raised from the dead. If you want to disagree, then you must produce some convincing alternative explanation.

If the resurrection did take place, then it makes the fact of other miracles highly likely. For, first, it establishes the possibility of the miraculous taking place at all. It means that God can act in the natural order in an unusual manner. Second, the resurrection is God's 'Yes' to the life of Jesus – including Jesus' own claim to work miracles (Luke 7:21f.; 11:19).

This evidence is confirmed by the reliable historical tradition that Jesus did work miracles, which is found in the Gospels. To be sure, we cannot test and affirm on purely historical grounds the truth of every single miracle story. In some cases, what seemed miraculous to 1st-century people may be explicable in natural terms (e.g. in the psychological healing of a psychosomatic disease); in other cases there may not be enough evidence to confirm or disprove the Gospel story.

The purpose of the miracles

One important point often raised against the historicity of the New Testament miracles is that similar stories are told of other great men of the period. Hence it is likely that Christians, who shared the superstitions of their day, would invent similar stories about Jesus.

One could reply that if it was necessary for Jesus to be a miracle-worker in order to be seen to be 'the greatest' in 1st-century terms, then God could and would do mighty wonders through him. More important is the fact that the stories of Jesus display some important differences from those told about other men. The importance of Jesus' miracles lies not so much in the miraculous power which he displayed in them, as in the significance attached to them.

— In general they were effected by his simple word (Mark 1:27; 2:11) or touch (Mark 5:41) rather than by the use of magical devices.
— They did not bring glory to him, but were meant to bring glory to God (Luke 7:16).
— They testified to God's love for suffering humanity (Mark 1:41; 8:2).
— They fulfilled the Old Testament promises of the coming time of salvation when God would heal men's bodies as well as their souls (Luke 7:22; Isaiah 29:18-19; 35:5-6; 61:1).
— They were done in order to lead men to faith in the saving power of God at work in Jesus (Mark 9:23f.). They were not compelling signs of God's power: the Pharisees felt able to attribute them to the power of Satan (Mark 3:22). But to those with the eyes to see, they constituted the sign that God was at work in Jesus in fulfilment of his promises, and were meant to awaken and confirm faith in him.

All this applies to the miracles of Jesus himself. It also applies to the miracles in the early church. The early Christians displayed powers similar to those of Jesus. We hear of sick people being cured, the dead being raised, the miraculous release of prisoners and even the power to inflict physical judgement. These were signs that the same power of God which was at work in Jesus was still at work in his disciples, confirming their message of salvation, and also warning of the reality of God's judgement.

Verses 37-49: see on Matthew 7.

7:1-10 The centurion's slave

See on Matthew 8:5-13.

7:11-17 Jesus brings the widow's son back to life

We have no other record of this incident. It is a further example of Luke's concern for the under-privileged. The widow's son is her only means of support. Once again Jesus shows himself Lord of life and death.

Nain (11): a village south of Nazareth. See map.

Verse 13: Luke is the only Gospel writer to refer to Jesus as 'the Lord', a term probably not much used during his lifetime.

7:18-35 Messengers from John the Baptist

See on Matthew 11:1-19.

Verse 35: 'God's wisdom, however, is shown to be true by all who accept it'. People turned to God in response to the preaching of both John and Jesus.

7:36-50 In the Pharisee's house

This is a different incident from the one recorded in the other Gospels. Simon shows Jesus no special courtesy. But a common prostitute, to whom he has opened up the possibility of forgiveness, pours out her gratitude in lavish love – not caring what anyone thinks. Her love does not *earn* forgiveness (47), it follows it.

8:1-21 'If you have ears ... then hear'; Jesus teaches in parables

Verses 1-3: only Luke tells us the part the women played in Jesus' mission. Susanna is not mentioned again. Mary Magdalene stood watching at the crucifixion, and she and Joanna were at the tomb and saw the Lord on the resurrection morning. Their love, and that of many other women who followed him from Galilee, never wavered. Mary is not the woman of 7:36ff., but there was a real battle in her heart before she became a disciple.

Verses 4-15: see on Matthew 13:1-52. See also Mark 4:1-20.

Verse 19: see on Matthew 12:49.

8:22-39 The stormy crossing; the man possessed by demons

See on Mark 4:35-41; 5:1-20.

Verse 32: pork was forbidden food for Jews. But the country east of the lake was largely non-Jewish.

8:40-56 Jairus' daughter; the woman with a haemorrhage

See on Mark 5:21-43.

9:1-17 The Twelve sent out; Herod is puzzled; 5,000 fed

Verses 1-6: see on Matthew 9:35 - 10:42.

Verses 7-9: Luke seems to have a special source of information about Herod, perhaps through Joanna (8:3).

Verses 10-17: see also Matthew 14:13-21; Mark 6:30-44; John 6:1-14. This is yet another example of Jesus' power.

9:18-27 'Who do you say I am?'; Jesus speaks about his suffering

See the fuller version in Matthew 16:13-28, and Mark 8:27 - 9:1. Luke abridges at this point.

9:28-36 Jesus is transfigured

See on Mark 9:2-13.

9:37-50 The epileptic boy; 'Who is the greatest?'

Verses 37-43: see on Mark 9:14-29. Verses 46-48: see on Matthew 18 and Mark 9:30-50.

9:51 - 19:27 ON THE MOVE TOWARDS JERUSALEM: TEACHING AND HEALING

In this section Luke groups incidents and teaching from various periods of Christ's ministry, on the general theme of discipleship. He may have had several journeys to Jerusalem in mind. Much of what is recorded in these chapters is unique to Luke.

9:51-56 The Samaritan village

Jesus' insistence on going to Jerusalem was red rag to a bull to the Samaritans (see article 'Religious Background' and on 10:29ff.).

Verse 54: no wonder Jesus nicknamed these two brothers 'sons of thunder'!

9:57-62 No turning back

See on Matthew 8:18-22.

10:1-24 Jesus sends out the seventy

Compare this with Jesus' instructions to the Twelve (Matthew 10:5-15). See also Matthew 11:20-27. Those entrusted with God's good news are entitled to support from the people they go to. But they are not to look for luxury (the 'going from house to house', 7, is with a view to a better living). Time is too precious to waste on endless social formalities (4). There is work to be done, a message to be made known. And God himself will judge those who reject it. The seventy are overjoyed at their new power. But greater cause for joy is the certainty of eternal life (20).

Son of peace (6): a peace-loving man.

Verses 13-17: for the places mentioned, see map. Tyre and Sidon: heathen cities denounced by the Old Testament prophets. 'Hades': the place of the dead – a metaphorical phrase, 'brought down to the depths' (New English Bible).

I saw Satan fall (18): their ability to exorcise evil spirits is a sign that Satan's power is broken. The preaching of the new age means that the power of evil is to be defeated at last. Jesus rejoices in this fulfilment of his ministry.

10:25-37 A test question; the good Samaritan

Only Luke tells this story. Jesus gives a textbook answer to the question. The lawyer, chagrined, in an attempt to save face asks another. Instead of answering directly, Jesus replies with a parable. There was a long history of hatred between Jew and Samaritan (see article 'Religious Background'). The Samaritans were regarded as scum – untouchables. Yet Jesus shows this one carrying out the law whereas the injured man's fellow Jews – even the religious leaders – fail. A real 'neighbour' is one who gives help wherever it is needed, even to someone who yesterday, so to speak, kicked him in the teeth.

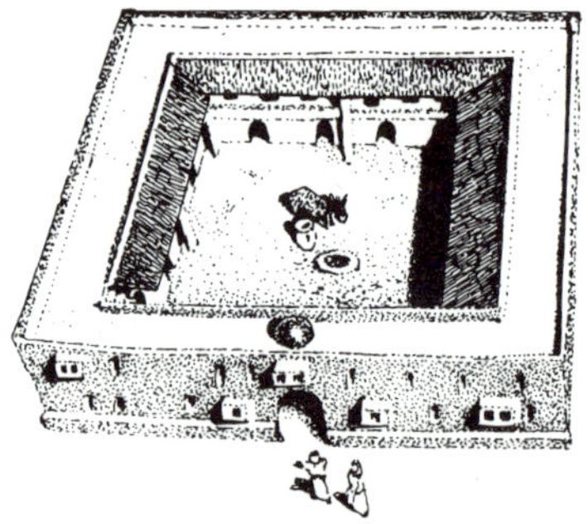

A model of an eastern inn, built around a courtyard.

Verse 30: the road which winds its way down from Jerusalem to Jericho (dropping 3,300 feet in 17 miles) passes through lonely, desolate, rocky terrain – ideal brigand country.

10:38-42 Martha and Mary

The two sisters and their brother Lazarus lived at Bethany, near Jerusalem. Martha gets into a state slaving to prepare an elaborate meal. She would have done better to keep the menu simple and leave time to listen to Jesus.

11:1-13 Jesus teaches his disciples how to pray

Matthew (6:9-13) gives the longer form of the Lord's Prayer. Jesus is not supplying just a form of words. His prayer provides us with a pattern. It teaches us to come to God simply, talking to him as we would our own father, both sharing his concerns and confidently telling him of our own needs. And we are not to be discouraged if time goes by and we see no answer. Persistence will in the end win over even the most reluctant friend – and there is no reluctance to answer on God's part. See also Matthew 7:7-11.

Verse 7: a poor family slept all together on thin mattresses on a raised section of the one all-purpose room.

Verses 11-12: fish and serpents look alike, so do eggs and rolled-up scorpions.

11:14-36 Opposition; Jesus slates his contemporaries

Verses 14-23: see on Matthew 12:15-37. Verses 24-26: see on Matthew 12:43-45. Verses 29-32: see on Matthew 12:38-42. Verses 34-36: see on Matthew 6:22-23. Only Luke includes 27-28.

Verse 24: dry, desert places were thought to be the natural home of evil spirits.

11:37-54 Jesus' rebuke infuriates the Pharisees

Verses 37-41: see on Matthew 15:1-20. Verses 42-52: see on Matthew 23.

12 - 13:9 Warning and reassurance; be ready

A collection of Jesus' teaching about the future, and the way future events should affect life here and now. The consequences of following a short-sighted materialist philosophy will in the end prove disastrous. Much of this section is paralleled in Matthew.

Verses 1-12: see on Matthew 10:26ff.

Verses 13-21: the parable of the rich fool – unique to Luke.

Verses 22-34: see on Matthew 6:9-34.

Verses 35-48: see on Matthew 24:42-51.

13:1-9: Roman troops had slaughtered some Galilean pilgrims in the temple at Passover. People assumed that the victims of the two disasters must have been specially wicked – but that was not true. The whole nation is ripe for judgement and will meet an equally horrible fate if present opportunities for a change of heart are let slip.

Verse 10: see on Matthew 12:15-37.

Verse 35: for freedom of movement

at work the long tunic was drawn up through a belt.

Verses 49-50: the good news of the gospel will run through the earth like fire. But first Jesus must plumb the depths of suffering.

13:10-17 The woman with arthritis

Only Luke records this story. It is one of numerous clashes with the Pharisees over healing on the sabbath. See also Mark 3:1-6.

Verse 16: Satan bears ultimate responsibility for bringing suffering into the world along with sin.

13:18-21 Pictures of what God's kingdom is like

See on Matthew 13, and article 'The Kingdom of God and the Kingdom of Heaven'.

13:22-35 The narrow door

Verses 22-30: speculation over how many will be saved is futile. The important thing is for each individual to make sure of his own place. It is not enough merely to recognize Christ. He requires response – and there is a time limit.

Verses 31-35: Jesus is not bothered by Herod's threats. He knows what lies ahead, and grieves at the fate of the city that will destroy him.

14:1-24 Jesus dines out; two parables

Verses 1-6: another sabbath healing – see 13:10-17; Mark 3:1-6. Human life is cheap, livestock precious!

Verses 7-11: guests were carefully seated according to rank and status (as at a formal banquet today), but everyone wants a seat at the top table. Jesus is commending a genuinely humble spirit, not false modesty.

Verses 12-14: real generosity does not look for returns.

Verses 15-24: the story illustrates how people react to the invitation God makes through Jesus. Many reply with a snub. It is not really a case of 'I *cannot* come', but 'I *will* not come'. The 'reasons' are no more than excuses.

Dropsy (2): fluid collecting in parts of the body and causing swelling and pain.

14:25-35 Counting the cost of discipleship

The guests in the story had their priorities wrong. Jesus' claim must take precedence over all others. No one can follow him unless he is prepared for all that this means. Too many people start to build in fine style and then run out of funds (28-29).

Verse 26: Jesus teaches us to love even our enemies. He is not telling us to hate our family! He means we must love him more than anyone or anything else (33). The black-and-white contrast was a figure of speech.

15 The lost sheep; the lost coin; the drop-out son

These three stories contrast strongly with the severity of chapter 14. God cares for those who have gone wrong in life. He is always ready to forgive any who turn to him. The men of religion (1-2), like the elder son in the story, show neither love nor pity for those who fail to meet their standards. But God rejoices at their rescue.

Verse 8: the silver coins were probably the woman's dowry, worn round her neck or on her headdress.

16 The dishonest manager; the danger of being taken up with money

Verses 1-13: Jesus commends the manager's astuteness, not his dishonesty. He knows how to make money work for him.

Verses 16-17: compare Matthew 11:12-13. The emphasis here is different.

Verse 18: see on Matthew 19:1-15.

Verses 19-31: the rich man and Lazarus. Jesus uses popular picture language (Abraham's bosom, the great chasm, etc.). But the story makes it clear that if we will not respond to the message God has already clearly given in the Bible, we will not respond at all. No amount of miracle-working would make any difference. Our future is determined by our present response, or lack of it.

Verse 9: New English Bible gives a plausible rendering of a difficult verse. Friends bought by money *cannot* get us to heaven. But the way we use our money now may affect our eternal destiny. It is a test of how we could handle wealth of a different kind. Is God, or money, our master?

17:1-10 Forgiveness; faith; duty

17:11-19 The ten lepers

The men are sent to the priests in order to be declared fit to return to normal society. By going, they demonstrate their faith in Jesus' word. All are cured, but only one takes the trouble to say thank you.

Samaritan (16): see article 'Religious Background'.

17:20-37 Teaching about Jesus' return

See on Matthew 24. No amount of calculation can fix the time (20-21) or place (37) of Christ's return in judgement. The world will be caught unprepared, as it was by the flood.

18:1-14 More about prayer

Two parables which appear only in Luke. Like all Jesus' parables, these are stories from life.

Verses 1-8: God is no unjust judge. If a woman could persist with her plea against such odds, surely we can pray on if the answer does not come at once.

Verses 9-14: the Pharisee 'prays' simply to give himself a pat on the back. It is the tax collector, who can find nothing in himself to be proud of, whom God hears.

18:15-17 Jesus and the children

See also Matthew 19:13-15; and on Mark 10:13-16. To the disciples, the children were a nuisance. But Jesus loved them. Verse 17 makes the same point as the story of the Pharisee and the tax collector. Admission to God's kingdom is never denied to those who come in humble trust.

18:18-34 The rich ruler's question; Jesus again predicts his death

See on Matthew 19:16-30; 20:17-19; see also Mark 10:17-34.

18:35 - 19:10 At Jericho: the blind beggar; Zacchaeus

18:35-43: see on Mark 10:46-52. 19:1-10: Zacchaeus, like Matthew, was a social outcast because of his job. He made himself a fat living by fleecing his own people of money to pay the Roman taxes. But when Jesus chose to stay at his home, Zacchaeus became a new man.

19:11-27 The parable of the pounds

This story is similar to the parable of the talents in Matthew. Verse 11 is the key. Herod's son, Archelaus, did just what the nobleman in Jesus' story did – went to Rome to be given his title to the kingdom of Judea. (He was followed by a delegation of Jews opposed to his rule.) Jesus is no despot, like Herod, but he too is about to leave his people for a time. In his absence they must faithfully carry out the work given them to do. For he will return with authority to judge every man.

The pound (13): the Greek mina.

19:28 - 21:38 JESUS IN JERUSALEM

19:28-48 The triumphant ride into the city; Jesus in the temple

See also Matthew 21:1-17; Mark 11:1-19. Jesus rode in on an ass (Zechariah 9:9), not a war-horse. He came on a peace mission. But Jerusalem would have none of it, choosing instead the violent course which led to total destruction at the hands of the Romans in AD 70.

Bethphage and Bethany (29): villages east of the Mount of Olives, two miles from Jerusalem.

Verse 38: Luke paraphrases for his non-Jewish readers.

Verse 45: see on Matthew 21:12-17. Luke, like Matthew, compresses the events; compare Mark 11:11 and 15ff.

20:1-18 On whose authority ... ? The parable of the vineyard

See on Matthew 21:23-46. See also Mark 11:27 - 12:12.

20:19 - 21:4 Jesus' enemies set traps

See on Mark 12:13-44. See also Matthew 22:15-46.

21:5-38 Jesus talks about the destruction of the temple and the end of the world

See on Matthew 24. See also Mark 13.

Verses 8-11: signs of the end.

Verses 12-19: suffering and witness of the disciples.

Verses 20-24: the fall of Jerusalem: phase 1 of the end.

Verses 25-28: cosmic upheaval and Jesus' return: phase 2 of the end.

Verses 29-33: the certainty of these events. 'All' (32) must refer to the warning signs, including the fall of Jerusalem. All the indications are that Christ's coming is near: yet God still delays, giving time for the good news to be made known throughout the world. The fig-tree is the first to come into leaf in Palestine.

Verses 34-36: the need to be ready.

22 - 24 JESUS' LAST HOURS: THE CROSS AND RESURRECTION

22:1-38 Judas turns traitor; the Last Supper

See on Matthew 26:14-29. See also Mark 14:12-25; John 13 - 14.

Verse 10: it was usually the woman's job to carry water, so this man would have been conspicuous.

22:39-53 On the Mount of Olives; the arrest

See on Matthew 26:30-56. See also Mark 14:26-52.

22:54-65 Peter denies Christ; the mockery of the soldiers

Only Peter and one other disciple had the courage to keep within sight of Jesus. But with nothing to do but wait, courage oozes away and fear

A model of the Fort of Antonia, in the Ecce Homo Convent, Jerusalem. Here Jesus was taken to be tried by Pontius Pilate, the Roman Governor.

takes control. Three times Peter says what he swore he would never say (22:33; Mark 14:29-31). Even Peter, leader of the disciples, denies him. Afterwards one look from Jesus is enough to break the big fisherman's heart.

22:66 - 23:12 Jesus before the Sanhedrin; before Pilate; before Herod

See also on Mark 14:53 - 15:15. Blasphemy is a capital charge under Jewish law. But the accusation and charge is rephrased for Pilate in order to get Jesus convicted of treason. The Roman governor is not interested in offences against Jewish religious law.

Herod was in Jerusalem for the Passover. If Pilate was attempting to pass the buck by sending his prisoner to Herod, it did not work. It is strange that the exchange over Jesus should have brought these two old enemies together.

Verse 3: the answer is non-committal. What Jesus would mean by the title, and what Pilate would understand, are two very different things. See the fuller record in John 18:33-38.

23:13-31 Sentenced to death

Although acquitted by both Herod and Pilate, Jesus is condemned to death – because Pilate dare not risk another unfavourable report reaching the emperor (John 19:12). So a convicted murderer is freed, and an innocent man scourged and crucified.

23:32-49 On the cross; the two criminals; Jesus' last words

See on Mark 15:16-41. Only Luke tells us that one of the mocking robbers repented and was forgiven.

Verse 45: the curtain divided the sanctuary from the body of the temple. Only once a year could the high priest pass through and intercede for the people (Hebrews 9:7). Now no intermediary is needed – all may have access to God (Hebrews 10:19-22).

23:50-56 Joseph sees to the burial

See on Mark 15:42-47.

24 Christ is risen!

In the stillness of that Easter morning the extraordinary news gradually broke, the light dawned. The tomb was empty. Jesus was alive! The details given in the four accounts of what took place on that momentous morning are difficult to harmonize. The fact that it happened is clear, and has stood up to the most searching examination. Like reports of any major event, it is difficult to piece together the information of a number of independent witnesses. A rough sequence of events is set out in the article 'The Accounts of the Resurrection'.

No matter what the variation in detail, the main facts are absolutely clear. As day broke on that Sunday morning, Jesus' followers were shadow-men. When Jesus died the group became a body with the heart wrenched out. They were terribly afraid. They were without hope. They did not expect a sequel to the story. Peter, the natural leader, was crushed beyond bearing by the knowledge that he had denied Christ. The two on the Emmaus road were typical of the rest.

Yet within twelve hours everything is changed. Not only is the tomb empty – Jesus himself has been seen on at least five different occasions, by more than 16 of his followers. And it really was Jesus, not a ghost. They recognized him. They saw the crucifixion scars. And he ate with them. Peter is a new man. Despondency and mourning are things of the past. Fear is gone and in its place, indescribable joy. On the concrete certainty of the resurrection rests the whole of subsequent Christian history. Nothing else can account for the facts.

Verses 50-52: Luke compresses events. As he makes clear in Acts, his sequel, the ascension took place 40 days later.

THE ACCOUNTS OF THE RESURRECTION

David Wheaton

A superficial reading of the accounts of the resurrection in the four Gospels may suggest that there are many points of disagreement among them. Closer examination reveals a remarkable degree of unanimity, and suggests that in fact the apparent discrepancies provide evidence that although the Gospel writers obtained their information from different sources in the early Church, all four had the same basic tale to tell. Anyone who has heard evidence from different witnesses to an accident knows how in that situation people with different interests, backgrounds and emotional make-up tend to notice and remember different elements in a composite picture.

The main witnesses who first saw the empty tomb were a group of women who had recently been under severe emotional strain. Immediately after the momentous discovery they would appear to have scattered in order to take the news to different people. So it is not surprising that the accounts vary in detail. The variation suggests that the writers collected their evidence from more than one source, which makes the over-all agreement of the four accounts all the more impressive. The events in the records can be set out more or less as follows.

The Bible evidence

A group of women go to the tomb early on the first day of the week to embalm the body of Jesus (Matthew 28:1; Mark 16:1-2; Luke 24:1; 10; John 20:1a).

They discover that the stone has been rolled back (Matthew 28:2-4; Mark 16:3-4; Luke 24:2; John 20:1b).

The body of Jesus is no longer in the tomb; instead they see an angel who explains the situation and gives them a message (Matthew 28:5-7; Mark 16:5-7; Luke 24:3-7).

The women run back to Jerusalem to tell the other disciples, and are greeted in the main with disbelief (Matthew 28:8; Luke 24:8-11; 22-23; John 20:2).

Peter and the 'other disciple whom Jesus loved' go to the tomb and find it empty; they then return home (John 20:3-10; see Luke 24:24).

Mary Magdalene follows them back to the tomb, and remains there after they have left. Jesus then makes his first appearance to her (John 20:11-18; Matthew 28:9; Matthew names Mary Magdalene and the 'other Mary').

On that same day he appears to Peter (Luke 24:34; 1 Corinthians 15:5), to the two going to Emmaus (Luke 24:13-32; see Mark 16:12-13), and then to the rest of the disciples apart from Thomas back in Jerusalem (John 20:19-23; Luke 24:36-43; Mark 16:14). Other appearances, outside the scope of this article, are recorded in the four Gospels, Acts 1 and 1 Corinthians 15. What emerges from all the accounts is a remarkable consistency on two points – that Jesus could now reveal himself and disappear at will and that he only showed himself to his followers.

Apparent discrepancies

Which women went to the tomb? Apparently Mary Magdalene, Mary the mother of James, Salome, Joanna, and 'the other women from Galilee' (Luke 23:55). John singles out Mary Magdalene for mention (20:1) presumably because it was she who brought information back to Peter and the other disciples: she herself implies in 20:2 that there were others with her – we do not know. So the writers could each be mentioning by name those of the party whose behaviour made an impact on those from whom the writers gained their information.

When was the stone rolled back? Mark 16:3-4 and Luke 24:2 imply that it had been rolled back before they arrived on the spot. Then Matthew 28:2-4 could have happened before their arrival, and as a result the guards went off back to the city (in 28:11-15 the guards have presumably already reached the city and are busy spreading their tale by the time the women are on their way back from the tomb).

How many angels were there? When the women arrive, the angel who descended to roll back the stone (Matthew 28:2) has moved inside the tomb and been joined by another (Luke 24:4 – Mary Magdalene also sees two, John 20:12). Matthew and Mark may refer only to the one who acted as spokesman, and therefore engaged the attention of their informants, and the plural in Luke 24:5 ('the men said') may refer loosely to the fact that while one spoke the other corroborated.

What did the angels say? Again, the accounts can be put together to help us see the full picture:

> Do not be afraid: we know why you have come. Jesus is not here because he has risen. Look at the empty tomb. Tell his disciples; he is going to meet you in Galilee. Remember how he foretold all this.

Who was the first to see Jesus? Mark 16:9 says he first showed himself to Mary Magdalene, and this agrees with John's story. Luke has nothing to conflict with this. In Matthew 28:9 Jesus appears to Mary Magdalene (the key figure) and 'the other Mary'. It seems likely that this is the first appearance, and natural that when the story went round Mary Magdalene was named.

It has been pointed out that Matthew and Mark both record appearances of Jesus to the disciples in Galilee, and Luke and John in Jerusalem. In fact, of course, John 21 takes us back to Galilee; and Mark in his postscript refers to the Jerusalem appearances. In the case of Matthew and Luke, it accords with the purpose and structure of the writers for Luke to conclude his Gospel where he began – in Jerusalem – and for Matthew to conclude with the King's final proclamation on a mountain (28:16-20).

THE GOSPELS AND MODERN CRITICISM

Leon Morris

The Gospels are not biographies, though they contain much biographical information. They are books written by convinced Christians to commend and explain their faith to others (see Luke 1:3-4; John 20:31). They are quite unlike any other type of ancient literature. This means that they cannot be approached in quite the same way as other documents. We must bear in mind, first and foremost, that they are documents of faith; and second that they convey historical information.

The New Testament scholar comes to the Gospels with such questions as these: What purpose were these writings meant to serve? How accurate is the history recorded in them? What can we learn about their method of composition and what light does this throw on their authors' intention and achievement?

Some scholars consider it possible that writers seeking to commend their faith may not be very interested in historical accuracy. They have sometimes concluded that there is very little history in the Gospels at all. They feel that theology is all-important to the Gospel writers, and that they never intended their history to be taken seriously.

Others think that this approach is too subjective. A more objective approach finds good evidence that the Gospel writers do take their facts with the utmost seriousness; Luke, for example, claims to have made a careful examination of the evidence before writing his Gospel (Luke 1:1-3).

Textual criticism

The scholar's first task is to establish the text. Textual criticism, as this is called, is a patient study of the manuscripts, the versions (that is, translations into languages other than the original), the quotations in early writings, the lectionaries used in worship and anything else that can help establish the text.

Behind all this is the fact that it is a trying process to copy out by hand a book as long as a Gospel, and mistakes are liable to creep in. But a careful comparison of the manuscripts, and a study of the methods of scribes, helps the textual critic to distinguish between early and later readings, and so to establish the text.

With thousands of manuscripts involved, textual criticism is an arduous business. But those engaged in it are agreed that the text of the New Testament is in surprisingly good shape (much better than the text of most of the classics). Although we may be uncertain of the original reading here and there, this rarely affects anything important. None of the basic Christian doctrines is in any doubt. And we may now be confident that we have the text of the New Testament substantially as it was written.

Source criticism

Having established the text, critics go on to observe that there are important similarities between the first three Gospels, over against the fourth. Matthew, Mark and Luke all describe a ministry of Jesus in Galilee, with a journey to Jerusalem at the end, at which time he is arrested and crucified. The passion story, with its sequel, the resurrection, occupies a large proportion of each account. But apart from this and the stories of Jesus' birth in Matthew and Luke there is not much that can be confidently located in Judea. John, on the other hand, speaks of a longer ministry (this is clear from his references to Passover feasts), and he describes many incidents which took place in Judea.

The resemblances between the first three Gospels led to their being given the name 'Synoptic Gospels': they can be set side by side and studied together. When this is done, however, differences as well as resemblances come to light, and the problem of the relationship between these Gospels (the 'Synoptic problem') has teased scholars for generations.

At one time it was commonly held that Matthew wrote first and that Mark has abbreviated him. A few still hold this view. But most scholars these days are impressed with the greater freshness of Mark, and by the fact that Mark's order seems always to be followed by either Matthew or Luke. They also point out that, although Mark is the shortest of all the Gospels, it is usually longer than Matthew in the narratives they have in common, which does not look like abbreviation. There is also very little indeed in Mark that is not contained in Matthew or Luke, so why should this Gospel have been written after the others? For these reasons it is now commonly held (though it has not been proved beyond doubt) that Mark was written first and that both Matthew and Luke made use of our second Gospel.

There is also a certain amount of material common to Matthew and Luke but absent from Mark. This is usually thought to represent another source, which has not survived, denoted by the symbol Q. Most see Q as a collection of sayings, with little narrative material. Many scholars think of it as a single document. Others point out that the amount of resemblance in the sections common to Matthew and Luke varies greatly. Sometimes the two are almost word for word (e.g. Matthew 3:7-10 = Luke 3:7-9), but in other places there are considerable differences (e.g. the Beatitudes). They therefore think in terms of several documents (see Luke 1:1), and use Q to denote the shared material in general, without committing themselves to any particular theory of documents.

Other material appears in only one Gospel, and clearly each of the Gospel writers had sources of his own. Symbols used for these are M for material that occurs only in Matthew, and L for material only in Luke. It has been suggested that in the case of Luke this is particularly important. Luke has his material from Mark in blocks, sometimes with long stretches in between. Some scholars hold that he first combined L and Q into a Gospel which has been called 'Proto-Luke'. Later he came across Mark's Gospel and incorporated a good deal of it to make up our present third Gospel. This view of Gospel origins takes the Lukan material very seriously and sees Proto-Luke as quite old and reliable.

Form criticism
That is about as far as source criticism has been taken, perhaps as far as it can go. In recent times attempts have been made to get behind the written sources to the time when the tradition was transmitted by word of mouth. The form critics pay attention to the form of the units which make up the Gospels and identify miracle stories, 'pronouncement stories' (i.e. stories leading up to some memorable saying) and so on. They point out that these units must have been passed on orally for many years.

Why were these particular stories preserved, out of the vast amount of material originally available? The answer, according to the form critics, is that they met the needs of the early Christians; it was the requirements of preaching that determined what would be preserved. Many form critics are rather radical and think that the preachers manufactured stories when they did not have suitable ones, under the belief that the Spirit of God was inspiring them to say what Jesus would have said in the circumstances confronting them. Usually they feel that the Gospels tell us more about the faith of the early church than they do about the teaching of Jesus. This is a highly subjective judgement, and form critics have often been criticized for propounding bold hypotheses on very little actual evidence.

Redaction criticism
The redaction critics take up where the form critics leave off, concentrating on the editorial framework which links together the various units of the Gospel story. Redaction critics find these links highly important, for they help us to see the evangelists' purpose as they wove the stories into their complete accounts. Thus the critics conclude that Matthew was interested in the church and provided a manual for teachers; that Mark used the 'messianic secret' to show that Jesus' true nature was not known until it was revealed by the cross and associated events; and that Luke was the theologian of 'salvation history'.

It is not easy to compare the fourth Gospel with the Synoptists and some feel that the Jesus of John's Gospel is so different from the Jesus of the other Gospels that we must reject one or the other. But Jesus must have been so great a figure that no one evangelist could be expected to capture his whole personality. It has been suggested that the Synoptists reflect the public teaching of Jesus, whereas John reflects Jesus' informal teaching of his disciples and his disputes with his enemies. The two portraits are not irreconcilable.

Probably no other documents in any language have been subjected to such detailed critical examination as the Gospels. The most minute details of vocabulary and syntax have been critically weighed for their bearing on the larger questions. That this searching examination has disclosed difficulties need not surprise us. It could scarcely have been otherwise. But in the judgement of many competent scholars the difficulties are by no means insuperable. They should certainly not deter us as we approach the Gospels. It requires no intellectual compromise, even today, for a humble man to read these books and find his Saviour there.

See further 'The Gospels and Jesus Christ'.

New Testament 1.4

JOHN

John's Gospel is strikingly different from the other three. It was the last to be written – probably about AD 90 – and seems to assume that the readers already know the facts about Jesus' life. John supplements the other accounts, and concentrates on interpreting and bringing out the meaning of what took place. He selects from Jesus' many miracles certain 'signs' which show most clearly who he was. Everything he writes is subordinated to the main aim of bringing the reader to faith (20:30-31). He records mainly what Jesus said – especially about himself – in a style very different from Matthew, the other Gospel which concentrates on Jesus' sayings. There are no parables in John. Most of the events recorded take place in and around Jerusalem at the various festivals. And it may well be that Jesus adopted a different teaching method for the nation's capital city and theological centre. The keynote of John's Gospel is Jesus as Messiah and Son of God.

The author (who may, like Paul, have used a secretary) refers to himself simply as 'the disciple whom Jesus loved' (21:20, 24). He is one of the Twelve, and one of those closest to Jesus and also to Peter. These facts – and the fact that this Gospel makes no mention of the apostle John and describes the Baptist simply as 'John', make it likely that he is himself John, son of Zebedee, brother of James, and business partner of Peter and Andrew. The early church certainly thought so – and taught that the aged apostle wrote or dictated this 'spiritual' Gospel from Ephesus in present-day Turkey. John may have been Jesus' cousin (his mother, Salome, being Mary's sister: Matthew 27:56; Mark 15:40; John 19:25).

The Capernaum fishing business must have been a flourishing one, as the household had hired servants, and a house in Jerusalem. If the 'other disciple' of 18: 15-16 is John it may have been through the business that John was acquainted with the high priest (John 18:15-16). He may also be the unnamed disciple of John the Baptist referred to in John 1:35, 40.

John and James (nicknamed by Jesus 'sons of thunder') with Peter were the leaders of the Twelve disciples and later of the Jerusalem church. They were the inner circle of three who were allowed to see Jesus transfigured, who saw him restore Jairus' daughter to life, and who were near him in the garden of Gethsemane. Jesus committed his own mother to John's care as they stood near the cross. It was not given to many to know Jesus as closely as John did.

1:1-18 PROLOGUE

John begins his Gospel with a tremendous statement about Jesus Christ: on these truths his whole case rests. In him (the Word) God speaks to man. He is the most perfect and complete expression of the Person of God we can ever know. He is far and away above all humanity – God's executive in creation. When God spoke (see Genesis 1), his Word brought life itself into existence. And it was this Supreme Being who became man – the man we know as Jesus Christ. His life shone out – and still shines – against the darkness of a world which failed to recognize him. But to individuals who give him their allegiance he makes available all God's loving forgiveness (grace, 16). And he makes a new, transformed life possible (12).

John (6): John the Baptist (see on Luke 1, Matthew 3, Mark 1), the herald sent by God to tell people of the coming Christ and prepare for his arrival.

Verse 14: John may be thinking especially of the transfiguration – the time when he and Peter and James saw something of Jesus' supernatural splendour (Matthew 17:1-8).

1:19 - 2:12 EARLY DAYS

1:19-34 John the Baptist identifies Jesus as Messiah

John's dramatic preaching attracted

much attention. But he directs it away from himself. He is not Messiah. Nor will he admit to being the predicted second Elijah (Malachi 4:5; in contrast, Jesus leaves us in no doubt that this prediction was realized in John, Matthew 17:10-13). Nor is he the prophet like Moses (Deuteronomy 18:15). As soon as God has shown him the Messiah (32-34) he directs men to Jesus.

Pharisees (24): see article 'Religious Background'.

The Lamb of God (29): a phrase from the Old Testament sacrifices (Leviticus 4:32-35; see also Isaiah 53:4-12). Sin puts every individual under sentence of death – separation from God. But in Old Testament times God accepted the death of an animal as substitute for the death of a person. Further sin meant repeated sacrifices. Jesus was to die to give his life once and for all, sacrificed like a lamb for human sin throughout the ages.

1:35-51 Jesus' first followers

See also on 'The Twelve', Mark 3:7-19. At John's words, two of his followers leave him for Jesus – Andrew, the fisherman (see also 6:8-9; 12:22) and an unnamed follower, possibly the apostle John. The news is too good not to share; so first Andrew brings Peter, and then Philip (see also 6:5; 12:21; 14:8) brings the intellectual Nathanael.

Verse 39: it seems likely, judging by 19:14, that John uses the Roman (and modern) method of reckoning the hours, in which case the time here is 10 a.m.

Verse 42: 'Cephas' and 'Peter' both mean 'the rock-man'.

Verse 48: Nathanael was following the Jewish custom of meditating on the scriptures under his fig-tree. It seems likely, from Jesus' words in verse 51, that he was thinking about Jacob's dream of a stairway between heaven and earth (Genesis 28:12). Jesus is himself a 'ladder' giving man access to God.

The Son of man (51): Jesus' favourite description of himself. The title was one applied to the Messiah (Daniel 7:13-14).

2:1-12 Jesus at the wedding

Jesus' first miracle has a homely setting. The wedding festivities lasted several days, and when the wine ran out the bridegroom (who footed the bill) must have been highly embarrassed. This is the first of seven 'signs' selected by John. All

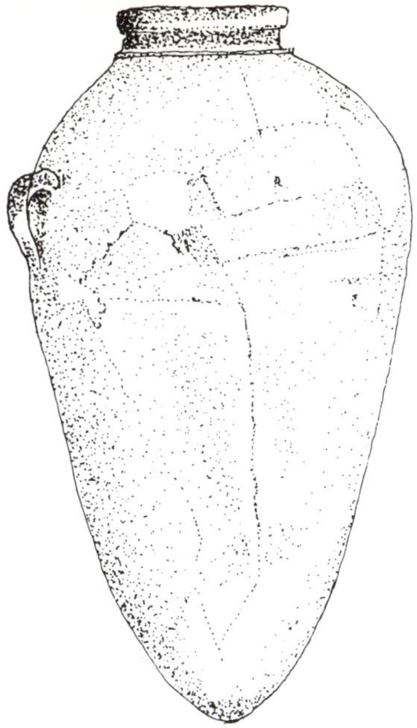

A large water-pot at the Rockefeller Museum, Jerusalem, of the type used for Jewish rites of purification.

have a purpose – they actively support the claims Jesus made, and are intended to lead to faith. Here the new wine of the Gospel is contrasted with the water of the old faith (see verse 6). Jesus had come to bring something really new.

Cana (1): Nathanael's home town (21:2); a few miles north-east of Nazareth.

Verse 4: no one, not even his mother, has the right to put pressure on Jesus. But his reply is not as harsh as some translations make it sound. New English Bible 'Your concern, mother, is not mine' is better.

Verse 6: the water-pots were there for the ritual washing of hands and utensils.

2:13 - 3:36 JESUS' PUBLIC MINISTRY BEGINS: JERUSALEM

2:13-25 Jesus ejects the traders from the temple

See on Matthew 21:12-17. John places this at the beginning of Jesus' ministry, the other Gospels at the end. Jesus may, of course, have turned the traders out of the temple on more than one occasion. But it seems more likely that John overrules strict chronology for more important considerations. The incident illustrates the dishonesty, hypocrisy and prejudice at the heart of Israel's religious life. It makes us see that a head-on clash between Jesus and the religious authorities is inevitable.

Passover (13): see on Matthew 26:14-29.

Verses 20-21: the temple was in a special sense the place of God's presence – the closest man could come to God himself. With the coming of Jesus that changed: he could accurately describe himself as the Temple of God.

3:1-21 The interview with Nicodemus

Nicodemus comes secretly; later he comes out openly on the side of Christ (7:50-51; 19:39). Men need an entirely new spiritual re-birth in order to enter God's kingdom. The new age Jesus was announcing was not to be bound by the old cycle of physical birth and death. It was to be a radical new beginning, a new quality of life – eternal life.

Verses 16-21 may be Jesus' words (New English Bible), or John's comment (Revised Standard Version). They contain the heart of the Gospel message. Jesus comes to save – but the consequence of his coming, for those who refuse him, is judgement.

Verse 14: see Numbers 21:4-9; Jesus is referring to his crucifixion.

3:22-36 John the Baptist steps down

For a while Jesus' ministry overlaps with John's and Jesus draws the bigger crowds. John's reaction, in a situation which goes very much against the human grain, is absolutely right. He allows no trace of bitterness or jealousy to sour his gladness at Jesus' God-given success.

Verses 31-36 may be the Baptist's words or the apostle's comment.

Verse 24: see Mark 6:17-29. The writer here as elsewhere assumes that his readers know the basic facts.

4:1-42 SAMARIA: THE WOMAN AT THE WELL

Jesus chooses the short route from Jerusalem to Galilee which takes him through Samaria – normally avoided by Jews, for over 700 years of religious and racial prejudice separated the Jew from the Samaritan (see article 'Religious Background'). Add to this the Jewish prayer, 'Blessed art thou O Lord ... who hast not made me a woman' and one can understand the Samaritan woman's surprise (9) when Jesus talks to her. Tired and thirsty though he is, he can never ignore human need. As the conversation develops he makes it clear that the woman's need is spiritual rather than physical (7-15), moral rather than 'theological' (16-26). As a result of this seemingly insignificant encounter, many others believe – some through the woman's testimony, more through Jesus' own words.

Verse 20: for the Samaritan, Mt Gerizim was the centre of worship; for the Jew, Jerusalem. Jesus says that the place is unimportant. What matters is that worship should be genuine and spiritual.

4:43-54 GALILEE: HEALING OF THE OFFICIAL'S SON

This is the second of the signs recorded by John (see on 2:1-12 above). Jesus never performed miracles simply to impress. They were intended, as here (verse 53), to lead to faith. John's purpose in recording them is precisely the same.

Verse 44: Jesus was speaking about Nazareth (Mark 6:1-6). John may be giving the words a wider reference, to lack of response in Judea.

5 JERUSALEM AGAIN

5:1-18 Trouble over healing on the sabbath

This is the third sign (see above). Jesus clashed with the religious authorities a number of times over healing on the sabbath (Mark 3:1-6; Luke 13:10-17; 14:1-6; John 9). It was not the general principle of the sabbath that he disagreed with (he regularly attended the synagogue) but the petty restrictions imposed by the religious authorities, which often worked *against* God's purpose in giving man a weekly day of rest. Here the Jews attack him on two counts – sabbath-breaking and blasphemy – because he puts his own work on the same level as God's (17). God's activity in the world did not finish with the creation.

5:19-47 The claims of Jesus

The Jews were right. Jesus *was* making himself God's equal (18) – though this did not mean setting himself up as an independent authority (19). In this passage alone he claims to have:

- knowledge of God's plan (20)
- God's authorization for all he says and does (19, 30)
- power to give eternal life (21, 24, 40)
- the right and authority to judge all men, living and dead (25-29).

A man who makes these claims must be 'mad, bad, or God'. What support can he give them?

- the word God spoke at his baptism (37)
- the testimonial given by John the Baptist (33-35)
- the evidence of his own miracles (36)
- the words of Old Testament Scripture (39).

6 GALILEE

6:1-21 Food for 5,000; Jesus walks on the lake

See on Mark 6:30-56. See also Matthew 14:13-36; Luke 9:10b-17. These are the fourth and fifth signs. The events stand out clearly in John's mind. He remembers which disciples replied to Jesus' question; he recalls the lad; he remembers how far they had rowed from shore when they saw Jesus.

6:22-59 The crowd tracks Jesus down; Christ, the bread of life

The crowd is all in favour of a Messiah who can provide free meals for the asking (26, 34). No one can live without food. But life is more than physical existence (27). Jesus comes to provide bread for the spiritually starving. He is the giver *and* the gift itself. He is the bread of the new life; the one on whom we depend entirely for existence. And the bread we feed on – the source of life for us – is his death (51). Because sin has placed us under God's sentence of death, we live only because of Christ's death on our behalf. We know life only as we make his death and all it means our own. The forgiveness his death has bought is the meat and drink of Christian living. Each one of us must receive it for himself (52-58). The Lord's Supper proclaims this same fact in visual terms (Matthew 26:26-28).

Manna (31): see Exodus 16 and Deuteronomy 8:3.

6:60-71 Reaction

Those who put a crudely literal interpretation on Jesus' words were disgusted. The law forbade the drinking of blood. Meat had to be specially butchered to meet the law's requirements. Yet had they bothered to think back to the reason for the rule they would have understood. Leviticus 17:11 says, 'it is the blood that makes atonement, by reason of the life.' Jesus is saying, 'I am atoning for your sin; avail yourselves of my sacrifice.' The crowd turn away – they do not want this sort of Messiah. But the Twelve remain, in growing faith.

7 - 10:21 TO JERUSALEM FOR THE FEAST OF TABERNACLES

7:1-13 Danger

Last time Jesus visited Jerusalem there was trouble, ending in a plot against his life (chapter 5). This time he avoids publicity.

Tabernacles (2): September/October – the 8-day Jewish harvest festival, commemorating the nation's desert wanderings. See 'Feasts and Festivals'.

Not going (8): some manuscripts add 'yet', showing that Jesus did not intend to mislead. He waited for the opportune moment and then seized it.

7:14-52 Jesus' message gets a mixed reception

As opposition mounts, individuals take sides. Jesus' teaching (40) and his miracles (31) convince some. Others raise difficulties (27, 41-42). But no one who genuinely wants to do God's will is left in doubt (17). Jesus draws his imagery from the ceremony appointed for each day of the festival, when water from the Pool of Siloam was offered to God. Jesus is a bubbling spring, reviving and transforming the thirsty human heart.

Dispersion (35): the Jewish communities abroad.

Verse 42: they cannot have heard the story of Jesus' birth. The Old Testament reference is Micah 5:2.

7:53 - 8:11 The woman guilty of adultery

Although this story is quite genuine, it is unlikely that it originally belonged here (some manuscripts place it at the end of John's Gospel, others insert it after Luke 21:38). The lawyers were trying to trap Jesus. They intended to push him either into contradicting the Mosaic law, or into falling foul of the Roman authorities, who did not allow Jews to carry out a death sentence. But Jesus did neither – nor did he condemn, or condone, the woman's conduct. He gave her a second chance.

8:12-59 Jesus, the light of the world

Jesus again uses one of the ceremonies of the feast to explain his own mission. At dusk they lit four great golden candelabra to symbolize the pillar of fire by which God guided his people through the desert by night (Exodus 13:21). Jesus lights the way through life for all who follow him. He strengthens his claim to be, in a unique sense, God's Son (see also on 5:19-47).

Jesus taught in the porticos of the temple area in Jerusalem.

Verses 12-30: unlike the rest of us, he knows where he comes from and where he is going. He knows the future. The Jewish people have their origin and ancestry in this world, but not Jesus.

Verses 31-47: other men are held in the grip of sin. Jesus is free, and has the power to free others.

Verses 48-59: Jesus asserts his control over death and the eternal destinies of men. Only God has these powers.

9 The blind man sees; the sighted shut their eyes

Jesus really is the light of the world. This sixth sign makes that plain. It also gives us some insight into the problem of human suffering.

- Although there is a direct connection between human suffering and man's sin, the individual is not necessarily suffering because of his own or his parents' sin (3).
- There are times when God allows suffering for a purpose. And he brings good out of it, for the individual himself and all he comes into contact with.

Here the man's blindness leads to an encounter with Jesus. His eyes were opened and he saw (7). His mind was opened and he believed (35-37). By contrast, the sighted men allow prejudice and pride to blind them to the truth (40-41). Confronted by a miracle, all they can see is a broken rule (16). Their minds are closed. They will not listen to the simple logic of the man in the street (30-34).

Verse 6: Jesus uses the methods of popular medicine (saliva was thought to have healing properties). But the method is not the important thing. What counts is the man's faith, demonstrated by his ready obedience (7).

Sent (7): because the water was channelled from another source.

Verse 22: anyone who followed Christ faced excommunication.

10:1-21 Jesus, the good shepherd

This passage follows straight on from chapter 9. The shepherd was a familiar figure in Palestine. He spent much of his life with his flock. His own sheep knew and responded to his voice. He led (not drove) them to fresh grazing, and guarded them from wild animals by lying across the entrance to the sheepfold at night, so becoming its 'door'. In the Old Testament God is often called the shepherd of Israel. And his chosen leaders are also the nation's 'shepherds'. Now Jesus chooses to describe himself as the *true* shepherd. The phrase sums up so much: the close, personal relationship between himself and each of his followers; the absolute security we have in him; his leadership and guidance; his constant company; his unfailing care; his sacrificial love.

Verse 16: Jesus' concern goes out beyond the Jewish nation to the waiting world. Jew and non-Jew, slave and free man, man and woman, all are one flock (see Galatians 3:28).

10:22-42 JERUSALEM: THE FEAST OF DEDICATION

This eight-day feast – the festival of lights – took place in December. It commemorated the great Jewish victory under the Maccabees and the rededication of the desecrated temple.

The Jews remain in suspense because they will not believe (24-26). They are ready to stone Jesus as a man making himself out to be God (33). But they have it back to front. Jesus is not man made God, but God made man (30).

11 LAZARUS RETURNS FROM THE DEAD; JESUS, THE RESURRECTION AND THE LIFE

This is the seventh sign. Lazarus' death is permitted for the same reason as the man's blindness (4 and 9:3). Time and again we see how

Jesus' miracles back up the claims he made. No wonder he so often referred his critics to the work he was doing. He claims he can give men new, spiritual life. What clearer assurance that this is so than Lazarus' return from the dead after four days in the grave? So we too can take him at his word. Neither the disciples nor the two sisters could understand Jesus' behaviour, but the result for all of them was renewed trust in him (15, 27, 42). The event is decisive – for faith and life on the one hand (45); for hatred and death on the other (53).

Thomas (16): see also 20:24-29.

Verse 50: the high priest's words took on a significance he never dreamed of.

12 FINAL DAYS OF PUBLIC TEACHING IN JERUSALEM

12:1-8 Mary's precious flask of perfume

See on Mark 14:1-11.

12:9-11 The plot to kill Lazarus

12:12-19 Jesus rides in triumph into Jerusalem

See on Luke 19:28-48 and introduction to Matthew 21. See also Mark 11:1-11.

Branches of palm (13): the symbol of victory.

12:20-36a The Greeks search Jesus out

The arrival of the Greek converts brings Jesus face to face with his destiny. The time has come for him to buy life for mankind with his own death. Verses 20-36 and 44-50 record his last public statement. It is full of paradox: life through death; glory through the ignominy of the cross; the world judged in the execution of judgement.

Verse 25: Jesus is not advocating a death-wish. But love for him and concern for eternal things must far outweigh all selfish, material concerns.

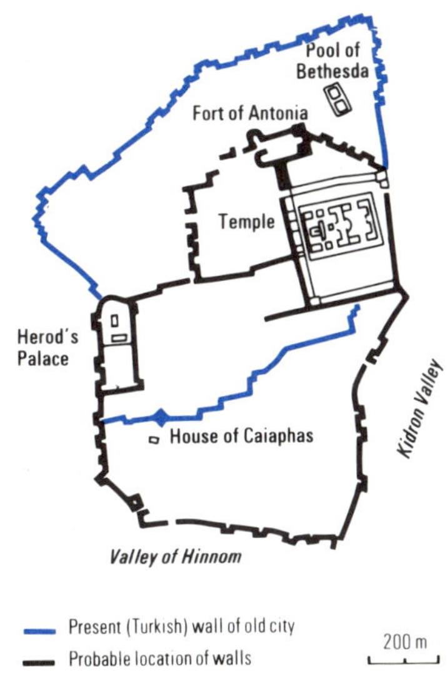

JERUSALEM IN NEW TESTAMENT TIMES

12:36b-50 Jesus steps out of the limelight

Verses 36b-43: at the end of Jesus' public ministry and despite all his miracles the Jews remained unconvinced. And many of those who did believe were too afraid to say so openly.

Verses 44-50: it matters how each of us reacts to Christ. Because he comes on God's authority, it is all-important whether we believe in him or not.

Verse 40: God never hardens the heart of someone willing to respond. But in the end, if we choose to be blind and persistently reject his truth, he lets us become immune to it.

13 - 17:26 JESUS' LAST WORDS TO THE TWELVE

13:1-20 Jesus washes the disciples' feet

The occasion is the Last Supper (see on Matthew 26:14-29). The disciples have been arguing over who is greatest (Luke 22:24). Jesus gives them the answer in this simple action. The Master, conscious of who he is and in his love for men, has willingly made himself their slave (Luke 22:27). His followers must do the same.

13:21-30 Judas, the traitor

Judas has already volunteered to help the priests make a secret arrest (Luke 22:3-6). Now the moment has come. The rest of the disciples have no idea of what is afoot. But Jesus knows. 'It was night' – quite literally. But light and darkness acquire a special meaning in this Gospel (1:4-9). These were Jesus' darkest hours, but nothing could extinguish the light of his life (1:5). Judas, by contrast, stepped from the light into darkness so intense it destroyed him (3:19-20; Matthew 27:3-5).

Verse 23: most probably John himself; see introduction.

13:31-38 The command to love one another; Jesus predicts Peter's fall

The prospect of death on the cross, cut off from his Father by the colossal burden of the world's sin, appalled Jesus (Luke 22:42-44). Yet because of all it would achieve, he could describe it in terms of triumph and glory. It was his love for others that took him there. And it is love of this same calibre he looks for in his followers.

14 Jesus reassures his disciples; 'I am the way, and the truth, and the life'

The disciples are worried and upset by the talk of betrayal and the thought of Jesus leaving them. Jesus himself is concerned at the effect his death will have on them all. And so he tries to get them to understand why it has to happen.

His death means his return to the Father (12, 28). He is making the approach-road for men to come to God (6). He is going to get a permanent home ready for his disciples, and in due course he will come for them (2-3). Meanwhile his return to God will be to their good: it will bring new power in action, new certainty in prayer (12, 14). Best of all, the Holy Spirit will come to be with them always and everywhere (not limited by a physical body as Jesus had been). He will teach and counsel and bring to mind all that Jesus has said (16-17, 26). And Jesus' own unshakable peace will be theirs (27).

For their part, the disciples must continue to love and trust him (1). And the way to show their love is to do all that he says (15, 21, 23).

15 - 16 Jesus, the true vine; opposition; the promise of the Holy Spirit

The conversation continues as they make their way to Gethsemane (14:31). There is not much time left.

15:1-17: in the Old Testament, Israel is the vine – so often failing to yield fruit (see Galatians 5:22-23). But Jesus was the true vine, the fulfilment of God's purpose where Israel had failed. Those who believe in him are branches. Every branch of a vine grows directly from the main 'stock'. When they are cut back, branches which have borne fruit are pruned to within an inch or two of the stock. They then 'abide' in the stock for most of the year as it grows round them. Then the branches grow out rapidly to bear fruit again. Branches which have not borne fruit at all are cut right back, and are fit only for burning.

15:18 - 16:4a: those who belong to Christ will inevitably encounter the hatred of self-centred humanity, just as Christ himself did. They will even be hounded by men who (like Paul) consider themselves to be doing God a service.

A vine, with the main 'stock', branches growing from it, bunches of grapes on the fruitful branches, and the unfruitful ones cut off to be burnt.

16:4b-15: Jesus' going means the coming of the Holy Spirit to convict men of the truth and lead them into deeper understanding of it.

16:16-33: at Christ's death there will be grief, but only for a little. With the resurrection will come lasting joy.

16:25, 29: 'figures of speech', New English Bible.

17 Jesus' prayer; for himself and for his followers

Jesus has accomplished all he set out to do during his lifetime. He has passed God's message on. He has made God known. Now there remains only death, and beyond it the glory he renounced to become man. But his followers will be left bereft in a hostile world. So he prays that God will protect them; that their lives may be shaped by the truth of God's word; that they may display such unity among themselves that the world will be shaken out of its disbelief; and that they may, in the end, go to be with him and see his glory for themselves.

Verse 12: the reference is to Judas.

18 - 21 TRIAL, DEATH AND RESURRECTION

18:1-12 Betrayal and arrest

See on Matthew 26:30-56. See also

Mark 14:26-52; Luke 22:39-53. John omits Jesus' prayer in the garden. But he tells us the name of the slave, and that the swordsman was Peter.

18:13 - 19:16 Jesus before Annas and Caiaphas; Peter's denial; Jesus before Pilate

See on Mark 14:53 - 15:15; Luke 22: 54 - 23:31. See also Matthew 26:57 - 27: 26. The detail John fills in shows his close knowledge of what happened – the cold night; the charcoal fire (18:18); the blow to the prisoner (18:22); Jewish religious scruples over entering the Roman's house at such a time (18:28); the exchanges between Jesus and Pilate, and Pilate and the Jews; the terrible national apostasy as God's people declare they have no king but Caesar.

19:14: unlike the other Gospel writers, John probably uses Roman time, counting as we do from midnight. Unless, as some believe, John dates the Passover one day later than the other Gospel writers (see Mark 14:12), the reference here is to the preparation for the sabbath of Passover week (19:31).

19:17-37 The crucifixion

See on Mark 15:16-41; Luke 23:32-49. See also Matthew 27:27-56. Again John shows his vivid recollection of events – the details of the inscription (20-22); the seamless tunic (23-24); the moment when Jesus entrusted his mother to John's care (26-27); the incontrovertible evidence of Jesus' death (34).

Verse 31: Jewish law said that the bodies of criminals must not be left hanging after sunset (Deuteronomy 21:23).

Verse 34: John is implying more than that Jesus was without question dead. As a Jew, he could not help seeing special significance in the flow of blood (for sacrifice) and water (for cleansing). The blood atones for man's sin, the water gives him a clean, new start. Jesus' death brings us forgiveness and new life.

19:38-42 Burial

See on Mark 15:42-47. See also Matthew 27:57-66; Luke 23:50-56. The death of Jesus brings two secret disciples out into the open. Only John mentions the part played by Nicodemus (see 3:1-15).

20 The resurrection; Jesus appears to the disciples in Jerusalem

See on Luke 24. See also Matthew 28; Mark 16. John gives his own personal account of what happened – what he heard and saw for himself, and what he learnt from Mary Magdalene. Thomas the realist's momentous declaration of faith – 'My Lord and my God!' – is the climax of the whole Gospel. John's purpose in writing is to bring men to just such assured and clear-cut belief in Jesus (31).

Verse 7: John sees the grave-clothes and head-cloth lying undisturbed, still in place. But now an empty space separates the head-cloth from the rest. No one could steal a body and leave the grave-clothes like that. Jesus' body can only have passed through them. So John took note, and believed.

21 Jesus appears again in Galilee; the author's final word

Only John tells us how Jesus came to the seven of them as they were fishing, just as in the old days. John was there. He remembers how many fish they caught, and their surprise and relief at finding the net intact. He remembers how Jesus gave Peter the chance to cancel out his three-fold denial with the three-times-repeated question 'Do you love me?'; how he restored Peter to his old place as leader, and gave him the task of caring for his people. He remembers Peter's question about his own destiny – and sets the record straight.

And having remembered it all, he closes his Gospel with an affirmation of the truth of what he has written.

Verse 18: a prediction of Peter's death – stretched out on a cross, like his Master.

New Testament 1.5

ACTS

The book of Acts covers a period of some 30 years, from the birth of the church on the Day of Pentecost to the close of Paul's imprisonment at Rome. It describes the spread of Christianity around the northern Mediterranean – through present-day Syria, Turkey and Greece, to the heart of the Roman Empire. The 'acts' related are mainly those of the apostles Peter and Paul, though the book might well be called 'the acts of the Holy Spirit'. It is under his direction that the new-born church bursts through the national frontiers of Israel to become an international, world-wide movement.

Who wrote it? All the evidence, from earliest times, points to Paul's 'dear friend Luke, the doctor'. He wrote Acts as a sequel to his earlier volume, the third Gospel. Luke is the only non-Jewish writer in the New Testament. He came from Antioch, or possibly Philippi. Although we have a few facts about his life, his writings prove him a fine and reliable historian. We know, from the way he changes from 'they' to 'we' in Acts (16:10; 20:5; 27:1), that he was present at many of the events he describes. He was with Paul at Philippi. He made the fateful journey with him to Jerusalem, stuck by him during the two years at Caesarea, and shared the voyage and shipwreck on the way to Rome. He had plenty of opportunity to obtain his other information first-hand – from Paul and Barnabas and others in the church at Antioch; from James, the Lord's brother, among others at Jerusalem; and from Philip and his daughters at Caesarea. And we know from Luke 1:1-4 just how concerned he was to get at the facts.

Why did he write? It was in order to give the Roman Theophilus an accurate record of the true facts about Christianity (Luke 1:1-4). There were plenty of strange and distorted rumours flying about. This explains Luke's emphasis on the spread of the gospel to the Gentiles, who, unlike many Jews, were eager to hear (28:28). He is also concerned to account for the disturbances which so often followed the preaching. In every place the troubles are fomented either by Jewish jealousy, or vested interest. Time and again he relates how the Roman authorities cleared the Christians of all charges of subversion and sometimes protected them from the fury of the mob.

When was Acts written? Most probably at the close of Paul's two-year imprisonment in Rome, in the early or mid-sixties. There is no hint of Nero's persecutions, or the Jewish revolt (AD 66-70), or Paul's death (about AD 67). On the contrary, the

TIME-CHART

There are not enough fixed points to be exact, but the dates below are accurate within a year or two either way.

AD 30 The founding of the church in Jerusalem (Acts 1 - 2)
32/35 Paul's conversion (Acts 9)
34/37 Paul's first visit to Jerusalem (Acts 9:26ff.)
45 or 46 Famine relief sent to Jerusalem from Antioch (Acts 11:27ff.) Death of James
46 or 47 First missionary journey (Acts 13 - 14)
48 Apostolic Council at Jerusalem (Acts 15)
48-51 Second missionary journey (Acts 15:36 - 18:22)
50 Paul reaches Corinth (Acts 18)
53 Third missionary journey begins (Acts 18:23)
54-57 Paul's stay in Ephesus (Acts 19)
57-58 Paul in Greece (Acts 20)
58 (June) Paul reaches Jerusalem (Acts 21)
58-60 Imprisonment at Caesarea (Acts 24 - 26)
60-61 Appeal to Caesar and voyage to Rome (Acts 27)
61-63 Imprisonment in Rome (Acts 28:30)

EARLY CHRISTIAN PREACHING

Michael Green

The truly amazing thing about early Christian preaching is that it did not proclaim religious duties or moral standards, or even a reforming programme, but a person: one Jesus who was crucified and whom the Christians knew to be alive. They devoted their energies to understanding him better (from studying the Old Testament) and making him real to people who had never met him. Common belief and varied presentation are the keynotes of their achievement. Above all it is crucial to recognize that both the content and the dynamic of their preaching was the Risen One, whom many of them had known and followed for several years while he had been a carpenter and rabbi.

It has been shown that the early Christians had a broadly uniform pattern for preaching Jesus Christ. It ran something like this:

> 'The ancient prophecies have been fulfilled and the new age has been inaugurated by the coming of Christ. He was born of David's family, died according to the scriptures in order to deliver us from the present evil age. He was buried, rose again the third day as scripture foretold, and is now exalted at God's right hand as Son of God and Lord of the living and the dead. He has given his Holy Spirit to his followers as an assurance of his Lordship and as a foretaste of his return to be the Judge and Saviour of men at the Last Day.'

This pattern of teaching was already developed from an early date. This can be seen in the pieces of early preaching, or hymns, or creeds, incorporated into the Letters. For instance, Philippians 2:4-11 is very early, possibly coming from the Aramaic-speaking church; yet it is as doctrinally advanced as anything in the New Testament. Other fragmentary statements of belief from very early days have been preserved in such passages as 1 Corinthians 15:3-4; Romans 1:3-4 and 1 Timothy 3:16.

Slight variations in emphasis may also be detected. When speaking mainly to Jews, the deliverance Christ gives from the broken law of God is stressed. Forgiveness, justification, cleansing are the important things. When the readers are predominantly pagan in background, stress is laid on the deliverance Christ gives from the demonic powers of which men of the ancient world were so acutely aware.

So to the Jews Jesus was shown as Christ, the messianic Deliverer, the climax of the Old Testament revelation. To non-Jews, to the pagan world, he was presented as Lord and conqueror of all the forces of evil.

When preaching to the pagan world, without the background of the Old Testament revelation of God, the early missionaries also had to start further back in their teaching. Acts gives us two examples, one of preaching to unsophisticated people (14:15-17), the other the approach to the cultured (17:22-31). In both cases the Christians seek to establish the fact that there is one God, discredit idolatry and through the light of natural revelation (God the Creator and Sustainer) to prepare the way for the special revelation of God contained in Christ. This way of proceeding had been used by Jews in the previous century or so, when seeking to commend the ethical monotheism of Israel to an immoral and idolatrous but wistful pagan world. It formed a useful introduction to the specifically Christian proclamation, and it remained the staple approach for centuries.

Whether preaching to Jews or Gentiles, the early Christians emphasized not only what God had done for men through Christ, but what he offers (new life by the Holy Spirit, forgiveness of sins) and what he requires (repentance, faith and commitment). This commitment involved three strands which must be held onto together: baptism, faith and reception of the Holy Spirit. These three make a man a Christian.

Acts makes a point of the depth at which this early preaching was carried on. Words are used which indicate that the Christians acted like heralds, like teachers, like debaters. They discussed this good news, argued it, gave testimony to it, and showed how it fitted in with the Old Testament scriptures. It was the task of no single category of Christians; women chattered it at the laundry, philosophers argued it at the street corner, prisoners told their fellows. Men of every background and culture demonstrated its power by their transformed lives (see 1 Corinthians 6:9-11) and their willing acceptance of suffering and death (e.g. Acts 20:22-24).

It was these qualities which commended the new message, with the power of the Spirit in their social and personal lives which backed up their claims. There was also an intellectual characteristic which contributed largely to their success. They discovered how to interpret Jesus in varying ways to meet varying needs – they were not rigorously hidebound. Neither were they 'syncretists': they did not say that other religious insights were equally true and could be merged with the new faith. Christianity, like Judaism, would have nothing to do with the syncretism of the pagan world. But Christians succeeded, as Judaism never did, in giving great flexibility to the expression of their faith while retaining the main common pattern and content which we have seen.

For instance, Jesus' preaching of 'the kingdom of God' might be meaningful in a Jewish constituency but could be politically inflammable elsewhere. So the early preachers preferred to use Jesus' other expressions 'eternal life' or 'salvation'.

Again, 'Son of man' was a peculiar form of address with highly apocalyptic associations understood in some circles in Judaism but meaningless elsewhere. Words which rang a bell with pagans – such as 'Son of God' or 'Lord' – were used instead by these versatile early preachers.

When engaged in interpreting the person of their Master, they used the language and thought-forms familiar to those they sought to reach. Their aim was to make crystal clear the unique saving work of the divine, crucified and risen Jesus who was both the Lord they served and the message they proclaimed.

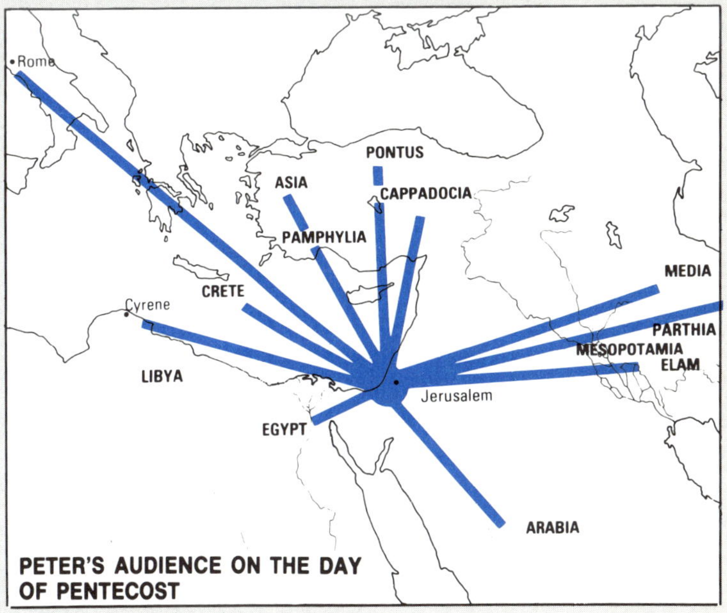

PETER'S AUDIENCE ON THE DAY OF PENTECOST

book ends on an optimistic note. It must have been written after the Gospel, which some date later than AD 70. But the evidence points to a date about AD 60, which makes 63 or thereabouts a likely date for Acts.

1 - 8:1a THE BIRTH OF THE CHURCH: JERUSALEM

1:1-14 Introduction; the 40 days from resurrection to ascension

Luke's 'first book' (his Gospel) is an account of all that Jesus 'began to do and teach' during his life on earth. Acts continues the story of his work after the ascension, by the power of the Holy Spirit in the lives of the apostles. It shows how the promise in verse 8 was fulfilled: in Jerusalem (2:1 - 8:1a), Judea and Samaria (8:1b - 11:18) and way beyond (11:19 to the end).

A cloud (9): all that human eyes could see of the glory of God's presence (compare also Exodus 40:34 and Luke 9:34-35).

Sabbath day's journey (12): the law limited travel on the sabbath to 2,000 cubits – about two thirds of a mile.

Mary ... and his brothers (14): this is the last time Jesus' mother is mentioned in the New Testament, and the first time his brothers are associated with the disciples. We know at least one of them – James – had seen the risen Jesus (1 Corinthians 15:7).

1:15-26 A twelfth apostle is chosen

As far as we know, this is the last time the apostles use the time-honoured method of casting lots. It is not just a 'lucky dip' – the decision is made after much prayer. The twelfth man had to have been with Christ throughout his earthly ministry, and to have seen him after the resurrection.

2:1-13 Pentecost: the coming of the Holy Spirit

With the coming of the Holy Spirit – made unmistakably evident by inward transformation and signs that all can see and hear – the waiting is over. The apostles and disciples become the new church, full of life and power, as different from their former fearful selves as can be imagined.

Pentecost (1): the old Jewish festival of firstfruits, which took place at the beginning of the wheat harvest. It was 50 days after the Passover, the time of Jesus' crucifixion.

Each heard in his own language (6): the audience of Jews and converts were from many countries, though all would speak either Greek or one of the Aramaic dialects. Normally the apostles' difficult Galilean speech would have been hard to follow. Now, to their astonishment, everyone in this mixed audience heard his own language being spoken. The curse of Babel (Genesis 11) is dramatically reversed.

2:14-47 Peter's sermon and what follows

The sermon evokes an immediate response. Baptism is followed by a new, joyous sense of community. And spiritual unity finds practical expression in readiness to share money and possessions.

The third hour (15): 9 a.m., and on that day there was fasting till mid-morning.

3-4:31 Healing of the lame man; Peter and John taken into custody

Healing and teaching, as in Jesus' ministry, go together, both made possible by the power of the Spirit of God. It is the teaching, centring as always on the risen Christ, which annoys the Sadducees – naturally enough, as they denied the possibility of resurrection. Paul, in his turn, divided the Pharisees and Sadducees over the very same question (23:6). The resurrection was the core of the Christian message from the very earliest days. Everywhere the apostles spoke about Jesus and the resurrection – so much so that the Athenians thought Paul was talking about *two* new deities (see on 17:18).

The ninth hour (3:1): 3 p.m. Prayer times were early morning, afternoon (as here) and sunset. The first two coincided with the morning and evening sacrifices.

Annas ... Caiaphas (4:6): Annas was senior ex-high priest, his son-in-law, Caiaphas, ruling high priest (AD 18-36).

This is the stone (11): a quotation from Psalm 118:22.

Uneducated, common men (13): 'untrained laymen', New English Bible.

4:32 - 5:11 Ananias and Sapphira

The pooling of property was quite voluntary, but some were prompted less by real generosity than by a desire to impress. In lying to the church, Ananias and Sapphira were practising deceit against God himself. The terrible consequences served as an example to the whole church.

Barnabas (4:36): later chapters show how aptly he was named. A leader in the church at Antioch, he and Paul were sent out together as missionaries. Paul benefited from Barnabas' encouragement – so too did his young cousin, John Mark.

THE NAZARETH DECREE

This remarkable inscription most probably dates from the first century AD. It was sent to a French collector from Nazareth in 1878. Was it the rumour that Jesus of Nazareth had risen from the dead that made the decree necessary?

ORDINANCE OF CAESAR. It is my pleasure that graves and tombs remain undisturbed in perpetuity for those who have made them for the cult of their ancestors, or children, or members of their house. If, however, any man lay information that another has either demolished them, or has in any other way extracted the buried, or has maliciously transferred them to other places in order to wrong them, or has displaced the sealing or other stones, against such a one I order that a trial be instituted, as in respect of the gods, so in regard to the cult of mortals. For it shall be much more obligatory to honour the buried. Let it be absolutely forbidden for anyone to disturb them. In the case of contravention I desire that the offender be sentenced to capital punishment on charge of violation of sepulture.

5:12-42 The apostles before the council

It was like the days of Jesus in Galilee all over again, so many were being healed by the apostles. No wonder the Jewish authorities grew jealous of their enormous influence. But threats, imprisonment, even the lash are no weapons with which to resist the power of God.

Solomon's Portico (12): it was common practice for groups to meet for teaching and discussion in the courts of public buildings, and for disciples to listen to their teachers in the courts of the temple. The Christians met in Solomon's porch – but knowing the authorities' hostility towards them, the bystanders kept their distance.

This man's blood (28): the apostles openly held the council responsible for Jesus' death, and they fear reprisals.

Hanging him on a tree (30): the upright of the cross was a fixture, and might well be a sawn-off tree-trunk. See also Deuteronomy 21:22-23.

Gamaliel (34): leader of the Pharisees; Paul's teacher. His is wise advice.

6 Seven assistants appointed; Stephen arouses opposition

Complaints come from the Greek-speaking, non-Palestinian Jews of unfairness in the daily share-out. The apostles' answer is to let them choose seven of their own number – men of spiritual calibre – to oversee these practical matters. At least two left a permanent mark on the young church: Stephen, a powerful preacher, the first martyr, and Philip the evangelist.

The charge against Stephen is blasphemy – the very same charge that was brought against Jesus. Stephen seems to have been among the first to foresee the inevitable break with Jewish worship which the new teaching entailed.

The synagogue of the Freedmen (9): probably attended by freedmen from the places mentioned.

7 - 8:1a Stephen's defence and death

The defence takes the form of a review of the nation's history. The court knows the facts, but the interpretation is revolutionary. And the sting lies in the tail (51-53). Israel of old rejected the prophets from Joseph and Moses onwards. The present generation has rejected the Messiah himself. Verses 44-50 are Stephen's answer to the charges about the destruction of the temple. A permanent building to 'house' God was never more than second-best.

Delivered by angels (53): Galatians 3:19 and Hebrews 2:2 also connect angels with the giving of the law, but there is no mention of this in the Old Testament.

The witnesses ... Saul (58): the prosecuting witnesses, by law, had to cast the first stones – though in other respects this particular affair was little more than a lynching. The 'young man' Saul was probably in his thirties. He appears here for the first time. As the apostle Paul (the Roman version of his name) he is the central figure in the later chapters of Acts. Here he shares the responsibility for Stephen's death. ('Consenting' may mean that as a member of the Sanhedrin he cast his vote against Stephen.) But the scene at Stephen's death burnt into Saul's mind (22:20), and must have played its part in preparing him for the encounter on the Damascus road.

8:1b - 11:18 PERSECUTION: THE GOSPEL SPREADS TO JUDEA AND SAMARIA

8:1b-25 The response among the Samaritans

The persecution following Stephen's death led to the first broadening of the church's outreach. The attack seems to have concentrated on Stephen's fellow Hellenists (Greek-speaking Jews), leaving the apostles free to remain in Jerusalem. Wherever the scattered believers went they preached the good news – in Philip's case with such marked success that two of the apostles came down to see what was happening.

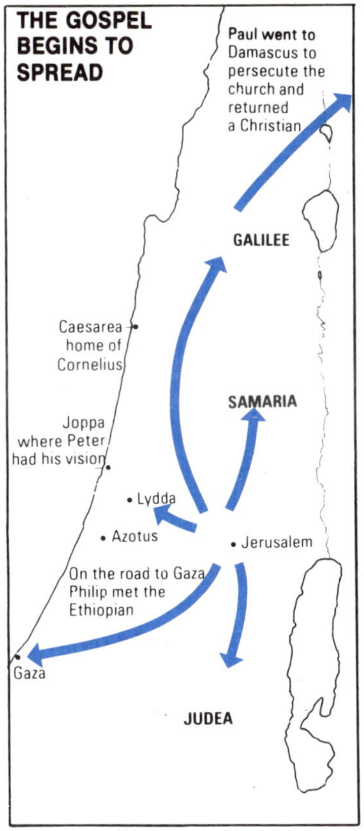

That power of God which is called Great (10): Simon saw himself as the sole agent of the supreme God.

That they might receive the Holy Spirit (15-17): every believer has the Spirit of God – see Romans 8:9; 1 Corinthians 12:13. But the visible sign of the coming of the Spirit – given when the apostles officially recognized that these members of the despised enemy nation had become God's children – underlines the special significance of the Samaritans being welcomed into the church.

8:26-40 Philip and the Ethiopian treasurer

At the height of Philip's flourishing Samaritan campaign God calls him away to meet the need of an individual.

An Ethiopian (27): the man, a Jewish convert, was treasurer not of present-day Ethiopia, but of the old kingdom in northern Sudan.

Candace (27): the title of the queen mother who ruled the country on behalf of her son. The king himself, deified as the child of the sun-god, was considered too holy for such secular functions.

The scripture (32): Isaiah 53:7-8. The quotation is from the Greek (Septuagint) text which differs slightly from the Hebrew (massoretic) text on which our Old Testament is based.

Caesarea (40): Philip seems to have settled at this sea-port and brought up a family. See 21:8-9.

9:1-31 The Damascus road: Saul's conversion

Saul's conversion marks a turning-point in the history of the early church. The story is told three times in Acts, once, here, by Luke, and twice by Paul – 22:5-16; 26:12-18. Never has any conversion meant a more complete about-face and radical change of thinking. The encounter with Christ was followed by three sightless days: Saul was identified with Jesus in his death and three days in the grave, and identified with him too in baptism and newness of life. By the time Ananias reached him, Saul the persecutor had become 'Brother Saul' – a man to be hunted down, in his turn, by those whose cause he once led. With his conversion, the church for a while had peace.

The Way (2): the church was known by this name before the people of Antioch invented the new name 'Christian' (11:26).

Tarsus (11): a university city with a population of half a million; meeting-place of East and West, Greek and Oriental.

9:32-43 Peter at Lydda and Joppa: Tabitha raised from the dead

With peace at last, Peter is free to visit the Christian groups. He settles for a time at Joppa (the port from which Jonah, another reluctant missionary to the Gentiles, embarked). His host's job is the 'unclean' one of tanning – perhaps an indication that Peter is already to some extent emancipated from his religious taboos. But a far more radical challenge is to follow.

The first stop for Paul and his companions on their first mission was Salamis in Cyprus. Here they confronted the power of the contemporary Roman civilization.

10 Peter and Cornelius

Up to this point the gospel has been preached only to Jews, converts to Judaism (proselytes) and Samaritans (who observed the law of Moses). Now God steps in to make it plain that the message is for all men (34-35). He prepares Cornelius, and he prepares Peter. Three times the vision and message come – apparently instructing Peter to break the Jewish food-laws (see Leviticus 11). But when the men from Cornelius arrive, he is quick to realize the far deeper, human implications of his dream (28). A second Pentecost – the coming of the Holy Spirit on the Gentiles – follows his teaching. No one could then deny baptism to those who had received such an obvious mark of God's favour.

Cornelius, a centurion (1): one of those who formed the back-bone of the Roman army. The centurions stationed in Palestine appear in a very favourable light in the New Testament. Cornelius was an adherent to Jewish faith and worship, but not a circumcised convert. (See article 'Roman Soldiers'.)

Peter's trance (9-16): it was midday when Peter fell into his waking dream – and Cornelius' men were already nearing Joppa. Peter's hunger, and perhaps the leather awning overhead, shape the images of a vision which God uses to convey his message.

11:1-18 The apostles approve Peter's action

This repetition of the events at Caesarea underlines their significance. The criticism Peter faces from a particularly narrow faction of Jewish Christians in Jerusalem is to dog every stage of Paul's missionary work. The admission of Gentiles to full membership of the church, without circumcision, is the most controversial question of the apostles' generation. But Luke makes it clear that the apostles and leaders had a full report from Peter and fully approved his action – the hand of God was so evident in it all.

11:19 - 16:5 ANTIOCH AND THE MISSIONARY EFFORT: ADVANCE INTO PRESENT-DAY SYRIA AND TURKEY

11:19-30 Antioch: the first Gentile church

At about the same time as the events in Caesarea, things are moving in the north, at Antioch, third largest city in the world (after Rome and Alexandria), busy commercial centre and

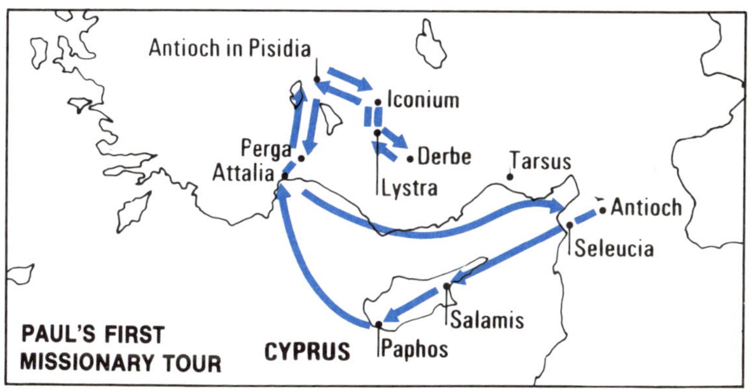

capital of the Roman province of Syria. The warm response of the Greeks to the Christian message brings Barnabas back from Jerusalem. He in turn tracks Saul down at his home city of Tarsus. And the stage is set for the next great advance, described from chapter 13 onwards.

A great famine ... in the days of Claudius (28): Claudius was emperor AD 41-54. The famine hit Palestine about AD 46.

12 Death of James; imprisonment of Peter

While Paul and Barnabas are in Jerusalem, handing over Antioch's donation for the famine relief, Herod (posing as a champion of the law) instigates a new wave of persecution. James, one of the three apostles closest to Jesus, dies. But God has other plans for Peter. Even a maximum security prison presents no problems to God.

Herod the king (1): Herod Agrippa 1, grandson of Herod the Great (Luke 1:5). The kingdom was given him by his friend, the Emperor Caligula, and extended by Claudius. His sudden death (23) in AD 44 is also described by the Jewish historian Josephus.

Unleavened Bread (3): the seven-day feast immediately following Passover, and regarded as part of that festival (4).

Four squads of soldiers (4): one squad of four soldiers for each watch of the night, two with Peter, two at the door.

13 - 14 Barnabas and Saul sent out: the first missionary journey

The church, directed by the Holy Spirit, selects its best men for pioneer work.

The tour begins with **Cyprus** (Barnabas' native island; 13:4-12) where they encounter Elymas, the magician, and make a notable convert, the proconsul Sergius Paulus. Saul adopts the Roman version of his name, Paul, and becomes the natural leader of the company.

At **Perga** (13:13) John Mark returns home – for what Paul considers insufficient reason (15:37ff.).

Pisidian Antioch (13:14-52): Paul's first reported sermon; opposition from the Jews.

Iconium (14:1-6): a mixed reception followed by attempted stoning.

Lystra (14:6-20): the cripple healed; Paul and Barnabas acclaimed as gods.

Derbe (14:20-21): a good reception after Paul's narrow escape from death by stoning at Lystra. This does not deter him from a follow-up visit there and to each of the other towns on his way to the coast.

15:1-35 The Council at Jerusalem

Ten years or more have passed since the apostles approved the admission of Cornelius' gentile household to the church (chapters 10-11), and opposition has hardened. When reports of Paul's successes amongst the Gentiles reach the 'salvation by faith *and* circumcision party', they see the red light and openly oppose his teaching. On such a vital matter an authoritative decision by the apostles and elders is essential to avoid a complete split. Peter's reminder of the earlier events, and the account given by Paul and Barnabas of God's work among the Gentiles, carry the day. The final summing-up and verdict given by James, the Lord's brother and leader of the Jerusalem church, finds general acceptance. The Gentiles are asked only to accommodate the Jewish Christians in certain social matters, so that the church may meet together as one.

15:36 - 16:5 Paul and Barnabas separate; the second missionary journey begins; churches in present-day Turkey revisited

The dispute over Mark results in two missionary journeys instead of one. Barnabas' special gift of encouragement no doubt helped his young nephew to make the grade and win Paul's approval later (2 Timothy 4:11).

Silas (Silvanus) (15:40): representative of the Jerusalem church (15:22). Like Paul, he was a Roman citizen. He travelled with the apostle as far as Beroea (17:14) and rejoined him at Corinth. Silas was associated with Paul in the writing (from Corinth) of 1 and 2 Thessalonians; also with Peter in the writing of his first letter.

Timothy (16:3): the decision to circumcise Timothy was taken in order to regularize his position as a Jew, not in order to secure his salvation. Paul had a special affection for his loyal, though timid, companion and successor. He came to regard him almost as his own son.

16:6 - 19:41 PAUL TAKES THE GOSPEL TO EUROPE

16:6-40 At Philippi

At Troas, close to ancient Troy, Luke joins the party for the first time, and Paul receives his call to cross to Europe. It is tempting to think that Luke himself was the man in Paul's dream.

The church at Philippi is born from a bunch of oddly assorted converts – a business woman and her household, a slave-girl and a gaoler. But the Philippian Christians brought Paul much joy down the years by their loving, faithful support and unfailing concern for him (Philippians 1:3ff.; 4:10ff.; 2 Corinthians 8). When Paul moves on, Luke the doctor remains behind. Philippi was a medical centre. See also on Philippians.

A place of prayer (13): small groups of Jews would often meet for prayer. A minimum of ten men was required to constitute a synagogue proper. The riverside at Philippi was a quiet place near the town.

Thyatira (14): a church was later formed in Lydia's home town (see Revelation 2:18ff.).

17:1-15 Thessalonica and Beroea

Thessalonica (1-9): the response to Paul in this sea-port and capital city of Macedonia was no mere flash in the pan (see 1 Thessalonians 1:2-10; 2 Thessalonians 1:3-4). The Jews were 'jealous' because here as elsewhere Paul won over the 'devout Greeks', those already attracted to Judaism – the very people they themselves hoped to win as converts.

Beroea (10-15): the Jewish group here were notable for their open-minded study of the scriptures.

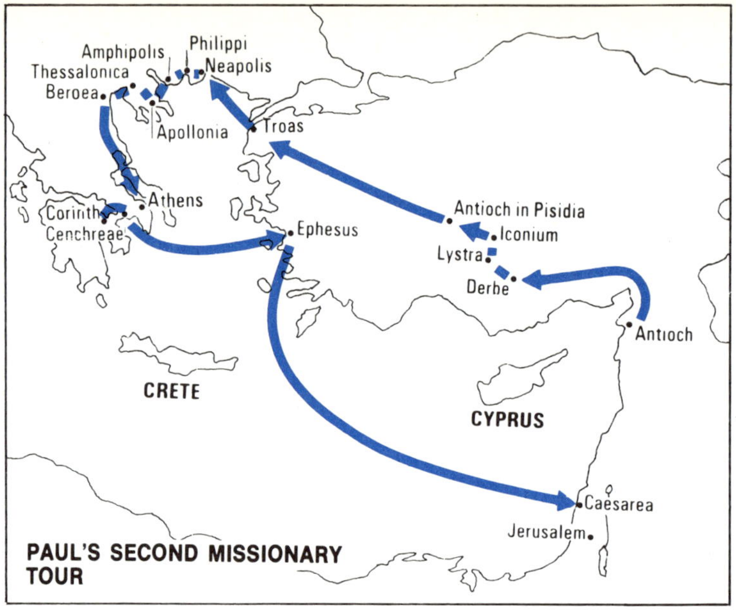

Rutted by chariot wheels, the Via Egnatia is the road Paul and his companions trod on their journey from Philippi to Thessalonica.

The acropolis and Parthenon temple at Athens. Here, where countless gods were worshipped, Paul made known the one true God, the Creator.

17:16-34 Paul at Athens

The apostle Paul was a strategist. He campaigned in the great cities of the Roman world. He selected centres on trade-routes, sea-ports, places where there was much coming and going. From these centres the message would run like fire far and wide. He started with present-day Turkey, moved on to Greece and then set his sights on Rome, and beyond that, on Spain. So he came from Beroea to Athens, a city with 1,000 years of history, glorying in past greatness; Athens, the founder of democracy, home of Aeschylus, Sophocles, Euripides, Thucydides, Plato, Socrates; the greatest university of the world, centre of philosophy, literature, science and art – but hard ground for the gospel.

The Epicureans (18): materialists whose philosophy often amounted to little more than the pursuit of pleasure.

The Stoics (18): rationalists, propounding a philosophy of self-sufficiency and dogged endurance.

Foreign divinities (18): so inseparably did Paul speak of Jesus and the resurrection *(anastasis)* that the Athenians took these to be the names of two new-fangled deities. Several philosophical schools believed in the immortality of the soul, but the Greeks regarded the idea of *bodily* resurrection as completely ludicrous (32).

The Areopagus (19): an ancient court of great prestige, possibly responsible for licensing public lecturers.

In him we live and move ... (28): Paul quotes the Cretan poet Epimenides. According to legend, it was he who advised the Athenians to erect 'anonymous' altars.

18:1-17 Paul in Corinth

See on 1 Corinthians for background. Paul was there during Gallio's pro-consul-ship, probably arriving in AD 50. Gallio's decision was an important one for the Christian faith.

Aquila and Priscilla (2): tent-makers or leather-workers. They became staunch friends of Paul. Travel took them to Corinth, Ephesus and back to Rome. Everywhere this hospitable pair were a great support to the young churches.

Claudius' edict (2): issued about 49-50 against the Jews for 'constantly rioting at the instigation of Chrestus'. No doubt an allusion to disputes between Christian and non-Christian Jews in Rome.

18:18-28 Paul returns to Antioch; start of the third missionary journey; Apollos meets Aquila and Priscilla

Apollos (24): thanks to Aquila and Priscilla this eloquent Alexandrian became a man of great influence in the Corinthian church (see 1 Corinthians 1:12; 3:4ff.).

19 Paul at Ephesus

Ephesus was another great commercial centre, although its fine harbour was already beginning to silt up by Paul's day. Situated at the end of the Asiatic caravan-route, the city was a bridgehead between East and West. The tradition is that the apostle John made his home there. So effective was Paul's ministry that it actually affected the takings of the silversmiths. Probably all seven churches mentioned in Revelation 1:11, as well as those at Colossae and Hierapolis, were also founded during this period.

Hall of Tyrannus (9): a lecture-hall which Paul probably used during siesta-time, from 11 a.m. to 4 p.m. (See the Revised Standard Version footnote.)

Magic arts ... books (19): such was the city's name for magical papyrus scrolls of spells that these were known in the Roman world as 'Ephesian letters'.

Artemis (Diana) (24): the cult adopted the name of the Greek goddess, but continued to worship the many-breasted mother-goddess figure of the ancient religion of Asia Minor. The temple was one of the seven wonders of the world, four times the size of the Parthenon. The 'sacred stone' (35) was a meteorite, supposed to resemble the goddess, and kept in the temple.

The theatre (29): an ideal place for the crowd to gather, since it could hold 25,000 people.

The Asiarchs (31): important officials specially responsible for maintaining order at religious functions.

The town clerk (35): the leading civic official, answerable to the Romans for such an illegal assembly.

20 - 28 HOW PAUL EVENTUALLY REACHES ROME

20:1-16 Paul sets out for Jerusalem

2 Corinthians fills in some of the details for the period covered in 20:1-6. The apostle is preoccupied with the collection for the poverty-stricken Christians in Jerusalem (the men listed in verse 4 are delegates from the Gentile churches). His mission to the Gentiles has been much criticized by the Jews. This is his great gesture – a practical expression of the unity of Jew and Gentile in the church of

THE HOLY SPIRIT IN ACTS

G. W. Grogan

The Acts of the Apostles is a book in which the Holy Spirit is especially prominent. Indeed his activity dominates it. The book might well be called 'The acts of the risen Christ by the Holy Spirit through the apostles'.

A divine Person

It is quite clear from the book that the Spirit is personal, for he did what only a person can be said to do. He spoke (1:16; 8:29; 10:19; etc.), and caused others to speak (2:4; 4:8; 31; etc.). He bore witness (5:32), sent out Christian workers (13:4), forbade certain courses of action (16:6-7) and appointed men to office in the church (20:28). He is associated with other persons (15:28) and is clearly believed to be equal with God (5:3, 9).

The agent of Christ

Acts 1:1 may imply that Jesus continued his work after the ascension through the Holy Spirit. He is the gift of the ascended Christ to his disciples (2:33) and is called 'the Spirit of Jesus' (16:7). He is also described as 'the promise of the Father' (1:4).

The creator of the church

The church as we know it today was created at Pentecost. Wind and fire (2:2-3) are Old Testament symbols of deity (see Exodus 19:18; 1 Kings 19:11-12). The gift of tongues (2:4-13) may have been deliberately chosen by God to symbolize the ultimate universality of the church, its presence among men of every language. The Spirit created a fellowship of love and unity (2:43-46) and he was promised to those who responded to the Christian message (2:38; see also 5:32).

The uniting force of the expanding church

Luke is vitally interested in the progress of the gospel and the consequent expansion of the church through the activity of the Spirit. The church at Pentecost was composed of *Jews* and *proselytes*, Gentiles who were committed to Judaism and so reckoned as if they were Jews (2:10). Jews hated Samaritans, who were of mixed race and schismatic religion, but in Acts 8:14-17 the Spirit came upon *Samaritan believers*. It is significant that this happened only after the (Jewish) apostles had laid their hands on them, indicating an attitude of love and fellowship on their part as well as the fact that 'salvation is from the Jews' (John 4:22). The barrier between Jew and Gentile was broken down in Acts 10:44-48 (see also 11:1-18) when the phenomena of Pentecost were repeated by the Spirit as Peter preached the gospel to *Gentiles*. It was through John the Baptist that the promise of the Spirit had first been given (Matthew 3:11-12; see Acts 1:5; 11:16), so Luke records how a group of *John's disciples* also received the Spirit (19:1-7). These passages reveal how the Spirit bound these divergent groups together and prevented division.

The power behind the church's witness

The Holy Spirit was given to the church to enable it to witness for Christ (1:8; compare 4:33). The church was directed by the Spirit when they sent Barnabas and Saul to evangelize the Gentiles (13:1-4), just as he had earlier guided Peter to preach the gospel to Cornelius and his friends (10:19ff.; compare also 8:29; 16:6-7). Filled with the Spirit they spoke with power (4:8, 31; 6:10) and undertook the various aspects of the new church's life and witness (6:3, 5; 11:22-24). The Holy Spirit gave men power to reveal Christ both by their lips and by their lives.

The life of the church

The Spirit of God is concerned with the inner life of the church in every place (9:31). It was the Spirit who appointed elders of the church as its guardians (20:28). The new age was to be one of prophecy (2:17-18), concerned with the instruction and upbuilding of the church itself (15:32) and prediction of things to come (11:28; 21:4). The church in council sought guidance and believed that this was given through the Holy Spirit (15:28).

So Acts occupies a unique position in the revelation of the person and role of the Holy Spirit. It records a fulfilment which is also a new beginning. The prophecies of the Old Testament and the promises of the Lord Jesus about the Holy Spirit find their fulfilment at Pentecost. The new age, the age of the Spirit, preached by Jesus, so evident in the Letters, had begun.

Christ. It is supremely important to him – hence his determination to get to Jerusalem.

Before he left Ephesus, Paul wrote 1 Corinthians. From Macedonia (1) he wrote 2 Corinthians. From Corinth he wrote the letter to the Romans. It is likely he also visited present-day Albania and Yugoslavia ('Illyricum', Romans 15:19) at this time. Back in Philippi, Luke joins the party to Jerusalem.

A Roman legionary

Troas (7-12) provides an interesting glimpse of early church worship – the meeting on a Sunday evening for the Lord's Supper followed by a meal together (11); the length of time given to Paul's preaching (they had no New Testament); the private house, lit by torches; the effort to listen for so long, so late at night, which proved too much for the weary Eutychus.

20:17 - 21:14 Paul addresses the Ephesian elders; Miletus to Caesarea

This is the only address we have in Acts which was given to Christians – and the only recorded address by Paul which Luke actually heard him give. The apostle foresaw so clearly the troubles the church would face, from inside and out. Revelation 2:2 shows what notice the elders took of his warning.

Trials (20:19): there was serious trouble in Asia quite apart from the riot at Ephesus (see 2 Corinthians 1:8-11).

Philip ... one of the seven (21:8): see Acts 6:5; 8:4-40.

Agabus (21:10): acted prophecy of this kind is familiar from the Old Testament (e.g. Ezekiel).

21:15 - 23:35 Paul in Jerusalem: the arrest

Garbled tales have reached the Jewish Christians in Jerusalem that Paul has been teaching *Jews* to abandon circumcision and the law. The troubles loom so large that the relief fund on which Paul set such store is not so much as mentioned by Luke.

The vow (21:23): compare Numbers 6:13-21. By identifying with these men Paul openly shows his respect and conformity to the law.

Brought Greeks into the temple (21:28): anyone might go into the outer court, but notices in Greek and Latin forbade Gentiles, on pain of death, to enter the inner courts.

The barracks (21:34): the cohort was stationed in the fort Antonia. Two flights of steps led down from the

fort to the outer court of the temple.
The Egyptian (21:38): leader of the 'dagger-men' who specialized in assassinating Romans and pro-Roman Jews. They murdered Ananias the high priest in AD 66.
Is it lawful ...? (22:25): the Roman citizen had a right to a fair trial, and even if guilty he was spared the scourge. This horrible whip of several thongs armed with pieces of lead or bone was a far more deadly instrument than the Philippian 'rods'.
Caesarea (23:23): headquarters of the administration of the Roman province of Judea. The size of the escort provided for Paul and his friends – heavy-armed infantry, cavalry, light-armed troops – is an indication of the restiveness in the province.
Felix (23:24): Pilate's successor; governor of Judea AD 52-59. His residence was the palace built by Herod the Great (35).

24 - 26 In Caesarea: the defence before Felix, Festus and Agrippa

Paul spends two years in custody in Caesarea, probably AD 58-60. Three times he is called before the authorities, and the skill with which he conducts his case is some measure of the apostle's ability. So effectively does he answer the charges that his hearers are compelled to admit there is no case against him – no case, that is, apart from the theological question of the resurrection.
Before Felix (chapter 24). A violent but ineffective governor, Felix was eventually recalled (about AD 59) for mishandling riots in Caesarea. Drusilla, a Jewess, daughter of Herod (Acts 12:1), was his third wife. She was presumably the source of Felix' information about 'the Way'. Paul's talk of 'justice and self-control and future judgement' was too near the bone for this pair, especially as Felix was hoping for a fat bribe from his prisoner (26).
Before Festus (25:1-12). Festus was not governor for long: he died in AD 62. His attempt to curry favour with the Jews compelled Paul to appeal to Caesar. He had more hope of justice from Nero than from the Sanhedrin!
Before Agrippa (25:13 - 26:32). This is Agrippa II, son of the Herod of Acts 12:1, great-grandson of Herod the Great. Bernice, his sister and acting wife, went on to complete an inglorious career by becoming mistress to the emperors Titus and Vespasian. The mention of resurrection strikes the pagan Festus as completely crazy. Agrippa laughs it off – to avoid either losing face with Festus or annoying the Jews by denying the prophets.

Paul's conversion story in chapter 26 differs in emphasis from the account in chapter 22. The 'goads' are the pressures compelling Paul to a complete change of direction in life. Verses 16-18 summarize the Lord's words on the Damascus road, what Ananias said, and the message which came to Paul in the temple (22:17ff.).

27 - 28 Paul's journey to Rome: shipwreck and house-arrest

The voyage is made in three ships: a coaster from Caesarea to Myra; a cargo vessel (carrying grain on the regular run from Alexandria to Rome) from Myra to Malta; and another from Malta to Puteoli in the Bay of Naples. Luke gives a superb account of the eventful passage, and a vivid impression of the outstanding courage and leadership of Paul under strain. So Paul reaches Rome at last, though hardly in the way he imagined
The fast had already gone by (27:9): i.e. the Atonement, September/October. These were dangerous months for sailing, which ceased for winter in mid-November.
Secure the boat (27:16): the dinghy had been towed behind – now they brought it on board.
Undergird the ship (27:17): by passing ropes round the hull.
The Syrtis (27:17): quicksands and whirlpool off the North African coast.
Neither sun nor stars (27:20): without which they were unable to set a course or calculate their position.
The Twin Brothers (28:11): Castor and Pollux, the sailors' patrons.
Two whole years (28:30): Paul made good use of his free custody. It is not known what happened after this time. Most probably he was released, went to Spain as planned, and then back east before further imprisonment and execution in about AD 67.

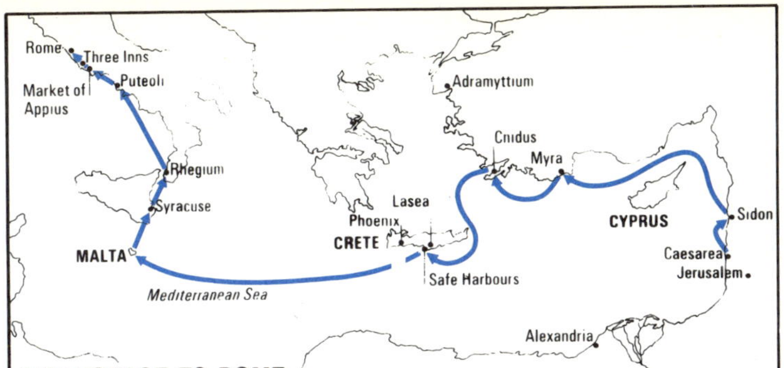

THE VOYAGE TO ROME

A model of a Roman corn ship, at the Haifa Maritime Museum. Paul travelled to Rome on a ship like this.

THE HISTORICAL AND POLITICAL BACKGROUND OF THE NEW TESTAMENT

Colin Hemer

The Persian Empire was overthrown by the spectacular conquests of Alexander the Great (336-323 BC). Alexander aimed to unite the cultures of Greece and the East, and from his time Greek influence spread in the eastern Mediterranean. After the conqueror's untimely death his enormous dominions were divided. His general Ptolemy took Egypt and also established control over Palestine. The country was of strategic importance to Ptolemy and his successors, but he allowed it a large measure of autonomy in religious affairs. Many Jews actually migrated to Alexandria, his new capital in Egypt, and their community received limited political rights in that brilliant and successful city.

Greek influence

The whole succeeding period is often called the Hellenistic age (*Hellen* = 'Greek'). The *Koine* ('common') dialect of Greek became an international language. The 'Dispersion' (expatriate) Jews, particularly in Alexandria, adopted it, and a Greek translation of the Old Testament, the Septuagint, was made there, commissioned originally, it is said, by King Ptolemy II himself, and completed by the middle of the 2nd century BC.

The Hellenizing movement was also strong among the Jews, though the Hasidim ('pious'), and later the Pharisees, resisted Greek influences in the name of devotion to the Jewish law.

When the power of the Ptolemies declined, Palestine finally fell in

The theatre at Ephesus was the scene of the demonstration against Paul and his companions described so dramatically in Acts 19.

200 BC to Antiochus III ('the Great'), one of the Seleucids, the rival Macedonian dynasty of Syria. The Seleucids at first treated Jewish institutions with respect. But Antiochus made a fatal error. His ambitions in Asia Minor and Greece provoked a clash with the rising power of Rome. He was decisively beaten in 190 at Magnesia in western Asia Minor, and forced to surrender large territories and to pay punitive reparations. So Rome became a force in the East.

Antiochus IV Epiphanes ('god manifest') (175-164 BC) tried to restore the fortunes of his kingdom. He profited from intrigues among the Jewish factions to force upon the Jews a Greek culture and then a pagan altar and cult actually in the temple in Jerusalem.

This act provoked a violent response. The Jewish patriots found a leader in the priest Mattathias and then among his five sons. The family are known collectively as the Maccabees, from Judas Maccabaeus, the third son, who first assumed the leadership upon his father's death.

After a long struggle the brothers achieved religious freedom for their people and eventually established a virtually independent Jewish state, ruled by a succession of high priests of the Maccabean family. These rulers are known by the dynastic name Hasmoneans, and they later took the title of 'kings'. They cultivated good relations with Rome, conquered Samaria and Galilee to the north, and remained in power until 63 BC. In that year Pompey, the Roman commander in the East, intervened in a dynastic dispute, occupied Jerusalem, and added Palestine to the Roman province of Syria, newly organized from the former Seleucid dominions.

Rome: from Republic to Empire

The Roman state itself was deeply divided by social and party strife. It had become evident that its municipal institutions were hopelessly unequal to the government of its huge conquests. A series of Roman civil wars had repercussions throughout the East. Julius Caesar defeated Pompey and became dictator until murdered by republicans in 44 BC. His faction, now led by Antony and Octavian, overthrew the republicans under Brutus and Cassius at Philippi in Macedonia in 42. Antony and Octavian in their turn fought for supremacy, and Octavian won the decisive victory at Actium in western Greece in 31.

The new master of the Roman world was still a young man, the great-nephew and adopted son of the great Julius Caesar. In 27 the Roman Senate conferred upon him the title 'Augustus'. He was careful to disguise the extent of his power by a scrupulous appearance of legality. He claimed to have restored the Republic, but in fact founded what we must call the 'Empire', though in theory the idea of hereditary monarchy was abhorrent to the Romans. He and his immediate successors gave a new peace and prosperity throughout the Mediterranean world. He died in AD 14.

Among the New Testament writers only Luke ever names a Roman emperor. His references give us in outline a framework for the events of the Gospels and Acts. Jesus was born in the time of Augustus (Luke 2:1). The preaching of John the Baptist (Luke 3:1-2) and the ministry, death, resurrection and ascension of Jesus happened under Tiberius (AD 14-37). Paul's journeys occupied much of the reigns of Claudius (AD 41-54; mentioned in Acts 11:28 and 18:2) and Nero (54-68), the Caesar to whom Paul appealed. Paul reached Rome about AD 60.

The fullness of time

The times were ripe for the coming of Jesus and the spread of the gospel. Augustus had given his world respite from war. A great network of new roads united the civilized world, with its focus in Rome. Communications became easier than ever before. Latin and Greek became official languages, with Greek spoken everywhere in the East. It was already the language of the Septuagint translation of the Old Testament, and now was to become the natural vehicle of the new scriptures.

Among the Jews there was fervent expectation of the prophesied Messiah (see 'The Religious Background of the New Testament'), and among the Gentiles a less articulate reaching after a personal 'salvation'. Meanwhile the communities of Dispersion Jews scattered in strategic centres throughout the Empire provided a ready-made audience for the future preaching of Paul and others.

Rulers of Palestine

The more immediate political background to the Gospels goes back to a dominant figure in Palestine before the Roman occupation, an unscrupulous, half-Jewish adventurer named Antipater. He and his son Herod courted the favour of successive Roman rulers, and Herod ('the Great') was made king of the Jews by them. He reigned 37-4 BC: Jesus was born just before he died (see Matthew 2; Luke 1:5).

At his death his kingdom was divided among three of his sons. Herod Archelaus, the ruler of Judea and Samaria (Matthew 2:22), was deposed in AD 6 and replaced by direct Roman rule under 'procurators', junior governors subject to the governors of Syria. Galilee and other territories continued for the most part to be ruled by the Herods. Herod Antipas, ruler of Galilee (4 BC-AD 39), was responsible for the death of John the Baptist (Matthew 14 and parallels). In the Acts we read of Herod Agrippa I (died AD 44; Acts 12), under whom all Palestine was again briefly united, and his son Herod Agrippa II (Acts 25 - 26).

The best known of the procurators is Pilate (26 - 36), known from other sources as a tactless, violent offender of Jewish scruples. Paul later appeared before the procurators Felix and Festus (Acts 23 - 26).

Political tensions

Palestine was an occupied country, and a strong resistance movement emerged. Nationalists looked for a political Messiah who would liberate his people from the Romans. There were messianic pretenders, especially in turbulent Galilee. The Zealot party of extreme nationalists resisted payment of taxes to Rome.

Meanwhile the high priests and their Sadducee followers collaborated with the Romans. Annas and his family in particular had a vested interest in co-operating with the authorities to whom they owed their position. The Herods too were servile in their dependence on Rome. And the 'publicans' and their tools enriched themselves in the process of collecting taxes for the Romans.

There were evidently many who expected Jesus to fulfil the role of nationalist leader and who were alienated when he showed no intention of fitting in with their plans for him (see John 6:15, 66). But the tenseness of the whole political situation emerges in the manoeuvres at the time of his trial. Pilate was only impelled to action by the supposed political implication of the charge presented.

The gospel in the Roman world

The history of the times is too often viewed exclusively through the perspective of Roman imperial affairs. The Acts of the Apostles stands in its own right as a most important document of the neglected aspects of provincial life and administration. There we have vivid glimpses of provincial governors, client kings and Greek city magistrates. Asia Minor, the land where so much of the narrative is set, was the real centre of the Greek civilization of the period, and it became a strategic focus of Gentile Christianity. There Rome worked through the institutions of Greek civic life, while also accepting and finally authorizing as a bond of loyalty the ruler-cult congenial to the oriental mind. In many of the strategic cities there were wealthy Jewish communities, with privileges guaranteed by the Romans.

Paul of Tarsus was at once Jew, Greek and Roman, a man singularly fitted to communicate the gospel across racial and cultural barriers. We may trace his route along the great roads, and see him adapting his approach to the individual character of each audience. The record of Acts notes the various local institutions with minute correctness: the 'town clerk' at Ephesus, the 'politarchs' (Authorized Version 'rulers of the city') at Thessalonica, the court of 'Areopagus' or 'Mars' Hill' at Athens. The pride of Philippi in its status as a 'colony' of Roman citizens comes over clearly and with an ironic humour (Acts 16:12, 20-21, 37-39; compare Philippians 3:20, Revised Version). The confirmation of many details of this kind is preserved for us on stone in contemporary inscriptions from these cities.

The cosmopolitan Paul found in Roman institutions a protection and aid for the gospel. Judaism was a legally recognized and licensed religion, and in Jesus was the messianic fulfilment of Judaism. At Corinth this view faced a severe challenge. It was a test case and a potential legal precedent. Paul was accused before Gallio, the new Roman governor, of teaching a religion contrary to the law (Acts 18:13). Gallio, brother of the famous philosopher Seneca, the tutor of the future Emperor Nero, was not impressed. In his view the whole thing was a matter of Jewish sectarian theology, in which he took no interest. But by dismissing the case he implicitly acknowledged that Paul's message was entitled to the same standing as other forms of Judaism. This event may probably be dated in 52: an inscription from Delphi in Greece mentions Gallio and gives a fixed point for the chronology of Paul's life.

Paul made full use of the advantages of being a Roman citizen, an unusual privilege at this period for a provincial Jew. At a time of increasing tension in Palestine he exercised his ultimate right of appeal to the emperor. He finally reached Rome as a prisoner, but apparently confident of gaining justice and a vindication of the gospel before the highest tribunal of Nero. The narrative of the Acts breaks off suddenly without telling us the outcome.

Crisis and persecution

The history of the following years was marked by events of far-reaching consequence. In 64 Nero made the Christians the scapegoats for the great fire which destroyed much of Rome. He killed a great number of them with every refinement of cruelty. This was, however, no part of a considered policy, but an irrational, and perhaps quite localized, outburst.

Meanwhile events were moving to a tragic climax in Palestine. The misdeeds of the later procurators and the defiance inspired by the Zealots culminated in a desperate rebellion and war against Rome (66-70). The Roman commander Vespasian was proclaimed emperor in 69 and left his son Titus to finish his campaign. In 70 Titus captured Jerusalem, utterly destroyed Herod's temple and laid waste the city.

The disaster was fraught with profound consequences for Jews and Christians alike. The two faiths became much more decisively separated. Judaism lost some of its privileges and Christianity was faced with new problems and the renewed peril of official persecution.

The relation of some of the later New Testament books to the fall of Jerusalem and the early persecutions is often debated. There are strong reasons for believing at least that Revelation belongs to the last years of the Emperor Domitian, Vespasian's younger son (81-96). Rome was not now a protector, but a mortal adversary. Domitian demanded as a test of loyalty the worship of himself as 'Lord' and 'God'. People were faced with a fundamental choice between Christ and Caesar.

New Testament section 2

THE LETTERS

Introduction/Donald Guthrie

The letters make up about a third of the New Testament. Their contents are varied, but all are important because they represent what the apostles and their associates taught. They combine teaching about God and the Christian gospel with instruction on life and behaviour. They also give an insight into the problems of the early church and how they were met.

As letters they were written by real people because of real situations or needs. So it will help to trace the story which lies behind them. It will also help us to understand them to know the ideas which were held at the time. Then we can gather together some of the main themes.

THE LETTERS IN GROUPS

The obvious way to group the letters is by author, and this is in fact already done for us in the New Testament. There are thirteen letters under Paul's name, one anonymous letter (Hebrews), one by James, two by Peter, three by John, one by Jude.

Paul's letters fall naturally into four groups:

— 1 and 2 Thessalonians are probably the earliest, and are particularly concerned about Christ's return.
— Romans, Galatians and 1 and 2 Corinthians share a common emphasis on the gospel which Paul preached.
— The 'captivity letters', in all of which Paul mentions that he is a prisoner, consist of Ephesians, Colossians, Philippians and Philemon. Some of his most profound teaching is included in these letters.
— The 'pastoral letters', 1 and 2 Timothy and Titus, are concerned with practical matters of church leadership and organization.

The other letters are often grouped under the title of 'General Epistles'. They are addressed to a more general, less precisely defined, readership than Paul's letters. Exceptions are Hebrews, which really stands on its own, and 2 and 3 John addressed to a specific individual or church.

THE SETTING OF THE LETTERS

It is not always easy to reconstruct the historical setting of the letters. They were the products of the life of the early church, not written systematically. They supply much basic Christian teaching, but not in a formal way as theological or ethical treatises. The fact that the letters grew out of the life of the church in this way is also their strength: Christian teaching was dynamic, not stereotyped.

The book of Acts is our only other source of historical information about the early church. But Acts was selective. It did not claim to be a complete record of the events, so there are many gaps in our knowledge.

This creates a problem when it comes to trying to decide the setting of the letters. There are many issues about which we cannot be dogmatic. But the following possible reconstruction may help by showing in outline the story behind the letters.

The first letters

We can be certain of the rough dates of the first letters at least.

1 and 2 Thessalonians were written during Paul's time at Corinth on his second missionary journey. An inscription at Delphi helps to fix this date at about AD 50-51.

After his remarkable conversion Paul had spent some years at Tarsus. He had had time to think over the implications of his new faith. He had also spent a year teaching at Antioch, and about two years in missionary work, when many churches were established in non-Jewish areas.

So Paul's first letters were from someone whose Christian thinking had already matured. They were also essentially practical, and did not call for the great assertions of Christian truths which are so characteristic of some of his later letters.

The 'gospel' letters

The next group may fairly confidently be placed during the third missionary tour, though there is a good case for assigning **Galatians** to the period between the first and second tours.

Paul had sailed from Corinth in Greece to Ephesus. He had spent some time there when he heard reports of difficulties in the church back at Corinth. He also received a letter from the church itself. **1 Corinthians** was his reply. Again this is essentially a practical letter which throws light on the many problems facing a newly established community in a pagan environment notorious for its immorality.

Paul's various contacts with the church at Corinth are not easy to unravel, though **2 Corinthians** provides some information. Paul may have visited Corinth after writing his first letter, and have written another letter which has not been preserved. At any rate, it is plain that he was not too happy about the Corinthians' attitude to him. Then Titus was sent to Corinth, and gave Paul better news of the situation. So in 2 Corinthians Paul expresses his relief, his anxiety to restore good relations, and warns and encourages the church.

Shortly afterwards Paul visited Corinth again himself. While there he wrote his famous letter to the **Romans,** the nearest of all his letters to a theological treatise. In it he works out in some detail the great theme of righteousness by faith and shows the practical outcome of the doctrine.

It is not certain why he wrote in this way to the Romans. He expected to be visiting them soon, so may have wanted them to know the basics of his thinking. He may also have wanted to lay the foundation of further outreach to Spain.

But it was not to work out as Paul had planned. Soon afterwards he travelled to Jerusalem, where he was arrested. He was held captive for some time at Caesarea. Then he claimed his right to be tried before the emperor. He arrived in Rome – as a prisoner.

The prison letters

Tradition favours Rome as the place from which Paul wrote a number of his letters. However some believe these 'captivity letters' were written at Caesarea. There is also growing support for Ephesus as the place of origin of the letter to the Philippians, if not of the others too. If it was in Rome, this would agree with what is said in Acts: Paul was allowed considerable freedom during his imprisonment there. This would also agree well with the allusions in these letters to frequent communication between himself and his associates.

Ephesians and **Colossians** are close in content. The former seems to deal in general terms with a situation seen more specifically in the latter. A heresy was threatening the churches in the Lycus Valley east of Ephesus, and Paul writes his letter to Colossae there to strengthen the Christians and give them positive teaching about the person and work of Christ to help them resist the error. Many of the same themes are echoed in Ephesians, often in similar words, but applied more to the doctrine of the church. In spite of its title, this letter may well have been a circular letter sent round to many churches in the province of Asia.

The little letter to **Philemon** belongs to the same period. Paul writes tactfully, pleading for leniency towards a runaway slave. Many of Paul's associates mentioned in Colossians are also mentioned in Philemon.

Philippians deals with a different situation. Paul wants to thank the Christians at Philippi for the concern they have shown in sending him gifts. The main reason for writing is because he wanted to return to Philippi. He also wanted to prepare the way for Timothy's coming visit.

The remarkable feature of these 'captivity letters' is the depth of Christian understanding Paul shows in them. Perhaps it was a by-product of a period when physical freedom was denied him.

The pastoral letters

If Paul wrote these letters in his old age, he must have been released from his captivity in Rome. **1 and 2 Timothy** and **Titus** show something of his care and concern for the churches and their organization. Some have queried whether in fact Paul was the author of the letters as stated, partly because they require a period of further activity in Ephesus and Crete of which there is no hint in Acts.

Hebrews

The letter to the **Hebrews** seems to have originated in, or been addressed to, Rome, although it is impossible to be certain about this. The letter is not addressed to a specific church, but to a group of Christian Jews who, it is generally supposed, were segregating themselves from the main church and were hankering after the glories of Judaism. The unnamed author shows the superiority of Christ to the old religion.

The general letters

It is difficult to be certain of the precise historical setting of the general letters.

1 Peter is the most specific, mentioning Christians in five provincial districts of Asia Minor who were threatened with persecution. The letter is intended to encourage those who are suffering for Christ's sake, and the basis of that encouragement is found in the sufferings of Christ himself.

2 Peter was presumably sent to the same general circle of readers. It warns against a particular heresy which encouraged immorality, and gives an idea of the influences which threatened the teaching and conduct of the early church.

1, 2 and 3 John are generally thought to be among the latest of the New Testament writings. They probably date from the last decade of the 1st century. According to tradition John lived in Asia Minor, so the background to the letters is probably the church life there. For instance 'Docetism', a heresy which regarded Christ as a heavenly being incapable of suffering, and so denied his incarnation, was beginning to take root and spread.

Of the remaining letters, **James** is almost wholly practical, concerned with encouragement and warning. There is some uncertainty about the setting of this letter, but there seems no reason to doubt that it reflects early conditions within the church. It could even belong to a period before the fall of Jerusalem in AD 70. It appears to come from the Jewish Christian section of the church. The brief letter of **Jude** is closely linked to 2 Peter since much of the material about the heresy occurs in both, often in similar language. Jude describes himself as James' brother. It is reasonable to suppose that both were brothers of Jesus.

THE BACKGROUND OF THE LETTERS

It seems clear, then, that all the letters belong to the second half of the 1st century, the formative period of early church development. They are therefore our only source of information on what the apostles taught.

To interpret them properly we need to understand their background. We have to know something of the thought and practice against which the letters were written for many of their ideas to be meaningful. The following paragraphs simply draw attention to the main areas, to indicate the methods by which light can be thrown on problems of interpretation.

The Old Testament

Although some letters make more direct use of the Old Testament than others, there is a basic assumption that Christianity is essentially a fulfilment of what the Jewish scriptures predicted. The writers therefore appeal to the Old Testament as their authority. Paul frequently uses it to support his arguments. Sometimes he strings quotations together as the rabbis did, with little consideration for the original context (for example in Romans 3), but more often he cites separate passages to lend authority to his argument.

Much of the imagery of the letters is drawn from Old Testament sources: for instance, the 'redemption' and 'priesthood' themes in 1 Peter and the allegory of Sarah and Isaac in Galatians. Many of the phrases in a letter such as James are echoes of Old Testament language. There can be no doubt that since the church took the Old Testament as their scriptures it played a dominant part in the thinking of those who wrote the New Testament letters. All these writers were Jews who had become Christians.

Hellenism

How far Greek thought influences the writers has long been a matter of debate. Certainly much of the earliest missionary activity took place in areas where Greek influence was very strong. When Paul discusses 'wisdom' it is not necessary to see this as evidence of Hellenistic influence. Even so, his Christian interpretation of wisdom cannot properly be understood except against the kind of debate common in his time. Similarly, his idea of 'fullness' must be understood against the Greek philosophical background.

The method of argument in Hebrews is in some respects similar to that of Philo of Alexandria (although there are even more striking differences). In 1 John some find echoes of Greek catchwords which have been taken up and used in a Christian sense. The ideas of light and life, for example, have parallels in contemporary thought.

Paganism

The New Testament church grew up in a pagan environment. Some of the problems discussed in the letters stem directly from this. The situation behind 1 Corinthians is a classic example of the practical difficulties which arose in the church as a result of the previous pagan background of the converts. Some Christians were taking legal action against each other before pagan judges, and Paul had to point out the incongruity of this. There was even a problem from the market-place: meat offered to idols was the only meat sold and this posed a dilemma for sensitive consciences.

The immorality of the Gentile world is vividly painted by Paul in the opening chapter of his letter to the Romans. When the developing church is set against its environment, the grace of God – such a dominant theme in the New Testament letters – is most triumphantly seen.

Judaism

In the ancient world, before the rise of the Christian church, the most ethical form of religious teaching was undoubtedly Judaism. It was because they were dissatisfied with pagan religions that many of the more thoughtful Gentiles became proselytes, adherents of the Jewish faith.

From this growing group of interested Gentiles Paul won many converts on his missionary journeys. The letter to the Hebrews points out Christ's superiority to Judaism by showing that the old system of worship has its spiritual fulfilment in Christianity.

THE MAIN THEMES OF THE LETTERS

It is not possible to summarize here all the themes of such a varied collection of letters. In some letters important doctrines are carefully discussed. In others they are merely stated, and in yet others no more than implied. Nevertheless, in spite of the variety, there is a basic uniformity in the teaching – explicit or implicit - which runs through them all

God

The letters teach that God is a holy God who expects holiness. He is himself the pattern for Christian behaviour. He is moreover sovereign. The Christians were in no doubt that he controls the world. But the most characteristic view is that which Jesus taught, echoed many times in the Epistles: that God is Father. The intensely personal view of God which the letter-writers all share springs from this conviction. God is both Creator and author of the new creation. Paul describes the cosmic reconciliation of the world to God through his action in sending Christ.

Christ

The early Christians expressed their view of Jesus in a variety of ways. This is reflected in the letters, and shows the impossibility of reducing the person of Christ to a single formula.

They use various titles to describe him. 'Jesus Christ' is used to show Jesus as the fulfilment of the promised Jewish Messiah (Christ). But the fuller title, 'Lord Jesus Christ', is also frequent, and shows that the Christians at once acknowledge his sovereignty.

The most characteristic passages of Paul's letters are those which show his exalted view of the person of Christ. He existed before the world was made. He set aside his riches to become poor for our sakes (2 Corinthians 8:9). He humbled himself to become a man in spite of his position of equality with God (Philippians 2:5-11). He was the exact 'image' of God (Colossians 1:15).

The other letters demonstrate a similar view of Christ. Hebrews shows him as fully God (chapter 1) and at the same time fully man (chapter 2), able to represent his people as their High Priest before God the Father. The letters of Peter and John show no essential difference. Through Christ God the Father brings salvation to men. He is the supreme expression of God's love.

Man and his salvation

The world is corrupt and evil. The completely new start, the new era brought in by Christ, is the only answer. The new creation, salvation, eternal life, this is the main theme of the Letters, expounded in them or simply reflected and expressed. Life in Christ demands a new morality, living not according to the old pagan ways but according to God's law of love, and this must be worked out not only in church life, in the new community, but in the world.

New Testament 2.1

ROMANS

Paul, the traveller and Roman citizen, had still not been to Rome when this letter was written (about AD 57). He had made three prolonged and extensive journeys, pioneering the Christian message throughout the eastern provinces of the Empire and establishing churches. Now, probably in Corinth, about to take the relief fund to Jerusalem (see on Acts 20), Paul felt free at last to turn his eyes west – to Spain. And on the way he would fulfil the ambition of years and visit the Christians at Rome. He was not to know that three weary years would elapse between the letter and the visit, or that when he eventually entered Rome it would be as a prisoner (Acts 28).

The city and the church. Rome in Paul's day was the capital of an empire which stretched from Britain to Arabia. Wealthy and cosmopolitan, it was the diplomatic and trade centre of the then-known world. There was constant coming and going. The Roman Peace made travel safe; Roman roads made it relatively swift and easy. Visitors from Rome heard Peter's first sermon in Jerusalem on the Day of Pentecost. So it is not surprising that there was a large and flourishing Christian community there by the time Paul wrote. It was the usual mixture of Jews and Gentiles. There was no serious rift between the two sections, as there had been in the Galatian churches. But there was a tendency for each to criticize and look down on the other.

Some time earlier there had been trouble with the authorities. And although all was now quiet, the Christians were still suspect. Their Founder had, after all, faced a charge of treasonable activity against the emperor. And despite their efforts to live as loyal citizens of Rome, only a few years after this letter (in AD 64) Nero was able to make a scapegoat of the Christians, laying the blame on them when the city went up in flames. Tradition says that Paul – and Peter too – died in the ferocious persecution that followed.

The letter. Romans takes pride of place among the New Testament letters. In point of time, it follows the Thessalonian and Corinthian letters and Galatians, and precedes Colossians and Ephesians. Some of the themes of the earlier letters are taken up again in Romans, which is the fullest and most closely reasoned statement we have of the basic Christian truths. It is Paul's gospel manifesto. What impelled him to write this unique document we do not know. Perhaps he already sensed he was risking his life by going to Jerusalem, and felt he might never give his message to the Roman Christians in person.

The great theme of Romans is faith in Christ as the only ground of man's acceptance by God, who treats all men alike, Jew and Gentile. Paul pulls no punches in describing the state the world is in (1:18-32). Every one of us stands condemned by God's standards. Even the Jew, who has the unique privilege of knowing God's law, cannot keep it (2 - 3:20). But God offers us free pardon and new life. Jesus has served our sentence for us (chapter 5). We are free to make a fresh start – this time with all the power of God at our disposal (chapters 6 - 8). Why, then, when the Gentiles respond to God's offer of salvation, do the Jews reject it? It is because they see salvation in terms of works. But in the end they too will come in (chapters 9 - 11). God's forgiveness and love spur us on to live up to our new calling – to reshape our whole way of thinking and manner of life. God's 'good news' is not an end in itself. It is meant to transform human relationships – making it possible for Jews and Gentiles to treat one another as equals in the church – and to permeate every aspect of daily living (chapters 12 - 15).

The impact and influence of Romans is immeasurable. It has fired great men – Augustine, Luther, Bunyan, Wesley – and through them shaped the history of the church. But

God has also touched the lives of countless individuals through this letter – ordinary men and women who have read and believed and acted on the apostle's teaching.

1:1-15 INTRODUCTION

The apostle's whole life-mission is captured in this first, typical, aside (1-6). Paul, Christ's slave and emissary, whose commission is to carry God's good news to the nations, writes to his fellow Christians in Rome. His 'grace' and 'peace' blend the traditional Greek and Jewish greetings into something uniquely Christian. Romans is the product of an intellectual, someone with a keen mind – but also a warm, human personality. That much is clear from verses 8-15. Paul is full of appreciation, longing to see and share with a group of Christians he has not yet met.

Saints (7): not a special, super-grade elite, but all who belong to Christ.

Barbarians (14): New English Bible, 'non-Greek' – and therefore uncivilized!

1:16 - 8:39 THE CHRISTIAN GOSPEL

1:16-17 The gospel in a nutshell

Paul glories in his message: that God is able to save – and will save – anyone prepared to rely completely on him.

Verse 17: the first part means that salvation is a matter of faith, from beginning to end. The quotation from Habakkuk is open to more than one interpretation. Here the meaning is: 'he who is put right with God through faith shall live' (Good News Bible).

1:18 - 3:20 The old humanity

Why should anyone need to be 'put right with God'? Paul begins his thesis with a penetrating analysis of the human situation.

The pagan world (1:18-32). Here man is caught in a downward spiral. Evidence of God is all around him, in the natural world that God has created. But man closes his mind to the truth. Because of this his whole mental process becomes warped. He is determined to go his own way, and in the end – since he has been given real freedom of choice – God lets him. So he sinks deeper and deeper into the morass of his own perverse and perverted behaviour. Wrong thinking (irrationality) and wrongdoing go hand in hand. The man who rejects reason (25) will not listen to conscience either (32).

The forum at Rome as it looks today. When Paul wrote his letters, Rome was the proud and glorious capital of a great empire.

Moralist and Jew (2 - 3:20). There were some high-principled individuals, even among pagans. And there were the Jews, who prided themselves in possessing and knowing God's law. Both would be quick to condemn the vices of the pagan world. But are they in any better position? Does the moralist actually live up to his high standards? Is his conscience clear? Does the Jew actually keep the law he is so proud of? If not, he is as morally bankrupt as the pagan. God judges with strict impartiality.

Paul can imagine the questions the hecklers will fling at him. He meets their points one by one:

— Has the Jew any advantage, then? Yes, the fact that God has entrusted him with his revelation (3:1-2).
— If the Jews have failed in their trust and will be judged, what about all God's promises to them? God still keeps his word (3:3-4).
— It seems human sin serves a good end, then, by throwing God's goodness into relief. So why should it be punished? Why not go on sinning so that people can see God's goodness all the better? Because God is a just Judge – and the end does not justify the means (3:5-8).
— Are the Jews any better off than other people? No. Everyone is in the grip of sin. And the law makes man accountable – it is powerless to put anyone in the right with God (3:9-20).

2:6-10: the point is God's impartiality, not that salvation can ever be earned, as 3:20 makes clear.

Circumcision (2:25): see on Genesis 17.

2:29: there is a play on words here. 'Jew' is derived from 'Judah', which means praise.

Justified (3:20): Paul often uses this legal term. It means acquittal or free pardon. See 4:25.

3:21 - 5:21 Acquittal

Free pardon on the ground of faith (3:21-31). Since God is just, the man who infringes his law must be punished. The whole human race stands under sentence of death unless the demands of justice can be met some other way. Jesus has provided that other way by standing in for us at the cost of his own life (chapter 5 explains how this was possible). God will now forgive and receive *anyone* who comes to him trusting in Jesus. This opens up a new life. It is the essence of the good news Paul was commissioned to preach, and the heart of the Christian message still.

The case of Abraham (chapter 4). Paul picks up on his statement in 3:21-22 that this same faith-principle is inherent in the Old Testament scriptures. If he can prove his point in the case of Abraham – father of the Jewish nation, and the prime example of an upright man – surely the Jewish objectors will be convinced. And he can. God accepted Abraham not because of his good life, but because of his faith (4:3; Genesis 15:6) – because against all the odds Abraham stuck to his conviction that God would do what he promised (21). The covenant-agreement, of which circumcision was the outward sign, came later (Genesis 17). So it is to those who share Abraham's faith, not simply his national identity, that God extends his friendship still.

Christ and Adam (chapter 5). The death and resurrection of Jesus has given us a new standing before God. We have life. We have peace. We have hope. We have the presence of the Holy Spirit. There is point and meaning now to the rough and tumble of life (1-5). But how can one man's death result in pardon for millions of others? The key lies in the solidarity of the human race. Sin, disobedience, began with one man (Adam) and spread to all his descendants. We all share the 'disease' and its inevitable consequence, death – being cut off from God. On the same principle, Jesus has made acquittal and life available to all. Adam was the head of the old humanity; Jesus is the head of the new, reborn humanity. We were 'in' Adam when he sinned. We are 'in Christ' when we put our trust in him.

Grace (5:2): another of Paul's favourite words. It means the (wholly undeserved) favour of God.

5:20: we all have an innate tendency to feel that laws were made to be broken. The fact that something is forbidden actually makes us want to do it more (see 7:8).

6 - 8 The new humanity

The old life and the new (chapter 6). God's forgiveness is 'big' enough to deal with any amount of human sin. Does that mean Christians have an insurance policy to go on as before? What an absurd idea! Becoming a Christian means identifying ourselves with Christ – becoming one with him – and so sharing in his death and resurrection. Baptism – going down into the water and coming up again – gives us a living picture of what has actually happened. there is as complete a break between the old life and the new as if we had actually died and been reborn. We were dead to God before – now we are alive to him (11). We have been given a new inclination to obey, with which to fight the old tug of sin (17). And we must act on it. Sin is not our master any longer. We are in the service of God. The result of serving sin is death (21), but the result of serving God is life – God's life at work in us, transforming us (22).

The law and its limitations (7 - 8:4). In order to counteract the widespread belief that men can 'work their passage' to heaven, Paul has said some harsh things about the law. Now he stops to set the record straight. For Jews like himself, who took the matter seriously, the law could be a real tyrant. Christ sets us free from the killing struggle to get right with God by keeping the law to the letter – but not free to do as we please. There is nothing wrong with God's law in itself. It is wholly good. And the Christian, with the new power at his disposal (6, and 8:4) has the potential to keep it. The root of the trouble, as Paul shows from his own experience, is not the law but our own bias to sin (7:14). And conversion does not end the tension (22-23). Left to ourselves we are still helpless to obey. But we are not now left to ourselves. The law serves its purpose when it makes us despair of our own efforts. Only at this point are we ready to ask Christ to do for us what we cannot do for ourselves.

The Holy Spirit – and God's eternal purpose (8:5-39). The Holy Spirit of God is alive and actively at work in everyone who belongs to Christ (9). He helps us to keep God's law. It is his presence that convinces us we really are God's children (16). He is our foretaste (first instalment, 23) of glory to come – a living spring of hope within us. And he turns our inarticulate longings into prayer (26-27).

It is God's intention that every one of us should be like Christ (29). Like him in character now. Like him in glory eventually. In other words, God is recreating us 'in his own image' (Genesis 1:27). And every little circumstance of life is worked into this great overall purpose (28). Nothing can shake it. No one can ever make him write us off – we have Christ in heaven to plead our cause. And there is no power in heaven or earth that can cut us off from his love. So whatever life may bring, we can win through. These are the great certainties of the Christian life.

Sinful body (6:6): not the human body, but the 'sinful self' (New English Bible).

Verse 11: this is not a matter of playing games, pretending to be what we are not – but of being what we are. 'Dead to sin': in the sense that the score for the old life has been settled, not that we no longer feel its pull.

Flesh (7:5, etc.): Paul often uses this word, in distinction from the 'spirit'. He means 'self' – the old, sinful nature.

Body of death (7:24): human nature, subject to the laws of sin and death.

Likeness of sinful flesh (8:3): Paul chooses his words with care. Jesus was a real man, but in one respect he was not identical to other men. He did not share the sinfulness that ordinarily goes with human nature.

Your bodies are dead (8:10): i.e. we still die physically.

8:11: Christians are promised a resurrection like Christ's.

Abba (8:15): the ordinary word a Hebrew-speaking child still uses for his 'daddy'.

Creation (19ff.): because man is part of nature, when he sinned he brought pain and death not only on himself but on the whole created world. So in the day man is transformed, the creation will share his transformation. There will be 'a new heaven and a new earth' (Revelation 21:1).

Predestined (8:29): see the note on Election.

9 - 11 THE NATION OF ISRAEL

As Paul dwells on God's glorious provision for all who are 'in Christ', he is filled with distress for Israel, God's own specially chosen and privileged people. How could they refuse to believe in their own, promised Messiah? The Gentiles responded eagerly to the gospel – but not the Jews. And Paul would have sold his own soul to have had it otherwise.

How can he account for this strange anomaly? God has not broken his word (9:6). All along he exercised his sovereign right of choice (9:6-13). And we can hardly call him to task for it. The Maker has an indisputable right to do as he pleases with what he makes (9:14-21). It is only by virtue of his patience and mercy that even a remnant of stubborn, rebellious Israel survived his judgement (9:22-29). People of other nations, knowing their failure, welcomed God's offer of acceptance through faith. The Jews, thinking they could earn salvation by keeping the law, refused to consider it (9:30-33).

Paul himself once shared this misplaced zeal. Now he longs for the Jews to share his faith (10:1-4). God offers salvation – life – to men and women on only one condition: an open declaration of belief in the risen Christ as Lord (10:5-13; and see Philippians 2:11). It is the preacher's task to see that everyone hears about it. And Israel *has* heard, and understood – yet still refused to believe (10:14-21).

Is this the end for Israel, then (11:1)? No. The very fact that Paul and some of his fellow Jews had become Christians is living proof God has not given Israel up. The nation's blindness is partial and temporary. And it has given the Gentiles their opportunity all the sooner. They owe the Jews a great debt; they should never disparage them. And in due course their own faith will lead to a great turning to God among the Jews. God's ways are beyond us, but his purpose is forgiveness through Christ for Jew and Gentile alike.

9:12-13: the quotations are from Genesis 25:23 and Malachi 1:2-3. Both refer to nations – Israel, descended from Jacob; Edom, descended from Esau – rather than individuals. See on Obadiah.

9:18, 22: see the note on Election.

Like Sodom ... like Gomorrah (9:29): i.e. utterly obliterated. See Genesis 19:24ff.

10:6-10: in the style of a rabbi of his day, Paul gives a running commentary on Moses' words in Deuteronomy 30:11-14.

11:7: see the note on Election.

11:17: it was the ancient practice, when a cultivated olive failed to yield, to graft in a slip of wild olive to give the tree new vigour.

All Israel (11:26): the phrase means Israel as a whole, rather than every Jew without exception.

Mercy upon all (11:32): without distinction, rather than without exception.

ELECTION

In Romans 9 and 11 we have perhaps the most forthright treatment of this subject in the whole Bible. Paul's starting-point is that no one has any claim to God's mercy. He shows how God in his love has chosen certain individuals down the ages to play a special role in his purpose for the world (9:6-13). And he emphasizes the wideness of God's mercy (11:28-32). God the Creator has the right to choose, and we have no right at all to question his choice or doubt his justice.

If God selects some men for forgiveness, does he select others for destruction? Paul is much more cautious about this ('What if ... ?'). He contents himself with asserting God's right to do so – but at the same time stresses God's patience (9:22). He talks about God hardening men's hearts (9:18; and see 1:28), but in every instance these are people who have deliberately refused to listen to him. God never hardens someone's heart against his will.

Human beings are not helpless pawns in the hands of a capricious god. The Bible teaches God's election. It also teaches man's responsibility: his freedom to choose. It may be beyond our understanding how both can operate simultaneously (just as it is hard to understand how scientists can describe light in terms of both waves and particles – two ideas which seem mutually contradictory). God is outside time: we cannot imagine anything beyond our limited range of understanding. So we can only take God's word for it, and hold on to both God's sovereignty and man's freedom to choose – not try to find a compromise between them.

12 - 15:13 THE CHRISTIAN LIFE

Out of sheer love, and at great cost, God has saved our lives. What stronger motive could we have for turning them over to him from now on? This means complete mental re-orientation affecting our whole character, our motives and our behaviour (12:1-2).

12 Human relationships

This is where the transformation begins, as every individual takes his place in the new 'family' of Christ. His own stock goes down. His opinion of others goes up. And individual gifts are pooled for the good of the whole Christian community. We put ourselves at God's disposal, and we don't pull out when the going gets hard. Old attitudes change – not only towards fellow Christians but towards the outside world. Instead of giving tit-for-tat when we are wronged, we treat the enemy as if he were our best friend, and leave God to do the judging.

Burning coals (20): in Egypt people went through the ritual of carrying a pan of burning charcoal on their heads as a token of their penitence.

The Colosseum at Rome was built in AD 80. Here spectators could watch fights between gladiators – and Christians were thrown to the lions.

13 The powers that be

God delegates his power to the authorities for the public good. Christians must therefore respect them. Taxes are to be paid, and laws observed. The Christian has a duty to meet all 'Caesar's' authorized demands. Only when these demands directly conflict with the commands of God is it right to say 'No' (Acts 5:29).

We must incur no debt, other than our permanent obligation to love – and not to wrong – our fellow men. The time we have left is short, and we must live accordingly (11-12 – Paul is alluding to Christ's return).

14 Freedom and responsibility

There are some matters of conscience over which Christians disagree. (Paul instances the eating of meat, 2-3 – see on 1 Corinthians 8 – and observance of Jewish feast-days, 5.) We should not try to force agreement, and so create division. We ourselves may feel free to do things that would give a weaker Christian a bad conscience. That is no reason to despise him. We are answerable, not to one another, but to Christ. It is better to limit our own freedom than exercise it at a fellow Christian's expense.

14:2, 14: there was the problem that meat sold in the market had been sacrificed to pagan gods; and there were also the Jewish food-laws about 'clean' and 'unclean' animals and the method of slaughter. If Jewish Christians insisted on the letter of the law, and Gentile Christians stuck out for freedom, the two sections would never share a meal together.

15:1-13 The example of Christ

There is nothing Christian about pleasing ourselves. Good relations between Christians are far more important than 'my rights'. We must do all we can to promote real oneness, regardless of former background.

15:14 - 16:27 EPILOGUE

15:14-33 Personal

In more than 20 years as apostle to the non-Jewish world, Paul has seen churches established all over the countries we now call Cyprus, Syria, Turkey and Greece. Now he has discharged his responsibilities. And once the Jerusalem trip (about which he has real misgivings) is over, he can look west.

Illyricum (19): present-day Yugoslavia.

Macedonia and Achaia (26): northern and southern Greece.

16 Greetings to friends

It is in one way surprising to find such a long list of friends in a church which Paul had never visited. (For this reason some believe this chapter originally belonged to a copy of Romans which was sent to Ephesus.) Yet all roads led to Rome, and many Christians from the eastern provinces must have passed through the capital at one time or another. It is obvious that despite his busy life Paul did not lose interest in people or lose touch with them.

His last word is one of warning against a set of troublemakers whose disruptive influence on the churches he knew all too well (17ff.). But, as always, at the close his thought returns to the wisdom and glory of the eternal God.

Phoebe (1): it was probably Phoebe – travelling from Cenchreae, the port of Corinth – who carried Paul's letter to Rome.

Prisca and Aquila (3): a couple whose home was in Rome, but who travelled extensively in the course of their leatherworking business. They did sterling Christian work at Corinth and Ephesus (Acts 18:2-3; 18-28).

Rufus (13): may be the son of Simon of Cyrene (Mark 15:21).

Verse 21: Timothy is well known in the letters. He was like a son to the ageing Paul. Jason may be Paul's host from Thessalonica (Acts 17:5-8). Sosipater may be Sopater from Beroea (Acts 20:4).

Tertius (22): the Christian who acted as Paul's secretary in writing this letter.

Erastus (23): this may be the same public official whose name has been found inscribed on a marble paving-block at Corinth, dating from this time.

New Testament 2.2

1 CORINTHIANS

Paul probably wrote this letter from Ephesus, about AD 54. Acts 18 recounts Paul's 18-month stay at Corinth on his second missionary journey – and describes the founding of the church.

The city. The old Greek city of Corinth was destroyed and rebuilt by the Romans. It stood in a strategic position to control trade across the narrow neck of land between Aegean and Adriatic. A thriving centre of commerce and a cosmopolitan city where Greeks, Latins, Syrians, Asiatics, Egyptians and Jews rubbed shoulders, it was an obvious target for Paul. Establish a church here, and the Christian message would quickly spread far and wide.

Yet in other ways it is hard to imagine a less likely place for Christianity to take root. The town was dominated by the temple of Aphrodite (goddess of love; what a contrast to 1 Corinthians 13!), built on the heights of the acropolis. Thousands of temple prostitutes, a large floating population, and the general racial hotch-potch, all contributed to Corinth's unsavoury name. The city was a by-word for excess and sexual licence. There was even a word for it: to 'Corinthianize'.

The church. The Christian church, like the city, was a racial and social mixture. There were a few Jews, but more Gentiles: some men of wealth and position, but most from the lower classes. Many were converts from a permissive pagan background. They had little to boast of – yet, in Greek fashion, they prided themselves in their intellectual prowess. They bandied about such slogans as 'Liberty' and 'Knowledge'. It was a group which had little cohesion.

The letter. Two factors lie behind the writing of 1 Corinthians.

1. Paul had received reports of the church which made him very uneasy (1:11;5:1).

2. A delegation arrived from Corinth, and (or with) a letter seeking his advice on various questions (7:1;16:17).

The great Temple of Apollo at Corinth. The fact that meat on sale in the markets had been offered to idols in the temples was a real problem of conscience for the Corinthian Christians.

In the letter, Paul takes up five of the matters reported to him:
- divisions in the church;
- a case of incest;
- court-cases between members;
- the abuse of Christian 'freedom';
- the general chaos reigning in church services, even in the Lord's Supper.

He also answers questions the Corinthians have written about:
- questions about marriage and single life;
- problems over food consecrated to idols and social functions held in the temples;
- whether or not women should be veiled, and their place in public meetings;
- the matter of spiritual gifts;
 the meaning of the resurrection of the dead.

His reply takes the lid off one of the early churches, and gives us a fascinating glimpse of the none too edifying contents.

1:1-9 Greeting and prayer

Opening and thanksgiving (1:4-9) are characteristic. Paul believes in

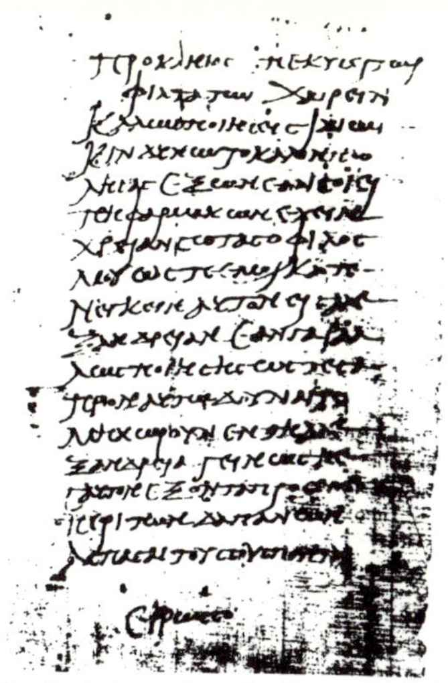

Paul's letters played a key role in his relations with the churches. This papyrus letter from the 1st century AD begins, 'Prokleios to his good friend Pekysis, greetings...'

encouragement. Only Galatians, of all the letters to churches, lacks this note of praise.

Sosthenes (1): possibly the synagogue leader mentioned in Acts 18:17. He may be acting as Paul's secretary.

1:10 - 4:21 Rival cliques

In a day before church buildings, when Christians met in houses or halls, and a large group might well have to split up, it is easy to see how divisions could arise.

Paul mentions three sects centred on rival 'leaders': Paul (their founder), Apollos and Cephas (Peter). A fourth sect, in their pride, claimed exclusive rights to the label 'Christian'.

Apollos (1:12) was a Jewish Christian from Alexandria (Egypt). When he arrived in Ephesus, Aquila and Priscilla took him home for fuller instruction (Acts 18:24ff.). He travelled to the province of Achaia (of which Corinth was capital), where he proved a powerful and eloquent teacher.

The mention of Peter (Cephas, 1:12) does not necessarily mean he visited Corinth. As leader of the twelve apostles it would be natural for him to have a following, particularly among Jewish Christians.

It is clear from these chapters that the groups were making invidious comparisons between Paul and the more eloquent Apollos. Paul, although a trained scholar, had had his troubles at Corinth (Acts 18:9-10; 1 Corinthians 2:3). God's message, not polished speech, was his main concern.

But the Corinthians were infected with something of the spirit of nearby Athens. They fancied themselves as thinkers and took a pride in their supposed intellectual superiority. In fact, as Paul points out (3:1-4), their argumentative, judgemental attitude shows they are still bound by the world's way of thinking. They stand in need of teaching. They have to be reminded that human cleverness is a far cry from God's wisdom (1:18 - 2:16). It is not proud and clever people who appreciate the wisdom of God's plan of salvation through Christ's death on the cross, but those who are spiritually wise. This kind of wisdom, and with it true values and real judgement, is God's gift to man through his Holy Spirit. A man must become a fool in the world's eyes in order to be really wise (3:18).

So Paul and Apollos are not rivals but partners, sharing the work of building God's church (3:5-9). Once the basic foundation of faith in Christ is laid, every Christian is responsible for what he does with the new life he has been given. We must see to it that we build to last (3:10-17).

There should be no place for pride among Christians and no looking down on others. The greatest Christians regard themselves as no more than God's slaves. We are to follow their example (chapter 4).

Chloe's people (1:11): presumably members of Chloe's household.

Stephanas (1:16): a founder-member of the church at Corinth, and one of the delegation sent by the church to Paul at Ephesus (16:15ff.).

Jews and Greeks (1:22): national characteristics show through. The Jews always wanted miracles as concrete evidence. The Greeks saw salvation in terms of wisdom.

The Day (3:13): when Christ returns; the day of judgement.

5 Incest

In the name of their boasted 'liberty' the church is condoning incest. It is a case which would shock even the pagans in that notorious city. The old immorality - and worse - has gained a foothold and the whole church is endangered (as Paul had warned in a previous letter, 5:9).

His father's wife (5:1): presumably his step-mother, or Paul would have said 'mother'.

Deliver ... to Satan (5:5): Paul is expressing God's judgement on the man for abusing his body through gross sexual immorality. Short-term discipline is to be exercised for long-term good. Such discipline would certainly include expulsion from the church.

Leaven (5:6-8): yeast - often (though not always) used as a picture of the corrupting power of evil. Bread for the Passover was made without leaven, as a reminder of the Israelites' hasty departure from Egypt. Christ has become our Passover sacrifice, says Paul; it is time we got rid of the old yeast of evil in our lives.

6:1-11 Lawsuits

Even Jews would not take cases before Gentile courts - not because the courts were corrupt, but because it would be an admission of Jewish inability to operate their own laws. Surely the Christian community - these 'wise' Corinthians - should be capable of settling internal disputes. Better to be wronged than drag one another to court.

The saints will judge the world (6:2): a development from Christ's teaching in Matthew 19:28. The angels are mentioned as the highest order in the created universe.

6:12-20 Freedom or licence?

The Corinthians claim they are free to do anything. 'No doubt,' says Paul, 'but I for one will not let anything make free with me' (6:12). Sexual needs, they argue, are like hunger: they must be satisfied. The body is not important anyway. But this is wrong thinking, a carry-over of the old Greek ideas. For the Christian the body is part of the whole personality. Body *and* soul are the Lord's. You cannot sin with the body and keep the 'soul' untarnished: man is a unity.

7 Questions about marriage

The Corinthians have raised six questions about single and married life. Several reflect the Greek tendency to regard the physical side of existence as evil.

— Are married couples to continue normal sexual relations after conversion? Yes (7:1-7).
— Should single people marry? Paul prefers the single life - but only for those with the gift of self-control (8-9).
— Is divorce between Christians permissible? No (10-11).
— What about the unconverted husband or wife? The Christian is to stick to his pagan partner unless that partner wants a separation (12-16).
— This question is not so clear. Most likely it is: 'Should engaged couples marry?' This must be a matter for personal decision, but in the very troubled times Paul sees ahead, single people will find it easier to work out their Christian priorities (25-38).
— May widows remarry? Yes, but Paul qualifies this (39-40).

8 Food offered to idols: problems over social customs

It was hard in Corinth to make a clean break with paganism. Trade groups and clubs held their social functions at the temples. Most of the meat sold in the shops had first been offered to idols. Some Christians maintained that 'idols were nothing'. They were free to eat meat and attend club dinners. But others were worried. Freedom is right, says Paul. But no one should exercise personal freedom at the expense of another man's conscience.

9 Forgoing rights

Paul takes examples from his own life to push this lesson home. If anyone has rights, surely it is the apostle. Yet he has gladly given up his right to take a wife with him on his trips and expect the church to provide for her keep. There are more important things than rights. He willingly restricts his freedom to help him win men for Christ.

In a race ... (24-27): the Isthmian Games (second only to the Olympics) were held every three years at Corinth. Each competitor underwent 10 months' stiff training, hoping to be crowned with the victor's pine wreath. Paul was afraid, not of losing his salvation, but of forfeiting his 'crown'.

10:1-13 A warning from history

It is easy to be over-confident, especially when life is smooth (10:12-13). The fate of many of the children of Israel during the wilderness wanderings stands as a solemn warning. (Hebrews 3:7ff. draws similar lessons from the same events.)

10:14 - 11:1 Paul's appeal and summary

Christians must choose between the Lord and idols (empty in themselves, but behind them, real demonic powers). There can be no compromise. It is playing with fire to have any part in pagan sacrifices. As far as meat is concerned, the rule is unselfish concern for the good of others.

The cup of blessing (10:16): the name given to the third cup in the Passover feast, over which a prayer of thanksgiving was said. This may well have been the cup with which Jesus instituted his memorial Supper – hence the thought here.

11:2-16 Women and the veil

No decent woman would appear unveiled in public at this time. The veil guaranteed safety and respect in the streets. But there were differences in Greek and Hebrew custom when it came to prayer. Greek women, as well as men, prayed bareheaded. Roman and Jewish men and women prayed with their heads covered. The church needed a ruling.

The ruling Paul gave rested on the relative roles of men and women in the created order. He was also concerned not to flout current social convention and so bring the Christians into disrepute. Men, because they are the 'head' of creation, are under no authority but Christ's. They were therefore to pray bareheaded. Women were to pray veiled, the veil being a token both of their acceptance of their husband's authority and of the current standards of decency.

Dishonours his head (4-5): i.e. Christ (3). The veil was a token of submission to another person; he should submit only to Christ. *Dishonours her head:* i.e. her husband (3). By discarding the veil she discarded her husband's authority, as if she were a prostitute.

Shorn or shaven (6): the punishment for a prostitute at that time.

The image and glory of God (7): Genesis 1:26-27 includes both sexes in God's 'image', but does not mention 'glory'.

Because of the angels (10): the angels, representatives of order, would not want to look on immorality, or even the appearance of it.

11:17-34 Disorder at the Lord's Supper

In the early days the Lord's Supper took place in the course of a communal meal. All brought what food they could, and it was shared together. Not so in Corinth. There they could not even wait for everyone to arrive before they began eating. And some got drunk while others went hungry. It is not surprising that Paul could not 'commend' them – it was a disgrace. He pulls them up short with a reminder of the circumstances in which the first Lord's Supper took place. Their offence is serious.

This is my body (24-25): this is the earliest record we have of Jesus' words.

Unworthy (27-30): no Christian is ever 'worthy' to come into God's presence, but that is not the point here. Judgement has overtaken the Corinthians not for insufficient self-examination, but for stuffing themselves at the meal as if it had no connection with the Lord's death.

12 - 14 Spiritual gifts

In contemporary religions trances or strange, ecstatic speech showed a man's spiritual status. It was therefore not surprising that the Christian church at Corinth, to whom God gave a variety of gifts by his Holy Spirit, should have been specially taken up with the more spectacular ones, among which was the ability to speak in unknown 'tongues'.

Paul does not underestimate these gifts. He would have them all speak in tongues, he says (14:5); and he himself excels in this gift (14:18). But it does not top the list on his scale of values. Those seeking experiences for themselves needed to be reminded that the life of the church was more important. There are other gifts Christians should seek even more strenuously.

Christian unity does not imply uniformity. The gifts come from a single Source, and are given for the good of the whole church. Every individual has an indispensable part to play in the life of the one body. This should prevent a universal scramble for the same gifts. The important thing is not which gifts are most impressive, but which best serve to build up the church. This means that prophecy – a message from God which everyone can understand – is of more value than tongues.

Yet there are things more important still. Three qualities of life – faith, hope, love – will outlive all the gifts. And these are for everyone. Without them no one is anything. And Christian love outshines all. This is the best way of all; this is what we should really set our hearts on. Paul bursts into a great hymn on the theme (chapter 13), one of the most glorious passages in the whole Bible. And as he paints his picture of what love is, he consciously or unconsciously draws us a portrait of a person – Jesus himself. He is the living embodiment of this outgoing, long-suffering, self-giving, self-effacing love. Without it – without him – there would be no church.

14:26-33 provides a glimpse into an early-church service. Again Paul stresses the need for order. Paul forbids the women to disturb the service by talking (34-35). From verse 35 it seems that some were calling out questions and comments (they sat apart from the men). Their new liberty was not to be abused. But it is clear from 11:5 that he did not condemn the women to absolute silence: the gift of prophecy was exercised in public.

12:8 'One man ... has the gift of wise speech, while another ... can put the deepest knowledge into words' (New English Bible).

Faith (12:9): not saving faith, but faith in special measure.

Prophecy (12:10): inspired speech, conveying the message of God to the hearers. *Tongues:* inspired speech to express the praise of God or other deeply-felt emotion; the person uttering it did not know its meaning, hence the need for interpretation.

15 The resurrection

This chapter is the classic Bible passage on the subject. Most of the Jews believed in the resurrection of the body (the same body that had died). To the Greeks it was the soul that was immortal. The very idea of resurrection seemed ridiculous to them (see Acts 17:32).

Paul declares that Christ's resurrection is of the first importance: it is no optional extra. On it the Christian faith stands or falls. What is more, it is a fact and a well-attested one. Most of those who saw the risen Lord are still alive (about 25 years after the event). Christ's resurrection implies resurrection for the Christian. But the body which is raised will be better than the body which is buried. The old was physical, the new will be spiritual and immortal – but still a body. It will as far outshine the old body as a full-grown plant outshines the shrivelled seed from which it grows.

Baptized on behalf of (or for) the dead (29): possibly by proxy for those who died unbaptized. But the meaning may be that people became baptized in order to be reunited with Christian friends and relatives who had died.

Beasts at Ephesus (32): one of the spectacles at the arena was to watch men fighting savage wild animals. But Paul is probably speaking metaphorically about what he went through there. Ephesus had a magnificent theatre but no arena as such.

16 Practical matters

Paul gives directions for collecting money for the poor at Jerusalem (the Gentile churches were contributing). He looks forward to an extended visit to Corinth. And he gives news and instructions about various individuals. The letter closes with greetings from the Asian churches (Ephesus was the provincial capital), especially from Aquila and Priscilla, the leatherworkers in whose house Paul lived during his stay in Corinth. The final greeting he writes himself (the rest presumably having been dictated to a secretary).

Macedonia (5): Philippi and Thessalonica were both in this province.

Apollos (12) is probably reluctant to return because of the split (3:4).

New Testament 2.3

2 CORINTHIANS

The road leading down from Corinth to its port. Behind the ruins of the ancient city is the fortified acropolis.

An interval of not much more than a year separates Paul's two letters to Corinth. The second letter was probably written about AD 56, from a town in Macedonia (the Roman province in northern Greece whose capital was Philippi).

After 1 Corinthians was written, affairs seem to have come to a head, and Paul paid a swift unscheduled visit (his second; on his first visit to Corinth the church was founded) which proved unpleasant both for him and for the church (2:1). He promised to return (1:16). But instead, to avoid an even more painful visit (1:23), he returned to Asia (where he ran into grave danger, 1:8ff.) and wrote them a sharp letter which caused him a great deal of anguish (2:4). He could enjoy no peace of mind until he heard their reaction, so he left for Troas, on the coast, hoping for news. Although things were going well there, he could not bear to wait, and crossed the Aegean into Macedonia (2:12-13) where at last Titus reached him with the news that the letter had brought the Corinthians to their senses (7:6ff.). His relief knew no bounds.

Now, as he writes again, the worst is over. He looks forward to a third visit, which he hopes will be a happier one. So the final part of the letter is specifically intended to clear the air (13:10). (He did pay his visit, and wrote to the Romans during his stay at Corinth. So there was presumably a happy ending to the troubles.)

2 Corinthians is perhaps the most intensely personal of all Paul's letters. We feel for ourselves the weight of his burden of care for all the churches (11:28): the depth of his love for them and his anguished concern for their spiritual progress. We see in personal terms the cost of his missionary programme: hardship, suffering, deprivation, humiliation, almost beyond human endurance. And we see unshakable faith shining through it all, transforming every circumstance.

The personal nature of the letter makes it difficult to analyse. Paul's thought flows on, almost unbroken (apart from the break before chapter 8, when Paul turns to the matter of the relief fund for Jerusalem; and again before chapter 10, when he takes up the accusations made by his critics), and themes are often recurring. In the main, Paul writes in defence of his ministry and his God-given authority as an apostle.

1:1-7 Greeting and thanksgiving

Paul's associate in this letter is Timothy. His readers are the Christians at Corinth and the surrounding province of Achaia, which would include the groups at Athens and Cenchreae.

His prayer strikes a more personal note than usual. Instead of praise for the church, Paul thanks God for his special goodness during recent trials. His suffering has had two wholly good side-effects:

— the experience of God's comfort in it all;
— a new ability to help and comfort those in similar circumstances.

1:8 - 2:17 News and explanations

Facing death (1:8-14). The reason for Paul's prayer is now explained. While in the province of Asia (capital city, Ephesus) Paul ran into trouble so serious it seemed likely to cost him his life. At first sight this looks like a reference to the uproar at Ephesus recounted in Acts 19:23-41. But there Paul's life was not in danger. It is perhaps more likely he was either seriously ill, or in danger from mob violence somewhere in Asia Minor.

Paul accounts for his changes of plan (1:15 - 2:11). In his first letter (1 Corinthians 16:5) Paul promised to come to Corinth via Macedonia. Later he decided to make two visits, on the way to and from Macedonia (1:16). In the event he has done neither, and the Corinthians have criticized him for shilly-shallying. But this is not the reason for the changes of plan. He took his decision because of the state of affairs in the church. Having had one head-on clash, he wanted to delay visiting them again until relations were happier. So he tried to sort things out by letter – a letter he feared would hurt them, and which cost him a great deal to write.

The trouble seems to have been personal antagonism to Paul on the part of one man (2:5-11; not the man guilty of incest, 1 Corinthians 5:1). Now that the church has dealt with him, Paul urges his forgiveness.

Paul's recent travels (2:12-17). After writing the letter, Paul could not rest. He went to Troas hoping to meet Titus on his way back from Corinth with news of the church's reaction. Not finding him there he crossed the Aegean to Macedonia. The reason for the thanksgiving of verses 14-17 becomes clear in chapter 7. In Macedonia he met Titus, and the news from Corinth was good.

Leads in triumph (14): Paul takes this picture from the triumphal procession accorded to a victorious Roman general. He headed a parade through the streets of Rome, accompanied by incense-bearers and followed by his captives and the spoils of war.

3 - 6:10 Paul's ministry

Past, present and future interweave in these chapters. As for the past, the old covenant has been replaced by a new life-giving one (3:6-18). The present is an anomaly: on the one hand the apostle is appointed ambassador of God himself, charged with his amazing message to mankind (3:4-6; 4:1ff.; 5:16 - 6:2); on the other, he is subjected to every kind of human weakness, persecution and suffering (4:7-12; 6:3-10). But the future, in all its glorious certainty, eclipses any suffering the present can hold (4:13 - 5:10). Weigh the cost of discipleship, incredible though it seems, against the 'eternal weight of glory' being made ready for the Christian and you have the true balance of things.

Letters of recommendation (3:1): in the early days, Christians moving to a new town often took with them such letters from the old church to the new. Paul has no need of such a letter – the very existence of the Corinthian church is sufficient testimony.

Moses' face (3:7ff.): when Moses came down from Mt Sinai with the tablets of the law, his face dazzled the Israelites, so close had he been to God. In order to overcome their fear he veiled his face (Exodus 34:29ff.).

Reflecting the glory (3:18): the 'glass' or 'mirror', being made of polished metal, gave only an imperfect reflection.

In Paul's day mirrors were made of polished metal (like the bronze mirror pictured here) and gave only a dim and imperfect image (3:18).

Earthenware vessels (4:7): cheap pottery lamps (see verse 6), or, if Paul is picturing the Roman triumphal procession, earthenware pots deliberately chosen as a foil to the magnificent treasures inside.
The earthly tent (5:1): our physical body. Paul uses an ordinary Greek expression, which at the same time reminds us of the body's impermanence.
Found naked (5:3): as a disembodied spirit.

6:11 - 7:1 The need for a clean break

Paul's feelings are deeply stirred (6:11-13). He longs for the Corinthians to match his own complete open-heartedness towards them.

The change of tone at 6:14 is abrupt – but there is no evidence that this section has been misplaced, as some argue. Paul's love for his churches always holds them to the highest standards. He has warned them before of the dangers of compromise with the pagan world (1 Corinthians 8:10). Now he stresses the utter incongruity of permanent relationships between Christians and heathen.

7:2-16 Paul's joy at the good news from Corinth

He had reached this point in the story at 2:13. Now he takes it up again. At last Titus is able to set Paul's mind at rest. The Corinthians' reaction to his letter is all he could have hoped. The result has been entirely good. The apostle's relief and joy are overwhelming. His faith in them has been completely vindicated.
Not on account of ... (12): a Jewish idiom meaning 'Not so much on account of'.

8 - 9 Money matters

Now that confidence is restored, it is possible to raise the matter of the relief fund for the poor in Jerusalem. Titus had helped the Corinthians make a start, following Paul's instructions in his earlier letter (1 Corinthians 16). Now he is to return and supervise the completion of the collection, accompanied by delegates from the Macedonian churches (8:18, 22) as a safeguard against any charge that Paul was embezzling the fund (8:20-21; 12:16-17).

The Jerusalem church seems to have been in financial trouble almost from the start, probably because the break with Judaism cut the convert off from his family and often cost him his job. Converts from Islam face the same problems today. Paul was quick to encourage the Gentile churches in Galatia, Macedonia and Corinth to help their Jewish fellow Christians. By doing so they would learn the duty and blessing of systematic Christian giving, and at the same time show their appreciation of what they owed the Jewish parent-church.

Practical instructions rub shoulders with spiritual principles in these chapters. Christian giving is a loving response to the self-giving of the Lord Jesus. Christians should need no urging to give cheerfully and generously. Those with more than they need will make up the incomes of those with too little, so that all have enough.
The churches of Macedonia (8:1) included Philippi (see Philippians 4:15ff.), Thessalonica and Beroea. Harsh treatment from the Romans and a succession of civil wars had impoverished the province, and the persecuted Christians must have been worse off than most.

10 - 12:13 Paul answers his critics

Paul now turns his attention to the hostile minority at Corinth who have challenged his authority and criticized his behaviour. This sounds very like a continuation of the old rival cliques of 1 Corinthians 1 - 4, particularly the pro-Jewish faction. They show the same conceit, the same old mistaken standards of judgement. They have attacked Paul on a number of counts:

— He may be a brave letter-writer, but meet him face to face and he's a coward (10:1, 9-11).
— He is no speaker (10:10; 11:6).
— He is a second-rate apostle (11:5; 12:11) – his insistence on earning his own living underlines this (11:7ff.).

Paul answers every charge, showing the hollowness of their standards of judgement.

— When he comes, they will discover he is as ready to act as he is to write: but he would much rather use his authority to build up the church (10:1-11).
— Their boasting counts for nothing: it is God's commendation which is all-important (10:12-18). Yet he can surpass them all in boasting, though he will make suffering and weakness his boast, and the vision and revelation God has given him (11:16 - 12:10).
— Apostleship does not consist in oratory and lording it over the church (11:6, 13-15, 19-20). Paul is not lacking in any of the qualities of true apostleship (11:6; 12:12). As for earning his own living, he was concerned that no one should think him a sponger, and anxious not to burden them (11:7ff.).

King Aretas (11:32): Aretas IV ruled the Nabataean kingdom (stretching from the Euphrates to the Red Sea) from his capital, Petra, from 9 BC to AD 40. The Jews were behind the governor's action – see Acts 9:22-25.
Visions and revelations (12:1): we know of three early visions from Acts: on the Damascus road (9:4ff.); at the house of Judas (9:12); and in the temple at Jerusalem (22:17ff.).
A man in Christ (12:2-3): i.e. a Christian. Paul is speaking of himself. *Fourteen years ago:* AD 41-42, six or seven years after Paul's conversion, but before the great Gentile missions. The *third heaven* is a Jewish expression meaning to be actually in the presence of God. Paul is describing the most sublime experience imaginable.
A thorn ... in the flesh (12:7): this may be some physical illness (a painful eye disease, or malaria) or a reference to the unremitting opposition he encountered. Either way it was a constant source of pain and depression – Satan's work – yet the means God used to keep Paul humble and to demonstrate his power.

12:14 - 13:10 The coming visit

Paul looks forward to his third visit to Corinth. And the reason for the tone of these last chapters becomes clear. He is afraid he will find the same bickering splinter-groups, the same cockiness and general disorder that made him write the first letter. He is afraid his pride in them will take a knock, in the face of typical 'Corinthian' sins: sexual promiscuity, bitter quarrels and disorder (12:20-21). And so he calls them to put things right before he comes, so that he may not have to discipline the church severely.
Two or three witnesses (13:1): the procedure laid down under Jewish law (see Deuteronomy 19:15).

13:11-14 Conclusion

After last-minute instructions, and farewell, Paul closes with the lovely words of 'the grace'.
A holy kiss (12): a kiss on the cheek had become the customary Christian greeting, expressing a loving family relationship.

New Testament 2.4

GALATIANS

Galatia was a huge Roman province extending almost from coast to coast through the mountain and plain of central Turkey. How much of it Paul evangelized we do not know. But Acts 13 and 14 record how he founded churches in the southern cities of Antioch, Iconium, Lystra (Timothy's home town) and Derbe on his first missionary journey. And we know of two follow-up visits made later on (Acts 16:6; 18:23).

Not long after Paul's first visit, other Jewish teachers arrived in Galatia. Whereas Paul had taught that repentance and faith were all that was needed in order to receive God's forgiveness and the gift of new life, these men insisted that non-Jewish converts must also be circumcised and observe the Jewish law – virtually become Jews – in order to be saved. (The same thing happened at Syrian Antioch, Acts 15:1.) When Paul heard this he was distraught (Galatians 4:20). He saw that it struck at the roots of the Christian message. Salvation – new life – is God's gift to all who believe. No man can earn it by living the perfect life God's standards demand. But these men were saying that faith is not enough; there are things we must do to merit salvation. And the Gentiles in Galatia were being taken in. It was a desperate situation, requiring the most strongly worded of all Paul's letters.

The date is probably about AD 47, shortly before the committee of enquiry met in Jerusalem to resolve this very issue (Acts 15). Paul raises many of the same points nine or ten years later, in the letter to the Romans, when less extreme circumstances allowed a more dispassionate consideration of the issues. But the letter to the Galatians stands out, none the less, as the great charter of Christian freedom.

1 The God-given gospel

We can sense Paul's urgency right from the start. The abrupt assertion of authority (1) and lack of any word of praise are most unlike him. He gets straight to the point (6) – and he does not mince his words. The matter is serious. The whole fabric of the Christian gospel is threatened. As if this were not enough, the Jewish troublemakers have tried to undermine confidence in Paul himself. They have accused him of currying favour (10). They have called him a bogus apostle, and he is forced to defend himself (1, 11ff.). In flat contradiction of the charges, Paul asserts his God-given commission and authority. The very gospel he preaches was revealed to him, not by man – not even the other apostles – but by God. This is the point of his brief autobiography (13-24).

Verses 4-5: Paul stresses the fact that the initiative was God's.

My former life ... (13): see Acts 8:1; 9.

Arabia (17): probably the Nabataean kingdom whose capital was Petra in present-day Jordan. Acts 9:22-23 does not mention this. This 'three years' may have been one full year and part of two others. Paul does not say why he went. Perhaps after the dramatic about-turn of his conversion, he needed a time away on his own to reorientate his thinking.

Cephas (18): Peter. This seems to be the visit of Acts 9:26ff.

Syria and Cilicia (21): Antioch was in Syria, Tarsus (Paul's home town; Acts 9:30) in Cilicia – the south-east corner of the coast of modern Turkey.

2 The apostles sanction Paul's mission

Paul's next visit to Jerusalem seems to be the one mentioned in Acts 11:30. He took the opportunity to raise the matter of his own position with the other apostles. This attack of self-doubt seems rather out of character but Paul had, after all, been working very much on his own. And he was under attack (4). The apostles had no hesitation in approving his work among the Gentiles – God's hand was so clearly in it (7-9). But Peter later failed to practise what he preached, and had to be called to task over his inconsistency (11ff.). As Jews, Peter and Paul both knew that it was hopeless for any man to try to earn acceptance with God (15-16). Having once gained their freedom through faith in Christ, how could they put their heads back in the noose of the law? If good deeds had been enough to save a man, Christ need never have died.

From James (12): James did not share their view, see Acts 15:13-21.

Ate with the Gentiles (12): see on Romans 14:2, 14.

Verses 17-18: Paul is saying that the real sin lies not in breaking Jewish food-laws, but in turning back to the law for salvation.

Verses 19-20: see on Romans 6-7.

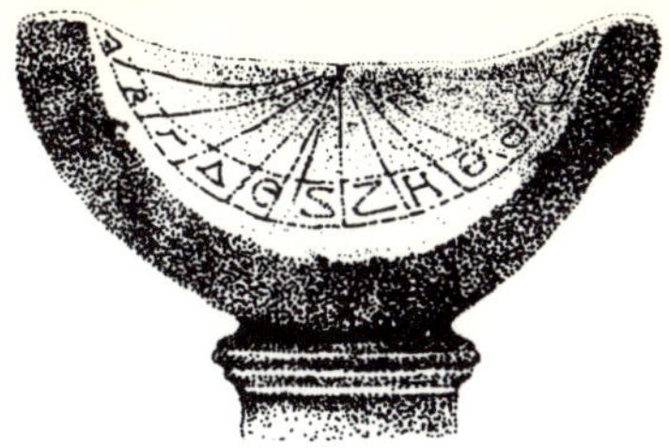

A sundial inscribed with Greek symbols at Ephesus. Paul was concerned that the Galatians, delivered from being slaves of the 'elemental spirits of the universe', should not fall into the new bondage of observing 'days, months and years'.

3 - 4 Slavery under the law

Anyone willing to exchange Christian freedom for the Jewish law is a fool. The Jews talk about making the Gentiles sons of Abraham through the rite of circumcision. But Gentile Christians are already Abraham's sons and heirs – because they share his faith (3:7, 29). God accepted Abraham centuries before the law was given through Moses. So how can the law win man free pardon (3:15-18)? The law operated as a temporary restraint until the promise made to Abraham was fulfilled in the coming of Christ (3:19-24). Now, by faith in him, we are all God's children – regardless of race or status or sex.

The Galatians had responded eagerly to Paul's preaching. What happened to make them change (4:12-20)? Can they really want to throw their freedom away (4:8-9)? Those under the law are like the son Abraham had by his slave-woman, Hagar. But Christians are free-born – heirs, like Isaac, to all God's promises.

Elemental spirits (4:3, 9): the forces that once controlled them; the pagan no-gods they once served.

Days ... (4:10): Jewish feast-days.

Bodily ailment (4:13): see on 2 Corinthians 12:7.

Mt Sinai (4:24): where the law was given to Moses.

5 - 6 Freedom in Christ

It is not circumcision that matters, but what it stands for. Paul is so incensed by those who have unsettled his young converts that he could wish they would go the whole hog and castrate themselves (5:12)! Christ has saved us to set us free – free, not to live permissive, self-indulgent lives, but to put ourselves at God's disposal. We harvest what we sow in life (6:7-9). When we live to please ourselves it shows in the way we behave (5:19-21). When we live to please God we harvest a life and character produced in us by the Holy Spirit (5:22-24). And there is no mistaking the two. Christ has dealt with the old life (24) and made us new. Now we have to act accordingly, letting his Spirit control our everyday life and transform our relationships (5:25 - 6:10).

At this point (6:11) Paul takes over from his secretary to pen the last lines himself. For him there is only one thing worth glorying in: the power of the cross of Christ to recreate and transform human lives.

The marks of Jesus (6:17): the scars Paul's Christian service has earned him (see 2 Corinthians 4:7-12; 6:4-10; 11:23-29); living proof, if proof is still needed, that he is Christ's true apostle.

New Testament 2.5

EPHESIANS

Paul's letter to the Ephesians differs considerably from his other letters. There are none of the usual personal greetings, although Paul had spent some years in Ephesus and had many friends there (see on Acts 19). Nor does Ephesians deal with particular problems or news. Even the words 'at Ephesus' (1:1) are missing from some of the early manuscripts. So it seems likely that Ephesians began as a circular letter written to a group of churches in what is now western Turkey – of which Ephesus itself was the most important. John's 'seven churches' (Revelation 1:11) were in this general area, as was the church at Colossae.

The fact that Paul wrote from prison (probably in Rome in the early 60s) links this letter with Philippians, Colossians and Philemon – the other 'letters from prison'. Of the three, Ephesians is closest in thought to Colossians. Because of its general nature the letter provides few clues to the situation in the churches. But it is clear that the Gentile Christians predominated, and that they tended to look down on their Jewish fellow Christians. Paul had been specially commissioned to work among the Gentiles, but he held no brief for a divided church. And so his great theme in this letter is God's glorious plan to bring men of every nation and background together in Christ (1:10). As Christians, all are on equal terms. We are one. And we must see that we express that oneness in personal relationships and the way we behave.

Temple dedicated to the Roman Emperor Hadrian at Ephesus.

1 - 3 GOD'S GREAT PLAN

1:1-14 The eternal purpose of God

Paul catches his breath in wonder at the very thought of it. God has poured out his love on us. From the very beginning he determined to share his spiritual riches and glory with us – 'in Christ' (the key phrase of Ephesians). Christ stands at the very heart of God's plan. As we believe in him, his death sets us free: we can be forgiven. We can also share his new, risen life. We are made one with him, part of him. And in him we too are caught up in God's great world-plan as we live to his glory.

Saints (1); grace and peace (2): see on Romans 1.

Mystery (9): no human mind could have guessed God's intention. Paul usually uses this word to mean the 'open secret' of the gospel.

1:15-23 Paul's prayer

It warms Paul's heart to hear of the faith and love of these Christians. He prays that they may have greater understanding, a surer grasp of their glorious destiny, and increased awareness of the power at their disposal. The power God exercised in raising Christ from the dead and setting him in supreme control of the universe is at work in us, too!

2:1-10 From death to life

Because of our sinful nature we could not have fellowship with God: and to be cut off from him means death. But Christ has taken our death himself. God in his goodness – through no effort of our own – has given us new life in Christ. He has made us part of his new creation, set us off on a new life with power to carry out what he intends.

Prince of the power of the air (2): Satan, whose rebellious spirit is actively at work in the world of men.

2:11-22 Broken barriers

In the ancient world the Jew was separated from the Gentile by racial, religious, cultural and social barriers. If Christ could bring these two together, there was, and is, no human gulf too great for him to bridge. And he did. His death on the cross is the one means of peace with God for all men, without distinction. And all who belong to him have a common bond which is deeper and stronger than any of their former differences – of race or colour or status or sex or background. Jew and Gentile are one in Christ.

The circumcision (11): i.e. the Jews. See on Genesis 17.

Verse 12: the Gentile Christians have no cause to give themselves airs. Up till now they have been outsiders. The Jews, as God's people, were the only ones for whom there was hope.

3:1-13 Paul's mission to the Gentiles

Before Christ came, God's promises had been largely confined to the Jews. His purpose for the world at large had remained a secret (4-6, 8-9). When Paul was commissioned to take the message of salvation to the Gentiles, a new phase in God's plan was opened up. As men of all nations are brought together in Christ they demonstrate God's power and wisdom, not just to the watching world (see John 17:21), but to the cosmic powers beyond and behind it (10). The scope of God's purpose is breathtaking. In the light of it, Paul could keep his own troubles in perspective – and so can we.

Verse 3: not necessarily a separate letter – Paul had just told them how God had revealed his 'secret plan' to him (1:9, etc.).

3:14-21 Paul prays again

Paul has prayed that the church might have understanding (1:15-23). Now he prays more urgently than ever that they may have love; that they may be strong; that Christ may make his home in their hearts; that God may fill them completely. He can do all this and more.

4 - 6 CHRISTIANS IN ACTION

4:1-16 Unity – in practice

Christian unity is a fact. We are bound together by a common faith, a common life, common loyalty, common purpose. We serve one Master. He is the head, we are the limbs of a single body (see also 1 Corinthians 12 - 13). But we are not identical in temperament, personality or gifts. We must constantly cement the bond by a loving, forbearing attitude to one another, and by using our different gifts for the common good. We have to grow up together until we are all Christ wants us to be – until we are really like him.

Verse 8: following his ascension Christ gave gifts to men (see verse 11).

4:17 - 5:20 The new life

Salvation is God's free gift, but it carries with it the obligation to live and behave from that point on as God wants (4:1). This means deliberately discarding the old, selfish way of life, shedding former habits – and letting the new life change our thinking and remould our pattern of behaviour. This calls for truth and honesty; no harboured grudges, no spite and bitterness – instead kindness and a new readiness to forgive. In a word, we are to copy God's character. All that we think and do and say must be able to stand his searchlight.

5:21 - 6:9 Christian relationships: family and household

If everyone subordinates his own interests (21), no one can lord it. The Christian wife gives her husband complete respect and loyalty. The Christian husband cares for his wife with unselfish, undemanding love. Each depends on the other, and both model themselves on Christ. Their relationship, in turn, reflects the relationship between Christ and the church. In the family, children owe their parents respect and obedience. Parents must exercise discipline – not behave like petty tyrants; Christian slaves (and, presumably, employees) serve their masters as willingly and well as they serve Christ. Christian masters (and employers) will not bludgeon or bully, knowing that they must answer to a Master themselves.

5:32: the close physical bond between husband and wife is an illustration of Christ's spiritual oneness with his church.

6:10-24 The armour of God

Paul does not pretend it will be easy to maintain these standards – to keep our feet in the Christian life. The fight is on. And we are up against powerful external forces. It is a spiritual struggle for which we need spiritual weapons. But we are not left helpless. The whole armoury of God is at our disposal – and with this defence we can stand.

New Testament 2.6

PHILIPPIANS

Philippi was a Roman colony, on the Egnatian Way – the great northern east-west highway. It was occupied by Italian settlers following Octavian's great battles, first against Brutus and Cassius, then against his former ally Antony. The colonists were proud of their special rights and privileges, and intensely loyal to Rome. In Philippi, as in the province of Macedonia as a whole, women enjoyed high status. They took active part in public and business life – a situation which is reflected in the church.

The church was founded about AD 50, during Paul's second missionary journey (see Acts 16:12-40). When Paul, Silas and Timothy left, Luke, the doctor, stayed on. Philippi was a medical centre, and may possibly have been Luke's home town. He no doubt did much to put the group on its feet and continue the evangelistic outreach. The letter reveals a church taking its share of suffering (1:29), and in some danger of division (1:27; 2:2). There may have been some leaning to a doctrine of perfectionism (3:12-13). And the arrival of the Judaizers (see on 3:2ff.) introduced a new threat. But Paul loved this church and rejoiced over its progress.

The letter. Paul wrote from prison (1:12). If this was in Rome (Acts 28:16, 30-31), the date was about AD 61-63. But conditions are harsher than they appear in Acts; judgement is imminent, and there is a real possibility of death. Timothy, but not Luke (to judge by 2:20-21), is with him. It may therefore be that the imprisonment is an earlier one not recorded in Acts. A good case has been made out for Ephesus, which would make the date of writing about AD 54. We cannot be certain either way.

There are several reasons for writing. Paul wanted to explain why he was sending Epaphroditus back. He wanted to thank the Philippians for their gift. He had news for them. And what he had heard about them made him long to encourage and advise. Further news reached him while he was writing that made it imperative to add a word of warning (3:1b).

1:1-2 Opening greetings

The letter comes from Paul 'and Timothy' – the young man who was with Paul when the church was founded, and who would shortly be coming to Philippi again (2:19). The 'slaves of Christ Jesus' write to the 'saints': not an elite, but all the Christians, as men and women set apart for God's service. The 'bishops' (overseers) and 'deacons' (administrators) receive special mention.

1:3-11 Paul's prayer for the church

Paul's prayer is full of love, joy (a keynote of the whole letter) and thankfulness. He longs for them to enjoy progressively richer and deeper spiritual knowledge which will mould their lives to God's pattern.

The first day (5): see Acts 16:12-40.

My imprisonment (7): see introduction above.

1:12-26 Personal news

Paul speaks of the past (12), present (13-18) and future (19-26), weighing the alternatives of life and death.

What has happened to me (12): if Paul writes from Rome, this includes mob violence, injustice, plots, prison, shipwreck and long detention under constant guard.

The whole praetorian guard (13): the crack imperial force from which Paul's warders were drawn.

Deliverance (19): if the judgement goes against him, death will deliver him into Christ's presence; if it goes for him, his captors will release him to serve the church.

To live is Christ ... (21): possessing more and more of him, becoming more and more like him, until on his death the process is completed in one glorious moment.

1:27 - 2:18 A plea for a united stand

There is more than a hint of division in the church (see for example 4:2). Paul urges them all to pocket their pride, and to live and work and think as one. Anything less lets down the gospel and the Lord, whose life on earth is the supreme example of humility. It is because Jesus gave up all that was his by right – even his life – that God has given him the highest place of all. (2:5-11 is probably a quotation from an early hymn in praise of Christ.)

Have this mind ... (2:5): 'The attitude you should have is the one that Christ Jesus had' (Good News Bible).

The form of God (6): the actual nature, not just the appearance (as also in verse 7).

Emptied himself (7): New English Bible, 'made himself nothing'. In becoming man the Lord stripped himself of his glory: he lived a life of humble obedience. But he cast off none of his essential deity.

Day of Christ (16): the day of his return.

A libation (17): Paul's death adds only the finishing touch to the real offering, the faith and life of the church.

2:19-30 Paul commends his fellow workers

Verses 19-23: Timothy (see on 1:1-2). Verses 25-30: Epaphroditus. The Philippians had sent him to help Paul. In sending him home, Paul is anxious to make it clear he has not fallen down on his job. Far from it.

3 Warning and example

Paul had been rounding off his letter (3:1a), but fresh and alarming news compelled him to take up his pen again. He does not mind repeating former advice, as a safeguard (3:1b). They must beware of those 'dogs' the Judaizers – that group of Jewish Christians who followed Paul everywhere, insisting that Gentile converts must be circumcised and keep the law (despite the official edict of Acts 15:19ff.). They are in fact altering the whole basis of salvation, making it 'by faith *and* ...', instead of 'by faith only': hence Paul's anger.

The true circumcision (3): the true Israel, the true people of God.

Gain ... loss (7-8): God does not operate a credit and debit account. The finest human achievement is garbage compared with the standard of life he demands, and provides for us, in Christ.

I press on ... (12ff.): like the athlete or charioteer, who does not waste time looking back, but strains every nerve and concentrates every effort to cross the line or pass the post. Paul counters the idea that perfection can be reached here and now.

'I press towards the goal to win the prize': whether Paul is thinking of the athlete, or of the Roman chariot race, pictured here, the point is the same.

Their god is the belly (19): i.e. appetite; whatever they want; revelling in things they should be ashamed of.

Our commonwealth (20): 'state' or citizenship. They are to regard themselves as a colony of heaven. The Philippians, being intensely proud of their status as a Roman colony, would be quick to grasp all that that meant.

4 Advice and encouragement: grateful thanks

Verse 1: a general appeal. Verses 2-3: personal appeals. Euodia and Syntyche are two women who have quarrelled.

Verses 4-9: rejoice, rejoice. The advice comes from a man in prison, facing death; a man who had been stoned and beaten and hounded by the mob. Yet experiences which leave others sour and bitter leave Paul overflowing with joy! The secret is in verses 6-7: learning how to offload all our cares on the One who cares for us (1 Peter 5:7). Nothing is beyond him. Having emptied our minds of worry, the next step is to fill them with the sort of things that will shape a truly Christian character (8).

Verses 10-20: the apostle's appreciation of the church's gifts. From the very first they have supported him (15), with a generosity that extends to all in need (2 Corinthians 8:1-5). At real cost they have given themselves and all they possess. No wonder Paul loves these Christians: a group of faithful, loyal, thoughtful, generous, outgoing men and women.

Caesar's household (21): Christian members of the imperial staff (the palace staff, if Paul is at Rome).

New Testament 2.7

COLOSSIANS

Colossae was a small town in the beautiful Lycus Valley, about 100 miles east of Ephesus, near Denizli in modern Turkey. Its near neighbours were the more prosperous Laodicea (Colossians 4:16; see on Revelation 3:14ff.) and Hierapolis. There were Christian groups in all three towns.

The church. We have no record of how it began. But it was probably during Paul's three years in Ephesus (Acts 19) that two prominent men from Colossae – Epaphras and Philemon – became Christians. And they were active in spreading the Christian message in their home area (Colossians 1:6-7; 4:12-13; Philemon 1-2, 5).

The letter. Although Paul had never visited the group at Colossae, he had heard all about it from Epaphras. There was much to be thankful for, but some of the news was worrying. So he wrote to them from prison – probably in Rome, about AD 61. He had a ready-made opportunity to send the letter with Tychicus (who may well have carried the letter to the Ephesians at the same time) and Philemon's runaway slave Onesimus, whom he was sending home (see on Philemon).

The problem. The trouble at Colossae was 'syncretism' – that tendency to introduce ideas from other philosophies and religions on a level with Christian truth, which is also perhaps our greatest temptation today. It was understandable. There were Greeks and Jews in the Colossian church, as well as 'native' Phrygians. It was natural that they should cling to their own ideas and want to incorporate them into Christianity. It seemed harmless enough. But Paul knew that it struck at the heart of the Christian faith. By trying to retain circumcision, their food-laws and festivals (2:11, 16), the Jewish Christians brought the whole basis of man's acceptance with God into question (see on Galatians). The idea of angel intermediaries (2:18) was a direct challenge to the supremacy of Christ. And the introduction of asceticism and high-flown philosophy threw man back on himself and on human wisdom (2:18-23) – which had already been proved a failure. Although Paul does not deal with these issues point by point these are the thoughts that lie behind his letter. The Colossians needed to take fresh hold on Christ, on his complete supremacy and utter sufficiency. This is Paul's theme.

1:1-14 Opening greetings and prayer

It is characteristic of Paul to begin with thanksgiving. He has his Christian priorities – and his psychology! – right. But his warm-hearted praise is genuine, not just sugar to coat the pill of the lecture to follow. His loving care (and his prayer-list) extended beyond the churches he himself had brought into being, to groups of Christians he had never even met (2:1). It cheered him immensely to hear of their faith and love and hope. And he longed for God to give them fuller understanding and spiritual maturity.

1:15-23 Jesus Christ the Lord

Jesus is the living expression of God himself – active in the creation and holding together of all that exists. He was first, he is first – in existence, in power, in position. He has first place in God's new creation and his new people, the church. He brought it into being. He is its Head. Through his death it is possible for us to become God's friends – this is the good news of the gospel.

Firstborn (15): not first to be created, but the heir whose position is unique.

Thrones ... (16): unseen beings and powers outside our visible world.

1:24 - 2:5 Paul's own task

The apostle's job is to make God's message known. The philosophers hint at secrets, at deep things known only to the initiated. This is God's open secret: Jesus Christ – at home in every Christian, preparing him for a glorious future. And Jesus really is a 'secret' worth knowing. This makes all Paul's efforts worthwhile.

What is lacking ... (1:24): Paul is not implying that Christ's suffering was not enough for our salvation. But the church – Christians – cannot be perfected without suffering too.

2:6 - 3:4 Wrong teaching and right attitudes

False argument was filtering into the Colossian church from various quarters (see introduction above). It was misleading and dangerous. The Christian cannot afford to compromise either with philosophy or with legalism. Both of these are man-centred. Christianity is Christ-centred – or it is nothing at all. We have all we need in him. We do not need to invoke other spiritual powers or intermediaries (2:8, 23), because Christ is infinitely greater. No religious rite (2:11) can give us more than we already have. Old Testament practices are no more than a shadow of the reality – which is Christ (16ff.). He is our life. He is the One we must hold on to. We depend on him, not on ourselves, our spirituality, our asceticism.

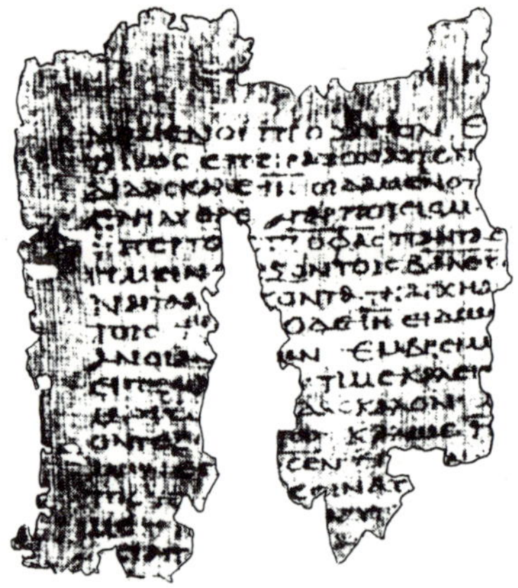

Paul warned his readers against those bringing false teaching and writing letters which claimed apostolic authority. 'Embroidered' stories of the life of Jesus have survived. These fragments of an unknown 'Gospel' date from the first half of the 2nd century.

2:12: see Romans 6.

Food and drink ... (2:16): despite all that the Jews said, salvation does not depend on things like these.

Elemental spirits (2:20): Christians must throw off the old pagan superstitious idea that spirits control the world.

3:5 - 4:6 The old life and the new

Becoming a Christian means a definite break with the old selfish way of life. It means determination to let the new life which is in us govern all we think and say and do. It means a permanent resolve to become like Christ, to take on his character (3:10). His life – his love and forgiveness – is our model (3:12ff.). His word (3:16) shapes our thinking. The hallmark of the Christian life is prayer and thanksgiving to God, and outgoing unselfish love in all our human relationships. Our concern is no longer to get, but to give.

3:18 - 4:1: see on Ephesians 5-6, where Paul treats the same subject more fully.

4:7-18 Personal news

The reference to Tychicus and Onesimus links this letter with Ephesians (see 6:21-22) and Philemon. All three letters would seem to have been sent at the same time by the same messenger. (The letter from Laodicea, 16, may be Ephesians.) It is good to find Mark reinstated after the trouble he once caused between Paul and Barnabas (Acts 13:13; 15:36-40). Aristarchus, who though a Jew came from Greece, was another long-standing companion of Paul's and had been involved in the riot at Ephesus (Acts 19:29). Luke stayed with Paul to the end, but Demas defected (2 Timothy 4:10-11). Epaphras, the Colossian, has been mentioned already (1:7, and see introduction). Archippus may be Philemon's son (Philemon 2). Nympha, in Laodicea, is only one of those who opened their homes to the local Christian group long before there were church buildings. Aquila and Priscilla at Ephesus (1 Corinthians 16:19) and later at Rome (Romans 16:5), Philemon at Colossae and Gaius at Corinth (Romans 16:23) all did the same. The whole church is deeply in their debt.

New Testament 2.8 and 9

1 AND 2 THESSALONIANS

Thessalonica was a free city, capital of the Roman province of Macedonia (northern Greece). It was a prosperous port on the Aegean Sea, across the bay from Mt Olympus. It also stood on the Egnatian Way, the land trade-route from Dyrrachium on the Adriatic to Byzantium (Istanbul). Thessaloniki is today a flourishing modern city, centre of government for northern Greece, and second only to Athens.

The church was founded about AD 50, after Paul (with Silas and Timothy) left Philippi on the second missionary journey. See Acts 17:1-9. Paul did not stay in Thessalonica long: three successive sabbaths preaching in the synagogue, followed by a short time based at Jason's house. Then the Jews stirred up trouble. Jason and the other Christians were hauled before the magistrates and bound over to keep the peace. For safety's sake the newly-formed church sent the missionaries away. But persecution continued, from Jews and others.

The letters. From Thessalonica, Paul and his party went to Beroea, then Paul continued alone to Athens. It seems Timothy joined him there (1 Thessalonians 3:1-2), but was almost immediately sent back to Thessalonica for news. Paul was acutely anxious to know what had become of the Christians. He was in Corinth by the time Timothy returned with good news. 1 Thessalonians, written at this point, is full of relief and joy. Paul answers questions that had arisen, and repeats his teaching on matters where the church was weak. The second letter followed a few months later, reinforcing the teaching and clearing up misunderstandings, particularly over Christ's return. These two letters are the earliest of Paul's surviving writings (with the possible exception of Galatians). They were written only 20 years after the crucifixion of Jesus.

1:1 Opening greetings

Paul is the author of the letter. But he writes in association with Silvanus (=Silas, see on Acts 15:40) and Timothy, his companions on the mission to Thessalonica, and now in Corinth.

1:2-10 Paul thanks God for good news of the church

What happened at Thessalonica was the work of God. What else could account for the way this little group – persecuted, deprived of their teachers from the word go – stood firm? More than that, within months they have become an example of unwavering faith to the rest of Greece (7), spreading the good news far and wide by word and life. No wonder Paul has cause for thanks.

They themselves (9): the people of Macedonia, Achaia, etc.

Verses 9-10: the gospel in a nutshell. Paul had preached the character of God; Jesus, his Son, who died to deliver man from judgement; the resurrection; and the return of Christ from heaven. The promise of the Lord's return is specially precious to all who suffer. These letters are shot through with it.

2:1-16 Paul recalls his visit

It is clear that Paul's enemies have been pursuing a campaign of vilification. The apostle clears himself of their charges by reminding the Christians of what actually happened when he was with them. He did not come as an itinerant quack teacher peddling dubious wares, and out to deceive (3). Nor was he on the make, in any sense (5). He came to give, not get (8), willing to face more trouble while still smarting from the wounds of Philippi (2; see Acts 16:22ff.). He even refused financial support (9).

Each one of you (11): Paul counselled enquirers personally, individually.

Verses 15-16: nowhere does Paul speak so harshly of his own people. His tone is prophetic. There is a point of no return for those who implacably oppose God. Judgement is as certain as if it had come already (16b).

2:17 - 3:10 Subsequent events

Paul is as close to his converts as parent to child. No matter how far away, they are deep in his heart and thoughts. The knowledge that they are in trouble fills him with unbearable anxiety. Paul's happiness – his life, even – depends on their continuance and progress in the faith. So he longs to see them and hear from them. He is even prepared to face Athens alone, rather than do without news. So Timothy's welcome report brings the apostle an influx of joy, a new lease of life.

Little remains of ancient Thessalonica today. As Thessaloniki, it is the second largest city in Greece. In later Roman times the Via Egnatia passed under the Arch of Galerius, pictured here. The street is still called by the same name.

Satan hindered us (2:18): it is in his interest so to engineer circumstances that the missionary and his converts are kept apart.

We told you beforehand ... (3:4): 1st-century Christians were taught from the outset to expect trouble and suffering.

3:11-13 Paul's prayer

Paul prays for reunion, and for love and holiness in the church.

4 - 5:22 Specific teaching

On sexual matters (4:1-8). Pagan standards of sexual behaviour fell far short of Jewish and Christian ones. The pull of the old ways was strong for the young converts.

On Christian love and right living (4:9-12). Even where love already exists there is always room for more. The Greeks despised manual labour. And there were idlers in the church quite happy to sponge on the generosity of fellow Christians. But Paul worked with his hands and encouraged others to do the same. The prospect of Jesus' return was a great temptation to opt out of hum-drum daily work (see also 2 Thessalonians 3:11-12).

On the Lord's return (4:13 - 5:11). Two problems have arisen out of Paul's teaching on the subject:

1. Some had died in the months between Paul's departure and the writing of this letter. So will Christians who die before Christ comes lose out (13-18)? Far from it, says Paul. They will be raised first when Christ comes. And dead and living together will join in the Lord's triumph and enjoy his presence.

2. When will the Lord come (5:1-11)? No one knows. But he will come suddenly and unexpectedly – and we need to be ready.

On general matters (5:12-22). Time, or space, is running out. But Paul manages to pack seventeen practical and characteristic commands into these few verses.

Wrong his brother (4:6): the same principle applies before and after marriage – sexual promiscuity deprives a fellow man of what is rightly his.

Asleep (13) ... fallen asleep (14): for the Christian, death is merely a sleep from which he awakes to the presence of Christ.

The breastplate (5:8): faith, love and the certainty of future salvation are the Christian's defences against all attack. Compare Ephesians 6:14ff.

5:23-28 Conclusion

Paul's prayer is comprehensive: for the whole man in every aspect ('spirit, soul, body'). Authority (the stern command to read the letter to the whole church) sits beside humility. The apostle, who never ceases to pray for his readers, knows how much he needs their prayers.

A holy kiss (26): see on 2 Corinthians 13:12.

2 THESSALONIANS

1:1-2 Opening greetings

1:3-12 Praise and encouragement

Verses 3-4: the Thessalonians seem to have protested against the extravagant praise of Paul's first letter (chapter 1). He replies that it is only right to thank God for their growing faith and love, and their firm stand in face of persecution.

Verses 5-12: the universe is a moral universe; God is a just God. It is therefore certain that those who make his people suffer, and reject his truth, will themselves be eternally, irrevocably punished at his coming. This is a fact no Christian gloats over.

2:1-12 The events leading up to Christ's return

This passage is one of the most difficult in all Paul's letter; and even Peter found Paul hard to understand (2 Peter 3:16)! He alludes to teaching of which we have no surviving record, so that much which was clear to his first readers is now obscure. It is better, in some cases, to admit we do not know the meaning, than to speculate.

Some of the Thessalonian Christians thought the day of the Lord had already begun. But Paul has never said (or written, 2) so. Before this happens, he explains, there will be a great, final rebellion against God, headed by an individual utterly opposed to him. (Compare Revelation 13, and 1 John 2:18-25). At present there are forces at work restraining evil – but in the end these will be swept away. Victory will come only through Christ, at his coming.

Man of lawlessness (3): not Satan himself, but the leader of the anti-God forces, who sets himself up as God. ('Son of perdition' is Hebrew idiom, meaning 'the one who is doomed to destruction'.)

He who now restrains it (7): perhaps Paul personalizes the principle of law and government which holds evil in check; perhaps he means an angelic being. We really do not know.

Those who are to perish (10): because they do not welcome the gospel. They turn their backs on the truth which offers salvation. In effect, like Satan, they say 'Evil be thou my Good' (12).

2:13 - 3:5 Thanksgiving and prayer

Paul turns, with tremendous contrast, to the Thessalonians. They responded gladly to the truth. And now all the glory of the Lord awaits them.

From the beginning (13): from eternity (see Ephesians 1:4).

The traditions (15): not customs, but the truth about Jesus and his teaching, faithfully handed down by the apostles: the same truth that we possess in written form in the New Testament.

Comfort (17): in the old sense of strengthen.

3:6-15 The need to work for a living

Paul stressed this in his first letter (4:11). But excitement about Christ's coming seems to have made the situation worse, not better. So Paul speaks out in strong terms against those who idle their life away and sponge on others. They can find no warrant for this in his own behaviour.

3:16-18 Conclusion

The present is tough, the future will be tougher (2:3-12). But no matter what times may be like, no matter what may be going on around, the Christian has an inexhaustible, unfailing source of peace.

At verse 17 Paul takes over from his secretary. His own signature authenticates this letter (see 2:2). He added his personal signature to each of his letters in the same way.

New Testament 2.10 and 11

1 AND 2 TIMOTHY

Timothy was the child of a mixed marriage – his mother being Jewish, his father Greek. His home was at Lystra in the Roman province of Galatia (not far from Konya in present-day Turkey). Paul came to Lystra on his first missionary journey, and it must have been then that Timothy was converted. He made such strides as a Christian that when Paul called again he decided to take Timothy with him on his travels. The local church leaders formally commissioned the young man and gave him their blessing. And from then on he became Paul's constant, loyal, trusted and greatly loved companion.

Timothy was not naturally brave, and he was often unwell. He needed a good deal of encouragement. But Paul's confidence was not misplaced. In the letters to the different churches he speaks most warmly of this 'son in the faith'. Timothy not only travelled with Paul and was associated with him in many of his letters, he frequently acted as Paul's envoy to the churches. Very early on he was left behind in Beroea to consolidate and follow up Paul's work there and at Thessalonica. He was sent to Corinth when Paul heard of the troubles in the church there – no easy assignment. And at the time Paul wrote to him he was in Ephesus, supervising the local Christian groups and responsible for choosing and training church leaders.

The letters. 1 and 2 Timothy and Titus belong to the end of Paul's life. Paul was free when he wrote 1 Timothy and Titus, and had recently been engaged in further evangelism in Greece and what is now Turkey. This does not tally with anything we know from Acts, and it may be assumed that Paul was released from the imprisonment described in Acts 28, resumed his preaching for some time, and was then re-arrested and taken to Rome for trial. In 2 Timothy he is in prison and expecting to be executed.

In these 'pastoral letters' – the general title for the three letters – we have a directive from Paul on the way Timothy and Titus should handle the various problems they encountered in the oversight of the churches in their charge. Paul sets out the qualities to look for in appointing church leaders. He gives advice on personal conduct. And in the face of much false and misleading teaching he urges them to concentrate on essentials and not be side-tracked. The best way to counter wrong ideas is to teach the truth.

The early church had no doubt that these letters were genuinely written by Paul to the two men named. Mod-

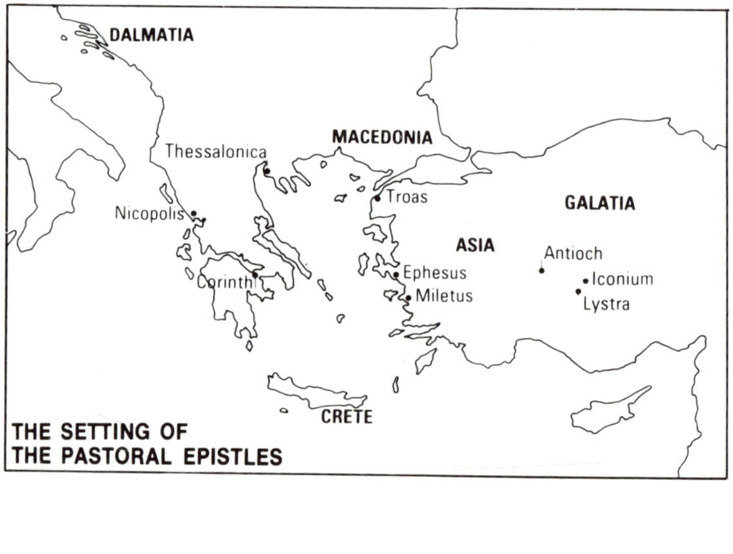

THE SETTING OF THE PASTORAL EPISTLES

ern scholars have questioned this on the grounds that they differ in language and content from Paul's other letters, and that they counter 2nd-century heresies. Some suggest they are the work of a later writer who incorporated some genuine Pauline material. This raises fresh problems, however, and there may be a simpler explanation.

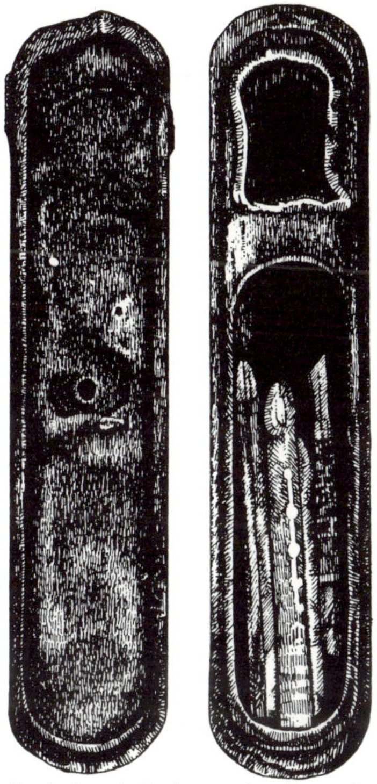

Paul signed the letters he dictated, adding a greeting. The wooden pencase containing reed pens, with an ink-well half-filled with black ink, dates from the 1st century.

We know that Paul often used a secretary, for instance, and if he was given a good deal of freedom this would make arguments based on vocabulary very uncertain (even with computer analysis!). The problem over content is that Paul tells Timothy and Titus things they must surely have known already. The reason may be that the instructions were meant to be read to the churches over which the two men ministered. Even the point about heresies is by no means certain. There is nothing in the letters that we can categorically say Paul could not have written.

1 The trouble at Ephesus; Paul and Timothy

There had been a tremendous response to Paul's preaching in and around Ephesus (Acts 19). A great many Christian groups had sprung up almost overnight. And Paul was quick to realize how vulnerable they were to wrong teaching (Acts 20: 29-30). Ten years later his fears had materialized. Apocryphal Jewish legends and family-trees (4) were being made the basis of strange teaching. This was a wrong approach to the Old Testament law, and Timothy must stop it spreading. The Christian message should result in faith and love and a clear conscience – not idle speculation. It has always seemed more exciting to argue over abstruse topics than to live the Christian life.

Paul had been a Christian for over 30 years. He had been on the road with the gospel message for 20. Yet he never forgot that he had once gone all out to destroy this sect (13; Acts 8:1-3; 9). He never ceased to be amazed that God should have taken a man like him into his service. Paul's directive is a good one: 'hold to your faith; obey your Christian conscience'.

Prophetic utterances (18): the indication (given either to Paul, or at Timothy's commissioning) that God had chosen Timothy for this work.

Delivered to Satan (20): we do not know exactly what this means – but see on 1 Corinthians 5:5.

2 Prayer; the place of women

The first duty of the Christian church is prayer. It is in answer to prayer that God gives conditions in which Christians can lead peaceable lives and put all their energy into making his good news known to the whole world (4).

The Christian message upgraded the status of women (see e.g. Galatians 3:28). But God did not intend them to take over. Men and women are equal in his sight, but their roles in life are not identical. So Paul's word to Christian women is to be conduct-conscious, not clothes-mad, and not to lord it over the men.

Verse 15: Paul could never have meant that women win eternal salvation through childbirth (compare verse 5)! The thought may follow on from verses 13-14 – i.e. though woman was the first to sin, it was through woman that the Saviour was born (Revised Standard Version margin). Or he means that women will be 'brought safely through' childbirth ... (New English Bible margin).

3 Church leaders

It was Paul's practice to appoint several elders (the same thing as bishops, 1) to take charge of each church (Acts 14:23). These in turn were assisted by 'helpers' (deacons, 8). His list of qualifications for these leaders makes sound sense. They must be men (and women, 11, unless these are deacons' wives) who can control themselves and their families, who have proved to be stable Christians, and who have the respect of the outside world. Timothy was not a naturally forceful character. To have Paul's written authority was the next best thing to having the apostle with him (14ff.).

Mystery (9): God's revealed secret in Jesus Christ; the Christian faith is God-given, not man-made.

Verse 16: Paul seems to be quoting a Christian hymn.

4 False teachers – and true

The ultimate source of false teaching is the devil himself. It is promoted by men who are dead to conscience. They ban marriage and lay down rigid rules about diet – things God has designed for man's good. They claim that their thinking is super-Christian. In fact it is sub-Christian. Timothy, as a true teacher, has to make this clear. And this does not stop at words. His whole life must bear out what he teaches others. So he has to let the truth mould his own life (6); he has to keep spiritually fit (7, 8). He has always to watch himself, and watch his teaching.

5 - 6:2 Dealing with people; widows; elders

To treat other people as we would our own family (1-2) is sound advice. There was no welfare state in Paul's day and the widow's lot was unenviable. The church was quick to realize and accept its responsibility to help (Acts 6:1). It soon had a sizeable problem, and not all of the cases were equally deserving. Paul's rule is that the church should reserve its help for those who are really destitute. It should take on to its books only older widows of good Christian character, and committed to Christian work. The younger ones should remarry. And wherever possible widows should be cared for by their own relatives. In the city where the goddess Diana was served by a host of prostitutes, the reputation of those who serve Christ must be beyond reproach.

Elders must be carefully chosen, treated with respect, and paid for their work.

As Christians, slaves are free men – but they are not to drag Christ's name in the mud by turning on their masters (see also on Ephesians 6:5ff.; Philemon).

5:9: not 'only married once', but 'faithful in marriage to one man' (New English Bible).

5:22: 'lay hands on': i.e. commission men for Christian service.

5:23: sound medical advice at the time; wine counteracted some of the harmful impurities in the water.

6:3-21 Real wealth; personal instructions

The subject of false teaching comes up yet again. The superior 'knowledge' (*gnosis*, 20) claimed by these men soon grew into the full-scale heresy of 'Gnosticism', whose initiates felt free to discard some of the cardinal Christian truths, including the fact that Christ was a real man.

Some men see Christianity as a road to riches. And Christians *are* rich – though not in money. Not that money is wrong in itself. It can and should be put to good and generous use. It is the *craving* for money that leads to all kinds of evil. The 'man of God' (11) craves for a truly Christian character, and all his effort is directed to this end. He knows that Jesus will one day return in glory, and he lives in the light of that fact.

The root (10): more accurately, '*a* root'.

2 TIMOTHY

This is Paul's last and most moving letter. After a lifetime of service and suffering for Christ he is in prison again, and death is imminent. He is alone except for Luke, and longs to see Timothy again. Yet there is no hint of self-pity; there are no regrets. His last word is one of encouragement to all who follow after. He can face death without fear and without doubt. The race is over – ahead is his reward.

1 'I thank God'

Gratitude was the habit of Paul's Christian life. He had long since ceased to grumble about his own discomforts. Deep thankfulness fills his heart now as he thinks of Timothy. And he longs for this man of many fears, as well as real faith, to share his own confidence. The secret is simply to *know* Christ (12; and see Philippians 3:10). We have good news

for the world – a gospel that brings men life. We need neither apologize for it, nor try to improve on it.
Tears (4): shed when they parted.
That day (12): the day of the Lord's return; the day of judgement.
All ... in Asia (15): false teaching took such a hold in Ephesus (see on 1 Timothy 1) that Christians rejected the very man to whom they owed their faith. It must have been a bitter moment for Paul.

2 On active service

It costs something to be a Christian – no man knew this better than Paul. Timothy will need single-minded determination not to get sucked in by the demands of life (4) or side-tracked by fruitless, divisive argument (16, 23). Not everyone who makes a good beginning stays the course. The way we live must demonstrate the truth of what we say. We are not to bicker and fight over words, but hold to the truth with gentleness and love.
Verses 11-13: Paul is probably quoting a hymn.
The resurrection (18): they 'spiritualized' the teaching and denied any future bodily resurrection.

3 Troubled times ahead

Paul warns that as the time for Christ's return draws near evil will intensify – even within the church (5-6). Those who are true to Christ will go through persecution – as Jesus himself predicted (John 15:20). Timothy must stand firm in the truths taught him from the scriptures. They contain all that is necessary for salvation and for right living.
Jannes and Jambres (8): in Jewish tradition, the names of Pharaoh's magicians (Exodus 7).
Verse 11: see Acts 13-14. Timothy would vividly recall these events since they took place near his home. Paul was stoned and left for dead at Lystra, Timothy's home town.

4 Final instructions

Paul may be put to death any time now. The prospect does not ruffle him. But he has a last charge for Timothy: to go on declaring God's message, come what may; though, sadly, this is not what men are itching to hear.

Personal news is left till last. Paul's fellow missionaries – Titus, Tychicus, Trophimus – are all away. One is ill, and one (Demas) has defected. At the first stage of his trial (16) Paul, like the Lord, stood alone. All his friends deserted him, and his enemies were not slow to make capital. Now winter is coming and he wants his books and papers, and his thick cloak. He has only Luke's presence, and the faithful Christians in Rome (21) to warm his heart – and the hope that Timothy and Mark will reach him in time.
Endure suffering (5): despite his fears, Timothy did just that (see Hebrews 13:23).
Books and parchments (13): possibly copies of Old Testament books, Paul's own notebooks, or personal papers.
Alexander (14): see 1 Timothy 1:20.
The lion's mouth (17): this may just be a manner of speaking; or it may refer to the lions in the arena, to Nero, or to the devil.

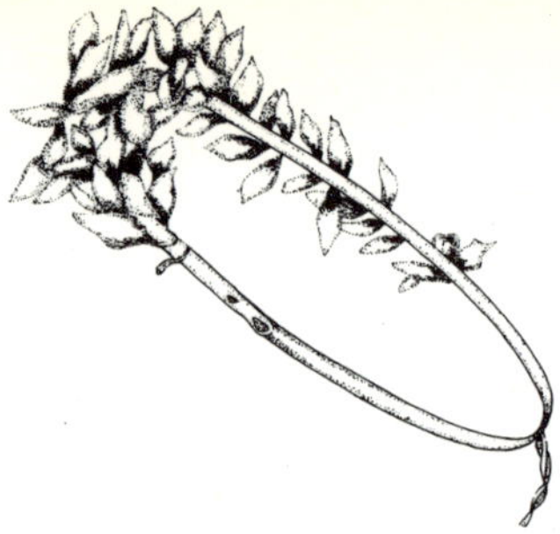

'I have finished the course, the victor's wreath awaits me' – Paul uses the vivid picture of the athlete's crown. This gold wreath was found at Pergamum.

New Testament 2.12

TITUS

See introduction to 1 and 2 Timothy.
Titus is not mentioned in Acts, but it is clear from the letters that he was one of Paul's trusted inner circle. As a Greek he was made a test case on the visit to Jerusalem, to clarify the position of non-Jewish converts (Galatians 2:1-4). Later when, despite Timothy's work, trouble flared up in Corinth Paul chose Titus as the man for the job. He not only sorted things out, but established really good relations with the church – no small tribute to his tact and strength of character (2 Corinthians 2; 7; 8; 12). Some years later again, when Paul wrote this letter, Titus had been left to consolidate the apostle's work in Crete. He faced a situation very similar to Timothy's at Ephesus (see 1 Timothy). The last mention of Titus is in 2 Timothy 4:10, when he was away (presumably still furthering the Christian cause) in Dalmatia (Yugoslavia).
Crete was probably one of the first places to hear the Christian gospel. There were Jews from Crete in the crowd that listened to Peter on the Day of Pentecost (Acts 2:11). But the message fell on rough ground. The Cretans were such habitual liars (1:12) that the Greeks coined a special verb for lying – 'to Cretize'. And it is plain from Paul's letter that even the Christians were an unruly, hot-headed, volatile bunch who needed firm handling.

1 Elders – and trouble-makers

It is the thought of the Cretans and their lies (12) that makes Paul dwell on the dependability of God's word. When he holds out the promise of eternal life, we can rely on it. He tells us the truth – we can pass it on with absolute confidence.

For the qualifications of church leaders (5-9) see on 1 Timothy 3.

False teachers have produced a situation so bad it calls for a really strong line. Physical force is never justified, but there are times when forceful words certainly are. The worst heretics were Jewish – but there were others too (10, 14; and see on 1 Timothy 1).
Verse 12: a quotation from the poet Epimenides.
Verse 16: the acid test of faith is how we live. It is not enough simply to call ourselves Christians.

2 - 3:11 Christian conduct

By the way we behave we can discredit, or reinforce, the Christian message. Paul's instructions throw no flattering light on the Cretan temperament. They were a naturally belligerent, argumentative people, uncontrolled, resentful of authority and partial to the bottle! But the Christian life calls for discipline, obedience and respect for others – within the family and household, within the church, and in relation to the authorities. Jesus gave his life to buy us back from our old sinful ways and make us into people whose consuming passion is to do good (2:14). The Christian teacher must use his authority to insist on Christian standards – and he must set a good example. Doing good results *from* (not *in*) salvation (3:3-7).
Washing (3:5): a picture of the cleansing, renewing work of the Holy Spirit which is symbolized in Christian baptism.
Genealogies (3:9): see on 1 Timothy 1.

3:12-15 In closing

When his 'relief' arrives, Titus is to join Paul at Nicopolis on the west coast of Greece. Tychicus is another member of Paul's inner circle of partners in the gospel (Ephesians 6:21, etc.). Zenas and Apollos (see Acts 18:24-28) may have been the ones who brought Paul's letter to Titus.

New Testament 2.13

PHILEMON

This is a private letter from Paul to Philemon, one of his converts and a good friend. Philemon was a man of some standing. A group of local Christians regularly met in his home at Colossae. One of his slaves, Onesimus, had stolen some money (18) and run away to the big city (probably Rome) where he could easily escape detection. There he somehow came into contact with the imprisoned apostle, and through him became a Christian. Paul loved this young man like a son, but he was Philemon's legal property. It was hard for Paul, and hard for Onesimus – who was liable to terrible punishment for what he had done – but he must go back and make amends. Paul could not keep him without Philemon's willing consent. So he wrote this 'covering note' for Onesimus. And Tychicus went with him for company and moral support, taking the latest news and a letter from Paul to the Colossian church (Colossians 4:7-9).

Paul's intention in writing is to ask Philemon to be lenient. A very different Onesimus is returning from the one who ran away. He is not just a slave now, but a brother-Christian. And Paul wants Philemon to welcome him as such. He could have insisted. He had the authority – and Philemon was deeply indebted to him. But instead his letter is loving and tactful, considerate and full of warm praise. He knows this man. He knows his faith and his Christian love. There is no need to make demands. Philemon will do all that he asks – and more.

Apphia (2): probably Philemon's wife. Archippus may be their son.

No use ... (11): Paul plays on Onesimus' name, which means 'useful'.

Verses 15-16: it is not clear whether Paul has any thought of Onesimus being set free. But the ideas expressed here are radical enough to have a far-reaching effect. Slavery was such an integral part of the social structure of the day that to preach freedom would have been tantamount to revolution. Paul's brief was not to engage in political campaigning but preach a gospel capable of transforming human life from within.

Verses 18-19: Paul's 'IOU' recalls the Samaritan's good neighbourliness (Luke 10:35).

Epaphras, Mark ... (23-24): see on Colossians 4.

New Testament 2.14

HEBREWS

Who wrote the letter? The origin of Hebrews is something of a mystery. The oldest manuscripts are anonymous, and there are none of the conventional greetings with which a 1st-century letter usually began. In fact it is more a treatise than a letter. Even in the first few centuries AD no one knew for certain who the author was, though many people attributed it to Paul. Today this is considered very unlikely. Hebrews reflects neither Paul's style nor his thought. But having said that, we are no nearer to solving the puzzle. From the letter, we know that the author knew Timothy (13:23). He writes extremely polished Greek. And he is plainly an able teacher. He knows the Old Testament inside out. And the version he quotes is the Greek Septuagint – which means he is probably a Greek-speaking (Hellenistic) Jew, writing to fellow Greek-speaking Jews. He is a Christian who has thoroughly thought through the relation of his faith to Judaism.

To whom was it sent? The title 'To the Hebrews' is very old, but may not be original. It is a fair inference from the letter – with its discussion of priests and sacrifice and its many Old Testament quotations – that it was written to a group of Jewish Christians. They were men of some intellectual ability. The group had been established a good many years (2:3; 13:7), and had a history of persecution. They should have been mature Christians by this time, capable of teaching others (5:11 - 6:2). Instead they are withdrawn and inward-looking. And they seem to have half a mind to turn back to Judaism. They need a forceful reminder that what they possess in Christ is far better.

When was it written? The most likely date is the late 60s. If Jerusalem and the temple had already fallen to the Romans the author would have been almost bound to mention it when he referred to the priests and sacrifices. So it is fairly certain it was written before AD 70. If the letter was written to Rome (see on 13:24) and alludes to Nero's persecution this places it sometime between AD 64 and AD 70.

What is it about? Hebrews was written for a group of Christian Jews wavering between Christianity and Judaism. It is in a sense the counterpart to Paul's letter to the Romans, this time directed to a Jewish audience and explaining Christ's relationship to all that had gone before in the religious history of Israel. So the writer compares and contrasts the person and the achievements of Jesus with the Old Testament priesthood and sacrificial system. He is not only incomparably greater and better than these, he is the ultimate realization of all they stand for. He is the perfect priest, offering the perfect sacrifice. He has finally removed the barrier of sin and given men access to God in a way the sacrificial system could never do. That was the copy: he is the original pattern. That was the shadow: he is the reality men have always been searching for. If we turn away from him – back to an inferior substitute, back to a proven failure – we lose everything.

1 Jesus Christ – the Son of God

The letter begins with a tremendous affirmation of the deity of Christ (1-4). Through Jesus, God has made his supreme and final revelation of himself to man. Jesus is the living embodiment of the character and majesty of God. He has dealt with the problem of human sin, once and for all. He is now at God's side, in the position of supreme power.

The angels – whom the Jews came near to worshipping – themselves worship Christ (6). They are spiritual beings, but no more than God's servants (14). The Son is far and away above them – as the scriptures prove.

The writer's use of the Old Testament. The quotations in Hebrews are from the Greek Septuagint version, which differs in some respects from our own Old Testament. And the writer is in any case more taken up with the meaning than with the precise words used. Comment and quotation are often merged, as was then quite customary. And if we look the references up, we find that the writer – like other New Testament writers – exercises a surprising freedom of interpretation. Some verses are filled with meaning far beyond their original context. See 'New Testament Quotations from the Old Testament'.

The quotations in this chapter are from Psalm 2:7; 2 Samuel 7:14; Psalm 97:7 or Deuteronomy 32:43; Psalm 104:4; Psalm 45:6-7; Psalm 102:25-27; Psalm 110:1.

2 Jesus Christ – the Son of man

If the message of the angels – that is the law of Moses, Acts 7:53 – proved true, how much more important is the Son's message of salvation (1-4).

We are not to underestimate Christ because he shared our human nature. God created man for a great destiny (7-8) – a destiny we can now realize, because Christ has suffered and died for all men (9-10). He became man to win forgiveness for us. He became man to help us.

Verses 6-8, 12, 13: the texts quoted are Psalm 8:4-6; Psalm 22:22; Isaiah 8:17-18.

Perfect (10): the idea is not moral improvement, but that through suffering Jesus was perfectly able to do the task God gave him. Only by this means could he make man's salvation possible.

Verse 17: this idea is more fully explained in chapter 5.

3 Jesus Christ – greater than Moses

Moses made Israel into a nation. He led them out of slavery in Egypt and through the desert. He gave them God's law and their forms of worship. No man was more revered by the Jews, and rightly so. But he could never be more than God's faithful servant. Jesus is God's Son (1-6).

The readers are in a very similar position to Israel at the time of the exodus. Both have seen God at work in an amazing way. But despite this the Israelites rebelled against God in the desert – and never entered the promised land (11). What happened to them can happen to us if we now turn our backs on God.

Verse 8: see Exodus 17:1-7; Numbers 20:1-13.

4:1-13 God's rest

The parallel is made more explicit. The 'rest' God spoke of was more than just a stable and secure life in the land he had promised. Through the psalmist (Psalm 95), hundreds of years after Joshua's day, God was still appealing to people to enter his rest. There is a spiritual counterpart to the promised land, and the passport to it is faith. We enter into God's eternal rest, his peace, as we trust him and take him at his word (3). Salvation is his gift, not a reward for our own hard work (10). And we cannot hope to conceal our real attitude from him.

4:14 - 5:10 Jesus – our great high priest

Aaron (5:4) was the first high priest of Israel appointed by God. He was the intermediary between a holy God and a sinful people, the go-between who represented each to the other. The Jewish religion – the system these Jewish Christians were tempted to return to – still had its high priest. But in Christ we have a high priest who fulfils all the statutory requirements, and far more, because he has no need to atone for his own sins. He is the perfect high priest appointed by God as mediator for all time.

Under the Jewish law the same sacrifices were offered year after year. Jesus' sacrifice of himself was made once and for all.

Melchizedek (5:6, 10): the king/priest of Salem to whom Abraham gave a tenth of his possessions (Genesis 14:18-20). Chapter 7 develops the thought of these verses.

5:8: not learning to obey, but learning the full cost and meaning of obedience through suffering.

5:9: see on 2:10.

5:11 - 6:20 Warning – and encouragement

The writer breaks off to do some plain speaking. His readers have got stuck at the ABC of Christianity (5:11 - 6:3). Their lack of progress is bad enough in itself. But it is symptomatic of something much more serious. They are in danger of throwing the whole faith overboard. The situation calls for shock tactics. So the writer spells it out. If, despite all their Christian knowledge and experience, they deliberately reject Christ there is no hope for them. It is not that God refuses to forgive, but that they refuse the one available means of forgiveness. And their thinking is leading them in this direction, though they have not yet reached the point of no return.

But he is quick to comfort. He cannot believe they will go so far – or that God will allow it. Faith and perseverance will lead to the realization of all God has promised. The presence of Jesus in heaven guarantees that hope (6:19-20).

6:2: 'baptisms' – not the usual word for Christian baptism. The teaching may be on the difference between Christian baptism and Jewish ritual washings. 'Laying on of hands', at baptism and commissioning for special service, symbolized the empowering of the Holy Spirit.

7 A new high priest

6:20 brings us neatly back to the point made in 5:10 – this chapter carries it forward. Jesus has superseded the Levitical priesthood by becoming high priest for all time. This fact is anticipated in Psalm 110, where the Messiah is described as priest of a different order. The shadowy figure of Melchizedek (Genesis 14:18-20) reflects something of the nature of Christ's priesthood – the dual role of king *and* priest; the timelessness of it; its superiority to the old order. Levi in a sense acknowledged this by paying Melchizedek tithes through his ancestor Abraham! If the priesthood of Aaron and his fellow Levites had been good enough, no change would have been needed. Neither these men nor their work was perfect. Jesus is. They were not able to meet our needs. Jesus can and does.

8 A new covenant

The Old Testament is constantly pointing forward. David anticipated a new priesthood. Jeremiah (31:31-34) spoke of a new covenant – because the old agreement God had made with his people (Exodus 34:10-28; 20) had already broken down. The system of sacrifices instituted by Moses, and the tabernacle he had built, are only copies. In Jesus we have the original – the pattern – the reality. When Jesus offered up himself as the one final sacrifice (7:27) he arranged a new and better covenant between God and men – the one Jeremiah looked forward to. And the new supersedes the old.

9 - 10:18 Shadow and reality; the perfect sacrifice

The writer's thoughts are again back in the time of the exodus, when God made his covenant with Israel through Moses and gave them the pattern on which to construct the tabernacle. (The temple was later modelled on it – but it is not the temple he has in mind here.) Although God had chosen to live with his people, in a tent like their own, they had no right of access to him. The layout of the tabernacle and the whole system of animal sacrifice emphasized God's apartness and the people's sin. Only one man (the high priest) once a year (on the Day of Atonement) was allowed to enter the inner sanctuary (9:7). And the very repetition of the sacrifice made its ineffectiveness all too clear (9:25).

These things are the shadow. They point forward and prepare men for Christ, who is the reality. When Christ came, the whole system was reformed (9:10). As perfect high priest he offered himself as the perfect sacrifice (9:14) – a single offering for sin, valid for all time. He has dealt with human sin once and for all, removing the stain completely – something the Old Testament animal sacrifices lacked the power to do (10:10-12). And his death brought the terms of his will (the new covenant) into effect (9:16ff.). We are forgiven. We can come to God. No further sacrifice is needed (10:9).

10:19-39 No turning back

The way is open. We can come right into God's presence – if only we will. Christ's death has made it possible (19-22).

If we reject that sacrifice there is no other. We condemn ourselves to God's judgement. He holds us accountable for our actions (26-31).

No one pretends the Christian life is easy (32ff.). It calls for courage and perseverance. But it is infinitely worth while. If we turn back, we are lost – eternally. If we hold on, and keep trusting, God will give us all he has promised.

Through the curtain (20): see Mark 15:38.

11 Faith

The faith under discussion here – following directly on from 10:38-39 – is not man's first unsteady step towards

God. It is a life-long attitude of confident reliance on God's word. To have faith is to be certain – not of the here and now, the tangible things – but about things future, the unseen realities (1). The Old Testament abounds in examples of men who possessed a faith like this, and who lived and died accordingly. God has given us their record – he is proud to own them and be known as their God (16). They all looked forward to the time when God would fulfil his promises, but none of them lived to see it (13). Because God planned to include us too – to save and perfect every one of his people through Christ (39-40).

Abel demonstrated his faith – and was killed (Genesis 4). Enoch walked by faith – and lived (Genesis 5:21-24). Noah's faith saved his whole family (Genesis 6-8). Abraham's took him away from his settled life at home (Genesis 12:1-7) and made him an alien and refugee. Faith made him willing to offer up his only son, trusting that God would bring him back to life (Genesis 22). Isaac, Jacob and Joseph in turn all demonstrated their belief in God's promise (Genesis 27; 48; 50:24-25). Faith overcomes fear (23). It determined Moses' choice to leave court and throw in his lot with a nation of slaves (Exodus 2; 12; 14). Jericho was taken by faith, not superior force (Joshua 2 and 6). And so on through the Judges – Gideon (Judges 6 - 7); Barak (Judges 4); Samson (Judges 15 - 16); Jephthah (Judges 11 - 12) – through King David and the prophets. Daniel's faith saved him from the lions (33; Daniel 6). Elijah and Elisha brought the dead back to life (35; 1 Kings 17; 2 Kings 4). In answer to faith, God has given men remarkable triumphs and victories. But not always. Faith is demonstrated – equally – through those who have endured imprisonment, torture and death. Jeremiah was beaten and imprisoned (36; Jeremiah 38); Isaiah, it is said, was sawn in half (37); Zechariah was stoned (37; 2 Chronicles 24). And there were many more.

12 The incentive to go on

We are being watched by these great heroes of faith. They are crowding round the track to see us run. Let us strip off everything that hinders, and run the Christian race with all we have. Christ did not give up when the going got hard; neither must we. When we suffer, it is not because God does not care – but because he

The people of Israel came to Mt Sinai in fear, to the blast of the trumpet. The Christian, by contrast, comes to 'Mt Zion, the city of the living God'.

cares enough to discipline us for our own good. We must not be discouraged and give up.

We have come to God by a better way than the terrors of Sinai (18-21; Exodus 19) – through Christ himself. But we must not forget who God is. We do well to listen carefully to what he says (25) and take his warnings to heart (15-17), because our life depends on it. One day the world as we know it will cease to exist. We need to be sure we have put first things first.

Esau (16-17): see Genesis 25:29-34; 27:34-40.

13:1-17 Pleasing God

God is concerned with the whole of life – with how we use our homes; how we respond to the need of others; with marriage; with our use of money. We grow strong as Christians, not by a code of religious observance, but by obeying God. Those who depend on the Jewish sacrifices cannot benefit from Christ's sacrifice. It is a straight choice – and the principle still holds good. Christ offers salvation to all, but there is an exclusiveness at the heart of Christianity which men have always found hard: one, and only one, sacrifice for sin; one, and only one, way of coming to God. He calls us to identify ourselves unashamedly with him (13).

13:18-25 Personal messages

The writer closes with a deeply moving prayer and blessing (20-21). He has intended his letter to be one of encouragement, not censure. He hopes to see the readers soon.

Verse 24: this may mean the letter was sent *to* Italy; equally it may mean *from* Italy.

New Testament 2.15

JAMES

James is the first of a group of letters addressed to Christians in general (see on 1:1), rather than to a particular church. It is an extremely practical letter about the Christian life. Christian freedom can be a heady thing to people previously bound by a strict legal code of conduct. If salvation is God's free gift, what does it matter how we live? There is no question in James' mind – it matters immensely. In fact we can tell whether someone's faith is real by how they behave. Genuine faith in Christ *always* spills over into the rest of life. It affects our basic attitude to ourselves, to other people, and to life in general. There should be no discrepancy between belief and action. James reminds us of the need for genuinely Christian standards and values in every area of life. It is so easy to let things slip; so easy for the world around to squeeze us into its own mould, to convince us that there are no absolutes, no black and white, only grey. The early Christians needed the letter of James – and so do we.

We know little or nothing of how the letter came to be written, or who it was sent to. We are not even sure who the author was. But the most likely candidate is the James who was Jesus' brother. He became a Christian when he saw the risen Jesus (1 Corinthians 15:7) and went on to become a leader in the church at Jerusalem (Acts 12:17; 15:13ff.; 21:18). The letter was written early, but the exact date is unknown.

1 Deeds not words

This somewhat staccato chapter mentions almost all the topics dealt with more fully later: testing (2, 12-15), endurance (3; 5:7-11), wisdom (5; 3:13-18), prayer (5-8; 4:2-3; 5:13-18), faith (6; 2:14-26), riches (9-11; 2:1-13; 5:1-6), the tongue (19, 26; 3:1-12; 4:11), Christianity in action (22-25; 2:14-26). The crisp, succinct style and some of the themes remind us of Proverbs in the Old Testament and the Sermon on the Mount in the New (Matthew 5 - 7).

James' comments in this chapter provide us with a fair idea of what a Christian should be like. He has a positive attitude to the difficulties of life, knowing their value. He does not blame God when things go wrong. He knows where to turn for help and guidance. His values are right. He has control of his tongue and his temper. He sets himself to discover God's standards and to live them out. He puts faith into practice – and it shows.

Twelve tribes in the dispersion (1): the Dispersion was a technical term for the Jews scattered abroad. Here the phrase symbolizes all God's people.

Verse 27: real religion shows itself in care for the needy and in an exem-

Two superior Greeks are pictured on these coins: James criticized his readers for snobbery, paying more attention to the rich than the poor.

plary life. But James is not saying that these things are all God looks for.

2:1-13 Social distinctions

We all have a natural tendency to play up to social superiors and despise those below us on the social scale. But Christians must not make these distinctions. We are to treat everyone with equal respect – regardless of status, intellectual ability, race or colour. When we fail to do so we are breaking one of God's greatest commandments (8; Mark 12:28-31).

Law of liberty (12): the law of Christ, under which we are forgiven and set free from sin – something the law of Moses could not do.

2:14-26 Faith and actions

Faith that stops at words is not faith at all. Even the devil believes in God in that way, but it won't save him from God's judgement. Faith is proved – and develops – as we act on it. God accepted Abraham (Genesis 15:1-6; 22) and Rahab (Joshua 2) not because they *said* they believed him, but because they proved it by what they did. It is a good test.

Verse 24: only by taking this right out of context can James be made to contradict Paul (Romans 4). James is discussing the difference between real faith and mere words; he is not saying we can earn salvation.

3:1-12 The ambition to teach – and controlling our tongues

The man who wants to be a teacher in the church must first learn to control his tongue. A wrong word in public can have serious repercussions. James' terrible description is no exaggeration. Words can be so destructive – wrecking character, reputation, relationships, undoing years of good work. By one careless, venomous, inflammatory remark we can unleash forces we are powerless to stop. What is said can never be unsaid. If we can iron out the contradictions here, we have our whole personality under control.

Cycle ... (6) 'the entire course of our existence' (Good News Bible).

3:13-18 True wisdom

Christian wisdom is a very different thing from being worldly-wise. The worldly-wise are full of selfish ambition, eager to get on, asserting their own rights. God reckons a man wise when he puts selfishness aside and shows disinterested concern for others. This kind of wisdom is seen in a man's personality and behaviour – not in mere intellectual ability.

4 - 5:6 God's way – or the world's?

Christians can sell out to the world – the hostile, unchristian, anti-God world – and not even realize it. It happens every time we let the things we want from life overpower our judgement and Christian principles. This is the stuff wars are made of. It happens when we try to use prayer to further our own ends. It happens when we set ourselves up as judges of other people. It happens when we plan our lives without reference to God. It happens when wealth and pleasure become an end in themselves and justice flies out of the window.

How can we avoid it? By prayer – the right kind of prayer. By continually resisting the things we know are wrong. By seeking God out; by seeing ourselves as we really are and submitting whole-heartedly to him. By realizing we can count on nothing in this life – not even tomorrow – and depending on him. 4:15 expresses our whole attitude to life – not just tacking an automatic 'God willing' on to our own plans.

There is a special danger in affluence (5:1-6; 2:6-7). It cocoons people in false security. They are so well-insulated that they cease to feel for those who are cold and hungry. And values become warped. This life is so pleasant they lose sight of eternity. But God sees it all – and judges. Compare this with Jesus' parable of the rich fool (Luke 12:16-21).

5:7-20 Patience and prayer

Job is our model of patient endurance of suffering, and its reward; Elijah our example of the power of prayer (1 Kings 17:1; 18:1, 4). The Christian life is God-centred. In trouble we pray; in joy we praise. Believing prayer is a force to be reckoned with. God heals the sick and forgives sin in response to it. It is the prayer, not the oil, that is important. And there is nothing more worth while than bringing a man back to Christ, who can cover all his sin. Heaven itself rejoices (Luke 15:7).

New Testament 2.16 and 17

1 AND 2 PETER

Peter met Jesus first of all through his brother Andrew (John 1:40-42). The two brothers came from the fishing-village of Bethsaida. But they were living at Capernaum, at the northern end of the Lake of Galilee, when Jesus called them to leave their fishing business and become his disciples. Peter quickly became the leader and spokesman of the group of twelve men who were with Jesus right through his ministry. He was one of the inner three who saw some of Jesus' greatest miracles and who were allowed to see him in his true glory (Mark 9; 2 Peter 1:16-18). But when Jesus stood trial, Peter, for all his fine words, denied all knowledge of him – a fact he never forgot. Knowing his remorse, Jesus appeared to Peter before any of the other apostles after the resurrection. And he became the leader of the new-born church, as Jesus had predicted (Matthew 16:13-20) – the very first to preach the gospel (Acts 2). After a lifetime of preaching and teaching (accompanied in his travels by his wife), tradition has it that Peter was crucified head downwards in Rome during the Emperor Nero's terrible persecution which began in AD 64.

The letters. The first letter was sent to scattered groups of Christians in the five Roman provinces which covered the greater part of modern Turkey, north of the Taurus mountains. Peter most probably wrote from Rome (see on 5:13), at the outbreak of Nero's persecutions. He had John Mark with him, and Paul's companion Silvanus (Silas) to help him write. Christians in other parts of the Empire would soon be suffering as they were in Rome. Peter's message is one of comfort, hope and encouragement to stand firm.

The second letter mentions neither place of writing nor destination. Scholars have very great doubts whether the letter is really Peter's. It certainly differs in language and subject from 1 Peter – and some scholars point out anachronisms and believe the writer 'borrowed' from Jude. It is possible that a disciple of Peter wrote in his name, incorporating his teaching, but there is no conclusive proof. Longstanding tradition, and the care taken by the early Councils to exclude documents they regarded as forgeries incline us to assume the letter is Peter's. He is facing death as he writes (1:14). The church is beset and confused by false teaching – about Christian behaviour, and about Christ's return. His theme, therefore, is true knowledge.

1 Faith and hope

Christians can be glad, even in times of suffering. This is the way faith is tested and proved genuine. The dark days are short in comparison with the joy that lies ahead, when hope will be realized and we shall come into our promised inheritance. These are the realities nothing can change. One day soon we shall see the Lord we love and trust – and then what inexpressible joy and blessing. What greater impetus could there be to live as we should, modelling our behaviour on what we know of God's own character?

Dispersion (1:1): see on James 1:1.

Verses 10ff.: the Old Testament prophets had a message for their own generation – but they also looked to the future, when Christ would come. The author of Hebrews writes in very much the same vein (11:39-40).

2 - 3 Instructions for living

Remember who you are (2:1-10) – God's own people, chosen to make known the wonderful things he has done and still does. We are all being built into the fabric of a living temple which rests on the work of Christ. The world sees God in the lives of his people, individually and collectively.

The world at large and the powers that be (2:11-17). The Christian will always be suspect because he is a 'foreigner' in the world – but he must ensure that the accusations are groundless. Civil authorities must be obeyed – even if Nero is emperor! (See also Mark 12:17; Romans 13:1-7.) Christians in Peter's day had to live down unsavoury rumours that they practised incest, held sexual orgies and even indulged in cannibalism.

Slaves (2:18-25). The emphasis all through this section is on accepting authority and giving respect and loyal service where it is due, no matter what the other man is like. If we suffer unjustly, we have Christ's example before us.

Wives and husbands (3:1-7). In every case Christians are to do what is right, not insist on their own rights. Love and respect – sheer quality of life – is the surest way to win over a non-Christian partner. Christian character is more important in a woman than the latest fashion. The Christian husband, for his part, will be considerate. Prayer withers in an atmosphere of friction.

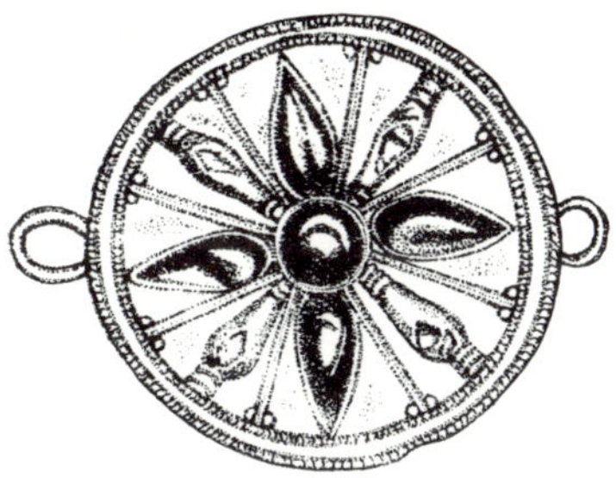

First-century ornament from a necklace; Peter exhorts his readers to avoid ostentatious dress.

In summary (3:8-22). Be at one. Be loving. Be humble. If suffering comes, let it be undeserved, let it be for doing good.

Living stone (2:4): a favourite New Testament metaphor for Christ (see Mark 12). The quotations are from Isaiah 28:16; Psalm 118:22; Isaiah 8:14-15.

Spiritual sacrifices (2:5): see, e.g., Romans 12:1; Hebrews 13:15-16.

Spirits in prison ... (3:19-22): Peter seems to say that between his death and resurrection Jesus preached (or proclaimed his triumph) to the spirits of the disobedient men (or fallen angels – see 2 Peter 2:4-5; Genesis 6:1-8) of Noah's day. The flood-water which destroyed the world saved Noah and his family by floating the ark. Similarly, Peter sees the water of baptism as a symbol of rescue from death. Of course it was the ark, not the water, which really saved Noah. So it is the risen Christ, not baptism in itself, who saves those who trust him and are cleansed from sin.

4 - 5 When suffering comes

Peter anticipates a time of suffering and persecution for his readers. When it comes, they must be ready – level-headed, alert, prayerful and unfailingly loving to others. It should come as no surprise to Christians to suffer for Christ's sake. It is a cause for joy, not discouragement! Christ's suffering was the prelude to glory. So it is for the Christian. God always keeps his promises.

As a leader himself – and a witness of the crucifixion – Peter appeals for a real 'shepherd spirit' in all church leaders (5:1-4; and see John 10 and 21:15ff.). And the younger people must respect their authority. Every Christian needs to acquire a genuinely humble spirit, like Christ's. He also needs a stout heart to face formidable and unrelenting opposition (8-9). But God cares for us. He perfects our Christian character through the things we suffer. He is in control!

Head of Nero, the Roman Emperor behind the persecution which was the subject of Peter's first letter.

4:1-2: the reference may be to the Christian's identification with Christ in his death, and the freedom from sin – the new life – that follows.

To the dead ... (4:6): i.e. Christians who are now dead. They suffered the judgement of death, like other men, but they will live.

Love covers ... (4:8): a proverb also quoted in James 5:20.

Judgement (4:17): the thought may link with 4:6, see above.

5:5ff.: these verses echo the thought in James 4:6ff. The 'roar' is intended to frighten, but Satan no longer has the power to destroy the Christian.

Silvanus (12): Silas, companion to Paul on his second missionary journey (Acts 15:22, 32ff.), and his associate in writing to the Thessalonians.

Babylon (13): probably a code-name for Rome (see on Revelation 17).

Mark (13): see introduction to Mark's Gospel.

2 PETER

1 Knowing God and his message

The purpose of our salvation is that we should become like Christ (4). And Christian growth depends on knowledge (2-3) – the kind of knowledge which gets translated into action (8). Peter shares Paul's determination to know Christ, and to put every effort into growing like him (see Philippians 3:10-16). Like James, he stresses the fact that real faith shows itself in the quality of life, in love and goodness (5:11; see James 1:26-27; 2:14-17).

The Christian message does not rest on myth and legend, but on the evidence of eye-witnesses (16). Peter actually saw Jesus in all his glory – transformed (see Mark 9:2-8). We have in addition the written testimony of the prophets – not simply human opinion, but a word from God himself.

Verse 14: Peter, facing death, recalls the Lord's words: John 21:18-19.

Verse 19: the scriptures light our path through life until the dawning day of Christ's return. Psalm 119:105; Revelation 22:16.

Verse 20: this may mean either 'it is not the interpretation that authenticates the prophet's message', or 'the true interpretation, like the message itself, is God-given'.

2 False teachers

The argument of this chapter is closely paralleled in Jude 4-16. To be forewarned is to be forearmed – so Peter warns his readers against the false teachers who have already disrupted other Christian groups. They are anti-authority. They respect no one. They teach self-gratification, and their dissolute lives deny the Lord and shame his church. They are out to exploit others for profit. And they are merchants of false hope, like a dried-up spring in the desert, or clouds that promise rain but blow over (17). Their punishment is certain. The Old Testament affords plenty of examples of God's punishment of wicked men, and his ability to rescue those who are his: the flood, and the saving of Noah (Genesis 6-8); the destruction of Sodom and Gomorrah, and the rescue of Lot (Genesis 19).

Angels (4,10-11): see on Jude.

Balaam (15): it seems this true prophet turned traitor when the price was high enough (Numbers 31:16).

Verses 19-22: for all they had learned of Christ, their conduct makes it clear that their basic nature remained unchanged.

3 The certainty of Christ's return

There will always be men who scoff at the idea of Christ's return – the more so as time passes. But Peter and Paul are unanimous on the subject (15-16; see e.g. 1 Thessalonians 4:13 - 5:11; 2 Thesalonians 2). We have God's word that it *will* happen; a word of such power that it brought our whole world into being (5; Genesis 1:3). If God 'delays' it is out of mercy, not weakness. The certainty that Jesus will come, and that it could happen any day, is our strongest incentive to Christian living. We want to be ready. We want him to be pleased with what he finds – and we may have only today.

Second letter (1): the first may be 1 Peter, or some other letter now lost.

Follow their own passions (3): 'live self-indulgent lives', New English Bible.

The fathers (4): either the Old Testament fathers, or the first Christians. *Fell asleep:* this is the way Jesus talked of death.

Verse 16: it is a comfort to know that Peter sometimes found Paul hard to understand! But he had a high regard for Paul's writings – placing them alongside the other scriptures. Romans 3 shows how people twisted Paul's words – they took his teaching on freedom, for example, as carte-blanche for licence.

New Testament 2.18,19 and 20

1, 2 AND 3 JOHN

John's Gospel was written to bring men to faith. 1 John, clearly by the same person, is intended to reassure Christians about their faith – to renew confidence shaken by false teaching. Both Gospel and letter belong to the close of the 1st century. The Christian faith was 50 or 60 years old by this time and had spread throughout the Roman Empire. John, living out his last years at Ephesus in modern Turkey – a strategic centre of the Christian church – was probably the only apostle still alive. There was pressure on many Christian groups to incorporate ideas from other philosophies as part of the faith.

John's letter was written to counter some early form of 'Gnosticism' being propounded by men who were once church members but had now withdrawn from the group. They liked to think of themselves as intellectuals – possessing a superior knowledge of God. They made a complete distinction between the spiritual (which was pure) and the material (which was evil). In practice this often led to immorality – because nothing the body did could tarnish the purity of the spirit. It also led to a denial of Christ's human nature – which was either 'make-believe' or only temporary. The Christ – being spirit – could not have died.

In this strong but tender appeal to his 'little children' in the faith, John makes it plain that these ideas cut the heart out of Christianity. If Christ did not become man and die for human sin there is no Christian faith. If any man sins deliberately and habitually he is not a Christian. God is light, and he calls men to walk in the light of his commands. He is love, and he requires his people to love one another.

1 JOHN

1 God is light

John writes as one who knew Jesus, the life-giving Word of God (see John 1:1-5), personally. He knew that Jesus was both Son of God and real man: no apparition but a person you could see and touch.

Jesus, the 'light of the world' (John 8:12), shows us that God is light. By 'light', John means not just the blinding radiance of his presence, but truth, purity, moral perfection. No one who has access to him can live in 'the dark' – dealing in sin and evil and lies, qualities opposed to his very nature. This is not to say that Christians are perfect. The searchlight of God's presence shows us up. Friendship with him involves seeing ourselves as we really are, and constantly asking his forgiveness.

2 To know God is to obey him

We are not perfect, but that is our constant aim: to become, to behave just like Christ (6). And when we fail, he has provided the remedy (1-2). Being a Christian means obeying God; doing what is right; loving, not hating, our fellow men. This is the real test of any man's claim to know God. To know is to obey.

The early Christians were taught that an arch-enemy of Christ – the embodiment of evil – would come on the scene when the Lord's return was imminent (18; the actual word 'antichrist' occurs only in John's letters, but 2 Thessalonians 2 makes the same point). John sees the 'explosion' of false teachers – who deny that the man Jesus was the Messiah and Son of God – as a sign that the time is near.

Abiding (6, 28): see on John 15.

Children ... fathers ... young men (12-14): the threefold address is probably used for emphasis. Forgiveness, knowledge of God and victory over evil are things all Christians possess.

The world (15): man organized for some end of his own without thought of God, or in open hostility to him. God, of course, loves the world of mankind (see John 3:16), despite its rebellion.

Anointing (27): John refers to the discernment the Holy Spirit gives to Christians. See also 4:4-6. He is talking about false teachers, not saying that Christians have no need of teaching.

3 Right living; true love

For the Christian – the child of God – sin is no longer inevitable. On the contrary, it is a denial of his new nature. Christ has really given us the freedom not to sin, and we are to live in the light of that fact. It is not possible for anyone born into God's family to go on breaking his law deliberately and habitually (the Greek John uses conveys the sense more clearly than our English translations: verses 6 and 9, in the light of 1:8 - 2:2). A man who behaves like this cannot be a Christian, no matter what he may say.

The Christian life-style can be summed up in the one word 'love'. The command to love one another rolls up into one all God's instructions about human relationships. But Christian love – Christ's love – is more than just words or feelings. It will inevitably touch our pocket and possessions – it may cost us life itself. We can measure the reality of our love for God by our determination to do as he says and love our fellow men. If our conscience is clear on this score, we can be confident that God will answer our prayers.

4 Distinguishing false from true; God is love

There is one basic test by which to judge any teacher – his recognition of Jesus Christ as man (emphasized here because this was the particular heresy of the day) and God. No man who denies this can possibly come with a message from God. The Holy Spirit enables the Christian to recognize truth when he hears it.

God is love. In the death of Christ for human sin he has shown us what love is (10). And if we really share his life – his nature – that love must flow through us to all around. Genuine love for God is bound to show itself in action towards others. This is John's favourite theme. But love is not trite or sentimental, nor inconsistent with plain speaking (of which verse 20 is a sample!). Love and obedience are bound up together (21). If we love and obey God we need not dread the day of judgement (17-18).

5 We can be sure

To know God is to love God. To love God is to obey God. To be his child is to love his children. Eternal life (the life of God), and the ability to defeat the anti-God forces of the world we live in, are ours as we believe in Jesus Christ as God's Messiah. God himself stands witness that Jesus is his Son. 'To believe is life, to disbelieve is death' (12). We can be sure of these things. We know he hears all we ask. We know he always answers.

The false teachers loved to talk about 'knowledge'. John makes his own list of things Christians know for a certainty. We know the gravity of sin. We know it is no longer the norm for Christians. We know we are absolutely secure in Christ. We know we belong to God in an alien world. We know that through the Son of God we know God himself, and real life.

Verses 6-8: the Authorized Version incorporates words that do not form part of the original letter, but are a late addition. These are omitted in all modern versions.

Three witnesses (8): the Holy Spirit, the baptism of Christ and the death of Christ – of which Christian baptism and the Lord's Supper stand as permanent reminders.

Verse 16: John does not say what this deadly sin is. The New Testament knows only one 'unforgivable' sin – that which attributes the Holy Spirit's work to the devil, and persistently rejects the One who makes forgiveness possible (see Matthew 12:31-32; Hebrews 6:4-6; 10:26).

2 JOHN

There is little doubt that all three letters are the work of one author – traditionally the apostle John since we know of no other apostle still alive at this time. As an apostle and senior elder of the church at Ephesus John's choice of the term 'Elder' is appropriate enough. The 'lady' is most probably a local church, rather than an individual. The 'children' would then be church members (as in 1 John); the lady's 'sister', John's own church.

Here again we have John's favourite theme: Jesus' command that those who follow him should love one another (5; John 15:12-17). To love others as Jesus loves us means keeping all God's commands. 'Love' which breaks any of the basic rules God has set to govern human relationships is not love at all. The love of Jesus is self-giving, not self-seeking.

For the Christian, love and truth go hand in hand. But he should content himself with what Christ taught. Only the false teachers are compelled to eliminate or elaborate (9-10). John is combatting the same sort of trouble here (7) as in his first letter. There had been travelling evangelists and teachers from the very start of the Christian mission, usually responsible to one of the apostles. The time had come to tighten up and refuse hospitality to anyone whose teaching contradicted the fundamental truth about Jesus Christ. It was essential for survival.

3 JOHN

See on 2 John above. This is a personal letter to an individual. **Gaius** was a common name, and it is not likely that this Gaius is the same as any of the others mentioned in the New Testament. If tradition is anything to go by, he may have been a leader of the church at Pergamum. What matters more, Gaius was a man who 'lived in (and therefore lived out) the truth'. His words, his deeds, his character were all of a piece. His life and conduct are in striking contrast to that of another local leader, **Diotrephes**. Gaius, a man of integrity, is doing all in his power to help his fellow Christians, especially the travelling evangelists and teachers who depended on Christian hospitality and support. Diotrephes is damaging John's own character, suppressing his letter, spreading lies, hugging his own position as leader and hindering missionary outreach. It seems the church has always had its petty dictators, men like Diotrephes who consider themselves indispensable. The third character in the letter, **Demetrius,** may have been John's messenger (there was no postal service!). This man's life speaks for itself. He richly deserves the high regard in which John holds him.

New Testament 2.21

JUDE

The author is Jude, the younger brother of Jesus and James, now an old man (the date is uncertain, but may be around AD 80). He was already thinking of writing, when alarming news of false teaching (see below) made him pen this short, vigorous letter with all speed. The letter is obviously Jewish – full of Old Testament references and allusions, and drawing its illustrations from at least two Jewish apocryphal writings (see below). Jude is dealing with a situation very like that dealt with in 2 Peter. And in fact the bulk of Jude's letter is paralleled in 2 Peter 2. The two are so similar that either one made use of the other, or both drew on an existing tract which countered false teaching.

Jude writes to a group of Christians threatened from within by men who have 'slipped in' and are now creating division by their false teaching. These men are characterized by arrogance and immorality, and their claim to superior knowledge. They are anti-authority. They are out for what they can get. And they are self-indulgent to a degree. They will argue black is white if it suits them.

But they are marked out for destruction – as Sodom and Gomorrah were for their sexual immorality and perversion (Genesis 19); as Cain was for murdering the brother whose life showed up his own (Genesis 4); as Balaam was for betraying his position as a prophet (Numbers 31: 8, 16 – see on 2 Peter 2:15); and as Korah was for his rebellion against God-given authority (Numbers 16). The examples are carefully chosen. These are the very things of which these teachers are guilty.

Jude's intention is to stiffen the resistance to such teachers. The Christians are not defenceless, but they must make full use of their defences. They must build on 'the faith' – that definite body of truth they have been given. They must pray and use the power of the Holy Spirit. They must live in the light of Christ's coming again. There is no need to be afraid or despair, for God is indeed able to keep them from falling.

The angels (6): the statement about the 'sons of God' in Genesis 6:1-2 led to a belief in an earlier war in heaven between good and evil angels whose pride and ambition led to their downfall. It was an apt illustration for Jude's argument.

Verse 9: the story comes from the apocryphal *Assumption of Moses*. Michael was sent to bury Moses, but the devil challenged his right to the body, on the ground that Moses had murdered an Egyptian. Jude uses Michael's circumspect reply as a lesson to men to watch their words, and not to treat the devil lightly.

Verses 14-15: a quotation from the apocryphal *Book of Enoch*. Jude takes his illustrations from books he and his readers know and respect, as well as from the scriptures themselves.

New Testament 2.22

REVELATION

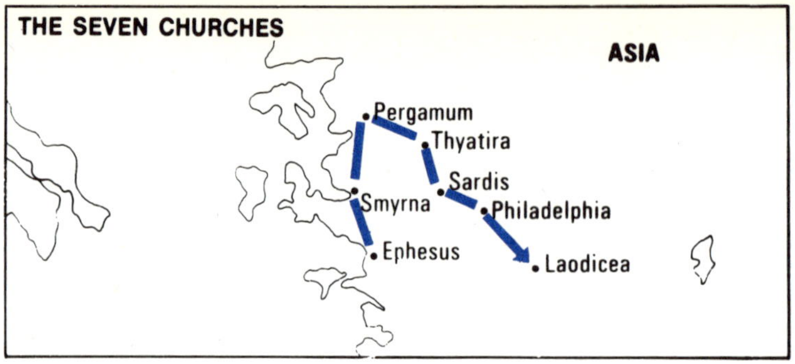

Revelation was written about AD 90-95, though some say earlier. The author is named as John. The style and language of Revelation is so different from John's Gospel that many have concluded this writer must be a different John. But we do not know of anyone apart from the apostle so well known that he could simply describe himself as 'John'. And tradition says that the apostle left Israel to make his home in Ephesus – capital city of the Roman province of Asia, in which the seven churches of Revelation 2 - 3 are located, and itself the recipient of one of the letters.

The book was written during a time of persecution. John's own exile on Patmos (1:9) probably entailed hard labour in the island's quarries. Some Christians had been killed (2:13) and others imprisoned for their faith. And there was worse to come (2:10), as worship of the Roman emperor became obligatory. The early Christians lived in eager expectation of Christ's return. But 60 years after his death this hope was still unrealized. It was only human for some to waver. So the letters to the churches, and the book as a whole, were needed to encourage them to stand firm. God is in control, no matter how things may look. Christ, not the emperor, is lord of history. He has the key of destiny itself. And he *is* coming again to execute justice. There is a glorious, wonderful future for every faithful believer – and especially those who lay down their lives for Christ. This world and all that happens in it is in God's hands. His love and care for his people is unfailing.

John's message was conveyed in a form designed to inspire as well as instruct. The vivid symbols, only too clear to those who first heard his circular letter to the churches, would have meant little to the authorities (who were always ready to pounce with a charge of sedition). More important, they would be equally vivid to Christians of every age. Christians are still enduring the pressures of totalitarian regimes. The victory of Christ and his people is vitally relevant today, when the machine, or the state, so often takes the place of God.

In our own materialistic age it has been only too easy to miss the spirit of the book. On the one hand, instead of seeing it as something to catch the imagination, we reduce it to a timetable of events. On the other, reacting against the rational, we reduce it to fantasy and mysticism. But to understand Revelation we must see it both as a book of vision and imagination *and* as a book firmly rooted in history, proclaiming Christ as Lord of history. Today – perhaps more than ever – we need its eternal, timeless realities. And we need its perspective.

A few basic pointers to the interpretation of the book may help those coming fresh to it:

1. The first thing to establish about any Bible passage is what it meant to the original readers; to see it in the light of contemporary history.

2. Revelation belongs to a particular type of literature – apocalyptic (see note). It is poetic and visionary, expressing its meaning through symbols and imagery. To take this picture-language literally, or treat the book as a logical treatise or timetable, is to go against the whole spirit of it.

3. Revelation is rooted in the Old Testament. This is where we find the clues to the meaning of the various symbols – comparing scripture with scripture.

4. Obscure passages must always be understood in the light of passages that are clear – never the other way round.

5. This is a book of visions. The fact that John is not over-concerned about harmonizing details makes it clear that it is the main thrust of each picture which is important. We should treat visions as we do parables, looking first at the whole picture and trying to discover the main idea.

6. We are not necessarily meant to take John's visions as a sequence of events which follow on one after the other. The eastern mind is not so preoccupied with chronology as we tend to be.

1 INTRODUCTION: JOHN'S VISION OF CHRIST

In more than one sense this book is 'the revelation of Jesus Christ' (1). He is John's source *and* his subject. Jesus draws back the veil on future events for John to make them known. There is nothing speculative about it. These are certainties, things that will take place 'soon'. The vision of Christ is at one and the same time for John's immediate audience – the seven churches in the Roman province of Asia (western Turkey) – and for Christians down the ages. No true Christian group is ever alone and abandoned. Jesus stands among his people (12-13, 20): the living Christ in all his power and glory; the Master of life and death and human destiny.

Soon (1): we do not know God's time-scale, and the prophets tend to foreshorten the future. The word serves to remind us to be ready.

Reads aloud (3): this was how the scriptures were made known in John's day.

Seven churches (4, 11): John makes great use of the number seven (seven seals, seven trumpets, seven bowls, etc.), which usually in this book stands for completeness, perfection. Here the number is also literal. Of the seven churches only Ephesus is well known (Acts 19). Acts 16:14 mentions Thyatira as Lydia's home town. The church at Laodicea is mentioned in Colossians 4:15-16. The rest occur nowhere else in the New Testament.

Alpha and Omega (8): the first and last letters of the Greek alphabet.

Patmos (9): a small Greek island off the west coast of Turkey (see also introduction).

Lord's day (10): usually taken to mean Sunday.

Sword (16): see Hebrews 4:12. Jesus' words are double-edged. They can cut a man free, or administer judgement.

Hades (18): the place where the dead await resurrection and judgement.

Angels (20): some see this as a reference to pastors, some to guardian angels, some to the essential spirit of each church. Elsewhere in Revelation angels are always heavenly beings.

2 - 3 SPECIAL MESSAGES TO THE SEVEN CHURCHES

The letters are addressed to particular churches, but the message is for the whole church. It is worth noting that – with the exception of Smyrna and Philadelphia – the danger from within each church is more destructive than the danger from without. Jesus knows the strength and weakness of each one. The opening description reminds each church of some specially relevant aspect of his person and work.

2:1-7 Ephesus

See on Acts 19. The church at Ephesus was firmly established and possessed spiritual discrimination. There was sound teaching but an absence of the love – for Christ and one another – which had been their hallmark to begin with.

Nicolaitans (6): unknown outside this book. Their abhorrent behaviour sprang from false teaching (15), which had infiltrated the church at Pergamum.

Tree of life (7): the ban of Genesis 3:22-24 is lifted for all who are faithful to Christ. Eternal life is his to give.

2:8-11 Smyrna

The little church at Smyrna was poverty-stricken – but rich in all that

mattered. Jesus' word to them is all encouragement. He has set a definite limit to their suffering – and he holds out to them the gift of life beyond the grave.
Synagogue of Satan (9): those Jews who harass the church are not God's people. See John 8:39-44.
Second death (11): explained in 20:14-15.

2:12-17 Pergamum

At Pergamum the church had made a brave stand despite external pressure, but some members had become addicted to false teaching. As a result, old pagan practices were creeping in.
Satan's throne (13): Pergamum was the principal centre of emperor-worship in the region. An immense altar to Zeus dominated the town from its acropolis. And people flocked to be healed at the Temple of Asclepius. One or all of these may be referred to.
Balaam, Balak (14): see Numbers 31:16; 25.
Food sacrificed to idols (14): see on 1 Corinthians 8.
Verse 17: *manna* (Exodus 16) – i.e. food which God supplies. The meaning of the *white stone* is unknown. The *name* stands for the whole character. In the ancient world, to know a man's name was to possess power over him.

2:18-29 Thyatira

This was another very mixed church. In many ways it was healthy. But within the fellowship there was an influential woman advocating easy compromise with the immoral, idolatrous pagan world. And many fell in with her way of thinking. There were 'Christians' who plunged deep into evil – perhaps to demonstrate their moral superiority; perhaps because they drew a false (Greek) distinction between soul and body. Those who remain faithful are promised Christ's power and his presence (the morning star – see 22:16).
Jezebel (20): King Ahab's evil wife; see 1 Kings 21:25-26.

'Smyrna' is modern Izmir, main city and port on the west coast of Turkey. The most important remains from Roman times is the Forum, pictured here. It was at Smyrna, in about AD 155, that the aged bishop Polycarp refused to renounce Christ and was martyred.

3:1-6 Sardis

For all its reputation, the church at Sardis was dying on its feet. It was not opposition this church had to overcome but apathy, indifference and self-satisfaction.
Verse 2: it is by his life that a man demonstrates the reality of his faith. A formula of words will not save him – see Matthew 7:21.

3:7-13 Philadelphia

This letter, like the letter to Smyrna, contains no word of blame. To judge by these letters, it is not the biggest, most impressive-looking churches, or those with most prestige, which are necessarily in best spiritual shape. Christ opens the door for effective work (8 and 1 Corinthians 16:9), not to those who are strong, but to those who are faithful.
Verse 9: see on 2:9.

3:14-22 Laodicea

The worst case of all seven is a church so self-satisfied as to be totally blind to its true condition. It is so far from what it should be that Jesus stands *outside*, knocking for admittance to the lives of individuals who call themselves Christians (20). This letter is full of local colour. Banking and the manufacture of black woollen clothing made Laodicea affluent (17-18). The town was proud of its medical school, and renowned for a special ointment for sore eyes (18). Laodicea's water-supply was channelled from hot springs some distance away, reaching the town tepid (16). The church was like its water – lukewarm. There was nothing to commend it.
Beginning (14): 'the origin' (Good News Bible) or 'prime source' (New English Bible).

4 JOHN'S VISION OF HEAVEN

The scene shifts, characteristically, from what is happening on earth to what is happening in heaven. John is constantly getting this life into perspective by turning to the eternal realities. So the picture of the struggling churches fades before this sublime vision of the throne: God in control of all that goes on. Everything speaks of his power and glory, his utter faithfulness (3, and see Genesis 9:12-17), and purity (the white garments, the shining, transparent 'sea'). The 'elders', who represent all his faithful people, join with the 'living creatures', who represent the whole creation, to honour him.
Seven spirits (5): the Holy Spirit. See on 1:4 for the meaning of seven.
Four living creatures (6): similar, but not identical, to Ezekiel's 'cherubim' (Ezekiel 1 and 10).

5 - 8:1 THE SEVEN SEALS

5 The sealed scroll

At this point John begins to see the things which must take place (4:1). The scroll contains the world's destiny, revealed to John in a series of pictures (6:1 - 8:1). Only Christ has the right to set these things in motion – not by virtue of his power (the Lion) but through his sacrificial death (the slain Lamb). Chapter 4 pictured God the Creator. This chapter pictures God the Redeemer. The response to both is universal praise and worship (4:8-11; 5:8-14, and see Philippians 2:8-11).
Seven horns, seven eyes (6): i.e. all-powerful, all-seeing.

6 The breaking of the seals

The breaking of the seals sets in train a series of disasters. On the heels of conquest (2) come slaughter, famine and disease (4-8) – the classic judgements of God so often predicted by the prophets (see on Jeremiah 14:12; Ezekiel 14:21; the riders come from Zechariah 1:8). But no matter what the disaster, God is in control. His love and care for his people never fails (9-11). Verses 12-17 picture the cataclysmic events which usher in God's great day of reckoning. In apocalyptic language John depicts the disintegration of the fixed and stable world we know. See also Matthew 24:29; Joel 2; Zephaniah 1.
Verse 2: not the same figure as in 19:11.
Verse 6: the price of basic essentials is so inflated that ordinary people must give their day's wage for bread.

7 - 8:1 The people of God; the seventh seal

The four winds may be the same as the four horsemen of chapter 6 (see Zechariah 6:5). If so, John sees the forces of destruction held back while God sets his mark of ownership on everyone who belongs to him. The Christian is not promised a trouble-free life on earth. But he will come through it to the permanently trouble-free life of heaven (14-17). Solemn silence follows the breaking of the last seal. We are brought to the time of the end.
After this (1,9): indicates a new vision, not time in relation to the events of chapter 6.
144,000 (4): this number has been much debated, but it seems best to take it symbolically, as the complete total of all God's people (12 x 12 x 1000), identical with the 'great multitude' (9). We take Israel to mean, not the nation, but God's people – Old Testament believers and New Testament Christians alike.

8:2 - 11:19 THE SEVEN TRUMPETS

8:2-13 The first four trumpets are blown

The trumpets follow the pattern of the seven seals, but the judgements are intensified. The prayers of God's people play a significant part in all this (5:8; 8:3-4). The trumpets sound a note of warning. The judgements, though severe, are not total. They are intended to bring men to their senses (9:20-21). In symbolic picture-language John describes four calamities affecting the natural world – earth, sea, water and the heavens. The 'woes' of the lone eagle imply that there is worse to come. The remaining judgements directly affect mankind.

9 The fifth and sixth trumpets

Demonic forces (monstrous locusts-cum-scorpions), servants of 'the Destroyer' (Apollyon/Abaddon, 11), are next unleashed. But God sets them a time-limit (five months is the approximate life-span of the real locust). Though men are their target they have no power to touch those who belong to God (4).

The 'locusts' torture; the angel army has power to kill – within limits. Yet even in the face of the most fearsome warnings men stubbornly refuse to change their ways (20-21). This is the world we live in: a world that resists God to the bitter end; a world that prefers to make its own 'gods', to choose its own standards of behaviour.

200,000,000 (16): there were so many, John had to be told the number. He could not count them. God has colossal powers at his disposal.

10 - 11:13 Interlude; the little scroll and the two witnesses

There is a break between the sixth and seventh trumpets, as there was between sixth and seventh seals. God delays his final judgement, but not for ever (6-7). The glorious angel brings John a message for the world – a message which is 'sweet' to him as a Christian (9; and see Jeremiah 15:16; Ezekiel 3:1-3). But he derives no joy from the bitter message he must make known to those who refuse God.

Chapter 11 is difficult. John draws his symbols from Ezekiel 40-41 (the measuring of the temple) and Zechariah 4 (the olive-trees). The measuring indicates God's protection and care for his people. The two olives represent the church, faithful to the death. (The Old Testament law required that evidence must be attested by at least two witnesses – Deuteronomy 19:15.) Warring against them are the anti-God forces of the Satanic 'beast', with power to kill and dishonour, but not destroy or prevent their triumph.

10:4: John is under orders about what he writes. Not all he sees is for public knowledge.

Forty-two months (11:2): equal to 1,260 days (3), and 'a time (1 year), times (2 years) and half a time (6 months)' (12:14). This may be derived from the length of Antiochus Epiphanes' tyranny in Jerusalem, or from Israel's 42 encampments in the desert. But the precise length of the trial is less important than the fact that God has set a definite limit to it.

Sodom and Egypt (11:8): bywords for evil and oppression. The final phrase suggests Jerusalem, but it is more likely that the 'great city', stands for the city of rebel man.

11:14-19 The seventh trumpet

The seventh trumpet announces the end. Jesus reigns: the world is his kingdom. Praise God! The ark, once hidden away in the most sacred and inaccessible part of the temple, is now visible to all (19). The way into God's presence is wide open.

12 - 14 VISIONS CONNECTED WITH THE TROUBLES OF THE CHURCH

12 The woman and the dragon

John was writing for a persecuted church, and these chapters are full of encouragement to take heart. The woman (1, and contrast 17:3ff.) stands for God's chosen people, from whom first the Messiah (5), and through him the church (17), was born. The dragon bent on destruction is Satan himself (9). Verses 7-12 are a reminder that the struggle Christians are caught up in is part of a much greater conflict (Ephesians 6:11-12).

The main message is clear. Although Satan is strong and powerful – his attack fierce – his time is short. He has been overpowered by Christ: he can be overcome by Christians. He is destined for destruction, the church for triumph. God's people are at all times and everywhere under his protection.

13 The two beasts

The beast from the sea (an evil place in Jewish thinking) is a composite creature drawn from the four beasts which represent successive world empires in Daniel 7. With its crowns and horns (sovereignty and power) and its open defiance of God, it stands for the authoritarian anti-God state. It derives its power from the evil one (2, 4) and it is seemingly indestructible (3). It dupes the world, but not the Christian (8).

The second beast – the pseudo-lamb which speaks with Satan's voice (11) – is state-sanctioned, state-dominated religion. 16:13; 19:20 identify it as the 'false prophet'. It apes the real thing, and misdirects men's worship. Refusal to worship cost some their lives (15), others their livelihood (17). For John, the two beasts were the Roman Empire and emperor-worship. But every age – our own included – has its equivalents.

Forty-two months (5): see on 11:2.

The mark (17): indicating ownership, and acceptance of the beast's authority. Men bear either the 'mark' of the world or the 'seal' of God – and it shows (16; 7:3).

The number (17-18): many have tried to identify an individual (e.g. Nero Caesar), since the letters of the alphabet doubled as numbers in ancient times. But the key may lie in the symbolism of the numbers, 6 being 'a human number', the number of man. No matter how many times repeated, it always falls short of 7, God's number. No matter how powerful the 'beast', it is not God.

14 The joy of the redeemed; the harvest

This chapter stands in dramatic contrast to chapters 12-13. In the world God's people can expect implacable hostility. In God's kingdom the tables are turned (compare 9-11 with 13:15-17). The world sets its face against God; God sets his face against evil. He offers men a gospel which is timeless (6); the greatest of world-powers is temporary (8). In the end there will be absolute justice. All that is good will be lovingly harvested; all that is evil, totally crushed (13-20).

Verses 3-4: see on 7:4. The Bible nowhere implies that sexual intercourse is in itself defiling, or that it is more godly to be celibate than married. Verse 4 must therefore refer to those who are faithful to God. The prophets frequently use the same figurative language: idolatrous Israel is a 'prostitute', an 'adulteress'. The 'first-fruits' are that part of the world harvest which belongs to God.

Babylon (8): see on chapter 17.

One like a son of man (14): since he is under orders (15) this must be an angel, not Christ himself.

1600 stadia (20): the *stadion* was about 202 yards. But *1600 stadia* is clearly another symbolical number – 4 (which stands for the earth) x 4 x 10 x 10 – the complete destruction of the wicked throughout the earth.

15 - 16 THE SEVEN LAST PLAGUES

The great disasters of human history are warnings of the final, total calamities which will overtake those who refuse to listen. The plagues John describes here vividly recall those which fell on Egypt at the time of the exodus. But first we see the joy and security of God's people. They are not subjected to the final terrors, which are specifically directed against evil (16:2, 9, 11). Again and again in Revelation heaven is seen as a place of song – not everlasting, lugubrious, dutiful hymn-singing, but spontaneous song. In heaven life is so good, people so utterly happy and carefree that they just cannot help singing. Praise, at last, comes naturally.

Song of Moses (15:3): the great rejoicing after the crossing of the Red Sea (Exodus 15). Both songs are songs of deliverance and freedom.

16:12: the Euphrates separated the civilized world from the barbarian hordes beyond.

Armageddon (16): the hill (mound) of Megiddo, the famous fortress on the edge of the plain of Jezreel which guarded the pass through the Carmel range. The scene of so many battles, it came to stand for battle itself.

The great city ... great Babylon (19): see on chapter 17.

17 - 20 GOD'S FINAL TRIUMPH

17 - 19:5 The fall of Babylon

So often and so vigorously did the Old Testament prophets denounce the literal Babylon (see references below) that it became a byword for human pride and vainglory. For John and his readers, Babylon, the luxury-loving prostitute, was Rome, city of the seven hills (see verse 9) – pampered, decadent Rome; Rome, where Christians were thrown to the lions and burnt alive as public entertainment; Rome, the cess-pit of the Empire. But every age has its 'Babylon', the personification of all the greed and luxury and pleasure which entice men away from God; the things that promise so much and give so little. And Babylon, the epitome of all that cheats, is doomed!

Chapter 18, describing Babylon's fall, echoes the spirit and language of all the great 'downfall' prophecies of the Old Testament. (Isaiah 13-14, 24; Jeremiah 50-51; Ezekiel 26-28.) It is one final, comprehensive pronouncement of doom on every power in every age that grows fat on evil and treats men as mere commodities to be bought and sold (13). God's people are tempted to come to terms with the world. But they are called to take an uncompromising stand (4). They will be vindicated. Justice will be done. It is so certain, it can even be said to have happened already. Babylon *has* fallen!

Was and is not (17:8): at times evil powers rampage through human history; at times they go underground – but they always return.

Seven kings (17:10): these may be emperors, or empires.

Ten kings (17:12): sometimes taken to mean Roman emperors, but John is describing a future coalition.

19:2-3: this is not sheer vindictiveness, or gloating over the fate of others. God's people stake their lives on his truth and justice. They rejoice to see militant, unrepentant evil overthrown.

19:6-10 The wedding-feast of Christ and his bride, the church

John paints a lovely picture. The bride's wedding-dress has been woven out of all those truly Christian acts in which the Lord himself takes pleasure.

Verse 10: John would hardly need to be told to worship only God (here and again at 22:9). But presumably some in the church needed this lesson (compare Hebrews 1).

19:11-21 Christ victorious

Satan's two henchmen and their allies are now seized and destroyed – in a 'war' without weapons, armour, or battle, so great is the power of Christ.

A name (12): see on 2:17.

20 Evil eradicated; the overthrow of Satan; the last judgement

There has been a great deal of argument over the meaning of this chapter – which contains the Bible's only mention of a 'millennium'. But first the things that are clear.

John sees Satan under God's firm control (1-3). He sees the souls of the martyrs, not every Christian (and this is important for the persecuted early church), resurrected to reign with Christ 1,000 years (4-6). At the end of it the forces of evil muster to attack God's people, but are utterly destroyed – even Satan and his henchmen (7-10). There is a general resurrection, when all men stand before God and each is judged on his own record. The verdict is life or death. And for those who live there will be no more death (11-15).

With regard to detail it pays to be cautious. The same rules of interpretation apply here as for the rest of the book (see Introduction). To ask 'where' the reign takes place, and work out a time-table of events, is to miss the spirit of the book. The idea of an earthly millennium belongs to the Old Testament, not the New. Peter simply speaks of 'new heavens and a new earth'. John himself gives no location (elsewhere in Revelation thrones, 4, are in heaven). Nor does he mention timing, or the relation of all this to Christ's return.

1,000 years (2): other numbers in Revelation are symbolic figures. 1,000 years is long enough to show God's complete authority over Satan, and to far outweigh the earthly sufferings of the martyrs.

Gog and Magog (8): see on Ezekiel 38.

Beloved city (9): the community of God's people in contrast to the 'great city' of Babylon.

21 - 22:5 GOD'S NEW WORLD

With everything evil gone, and death destroyed, what is the new age like? What John describes is a heaven-on-earth. The new life is one long unclouded wedding-day for all God's people – the happiest, most joyful time imaginable. And there is never anything to spoil it: no sorrow; no pain; no parting with loved-ones; no night even. For God is always there. He is *near.* There is no sin, outside or in, to drag us down, to spoil the perfect relationship, to leave us groping for God or to fill us with shame. The cities of the world have their riches and beauty, but they are nothing to the glorious splendour, the shining radiance, of the city of God's people. There is peace there, too, and freedom and security. It is all infinitely precious, infinitely worth while.

12,000 stadia (21:16): 1,500 miles. But this is not intended to be taken literally. It is 12x1000 (see on 7:4 and 14:20). On earth God's people seem few and scattered. But they are part of a vast community – a great heavenly city.

21:19-20: the list of jewels echoes those which were set into the high priest's breast-piece, to represent Israel.

22:2: fallen man was denied access to the 'tree of life' (Genesis 3:22-24). Now the edict is reversed. Redeemed man will never again abuse his freedom.

22:6-21 EPILOGUE

The final statements may be somewhat disjointed, but they lack nothing in vigour. John affirms the truth of what he has written. In the sternest terms of his day, he warns against tampering with it. His closing words are full of urgency. The things he has described will happen soon. Christ's coming is imminent. And men will then be fixed in their attitudes. It will not be possible to change. In the end, those who are not saved will be lost; those who do not enter into eternal life and the presence of God will be shut out for ever. So 'let him who is thirsty come'. Let him 'take the water of life' which is 'without price'.

PART FOUR

A-Z Bible Encyclopedia

A

Aaron
Elder brother of Moses and Miriam, born when the Israelites were slaves in Egypt. Moses was not good at speaking, so Aaron spoke for him to the Egyptian Pharaoh, pleading with him to obey God's command and let the people of Israel go. Pharaoh refused, and it was Aaron, with Moses, who warned him of the ten plagues God would send. Aaron gave Moses his loyal backing during the escape from Egypt. But at Mt Sinai Aaron gave way to the people's demands and made them a golden calf-idol to worship. Even so, God forgave him and made him the first high priest of Israel. Aaron was in charge of a special tent used for worship (the tabernacle). There he offered sacrifices to God for the sins of the people and prayed for them to be forgiven. But at times Aaron was jealous of Moses' position as the people's leader. He died before the Israelites entered Canaan and his son Eleazar became high priest after him.
Exodus 4:14; 5–12; 28:1; 32:1; Numbers 20:23-29

Abana
Now called Barada, 'cool'. One of two rivers which flow through Damascus in Syria. When Elisha's servant told Naaman to bathe in the River Jordan and be healed, the Syrian general despised the muddy Jordan compared with the clear, fast-flowing waters of Abana and Pharpar.
2 Kings 5:12

A lion from the walls of Babylon's main street.

Abednego
The Babylonian name given to one of three Jewish exiles chosen for special service by King Nebuchadnezzer of Babylon. Shadrach, Meshach and Abednego, led by Daniel, courageously refused to eat the court food because, even in a foreign country, they were determined to obey the food-laws God had given the Jewish people. Later they refused to bow before an idol the king had set up. All three were thrown into a blazing furnace. But God protected them, and they came out unharmed. The king was most impressed. 'No other God can do what this one does,' he said.
Daniel 1–3

Abel
Adam and Eve's second son: brother of Cain. Abel became a shepherd when he grew up, and offered a lamb to God as a sacrifice. This pleased God. But Cain was jealous because God did not accept his gift of fruit, and he killed his brother. The New Testament explains that it was because of Abel's faith that he, and not his brother, won God's approval.
Genesis 4:1-8; Hebrews 11:4

Abel-beth-maacah
A town in the north of Israel, near Lake Huleh, to which Joab pursued Sheba. Captured by Aramaeans of Damascus and recaptured more than once.
2 Samuel 20; 1 Kings 15:20; 2 Kings 15:29

Abiathar
The son of Ahimelech the priest in the days of King Saul. When David became king, Abiathar was made joint high priest with Zadok. But after David's death he conspired to put Adonijah on the throne, instead of Solomon, and was banished.
1 Samuel 22:20ff; 2 Samuel 8:17; 15:24ff; 1 Kings 1 and 2

Abihu
See *Nadab.*

Abijah
The son of King Jeroboam I of Israel. He died as a child.
1 Kings 14

Abijah/Abijam
Son of King Rehoboam of Judah; he reigned for three years, about 913-911 BC.
1 Kings 15; 2 Chronicles 13

Abilene
The region north-west of Damascus, governed by Lysanias.
Luke 3:1

Abimelech
1. Because he was afraid for his life, Abraham pretended that his wife, Sarah, was only his sister. Abimelech, king of Gerar, wanted to make her his wife, but God showed him the truth and prevented it.
Genesis 20; 26 (this story may be about another king of the same name who had a similar experience with Isaac)
2. A son of Gideon who killed his brothers to become king.
Judges 8:31ff; 9

Abishai
A nephew of King David, brother of Joab, and one of the king's generals.
1 Samuel 26:6-12; 2 Samuel 10:9-10; 16:9, 11-12; 18:2

Abner
A first cousin of King Saul and commander of his army. When Saul was killed, Abner put Ishbosheth, Saul's son, on the throne. This led to war between the tribes who accepted Ishbosheth and the tribe of Judah, where David reigned. Abner became angry at the way Ishbosheth treated him and decided to support David as king of the whole of Israel. But he was murdered by David's army commander, Joab, whose brother he had killed.
1 Samuel 14:50; 2 Samuel 3

Abraham/Abram
Abram's name was changed to Abraham (father of nations) when God promised to make him the founder of the Hebrew nation. Abraham's original home was the rich and splendid city of Ur on the River Euphrates. He lived there for many years with his father Terah and his three brothers. He married Sarah, his half-sister. Terah and all his family moved from Ur to Harran, several hundred miles to the north-west. Terah died there, and God called Abraham to move on to Canaan.

Abraham obeyed. He lived as a nomad, moving from place to place with his flocks and herds. Wherever he camped, he built an altar and worshipped God. Famine drove him south to Egypt. But God told him to go back to Canaan. This was the land God promised to give the new nation. Abraham grew old, and still Sarah had no children. Following the custom of his time he had a son by Sarah's servant-woman, Hagar. But this son, Ishmael, was not the child God had promised.

When Abraham and Sarah were both old, God gave them a son–Isaac. The new nation was to come through him. Isaac was still only a boy when God tested Abraham's faith as never before. He was told to take Isaac to a distant mountain and sacrifice him there. With a heavy heart Abraham obeyed, trusting God to keep his promise about his son. Isaac was bound on the altar. The knife was raised ready to strike. Then God's angel called out, 'Do not harm the lad...Now I know you will obey God whatever the cost.' A ram, caught in a bush, was offered instead. Then God repeated all his promises to

Abraham and his family lived in tents, moving from place to place to find fresh pasture for their flocks.

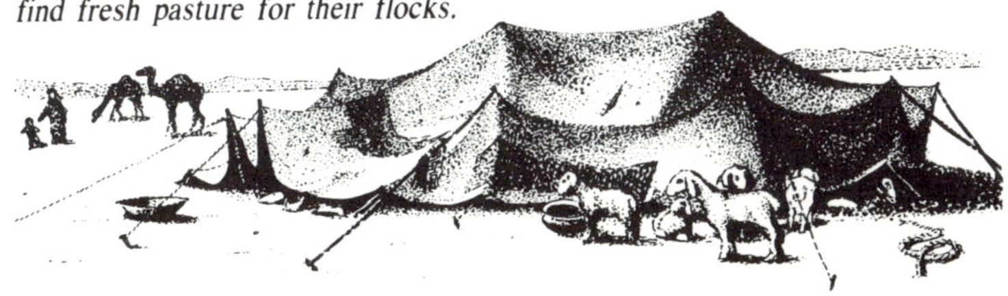

Abraham. 'Your descendants will be as many as the stars in the sky. And all the nations of the earth will be blessed, because you obeyed me.'

After Sarah's death, Abraham sent his trusted servant Eliezer to choose a wife for Isaac from his own family in Harran. Abraham is one of the really outstanding men of the Bible. His faith in God has made him an example for all time.
Genesis 11:31-32; 12:1ff; 17:1-8; 21:1-3; 22:1-14; Roamans 4:1-3; Hebrews 11:8-19; James 2:21-23

Absalom
Favourite son of King David. He rebelled against his father and plotted to become king. David's men defeated Absalom's army in the forest of Ephraim. Absalom, escaping on a mule, was caught by his head in the branches of an oak. Joab, David's general, killed him–against the king's orders.
2 Samuel 15–19

Acacia/shittim
The wood from which the Covenant Box (ark) was made for the tabernacle. The acacia is one of the few trees to grow in the Sinai desert.
Exodus 25:10

Acacia tree.

Accad
Name of a region and a city in ancient Babylonia, founded by Nimrod. See *Babylonians*.
Genesis 10:10

Achaia
The Roman province of southern Greece governed from Corinth.
Acts 18:12, etc.

Achan
When the Israelites conquered Jericho, Achan disobeyed God's orders and took gold, silver and fine clothes for himself. Because of this the Israelites were defeated at their next battle.
Joshua 7–8

Achish
A king of Gath. Twice David fled to Achish from King Saul.
1 Samuel 21; 27–29

Achor
'Trouble Valley', near Jericho, where Achan was killed because he disobeyed God's command.
Joshua 7:24

Acts
The Book of Acts continues the story begun in the Gospel of Luke, and is by the same author. It tells of the 'acts' of (mainly) the apostles Peter and Paul. Because of its emphasis on God's power, it has often been called the 'Acts of the Holy Spirit'.

The book tells how the followers of Jesus spread the good news about him first in Jerusalem, then all through the local provinces of Judea and Samaria, and beyond 'to the ends of the earth'. It covers roughly thirty years, from the beginnings of the Christian church on the Day of Pentecost, to Paul's imprisonment at Rome.

Acts may have been written any time between AD 60 and 85. The author wanted to stress that the good news was for all people–not only for the Jews. He often takes care to show that Christianity is not a political threat to the Roman Empire.

The first seven chapters of Acts tell how the Christian movement began in Jerusalem itself, with the coming of the Holy Spirit in power on the Day of Pentecost. Filled with this new power the Christian group began to carry out Jesus' command to preach and teach. The church grew and spread. This section also records how Stephen, one of the first Christians, died for his faith.

Chapters 8–12 describe how, at first because of persecution, Christianity spread into Judea (the province around Jerusalem) and Samaria (where people belonging to a despised enemy nation were welcomed into the church). Saul's (or Paul's) dramatic conversion on the way to Damascus is followed by the account of how Peter learnt that the Christian message was for all nations, not only Jews.

The rest of the Book of Acts is taken up with the missionary work of Paul and his fellow-workers–his journeys in the Mediterranean world, his trials and his imprisonment in Rome (chapters 13–28). The message of the Christian faith is well summed up in several of the sermons recorded in Acts.

Adam
1. The first man (the word 'adam' means mankind), created by God to be like himself. Adam was put in charge of all the other animal life on earth. He was to live and work in the garden God had planted in Eden, and enjoy its fruits. Only the fruit of one tree was forbidden him–the 'tree that gives knowledge of what is good and what is bad'.

God never intended the man to live alone. He made Eve–the woman–to share his life. Tempted by the thought of being wise like God, Eve took the fruit, and she and Adam both ate it. Knowing they had done wrong, Adam and Eve tried to hide from God. Their friendship with him was spoilt. Because they disobeyed God, from that day to this the whole created world has felt the effects. And every life has ended in death.

Adam and Eve were driven out of Eden. They had children. But their family brought them pain as well as joy.
Genesis 1:26-27; 2–5:5
2. The place where the River Jordan was blocked, allowing the Israelites to cross into the Promised Land. In 1927 earth tremors caused the high clay banks to collapse at the same spot, and the Jordan was dammed for twenty-one hours.
Joshua 3:16

Admah
One of a group of five cities, of which Sodom and Gomorrah are best-known, now probably under the southern end of the Dead Sea. The kings of these cities formed an alliance and rebelled against four northern kings in Abraham's day. In the battle that followed, Abraham's nephew Lot was taken captive.
Genesis 10:19; 14:2

Adonijah
The fourth son of King David. When David was old, and the elder brothers were dead, Adonijah tried to seize the throne. But David had promised his wife Bathsheba that her son Solomon would succeed him. Adonijah's attempt failed. David forgave him but when Solomon was king he had Adonijah executed when he seemed once again to be trying to seize the throne.
1 Kings 1–2

Adramyttium
A port near Troy (Troas) on the west coast of what is now Turkey. A ship from Adramyttium took Paul and his fellow prisoners on the first stage of their journey to Rome.
Acts 27:2

Adullam
David, on the run from King Saul and fearing King Achish of Gath, took refuge in a 'cave' (probably a fort) near this town. His family and a group of 400 outlaws joined him in hiding. While he was there, three of David's bravest soldiers risked their lives to bring him water from the well at Bethlehem, which was held by the Philistines.
1 Samuel 22:1; 2 Samuel 23:13

Agabus
A Christian prophet from Jerusalem who told the church at Antioch that a great famine was coming. Later he also warned Paul that he would be imprisoned if he went to Jerusalem.
Acts 11:27-30; 21:7-14

Agrippa
See *Herod*

Ahab
Seventh king of Israel (about 874-853 BC). He reigned from the capital city of Samaria. Ahab went to war against Syria three times, and the third time he was killed. He was a successful ruler, but the Old Testament sees him as a wicked king who did more to anger God than all the kings of Israel before him. He married Jezebel, daughter of the king of Sidon, and began worshipping Baal (Melkart), the god of Jezebel's people. This involved him in a number of clashes with the prophet Elijah. On Mount Carmel Ahab watched Elijah stage a contest with the supporters of Baal, and win a great victory for God. When Ahab had Naboth killed so that he could take his vineyard, Elijah denounced him. Ahab died in battle at Ramoth-gilead. It was God's punishment for his sin.
1 Kings 16:29-34; 18; 21; 22

Ahasuerus
1. Hebrew form of the name of a Persian king known to us in its Greek version as Xerxes. Xerxes I (486-465 BC) divorced Vashti to marry Esther, a Jewish girl, and make her his queen. Ahasuerus is also mentioned in the Book of Ezra. The people of the land complained to him when the returned Jewish exiles began to rebuild Jerusalem.
Esther; Ezra 4:6
2. Father of Darius the Mede.
Daniel 9:1

A 'relief' of Xerxes I (Ahasuerus) from the treasury at Persepolis, Iran.

Ahava
The name of a canal and a region in Babylonia where Ezra assembled the second party of returning Jewish exiles. Here they fasted and prayed for God's protection on their 900 mile/1,448 km journey to Jerusalem.
Ezra 8:15, 21, 31

Ahaz
King of Judah about 732-716 BC (co-regent from 735 or earlier). He introduced pagan worship and even sacrificed his own son. Ahaz was defeated when Israel and Syria launched a combined attack on Judah. Rejecting the prophet Isaiah's advice, he appealed to the Assyrian King Tiglath-pileser III for help but by doing so became his subject.
2 Kings 15:38ff.; 2 Chronicles 27:9ff.; Isaiah 7

Ahaziah
1. The son of Ahab and Jezebel. He was king of Israel after Ahab but only for a short time (about 853-852 BC). He followed in his father's evil ways and worshipped Baal.
1 Kings 22:40ff.; 2 Kings 1;
2 Chronicles 20:35-37
2. A King of Judah, the son of Jehoram (841 BC). He and his uncle, King Jehoram of Israel, with whom he had made an alliance, were murdered by Jehu.
2 Kings 8:24ff.; 2 Chronicles 22:1-9

Ahijah
A prophet from Shiloh. Ahijah tore his dress into twelve pieces before King Jeroboam I to show how Solomon's kingdom would be divided. He told Jeroboam to take ten of these pieces, because God had chosen him to rule ten of the twelve tribes of Israel.
1 Kings 11:29ff.; 14

Ahithophel
King David's trusted adviser who turned traitor and supported Absalom in his rebellion. When Absalom ignored his advice Ahithophel committed suicide.
2 Samuel 15:12–17:23

Ai
The name means 'the Ruin'. After capturing Jericho, Joshua sent a small force against nearby Ai–and was beaten. The reason was because Achan had defied God's command by taking spoil from Jericho. Achan was punished, and Joshua attacked Ai again. He lured the men of Ai out by pretending to run away, and a hidden ambush force moved in and set fire to the stronghold.
Joshua 7 and 8

Aijalon
1. An Amorite town belonging by right to the tribe of Dan, but given to the Levites. Much later King Rehoboam fortified the city and kept stores and arms there.
Joshua 19:42; 21:24; Judges 1:35;
2 Chronicles 11:10
2. A valley through which an important trade-route passed; near to the town of Aijalon. In this valley Joshua fought a great battle against the Amorites, and 'the sun stood still'.
Joshua 10

Alexander
The name of several men (not all necessarily different) in the New Testament.
1. Son of Simon of Cyrene, the man who carried Jesus' cross.
Mark 15:21
2. A member of the high priest's family and one of the Jewish leaders in Jerusalem.
Acts 4:6
3. A Jew who tried to speak to the crowd during the silversmiths' riot at Ephesus (see *Demetrius*).
Acts 19:33
4. A Christian who lost his faith, at least for a time.
1 Timothy 1:20
5. A coppersmith who was bitterly opposed to Paul and the gospel. Paul warned Timothy against him.
2 Timothy 4:14

Alexandria
A great Egyptian seaport on the Nile Delta founded by Alexander the Great. The famous Pharos light-house tower stood at the harbour entrance. Alexandria was the capital of Egypt under the Ptolemies, and remained a great centre of Hellenistic culture.

In Roman times grain-ships loaded up at Alexandria so that the people of Rome could have cheap bread. The city had a 'museum' of arts and sciences and a famous library containing thousands of papyrus scrolls. There was a strong Jewish community, and it was here that the Old Testament was translated into Greek–the Septuagint version. Apollos, who became an important teacher in the early church, came from Alexandria.
Acts 6:9; 18:24; 27:6; 28:11

A Greek medallion showing the Pharos light-house at Alexandria. It was built of white marble and completed in about 280 BC. A beacon at the top burned day and night.

Almond
The almond was the first fruit-tree to blossom in Israel each year, sometimes as early as January. As well as being a favourite food, the nut also produced oil. The most famous Bible reference is Aaron's almond rod which flowered and produced fruit overnight.
Numbers 17:8

Amalekites
These people were related to Edom and Israel (like the Edomites they were descendants of Esau). They were a nomadic tribe and at the time of the exodus attacked Israel in the Sinai desert and further north. In the days of the Judges they often raided Israel. They were bitter enemies of Israel for many centuries.
Genesis 36:12,16; Exodus 17:8-13; Numbers 14:43, 45; Judges 3:13; 6; 7:12; Deuteronomy 25:19; 1 Samuel 15; 30:1-20; 1 Chronicles 4:43

Amasa
King David's nephew, chosen by Absalom to lead his rebel army. After Absalom's defeat, David pardoned Amasa and made him commander of his own army in place of Joab. In revenge Joab murdered him.
2 Samuel 17:25; 20

Amaziah
1. The son of King Joash of Judah, who came to the throne when his father was assassinated. Amaziah (796–782 BC) was a good man, but victory over Edom went to his head. He challenged Israel and lost. He also brought back idols from Edom and refused to listen to God's prophet. The people plotted against him and eventually he was murdered at Lachish.
2 Kings 12:21-14:21;
2 Chronicles 24:27ff.
2. A priest at Bethel who opposed the prophet Amos. (See *Amos*.)
Amos 7:10ff.

Ammonites
North of the Dead Sea, between the Arnon and Jabbok rivers, lived the Ammonites. They were related to the Israelites through Lot, and did not stand in their way on the march to the Promised Land. But they did attack later, during the days of the Judges and of Saul. King Nahash made peace with David. But his son insulted David's messengers and hired men from Aram to fight for him. David's generals captured his capital, modern Amman, and took control of the land. In the reigns of later kings, Ammonites often raided across the Jordan, and were again

made subject when Judah was strong. After the exile, the Ammonite Tobiah interfered with Nehemiah's work.

The Ammonite kingdom was protected from raiders by a series of stone watch-towers. Excavation done in Ammon reveals ruined houses and tombs with pottery like that of the Israelites, stone statues, seals engraved with their owners' names, and a few brief inscriptions, which show that their language was similar to Hebrew. The main road east of the Jordan–the King's Highway–brought traders through the Ammonite kingdom on their way from Damascus to the Gulf of Aqaba. These were a source of wealth and a strong cultural and religious influence.
Genesis 19:38; Judges 3:13; 10; 11; 1 Samuel 11; 12:12; 14:47; 2 Samuel 10; 12:26-31; 2 Chronicles 20:1-30; 26:8; 27:5; Nehemiah 2:10, 19; 4:3, 7

Amnon
The eldest son of King David. He raped Tamar, his half-sister, and in revenge Absalom had him killed.
2 Samuel 3:2; 13

Amon
King of Judah after Manasseh, his father (642-640 BC). Amon refused to obey God and worshipped idols instead. After only two years he was murdered by his palace servants.
2 Kings 21:18-26;
2 Chronicles 33:20-25

Amos
One of the first of God's prophets to have his messages permanently written down. Amos lived in the eighth century BC. He kept sheep and tended fig-trees at Tekoa, a hill village in Judah. But God sent him north to Bethel in Israel, where King Jeroboam I had set up a golden calf-idol. Here he bravely gave God's message of justice and judgement against oppression and greed. The cheating traders could not make up for their dishonesty simply by offering sacrifices to God.

Amaziah, the priest at Bethel, who was in the pay of the king of Israel, told Amos to pack up and take his message back to Judah. But Amos continued to warn the people of Israel of judgement and exile if they did not repent.
Book of Amos

Ananias
1. Ananias and his wife, Sapphira, gave the apostles only part of the money they received from the sale of land, though they pretended to give it all. Because of that lie, both died.
Acts 5:1-11
2. A Christian who lived in Damascus. Just after Saul (Paul) was converted, God told Ananias to go to the house where he was staying. Ananias restored Saul's sight when he had been blind for three days after seeing Jesus on the road to Damascus.
Acts 9:10-19
3. A high priest present when Paul was being questioned by the Jewish council (the Sanhedrin), and who ordered the guard to hit Paul. When Paul was tried by Felix, Ananias was the prosecutor. Acts 23:2-3; 24:1

Anathoth
A town 3 miles/4km north of Jerusalem belonging to the Levites. The birthplace of Jeremiah.
Joshua 21:18; Jeremiah 1:1

Andrew
One of the twelve apostles chosen by Jesus. Andrew and his brother Simon Peter were fishermen from Bethsaida on the Lake of Galilee. John the Baptist told Andrew that Jesus was the 'Lamb of God'. Andrew recognized him as the Messiah (Christ) and brought his brother Peter to hear Jesus teach. Later, when they were fishing, Jesus called both brothers to follow him. Andrew brought the boy with the loaves and fishes to Jesus when he fed 5,000 hungry people. When some Greeks who had come to worship at Jerusalem wanted to see Jesus, Andrew and Philip told him about them. Andrew was with the other apostles in Jerusalem after Jesus ascended to heaven.
John 1:35-42; Matthew 4:18-19; 10:2; John 6:6-9; 12:22; Acts 1:13

Angel
The word means 'a messenger'. In the Bible it is used of the supernatural beings who surround the throne of God. Jesus tells us that they share in God's joy 'over one sinner who repents'.

Angels are also referred to as 'sons of God' or 'heavenly beings' and 'heavenly powers', the 'servants of God'. Their work is to serve God. In heaven they worship God and on earth they act as God's messengers, bringing his word to men and women. They also help people. They took care of Jesus after his temptations and they care for his followers.

The Jews believed there was a complex hierarchy of angels, all of whom had their own names. The Bible has no clear reference to such a system. It names only two angels–Gabriel and Michael. It was Gabriel who brought news of the birth of Jesus.

The phrase 'the angel of the Lord' is often used in the Old Testament as a way of describing how God sometimes came to people in human form to give them a special message. The 'angel of the Lord' is also God's agent of judgement.

See also *Heaven.*
Luke 15:10; Job 1:6; 1 Kings 22:19; Psalm 103:20-21; Daniel 12:1; Luke 1:26-38; Matthew 1:20; 4:11; Hebrews 1:14; Genesis 16:7-14; 22:11-12; 31:11; Judges 6:11-21; 13:3-21, and many other places

Anna
An old prophetess who was in the temple when Joseph and Mary brought Jesus there as a baby to dedicate him to God. Like Simeon, she recognized Jesus as the Messiah, and told others about him.
Luke 2:36-38

Annas
Former high priest, with his son-in-law Caiaphas, when Jesus was arrested. He questioned Jesus before sending him to Caiaphas.
Luke 3:2; John 18:13-24

Antioch ('Pisidian')
A town in the heart of Asia Minor (present-day Turkey) visited by Paul and Barnabas on their first missionary journey. They preached first in the synagogue, but when non-Jews responded to Paul's message the Jews stirred up trouble and threw Paul and Barnabas out of the city. Two or three years later, Paul visited Antioch again, on his second missionary journey, to encourage the Christians in their new faith.
Acts 13:14-52

Antioch in Syria
Modern Antakya, on the Syrian border of Turkey. The most famous of sixteen cities with this name, founded by one of Alexander's generals in honour of his father. Antioch, on the River Orontes, had its own sea-port. Under the Romans it became the capital of the province of Syria and third largest city of the Empire, renowned for its culture. It had a large Jewish community. After the death of Stephen, persecuted Christians fled the 300 miles/483 km from Jerusalem to Antioch.

This was the start of one of the largest and most active of the early Christian churches. Many local people were converted, including a large number of Greeks, and it was here that they were first called 'Christians'.

Barnabas, who had been sent from Jerusalem to find out what was happening, set off to find Paul and ask him to help teach the new converts. They taught together in Antioch for over a year. Some time later the church at Antioch sent Paul and Barnabas out to teach in Cyprus and beyond. Antioch remained Paul's base, and for a long time the church there was second only to Jerusalem. The ancient city was levelled by an earthquake in AD 526.
Acts 11:19-26; 13:1; 15:35

Antipas
See *Herod.*

Antipatris
A town rebuilt by King Herod and named in honour of his father, Antipater. When Paul's life was threatened he was taken under escort from Jerusalem to Caesarea on the coast. On the way they spent the night at Antipatris.
Acts 23:31

Apollos
A Jew from Alexandria who went to Ephesus and taught in the synagogue after Paul's visit there. Aquila and Priscilla, friends of Paul, were able to teach him more about Jesus. Apollos then went to Corinth, where he spoke to the Jews with great power about Jesus as the Messiah.
Acts 18:24-28; 19:1;
1 Corinthians 16:12

Apostle
The word means 'a person who is sent'–a messenger or representative. In the New Testament it is mainly used to refer to Jesus' twelve disciples, to Paul, and to other Christians who were involved in missionary outreach.

Jesus chose twelve apostles to be with him, to preach and to heal. After he rose from the dead Jesus told them to go and tell the whol world what they had learnt about him.

When the disciples were looking for an apostle to replace Judas Iscariot, Peter told them that they must choose someone who had been with Jesus from the very start of his ministry, and who had seen him after he rose from the dead.

Paul claimed that he was an apostle, because he believed that his experience on the Damascus road was not just a vision but a meeting with the living Jesus. He had been chosen by Jesus as his special messenger, particularly to bring his message to the non-Jewish world (the 'Gentiles').

Luke 6:12-16; Acts 1:12-26; 14:1-4; 1 Corinthians 15:5,7; Galatians 1:1; 2:7,8

Aquila

A Jewish Christian who was a friend of Paul. Aquila and his wife, Priscilla (or Prisca), were forced to leave Italy when the Emperor Claudius expelled the Jews from Rome (AD 48). Like Paul they were tentmakers and for a time Paul stayed and worked with them in Corinth. When Paul travelled to Ephesus, Aquila and Priscilla went with him (see *Apollos*). Later, Aquila and Priscilla moved back to Rome. In both places Christians met in their home.

Acts 18:1-3, 18-26; Romans 16:3; 1 Corinthians 16:19; 2 Timothy 4:19

A Roman man and his wife.

Ar

Capital of Moab, on the River Arnon. During their time in the desert after leaving Egypt the Israelites were told to leave this city in peace. God had given it to the Moabites, Lot's descendants.

Numbers 21:15; Deuteronomy 2:9; Isaiah 15:1

Arabah

The rift valley of the River Jordan, stretching from Lake Galilee in the north to the Dead Sea in the south and continuing on to the Gulf of Aqaba. The 'Sea of Arabah' is the Dead Sea.

Aram

A group name for various states in southern Syria, especially Damascus. See *Aramaeans*.

Aramaeans/Aramaic

At the time when Israel was moving into Canaan, a group of Semitic tribes settled into the land to the north. These were the Aramaeans (Syrians in the Authorized/King James' Version). We know some of their history from Hebrew and Assyrian records, and a few inscriptions written in Aramaic. There were several tribes, each centred on one city. They were scattered throughout Syria, across to Assyria, and down the River Euphrates into Babylonia where one branch became the nation of the Chaldaeans. Smaller kingdoms north of Galilee were soon absorbed by Israel and by the major Aramaean kingdom, Damascus.

In the reign of Solomon Damascus won independence from Israel, and a strong line of kings built up power there (see 1 Kings 11:23; 15:18). Until the Assyrians made Damascus a province in 732 BC its kings (including Ben-Hadad and Hazael who feature in the Bible stories) were often at war with Israel and Judah, trying to control the roads to Egypt and Arabia. From time to time they were able to dominate their fellow Aramaean rulers to the north, and in the sea-ports.

Because they were so widespread (this increased even more when Assyrian kings conquered and deported many of them to Assyria and Persia), their language–Aramaic–became the common language for diplomats and traders all over the Near East from about 750 BC. When King Sennacherib's Assyrian officials came to threaten Jerusalem, King Hezekiah's men begged them to speak in Aramaic. The decrees of the Persian kings were written in Aramaic. When the people living in the land had complaints against the Jews who returned with Zerubbabel, they wrote to the king in Aramaic. Part of the Book of Daniel is also in Aramaic.

After Alexander brought Greek to the Near East, Aramaic took second place for official purposes. But it remained the common language over a wide area and was spoken by the Jews in Israel in New Testament times. The New Testament contains several Aramaic phrases, for example: *talitha koum (cumi)*, *abba* (the everyday word for 'father'), and *Eli, eli lema sabachthani* (Jesus' words from the cross).

2 Kings 18:26; Ezra 7:12-26; 4:7–6:18; Daniel 2:4–7:28; Mark 5:41;14:36; Matthew 27:46

Two Aramaeans dressed in caps and fringed robes, from an eighth-century BC relief discovered at Zinjirli, to the north of ancient Syria.

Ararat

The mountain country where Noah's ark came to rest when the flood waters drained away. The area, called Urartu in Assyrian inscriptions, is Armenia, on the borders of present-day Turkey and Russia. Mount Ararat itself is an extinct volcano nearly 17,000ft/5,214m high.

Genesis 8:4; Jeremiah 51:27

Araunah/Ornan

A man from Jerusalem who sold his threshing-floor to King David. Because of David's wrongdoing, Israel was suffering from a plague. David realized he was to blame for the trouble and obeyed God by building an altar on Araunah's threshing-floor. God saw that David was sorry for what he had done and the plague stopped. The temple was later built on this site.

2 Samuel 24:16-25; 1 Chronicles 21:18-30

Archaeology

The first notable steps in learning about the ancient world were taken in 1798 when Napoleon's invasion of Egypt included a survey of monuments there. During this invasion the Rosetta Stone was discovered. This is a stone block on which the same text was engraved in Greek and Egyptian writing. It helped people to decipher ancient Egyptian hieroglyphs for the first time (1824). Within a few years, a British diplomat in Baghdad, *Claudius James Rich*, had made the first accurate surveys of the sites of ancient Babylon and Nineveh. He also made the first representative collection of Assyrian and Babylonian seals and inscriptions.

Places in Israel were better known, because pilgrims had visited the 'Holy Land' for centuries. In 1838 *Edward Robinson*, an American professor of Biblical Literature, undertook the first careful study of the country. From its geography and the way in which place-names survived, he was able to identify many of the towns named in the Bible. Most of his identifications remain satisfactory even today.

Egypt and Assyria In Egypt the task of clearing mounds of sand and tumbled stone from tombs and temples continued throughout the nineteenth century, and during this period a great many stone sculptures were taken out of the country.

Excavations began in Assyria when the French consul, *Paul-Emile Botta*, opened trenches in the mound of rubble that was ancient Nineveh. His work there was unrewarding, but nearby he discovered an Assyrian palace whose walls were lined with carved stone slabs (1842-43).

An English traveller, *Henry Layard*, was also interested, and in 1845 he found similar carvings in Nineveh, where Botta had failed to do so. Writing cut into the stonework and impressed on small tablets of clay was deciphered by 1850. This was the Babylonian cuneiform script. Documents written in this script have proved particularly valuable for biblical study.

The digging in Egypt, and in Assyria and Babylonia, was carried

Excavation of a 'tell', the mound of an ancient town.

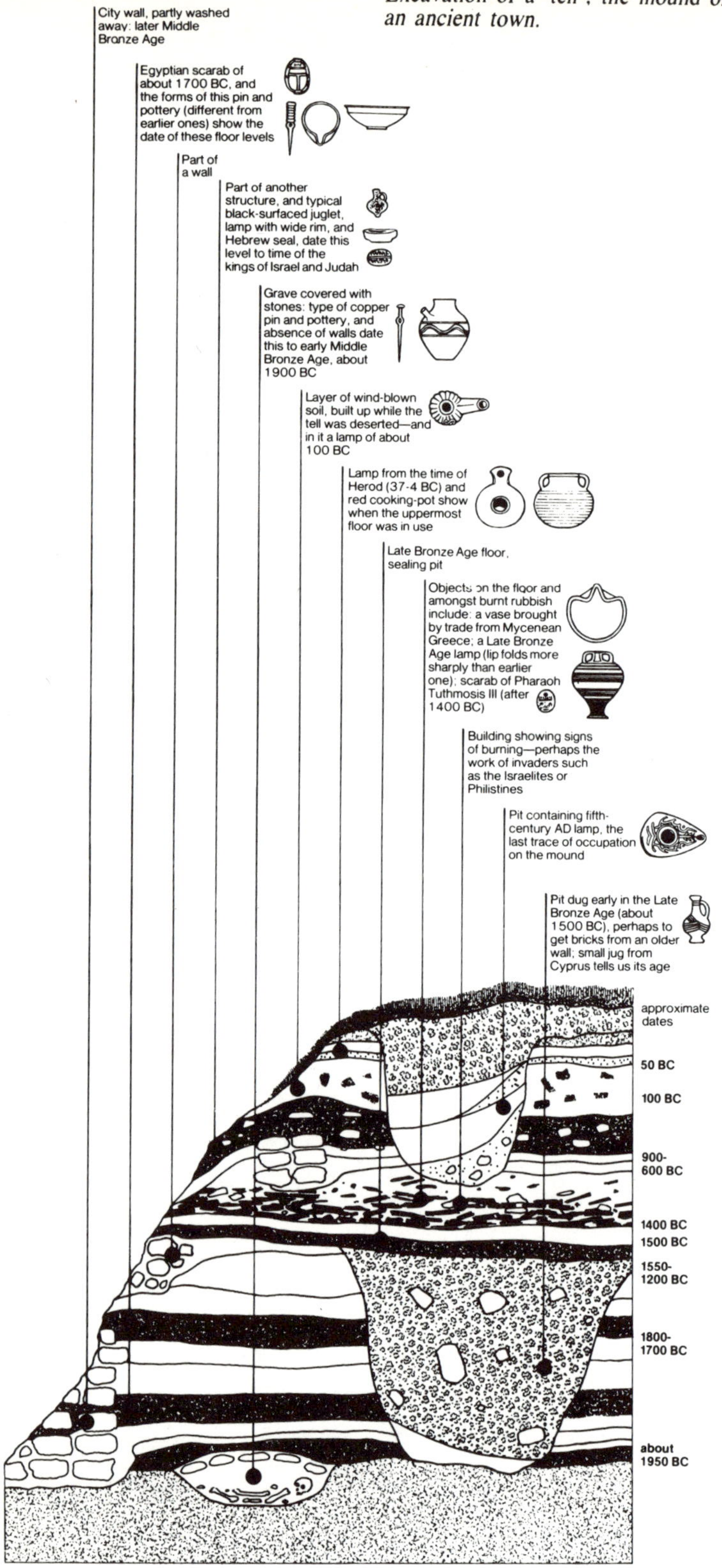

out by British, French and Italian expeditions, quickly joined by teams from Germany and the United States. Most of the money raised for excavation came from museums, and some were intent only on acquiring spectacular exhibits for their sponsors. Others carefully noted many details and collected examples of the less exciting finds–pottery, knives, and so on. They measured buildings and drew plans on which they marked the positions of the objects they unearthed.

International expeditions still carry out this work, with permission from local departments of antiquities. Egyptian and Iraqi scholars also excavate independently. They pay special attention to preserving their national heritage. Even after a century and a half of exploration in those lands, it is clear that there is a great deal still to be found.

Palestine and Syria The early excavators were mostly concerned to find great monuments of imperial power to impress the western public, and so the cities of Palestine and Syria were by-passed. Apart from a few isolated trenches at Jericho and other sites (1866-69), the first digging was confined to Jerusalem. There *Charles Warren* traced the foundations of King Herod's temple wall and surveyed other ancient remains (1867-70). He cut through masses of fallen stones and rubbish (sinking shafts 211ft/65m deep and burrowing along the natural rock surface) to show how the shape of the city had changed over the centuries.

Into the twentieth century Near Eastern archaeology took a major step forward in 1890 when *Flinders Petrie* started to excavate at Tell el-Hesi, near Gaza in southern Israel. He realized that, on any given site, the things he found at one height above sea-level were different from things found at another height.

This was most obviously true of the broken pottery. Taking care to separate the pieces according to their levels, he managed to work out a series of pottery styles that followed in order of time. He then gave dates to each style, by comparing them with Egyptian objects found in the same places. (The ages of the Egyptian objects were known from the discovery of similar pieces in Egypt, where inscriptions related them to the reigns of individual kings.)

Petrie's observations have become

Sir William Flinders Petrie, whose work in Israel led to a break-through in methods of dating discoveries.

basic to all archaeological excavation. For several decades other archaeologists working in Palestine failed to realize their importance, and because of this many of their own conclusions have been proved wrong. But the basic idea of using pottery styles as a guide for dating other objects is now adopted by all archaeologists–though, of course, there have been some further important developments since.

As people's interest in the subject grew, museums and universities began to pay attention to sites in the land of Israel. Regrettably, the standard of excavation was often poor. Better techniques for observing and recording finds were developed by *G. A. Reisner* and *C. S. Fisher* during their excavation at Samaria in 1908-11. Following Petrie's example, the American, *W. F. Albright*, established the basic system of dating Palestinian pottery (at Tell Beit Mirsim from 1926 to 1936).

British archaeology had progressed by developing 'stratigraphy', the close examination of the soil inside, and underneath ancient remains. *Kathleen Kenyon*, working at Samaria, was the first to apply this approach to an excavation in Palestine (1931-35). From 1952 she used it with conspicuous success at the difficult sites of Jericho and Jerusalem. So far this method of excavation is unsurpassed, although it makes far more demands on the excavator during the digging, and afterwards in interpreting his finds.

The work of excavation Mud is the commonest, and one of the earliest, building materials in the Near East. Walls made of mud-bricks dried in the sun will last for thirty years or so if they are plastered regularly to keep out the damp. Bricks baked in kilns were expensive in ancient times, so they were used only for important buildings. Foundations were built of stone wherever it was available, and in very stony areas entire houses were stone-built. Roofs were normally made of wooden beams with matting and mud plaster laid over them.

These buildings easily collapsed through neglect, old age, fire, earthquake, or enemy attack. When they fell, people re-used the best pieces from the heap of debris, but most of it was left where it had fallen. In the course of time, new houses were built on top of the old ones. This meant that street levels became higher, and over the centuries the level of the whole town gradually rose. The results of this process can be seen all over the Near East in the ruin-mounds called *tells*.

Cities that once surrounded an inner fortress with heavily defended palaces and temples may leave an extensive area covered with low mounds, the fortress standing up as a great hill. Or the whole city may be a single mound. These tells can be 90-130ft/30-40m high, and 540yds/500m or more in length.

The most recent remains lie at the top of the mound. They may not be the ruins of the last buildings that stood there, because winter wind and rain quickly erode the dry mud-brickwork once the site is no longer occupied. At the lowest level, on the original soil, will be traces of the first town. There are many reasons why ancient towns were abandoned. The town may have grown up around a spring or well, at a ford of a river, or at a crossroads. If the spring dried up or the roads changed, the town may have died. Some political turn of events may have deprived a place of its influence and prosperity. Or the mound may have grown too high for people to live on top of it conveniently.

Cities like Jerusalem and Damascus, however, have never lost their importance, and they can be excavated only when buildings are demolished or areas are left undeveloped.

The dig The archaeologist digs into the mound from the top or at one side. As he cuts into it, so the remains of one period appear on top of another, much like the layers in a large cake sliced down the middle. Once he has disturbed the earth and the objects in it, they can never be replaced in exactly the same way. So his first job is to note where and in what layer of soil, each item is found.

A plan of the area will show horizontal positions of walls and other things. But the remains are rarely in absolutely even levels. A street may slope, or a wall may stand much higher at one point than another. Very often people of a later period will have dug a pit, for storing food or for rubbish, and that will go down from their own floor level deep into earlier ruins. Recording things by absolute levels (metres above sea level) would put rubbish from the bottom of the pit with bits and pieces from the earlier periods it had broken into. So the depth of any discovery has to be linked to the layer of earth in which it was found.

When the trench has cut into the earth the layers can be clearly seen in the vertical side of the excavation. Pottery lying on the floor of a room will belong to the last period the room was lived in. Pottery found underneath the floor will be older than the floor. The archaeologist has to note how the floor joins a wall, because a later wall may have cut through an earlier floor. If he does not notice, he could produce a wrong plan of the building, with the wall dated by objects on the floor.

Expert knowledge is necessary at every stage. Before any earth is removed, a surveyor has to measure the whole site and fix points from which measurements can be made. As work goes on he will plot the edges of the trenches and any other noteworthy features. A photographer is needed to record the stages of excavation, to picture important or fragile objects in position in the soil, and afterwards to photograph them and other pieces for publication.

Studying the finds Every object has a label fixed to it, or a mark written on it as soon as it is discovered, to show where it was dug up. Individual finds, such as pins, knives, jewellery, but not usually broken pottery, are listed and described. The pottery is sorted according to the place and level or layer of discovery. Someone who knows the whole range of discoveries can then choose significant pieces for detailed records.

Some pottery will need to be mended, and metal things will need treatment for rust or corrosion. Woodwork and other fragile objects will require special care to ensure that they do not decay any more. Samples of all sorts of natural remains can also give us information about the ancient environment, so shells, bones, and earth containing seeds, are all carefully collected.

Results Archaeology's main service is to illustrate the general context of the Bible and to show us what the biblical world was like. It may sometimes throw light on a particular verse; it may guide interpreters along some paths and bar others. It may appear to support historical statements in the Bible, or make it less difficult to accept them. But we must always remember two important facts. One is that much of our knowledge of the ancient world from archaeology is tentative and subject to change. Today's 'assured results' may tomorrow be little more than a curiosity. Then we should also remember that ultimately it is pointless to speak of archaeology either 'proving' or 'disproving' the Bible. For the Bible's message is about God and his scope of archaeology to say anything about that.

Archelaus

See *Herod*.

Areopagus

'Mars hill', north-west of the acropolis in Athens, from which the Council of the Areopagus (which originally met there) took its name.
Acts 17

Aretas

An Arabian king whose capital was Petra (in present-day Jordan). For a time Damascus was part of his territory. When Paul was in Damascus, Aretas's governor planned to arrest him, but he escaped by being lowered over the walls in a basket.
2 Corinthians 11:32

Argob

Part of the kingdom of Og in Bashan, east of the Jordan. It was given to the half tribe of Manasseh, and was a fertile region with many strong towns.
Deuteronomy 3; 1 Kings 4

Arimathea

The home of Joseph, a secret disciple of Jesus, in whose new rock-tomb the body of Jesus was placed after he was crucified.
Matthew 27:57; Mark 15:43

Aristarchus

A Macedonian Christian, a friend and fellow-worker of Paul. He was with Paul when the Ephesian silversmiths started a riot. Aristarchus went with Paul to Jerusalem and later set off with him to Rome. When Paul was in prison in Rome he stayed with him.
Acts 19:29ff.; 20:4; 27:2;
Colossians 4:10

Armaggedon

See *Megiddo*.

Arnon

A river which flows into the Dead Sea from the east (now Wadi Mujib). It formed the border between the Amorites and Moabites. The invading Hebrews defeated the Amorites and their land was settled by the tribe of Reuben. The River Arnon remained the southern border.
Numbers 21:13ff; Isaiah 16:2

Aroer

A town on the north bank of the River Arnon, east of Jordan. The southern limit of the Amorite kingdom and later of the tribe of Reuben. Under Moabite rule from the time of Jehu to Jeremiah's day. Also the name of a town in the Negev, south of Beersheba.
Deuteronomy 2:36, etc.;
2 Kings 10:33

Artaxerxes

Name of several kings of Persia. Ezra and Nehemiah probably returned to Jerusalem from exile during the reign of Artaxerxes I (464-423 BC).
Ezra 4:6-7

Asa

The son of Abijah and third king of Judah. He reigned for forty-one years (about 911-870 BC). When Asa became king he tried to wipe out pagan worship. He won a great victory when a huge Ethiopian army led by Zerar attacked Judah.
1 Kings 15:8ff; 2 Chronicles 14:1ff.

Asahel
A nephew of King David. Asahel was one of David's bravest soldiers and commander of a large division of the army.
2 Samuel 2:18ff; 23:24

Asaph
A Levite who led the singing in King David's reign. His descendants served in the temple choir. Asaph wrote a number of psalms.
1 Chronicles 15:17ff.; 25:1ff.;
2 Chronicles 29:30; 35:15

Levite musicians playing harps and cymbals, drawn from a model.

Ascension
For forty days after Jesus rose from the dead he often visited his disciples. Then he returned to heaven. The disciples were with him on the Mount of Olives when Jesus gave them his final message. As they watched, they saw him 'taken up to heaven...and a cloud hid him from their sight'. This is what we call the 'ascension'.

Although the ascension was the end of Jesus' ministry on earth, it was not the end of his work. As the disciples watched Jesus being taken from them two heavenly messengers asked them, 'Galileans, why are you standing there looking up at the sky? This Jesus, who was taken from you into heaven, will come back in the same way that you saw him go to heaven.' The rest of the New Testament makes it clear that between Jesus' ascension and his return at the end of time he is with God, his Father, in the glory of heaven. He reigns over the whole universe. He represents his followers before God and sends the Holy Spirit to help them.
Luke 24:50-53; Acts 1:6-11; Hebrews 1:3; 4:14-16; 7:24-26; John 16:5-15

Ashdod
One of five Philistine strongholds in Old Testament times. When the Philistines captured the Covenant Box (ark) they took it to the temple of their god Dagon at Ashdod. Next morning they discovered the statue of Dagon flat on its face; the following day it was broken in pieces. Ashdod fell to King Uzziah of Judah in Isaiah's time. In New Testament times the city (called Azotus) was restored by King Herod.
1 Samuel 5; 2 Chronicles 26:6; Isaiah 20:1, etc.; Acts 8:40

Ashkelon
An ancient city on the coast of Israel, between Jaffa and Gaza. It became one of the main strongholds of the Philistines. Samson made a raid on Ashkelon, killing thirty men to pay what he owed in a bet. In the centuries that followed, Ashkelon was ruled in turn by Assyria, Babylonia and Tyre. In New Testament times Herod the Great was born at Ashkelon.
Judges 1:18; 14:19; 1 Samuel 6:17; Jeremiah 47:5-7, etc.

Ashtaroth/Ashteroth-karnaim
A city east of the Jordan, named after the Canaanite mother-goddess. It was captured by Chedorlaomer in Abraham's time and later became a capital of King Og of Bashan. One of the cities given to the Levites.
Genesis 14:5; Deuteronomy 1:4; 1 Chronicles 6:71

Asia
The western part of Asia Minor (modern Turkey) including a number of important Greek city-states. Later the Roman province of Asia, including the whole west coast, whose most important city was Ephesus. Much of Paul's missionary work took place in this region.
Acts 2:9; 19:10; Revelation 1:4,11

Ass (donkey) and mule
The most common of all pack animals, used for carrying heavy loads, and also for riding by rich and poor alike. The donkey is a descendant of the North African wild ass. The mule is cross-bred from a donkey (male) and a horse. Both ass and mule are sure-footed and can live in much rougher country than horses. The ass is the 'hero' of the story of Balaam. Lost asses led Saul to a vital meeting with Samuel. And it was an ass which Jesus rode into Jerusalem on Palm Sunday, as a king coming in peace.
Numbers 22; 1 Samuel 9 and 10; Zechariah 9:9; Matthew 21:1-11

Assos
The sea-port on the west coast of modern Turkey from which Paul set out on his last journey to Jerusalem.
Acts 20:13

Assyria
Assyria is the northern part of modern Iraq, along the Tigris river and eastwards to the foot of the Zagros mountains. The winter rains and the rivers that run into the Tigris provide enough water for farming. Barley and wheat grow on the plains. Grapes, olives, apricots, cherries and other fruit are grown on the hills. The countryside is covered with grass in winter and spring, unlike the land west of the Tigris. There, much of the land is desert, with craggy forested mountains to the east, which in winter are covered with snow. Assyria looked attractive to the wild tribesmen of the desert and mountains. The story of the land is one of constant war with these envious neighbours.

The Assyrians called their capital city, their country, and their national god by one name, Ashur. The city of Ashur is in the south of the country, on the west side of the Tigris. The second city, Nineveh, lies east of the river, opposite modern Mosul, 68 miles north of Ashur. Both cities were prosperous as early as 2500 BC and probably long before.

The Assyrian people First-hand records from Assyria begin soon after 2000 BC. The Assyrian king-list, an important record from a later date, shows that the Assyrians were in their land about 2300 BC. The texts prove that the Assyrians were a Semitic people. They used a language very closely related to Babylonian. They also show, as we would expect from the situation of the country, that the population was very mixed. Many non-Semitic people came in from the east and north. This seems to have happened peacefully, and, in later times, men who were not Assyrians by origin held important government posts.

Assyrians are commonly thought of as cruel imperialists. This picture, which comes partly from their wars with Israel reported in the Old Testament, has to be balanced against the situation of Assyria. Even when the frontiers seemed secure, threats existed, or could be imagined, from foreign rulers a little further away. These threats could only be dealt with by new campaigns. No doubt success encouraged further military adventures. But the Assyrians, like most people, prized peace and prosperity.

The Assyrian Empire Between 1500 and 1100 BC Assyria became a leading state in the Near East, ruling as far west as the River Euphrates. Her kings wrote letters, as equals, to the kings of Egypt. Then Aramaean invaders from the desert almost completely overran the Assyrian homeland. This began a period of weakness that lasted until about 900 BC.

Then a line of vigorous kings began to regain their lost lands. They also tackled the problems of maintaining control over them. The warrior-kings Ashurnasirpal II (883-859 BC) and Shalmaneser III (858-824 BC) captured many cities and made their kings vassals. But as soon as the Assyrian army had gone home the subject kings rebelled. Tiglath-pileser III (745-727 BC) was the first to establish an effective system of provincial governors with firm control.

Exile A common way of trying to break resistance was to take hos-

King Ashurbanipal of Assyria hunting lions. One of a series of lion-hunt scenes which decorated his palace at Nineveh.

tages. After a major rebellion large numbers of the population were deported to other parts of the empire and replaced with strangers from far away. (This happened in Israel when the Assyrians captured Samaria– 2 Kings 17:6, 24ff; see too 18:31, 32.) The famous emperors Sargon (721-705 BC), Sennacherib (705-681 BC), Esarhaddon (681-669 BC), and Ashurbanipal (669-627 BC) all followed this policy. Under the last two the empire grew too large, covering Egypt, Syria, the land of Israel, north Arabia, parts of Turkey and Persia. The frontiers could not all be defended, nor all rebels defeated. Babylon won independence in 625 BC, and, with help from the Medes, destroyed Nineveh in 612 BC.

Works of art Assyria's great empire brought enormous wealth. Some of it came as tax, some through trade. The kings were able to build great palaces and temples, each aiming to do better than ever before. From those excavated at Nineveh and at Nimrud (ancient Kalah, about 20 miles south) and at other places, we have recovered some fine works of art. Walls were lined with stone slabs carved in low relief to depict the king in religious, military, and sporting life. Furniture was decorated with ivory panels, carved or engraved, often plated with gold.

Many different influences–Egyptian, Syrian, Iranian–can be seen in the workmanship of these objects. But the basic culture of Assyria was drawn from the south, from Babylonia (see *Babylonians*). The most important of all Babylonian customs in Assyria was the cuneiform writing system on clay tablets. Thousands of these tablets have been found in the Assyrian ruins. Some deal with the administration of the empire. Some are diplomatic documents. Some are private legal deeds. Some are the records of the deeds of kings. Most outstanding of all is the library collected by King Ashurbanipal. This library held copies of every piece of literature and knowledge that had been handed down from the past. With its recovery, from 1849 onwards, modern study of Assyria and Babylonia began.

The Assyrians and the Bible story The Assyrians come into the Bible story at the time of the last kings of Israel, when the prophets Amos and Hosea were at work in the north, and Isaiah was coming into prominence in Judah. They were the major world power, and the people of less powerful countries lived under constant threat of invasion.

'I will bring upon you...the king of Assyria', says Isaiah. The prophet's prediction to King Ahaz of Judah was terrifying. Ahaz was trying to win Assyrian help against his enemies, the kings of Damascus and Samaria (Israel). But God's messenger was telling him that this, the greatest power of the time, would soon overwhelm his own country. The Assyrian king was Tiglath-pileser III (745-727 BC). He did accept Ahaz and Judah as his vassal. Then he relieved the pressure by conquering Damascus and most of Israel and making them provinces of his empire.

It was Assyrian practice to make pacts with subject nations all around. If a subject stopped keeping the terms of the pact–if they failed to send an annual tax, or made friends with an enemy of Assyria–the Assyrians would try to change the situation by diplomacy. If that failed, they sent an army.

This happened to Judah. Ahaz kept the treaty, but his son Hezekiah–and King Merodach-Baladan of Babylon–joined a general rebellion when the Assyrian King Sargon died in 705 BC. Hezekiah took control of the Philistine cities which were subject to Assyria. After crushing the trouble in Babylon, Sennacherib, the new Assyrian king, naturally turned to deal with the rebel Hezekiah. His army overran Judah, as Isaiah predicted. Sennacherib's records claim: 'forty-six of (Hezekiah's) strong towns...I besieged and conquered. I brought out from them 200,150 people...(Hezekiah) I shut up like a bird in a cage in Jerusalem his capital city...the awful splendour of my lordship overwhelmed him...he sent 30 talents of gold, 300 talents of silver...to Nineveh.' Jerusalem, however, remained uncaptured. In fact, the Assyrians never attacked Jerusalem again, although Manasseh, Hezekiah's son, joined an Egyptian-inspired revolt, and was kept captive for a while (about 671 BC).

Isaiah 7:17-25; 2 Kings 15:27–16:9; 18:7, 8; 19; 20:12ff.; 2 Chronicles 33:11-13

Assyrian and Babylonian religion

Like most peoples in the ancient world, the people of Babylon and Assyria honoured the great powers of the universe, and had favourite gods or goddesses of their own. They told stories about their gods, gave offerings to them in great temples and small shrines, asked for their help, and hoped for their good will. The gods were in control of everything, and their behaviour unpredictable.

Anu, king of heaven, was the chief of the gods. He was a remote figure. His son, Enlil, ruled over the earth's surface, and was treated as the king of the gods. Enki, or Ea, had charge of the fresh waters that gave life. Each had a wife and family. Ishtar was the wife of Anu, and far more prominent than he was in religious life. She was in charge of war and of love. Enki was given a son– Marduk– who became very important.

Marduk, also known simply as Bel, 'lord', was the patron god of Babylon. His worship began to grow as Babylon's power increased during the period 2000-1000 BC. As time passed he was raised to be king of all the gods (see below). Marduk's son, Nabu, god of Borsippa near Babylon rose to high honour in turn.

There were other gods separate from these: Shamash, the sun, god of justice; Sin, the moon, worshipped especially at Ur of the Chaldees and at Harran; Adad, the god of rain and storm. Ideas such as fairness, truth, justice, and time, were also given the status of gods from soon after 2000 BC. In Assyria there was also the national god, Ashur, whose name was the same as the capital city and the land it ruled. Ashur's origin is unknown. As Assyria grew strong, her theologians identified him with Enlil, as king of the gods.

The Babylonian world was full of shadows. Evil spirits and demons lurked to catch anyone they could. They would slide under the door to attack a man in his sleep, or to snatch a child from its mother's lap, or bring diseases with the wind. Special priests recited prayers and spells over the sick or injured person, calling on the gods for help. Sometimes the affliction would be transferred by a ritual to a goat or some other substitute, which would then be killed or destroyed. People wore charms and amulets to ward off these evils. They also hung them in the doorways and buried them under the doorsteps. These last were sometimes model dogs inscribed with words such as 'Don't wait, bite!'

Worship Each city had a main temple where the patron god of the city was worshipped. Here the people would gather for major festivals at the New Year and on the god's own special day. They lined the streets when the god's statues were carried in procession, taken on tour from one shrine to another. Usually, it seems, ordinary citizens worshipped at small shrines set amongst the houses of a town. There they could ask the god or goddess for a son, pray for success in business, give him 'thank-you presents', or make offerings to win attention, or persuade the deity to rid them of some misfortune. A priest would perform rites, speak the correct prayers, and accept the animal or goods offered in sacrifice.

The Assyrian king Tukulti-Ninurta I (about 1240 BC) depicted on an altar, standing and kneeling before the symbol of Nusku, the fire-god.

Divination The gods had control of everything, according to Babylonian thought, but they did not reveal the future. People could not be certain about anything. So the Babylonians consulted omens. The livers and other parts of sacrificed animals were inspected for unusual symptoms, to see if the gods had 'written a message' in them. They also used other unpredictable things–the flight of birds, or patterns of oil on water.

Astrologers worked out 'omens' from the movements of the stars. The clear night skies made observation easy. And because each star was linked to a god or goddess, it was possible to make all sorts of deductions about the will of the gods. Some of these arts passed to the Greeks, and so to modern astrology. The zodiac is one legacy of the Babylonian astrologers. The 360-degree circle, and the 60-minute hour, were also first worked out by the Babylonian star-gazers.

Death and the afterlife All the dead

were thought to inhabit the underworld. There they lived in a land of dust, fed by offerings of food and drink made by their descendants. If no offerings were made, the ghosts of the dead would come back to haunt their families. So, too, would the ghosts of those who were not properly buried. Apparently the wicked had a worse time than the good, for some of the ancient kings served as judges in the underworld. Ideas of life after death were very vague, and offered the Babylonians no hope.

Athaliah

The only woman to rule over Judah (841-835 BC). She was a cruel, evil queen–like Jezebel, her mother–and put to death all the royal children except the baby Joash who was hidden by his aunt. When he was seven there was a coup. Joash was crowned king and Athaliah was killed.
2 Kings 11:1-16;
2 Chronicles 22:10–23:15

Athens

The capital of modern Greece which first became important in the sixth century BC. The city was at the height of its greatness in the fifth century BC when its most famous public buildings, including the Parthenon, were built. Athens was then a model democracy and centre of the arts, attracting playwrights, historians, philosophers and scientists from all over Greece. In 86 BC the city was besieged and stripped by the Romans.

Although it lost its power and wealth as a centre of trade Athens still had a great name for learning in the mid-50s AD when Paul arrived on his second missionary journey, preaching about Jesus and the resurrection. The Athenians loved a discussion and called him to speak before their council. Paul used their altar, dedicated 'To an Unknown God', as his starting-point. He spoke about the God who made the world and is near to each one of us.
Acts 17:15-34

Athens is dominated by the acropolis, surmounted by the Parthenon temple.

Atonement

The people who wrote the Bible were concerned with one problem above all others. How can men and women enjoy friendship with God? Because of sin they are separated from God, and their basic need is to be made 'at one' with him. This is what the word 'atonement' means.

However hard people try they can never make themselves acceptable to a holy God. We always fall short of God's standards.

In Old Testament times, sacrifices were offered in order to atone for sin. But this system could not be the final answer. A number of Old Testament writers saw that God himself would have to deal with the problem of sin. Isaiah wrote of the coming of God's servant to solve this problem: 'All of us were like sheep that were lost, each of us going his own way. But the Lord made the punishment fall on him, the punishment all of us deserved.'

The New Testament describes how God sent Jesus, his Son, to do just this. His death was the complete sacrifice for all men. When Jesus died on the cross he died in our place and suffered the death-penalty due for our sin. On the cross he became acutely aware of the agony of separation from God, and cried, 'My God, my God, why did you abandon me?' Matthew goes on to tell us that the curtain hanging in the temple was torn from top to bottom. The fact that the curtain was torn in two announced in a dramatic way that we need no longer be cut off from God. Jesus had atoned for the sin of the world.

See also *Cross, Feasts and Festivals, Reconciliation, Redemption.*
Genesis 3; Leviticus 16; Isaiah 53; John 3:14-17; Mark 10:45; 15:34, 38; 2 Corinthians 5:14-21; Ephesians 2:14; Hebrews 7:26-9:28; 10:19-20

Attalia

Modern Antalya, a port on the south coast of Turkey, used by Paul on his first missionary journey.
Acts 14:25

Augustus Caesar

A statue of the Emperor Augustus.

The first Roman emperor, successor to Julius Caesar. He ruled from 31 BC to AD 14. Augustus ordered the census which brought Mary and Joseph to Bethlehem.
Luke 2:1

Azariah

Best-known of several Azariahs is the king of Judah, also called 'Uzziah' (791-740 BC). Azariah was a good king, strong and powerful, who served God. But he still allowed his subjects to worship idols, and fame made him proud. He went into the temple to offer incense, which only the priest was allowed to do. His punishment was a severe skin disease which forced him to live in isolation and make Jotham, his son, acting king.
2 Kings 14:21ff; 2 Chronicles 26

B

Baal

See *Canaanite Religion.*

Baasha

A man from the tribe of Issachar who seized the throne of Israel from Nadab, son of Jeroboam, and ruled from about 909 to 886 BC.
1 Kings 15:16ff.

Babel

(Predecessor of ancient Babylon) After the flood, when people still spoke one language, they planned to build a city on the plain of Shinar (Sumer) in the land of the two rivers (Mesopotamia)–and a tower that would reach to heaven. God saw their pride and brought the work to a standstill by confusing their language, so that they could not understand one another.
Genesis 10:10; 11:1-9

Babylon

A city on the River Euphrates, 50 miles/80 km south of modern Baghdad. Babylon was founded by Nimrod 'the mighty hunter'. It later became the capital of Babylonia and the Babylonian Empire. About 1750 BC, Hammurabi, one of the early kings of Babylon, wrote down on stone a great code of laws which it is interesting to compare with the later laws of Moses.

After the defeat of Assyria in 612 BC Babylon became capital of a powerful empire extending from the Persian Gulf to the Mediterranean. In 597 and 586 BC King Nebuchadnezzar of Babylon conquered rebellious Jerusalem. On each occasion, many of the people of Judah were taken into exile to Babylon–among them the prophets Ezekiel and Daniel.

The city covered a huge area on both banks of the Euphrates. Both inner and outer city were protected by double brick walls 11-25ft/3-7m thick. Eight great gates led to the inner city, and there were fifty temples. The 'hanging gardens' of Babylon was one of the wonders of the ancient world. These were terraces on different levels laid out with palms and many other trees and plants, providing colour and shade in a flat land.

In 539 BC the Persians, under Cyrus, took the city. Herodotus, the Greek historian, says they diverted the River Euphrates and marched along the dried-up river bed to enter the city. From that time on, Babylon declined. Nothing remains today but a series of widely scattered mounds, for the archaeologists to work on. Genesis 10:10; 2 Kings 24:1; 25:7-13; Isaiah 14:1-23; Daniel 1–6

Babylonians

The southern part of modern Iraq was the ancient kingdom of Babylonia. The city of Babylon first rose to power about 1850 BC for a few generations, then again under Nebuchadnezzar, 1200 years later, for an equally short time. It was the glory of Nebuchadnezzar's city that made Babylon famous in world history.

Civilization began in Babylonia long before Babylon became important. Cities grew up there soon after man learnt how to use the river waters to irrigate the land. Massive temples of mud brick have been excavated at Uruk (modern Warka, Old Testament Erech–Genesis 10:10). Their freestanding pillars are decorated with coloured mosaics.

Writing Here the oldest known writing was found, the beginning of the Babylonian cuneiform script, in which 800 or more simple pictures stand for common objects or ideas. The pictures quickly changed from representing objects to being used as syllables, for their sound values alone. (For example, drawings of a thin man and a king might mean 'the king is thin' or 'the thin man is king' as pictures; but they could be used as sounds to write the word 'thinking'.) Soon extra signs were included to show grammatical classes, subject, object and so on.

We cannot understand the very earliest clay tablets. But those of the next stage–about 3200 BC–are clearly written in a language we call Sumerian. They include lists of words by groups (stones, animals, professions), and the first meagre examples of literature, as well as accounts and deeds of sale. From the recognizable pictures, the signs quickly developed into groups of lines (these were easier to inscribe on clay), producing the wedge-shaped cuneiform script. The clay tablets survive well in the soil. They have given us more information about Babylonia than we have about almost any other ancient culture.

Sumerians and Akkadians The Sumerians may not have been the first people to live in Babylonia. But because they have left these documents, they are the first we can identify and name. Their origin is unknown, and we cannot relate their language to any other in the world. Side by side with them in the north lived Akkadian tribes. Their Semitic language was an early form of Babylonian, related to Arabic and Hebrew. The scholars of ancient Babylonia made translations from Sumerian into Akkadian, and these enable modern students to translate Sumerian.

Whoever the Sumerians were, their genius seems to have led to the invention of writing, perhaps of wheeled vehicles, and of city life in Babylonia. Stories copied out about 2000 BC recount the exploits of Sumerian heroes and gods. The most famous of these was Gilgamesh, king of Uruk soon after 3000 BC, who marched to the Lebanon mountains to fetch cedar wood, and perhaps into Turkey, too. His search for eternal life led him to the Babylonian Noah, who told the king how he was given immortality after surviving the flood. Gilgamesh was given two chances of gaining his goal. But he lost both, and returned home. He concluded that only through fame could a man's name live after him. Recent research has shown that some of these stories probably have a factual basis, even though they have mythical episodes.

About 2300 BC the Semites gained control of Babylonia under King Sargon. His capital was at Akkad, a place we have not yet discovered. His rule extended into north Syria, where he fought the king of Ebla. From this time on, the Sumerian language was less important than Akkadian. Sargon's family maintained his empire for about a century until attackers from the east broke their power. From about 2100 to 2000 BC a line of kings based at Ur had a kingdom which was almost as large.

Works of art Craftsmen in the third millennium (3000-2000) BC made fine jewellery in gold, silver, and semi-precious stones imported from the east and south. Smiths cast copper and bronze for weapons and statues. Stone carvers produced some of the finest pieces of Babylonian art–from great monuments to tiny cylinder seals (¾-2 ins/2-5cms high) which were rolled acros clay to leave impressions of the pictures engraved on them. Outstanding examples of these skills were found in the Royal Tombs at Ur (dated at about 2400 BC). The local princes were buried in these tombs with their courtiers, dressed in their finery, and with chariots and wagons.

Inscriptions The small tablets which list rations and accounts seem least interesting of all the inscriptions. Yet they are of great value for the names they contain. By careful study we can separate Sumerian, Akkadian, and foreign names. From 2400 BC there are more names of the sort used later by Semites in the west (Canaanites, Hebrews). By 2000 BC large numbers of these 'westerners' (Amorites) were pouring into Babylonia, and they took over the rule of the ancient cities.

Hammurabi The most outstanding of their kings was Hammurabi of Babylon, about 1792-1750 BC. He gained power for his city by war and by diplomacy. During his reign he revised the laws of the land and had them engraved on stone. These are 'case laws' like those of Exodus 21 and 22. They begin: 'If a man...' In Hammurabi's laws things are not forbidden on moral grounds, as they are in the Ten Commandments. Despite royal authority, these laws soon fell into disuse, but they were copied in schools for another thousand years.

Hammurabi's line (dynasty) collapsed when a Hittite army raided Babylon in 1595 BC. Kassite kings from the east took over, and, although they were not Semites, they quickly adopted Babylonian culture. The land was peaceful for 400 years, then a native dynasty arose.

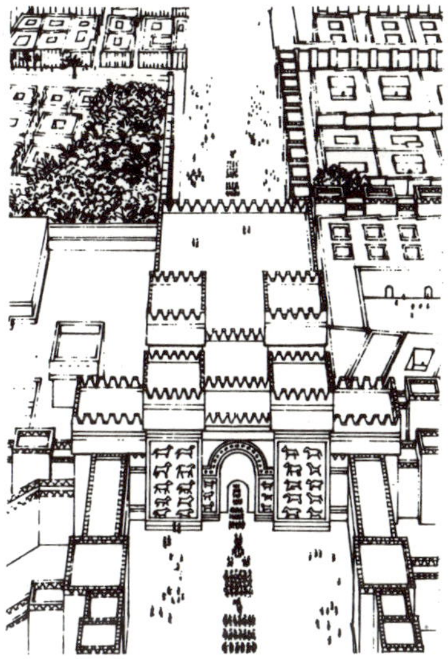

The Ishtar gate, Babylon, and processional way leading to the temple of Marduk.

Nebuchadnezzar and the empire Chaldaeans and Aramaeans from the west caused turmoil until the Chaldaean King Nabopolassar defeated the Assyrians (612 BC). His new empire contained most of the Assyrian provinces, although his son Nebuchadnezzar (605-562 BC) had to crush rebels in the west, including Judah. The wealth of the empire enabled these two kings to rebuild Babylon on an immense scale, with lavish decoration. The Book of Daniel describes how Nebuchadnezzar was struck down while boasting of his works (Daniel 4). His son was killed by a General Neriglissar (Nergal-Sharezer, Jeremiah 39:3), but Nabonidus in turn displaced Neriglissar's son. This king held strong religious convictions. He left Babylon in the care of his son Belshazzar, and lived for ten years in Arabia. After his return, the army of Cyrus the Persian took Babylon. The centre of world history moved away from the city for the last time.

Babylonian contributions to the world at large stem from the period about 3000-1600 BC, when the Baby-

lonian writing system spread throughout the Near East. It took with it the knowledge of astronomy and mathematics (the divisions of the circle, the hour, and the day), which the Greeks borrowed. Other influences are harder to trace, but were undoubtedly strong.
See also *Assyrian and Babylonian religion.*

Balaam

A prophet from Mesopotamia who was asked by Balak, king of Moab, to curse the Israelites at the time of their desert wanderings. They had just defeated the Amorites and Balak was afraid his country would suffer the same fate. At first Balaam refused to go and meet the king, but the second time he agreed. On the way, God's angel stopped Balaam's donkey and warned Balaam only to say what God told him. Instead of cursing the Israelites, Balaam blessed them three times. Later he tried to bring about the Israelites' downfall and gain the reward he had been promised by encouraging them to worship Baal. He was killed when the Israelites attacked the Midianites.
Numbers 22–24; 31

Balak

A king of Moab who reigned at the time when the Israelites were waiting to conquer Canaan. (See *Balaam.*)
Numbers 22:2–24:5

Baptism

Jesus commanded his followers to be baptized to show they had become Christian converts. This practice had a Jewish background. In the time between the Old and New Testaments, people who became converts (proselytes) to the Jewish religion were baptized, or immersed in water, usually a nearby river, as a sign of cleansing. John the Baptist also baptized many people as a sign of their repentance and their inner cleansing by God.

But Christian baptism was not usually regarded as a 'washing' from sin. Paul explains that when the person being baptized disappears beneath the water and then reappears, he or she has undergone a symbolic death, burial, and resurrection. Christians share in the death and resurrection of Jesus by the act of baptism: 'By our baptism, we were buried with him and shared his death, in order that, just as Christ was raised from death...we might live a new life.'

The fullest account of a baptism in the New Testament is in the story of Philip and the Ethiopian. Acts 8:37 shows one form of words that the early Christians would have used. The preacher says: 'If you believe with all your heart you may be baptized.' The person being baptized replies: 'I believe that Jesus Christ is the Son of God.' People were baptized sometimes 'in the name of Jesus Christ', sometimes 'in the name of the Father, Son, and Holy Spirit'.
Matthew 28:19; Mark 1:4-11; Romans 6:3-4; Acts 8:26-39; 2:38; 19:5

Barabbas

A robber and murderer accused of rebellion, in prison at the time of Jesus' arrest. The Roman governor, Pilate, knowing that Jesus was innocent of any crime and wishing to set him free, offered to release him. But the religious leaders stirred up the crowd to ask for Barabbas instead. So Barabbas was set free and Jesus was crucified.
Matthew 27:15-26

Barak

An Israelite from Naphtali chosen by Deborah, the prophetess, to recruit a large army to fight Jabin, a Canaanite king at the time of the Judges. Barak's men won a great victory for Israel which ended twenty years of Canaanite rule.
Judges 4–5

Barnabas

The nickname ('son of encouragement') of a Jewish Christian, born in Cyprus, who was a member of the church at Jerusalem. He was generous and warm-hearted, and he sold his land to give the money to poor Christians. When Paul came to Jerusalem after his conversion the Christians were still suspicious of him. But Barnabas welcomed him and introduced him to the apostles. The Jerusalem church sent Barnabas to Antioch to help the new Christians there, many of whom were not Jews. He went on to Tarsus to find Paul, and asked him to share in this work.

Barnabas and Paul set out together from Antioch on their first missionary journey and took John Mark, Barnabas' cousin, with them. On their return they reported to an important meeting of church leaders in Jerusalem. The two men later disagreed about asking Mark to come with them a second time. So Barnabas went back to Cyprus with Mark while Paul went on to Asia Minor (Turkey). Barnabas and Paul continued to be good friends and in his letters Paul speaks highly of Barnabas.
Acts 4:36; 9:27; 11:22ff.; 12:25ff.; 15; 1 Corinthians 9:6; Galatians 2

Bartholomew

One of the twelve apostles. He was with the other apostles after Jesus ascended into heaven, but we know nothing more of him. It is possible that he was the same person as Nathaniel, the man whom Philip brought to Jesus.
Matthew 10:3; Acts 1:13

Baruch

A loyal friend of Jeremiah, the prophet, during the last days of Jerusalem, just before the Babylonians captured the city in 586 BC. Baruch wrote down the messages God gave Jeremiah. He stayed with Jeremiah after Jerusalem was destroyed, even when he was forced to go to Egypt. One of the books in the Apocrypha is named after him.
Jeremiah 36; 43:6

Bashan

A fertile region east of Lake Galilee, famous for its cattle, sheep and strong oak trees. On their way from Egypt to Canaan the Israelites defeated King Og of Bashan, and his land was given to the tribe of Manasseh.
Deuteronomy 3; Psalm 22:12; Isaiah 2:13

Bathsheba

Wife first of Uriah the Hittite and then of King David. (See *David.*)

Beans and lentils

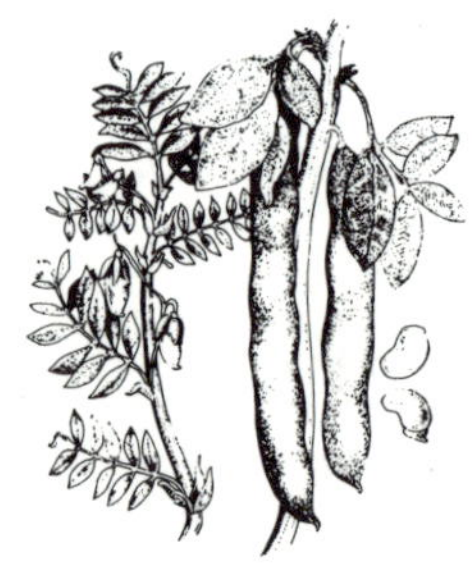

Lentils (on the left) and beans.

Broad beans can be cooked as a vegetable, or dried and ground into flour. The lentil grows in a small flat pod, like a pea. It is red-coloured and is usually made into soups and stews (such as Jacob made for Esau), but can also be dried and ground into flour.
2 Samuel 17:28; Ezekiel 4:9; Genesis 25:34

Bear

The Syrian brown bear was quite common in the hilly and wooded parts of Israel in Bible times. Bears will eat almost anything. They usually live on fruit, roots, eggs, bees' and ants' nests. But when they are hungry they may take a lamb from the flock. David, as a shepherd, had to protect his flock against them; and the Bible tells how bears attacked a mob who were jeering at the prophet Elisha. The Syrian brown bear still lives in the Middle East, but not in Israel.
1 Samuel 17:34-36; 2 Samuel 17:8; 2 Kings 2:24

A Syrian bear.

Beatitudes

See *Jesus' teaching.*

Beersheba

The southernmost town to belong to the Israelites, on the edge of the Negev Desert, and on the trade route to Egypt. The well (*be'er*) which gave the town its name was dug by Abraham. Hagar came near to death in the desert of Beersheba. It was from this place that Abraham set out to offer up Isaac. Isaac himself was living here when Jacob left for Harran. Beersheba is also mentioned in connection with Elijah and Amos. The phrase 'from Dan to Beersheba'

became a common way to speak of the whole land, from north to south.
Genesis 21:14, 30-32; 26:23-33; 1 Kings 19:3; Amos 5:5

Belshazzar

Ruler of Babylon, killed when Babylon was captured in 539 BC by the Medes and Persians. He had been acting king, ruling in the absence of his father Nabonidus. During a great banquet he was frightened by strange writing on the wall of his dining-hall. Daniel was called to translate the words. He warned Belshazzar that God had judged his kingdom and it had failed. Belshazzar would lose his life and Babylon would be conquered. That very night the Persian army took the city by surprise.
Daniel 5

Belteshazzar

This Babylonian name was given to Daniel. (See *Daniel*.)

Benaiah

The best-known of serveral men of this name is the captain of King David's bodyguard who remained loyal when Adonijah tried to seize the throne. Benaiah played a leading part in proclaiming Solomon king, and became commander of his army.
2 Samuel 8:18; 1 Kings 1–2

Benhadad

Name of three kings of Syria, probably meaning 'son of Hadad (the Syrian storm-god). Benhadad I (about 900-860 BC) helped Asa, king of Judah, against Israel. Benhadad II (about 860-843 BC) was an enemy of Ahab, king of Israel. Benhadad III (about 796-770 BC) went to war against Israel in the time of Elisha, the prophet. God freed the Israelites from the Syrians several times in answer to Elisha's prayers. He revealed to Elisha that Benhadad would die at the hands of his servant, Hazael.
1 Kings 20; 2 Kings 6–8

Benjamin

Youngest son of Jacob and Rachel. His mother died when he was born. With his brother Joseph he was the special favourite of his father. Their jealous half-brothers sold Joseph into Egypt. Later, when the brothers were in Joseph's power in Egypt, he tested them to see if they would be equally cruel to Benjamin. But the brothers were changed men. They would not leave Benjamin behind in Egypt, even to save themselves. One of the twelve tribes of Israel was named after Benjamin.
Genesis 35:18-20; 43–45

Bernice

The sister of Herod Agrippa II. (See *Herod Agrippa II*.)
Acts 25:13ff.

Beroea

A town in northern Greece (Macedonia), 50 miles/80km from Thessalonica. Paul preached here on his second missionary journey. The Beroeans welcomed him because they studied the Scriptures. When Jews from Thessalonica stirred up the mob against him he had to leave. But Silas and Timothy stayed behind to teach the Beroeans more about the Christian faith.
Acts 17:10-15; 20:4

Bethany

A village about 2 miles/3km from Jerusalem on the far side of the Mount of Olives, and on the road to Jericho. Mary, Martha and Lazarus lived here, and Jesus stayed with them when he visited Jerusalem. Jesus raised Lazarus from the grave at Bethany.
Matthew 26:6-13; Luke 10:38-42; 24:50; John 11; 12:1-9

Bethel

A place 12 miles/19km north of Jerusalem where Jacob dreamed of a staircase from heaven to earth. God promised to protect him, and said he would give the land to Jacob's descendants. Jacob called the place 'Bethel' (house of God). Centuries later, when the Israelites invaded Canaan, they captured Bethel and settled there.

When the kingdoms of Israel and Judah split up, King Jeroboam of Israel set up an altar and golden calf at Bethel, so that people could worship there instead of at Jerusalem. The prophets condemned this, and when the Israelites were taken into exile Bethel was settled by Assyrians. When the exiles returned, some of them lived in Bethel.
Genesis 28:10-22; Judges 1:22-26; 20:18; Kings 12:26-30; 2 Kings 2; 17:28; Nehemiah 11:31

Bethesda/Bethzatha

A large pool in Jerusalem. At the time of Jesus it was sheltered by five porches, and it is probably the five-porched pool that has been unearthed by archaeologists in the north-east of the city. The pool was fed by a spring which bubbled up from time to time. Many sick people gathered there, hoping to be healed if they were first into the water after this bubbling. It was here that Jesus healed a man who had been ill for thirty-eight years.
John 5:1-15

Beth-horon (Upper and Lower)

These two towns controlled the Valley of Aijalon and the ancient trade-route which passed through it. Many armies took this route in Bible times. Here Joshua pursued the Amorite kings who had attacked the town of Gibeon. Philistines, Egyptians and Syrians also came here.
Joshua 16:3-5; 10:10; 1 Samuel 13:18

Bethlehem

The city of David, 5 miles/8km south-west of Jerusalem, in the Judean hills. Rachel, Jacob's wife, was buried nearby. Ruth and Naomi settled here. Bethlehem was David's birth-place, and the place where the prophet Samuel chose him as the future king, to succeed Saul. The prophet Micah foretold the birth of the Messiah at Bethlehem, although it was only a small town.

Centuries later the Roman census brought Mary and Joseph to Bethlehem. Shepherds and wise men came to kneel before their baby, Jesus –born in a stable in the 'city of David'. Not long after, jealous King Herod gave orders to kill all the boys in Bethlehem under two years old.
Genesis 35:19; Ruth; 1 Samuel 16; Micah 5:2; Matthew 2; Luke 2

The small town of Bethlehem straddles a ridge in the hills to the south of Jerusalem.

Bethphage

A village near Bethany, on or near the Mount of Olives, on the east side of Jerusalem. When Jesus came here on his last journey to Jerusalem, he sent two disciples to a nearby village to fetch the young colt on which he rode in triumph into the city.
Matthew 21:1; Mark 11:1; Luke 19:29

Bethsaida

A fishing town on the north shore of Lake Galilee, near the River Jordan. The home of Jesus' disciples, Philip, Andrew and Peter. Jesus restored the sight of a blind man at Bethsaida, and warned the peóple of God's judgement. Although they saw his miracles they would not change their ways.
John 1:44; Mark 8:22; Matthew 11:21

Beth-shan

A very ancient city in northern Palestine where the Valley of Jezreel slopes down to the west bank of the River Jordan. The Israelites failed to drive the Canaanites out of this district. After Saul and Jonathan were killed by the Philistines on Mt Gilboa, their bodies were fixed on the walls of Beth-shan, but later rescued and buried by men from Jabesh-gilead. In New Testament times Beth-shan was known by the Greek name Scythopolis, and became one

of the cities of the Decapolis, the only one west of the Jordan (see *Decapolis*). The modern town of Beisan stands close to the mound of the old site.
Joshua 17:11, 16; Judges 1:27; 1 Samuel 31:10-13; 2 Samuel 21:12; 1 Kings 4:12

Beth-shemesh

A town about 12 miles/19km west of Jerusalem, given to the priests. It was near the borders of the Philistines. When the Covenant Box (ark) was returned by the Philistines, it came to Beth-shemesh. But some of the people here were punished for not treating it with respect. Later Jehoash, king of the northern kingdom of Israel, defeated and captured Amaziah, king of Judah, at Beth-shemesh.
Joshua 21:16; 1 Samuel 6:9-21; 1 Kings 4:9; 2 Kings 14:11-13

Beth-zur

A city of Judah, 4 miles/6km north of Hebron. Beth-zur was settled by the family of Caleb. Later it was one of fifteen cities fortified by King Rehoboam. Men from here helped to rebuild Jerusalem under Nehemiah's leadership. The place stood on one of the highest hill-tops in the land, and was the scene of one of the great Jewish victories in the Maccabean revolt (*1 Maccabees* 4:26-35).
Joshua 15:58; 1 Chronicles 2:45; 2 Chronicles 11:7; Nehemiah 3:16

Bible: interpretation

Some of the stories in the Gospels are so clear that anyone can understand them. But it is not so easy to get the meaning of some other parts of the Bible. The Bible is an ancient book made up of many parts. It has many different writers, different audiences, different styles of writing and language. When we read a passage from the Bible it is useful to ask three questions:

What does the passage actually say?
What does the passage mean?
What does the passage mean today?

What does the passage actually say? To understand what the passage says we need to ask some further, more detailed questions. For example, it is important to ask: **when** and **where** the book, or passage, was written.

Was it before or after the birth of Christ?
Before the exodus or after?
When Israel was ruled by kings, or during the Roman occupation?
Where was it written?
In exile in Babylon?
In a prison cell in Rome?
At the royal court as an official record?

If we find out the answers to these questions we shall discover the setting of the passage in history. This helps us to understand what the writer intended.

A second useful question is: **why** was this passage written? If we can discover the purpose of the writer, we will begin to understand better some of the things he says. For example, some of Paul's letters were written to try to correct errors among groups of Christians. He points out their mistakes, and shows them a better way for the future. Similarly, it helps to know that the writer of the Book of Revelation wanted to encourage his readers who were suffering persecution for their faith.

It also helps to ask generally: **what** is this book about? The answer to this question will help us to read the book in the right way.

Is it the account of events in the life and death of Jesus?
Is it a list of the religious duties of the Hebrew people?
Is it a collection of religious poetry?

Sometimes it is important to ask what particular words mean. There are some special terms in the Bible–'atonement', for example, or 'sin'. It is important to understand their special meaning if we are to get the writer's message.

We need, especially, to ask: what *sort* of writing is this? In what form has it been written.

Is it history?
Is it poetry?
Is it a letter?

Then we can go on to ask the questions that apply to that kind of writing.

If we are reading a book of history, we can ask: what actually happened? What other important events were occurring at the same period? Why has the writer chosen these events to recount? And why does he recount them in the way he does?

But if it is a book of poetry, we should look at the writer's use of picture-language. What does he mean by his pictures? How was the poem or hymn used in worship?

It is worth looking in more detail at some of the forms of writing in the Bible.

History and biography The Old Testament has many books of history, such as Samuel and Kings, and we find New Testament history in the Gospels and Acts. If we are reading history, we need to enquire about the background to events.

What was going on in the wider world at the time?
What important affairs were taking place?

Then we need to look at the passage itself carefully.

What actually happens?
Who are the principle characters?
Where did this all occur?

Sometimes history books are written to prove or make a particular point. So it is important to ask what the writer was trying to show.

Law The main law-books of the Old Testament are Exodus, Leviticus, Deuteronomy and Numbers. These books contain long passages listing laws which cover many different aspects of life. It is useful to ask what part of life particular laws apply to.

Does the law deal with matters of behaviour and morals?
Are they state laws or social rules?
Are the laws about hygiene or family life?
Or are they religious laws–about worship, ritual and sacrifice?
Are they solemn ritual blessings and cursings related to Jewish religion?

When we read passages of the law, it is important to relate them to the particular periods in Israel's history to which they applied. When we come to the New Testament, we need to understand how far Jesus' teaching overruled the law. Galatians and Hebrews, for example, show how the first Christians believed the scope of the law was altered.

Poetry Some Old Testament books are largely made up of poetry. Job, Psalms and the Song of Solomon are good examples. There are also passages of poetry in the prophets and shorter ones in the New Testament – for example Mary's song of praise, the Magnificat. We need to read these passages as poetry, not as prose.

Is the book written rather like a play, with characters? (The Book of Job can be looked at like this).
Or is it the writer's personal feelings, which we can sometimes share? Examples of this include some of the psalms.
Or does the poetry have much picture-language?

Some Old Testament poetry was written for official temple worship. A psalm, for example, may retell the great events in Israel's history. Sometimes it is important to know the history behind a particular poem–for example, David's lament over the death of his friend Jonathan. There are some special effects in Hebrew poetry. The one we see most often is the way the poet makes the same point in two slightly different ways in consecutive lines.

Wise sayings Some Old Testament books–particularly Proverbs and Ecclesiastes–are made up of 'wise sayings'. Some of these stand on their own: sometimes they are grouped into sayings with a common theme. Some of the sayings are common-sense comments on everyday living, often with a touch of humour. Others try to draw out general principles about human life. Some talk about life without God; others about the true source of happiness.

Prophecy A large section of the Old Testament is made up of 'books of prophecy'. This does not necessarily mean that they foretell the future. The prophets who wrote the books were usually concerned to speak out against evils, or the disregard for God and his rules which they saw in society around them. But they also occasionally looked forward to what God had in store for the future.

When we read the prophets, we need to find out their background in history. There are other useful questions.

Is the writer using picture-language?
Is he writing a kind of poetry?
What do his word-pictures mean?
What was the prophet's purpose in speaking as he did?
Was the prophecy understood in a special way by the New Testament writers?

Parables Many of Jesus' parables are written down in the Gospels. We also find parables, or picture-stories, in some of the Old Testament books of history and prophecy. We need first to find out what the main point of the parable was. Do the details of the parable have any special meaning–or are they there just to set the scene for the story? Many of Jesus' parables were told to help ordinary people understand what God's kingdom was like, and how he deals with men and women.

Letters Many of the later books of the New Testament are letters from apostles or other Christians in various places. When we read these letters we must ask:

Who wrote this letter?
To whom?
What was his purpose in writing?
What is the main theme of the letter?

What did the passage mean to its first readers? If we have answered all the questions, and know what the passage actually says, it is not so difficult to find out what it meant to its original readers. We can try to find out what the main point of the passage is. What does it teach? If the passage was written to answer a specific need or situation, we can ask: Is there a general principle behind these events?

When we feel we know what the passage actually says, and what it meant for its original readers, we can confidently ask our final question.

What does the passage mean for us today? Is there a modern situation like that of the original reader? What would the writer have to say to such a situation? If not, is there a principle that still applies? What specific teaching is there in the passage? (It is often useful to compare it with other Bible passages dealing with similar subjects. Sometimes they may set it out more clearly–or add to the meaning of the passage we are reading.) Is there something we can learn?

About God?
About man?
About the world?
About the church?
About some other specific theme?

Can we find some example to follow? Is there a warning? Does it contain a promise that applies to us? Is there some action we should take in the light of this passage? Does it make us want to pray? Or to praise? Can we use the writer's words to express our own feelings about God? How does this passage, and its meaning, fit in with other passages we know with similar themes?

See also *Old Testament text, New Testament text*

Bible translations

For many Christians in the first century 'the Bible' was the Greek translation of the Old Testament (the *Septuagint*) which was begun in the third century BC. Soon after the New Testament was completed, translation work began. The first translation was probably into Latin. This was the official language of the Roman Empire, though Greek was the most widely spoken language among Christians, even in Italy. At first Greek was used in most churches.

For centuries the Bible manuscripts were copied by hand. This print from about AD 1340 shows a court secretary copying a manuscript in his library.

From the second century on, there were many local translations of the Bible. But people felt that there should be a standard text that could be recognized and used by everyone. So in about AD 384 Pope Damasus instructed his secretary to revise the Latin New Testament. This man was Jerome. He is the first Bible translator whose name has come down to us (we know of earlier Jewish scholars who revised the Greek Old Testament). His Latin translation, the Vulgate (or Common Version), has been the standard Bible of the Roman Catholic Church ever since. Scores of other translations have been made from it including the first English ones.

Jerome was a good scholar and he did his work well. In order to translate the Old Testament he learnt Hebrew, living for many years in Bethlehem. Through his work, copied out by hand in many lands, God's word brought hope and new life to countless people.

In the second century, translators began work in Syriac, a dialect of the Aramaic language which Jesus himself spoke. Although old Syriac is no longer spoken, the fourth-century translation (known as the Peshitta) is still used in worship by Nestorian and Syrian Christians in Syria, Iran, India and other lands.

In Egypt the church at first used the Greek language. But as Christianity spread south, an Egyptian (or Coptic) version was needed. Translation began in the third century. The Coptic Bible is still used in worship.

After the Roman Emperor Constantine was converted (AD 312) Christianity spread rapidly, and new translations were soon needed. The Goths, who invaded the Empire in the River Danube basin, received almost the whole Bible in their own language from the missionary translator, Ulfilas. Much of the text survives in manuscripts, although the language has long been extinct.

St Mesrop worked out an alphabet for the Armenians, the first Christian nation in the world, and gave them their Bible in the fifth century. This is still the standard version of the ancient Armenian Church, both in the Armenian SSR (part of the USSR) and in the many lands where Armenians are scattered. The Ge'ez and Georgian Bibles, used to this day in the churches of Ethiopia and Georgia (USSR), probably also date from the fifth century.

Later there was a translation in Old Slavonic, the language spoken in Bulgaria, Serbia and southern Russia in the ninth century, when the Slavic tribes became Christians through the work of St Cyril. He invented the Cyrillic alphabet, and before long the whole Bible had been translated. This version is still the official version of the Russian Orthodox Church.

As well as these church translations, we know of at least one 'missionary' version made *before* a church had been established. In about AD 640 a group of Nestorian missionaries, whose language was Syriac, translated the Gospels into Chinese for the Emperor Tai Tsung.

The Dark Ages In the centuries following the break-up of the Roman Empire in the West, Christianity was spreading fast, especially in northern and eastern Europe. As the church grew, parts of the Bible were translated into many new languages.

The earliest real translation in England was Aldhelm's translation of the Psalms. Aldhelm was Bishop of Sherborne, in the south of England, AD 700. About the same time in the north of England the great historian, Bede, was concerned about priests who knew little or no Latin and so could not read the Bible. So he began to translate the Bible into Anglo-Saxon. He died in AD 735, working on his translation of John's Gospel on his death bed. Unfortunately, neither Bede's nor Aldhelm's work has survived. The English King Alfred (AD 871–901) was also a Bible translator, giving his people parts of Exodus, Psalms and Acts in their own language. Educated priests sometimes made their own versions, too. After the Norman conquest, various books of the Bible were translated into English, some in local dialects.

Other unofficial translations, mainly for church leaders and often in metre, were made in other languages. A translation of Matthew in Frankish (early German), made in AD 758, has survived. The earliest French texts date from the twelth century; Italian from the fourteenth. The first Bible translations in Arabic probably appeared in the eighth century, though there were Christians in Arabia in the fourth century.

Forerunners of the Reformation In the latter part of the Middle Ages a number of new Bible versions appeared. These were designed to be read by ordinary Christians and the work was supported by people who were critical of the official church leadership. About 1170, a merchant of Lyons, Peter Waldo, found new purpose in life through reading the New Testament. He arranged for the Bible to be translated into Provençal (southern French). His followers formed the Waldensian Church, which was bitterly persecuted for centuries.

Nearly 200 years later, an Oxford theologian, John Wycliffe, was studying his Bible. He became convinced that it was so important that it must be available to everyone. As a result, by 1384 the Latin Vulgate Bible had been translated into English. Nicholas of Hereford, John Purvey and others were the actual translators of most of it. They followed the Latin closely, even in its very un-English order of words! By 1395 Purvey had revised the work in better and clearer English.

Some copies carried notes expressing the controversial views of the Lollards (as Wycliffe's followers were called). In 1408 a synod of the church met at Oxford and banned the writing, circulation or study of these English versions. But the appeal of the English Bible was too great. Many hundreds of copies were still circulating when the first printed books of the Bible appeared over 100 years later.

A similar movement took place in Bohemia (Czechoslovakia). Jan Hus, Rector of the University of Prague, was influenced by Wycliffe's teaching. He was burnt at the stake in 1415, but his followers began the work of Bible translation. The Czech New Testament, printed in 1475, was the result.

Printing and the Reformation Around 1450, at Mainz in Germany, Johann Gutenberg pioneered the process of printing from movable metal type. His work began a new era in the history of books, and with them, of the Bible. The first major work to emerge from the press was the Bible (1456)–in Latin. Ten years later it was printed in German at Strasburg, from the text of an unknown fourteenth-century translator. In 1471 the first Italian Bible was printed and this was soon followed by the French New Testament. The first Dutch Scriptures appeared in 1477. Next came the whole Bible in Catalan (for Spain, 1478).

All these versions were based on existing manuscripts and translated from the Latin. But with the revival of learning, texts in the original languages began to be studied. Jewish scholars had preserved the Hebrew Bible and in 1488 they printed it in Italy. The Greek New Testament was first published by the great Dutch scholar, Erasmus, in 1516. Although he was not himself a translator (except into Latin) Erasmus, unlike many others, was very much in favour of translating the Bible into ordinary speech. He wrote:

> 'I wish that the Scriptures might be translated into all languages, so that not only the Scots and the Irish, but also the Turk and the Saracen might read and understand them. I long that the farm-labourer might sing them as he follows the plough, the weaver hum them to the tune of his shuttle, the traveller beguile the weariness of his journey with their stories.'

Meanwhile, in Germany, a young monk called Martin Luther was anxiously studying his Latin Bible. As he read, he was especially struck by Paul's words in Romans 1:17 'The gospel reveals how God puts people right with himself. It is through faith from beginning to end.' He describes the great release and freedom these words brought. 'I felt completely reborn ... My love for that sweetest word "righteousness of God" was henceforth as great as my hatred for it had been hitherto. In this way this passage of Paul was truly the gate of Paradise."'

Luther was a lecturer in the university at Wittenberg. He proclaimed this message, and made a close study of the Hebrew Old Testament and Erasmus' Greek New Testament. Then he undertook the task of making a new translation in German, in the clearest possible language. The New Testament appeared in 1522 and the task was completed in 1532. It has remained the best-known German Bible ever since.

The English Bible About the same time, William Tyndale, who had been a scholar at Cambridge soon after Erasmus, and was influenced by his writings, began to translate the New Testament into English. The church authorities gave him no encouragement. So he went to Germany to finish his work. The first New Testament printed in English appeared at Worms in 1526. Copies soon reached England and were eagerly studied. The authorities denounced them and the Bishop of London bought large quantities and burnt them. Tyndale's reaction was to publish a better version! He revised it twice, and by 1566 it had been printed forty times. He went on to write other books and to translate part of the Old Testament. But the New Testament is his great legacy to the English-speaking world, for the Authorized/King James' Version of 1611 follows it very closely.

In 1535 Myles Coverdale published the first whole Bible in English. It was printed abroad but soon found its way into England. In 1533 the clergy of the province of Canterbury had asked King Henry VIII for an official translation of the Bible. They wanted this 'delivered to the people for their instruction'. A dedication to the king was added to the Coverdale Bible. It seems that when the scholars assured him that it did not contain any heresies Henry authorized its circulation.

Coverdale did not work from the original Greek and Hebrew. He based his work on that of Tyndale, Luther and the Latin versions. His translation is still used today, in the version of the Psalms that is still printed in *The Book of Common Prayer.* Coverdale was the first to include chapter summaries, as in the Authorized/King James' Version, and to separate the Apocrypha from the Old Testament books. In the older versions the apocryphal books were set out in the same way as they are in the Greek *Septuagint.*

In 1537 came the first Bible actually printed in England. It had on it the name 'Thomas Matthew', the pen name of John Rogers, a fellow-worker of Tyndale's. It is made up mostly of Tyndale's translation, including his Joshua to Chronicles, not previously published, and contains a good deal of extra material in the form of indexes and notes. It was the first Bible to be published 'with the King's most gracious licence', a privilege granted to Coverdale's Bible in the same year.

In 1538 an order was issued with the king's authority that the clergy must provide 'a book of the whole Bible of the largest volume in English' to be set 'in some convenient place within the church, whither your parishioners may most conveniently resort to the same and read it ...It is the very living Word of God that every Christian person is bound to embrace, believe and follow if he look to be saved'.

The book the king intended was the Great Bible, Coverdale's revision of Matthew's version. It appeared in 1539. Its second edition contained a preface by Archbishop Cranmer, encouraging everyone to read the Bible. It also contained a note: 'this is the Bible appointed for the use of the churches.' One of the two bishops who had examined it for the king was Tonstall, who as Bishop of London had burnt Tyndale's New Testament. All controversial notes had been been dropped. Before Henry's death in 1547 Tyndale's and Coverdale's translations were forbidden and large numbers were destroyed. But the Great Bible remained in the churches throughout the reign of Edward VI and some even in the reign of the Roman Catholic Queen Mary (1553–58), although the church services were once more in Latin.

Meanwhile, in Geneva, scholarly English exiles were at work on a revision. This appeared in 1560, dedicated to Queen Elizabeth I. It contained the first translation of Ezra to Malachi directly from Hebrew. The Hebrew idiom was kept wherever possible, in the New as well as the Old Testament. The Apocrypha was included, with a note about its value. The Bible also contained some notes about its meaning. It became a very popular Bible. In Britain, as well as in Geneva, it was printed seventy times in Elizabeth's reign. In Scotland this was the Bible officially read in churches, and it continued to be used for some time after the Authorized/King James' Version had appeared. It is sometimes called the Breeches Bible, because in its translation of Genesis 3:7 it says that Adam and Eve made themselves 'breeches'.

Meanwhile the Great Bible was being revised. This was mainly the work of the bishops, with Archbishop Parker playing a leading part. So the new version which appeared in 1568 became known as the Bishops' Bible. The revisers aimed to improve the accuracy of the text, to change expressions offensive to public taste and to avoid controversial notes and interpretations. But the result was not so good as the Geneva Bible. Although it was used in churches, it proved to be less popular.

King James' (Authorized) Version When he came to the throne in 1603 James I of England (VI of Scotland) agreed to a new revision. He himself took a share in organizing the work, which was entrusted to six teams of scholars. After they had done their work, two scholars from each team worked over the whole Bible before it went to press. The work was based on the Bishops' Bible, but using the original Hebrew and Greek. Names were given their familiar forms, and familiar ecclesiastical words (like 'church' and 'bishop') were to be kept. Notes in the margins explained Greek and Hebrew words and linked parallel passages. Words added to complete the sense were printed in a different type. New chapter summaries were included.

This version enjoyed enormous prestige for 350 years. The main reasons for this are probably the beauty and rhythm of its language. All early editions included the Apocrypha. This was not omitted from the Geneva Bible till 1640, and much later from the Authorized Version. Since the first edition the spelling has been greatly modernized, the chapter summaries reduced and marginal references expanded. In 1701 Archbishop Ussher's dates were added in the margin and continued to appear for 200 years.

The Douai version One year before the Authorized Version, the standard Roman Catholic version, the Douai Bible, was published. This was the work of Gregory Martin and others at the English College at Douai, in France. His New Testament appeared in 1582 when the college was at Rheims. He tried to translate the Vulgate word for word, sometimes making little sense in English. Some unusual words taken over from the Latin are explained in a glossary. Full notes explain the text and points of doctrine.

Many found the language of the Douai Bible hard to understand, and so Bishop Challoner issued two revisions of the Old Testament and five of the New up to 1772, much influenced by the Authorized Version. His last revision came to replace the original Douai as the official Roman Catholic version.

Pioneer missionary Bible translators When missionary work began again after the Middle Ages, the first translations were made by Roman Catholics. They generally began with the Ten Commandments, the Lord's Prayer and selected parts of the Gospels or Bible story books, as well as the catechism. But in 1613 Jesuit missionaries published the whole New Testament in Japanese.

The first Protestant version was in Malay, and was made by employees of the Dutch East India Company.

The first whole Bible was John Eliot's 1663 version in 'Massachusetts'. This is a complex American Indian language, with some words 15-20 letters long.

Bible translation in India began in earnest with Danish Lutheran missionaries. Ziegenbalg's New Testament in Tamil appeared in 1711 and the Old Testament was added by Schultze in 1728. But a new era began when the first English missionary, William Carey, reached India in 1793. He spent forty years working at Serampore in Bengal with two colleagues and many Indian helpers. When he died, his press had produced translations of the whole Bible or New Testament in 37 different languages or dialects. These included Burmese and Chinese. He had also compiled grammars and dictionaries. It was an amazing achievement.

The Bible Societies In 1804 the British and Foreign Bible Society was founded 'for Wales, for the kingdom, for the world'. At first it issued existing Bible versions. But its members soon took an interest in new translations. They issued the Hindustani (Urdu) New Testament, translated by the pioneer missionary, Henry Martyn, in 1812 and the first modern African translation in 1816. This was in the Bullom language for Sierra Leone. Since then there have been translations into about 480 African languages. Christians were the first to write these languages down, using the Roman script. The first complete New Testament for Africa was in Amharic, for Ethiopia, in 1829. The first whole Bible in an African language was in Malagasy in 1835.

A similar process began in the Pacific (with Tahitian in 1818) and in Latin America (with Aymara, for Bolivia, in 1829).

By this time other societies had begun work. The Netherlands Bible Society, the American Bible Society and the National Bible Society of Scotland, all began the work of Bible translation. In India, Africa and the Arab lands Roman Catholic missionaries also worked on Bible translation.

The modern missionary movement grew all through the nineteenth century, and until 1939 translation went ahead at a great rate. Practically every missionary society had a part in it. The chief translators were generally missionaries, though nationals were also involved. Some played a major role. Nigerian-born Bishop Samuel Crowther, for example, worked on the Yoruba Bible (Nigeria, 1862) and Pandita Ramabai on the Bible in Marathi (1912). The Bible Societies helped set the work up. They gave money where it was needed. They had the translations printed and distributed and generally helped out with any problems. Only the Netherlands Society trained its own linguists and sent them out as translators.

Missionary Bible translation today There have been great changes in Bible translation since World War II.

The Wycliffe Bible Translators were founded in 1934 to bring people the Bible in their own language. Thousands of languages were still without it. This group has now expanded into the largest missionary society in the world. It has over 3,000 missionaries, who carry out a carefully organized programme in about 700 languages.

Each translator is first trained in linguistics. They usually have to give the language a written form for the first time. This is no easy task, especially when it contains sounds unknown in any European language. Then the translator has to write a grammar and a complete list of words used. He is usually helped by a national who has at least some knowledge of another language known to the missionary. Years may pass before he can begin even the simplest translations. Meanwhile the tribal people have to be taught to read. And then the translation must be tested all the time, to make sure that people can understand it.

A still larger programme, covering some of the major languages of the world (Hindi, Chinese, Arabic) has been carried on by the United Bible Societies. This organization unites sixty or so national societies all over the world. Both Roman Catholics and Protestants co-operate in this work. The second Vatican Council encouraged Roman Catholics to supply their people with the Bible in their own language.

Consultations are held to gain wide support for the new translation. Some people are bound to resent any changes in the Bible they have known from childhood, and their views must be taken into account. If a new translation is decided on, translators will be chosen and trained. They will make the first drafts, sharing them with each other and noting criticisms. Then their agreed draft will go to a team of experts on the Bible and the language, who will send their criticisms in writing. If the translators do not accept these, they will be discussed at a meeting of the experts. Church leaders will also receive drafts, so that when the work is finished they will support it and help churches to accept it. A Bible Society translations officer will keep in close touch with a number of projects like this. He will make regular visits, offering advice and suggestions and occasionally settling disputes.

Today thousands of people are working to make the Bible clear in terms which ordinary people can understand. There are still many hundreds of language groups, mostly small ones, with no existing translation that meets their need. And languages are always changing. United Bible Society scholars reckon that, to keep up with this change, some revision, if not a new translation, will be needed in every language every thirty years. Certainly there will be enough work to keep the Bible translators busy for many years to come, bringing God's message to everyone in his own language.

Bible: modern English versions

The Revised Version In 1870 the Church of England passed a historic resolution, to prepare a revision of the Authorized Version, making only necessary changes. Teams of Old and New Testament scholars were appointed, and Church of Scotland and Free Church scholars were invited to join. They were to make 'as few alterations as possible' in 'the language of the Authorized Version'. No changes in the Greek and Hebrew text were to be adopted without a two-thirds majority. Two parallel groups were formed in the USA to co-operate with suggestions and criticisms.

The Revised Version New Testament, printed in 1881 and telegraphed to Chicago, aroused great interest. It was based on a far more ancient Greek text than the Authorized Version, relying chiefly on the fourth-century Vatican and Sinaitic codices (see *New Testament Text*). Many marginal notes referred to the sources of the original text. Quite a number of well-known words and verses in the Authorized Version were left out because there was no good manuscript authority for them. This led to strong opposition, though without good reason. The translation is often over-literal or pedantic. But the Old Testament translation (1885) was a great advance on the Authorized Version. Many meaningless passages were made clear through new knowledge of the Hebrew; poetic passages were set out as poetry; paragraphs were used; and a good reference system was introduced in 1898.

The Revised Standard Version The American scholars who had been associated with the English Revised Version produced the American Standard Version in 1901. In 1937 the council which held the copyright for this decided on a revision. The New Testament appeared in 1946 and the Old Testament in 1952. Its language is a compromise between the outdated language made familiar by the King James' Version, and modern English. Most, but not all, of the out-of-date words have gone. Quotation marks are used for speech. In some places ancient translations have been followed where the Hebrew text seems clearly wrong. And in Isaiah some changes have been introduced in the light of the Dead Sea Scrolls.

In 1973 a new edition, known as *The Common Bible*, was issued. It was authorized by Roman Catholic authorities as well as the RSV committee.

The New English Bible In 1946 the Church of Scotland approached the main British churches and suggested an entirely new translation. The idea was welcomed and soon three teams of scholars were at work, with a further group to advise on questions of style. Dr C. H. Dodd was the general director. The New Testament appeared in 1961, the Old Testament in 1970. This is the first official inter-church translation in Britain and the first major version to depart from the Tyndale/Authorized Version tradition.

The New English Bible takes all the latest research into account. The Dead Sea Scrolls have thrown new light on the Old Testament text. Newly-discovered documents in languages related to Hebrew have revealed the meanings of some difficult words. It is intended to be in modern English without the old-fashioned 'biblical' language of the Authorized Version. But there are still frequent echoes of it. Some of the words are long and difficult and it did not capture the idiom of modern English.

The Jerusalem Bible In 1966 Roman Catholic translators published the Jerusalem Bible. This was a new version made from the original languages. It was similar to the French *Bible de Jerusalem*, and included the introductions and notes from the French translation. This translation has been widely used by Protestants as well as Roman Catholics. Its language is more lively and modern than that of the Revised Standard Version.

The Good News Bible (Today's English Version) The Good News Bible, produced by the American Bible Society (New Testament 1966, Old Testament 1976) has broken new ground. The aim is a reliable and accurate translation using words which make the meanings clear to everyone. This includes people who have no Christian background, people without much formal education, and people who use English as a second language. It is based on a careful study of linguistics and provides a pattern for translations in many other languages all over the world.

The basic aim is to provide in English the closest *natural* equivalent of the original language.

A second important aim concerns the level of language. Scholarly, poetical and technical religious terms are avoided. And so are all slang expressions. The result is a 'common language', which should be clear and acceptable to all readers of English.

Other modern English translations by groups and individuals are as follows:

1902 **The Twentieth Century New Testament**
The thirty or so translators included ministers but not textual experts. Easy to read and understand.

1903 R. F. Weymouth, **The New Testament in Modern Speech**
Long sentences are divided, and section headings added. Uses dignified and sometimes old-fashioned language.

1913 and 1924 J. Moffatt, **A New Translation of the Bible**
A good translation, especially in the Old Testament. Rearranges and changes parts of the text, for reasons which Moffatt explains elsewhere.

1923 and 1927 E. J. Goodspeed, **The Complete Bible: an American translation**
A very readable version. The Old Testament was the work of four other scholars.

1941 and 1949 **The Basic English Bible**
A successful experiment using a vocabulary of only 1,000 words.

1941 **The Confraternity Version**
A Roman Catholic translation made in the USA. A revision of Challoner's New Testament. The Old Testament translation is based on the Hebrew.

1945 and 1949 Ronald Knox, **The Holy Bible**
A Roman Catholic translation based on the Latin Vulgate, by a master of English style.

1947-1957 J. B. Phillips, **The New Testament in Modern English**
A free and racy version which has been very popular.

1945 and 1959 **The Berkeley Version**
The New Testament by Dr G. Verkuyl; the Old Testament by a team of scholars in the USA. A conservative version.

1958 K. S. Wuest, **Expanded Translation of the New Testament**
Designed to help Bible students who do not know Greek.

1958 **The Amplified New Testament**
Produced in the USA. Includes alternative and additional words to bring out the meaning.

1971 K. Taylor, **The Living Bible**
A popular American paraphrase into everyday language, designed for family reading.

1971 **New American Standard Version**
The American Standard Version of 1901 with modernized English.

1973 and 1978 **The New International Version**
A translation by a team of Protestant evangelical scholars mainly from the USA. Clear, dignified and readable.

Bilhah

Rachel's servant, who became the mother of Dan and Naphtali.
Genesis 29:29; 30:3-7

Bithynia

A Roman province in the north-west of Asia Minor (Turkey). Paul was forbidden 'by the Holy Spirit' to preach here. Yet Bithynia was not forgotten. Peter sent his first letter to Christian believers living in Bithynia, among other places. We know that this area soon became a strong centre of Christianity, for early in the second century the Roman governor Pliny wrote to the Emperor Trajan about the Christians there.
Acts 16:7; 1 Peter 1:1

Blood

The New Testament often describes the death of Jesus by the phrase 'the blood of Christ (or Jesus)'. The background to this unusual phrase is in the Old Testament, where the word 'blood' is used in a number of distinctive ways:

–When blood is shed a person's life is over: 'The life is in the blood.'
–Life is the gift of God, so no one must shed another's blood.
–The blood of animals was shed in sacrifice. It represents the animal's life poured out in death. Since life is the gift of God, this blood must not be used for food (this ruling applied to every animal killed, not only in sacrifice).

So when the New Testament uses the phrase 'the blood of Christ' it refers to the violent death of Jesus on the cross. Indeed, some modern versions simply translate the phrase as 'the death of Christ'.

See also *Atonement, Cross, Redemption*.

Genesis 9:4-6; Deuteronomy 12:15-16, 20-28; Ephesians 1:7;
1 Peter 1:18-19; Hebrews 10:19-22

Boaz

Hero of the Book of Ruth. Boaz was a rich and generous farmer in Bethlehem who married Ruth and became the great-grandfather of King David.
Ruth 2–4

Body

In the Bible the word 'body' is often used to stand for the whole person. So it can sometimes be translated as 'self'. For instance: 'Offer your bodies (your selves) as a living sacrifice.' The New Testament speaks of the 'resurrection body', the new form we will have when God raises us from death. This means a full, continued life for the whole person, not merely some disembodied existence as a spirit.

Paul uses the idea of the body–in which different parts have different functions–as a picture of the church. Christians are like the different parts which make up a body. Each has a different part to play in the church, working under the direction of Jesus.

The New Testament places great importance on the physical body. It is 'the body' which is the temple of the Holy Spirit, and our 'bodies' which are to be used for God's glory.

Romans 12:1; 1 Corinthians 15:35-49; Romans 12:4-5;
1 Corinthians 12:12-30;
Ephesians 4:15-16;
1 Corinthians 6:15-20

Bozrah

An ancient city in Edom, south-east of the Dead Sea, about 80 miles/128km south of modern Amman in Jordan. The prophets foretold that Bozrah would be utterly destroyed.
Genesis 36:33; 1 Chronicles 1:44; Isaiah 34:6; 63:1; Jeremiah 49:13, 22; Amos 1:12

Bread
See *Food.*

Building
Skill in building developed slowly in Israel. As slaves in Egypt the Israelites had made bricks for massive building projects. But when they entered the land of Canaan, they showed little interest in building. The spies reported 'large and well fortified' cities in Canaan (Numbers 13:28). But the Israelites destroyed many of these, and the buildings that replaced them were not very impressive.

It was not until the time of David and Solomon that real skill was used, and this must be due mainly to the help and instruction of Phoenician masons and joiners sent by King Hiram of Tyre (see 1 Chronicles 14:1). Buildings put up later, after the alliance with Phoenicia had broken down, reverted to the cruder style. The more elaborate buildings of later times still, owe much to Persian, Greek and Roman influence.

The materials available for building were mud, stones and boulders, limestone and wood.

Bricks were widely used where stone was not plentiful. Mud and straw were mixed, shaped–by hand or in wooden moulds–into squares or rectangles, and then dried in the sun. Mud was also used as mortar, sticking loose stones together to make a rubble wall.

The limestone of Palestine is soft and easily cut, but it was not much used for ordinary building work. Sites of old quarries have been found, showing the marks of picks, and unfinished blocks of stone. Hammers, saws, picks, and axes were used as tools. To detach a large block of stone, the rock was split with hammers along the natural faults and wooden wedges hammered in and then soaked. As the wood expanded, the rock cracked.

Stones were roughly finished in the quarry, but then sent to the building sites for final trimming. This accounts for the piles of stone chips excavators have found at the palace of Lachish and the later citadel in Jerusalem. But for Solomon's temple, as 1 Kings 6:7 records, the stone was prepared at the quarry, so that there was no sound of hammer, axe or iron tool in the holy place.

Forests were plentiful in Israel at that time, particularly in Galilee. For building purposes conifers were often used.

Builders' tools found in Egypt, dating back to about 2,000 BC: a wooden mallet, bronze chisels and plumb-bob.

Building work meant mainly constructing houses and city walls, and digging wells, cisterns, water tunnels and grain silos. These were usually an individual or village community effort. (Compare the building of the walls of Jerusalem by united effort under Nehemiah–Nehemiah 3–6.) There was no question of skilled craftsmen doing all the work.

Houses were built on a stone foundation, but the walls were made of brick, plastered on both sides with mud. Sometimes long stones were used as reinforcements and wooden columns were put up on a stone foundation, as supports to extend the reach of the house. Rubble walls were then built between these columns, making small rooms which led off an open court. But normally the house had only one room. Wooden beams were laid across the top of the walls and the roof was made of matting, covered with a plaster of straw, mud and lime. There was usually only one storey, but the roof itself became an extra working-space. A staircase outside the house, or a ladder inside, led up to it. There was a railing round the edge of the roof to prevent accidents.

Town walls were made of rubble or boulder masonry, sometimes plastered and strengthened by towers. The boulders were only roughly shaped, but carefully fitted together. Houses were built along the inside of these walls, but beyond that there was little attempt at town planning. Houses were built wherever there was a space.

As time went on, many houses had a cistern underneath to store rain water. These were dug out of solid rock, but needed to be lined with slaked lime to stop the water leaking away. Pools for storing water were often cut out of rock and in several cities excavations have revealed tunnels cut to make water more accessible. One at Megiddo is from Israelite times.

Masons and carpenters also made things for everyday use–stone basins, water jars, loom weights, millstones; wooden yokes, ploughs, threshing-boards, carts and furniture.

Special projects Special building projects of Bible times include David's palace; Solomon's fortifications; the temple and buildings around it in Jerusalem; Ahab's palace at Samaria; Hezekiah's water tunnel in Jerusalem; the rebuilding of Jerusalem after the exile; then the many buildings of Herod the Great and his successors (the temple, Herod's palace, the fortress of Machaerus, the Herodium, Massada, and the harbour at Caesarea). Under Pontius Pilate, an aqueduct was constructed to bring water into Jerusalem.

The temple built by Solomon at Jerusalem must have been the most spectacular early project. Cedar-trees were supplied by Hiram, king of Tyre, who was one of Solomon's allies. Hiram also sent skilled craftsmen. And at this point, for the first time since the Israelites occupied the land, we find finely dressed and shaped stones–ashlar masonry. The corners are well jointed, and bonded; blocks are closely aligned without the use of mortar; and the technique of 'headers' and 'stretchers' is used (stones laid alternately widthwise and lengthwise for extra strength).

The walls of Solomon's temple had three courses of finished stones, surmounted by brick on a row of cedar beams. The wood helped to absorb shock in case of earthquakes. The roof and doors were timber; the floor, walls and ceiling were lined with boards of fir and cedar, decorated with carvings. (See 1 Kings 6.)

The fortifications of Solomon's cities at Hazor, Megiddo and Gezer had city walls of the casemate design (two walls with partitions across, the hollows filled with rubble, or left as store-rooms) and city gates with three guard-rooms either side. Under the paved floor of the gate there was a stone drain.

Hezekiah's tunnel was built to bring water from the Gihon spring into the city of Jerusalem. In 1880 an interesting inscription made by the workers was found. It describes two groups of quarry-men, 150ft/45m underground, about to meet in the middle after a long (1750ft/530m) and winding route from each end. They can hear one another's picks.

'On the day of the piercing through, the stone-cutters struck through each to meet his fellow, axe against axe. Then ran the water from the spring to the pool...'

Because of King Herod's building programme the building trade at the time of Jesus had an important position in Jerusalem. Herod is said to have prepared 1,000 wagons for transporting stones, some of which may have been quarried from the caves under the city itself. Stones 5-10 tons in weight were produced and were moved to the buildings, perhaps on rollers. Arches and vaults were constructed on the Roman pattern.

Jerusalem in Herod's day was also a typical city of the Roman Empire. Excavations of first-century Jerusalem have uncovered large houses built on a lavish scale. There is underfloor heating and piped water. A paved Roman road in a village nearby is flanked by stone holders for torches, to serve as street lights. The houses of the poor continued to be simple, but probably most had more than one storey.

C

Caesar
The title of Roman emperors in New Testament times. Augustus reigned when Jesus was born. Tiberius reigned after him. Peter and Paul were probably martyred when Nero was Caesar. Jesus sometimes used the word to mean 'the ruling power'. Mark 12:14-17; Luke 2:1; 3:1; Acts 25

Caesarea
A Mediterranean port built by Herod the Great. He named the town after the Roman Emperor Augustus Caesar. Statues of the Emperor stood in a huge temple dedicated to him

A section of the aqueduct built by Herod the Great to carry water to Caesarea.

and to Rome. Traders on their way from Tyre to Egypt passed through Caesarea. So it was a centre of inland as well as sea-trade.

Caesarea was the home town of Philip the evangelist. It was also the home of Cornelius, the Roman centurion who sent for Peter, asking him to explain God's message. It was here that Peter learned that 'the Good News of peace through Jesus Christ' was for non-Jews as well as Jews.

Paul several times used the port on his travels. The Roman governors lived at Caesarea, rather than at Jerusalem, so it was here that Paul was taken for trial before Felix after his arrest. He spent two further years in prison here. From Caesarea he sailed for Rome after his appeal to Caesar.
Acts 8:40; 21:8; 10; 11; 9:30; 18:22; 23:33–26:32

Caesarea Philippi

A town at the foot of Mt Hermon and close to the main source of the River Jordan. Herod the Great built a marble temple here to Augustus Caesar. And one of his sons, Philip, changed the town's name from Paneas to Caesarea. It was known as Philip's Caesarea to distinguish it from the port.

Jesus had taken his disciples to this part of the country when he asked them, 'Who do you say I am?' The answer came from Peter: 'You are the Messiah, the Son of the living God.'
Matthew 16:13-16

Caiaphas

High Priest in Jerusalem AD 18-36. At the trial of Jesus he and his father-in-law, Annas, found Jesus guilty of blasphemy and sent him to Pilate for sentence. Caiaphas was the high priest mentioned in Acts, who persecuted the first Christians.
Matthew 26:3, 57ff.; Luke 3:2; John 18:13ff.; Acts 5:17ff.

Cain

Eldest son of Adam and Eve. He worked as a farmer. His brother Abel was a shepherd. Because God was pleased with Abel's offering of a lamb, but not with Cain's offering from his harvest, Cain was furious. In a fit of jealous anger he killed Abel, and as punishment lived the rest of his life as a nomad.
Genesis 4; 1 John 3:12

Calah

A very ancient city of Mesopotamia on the River Tigris, later a leading city of the Assyrian Empire. Excavations at the site, now Nimrud in Iraq, have unearthed inscriptions and ivory-carvings which throw light on the times of the kings of Israel.
Genesis 10:11-12

Caleb

A spy sent by Moses to find out all he could about Canaan and the people who lived there. Of the twelve spies who reported on what they had seen, only Caleb and Joshua believed God would make it possible to conquer the land. Because of their confidence in God, Caleb and Joshua were allowed to settle in Canaan–all the other Israelites born in Egypt died in the desert.
Numbers 13-14; Joshua 14:6ff.

Call

The God of the Bible is a God who calls people and speaks directly to them.

In the Old Testament the story of the nation of Israel begins with the call of Abraham, and shows how the Israelites were God's people, not because they had earned the right to be his children, but because God himself decided to 'call' them.

It is the same in the New Testament. Jesus called people to follow him, to respond to his teaching about his new kingdom, and the early church did the same. Christians are 'called' to salvation, to eternal life, to a life of endurance, to a life of peace, to go on being changed by the Holy Spirit.

In both Old and New Testaments the personal nature of God's call to his people is often emphasized. God calls men and women to specific tasks: Abraham, Moses, Samuel, David, Isaiah, Jeremiah, Ezekiel and many others. In the New Testament Paul was 'called to be an apostle', and to travel abroad to preach the gospel.

See also *Election, Grace.*
Genesis 12:1; Hosea 11:1; Matthew 11:28-30; Mark 1:20; 2:14; Acts 2:39; 2 Thessalonians 2:13-14; 1 Timothy 6:12; 1 Peter 2:21; 1 Corinthians 7:15; 1 Thessalonians 4:7; Exodus 3; 1 Samuel 3; 16; Isaiah 6; Jeremiah 1:4-10; Ezekiel 1–3; Romans 1:1; Acts 9; 13:1

Camel

In the Old Testament, usually the one-humped Arabian camel, invaluable to desert nomads. It can live on poor food and go for several days without drinking. In ordinary use it can carry a load of about 400 lbs/180 kgs, as well as its rider. Camels are mentioned in the stories of Abraham, Jacob and Job. The Israelites were not allowed to eat camel-meat.
Genesis 12:16; 30:43; Job 1:3

One-humped Arabian camels.

Cana

The village in Galilee where Jesus turned the water into wine at a wedding. During another visit to Cana, Jesus healed the son of an official from Capernaum. Nathanael, one of Jesus' twelve disciples, came from Cana.
John 2:1-12; 4:46-53

Canaan

Son of Ham. Because of his disrespect, Noah, his grandfather, put a curse on Canaan and his descendants (the Canaanites).
Genesis 9:18-27

Canaanite religion

At Mount Sinai God had commanded Israel to have no other gods but him. The Israelites, when they invaded Canaan, must therefore avoid all contact with Canaanite religion. But even before the Israelites invaded Canaan they had begun to worship Baal, the Canaanite god. When they settled in the Promised Land, Baal became a serious rival to Israel's own God.

Baal was the Canaanite god of weather and fertility.

The Book of Judges describes the troubles this caused, and how men like Gideon opposed Baal-worship. Although little is said about it in the time of King David and King Solomon, later, when Ahab became king of the northern kingdom of Israel, Baal almost ousted the God of Israel. This was the work of Ahab's queen, Jezebel, who came from the Canaanite city of Sidon and brought many priests of Baal with her.
Exodus 20:3; 23:23,24; 1 Kings 16:29 and the chapters that follow

Canaanite gods Canaanite gods and goddesses were the powers of nature personified. Baal, which means 'lord', was the title of Hadad, the weather-god (his name probably has the sound of thunder). He controlled the rains, mist, and dew, and so held the key to the good harvests which were essential if the Canaanites were to survive.

Baal's wife was Astarte, also known as Anat, goddess of love and war. His father was El, the chief of the gods, but at the time of the Israelite conquest he had become a shadowy figure. El's wife was Asherah, mother goddess and goddess of the sea. Both Asherah and Astarte were often simply called 'Mistress' (Baalat).

Other leading deities were Shamash, the sun; Reshef, lord of war and of the underworld; Dagon, the corn; and many lesser ones who made up the families and courts of each senior god. This general picture varied from place to place, as each town had its own patron or favourite deity, often called 'Lord' or 'Mistress' of such-and-such a place.

Stories of the gods Stories of these gods and goddesses are known from Canaanite (Ugaritic) and foreign sources. They were brutal and bloodthirsty, delighting in battle with each other, and in uncontrolled sexual relationships. They interfered in human affairs simply to satisfy their whims, regardless of the suffering caused. At the same time, they could be kind and generous. They were no more than reflections of their worshippers, dressed up as gods.

Naturally these stories had their effect on the worship of the Canaanites. Religious festivities became a degraded celebration of the animal side of human nature. Even Greek and Roman writers were shocked by the things the Canaanites did in the name of religion. So it is hardly surprising that the Bible totally condemns their wickedness.
Deuteronomy 18:9; 1 Kings 14:22-24; Hosea 4:12-14

Temples and priests The important gods had richly endowed temples in the leading cities, with priests, choirs, and temple servants. On holy days the kings would go in procession to offer sacrifices. Some of these were burnt entirely; some were shared between the god and his worshippers. On occasions of great celebration the ordinary people probably joined the processions and watched the ceremonies from a distance. But the temple buildings were not large, and only the privileged could go into them.

It was a matter of pride for a king to make the temple as grand as he could, covering the statues of the gods and the walls of the shrine with precious metal, and supplying golden dishes for the god's food. As well as a statue of the god, or of an animal that was his emblem (Baal was represented by a bull, Asherah by a lion), there was also an altar for the sacrifices, an altar for incense, and perhaps a number of stone pillars inside the temple. The pillars were thought to be the homes of gods or spirits. There were also stone pillars, altars, and a wooden pole or tree trunk in simpler open-air shrines ('high places'), where the ordinary people could easily go to make a sacrifice, or to pray. The pillars sometimes stood for Baal, and the post for Asherah (see Deuteronomy 12:3).

When a sacrifice was offered, the priest often examined the entrails of the animal to forecast the fortune of the worshipper (see *Assyrian and Babylonian Religion*). Other ways of telling the future were by looking at the stars, by making contact with the dead, and by prophetic trances. The priests were also in demand to heal the sick by prayers and incantations.

Sacrifices The sacrifices offered to the gods were normally animals and foodstuffs. The fact that Israel was commanded to avoid human sacrifice, and later information from Greek and Roman writings, shows that this was practised, but it is not clear how common it was. Probably it was a rite used in extreme circumstances, when only the greatest sacrifice was thought adequate to persuade the god to act favourably. The god Molech, who is named in connection with this sacrifice, seems to have been a god of the underworld.

The Canaanite and Hebrew languages share several words for sacrifices, priests, and other religious matters. There are some other expressions that are similar, too. There was obviously a common stock of words; but the ideas indicated by them differed from place to place and from faith to faith.
Leviticus 18:21; Deuteronomy 12:31; 2 Kings 3:27

Israelite and Canaanite religion The religion of the Canaanites was totally different from Israelite religion. No evidence for a series of rules of conduct like the Ten Commandments has been found among the Canaanites. There is no known mention of love for any god and there seems to have been little joy and happiness in Canaanite worship. On the other hand, our information is limited, and it should be noted that kings were expected to care for the poor, the widow and the orphan.

It was a strong temptation for the invading Israelites to respect the gods already in the land, and supposedly responsible for its fertility. As well as this, worship of the Canaanite gods was much less demanding than the strict Israelite laws and rituals. Many of God's people gave in to the temptation. The result was the gradual slide towards disaster recounted in the books of Kings. The God of Israel demanded total loyalty.

Canaanites

About 1300 BC 'Canaan' was an Egyptian province covering Lebanon, Syria and what later became the land of Israel. The name may have belonged at first to the coastal plain, then have been extended to include the people of the forested hills–the Amorites (see Numbers 13:29; 35:10; Joshua 5:1). Besides Canaanites and Amorites, there were other groups living in the land. Deuteronomy 7:1 lists five others. So the term 'Canaanites' came to include a mixture of peoples.

Trade Those living on the coast were traders. In fact, trade was so much a part of Canaanite life that the word Canaanite came to mean 'merchant' in Hebrew (it is used that way, for instance, in Proverbs 31:24). The major ports were Tyre, Sidon, Beirut and Byblos, in the tongue of Canaan that stretched northwards (the coast of modern Lebanon). From them cedarwood, jars of oil and wine and other goods were exported to Egypt, Crete, and Greece. In return came Egyptian luxuries and writing paper, Greek pottery, and metal ores. Beyond the boundary of Canaan, but sharing many Canaanite characteristics, was the great city of Ugarit (near modern Latakiya). This city too, was a wealthy commercial centre.

The position of Canaan as a bridge between Asia and Egypt, as well as her trading activities, laid the people open to cultural influences of all sorts. Palaces and temples might be built in Egyptian style for a resident governor or garrison in one city. Syrian styles might be followed in another. Scarabs and other Egyptian jewellery were fashionable–alongside Babylonian cylinder seals and Hittite goldwork from Turkey. These influences are seen most plainly in the way the Canaanites used both Egyptian ('hieroglyphic') and Babylonian ('cuneiform') writing.

The alphabet Canaan's great legacy to the world is almost certainly the alphabet, invented here between 2000 and 1600 BC. Egyptian influence led to paper (papyrus) becoming the normal writing material. Because this has not survived the centuries in Canaan, examples of the infant alphabet are very rare. They are limited to more durable items–names scratched on cups, for instance.

Cities and rulers Canaanite cities were surrounded by defensive walls of earth and stone to keep out raiders and wild animals. Inside, the houses were crowded together, as they are in the old cities of the Near East today. The ordinary people worked for themselves on small patches of land, or at various crafts, or were employed by the king, landowners, and merchants. Beyond the city lay scattered villages of farmers and herdsmen.

The rulers of the cities were constantly quarelling and fighting with each other. And some were liable to attack by bands of brigands and outlaws who hid in the forests. The Amarna Letters, found in Egypt, describe this state of affairs in about 1360 BC. And the Bible books of Joshua and Judges show that it was much the same a century or two lat-

A Canaanite ruler celebrates a victory. This scene is carved on an ivory found at Megiddo, dating from between 1350 and 1150 BC.

er. This made the conquest easier for the Israelites. A united Canaan would have been much more difficult (see the lists of kings in Joshua 10 and 12).

Canaanites and Israelites The language of the Canaanites was closely related to Hebrew, perhaps even the same. The life of the Canaanite farmers was not very different from the life of the Israelites in Egypt before they became slaves. So the Israelites were able to settle easily into their Promised Land. It was tempting to fall in with other Canaanite ways, too. But the Canaanite religion was a far cry from the love of God and obedience to his clear, moral laws. So the Israelites were forbidden to mix and marry with these peoples.

Capernaum
An important town on the north-west shore of Lake Galilee at the time of Jesus. It was Jesus' base while he was teaching in Galilee. Levi (Matthew) the tax-collector lived at Capernaum. So too did a Roman army officer whose servant Jesus healed. There may have been an army post here. Many of Jesus' miracles took place at Capernaum, including the healing of Peter's mother-in-law. Jesus also taught in the local synagogue. But despite all this, the people of the town did not believe God's message, and Jesus had to warn them of coming judgement.
Mark 1:21-34; 2:1-17;
Luke 7:1-10; 10:13-16, etc.

Cappadocia
A Roman province in the east of Asia Minor (Turkey). There were Jews from Cappadocia among those who heard Peter in Jerusalem on the Day of Pentecost. Later the Christians in Cappadocia were among those to whom Peter sent his first letter.
Acts 2:9; 1 Peter 1:1

Carchemish
An important Hittite city from early times, on the River Euphrates. The ruins now lie on the border between Turkey and Syria. When the Egyptian Pharaoh (king) Neco went to attack Carchemish, Josiah, the king of Judah, made a needless attempt to oppose him, and was defeated and killed in the plain of Megiddo. In 605 BC Neco himself was defeated at Carchemish by Nebuchadnezzar, king of Babylon.
2 Chronicles 35:20; Isaiah 10:9; Jeremiah 46:2

Caria
A small state in south-west Turkey which emerged after the fall of the Hittite Empire. The Indo-European Carians remain virtually unknown. We are not yet able to read their alphabet. They served as mercenary soldiers in Egypt, where their inscribed gravestones have been discovered, and in Judah.
2 Kings 11:4, 19

Carmel
A mountain range which juts into the Mediterranean Sea close to the modern port of Haifa. The ancient city of Megiddo guarded one of the main passes through the hills some miles inland. It was on Mt Carmel (1,740ft/535m at the highest point) that Elijah, God's prophet, challenged the prophets of Baal to a contest. Elisha, who followed Elijah as prophet, also seems to have made a base there.
1 Kings 18:19-46; 2 Kings 2:25; 4:25

Cattle
Long before Abraham came to Canaan, herds of cattle were kept to provide milk and meat, and leather from skins. The ox pulled the farmer's plough and his threshing-sledge, and was harnessed to wagons and carts. Cattle were killed in the tabernacle and temple sacrifices. A man's wealth was reckoned by the numbers of cattle and sheep he owned. Bashan, to the east of the Jordan, was famous for its cattle.
Genesis 1:24; 13:2; Leviticus 1:2

Cedar
The cedar of Lebanon.

The beautiful, giant cedar of Lebanon, which once grew in great forests. Although the cedar is still the national symbol of Lebanon only a few of these trees remain, high in the mountains. In Solomon's day King Hiram of Tyre exported vast quantities of cedar. The wood is a warm red colour, and long-lasting. It could be carved and decorated, and was used to panel Solomon's temple and palace.
1 Kings 6:15–7:12

Cenchreae
The eastern port of Corinth in southern Greece, from which Paul sailed to Ephesus.
Acts 18:8; Romans 16:1

Cephas
See *Peter.*

Cereals
Barley, wheat, millet and spelt were a major part of the normal diet in ancient Israel. Wheat made the best flour and bread; it was used to make the bread the priests offered to God. Barley, which ripens before wheat and is harvested in early summer, was the food of the poorer peasants. When Egypt's barley crop was ruined by the plague of hailstorms, the wheat, which came up later, was saved. Spelt is a poor kind of wheat; and millet, which is rather like rye, makes the worst bread of all. It is mentioned in Ezekiel as food fit for a time of famine.
Exodus 9:31-32; Ezekiel 4:9

Chaldea
South Babylonia; Abraham's family home. See *Aramaeans.*

Chebar
A canal running from the River Euphrates in Babylonia (S. Iraq). It was by the Chebar that the prophet Ezekiel, in exile with the Jews in Babylonia, saw some of his great visions of God.
Ezekiel 1; 3; 10; 43

Chedorlaomer
A king of Elam.
Genesis 14

Cherith
A desert stream east of the Jordan. Here God provided food and water for Elijah during years of drought and famine, until the stream itself dried up.
1 Kings 17:3-7

Children
See *Family Life.*

Chinnereth
The Old Testament name for Lake Galilee, from a place on its western shore. The name is used in descriptions of the boundaries of lands belonging to the tribes of Israel, and of nearby kingdoms. See *Galilee.*
Numbers 34:11; Deuteronomy 3:17; Joshua 11:2, etc; 1 Kings 15:20

Chorazin
A town where Jesus taught, near Capernaum, on a hill above Lake Galilee. Jesus was deeply troubled that these places which heard his teaching did not show any change of heart and life as a result. The site of Chorazin is now a deserted ruin.
Matthew 11:21; Luke 10:13

Chronicles
At first glimpse, the books of Chronicles seem to retell 2 Samuel and Kings in a duller way. The writer was in fact repeating the account for readers who knew the earlier books. He had two main reasons for writing his own history of the kings of Israel:

He wanted to show that, in spite of the disasters, God was keeping his promise to look after his people. The writer pointed to the nation's success under David and Solomon, and to the good reigns of kings Jehoshaphat, Hezekiah and Josiah.

He wanted to describe how the temple worship in Jerusalem began, to set out the duties of the priests and Levites, and to show that David was the true founder of the temple (although Solomon had actually built it).

The author, the 'Chronicler', was probably writing specially for the Israelites who had returned from exile to rebuild Jerusalem. They needed to understand their past. He underlined the fact that the nation's success depended on its loyalty to God.

1 Chronicles begins with a section of family trees, from Adam to King Saul (chapters 1–9). The remainder of the book is taken up with the reign of King David, and his preparations to build the temple (chapters 10–29).

2 Chronicles opens with the reign of King Solomon and the building of the temple (chapters 1–9). After

recounting the revolt of the northern tribes under Jeroboam, chapters 11–36 deal with the history of the southern kings of Judah up to the destruction of Jerusalem in 587 BC.

Church
The church is the community of those who believe in Jesus. In the New Testament the word always refers to people, never, as it often does today, to a building. In fact for several generations Christians had no purpose-built meeting-places.

Jesus promised Peter that he would establish the church, and it was Peter's sermon on the Day of Pentecost that led to the first 3,000 people being baptized and joining the Christian group. In the Old Testament God had chosen the Israelites to be his special people. The New Testament states that all those who believe in Jesus–whatever their race–are now God's chosen people, his 'church'. They are being prepared for the day when he returns–the great 'wedding-day' of Jesus and his people.

In the New Testament, the word for church refers both to a local group of Christians and to all Christians throughout the world. Paul teaches that Jesus Christ is head of the church, and that no Christian stands alone but is part of the whole: 'Though we are many, we are one body in union with Christ, and we are all joined to each other as different parts of one body.'

In New Testament times there was no organization of the local church comparable with what we know today. Some churches had leaders, sometimes called 'elders' or 'bishops' who taught and looked after the members. But many others had no 'official' leaders, and special gifts, such as preaching or healing or caring for others, were exercised by different members. There must have been great variety in the gatherings of these churches, as different people took part.
Matthew 16:18; Acts 2; 13:1; 1 Corinthians 12:12-28; Romans 12:5; Colossians 1:18; Ephesians 4:11-16; 1 Corinthians 12:1-11; Acts 2:42-47; 4:23-25; 1 Corinthians 11:13-34; 1 Timothy 2-3; Titus 1:5-9; Revelation 19:5-9

Cilicia
A region in south Asia Minor (modern Turkey) which became a province of the Roman Empire in 103 BC. Tarsus, where Paul was born, was the chief town of Cilicia. Behind it, running north-east, lay the wild Taurus mountains, cut through by an impressive pass known as the Cilician Gates.
Acts 21:39; 22:3; 23:34

Cinnamon
Oil distilled from the bark of the cinnamon tree, and used to flavour food and wine.
Song of Solomon 4:14; 8:2

Flowers of the cinnamon tree

Circumcision
Circumcision is a minor operation to cut away the loose skin covering the end of the penis. It is widely practised by primitive peoples, and was carried out on every Israelite baby boy on the eighth day after his birth.

When God promised Abraham that he would be the founder of a great nation, the nation of Israel, he commanded that all his male descendants should be circumcised. This was to be the physical sign that they belonged to the people of God.

As time went on, the sign came to be more important than what it represented, and the prophets often had to remind the people that the outward sign on its own was not enough. It should be matched by love of other people and obedience to God.

The New Testament makes a similar point. 'True circumcision', or membership of the people of God, is really a matter of what we believe and how we behave. Therefore non-Jews (Gentiles) who become Christians do not need to be physically circumcised. Christians are sometimes called the true circumcision, for they have come into a right relationship with God and are now the heirs to the promises of God alongside the believing people of Old Testament times.
Genesis 17; Luke 2:21; Jeremiah 9:25-26; Romans 2:25-29; Galatians 5:2-6; Philippians 3:2-3; Colossians 2:11-15.

Cities
See *Towns.*

Claudius
The fourth Roman emperor. Claudius reigned AD 41-54. During this time the famine predicted by the Christian prophet Agabus took place. Towards the end of his reign Claudius forced all Jews to leave Rome.
Acts 11:28; 18:2

The Emperor Claudius.

Claudius Lysias
A commander of the Roman garrison at Jerusalem who rescued Paul when an angry crowd of Jews was about to kill him. Claudius Lysias arrested Paul and allowed the Jewish council (the Sanhedrin) to question him, but the session ended in chaos. When he heard about a plot to murder Paul, Claudius Lysias sent him to Caesarea for trial by Felix, the Roman governor.
Acts 21:31–23:30

Cleopas
On the day Jesus rose from the dead Cleopas and a friend were walking from Jerusalem to Emmaus. They had thought Jesus was the Messiah and were puzzled about his death and the report that he was alive again. A man joined them. As he explained the Old Testament passages about the Messiah it was as if 'a fire burned within them'. At Emmaus, Cleopas and his friend invited the stranger to join them for a meal. As he asked God's blessing on the food and broke bread they realized it was Jesus. They went to Jerusalem at once to share the news with the other disciples.
Luke 24:13-53

Clothes-making
The main materials used for making clothes were linen (from flax), sheep's wool, goats' hair and animal skins. Cotton was not used in Israel until they began to import it, probably after the exile. The Israelites loved to decorate their clothes with brightly coloured fringes, borders, and tassels. Gold thread was used to embroider very special clothes–for example, for the high priest (Exodus 39:3).

Linen In Israel flax grew only on the southern coastal plain, near Jericho, and in Galilee, though in New Testament times the amount grown in Galilee was greatly increased. The Egyptians grew a great deal of flax and, by soaking the flax in running water, were able to produce a very soft kind of linen. The Bible calls this 'fine linen'. It was a 'fine linen robe' that Pharaoh gave to Joseph when he appointed him governor (Genesis 41:42). Linen was used for making clothes and ships' sails. Rahab, in Jericho (Joshua 2:6), hid the spies beneath flax spread out on her roof.

After the flax was cut and dried, the seeds were removed. It was then soaked and dried again in an oven. The fibres were separated and then it was ready for spinning and weaving. Linen was not usually dyed, though occasionally blue threads were woven in. (The blue linen robe which the high priest wore was very special–Exodus 28:31.) So, when the Bible talks about coloured clothes, it usually means woollen ones.

Wool After being dipped, the sheep were shorn in the spring. The new wool was washed, or sent to the fuller to be cleaned of natural oils. He would do this by treading out the wool on a rock in water. The wool was then spread out to be dried and bleached in the sun. We read of the 'fuller's field' in 2 Kings 18:17, beside a water supply and–as it often was–outside the city because of the smell. The fuller also worked on the newly woven cloth to shrink it, and sometimes he was responsible for dyeing the wool.

Dyeing In Genesis 30:32 Laban's flock included black and white, striped and spotted sheep! This is a reminder that wool can have many natural colours. So the basic dyes will produce a variety of shades. The colours the Bible refers to most often are blue, scarlet, and purple. These may have been the basic dyes. Purple clothes were a sign of royalty and wealth. A poor quality purple may have been produced by dyeing, first with blue, then with red. The best purple came from Tyre and was very expensive. It was made from molluscs (sea snails) found on the east Mediterranean coast. The industry was firmly in the hands of the Phoenicians, and the Israelites probably had to import all their purple clothes.

Certain places in Israel–where there was a good water supply and good grazing for sheep–became centres for dyeing. Among these were Gezer, Bethshemesh, Bethzur and Debir. At Debir excavations have shown that about thirty homes had rooms specially designed for dyeing. Each contained two stone vats with small openings on top. Potash and slaked lime were probably put into the vat and dye added later, with more dye in the second vat. The wool was given two baths. The potash and lime fixed the dye, and the wool was laid out to dry. It was then ready for spinning and weaving. Almost every home at Debir also had a loom.

Spinning and weaving After being combed, the wool was spun into yarn. Spinning was usually the women's work. It was probably done on a simple hand spindle, although only the stone, clay and bone whorls of these have been found. Two main types of loom were used in Israel: a vertical loom and a horizontal loom.

A woman using her right hand to twist combed wool into yarn which is then wound onto the shaft of her spindle.

The weaver stood in front of the vertical loom, with the down-ward threads (warps) attached to a beam across the top (Goliath's spear is said to have been as thick as a weaver's beam–1 Samuel 17:7) and held down with weights. As the weaver worked, the cross-wise threads were beaten upwards. Five or six warps could be worked on at a time, which made it possible to produce patterns. Because the weaver could move about, he was able to make wide pieces of material. Later a rotating beam was made for the bottom of the loom. The web was begun at the bottom and the finished cloth rolled up. This made it possible to make quite long lengths of cloth.

The horizontal loom was made of two beams, held in place by four pegs in the ground, and the weaver sat in front. The loom could be no wider than the reach of the weaver's arms, although the Egyptians seem to have had a system of two people working this loom. Both wool and linen were woven on this type of loom, and sometimes also the coarser goats' or camels' hair for thick shepherds' cloaks and for tents.

When the Bible talks about embroidered cloth (see Judges 5:30; Ezekiel 26:16) it may refer to different cloths sewn together, or woven patterns, although the Israelites did have embroidery and tapestry.

Shaping clothes There were two main ways of shaping a garment. If the loom was wide enough, the whole garment could be made in one piece (Jesus had a seamless robe–John 19:23). The weaver started at the sleeve edge and worked across to the other sleeve edge, leaving a hole for the neck.

Sleeves could be as long or short as the person wanted, and the striped pattern was easy to make. When cut off, the free warps were twisted into cords which strengthened the sides. Sometimes they were left as tassels at the bottom corners.

If the loom was narrow, the garment was made in three pieces; the main bodice and sleeves; the front skirt; and the back skirt. The neck opening was given a woven binding to strengthen it.

Sometimes circular garments were made. The weaver began in the middle and the web was broadened a warp or two at a time.

See also *Dress.*

Colossae

A town in the Lycus Valley, in the Roman province of Asia (now south-west Turkey). It stood just a few miles from Laodicea, on the main road east from Ephesus. The Christian message probably reached Colossae when Paul was staying at Ephesus, though he himself never went there. Paul wrote a letter (Colossians) to the church there.
Colossians 1:2

Colossians

Paul wrote his letter to the Christians at Colossae from prison–probably in Rome about AD 61. Although he had not begun the church in Colossae (in western Turkey) Paul had a great interest in it. Its founder was one of his own converts, Epaphras, and in Rome he had met a runaway slave from the city (see *Philemon*). He heard that false teachers were at work there. They claimed that to know God, people had to worship other spiritual powers–and observe rites and regulations. They were introducing ideas from other philosophies and religions.

Paul clearly sets out the true Christian message (1:1–2:19). Only Jesus–and Jesus alone–can save a person and give new life. Through Jesus Christ, God created the world.

Paul then goes on to show what this new life means in practical terms (2:20–4:6). It affects everything we do and say; feelings and relationships–in the home, at work, and in the church.

He closes with personal news (4:7-18).

Commandments

See *Law.*

Communion

See *Lord's Supper.*

Cooking

Food was normally cooked by boiling, in a pot over a fire. Some foods were poached in oil. And bread, of course, was baked. There were several methods of baking bread. The simplest was to scoop out a hole in the ground, make a fire in it, then remove the ash and stick the flat 'pancakes' of dough on the sides of the hole. Sometimes stones were put into the fire, and when the dough was ready for baking, the hot stones were taken out and the dough placed on them to cook. Or a large shallow earthenware bowl was placed upside down over the fire, and the dough placed on that.

Wealthier homes had a pottery oven. This consisted of a beehive-shaped funnel. The fire was lit in the bottom of the funnel, and the bread was stuck on the inside towards the top. Not until Roman times was a divided oven invented, with the fire separate from the cooking area. None of these methods of baking was very hygienic.

Many vegetables (such as the cucumber), were eaten raw. Lentils and beans were boiled in water or oil. Corn porridge was made with water, salt and butter.

Corinth

An old Greek city destroyed by the Romans in 146 BC and rebuilt by them a hundred years later. Corinth stood on the narrow neck of land connecting mainland Greece with the southern peninsula, between the Aegean and Adriatic seas. It was a good position for trade.

The town attracted people of many nationalities. It was dominated by the 'Acro-corinth', the steep rock on which the acropolis and a temple to Aphrodite (goddess of love) was built. Temple prostitutes and a large 'floating' population helped to give Corinth a very bad name for all kinds of immoral behaviour.

Paul stayed in Corinth for eighteen months, on his second missionary journey. During that time he founded a church to which he later wrote at least two letters now in the New Testament (1 and 2 Corinthians).
Acts 18

Corinthians

1 Corinthians This is a letter from Paul to the Christians at Corinth. Corinth was a Greek city teeming with people of many different nationalities. It was well known for its trade, culture, its many religions–and its low moral standards.

The church there had been started by Paul during his eighteen-month stay in the city on his second missionary tour. Now he had received bad reports about the church. When some of the members came from Corinth to ask for advice, he wrote this important letter. He tried to deal with the main problems in the church: division (chapters 1–4), and problems of morals and family life (chapters 5–7). There were even reports of a case of incest and Christians taking one another to court.

Paul tackled the problem of conscience which Christians were facing over food (chapters 8–10). Most of the meat sold in the shops had been offered to idols. Was it wrong to eat it?

Chapters 11–14 lay down principles for orderly worship in the church, especially at the Lord's Supper, and discuss the special gifts God gives to his people. The letter gives a clear–not always impressive–picture of the way in which early Christians met and behaved.

Paul also explains the meaning of the resurrection of Jesus, and of all who die trusting him (chapter 15).

In the last chapter he tells the Corinthian church about a collection he is making for needy Christians in Judea. He ends with personal greetings.

Chapter 13, in praise of love–God's best gift to his people–is one of the most famous passages Paul wrote.

2 Corinthians Paul wrote his second letter to Corinth a year or so after the first (about AD 56) when relations between him and the church there were at crisis point. During that year, some of the Corinthian Christians had strongly attacked him. And he had apparently paid a quick visit to Corinth. The letter shows how much he longed to be at one with the church in Corinth.

In chapters 1–7 Paul begins with his relations with the church at Corinth. He explains his previous severe words, and how grateful he was for their change of heart. He looks forward to a third, happier visit.

Paul appeals for a generous response to the needs of the Judean Christians (chapters 8–9).

The last chapters (10–13) are taken up with his defence of his claim to be an apostle. Several Christians at Corinth had questioned his right to the title.

2 Corinthians, with its range of moods, sometimes stormy, sometimes joyful, is one of the most personal of Paul's letters. His loving concern for the church, his suffering and his unshakable faith shine through it all.

Cornelius

A Roman army captain (centurion) stationed at Caesarea. He worshipped God and gave generously to poor people. In a dream, an angel told Cornelius to send for Peter, who was at Joppa (see *Peter*). At Cornelius' house Peter found a crowd of the soldier's friends and relatives eagerly waiting to hear him. They believed and were baptized: the first group of non-Jewish converts to Christianity.
Acts 10

Covenant

The basic meaning of 'covenant' in the Bible is summed up in the words of Jeremiah 31:33: 'I will be their God, and they will be my people.' God enters into a special relationship with men and women. He commits himself to protect his people, and in return he expects obedience from them. Most covenants mentioned in the Bible are between God and man, but there are also 'man-to-man' covenants in the Old Testament.

The Bible itself is arranged into two major 'covenants', the Old and the New. They are more often called the Old and New 'Testaments' (which means the same thing). The old covenant is the one made with Moses on Mt Sinai, when the Ten Commandments were given to God's people as the basic rules for living. This covenant forms the basis of Israel's religion. Some archaeological discoveries suggest that the way the covenant is set out may be based on the pattern of treaties made between certain Near Eastern nations at that time.

There are also other covenants in the Old Testament. There is the one made with Noah after the flood, when God promised never again to destroy the earth with a flood. This is God's general covenant with all people.

Then there is the covenant with Abraham, in which God promised his descendants a land of their own, and urged them to share their blessings with the other nations of the earth. This is God's covenant with his special people, renewed in the covenant with Moses on Mt Sinai.

The New Testament writers show that the new covenant between God and men, to which the Old Testament looks forward, rests on the death of Jesus. Jesus himself spoke of this at the last supper: 'This cup is God's new covenant, sealed with my blood.' The letter to the Hebrews compares the old and new covenants. The new covenant offers something the old covenant could never secure–release from the power of sin; the freedom to obey God.

See also *Election*.
Exodus 19:3-6; 20:1-17; Genesis 9:1-17; 12:1-3; 15:7-21; Jeremiah 31:31-34; 1 Corinthians 11:25; Hebrews 8:13; 10:4

Crafts and trades

In Old Testament times Israel had few if any craftsmen who made beautiful things for their own sake. Even when it came to making places of worship, they often had to bring in foreign artists to complete the decoration. It was a poor country and skills were limited to making strictly useful objects. However, certain trades were regarded as skilled from an early period. These were the crafts of certain families, who probably handed down 'trade secrets' from father to son.

Special areas became linked with a particular trade, perhaps because necessary materials were ready to hand. So Succoth became known for the casting of metal utensils; Debir for weaving and dyeing. It is likely that some form of trade guilds came into being fairly early, especially in the cities, where the different crafts seem to have had their special quarters. The Bible mentions the carpenters' quarters, the linen workers', the potters', the goldsmiths' and the perfumers' sections.

In New Testament times trade guilds were well known in the Roman Empire. But they had to have a licence from the emperor to make sure they were not simply a cover for undesirable political activities.

Crafts were held in high regard by the Jews at this time. Craftsmen were exempt from the rule that everyone should rise to his feet when a scholar approached. Most of the scribes probably had a trade. The writings of the rabbis mention a nailmaker, a baker, a sandalmaker, a master builder, a tailor. But some trades were despised: among others, tanning, because 'it was dirty'; being a tax collector (publican), because it gave scope for trickery; weaving, because it was women's work. The weavers worked in one of the poorest areas of Jerusalem, close to the Dung Gate.

Leatherwork Bible references to articles made with leather (from sheep- and goatskins) include clothes, belts and footwear. The complete hides of small animals were sewn together to make bottles for wine, water and milk. Tents were originally made of leather covering, but later felt or woven goats'-hair was used, as it is today by the Bedouin. Leather was also used as a writing-material. The Isaiah manuscript of the Dead Sea Scrolls, dating from 150 BC, was written on seventeen sheets of leather, the skins sewn together. The details of how leather was processed and worked are not known, but two or three different trades may have been involved.

There was the job of skinning the animals. Knives have been found which may have been used for this.

Then there was job of tanning. In early times this may simply have been a process of drying the hides in the sun, or perhaps treating them with the juice of certain plants. But tanners were expected to live outside a town because their work was smelly.

Finally there was the work of shaping and sewing the leather. Paul, Aquila and Priscilla are said to have been 'tentmakers', but some think that this word may mean 'leather-workers'.

Genesis 3:21; 2 Kings 1:8; Ezekiel 16:10; Exodus 26:14; Acts 18:3

Gem-cutting The Israelites used semi-precious stones such as agate, jasper, carnelian and rock-crystal. These were cut and polished to make beads, or engraved with designs, and sometimes the owners' names, to serve as seals. The Bible mentions many different stones, although not all can be identified. Engraving stones and setting them in gold for the high priest's breastplate are described in Exodus 28:9-14.

Glass-making The art of making articles of glass never seems to have been common in Israel. Long before the Israelites entered Canaan the Egyptians and Babylonians had discovered how to make an opaque form of glass and to shape it over a core of sand. By New Testament times the Romans were making transparent glass and 'blowing' it into shape. Many of the glass articles which have been found in Israel were clearly imported.

Ivory-carving No list of the crafts in Israel would be complete without a mention of ivory carving, although probably not many craftsmen were involved in it, and those who were may have been mostly foreigners. Ivory was rare. It had to be imported

A carved ivory of a man saluting with one hand and holding a lotus tree with the other; from Nimrud, eighth century BC.

from Africa (or from Syria in the early times). It was a favourite with the kings, but the prophets condemned its use as a symbol of extravagance and idle living.

Solomon probably used ivory carvings and inlay in the temple decorations, but the only detail mentioned in the Old Testament is that he had an ivory throne. King Ahab of Israel built an 'ivory house' in Samaria, his capital. It is at Samaria that the largest Israelite collection of ivory has been found. Excavations have shown that the art flourished among all the Near Eastern nations. Objects found consist mostly of small carvings, inlays and sculptures.
1 Kings 10:22; Ezekiel 27:15; Amos 3:15; 1 Kings 22:39
See also *Building, Clothes-making, Mining, Pottery.*

Crane

Crane.

A regular migrant and winter visitor to Israel. A large grey bird with a wing-span of 8ft/2.5 metres, the crane feeds mostly on seeds and leaves.

Creation

The Bible teaches that everything was made by God. He was the Creator in the very beginning, and his work continues as he maintains, and occasionally intervenes, in his creation. The Bible has nothing to say about which scientific theory of creation is most likely to be true. This is not surprising, since it was never intended to be a book of science. Its purpose is to tell us about God, and his dealings with men and women and the world they live in.

In Genesis 1 we learn that God created the world perfect. He created plants and animals, able to reproduce themselves. And he placed man and woman at the centre of creation to take care of it. According to Genesis 2 the world as God created it was a delightful place in which to live, especially since the man and his wife enjoyed a free and open relationship with God.

The first perfection of creation is now gone, because people chose to disobey God. But the Bible continues to speak of God as Creator. Again and again it reminds us of his greatness, and the smallness of man in comparison. Yet he cares for people and provides for all his creation. So:

'Fear the Lord, all the earth!
Honour him, all peoples of the world!
When he spoke, the world was created;
At his command everything appeared.'

Paul also speaks of a 'new creation'. By Jesus' death and resurrection God made it possible for people to be forgiven and to share in the new life of the new creation. Christians already know something of this new creation and one day they will be fully part of it, when the universe spoilt by sin exists no more and all things are made new.
Genesis 1–3; Job 38–42:6; Psalms 8; 33:6-22; 104; Isaiah 40:21-26; Matthew 6:25-33; Acts 14:15-18; Romans 1:18-23; 8:18-23; Colossians 1:15-20; Hebrews 1:1-3; Revelation 21–22

Creeds and hymns

The New Testament church was a community which believed certain basic truths–'the apostles' teaching', or 'the true teaching', or 'true words'. These beliefs were expressed not only in the New Testament writings, but also in worship, often sung as hymns.

Some of the early Christian creeds were very simple and short. 'Jesus is Lord' was the basic one. These were probably words each new convert spoke. Some creeds contain two or three statements of faith. 'There is one God, and there is one mediator between God and men, the man Christ Jesus'; 'one Lord, one faith, one baptism'.

At times, New Testament writers clearly quote early Christian statements of faith. 1 Timothy 3:16 is a creed in the form of a hymn (like the *Te Deum* in later Christian worship):

'He appeared in human form,
was shown to be right by the Spirit
and was seen by angels.
He was preached among the nations,
was believed in throughout the world,
and was taken up to heaven.

An even more detailed confession of the person and work of Christ was used by Paul in Philippians 2:6-11. The hymn ends with the confession of the new convert: 'all will openly proclaim that Jesus Christ is Lord'. It may have been sung at a baptism service.
Acts 2:42; 1 Timothy 4:6; 2 Timothy 1:13; 1 Corinthians 12:3; 1 Timothy 2:5; Ephesians 4:5

Crete

Crete is known in the Old Testament and other ancient texts as Caphtor. The Minoan civilization flourished there from 2000 BC, merging with the Mycenaean. It fell in the twelfth century BC. The Cretan scripts Linear A and Linear B represent a local form of writing. Linear B was adopted for an early form of Greek. Caphtor was one of the places from which the Philistines came. Later inhabitants probably supplied David's bodyguard of Cherethites. One Cretan poet–Epimenides–had some strong words to say about the Cretans. But some responded to the Christian message.
Jeremiah 47:4; Acts 18:28; Titus 1:12.

Crispus

Chief official of the Jewish synagogue in Corinth. He and his family were converted and baptized by Paul.
Acts 18:8; 1 Corinthians 1:14

Cross

The cross has come to be the universal symbol of the Christian faith, because it reminds us of the most astonishing and important event in the story of Jesus of Nazareth.

It was astonishing because Jesus the Messiah (God's chosen one) was executed like a common criminal. The Jews found it impossible to accept that such a person could really be the Son of God–and many ordinary people just could not understand how the world could be saved by a person who had met such a bizarre end.

Yet to the early Christians the cross had a deep meaning. It was at the heart of all that God had planned for his people. Paul was quite sure that the cross was all-important–so much so that he wrote to the Corinthian Christians: 'While I was with you, I made up my mind to forget everything except Jesus Christ and especially his death on the cross.'

The New Testament makes it clear that Jesus died on the cross, not because of his own wrong-doing (the charges against him were false), but in the place of ordinary sinful men and women. He experienced the separation from God which they deserved, and so made possible forgiveness and new life for all who will trust their lives to Jesus as the one who died for our sins and rose again from death.

In Jesus' death on the cross we see the depths of God's love. As a result of this, men and women can be reconciled both to God and to each other. In the cross God defeated all the powers of evil.

The cross is also a dramatic symbol of the sort of life Christians ought to live. Jesus called people to 'take up their cross' and follow him. He called them to a life of self-sacrifice. They must give up their own claims over their lives, and live in the power of the new life which God gives them. And Paul understood what this meant in his own experience: 'I have been put to death with Christ on his cross, so that it is no longer I who live, but it is Christ who lives in me.'

See also *Atonement, Reconciliation, Redemption.*
1 Corinthians 1:18–2:5; Romans

5:6-11; Ephesians 2:16-18; Colossians 2:14-15; Galatians 2:20; 1 John 4:7-10

Cummin and dill
Cummin seeds were used to spice meat, also in eye medicine. Dill (or anise) seed flavours bread or cakes. The Pharisees gave God a tenth of everything, even their seasoning herbs–mint, cummin and dill–but Jesus said they neglected more important things: honesty, justice and mercy.
Isaiah 28:25-27; Matthew 23:23

The herbs cummin and dill.

Cush (Sudan)
To the south of Egypt lies the Sudan (Old Testament 'Cush', sometimes translated as 'Ethiopia'). Pharaoh Tirhakah came from Cush. But usually Egypt dominated, and Cushite soldiers served in her armies. Ebed-melech, who rescued Jeremiah, was a Sudanese. An independent kingdom existed there in Hellenistic and Roman times, with its capital at Meröe. Queens, entitled Candace, often ruled this state and it was the chancellor of one of these whom Philip met going home from Jerusalem.
2 Kings 19:9; Jeremiah 38:7; Acts 8:27

Cyprus
The Cypriotes had close links with Syria and Israel/Judah through trade ('purple from the island of Cyprus', Ezekiel 27:7). In early times the island was known as Elisha or Alashiya, and was a major source of copper. Flourishing cities with colonies of Myceneans from Greece were destroyed by the Sea Peoples (see *Philistines*) about 1200 BC. One city that revived afterwards was Kition, modern Larnaca (Old Testament 'Kittim'), whose name was sometimes used for the whole island, and even for the opposite coasts. As a distant place, the name was used to stand for Rome in Daniel 11:30.

Cyprus came under the rule of Rome in 58 BC, and was governed by a proconsul from 27 BC. It was a natural stopping-place for ships passing from the eastern Mediterranean coast to Turkey or Rome.

In the New Testament Cyprus features as the home of Barnabas. It was the first place Paul and Barnabas visited when they set out to take the good news of Jesus to the non-Jewish world. Here they met the governor, Sergius Paulus, and his magician friend. Barnabas later returned to Cyprus with Mark.
Acts 4:36; 13:4-12; 15:39; 27:4

Cyrene
A Greek city on the north coast of Africa, in modern Libya. A man from Cyrene, Simon, was forced to carry Jesus' cross. Jews from Cyrene were among those present in Jerusalem on the Day of Pentecost. Other Cyrenians became involved in the earliest mission to non-Jews, at Antioch.
Matthew 27:32; Mark 15:21; Acts 2:10; 6:9; 11:20; 13:1

Cyrus
The Persian king who captured Babylon in 539 BC. Cyrus allowed the Jews exiled in Babylon to return to Jerusalem to rebuild the temple. He sent back with them all the treasures taken from the temple by Nebuchadnezzar and gave them a large sum of money to help with the work. Isaiah declared that Cyrus was chosen by God to be king and to free the Jewish captives. The later stories about Daniel took place in the reign of Cyrus.
Ezra 1:1ff.–6:14; Isaiah 44:28ff.; Daniel 6:28

D

Daily life
In Bible lands there have always been 'nomads'–people who move from place to place–as well as those with settled homes.

Abraham exchanged a settled, civilized city life at Ur in Mesopotamia for a semi-nomadic lifestyle when God called him to leave his home. Like the modern Bedouin, he lived in a goats'-hair tent. The black and brown striped material was woven from goats' hair after shearing time, on a loom pegged out on the ground. Wooden rings were stitched along the edge and in the centre to take nine poles in three rows. The middle row of poles was about 6ft/1.8m high, and the two outer rows a little less.

The tent house was made by propping up a long length of goats'-hair cloth about 6ft/1.8m wide, and living in the area underneath it. The women did the hard work, putting up the tent and securing the poles with guy ropes. The area under the curtain was closed in at the back with a screen made of goats'-hair cloth, or reeds and twigs woven together, and the area was then divided into two 'rooms'. One formed an open porch where visitors could be received, and the remainder was curtained off for the use of the women and for the household stores. The only adult male who could enter this part was the head of the family. Sometimes the ground under the tent was covered with woven matting but more often it was left as bare earth. Tents were pitched in groups for protection. Women very rarely had a tent of their own, unless the family was very rich.

For hundreds of years Abraham's descendants lived in tents: first in Canaan, then in Egypt, then in the desert. When they conquered the Canaanites, they took over the Canaanite cities, patched up the ruins and copied their building style.

House-building The poorer people in Old Testament times lived in very small houses. There was one square room with an outside yard. Houses were built by groups of neighbours, and by skilled builders who went from place to place.

If the house was built on the plain or in a valley, the walls were made of mud brick. Rooms could be added alongside or as another storey as people grew better off, and building skills increased. Mud bricks were quite large–about 21in x 10in x 4in/53cm x 25cm x 10cm–and were made in wooden moulds.

The fathers and grandfathers of the Israelites who settled in Canaan had had plenty of practice at making mud-bricks when they were slaves in Egypt. They began by digging a hole in the ground and filling it with water, chopped straw, palm fibre and bits of shell and charcoal. The workmen then trampled the mixture until they had a soft and pliable mud. Most bricks were laid out to dry in the hot sun. Kilns produced stronger bricks which were used for the foundations. Mud was also used to cement the bricks together and to plaster the finished walls. It is not surprising that in wet weather the houses tended to leak. They were not very strongly built and it was easy for a thief to break in just by digging a hole through the wall.

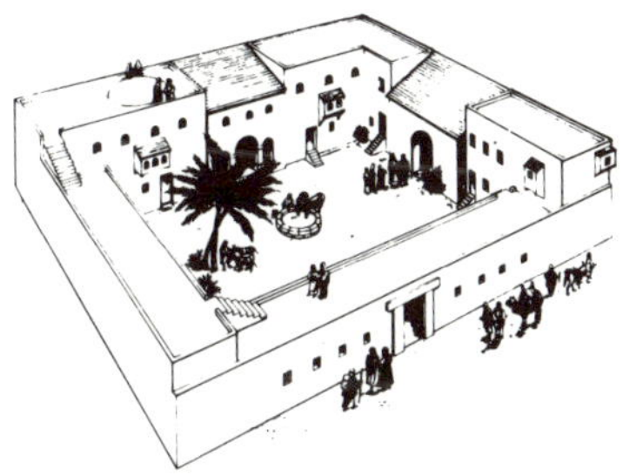

The type of house owned by wealthy Jews in New Testament times.

In the mountains, where limestone and basalt were ready at hand, and on the coast where sandstone was found, roughly squared stone was used for the foundations, with rough stone or brick walls nearly 3ft/91cm thick built on top. These thick walls could be hollowed out and alcoves made for storage. In early days the walls were little more than rubble, but as iron tools became available for shaping stone more easily, the stones were roughly squared.

Windows were few and tiny, set high up in the wall for coolness in summer, warmth in winter. There was no glass. Instead, a lattice shutter was put across the hole to keep intruders out. Thick woollen curtains were used in the cold, wet season, to keep the weather out. Doors at first were made of woven twigs. Then, as skills developed, of wood and metal.

The roof was made by laying beams across the width of the walls, and smaller beams at right angles across them. The kind of wood depended on how rich you were: sycamore for ordinary homes, cypress and cedar for those who could afford it. Layers of brushwood, earth and clay were then added and the whole thing made firm by using a stone roller 2ft/60cm long, which was kept on the roof.

After the rain the roof often sprouted grass and the smaller animals might be sent up to graze! Gutters took the precious, but not very clean, water to a storage cistern, waterproofed with a mortar made from ashes, lime, sand and water. To have your own stored water was something of a status symbol in Old Testament times. But it cannot have led to very good health.

The roof was a very important part of the house. Poor people probably climbed up by ladder. The better off had a flight of steps built into the walls, leading from the yard to the roof-space. The roof was used for drying fruit and grain (Rahab hid the spies under the flax which was drying on her roof–Joshua 2:6), and was a cool place on a hot evening. Sometimes the family made a tent of branches and slept out on the roof.

As building skills improved, permanent upper storeys became more common. The rich woman at Shunem built on a special guest-room for the prophet Elisha (2 Kings 4:10). Sometimes trellis was put on the roof and vines trained over it. If the house was built into a steep hillside, the roof was sometimes used as a threshing-floor. Householders would shout their news from roof to roof ('from the housetops') above the noise from the streets below. The roof-space was so much part of the life of the house that the law insisted it must have a railing round the edge for safety (Deuteronomy 22:8). Tiled and pitched roofs began to be built shortly before New Testament times.

Inside the house the floor area was divided into two, like the nomad's tent. The animals were brought into the lower area of the house near the door during winter. This floor area was of beaten earth. The family lived on a raised platform, farthest away from the door. The space underneath may have been used for storing tools and jars–and even keeping small animals. Cooking things, clothes and bedding were kept on the platform.

Sometimes stone chippings were worked into the earth floor. But it was only under Greek influence, after about 300 BC, that the art of making mosaic floors was developed. Even then this was frowned on for religious reasons, and the only mosaic floors found in Israel during Bible times were in the palace of King Herod the Great at Masada and rich houses in Jerusalem.

Life in the home What was life like for families living in the ordinary small house? During the hot summer, the house was alive with insects. When the weather grew cold, the house was filled with smoke from the fire. There was no real fireplace. The fire smouldered in a hole in the earth floor. If the family was wealthy enough, they warmed themselves around a brazier. But there was no chimney.

When it rained hard and continuously the roof and the walls leaked. The writer of the Old Testament proverb knew just how miserable that was. 'A nagging wife,' he wrote, 'is like water going drip-drip-drip on a rainy day' (Proverbs 27:15). There were no facilities for bathing, and the house of the ordinary person was so dark that a lamp had always to be kept lit. It was placed on a stand, or in a niche in the wall, in the area farthest from the door.

From the time of Solomon, however, a wealthy class began to emerge, and for them life was very different. Rooms were extended around courtyards and gardens which provided shade and cool currents of air in the summer. In winter it was possible to use rooms in a warmer, sunnier position. The whole house was built on a much larger scale, with pillars to support roof beams. Once pillars were used it was possible to have porches and colonnades. The prophet Amos talks about the 'winter houses and summer houses' enjoyed by the rich (Amos 3:15).

In the time between the Old and New Testaments wealthy people even began to add special bathrooms, with tubs set into the floor. (Sergius Orata is said to have invented a centrally heated bathroom, with a hot water supply, in about 70 BC!) By New Testament times rich people in Palestine had houses built Roman-style, with two rectangular courtyards, one behind the other, each surrounded by rooms.

Furniture People in the east, even today, have much less furniture than many in western countries. The style, even for the rich, is cool, simple and uncluttered–with just a few mats for the floor, seating, small tables and some kind of heating for winter.

Throughout Bible times the poor possessed very little by way of furniture and furnishings. The 'bed' was a thin wool-filled mattress, spread out each evening on the raised part of the floor. The whole family slept there, under goats'-hair quilts. In the morning they rolled or piled up the bed and bedding and stacked it away. The furniture which the woman at Shunem provided for Elisha was better than average: a bed, a table, a chair and a lamp (2 Kings 4:10). The table was often simply a straw mat laid out on the raised floor. In some homes, but by no means all, there were stools to sit on.

Every house had stone or clay storage bins in which they kept fodder for the animals as well as food stores for the family. There were special jars for storing flour and olive oil, earthenware pots for carrying and storing water. There were cooking pots, too, and bowls for serving food.

Cooking things One of the most important things in the home was the grinding mill. This was made from two circular stones. The larger, lower stone had a spike which pierced the centre of a smaller one, which was turned round on top of it. Corn was poured through the central hole and as two women turned the top stone with a handle, flour ran out at the edge between the two stones. It was hard work! A fire for cooking was made simply in the earth floor, or sometimes in an earthenware pot. Charcoal, thorns or dried animal dung provided the fuel. A convex baking-sheet, which could be put over the fire, and a cooking-pot which could stand in the fire, made up the remainder of the basic cooking things.

Lamps Because the houses were so dark, one of the most important items in any household was the lamp. Throughout the Old Testament period lamps were simply pottery dishes with a lip at one side. Oil was poured into the dish and a wick laid from it to the lip. Such a lamp might stay alight for two or three hours, then need refilling. By New Testament times potters had learnt how to make lamps in moulds, completely covered over, with a small hole for the oil and a spout for the wick. This was safer and more efficient. The wicks were usually strips of flax or rag. Olive oil or animal fat was commonly used, oil from other seeds and vegetables being introduced by New Testament times. Lamps were small enough for a traveller to carry in his hand. This may have been the picture in the psalmist's mind when he wrote, 'Your word is a lamp to guide me and a light for my path' (Psalm 119:105).

Household goods Brooms for cleaning were made of corn stalks. They were kept with the tools the father needed for his trade. Most of the jars and bowls in everyday use were made by the potter. But in wealthier homes they had things made from metal. By New Testament times glass, moulded on a core, and produced in Egypt, was used. In about 50 BC, the art of glass blowing was developed in Syria. But although this made glass cheaper, it was still beyond the reach of most people. There were no 'ornaments' as such in the ordinary home. People used their artistic skills in making and decorating the things they used every day.

The rich The rich had a good many extra comforts: high beds, tables, chairs and couches. These were often made of fine wood, carved and inlaid with bone or ivory. There were pillows for their beds, and fine wool blankets. Extra clothes and bedding were stored in chests. In New Testament times wealthy people ate their meals Roman-style, reclining on a three-sided couch (*triclinium*) around a square table.

The greatest luxury of all was to be found in the royal palaces, from King Solomon–who built in well-cut stone and lined his walls with cedar–and King Ahab (with a palace at Samaria which boasted beautiful carved ivory inlays and expensive furniture), to Herod the Great. Herod had a summer palace with lovely gardens at Jerusalem, and a winter one at Jericho.

See also *Building*.

Dalmatia

A Roman province on the east coast of the Adriatic Sea, along the coast of modern Yugoslavia. Paul's second letter to Timothy shows him almost alone at the end of his life. His friends have left him for various reasons. Titus has gone to Dalmatia.
2 Timothy 4:10

Damascus

The capital of Syria (see *Aramaeans*). Damascus was already well known in Abraham's day, and is often mentioned in the Old Testament. King David captured the city, but it soon regained its independence. Damascus was the home of Naaman, who came to the prophet Elisha for healing. The prophet later went to Damascus to advise on the king's health.

Isaiah predicted the destruction of Damascus. And after a series of attacks the Assyrians captured the city in 732 BC, carried away its treasures and many of its people, and reduced its power. From 64 BC to AD 33 Damascus was a Roman city.

Paul was on his way to Damascus to persecute the Christians when he met with Jesus himself, and the whole direction of his life was changed. He had to escape from the city later, when the Jews persecuted him.

Genesis 14:15; 15:2; 2 Samuel 8:5; 1 Kings 20:34; 2 Kings 5; 8:7-15; Isaiah 17; Acts 9

Dan

The land belonging to the tribe of Dan, and a town (Laish) in the far north of Israel. Dan was the northernmost city of Israel, and the expression 'from Dan to Beersheba' meant 'from one end of the land to the other'. When the kingdom was divided, Jeroboam I tried to keep the loyalty of the northern tribes by giving them two golden calves to worship: one was at Dan.

Joshua 19: 40-48; 1 Kings 12:25-30

Daniel

Best-known of several Old Testament Daniels is the high- born Jew who was taken captive to Babylon, probably in his teens. At the court of King Nebuchadnezzar Daniel and his three friends, Shadrach, Meshach and Abednego, were trained to be counsellors to the king. Daniel was determined still to obey God. He refused the rich food he was given and instead grew strong on the simple diet allowed by Jewish food-laws. God gave Daniel great wisdom. Twice he was able to tell Nebuchadnezzar the meaning of strange dreams. Daniel later explained to Belshazzar (who held power after Nebuchadnezzar) the writing that appeared on his wall: the kingdom was about to be overthrown. That same night Belshazzar was killed and the Persians captured Babylon. They made Daniel an important official, but the other leaders were jealous of his power and plotted his downfall. Daniel was thrown into the lions' den, but God saved his life. Daniel also recorded a number of dreams in which God told him of his plans for the future.

The Book of Daniel was written at a time when the Jewish people were being oppressed, perhaps during the persecution of Antiochus Epiphanes in 168 BC. Stories and visions included in the book encouraged them. God would destroy the oppressor and restore his people.

Chapters 1–6 record stories about Daniel and some of his friends in exile at the time of the Babylonian and Persian Empires. Because they trusted and obeyed God no matter what the cost, they triumphed over their enemies.

The rest of the book (chapters 7–12) is a series of Daniel's visions. They describe in picture form the rise and fall of empires. The pagan persecutors will fall, and God's people will be victorious.

The impression made by a tiny cylinder seal of Darius, probably Darius I, showing the king hunting lions.

Darius

1. Darius the Mede is named in the Book of Daniel as ruler after Belshazzar. Darius is not otherwise known from contemporary records (which give a far from complete picture). Cyrus may have made Darius ruler of Babylon, or may even have used the name Darius himself.
Daniel 5:31ff.
2. Darius I of Persia (522–486 BC), who encouraged the Jews to finish rebuilding the temple.
Ezra 4:5; Haggai 1:1; Zechariah 1:1
3. Darius II of Persia (423–408 BC), mentioned in the Book of Nehemiah.
Nehemiah 12:22

David

Youngest of the eight sons of Jesse, a farmer at Bethlehem. David was a shepherd. He was looking after the flocks when Samuel the prophet came to Bethlehem, sent by God to anoint one of the sons of Jesse as king in place of Saul. When David was chosen his brothers were jealous.

David's skill in playing the harp took him to Saul's court, to soothe the king in his fits of madness. Later, when he was sent to take food to his brothers in the army, David took up the challenge to fight Goliath, the giant champion of the Philistines. He killed him with a stone from his shepherd's sling. After the battle the women came out to meet Saul. 'Saul has killed thousands, but David tens of thousands,' they sang. From then on Saul became very jealous of David and several times tried to kill him. Jonathan, Saul's son and David's close friend, warned him to escape and he became an outlaw. Saul hunted him without mercy, although David twice spared his life.

Saul and Jonathan were killed in battle against the Philistines, and David was crowned in Judah. But it was two years before all Israel accepted him as king. David was a brave soldier and won many victories. He was very popular with the people and ruled them well. When he had captured Jerusalem from the Jebusites David made it his capital. He brought the Covenant Box (the ark) there and planned to build a temple but God forbade it.

David made love to Bathsheba, wife of Uriah, one of his soldiers. When Bathsheba became pregnant David ordered Uriah to the front line and made sure he was killed. David then married Bathsheba. The prophet Nathan denounced his sin and although the king was genuinely sorry and God forgave him, Bathsheba's child died. Their next son, Solomon, was David's heir.

Later there was trouble between David's sons. Absalom, his favourite son, tried to seize the throne. David was forced to leave Jerusalem, but Absalom was defeated and killed, to David's great distress. When he was old, Adonijah, another son, plotted against him.

David was a great king, a great soldier and a great poet, who wrote many beautiful psalms of praise to God. Although he made mistakes and did wrong, he never failed to repent and ask God to forgive him. The Bible describes him as 'a man after God's own heart'.

1 Samuel 16ff–1 Kings 2;
1 Chronicles 11–29

Dead Sea

See *Salt Sea* and *Arabah*.

Dead Sea scrolls

The most exciting discovery from New Testament times has been the Dead Sea Scrolls. No one had expected that ancient papers would last in Palestine. Yet in 1947, in a cave near the north-west shore of the Dead Sea, a shepherd boy happened to find jars containing old leather rolls. He did not know what they were, and sold them for next to nothing. Eventually archaeologists heard about the find and where it had been made. Between them, shepherds and archaeologists collected pieces of over 400 rolls.

These books belonged to the library of a religious commune at Qumran on the edge of the Dead Sea. Their owners had hidden them in caves when the Roman army advanced against the rebel Jews in AD 68. The dry heat of the region preserved them. They are less valuable than the papyri for understanding the text of the New Testament. But the scrolls, mostly written in Hebrew or Aramaic, bring a mass of new information about Jewish religious life in the New Testament period.

Old Testament books were favourites in the library. Every one of them is there, except Esther. Many copies show that the traditional Hebrew text (only available in copies made about AD 900 before this discovery) was current in the first century AD, and earlier. There are also other Hebrew texts amongst the scrolls, though they are in a minority. These have variations, some of which are reflected in the Greek translation (the Septuagint) and in the New Testament (the quotation of Deuteronomy 32:43 given in Hebrews 1:6 is one of them).

The Qumran community Other books are commentaries on sections of the Old Testament. Commentators explained ancient names of people and places in the light of current affairs. They believed the prophets had spoken about them, not about their own days. From these remarks, and from other writings, we learn of the community's early leader, the Teacher of Righteousness. He disagreed with most Jews about the dates of major festivals and withdrew from Jerusalem to set up the strictly ruled community by the Dead Sea.

Enemies were called the 'Sons of Darkness'; the people of the Dead Sea community considered themselves 'Sons of Light'. They looked forward to a day when God's Messiah would lead them to a great victory over their opponents. Then they would worship as they thought right in the temple.

Their hopes were disappointed. Their Messiah did not come, and the Romans broke up their commune. The men of Qumran and the early church were very different. The owners of the scrolls were thoroughly Jewish. They had no direct connection with early Christianity. Some ideas are shared by both–for example, contrasting good and bad, light and darkness–but these are common Jewish ideas of the time. In some cases the similarities–which have been heavily emphasized in recent books–seem striking because there is no other material from Jewish groups of the same date. A study of the attitude to the Old Testament shown in the Scrolls has given a clearer view of the way Jesus and his followers treated it.

Jesus attacked Jewish leaders for strict obedience to details of the Law without understanding its real meaning. The Scrolls reveal a Jewish sect as strict as these leaders, if not more so. The 'phylacteries' that have been found are an indication of this. In order to obey God's command to remember his laws they actually tied them to their hands and foreheads (see Exodus 13:9, 16). Passages of scripture were written on minute pieces of parchment, bound in leather cases (phylacteries), and strapped on the head and left hand at prayer time. An example from Qumran is $\frac{3}{4}$ x $\frac{1}{2}$ in/ 20 x 13mm. The parchments, unfolded, are about $1\frac{1}{2}$ x $1\frac{1}{4}$in/ 40 x 27mm. On one piece Deuteronomy 5:22–6:9 was written in twenty-six lines. Jesus accused the Pharisees and teachers of the Law of showing off by wearing phylacteries for others to see (Matthew 23:5).

Death

When Paul was facing possible death, he was able to write in his letter to the Philippian Christians: 'What is life? To me, it is Christ. Death then will bring more. I want very much to leave this life and be with Christ.' He knew that for a Christian there is a wonderful life beyond death, made possible by the death and resurrection of Jesus. But the Jewish people had not always believed in life after death.

Jewish beliefs In the early days of the Old Testament, the Israelites believed that when a man died, he went down into a shadowy place under the earth called *sheol*. It was not until much later that people began to ask how a just God could let good people die like this. So they reasoned that *sheol* could not be the end. Surely there would be a resurrection, and a person's final destiny would depend on how he had lived in this life. The prophet Daniel writes: 'Many of those who have already died will live again: some will suffer eternal life, and some will suffer eternal disgrace' (Daniel 12:2). In New Testament times, the Pharisees believed in a resurrection but the Sadducees did not.

Funeral customs The funeral arrangements were much the same as they are today. When someone died, his eyes were closed. The body was washed and wrapped in strips of cloth for a quick burial, because of the hot climate. It was not put in a coffin, but carried on a wooden stretcher (a bier) to the burial-place.

A decorated limestone ossuary in which the bones of the dead were kept. It dates from about the time of Jesus, and was found in the Jerusalem area.

Family and friends made a great show of mourning: weeping, wailing, wearing uncomfortable clothes, walking barefoot, putting ashes on their heads, tearing their clothes and shaving off their beards. Sometimes professional mourners were hired to add to the wailing. Mourning normally lasted for seven days, but longer for an important person (seventy days for Joseph; thirty days for Moses). A time of fasting went with the time of mourning. But there was a funeral feast which often took place at the tomb. In countries outside Israel–particularly Egypt–the body was embalmed. The insides and brain were removed and the space filled with a gummy paste.

Burial The people of Israel often buried their dead in caves. Some caves were large enough for all the members of a family (Genesis 50:13), but if necessary, they could be enlarged to form corridors with shelves cut out of the rock on which the bodies could be placed. Rich people were able to have tombs specially constructed with a stairway leading down through the solid rock to the burial chamber. A slab of stone was put at the entrance with a boulder against it. In New Testament times a large circular stone was sometimes set in a groove and rolled across to cover the opening. But of course the number of caves, even man-made ones, was limited. So the bones were often removed and stored in chests of wood or stone called 'ossuaries'.

The poor were buried in shallow graves in open ground. A row of stones was placed round the body and the spaces in between were filled up with small stones and earth. A slab of stone was then put on the top. All graves were painted white to draw people's attention to them. For they must not be touched: any contact with the dead made a person ritually 'unclean'.

Christian beliefs Throughout the Bible there is a close link between death and sin. Death is part of the judgement that comes to Adam after his disobedience. Paul regards death as the inevitable consequence of the presence of sin in the world. For God is 'holy', and cannot tolerate evil. If we die with sin unforgiven, our death is not only physical but spiritual: it is separation from God. The New Testament often speaks of non-Christians as being physically alive, but 'spiritually dead because of disobedience and sins'.

When Jesus died on the cross he took the ultimate consequences of sin on himself. His resurrection showed that he had defeated death. So although our human fate is to die, by faith in Christ we can have 'eternal life'. The Christian is already lifted out of spiritual death to new life and looks forward to the end of the age when physical death, 'the last enemy', will also be overcome.

See also *Heaven, Hell, Judgement, Life, Resurrection, Second coming of Jesus.*

Psalm 144:4; Deuteronomy 30:15,19; Psalm 55:4; Genesis 3:19; Romans 6:23; Matthew 7:23; Ephesians 2:1; Hebrews 2:14-15; 1 Corinthians 15:21, 26; 2 Corinthians 5:1-10

Deborah
The only woman who was a Judge of Israel. Deborah encouraged General Barak to fight against Sisera, commander of the army of Jabin, a Canaanite king. The resulting victory ended twenty years of Canaanite oppression.
Judges 4–5

Decapolis (the Ten Towns)
An association of ten Greek towns gave this region its name. The Decapolis was an area south of Lake Galilee, mostly east of the River Jordan. Many of the people living there were non-Jews, but they joined the crowds that followed Jesus. Jewish Christians fled to Pella, one of these towns, before the war with the Romans in AD 70.
Matthew 4:25; Mark 5:1-20; 7:31-37

Dedan
Within the general area of Midian the city of Dedan (now Al-'Ula) later grew up. This major trading centre was known even to the Babylonians.
Isaiah 21:13; Jeremiah 25:23; 49:8; Ezekiel 27:20

Deer and gazelle
These graceful animals provide the Bible writers with a picture of swiftness and gentleness. Fallow and roe deer, gazelles and ibex, whose sandy colouring makes them difficult to spot, were a major source of meat.
Deuteronomy 12:15; Song of Solomon 2:8-9

Delilah
A beautiful Philistine woman who betrayed Samson. (See *Samson.*)
Judges 16

Demas
A Christian who was with Paul when he was a prisoner in Rome. He later deserted Paul and went off to Thessalonica.
Colossians 4:14; 2 Timothy 4:10

Demetrius
1. A silversmith in Ephesus who made souvenirs at the temple of Diana (Artemis)–see below. He was afraid that as a result of Paul's preaching the visitors would no longer buy these models, and so he encouraged other men in the same business to riot.
Acts 19:24ff.
2. A Christian mentioned in John's third letter, of whom everyone spoke well.
3 John 12

Derbe
A city in Lycaonia, in southern Asia Minor (modern Turkey), where Paul preached on his first and second journeys.
Acts 14:20-21; 16:1

Deuteronomy
The book of Deuteronomy consists of a number of speeches given by Moses to the Israelites in the plains of Moab, just before they entered the Promised Land.

The name of the book means a 'second law-giving'. But it is in fact a new statement of the laws God gave at Sinai (recorded in Exodus, Leviticus and Numbers), applying them to the settled life of the land of Canaan.

In the course of his speeches, Moses retells the great events of the last forty years. He repeats and underlines the Ten Commandments, and appoints Joshua as his successor to lead the Israelites.

The great theme of Deuteronomy is that God has saved and blessed his people. They must always remember this, and love and obey him.

The words that Jesus called the greatest commandment: 'Love the Lord your God with all your heart, with all your soul, and with all your strength,' come from the Book of Deuteronomy (6:4-5; Matthew 22:37).

Diana

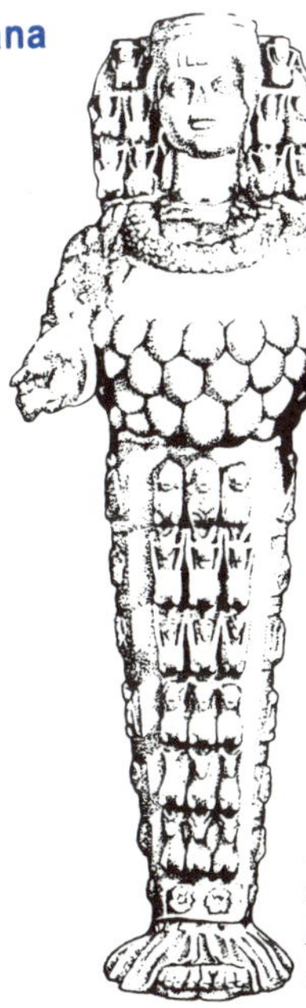

A statue of the goddess Diana, found at Ephesus.

Roman goddess of the moon and hunting, called Artemis by the Greeks. Her magnificent temple at Ephesus was one of the wonders of the ancient world. (See *Greek and Roman religion.*)
Acts 19

Dibon
A Moabite town east of the Dead Sea and 4 miles/5.5km north of the River Arnon. The Israelites captured it at the time of their entry into Canaan. It was given to the tribes of Gad and Reuben, but changed hands several times in the course of its history.
Numbers 21:30; 32:34; Isaiah 15:2

Dionysius
A member of the Areopagus, a powerful council at Athens set up to hear religious cases. Dionysius was converted to Christianity when Paul was asked to address the council.
Acts 17:34

Distances
New Testament **orgyia** (fathom) = 6ft/1.85m
New Testament **stadion** (furlong) = 202yd/185m
A sabbath day's journey, the maximum distance allowed by the Jewish law, was fixed at 2,000 cubits/1,000 yd/914m
New Testament **milion** (mile) = 1,000 paces (Roman measurement) 1,618 yd/1,478m

Divorce
See *Marriage.*

Dorcas/Tabitha
A Christian from Joppa who helped the poor by making clothes for them. When she died her friends sent for Peter, and he brought her back to life.
Acts 9:36-41

Dothan
A town on the route from Beth-shan and Gilead to Egypt. Here Joseph's brothers sold him to the Ishmaelite traders. At Dothan, Elisha was rescued from the surrounding Syrian army.
Genesis 37:17-28; 2 Kings 6

Doves and pigeons
The most common and important of all the Bible birds. Several kinds are native to Israel; others come as winter visitors. They were widely kept as domestic birds, for food. Poor people, who could not afford to sacrifice a sheep or goat would offer two pigeons–which they could buy in the temple courts–instead. It was a dove that brought back to Noah the first green leaf after the flood.
Genesis 8:8-12; Psalm 55:6; Matthew 3:16; 21:12

A Stock Dove (on the left) and Turtle Dove.

Dress
The Bible covers about 2,000 years of history. But because of the hot climate and the limited number of materials available, dress remained fairly standard in Israel for most of that time.

The main differences in dress were between the rich and poor. The poor peasant had only the woollen or goats'-hair clothes he stood up in. But rich people had clothes for winter and for summer; clothes for working and clothes for leisure; clothes of different materials–fine linen, or even silk. Some of them spent so much time and money on clothes that they needed Jesus' words to remind them of the really important things in life. 'Why worry about clothes?' he said. 'Look how the wild flowers grow...It is God who clothes the wild grass... Won't he be all the more sure to clothe you?' (Matthew 6:28-30).

Because the names have changed, we do not know which clothes some Hebrew words mean. We have to make careful guesses.

The first thing a man put on was either a loincloth or a short skirt from waist to knee. This was all he wore when he was doing heavy work.

Over the top of this came a shirt or tunic made of wool or linen. This was like a big sack: a long piece of material folded at the centre and sewn up the sides, with holes for the arms and a slit at the folded end for the head to go through. The shirt was calf-length for a man and coloured, usually red, yellow, black or striped. A woman's tunic came down to her ankles and was often blue. Often it was embroidered on the yoke with a special pattern. Each village had its own traditional pattern of embroidery. Apart from these features a woman's tunic would be very similar to a man's.

The tunic was fastened round the waist with a girdle or belt. This was a piece of cloth, folded into a long strip to make a kind of pocket to hold coins and other belongings. If a man was rich he might have a leather belt with a dagger or an inkhorn pushed into it. When a man needed to be able to move more freely, to work, he would tuck his tunic into his belt to make it much shorter. This was called 'girding up the loins'. It meant getting ready for action. A woman could lift up the hem of her long dress and use it as a large bag, even for carrying things like corn.

Out of doors, a rich man would wear a light coat over his tunic. This came down to his knees and was often gaily striped or woven in check patterns. Rich people wore lightweight coats indoors as well, perhaps made from imported silk. In Joseph's time, a long-sleeved coat of many pieces was worn by the future leader of the clan (see the story of Joseph, Genesis 37:3).

There was also a thick woollen coat or cloak to keep out the cold, called a *himation* in New Testament times. This was made from two pieces of material, often in stripes of light and dark brown, stitched together. The joined material was wrapped round the body, sewn at the shoulders, and slits were then made in the side for the arms to go through. The shepherd lived in his. It was his blanket when he slept in the open at night. It was also thick enough to make a comfortable seat.

Israelites shown on the 'Black Obelisk' of Shalmaneser III of Assyria. They are wearing pointed caps and shoes and fringed cloaks.

A poor man's cloak was so important to him that if it was handed over to guarantee repayment of a debt, it had to be returned to him at sunset.

Headgear In Israel the sun was so hot that some covering was needed to protect the head, neck and eyes. This was usually a square of cloth folded diagonally, with the fold across the forehead. A circle of plaited wool held it in place over the head, and the folds protected the neck. A cap was sometimes worn, and a fine wool shawl or *tallith* over it, especially during prayer. Women put pads on their heads to steady the jars of water and other things they carried.

Footwear Although many poor people probably went barefoot, sandals were the normal footwear. The simplest design was a piece of hide the same size as the foot, with a long leather strap which passed between the big and second toe, and was then tied round the ankle. Sandals were cool to wear, but people's feet got very dusty. Sandals were always taken off before going into someone else's home. It was the lowliest servant's job to take off the visitor's sandals and wash his feet. Sandals also were removed before entering a holy place. According to custom the right sandal was always put on and taken off before the left. A man selling property took off his sandal and gave it to the buyer as a token that he gave up his right to the property (as Boaz' relative did in the story of Ruth–Ruth 4:7).

It is interesting that despite the strict rules against all work on the sabbath the Jewish law book allowed for a man to take certain clothes from a burning house on the sabbath day. Most people had few clothes, and they had to make them last. They were carefully washed with soap made from olive oil, and rinsed in fast-flowing water so that the current could run through the material and loosen the dirt. If someone tore his clothes as a sign of mourning, it was out of real grief!

There were no nightclothes. At night people simply lay down and loosened their day clothes.

These basic clothes were influenced to some extent by styles from other countries. But fashions did not change much. A painting of Asiatic nomads who visited Egypt, can be seen on the wall of a tomb at Beni-Hasan (about 1890 BC). They have cloaks of coloured wool which reach below the knee, with a loose end thrown over the shoulder. This was probably the type of clothing worn by Abraham.

See also *Clothes-making, Hair, Jewellery, Make-up.*

Drink

Although water was the basic liquid used in cooking, it was not very good for drinking. Water from the local well or spring was generally safe enough. It was collected in porous earthenware jars in which the water remained cool by a process of slow evaporation. Water from the family cistern, a conical shaped pit in the ground with a waterproof lining, was far from safe. Because the water came from the roof and ran down into the cistern through gutters, it was often dirty and full of germs. In Roman times when water was brought to the towns by aqueduct (as it was to Caesarea and Bethlehem) or mixed with olive oil to clean and heal wounds. (The Good Samaritan poured oil and wine on the wounds of the injured man–Luke 10:34.) by pipeline (as it was to Jerusalem), the water was still not fit to drink. For this reason other liquids made better drinks.

There was milk, often straight from the family goat, or brought to the door by the 'milkman'. But wine was the commonest drink. At the time the grapes were picked, there was fresh grape juice, pressed straight from the bunch into a cup. But most of the juice had to be fermented so that it would keep. The first wine of the year was made from the juice extracted when the grapes were trodden in the press. A second batch was made by squeezing the remainder in a press. Wine was sometimes mixed with gall or myrrh to relieve pain. (This was offered to Jesus at the crucifixion–Matthew 27:34.) It was also

Although wine was the normal drink–Jesus himself provided wine for the wedding at Cana, and drank enough to be called a 'tippler' ('winebibber') by the Pharisees–people under a vow to God, or engaged on special service, sometimes gave up drinking it (Leviticus 10:9; Numbers 6:3). And any drunkenness or excess was always condemned. The Rechabites avoided drinking wine as part of their calling to keep the nomadic way of life. Planting vineyards and producing wine was considered part of a settled life.

Wealthy homes in New Testament times had cellars of fine wines from all over the Mediterranean world. They were kept in narrow jars (*amphorae*) with a pointed end, so that they could be pushed deep into earth or sand to keep the wine cool. But wine was usually stored in leather bottles (wineskins).

Drusilla

The youngest daughter of Herod Agrippa I and wife of the Roman governor Felix. (See *Felix.*)
Acts 24:24

E

Eagles and vultures

The word usually translated 'eagle' also includes the Griffon-Vulture. From a distance both look alike. Isaiah and the Psalmist both speak of the eagle's strength and vigour. The 'eagle' was the badge of the Roman legions. Matthew probably had that in mind when he described the eagles waiting for Jerusalem to fall.
Isaiah 40:31; Psalm 103:5; Matthew 24:28

Ebal

A rocky mountain in Samaria, opposite the wooded height of Mt Gerizim, close to ancient Shechem and modern Nablus. Here Joshua carried out a command given him by Moses before the conquest of the land. He built an altar on Mt Ebal and gave

A Golden Eagle (on the left) and Griffon Vultures; two birds of prey–forbidden foods for the Israelites.

the people a choice–to obey God and enjoy his blessing, or to disobey and be punished. Some of the people stood on Mt Ebal, whose bare, scorched height represented God's curse, and others on Mt Gerizim.
Deuteronomy 11:29; 27;
Joshua 8:30, 33

Ebed-melech
An Ethiopian who was one of King Zedekiah's palace officials (sixth century BC). Because he saved Jeremiah's life God promised that Ebed-melech would not be killed when Jerusalem was destroyed.
Jeremiah 38; 39:16-18

Ecclesiastes
This book gathers together the 'wisdom'–wise observations, thoughts and sayings –of 'the Philosopher' (Qoheleth). This kind of writing was popular in the ancient Near Eastern countries at the time.

The writer looks at human life. He finds it short and meaningless, and concludes that it has no point. He cannot understand the purpose of it all. But he ends by recommending hard work and enjoyment of pleasure while it lasts. Much of the book seems depressing and destructive, because it looks at 'life under the sun'–from a purely human viewpoint. Life without God lacks purpose and meaning. But wisdom and justice inject at least some nobility into man's existence.

Eden
The garden God made, in the beginning, as a place for his people to live in. After they had disobeyed him, God sent Adam and Eve out of the Garden of Eden. Two of the rivers in it were the Tigris and the Euphrates.
Genesis 2:8-14

Edom
The land of Edom lay south of Moab, stretching down to the Gulf of Aqaba. The Edomites lived here, ruled by kings, from an early date. Some Edomites travelled as traders; others worked at copper mining and farming. Like their neighbours they were hostile to Israel. They were conquered more than once, but often broke free again. Their Red Sea port, Ezion-geber (Elath) was used by Solomon and later kings. Many Hebrew prophets spoke bitter words against Edom. The Edomites took advantage of the exile to occupy much of southern Judah. This area, known later as Idumaea, was the home of the Herod family who ruled Judea in New Testament times.
Genesis 36:1-19, 36-39; 1 Kings 9:26; 22:48; 2 Kings 14:22; Amos 1:11-12; Jeremiah 49:7-22; Obadiah

Education
As far back as Abraham's time certain nations were developing education. In Sumer, Abraham's homeland, there were schools to train future secretaries for work in the temples, palace and business life. This education was voluntary. The pupil's family had to pay and so it was usually only the privilege of the rich. But the range of subjects was wide. Botany, geography, mathematics, grammar and literature were all studied.

Excavations have unearthed many clay tablets containing exercises to be copied, while others record the pupils' attempts and their teachers' corrections. In the palace of Mari, two schoolrooms with benches and desks have been found. School staff included a professor (often called 'the school father', with pupils called the 'school sons'), an assistant who prepared the daily exercises, specialist teachers, and others responsible for discipline (one called 'big brother').

There was a similar system in Egypt, where schools were often attached to the temples. After the beginners' course pupils transferred to a government department where they studied composition, natural science and the duties of office. There was special training in letter-writing and 'model letters' have been found. If they were being trained to be priests, they studied theology and medicine. Discipline was strict: no wine, no music, no women.

Systems like these must have influenced the people of Israel at certain points in their history. Abraham may have been a man of some learning. Joseph would have relied on secretaries for his work as a chief minister of Pharaoh. And Moses had an Egyptian education–so it was a man with a trained mind who was chosen to teach God's law to the people of Israel. But education in Israel itself took a very different course.

The basic idea in Israel and all through the Bible is that all knowledge comes from God. He is the greatest of all teachers. All wisdom and learning should begin with 'the fear of the Lord'. Its aim is to understand the Creator and his work better. So learning leads to praising God (as in Psalm 8). It is not enough simply to satisfy human curiosity. It also helps people to use their God-given abilities to the full. So elementary mathematics was needed for surveying land and calculating the harvest, and for large building works. Studying the movements of the sun, moon and stars helped in working out the calendar. Many of these things were learnt by experience, or, as in other crafts, in an apprenticeship.

At the same time, the education of children was given an important place. It was every parent's duty to make sure that his children were taught. But the content of this teaching was almost entirely religious.

They were to be taught the story of God's dealings with Israel.

They were to be instructed in God's laws. God is holy and requires holiness from his people. Children must therefore be taught how to 'keep the ways of the Lord'.

They were to be given instruction in wise dealing. The Book of Proverbs is full of maxims on the subject of 'how to get along with people' and is written for 'sons'. This type of teaching Israel had in common with other nations.
Exodus 20:4; Proverbs 1:7; 9:10; Job 28:28; Deuteronomy 4:9-10; 6:20-21; Exodus 13:8-9; 12:26-27; Joshua 4:21-22; Leviticus 19:2; Genesis 18:19; Proverbs 1:8; 4:1

How education developed Education began at home. Abraham was instructed to teach his children. It was important that the truth of God's acts for his people was passed from father to son, from generation to generation. Mothers also probably shared in this when the children were young.

Opinions differ about how many people could read and write in Old Testament times. Some think that only the nobles could. But, on the other hand, Joshua expected written reports on the land of Canaan; Gideon expected a young passer-by to be able to read; and in the time of Hezekiah it was presumably a workman who wrote on the wall of the tunnel dug to bring water into Jerusalem (see *Building*). Enough other examples of ancient Hebrew writing have been found to show that there was widespread knowledge of the skill.

It is not known when schools for children started. They are not referred to until 75 BC, when the country came under Greek influence and there was an attempt to enforce elementary education. But there may have been voluntary schools before this. The boy Samuel was handed over to the priest's keeping and was presumably taught by him. This kind of thing may have been a regular practice. The 'Gezer calendar' (see *Farming*) may also be evidence of a more formal type of education. Certainly the young men had the chance to become pupils of the prophets, and probably also of the priests and Levites. Isaiah gave private teaching to a group of disciples and Elisha was very concerned for the welfare of his pupils and their families. But none of this was 'education' either in the modern sense, or in the way we find it in Egypt or ancient Babylon. It was learning about religion in order to serve God better.

After the people returned from exile, a specialized class of Bible scholars, known as 'scribes', came into being. This term had been used earlier to mean secretaries, but some of the Levites were scribes, and even before the exile they were recognized as experts in God's law. According to Jewish tradition, after the exile these scribes were the equivalent of the earlier prophets, and were called 'men of the great synagogue'. They came to be known as 'lawyers', 'doctors of the law' and 'rabbis'. Simon the Just, Shammai, Hillel and Gamaliel were some of the most famous. They taught and explained the written Law of God, and they applied the Law to contemporary life. These teachings built up into large collections of rules. At first they were taught by word of mouth, but eventually they were written down to form the *Mishnah*, about AD 200. They were regarded as having the same authority as the Old Testament itself.

A Greek vase-painting showing a teacher hearing a boy read.

It was during these last centuries before Christ that the group later known as the Pharisees seems to have organized a school system. Children first went to school in the synagogue, 'the house of the book'. Further education then took place in 'the house of study'. Many of these were under the direction of famous rabbis.

We can only guess at educational methods. Isaiah may throw some light on this. He writes that the people think his message is only for babies: 'He is trying to teach us letter by letter, line by line, lesson by lesson.' This may reflect the practice of teaching a little at a time, or it may represent the first letters of the alphabet being learnt by repetition. Most instruction was given by word of mouth, and various devices were used to make it easy to memorize. Jesus himself used catchwords, repetition, and parables.
Psalm 78:3-6; Proverbs 31:1; 1:8; 6:20; Joshua 18:4, 8-9; Judges 8:14; Isaiah 8:16; Jeremiah 36:26; 1 Chronicles 24:6; Jeremiah 8:8; Mark 7:6-9; Isaiah 28:10; Proverbs 1:8; Mark 9:42-50; Matthew 6:2-18

Adult education Education in the Bible was not only for children. Abraham was told to teach the whole of his household. Moses taught the people of Israel the Law of God, and the Levites were commanded to pass on this teaching. The kings sent Levites throughout the land to teach, though the prophets complained that this duty was often done badly, and regarded as a way of making money. The custom of regular teaching of the people probably developed only after the exile.

Ezra was a priest and scribe 'with a thorough knowledge of the Law'. He 'devoted his life to studying the Law of the Lord...and to teaching all its laws and regulations to the people of Israel.' Nehemiah 8 pictures him standing in a wooden pulpit, with all the people gathered to hear him.
Genesis 18:19; Leviticus 10:11; 2 Chronicles 17:7-9; 35:3; Micah 3:11; Malachi 2:7-8; Ezra 7:6, 10

Greek education By the time of Jesus Greek education had become world-famous. Body, mind and soul, it was thought, needed room for expression, so the syllabus included athletics, philosophy, poetry, drama, music and rhetoric. Boys would attend elementary school between the ages of seven and fifteen. They would then go to a 'gymnasium' for a wider education (not just for athletics). Members of the public were welcome to come and join in the students' discussions. Standards in the gymnasia had declined by the time of Jesus, but these schools still represented the best of Greek culture. They were set up wherever Greeks came to live, and one was started in Jerusalem in 167 BC.

Most Jews thoroughly disapproved of the Greek view of education. The gymnasia were also condemned because Greek athletes practised and competed naked. Foreigners, were, however, welcome, and since Paul's home-city of Tarsus was also famous for its gymnasium we may wonder if Paul ever went there. He certainly refers to the Greek games, and shows a knowledge of Greek culture in his letters.
1 Corinthians 9:24-27
See also *Writing*.

Eglon

1. A king of Moab in the time of the Judges. He defeated Israel and captured Jericho, keeping the Israelites subject for eighteen years. He was murdered by Ehud.
Judges 3:12-26
2. One of a group of Amorite cities conquered by Joshua in his first vigorous campaign. It was probably Tell el-Hesi near Lachish, in the Shephelah, the low hill-country west of Jerusalem.
Joshua 10; 12:12; 15:39

Egypt

The huge Sahara Desert sweeps across North Africa from the mountains of Morocco in the west to the Red Sea in the east. From the lakes and highlands of tropical East Africa, the River Nile flows north across the dry deserts all the way to the Mediterranean Sea. For the last 600 miles to the sea, the river flows through a valley bordered by cliffs on either side. Then, 100 miles from the sea, it splits into two streams. They enclose a great triangle of flat land called the Nile Delta, because its shape is like the Greek letter 'D', *delta*, a triangle.

The Nile flood Every year, tropical rains in East Africa cause the river to flood its banks, bringing down masses of mud in the flood-waters. Until modern times, that fertile mud was deposited fresh each year along the valley and in the great Delta triangle, which was entirely formed of this mud. This is Egypt: rich green crops on black soil along the narrow ribbon of valley and river, and across the broad Delta. On either side, the yellow-brown deserts stretch away beyond the cliffs. Nowadays, great dams control the Nile floods, and hold back the mud. In ancient times, there was no control. A small flood meant no water for crops, and so nothing to eat. Too big a flood swept away villages and farm animals. To spread the water as far as possible, the ancient Egyptians cut canals and irrigation channels among the fields.

Transport The Egyptians quickly learned to make boats. At first, they made canoes out of papyrus-reeds, then larger boats of wood. With these they could travel easily on the River Nile along the whole valley, or through the Delta. Going north, they simply rowed with the current. Going south, the north wind would fill their sails to travel against the river's flow. So the Nile has always been Egypt's 'main road'.

The other parts of the country were also important. The deserts and the Sinai peninsula contained valuable metals (copper, gold), and stone that was used for building the giant pyramids and the temples in the Nile Valley.

A land of history To begin with there were two kingdoms in Egypt: the Nile Valley (Upper Egypt) and the Nile Delta (Lower Egypt). But before 3000 BC a king of the Valley managed to defeat the king of the Delta and become the king of all Egypt. To rule both lands, he built his capital city, Memphis, at the point where the valley widens into the Delta. Menes, this first king of all Egypt, began a line of kings or 'pharaohs'. For the next 3,000 years, thirty such families of kings (dynasties) ruled Egypt, mainly following one after the other. During that long span of time, Egypt enjoyed three periods of greatness.

The Pyramid Age The first great age in Egypt was the 'Old Kingdom' (about 2600-2200 BC), or 'Pyramid Age', from the huge, pointed stone tombs that the kings built. After the strong kings of the Pyramid Age, Egypt became poorer under less able leaders. Once more rival kings came to power in south and north, until a prince from Thebes again re-united Egypt.

The Middle Kingdom This prince's family, and the one after it (the 12th Dynasty) were Egypt's 'Middle Kingdom' (about 2060-1786 BC). Its new, strong pharaohs took over the river-valley and deserts of Nubia, south of Egypt, to obtain gold and other African products. By improving the use of the Nile-waters for farming, these kings also increased the crops grown, and the wealth of the people. It was probably about this time that Abraham visited Egypt because of famine in Canaan. Many others like him came from Canaan into Egypt. Some stayed, and were even promoted to important posts in the government of

Egypt: others were less fortunate and became servants or slaves.

After the 12th Dynasty, from about 1780-1550 BC weaker kings ruled. This was perhaps the time when Joseph was sold as a slave into Egypt, to be followed some years later by his family. From amongst the foreigners living in the east Delta, princes arose who made themselves kings of all Egypt. They are known as the Hyksos, or 15th Dynasty. But it was not long before Egyptian princes from Thebes in the south again came north, to expel the Hyksos rulers and re-unite Egypt once more.

The Empire These pharaohs also won control over Canaan, to the north of Egypt, as well as Nubia to the south. This period, the 'New Kingdom', is often called the 'Empire'. It includes the 18th-20th Dynasties, and covers the period from about 1500 to 1070 BC. These kings fought many battles in Canaan and Syria. In Egypt, they built many huge temples, the most important at Memphis (their capital) and Thebes (their sacred city).

In the meantime the Hittites in the far north conquered part of Egypt's empire in Syria. A new line of pharaohs tried to win back the lost provinces, especially kings Sethos I and Ramesses II (19th Dynasty, thirteenth century BC). These kings were great builders. Being a Delta family, they built a new royal city, Pi-Ramesse–the Raamses (Rameses) of Exodus–in the east Delta. This was the climax of the 'oppression' of the Hebrews–who were used as slave-labour by the pharaohs–and the time when Moses was sent to lead the Hebrews out of Egypt (the 'Exodus'). Shortly before 1200 BC another pharaoh, Merenptah, sent soldiers to Canaan and defeated several groups of people there. One of these was the Israelites, who obviously must have been in Canaan by that date.

Soon after 1200 BC, the ancient world had much trouble. The 'peoples of the sea' and others overthrew the Hittite Empire and most of the kingdoms in Syria and Canaan. Ramesses III pushed the invaders back from Egypt's borders in two fierce battles on land and sea. One of these peoples was the Philistines. After Ramesses III, Egypt's 20th Dynasty and empire lost power under weak kings. They governed badly and low Niles brought famines.

The Late Period From about 1070 BC to 330 BC, Egypt went through her 'Late Period'. Egypt was never again as powerful as in earlier times. In 925 BC, Shoshenq I (Shishak) subdued King Rehoboam of Judah and King Jeroboam of Israel. The Egyptians recorded this victory in their temple of Karnak. But their power did not last long: 200 years later neither So nor Tirhakah could help the Hebrew kings against Assyria. Nor did Hophra in 588 BC really help Zedekiah against the Babylonians.

King Tutankhamun and his queen. The scene is created in gold, silver and coloured glass on the back-rest of his throne.

A jackal representing Anubis, the Egyptian god of embalming, on a funerary chest.

From 525 BC Egypt, like her neighbours, was part of the Persian Empire, sometimes rebelling and becoming free again (28th-30th Dynasties), until finally Alexander the Great took over (332-323 BC). After him, the Greek Ptolemies ruled Egypt until the coming of the Roman Empire.

Genesis 12:10-20; 37-50;
Exodus 1:11 and chapters 1-14;
1 Kings 14:25-27; 2 Kings 17:4;
19:9ff.; Jeremiah 37:5-7 and 44:30

Life in ancient Egypt The pharaoh was supreme ruler of Egypt. He was assisted by his great men, including wise men like those the king sent for to explain his dreams. The land was divided into provinces. Each had its chief city for local government and supplies. Most Egyptians were farmers, growing grain, keeping cattle, depending on the Nile. These are all features of the dreams of Joseph's pharaoh. Dreams mattered to all classes (prisoners as well as kings) and the Egyptians even wrote textbooks to interpret dreams.

Egyptian writing began as pictures ('hieroglyphs'), used to write the sounds of their language. An owl was *m*, a mouth was *r*, and so on. For use on papyrus sheets (an early form of paper), flowing forms of script were used ('hieratic', 'demotic'). The Egyptians wrote stories, poetry, books of wisdom (like the Bible book of Proverbs), as well as everyday things like lists, letters and accounts.

Both Egyptians and foreigners had to work as labourers on building-sites, especially making bricks. For these, straw was needed to mix with the clay to make better bricks. The papyri also mention straw, and fixed work-targets. Like Moses, many young foreigners were brought up at court, were well educated, and had all kinds of jobs. Like Moses and the Hebrews, others, too, tried to escape from Egypt. The papyri mention slaves who ran away to gain their freedom.

Genesis 40 and 41; Exodus 1-14

Egyptian religion

The Egyptians had many gods. Some came from nature: Re, the sun-god; Thoth, Khons, moon-gods; Nut, the sky-goddess; Geb, the earth-god; Hapi, the god of the Nile-flood; and

Amun, the god of hidden life-powers in nature. Some stood for ideas: Maat was goddess of truth, justice, and right order. Thoth was also the god of learning and wisdom. Ptah was the god of craftsmanship. Most Egyptians turned to Osiris for hope of a life after death. Osiris was said to have been slain by his brother and then made king of the underworld.

Animals noted for special qualities were treated as sacred to particular gods. They could act as 'live images' for their gods. So the Apis-bull was sacred to Ptah, the ibis-birds to Thoth, falcons to Horus, cats to the goddess Bastet. A god was sometimes shown wearing the head of his sacred animal, to make him easier to recognize.

With so many different gods controlling their world, the Egyptians tried to link these to one another. They produced 'myths' (stories about the gods), in which gods were often grouped as 'families'. There would be a chief god and goddess as husband and wife, with a lesser god or goddess as their son or daughter.

In the fourteenth century BC, Pharaoh Akhenaten tried to make all his subjects worship the sun-god only (as seen in the sun's disc–Aten). But he failed, and after about ten years the Egyptians returned to the gods they had worshipped before.

Worship at the great temples The life the Egyptians imagined for the gods was modelled on their own daily life. The huge stone temple, hidden behind great brick walls, was the home of the god. The priests were his servants. Each morning, they woke him up with a morning hymn, broke the seal on his shrine, redressed his image, and gave him food and drink offerings for 'breakfast'. These offerings were then placed before statues of Pharaoh's ancestors (earlier kings of Egypt) and the great men of Egypt) before being finally eaten by the priests. At midday, a shorter service and offerings made up the god's 'lunch'. An evening hymn sent him to rest, after a third offering ('supper'). On special festival days, smaller images of the gods were carried in procession from temple to temple. These were days on which the gods 'went visiting', sometimes to celebrate events mentioned in the stories about them. People believed that the 'spirit' of the god lived in his image in the temple.

In theory, Pharaoh himself was high priest of all the gods. In real life, his deputies were high priests in the various temples, assisted by other priests. Only the king, priests and higher officials could go beyond the first sunlit court into the dim, pillared halls and the darkness of the sacred inner room of the temple. Akhenaten's sun-god religion worked in the same way, but in open-air temples. There is a famous hymn, praising the Aten as the creator who provides for the world. People have compared it with Psalm 104. But there are no links between the Egyptian hymn and the psalm, or the Hebrew worship of one holy God.

The religion of the people Pharaoh was the go-between for gods and people. Through his deputy priests he made offerings to the gods on behalf of the people in order that, in turn, the gods might shower their gifts on Egypt (good Nile-floods, rich crops). He also appeared as the representative of the gods to the people. He directed the building and upkeep of the temples which were always built in his name.

The mass of the ordinary people could not enter the great state temples. They only saw the great gods on festival days, when their veiled images were carried in procession in small sacred boats by the priests. Instead, ordinary people worshipped at small, local shrines, or the chapels at the gateways of the great temples. Their worship was mostly to present offerings, following certain set rituals. The people were allowed to make merry at the great festivals. They also sometimes got time off to worship their own god (this was what Moses asked Pharaoh's permission to do, Exodus 5:1,3). When troubles such as illness struck them, the Egyptians sometimes thought this was punishment from the gods for wrong-doing. They then confessed their sins and prayed for healing and help. If healing came, they often set up little inscriptions, with a short hymn to the god or goddess, to record their thanks.

Like most peoples, the ancient Egyptians had a moral sense of right and wrong. Murder or theft were wrong then, as now. But magic was used to grasp at supernatural power. Good or 'white' magic was designed to ward off life's troubles. Harmful or 'black' magic was a crime, and was punished as such. Magic usually meant the exact reciting of spells, often over small images or drawings connected with the subject of the magic. People often wore lucky charms, or amulets. The symbol of life, or the scarab-beetle for renewal, was popular.

Life after death The early Egyptians buried their dead along the edges of the dry deserts that bordered the Nile Valley. The dry sand and hot sun often dried up and so preserved the bodies of those early people in their shallow graves. The Egyptians came to believe that the body was a home for the soul, and that the soul needed its personal belongings in a life after death something like earthly life. So, when tombs became too big and deep for the sun's heat to dry the body, the Egyptians did this artificially. They packed the body in salt to dry it up, stuffed it and bandaged it (mummification). The mummy was then buried in a coffin in the tomb with the other belongings. Joseph was embalmed in this way, and put in a coffin in Egypt (Genesis 50:26).

Most Egyptians hoped to have a pleasant after-life in the kingdom of Osiris. They had papyrus-roll books of magical spells to help them pass the judgement of the dead. This bypassed the moral test of that judgement. The most famous collection of spells is the *Book of the Dead*.

Souls of dead kings spent their after-life with the sun-god, crossing the sky in his heavenly boat by day. Then, at night, they passed through the realm of Osiris, providing for their dead subjects. The emphasis on mummification, magic, and richly furnished tombs led to very materialistic views of the after-life.

Egyptian religion and the Bible Egyptian religion was very different from that of the Hebrews. Israel's God dealt with his people in actual history. He required obedience to his just laws more than rituals or sacrifices (1 Samuel 15:22). Ritual without right living was useless. (The Egyptians also admitted this sometimes.) Unlike the gods of Egypt (who needed three meals a day), the God of Israel had no personal need of food or of anything that human hands might provide (see Psalm 50:11-13). Egyptian rituals were symbols, and magical acts. The rites which took place in the Hebrew tabernacle and temple were intended to instruct the people in the nature and purity of their God. Egyptian rites were complicated and for the special few. The Hebrew ones were far simpler, designed mostly for the instruction of people as well as priests.

Ehud

A left-handed Israelite from the tribe of Benjamin. Ehud thought up a cunning and daring plot to kill King Eglon of Moab who had oppressed part of Israel, including the eastern section of the land belonging to Ehud's tribe, for eighteen years. With Eglon dead, Ehud gathered an army to defeat the Moabites and free his people.
Judges 3:15-30

Ekron

One of the five main cities of the Philistines. It was given to the tribe of Judah in the early years of conquest. But the Philistines on the coastal plain were too strong for them to keep it. When the Philistines defeated Israel and captured the Covenant Box (ark), plague broke out in each of the Philistine cities to which the ark was taken. When the plague reached Ekron, the Philistines finally decided to send the ark back to the Israelites.
Joshua 15:11,45-46; Judges 1:18; 1 Samuel 5:10-6:17; 7:14; 17:52; 2 Kings 1:3-6; Amos 1:8, etc.

Elah

1. Best-known man of this name in the Old Testament is the son of King Baasha. Elah was an evil king who reigned over Israel for less than two years (886-885 BC). While drunk he was killed by Zimri, a general in his army.
1 Kings 16:8-14
2. A valley south-west of Jerusalem. The Philistines marched through the Valley of Elah to invade the land of Israel. Here David fought the Philistine champion Goliath.
1 Samuel 17:2

Elam

The Elamites were an isolated nation whose chief city was Susa. They had lived there from prehistoric times. Their culture shared with the Sumerians (see *Babylonians*) in the earliest cities and writing. Their king, Chedorlaomer, joined the attack on cities in the Jordan Valley, and was defeated by Abram. The Elamites were often under the thumb of their western neighbours. The Assyrians sent some of the citizens of Samaria to Elam and Elamites were sent to

Israel to replace them. Elam became part of the Persian kingdom.

Jews from 'Elam', the semi-independent kingdom called Elymais in Greek, heard Peter in Jerusalem on the Day of Pentecost.
Genesis 14:1; Ezra 4:9; Isaiah 11:11; 21:2; Jeremiah 25:25; Acts 2:9

An Elamite archer of the Persian royal guard: from the palace at Susa built in the fifth century BC.

Elath/Ezion-geber

A settlement (later a town) at the head of the Gulf of Aqaba on the Red Sea. The Israelites camped there on their way from Egypt to Canaan. King Solomon based a Red Sea trading fleet there. King Jehoshaphat later tried to revive this, but his ships were wrecked. The town eventually came under Edomite control.
Numbers 33:35-36;
Deuteronomy 2:8;
1 Kings 9:26-27; 22:48;
2 Kings 16:6

Eleazar

The most important of several Eleazars was Aaron's third son. Eleazar's two elder brothers were killed, so he became high priest when Aaron died. He was in charge of the Levites and supervised everything to do with the worship tent (tabernacle).
Exodus 6:23; Leviticus 10;
Numbers 3ff; Joshua 14, etc.

Election

'You did not choose me; I chose you', said Jesus. These words sum up the Bible's teaching on election (choice). Because God is the all-powerful Creator he is the one who makes the ultimate decisions–not man.

The Old Testament records how God chose people. He chose Abel and not Cain; Isaac and not Ishmael; Jacob and not Esau; Joseph and not his brothers. They were not chosen for their own goodness or greatness. Moses tells the people of Israel, 'The Lord did not love you and choose you because you outnumbered other peoples...But the Lord loved you.' 'Do not say to yourselves that he brought you in to possess this land because you deserved it.' The reason for God's choice is hidden within his own mind and no human being can understand it.

It is clear, however, that those who accept the challenge of God's choice are expected to obey him and give their lives in his service. This was so for Abraham and the people of Israel. It is now true of Christians: 'You are the chosen race, the king's priests, the holy nation, God's own people, chosen to proclaim the wonderful acts of God, who called you out of darkness into his own marvellous light.'

For God's choice of individuals see *Call*; see also *Covenant*, *Grace*.
John 15:16; Deuteronomy 7:7-8; 9:4-5; Romans 9:18-29;
1 Peter 2:9

Eli

A Judge and priest in Israel. Samuel's mother (see *Hannah*) took her son to Eli to be trained in the shrine at Shiloh. Eli's two sons, Hophni and Phinehas, were a disgrace. They would not listen to their father, and God warned Eli of their terrible fate. Later, they were both killed in a battle against the Philistines and God's Covenant Box (the ark) was captured. When Eli heard the news he collapsed and died.
1 Samuel 1–4

Eliah

Jesse's eldest son, the brother of David.
1 Samuel 16:6ff.; 17:13, 28

Eliakim

The most important man of this name was the son of Hilkiah, King Hezekiah's chief palace official. When King Sennacherib of Assyria threatened to besiege Jerusalem Hezekiah sent Eliakim, along with Shebna and Joah, to hear the Assyrian spokesmen.
2 Kings 18:18ff.;
Isaiah 36–37:6

Eliezer

Abraham's chief servant. Before Abraham had a son, Eliezer was his heir. It was presumably Eliezer who was trusted with the task of going to Mesopotamia to choose a wife for Isaac.
Genesis 15:2; 24

Elihu

The angry young man in the story of Job who wrongly insisted that the reason for Job's suffering must be Job's own sin.
Job 32-37

Elijah

A prophet who lived in Israel during the reign of King Ahab. Ahab and his foreign queen, Jezebel, sinned against God by worshipping Baal and killing God's prophets. Because of this, Elijah was sent to tell Ahab that God was sending a drought. Then Elijah went into hiding by the Brook Cherith, where ravens brought him food. When the brook dried up, he went to Zarephath in Sidon and stayed with a widow and her household. She shared the last of her food with Elijah, but God renewed her supply of flour and oil until the famine was over. When the widow's son died, God answered Elijah's prayer and brought him back to life.

In the third year of the drought Elijah went back to Ahab. The king accused him of causing Israel's troubles. 'I'm not the troublemaker,' Elijah replied. 'You are–you and your father. You are disobeying the Lord's commands and worshipping the idols of Baal.' He told Ahab to send the prophets of Baal and Asherah to Mt Carmel. There Elijah challenged them to prove that their god was real. If Baal could set fire to their sacrifice then the people should worship him; but if God sent fire to burn up Elijah's sacrifice, that would prove he was the true God. The prophets of Baal danced, prayed, and cut themselves all day, but nothing happened. When Elijah prayed to God the fire feli and burnt his sacrifice. All the people shouted, 'The Lord, he is God.' The priests of Baal were killed–and that same day the drought ended.

Jezebel was furious when she heard her prophets had been killed. Elijah ran away south into the desert to save his life. He felt alone and near to despair. But God spoke to him. He told Elijah there was work still to do. He was to anoint a new king and train Elisha to take over his work.

Later, when Ahab had Naboth killed in order to seize his vineyard, Elijah warned the king that God would punish his whole family. Ahab was killed in battle, but God protected Elijah. When his work was finished, God took him to heaven in a chariot of fire.

The prophet Malachi foretold that Elijah would return: much later he appeared with Moses when the disciples saw Jesus' glory (the transfiguration).
1 Kings 17–2 Kings 2;
Malachi 4:5–6; Luke 9:28ff.

Elimelech

See *Naomi*.

Elisha

Elisha carried on Elijah's work as God's prophet in Israel for more than fifty years. Before Elijah was taken up into heaven, Elisha asked for the share of his power that would make him Elijah's successor. This request was granted. Elisha worked a number of miracles. He brought the Shunammite woman's son back to life and healed Naaman, the Syrian general, of leprosy. Elisha lived through the reigns of six kings of Israel.
1 Kings 19:16ff.; 2 Kings 2–9; 13:14ff.

Elizabeth

Wife of Zechariah, the priest. Elizabeth had been unable to have children. But to her joy, in old age she became the mother of John the Baptist. Mary, Jesus' mother, was a relative of Elizabeth and visited her before the babies were born. Elizabeth knew at once that Mary's child was the long-awaited 'Lord' (Messiah).
Luke 1

Emmaus

A village within 8 miles/13km of Jerusalem. It was probably modern El-Qubeibeh. On the day of his resurrection Jesus appeared to two of his followers who were on their way to Emmaus.
Luke 24:13

Endor

A place in northern Israel, near Mt Tabor. King Saul made a secret journey to Endor on the night before his last battle. He wanted to ask the

witch (or medium) there to call up the spirit of the dead prophet Samuel, to advise him. Saul and his son Jonathan were killed next day in the disastrous defeat at nearby Mt Gilboa.
1 Samuel 28

Engedi
A spring to the west of the Dead Sea where David hid out.
Joshua 15:62; 1 Samuel 23:29, etc

Enoch
A descendant of Adam's son, Seth. He lived in such close friendship with God that the Bible says he did not die. Instead 'God took him away'.
Genesis 5:22; Hebrews 11:5

Epaphras
A Christian who founded the church at Colossae. Epaphras visited Paul when he was in prison in Rome and gave him news about the Colossian Christians. As a result Paul wrote his letter to them.
Colossians 1:7-8; 4:12; Philemon 23

Epaphroditus
A Christian from the church at Philippi. When Paul was in prison in Rome, members of the Philippian church sent Epaphroditus to Rome with a gift.
Philippians 2:25-30; 4:18

Ephesians
The letter from Paul to the Ephesians was probably a 'circular' to a group of churches in what is now western Turkey. The church at Ephesus–the main city of the whole region–was most important of the group. Paul wrote this letter (as he did Philippians, Colossians and Philemon) from prison–probably in Rome in the early sixties.

The great theme is 'God's plan ...to bring all creation together, everything in heaven and on earth, with Christ as head' (1:10).

The letter opens up this idea of unity (chapters 1-3). God the Father has chosen his people. Jesus, the Son, has freed them from their sins and broken down the barriers of race, religion and culture. God's Spirit is at work in their lives leading them from strength to strength.

The second part of the letter (chapters 4-6) calls on Christians to live so that their oneness in Christ may be seen in their love for each other. We must come out of the dark, and walk in the light!

Paul uses a series of pictures to illustrate this oneness with Christ: the body, the building, the relationship of husband and wife. Everything in human life and experience is seen in the light of Christ: his love, his death on the cross, his forgiveness and his purity. Paul ends by encouraging Christians to put on the 'whole armour of God, ready to do God's will and stand firm against evil'.

Ephesus
The most important city in the Roman province of Asia (western Turkey). Ephesus was a bridgehead between East and West. It stood at the end of one of the great caravan trade routes through Asia, at the mouth of the Cayster River. By Paul's day the harbour was beginning to silt up. But the city was magnificent, with streets paved in marble, baths, libraries, a market-place and theatre seating more than 25,000 people. The temple to Diana at Ephesus was one of the seven wonders of the ancient world, four times the size of the Parthenon at Athens. There had been a settlement at Ephesus since before the twelfth century BC. But by New Testament times the population had grown to something like a third of a million, including a great many Jews.

Ephesus soon became an important centre for the early Christians, too. Paul made a brief visit on his second missionary journey, and his friends Aquila and Prisca stayed on there. On his third journey he spent over two years at Ephesus, and the Christian message spread widely throughout the province. Sales of silver images of Diana began to fall off. People's incomes were threatened and there was a riot.

Paul wrote his letters to Corinth from Ephesus. And some of his letters from prison (Philippians, etc.) may have been written from Ephesus. Timothy stayed behind to help the church when Paul left. Paul later wrote a letter to the Christians at Ephesus. One of the letters to the seven churches in Revelation was also addressed to them.

There is a tradition that Ephesus became the home of the apostle John.
Acts 18:19; 19; 20:17;
1 Corinthians 15:32; 16:8-9;
Ephesians 1:1; 1 Timothy 1:3;
Revelation 2:1-7

The theatre is one of the splendid remains of the major Hellenistic city of Ephesus: here Paul and his companions were taken by the angry mob.

Ephraim
The younger of Joseph's two sons, born in Egypt. Ephraim was adopted by Jacob, his grandfather, and received a greater blessing from him than Manasseh, his elder brother. The tribe which descended from him was an important one. Israel is sometimes called Ephraim by the prophets
Genesis 41:52; 48

Erastus
1. An assistant of Paul who went with Timothy to work in Macedonia (Greece) while Paul stayed on in Asia Minor (Turkey).
Acts 19:22; 2 Timothy 4:20
2. The city treasurer at Corinth. Erastus was a Christian and sent his greetings to the church in Rome.
Romans 16:23

Erech
One of the great Sumerian cities, in southern Babylonia, about 40 miles/64km north-west of Ur. It is mentioned in Genesis in the list of nations.
Genesis 10:10; Ezra 4:9

Esarhaddon
Son of Sennacherib. He became king of Assyria (680-669 BC) when his father was murdered. Manasseh, king of Judah, was one of many minor kings who were subject to Esarhaddon.
2 Kings 19:37; Ezra 4:2

Esau
The (elder) twin brother of Jacob; son of Isaac and Rebekah. He became a hunter, and cared so little about the promises of God that one day when he came in hungry Esau 'sold' Jacob the rights of the elder son in return for food. When Jacob also gained Isaac's blessing by a trick, Esau was angry. Afraid of what he might do, Jacob left home. In the years that Jacob was away, Esau settled in the area around Mt Seir and became rich. When they met again Esau greeted his brother warmly and accepted his gift of livestock. Esau went back to Seir and founded the nation of Edom, while Jacob went into Canaan. But there was continued trouble between their descendants.
Genesis 25:21ff.; 27-28:9; 32-33;
Hebrews 12:16-17

Eshcol
A valley near Hebron. The name means 'a cluster of grapes'. When Moses sent spies into the Promised Land they brought back samples of the fruit of the country, including a huge bunch of grapes from this valley.
Numbers 13:23-24; 32:9;
Deuteronomy 1:24

Eshtaol
A place about 10 miles/16 km west of Jerusalem, on the borders of the land belonging to the tribe of Dan. This was the home district of Samson. Here he grew up, and the Spirit of God first moved him to go out against the Philistines in the lowlands to the west. In spite of Samson's exploits, the Danites never occupied their inheritance.
Joshua 15:33; 19:41; Judges 13:24-25; 16:31; 18

Essenes
The Essenes were a small and fairly exclusive sect, never numbering more than a few thousand. They had

grown up in the second century BC as a protest movement–against Greek influence on the Jewish religion; against corrupt kings; and against the growing carelessness among Jewish people about keeping the Law. They were even stricter than the Pharisees, whom they denounced as 'givers of easy interpretations'! They were so disgusted with Jewish society that many of them opted out of it and went to live in monastic communities.

The community at Qumran, the people who wrote the Dead Sea Scrolls, probably belonged to the Essene movement. See *Dead Sea scrolls.*

Esther

A Jewish girl who became queen of Persia. Esther was an orphan brought up in Susa, capital of Persia, by her cousin Mordecai. After King Ahasuerus (Greek Xerxes) had divorced Vashti he chose Esther as his new queen. Esther kept secret the fact that she was a Jewess. When Haman, the king's chief minister, planned to wipe out all the Jews because he so hated Mordecai, Esther pleaded with the king and uncovered the plot. Instead of being destroyed, the Jews were allowed to kill all their enemies. This event is remembered at the annual Feast of Purim.

The book of Esther records this story and shows how, once again, the Jewish nation was saved from being destroyed.

Ethiopia

This is Sudan, not modern Ethiopia, and is called Cush in many translations of the Old Testament. See *Cush.*

Eucharist

See *Lord's Supper.*

Eunice

Mother of Timothy.
Acts 16:1; 2 Timothy 1:5

Euphrates

In the Old Testament this great river is often referred to simply as 'the river'. It is 1,200 miles/1,931km long. It rises in eastern Turkey and flows south east to the Persian Gulf. Its course through the Babylonian plains has moved west, leaving many of the ancient cities which once stood on its banks now 3-4 miles/5-6km to the east. The route to Syria followed the Euphrates north to Carchemish, then turned south towards Damascus, Israel and Egypt. The Euphrates is mentioned as one of the four rivers of Eden.
Genesis 2:14; 15:18; etc;
Revelation 9:14; 16:12

Eutychus

A young man who went to hear Paul preach in Troas. It was late and Eutychus went so sound asleep that he fell to his death from the third-floor window where he was sitting. Paul went down and brought him back to life.
Acts 20:7-13

Eve

The first woman, and companion to Adam. She and Adam disobeyed God's command not to eat the fruit of the 'tree that gives knowledge'. Because of this, death came into the world and God sent them out of the Garden of Eden. Genesis names three sons of Eve: Cain, Abel and Seth.
Genesis 2:18–4:2; 4:25

Evil-Merodach

King of Babylon 562-560 BC. When he came to the throne he released King Jehoiachin of Judah from prison in Babylon.
2 King 25:27-30;
Jeremiah 52:31-34

Exile

The Jewish exile began in 597 BC when the Babylonians first took thousands of Jews captive to Babylon. Ten years later they destroyed Jerusalem completely and the kingdom of Judah ceased to exist. The Jewish people were exiles in a foreign country.

Israel They had long been warned that this would happen. Even before the people entered Canaan Moses told them that if they did not listen to God and keep his laws they would lose their land. For 200 years before Jerusalem fell, the prophets had been repeating the warning. In the eighth century BC Amos and Hosea told the northern kingdom of Israel how they would suffer if they did not keep their promise to obey God. They ignored the warning, and in 721 BC the Assyrians captured Samaria, their capital city. The people were deported and scattered in other provinces of the empire. Foreigners were settled in the land and it became the Assyrian province of Samaria. The ten tribes of Israel were never heard of again.
Deuteronomy 8:19-20; 2 Kings 17; Amos 2–9; Hosea 9

Judah In the south Judah, too, was threatened by the Assyrians. The Assyrian King Sennacherib took many Judean cities and besieged Jerusalem. But King Hezekiah trusted God and obeyed God's laws. He listened to the prophet Isaiah's messages from God. When the Assyrians called on him to surrender he turned to God for help and God saved them from defeat.

The people of Judah learned only half the lesson. The idea grew that Jerusalem, the city of God, was unconquerable. With the city and the temple they were safe from any enemy. It did not matter what they did. For a time they were safe because they paid tribute to the Assyrians who were fighting other enemies, and at the end of the seventh century BC that empire broke up.

But a new danger loomed–from Babylon. In the reign of King Josiah, the prophet Jeremiah began to warn the people of Judah. Only if they gave up their selfish ways and obeyed God would they be safe. But no one listened.

In 604 BC the Babylonians took control of Syria and the land to the south. King Jehoiakim of Judah was one of the kings who had to pay tribute to them. The Babylonian King Nebuchadnezzar also took hostages back to Babylon. Before long King Jehoiakim thought he would be better off on the side of the Egyptians, and he rebelled against Babylon. He died before the Babylonians reached Jerusalem. After a short siege the new king, his son Jehoiachin, surrendered, on 16 March 597 BC. Nebuchadnezzar stripped Jerusalem of its treasures and took the king and many leading citizens to Babylon. The exile had begun.
Isaiah 36–37; Jeremiah 7;
Daniel 1

The fall of Jerusalem Nebuchadnezzar left Zedekiah, the king's uncle, as a vassal king in Judah. Jeremiah told the people again and again that to be safe they must accept Babylonian rule. But false prophets said Babylon would soon fall and encouraged Zedekiah to rebel. Quickly the Babylonians marched against Judah and again besieged Jerusalem. Other cities fell until only Jerusalem was left. It held out for eighteen months. Food supplies were used up and the people were starving when Nebuchadnezzar's army broke through the walls in the summer of 587 BC. Zedekiah tried to escape by night but was captured. The Babylonians looted the city and left it and the temple a burnt-out ruin. Many important men from Jerusalem were executed. Other survivors were taken to Babylon to join the earlier exiles.

Very little remained of the kingdom of Judah. Settlers from Edom were already taking over the land south of Hebron and Beth-zur. Nebuchadnezzar appointed a governor, Gedaliah, to rule the rest of the country in the name of Babylon. The Book of Lamentations describes the horror of it all. The cities were in ruins. Apart from the thousands exiled to Babylon many people had died in the fighting. Many more died of starvation and disease in the siege. Now few remained to farm the land the invaders had ruined.

Gedaliah made his headquarters at Mizpah and tried to rule well. But

A city under siege, with a battering-ram against its walls, and refugees with their possessions leaving in carts drawn by oxen, is depicted on this Assyrian relief.

some still refused to accept the Babylonian rulers. They plotted against Gedaliah and murdered him. His supporters were afraid and fled to Egypt, taking the prophet Jeremiah with them. The Babylonians carried off still more of the people in 582 BC, and joined the land to the province of Samaria.
Jeremiah 27-28; Lamentations; 2 Kings 25:22-26; Jeremiah 40–43

The exiles In Babylon the Jews lived in their own settlements in the capital and other towns. They were free to build houses, earn a living and keep their own customs and religion. They could not go back home but they were not ill-treated. King Jehoiachin and his family were 'guests' in the king's household. Some Jews, like Daniel, rose to high positions in government service. Skilled Jewish craftsmen were among the workmen Nebuchadnezzar employed. Many became so much at home in Babylon that when the opportunity came to rebuild Jerusalem they did not want to go. But some Jews longed to return to Judah and in exile they clung to their religion and their way of life.

Ever since Solomon had built the temple it had been the centre of Jewish faith and worship. Now it was gone. There was nowhere to offer the temple sacrifices. So the people began to lay new stress on those parts of their religion that they could observe. Keeping the day of rest, the sabbath, became very important. So also did circumcision, the sign of God's covenant with them, and the laws about what was clean and unclean. And they began to value the written records of God's message as never before. Some of the priests, such as Ezra, began to study the law of God in every detail (they were called 'scribes'). Many of the books that make up our Old Testament were given their present form during the time of the exile.

Return from exile In 539 BC, nearly fifty years after King Nebuchadnezzar of Babylon had captured Jerusalem, Cyrus king of Persia conquered Babylon. The Babylonian Empire passed to the Persians. They put a Persian governor (a satrap) in control of each province of their new empire. But they gave the people of these provinces much more say in their own affairs. They were encouraged to keep their own customs and religion–and nations exiled by the Babylonians, including the Jews, were allowed to go back home if they wanted to.

In 538 BC Cyrus issued a decree saying that the Jews could 'go to Jerusalem and rebuild the Temple of the Lord, the God of Israel'. They were to be given money and all the supplies they needed. Cyrus gave them back the gold and silver bowls and other things that Nebuchadnezzar had taken from the temple. The first party of exiles made the long journey back home.

Exodus

The word Exodus means a 'going out'. The Book of Exodus tells how the people of Israel left Egypt, where they had been slaves, and how they emerged as a nation. They are set free and given hope for the future.

The book centres on Moses, the great champion of Israel. He is called by God to lead the people of Israel out of Egypt.

Exodus falls into three parts.

Chapters 1-19: the Hebrew people are freed from slavery in Egypt. Moses leads them through the desert to Mt Sinai.

Chapters 20-24: God makes a binding agreement with his people at Sinai. He gives them rules which they must live by, both while in the desert and when they reach the Promised Land. These rules are summed up in the Ten Commandments in chapter 20. God's laws affect the whole of life: how people behave towards one another; how they are to live together, and how they must behave towards God himself.

Chapters 25-40: God instructs the people of Israel to build and furnish a movable tent (the tabernacle) where they can worship him. Laws are drawn up for the priests and for the worship of God.

The Exodus The 'going out' of Egypt, the exodus, was the key event in the history of Old Testament Israel. All future generations were to look back to it. Annual religious festivals commemorated it. Parents were to make sure their children learned what it meant. Through Moses God led the Hebrew slaves out of Egypt and began to make them into the nation of Israel. The date was probably early in the thirteenth century BC, about the time when Ramesses II was pharaoh of Egypt.

When Moses first asked the Pharaoh to free the Hebrew slaves, his reply was not encouraging. Pharaoh was not moved by the signs Moses did or by anything his brother Aaron could say. He immediately tightened his grip on the discontented workers. But then God took direct action. In the course of some eight or nine months ten disasters (the 'plagues') struck the country. Some of these troubles had been experienced before in Egypt, but not all, and never one after the other in such a short space of time.

The plagues Under God's direction Moses warned Pharaoh when each disaster was going to strike–and at the expected time it happened. Some came to an end when Moses prayed. Several times the Hebrews living in the Nile Delta region escaped, so that when Egyptian cattle died of disease the Hebrew slaves lost none of their animals. When hail destroyed crops and herds alike, when it stayed dark for three long days, again the people of Israel were not affected.

In all this, too, the Egyptians saw their gods defeated. When the God of the Hebrews took action the Nile-god, for example, who should have made the land fertile, brought only ruin. Even the powerful sun-god Ré was overwhelmed in unnatural darkness. The king's magicians could do nothing about it. Nine plagues came and went: the Nile water was polluted; then came frogs, gnats and flies; animals died; the people had boils; hail was followed by locusts, and after that a terrible darkness.

But it was the tenth 'plague' that gained Israel's freedom, and this was something different. 'All through Egypt,' Moses announced, 'on a certain night, the firstborn sons in every household will die.' The firstborn sons of the Hebrews would be safe if the people carefully followed the instructions Moses gave them. They must mark their doorposts with the blood of a lamb killed in sacrifice. They must cook the lamb (again as instructed) and eat it that night, with bitter herbs and bread made without yeast. They must pack their belongings and get dressed, ready for a journey. It all happened as God said.

Every year afterwards the people of Israel kept the anniversary of this event as the Festival of the Passover: for after this (when death 'passed over' the families of Israel) Pharaoh let them go.

At midnight the firstborn died. Before morning the king ordered the Hebrews out of his country. With gifts of gold and jewellery from their neighbours–and anything else they asked for–the Hebrews began to move. But their troubles were not yet over. As the long, straggling line of families with their goods and cattle began the slow journey eastwards, Pharaoh summoned his charioteers and set out to bring them back. He sighted the runaway slaves camped by the sea, at a point the Old Testament calls 'the Sea of Reeds'. It was probably a part of Lake Menzaleh near present-day El Qantara on the Suez Canal. The sea blocked the way of escape. They were trapped between it and an armed, fast-moving enemy.

Again God intervened. He opened a path for them across the sea. When the Egyptians tried to follow, the waters returned and drowned them. The people of Israel were safe on the other side.
Exodus 5–15

The commandments at Mt Sinai With no more to fear from the Egyptians, the refugees turned south-east towards Sinai and the planned meeting with God. After travelling for nearly three months they camped before Mt Sinai, one of the mountain peaks in the south of the Sinai peninsula. There, in an awe-inspiring setting, God completed what he had begun when he rescued the people from Egypt. He made his agreement (covenant) with them. He formally declared that the rabble of ex-slaves were his people, the nation of Israel.

For their part they must listen to him and obey his laws, summed up in

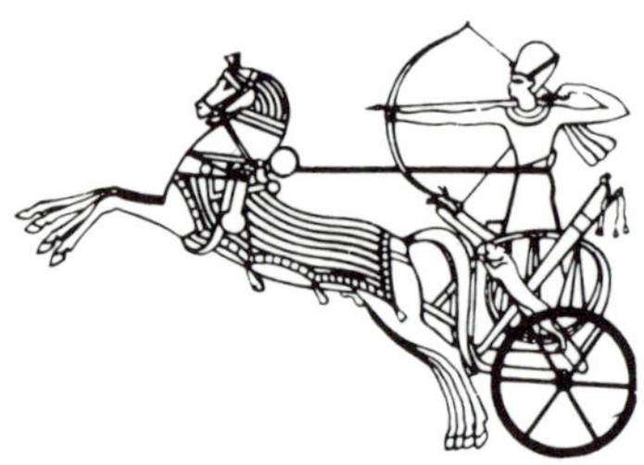

An Egyptian pharaoh stands in his chariot, firing arrows at the enemy.

the Ten Commandments which he gave to Moses on two stone tablets. They set out the basic principles that would govern the people's lives. Their promise to obey was confirmed in a solemn ceremony under the shadow of the mountain. Animal sacrifices were offered and the blood was sprinkled on the people and on the altar. So the agreement was sealed. God then told them how to build a special tent (the tabernacle) that would be the sign of his presence with them all the rest of their journey.

They spent almost a year at Sinai Then they turned north to go through the Wilderness of Paran until they came to Kadesh-barnea. There they camped on the southern borders of Canaan.

There were problems all the way. Very soon after they left Egypt their food supplies began to run out and it was obvious that the desert scrub land could not supply them. More than once they had no water because there was no oasis anywhere near, or because the spring they found was polluted. Each time the people turned on Moses and blamed him and Aaron for leading them to their deaths. Soon, too, they looked back at the slave-ghetto in Egypt through a rosy glow–'At least we had plenty to eat there'! Yet each time God met their need. He fed them with 'bread from heaven' (manna) every day throughout the long years until they came to Canaan, and he supplied water even in unlikely places.
Exodus 16–40; Numbers; Deuteronomy

On the borders of Canaan At Kadesh-barnea the people's grumbling had serious results. Spies were sent into Canaan and they came back with reports of the great and powerful people who lived there. When they heard this the frightened Israelites rebelled. Moses' life was threatened and some began calling for a leader to take them back to Egypt. The trouble was eventually overcome. But they had to spend another thirty-eight years of aimless wandering in the desert–until the people who were afraid to go on into Canaan had died. Only then did the nation again come in sight of their Promised Land.

They made their way through the wilderness of Zin, bypassing the country of Edom. They defeated other kings who would not let them pass and finally camped opposite Jericho ready to cross over the River Jordan into the land God had promised to give them. Moses, on the point of death, appointed his assistant, Joshua, as the people's new leader. 'There has never been a prophet in Israel like Moses; the Lord spoke with him face to face. No other prophet has ever done miracles and wonders like those that the Lord sent Moses to perform against the king of Egypt.' The people mourned his death.
Deuteronomy

Ezekiel

One of the great Old Testament prophets. Ezekiel was the son of a priest called Buzi and lived in Jerusalem until Nebuchadnezzar invaded the city in 597 BC. Along with King Jehoiachin and other important citizens he was taken captive to Babylon. There he was allowed to have his own house and lived in a settlement of Jewish exiles at Talabib on the River Chebar. After about four years he was called by God to be a prophet. Until Jerusalem was completely destroyed in 586 BC his main message was a call to repentance. The Jews had disobeyed God and must seek forgiveness. After the Babylonians had overthrown Jerusalem Ezekiel looked forward to the day when God would allow the Jews to rebuild the city and God's temple.

The book Ezekiel was called to be a prophet at the age of thirty. He gave God's message both to the exiles in Babylonia and to his people still living in far-off Jerusalem. When his call came to be a prophet he was also given a vivid vision of the holiness of God (chapters 1–3). This affected his whole life.

Chapters 4–24 consist of warnings to Israel of God's judgement. Jerusalem will be destroyed.

Ezekiel also brought a message of God's judgement on the nations who were threatening his people (chapters 25-32).

When Jerusalem finally fell in 587 BC Ezekiel's message took on a new note (chapters 33–39). He brought comfort to the people, and a promise of hope for the future. God would restore his people.

Finally Ezekiel described his visions of the time to come, when God's people would offer his perfect worship in a new temple (chapters 40–48).

Ezekiel underlined that each individual has a responsibility towards God. He stressed the need for people to be made new from the heart. He was a dedicated prophet. Holiness is his constant theme. He gives his message in pictures, much more than most other prophets.

Ezion-geber

See *Elath.*

Ezra

A priest and teacher of the Law at the time of the exile. Ezra was given permission by King Artaxerxes to lead a large group of Jewish exiles back from Babylon to Jerusalem. The temple had been rebuilt, but when Ezra arrived he was distressed to find that the people no longer obeyed God's laws, even after all that had happened. Many Jews, including priests, had married women from nations that did not worship God. Ezra put an end to these mixed marriages. He taught the people God's laws and they turned to God again with new joy.
Ezra 7-10; Nehemiah 8–9

Book of Ezra

The Book of Ezra follows directly on from Chronicles. It describes the return of some of the Jews from exile in Babylon. They brought back life and worship to Jerusalem. The account covers roughly the years 538-433 BC. Some of the book may consist of the leader Ezra's own writings.

The return to Jerusalem is presented in three stages:

Chapters 1-2: the first party returns, with Zerubbabel, on the orders of Cyrus, emperor of Persia.

Chapters 3-6: the temple is rebuilt and worship at Jerusalem begins again, despite local opposition.

Chapters 7-10: Ezra leads another group back to Jerusalem. He helps restore the religion and way of life of Israel.

F

Fair Havens

A small port on the south coast of Crete. Paul's ship called in at Fair Havens on the voyage to Rome. Here Paul conferred with the centurion Julius and the owner and captain of the ship, who wanted to reach a more attractive harbour in which to spend the winter. In spite of Paul's advice they put out to sea, and were caught in the violent wind which drove them to shipwreck on Malta.
Acts 27:8-12

Faith

Paul carefully explains in his letters to the Christians in both Rome and Galatia that a person can find a right relationship with God, not through his own good deeds (as people often think), but only through faith or believing.

'Faith' means having confidence and trust in God. It is not a 'leap in the dark' which a man must take without thinking. It is trust in a God whom we believe to be trustworthy. Confident in this knowledge, a person can believe and entrust his life to Jesus Christ. As sinful people we can do absolutely nothing to save ourselves. We have to depend totally on what God has already done for us through Jesus.

This is the start of a 'life of faith'. No one can be certain of living aright by his own efforts. We need to continue to trust wholly in Jesus and the Spirit he gives to help us live in a way that pleases God. This life of dependence on God goes right back to the beginning of God's dealings with man, as Paul shows when he traces it back to Abraham.

The New Testament also refers to 'the faith', meaning the basic teaching about Jesus on which our trust is grounded.
1 John 5:1-5; John 1:12; 3:16; 5:24; Romans 1:17; 5:1; 10:9-10; Galatians 3; Ephesians 2:8-9. See also Genesis 15:6; Psalm 37:3-9; Proverbs 3:5-6; Jeremiah 17:7-8; Habakkuk 2:4; Hebrews 11; James 2; 1 Timothy 3:9; 5:8.

Fall

Sin is present in the world because mankind has rebelled against God. There has never been a person (except Jesus) who was not a sinner. The Bible traces this back to the very beginning of history. The story of Adam and Eve depicts the dramatic 'fall' of men and women from the high place they once had as friends of God and the crown of his creation.

Adam and Eve originally lived in full and open fellowship with God and each other. There was no sin to spoil their lives. This was how God meant it to be. But in Genesis 3 we learn that all this changed drastically. The couple listened to the serpent and decided to rebel against God by doing what he had forbidden. As a result of this disobedience Adam and Eve were banished from God's presence. They were told that from then on life would be hard work. They would know sorrow, and life would end in death.

Since the fall of Adam and Eve the whole creation has been affected by their rebellion against God. 'Sin came into the world through one man, and his sin brought death with it. As a result, death has spread to the whole human race because everyone has sinned.'

Every part of the universe is affected by sin–both people and the natural world in which we live. Although we still have much of the original nature God gave us, and we still know and search for God, yet we have an inbuilt bias towards sin.

See also *Death, Judgement.*
Genesis 1-3; Romans 1:18-32; 5:12-19; 7:14-25

Family life

The 'family' of Abraham's time was what those of us who live in small family units would call the 'extended family'. It consisted not just of parents and children, but grandparents, aunts, uncles and cousins–and servants, too. It could be very large. Abraham was able to take 318 fighting men with him when he went to rescue Lot from the raiding kings who had taken him prisoner (Genesis 14:14).

In this kind of family group the grandfather had complete authority, not just in practical matters but in religious ones, too. When he died, his eldest son took over by right of birth. The leader's word was law. Abraham's family clan accepted the fact that God had made himself known to Abraham in the silence of the desert. His God was their God, even though they did not always share the kind of faith he had.

God had made a promise to Abraham. He made the same promise again to Isaac and to Jacob. He would be their God, caring for them and protecting them. In return they must live by his rules. Those rules were spelt out in detail to a later generation, when God gave the 'commandments' to Moses at Mt Sinai. So, from the very beginning, ordinary life in Israel was bound up with religious life. The two were one and could not be separated. Everything the family did was based on God's law. If they treated one another badly, they broke God's law. Things had to be put right between them, and a sacrifice was needed to put them right with God (Leviticus 6:1-6).

Parents and children Religion and family life were woven together in the way parents brought up their children. Children were encouraged to ask questions and find out about their religion and history (Exodus 13:14). Places where God had done something special for his people were marked with large stones. When the children asked what they were for, the parents would explain (Joshua 4:5-7).

The regular weekly rest-day (the sabbath) was intended also to be a day when God could be remembered and worshipped (Exodus 31:15-17). In early Old Testament times parents and children would visit the local shrine. There they would offer a sacrifice and the priest would teach them. In New Testament times the sabbath day began on the Friday evening with the best meal of the week. Then came a visit to the meeting-house ('synagogue') to hear the law explained by the teacher.

The inside of a simple peasant house, with women grinding corn and spinning.

Parents taught their children the laws of God. They also learned by heart other parts of the Bible. David's great poem on the death of Saul and Jonathan was a favourite. In the evenings, members of the family recited many of the stories now written down in the Bible.

Festivals The meaning of the great religious festivals was clearly shown by special ceremonies. At Passover, for example, the eldest child was asked by the father, 'Why do we have this service?' And the child explained how it had come about, as he had been taught. There was the Day of Atonement, followed by the Harvest Festival (Tabernacles), when everyone lived in tents made of branches to remind them of the way their ancestors lived in the desert. Later in Israel's history the children acted the story of Esther at the Festival of Purim. All the festivals were so full of life and action that children wanted to know what they were about. In this way they learned the history of their nation as the people of God.

Teaching There were no schools as such in Old Testament times. The children were taught at home, first by their mother, then by their father. In addition to religion and history, which was learned through stories and by question and answer, and memorized, the girls learnt homemaking skills–baking, spinning, weaving–from their mother, while the boys learned a manual trade from their father. The Jews had a saying 'He who does not teach his son a useful trade, is bringing him up to be a thief'. The father's work, tools and (in later Old Testament times) fellow members of his trade guild, were all important for a boy's education. (See *Education.*)

Land and animals Everyone owned some land so both boys and girls had outdoor work to do. There was always plenty to do in looking after the vines, ploughing and threshing.

The children also looked after any animals the family kept–usually sheep and goats. Every family, even the poorest, hoped to be able to buy two lambs at Passover time. One was killed and eaten, but the other became a playmate for the children, giving its wool for their clothing. In a poor home there was no separate shed for the animals, and the lamb often slept with the children and fed from the same dishes (2 Samuel 12:3). At the end of summer it was killed and the meat was preserved in the fat from the sheep's tail. Most families would also have at least one goat which was kept for milk. Some of the milk was allowed to go sour to produce goats'-milk cheese.

Although some households had dogs they were not common and were regarded as scavengers.

The donkey (ass) was the most common form of transport. It could carry heavy loads as well as people. Richer farmers used oxen for farm work and camels for transport.

Nomads and settlers In the early days of the Old Testament –before the years in Egypt–the people lived in tents. Abraham left a settled, civilized city life in Ur on the far-off River Euphrates to obey God's call. For the rest of his life he was, at least from time to time, on the move. His son Isaac and grandson Jacob also lived in tents–like the Bedouin today. Water was scarce, particularly in the summer or during a time of drought, and the people who lived in Canaan defended their wells against these wanderers, who took water not only for themselves, but for their animals as well. The dispute between Abraham and Abimelech over the well at Beersheba is one example (Genesis 21:25-31).

Although they had no permanent home, Abraham and his family were settled enough to grow crops. And they never moved far from the big centres of population. After the time of Moses the people of Israel wanted to settle more permanently, and then for some years there was war. When the Israelites had won their land, other groups of nomads wanted to settle there too. So the Israelites in their turn had to learn to deal kindly with these landless strangers, who soon came to form the working class of the population.

The pattern of each day did not vary much. The basic pattern of family life changed little over many centuries. It was interrupted now and then by invading armies, but otherwise peaceful. The people lived close to the land. Each family looked after its own small farm. There were always some animals to care for. Then there was the daily cleaning, baking, spinning, weaving and dyeing, as well as the work of the farm itself.

Family relationships Family life grew more important during the course of Israel's history. When the clans began to settle in permanent homes the normal family unit became smaller.

The father Within this smaller unit, as before, the father had complete authority. He could, if he wished, even sell his daughter into slavery. In early Old Testament days it was possible for a father to have disobedient children put to death. He could divorce his wife without any reason and without providing for her. And he could arrange the marriages of his sons.

Women The woman was *owned* by her husband, and looked up to him as her master. This attitude was still found even in New Testament times.

Though women did much of the hard work, they had a low position both in society and in the family. But the law did protect a divorced woman, and her children were taught to respect her.

Jesus' dealings with women–for example, his readiness to speak to and help the Samaritan woman (see John 4)–contrast strongly with prevailing attitudes. And Christian teaching is clear: 'There is no difference...between men and women; you are all one in union with Christ Jesus' (Galatians 3:28). There are no second-class citizens in Christ's kingdom.

Inheritance Normally only sons could inherit–and the eldest son in a family had a special position. He had the right to a double share of his father's property. Only if there were no sons could daughters inherit. If there were no children at all, the property passed to the closest male relative.

Respect and discipline The Book of Proverbs speaks of family relationships more freely and directly than any other Bible book. For their own good, children were expected to respect their parents and pay attention to their teaching and advice. Parents who really love their children will discipline and correct them, especially when they are young. 'A good spanking will teach them how to behave.' 'If a child has his own way, he will make his mother ashamed of him.' The happiness of parents and children are bound up with one another. And reverence for God is the starting-point.

The New Testament builds on the same foundation. It is the Christian duty of children to obey their parents, and of parents to bring their children up with Christian discipline and teaching.

Some Bible passages on family relationships: Exodus 20:12; 21:7-11; Deuteronomy 21:15-21; 24:1-4 (compare with Matthew 19:8-12)

The teaching in Proverbs on parents and children: 1:8-9; 4 and 5; 6:20ff.; 10:1; 13:1, 24; 17:21, 25; 19:13, 18, 27; 20:11; 22:6, 15; 23:13-16, 19-28; 28:7, 24; 29:15, 17; 30:11, 17

In the New Testament see especially: Ephesians 5:21-33; 6:1-4; Colossians 3:18-21

Worship in the home At home every Jew was expected to pray the 'Eighteen Benedictions' every morning, afternoon and evening. Each benediction begins, 'Blessed art thou, O Lord, king of the universe'. They all praise God–for the promise of a redeemer, or the resurrection of the dead, or the gift of repentance, or healing the sick, and so on.

Before every meal the father of the household said a blessing: 'Blessed art thou, our God, king of the universe, who createst the fruit of the vine' (or, 'who bringest forth food from the earth'; or, 'who createst the fruit of the tree').

A new baby 'Children are a gift from the Lord;
they are a real blessing.
The sons of a man when he is young
are like arrows in a soldier's hand.
Happy is the man who has many
such arrows.'

These words from Psalm 127 show how the people of Israel felt about children. A big family was a sign of God's blessing. If no children came, people thought God must be displeased–and this could be very hard on a couple who had no children (see for example the story of Hannah in 1 Samuel).

Children were important for a number of reasons. Boys were the most valued. It was so important to have a son that the woman's name was changed to 'Mother of...' when her first son was born. As they grew up boys were able to help work the family's land. Girls were much less important, but still useful workers. A wedding-gift had to be paid to the parents to make up for the loss of the daughter's work when she left to be married. Sons were also needed to carry on the family name. In the earliest times, before people were sure that there was a life after death, they liked to think they would live on through their children, so without children there was no future. This was why, if a man died without a child, it was the duty of his closest relative to marry the wife. Their first son would then take the dead man's name and inherit his land (the 'Levirate law'–Deuteronomy 25:5-6).

Customs The new-born baby was washed and rubbed over with salt (it was thought this made the skin firm). Then it was wrapped in 'swaddling cloths'. The mother or her helper placed the baby on a square of cloth. Then she folded the corners over its sides and feet, and wrapped bandages (often embroidered) round the whole bundle to keep the baby's arms straight by its sides. The bandages were loosened several times a day and the skin was rubbed with olive oil and dusted with powdered myrtle leaves. This went on for several months. The wrappings made it easy for the mother to carry her baby in a woollen 'cradle' on her back. At night the cradle was hung from a beam in the house, or between two forked sticks.

Babies were normally breast-fed for two or three years. But there was a very high death-rate amongst babies because of the poor conditions in most houses.

In Old Testament times the baby was named when it was born. The name always had a meaning. It might say something about how the baby was born, his character, or the family's feelings towards God. For example, Jacob's wife, Rachel, who had waited so long for her first son, called him Joseph–'may God add sons'. The name Barak means 'lightning'; Elijah means 'the Lord is God'; Isaiah means 'God is salvation'.

Ceremonies In New Testament times a baby boy was not named until the eighth day after birth. At the same time he was 'circumcised' (the loose skin was cut off the top of his penis). In many other nations boys were circumcised when they were recognised as adult members of the clan. But as far back as the days of Abraham God had made circumcision on the eighth day after birth the physical sign of the promise he had made to Abraham and his descendants for all time. This ceremony reminded them that every child in Israel was one of God's own people. Sadly, the real meaning of the ceremony was often forgotten, and by the time of the exile to Babylon it was looked on simply as a sign of being a Jew.

Two other ceremonies sometimes took place at the same time. If the baby was the 'firstborn' in the family he belonged to God in a special way and had to be bought back (redeemed). This was because at the time of the exodus, when all the firstborn children of the Egyptians had died, God saved the firstborn sons of Israel. From then on the firstborn belonged to him. 'You must buy back every firstborn male child of yours.' 'This observance will be a reminder...it will remind us that the Lord brought us out of Egypt by his great power' (Exodus 13:13ff.). The first generation after the exodus were redeemed by dedicating the Levites for God's service. After that each family paid five pieces of silver to the priest to buy back their firstborn.

The other ceremony was a sacrifice made by the mother for her 'purification' (see Leviticus 12). According to the law of Moses a person had to be ritually 'clean' to worship God. Certain things–contact with a dead body, for example, or having a baby, or eating forbidden foods which might carry disease–barred people for a time from joining in worship. To be 'clean' again the mother had to sacrifice first a pigeon and then a lamb. If, like Jesus' parents, Joseph and Mary, they were too poor to afford a lamb, they could offer a second pigeon instead. In New Testament times money was put into the offering boxes of the temple to pay for the sacrifices, and the women gathered on the steps near the altar for the ceremony.

In New Testament times, too, a boy became a man on his thirteenth birthday. This was marked by a special service called the Bar Mitzvah ('son of the law'). In the months before his birthday he learned to read the passages from the Old Testament Law and Prophets that were to be read in the synagogue that day. He had to recite them at the service. The minister ('rabbi') then spoke to the boy and asked God's blessing on him in the beautiful words of Numbers 6:24-26:

'May the Lord bless you and
take care of you;
May the Lord be kind and
gracious to you;
May the Lord look on you with
favour and give you peace.'

The boy was now a grown-up member of the community. Sometimes his parents took him to watch a service like this the year before his own thirteenth birthday.

Farming

In the main, the people of Palestine have always been farmers, although the nature of the soil, the climate, and other factors made farming a life of constant toil and hardship. A large part of the land was desert and rock, and could not be farmed. When the Israelites first settled in the Promised Land each household was given a plot of land and also, perhaps, grazing rights on land held in common. But, as time passed, those who were well off tried to 'buy out' the small farmers (see Isaiah 5:8), and it was a constant struggle for poor people to hold on to their land.

A typical Israelite farmer did not live on his farm but in a nearby village or town, which was often close to a fortified city. It was important to be within reach of water supply and protection, in case of enemy invasions. He owned no more land than he and his family could manage by themselves, perhaps with the help of a few servants or hired labourers. Everyone in the farmer's family shared in the work. He might grow arable crops, as well as grapes and olives. He might possess a few sheep and goats, with one of his sons or a hired shepherd to care for them. Or a farmer might decide to specialize.

The farmer had four main problems: drought; strong winds from the east (the 'sirocco') which could take away his dry soil; locust plagues; and invading armies.

The main crops were grain, grapes (for wine) and olives (for oil). These three are mentioned together over and over again in the Bible (for example, Deuteronomy 7:13; Nehemiah 5:11; Hosea 2:8). But this list of crops can be expanded.

Grain In the few fertile valleys, the Philistine plain, the Jordan Valley, and the Plain of Jezreel, a valuable crop of wheat was grown. Barley was grown more widely, as it needed a shorter growing season and flourished on poorer soil. Spelt and millet were also grown. Bread was the basic item of diet for everyone, and every available valley and lowland area was used for these crops. The many rocks and stones lying about were built into terraces on the hillsides to keep the precious soil from being lost.

Vegetables There were small harvests of vegetables–lentils, peas, beans, onions, cucumbers, garlic and herbs. These were grown near the house or between the vines.

Fruit Wine and raisin cakes were made from grapes. Other fruits included melons, figs, dates, pomegranates and nuts. Many of these provided a useful source of water during the six-month summer drought from May to October. The oil from olives was used for cooking, lighting, medicine and washing. Vines and olives grew on the hillsides.

Flax Some flax was grown for making linen cloth.

The farmer's year Some time ago a limestone plaque was discovered dating from about the time of King Solomon, on which was written a kind of schoolboy rhyme. It is called the Gezer calendar.

The two months are (olive) harvest
The two months are planting (grain)
The two months are late planting
The month is hoeing up of flax
The month is harvest of barley
The month is harvest and feasting
The two months are vine tending
The month is summer fruit

Here is the farmer's year at a glance.

Olive harvest From September or October to November there was time for the olives to be picked and pressed for oil. Olive-trees can stand long periods of drought and can grow in very shallow soil. They take two years to mature and, because the fruit ripen slowly, the farmer could pick them whenever he had time. They were carried in baskets to the vats and, in earlier times, the oil was squeezed out by treading, or pounding with a pestle. Later, a millstone was developed. The olives were placed on a grooved stone wheel, and another stone was turned over them, worked by a beam. The pulp was then pressed under weights.

Large olive presses have been found from the time of David, consisting of a beam which would press on the baskets of olives. The upper end had weights attached, while the lower end was fixed in a hole in the wall. The oil ran into stone vats, where it was left for some time to settle and clear.

Ploughing and planting In October/November came the precious 'early rain' after the long summer drought. From then till January was the time for ploughing and planting. The plough was usually a simple wooden stake with a handle and a point of iron (bronze before the time of David). It was attacked to a yoke, and drawn by one or two oxen. The farmer could hold the plough with one hand while the other held a stick for beating the oxen. Since it was light the plough could easily be lifted over any large stones. It left a furrow 3-4ins/80-100cms deep. The seed (wheat, barley, flax) was scattered by hand and then the plough was sometimes used again to cover the seed with earth. Occasionally branches were dragged along to smooth the ground, and a hoe used to remove weeds.

Late planting From January to March the winter rains fell and planting continued–millet, peas, lentils, melons and cucumbers.

Flax and grain harvests In March and April the later rains came. These developed the grain to the point where harvesting could begin.

Flax was harvested first, in March and April. The plant was cut with a hoe near to the ground and the stalks were dried, ready to be made into cord and linen cloth.

Then in April, May and June came the harvests of barley and wheat. The stalks were cut with sickles (a small wooden handle with a curved iron or copper blade) and the bundles were tied into sheaves. These were loaded on to donkeys or carts and taken to the 'threshing-floor'. This seems to have been common property and a centre of village life at this time of year. It was usually a rocky outcrop, or clay-covered patch, in a windy spot outside the village. Stones were put around the edge and the sheaves were spread out on the floor about a foot deep.

Threshing was done by beating with a stick, or by driving animals round, or by using a threshing-sledge. This was simply a board, or a board on wheels, with bits of stone or iron fixed to it. The stalks were chopped and the grain loosened.

The farmer would then 'winnow', tossing the stalks in the air with a wooden fork or shovel. The straw was blown aside (and in winter used to feed the animals), but the heavy grain fell back on the floor. This was probably then sifted and stored in large earthen-ware jars, in dry cisterns (silos) dug in the floor, or in 'barns'. There seem to have been large national silos, and the farmer probably paid his 'income tax' (and debts) in grain at this time.

Vines In June, July and August the vines were pruned and tidied up. Isaiah 5 and Mark 12 provide pictures of how a new vineyard was prepared. A boundary trench was dug, and posts driven in to support a hedge or fence. The young vines were planted in rows and the branches raised up on supports. Then the pruning was done. When the fruit began to form, a shelter of branches or a stone tower was put up, and the household kept watch against thieves, or raiding foxes or jackals.

Fruit harvest In August and September the summer fruits were harvested–figs, sycomore figs, pomegranates and grapes. Baskets of grapes were taken to small vats, whose floors sloped towards jars. The grapes were trodden to squeeze out the juice. Great numbers of these vats have been found in the 'Shephelah' (the foothills of Judah).

The picking and the treading of the grapes was all done in holiday mood. The fruit could be eaten at the same time. 'When you walk along a path in someone else's vineyard', says Deuteronomy 23:24, 'you may eat all the grapes you want, but you must not carry any away in a container.' Forty days were needed for the 'lees' or sediment to settle. Then the fermenting wine was stored in new goatskin bags or pottery containers.

In some places wine-making became something of an industry. At Gibeon, fifty-six jar handles have been discovered inscribed with the name of the town and the vineyard

A farmer using a simple plough: a wooden stake with a metal tip at the bottom.

owners. In addition there were sixty-three bell-shaped vats used as wine cellars during the time of the kings, together with fermenting-vats and wine presses.

Animals 'Cattle' in Hebrew includes sheep, goats, oxen and asses, but not pigs. Asses were kept for carrying loads, and oxen for ploughing. Only on special occasions were oxen killed for meat. Sheep and goats were always kept together. Sheep mainly provided wool for clothes. They were occasionally eaten as meat–in Israel their distinctive fat tail was considered a rare delicacy. They also provided milk in the form of curds for the very poor. Goats were valuable for meat and milk. Their hair made coarse cloth and their skins made bottles.

The life of the shepherd seems to have altered little from the time of Abraham to that of Jesus. The shepherd led his sheep, knew each one, and watched over them night and day (see John 10:1-6). Despite the rough stone enclosures which served as folds, there was constant danger from thieves and wild beasts–lions, leopards and bears (until they became extinct), wolves and hyenas, jackals, snakes and scorpions. The shepherd carried a staff to catch hold of any sheep which fell, and was armed with a wooden club. If sheep were stolen he had to repay his master. If they were attacked by wild beasts he had to bring back evidence (see Exodus 22:12-13).

New Testament times Farming changed little in the land of Israel throughout the Bible period, though in other Mediterranean countries notable progress was made. Pharisees often referred to those with no religious education as 'people of the land', which perhaps suggests that the farmer was not held in very high regard. However, the country was being farmed more intensively. A writer of the time described Israel's fruit as being better than that of any other land. Fertile Galilee was producing more flax, and probably some attempts were being made at irrigation. It had, by then, become quite common to keep poultry.

Fasts

Only one day in the year is set apart for a national fast in the Old Testament laws. That is the Day of Atonement, on the 'tenth day of the seventh month' (end of September/beginning of October). During the exile in Babylon, special fasts were also held in the fifth and seventh months to mourn the destruction of the temple and the murder of Gedaliah, governor of Judah.

After the exile two other regular fasts were held: in the tenth month, to remember the start of the siege of Jerusalem, and in the fourth month, marking the final capture of the city. Fasts were also kept by the nation and by individuals at times of special need.

Prayer and fasting often went together. People fasted as a sign of genuine repentance. During the time of fasting they did not eat or drink. Other customs were to tear their clothes, dress in coarse sackcloth, throw dust and ashes on their heads, and leave their hair uncombed and their bodies unwashed. But the prophets, and Jesus himself, made it plain that these outward signs of fasting were not enough. A real change of heart was what mattered most.
Leviticus 16:29; Zechariah 7:5; 8:19; Judges 20:26; Nehemiah 1; 2 Samuel 12:16, 20; Esther 4:16; Isaiah 58:3-5; Joel 2:13; Jonah 3:5; Matthew 6:16-18

Feasts and festivals

The sabbath and most of the great festivals of the Jewish religion were kept from the very earliest period of Israel's history. But two of the festivals described here began to be observed much later–Purim (from the time of the Persian Empire, fifth century BC) and Dedication/Lights (from the time of the Maccabees, second century BC).

Israel's main religious festivals were connected with the seasons and the farmer's year in Canaan. They were held in the spring, the early summer, and the autumn. On each occasion the men were expected to go to their local shrine and present their offerings to God. After the seventh century BC these 'pilgrim' festivals were held only in Jerusalem. By the time of Jesus, the city's normal population of 40,000 or so was swollen to about 150,000 by the pilgrims who came for the Passover. Festivals were times of thanksgiving to God for harvests, occasions for remembering outstanding events in Israel's history, and opportunities for great rejoicing and feasting.

The sound of the ram's-horn trumpet, the 'shofar', announced the start of all the religious festivals in Israel.

Passover and Unleavened Bread Passover was one of the most important annual festivals. It took place the evening before the fourteenth of Nisan. On that night every family sacrificed a lamb. It was a reminder of the first such sacrifice, which took place just before God rescued the Israelites from Egypt. On that occasion God 'passed over' the Israelite houses where the blood of the lamb had been sprinkled on the door-posts and lintel, and he spared the lives of their firstborn.

Bread, made quickly and without yeast ('unleavened bread') was eaten at the Passover meal and all through the following week. This, too, was a reminder of the hurried preparations made when Pharaoh finally allowed the Israelites to leave Egypt. It also recalled the first bread baked from new corn, four days after the Israelites entered Canaan.

At first the Passover was held in people's homes, but by New Testament times it was the main 'pilgrim' festival celebrated in Jerusalem. It remains one of the most important Jewish festivals today.
Exodus 12; Joshua 5:10-12; Mark 14:1-2

Firstfruits This ceremony was held on the last day of the Festival of Unleavened Bread. The first sheaf of the barley harvest was presented to God. The main harvest festival (Weeks) came later.
Leviticus 23:9-14

Weeks (later **Pentecost**) At the end of the grain harvest the priest offered two loaves of bread made from the new flour, along with animal sacrifices. This took place fifty days (or seven weeks plus one day) after Passover and the start of the harvest. The festival later came to be known as 'Pentecost', from the Greek word meaning 'fiftieth'. It was a time of great rejoicing and thanksgiving for God's gifts at harvest.
Exodus 23:16; Leviticus 23:15-21; Deuteronomy 16:9-12

Trumpets (later **New Year**) The beginning of every month, as well as every festival, was signalled by a blast of trumpets. But on the first day of the seventh month the trumpets sounded for a special celebration. It was a day for rest and worship, more important even than the sabbath, judging by the offerings made. It marked out the seventh month as the most solemn month in the year. After the exile it was treated as a religious New Year festival *(Rosh Hashanah)*, but the months were still counted from Nisan (March/April).
Numbers 10:10; 28:9; 29:1-2

Day of Atonement On this day (*Yom Kippur*) the whole nation of Israel confessed their sin and asked for God's forgiveness and cleansing. The high priest, dressed in white linen, first offered a sacrifice for his own sin and the sin of the priests, and then offered another sacrifice for the sin of the people. It was the only day in the year when the high priest went into the 'holy of holies'–the inner, most sacred part of the tabernacle (worship tent) or temple. There he sprinkled blood from the sacrifice. Then he took a goat, known as the 'scapegoat', and, after laying his hand on its head, sent it off into the desert as a sign that the people's sins had been taken away.

See also *Atonement, Priests and Levites, Sacrifices.*
Leviticus 16

Ingathering/Tabernacles/Booths/Shelters This was the most popular and joyful of all the festivals. It was held in the autumn when all the fruit crops had been harvested. The celebrations included camping out in gardens and on roof-tops in tents or huts made from the branches of trees. These tents (or 'tabernacles') were a reminder of the time when Israel had lived in tents in the desert.

This festival included a ceremony in which water was poured out and prayers made for good rains for the coming season. It was at this festival, perhaps following this particular ceremony, that Jesus stood up and declared: 'Whoever is thirsty should come to me and drink. As the scripture says, "Whoever believes in me, streams of life-giving water will pour out from his heart."'
Exodus 34:22; Judges 21:19-21; Nehemiah 8:14-16;
Leviticus 23:39-43; John 7:37-38

Dedication/Lights This festival commemorated the cleansing and re-dedication of the second temple by Judas Maccabaeus in 165 BC, after it had been defiled by the Syrian ruler Antiochus IV Epiphanes. It was also called 'Lights', as each evening lamps were placed in houses and synagogues. This festival, called Dedication in John 10:22, is celebrated today as *Hanukkah.*
1 Maccabees 4:52-59

Purim An excited and noisy celebration, traced back to the time when Esther and her cousin Mordecai saved the Jewish people from massacre during the reign of the Persian King Xerxes ('Ahasuerus'). Purim means 'lots' and the name refers to the lots cast by Haman, the king's chief minister, to decide on which day he should massacre the Jews.
Esther 3; 7; 9:24, 26

The sabbath The sabbath was Israel's most distinctive festival. Other nations had their harvest festivals and new moon rituals. Only Israel had the sabbath, which cut across the rhythm of the seasons. Every seventh day was set aside for rest. This was the 'sabbath' and it belonged to God. The fourth commandment instructed the people of Israel to stop work on this day. The pattern of six days' work followed by a day of rest was also traced right back to creation, when God 'rested' on the seventh day. On the sabbath people were to remember all that God had done, especially in rescuing them from slavery in Egypt.

'If you treat the Sabbath as sacred,' God said through the prophet Isaiah, 'and do not pursue your own interests on that day; if you value my holy day and honour it by not travelling, working or talking idly on that day, then you will find the joy that comes from serving me.'

By New Testament times, keeping the sabbath had become so complicated with rules and regulations that Jesus had to remind people that 'the Sabbath was made for the good of man; man was not made for the Sabbath'.
Genesis 2:2-3; Exodus 20:8-11; 31:12-17; Deuteronomy 5:12-11; Isaiah 56; 58:13-14; Matthew 12:1-14; Mark 2:23-27

New Moon The day of the new moon signalled the start of each month. Trumpets were blown and special sacrifices made. The arrival of the new moon was understood as a reminder that God had created an orderly world. No work was done on this day, but there were special meals and religious teaching.
Genesis 1:16; Numbers 10:10; 28:11-15; Psalm 104:19;
1 Samuel 20:5, 24; 2 Kings 4:23

Sabbatical year Just as every seventh day was to be a day of rest, so every seventh ('sabbatical') year was 'to be a year of complete rest for the land, a year dedicated to the Lord'. Obviously the whole land could not lie fallow at the same time. Probably each field lay fallow every seventh year after it was first sown. Anything which did grow in this year could be harvested free by the poor. This arrangement was a sign to the Israelites that the land was not their own. It was 'holy' (belonging to God). Also, each seventh year all Israelite slaves were set free and all debts cancelled.
Leviticus 25:1-7; Exodus 23:10-11; 21:2-6; Deuteronomy 15:1-6

Jubilee year The law said that in every fiftieth year–the year after seven 'sabbatical' years–land and property (except for town houses) was to be returned to its original owners, Israelite slaves were to be set free, debts cancelled and the land allowed to lie fallow. The jubilee law may have proved too difficult to keep, so it was looked forward to as a time that only God could introduce. It was the 'year' promised by Isaiah, and announced by Jesus.
Leviticus 25:8-17; 23-55; Isaiah 61:1-2; Luke 4:16-21

Felix
The Roman governor before whom Paul was brought for trial at Caesarea. He kept Paul in prison for two years, hoping for a bribe.
Acts 23:24; 24:1-27

Fellowship
The 'sharing' companionship which is at the heart of Christian experience. Man was made to live in 'fellowship' with God. Man's disobedience broke this friendship. Jesus came to restore it by dying to deal with the sin which separates us from God.

So Christians can begin to know the companionship with God for which every man and woman was created. A Christian shares, with Jesus, in the love of God himself, 'the fellowship that we have with the Father and with his Son Jesus Christ'. Jesus pictures the closest possible 'sharing' between himself and his followers. 'I am the vine,' he said, 'and you are the branches.'

Just as we share Jesus' life, so we share in the lives of our fellow-Christians. The Christian is not just an individual joined to Christ, he also shares a new life with fellow-Christians and with Christ himself. 'We are all joined to each other', and the hallmark of this Christian 'fellowship' is love.

This sharing and love which characterizes the Christian church shows itself in action. The early church in Jerusalem showed their oneness by sharing all their possessions with one another. The non-Jewish churches showed their love for the needy church in Jerusalem by sending money.

See also *Body, Church.*
1 John 1:3; John 15:1-17; Romans 12:4-13; John 13:34-35; Acts 2:44-47; 4:32-37; Romans 15:25-27

Festus
The Roman governor of Palestine after Felix. He listened carefully to Paul and called him to defend himself before King Herod Agrippa II and Bernice. He agreed with them that Paul was innocent of any crime. But Paul had appealed to Caesar, and would have to go to Rome for trial.
Acts 25-26

Fig and sycomore fig
The fig was an important fruit in Bible times. The ideal of peace and prosperity was summed up as 'everyone able to sit down under his own vine and fig-tree'. Figs are slow-growing trees, bearing fruit for about ten months of the year. The large leaves make useful wrappings. Cakes of dried figs made excellent food–compact 'iron rations' which were easy to carry. Amos the herdsman and prophet also 'took care of fig-trees'. The tree Zacchaeus climbed to get a better view of Jesus was a sycomore–another kind of fig-tree.
Amos 7:14; Luke 19:4

Fishing

A fisherman casts his net.

The Israelites were not much involved in the fishing trade until New Testament times. There is only one Hebrew word for fish–to cover everything from the smallest 'tiddler' to the great fish that swallowed Jonah. The main fishing industry in Old Testament times was in the hands of the Phoenicians, though the presence of a 'Fish Gate' is probably an indication of a market for imported fish in Jerusalem.

By the time of Jesus, however, a flourishing industry seems to have developed on the inland Sea of Galilee. The name of the lakeside town, Tarichaea ('pickling'), probably indicates that it was a centre for salting and preserving fish. The Gospels describe the fishermen working in family groups, and often using hired helpers. They mended nets and sails, repaired boats and often fished by night. This was dangerous, for storms could quickly blow up on the lake.

Bone or iron fish-hooks were used from early times. Isaiah refers to a hook and line (no rod was used) and Job mentions a spear, but fish were usually netted. There were two kinds of nets. One was a net thrown by hand while the fisherman stood on

the shore. The other was a large net (dragnet) used from the boats, with floats and weights attached so that it moved vertically through the water, bringing the fish to the boats or to shallow water in smaller and smaller circles. The fish were brought to the shore and sorted before being sent to market.
Nehemiah 13:16; Mark 1:20; Isaiah 19:8; Job 41:7; Ecclesiastes 9:12; Matthew 13:47-48

Flax

Linen cloth is made from this pretty blue-flowered plant which grows about 1½ft(45cm) high. After the plants are pulled up, the stem fibres are separated by steeping them in water (retting). They can then be combed and woven like threads. The fibres are also used for string, nets and lamp-wicks. Linen was used for sails. It was also wrapped round dead bodies, and made into fine clothes, in Egypt and Israel.
Exodus 26:1; Joshua 2:1, 6; Proverbs 31:13; Ezekiel 27:7; Mark 15:46

The attractive flowers of the flax plant ripen into seeds used to produce linseed oil.

Flesh

The word 'flesh' in the Bible is often used to refer to people as physical beings–'mortal flesh'. In this sense it can be used to show the weakness of man, who is 'only human', in contrast with the strength of God. When Jesus' disciples fell asleep in the Garden of Gethsemane he told them to watch and pray: 'the spirit is willing, but the flesh is weak'.

Paul used the word 'flesh' ('lower nature' or 'human nature' in some recent translations) to refer to the life non-Christians live under sin's domination.

The Christian, on the other hand, is both 'in the flesh' and 'in the Spirit'. He is caught in a battle between his own inborn bias to sin and the presence of God's Spirit in his life, working to make him more like Christ. He has to say 'no' to the sinful desires which are part of his fallen nature, and allow the 'fruit' of the Spirit to grow in his life.

See also *Body*.
Psalm 78:39; Isaiah 40:5; Mark 14:38; Romans 7:13-25; 8; Galatians 5:16-24

Flood

The flood was a tremendous disaster from which only Noah's family and the birds, animals and reptiles he took with him into the 'ark' (the boat God had instructed him to make) were saved. The flood was sent by God because the human race had become so wicked that he was sorry he had made men and women. The flood waters covered everything for a whole year.

Rain fell for forty days. The floods were swollen by water released from underground sources. For five months (150 days) the waters went on rising. It was nearly eight months before any dry land was seen again. The growing population and civilization described in the early chapters of Genesis were destroyed.

Noah, his wife, his three sons and their wives were saved in the ark. God gave Noah the plan for this gigantic basket-boat which would float on the rising waters. The measurements given are enormous: about 450 x 76 x 45ft/137 x 23 x 14m.

It had a wooden framework bound with reeds and sealed with a thick layer of tar to keep out the water. It was roofed and had an opening to let the light in all around, just below the roof. The people and the animals went in through an opening in the side. There were three decks and presumably some means of separating the various creatures. Noah took on board one pair of all living creatures–seven pairs of the ones used for sacrifice and for food–and stocked the ark with food for them all.

When the flood began to go down the ark grounded on one of the mountains in the country of Ararat (Urartu) in eastern Turkey. But the land dried slowly. It was over two months before Noah could see the mountain tops. Forty days later he sent out a raven, and after another week a dove, to try to get some idea of the situation further away. The raven never came back. The second time the dove went out it returned with a fresh green leaf. The plants were beginning to grow again. A week later the dove flew off again and did not return. Still Noah waited. In another month the water had gone, but it was nearly two months more before God told them they could safely set foot on dry land again.

As soon as they left the ark Noah built an altar and expressed his thanks to God by offering sacrifices. God promised that he would never again destroy the earth and its inhabitants in such a flood. He made the rainbow a sign of his promise, to reassure them. 'Whenever I cover the sky with clouds and the rainbow appears, I will remember my promise,' God said.
Genesis 6–9

Other stories Besides the Bible account of the flood, there are many other fascinating stories of an ancient flood from various parts of the world. Folk tales of a great flood are worldwide.

In one Babylonian story the gods sent the flood in order to get some rest from the noise of mankind. The god who made man warned the hero, and he built a boat in which he and his family and animals escaped. After seven days the gods missed the food supplied by sacrificial offerings and called a halt

The Genesis flood story is set against a Mesopotamian background and in view of the similarities may well look back to the same event.

Archaeologists have found evidence of floods in southern Mesopotamia, but these were only local disasters. They came much later (about 3000 BC) than the flood described in Genesis.

Food

For ordinary people, food and clothing have always been two of the main concerns. 'Don't start worrying,' Jesus said, '"Where will my food come from? or my drink? or my clothes?"' He knew how easy it is to worry when there is only just enough to live on. In Bible times this was how most of the people in Israel lived. For this reason their enemies attacked during the growing season. If the crops were destroyed, the people could not survive. In Gideon's time, 'wherever the Israelites sowed any seed, the Midianites would come...and attack them...and destroy the crops' (Judges 6:3-4). Unreliable rainfall, drought, and pests such as locusts, made the crops uncertain. Famines were expected as a normal part of life. It is not surprising that the Israelites saw the golden age of the future as an age of plenty with more than enough for all.

There were a number of sources of food: mainly cereal crops, fruit and vegetables. Bread was the basic item of everyone's diet. The word 'bread' in the Lord's prayer stands for food in general. And Jesus called himself 'the Bread of Life', meaning 'the food of life'.

Bread Barley bread–the bread the boy with the five loaves and two fish gave to Jesus (John 6:9)–was probably the most common. Wheat gave the best flour and was also quite common, and spelt, too, was sometimes used.

The grain was first sorted in a shallow basket, to remove poor grain and any poisonous seeds such as darnel ('tares'), weeds which grew with the corn and looked very similar. Then it was ground. In early days this was done by rubbing between a small stone and a larger one. Later it was ground between two small millstones. The lower one was fixed; the upper one turned round on top of it.

For each baking, forty litres of flour (Matthew 13:33) were mixed with water (or sometimes olive oil) to form a dough. People seldom had fresh yeast, so a piece of fermented dough ('leaven') from the previous baking was kneaded into the new dough and the whole left to rise. Before it was baked, part of the dough was put aside for the next day's 'leavening'. The bread was baked as a flat cake. This was appetising when fresh, but soon went dry. 'Parched' corn–fresh ears put on a metal sheet over the fire and 'popped'–was a popular alternative. For special occasions cakes and pastries were included in the baking.

Fruit and vegetables Fruit was another important food. The grape vine did more than produce juice. Many grapes were eaten fresh at harvest time, and many more were dried and used as raisins. Figs, too, were eaten fresh, and also dried and pressed together to make fig cakes. When

Abigail gave David supplies for his men they included 'a hundred bunches of raisins and two hundred cakes of dried figs' (1 Samuel 25:18). They were specially useful for taking on a journey. The prophet Isaiah prescribed a paste made of figs to heal King Hezekiah's painful boil (Isaiah 38:21).

Dates are not mentioned by name in the Bible, but they were certainly grown. The crowd waved date palm branches to welcome Jesus to Jerusalem, the week before he died. Dates were also used in the special sauce (*charoseth*) in which everyone dipped their bread at the Passover meal. The sauce was made from dates, figs, raisins and vinegar.

Olives were also eaten–some fresh, in October, and others after pickling in salt water. The most important produce of the olive was its oil, which was used in cooking. Pomegranates, almonds and pistachio nuts were also available, and citrus fruits were just coming in in New Testament times.

There were fresh vegetables in season. Beans, lentils and peas were dried and stored in jars. There were also onions and leeks, melons and cucumbers. Vegetables were used to make soups. Esau exchanged his birthright for a bowl of red lentil soup (Genesis 25:29-34). Farm products were also available. Butter was not much used because it would not keep in the hot weather. But cheese and yoghurt were popular, and in in New Testament times people kept hens and poached the eggs in olive oil.

Meat and fish Not much meat was eaten. Mutton and meat from the goats was the most common, and birds were caught for food, although the wealthy, even in Old Testament times, fed on lamb, veal and beef. Meat was normally boiled. The lamb roasted for the Passover Festival was an exception. Ordinary people ate meat only on special occasions such as a celebration party, or when entertaining guests at a religious festival, or special sacrifice at the local shrine. On this occasion the family gathered together to eat some of the animal that had been sacrificed at the shrine, as a sign of their renewed friendship with God.

Fish was certainly an important food in New Testament times. (At least seven of Jesus' twelve disciples were fishermen.) Small fish were dried and salted and eaten with bread, as at the feeding of the 5,000. Or they could be cooked over an open fire and eaten fresh, as at the breakfast Jesus prepared for his followers (John 21).

Sweetening and seasoning The Israeiites had no sugar. Honey from wild bees was the main sweetener (see the story of Jonathan in 1 Samuel 14:25-27 and of Samson in Judges 14:8). But another kind of 'honey' may have been produced by boiling dates and locust beans to make a syrup.

Seasoning was important, too. There was plenty of rock salt on the south-west shores of the Dead Sea. Salt was also obtained by evaporation. The outer layer of rock salt was often impure and hard. It had no flavour and was used to spread on the temple courtyards in wet weather to make them less slippery.

Salt was used for seasoning food, but it was much more important for preserving it. In New Testament times the main industry at Magdala, on the Sea of Galilee, was the salting of fish. Mint, dill (anise)–and cummin (seeds like caraway but used in place of pepper) were also used to give food the strong flavouring which everyone liked. They also helped give variety and interest to an otherwise boring diet. Rarer spices, imported from Africa and Asia, were used only by the wealthy.

See also *Meals.*

Food laws

Strict laws about diet are laid down in the Old Testament saying what may, and what may not, be eaten. The general rule was that animals which chew their cud and have divided hoofs could be eaten. This ruled out the pig. Fish were allowed, but only those with fins and scales. Many birds were not to be eaten, particularly if they were scavengers. It was also laid down that the blood must be drained from a carcase before it was cooked and that meat and milk dishes were not to be cooked or eaten together.

These two rulings meant that a Jew could not eat at the home of a non-Jew, where these restrictions were not normal. They resulted in a division between Jewish and non-Jewish Christians in New Testament times. Paul needed to teach the Christians at Corinth about their Christian freedom in this respect. In New Testament times, too, a family which followed the teaching of the Pharisees was not allowed to buy or eat food which had been killed in a pagan temple as an offering. For three days before a festival they were not allowed to buy any food at all from a non-Jew.

The reason for these strict laws on diet was never explained. They may have been God's way of protecting the health of the people. They may have been intended to avoid cruelty to animals: for example, the law which forbade the boiling of a kid in its mother's milk; and the draining of the blood, which prevented the practice of cutting a limb off a live animal for meat. Or they may have been given for more strictly 'religious' reasons. This was certainly the reason for forbidding meat which had been offered to an idol. And boiling a kid in its mother's milk may have been a Canaanite religious practice which the Israelites were to avoid. We cannot always be sure in any particular case whether one or all of these reasons holds good.

Leviticus 11;17:10-16

Forgiveness

It is one of the most extraordinary things that God loves sinful human beings and delights to forgive them.

'If you kept a record of our sins,
who could escape being condemned?
But you forgive us,
so that we should stand in awe of you.'

Yet from start to finish the Bible makes it clear that when we repent and turn from our sinful past to God, he will forgive us.

As Christians we enter a new life; we become children of God; we have been forgiven. Christians will forgive others because they have been forgiven, and although there may still be times when they fall into sin, they have only to turn to God in repentance and God will forgive and restore them.

See also *Repentance.*

Exodus 34:6-7; Psalm 51; Psalm 130:3, 4; Isaiah 1:18; 55:6-7; Hosea 14; Matthew 6:12-15; 26:26-28; Luke 7:36-50; Acts 2:38; Ephesians 4:32; 1 John 1:9

Fox and jackal

These are smaller cousins of the wolf. The fox, who hunts alone, likes fruit and often damages the low vines. Jackals go about in packs, scavenging at night. The foxes in the story of Samson were probably jackals.

Judges 15:4

A fox (in the foreground) and jackal.

Frankincense

Gum collected by peeling back the bark of the frankincense-tree (*Boswellia*) and cutting into the trunk. The resin gives off a sweet scent when warmed or burned, and was used as incense in Bible times. Frankincense was one of the gifts brought to Jesus by the three wise men.

Exodus 30:34-38; Leviticus 2:1, 15-16; Matthew 2:11

Freedom

In any society where some men rule harshly over others one of man's greatest longings is for physical freedom. So it is not surprising that this idea has a large place in the Bible. Freedom is the central theme in the quotation from Isaiah which Jesus used to describe his own work. 'The Spirit of the Lord is upon me ...he has sent me to proclaim liberty to the captives.'

Many hoped that Jesus had come to set Israel free from the Romans. But he made it plain that his first concern was to deal with a far more cruel slavery. He had come to set men free from the power of evil, and he demonstrated this by releasing people from the grip of evil spirits, and healing the sick.

In his letters to Rome and Galatia Paul is anxious to show how important this freedom is. It is freedom from the penalty of our sin, and freedom from the effort of trying, and failing, to please God. The Christian knows he is saved by God's grace, not by anything he can do himself.

Paul saw two main ways in which Christians abused this precious gift of freedom. Some hankered after the rules and regulations of the old Jewish religion. This was happening in

the churches of Galatia, and Paul wrote his letter to them to show how Christian faith was entirely different from a religion of rules. Others thought that because Jesus had set them free they could do what they liked, even sin as much as they wanted. This was quite wrong: they were freed *from* sin, not to go on sinning. They gladly serve a new master–Jesus Christ. True freedom is found in serving God and in serving others.
Luke 4:18; John 8:31-36, 41-44; Mark 3:22-27; 5:1-13; Luke 13:10-16; Romans 6:16-23; 8:2, 21; Galatians 3:28; 5:1, 13; Romans 1:1; 6; Matthew 11:28; James 1:25; 2:12; 1 Peter 2:16

Furniture
See *Daily Life.*

Future destiny
Apart from the certainty of judgement at the second coming of Jesus, the Bible says very little about what happens after death.

The Old Testament writers generally expected a continued existence in *Sheol.* This was simply a place of rest and silence when the blessing of life had been taken away. But as time went on people began to understand more clearly that God had a glorious future in store for them beyond *Sheol.* God does not abandon his people in *Sheol* but will lead them into life and joy. Job and Daniel both express confidence about the future. Job is certain he will see God. And Daniel speaks of the dead living again.

Hades is the New Testament equivalent of *Sheol.* Peter, speaking of the death of Jesus, said that David 'spoke about the resurrection of the Messiah when he said, "he was not abandoned in the world of the dead (*Hades*); his body did not rot in the grave".' In another context Peter says that Jesus went to preach to the dead, 'the imprisoned spirits', presumably in the time between his crucifixion and his resurrection.

The New Testament often talks of death as a sleep. 'Paradise' is the word used by Jesus to describe the pleasant existence of those who die at peace with God. And Paul was confident that when a Christian dies he is in the presence of Jesus. It is impossible for us to imagine an existence outside time; but the New Testament writers were confident that Christian believers, whether dead or living, would meet with Jesus, and enter into the glory of heaven, being given new 'resurrection' bodies no longer subject to death.

See also *Death, Heaven, Hell, Judgement, Second coming of Jesus.*
Psalms 94:17; 16:9-11; Job 19:25-27; Daniel 12:2, 3; Acts 2:31; 1 Peter 3:19-20; Matthew 9:24; 1 Corinthians 15:20, 35-58; Luke 23:43; 1 Thessalonians 4:13-17; Revelation 20:11-22:5

G

Gabriel
An angel who was God's special messenger. Gabriel was sent to Daniel twice: once to tell him the meaning of a dream and later to predict what was going to happen to Jerusalem. Gabriel was also sent to announce the birth of John the Baptist to Zechariah, and of Jesus to Mary.
Daniel 8:16; 9:21; Luke 1:11-20, 26-38

Gad
Seventh son of Jacob, who gave his name to the tribe of Gad.
Numbers 32
2. The land belonging to the tribe of Gad. Part of the former Amorite kingdom, east of the River Jordan (south Gilead).
Joshua 13:8-13

Gaius
1. A Macedonian Christian who was with Paul on his third missionary journey. Gaius was dragged into the amphitheatre during the Ephesian silversmiths' riot. (See *Demetrius.*)
Acts 19:29
2. A Christian from Derbe who travelled with Paul to Jerusalem.
Acts 20:4
3. One of the few Christians Paul baptized at Corinth.
1 Corinthians 1:14
4. The Christian friend to whom John addressed his third letter.
3 John 1
These may not all be different people.

Galatia
A Roman province in central Asia Minor. Its capital was Ancyra (now Ankara, the capital of modern Turkey). Several cities visited by Paul–Pisidian Antioch, Iconium, Lystra and perhaps Derbe–were in the southern part of Galatia, and Paul's letter to the Galatians was probably addressed to them. Galatia was also one of the areas to which 1 Peter was sent.
Acts 16:6; 18:23; Galatians 1:1; 1 Peter 1:1

Galatians
This letter is the earliest of Paul's New Testament letters, written in about AD 47-48. It was sent to a group of churches in the Roman province of Galatia (central Turkey), some of which, at least, Paul had visited. He had taught, simply, that God's gift of new life is for all who believe. And many people had responded. But since then Jewish teachers had come, arguing that Christians must keep the Old Testament laws.

So Paul's letter answers a vital question. Did non-Jews have to obey the Jewish law of Moses to be true Christians?

He begins by defending his claim to be an apostle who speaks with God's authority, and with a special mission to non-Jews (chapters 1–2).

Paul then puts forward his argument (chapters 3–4). People are put right with God by faith in Christ on its own. New life is God's gift to all who believe. We can do nothing to *earn* it.

Paul finishes his strongly-worded letter by showing that the way Christians behave springs from the love that comes from belief in Christ (chapters 5–6).

His letter is a great defence of Christian freedom: 'Christ has set us free. Stand, then, as free people, and do not allow yourselves to become slaves again' (5:1).

Galilee
The name of an area and large lake in northern Israel. The home area of Jesus and a number of his disciples. When his public work began, Jesus spent much of his time here.

Galilee is mentioned occasionally in the Old Testament. It was surrounded on three sides by other nations and strongly influenced by them. Most of Galilee is hilly, but the land falls steeply to 600ft/184m below sea level around the lake.

At the time of Jesus several major roads of the Roman Empire crossed Galilee. Farming, trade and the lakeside fisheries were the main industries. Many of the towns and villages mentioned in the Gospels were in Galilee, including Nazareth (where Jesus grew up), Capernaum, Cana and Bethsaida. The lake, which is liable to sudden fierce storms as the wind funnels through the hills that ring it round, is also a focal point in the Gospel stories.
1 Kings 9:11; 2 Kings 15:29; Isaiah 9:1; Luke 4:14; 5:1 and following; 8:22-26; John 21, etc; Acts 9:31

Gallio
The Roman governor of Achaia, about AD 51-53. Gallio was the Emperor Nero's tutor and the brother of Seneca, the philosopher. While Gallio was governor of Achaia he was based at Corinth. When Paul was in Corinth Jews who were worried about the success of his preaching tried to persuade Gallio to condemn him. However, Gallio refused to get involved with Jewish laws, and as a result Paul was able to continue his work.
Acts 18:12-17

Gamaliel
A famous Pharisee, Paul's teacher, and a member of the supreme Jewish council, the Sanhedrin. When the apostles were arrested and questioned, some of the council wanted to put them to death. But Gamaliel advised caution. 'Leave them alone!' he said. 'If what they have planned and done is of human origin, it will disappear, but if it comes from God, you cannot possibly defeat it.'
Acts 5:34ff.; 22:3

Games and sport
Children's games seem to have changed very little. We know that children in Bible times had toys which made a noise–such as rattles and whistles. These have been found in many places by archaeologists. Some rattles were shaped like boxes with small holes in each side, others like dolls and birds, though they were rather heavy to handle.

Girls played with dolls' houses, too. Miniature cooking pots and furniture, made out of pottery, have been found dating from between 900 and 600 BC. Some dolls had jointed arms and legs, and hair of beads and mud. They had holes in their shoulders for puppet strings. But whether these were really used for play, or in religious ceremonies, is not quite certain.

Israelite children, like children everywhere, also played 'imitating' games, copying the grown-ups. Matthew 11:16-17 describes groups of children in the market-place, playing at weddings and funerals.

The game played by the soldiers at the trial of Jesus was also a dice game. As a four-sided dice was used, they moved a skittle from a central mark to positions where it could be 'robed', 'crowned' and 'sceptred', and the soldier whose move completed the 'ceremony' called 'king' and collected the stakes which had been put down. In this instance the prisoner was used as a human skittle (Matthew 27:28-29). Although dice games were so popular amongst the people, the religious leaders strongly disapproved of gambling, and Jewish law disqualified a gambler from testifying before a court of justice.

As time went on some people began to make a living by entertaining others. This kind of entertainment –what Paul calls a 'spectacle' in 1 Corinthians 4:9–became very popular in Greek times. It was one of the areas of disagreement between the Sadducees, who enjoyed it, and the Pharisees, who believed it to be wrong. King Herod built a stadium (for fights between gladiators–who were trained captives taken in war, or criminals– and between men and animals) and an amphitheatre (for chariot-racing) in Jerusalem. He built theatres at Caesarea and Sebaste which can still be seen.

Greek-style athletics were also performed in the stadium and in the gymnasium. The Greeks believed that exercise of this kind was necessary for a healthy body. But Greek athletics were not very popular with the Jewish people. They found it offensive that the athletes competed naked. And the close link with Greek religion was a further obstacle. The sporting events mentioned in Paul's letters are all linked to the Greek games. He uses the strict training of the athlete as an example (1 Corinthians 9:24-27), and writes of runners competing to win a crown of laurel, pine or olive leaves. He also refers to boxing, with arms and hands bound with studded leather, so that a blow must be avoided rather than parried! Philippians 3:13-14 pictures a race, and Hebrews 12:1-2 reflects the long-distance foot race, where weight has been lost in training and clothes are shed for the race.

A Greek discus-thrower.

Gath
One of five Philistine strongholds in Old Testament times. When the Philistines captured the Covenant Box (ark) it was taken to Gath, but plague followed. Goliath came from Gath, the home of other 'giants', too. Later, when David was on the run from King Saul, he escaped to Gath. Soldiers from Gath helped him when his son Absalom led a rebellion against him. The city was subject to the kingdom of Judah for some time and eventually fell to the Assyrians in the eighth century BC. The site is still not certain.
Joshua 11:22; 1 Samuel 5; 17:4; 21:10-22:1; 27; 2 Samuel 15:18; 2 Kings 12:17; 2 Chronicles 11:8; 26:6

Gath-hepher
A place in Galilee on the borders of the lands belonging to the tribes of Zebulun and Naphtali. It was the birth-place of the prophet Jonah. It lay close to the later town of Nazareth.
Joshua 19:13; 2 Kings 14:25

Gaza
One of five Philistine strongholds in Old Testament times, on the coastal plain. Joshua conquered and then lost the city. The town features in the story of Samson. He was put in prison here, and finally died when he brought about the collapse of a great building. Gaza suffered with the other Philistine cities when they captured the Covenant Box (ark).

The town was an important one on the trade route to Egypt. It was conquered by King Hezekiah of Judah, and later by the Assyrian armies and the Egyptian pharaoh.

In the New Testament, Philip was on the road from Jerusalem to Gaza when he met the Ethiopian official
Joshua 10:41; Judges 16; 1 Samuel 6:17; 2 Kings 18:8; Jeremiah 47; Acts 8:26

Geba
Modern Jeba', opposite Michmash, 6 miles/10km north of Jerusalem. A city belonging to the tribe of Benjamin. Saul's army camped here in front of his capital at Gibeah when the Philistines held Michmash. Later Geba became the northern limit of the southern kingdom of Judah, and was fortified by King Asa. Like Michmash, it was on the route of the Assyrian approach to Jerusalem, and was resettled after the exile.
Joshua 18:24; 21:17; 1 Samuel 13:16; 1 Kings 15:22; 2 Kings 23:8; 1 Chronicles 6:60; Isaiah 10:29; Ezra 2:26; Nehemiah 7:30; Zechariah 14:10

Gebal
A very ancient Phoenician city, often known by its Greek name Byblos. It was on the coast of modern Lebanon, north of Berytus (Beirut). 'There is still much land to be taken,' God told Joshua in his old age. Gebal was one of the areas included on the list. Later, workmen from Gebal helped to prepare the timber and stone for building Solomon's temple. Ezekiel prophesied against Tyre and other Phoenician towns, including Gebal.
Joshua 13:5; 1 Kings 5:18; Psalm 83:9; Ezekiel 27:9

Gedaliah
Best-known of several Gedaliahs is the man appointed governor of Judah by King Nebuchadnezzar of Babylon after he had captured Jerusalem. After seven months he was murdered by Ishmael, a member of the royal family. The Jews still living in Judah were afraid that the Babylonians would treat this murder as rebellion, and fled to Egypt.
2 Kings 25:22-26; Jeremiah 39:14-41:18

Gehazi
Servant of the prophet Elisha. When Naaman came to Elisha to be cured of leprosy, Gehazi took the gift which the prophet refused. He lied to Elisha and as punishment became a leper himself. He continued as Elisha's servant and spoke to King Jehoram about the wonderful things Elisha had done.
2 Kings 4–5; 8:4ff.

Genesis
Genesis, the first book of the Bible, is a book of beginnings. The name Genesis itself means 'origin'.

The book tells about the creation. God made the universe. Genesis also tells of the origins of man and woman, how things began to go wrong, and God's good purpose for his creation.

There are two main parts to the book. Chapters 1–11 tell the story of the creation of the world and of the human race. We read about Adam and Eve, Cain and Abel, Noah and the flood, and the tower of Babel.

God's good creation is gradually spoilt by the selfishness, pride and wickedness of men and women. The book tells of the beginnings of sin and suffering–and God's promise of hope.

Chapters 12–50 narrow down from the general story of the human race to one person–Abraham–and his family. Abraham trusted and obeyed God: God chose him to found the nation of Israel. The following chapters tell the stories of his son, Isaac, his grandson, Jacob (also known as Israel), and of Jacob's twelve sons, the founders of the twelve tribes of Israel.

The story then focuses on one of Jacob's sons, Joseph. He is imprisoned in Egypt, and later his whole family comes to live there. The book ends with God's promise to care for his people. All through its chapters, God is active, judging and punishing people who do wrong; guiding and keeping his people, moulding their history. Genesis tells the stories of some of the great men of faith.

Gennesaret
A place on the western shore of Lake Galilee. The name is also used of the lake itself.

See also *Galilee, Chinnereth.*
Mark 6:53; Luke 5:1

Geography of Israel

The land of Israel is very small. From north to south–'from Dan to Beersheba' as the Bible puts it–it is less than 150 miles, barely 230 kms, long. The northern end of the Dead Sea is only 50 miles/80 kms from the coast (though about 1,300ft/400 metres below sea level). The land is, in fact, rather like the roof of a house. It rises gently from the Mediterranean to about 3,200ft/1,000 metres above sea level, and then plunges steeply down to the great gash of the Jordan rift valley. There the earth's surface has cracked and dropped to form a trench which we can trace south all the way into East Africa. East of the Jordan and north of Galilee the mountains rise to greater heights–to nearly 6,500ft/2,000 metres in Edom on the eastern desert fringe, and over 9,800ft/3,000 metres in Lebanon and Mt Hermon to the north.

To surrounding nations, therefore, the people of Israel in their land seemed like hill tribes. 'The gods of Israel are mountain gods', say King Benhadad's officials. The heart of their kingdoms lay along the mountain spine between the coast and the Jordan rift. In these mountains they could hold off attacks from the Philistines on the coast. But they themselves never really conquered the coastlands. From time to time (especially under King David) they expanded north into Syria or east beyond the Jordan where, at different times, they took control of Moab and Edom. But the Judean hills were their first base–and their last.

Geology Geologically, most of the materials making up these lands are young. Limestones or chalk occupy a large part of the surface. The structure is important in helping us understand the Bible.

There are certain characteristic landscape features wherever limestones occur. Water sinks through them (they are permeable), and there is little surface drainage. But they usually develop underground streams and the water can be tapped by sinking wells. Limestones contain many caves. And on the surface they often develop a kind of stony pavement which makes cultivation difficult and yields only a patchy soil. All these features are found in the hills of Palestine and all of them figure in the Bible story.

The desert climate also has its effects on the landscape and its structures. In the desert, regardless of rock type, there is usually a surface covering of sand, flintstone or salt. Much of the southern part of the land is covered by these infertile deposits. Wind and water are the forces which shape the desert rock. The wind scours the desert rocks into fantastic shapes. The force of water, made all the more powerful and dramatic because it is so rare, gouges out steep-sided valleys and overhanging crags. Occasional 'flash' floods can fill a dry valley several metres deep with water in a few minutes.

The rift The long, straight gash of the Jordan Valley, deepening at the Dead Sea, is one of several signs that the earth's surface is unstable. Volcanic activity and changes in the structure are still going on. The Jordan rift has slipped down between two parallel 'faults' to produce the deepest natural depression in the world. The shore of the Sea of Galilee is 660ft/200 metres below sea level. The deepest point of the Dead Sea is more than 2,600ft/800 metres below sea level, despite the deposits brought down by the River Jordan for thousands of years. Hot springs and mineral-stained rocks along the sides of the rift show that the area is still geologically active.

Climate The lands on the Mediterranean coast have a climate which is midway between temperate and tropical. The winters are wet, like those of northern countries. The summers are hot and dry, influenced by the tropical deserts that lie beyond the sea's southern rim. Thanks to this seasonal contrast, snow will lie on the coastal mountains but tropical fruits will ripen in the plain.

The climate varies a good deal in the different areas of the Middle East. But there are a few general factors.

Rainfall The amount of rainfall generally depends upon height above sea level. The mountains attract more rain than the lowlands. They also tend to cut off rain-bearing winds and prevent them reaching inland. In Israel/Syria, the result is more rain in the high mountains north of Galilee (29-60in/750-1,500mm each year) than in the hills of Judea (20-29in/ 500-750mm). The rainfall total lessens rapidly going south. By the time we reach Beersheba it is less than 8in/200mm. South again, desert conditions apply all the way into the Sinai peninsula.

The fall-off in rainfall going *both* inland *and* downhill to the Jordan Valley is even more rapid. The average rainfall for Jerusalem is about 20in/500mm, whereas at Jericho, 15 miles/25kms to the east but 3,200ft/1,000 metres lower, it is barely 4in/100mm. It then rises again on the east side of the Jordan, so that there is a tongue of desert extending north up the Jordan Valley from the Dead Sea, but a tongue of well-watered hill country extending south on the east side of the Jordan all the way from Lebanon to Edom. No wonder that two and a half of the original twelve tribes decided that the land on the east side of the Jordan Valley was as good for their cattle as the land on the west, and asked if they could settle there rather than across the river in the land God promised (Numbers 32). In later years, this land–the land of Gilead–became famous for its fertility. Its hills brought as much rain as that of the hills of Judea, which are nearer the coast but not as high.

Although the northern part of Palestine seems to have a good amount of rainfall (similar to that of southern Britain, for example) the average is very deceptive. There are in fact great variations in the total from year to year. In Jerusalem, where the average is 20in/500mm, there have been years with as little as 10in/250mm and as much as 42in/1,075mm during the past century. This means that the margin of the desert is not fixed. In some years the margin withdraws east and south. In other years it overruns the area and there is drought and famine. These exceptionally wet and exceptionally dry years play a great part in the Bible story. They constantly remind God's people that they depend on him.

Dew In places where there is not much rain, the dew may play an important part in watering the land. Most of the areas with heavy dews are on the coast. The moisture comes in from the Mediterranean during the summer days, then falls to the ground as dew when it is cooled at night. Some coastal areas may have dew on 200 nights each year, and it can give them as much as a quarter of their moisture. So it is not difficult to see why the dew plays so large a part in the life of Bible peoples. Elijah the prophet, for example, predicting a drought, says 'there will be no dew or rain' (1 Kings 17:1).

Winter rains In the Near East and northern Africa most of the rain for the year comes in the winter season. Between the middle of June and September, rain is unlikely to fall. The weather conditions are stable and predictable, dominated by a flow of air from the east. For example, for thirty years Tel Aviv, on the coast, has never recorded rain in June, July or August.

After such a dry summer, the coming of the rains is especially important for the farmer. They should begin in mid-September, but the start of the rainy season is sometimes delayed. This gives the farmer less time for ploughing, and there is also less time for the wells to fill up again after the summer's use. So the Bible pictures the farmer watching and waiting for the autumn rain (James 5:7), to begin work.

Once the rains really start, the winter months are wet. December, or January, has most rain. The rain blows in from the Mediterranean for two to three days at a time, followed by drier and brighter conditions. This pattern continues until, in late March or early April, drier weather sets in. But this is a very important time for the farmer. Plants are beginning to grow after the winter cold. It is vital that the rains continue for long enough into the spring for his crops to be watered during their growing period. He therefore looks for the 'later' rain in April, as well as the 'early' rain in October.

Temperature The temperature range in lands with seasonal rainfall is often very large. There are great contrasts–for example between a summer's day by the Dead Sea, with temperatures reaching 40 degrees C as a matter of course, and a wet winter's day a hundred miles away in Upper Galilee, where a freezing rain is falling. Winter weather on the uplands can be very unpleasant. There are 45-60 days of rain, and snow often falls in winter in Jerusalem. The daily changes can be trying in low-lying areas, too. Jericho has a January average temperature of 15 degrees C. But this is made up of high daytime temperatures and freezing nights.

Temperatures in summer on the coast and in the uplands average a pleasant 22-25 degrees C. They are affected generally by height above sea level and, from time to time, by the winds. In the daytime, in summer, cooling breezes blow in from the Mediterranean to make the heat less intense. But the effect of the *hamsin* is much less pleasant. This fiercely hot and dry wind blows from the south, out of Arabia, bringing a breath from the desert which can sometimes be felt even near the coast. It is well known to the people who live in Israel. 'When you feel the south wind blowing,' Jesus said, 'you say that it is going to get hot–and it does' (Luke 12:55).

The climate today does not seem to be very different from the time when Israel occupied the Promised Land, or when Jesus lived there. The landscape has certainly changed but this is not because of a change in climate.

Vegetation In an area with this sort of climate we would expect to find the following kinds of vegetation–starting in the heart of the desert and moving outwards to the coast and the mountains: desert scrub–steppeland with shrubs and grasses–grassland–transitional forest–forest at higher levels. We would also expect many of the plants to be specially adapted to store water from the wet to the dry season–plants with shiny, smooth, non-evaporating surfaces. All these types of vegetation are, in fact, found in the land of the Bible and its surroundings, the forests in Lebanon to the north, and the desert scrub to the south. The steppe and grassland forms just a narrow band around the uplands of Judea and east of the Jordan at middle levels. However, on the coastal slopes most of the original grassland has long since been ploughed and sown. And some of the desert was cultivated by irrigation agriculture in Roman times just as it is in modern Israel.

Changes But there have been great changes over the centuries. When Israel entered the Promised Land, most of the upland area was covered by forest. Even in the time of Jesus there seems to have been widespread tree cover. Many kinds of hardwoods and softwoods are referred to in the Old Testament, and the Romans laid out forest areas. Today, the landscape is quite different, and almost all the forest and woodland has disappeared.

Felling trees for building and firewood and to clear land for ploughing led to soil erosion. This meant that new trees could not grow, and the forest was gradually replaced by the kind of thorny scrub (*maquis*) which is so common in long-settled Mediterranean lands. This scrub clutters the ground and is quite useless (for example, for building). It contains few trees of any size, is a serious fire risk in summer and today may represent all that remains of once-splendid forests. In Israel there has also been deliberate destruction of trees in war after war and destructive grazing by goats. The same has happened on the now-bare hills of Moab, east of the Jordan, which was once a densely-settled woodland area.

Only in the past half-century have we begun to reverse this process of deforestation. This was just in time to save a few of the famous cedars of Lebanon and some of the mountain forest of the north. Landscape changes over the same time have been even more dramatic, because they have happened so much more quickly than those taking place in the long and dreadful period of destruction. Marshes have been drained and cultivated. Groves of fruit trees have been planted in place of the old oak forests. And irrigation has been extended into the desert, in some cases to the same areas once farmed under Roman rule in the time of Jesus. It is well known that some desert soils are fertile when watered. And the southern fringe, together with the lower Jordan Valley, is an area of oasis agriculture–for example at Jericho and Engedi.

The resources of the land God promised Israel a fertile land. In addition 'its rocks have iron in them, and from its hills you can mine copper' (Deuteronomy 8:9). Copper has been mined from very early times. Mining for iron came later, after the Hittites had discovered how to smelt it. The Philistines brought the secret with them. But not until the time of David and Solomon were the Israelites able to make their own iron tools. The copper mines just north of the Gulf of Aqaba were in full production in Solomon's time.

The country's other main resources are building stones, pitch, sands and clays, with a variety of chemical salts in the Dead Sea area where evaporation has left them bedded in thick layers. Today phosphate rock is extensively worked, and the waters of the Dead Sea themselves yield potash, bromine and magnesium.

The regions of Israel The Jews in the time of Jesus had a very precise idea of what was, and what was not, 'the land'. Their 'regional geography' was based on a scale which worked from the most sacred to the least sacred area. The Holy of Holies in Jerusalem came highest on the scale and, at the other end, the very touch of the dust of areas outside 'the land' was considered defiling. The heart of the country consisted of Judea and Galilee on the west side of the Jordan, separated by Samaria (which did not belong to it) but linked on the east bank by Peraea. The approved route from north to south without leaving 'the land' (avoiding Samaria) involved crossing the Jordan twice. Surrounding this core area was a kind of inner belt of lands which had once belonged to Israel. They were thought to be not quite as defiling as the heathen lands that were completely outside the boundaries.

The more usual regional geography, however, recognizes seven major natural divisions in the land.

The central highlands The core area of the Jewish kingdoms lay in the 'hill country' along the watershed–with the land sloping away to the coast on one side, and away to the Jordan Valley on the other. This upland rises to just over 3,280ft/1,000 metres at its highest points, near Hebron. The western slope is gentle, the eastern abrupt. The forest cover has long since gone and it has become a region of bare limestone slabs and poor soils. Cultivation is on terraces and in very small fields, much of the area is used for raising stock. The fortified towns of this hill-country made good defence points. The capitals of the southern and northern kingdoms (Judah and Israel) were both in this area. The northern kings of Israel used several different strongpoints before building the capital at Samaria.

At the northern end of this region a number of isolated hills look down on the neighbouring region, the Plain of Esdraelon. But the hill country continues north-westwards to the coast in the jutting promontory of Mt Carmel. The 1,970ft/600-metre ridge cuts the coastal plain in two, breaking the general north-south pattern of the regions. On the northern edge of Carmel lies the modern port-city of Haifa.

Even today the 'hill country' has few roads apart from the main Hebron–Jerusalem–Nablus (ancient Shechem) highway. The main highways of both the ancient and modern worlds pass north of the hills or run parallel with them along the coast. So, although this region contains Jerusalem, it has always stood a little apart from the everyday comings and goings through the land.

The Plain of Esdraelon Some distance back from the Mediterranean coast, mountain ranges run in a continuous line from Lebanon to Sinai. But there is one important break where a fault in the underlying rock has caused a section of mountain to drop to a height of 300ft/100 metres or less. This break divides the central highlands from Galilee and the northern mountains. It extends from Haifa Bay, north of Mt Carmel, to the valley of the Harod, a tributary of the Jordan. The watershed itself is cut through by the Valley of Jezreel.

The central plain forms a rough triangle, with each side about 15 miles/24kms long. Originally, the floor of the valley was marshy. It was here that Sisera lost his chariots and had to escape on foot–Judges 4:15. But it has been drained and today forms the most fertile agricultural area in the modern state of Israel.

Although the plain was infertile for many centuries before Jewish settlers began to reclaim it in 1911, it has always had great strategic importance. The principal north-south route of the ancient world (which the Romans called *Via Maris*, 'the way of the sea') cut through it on the way from Egypt to Damascus and Mesopotamia. It was an obvious route for trade–or for invasion. This may account for the long list of battles which have been fought in the plain, right up to modern times, in the Israeli War of Independence (1948). Megiddo lies at the western edge of the plain so the Hill of Megiddo, or 'Armageddon', became a symbol of the great battle in Revelation 16.

Galilee North of the Plain of Esdraelon, the upland ranges begin again. They stretch away northwards, gradually rising as they come nearer to the high mountains of Lebanon. They rise in a series of steps, with scarp edges facing generally south or south-east. The lower steps in the 'staircase' were and are fertile basin lands, separated from each other by the barren limestone edges. In the time of Jesus, these basins were known for their grain, fruit and olives. They formed a prosperous, well-populated area. But the higher steps rise to a bleak and windswept upland. This is isolated and infertile, and lacks the forests of the higher mountain slopes further north.

This whole area forms the region of Galilee, sometimes divided into Lower and Upper Galilee. The southern and eastern edges of the region are clearly drawn, but to the north, it merges into the mountains. In the past this northern boundary area was always the part of 'the land' where foreign influences were strongest. The Israelites seldom really had it under control. And the great trade routes which passed across it brought in many strangers. This was the region where Jesus spent his childhood years. It was a busy area, full of coming and going, with a very mixed community. Along its trade routes it was in touch with the outside world and aware of non-Jewish ideas. It lived off its fertile farmlands and its lake fisheries. And it was far more alert to the realities of life in the Roman Empire than the aloof Jews of Jerusalem–who despised their northern cousins as country bumpkins and because they were racially mixed.

The coastal plain When Israel occupied the Promised Land, they captured the central highlands and then made sporadic attempts to spread their control down to the Mediterranean coast. But this region was occupied by the powerful nation of the Philistines. And although, under David, Israel was able to gain control for a while, more often in Israel's history the Philistines were exerting pressure from their five cities on the coastlands up into the hills.

The coastlands were not, at this time, a particularly attractive area. They consisted of a belt of coastal sand dunes backed by forest, lagoons and swamp. There were no large natural harbours south of Carmel. The Philistines were not seafarers, and the first major port on this coast was the artificial harbour at Caesarea, built by King Herod the Great, not long before Jesus was born.

South of Mt Carmel, the plain was known as the Plain of Philistia and the Plain of Sharon. North of Carmel, it became the Plain of Asher. Going north, it narrows, but is much better provided with natural harbours. It was from here that the seagoing Phoenicians traded.

The 'Shephelah' or Piedmont Between the coastlands and the upland is an area of low foothills formerly covered by forests of sycamores. When the Philistines fought the Israelites the hills formed a kind of no-man's-land, where there were constant skirmishes. For either side to attack the other, it was necessary to pass through the Shephelah. Most of the routes through it were therefore fortified or guarded. Today, much of it is cultivated.

The Jordan Valley The River Jordan rises near Mt Hermon and flows south through Lake Huleh (now largely drained) and into the Sea of Galilee. At the southern end of the Sea it enters a deep valley known as the Ghor. Not only is the valley itself steep-sided but the river has cut into the floor and has created a winding, cliff-lined 'valley within a valley', filled with dense, jungle-like vegetation. This made crossing the river very difficult before the first modern bridges were built.

The Jordan valley is a geological rift. The sides follow parallel faults in the earth's crust. These faults carry on the line of the valley down to the Dead Sea and beyond it, through the depression known as the Arabah, which eventually leads to the Gulf of Aqaba. The faults are the reason why the valley is so deep. The shore of the Dead Sea is 1,270ft/388 metres below sea level. The distance from the mountain rim on one side of the valley to that on the other is 9-12 miles/15-20kms. But no major road follows the valley. One reason for this is the broken and difficult ground created by the Jordan and its tributaries. Another is the fact that inside the Ghor, the summer temperatures are so high that travellers are glad to cross as quickly as they can from the heights on one side to the heights on the other.

The land east of the Jordan (Transjordan) Here there are uplands, like those to the west, but higher. They are well-watered and provide good pasture for the huge flocks of sheep and herds of cattle formerly raised in Moab. At one time the king of Moab paid 100,000 lambs and the wool from 100,000 sheep every year to Israel as tribute (2 Kings 3:4). The mountains here rise from 1,900-2,300ft/600-700 metres east of Galilee to almost 6,560ft/2,000 metres south and east of the Dead Sea. They attract a rainfall which increases with their height and makes them a fertile belt between the dry valley on one side and the Arabian Desert on the other.

The fertility of parts of the region, such as Bashan and Gilead, the prosperity of the sheep raisers of Moab, and the success of the traders of Edom made all these areas powerful rivals of the Israelites west of the Jordan. It was, perhaps, just as well for Israel that the Jordan made it so difficult for these people to move into their land from the east. It almost completely separated two similar regions which lay within sight of each other across the valley.

Gerar

A place in the Negev, between Beersheba and Gaza, where both Abraham and Isaac stayed. For safety, Abraham said that his wife Sarah was his sister. Abimelech, king of Gerar, wanted to take Sarah as his wife. But God prevented this.

Genesis 20:26

Gerizim

The mountain of God's blessing, in Samaria, opposite Mt Ebal (see *Ebal*). Gerizim later became the Samaritans' sacred mountain, the place where they built their temple. It was the mountain which the woman of Samaria mentioned as the place where her ancestors worshipped. The site of the ancient Samaritan temple has recently been found on a spur of Mt Gerizim.

Deuteronomy 11:29; 27; Joshua 8:33; John 4:20

Gershon

Levi's eldest son. Gershon and his descendants formed one of the three groups of Levites.

Exodus 6:16-17; Numbers 3:17ff.

Geshur

A region and town in southern Syria King David married the king of Geshur's daughter. Their son, Absalom, fled to Geshur after he had killed his half-brother Amnon in revenge for the rape of his sister Tamar.

Joshua 12:5; 2 Samuel 3:3; 13:38, etc.

Gethsemane

A garden across the Kidron Valley from Jerusalem, close to the Mount of Olives (the name means 'olive press'). Jesus and his disciples often went there. So Judas knew where to take the soldiers on the night of the arrest.

Matthew 26:36-56; Mark 14:32-51; Luke 22:39; John 18:1-12

Gezer

One of the Canaanite towns Joshua campaigned against. It was in the low hills, on the road from Joppa (on the coast) to Jerusalem. Gezer belonged to Egypt for a while until one of the pharaohs gave it to his daughter, King Solomon's wife. Solomon fortified the town, with Hazor and Megiddo. It is the place where archaeologists discovered the 'Gezer calendar' (see *Farming*).

Joshua 10:33, etc.; 1 Kings 9:15-17

Gibeah

A hill-top town 3 miles/4km north of Jerusalem, which became famous as the home and capital city of King Saul. The place had been tragically destroyed as a result of a crime committed by its people during the time of the Judges. The site is at Tell el-Ful, overlooking the suburbs of Jerusalem.

Judges 19:12-20:48; 1 Samuel 10:26, etc.; Isaiah 10:29

Gibeon

A town about 6 miles/10km north-west of Jerusalem. After the fall of Jericho and Ai the Gibeonites tricked Joshua into a peace treaty. Saul later broke this. David's men fought the supporters of Saul's son Ishbosheth at the pool of Gibeon, to decide which should be king. The tent of worship (tabernacle) was kept at Gibeon, and King Solomon worshipped there. The people of Gibeon helped Nehemiah to rebuild the walls of Jerusalem.

Archaeologists have discovered a huge pit at Gibeon, with a stairway leading down to water. Inside it there were handles of a great many storage jars, each one inscribed with the name 'Gibeon' and the owner's name. The town seems to have been an important centre for wine-making in the seventh century BC.

Joshua 9; 2 Samuel 2:12-29; 20:8; 21; 1 Kings 3:4; 1 Chronicles 21:29; Nehemiah 3:7

Gideon

The 'Judge' of Israel who defeated

the Midianites, one of Israel's greatest enemies at that time. Gideon was secretly threshing his crop when God's angel messenger called to him to rescue Israel from the Midianites. To make sure that the call was from God he put it to the test. Twice God gave him the sign he asked for.

Gideon chose 300 men from the thousands who followed him. These were divided into three groups. Armed with an empty pitcher, a torch and a trumpet, they surprised the enemy at night with a tremendous shout, 'the sword of the Lord and of Gideon'. Panic broke out in the army of Midian. They turned on each other and then fled, with the Israelites in hot pursuit. Victory was complete and Gideon gave the land peace for forty years until his death.
Judges 6:11-23, 36-39; 7:1-23

Gihon

The name of one of the four great rivers which flowed out of the Garden of Eden.

Gihon was also the name of a spring at the foot of the hill on which the first city of Jerusalem stood. It was then the main source of water for the city. Solomon was anointed king at this spring by the command of his father David, to forestall the attempt of his rival Adonijah to seize the throne. The Gihon spring water was vitally important to the safety of the city and, later, King Hezekiah cut a tunnel to bring the water right through the hill and inside the walls. This tunnel still exists. The water comes out at the Pool of Siloam (see *Siloam*).
Genesis 2:13; 1 Kings 1;
2 Chronicles 32:30; 33:14

Gilboa

A mountain and range in the north of Palestine, overlooking the deep Valley of Jezreel which runs down to the River Jordan. King Saul and his army took their last stand against the Philistines on Mt Gilboa. Saul, Jonathan and his other two sons were all killed there.
1 Samuel 28:4; 31:1, 8; 2 Samuel 1; 21:12; 1 Chronicles 10:1, 8

Gilead

A large area east of the River Jordan, extending north from the Dead Sea. The tribes of Reuben, Gad and Manasseh each occupied part of Gilead. The region was good grazing-land, famous for its flocks and herds. It was also famous for a gum or spice known as the 'balm' of Gilead. This was used to heal wounds, and also as a cosmetic. Jair, Jephthah and the prophet Elijah all came from Gilead.
Genesis 37:25; Joshua 17:1;
Judges 10:3; 11; 1 Kings 17:1;
Song of Solomon 4:1

Gilgal

A place between Jericho and the River Jordan. The Israelites camped at Gilgal after crossing the river, and set up stones to mark the event. From Gilgal they set out to conquer Canaan. It became the site of an important shrine, and was on Samuel's circuit as a Judge. Gilgal is mentioned in the stories of Elijah and also of Elisha, who dealt with a pot of 'poisoned' stew there. The prophets Hosea and Amos condemned the worship at Gilgal as empty ritual.
Joshua 4:20; Judges 3:19;
1 Samuel 7:16; 10:8, etc;
2 Samuel 19:15; 2 Kings 2:1;
4:38-41; Hosea 4:15; Amos 4:4

Glory

When the word 'glory' is applied to people in the Bible, it usually refers to their wealth or position. But the 'glory of God' refers to his unique power and greatness: 'the King of kings and the Lord of lords. He who alone is immortal; he lives in the light that no one can approach. No one has ever seen him; no one can ever see him.' Though people cannot see God, they are sometimes allowed to catch a glimpse of his 'glory'.

In the Old Testament God's glory is seen in history, especially perhaps in the two major events of the exodus and exile. The Israelites were led through the desert by the glory of God seen in the cloud and fire which guided them on their journey. When Moses went up the mountain to receive the law of God the cloud of God's glory covered the mountain. Again, during the exile the prophet Ezekiel saw some amazing visions which showed the 'glory' of God.

The New Testament suggests that Jesus was the glory of God made visible on earth. God's glory was seen by the shepherds when they heard that Jesus was born. And those who saw Jesus recognized God's glory in him. 'We saw his glory,' writes the apostle John (see also *Transfiguration*). Jesus' way of life and his miracles 'revealed his glory'. But the glory of God was seen above all in Jesus' death on the cross. Jesus went to the cross, not as a defeated man but as the conqueror of sin and Saviour of the world. His resurrection was the living proof. Because of this there is a 'future glory' promised to all God's people as they share in the glory with which he will return to earth.
1 Timothy 6:15-16; Exodus 16:7, 10; 24:15-18; 40:34-38;
2 Chronicles 7:1-3; Ezekiel 1:26-28 and other passages;
Luke 2:8-14; 9:28-36; John 1:14; 2:11; 17; Romans 8:18-30;
Mark 8:38; 13:26

God

In the Bible, God is the all-powerful, personal, spiritual being who is beyond our understanding, but who has revealed himself to mankind in his work of creation and in his continuing activity in history. He created all life–and he is the one who keeps it going. We see him at work time and again in the Old Testament as he helps his people Israel. In the New Testament we see him at work especially in the life, death and resurrection of Jesus. He also continues to work in a personal way in the lives of Jesus' followers.

The Bible tells us what God is like by telling us what he does. It does not give us abstract philosophical descriptions of God's nature. But it is clear that he is all-seeing and all-knowing, present everywhere. His nature is both holy and just, loving and forgiving. The Bible takes the existence of God as a fact which needs no proof. It begins with the simple statement, 'In the beginning God created...'

People have always had many ideas about God. They have worshipped many different gods. One of the concerns of the Old Testament is to show that *Yahweh* (the Hebrews' name for God) is the only true God. He is the Creator, and King over all there is; the one who is 'light', who is utterly holy–and utterly loving.

The word *Yahweh*, the personal name for God in the Old Testament, is sometimes spelt Jehovah in English, and in many translations of the Bible is written LORD. The ordinary Hebrew word for 'God' is *Elohim*. The name *Yahweh* means 'the one who exists eternally', though the Jews have always referred to him by the Hebrew word *Adonai*, which means 'my Lord'.

In the Old Testament God was sometimes referred to as the 'father' of the people of Israel. Jesus gave this a new importance. God has made us for a parent-child relationship, made possible through faith in Jesus. God delights to work in the world through the people he has made for friendship with himself. He works with them through their prayer and action so that the whole world might come to know him.

See also *Trinity* and the many words which describe what God does.

The 'otherness' of God: the eternal spirit; the Creator: Genesis 1; Deuteronomy 33:26-27;
1 Kings 8:27; Job 38ff.; Psalms 8; 100; 104; Isaiah 40:12-28; 55:9;
John 4:23-24; Romans 1:19-20;
Revelation 1:8
The power of God: Genesis 17:1;
Exodus 32:11; Numbers 24:4;
Job 40–42:2; Isaiah 9:6; 45–46;
Daniel 3:17; Matthew 26:53; John 19:10-11; Acts 12; Revelation 19:1-16
–his knowledge: Genesis 4:10;
Job 28:20-27; Psalm 139:1-6;
Daniel 2:17-23; Matthew 6:7-8;
John 2:23-25; 4:25-29;
Ephesians 1:3-12
–his presence everywhere:
Genesis 28:10-17; Psalm 139:7-12; Jeremiah 23:23-24;
Acts 17:26-28
The character of God–his holiness and righteousness: Exodus 20;
Leviticus 11:44-45; Joshua 24:19-28;
Psalms 7: 25:8-10; 99; Isaiah 1:12ff.;
6:1-5; John 17:25-26; Romans 1:18-3:26; Ephesians 4:17-24; Hebrews 12:7-14; 1 Peter 1:13-16; 1 John 1:5-10
–his love and mercy: Deuteronomy 7:6-13 Psalms, e.g., 23; 25; 36:5-12; 103; Isaiah 40:1-2, 27-31; 41:8-20; 43; Jeremiah 31:2-4; Hosea 6; 11; 14;
John 3:16-17; 10:7-18; 13:1; 14:15-31; 15:9, 12ff.; Romans 8:35-38;
Galatians 2:20; Ephesians 2:4-10; 1 John 4:7-21
God the 'father': 1 Chronicles 25:10; Psalms 68:5; 103:13;
Matthew 5:48; 6:1-14; 28:19;
Romans 8:14-15

Gog

Described in the Book of Ezekiel as the ruler of Magog and the prince of Meshech and Tubal. He and his army invade from the north and Israel wins a great victory over them. In Revelation, Gog and Magog, led by Satan, are totally destroyed by God himself.

Ezekiel 38-39; Revelation 20:7-9

Goliath

The 9-ft (3-metre) Philistine giant from Gath who was killed by David. The stone from David's sling stunned the giant and he fell to the ground. David then drew Goliath's sword and cut off his head. The Philistine army fled.
1 Samuel 17

A shepherd-boy using his sling.

Gomer

Unfaithful wife of the prophet Hosea. (See *Hosea.*)
Hosea 1–3

Gomorrah

One of five cities probably now beneath the southern end of the Dead Sea. Gomorrah was violently destroyed with Sodom for deliberate, persistent and vicious sin.
Throughout the Bible, Sodom and Gomorrah are used as examples to warn God's people of his judgement. Jesus says that any town which refuses to hear his messengers is in a worse situation than Sodom and Gomorrah.
Genesis 14; 19; Isaiah 1:9-10; (Ezekiel 16:48-50); Matthew 10:15

Goshen

A fertile area of the eastern Nile Delta in Egypt. When Jacob and his family went to join Joseph, they settled in Goshen. It was a good place for their flocks and herds, and it was close to Pharaoh's court. In the time just before the exodus, the Israelites in Goshen escaped the plagues suffered by the rest of Egypt.
Genesis 45:10; Exodus 8:22, etc.

Gospel

The word 'gospel' means 'good news'. This good news, as far as the Bible is concerned, is the fact that we need not be cut off from God because of sins, for Jesus has come to bring forgiveness.

Mark's Gospel describes itself as 'the good news of Jesus Christ', and at its simplest Jesus himself *is* the good news, the 'gospel'. The facts of the gospel are simple: 'That Christ died for our sins, as written in the Scriptures; that he was buried, and that he was raised to life three days later, as written in the Scriptures.' We can have forgiveness and new life because of the death and resurrection of Jesus.

In fact the gospel is so simple that some sneered at it. It was not as complex as they thought it should be. Paul made it clear that it is never difficult to find God. The good news of Jesus Christ was not a system of philosophy, but the plan of God himself. Paul had proved in his own experience that it was 'God's power to save *all* who believe'.
Luke 2:10-11; Mark 1:1, 14; Luke 4:18-21; 1 Corinthians 15:3-4; 1:17-23; Ephesians 1:6-13; Romans 1:16-17

Government

The Bible does not put forward any one form of government as the right way to organize society. In fact the Bible reflects many different forms. The 'patriarchs', Abraham, Isaac and Jacob, lived in family clans. The nation of Israel was at first ruled by Judges, then by kings. And Christians in the New Testament accepted the Roman system of government under which they lived.

From the beginning Israel was meant to be a 'theocracy'–a nation with God as its king. But because of the sinful nature of men and women, it was soon clear that society also needed its human rulers to make laws and enforce them. The nation of Israel discovered this during the period of the Judges when there was no central government. 'There was no king in Israel at that time. Everyone did just as he pleased.'

God delegates authority to governments to uphold justice. 'Everyone must obey the state authorities, because no authority exists without God's permission, and the existing authorities have been put there by God.' God's people should pray for the government and support it as it tries to rule justly.

At the same time, the Bible shows that God expects rulers to uphold justice, not to pervert it. The Old Testament prophets–especially Amos–spoke out plainly against the injustices and tyrannical rule of many of the kings of Israel and Judah. And when governments oppress their subjects, the people of God must stand up fearlessly and condemn them. If it comes to a straight choice between what the government says and doing God's will, Christians 'must obey God'.
Judges 21:25; Romans 13:1-7; 1 Timothy 2:2; 1 Peter 2:11-25; Isaiah 56:9-12; Jeremiah 21:11-22:19; Daniel 3; Amos and many other passages from the prophets; Matthew 22:15-21; Acts 5:27-29

Gozan

Israelites from Samaria were taken captive to Gozan by the Assyrians. The town is modern Tell Halaf on the River Khabur in north-east Syria.
2 Kings 17:6; 19:12

Grace

Both the Old and New Testaments teach that God is good and kind to men and women. There is no need for God to be like this. We certainly do not deserve it. God is good to us because he loves us–this is the 'grace' of God.

The Old Testament is full of reminders of God's goodness, his constant love. But the grace of God is seen most clearly in the coming of Jesus. In the cross God has shown us how much he loves us–it was 'while we were still sinners that Christ died for us'. The human race did not deserve salvation, but God freely gave it. This is what the New Testament means by 'the grace of our Lord Jesus'.

But the New Testament also suggests that the Christian life, from start to finish, depends on God's grace. We obey God out of gratitude for his 'grace'. 'My grace', God says in answer to Paul's prayer for healing, 'is all you need, for my power is strongest when you are weak.' Paul's letters often begin or end with a prayer for God's grace.

See also *Covenant, Justification.*
Deuteronomy 7:6-9; Psalms 23:6; 25:6-10; 51:1; Jeremiah 31:2-3; Romans 5:8; 16:20; 3:19-24; 6:14; Ephesians 2:8-9; 2 Corinthians 12:9; 1 Timothy 1:2; 1 Peter 5:5-7; 2 Peter 3:18

Great Sea

The Bible often uses this name for the Mediterranean Sea.

Greece

The Greeks Until modern times the beginnings of Greece were a puzzle. *The Iliad* and *The Odyssey*, two great poems said to have been written by a blind Greek poet called Homer, about 800 BC, give hints of an even older way of life. Now modern discovery has built up a surprising picture of that early civilization. The Minoans in Crete had built great palaces long before, and traded with Egypt. But their empire fell suddenly, to earthquake or invasion. Its last rulers spoke Greek: tablets with the oldest known Greek language have been found in their palace.

The *Iliad* tells part of the story of the ten-year war when the Greeks attacked the city of Troy. We now know that there was a real Troy, and an early Greek civilization centred on Mycenae on the mainland of southern Greece. Homer echoes memories of what had really taken place long before.

Early history Greek-speaking people had entered Greece from the north. Greece is a poor and rocky land. The people lived in small towns separated by the mountains. After the great days of Mycenae, the land was never united. Town fought against town. It was often easier to travel by sea than by land. There was too little fertile land to support the people and the Greeks became adventurous sailors. The regular summer winds and the shelter of the many islands helped them to voyage across the Aegean Sea to Asia (modern Turkey). They imported food, and founded new cities on many parts of the Mediterranean coast, especially in Asia Minor. Greeks in Bible times lived over a far larger area than the land we now call Greece.

The 'golden age' In the fifth century BC the most famous of the Greek cities was Athens. The Athenians took a leading part in defeating two great attacks on Greece by the Persians in 490 and 480 BC. They became rich and powerful, and built many beautiful temples, including the Parthenon, which can still be seen today. Athens also became the home of some remarkable leaders, thinkers, writers and poets. The names of Pericles, Socrates, Plato, Sophocles, Euripides and others are still famous.

Alexander the Great riding to the rescue of a subject king. A detail from his tomb at Sidon.

These men have had great influence on the world.

Athens was the perfect example of the Greek way of life. It was a 'democracy'. That is a Greek word for a very Greek idea. To an Athenian it meant that every citizen ought to play his part in the affairs of his city. 'Politics' was the business of the 'city' (Greek *polis*). The Greeks were a very gifted people, clever and active, quick to argue, with a great love of freedom, and a feeling for beauty in art and writing. Although they were so divided, they were all very proud of being Greek. They thought of themselves as different from other races, whom they called 'barbarians'. Every four years all the cities met at Olympia in southern Greece for the Olympic Games, and wars between them stopped for that time.

Alexander Greece was divided and weakened by these bitter local wars. And after 336 BC Alexander the Great, king of Macedon (to the north), conquered the whole country. Alexander's people were Greeks, but had never been important until then. Alexander proved to be a brilliant soldier. He overthrew the great empire of Persia, and made conquests as far east as India. But he was also more than a conqueror. He aimed to spread Greek language and civilization through all this area.

Alexander's hopes were never fulfilled, for he died young, and his generals disputed his empire. It was divided from the start. Ptolemy won Egypt, and founded a line of Greek kings there. Seleucus tried to hold the East, and his line, the Seleucids, made their capital at Antioch in Syria. They struggled for Palestine with the Ptolemies. One of their kings, Antiochus Epiphanes (175-163 BC), became the bitter enemy of the Jews. In Asia Minor, Macedonia and Greece the situation was confused, as rival kings fought for power.

Greek influence The high point of Greek civilization belongs to the period before Alexander. The later period is known as the Hellenistic age (from *Hellen*, meaning 'Greek'). During this time Greek became an international language for the eastern Mediterranean and beyond. It was the language of trade, and of education and writing, even for people who still usually spoke their own languages. Even the Jews were influenced by it. In the second century BC the Old Testament was translated into Greek at Alexandria in Egypt, for the Greek-speaking Jews there.

This translation, called the Septuagint, was the version of the Old Testament best known to the first Christians.

As the power of Rome increased, the Romans became involved in the affairs of Greece. In 146 BC they destroyed Corinth, which had resisted them. This was the end of Greek political freedom. But their Roman conquerors took over Greek ways of thinking. Greek was established as the official language of the eastern half of the Roman Empire. It was natural for the New Testament to be written in Greek.

The New Testament The New Testament often mentions Greeks. It sometimes means simply non-Jews (Gentiles), Greek-speaking people of the Roman world. Very little of its story takes place in the land of Greece. Yet Paul, though a strict Jew, wrote in Greek and understood Greek ways of thinking. He knew, for instance, of the Greek interest in athletics, and pictured the Christian life as a race and a boxing match (1 Corinthians 9:24-27). Most of his work was in cities of the Greek kind, especially in Asia Minor (Turkey), which at that time contained some of the largest and richest Greek towns, such as Ephesus. These cities still had their rights, and lived a busy public life. There were meetings, markets, committees, elections, debates, sports, and theatres. They had trade-unions, and even strikes and demonstrations. But the real power belonged to the Roman governor.

Christian meets Greek The classic meeting of Christian with Greek took place in Athens itself. It was still a university town, though now living on its past glory. Paul found it a city full of religious images. He began to argue with those whom he met in the public square, and was called before the 'Court of the Areopagus' to present his new ideas. Paul spoke in terms they would understand. He quoted their poets. He dealt with the arguments of the Stoics and Epicureans, two leading parties among their thinkers. But he was deeply in earnest, and had more than this to say. For all the cleverness of their scholars they did not know God. He said boldly that God does not 'live in man-made temples' (Acts 17:24) like the beautiful ones that stood all around them. God called all people to change their way of life. He would judge all by Jesus, whom he had raised from the dead.

Most of the Athenians were unwilling to receive these teachings. Greeks, said Paul, looked for 'wisdom', but his message was foolish to them (1 Corinthians 1:22-23). Their thinkers took a different view of life after death. They were proud and did not care to open their minds to the evidence for such a disturbing challenge to their ways.

Greek and Roman religion

The Roman Empire covered a very large area, and included peoples with many different beliefs. Those living in the eastern Empire were the ones whom the early Christians first met. They were often influenced by eastern ideas which had been handed down from long before Greek civilization came to them.

The Minoans of Crete and the oldest peoples of Greece worshipped a fertility goddess. Like Baal in the Canaanite myths her consort-god was believed to die and rise again, like the seasons of the year. The details of this kind of religion varied from place to place, but many of these ideas were common throughout the eastern Mediterranean lands. They remained especially strong in country districts, where people's living depended on their herds and crops.

The gods of Greece and Rome The first Greeks brought with them a new group of gods. Their supreme god was Zeus. He ruled over the other gods who lived on Olympus, the highest mountain in Greece. The Greeks were a logical people, and tried to build complete family histories of the gods and fit all the older beliefs and local stories into the system. So these gods were pictured vividly. They were like people in the way they behaved–often jealous or vengeful, or immoral–but of course they were far more powerful.

Roman religion was really quite different. But when the Romans conquered the Greeks they took over all their gods and gave them Roman names. So Zeus became the Roman god Jupiter. His wife Hera became the Roman Juno, and his brother Poseidon, god of the sea, was given the name Neptune. Among the other gods were Ares (Mars), god of war; Hermes (Mercury) the messenger of the gods; Hades or Pluto (Dis), god of the dead; Hephaestus (Vulcan) the lame craftsman; and Apollo, god of wisdom. The best-known of the other goddesses were Artemis (Diana), the huntress and twin sister of Apollo; Athena (Minerva), patroness of art and war; Aphrodite (Venus), goddess of love; and Demeter (Ceres), goddess of the harvest. These names were remembered long after people ceased to believe in these gods. Some of them are still in use as the names of planets.

Festivals Greek religion was based on the city. There were great festivals in which everybody took part together, and social events were based on religion. The Olympic Games were first held as a religious event to honour Zeus. The plays in the theatre at Athens, tragedies and comedies, were performed at the festival of the god Dionysus. And the greatest works of Greek art all had a religious meaning.

Yet this religion did not satisfy people. It offered no real answers to the problems of good and evil, life and death. Life was uncertain. These gods had no power to save their cities from sudden disaster. People looked for purpose in life. Why should they live good lives if the gods could not give them justice?

The Maison Carrée at Nîmes in France was built as a Roman temple in 16 BC.

The philosophers Many thoughtful people turned to philosophy. Plato wrote down the discussions of his master Socrates, about subjects like justice and life after death, and built up a noble system of thought. Later the Stoics advised people to live in harmony with reason. And the Epicureans believed the world had come about by the chance meeting of atoms. They thought that men should live quietly without fear. Others made new moral lessons from the old stories of the gods. But many were near despair. They worshipped Tyche ('Chance'), and hoped that then the chances of life might favour them. Or they turned to astrology or magic.

New religions Others found hope in new religions, often from the East, which promised a personal 'salvation' to the worshipper. This idea was a very important one, but it meant very different things to people– being saved from evil or death, or from trouble or danger, or being given success in life. It was a fashionable word, rather as people speak of 'security' today. A victorious king was often honoured as the 'saviour' of his people. He was the one who could give them what they needed. It was only a matter of time before some of his less sophisticated subjects began worshipping him as a god.

The Romans Little is really known about the earliest Roman religion, but it was clearly then very different from that of the Greeks. The early Romans felt that a divine power (*numen*) existed in nature, and they wanted to harness it to their needs. So there were 'gods' for every area of life: gods of the house and of its doorway, of the fields, and so on. Most of these seem to us to have had a vague kind of existence. Only a few of the official gods of the state, like Jupiter, were clearly pictured as persons. But then Greek influence came, and the old Roman gods were fitted into the Greek system. Roman beliefs merged with Greek ideas in such a way that it is hard to separate out what is purely Roman.

Religion and the ordinary man Many things were always common to both Greeks and Romans. Both worshipped many gods, but their religion had little effect on the way the worshipper lived. Neither belief nor behaviour was really important. A person might believe what he wished, as long as he did what was expected of a good citizen, and remained loyal to the state. There was no great stress on a search for truth, nor was there any powerful body of priests. The gods were distant. They were to be paid due honour. But they were not deeply interested in human affairs.

Educated Romans in the time of Julius Caesar (first century BC) often had little regard for these gods. They would use the forms of religion for their own ends when there was some personal advantage or a political point to gain. But if they thought seriously about life they turned, like the Greeks, to philosophy or new religions.

The emperor Augustus (27 BC-AD 14) tried to revive Roman religion in a more splendid form. His chosen title, 'Augustus', had a sense of religious awe. He wanted to use religion to bind people in loyalty to his own government. In the East he was worshipped as a god in his lifetime, for he had brought peace and good government to a world torn by war. A great temple was built to Rome and Augustus at Pergamum (near the west coast of modern Turkey).

The mysteries Those who wanted a more personal faith went to the 'mystery' religions. Here the worshipper was admitted step by step into the secret inner spiritual knowledge of the faith. The mysteries at Eleusis in Greece had been known since early times. But many new foreign cults became popular in the Greek and Roman world of the first century AD. The Egyptian goddess Isis had many priests and an impressive ritual, and was thought to answer prayer. The Persian Mithras was the soldier's god. Men advanced from rank to rank in his service in the fight against evil. For a time Mithraism was one of the most serious rivals of Christianity.

Rome and the Christians Rome usually allowed these different beliefs to flourish. But groups which might not be loyal to the state were always banned. Judaism was specially allowed and, at first, Christianity was too, because it seemed to be a kind of Judaism. But, as time went on, the Romans began to use emperor worship as a test of loyalty. The Emperor Domitian (AD 81-96) required people to worship him as 'lord and god'. So the position of Christians changed and they had to be ready to suffer for their faith. That was the situation when the Book of Revelation was written.

The New Testament accounts of other religions are mostly set in the East (especially in modern Turkey). At Lystra, Paul and Barnabas were mistaken for Hermes and Zeus (Acts 14:12-13). At Ephesus the famous temple of Artemis was one of the 'seven wonders of the world' (Acts 19). She was really an eastern fertility goddess fitted to a Greek name. Paul answered these ideas at Lystra and at Athens: God creates, supplies, loves and judges all men.

Gnosticism Most of these religions easily became mixed. And about the time of the New Testament there arose a kind of thinking called 'Gnosticism'. Gnostics believed that 'spirit' was good and that material things were evil. Gnosticism came to be mixed with Christian and other ideas. But because it put other beings between God and man it denied the special place of Christ. Gnosticism, like the mystery religions, appealed to people who boasted of having a special inner knowledge (*gnosis*) that was better than the simple 'trust' that Christians talked of. Paul opposed the beginnings of this kind of thinking at Colossae. It became a serious problem for the church in the second century.

H

Habakkuk

A prophet to Judah who lived at the end of the seventh century BC, the time of Jeremiah. The Chaldaeans were becoming more and more powerful and Habakkuk found it hard to understand how God could use this wicked nation to punish his people. The answer came that God would one day judge all who were proud and wicked, including Judah's enemies.

Habor

The River Khabur in north-east Syria. A tributary of the River Euphrates. The town of Gozan was on the Habor River.
2 Kings 17:6

Hadadezer/Hadarezer

A king of Zobah in Syria. Three times King David defeated Hadadezer's troops. After the third defeat the people of Zobah became David's subjects.
2 Samuel 8–10; 1 Chronicles 18–19

Haggai

A prophet who probably returned from Babylon to Jerusalem in the party led by Zerubbabel. His message, recorded in the Book of Haggai, was given in 520 BC. Haggai was concerned to find that the people had built houses for themselves and were living in comfort while God's temple was still in ruins. He urged the people to rebuild it.

Hagar

Sarah's servant. Abraham took her as his secondary wife (concubine) when it seemed God's promise that his descendants would become a great nation could not come true because he had no children. Hagar became pregnant and ran away into the desert because Sarah treated her unkindly. An angel told Hagar to return and promised that her son Ishmael would be the founder of a nation. Ishmael was about fourteen years old when Sarah's son, Isaac, was born. When Ishmael made fun of Isaac Sarah asked Abraham to send Hagar and her son away. Hagar travelled through the desert until all her water was gone. Death seemed near, but instead an angel showed her a well and repeated God's promise about Ishmael.
Genesis 16; 21

Hair

A Roman lady, with her hair kept in place by a net.

The Israelites in the Old Testament normally grew their hair long. (See for example the stories of Samson and Absalom.) The Asiatic nomads shown as visitors to Egypt on the Beni-Hasan painting have long hair which came over their foreheads and hung down their backs. They also have beards which are neatly trimmed. Many years later, Assyrian inscriptions show the Israelites wearing beards. To shave off the beard was a sign of mourning. But by New Testament times, under the influence of the Greeks and Romans, hair was worn short and many men were clean shaven.

Grey hair was to be respected, as a sign of old age. 'One who had been living for ever'–presumably God himself–is pictured with white hair in Daniel 7:9. Men sometimes plaited their hair. At other times it was trimmed by the barber. The hair at the sides of the head, by the ears, was never cut. Leviticus 19:27 forbids it, as a pagan practice, a law still observed. Women plaited, braided or curled their hair. It was often kept in place by beautiful ivory combs. In Roman times the hair was piled on top of the head and kept in place by a net. The rich had nets of gold thread.

Ham

Noah's second son. Ham was the founder of the Egyptian, Ethiopian, Libyan and Canaanite nations.
Genesis 5:32; 6:10; 10:6-20

Haman

The chief minister of King Ahasuerus of Persia. He hated the Jew Mordecai for refusing to bow down to him, and plotted to kill Mordecai and all the Jewish people in Persia. Haman was hanged when Queen Esther revealed his plot to the king.
Esther 3–9

Hamath

Modern Hama, on the River Orontes in Syria. In Old Testament times Hamath was an important town, capital of a small kingdom, and on a main trade-route from Asia Minor (Turkey) south to Israel and Egypt. Hamath Pass, some distance to the south, was the 'ideal' northern limit of Israel. In the reigns of David and Solomon, Israel had a peace treaty with King Toi of Hamath. The town fell to the Assyrians and many of its people were moved into Israel. First Pharaoh Neco (before the Battle of Carchemish) and then King Nebuchadnezzar of Babylon made it their headquarters for a time.
Joshua 13:5; 2 Samuel 8:9-11; 1 Kings 8:65; 2 Chronicles 8:4; 2 Kings 17:24; 18:34, etc.

Hanani

Best-known of several Hananis is the man who travelled to Susa to tell Nehemiah that Jerusalem was still in ruins, even though the Jewish exiles had returned. When Nehemiah had rebuilt the walls of Jerusalem he made Hanani governor.
Nehemiah 1:2; 7:2

Hannah

Simple mud 'beehive' houses at present-day Harran.

The wife of Elkanah and mother of Samuel. For several years Hannah had no children. While she was making her annual visit to the shrine at Shiloh Hannah made a vow. She promised God that if he gave her a son, she would give him back to serve God. When Samuel was old enough Hannah took him to Shiloh where he helped Eli, the priest. Mary, the mother of Jesus, echoed Hannah's wonderful prayer of thanks in her great song of praise to God before Jesus was born. Hannah became the mother of three other sons and two daughters.
1 Samuel 1–2

Harod

The spring where Gideon chose his fighting-force by watching how the men drank from the stream. The 300 who showed their alertness by stooping and lapping the water were chosen. The place was in northern Palestine, probably by a stream which flows down the Valley of Jezreel.
Judges 7:1-8

Harran

A town in what is now south-east Turkey, on the River Balikh, a tributary of the River Euphrates. This was the place where Abraham's father, Terah, settled after leaving Ur, and where Jacob worked for Laban. Harran was on the main road linking Nineveh with Aleppo in Syria, and on south to the port of Tyre. It was fortified by the Assyrians as a provincial capital. For three years after the fall of Nineveh it was Assyria's capital city. Then in 609 BC it fell to the Babylonians.
Genesis 11:31; 12:4-5; 29:4, etc.; 2 Kings 19:12; Ezekiel 27:33

Hasidim

The name 'Hasidim' means 'pious ones'. This group was not an organized sect. It is the name given to those Jews who resisted the inroads of Greek culture (Hellenism) into Jewish life and culture. In the second century BC some of them joined the Maccabees in the armed struggle against the Greek rulers (1 *Maccabees* 2:42). Others were pacifists. All certainly were faithful followers of the Law, and many of them joined the sects of the Pharisees and the Essenes.

Hazael

An officer at the court of Benhadad II whom God told Elijah to anoint as king of Syria. Elisha wept when God showed him what Hazael would do to the Israelites. Hazael killed Benhadad and seized the throne. He made war against the kings of Israel and Judah.
1 Kings 19:15-17; 2 Kings 8ff.

Hazor

A bronze plaque of a Canaanite, found at Hazor.

A Canaanite city in the north of Israel. King Jabin of Hazor organized an alliance against Joshua. But he was defeated, and the city was burned. Another king of Hazor was defeated by Deborah and Barak. King Solomon rebuilt and fortified Hazor, with Megiddo and Gezer. In the eighth century BC the Assyrians destroyed the city.

Archaeologists have uncovered an upper and a lower city, which at its greatest may have housed as many as 40,000 people. The lower part was destroyed in the thirteenth century BC (about the time of Joshua). A city gate and wall from Solomon's time match others of the same design at Megiddo and Gezer. Hazor is mentioned in Egyptian and Babylonian texts, and in the Amarna Letters, as well as in the Bible itself.
Joshua 11; Judges 4; 1 Kings 9:15; 2 Kings 15:29

Healing
One of the results of evil in the world is illness. People become sick, age and die as a result of the 'fall', the coming of sin into the world.

This does not mean to say that a person is ill because he has sinned. This idea was commonly held in Jesus' day, but he did not agree.

Jesus came to announce a whole new creation in which sin and sickness and death would be no more. The new creation has already begun, with the resurrection of Jesus, but it remains to be completed in the future. Those who believe in him will share in it.

So the power of Jesus to heal sickness as well as to forgive sins was a way of showing what the new kingdom was like, and that it was real. He applied to himself the prophecy of Isaiah: 'The spirit of the Lord is upon me, because he has chosen me to bring good news to the poor. He has sent me to proclaim liberty to the captives and recovery of sight to the blind.' His healing of the sick in mind and body was a sample, a foretaste, of the coming age.

Christ's healing work has been continued by his disciples ever since. Paul describes a gift of healing given to every church. James considers it natural to call in the elders of the church to pray for a sick person. He advises Christians: 'confess your sins to one another, so that you will be healed.' The salvation Jesus brings is for the whole person.

But until 'all things are made new' at the end of time, the church cannot reverse the whole process of sickness, ageing and death. Healings will still be the occasional demonstration of the kingdom, of God's love and power, until the spiritual reality of the kingdom reaches its complete fulfilment.
Genesis 3:14-19. *Some Old Testament healings:* Numbers 21:4-9; 1 Kings 17:17-24; Deuteronomy 7:12-15; 28:20-23; 2 Kings 4:18-37; 5. *Some of Jesus' healings:* Matthew 8:5-13, 28-34; 9:32-33; 17:14-18; Mark 7:31-37; 10:46-52; Luke 4:18-19; 7:11-15; 8:41-42, 49-56; 17:11-19; John 9; 11. Acts 3:1-10 and other passages; 1 Corinthians 15; James 5:14-16; Revelation 21:1-5; 22:1-2

Heaven
The Hebrews used the word 'heaven' to refer to the sky. The phrase 'the heaven and the earth' means the same as our word 'universe'.

Heaven can also refer to where God is. So Jesus taught his disciples to pray, 'Our Father in heaven...' God is not alone in 'heaven'. He is surrounded by the 'angels of heaven' who serve him. Christians are promised a place 'in heaven' after this life. Jesus promised his disciples that he was going there to prepare a place for them. So 'heaven' is the experience in which all the angels and all the believers who once lived on earth join in unending worship of God.

What is heaven like? We are told that it will be 'home', where there will be rest, but also a share in God's work. In 'heaven' we shall be safe and happy in God's presence, with nothing to spoil things. In 'heaven' we shall meet all who have trusted Jesus in life–and we shall know them, as Jesus' disciples recognized him after the resurrection. 'Heaven' is a 'treasure-house', where more important things than money are kept for us. In heaven there are no tears, there is no pain, no weakness, no night or need for sleep. In God's presence there is joy for ever.

See also *Angel, Future destiny, Resurrection, Second coming of Jesus.*
Matthew 6:9; Nehemiah 9:6; Mark 13:32; Luke 6:21-23; 1 Peter 1:4; John 14:2; Romans 8; 1 Corinthians 15; Philippians 1:21-23; 3:12-21; 1 Peter 1:3-5; Revelation 4; 21–22

A letter written to a group of Christian Jews, some time in the first century. They seemed to be in danger of giving up their Christian faith.

The writer sets out to strengthen their faith. He shows Jesus as the one who truly and finally reveals God to man.

The writer shows that Jesus is far greater than the angels, or the great men of the Old Testament, Moses and Joshua (1:1-4:13). He shows that Jesus, as priest 'for ever', is far greater than the priests of the Old Testament (4:14-7:28). He shows that Jesus provides a better agreement between God and man, and a final once-for-all sacrifice, to which the Old Testament writers pointed forward (chapters 8-10). Jesus is the perfect priest, offering the perfect sacrifice, reconciling God and man.

The writer looks at the shining example of faith given by the great men and women in Israel's history (chapter 11). He urges his readers not to turn back, but to stay faithful to Jesus despite suffering and persecution (chapters 12-13).

It is not known who wrote the letter.

Hebron
A town high in the Judean hills (3,040ft/935m above sea level). The old name for Hebron was Kiriath-arba. Abraham and his family often camped near Hebron. He bought the cave of Machpelah from the Hittites at Hebron (see *Machpelah*). Moses' twelve spies came to Hebron, and it was later given to Caleb. Hebron was a city of refuge, and one of the Levites' towns. It was David's capital before he captured Jerusalem. Absalom staged his rebellion from Hebron. Much later, after the exile, Jews returned to live there.
Genesis 13:18; 23; 35:27; 37:14; Numbers 13:22; Joshua 14:6-15; 2 Samuel 2:1-4; 15:9-10; Nehemiah 11:25

Heliopolis
See *On.*

Hell
The teaching of Jesus is clear about the fact of hell as an eternal punishment for those who do evil. Jesus uses very vivid imagery to describe it–a rubbish tip; outer darkness; fire which never goes out; a fiery furnace where people will cry and grind their teeth; and the place where God destroys both body and soul.

These phrases are not to be taken as a literal description. They are meant as warnings. They emphasize the absolute and final nature of God's judgement and it is a mistake to draw exact meanings out of them. But it is also a mistake to dismiss the idea of hell as some medieval idea about little devils with pitchforks. Hell is an essential part of Jesus' own stern warnings about sin and its power. In fact Jesus said that he himself will pronounce sentence on the day of judgement–'Away from me, you that are under God's curse! Away to the eternal fire which has been prepared for the Devil and his angels!'

In English (for example in the Apostles' Creed) the word 'hell' has sometimes been used with a different meaning to describe the Hebrew word *Sheol* (Greek *Hades*). In this case it means, not the place of eternal punishment but the place of the dead.
See also *Death, Future destiny, Judgement.*
Matthew 18:8-9; 3:12; 13:42; Mark 9:48; Matthew 10:38; 25:41; Revelation 20:10-15

Hermon
A mountain on the Lebanon/Syria border. It is over 9,000ft/2,750m high. It is also called Sirion in the Bible. It is topped with snow almost all the year round. The melting snow and ice form a major source of the River Jordan. Mt Hermon is close to Caesarea Philippi and may be the 'high mountain' where Jesus' disciples saw him in his glory.
Joshua 12:1, etc; Psalm 42:6; 133:3; Matthew 17:1, etc.

Herod
1. Herod the Great. Son of Antipater, who was made procurator of Judea by Julius Caesar in 47 BC. Antipater appointed Herod to be governor of Galilee. After the death of his father and brother Joseph, who was governor of Jerusalem, the Romans gave Herod the title 'king of the Jews'. He reigned from 37-4 BC. Herod was hated by the Jews, although he spent large sums of money on the temple. He was not a Jew by birth and murdered members of the Jewish Hasmonaean family whom he saw as a threat to the throne. When the wise men came to worship the baby Jesus

he again felt threatened and ordered the murder of all male children in Bethlehem under two years old. After his death his kingdom was divided amongst three of his sons: Archelaus, Antipas and Philip.
Matthew 2. Luke 1:5
2. Archelaus, called Herod the Ethnarch, ruled Judea 4 BC-AD 6. When Mary and Joseph returned with Jesus from Egypt and heard that Archelaus was ruler of Judea they decided to settle in Galilee instead. Archelaus treated the Jews and Samaritans so cruelly that they complained to the Romans, who sent him into exile.
Matthew 2:22
3. Antipas, called Herod the Tetrarch, ruled Galilee 4 BC-AD 39. He imprisoned John the Baptist and as a result of a rash promise agreed to his wife's request to have him beheaded. Pilate handed Jesus over to Antipas for trial because he came from Galilee. Antipas treated Jesus with scorn and then sent him back to Pilate.
Matthew 14; Mark 6; Luke 23:7ff.
4. Agrippa I, called Herod the King, was son of Aristobulus and grandson of Herod the Great. He became ruler of Galilee, Judea and Samaria. To please the Jews he persecuted the Christians. He killed James, the son of Zebedee, and imprisoned Peter. Luke, the writer of Acts, records that Agrippa's death in AD 44 was a result of his pride.
Acts 12
5. Agrippa II was the son of Agrippa I. When he went to Caesarea to visit the Roman governor, Festus, he heard Paul's case. His verdict was that Paul could have been released if he had not appealed to Caesar.
Acts 25:13-26:32

Herodias
The wife of Herod Antipas. Herod married Herodias while Philip, her first husband, was still alive. Because John the Baptist condemned the marriage, Herodias had him beheaded.
Matthew 14; Mark 6; Luke 3:19

Hezekiah
King of Judah 716-687 BC (co-regent from 729) after his father, King Ahaz. As soon as he became king, Hezekiah re-opened and repaired the temple. He organized a national campaign to destroy everything to do with idol worship. Hezekiah rebelled against the Assyrians and refused to pay taxes to them. During his reign the northern kingdom of Israel was completely conquered by Assyria. Hezekiah realized that his country was also threatened. He cut a rock tunnel to ensure Jerusalem's water supply in the event of siege. King Sennacherib of Assyria captured several cities in Judah and surrounded Jerusalem. Judah was saved when death struck the Assyrian army overnight. Soon after this, Hezekiah became very ill but God answered his prayer and gave him another fifteen years to live.
2 Kings 18-20; 2 Chronicles 29-32; Isaiah 36-39

Hierapolis
A city in the Roman province of Asia, now in western Turkey. Paul mentions the Christians at Laodicea and Hierapolis in his letter to nearby Colossae. Over the centuries the hot-water springs at Hierapolis (modern Pamukkale), have 'petrified' to form amazing waterfalls of stone.
Colossians 4:13

Hilkiah
Best-known of several Hilkiahs is the high priest who lived in the reign of King Josiah of Judah. While the temple was being repaired he found an old scroll with God's laws written on it. This discovery led to a great reform in the worship at the temple.
2 Kings 22–23; 2 Chronicles 34

Hinnom
The name of a valley on the south side of Jerusalem, forming the boundary between the tribes of Judah and Benjamin. Here the kings Ahaz and Manasseh set up a shrine for the god Molech, and children were offered to him in sacrifice. It was destroyed by Josiah. Jeremiah denounced the evil of this place. Later, rubbish from the city was burned in the Valley of Hinnom. So it became a picture of hell. The word 'Gehenna', meaning 'Valley of Hinnom', became a word for 'hell'.
Joshua 15:8; 18:16; 2 Kings 23:10; 2 Chronicles 28:3; 33:6; Jeremiah 7:31; 19:2; 32:35

Hiram
1. A king of Tyre who was a friend of King David and King Solomon. He sent cedar-wood from Lebanon to Jerusalem for the building of David's palace and later for Solomon's temple.
2 Samuel 5:11; 1 Kings 5; 9-10
2. A craftsman sent by King Hiram to help King Solomon build his palace and the temple.
1 Kings 7

History of Israel
The Near East before 3000 BC had two quite separate centres of civilization. Each had its own culture, crafts and system of writing. One was in Mesopotamia, the land around the Tigris and Euphrates rivers, part of the 'fertile crescent'. The other was Egypt. The story of mankind begins in Eden, placed somewhere in Mesopotamia. Abraham came from the south Mesopotamian city of Ur. Some of his family settled at Harran in the north while he went on to Canaan.

So the world of Israel's early ancestors was one of rich and powerful kingdoms in the river valleys of Egypt and Mesopotamia. In the lands between were many walled cities and tiny kingdoms. These strongholds protected the settlers who farmed the country around. But there were also nomadic tribespeople who moved from place to place in search of good grazing for their flocks and herds. Abraham and his family were just one group among many on the move in the area.

This was the pattern in Canaan when Abraham arrived to set up camp at Shechem. The coastal plain and the Jordan Valley, where there was good farmland, were already settled. This looked attractive to Abraham's nephew Lot, who moved down from the hills to camp near Sodom. But life there had its dangers. Lot was only one of many who suffered when rebel kings tried to throw off the control of their distant overlords (Genesis 14).

Drought and famine often struck Canaan. So it was natural for the nomads to move down to the fertile land of Egypt. On one occasion (Genesis 12) Abraham was among them. A later famine took the brothers of Abraham's great-grandson, Joseph, to Egypt to buy corn. Soon the whole family of Israel (Jacob's twelve sons) were settled in Goshen, in the eastern Nile Delta.

The Exodus For nearly 400 years Jacob's people remained in Egypt. During that time they had grown into a nation–the nation of Israel. The Egyptians, now ruled by a less friendly dynasty of kings, began to see these people as a threat. They tightened their control, forcing the Israelites to work as slaves in the brickfields. To reduce their growing numbers, newborn Hebrew boys were drowned in the Nile. The people cried out to God–and he sent them a leader: Moses.

It took a series of terrible plagues before the king of Egypt would agree to let the Israelites leave his country. At the last minute he changed his mind and sent his army in pursuit–but the Israelites escaped across the 'sea of reeds' to Sinai. The 'exodus' had begun.

See *Exodus*.
Exodus 1-14

Semitic people arriving in Egypt. Part of a wall-painting at Beni-Hasan, Egypt, from about 1890 BC.

The conquest of Canaan Joshua took over leadership of the people as they entered the land across the Jordan. In front of them was the walled city of Jericho. The whole land God had promised them was waiting to be possessed. Canaan at this time was divided into a large number of small independent states, each centred on a fortified town with its own ruler.

Joshua took Jericho, and struck fear into the hearts of the Canaanites. At the second attempt, Ai fell. Men from Gibeon lost no time in sueing for peace. They tricked the Israelites into a treaty and this led to the next stage in the war. Joshua won a series of victories in the south and then turned north to defeat the king of Hazor's alliance. The Philistines remained in their cities on the coastal plain. And the Canaanites still controlled many inland towns. But it was possible for the Israelites to settle.

Lots were cast to share out the land among the tribes. Two and a half tribes settled east of the Jordan. The rest shared the land of Canaan. The Levites had no tribal land, but were given certain towns to live in. Six towns were set aside as cities of refuge, where people guilty of manslaughter were safe from revenge.
Joshua

The Judges The tribes settled into the areas allotted to them. They were scattered now, and surrounded by hostile neighbours. Joshua was dead. It began to seem impossible to gain full control of the land. Gradually the Israelites lost sight of the fact that God was fighting for them. They began to compromise with the nations around, and with their gods, for the sake of peace. Their enemies took advantage of their evident weakness. The Book of Judges relates the sad story.

The surrounding nations returned to the attack: the king of Mesopotamia from the north; Moabites and Ammonites from across the Jordan; Midianites from the east. The Canaanites at Hazor grew strong enough to make a second attack on the settlers. And from the coastlands the Philistines pushed the Israelites further and further into the hills.

As at so many times in their history, the Israelites cried to God for help in their need. Each 'Judge' won at least a temporary respite. The most famous of these freedom-fighters are Deborah and Barak, Gideon, Jephthah and Samson.

Israel's first kings The last and greatest of the Judges was Samuel–prophet and king-maker. When Samuel grew old, the people asked for a king to rule them, like the other nations. Samuel warned them that a king would mean conscription to the army, forced labour and oppression. But the Israelites insisted. And at last Samuel did as they asked.

The first king was a tall, handsome Benjaminite called Saul. To begin with all went well. But power went to Saul's head and he began to disregard God's clear instructions. Because of Saul's disobedience, his son Jonathan did not inherit the throne. Instead, during Saul's lifetime, God sent Samuel to anoint David as Israel's next king.

While still just a shepherd-boy, David killed the Philistine champion, Goliath. His popularity made Saul jealous, and for a number of years David was forced to live as an outlaw, in danger of his life. Then Saul and Jonathan were killed in battle against the Philistines. David became king.

David united the kingdom, captured Jerusalem, the Jebusite stronghold, and made it his capital. He was a soldier-king. During his lifetime he expanded the kingdom and drove off old enemies. His legacy to his son Solomon was peace and security.

David wanted to build a temple for God in Jerusalem, but he had to be content with getting materials together. It was Solomon who built the temple, and many other fine buildings. A strong, secure kingdom made it possible for Solomon to prosper through trade alliances. His wisdom was legendary. At Solomon's court there was leisure for culture and beauty. His reign was Israel's golden age.
1 Samuel 8–1 Kings 11

The two kingdoms Under King Solomon Israel became a rich and powerful kingdom, but the people were oppressed and burdened with heavy taxes and forced labour. When Solomon's son Rehoboam came to the throne they appealed to him to lighten their burdens. He refused. The ten northern tribes rebelled. They set up a new kingdom, the kingdom of Israel, with Jeroboam I ruling as king from his capital at Shechem. In the south, Rehoboam ruled the kingdom of Judah (the tribes of Judah and Benjamin) from Jerusalem.

Jeroboam also had to set up a new centre of worship for the northern kingdom, now cut off from Jerusalem. He chose Dan, in the north, and Bethel, an important centre when Samuel was alive. But pagan practices quickly became part of the worship. The historians who wrote Kings and Chronicles classified the kings as 'good' or 'bad' depending on whether they reformed religion or let the pagan practices continue.

Uzziah and Hezekiah were two of the reforming kings of Judah. King Ahab of Israel had one of the worst records. He and his foreign wife Jezebel opposed Elijah and persecuted those who worshipped God. The remains of his 'ivory house' at Samaria can be seen today. Assyrian annals record that he brought 10,000 men and 2,000 chariots to the Battle of Qarqar, where he joined forces with the Egyptians to resist the Assyrian King Shalmaneser (853 BC).

The rise of the northern powers Israel and Judah, in their strategic position between Egypt and the Mesopotamian powers, were very vulnerable to aggression. David and Solomon were successful partly because none of the larger nations were powerful enough to attack during their reigns. But after the division of the kingdom the nations were immediately around–Syria, Ammon, Moab–gave the subsequent kings of Israel and Judah increasing trouble. However, it was the growth of the major powers farther north-east that proved decisive.

The Assyrian Empire had an earlier period of power under Tiglath-pileser I. But the ruthless aggression for which Assyria was so much feared reached its peak in the period between 880 and 612 BC. The empire was based on three great cities: Asshur, Calah and Nineveh.

From the mid-ninth century BC, the time of Ahab in Israel, the kings of Assyria repeatedly attacked Israel and Judah. Soon King Jehu of Israel was paying tribute to Shalmaneser III of Assyria. A hundred years later Ahaz of Judah asked Tiglath-pileser III of Assyria to help him fight Syria and Israel (Isaiah 7; 2 Kings 16). He did so and defeated them both, but Judah had to become a subject kingdom of the Assyrians in return for their help.

When Israel refused to pay their yearly tribute, the next king of Assyria took Samaria, exiled the people and destroyed the northern kingdom (722/1 BC; 2 Kings 17).

King Jehu of Israel paying homage to Shalmaneser III of Assyria: from Shalmaneser's 'Black Obelisk'.

Soon after this, Egypt was defeated by the Assyrians. In 701 BC the powerful King Sennacherib besieged Jerusalem, but because of King Hezekiah's trust in God the city was saved (2 Kings 19).

The Assyrians had to fight many battles to defend their empire. In the next century several provinces regained their freedom. The empire lasted until Asshur fell to the Medes in 614 and Nineveh was destroyed by the Medes and Babylonians in 612.

Invasion and exile If Assyria in the Bible meant oppression, Babylon meant power. Nabopolassar, governor of the area around the Persian Gulf, freed Babylon from the Assyrians and in 626 BC was made king. He continued to gain victories over the Assyrians and in 612 BC the Babylonians and Medes captured the Assyrian capital of Nineveh. They were not content with taking over Assyria itself but set out to conquer the whole Assyrian Empire.

The Assyrians retreated to Harran but were soon driven out. The Egyptians, realizing that their own country might be in danger, marched north to support them. King Josiah of Judah intercepted the Egyptian army at Megiddo. In the resulting battle he was killed and Judah became subject to Egypt (2 Kings 23:29). Four years later, in 605 BC, the Babylonian army led by Nebuchadnezzar defeated the Egyptians at Carchemish (Jeremiah 46:1-2). The Babylonian Empire was spreading. Jehoiakim of Judah was one of the many kings who now had to pay tribute to Nebuchadnezzar.

After a fierce battle with the Babylonians in 601 BC the Egyptians encouraged Judah to rebel. Nebuchadnezzar sent troops to crush the rebellion and in 597 BC, shortly after Jehoiachin had become king, Judah submitted. The king and many of the country's leaders were taken into exile in Babylon. The policy of the invaders was not just to plunder and destroy, but also to weaken the subject nations and prevent further rebellions by deporting their leading citizens (2 Kings 24:10-17).

Despite this, ten years later Zedekiah, a puppet king placed on the throne of Judah by Nebuchadnezzar, appealed to the Egyptians for help. The Babylonians invaded Judah and laid siege to Jerusalem. The siege lasted eighteen months. Finally, a breach was made in the walls. In 586 BC the city was taken. King Zedekiah was captured and blinded. Valuable objects including the temple treasure were taken to Babylon. Jerusalem and its temple was destroyed and the citizens deported. Only the very poor were left to cultivate the land (2 Kings 25:1-21). See *Exile*.

Return to Jerusalem In the first half of the sixth century BC Babylon appeared all-powerful. But the prophets spoke of a God to whom kings were as puppets, and who could use even pagan powers to fulfil his purposes.

Cyrus the Persian united the two kingdoms of Media and Persia to the east of Babylon. He conquered lands as far east as India. Then he attacked Babylon. The city fell in 539 BC and he took over the whole empire.

The Persian kings extended their borders even further than the earlier empires. They took Egypt and all of what is now Turkey. When Babylon fell, Cyrus began to reorganize the empire. He divided it into provinces, each with its own ruler, called a 'satrap'. These were mainly Persians, but under them were local rulers who retained some power. The different peoples were encouraged to keep their own customs and religions.

As part of this policy, Cyrus sent the Jews back to Jerusalem to restore the city and rebuild the temple, as told in the books of Ezra and Nehemiah. Jews also settled in many other parts of the empire. In Susa, one of the Persian capitals, a later king, Xerxes I, even made a Jewess his queen, as told in the book of Esther. The 'dispersion', as Jews living in other lands came to be called, was significant later, in New Testament times. Because they were away from the temple, these Jews developed the local synagogue as a centre of teaching and worship. And this laid the basis for the later rapid spread of the Christian churches, which were formed on this model.

King Darius I (522-486), builder of the great new capital, Persepolis, and conqueror of western India, also pushed the empire westwards. In 513 he took Macedonia in northern Greece. In 490 the Persians were defeated by the Greeks at Marathon, and the stage was set for some of the greatest stories of Greek classical antiquity. Xerxes I (486-465) invaded Greece, even occupying Athens, but was defeated in the sea battle of Salamis. Artaxerxes, Darius II, and the kings that followed, took up the struggles. The fortunes of Persia and Greece, Media and Egypt ebbed and flowed until finally, in 333 BC, the Greek soldier Alexander of Macedon crossed the Hellespont to begin his meteoric career.

Alexander was only twenty-two when he set out on a campaign which swept across the ancient world. He 'liberated' Egypt from the Persians (founding the port of Alexandria), then marched east, to the heart of the Persian Empire. He pressed on as far as India, conquering all who stood in his way and founding Greek city-states wherever he went. His title 'Alexander the Great' was well earned. He died, when only thirty-three, in 323 BC.

Following his death, the great Greek Empire was divided up among his four generals. The Seleucid rulers, based on Antioch in Syria, controlled Palestine. The Ptolemies, based on Alexandria, ruled Egypt. Culturally, however, the Greek or 'hellenistic' world continued as a unity, with Greek as a common language and with a common pattern of civilization. This background played a vital part in events which were to follow: the events of the New Testament.

Israel in the New Testament By New Testament times the Jewish people had lived under foreign occupation for some 500 years since returning to their own land. Under Greek rule they had paid tribute to Ptolemy of Egypt and adopted Greek as the language of the empire. In 198 BC the Seleucid Greek ruler of Syria, Antiochus the Great, defeated the Ptolemies and took Palestine. But he in turn was defeated by the Romans at Magnesia in 190 BC.

The Romans taxed the Seleucid Empire harshly, and they in turn took any opportunity to loot cities and temples. Antiochus Epiphanes used the opposition of loyal Jews, the 'Hasidim' or 'pious ones', as an excuse to plunder the Jerusalem temple. Later he built a pagan Greek centre in the heart of the city and in the temple an altar to Zeus on which pigs (forbidden under Jewish food laws) were sacrificed.

This final affront resulted in the Maccabean Revolt. The Jews succeeded in freeing themselves for a time and were able to cleanse and rededicate the temple in 165 BC. The high priest Aristobolus, a later member of the Hasmonaean family which had led the revolt, declared himself king in 104 BC. But before long, rivalries among the Jews gave the Romans the chance to intervene. The last high-priest king was executed in 37 BC.

Judea became subject to Rome under the governor of the province of Syria. But the Jews kept the freedom to practice their religion and had their own ruler: from 37 to 4 BC an Idumaean Jew named Herod. Despite his ambitious building projects–including a new temple in Jerusalem–the Jews hated Herod the Great, and he is chiefly remembered for his tyranny and cruelty.

This was the background to the birth of Jesus. Luke records the fact that Jesus was born in the time of the first Roman Emperor, Augustus. He was succeeded by Tiberius in AD 14. Herod's act in putting the male children of Bethlehem to death was wholly in character with what we know of him otherwise. When he died, the kingdom was divided among three of his sons. One ruled so badly that the Romans removed him and appointed a 'prefect' for Judea. Pontius Pilate, who passed the death sentence on Jesus, was prefect AD 26-36.

The Jewish council, the Sanhedrin, tried to keep the peace with the Romans to protect its own position. Others, such as the hated tax collectors, profited from the Roman occupation to line their own pockets. Many looked forward to the day when they would be delivered, when they would be free. Like Simeon, who was in the temple when Jesus' parents came to present their baby, they were 'waiting for Israel to be saved'. So Jesus had to be careful to play down any claim to be the promised Messiah, the deliverer, for fear of raising people's hopes that he would lead a revolt against the Romans. The spirit of resistance was strongest among the Zealots (a guerilla group): and it was this spirit that led eventually to the disastrous events of the Jewish War, and the destruction of Jerusalem in AD 70.

But the time when the Jewish temple was destroyed and the Jewish nation scattered was also a time of a new beginning. After the death and resurrection of Jesus, it was made plain to his followers that the new kingdom was not just for the Jews but for all who believed in him. It offered a completely new start, not just for the Jewish people but for all who were to enter into the promises given to Abraham, which were based on faith. It was to mean liberation from sin and guilt and from the petty-fogging legalism of the Jewish Law. Jew and non-Jew ('Gentile') alike could begin a new life, filled with God's Spirit. The dynamic of this message was to turn the Empire upside-down, and change the world.

Hittites

Before the time of the Israelites and Aramaeans, Syria was controlled by the Hittites from Turkey. They were an Indo-European race who built up an empire which was very powerful from about 1600-1300 BC. Their capital city was Hattusha (now Bogazköy), near Ankara, the modern capital of Turkey. In its ruins the royal archives have been found. They are written in the Babylonian cuneiform script on clay tablets, but in the Hittite languages. Amongst the important documents are many treaties made with subject states. These follow a set pattern–the same pattern followed in Exodus and Deuteronomy, where God's treaties with his people, Israel, are set down.

The Hittites also developed a hieroglyphic writing of their own. In 1286 BC the Hittites fought the Egyptians at the Battle of Qadesh. Neither side won, so they drew up a treaty to agree a border. This was roughly the line followed by the northern boundary of Israel's Promised Land (see Joshua 1:4). About 1200 BC the Hittite Empire disappeared under the attacks of the Sea Peoples (see *Philistines*). Their culture was lost, except in a few outposts. These included some places in northern Syria (Carchemish, Hamath), where descendants of the Hittites mingled with other peoples. Hittite kings and Hittite women are still mentioned in the time of Solomon and even of Elisha–1 Kings 10:28ff.; 11:1; 2 Kings 7:6 (The Hittites living in Canaan very much earlier–at the time of Abraham, Genesis 23–may have been migrants from the north, or a separate group with a similar name.)

Holiness

The basic idea of holiness is 'separate (set apart) for God'. In the Old Testament, places, things, people and seasons were called holy when they were set apart for God. For that reason the seventh day, the sabbath, was holy.

The character of God himself shows what holiness is. He is different. He is the one who is absolutely separate from creation, and from all that is evil. Nothing compares with him. His very nature is different from our own: he is 'holy'. Because of this we should stand in awe of him. When someone realizes how holy God is, as Isaiah did, he is intensely conscious of his own sin that separates him from God.

The people of God have always been expected to reflect the holiness which they see in God. God wants his people to share his holiness. So in the New Testament the common word for Christians is 'saints'. This did not then mean an especially devout Christian. It meant 'the holy ones', those who are set apart and dedicated to God's service. And 'saints' are meant to grow in holiness and likeness to God–a process sometimes called 'sanctification'.

Genesis 2:3; Exodus 20:8; 30:22-33; Leviticus 19:1; Isaiah 6:1-5; 40:18-28; 10:20; Psalm 33:21; Isaiah 8:13; 6; Hebrews 12:10; Ephesians 5:25-27

Holy Spirit

The Spirit of God is one with God the Father and Jesus Christ (see *Trinity*). He is active throughout the history of God's work and God's people. But it is not until the New Testament and the 'age of the spirit' that we see the details of his work.

The Spirit of God was active in the creation of the world. As God, he is present everywhere–there is nowhere in the whole of creation outside his domain. Again and again we read of the Spirit of God giving people the power needed for special service. The Spirit of God gave the prophets their inspiration and communicated the word of God through them. But the Old Testament looked forward to the day when the Spirit of God would be poured out on all people.

When Jesus came, he was born by the power of the Holy Spirit. The Holy Spirit descended upon him at his baptism in the River Jordan. He was led by the Spirit into the desert where he was tempted by the devil. And at the beginning of his public work Jesus declared that he would carry it out through the power of the Spirit. John the Baptist declared that Jesus would baptize people with the Holy Spirit. And Jesus himself promised his disciples that after he had left them he would send the Holy Spirit to be with them all the time. After Jesus had returned to his Father, the Holy Spirit would teach and guide the followers of Jesus and give them power. 'He will give me glory,' Jesus said, 'because he will take what I say and tell it to you.'

The disciples were baptized with the Holy Spirit, as Jesus promised, on the Day of Pentecost. This was obvious to everyone because of a new note of praise and boldness, because they spoke in other languages, and because of their powerful preaching. As Peter told his listeners on the Day of Pentecost, the prophecy of Joel had come true. God had poured out his Spirit on all believers.

When someone becomes a Christian he or she receives the 'gift' of the Holy Spirit. The Holy Spirit lives within the Christian giving new understanding and direction, and making him aware that he really is a child of God. The Spirit is a guarantee of a future with God in heaven.

The Holy Spirit helps Christians to realize their oneness in Jesus Christ. He works to reproduce the character of Jesus in the life of every Christian–the qualities of 'love, joy, peace, patience, kindness, goodness, faithfulness, humility and self-control'. And he gives Christians the power and gifts needed to serve God.

See also *Trinity, Church.*

Genesis 1:2; Psalm 139:7-12; Judges 3:10; 14:6, and many other passages; Isaiah 11:1-3; 2 Samuel 23:2-5; Ezekiel 36:26-27; Joel 2:28-29; Micah 3:8; Luke 1:35; 3:22; 4:1-18; 3:16; John 14:16-17; 16:7-15; Acts 2; Romans 8; 1 Corinthians 12; Galatians 5:22-23

Hope

The Christian's hope is a confident looking forward to a future beyond this world, promised by God. It is something that keeps him joyful in troubles.

He has learned that God's promises can be trusted, and so he is confident about the future. 'I alone know the plans I have for you,' says God to Jeremiah, in the dark days of exile, 'plans to bring you prosperity and not disaster, plans to bring about the future you hope for.'

The resurrection of Jesus is the great foundation of the Christian's hope. 'Because of (God's) great mercy he gave us new life by raising Jesus from death,' wrote Peter. 'This fills us with a living hope.' This is confirmed by the gift of the Holy Spirit, who is the guarantee of the Christian's own future resurrection.

See also *Future destiny.*

Romans 4:18; 5:1-5; 8:24-25; 12:12; 15:4; Jeremiah 29:11; 1 Corinthians 15:19-20; Colossians 1:15; 1 Peter 1:3-6; 2 Corinthians 5:1-5

Hophni and Phinehas

Eli's two sons, priests at Shiloh. Because they showed open contempt for God, he forewarned Eli of their death. Hophni and Phinehas carried God's Covenant Box (the ark) into battle against the Philistines. It was captured and they were both killed.

1 Samuel 2:12ff.; 4

Horeb

Another name for Mt Sinai.

Horse

In Bible times horses were owned only by the rich. They were not kept in Israel until David's day. The country's geographical position made Solomon a convenient middleman, trading in chariots from Egypt and horses from Turkey (Cilicia). The horse was a 'weapon' of war and stood for power.

Exodus 14:23; Joshua 11:4; Esther 6:8, 10, 11

Hosea

Hosea lived at about the same time as Isaiah, the eighth century BC. But he lived in the northern kingdom of Israel. He prophesied during the troubled forty years before the fall of Samaria in 722 BC. Israel had six kings in just over twenty years, and was often turning to pagan religions.

Hosea was greatly concerned about this idol worship. He pictures the faithlessness of Israel in terms of his own marriage to an unfaithful wife (Hosea 1-3). Although God's judgement would come, his love would win his people back in the end.

Chapters 4-13 record his messages to Israel. They show how angry God was, and yet how he could never forget his love for his people. The final chapter pleads with the people to return to God. They would then be able to enjoy his promise of new life.

Hoshea
The last king of Israel. Hoshea made himself king by killing King Pekah. He was defeated by King Shalmaneser V of Assyria and as a result had to pay him tribute. When Hoshea rebelled he was imprisoned by Shalmaneser. Three years later Samaria, the capital of Israel, was captured and the people taken away to Assyria.
2 Kings 17

Huldah
A prophetess who lived in the reign of King Josiah. When Hilkiah the priest found an ancient scroll of God's Law in the temple Josiah asked her advice.
2 Kings 22:14ff.; 2 Chronicles 34:22ff.

Hunting

An Assyrian hunter; from a relief in the palace of King Sargon II at Khorsabad, eighth century BC.

Esau, we are told, hunted 'venison' (deer). The people of Israel had laws on the subject of hunting–particularly which animals and birds could be eaten and how they were to be killed. Israelite kings may have hunted for sport, as the Mesopotamians and Egyptians did, since 'deer, gazelles, roebucks and poultry' were brought to the table of Solomon. People hunted when hunger, or the attacks of wild animals on their flocks, drove them to it. But we do not know whether men regularly hunted for a living. The Old Testament references to catching animals are few.

However, the country lies on a main migration route for birds, so it is not surprising to find frequent mentions of the 'fowler' with his nets and snares.
Genesis 25:27; Deuteronomy 14:4-5; Leviticus 17:13; 1 Kings 4:23; Proverbs 1:17; Hosea 7:11-12; Proverbs 6:5; Psalm 124:7

Hurrians
One group which became part of the Hittite Empire was the Hurrian people. They are known from 2500 BC in Babylonia. But their origin is uncertain and their language–recorded in cuneiform texts–is not properly understood. Groups of them settled throughout the Fertile Crescent. They appear in Edom (the Horites, Genesis 14:6), in Shechem and in Gilgal (the Hivites, Genesis 34:2; Joshua 9:3-7). Hurrian names occur on cuneiform tablets of about 1400 BC found in Canaan, and Egyptian texts refer to Canaan as 'Huru'. At that time there was an important Hurrian state in upper Mesopotamia (Mitanni). These kings wrote letters to the pharaohs of Egypt. Among their gods they worshipped Mithra and others well known in India. The Hurrians had a strong influence on the Hittites, and they carried Babylonian culture wherever they went.

Hushai
A trusted friend of King David. During Absalom's rebellion Hushai pretended to go over to Absalom's side. His misleading 'advice' won time for David and he enabled him to escape by informing David's spies of Absalom's plans.
2 Samuel 15:32-17:15

Hymenaeus
A man who was thrown out of the church by Paul because he taught things which were not true and weakened the faith of some Christians.
1 Timothy 1:20; 2 Timothy 2:17

Hymns
See *Creeds and hymns*.

Hyssop
On the cross, Jesus was given vinegar in a sponge passed to him on a bunch of hyssop. In the Old Testament it was used in sprinkling the blood of the sacrifice, and on the eve of the Passover. It was obviously a bushy plant, and must therefore have been different from the herb we call by the same name today, and may have been either marjoram or caper.
Exodus 12:21-22; John 19:29

A sprig of marjoram, possibly the plant called 'hyssop' in the Bible.

I

Ibleam
A Canaanite town in the north of Israel, about 10 miles/14km south-east of Megiddo. Here Jehu killed King Ahaziah of Judah.
Joshua 17:11-12; 2 Kings 9:27; 15:10

Iconium
Present-day Konya in south-central Turkey. Paul preached at Iconium, then a town in the Roman province of Galatia, on his first missionary journey. He met with violent opposition.
Acts 13:51; 14:1-6, 19-22; 2 Timothy 3:11

Idumaea
The Greek name for the Old Testament Edom. By New Testament times many Idumaeans had settled west of the Jordan, in the dry country in the south of Palestine. This district was then called Idumaea. King Herod was an Idumaean. People came even from this area in the far south to see Jesus in Galilee.
Mark 3:8

Illyricum
The Roman name of a land stretching along the eastern shore of the Adriatic Sea. It covered much the same area as modern Yugoslavia. The southern part was also called Dalmatia (see *Dalmatia*). When Paul wrote to the Romans, he said he had preached the gospel from Jerusalem as far west as Illyricum. There is no other mention of Paul's work in this land.
Romans 15:19

Isaac
The son God promised to Abraham and Sarah. He was born when his parents were very old. A few years after Isaac's birth God tested Abraham's faith even more. He told Abraham to sacrifice his son. Just as he was about to kill Isaac, an angel stopped him. God rewarded Abraham and again promised that his descendants would be a great nation. When Isaac was forty he married Rebekah, a girl chosen for him from Abraham's family in Harran. After many years God answered Isaac's prayer for a son and the twins, Esau and Jacob, were born. God gave Isaac the same blessing he had given Abraham. When Isaac was old and nearly blind he was tricked into passing the blessing on to Jacob instead of Esau, the older twin. Jacob left home but returned several years later in time to see his father before he died.
Genesis 21-22; 24-28:9; 35:27-29

Isaiah
Isaiah lived in Jerusalem in the eighth century BC. The book named after him is one of the most powerful books of prophecy in the Old Testament. It has a strong picture of God's power and a message of hope for his people. Isaiah's own call to be a prophet is recorded in chapter 6. He continued to prophesy for more than forty years.

Chapters 1–39 belong to the period when the southern kingdom of Judah was under threat from Assyria–the great power of the biblical world at that time. But Isaiah warned the people that the real danger to the nation was their own sin and disobedience to God. They had failed to trust God. Isaiah called the nation to return to God, and restore justice and right action. If they did not respond, destruction would follow. Isaiah also looked forward to a time when there would be peace throughout the world. A descendant of King David would become the ideal king who would do God's will.

Chapters 40–55 picture the exile of Judah in Babylon. They are often thought to be the work of another prophet who was a follower of Isaiah. The people were without hope. But the prophet spoke of a time when God was going to free his people and restore them to Jerusalem. He emphasized that God controls history. He spoke of God's plan to use the nation of Israel to bring hope to all the nations. This section of the book includes a number of passages in which the prophet looks forward to the coming of the 'Servant of the Lord' who would bring hope to the nation.

Chapters 56–66 form a separate section and are mainly addressed to the Jewish people back in Jerusalem. The prophet reassures the people that God will keep his word. But he calls them, also, to justice and right living, and instructs them to keep God's sabbath, to offer sacrifices, and to pray.

Ishbosheth/Ishbaal
One of King Saul's sons. When Saul was killed by the Philistines, Ishbosheth was crowned by Abner, the commander of Saul's army. He reigned in Israel while David was king of Judah. For two years Judah and Israel were at war. Then Ishbosheth was murdered by two commanders of his army, and David became king of both Israel and Judah.
2 Samuel 2-4

Ishmael
Son of Abraham and Hagar. (See *Hagar.*)
Genesis 16; 21

Israel
The new name God gave to Jacob after he had wrestled all night with the 'man' at the River Jabbok. Israel means 'the man who fights with God'. The twelve tribes descended from Jacob were known as the children of Israel. For a full description of the other aspects of the life, land and religion of Israel see separate entries, especially *History of Israel, Religion of Israel, Geography of Israel.*

Issachar
1. Son of Jacob and Leah, who gave his name to one of the twelve tribes of Israel.
Genesis 35:23
2. The land belonging to the tribe of Issachar, south of Lake Galilee and west of the River Jordan.
Joshua 19:17-23

Ithamar
Aaron's youngest son. Ithamar was the priest who supervised the making of the worship tent (the tabernacle). He was in charge of two groups of Levites and founded one of the important families of priests.
Exodus 6:23; 38:21; Numbers 3ff.; 1 Chronicles 24:1

Ituraea
A name mentioned only in Luke's careful dating of the time when John the Baptist began to preach. Herod Philip was then ruler of Ituraea and Trachonitis. The Ituraeans were probably the descendants of the Old Testament people called Jetur. They were a wild tribal people in the hills west of Damascus, north of the headwaters of the River Jordan. See also *Trachonitis.*
Luke 3:1; compare 1 Chronicles 5:19

J

Jabbok
Now the Zerqa, a river that flows into the Jordan from the east, between the Dead Sea and Lake Galilee. Jacob wrestled with an angel beside the Jabbok. Adam–the place where the Jordan was dammed, allowing the Israelites to cross into the Promised Land–stands at the confluence of the Jabbok and the Jordan. The river is also mentioned in the Bible as a boundary.
Genesis 32:22-30; Numbers 21:24; Deuteronomy 3:16; Judges 11:13

Jabesh-gilead
A town on the east of the Jordan. When the wives of the Benjaminites were killed in a civil war at the time of the Judges, the town of Jabesh provided replacements. Saul answered an appeal for help when Jabesh was besieged by the Ammonites. Men from Jabesh later risked their lives to remove his body from Beth-shan.
Judges 21; 1 Samuel 11; 31:11-13

Jabin
1. King of Hazor defeated and killed by Joshua.
Joshua 11:1-11
2. A Canaanite king, also from Hazor, who oppressed the Israelites for twenty years. His army was defeated by Barak and Deborah.
Judges 4

Jacob
Son of Isaac and Rebekah; Esau's (younger) twin. When Esau was hungry after hunting, Jacob persuaded him to give up his rights as the elder son in exchange for a bowl of stew. Later Jacob gained his father's special blessing by pretending to be Esau. After that, Esau hated Jacob and planned to kill him. Jacob escaped north to his Uncle Laban in Harran. On the way he had a dream. He saw a staircase reaching from earth to heaven, with angels moving up and down it. God promised him and his descendants the land where he was sleeping. 'I will not leave you until I have done all that I have promised you.'

Nomads still use camels to travel across the desert, as Jacob did.

Jacob worked for Laban as a shepherd for twenty years. He loved Laban's daughter, Rachel, but was tricked into marrying her sister, Leah, first. While he was in Harran, Jacob became the father of eleven sons and one daughter. He waited long years for his first son by Rachel: Joseph. Later Rachel died giving birth to a second son, Benjamin. Laban cheated Jacob but in the end was outwitted. Jacob built up his own large flocks of sheep and goats, and then left for his own country. On the way he had a strange all-night wrestling-match with an unknown 'man', and would not let him go until he had been blessed. God gave him the new name of Israel which means, 'the man who fights with God'.

To Jacob's great relief Esau gave him a warm welcome. But afterwards they went their own ways. Jacob lived in the land of Canaan until Joseph invited him to settle in Egypt. Before Jacob died he blessed his sons, the ancestors of the tribes of Israel.
Genesis 25:21-34; 27-35; 37:1; 42–49

Jael
A woman from the nomadic Kenite tribe. After Sisera, commander of the Canaanite army, had lost his battle against the Israelites he ran away and hid in Jael's tent. While he was asleep she murdered him. Deborah praised Jael in her victory song.
Judges 4; 5:24-27

Jairus
The synagogue official at Capernaum who asked Jesus to heal his twelve-year-old daughter. By the time Jesus reached Jairus's house she was dead. But, to the amazement of her parents, Jesus brought her back to life.
Mark 5:22ff.

James
1. The son of Zebedee and a disciple of Jesus. Like his brother John, James was a fisherman. Jesus nicknamed the two stormy brothers 'men of thunder'! When Jesus called him to be one of his special followers James went with him at once. James was present when Jesus brought Jairus's daughter back to life, and at Jesus' glory (the transfiguration). He was killed for his faith by Herod Agrippa I.
Matthew 4:21ff.; 17:1ff.; Mark 5:37; 10:35ff.; Acts 12:2
2. Another apostle, the son of Alphaeus. He was probably the man called 'James the younger'.
Matthew 10:3; Mark 15:40; Acts 1:13
3. One of Jesus' brothers. James did not believe that Jesus was the Messiah until he saw him after the resurrection. He became a leader of the church in Jerusalem and probably wrote the Letter of James. The Jewish historian Josephus records that he was stoned to death in AD 62.
Matthew 13:55; Acts 12:17; 1 Corinthians 15:7; James

James, Letter of
A letter full of practical instructions for 'all God's people'. We are not

sure who wrote it, to whom, or exactly when, though it is often thought that it may have been James, Jesus' brother.

The writer uses colourful word-pictures to set out the behaviour and attitudes which should mark out Christians. The letter comments on faith and wisdom, property and wealth, testing and tempting, hearing and doing. We are to treat everyone with equal respect. Christians must guard their tongues and watch their attitudes towards the world around them. The writer emphasizes that without actions to match, faith is not faith at all. Genuine faith will affect the way we live.

Japheth

One of Noah's three sons. He survived the flood to become the founder of several nations.
Genesis 5:32; 9:18ff.; 10:1ff.

Jason

1. A Christian with whom Paul and Silas stayed when they were in Thessalonica.
Acts 17:5-9
2. A Jewish Christian mentioned by Paul.
Romans 16:21

Javan

One of the sons of Japheth. Javan is named as the father of a group of peoples, probably including those who lived in Greece and Asia Minor in early times. The name may be connected with the Greek 'Ionia', in western Turkey, and it is used in later parts of the Old Testament for Greece or the Greeks.
Genesis 10:2; 1 Chronicles 1:5; Isaiah 66:19; Ezekiel 27:13

Jebus

An early name for Jerusalem.

Jehoahaz

1. King of Israel 814-798 BC, after Jehu, his father. He led his subjects away from the worship of God and was defeated by Hazael and Benhadad, kings of Syria.
2 Kings 13:1ff.
2. Son of Josiah and king of Judah for three months in 609 BC. He was captured and taken prisoner to Egypt by Pharaoh Neco.
2 Kings 23:31-34

Jehoiachin

King of Judah for three months in 597 BC. He was taken prisoner to Babylon by Nebuchadnezzar. Many years later a new king of Babylon released Jehoiachin from prison and gave him a place at court.
2 Kings 24:8-16; 25:27ff.;
2 Chronicles 36:9-10;
Jeremiah 52:31ff.

Jehoiada

The most important man of this name was chief priest in Jerusalem during the reigns of Ahaziah, Queen Athaliah and Joash. Jehoiada was married to Jehosheba, sister of King Ahaziah. Athaliah, the queen mother, seized the throne when her son died and gave orders for all the royal family to be killed. But Jehoiada hid his nephew Joash, one of Ahaziah's sons. After six years he made Joash king and Athaliah was killed. Jehoiada ruled as regent until Joash was old enough to govern the country himself.
2 Kings 11-12; 2 Chronicles 23–24

Jehoiakim

Son of Josiah and king of Judah 609-597 BC. He was made king by Pharaoh Neco and had to pay taxes to Egypt. Jehoiakim undid all the good of his father's reign and was greedy and cruel. He burnt the scroll of Jeremiah's prophecies. When he rebelled against Babylon Judah was invaded.
2 Kings 24:1-7; 2 Chronicles 36:4-8; Jeremiah 22:18ff.; 26; 36

Jehoram/Joram

1. Son of King Ahab. Jehoram was king of Israel 852-841 BC, after the death of his brother, King Ahaziah. He ended Baal worship but did not wholly reform and was murdered by Jehu, who wiped out all Ahab's descendants.
2 Kings 3; 8-9
2. King of Judah 848-841 BC (co-regent from 853) after his father Jehoshaphat. Elijah warned that he would die from a terrible disease because he had murdered his six brothers and encouraged his subjects to worship idols.
2 Kings 8:16ff.; 2 Chronicles 21

Jehoshaphat

Best-known is the son of King Asa who became king of Judah 870-848 BC (co-regent from 873). He was a good king who destroyed idols and made sure his subjects learned God's laws. He improved the legal system and appointed judges in the major towns. But he made the mistake of forming an alliance with King Ahab and became involved in Israel's wars.
1 Kings 22; 2 Kings 3;
2 Chronicles 17-21:1

Jehosheba/Jehoshabeath

The sister of King Ahaziah of Judah. Jehosheba was married to Jehoiada, the priest. (See *Jehoiada*.)
2 Kings 11:1-3; 2 Chronicles 22:11-12

Jehu

A commander in the army of King Jehoram of Israel. He was king 841-814 BC. He was anointed king by Elisha and told to wipe out all King Ahab and Jezebel's descendants as punishment for their wickedness. This he did. Later in his reign King Hazael of Syria invaded Israel. Shalmaneser III of Assyria includes Jehu in a list of subject kings. Jehu may have asked Assyria to help him defeat Syria.
2 Kings 9–10

Jephthah

One of the 'Judges' of early Israel. Before he went into battle against the Ammonites Jephthah vowed that if he was successful he would sacrifice whatever came out of his house when he returned. Jephthah returned from defeating the Ammonites to be greeted by his daughter, an only child. Despite his grief Jephthah kept his vow. He ruled as a Judge for six years.
Judges 11–12

Jeremiah

The prophet Jeremiah lived about one hundred years after Isaiah. He was called to be God's prophet in 627 BC and died some time after 587 BC. While he was writing, the power of Assyria, the great empire to the north, was crumbling. Babylon was the new threat to the kingdom of Judah.

For forty years Jeremiah warned his people of God's judgement to come on them for their idol worship and sin. Finally, his words came true. In 587 BC the Babylonian army, led by Nebuchadnezzar, destroyed Jerusalem and the temple. Nebuchadnezzar took the people into exile. Jeremiah himself turned down the offer of a life of comfort at the Babylonian court. He probably finished his days in Egypt.

The chapters in the book do not follow the order in which events happened. The book opens with a description of Jeremiah's call to be a prophet. The first twenty-five chapters consist of messages from God to Judah during the reigns of the last kings–Josiah, Jehoahaz, Jehoiakim, Jehoiachin and Zedekiah.

Israelites being taken prisoner: from an Assyrian relief.

Chapters 26–45 are made up of the events in the life of Jeremiah and additional prophecies.

Chapters 46–51 record God's messages to several foreign nations. The final chapters describe the fall of Jerusalem and the exile to Babylon.

Jeremiah became very unpopular. He was labelled a traitor because he urged his people to give in to Babylon. But he loved his own people, and hated telling them of judgement. He had little self-confidence, but never softened the message God gave him. Although he is remembered as the by-word for pessimism, he also brought hope. He promised that God would restore his people to their homeland after the dark time of exile.

The book contains all sorts of writing–some poetry, some prose, acted parables, history and Jeremiah's own life-story.

Jericho

A town west of the River Jordan, 820ft/250m below sea level, about 5 miles/8km from the northern end of the Dead Sea. Jericho's freshwater spring makes it an oasis in the surrounding desert–the 'city of palm trees'. The town guarded the fords of the Jordan, across which Joshua sent his spies. It was well fortified, and the first main obstacle facing the invading Israelites. Joshua gained his first victory in the land when Jericho fell.

At the time of the Judges Ehud killed King Eglon of Moab at Jericho. At the time of Elijah and Elisha it was the home of a large group of prophets. After the return from exile, men from Jericho helped rebuild the walls of Jerusalem.

In the New Testament Jesus gave Bartimaeus his sight, and Zacchaeus became a changed man, at Jericho. The story of the Good Samaritan is set on the road from Jerusalem to Jericho.

Jericho has a very long history covering thousands of years. The first town was built here some time before 6000 BC. At the time of Abraham, Isaac and Jacob, life in Jericho was a civilized affair. In tombs from about 1600 BC, fine pottery, wooden furniture, basket-work, and boxes with inlaid decoration have been found. Some time after this Jericho was destroyed, but a small settlement remained.
Joshua 2; 6; Judges 12:13;
2 Kings 2; Nehemiah 3:2;
Mark 10:46; Luke 19:1-10; 10:30

Jeroboam I

A man from the tribe of Ephraim who became first king of Israel, the breakaway northern kingdom (931-910 BC). During Solomon's reign the prophet Ahijah predicted that Jeroboam would be the ruler of ten tribes. After Solomon's death his son, Rehoboam, succeeded him, but all the tribes except Benjamin and Judah rebelled against him and made Jeroboam their king. Jeroboam introduced idol worship and ordered two golden calves to be made. He put these in Dan and Bethel to stop his subjects returning to Jerusalem to worship. His bad example was followed by other kings of Israel and led eventually to Israel's total defeat and dispersion by Assyria in 721 BC.
1 Kings 11:26–14:20

Jeroboam II

Became king of Israel after his father, Joash, and reigned for forty-one years, 793-753 BC. He reconquered land which Israel had lost and during his reign the country became wealthy. Israel grew confident and careless. Neither king nor people took notice of the warnings of the prophets, Hosea and Amos. They continued to worship idols and to disregard God's covenant agreement.
2 Kings 14:23-29; Amos 7

Jerubbaal

Another name for Gideon.

Jerusalem

Capital of Israel's early kings, later of the southern kingdom of Judah, and one of the world's most famous cities. Jerusalem stands high (2,500ft/770m) in the Judean hills with no access by sea or river. The ground drops steeply away on all sides except the north. To the east, between Jerusalem (with its temple) and the Mount of Olives, is the Kidron Valley. The Valley of Hinnom curves around the city to the south and west. A third, central valley cuts right into the city, dividing the temple area and city of David from the 'upper', western section.

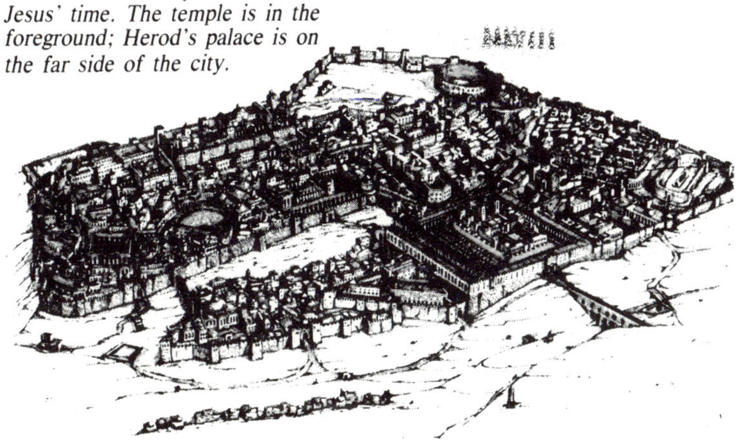

Jerusalem as it may have looked in Jesus' time. The temple is in the foreground; Herod's palace is on the far side of the city.

Jerusalem is probably the 'Salem' of which Melchizedek was king in Abraham's day. It was certainly in existence by 1800 BC. It was a Jebusite stronghold (called Jebus) when King David captured it and made it his capital. He bought the temple site and brought the Covenant Box (ark) to Jerusalem. Solomon built the temple for God, and from that time on Jerusalem has been the 'holy city'–for the Jews, and later for Christians and Muslims, too. Solomon added fine palaces and public buildings. Jerusalem was a political and religious centre, to which the people came for the great annual festivals.

The city declined to some extent after Solomon, when the kingdom became divided. In the reign of King Hezekiah (Isaiah's time) it was besieged by the Assyrians. The king had the Siloam tunnel built, to ensure his water supply. On several occasions powerful neighbouring kings were pacified with treasures from the city and its temple. The Babylonians besieged Jerusalem in 597 BC and in 586 they captured and destroyed both the city and the temple. The people were taken into exile.

In 538 BC they were allowed to return. Under Zerubbabel's leadership, the temple was rebuilt. With Nehemiah in charge they rebuilt the city walls. In 198 BC, as part of the Greek Empire, Jerusalem came under the control of the Syrian Seleucid kings. One of these, Antiochus IV Epiphanes plundered and desecrated the temple. Judas Maccabaeus led a Jewish revolt and the temple was rededicated (164 BC).

For a time Jerusalem was free. Then, in the middle of the first century BC, the Romans took control. Herod the Great, made king by the Romans, repaired Jerusalem and undertook new building work, including a magnificent new temple.

It was to this temple that Jesus' mother brought him as a baby. His parents brought him again when he was twelve, to attend the annual Passover Festival. When he grew up, Jesus regularly visited Jerusalem–for many of the religious festivals, and to teach and heal. His arrest, trial, crucifixion and resurrection all took place in Jerusalem.

Jesus' followers were still in the city several weeks later, on the Day of Pentecost, when the Holy Spirit made new men of them. So the Christian church began life in Jerusalem–and from there, spread out far and wide. The Christians at Jerusalem played a leading role in the early years. The Council that met to consider the position of non-Jewish Christians was held at Jerusalem.

In AD 66 the Jews rose in revolt against the Romans. In AD 70 the Romans regained Jerusalem. They destroyed its defences—and the temple. In the fourth century—the reign of Constantine—the city became Christian, and many churches were built.

In 637 the Muslims came–and Jerusalem remained under their control for most of the time until 1948, when the modern state of Israel came into being. Jerusalem was then divided between the Jews and the Arabs–Israel and Jordan. In 1967 the Jews won control of the whole city.
Genesis 14:18; Joshua 15:63;
2 Samuel 5; 1 Kings 6; Psalms 48;
122; 125; 1 Kings 14:25-26;
2 Kings 12:18; 18:13-19:36;
20:20; 25; Ezra 5; Nehemiah 3-6;
Luke 2; 19:28-24:49, etc.;
John 2:23-3:21; 5; 7:10–10:42, etc.;
Acts 2; 15

Jesse

Grandson of Ruth and Boaz, and father of King David.
1 Samuel 16–17

Jesus

The name (Old Testament 'Joshua') means 'saviour'. At the time when Herod was king of Judea and the whole country was under Roman occupation the angel Gabriel came to Mary in Nazareth. God had chosen her to be the mother of the promised Messiah. Mary's fiancé, Joseph, was told in a dream that they were to call him Jesus 'because he will save his people from their sins'. A census took Mary and Joseph to Bethlehem, where Jesus was born, in the town of King David, his ancestor. Herod was afraid that Jesus would be a rival king and plotted to kill him, but God guided his parents to take him to Egypt. After Herod died they went back to their home town of Nazareth. Here Jesus grew up and probably worked as a carpenter.

When he was thirty years old, Jesus was baptized by John the Baptist in the River Jordan. He chose twelve followers as his close companions to share his life and work. For three years Jesus taught the people and worked miracles, healing all kinds of diseases. Crowds followed him. But the Jewish leaders were afraid of his power and of his claim to be the Son of God. They wanted to kill him. Judas, one of the twelve, accepted a bribe and helped Jesus' enemies to capture him without the people's knowledge. Soldiers arrested Jesus in the Garden of Gethsemane, close to Jerusalem. He was tried and condemned by a Jewish court before dawn. Pilate, the Roman governor, had to ratify all death sentences. He found no fault in Jesus, but was afraid of a riot if he let him go free. So Jesus was crucified. He was buried in the tomb of Joseph of Arimathaea, a secret follower.

At dawn on the third day after Jesus' death a group of women found the tomb empty. Angels told them Jesus was alive again. His followers and many other people saw him during the next forty days. Now they knew he really was the Son of God. Then from the Mount of Olives Jesus returned to heaven. While the disciples were still looking at the sky an angel told them that one day Jesus would come back.
Matthew, Mark, Luke, John,
Acts 1:1-11

The Bible's teaching about Jesus is summed up in several titles used to describe him.

Jesus, the 'Servant of God'. Matthew gives Jesus this title, which comes from the prophecies of Isaiah. The character of the lowly, gentle servant of God who comes to bring justice was perfectly lived out in the person of Jesus. When Jesus said that he 'came to serve and to give his life to redeem many people', he was living out the work of the Servant of God, suffering to bear the sins of mankind, just as Isaiah describes him.
Matthew 12:15-21; Isaiah 42:1-4; 52:13-53; 12 and other passages; Mark 10:45

Jesus, the 'Son of David'. The angel who announced his birth told Jesus' mother that God would make her son a king 'as his ancestor David was'. By human birth Jesus was a descendant of King David. This title shows Jesus as the fulfilment of the hopes of the Jewish nation. It is the one used to describe Jesus in the opening sentence of Matthew, the most Jewish of all the Gospels. It was the title that the Jews used when they acknowledged Jesus as the Messiah. 'Praise to David's Son! God bless him who comes in the name of the Lord! Praise God!'
Luke 1:32; John 7:42;
Matthew 1:1; 21:9

Jesus, the 'Son of man'. This is the title Jesus most often used of himself, and it tells us much about him. He borrowed the phrase from Daniel's vision of someone who 'looked like a human being', yet had God's authority for ever. 'His kingdom,' Daniel says, would 'never end'. The Bible teaches clearly that Jesus was a real man. He identified himself completely with mankind. As the 'Son of man' he came to serve men and women and to give his life to save them. 'The Son of man must suffer... He will be put to death, but three days later he will be raised to life.' As the Son of man Jesus defeated sin and death and will come again 'with great power and glory'.
Daniel 7:13-14; Mark 10:45;
9:21-22; 21:25-28

Jesus, the 'Son of God'. At Jesus' baptism in the River Jordan a voice from heaven declared, 'You are my own dear Son. I am pleased with you.' Again, on the mountain, when Jesus' glory was seen, the voice came, 'This is my Son, whom I have chosen–listen to him.' John's Gospel explains what this phrase means. Jesus is God's 'only Son'. His whole life and purpose is to carry out the Father's work. 'The Father and I are one,' Jesus says. He was with the Father before the world was made. They are one for ever. Because Jesus shares God's nature and is free from sin, he was able to pay in full for the sins of the whole world for all time. And we now 'have someone who pleads with the Father on our behalf–Jesus Christ, the righteous one'.
Mark 1:11; Luke 9:35; John 1:14; 10:30; 17; Romans 1:3-4;
Hebrews 1; 1 John 1–2:2

Jesus, the 'Lord'. In the Gospels Jesus is often called 'Lord' in the everyday sense of 'master'. But after the resurrection the word took on a new meaning. 'My Lord and my God,' declared Thomas when he saw the risen Jesus with his own eyes. This was the way in which Jews often referred to God, and the first Christians publicly declared their faith in the words, 'Jesus Christ is Lord.' Paul, in his letter to the Philippians, looks forward to the time when Jesus will return as Lord, when 'all beings in heaven, on earth, and in the world below will fall on their knees, and all will openly proclaim that Jesus Christ is Lord, to the glory of God the Father'.
Luke 5:8; John 20:28;
1 Corinthians 12:3; Philippians 2:6-11
See also *Trinity, Judgement, Justification, Kingdom of God, Messiah, Redemption, Salvation,* and the events of Jesus' life: *Resurrection, Second coming of Jesus, Transfiguration.*

Jesus' teaching

Many people today think of Jesus' teaching as basically the Sermon on the Mount, summed up in the 'Golden Rule': 'Do for others what you want them to do for you' (Matthew 7:12). But the centre of Jesus' message was his announcement that the 'kingdom of God' had arrived.

The kingdom of God The 'kingdom of God' meant the rule of God breaking into human history, the new creation which would supercede the old creation spoilt by sin and death.

For a long time Jews had looked forward to the time when God would come in power to be their King. He would set his people free and judge the nations. 'No king but God' was in fact the slogan of the fanatical Zealots who hoped to drive the Romans out of their land by force. But the kingdom that Jesus announced and brought with him did not 'belong to this world'. It would not be brought about by brute force. The kingdom of God had in fact already arrived with the coming of Christ–for he was the first who fully obeyed the will of God. So he could say to the Pharisees: 'The kingdom of God is among you.' It was present in the words and works of Jesus.

Yet there is another sense in which the kingdom of God has not come, even yet. 'May your kingdom come', Jesus taught his followers to pray in the Lord's Prayer. So far the kingdom of God is still only partly in operation. In the future it will come 'with power'. Yet the future coming of the kingdom will not be a joyful event for everyone. For all who believe the good news of the kingdom there is 'salvation', a new life. But for many the coming of God's rule will be a judgement.

Jesus often used parables to explain what the kingdom of God is like. The kingdom turns the world's values upside down. It is the humble, the poor and those who mourn who are really happy. God's kingdom belongs to them. Rich people cannot buy their way in. For the first time in their lives they may find their riches a hindrance. Beggars are invited in–and they accept God's invitation when respectable people refuse and find themselves shut out.

Jesus' parables show God at work in the world, quietly, almost secretly. Yet 'the kingdom' goes on growing and spreading from small beginnings. It is like the tiny mustard seed which becomes a tree, or the yeast which makes a great batch of dough rise.

The 'Sower' goes out, making God's message known to people everywhere. Much of the 'seed' is wasted. People close their minds to what they hear. Or other things crowd in and they forget. But some listen, and their lives are changed. The seed comes to harvest.
John 18:36; Luke 17:21; Matthew 3:2; Mark 1:15; Matthew 6:10; Mark 9:1; 14:25; Luke 13:23-30; 14:15-24; Matthew 20:1-16; 19:23-24; 13:31-33; Mark 4:3-8

'Repent and believe' 'The kingdom of God is near!' said Jesus. 'Turn away from your sins and believe the Good News!' People must 'repent', have a total change of heart, if they are to accept the rule of God in their lives. They must *believe* the good news Jesus came to bring.

God offers new life to all who believe, who will leave their old way of life and follow him. This is worth everything anyone has. Finding it is like finding treasure hidden in a field–and selling everything to buy the field. It means giving up all we have clung to for security, and trusting God. It also means being sorry for our sins. This is not something we can manage just by trying hard enough. God actually comes to find the sinner. In the parables of the lost sheep and the lost son Jesus emphasizes the joy of being found by God.
Mark 1:15; Matthew 13:44-46;
Luke 15:1-7, 11-32

Jesus' teaching about himself Jesus knew that he was very close to God. He encouraged his disciples to call God their father, but he was God's Son in a unique way. John's Gospel especially presents us with this aspect of Jesus' teaching. He even said 'the Father and I are one'. So believing in God means believing in Jesus also. He is so close to God that people may rely on him as they do on God. But he said nothing to make himself more prominent than God. He was the 'way' to God. He did nothing of his own accord, but only as the Father directed him. He was mankind's 'bread' that the Father had sent down from heaven.

The way to 'eternal life'–the vital life of God that can be shared by human beings also–is to believe in (put our trust in) Jesus the Son of God. That is the same as true belief in the Father who sent him. It brings a person from 'death' to 'life'.
John 10:30; 14:1; 14:6; 5:19-20, 30; 6:32-33; 3:16, 18, 36; 5:24

Joy A note of joy runs all through the teaching of Jesus. The kingdom of God frees people and releases them to live a full life. Even when Jesus' disciples fast, he tells them they must make a festival out of it, anointing themselves with oil, not going about with dismal faces like most people. Among the Jews of Jesus' day, being good and obeying God's law was often a gloomy business. The religious leaders grumbled because Jesus enjoyed himself, and became angry when he was greeted with shouts of joy in Jerusalem. They were like the bitter elder brother in the parable of the lost son. But the boy's father says: 'We had to celebrate and be happy, because your brother was dead, but now he is alive; he was lost, but now he has been found.' God himself rejoices over every man and woman who comes back home to him, every 'sinner who repents'.
John 10:10; Matthew 6:16-18; 11:19; 21:15; Luke 15:11-32

The 'Beatitudes' Jesus pronounced blessings ('beatitudes') on the 'humble'–those who realized that spiritually they were 'poor'. In fact all those mentioned in the Beatitudes are 'poor' and 'humble' in one way or another. ('Blessed' means 'happy'.) These are the people God declares 'happy'. They will receive what God has promised. His kingdom belongs to them. They have nothing in the world, but they can expect everything from God.

Those who are 'hungry and thirsty for righteousness', 'whose greatest desire is to do what God requires', have their lives centred on God. They know they cannot survive without him. The 'merciful' are dealing with other people in the way God deals with them. Those who work for peace have no worldly power. They depend on the love of God which can change two enemies into friends. The persecuted are hunted out of the world of men.

It is to people like this that God's 'kingdom' belongs. They are the ones God will reward. All these are praised by Jesus. And so the Beatitudes turn the world's idea of 'happiness' upside down. They also set a standard. They represent a challenge, the demand the kingdom makes upon God's people.
Matthew 5:1-12; Luke 6:20-26

Jesus' followers To be a 'disciple' of Jesus, one of his students, was a great privilege. Unlike other teachers he did not lay great burdens on his followers. 'The yoke I will give you is easy,' he said, 'and the load I will put on you is light.' Yet he taught that 'the gate to life is narrow and the way that leads to it is hard'. His disciples must be like their master, ready to put themselves and their own interests last. Even family ties must not stand in the way of wholehearted obedience to him.

Jesus told his disciples to expect persecution. But they need not be anxious. God would give them the words they needed when they were on trial. Jesus called his followers to a life of service for others, yet he treated them as friends. They shared his confidences. They shared his sufferings. They would also share his life, his joy and his future glory.
Matthew 13:16-17; 11:30; 7:13-14; Mark 8:34; Luke 9:57-62; Matthew 10:16-25; John 13:4-17; 14-17

God and worship Jesus spoke of God as 'Father' in a new, more personal way than anyone before him. He taught that God was, in a special way, his own Father. But he also taught his followers to pray: 'Our Father in heaven'. He taught them to come to God as children to a loving, forgiving and wise Father. He gave his followers 'the right to become God's children'.

This teaching was new and revolutionary to many people. 'Religion' for many was a burdensome system of rules and ceremonies. Jesus showed that the basis of religion was a loving relationship with God himself. God, as Father, was concerned about every detail of life. He cared. This changed people's attitude to prayer.

As a result of what Jesus said and did, greater changes were to come. When the woman at the well asked where people should worship God, Jesus answered: 'The time will come when people will not worship the Father either on this mountain or in Jerusalem...by the power of God's Spirit people will worship the Father as he really is, offering him the worship that he really wants.' In the Book of Acts we see this beginning to happen, as the 'good news' is preached to non-Jewish as well as to Jewish people.

Jesus himself went regularly to the local synagogue and attended the festivals in Jerusalem. He did not set up a new system of religious ceremonies. He expected his disciples to follow his example, to meet to study the Bible, to pray and to fast. And he commanded them to baptize new believers and remember his death for them by sharing bread and wine together, as he had done with his disciples at the last supper.
Matthew 6:6-18, 31-32; 7:7-11; John 1:12-13; Matthew 9:14-17; John 4:19-24; Matthew 28:19; 1 Corinthians 11:23-25

Jethro/Reuel

A priest in the land of Midian and father-in-law of Moses. When Moses brought the Israelites to Sinai, Jethro came to see him, bringing Moses' wife and sons. He advised Moses to choose capable men to share the burden of leadership.
Exodus 2:16ff.; 2:1; 4:18-19; 18

Jewellery

The people of Israel were not as skilled at making jewellery as some of their neighbours–particularly the Egyptians. But jewellery has been worn from earliest times. Quite apart from its beauty, in the days before banks, a necklace was easier to carry from place to place than a bag of coins. It was certainly less trouble than a herd of cattle! Even before coins, jewels were a form of wealth which could be exchanged for other things–and taken as booty in war.

Bracelets, necklaces, pendants, anklets and rings–for ears and noses as well as fingers–were all worn. They were made from gold, silver and other metals, and set with precious or semi-precious stones, or even coloured glass. The stones were smoothed and polished, engraved and sculptured. Ivory was beautifully carved. It was often used for panelling and inlay in furniture-making, and also for hair-combs, brooches and plaques, and vases and flasks for cosmetics.

The jewellers and goldsmiths of Egypt were master-craftsmen. They produced some of the most colourful and beautiful jewellery the world has ever seen. Elaborate pendants (pectorals) hung on bead chains were made from semi-precious stones–deep blue lapis lazuli, turquoise, red carnelian, quartz–and coloured glass in dazzling blues and reds set in gold and silver. These pectorals were originally intended to give protection against evil spirits. The carved scarab beetles which decorate Egyptian rings and bracelets represent the belief that Re', the sun-god, took the form of a beetle, and are a symbol of eternal life.

When the Israelites left Egypt (the exodus), they took with them gold and silver jewellery as well as clothes. Gold ear-rings were melted down to make a gold bull to worship at Mt Sinai. But the people were soon sorry for this disloyalty to God, and 'both men and women brought decorative pins, ear-rings, rings, necklaces and all kinds of jewellery and dedicated them to the Lord', (Exodus 35:20ff.). Skilled Israelite craftsmen used the gold and jewels to beautify the tent of worship (tabernacle). The sacred breastplate worn by the high priest was set with precious stones, one for each of the twelve clans of Israel.

A Roman gold necklace from the first century AD.

The jeweller's skill was also used in making and engraving personal seals, sometimes worn as rings.

These were impressed on lumps of clay to secure and authenticate documents. Poor people had roughly engraved seals of terracotta. But the rich often had beautiful seals cut from carnelian, agate, jasper, rock crystal and other semi-precious stones.

Jewellery was worn in Israel for special occasions–such as a wedding. But to be obsessed with jewels and clothes was wrong and a sign of pride, condemned in both Old and New Testaments (Isaiah 3:16-24; 1 Timothy 2:9).

Jezebel

The princess from Sidon who married Ahab, king of Israel. Jezebel worshipped the weather and fertility gods Baal and Asherah. She persuaded Ahab and forced his subjects to accept her religion. She had God's prophets killed and replaced them with prophets of Baal. But the prophet Elijah escaped to challenge and defeat the prophets of Baal on Mt Carmel. After this Jezebel was determined to kill Elijah and he was forced to go into hiding. Jezebel signed her own death warrant when she urged Ahab to have Naboth killed so that he could take over Naboth's vineyard. Elijah predicted her violent death, and some time later she was thrown from an upstairs window at the command of Jehu.
1 Kings 16:31; 18:4, 13, 19; 19:1-2; 21; 2 Kings 9:30ff.

Jezreel

A town in the north of Israel and the plain in which it stood, close to Mt Gilboa. Saul camped at the spring in the Valley of Jezreel before the Battle of Gilboa. King Ahab of Israel had a palace at Jezreel. It was here that the sad story of Naboth's vineyard took place. King Joram of Israel went to Jezreel to recover from his wounds. Queen Jezebel was thrown down from the palace window and died here.
1 Samuel 29:1; 1 Kings 18:45-46; 21; 2 Kings 8:29; 9:30-37

Joab

King David's nephew and commander of his army. He was fearless but violent. Joab helped David become king of all the tribes of Israel. He remained loyal to David during Absalom's rebellion, but towards the end of David's reign supported Adonijah's revolt. After David's death King Solomon ordered Joab to be executed for taking part in the revolt and for the murders of Abner and Amasa, two other army leaders.
2 Samuel 2-3; 10–11; 14; 18–20; 24; 1 Kings 1–2; 1 Chronicles 11ff.

Joanna

The wife of an official of Herod Antipas. Joanna was healed by Jesus. She gave money to Jesus and his disciples. On the resurrection morning she was one of the women who found Jesus' tomb empty.
Luke 8:1-3; 24:10

Joash/Jehoash

1. Son of King Ahaziah, made king of Judah when he was seven years old. While he was a baby his life was saved by Jehoiada, the priest. In the early part of his forty-year reign (835–796 BC) he was guided by Jehoiada. He obeyed God's laws and repaired the temple. After Jehoiada's death he introduced idol worship and murdered Zechariah, Jehoiada's son. He stripped gold from the temple to appease the invading Syrians. Joash was murdered by his officials (see *Jehoiada*).
2 Kings 11-12; 2 Chronicles 24
2. King of Israel for sixteen years (798-782 BC) after King Jehoahaz, his father.
2 Kings 13–14

Job

The Book of Job is about a good man–Job–who meets complete disaster. The meaning of suffering is looked at from many angles.

The Book of Job stands alone in the Old Testament. We do not know who wrote it, or when, but its hero belongs to a 'patriarchal' society. The beginning and end are in prose, but most of the book is poetry.

Job, a prosperous and truly good man, loses all his children and possessions and is struck with a hideous disease. Job and the three friends who come to comfort him try to understand his terrible suffering (chapters 3–37). Job's friends assume that he must have sinned to have brought such suffering on himself. Job himself cannot understand how God can allow a good man to suffer like this.

Finally God responds to Job's challenge by appearing to him in power and wisdom. Job recognizes him humbly (chapters 38–42). He realizes at last that God is bigger than the religious thinking of his day allowed. The story has a happy ending as his health and his wealth are restored.

Joel

A prophet; the son of Pethuel. In his book Joel describes a plague of locusts and a terrible drought. These are pictures of God's coming judgement on those who disobey him–the 'Day of the Lord'. He called for repentance and spoke of a new age when God would send his Spirit upon all people.

Joel used the picture of a locust-plague to describe God's judgement.

Johanan

A Jewish leader who stayed in Judah after Jerusalem was captured by King Nebuchadnezzar of Babylon. Johanan warned Gedaliah, governor of Judah, about the plot to murder him. Afterwards, against Jeremiah's advice, he led the people to Egypt.
Jeremiah 40–43

John the apostle

Like his father, Zebedee, and his brother James, John was a fisherman. He was probably a follower of John the Baptist before Jesus called him to become his disciple. Jesus nicknamed John and James 'sons of thunder' because they were quick-tempered. Peter, James and John were especially close to Jesus. John was with Jesus when he brought Jairus's daughter back from the dead. He saw Jesus' glory at the transfiguration, and was with him in the Garden of Gethsemane just before his death. John's name is not mentioned in the Gospel of John, but he is almost certainly 'the disciple whom Jesus loved', the one who was close to Jesus at the last supper and to whom Jesus spoke from the cross, and told to look after his mother. After Jesus had ascended into heaven John, with Peter, became a leader of the church in Jerusalem. He was still in Jerusalem fourteen years after Paul was converted. There is a tradition that John lived in Ephesus until he was very old. If he is the same John who wrote the Revelation he must also have been exiled to the island of Patmos. The Gospel of John was written to bring men to faith. Three New Testament letters also bear John's name.
Matthew 4:21ff; 10:2; 17:1ff.; Mark 3:17; 5:37; 10:35ff.; 14:33; Luke 9:49ff.; John 19:26-27; Acts 3–4; Galatians 2:9

John the Baptist

The prophet sent by God to prepare people for the coming of Jesus, the Messiah. In their old age his parents, Zechariah and Elizabeth, were told by an angel that they would have this special son. John was related to Jesus and just a few months older. He lived in the desert of Judea until God called him to be a prophet. Crowds of people came to hear his fiery preaching. 'Turn away from your sins and be baptized,' he said, 'and God will forgive you.' Although Jesus had not sinned, he asked John to baptize him, too, in the River Jordan, to show his obedience to God.

Later John was put in prison by King Herod for his outspoken criticism. From prison he sent some of his disciples to Jesus to ask if he really was the person they were expecting. 'Tell John how I heal the sick and preach Good News to the poor,' Jesus answered. Then he told the crowds, 'John the Baptist is more than a prophet. He is greater than any man who has ever lived.' Not long after this, Herod's wife tricked him into having John beheaded.
Luke 1; 3; 7:18ff.; Matthew 3; 11; 14:1-12; Mark 1; 6

John's Gospel

John's Gospel–the fourth New Testament account of Jesus' life–stands apart from the other three. It was probably written last, possibly around AD 90. It is more concerned with the meaning of events than with the events themselves, which were presumably well known by that time.

John's Gospel begins with Jesus as

the 'Word' of God, existing before time itself, yet born in time as man.

In Jesus (the Word) God speaks to man. The Gospel was written 'in order that you (the reader) may believe that Jesus is the Messiah, the Son of God, and that through your faith in him you may have life' (20:31).

The Gospel probably contains the reminiscences of John, the brother of James and one of the closest of Jesus' twelve friends. In the Gospel John is not mentioned by name. He appears only as 'the disciple whom Jesus loved'. It may have been actually written down by a secretary.

After the opening passage presenting Jesus as the 'Word' of God (1:1-18) the Gospel goes on to describe a number of miracles which show that he really is the promised Saviour (chapters 2–12). The story of his preaching and teaching is arranged so that each miracle is followed by an explanation and discussion. John also shows how some people believed, but others rejected Jesus. He does not recount any of Jesus' parables.

Chapters 13–19 tell of Jesus' last days with his disciples in Jerusalem. They recall his words of encouragement and teaching to his followers before his death on the cross. Chapters 20–21 describe some of the times when Jesus was seen by his followers after he rose from the dead.

John understands the miracles as 'signs' showing who Jesus was. He also uses a series of common things to point to hidden truths about Jesus: water, bread, light, the shepherd and the vine. The famous 'I am...' statements come in John's Gospel. He presents Jesus as the way, the truth and the life.

John's Letters

1 John A letter written towards the end of the first century AD, probably by the apostle John, then living at Ephesus (in modern Turkey). His purpose was to encourage Christians to live in fellowship with God, and to warn against false teachers.

John was particularly concerned to counter the ideas of a group who believed they had special 'knowledge' about God (the 'Gnostics'). They also believed that the physical world was evil, and therefore that Jesus, the Son of God, could not have been a real man.

John writes as someone who knew Jesus, as the Son of God and also as a real man. Anyone who claims to know God must live as Jesus did (chapters 1 and 2). Christians are the children of God. They have his nature and cannot go on persistently sinning. Those who believe in Jesus will love each other, too (chapter 3). In chapter 4 John contrasts the true and the false. 'God is love,' John declares. 'We love because God first loved us.' Chapter 5 speaks of victory over the world, and of God's gift of eternal life.

2 John This letter is probably also by the apostle John. The 'lady' to whom it is addressed is probably a local church. The writer appeals to his Christian readers to love one another. He warns against false teachers and teachings.

3 John The third letter by 'the Elder' (John) is a private letter to a church leader named Gaius. The writer praises Gaius for his help to fellow Christians. He warns against a man called Diotrephes, who is behaving like a petty dictator in the church.

Jonah

Unlike the other books of prophecy, Jonah is written as a story.

The Book of Jonah describes the adventures of a prophet who tried to disobey God's orders. God told Jonah to go to Nineveh, the capital of Assyria–the great enemy nation–to denounce its people. Jonah finally delivered his message–and then sulked when God did not carry out his threat to destroy the people.

The book shows God's love and care. He would rather forgive and save than punish and destroy.

Jonathan

Eldest son of King Saul and a great friend of David. He was a brave warrior and distinguished himself in several battles against the Philistines. Although Jonathan knew David might become king in his place he was a loyal friend and saved him from being killed by Saul. Jonathan and Saul were both killed in battle when the Israelites were defeated by the Philistines. David was deeply grieved and wrote a lament in praise of Jonathan.

1 Samuel 13–14; 18–20; 23:16-18; 31:2; 2 Samuel 1

Joppa

The only natural harbour on the coast of Israel south of the Bay of Acre (Haifa): modern Jaffa, close to Tel Aviv. Joppa was the port for Jerusalem, 35 miles/56km away. The town has a long history and was mentioned about 1400 BC in the Egyptian Amarna Letters. Jonah set sail for Tarshish (Spain) from Joppa. Dorcas (Tabitha), the woman Peter restored to life, came from Joppa. Peter was there when he had his dream about the 'clean' and 'unclean' animals. He went from Joppa to the house of the Roman officer, Cornelius, and saw God at work amongst non-Jews.

2 Chronicles 2:16; Jonah 1:3; Acts 9:36-43; 10

Joram

See *Jehoram*.

Jordan

The main river of Israel, constantly referred to in the Bible. The Jordan flows from Mt Hermon in the far north, through Lake Huleh, and Lake Galilee to the Dead Sea. It is 75 miles/120km from Lake Huleh to the Dead Sea, but the river winds about so much that it is more than twice that length.

The name 'Jordan' means 'the descender'. It flows through the deepest rift valley on earth. Lake Huleh is 230ft/71m above sea level. Lake Galilee is nearly 700ft/215m *below* sea level, and the north end of the Dead Sea 1,290ft/397m below.

The northern part of the Jordan Valley is fertile; the southern end, approaching the Dead Sea, is desert, but dense jungle grows on the banks. The main tributaries of the Jordan are the Yarmuk and Jabbok rivers, both of which join it from the east. Many smaller tributaries dry up completely through the summer.

Joshua led the people of Israel across the Jordan from the east into the Promised Land near to Jericho. At the time of Absalom's rebellion, David escaped across the Jordan. Elijah and Elisha crossed the Jordan just before Elijah was taken up to heaven. Elisha told the Syrian general Naaman to wash himself in the Jordan and he would be healed. John the Baptist baptized people–including Jesus–in the Jordan.

Joshua 3; 2 Samuel 17:20-22; 2 Kings 2:6-8, 13-14; 5; Jeremiah 12:5; 49:19; Mark 1:5, 9, etc.

Joseph

1. Jacob and Rachel's first son after many years of waiting. Joseph was marked out as his father's favourite by the gift of a special coat. Joseph's brothers became jealous of him, especially when he told them his dreams, in which they bowed down to him. They planned to kill him but Reuben persuaded them to delay and Judah suggested that instead they should sell him as a slave. Joseph was taken to Egypt, and the brothers told Jacob he had been killed by wild animals.

In Egypt Joseph was bought by Potiphar, a high official, and put in charge of his household. Potiphar's wife claimed that Joseph had tried to rape her, and he was put in prison. There he was able to tell the butler and baker of the Pharaoh (king) of Egypt the meaning of their dreams. Two years later Pharaoh had dreams he could not understand. The butler remembered Joseph and Pharaoh sent for him. Joseph told him he must prepare for a long famine. Pharaoh made Joseph his chief minister and put him in charge of the preparations.

Joseph saw his brothers again when they came to Egypt to buy corn during the famine. He pretended to think they were spies and told them to come back with his younger brother, Benjamin, to prove their story. Then he tested them to see if they could be as cruel to Benjamin as they had been to him. When Joseph realized they really cared about Benjamin, he told them who he was.

Joseph invited his father and his brothers' families to live in Egypt. Jacob was overjoyed to see Joseph again. Their descendants lived in Egypt for four centuries.

Genesis 30:24; 37–50

2. Husband of Mary and foster-father of Jesus. Although Joseph was not Jesus' father physically, he was his legal father. Before Jesus was born an angel told him that Mary's child was God's Son. Joseph took Mary and the baby to Egypt when he was warned in a dream that King Herod planned to kill Jesus. After Herod's death Joseph brought his family back and they settled in Nazareth, where Joseph worked as a carpenter. When Jesus was twelve Joseph and Mary took him to the temple for the Passover. Nothing more is known about Joseph. He may have died before Jesus was grown up.

Matthew 1–2; Luke 1:27; 2

3. Joseph of Arimathea. A member of the Jewish Sanhedrin council and

a secret disciple of Jesus. After the crucifixion he asked Pilate for Jesus' body and placed it in his own unused tomb.
Luke 23:50-53; John 19:38-42

Egyptian officials measuring grain for tax purposes. An Egyptian tomb-painting from about 1400 BC.

Joshua

1. Leader of the Israelites after Moses' death. His name means 'God is salvation'. Joshua was chosen to lead the army while the Israelites were in the desert. Of the twelve spies sent by Moses to bring back a report on Canaan, only Joshua and Caleb believed the Israelites could conquer the land with God's help. God rewarded their faith. Of all the Israelites born in Egypt they were the only ones who lived to occupy Canaan. After Moses' death Joshua led the Israelites into Canaan. When the land had been conquered he divided it up amongst the twelve tribes. Before Joshua died he urged the Israelites to love and obey God. 'As for my family and me,' he said, 'we will serve the Lord.' And the people replied, 'We also will serve the Lord, he is our God.'
Exodus 17:9ff.; Numbers 13–14; Joshua
2. High priest immediately after the Jews returned from exile in Babylon. He started rebuilding the temple, but the work ground to a halt. When the prophets Haggai and Zechariah spurred the people into action, Joshua once again took charge.
Haggai; Zechariah 3

Joshua, Book of Joshua

The Book of Joshua tells how Israel invade Canaan, led by Joshua, Moses' successor. It is the first of the twelve 'books of history' in the Old Testament.

Chapters 1–12 tell of the conquest of Canaan, probably after 1240 BC. The stories may first have been written down during the lifetime of Samuel, though the book as a whole forms part of the great 'Deuteronomic history' that runs from Joshua to 2 Kings. It is not known who wrote the book. The account includes the crossing of the River Jordan, the fall of the city of Jericho and the battle of Ai.

Chapters 13–22 tell how the Israelites divided up and settled the lands they had conquered. The book ends with Joshua's farewell speech and the renewing of God's agreement and promise to his people at Shechem (chapters 23–24).

Josiah

Crowned king of Judah at the age of eight after the assassination of his father, Amon, in 640 BC. Josiah grew to be a strong, good king who led the nation back to God. He ordered the repair of the temple and while this work was being carried out a scroll was found on which were written the laws God gave to Moses. Josiah studied these laws and had them read to the people. Many reforms were made including the keeping of the Passover Festival. When Josiah was thirty-nine years old he was killed in battle against the Egyptians. Jeremiah the prophet mourned Josiah's death.
2 Kings 21:24–23:30;
2 Chronicles 33:25–35:27;
Jeremiah 22:15-16

Jotham

King of Judah 750–732 BC, after his father King Uzziah. He began to reign while his father was still alive but suffering from leprosy. Jotham worshipped God. He fortified Judah and defeated the Ammonites.
2 Kings 15:32-38; 2 Chronicles 27:1-6

Joy

Joy in the Bible is not an occasional emotional experience; it is a basic part of a personal relationship with God. As the Scottish *Shorter (Westminster) Catechism* says, 'The chief end of man is to glorify God and to enjoy him for ever.'

Living with the presence of God in one's life is a continuous experience of joy. And as this joy is a gift of God, it is possible for Christians to rejoice even in times of persecution. 'Rejoice in the Lord always,' wrote Paul to his readers at Philippi.
Psalms 16:11; 30:5; 43:4; 51:12; 126:5-6; Ecclesiastes 2:26; Isaiah 61:7; Jeremiah 15:16; Luke 15:7; John 15:11; 16:22; Romans 14:17; 15:13; Galatians 5:22; Philippians 1:4; 1 Thessalonians 2:20; 3:9; Hebrews 12:2; James 1:2; 1 Peter 1:8; Jude 24

Jubilee year

See *Feasts and Festivals.*

Judah

1. The fourth son of Jacob and Leah. Judah persuaded his brothers to sell Joseph to passing traders on their way to Egypt, instead of killing him. Jacob's last words to Judah promised him a future kingdom.
Genesis 29:35; 37:26-27; 38; 49:9-10
2. The Judean hills south of Jerusalem and the desert bordering the Dead Sea. The land belonging to the tribe of Judah. Later the name of the southern kingdom, with Jerusalem as its capital.
Joshua 15; 1 Kings 12:21, 23, etc.

Judas/Jude

There are several people with this name in the New Testament. Best-known are:
1. Judas, the son of James. He was one of the twelve apostles and was with the others after Jesus' ascension.
Luke 6:16; Acts 1:13
2. One of Jesus' brothers. Judas did not believe Jesus was the Messiah until after his death and resurrection. He may have written the letter of Jude.
Matthew 13:55; John 7:5; Acts 1:14
3. Judas Iscariot. The disciple who betrayed Jesus to the Jewish leaders. He looked after the disciples' money. He probably hoped Jesus would lead a rebellion against the Romans. When Jesus turned out to be a different kind of leader, Judas sold him to his enemies for thirty pieces of silver. Judas led the soldiers to arrest Jesus at night in the Garden of Gethsemane. When he realized how wrong he had been, he returned the money to the priests and committed suicide.
Matthew 10:4; 26:14ff.; 27:3ff.; John 12:4-6; 13:21-30; Acts 1:18-19

Jude

A letter 'From Jude'. He is sometimes identified as Jesus' younger brother, but we know nothing certain about him. The reason for writing was alarming news of false teachers. Jude describes their activities, and God's judgement on them. He refers again and again to the Old Testament and other Jewish writings. He encourages his Christian readers to keep the faith.

Almost the whole of this short letter is included word-for-word in 2 Peter 2:1–3:3.

Judea

The Greek and Roman name for Judah. Usually it refers to the southern part of the country, with Jerusalem as capital. But it is sometimes used as a name for the whole land, including Galilee and Samaria. The 'wilderness of Judea' is the desert west of the Dead Sea.
Luke 3:1; 4:44 ('the whole country' in *Good News Bible*), etc.

Judgement

Because God is Ruler of the universe he is also the Judge. The ruler makes laws and carries them out. This is what the Bible means by judgement.

Judgement in the Old Testament often meant 'good government'. The 'Judges' were national leaders before Israel had a king. God was the supreme Judge, the Ruler of all things.

So the 'last' judgement, as taught by Jesus, will be the final sorting out of good from evil. Because the Judge is God himself there will be no injustice. We can be confident that the Judge of all the earth will act fairly. God has given to Jesus the actual task of judgement.

Everyone will be judged according to what they know. Those who have never heard the written laws of God will be judged by what they know of God from creation, and what their own conscience tells them about right and wrong. But it is a fact that we all fail to live up to what we know of God and his standards, and we all stand condemned on the basis of the life we have led.

On the great day of judgement everything will depend on a person's relationship to Christ. Jesus himself said so. The early Christians were certain that the only way to be sure of life on the day of judgement was by believing in Christ. 'Whoever believes in the Son has eternal life,' wrote John, 'whoever disobeys the Son will not have life, but will remain under God's punishment.'

See also *Future destiny, Heaven, Hell, Second coming of Jesus.*
Psalm 96:10; Genesis 18:25; Romans 3:3-4; 1:18–2:16; 3:9-12; Matthew 10:32-33; John 3:18; 5:24-30; Acts 4:12; 10:42; 2 Corinthians 3:10-15; 5:10;

2 Thessalonians 1:5-10; Hebrews 12:22-27; Revelation 20:12-15

Judges
The Book of Judges is a collection of stories from the two lawless centuries from the time of the Israelite conquest of Canaan to just before the crowning of King Saul, roughly 1200–1050 BC.

The 'Judges' were local heroes of the tribes of Israel, usually military leaders, whose exploits are retold in the book. They include such figures as Deborah, Gideon and Samson. During this period only their shared faith in God held the tribes of Israel together. When they turned to local gods they became divided and weak, and a prey to the Canaanites. But even when they turned their backs on him, God was prepared to step in and save his people if they returned to him.

Julius
The Roman centurion in charge of Paul on his voyage to Rome to be tried before Caesar.
Acts 27:1, 3, 42-44

A Roman centurion.

Justification
There is nothing a person can do to get right (be justified) with God. Sin cuts us off from a holy God. However 'good' we try to be, we cannot escape its grip.

Therefore if a person is to be made right with God it can only come about by God's own action: by 'grace'. This is the point made by the doctrine of 'justification'. God accepts us as his children because of Jesus' death on the cross. 'Christ was without sin, but for our sake God made him share our sin in order that in union with him we might share the righteousness of God.' Christ took on himself the sentence on sin so that we could be acquitted. God now looks upon the Christian as 'in Christ'–a new person acquitted because of Jesus' obedience, and given the power to be obedient himself.

The Christian is therefore put right with God ('justified') by 'grace' on the basis of the death of Jesus. And his acquittal comes through faith in Christ.

See also *Atonement, Grace.*
2 Corinthians 5:21; Romans 3:24; 5:1,9

K

Kadesh-barnea
An oasis and settlement in the desert south of Beersheba. It is mentioned in the campaign of Chedorlaomer and his allies at the time of Abraham. It was near Kadesh that Hagar saw an angel. After the escape from Egypt, most of Israel's years of desert wandering were spent in the area around Kadesh. Miriam died there, and Moses brought water out of the rock. From Kadesh he sent spies into Canaan. It is later mentioned as a point on the southern boundary of Israel.
Genesis 14:7; 16:14; Numbers 20:13; 33:36; Deuteronomy 1:19-25, 46; Joshua 10:41; 15:23 (Kedesh)

Kedesh
A Canaanite town in Galilee conquered by Joshua and given to the tribe of Naphtali. It was the home of Barak. Kedesh was one of the first towns to fall to the Assyrians when Tiglath-pilezer III invaded Israel from the north (734–732 BC).
Joshua 12:22; 19:37; Judges 4; 2 Kings 15:29

The Kidron Valley, just east of the city of Jerusalem.

Kidron
The valley which separates Jerusalem and the temple from the Mount of Olives, on the east. For most of the year the valley is dry. The Gihon Spring, whose water King Hezekiah brought inside the city walls through the Siloam tunnel, is on the west side of the Kidron Valley.

David crossed the Kidron when he left Jerusalem at the time of Absalom's rebellion. Asa, Hezekiah and Josiah, kings who reformed the nation's worship, destroyed idols in the Kidron Valley. Jesus and his disciples crossed it many times on their way to the Garden of Gethsemane.
2 Samuel 15:23; 1 Kings 15:13; 2 Chronicles 29:16; 2 Kings 23:4; John 18:1

Kingdom of God
'God is King' is one of the constant themes of the Old Testament. And in one sense it was true. But it was only partially true and it was obvious that God would need to act decisively if the evils that man's sin had brought were to be put right. God promised that this would happen.

'The right time has come,' Jesus declared when he began to preach in Galilee, 'and the Kingdom of God is near! Turn away from your sins and believe the Good News.' God had sent Jesus to establish his new rule, to put an end to the evil mess into which the world had fallen, and to make a fresh start, a new age. God's rule is what the 'kingdom' means, rather than a *place* where God rules. The presence of God's rule was seen in Jesus' miracles and in the fact that he could drive out demons. Jesus was putting right both physical and spiritual illnesses to show the power of the new kingdom, in which evil would be completely destroyed.

The life and teaching of Jesus show that the kingdom of God has already arrived. He died for the sins of the old, sinful creation and rose again in the eternal life of the new creation, the life of the kingdom. But it is not yet fully established. This awaits the return of Jesus at the end of the age, when all things will be made new.

Jesus used parable stories to teach about the 'kingdom of God'. The Jews thought that it was going to be deliverance from the Romans. But Jesus made it clear that it was to be a slow growth of something which would eventually affect the whole world. It is worth all we have to enter it. It is not for the proud or self-centred, but for people who humble themselves before God–for sinners who repent.

People who believe in Jesus have his new life already. In the future, they will know the 'new heavens and the new earth', their bodies will be made new, when the new age, the kingdom, is completed.
Micah 4:6-7; Mark 1:15; Luke 7:18-23; Matthew 5:1-20; 6:10; 13; Mark 4; 9:45-47; Luke 8; 14:16-24

Kings
The two books of Kings cover 400 years of Israel's history: from the death of David to the destruction of Jerusalem in 587 BC.

It is not known who wrote these two books. But it is certain that, like 2 Samuel, they contain information that has been extracted from court records contemporary with the events they describe. They probably went through a number of editions and revisions, reaching their final form some time during the exile in Babylon (587–539 BC).

1 Kings can be divided into two parts:

Chapters 1–11: Solomon succeeds his father, David, as king of Israel and Judah. His golden reign includes the building of the temple in Jerusalem.

Chapters 12–22: the nation divides into northern and southern kingdoms. We are given the stories of the kings ruling each area, including Jeroboam (Israel), Rehoboam (Judah), Ahab (Israel), Jehoshaphat (Judah) and Ahaziah (Israel).

The prophets of God stand out as brave spokesmen, at a time when the people are turning to other gods. Elijah is the greatest of them all. His contest with the prophets of Baal on Mt Carmel is recorded in 1 Kings 18.

2 Kings continues the history of the two Israelite kingdoms where 1 Kings leaves off. It also has two parts:

Chapters 1–17: the story of both kingdoms from the mid-ninth century until the defeat of the northern kingdom by Assyria and the fall of Samaria in 722 BC. During this time the prophet Elisha, Elijah's successor, stands out as God's messenger.

Chapters 18–25: the story of the kingdom of Judah, from the fall of the kingdom of Israel until the destruction of the city of Jerusalem by King Nebuchadnezzar of Babylon in 587 BC. This includes the reigns of two great kings, Hezekiah and Josiah.

In the two books of Kings, the rulers of Israel are judged by their faithfulness to God. The nation succeeds when the king is loyal. When they turn to other gods, they fail. The northern kings are all failures according to this standard, but for a time the kings of Judah did a little better. The fall of Jerusalem and the exile of many Israelites was a major watershed in the history of Israel.

King's Highway
The road by which Moses promised to travel peacefully through the land of Edom and the land of Sihon, king of Heshbon. Both refused his request, and so the Israelites were forced to avoid Edom and to fight and defeat Sihon. The King's Highway was probably the main route north to south along the heights east of the Jordan, between Damascus and the Gulf of Aqaba.
Numbers 20:17; 21:22; Deuteronomy 2:27

Kiriath-arba
An earlier name for Hebron.

Kiriath-jearim
A hill-town a few miles east of Jerusalem. It was one of the towns of the Gibeonites, who tricked Joshua into a peace treaty. The Covenant Box (ark) was kept at Kiriath-jearim for twenty years before King David took it to Jerusalem.
Joshua 9; 1 Samuel 6:20–7:2; Jeremiah 26:20; Nehemiah 7:29

Kishon
A small stream which flows across the plain of Megiddo (Esdraelon) and into the Mediterranean Sea just north of Mt Carmel. In the story of Barak heavy rain raised the water level so high that the surrounding ground turned to mud and bogged down Sīsera's chariots, giving Israel victory. The prophet Elijah killed the prophets of Baal by the River Kishon after the contest on Mt Carmel.
Judges 4; 5:21; 1 Kings 18:40

Kittim
One of the sons of Javan in the Genesis 'table of the nations', and so the name of Cyprus and of its early city of Kition (modern Larnaca). See *Cyprus.*
Genesis 10:4; 1 Chronicles 1:7; Numbers 24:24; Isaiah 23:1, 12; Jeremiah 2:10; Ezekiel 27:6

Kohath
A son of Levi and grandfather of Moses. His descendants were known as the Kohathites and formed one of the three groups of Levites.
Exodus 6:16ff.; Numbers 3:17ff.

Korah
1. A Levite who led a rebellion against Moses and Aaron. He did not see what right they had to be leaders and was angry because the people had not reached Canaan quickly enough. Korah and the others died because they rejected God's chosen leader and rebelled against him.
Numbers 16
2. A son of Levi. His descendants were singers in the temple.
1 Chronicles 6:37; Psalms 44–49

L

Laban
The brother of Rebekah, Isaac's wife. He lived in Harran and welcomed his nephew Jacob when he had to leave home. Laban had two daughters–Leah and Rachel. Jacob agreed to work for Laban for seven years to marry Rachel. But Laban tricked him into marrying Leah and he had to work another seven years for Rachel. Jacob in turn outwitted Laban and as a result his flock of sheep and goats became larger and stronger than his uncle's. When Laban discovered that Jacob had secretly left for Canaan he chased after him. God warned Laban in a dream not to harm Jacob. They agreed to go their own ways and Laban returned to Harran.
Genesis 24:29ff.; 29–31

Lachish
An important fortified town in the low hills about 30 miles/48km southwest of Jerusalem. Lachish has a long history. It was a military stronghold before the sixteenth century BC.

The king of Lachish joined with four other Amorite kings to fight Joshua. But Joshua won. He attacked and captured Lachish and put everyone there to death. Solomon's son, King Rehoboam, rebuilt Lachish as a defence against the Philistines and Egyptians.

The town had an outer and inner wall, 19ft/6m thick. These walls were strengthened with towers. So too was the gateway. A well 144ft/44m deep ensured a good supply of water. Lachish had a palace and store-rooms approached by a street lined with shops.

King Amaziah of Judah fled to Lachish for safety. But his enemies followed and killed him there.

When the Assyrian King Sennacherib attacked Judah he besieged Lachish, cutting Jerusalem off from possible help from Egypt. He sent envoys from Lachish to demand Jerusalem's surrender. Lachish fell, and Sennacherib had the siege pictured on the walls of his palace at Nineveh. Archaeologists have also discovered at Lachish a mass grave from this time, holding 1,500 bodies.

The Babylonian army attacked Lachish at the time of the final siege of Jerusalem (589–586 BC). The 'Lachish Letters', written by an army officer to his superior, belong to this period. Lachish fell and the Babylonians burnt it. After the exile it was resettled, but was never again an important place.
Joshua 10; 2 Chronicles 11:5-12; 2 Kings 14:19; 18:14-21; Isaiah 36–37; Jeremiah 34:7; Nehemiah 11:30

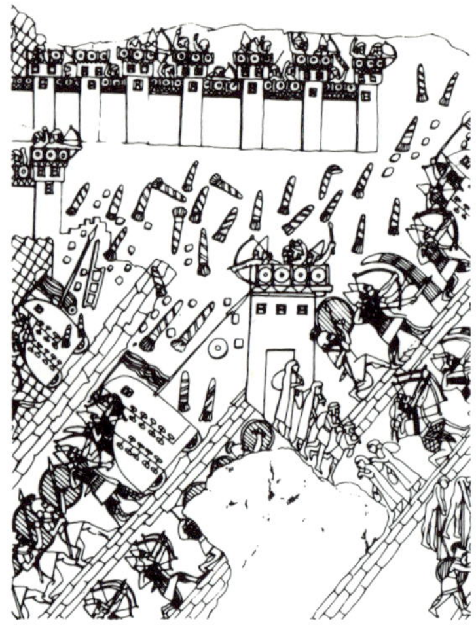

King Sennacherib's attack on Lachish; a relief commemorating his victory from his palace at Nineveh.

Lamech
1. A descendant of Cain. Genesis 4:18ff.
2. Son of Methuselah and father of Noah.
Genesis 5:28-31

Lamentations
The Book of Lamentations is a collection of five poems. They mourn the fall of Jerusalem in 587 BC, and the exile which followed. God's temple had been destroyed, and the nation saw this as a sign that God had given them over to their enemy. The prophet was mourning the sin of his people.

Although the book is mainly a lament, there is also the promise of hope. The author is not known. The poems are still read aloud in Jewish synagogues each July, when the Jews remember how the temple was destroyed in 587 BC and again in AD 70.

Laodicea

A town in the Lycus Valley of present-day western Turkey (the Roman province of Asia in New Testament times). Laodicea stood at the junction of two important main roads. It grew prosperous from trade and banking. The region produced clothes made of glossy black wool, and also medicines. Water for the town was piped from hot springs some distance away. A number of these points are reflected in the letter to the church at Laodicea in the Book of Revelation. Paul's letter to the Colossians was intended for Laodicea, too, although he had not been there. The Christian group there may have been started during the time when Paul was staying at Ephesus.
Colossians 2:1; 4:13-16;
Revelation 1:11; 3:14-22

Law

After their escape from slavery in Egypt, God led the Israelites through the desert to Mt Sinai. They camped at the foot of the mountain, while God gave Moses the laws his people were to obey. The promise (covenant-treaty) God had previously made with individuals–Abraham, Isaac, Jacob–he now renewed with the whole nation. They were his people; he was their God. He had rescued them and he expected them to respond by obeying his laws. These were not just rules for worship or religious occasions. They covered every aspect of life. And they are summed up in the Ten Commandments.

The Ten Commandments God spoke, and these were his words:
I am the Lord your God who brought you out of Egypt, where you were slaves.
Worship no god but me.
Do not make for yourselves images of anything in heaven or on earth or in the water under the earth. Do not bow down to any idol or worship it, because I am the Lord your God and I tolerate no rivals. I bring punishment on those who hate me and on their descendants down to the third and fourth generation. But I show my love to thousands of generations of those who love me and obey my laws.
Do not use my name for evil purposes, because I, the Lord your God, will punish anyone who misuses my name.
Observe the Sabbath and keep it holy. You have six days in which to do your work, but the seventh day is a day of rest dedicated to me. On that day no one is to work–neither you, your children, your slaves, your animals, nor the foreigners who live in your country. In six days I, the Lord, made the earth, the sky, the sea, and everything in them, but on the seventh day I rested. That is why I, the Lord, blessed the Sabbath and made it holy.
Respect your father and your mother, so that you may live a long time in the land that I am giving you.
Do not commit murder.
Do not commit adultery.
Do not steal.
Do not accuse anyone falsely.
Do not desire another man's house; do not desire his wife, his slaves, his cattle, his donkeys, or anything else that he owns.'

This is the best known collection of Israel's laws. It clearly has a special significance: in Exodus it is the first set of laws given on Mt Sinai, and in Deuteronomy it is said at the end of the Ten Commandments: 'These words the Lord spoke to all your assembly...and he added no more' (Deuteronomy 5:22), that is, there were no others of equal importance.

The Ten Commandments are addressed to the whole nation of Israel, not just to a particular group like the priests, and to every Israelite as an individual. All the same, though these Ten Commandments are unique as a collection, each one of them is found again in other places in the Hebrew laws.

The Ten Commandments were written on two stone tablets. This probably means two copies. The reason for having two copies of the Ten Commandments has only recently been understood. When a written covenant was made in the world of the Bible, each party making the covenant had a copy of its contents. If the covenant was between two nations, for instance the Hittites and the Egyptians, the two copies would be kept far apart, in the temple of a god of each land. In Israel, though, the covenant was between God and his people. Both copies of the Ten Commandments were kept in the Covenant Box (ark). This was the centre of Israel and it was also the place of God's presence. So God's copy and Israel's copy could be kept together. The Ten Commandments, then, were the terms of the covenant that God had made with his people. At Sinai, in response to all that God had done for them, the people of Israel accepted these terms.

The penalty for breaking any of the Ten Commandments is not mentioned. But if we compare these commandments with similar ones, it seems that the penalty was death (compare Exodus 20:13 with Exodus 21:12). This does not mean that the penalty was always carried out.

An ancient scroll containing the Pentateuch, the first five books of the Bible.

Other collections of laws Of course in any society many more detailed rules and laws are necessary. The basic laws need to be expanded. If the commandment says that you are not to do any work on the sabbath, who is meant by 'you' and what counts as 'work'? Already in Exodus 20:10 the simple command has to be spelled out in detail. It has to be made clear that 'you' is not just the father of the Israelite family, but also 'your children, your slaves, your animals...the foreigners who live in your country' (Deuteronomy 5:14). (We must assume and hope that 'your wife' was also included!) Later, the Jewish rabbis spent much time on defining exactly what was 'work'. Jesus was criticized by some because he and his disciples healed and picked grain on the sabbath (Luke 14:3-4; Matthew 12:1-2). This was against the Pharisees' definition of 'work'.

The Ten Commandments are God's 'covenant-law' for Israel. In addition to these, Israel's law-books (Exodus to Deuteronomy) contain many 'case-laws', some of them similar to those of other nations. There are three major collections of laws.

The first follows on from the Ten Commandments, in Exodus 21–23. It is sometimes called the 'Book of the Covenant'. It contains moral, civil and religious laws. Instructions about worship are followed by laws dealing with the rights of slaves; manslaughter and injury to human life; theft and damage to property; social and religious duties; justice and human rights. At the end come instructions for the three great religious festivals: Unleavened Bread, Firstfruits and Harvest. The laws show God's concern that life as a whole should be just and fair. They show his concern to protect the rights of those least able to help themselves–slaves, the poor, widows and orphans, foreigners.

Leviticus 17–26 contains a second collection of laws (the 'holiness' laws). These mainly concern how the Israelites should worship God, the rituals connected with the tabernacle. But they also deal with everyday behaviour. The keynote of the teaching is the command, 'Be holy, because I, the Lord your God, am holy' (Leviticus 19:2). Israel is to be 'holy' because the nation belongs to God.

The third collection of detailed laws is set down in Deuteronomy 12–25. They cover many of the same matters dealt with in Exodus and Leviticus. But they come in the form of a sermon given by Moses to the Israelites before they went into the Promised Land. They include frequent encouragements to keep the Law, and warnings of what will happen if the people disobey. Deuteronomy 17:14-20 is the only part of the Law which spells out the duties of the king.

The purpose of the commandments The Law was intended to be a guide to good relationships–with God and with other people. In it, God, the maker and rescuer of his people, tells them how they are to live–for their own good and well-being. The Hebrew word which is usually translated 'law' (*torah*) actually means 'guidance' or 'instruction'. These laws were never intended to be a long list of dos and don'ts to make life a burden.

The Law reflects God's character–his holiness, justice and goodness. It expresses his will. It gives his people the practical guidance they need in order to obey his command to 'Be holy, as I am holy.'

How far does the Old Testament Law still apply? Are Christians today bound by it as the Law of God? On the one hand, we have the sayings of Jesus. He has not come to abolish the Law; he has come to 'fulfil' it (that is, to fill it with fuller meaning). Until heaven and earth pass away, he says, not the least portion will pass from the Law. Whoever disobeys the least important of the commandments shall be called least in the kingdom of heaven.

On the other hand, Paul states that Christ 'has brought the Law to an end'. He sees the Old Testament Law as something that was 'introduced' at a certain point in history and was intended to be valid only till the time of the coming of Christ.

How do these two attitudes fit together? Some have thought the difficulty can be solved by distinguishing between the moral laws, which are still in force, and the ritual, ceremonial, and social laws of the Old Testament, which applied only to the Israelites. But for one thing it is impossible to say which laws are which, and, for another, although Paul acknowledges that the law is from God and is 'holy, just, and good', he speaks of even the moral law as 'cancelled' by the work of Jesus Christ. Christians are 'free' from the Law and are not subject to it–and in these passages Paul is thinking of the law as a whole, not just the moral law.

For Christians, then, Jesus Christ has taken the place of the Law. He has not put the Law aside or rejected it, but has summed it up. When Paul says that he is under Christ's law, he does not mean that he has accepted a new set of laws. Rather, he is a follower of Jesus and is filled with his spirit. By being linked with Jesus, sharing his new life and the power of his Holy Spirit, Christians are able to follow his example and obey his law. Christ's law is not a law that enslaves people because they are unable to keep it. It is the 'perfect law that sets people free'.
Deuteronomy 6:5; Leviticus 19:18; Matthew 5:17-20; Romans 10:4; 5:20; Galatians 3:19; Romans 7:6, 12; Colossians 2:14; Galatians 5:18; 1 Corinthians 9:21; Galatians 6:2; 5:1; James 1:25

Lazarus

1. Brother of Martha and Mary who lived in Bethany. When Lazarus became ill his sisters sent for Jesus. Although he loved them all, Jesus delayed until he knew that Lazarus was dead. (See *Martha*.) Jesus went with the weeping women to the cave tomb–and wept himself. He told people standing by to roll away the stone which blocked the door and then cried, 'Lazarus, come out.' Lazarus came, with the grave clothes still wrapped around him. Jewish leaders who saw this happen believed in Jesus. When the chief priests and Pharisees heard of Jesus' power over death they were afraid the whole nation would follow him, and plotted to kill him and Lazarus, too.
John 11–12:11
2. The name of the beggar in Jesus' story of the rich man and the beggar at his gate.
Luke 16:19-31

Leah

Elder daughter of Laban, married to Jacob through Laban's trick. She and Jacob had six sons, ancestors of the tribes of Israel, and a daughter.
Genesis 29:16–33:7

Lebanon

The modern country of that name and its mountain range. Lebanon in the Old Testament was famous for its forests, especially its great cedar-trees. The Bible refers also to the snows of Lebanon, and to the country's fertility. All kinds of fruit grow on the coastal plain and lower hill slopes: olives, grapes, apples, figs, apricots, dates and all kinds of green vegetables.

The great Phoenician (Canaanite) ports of Tyre, Sidon and Byblos were all on the coast of Lebanon and grew rich exporting its products. King Solomon sent to the king of Tyre for cedar and other wood from Lebanon to build the temple and royal palace at Jerusalem.
1 Kings 5:1-11; Hosea 6:5-7; Ezra 3:7; Psalm 72:16; Isaiah 2:13; 14:8; Ezekiel 31, etc.

Leopard

Isaiah and Jeremiah both mention the leopard, which was well known in Israel in Bible times. Its spotted coat helps it to creep up on its kill unseen, even in the open.
Isaiah 11:6; Jeremiah 13:23

Levi

1. Third son of Jacob and Leah. His descendants formed the tribe of Levi. The Levites were chosen to serve God in the tent of worship and, later, the temple.
Genesis 29:34; 34:25ff.; 49:5ff.; Numbers 3:5-20
2. See *Matthew*.

Leviticus

Leviticus is basically a rule-book. It contains the laws about religious ceremonies, worship and daily life which were designed to keep the people of Israel in a right relationship with God.

Leviticus gets its name from the priests (the members of the tribe or clan of Levi) who had the job of carrying out the rules for worship. It is always coming back to the theme of God's holiness–his utter goodness, so different from man. When Jesus summed up the law, he quoted from Leviticus: 'Love your neighbour as yourself' (19:18).

Leviticus contains the following sections of teaching:

Chapters 1–7: laws about sacrifice and offerings, and their meaning.

Chapters 8–10: laws about the men who could be priests, and how they were set apart for their work.

Chapters 11–15: laws for daily living. These concentrate on 'pure' and 'impure' things which barred people for a time from joining in God's worship.

Chapter 16: the Day of Atonement–an annual occasion when offerings were made to make the people 'clean' from sin.

Chapters 17–27: laws about holy living and worship, with promises for those who obeyed and warnings for those who disobeyed.

Libnah

A fortified lowland town not far from Lachish, taken by Joshua. In the reign of King Jehoram of Judah Libnah rebelled. The town survived a siege by the Assyrian King Sennacherib when plague hit his army.
Joshua 10:29-30; 2 Kings 8:22; 19:8, 35

Life

Life was 'breathed into man's nostrils' by God and he 'began to live'. God is in all the natural processes that keep us alive; and it is he who determines when life shall end. Life is a person's most valued possession, and one of his greatest desires is for God to bless him with a long life.

But there is more to life than just physical existence. A relationship with God enables people to live life on a new level. This is the full, abundant life that Jesus came to bring. It is 'eternal life', which Jesus offers as a free and permanent gift. Eternal life is life in a new dimension, 'God's life'. 'Whoever has the Son', says John, 'has this life.' It begins when a person becomes a Christian, and survives death. It is an eternal relationship with God.

See also *Death*, *Resurrection*.
Genesis 2:7; Psalm 104:29; Job 2:4; Psalm 91:16; Deuteronomy 8:3; 30:15-20; John 10:10, 28; 1 John 5:12; John 11:25-26; Romans 6:4-13, 22-23 and many other passages

Light

The Bible often uses the contrast of light and darkness to show the absolute difference between God and the forces of evil. 'God is light, and there is no darkness at all in him.' God is altogether good. His holiness is so utterly pure that he is said to 'live in the light that no one can approach'. In contrast to this the forces of evil are called 'the cosmic powers of this dark age'. John describes the spiritual battle between 'light' (God and goodness) and 'darkness' (Satan and everything evil). 'The light shines in the darkness, and the darkness has never put it out.' In the life, death and resurrection of Jesus light won its victory over darkness.

Jesus calls himself 'the light of the world' and promises 'the light of life' to all who follow him. Men and women need no longer walk in darkness, ignorant of the truth, cut off from God, and blinded by sin. They can 'live in the light–just as he is in the light'. To become a Christian is to move out of darkness into light. God's people are 'like light for the whole world'. They must let that light shine out to others.

At last, in the new heaven and earth, the light of God's presence will be a constant reality. There will be no darkness, no night, no lamps, not even sunlight. All God's people will be with him, and he will be their light.
1 John 1:5; 1 Timothy 6:16; Ephesians 6:12; John 1:4-9; 8:12; 1 John 1:7; Matthew 5:14-16;

Revelation 21:23-24; 22:5

'Lily of the field'
In the Old Testament the lily may have been the wild blue hyacinth, or the madonna lily (the bulb was also considered a delicacy to eat). When Jesus spoke of the lilies of the field he was probably thinking of wild flowers in general, rather than one in particular. In spring the hillsides of Galilee are ablaze with brightly coloured flowers: anemone, crocus, poppy, narcissus and yellow chrysanthemum.
Song of Solomon 5:13; 6:2; Matthew 6:28

Lion
The lion is mentioned many times in the Bible–although by New Testament times it was rare in Israel. Assyrian kings kept lions in pits, and enjoyed lion-hunts with their nobles. Lions lived in the thickets of the Jordan Valley and could be a danger to flocks and to humans. The strength and courage of the lion made him a symbol of power, so that Jesus himself is called 'lion of the tribe of Judah'.
Daniel 6:16-24; Revelation 5:5

Lord's Supper
Jesus instituted this communal meal at Passover time, at the last supper with his disciples before his death. At the Passover Festival people looked back to the deliverance from Egypt, and forward to the coming kingdom of God. The Lord's Supper, too, looks back. It reminds us, by the bread and wine, of the past event of Jesus' death. And it looks forward to the time when Jesus will come again. 'You proclaim the Lord's death until he comes,' says Paul.

The Passover meal began with a blessing–thanking God for the bread. Then pieces of the loaf were passed round to the guests. The same action in the Christian service was a reminder of the fact that Jesus' body had been 'given for you'. The meal ended with a shared cup of wine. In the Christian ceremony the wine was a token of the blood (the death) of Christ. His death was a sacrifice that sealed the new covenant agreement between God and man, just as the old covenant was sealed by the blood of sacrificial oxen (Exodus 24:5-8). So Jesus says, 'This is my blood... which seals God's covenant.'

Those who share in this sacred meal declare their loyalty to the Lord who has created the new covenant. The wine also points to the future kingdom of God, pictured as a banquet. Jesus said, 'I will never again drink this wine until the day I drink the new wine in the Kingdom of God.'

In Acts, the Lord's Supper is called 'the breaking of bread' ('fellowship meal'). This was the name used by the Jews for the blessing said over the bread. Originally it was part of an actual meal. The Christians at Corinth brought their own provisions for just such a meal together. Paul saw a further meaning in sharing the loaf. Christians share in Christ as they share the bread, and they also share in the 'body of Christ', the church. Division and disunity in the church denies the truth for which the one loaf stands.

Eventually the Lord's Supper moved from the homes of individual Christians to a special building, and was no longer part of an actual meal. Christian prayers and praises that had developed from the synagogue services were added to the ceremony. The earliest account we have of the prayers at the Lord's Supper (or Eucharist) come from the *Didache* ('The Teaching') written late in the first or early in the second century AD.
Matthew 26:26-30; Mark 14:22-26; Luke 22:14-20; Acts 2:46; 20:7; 1 Corinthians 11:20-34; 10:16-17

Bread and wine, shared by Christians at the Lord's Supper.

Lot
Abraham's nephew. He went with Abraham from Harran to Canaan but they parted after their herdsmen quarrelled. Lot went to live at Sodom in the fertile plain. Abraham rescued him from raiding kings. Later, when Sodom was destroyed for its wickedness, Lot just escaped. His wife, stopping to look back at the city, was caught in the disaster.
Genesis 11:31–14:16; 19

Love
'God is love'. This has always been the character of God. It is a mistake to think that the God of the Old Testament could not be described in this way. One of the most moving testimonies to God's love in the whole Bible is by the prophet Hosea. God's love was the reason why he chose and cared for the people of Israel. In return, God's people were expected to love him with their whole being, and show a similar love to their fellow men.

In the New Testament 'love' sometimes translates the usual Greek word for love, *philia*. This means 'intimate affection'. Far more important, however, is the word *agape*. This is not a sex word, although the Bible regards sex very highly. *Agape* is used to describe self-giving love, seen above all in Jesus Christ. It is in his death that we see the true depths of this love.

It is far greater than human love. It is the love that unites the Father and the Son. It is the love that God has for the world, and it becomes part of a Christian's life through the gift of God. It is in fact the mark of God's presence in the life of every Christian. 'If you have love for one another,' Jesus says, 'then everyone will know that you are my disciples.'
1 John 4:8; Hosea 11:1-4; 7-9; Deuteronomy 7:7-8; 6:5, Leviticus 19:18; Romans 5:5, 8; John 3:16, 35; 1 Corinthians 13; Galatians 5:22; John 13:34-35; see also John 14:15, 21-24; 15:9-14; 1 John 4:7-5:3

Lud
Lud, a son of Shem, gave his name to a people known later as the Lydians. They lived in the west of Asia Minor (Turkey) around Sardis. See *Lydians*.

Luke
A Greek-speaking doctor who wrote the Gospel of Luke and the Acts of the Apostles. He was a friend of Paul and travelled with him on some of his journeys, so he was able to describe at first-hand some of the things Paul said and did. On these journeys Luke was also able to learn about Jesus' life and the beginnings of the church from the apostles and first Christians. He sailed to Rome with Paul and stayed with him while he was a prisoner there.
Colossians 4:14; 2 Timothy 4:11; Philemon 24

Luke's Gospel
Luke's Gospel–third of the four accounts of Jesus' life in the New Testament–has by far the most detail. The story of the growth and spread of Christianity after Jesus returned to heaven is continued by the same writer in the Book of Acts (see *Acts*). Both books were written for a Roman official called Theophilus.

The Gospel writer has been careful to get his history and facts right. He sets out to tell what happened in Palestine during Jesus' life. Tradition suggests it was written by Luke, the doctor who went with Paul on some of his journeys.

Luke's Gospel presents Jesus as the promised Saviour of Israel–and as the Saviour of all people. It emphasizes how he preached this Good News to the poor.

The Gospel opens with the story of the birth and childhood of John the Baptist and Jesus (chapters 1 and 2). Many of these details are found only in Luke.

Chapters 3–9 deal with the baptism and testing of Jesus, and his preaching and teaching in Galilee.

His journey from Galilee to Jerusalem is covered in 9:51–19:46. Some of Jesus' parables, recorded in these chapters, are found only in Luke: for example the good Samaritan, the prodigal son and the rich fool.

His last week in Jerusalem is covered in 19:47–23:56.

Finally, chapter 24 tells how Jesus came back from death and returned to heaven.

Luke's Gospel is full of joy. It also stresses the need for prayer, the power of the Holy Spirit in Jesus and his followers, and God's forgiveness of sins. It is marked by a warm interest in people.

Luz
The older name of Bethel.

Lycia
A small, mountainous land in the south-west of Asia Minor (Turkey).

The ports of Patara and Myra, at which Paul landed, were in Lycia.
Acts 27:5

Lydda
A town about 10 miles/16km inland from Joppa. Peter healed a lame man, Aeneas, when visiting the first Christians here. The place is now again called by its Old Testament name, Lod.
Acts 9:32-35, 38

Lydia
A 'dealer in purple cloth' who came from Thyatira in Asia Minor (Turkey). She heard Paul preach in Philippi (Greece) and became a Christian.
Acts 16:14-15, 40

Lydians
On the west coast of Turkey lived an Indo-European people, the Lydians. Inscriptions and objects unearthed in their capital, Sardis, are beginning to reveal their culture and history. Gyges (Gog), who was king about 650 BC, was used by the prophet Ezekiel as a figure standing for a distant ruler. Obadiah refers to Sardis (Sepharad) as one of many places of exile. Lydia had rich deposits of gold. It was here that coinage began and the wealthy Croesus ruled. He was defeated by Cyrus the Persian in 546 BC. Lydia (Lud) is named as an ally of Tyre and Egypt in Ezekiel. From 133 BC it was part of the Roman province of Asia.
Ezekiel 38:2; Obadiah 20;
Ezekiel 27:10; 30:5

Lystra
A remote town in the Roman province of Galatia (not far from Konya in modern Turkey). Paul and Barnabas went on to Lystra after rough treatment at Iconium, on the first missionary journey. Paul healed a cripple at Lystra, and the people believed him to be Hermes (messenger of the Greek gods) and Barnabas to be Zeus himself. But Jews from Iconium stirred up trouble, and Paul was stoned and left for dead. Some of the people became Christians, and Paul returned to visit them on his second journey. Lystra (or possibly Derbe) was Timothy's home town.
Acts 14:6-20; 16:1-5

M

Maacah
A small Aramaean state to the south-east of Mt Hermon. It is mentioned in David's campaigns and one of his warriors came from here.
Joshua 12:5; 2 Samuel 10; 23:34

Macedonia
A region of Greece stretching north and west from Thessalonica. The Roman province of Macedonia included Philippi and Beroea as well as Thessalonica.

Paul crossed the Aegean Sea from Troas after seeing a vision of a Macedonian man asking him to come over and help them. It was the first stage in bringing the Good News of Jesus to Europe. Three of Paul's letters (Philippians, 1 and 2 Thessalonians) are addressed to Macedonian Christians. They gave generously to his relief fund for Christians in Judea. And several of them became his regular helpers.
Acts 16:8–17:15; 20:1-6;
2 Corinthians 8:1-5; 9:1-5, etc.

Machpelah
When Sarah died at Hebron, Abraham still owned no land. So he bought a plot of land with the cave of Machpelah from Ephron the Hittite. Abraham himself was later buried here, and afterwards Isaac and Rebekah, and then Jacob.

Much later, Herod the Great built a shrine round the place believed to contain the cave and the tombs, and this can still be seen.
Genesis 23; 25:9; 49:30; 50:13

Magog
See *Gog.*

Mahanaim
A place in Gilead, east of the River Jordan and near the River Jabbok. Jacob saw God's angels at Mahanaim, before the reunion with his brother Esau. For a short time it was the capital of Saul's son Ishbosheth (Ishbaal). It was King David's headquarters during Absalom's rebellion. One of Solomon's district officers was based at Mahanaim.
Genesis 32:2; 2 Samuel 2:8-10; 17:24-29; 1 Kings 4:14

Make-up

A Greek perfume bottle and jug made of multi-coloured glass.

From earliest times women have used beauty aids. In ancient Palestine, Egypt and Mesopotamia women put dark eyeshadow around their eyes. At first this was to protect their eyes against the strong sunshine. But it soon became a matter of fashion. Minerals were ground up in oil or gum with a small pestle and mortar. The women used their fingers, spatulas made of wood or bronze, or fine brushes to put on their eyeshadow. And they had polished metal mirrors in which to study the effect! Lead sulphide *(galena)* was used early on, and copper carbonate *(kohl)* gave a greenish tinge. By Roman times, antimony was more often used. Egyptian women used lipstick and powderpuffs. Their toe nails and finger nails were painted red with dye from the crushed leaves of the henna plant. Red iron oxide seems to have been used in Egypt as rouge.

Oil, rubbed into the body to soothe the skin, was almost as essential in a hot, dry climate. The only time it was not used was during times of mourning. But the oil, like the eye-paint, soon became part of the fashion scene and was perfumed. A heavy scent helped disguise body odour where there was not much water for washing! 'Good oil' was made from flowers, seeds and fruit, soaked in oil and water. This was then sometimes treated so that the essence could be extracted and strained out. Other perfumes came from gums or resins and were used either in powdered form, dissolved in oil, or mixed to make ointments. Most of these were imported into Israel and were a luxury. Because of their cost, they were kept in very expensive bottles and containers.

Malachi
The last of the Old Testament prophets (about mid-fifth century BC). The temple had been rebuilt after the return from exile but the people were not serving God wholeheartedly. 'Turn back,' said Malachi. 'Stop cheating God of his dues. Don't test his patience any longer.' Malachi's name means 'my messenger'. As God's messenger he spoke of the coming Messiah and the great day of God's justice and judgement.

Malta
The modern name of an island in the central Mediterranean Sea, between Sicily and the north coast of Africa. Its ancient name was Melita, and Paul's ship was wrecked here during his voyage as a prisoner to Rome. All the people on board reached land safely and were received kindly by the natives. They spent the winter on Malta before sailing for Italy.
Acts 28:1-10

Mamre
A place near Hebron. Abraham, and later Isaac, often camped by the oak-trees at Mamre. It was here that Abraham heard that Lot had been captured. At Mamre God promised him a son, and he pleaded with God to spare Sodom.
Genesis 13:18; 14:13; 18; 23:17; 35:27

Man and woman
Men and women are part of nature. They are 'animals'–yet different from the animals, because God made them to be 'like himself' and to enjoy his friendship. They were the crowning glory of his whole creation on earth.

The story of Adam and Eve in Genesis 2 shows the importance of men and women in God's creation. Adam is put in the Garden of Eden to look after it and to work in it. Work itself is not a necessary evil: it is part of God's original intention. Man was not meant to live alone. God made woman as the ideal partner for Adam, to work alongside him and to share his life. The relationship between man and woman, their sexuality, is part of God's perfect creation.

But when Adam ('man') and Eve ('woman') rebelled against God they lost the open fellowship with God and with one another which they had known. The results of their sin affected every area of their lives. The man's work became burdensome, and the woman's relationship with her husband brought pain as well as pleasure.

The rest of the Bible reflects both the glory and the fallenness of men and women. They are second only to God, crowned with honour. They care for all God has made, sharing his creativity in artistic achievement and caring for the earth's resources. But we see them, too, as spoilers, perverted and degraded, violent and evil.

The New Testament announces the dawn of a new age. Mankind 'in Adam' is the same as ever. But men and women are 'one in union with Christ Jesus'. Both are made new and share in the new creation as equal partners, to live life as God originally intended it.

See also *Fall, Future destiny, Life.*
Genesis 1:26-28; 2; 3;
Deuteronomy 5; 8; Psalm 8;
Romans 1-3; 5:12-19; 8:18-25;
2 Corinthians 5:17; 6:16-18;
Galatians 3:28

Manasseh

1. Joseph's elder son who was adopted and blessed by Jacob. His descendants formed the tribe of Manasseh.
Genesis 41:51; 48:1ff.

2. King of Judah for fifty-five years (696–642 BC) after his father, King Hezekiah. Manasseh led the nation astray, introducing all kinds of idol worship. He was taken prisoner to Babylon by the Assyrians. When he returned to Jerusalem he turned to God and changed his ways.
2 Kings 21:1ff.; 2 Chronicles 33

3. The land belonging to the tribe of Manasseh. West Manasseh was the hill-country of Samaria as far west as the Mediterranean Sea. East Manasseh was the land east of central Jordan.
Joshua 13:29-31; 17:7-13

Mareshah

A town in the low hills nearly 20 miles/32 km south-west of Jerusalem. It was fortified by Rehoboam. Later King Asa destroyed a great army from Sudan here. The prophet Micah foretold disaster for Mareshah.
Joshua 15:44; 2 Chronicles 11:8; 14:9-12; 20:37; Micah 1:15

Mark (John)

The writer of the second Gospel. John Mark lived in Jerusalem. His mother, Mary, allowed the first Christians to meet in her house. Mark later went with Paul and Barnabas, his cousin, to Cyprus on Paul's first missionary journey. He left them halfway through and Paul refused to take him when they set out again. Instead Mark went back to Cyprus with Barnabas. Later Paul and Mark were together in Rome, and Paul wrote of him as a loyal friend and helper. Peter describes him as 'my son Mark' and, by tradition, it was Peter who gave Mark much of the story of Jesus told in Mark's Gospel.
Mark 14:51; Acts 12:12, 25; 13:13; 15:36ff.; Colossians 4:10; 2 Timothy 4:11; Philemon 24; 1 Peter 5:13

Mark's Gospel

Mark–the second of the four Gospels which tell the life of Jesus–is a Gospel of action. It is full of life. Its author concentrates on what Jesus did, and where he went–rather than what he said and taught.

Mark is the shortest Gospel, with only sixteen chapters. It may also be the earliest. It was probably written about AD 65–70. Writers in the first centuries after Christ believed it was written down by John Mark from the account he heard from the apostle Peter. John Mark's name comes often in Acts and the New Testament letters. He shared part of Paul's first missionary tour and was later with Peter. In the Gospel, the writer often takes trouble to explain Jewish customs, so clearly he had non-Jewish readers in mind.

Mark keeps the pace of events moving. After a short introduction which covers John the Baptist and Jesus' baptism and testing, the first nine chapters deal with Jesus' healing and teaching in Galilee. Mark shows how Jesus' followers gradually began to understand him better. But his enemies became more and more hostile. Chapters 11–15 describe Jesus' last week in Jerusalem, and are followed by reports of his resurrection–how he came back to life (chapter 16). The ending, Mark 16:9-20, does not appear in many old texts and may have been added by early Christians, to make a less abrupt end to the book.

Mark shows Jesus as a man of action, a man of authority. He teaches powerfully, has power over evil spirits, and forgives people their sin. He is clearly more than an ordinary man. Yet he makes himself one with us. He came to give his own life to set people free from sin.

Marriage

The story of creation in Genesis 1 and 2 shows the pattern of marriage –one man to one woman for life–as God's original design. But it was not long before a code of rules was needed because standards had fallen.

Rules and customs The law-code of King Hammurabi of Babylon (about 1700 BC) implies that:

- A man would not take a second wife unless the first was unable to have children.
- The husband was allowed a secondary wife (a concubine), or his wife might give him a slave-girl, to have children by her.
- The children of the slave-girl might not be sent away.

It is clear from the story of Abraham that he, too, observed these customs. That is why he was so worried when Sarah insisted on sending away the slave-girl Hagar and her son (Genesis 16:1-6; 21:10-12).

The customs of Jacob's and Esau's time were less strict and allowed more than one wife. This practice grew until, by the time of the Judges and the Kings, a man could have as many wives as he could afford. But having several wives could lead to all kinds of problems. It must have been all too easy to have favourites. Deuteronomy 21:15 seems to recognize this problem when it says that a man must not take away the inheritance of his firstborn son to give to the child of his favourite wife. No doubt at first it made good economic sense to have more than one wife: more children meant more workers. But the time came when it cost more to keep several wives than the family gained by having more children.

By New Testament times the usual practice was once again to have only one wife (although at one time King Herod the Great had nine). In this respect the people had returned to the standard set out by Moses and the prophets.

It was very unusual for a man not to marry–there is no Hebrew word for 'bachelor'–and people in Israel married very young. The legal ages for marriage were thirteen and over for a boy, and twelve and over for a girl. It was probably because they were so young that marriages were arranged by parents, normally within the same clan in Old Testament times, and ideally with a first cousin. Marriage to someone from another nation worshipping other gods was forbidden. The law also forbade marriage between close relatives (Leviticus 18:6ff.). Arranged marriages did not always mean that the young people had no say. Shechem (Genesis 34:4) and Samson (Judges 14:2) both asked their parents to arrange a marriage with a particular girl. It was also possible to marry a slave or a war captive.

Marriage was a civil rather than a religious affair. At engagement (betrothal) a contract was made in front of two witnesses. Sometimes the couple gave one another a ring or bracelet. The engagement was as binding as marriage. During the waiting time before the wedding, while the girl was still living at her father's house, the man was excused from going to war (Deuteronomy 20:7).

A sum of money, a bride-price (called the *mohar*) had to be paid to the girl's father. It could sometimes be paid partly in work by the man. The father seems to have been able to use any interest the *mohar* could earn, but he was not allowed to touch the *mohar* itself. It was returned to the daughter on the death of her parents, or if her husband died. Jacob's father-in-law, Laban, seems to have broken with custom and spent his daughter's bride-price (Genesis 31:15).

The girl's father, in return, gave her, or her husband, a 'dowry' (wedding gift). This could be servants (as in the case of Rebekah and Leah), or land or property.

The wedding This took place when the bridegroom had the new home ready. With his friends, he went to his bride's house in the evening. She was waiting, veiled and in her wedding dress. She wore jewellery which the bridegroom had given her. Sometimes he gave her a head-band of coins. (It may have been one of these coins which was lost in the 'lost coin' story–told by Jesus–Luke 15:8.) In a simple ceremony, the veil was taken from the bride's face and laid on the bridegroom's shoulder. The bridegroom, his 'best man' (called a 'companion') and his friends (called the sons of the bridechamber) then took the bride back to his own or his parents' home for a wedding feast to which all their friends were invited. The friends waited at the roadside in their best clothes and went in torch-light procession to the new home, sometimes with music and dancing.

The law of Moses allowed a man to divorce his wife. But he had to write out divorce papers which gave the woman her freedom before he sent her away. In New Testament times the Jewish teachers often argued about the reasons for divorce. Some allowed divorce for anything which displeased the husband– even poor cooking! Others believed there must be a serious moral lapse, such as adultery. But, typically, there was a different standard for women. A wife could never divorce her husband, though under certain circumstances she could force him to divorce her.

When questioned about divorce, Jesus firmly reinstated the principle of God's original design for marriage. Paul, too, underlined the same point that in marriage two people become 'one flesh'.
Genesis 1:26-31; 2:7, 18-25; Deuteronomy 24:1-4 and Matthew 19:3-12; Proverbs 5:15-20; 12:4; 18:22; 19:13-14; 21:9, 19; 25:24; 31:10-31; 1 Corinthians 7; Ephesians 5:22-33; 1 Peter 3:1-7
Passages reflecting wedding customs: Genesis 24; 29; Judges 14; Matthew 22:2-14; 25:1-12; Luke 14:7-14; John 3:1-10; Revelation 21:2

Martha
The sister of Mary and Lazarus. She lived at the village of Bethany, close to Jerusalem. Jesus often visited their home. When Lazarus was ill the sisters sent for Jesus. Their brother died before Jesus came. Martha went to meet Jesus and said, 'If you had been here, my brother would not have died.' Jesus replied, 'I am the resurrection and I am life...Do you believe this?' 'Lord, I do,' Martha answered. And to her great joy, Jesus restored her brother to life.
Luke 10:38-42; John 11:20ff.

Mary
1. Jesus' mother. While she was engaged to Joseph, a carpenter, an angel told her she was to be the mother of Jesus, the Messiah and Son of God. Before Jesus was born, Mary visited her cousin Elizabeth. There Mary spoke the wonderful song of praise to God known as the *Magnificat.* Mary and Joseph went from Nazareth to Bethlehem to register for a Roman census. There Jesus was born. When the shepherds came, with their story of angels singing, 'Mary remembered all these things and thought deeply about them.' When Jesus was presented at the temple, a few days later, Simeon spoke to Mary about the future: 'Sorrow, like a sharp sword, will break your own heart.' While Jesus was still a baby, Mary and Joseph took him to Egypt because King Herod wanted to kill this rival. After Herod's death they returned to Nazareth.

When Jesus was twelve his parents took him to the temple for the Passover Festival. They were terribly worried when he stayed behind, alone, to talk with the teachers. Mary was with Jesus when he worked his first miracle at the wedding feast in Cana. At his crucifixion she stood by the cross, and Jesus asked one of his disciples (see *John*) to look after her. Mary was with the disciples when they met together to pray after Jesus' ascension.
Matthew 1:18-25; 2:11; 13:55; Luke 1–2; John 2:1ff.; 19:25-27; Acts 1:14
2. Sister of Martha. She lived in Bethany with her sister and brother Lazarus and loved to listen to Jesus. Just before Jesus' death she anointed him with precious oil and wiped his feet with her hair. (See also *Martha, Lazarus.*)
Luke 10:38-42; John 11; 12:3ff.
3. Mary Magdalene became a disciple of Jesus after he had healed her. She was the first person to see Jesus after the resurrection and ran to tell the apostles.
Mark 16:9; Luke 8:2; 24:10; John 20:1ff.
4. Mary, mother of James and Joseph. She was present at the crucifixion and was one of the group of women who found Jesus' tomb empty on the resurrection morning. This Mary is probably the same person as 'the other Mary' and Mary, wife of Clopas.
Matthew 27:56, 61; 28:1; John 19:25
5. Mary, the mother of John Mark. The first Christians met in her house in Jerusalem.
Acts 12:12

Matthew
One of the twelve apostles, and traditionally writer of the first Gospel. Matthew, also called Levi, was a tax collector before Jesus said to him, 'Follow me.'
Matthew 9:9; 10:3; Luke 5:27-32

Matthew's Gospel
There are four 'Gospels', telling the story of the life and teaching of Jesus. Each has its own special purpose. The Gospel of Matthew was written, in the first place, particularly for the Jews. It tells the good news that Jesus is the promised Saviour–the Messiah, or Christ, whom the Jews had been expecting for so long. With Jesus, all the promises God had made to his people in the Old Testament came true.

The Gospel does not give the name of its author. From very early on Matthew has been accepted as its writer. He was the tax collector who became one of Jesus' twelve close friends. If he did not write it all, he was almost certainly the author of a collection of Jesus' sayings included in the book. Matthew's Gospel was written some time between AD 50 and 100. Much of it is very similar to the story in Mark's Gospel. But there are ten parables and a number of incidents which come only in Matthew.

Matthew opens with the family tree and birth of Jesus (chapters 1–2). After describing John the Baptist's work, it records Jesus' baptism and his time of testing in the desert (chapters 3–4).

A large part of Matthew is taken up with Jesus' preaching, teaching and healing in Galilee. Matthew shows Jesus as a great teacher, with much to say about God's 'kingdom'–his reign in the world (chapters 4; 12–18). This teaching is presented in five main sections:

Chapters 5–7: the Sermon on the Mount. This answers many questions about the kingdom and gives us the basis of Jesus' teaching on moral questions.

Chapter 10: Jesus' instructions to his twelve disciples before sending them out.

Chapter 13: parables about the kingdom.

Chapter 18: Jesus' explanation about what it means to follow him.

Chapters 24–25: Jesus' words about the fall of Jerusalem, the end of this age, and the coming of a new age.

Matthew then describes Jesus' journey from Galilee to Jerusalem (chapters 19–20) and the events of his last week in that city (chapters 21–27). The account of Jesus' death on the cross is followed by the account of how he came back to life–the resurrection (chapter 28).

Matthias
Chosen by the disciples after the death of Judas Iscariot to take the traitor's place as one of the twelve.
Acts 1:21-26

Meals
In the peasant home, meals were very simple. There was no formal breakfast. If anything was eaten at all, it was as a snack carried and eaten on the way to work. The mid-day meal was usually bread and olives, and perhaps fruit. The evening meal was a vegetable stew, with a piece of bread used as a spoon to dip into the common pot. The whole family ate together for this meal, and if any important guests were present, meat might be added to the cooking-pot. The family sat on the floor to eat.

In a wealthy home it was different. There was more elaborate food with plenty of meat. In New Testament times guests reclined on couches round three sides of a square table. Instead of one dish, there were many.

A Roman, or Roman-style, dinner party followed this pattern: first came the hors d'oeuvres, and wine mixed with honey. Next, three main courses were served on trays. The guests ate with their fingers, though they used a spoon for things like soup! After this course, at a Roman meal, pieces of food were thrown into the fire as a token 'sacrifice'–a kind of 'grace'. Finally pastries and fruit were served as dessert. This was followed by drinks and entertainment. The 'religious' element–the offering to the gods–was one of the reasons why a Jew could never eat with a Gentile. The strict Jewish food-laws was another (see above). But God showed Peter in a vision that the old barriers between Jew and non-Jew must be broken down: Christians, whatever their nationality, belong to one family.

Among the nomadic, tent-dwelling people, a traveller was always welcome to stay–for three days and four hours!–the length of time the hosts believed their food sustained their guest. Flat loaves of bread, and milk, were basic to the meal. For the time of his stay the traveller became one of the clan. Both Old and New Testaments teach the importance of hospitality. As the author of the letter to the Hebrews writes: 'Remember to welcome strangers in your homes' (Hebrews 13:2).

Measures

See *Weights and Measures.*

Medes

The head of a Median noble, carved on the stairway of Darius' palace at Persepolis, Iran.

In north-west Persia, Assyrian kings met Median tribes from the ninth century BC onwards. They were on fairly good terms for two hundred years. Then the Medes joined with the Scythians, in alliance with Babylon, to bring about the downfall of Assyria (612 BC). The Medes had already been under Scythian pressure for some decades. But this time the Median king, Cyaxares, had built up his own strength, and was able to extend his rule as far as the Lydian frontier in Turkey, and over the Persians to his south.

Astyages, next king of the Medes, was overthrown by his son-in-law, Cyrus the Persian, in 549 BC. Media then became a province of the new Persian Empire. They played their part in the fall of Babylon. Media's capital, Ecbatana (modern Hamadan) became the Persian capital. Median officers held high positions in the Persian court, and Median words were adopted into Persian. Median influence was so strong in the Persian Empire that we find the joint phrase 'Medes and Persians' being used. And the Greeks called their great Persian war 'the war with the Medes'.

One tribe of Medes, the Magi, had a special religious position (like that of the Levites in Israel).
Jeremiah 25:25; 51:11, 28; Daniel 5:28

Mediator

A 'go-between' who brings together (reconciles) two people who are estranged from each other.

When Adam first disobeyed God his sin broke the friendship between them. The Old Testament therefore recognizes the need for a mediator between man and God. The Old Testament prophets spoke in God's name and made God real to their hearers. The priest who offered sacrifices to God represented the people before God. Moses combined both roles as Israel's mediator.

But, important as Moses was, he could never be the perfect mediator between God and the people, because he shared the sinful nature of every human being. Only Jesus, who was both man, but sinless, and the Son of God could be the perfect mediator who arranges a new covenant. This is the main theme of the letter to the Hebrews.

See also *Reconciliation.*
Exodus 32:30-32; 33:11; Leviticus 16; Numbers 12:6-8; Deuteronomy 5:4-5; Galatians 3:19-20; 1 Timothy 2:5; Hebrews 7:24-25; 8:6; 9:15; 12:24

Medicine

Even where symptoms are described in the Bible, it is not always possible to be sure what diseases were involved. Some form of leprosy was fairly common. Shortage of food in drought, combined with the heat and poor water supply, often led to dysentery, cholera, typhoid and beriberi ('dropsy'). The dust-filled air made blindness very common. Then there were the deaf and the crippled. The number of deaths among children was clearly quite high.

Mental illness was not uncommon. But the Bible often does not make any distinction between this and being possessed by evil spirits. There may also have been a popular belief that 'fits' could be caused by the moon. (In Matthew 4:24, 'epileptic' translates a word which literally means 'moonstruck'.)
2 Samuel 12:15; 2 Kings 4:20; 1 Kings 17:17; 2 Kings 5:1-14; 1 Samuel 19:9; Daniel 4:33

Attitudes to disease The attitude to illness in Israel was always quite distinct from that of Israel's neighbours. The Mesopotamians and the Egyptians in early times regarded illness as invariably caused by the malice of evil spirits. Treatment was therefore in the hands of exorcist-priests and involved incantations and magic, alongside other methods. Israel also regarded health as a religious matter, but this was because the people firmly believed that God was all-powerful. From him came both good and evil. Health was a divine blessing. Disease was a sign that the spiritual relationship between a person and God had broken down. Magic was therefore officially forbidden, although no doubt the ordinary people practised it to some extent. The discovery of many small images, probably used as charms, seems to indicate this.

This attitude to illness, however, also had its drawbacks. God was the only true healer. He had given his people a set of rules. If they obeyed, they would enjoy good health. If they disobeyed, they would not. Occasionally God would use his prophets as healers. But this was exceptional and there was no recognized place for doctors, no reason to explore the physical causes of disease, and little place for medical skills.

The Babylonian king, Hammurabi, had drawn up a code of laws in about 1750 BC. It fixed doctors' fees, and set out penalties for surgeons who were careless in performing operations. The Egyptians were also doing surgery, studying anatomy by dissecting dead bodies, and writing medical and surgical notes on papyrus. But this was unthinkable in Israel. The first reference to doctors in the Bible is critical: 'Asa was crippled by a severe foot disease; but even then he did not turn to the Lord for help, but to doctors.' The Book of Job, however, challenges the view that disease is always the direct result of a person's sin.

By the second century BC the prestige of doctors had increased. In Ecclesiasticus it is said that although God is the healer, he has given gifts of healing to men and has provided medicines for the cure of illness. Jesus resisted the view that it is specific sin which always causes illness. He saw disease as evidence of the power of evil in the world as a whole. In healing diseases he was attacking the kingdom of Satan, but this implied no criticism of the work of doctors. General attitudes, however, were hard to change, as certain recorded Jewish sayings show. 'Physician, heal yourself.' 'Live not in a city whose chief is a medical man, for he will attend to public business and neglect his patients.' 'Even the best among doctors is deserving of Gehenna' (hell).
Leviticus 26:14-16; Deuteronomy 7:12-15; 2 Chronicles 16:12; John 9:3; Luke 13:16; Mark 2:17; Luke 4:23

Treatment of disease It is interesting to notice how Israel's laws compensated for their general ignorance about hygiene. To obey these laws was part of their religious duty, but obedience obviously contributed to keeping them healthy as well.

First there must be one day of complete rest each week for physical and spiritual refreshment.

Then there were certain foods which must not be eaten. This included pork which, in a subtropical climate, carries a high risk of food poisoning. And water must be free from contamination.

All males must be circumcised–an operation believed to prevent venereal disease.

A man must not marry members of his own family.

Careful attention must be paid to cleanliness, in daily personal habits and in sexual relationships.

This is the earliest evidence we have of preventive medicine. The priests were expected to enforce these laws and to take special action in the case of 'leprosy' (though this may not have been the leprosy which we know today).

The prophets occasionally concerned themselves with health. Elisha neutralized poisonous herbs, purified the water of Jericho, and helped to cure Naaman and the Shunammite woman's son. In 2 Kings 20:1-7 Isaiah advises Hezekiah to apply a poultice of figs to a boil–the only real 'prescription' in the Old Testament.

Various oils and perfumes were used in personal hygiene–myrtle, saffron, myrrh and spikenard. Olive oil and 'balm of Gilead' (a spicy resin) were swallowed or put on wounds and sores. Isaiah's description of Judah throws light on the treatment of wounds: 'You are covered with bruises and sores and open wounds. Your wounds have not been cleaned or bandaged. No ointment has been put on them.' Certain herbs may have been used as painkillers, for example the 'wine mixed with a drug called myrrh' offered to Jesus on the cross. Many effective herbs must have been known, but there must also have been a good deal of superstition. It was widely believed, for example, that mandrake roots would help women to conceive children.

Broken arms and legs were bound up tightly and crutches may have been used. But there is no evidence of radical surgery being done in Old Testament times in Israel, except for the discovery of three skulls in eighth-century Lachish, with holes bored in them. This kind of operation was widespread to relieve pressure (or release demons).

There were, of course, Israelite midwives from the very earliest times. Even before the exodus they may have formed a kind of guild, with their own code of ethics and recognized leaders (two are named in Exodus 1:15). Mothers sometimes died in childbirth, but often the midwife was very skilled. Tamar successfully gave birth to twins who seem to have been locked in a difficult position (Genesis 38:27-30). Ezekiel, speaking about Jerusalem, throws light on what was normally done after a birth: 'When you were born, no one cut your umbilical cord or rubbed you with salt or wrapped you in a cloth.' Midwifery was perhaps the only honourable public duty in which a woman could be employed.
Exodus 20:8; Leviticus 11:13-23; 2 Kings 4:41; 2:19-22; 5; 4:18-37; Jeremiah 8:22; Luke 10:34; Isaiah 1:6; Mark 15:23; Genesis 30:14; Ezekiel 30:21; 16:4

New Testament times In Greece, medicine and surgery had become a highly developed skill, though still mixed with a certain amount of magic. It was the Greek, Hippocrates, who laid down the principles that the life and welfare of the patient should be the doctor's first consideration; that male doctors should not take advantage of women patients, or procure abortions; and that they should not reveal confidential information. At one time state doctors were employed, paid a salary and gave free medical attention.

Hippocrates, the Greek doctor who laid down principles for the practice of medicine. He lived from about 460 to 377 BC.

The Romans later adopted some of these practices. Surgical instruments and prescription labels have been found in excavations of Roman cities, and there was a school of medicine at Alexandria in Egypt. Paul's companion, Luke, was a doctor. The language he uses in Luke and Acts sometimes includes technical Greek medical expressions.

In Palestine itself the rabbis required that every town should have a physician and preferably a surgeon, too (the woman with the haemorrhage who came to Jesus had been to many doctors). There was always a doctor among the temple officials. His work was to look after the priests, who worked barefoot and were naturally liable to catch certain diseases.

Dentistry was practised even among the ancient Egyptians (some of the mummies have gold-filled teeth!), and the Greek historian, Herodotus, tells us that in 500 BC the Phoenicians were making false teeth. There is no evidence of such a practice in Israel.
Colossians 4:14; Luke 5:12; 13:11; 14:2; Acts 12:23; Mark 5:26

Megiddo

An important Old Testament city on the edge of the plain of Jezreel, guarding the main pass through the Carmel hills. About 20 miles/32 km from modern Haifa. So many battles took place here that the New Testament (Revelation 16:16) uses the name symbolically for the site of the great last battle: 'Armageddon', 'the hill of Megiddo'.

Joshua defeated the Canaanite king of Megiddo when the Israelites conquered Canaan. It was given to the tribe of Manasseh. They made the Canaanites who lived at Megiddo work for them, but did not drive them out. King Solomon chose Megiddo, with Hazor and Gezer, to be one of his main fortified cities, with stabling for large numbers of horses and chariots. King Ahaziah of Judah died at Megiddo after being wounded by Jehu's men. So too did King Josiah, attempting to stop the advance of Pharaoh Neco of Egypt.

Archaeologists have discovered twenty main levels of settlement on a mound now 70ft/21m high and covering, at the top, an area of more than 10 acres. The earliest settlement goes back to before 3000 BC. Excavation has uncovered, among other things, a Canaanite 'high place'; the city's water supply system; a fortified gateway built to the same pattern as others at Gezer and Hazor; a hoard of carved ivory objects; and a series of stables (probably from King Ahab's time).
Joshua 12:21; Judges 1:27-28; 5:19; 1 Kings 9:15; 2 Kings 9:27; 23:29

This remarkable seal, discovered at Megiddo, is carved with a roaring lion and inscribed 'Shema, the servant of Jeroboam'.

Melchizedek

A king and priest of God Most High at Salem (Jerusalem) who met and blessed Abraham after a battle. In the New Testament letter to the Hebrews Jesus is called a high priest 'for ever, in the line of succession to Melchizedek'. Like Melchizedek, Jesus is both king and priest–king of God's kingdom and a priest because he offered the sacrifice of his own life.
Genesis 14:18-20; Psalm 110:4; Hebrews 5:6-10

Memphis

The ancient capital of Egypt, on the River Nile not far south of modern Cairo. The pyramids at Giza are also near to Memphis. The city remained important for many centuries, up to the time of Alexander the Great. Several of the Old Testament prophets refer to Memphis when they condemn Israel's trust in Egypt.
Isaiah 19:13; Jeremiah 2:16; 46:14; Ezekiel 30:13

Menahem

One of the last kings of Israel (752–742 BC). When King Shallum had reigned for only one month Menahem killed him and made himself king instead. Menahem was a cruel and wicked king who worshipped idols. During his reign Tiglath-pileser III (Pul) of Assyria invaded Israel. Menahem paid the Assyrians a large sum of money to continue as king.
2 Kings 15:14-22

Mephibosheth

The son of Jonathan, David's great friend, and grandson of King Saul. When David was king he gave Mephibosheth a place at the palace and servants to wait on him.
2 Samuel 4:4; 9; 16:1ff.; 19:24-30; 21:7

Merab

A daughter of King Saul. Saul promised David he could marry her, but gave her to another man instead.
1 Samuel 14:49; 18:17ff.

Merari

One of Levi's sons. His descendants, the Merarites, formed one of the three groups of Levites.
Exodus 6:16ff.; Numbers 3

Mercy

The Hebrew word often translated 'mercy' occurs nearly 250 times in the Old Testament. It refers to God's loving patience with the people of Israel, his kindness and readiness to forgive. God had made his covenant-agreement with them, and although they often broke their side of the agreement, he did not disown them. He is faithful and has 'mercy' on them. Some English versions translate the word 'loving kindness'.

In the New Testament, 'mercy' is a loving pity for those in need. God is 'the merciful Father, the God from whom all help comes'. It is because of his mercy that we are saved. Jesus

himself was often moved with pity to respond to the needs of those around him. Christians are expected to show to other people the same mercy which they have experienced from God himself.
Exodus 34:6-7; Deuteronomy 7:9; Nehemiah 9:7, 31; Psalms 23:6; 25:6; 40:11; 51:1; 103:4, 8; Daniel 9:9; Jonah 4:2; Micah 6:8; Matthew 5:7; Luke 6:36; 18:13; Romans 9:15; 12:1; 2 Corinthians 1:3; Ephesians 2:4

Merodach-Baladan
A king of Babylon (in Babylonian, Marduk-apla-iddina II) who sent messengers to King Hezekiah in Jerusalem. Merodach-Baladan hoped to make Hezekiah join with Babylon against Assyria.
Isaiah 39

King Merodach-Baladan (on the left) granting land to an official; from a Babylonian boundary stone.

Meshach
See *Abednego.*

Mesopotamia
The land between the Tigris and Euphrates rivers. Harran and Paddan-aram, where some of Abraham's family settled, are in Mesopotamia. It was the home of Balaam, the prophet who was sent to curse the Israelites, and the country ruled by Cushan-rishathaim at the time of the Judges.

People from Mesopotamia were in Jerusalem on the Day of Pentecost and heard Peter and the apostles speak to them in their own languages.
Genesis 24:10; Deuteronomy 23:4 and Numbers 22; Judges 3:8, 10; Acts 2:9

Messiah
'Messiah' and 'Christ' both mean the 'anointed one'–Messiah is the Hebrew word and Christ is the Greek equivalent.

Throughout the troublesome history of the nation of Israel the hope gradually grew that God would one day send a great Messiah-king to establish his universal and everlasting kingdom. By the time of Jesus many Jews were longing for that day to come. So when they heard of his teaching and miracles they asked, 'Is he the Messiah?'

The New Testament shows plainly that the first Christians identified Jesus as the Messiah. At his baptism, 'God poured out on (anointed) Jesus of Nazareth the Holy Spirit and power.' Afterwards he applied to himself the prophecy of Isaiah that 'the time has come when the Lord will save his people'. But Jesus normally avoided directly calling himself the Messiah because the people understood it in political terms. The Gospels tell of only one occasion on which Jesus claimed to be the Messiah–to a poor, sinful woman at a well. When Peter told Jesus, 'You are the Messiah', he was asked to keep it quiet. Jesus wanted genuine disciples; he was no 'rabble-rouser', out to make a name for himself.

However, when the Jewish authorities began to put the pressure on Jesus, the key question asked by the high priest at his trial was, 'Are you the Messiah, the Son of the Blessed God?' 'I am', answered Jesus, and the high priest, enraged by this 'blasphemy' (insult to God) secured a unanimous verdict of guilty. Jesus was sentenced to death.

The verdict of the New Testament is that the Jewish court made a mistake. Jesus *was* the Messiah–and God proved this by raising him to life again. As Peter declared on the Day of Pentecost, 'All the people of Israel, then, are to know for sure that this Jesus, whom you crucified is the one that God has made Lord and Messiah!' See also *Jesus Christ.*
Deuteronomy 18:15-22; Psalms 2; 45:6-7; 72; 110; Isaiah 9:2-7; 11; 42:1-9; 49:1-6; 52:13-53: 12; 61:1-3; Jeremiah 23:5-6; 33:14-16; Ezekiel 34:22-25; Daniel 7; Zechariah 9:9-10; Matthew 1:18, 22-23; 16:16, 20; 26:68; Mark 8:27-30; 14:61-64; Luke 2:11, 26; John 4:25-26; 7:26-27, 31, 41-42; 9:22; Acts 2:36; 3:20-21; 4:26-28; 10:38; 18:28; 26:22-23

Methuselah
Remembered as the oldest man who ever lived. He died, in the year of the flood, 969 years old.
Genesis 5:22-27

Micah
The prophet Micah lived about the same time as Isaiah, Amos and Hosea, in the eighth century BC. He brought a message for both Israel and Judah. Like Amos, Micah denounced the rulers, priests and prophets. He attacked them for exploiting the poor and helpless, for business frauds and sham religion. God's judgement would fall upon Samaria and Jerusalem.

But Micah also brought a message of hope. He promised that God would give worldwide peace; that a great king would come from the family of King David, bringing peace with him. In one verse Micah sums up much of the message of the prophets: 'what God requires of us is this: to do what is just, to show constant love, and live in humble fellowship with our God' (6:8).

Micaiah
A prophet who lived in the reign of King Ahab. When Ahab planned to fight a battle against the Syrians he asked many prophets if he was going to win. Four hundred prophesied success, and only Micaiah foretold defeat. Ahab was angry at this answer and threw Micaiah into prison, but his prediction came true.
1 Kings 22

Michael
An archangel described in Daniel as the guardian of the Jewish people.
Daniel 10:21; 12:1; Jude 9; Revelation 12:7

Michal
King Saul's younger daughter and David's wife. She helped David to escape from Saul and saved his life, but Saul gave her to another man.
1 Samuel 14:49; 18:20ff.; 25:44; 2 Samuel 3:13-16; 6:16ff.

Michmash
A place about 7 miles/11km north-east of Jerusalem, at a village still called Mukhmas. It was separated from Geba by a deep valley. But an important route, 'the passage of Michmash', crossed an easy part of the valley. The Philistines invaded Israel and camped in force at Michmash, threatening King Saul's capital at Gibeah. Jonathan and his armour-bearer surprised the Philistine garrison by climbing across from Geba at a steep place down the valley, and in the panic which followed Saul defeated the Philistines. Michmash was on the route by which the Assyrians approached Jerusalem from the north. It was reoccupied after the exile.
1 Samuel 13-14; Isaiah 10:28; Ezra 2:27; Nehemiah 7:31; 11:31

Midian
The Midianites lived south of Edom along the Red Sea coast, engaging in trade and riding in on camels to raid the settled lands. Moses met them in the Sinai Desert and married a Midianite wife. The Midianites were descendants of Abraham through his second wife, Keturah.
Genesis 37:28; Judges 6-8; Exodus 2:16ff.; 3:1; Genesis 25:1-6

Miletus
A sea-port on the west coast of present-day Turkey. Paul stayed at Miletus on his way to Jerusalem at the end of his third missionary journey. To save time, the elders from the church at Ephesus came to meet him there and heard his farewell message. At another time Paul, writing to Timothy, says that he had left his helper Trophimus at Miletus because he was ill.
Acts 20:15-38; 2 Timothy 4:20

Mining and metalwork
In Deuteronomy 8:9 Moses promises the Israelites that the land of Canaan will be rich. 'Its rocks have iron in them, and from its hills you can mine copper.' In fact these are the only two metals native to the region of Israel. Gold, silver, tin and lead had to be imported.

Gold and silver Gold was probably the first metal known to man, because it is found in a pure state and needs no complicated process to cast it. When the Israelites left Egypt, the Egyptians had been using gold for many centuries. They took ornaments of gold and silver with them out of Egypt. And they knew how to work these metals.

To make solid objects the metal was melted and poured into moulds. Exodus 32:4 describes Aaron taking ear-rings, melting them and pouring the gold into a mould to make a gold bull. Gold could also be beaten into sheets, to cover objects, or beaten into a particular shape. The different Hebrew words for gold in the Old Testament, usually translated 'pure gold', 'fine gold', and 'choice gold', may indicate differences in colour and quality, but the exact meanings are unknown.

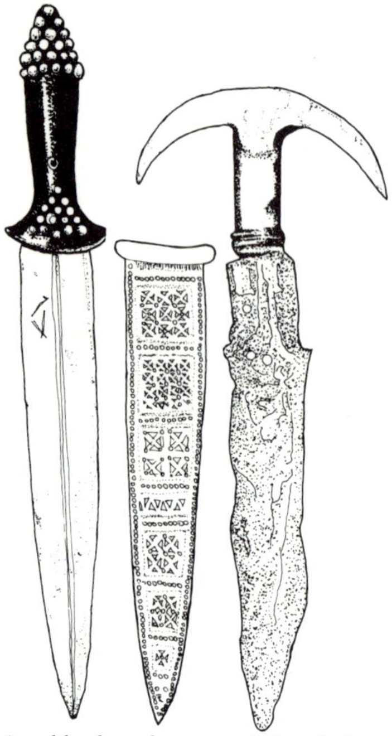

A gold adze, dagger and sheath from about 2600 BC, found in the Royal Graves at Ur.

When the Israelites entered the land of Canaan, gold and silver formed part of the spoils of war. Craftsmen probably made ornaments and jewellery for those who could afford them and, in times of religious decline, they adopted the practices of the surrounding nations and made idols of silver or overlaid with gold. (This custom was strongly criticized by the prophets.) Israelite craftsmen cannot have been very experienced. When Solomon needed intricate gold and silver work for the temple and other buildings, he employed experts from Phoenicia. He imported gold from 'Ophir' and is said to have made silver 'as common in Jerusalem as stone'.

The process of refining gold and silver–melting it to separate off the impurities–is often used in the Bible as a picture of the purifying effects of suffering.
Exodus 11:2; 32:4; 25:11, 31; Joshua 6:19; 22:8; Judges 17:1-4; Isaiah 2:20; 40:19; Hosea 8:4; 2 Chronicles 2:7; 1 Kings 10:1-27; Zechariah 13:9; Malachi 3:2-3; 1 Peter 1:7

Copper Copper was the most plentiful metal in early Israel. It was extracted from ore by heating (smelting) and, although the metal was rather spongy, it could be hardened and shaped by cold hammering. At some time before 2000 BC it had been discovered that if up to four per cent of tin was added, the copper was stronger and harder. Its melting-point was also lower, and it could be poured into a mould and cast into shape. The result is bronze. However, the Hebrew words for copper and bronze are the same, so it is not clear when the Israelites began to make bronze. It would certainly have been needed for the finely shaped work of Solomon's temple–the great bronze basin ('sea'), resting on twelve bronze bull-calves, and the bronze pillars whose tops were decorated with lilies and pomegranates.

Copper ore is to be found in the Sinai peninsula and in the Arabah, the desert area between the Dead Sea and the Gulf of Aqaba. Archaeology has shown that this area was being mined while the Israelites were in Egypt, and even much earlier. There is a site at Timnah, fifteen miles north of Elath, where the underground shafts penetrate for hundreds of yards in all directions and at several levels. The deeper workings are hundreds of feet below the surface, and ventilated through air channels.

Job 28 describes the work of mining for silver and, although they did not mine silver in Israel, the picture applies equally to mining for copper and iron. 'They search the depths of the earth and dig for rocks in the darkness. Men dig the shafts of mines. There they work in loneliness, clinging to ropes in the pits.'

Some have suggested that the Israelites learned the art of smelting and working copper from the Kenites (or Midianites), the desert tribe into which Moses married. Another suggestion is that there were travelling tinkers or smiths attached to communities from an early period. An Egyptian tomb-painting shows a group of Asiatics with what seem to be goatskin bellows.

A furnace from the Judges period has been found at Bethshemesh. Here copper was smelted on a small scale, and the heat was intensified, probably through pottery blowpipes or bellows.

Other furnaces dating from the time of Solomon have been found in Israel, some for treating copper, others for iron. The smiths would receive the metal, melt it in a clay pot over the fire and then shape the articles, sometimes using stone moulds. Their main products were for army and home use: arrow-heads, lances and spear-tips, swords, daggers, axes, plough-points, adzes, chisels, needles, safety pins, tweezers, bracelets, bowls and pails.

It is not clear how much mining and smelting activity went on in Solomon's time. At one time archaeologists thought that there had been a minor 'industrial revolution'. They had discovered a number of mining sites and small smelting furnaces in the Arabah. The furnaces were of different shapes–some round, some square and some with two compartments. There were also traces of encampments, where the workers, probably slaves, lived. Brick buildings discovered at a site at the head of the Gulf of Aqaba were identified with the town the Bible calls Ezion-geber. They were thought to belong to a giant smelting-plant to which copper was sent to be prepared for export, after the initial smelting on the site.

But these proposals are now seriously doubted. More recent excavations have shown that the most impressive mining works were used only at a much earlier period, even before the conquest of Canaan–while the brick buildings may have been a large fortified inn on an important trade-route.

Iron The use of iron spread very slowly in Israel. It needed to be heated as it was being worked, and so was difficult to produce. When the Israelites entered Canaan, the Canaanites already had chariots with iron fittings and other equipment. This put the Israelites at a disadvantage.

When the Philistines defeated the Israelites in the days of Samuel and Saul, they would not let them have blacksmiths of their own in case they made strong swords and spears. If the Israelites wanted their copper tools sharpened or repaired they had to go to the Philistines, who charged crippling prices. David, however, had great stores of iron. He 'supplied a large amount of iron for making nails and clamps'. And, from this time on, iron objects became more plentiful. Iron ore was also discovered and mined in the Arabah.
Joshua 17:16; 1 Samuel 13:19-22; 1 Chronicles 22:3

The New Testament period In New Testament times there was a smiths' bazaar in Jerusalem. But workers in bronze and iron were not allowed to work on certain religious feast days because of the noise they made. The extravagances of King Herod's court meant an increased trade in luxury goods.

In the temple that Herod built in Jerusalem the double gate, thresholds and lintel were overlaid with gold and silver. The walls inside were covered with gold plating. There were gold and silver lamps and bowls and there were even spikes of gold on the roof to keep the birds away! A thousand priests had to be trained to do much of this work, because no one else was allowed to enter the sacred temple area.

Miracles

One of the striking things about Jesus' life and work is the fact that he did miracles. Even his enemies agreed on this. The miracles described in the Gospels range from curing physical illnesses and casting out devils to calming a storm and bringing the dead back to life.

The miracles are sometimes described as 'mighty works'. They are done through the power of God. The most important display of God's power, the greatest miracle, is the resurrection of Jesus.

Jesus' miracles are also called 'wonders'. They often amazed those who saw them. But Jesus did not want to be seen as a mere wonder-worker. This was why he refused to jump from the highest point of the temple, as the devil suggested in his temptations. Jesus did not want people to follow him just to see his miracles. So he often told the people he cured to tell no one about it.

John's Gospel makes it plain that Jesus' miracles were above all 'signs'. They were signs that he was the Messiah, signs that the new age, the kingdom, had really come. When John the Baptist wanted to know if Jesus really was the Messiah he was told of the miracles Jesus did and left to draw his own conclusions. By doing miracles Jesus was showing people the kingdom of God. He was giving examples of the fact that in the new age sin and death and sickness would be no more.

Jesus gave his disciples power to do miracles. They continued to heal in the power of Jesus after Pentecost, and miracles remained part of the experience of the early church. One of the 'gifts of the Spirit' mentioned by Paul is the working of miracles, another the gift of healing. But the one who heals is always God himself, never the Christian, or the church.
Mark 10:27; Romans 1:4; Matthew 4:5-7; 11:2-6, 20-21; Luke 9:1; Acts 3:6; Galatians 3:5; 1 Corinthians 12:9-10
Jesus' healings: Matthew 8:2-3, 5-13, 14-15, 28-34; 9:2-7, 20-22, 27-31, 32-33; 12:10-13, 22; 15:21-28; 17:14-18; 20:29-34; Mark 1:23-26; 7:31-37; 8:22-26; Luke 13:11-13; 14:1-4; 17:11-19; 22:50-51; John 4:46-54; 5:1-9; 9
Jesus' command over the forces of nature: Matthew 8:23-27; 14:25, 15-21; 15:32-38; 17:24-27; 21:18-22; Mark 11:20-26; Luke 5:1-11; John 2:1-11; 21:1-11
Jesus brings the dead to life: Matthew 9:18-19, 23-25; Luke 7:11-15; John 11:1-44
Some Old Testament miracles: Exodus 14; Joshua 2; 1 Kings 17:17-24; 2 Kings 2; 4-5; Daniel 6 and many other passages

Miriam
Sister of Moses and Aaron. She watched over her baby brother Moses in the reed basket until he was found by the daughter of Pharaoh. After the Israelites had crossed the Red Sea, Miriam led the woman, singing and dancing for joy. Later she quarrelled with Moses, because she was jealous of him as leader. For a short time, as punishment, she suffered a terrible skin disease. But Moses asked God to heal her. Miriam died at Kadesh before the Israelites reached Canaan.
Exodus 2:4, 7-8; 15:20-21; Numbers 12; 20:1

Mitylene
The most important city and port on the Greek island of Lesbos, off the west coast of Asia Minor (Turkey). Paul stopped there overnight on his last voyage to Jerusalem.
Acts 20:14

Mizpah/Mizpeh
The name (meaning 'watchtower') of a number of different places. When Jacob and Laban made a peace agreement they called the place Mizpah. A Mizpah in Gilead (perhaps the same as Ramoth-gilead) features in the story of Jephthah, at the time of the Judges.

The most important Mizpah is a town a few miles north of Jerusalem. The Israelites met together here at the time of Samuel and the Judges. The town was on Samuel's circuit as a Judge. And at Mizpah he presented Saul to the people as their king. Later, King Asa of Judah fortified the town. After Jerusalem fell to the Babylonians the governor, Gedaliah, lived at Mizpah.
Genesis 31:44-49; Judges 10:17; 11; 20:1; 1 Samuel 7:5-16; 10:17; 1 Kings 15:22; 2 Kings 25:23

Moab
The Moabites lived south of the River Arnon, a river which flows into the east side of the Dead Sea. These people, related to Israel and Ammon–through Lot, Genesis 19:37–would not let Israel pass through their land when they wanted to reach Canaan. And they constantly harassed the Israelites for much of the Old Testament period. Moab is listed among the countries attacked by Ramesses II of Egypt (about 1283 BC). The city of Dibon was taken. Here, much later, King Mesha recorded his triumph over Israel on a famous stone (the Moabite Stone). The inscription shows that his language was similar to Hebrew. His belief that his god (Chemosh) acted in history was also very much like Israel's belief.
Numbers 21; Judges 11:17; 3:12-30; 1 Samuel 14:47; 2 Samuel 8:2, 12; 2 Kings 13:20; 24:2; 1:1; 3:4-27

Money
Money as we know it was first used in Bible lands in the eighth century BC, in Lydia (part of modern Turkey). Early coins were made of electrum (an alloy of silver and gold) and the weight of the metal was guaranteed by the stamp on the coin. From this time on the Jewish people rarely had their independence. They were exiled to Babylon, then subject to Persia, Greece and Rome–so not many Jewish coins were minted.

In the Greek period, coins were issued from Acco, on the coast of Israel. Roman coins were used throughout the Empire. The only Jewish coins minted were the small bronze coins first allowed by the Seleucid kings (the Syrian Empire which followed the death of Alexander the Great). The Jewish leaders (Hasmoneans) in Jerusalem coined these to their own designs. At the time of the rebellion against the Romans in AD 66 the Jews minted their first coins in silver. There were so many different coins about, that it was necessary for the buyer and the seller to know their equivalent values.

Old Testament gold and silver coins
Shekel (approx. 11.4 gm)
Mina (approx. 500 gm) = 50 shekels
Talent (30 kg) = 60 minas

New Testament coins There were three different currencies used in Palestine in New Testament times. There was the official, imperial money (Roman standard); provincial money minted at Antioch and Tyre (Greek standard); and local Jewish money which may have been minted at Caesarea. Money for the temple (including the half-shekel tax) had to be paid in the Tyrian coinage (the 2-drachma piece), not Roman. It is not surprising that money-changers flourished! Money was coined in gold, silver, copper and bronze or brass. The commonest silver coins mentioned in the New Testament are the Greek *tetradrachma*, and Roman *denarius*, which was a day's wage for the ordinary working man.

Jewish coins
lepton (bronze)
shekel
Greek coins
drachma (silver)
stater (or tetradrachma) (silver)
mina
Roman coins
quadrans
as (bronze) = 4 quadrans
denarius (silver) = 16 as
aureus (gold)

1 Jewish **shekel** = 1 Greek stater (tetradrachma) = 4 Roman denarii
30 Jewish **shekels** = 1 Greek mina = 100 Roman denarii

Mordecai
Esther's cousin and guardian. Mordecai was a Jew who lived in Susa, capital of Persia. When he heard about a plot to kill all the Jews he persuaded Esther, then queen of Persia, to plead with King Ahasuerus to spare them. Mordecai afterwards became the king's chief minister. (See *Esther*.)
Esther

Moresheth/Moresheth-gath
The home town of the prophet Micah, probably near Mareshah in the low country south-west of Jerusalem.
Jeremiah 26:18; Micah 1:1, 14

Moriah
The mountains to which Abraham was told to go for the sacrifice of his son, Isaac. The writer of 2 Chronicles says that the site of Solomon's temple was 'in Jerusalem, on Mount Moriah'. (The Samaritans claimed that the place of Abraham's sacrifice was not Jerusalem, but Mt Gerizim.)
Genesis 22:2; 2 Chronicles 3:1

Moses
The great leader who freed the Israelites from slavery in Egypt and led them through the desert to the borders of Canaan. Moses was born in Egypt, brought up by the daughter of the king, and educated as an Egyptian. When he was grown up, Moses was so angry at the cruel way the Israelites were treated that he killed one of the Egyptian overseers. When Pharaoh heard about it, Moses was forced to escape from Egypt. He lived as a shepherd in the desert and married a daughter of Jethro, the man who gave him a home.

After forty years God appeared to Moses. He saw a desert bush which flamed but did not burn up, and knew God was speaking to him. God told him to go back to Egypt and ask Pharaoh to let his people go. Pharaoh refused, and the Egyptians suffered ten plagues. Then Pharaoh let Moses lead the Israelites out of Egypt. But he quickly changed his mind; the Egyptians pursued the Israelites as far as the Red Sea. The Israelites escaped into the desert but Pharaoh's army was drowned.

After three months the people reached Mt Sinai. Here Moses the leader became Moses the law-giver. God gave him the Ten Commandments and instructions for building the worship tent (tabernacle). Moses led the people on to the oasis at Kadesh. From there, spies were sent into Canaan. Ten came back with frightening tales. The people shouted and rebelled against Moses, forgetting the power of God. Because they rejected God they were condemned to wander in the desert until all those who rebelled had died. Moses gave God's law to the new generation before he handed on the leadership to Joshua. When he had blessed the people Moses climbed Mt Nebo so that he could see Canaan, the land he was not allowed to enter because of his own earlier disobedience. Moses was 120 years old when he died in the land of Moab.

At the transfiguration, when they saw Jesus' glory, the disciples also saw Moses and Elijah, the two great Old Testament leaders, talking with Jesus about his coming death.
Exodus 2–Deuteronomy 34;
Luke 9:28ff.

Mount of Olives

A 2,700ft/830m hill overlooking Jerusalem and its temple area from the east, across the Kidron Valley. In Jesus' day it was planted with olive trees.

King David passed this way when he fled from Jerusalem at the time of Absalom's rebellion. King Solomon built an altar for idols on the Mount of Olives. Later, during the exile, the prophet Ezekiel saw the dazzling light of God's glory leave Jerusalem and move to the Mount of Olives. The prophet Zechariah foresaw God, on the Day of Judgement, standing on the Mount, which would split in two.

When Jesus rode in triumph into Jerusalem he came from the Mount of Olives. Seeing the city from the Mount, he wept over its fate. When he stayed at Bethany on his visits to Jerusalem he must have walked into the city round the shoulder of the Mount of Olives. The Garden of Gethsemane, where he prayed on the night of his arrest, was on its lower slopes. From the Mount of Olives Jesus was taken up to heaven.
2 Samuel 15:30; 2 Kings 23:13; Ezekiel 11:23; Zechariah 14:4; Luke 19:29, 37, 41-44; 21:37; 22:39; Acts 1:12, etc.

Music

Music and dancing have been part of life in all cultures, as far back in history as we can go.

There were three kinds of instrument in Israel–string, wind and percussion. They played together in unison rather than in harmony. And the music seems to have been strongly rhythmic rather than melodic, although there were set tunes to some of the psalms. Because the description of the instruments is rather vague it is not possible to identify them all. But we *do* know something about the following:

Strings The *kinnor* is normally translated 'harp' in the Bible. It may have been a harp or a lyre. It was a small, eight- or ten-stringed instrument with a wooden frame, and could be carried about. We do not know if it was played simply by plucking, or if a plectrum was used. The *kinnor* may be the instrument shown on ancient tomb-paintings at Beni-Hasan in Egypt.

An Egyptian timbrel made from wood and painted skin.

The *nebel*, called a 'psaltery', was another stringed instrument in a wooden frame, played by plucking with the fingers. The word *nebel* means a 'skin bottle' or jar, which suggests a swollen soundbox like a lute. David was able to play both *kinnor* and *nebel*.

Wind The *halil* (pipe) was the ordinary person's hollow pipe, made of cane, wood or bone. *Halil* means 'to bore', and describes the way the instrument was made. A reed was used in the instrument, and the player carried spare reeds about in a bag.

The *geren* (cornet, horn) was made from the horn of an animal and was used as a trumpet. If the horn used was a ram's horn, the instrument was called a *shofar*, also translated trumpet in some versions of the Bible. It was used on religious and public occasions.

The *hazozra* was a metal trumpet, which in Bible times was made of silver. A continuous call on two silver trumpets was the sign to gather at the tabernacle. One was sounded to call the chiefs together.

Percussion The *menaanim* is a percussion instrument and was probably made of discs rattled along metal rods, suspended in a wooden frame.

Meziltaim are copper cymbals. They were used by Levites in the temple to mark the beginning, ending, and pauses in the chapters which were sung.

The *tof* was a percussion instrument with a membrane, and is called a 'timbrel' or tambourine in English versions. It was used to accompany singing and dancing. At the time of the exodus Aaron's sister Miriam 'took her tambourine, and all the women followed her, playing tambourines and dancing' (Exodus 15:20).

Unfortunately, because the Israelites were not allowed to portray human figures in their art, we do not know exactly how these instruments were played. But pictures of similar instruments from Egypt, Assyria and Babylonia give us a fair idea. Instruments were made from a wide variety of materials–cedar-wood, sandalwood, leather, gut, ivory, shell, gold and silver.

Music had an important place in the worship at the temple. 1 Chronicles 15:16-24 describes how David organized the temple choir and orchestra 'to sing and to play joyful music'. In the temple the singing was often in parts– one line of a section being sung by one group, and the next sung in response by another. Dancing, too, was often part of the people's joyful expression of worship. When the Covenant Box (the ark) was brought to Jerusalem 'David and all the people danced with all their might to honour God' (1 Chronicles 13:8).

Two sistrums and a pair of rattles in plaited cane, from Egypt.

Mustard

God's kingdom, Jesus said, is like the tiny mustard seed, which grows into a great plant. He was probably talking about the black mustard, whose seeds were grown for oil as well as flavouring. Usually about 4ft (120cm) high, these plants can grow to 15ft (460cm).
Matthew 13:31-32

Flowers and leaves of the mustard plant.

Myra

A port in Lycia, in the south-west of modern Turkey, where Paul and his party changed ships on his voyage to Rome. Myra was a regular port for the corn-fleet which carried grain to Rome from Egypt.
Acts 27:5

Myrrh

Pale yellow gum from a shrub which grows in Somalia, Ethiopia and Arabia. Used as a spice and a medicine, and in making the holy oil for the tabernacle and temple. Myrrh was brought to Jesus by the wise men. It was mixed with the drink offered to him on the cross as a pain-killer. And Joseph and Nicodemus later embalmed Jesus' body with myrrh and aloes.
Exodus 30:23-24; Matthew 2:11; Mark 15:23; John 19:39-40

Myrtle

An evergreen with fragrant leaves and sweet-scented white flowers which were used as perfume.

Mysia

A land in the north-west of Asia Minor (Turkey), forming part of the Roman province of Asia. Paul came to this district during his second missionary journey, but God prevented him from crossing the border from Asia into Bithynia. He passed through Mysia, travelling west, and came to Troas before it became clear where he should go next.
Acts 16:7-8

N

Naaman
The Syrian general cured of leprosy by the prophet Elisha.
2 Kings 5

Nabataea
After the time of Alexander the Great, the Nabataeans, an Arab tribe made their home in Edomite and Midianite territory, building up a strong kingdom by controlling the trade which brought incense from southern Arabia to Damascus and across to Gaza. For a few years they ruled Damascus (2 Corinthians 11:32) but were conquered by Trajan of Rome in AD 106. Their chief city was Petra.

Naboth
Owner of a vineyard in Jezreel next to King Ahab's palace. Ahab tried to buy the vineyard from Naboth, but he refused to sell. The king sulked at this. Jezebel, his wife, promised Ahab that she would get the vineyard for him. She bribed two informers to say that Naboth had cursed God and the king. Naboth was found guilty and stoned to death. Ahab had the vineyard–but God sent Elijah to tell him that because of this murder his whole family would be wiped out.
1 Kings 21

Nadab
Aaron's eldest son. He became a priest but died when he and Abihu, his brother, dishonoured God.
Exodus 6:23; Leviticus 10

Nahor
1. The father of Terah and grandfather of Abraham.
Genesis 11:22-25
2. Abraham's brother.
Genesis 11:26-29; 22:20ff.; 24:10ff.

Nahum
A prophet from Elkosh, probably in Judah. His name means 'comforter'

The Book of Nahum is a poem. The prophet Nahum predicts that Nineveh, capital of Israel's enemy, Assyria, will fall. The prophet rejoices in the judgement of God on a cruel and arrogant nation.

Nineveh fell to the Babylonians and Medes in 612 BC, and the book was probably written about that time.

Nain
A town near Nazareth in Galilee where Jesus restored a widow's son to life.
Luke 7:11

Naomi
The mother-in-law of Ruth. Naomi and her husband Elimelech came from Bethlehem. They had two sons, Mahlon and Chilion. The family moved to Moab because of a famine. There Mahlon and Chilion married Moabite girls. After her husband and sons had died, Naomi returned to Bethlehem and Ruth went with her. Naomi arranged for Ruth to marry Boaz. Their son was King David's grandfather. Naomi looked after the child as her own son.
Ruth

Naphtali
The fifth son of Jacob; father of the tribe of Naphtali. Also the name of the land belonging to the tribe, in Galilee.
Genesis 30:8; 49:21 Joshua 19:32-39

Nathan
Best-known of several Nathans is the prophet who lived in King David's reign. David told Nathan he wanted to build a temple for God. 'God says, not you, but your son will be the one to build,' Nathan answered. After David had taken Bathsheba from her husband and engineered his death, Nathan confronted David with his crime. When David was old, he ordered Nathan and Zadok the priest to anoint Solomon king.
2 Samuel 7; 12; 1 Kings 1;
1 Chronicles 17

Nathanael
One of Jesus' twelve apostles. He is mentioned only in John's Gospel but may be the disciple known in the other Gospels as Bartholomew. Nathanael heard about Jesus through Philip.
John 1:45ff.; 21:2

Nazareth
A town in Galilee, the home of Jesus' parents, Mary and Joseph. Jesus grew up in Nazareth but made his base in Capernaum when he began his public work. His teaching in the synagogue at Nazareth made the people so angry that they tried to kill him.

Nazareth was close to a number of important trade-routes, and so in contact with the wider world. There are rock-tombs at Nazareth dating from New Testament times, and similar to the Gospels' description of the grave in which Jesus himself was buried.
Luke 1:26; Matthew 2:22-23;
Luke 2:39, 51; Mark 1:9; Matthew 4:13; Luke 4:16-30; John 1:45-46, etc.

Houses built in traditional style in the town of Nazareth.

Neapolis
The port for Philippi, in Macedonia (northern Greece). This was the place where Paul first set foot in Europe, in answer to a call for help from Macedonia. He later sailed from here on his last voyage to Jerusalem. The place is modern Kavalla.
Acts 16:11; 20:6

Nebo
A mountain east of the north end of the Dead Sea, in Moab. Before he died, Moses climbed Mt Nebo and saw the whole of the Promised Land spread out before him. Jebel Osha (3640ft/1120m high) has a viewpoint from which it is possible to see as far north as Mt Hermon, as well as the Dead Sea and the Negev. This is probably Mt Nebo.
Deuteronomy 32:48-52; 34:1-5

Nebuchadnezzar/Nebuchadrezzar
King of Babylon 605–562 BC. He was the son of Nabopolassar who conquered the Assyrian Empire. Nebuchadnezzar led his father's army against the Egyptians and defeated them at Carchemish in 605 BC. Babylon gained control of the countries which had been subject to Egypt, including Judah. For three years Judah paid tax to Babylon. In 597 BC King Jehoiakim rebelled. Nebuchadnezzar attacked Jerusalem. He took Jehoiachin, who was now king, prisoner to Babylon along with the most important citizens. Nebuchadnezzar made Zedekiah king instead. When Zedekiah rebelled he besieged Jerusalem. The city was destroyed in 586 BC and the leaders of the people taken into exile in Babylon. Daniel was one of an earlier group of Jews taken captive. He was trained at Nebuchadnezzar's court. When he was able to explain the meaning of Nebuchadnezzar's dreams, he was made his chief adviser. Nebuchadnezzar's success made him proud. 'Look how great Babylon is. I built it as my capital city to display my power and might. But God humbled him through a strange madness. When his sanity returned, he was a changed man. 'Now I, Nebuchadnezzar, praise, honour and glorify the King of heaven,' he said.
2 Kings 24–25; 2 Chronicles 36; Jeremiah 21:2-52:30;
Ezekiel 26:7ff.; 29:18ff.; 30:10;
Daniel 1–4

Nebuzaradan
The captain of King Nebuchadnezzar's guard. Nebuzaradan was responsible for sending the Judeans into exile in Babylon after Nebuchadnezzar had captured Jerusalem. He burned down the temple and reduced the city to ruins. However, he carried out Nebuchadnezzar's command to treat Jeremiah kindly and let him stay in Judah.
2 Kings 25; Jeremiah 39ff.

Neco
See *Pharaoh.*

Negev
A dry scrubland and desert area in the far south of Israel. The Negev merges with the Sinai Desert on the way to Egypt. Abraham and Isaac camped in various places in the Negev. So too did the Israelites, before they settled in Canaan.
Genesis 20:1; 24:62; Numbers 13:17; 21:1; Isaiah 30:6

Nehemiah

Nehemiah, a Jewish exile, was given permission by the Persian king, Artaxerxes, to lead a group of Israelites back to Jerusalem in 445 BC. The Book of Nehemiah, written as his memoirs, shows him as a born leader, and a man who trusted God completely. For Nehemiah it was almost as natural to pray as it was to breathe.

The book can be divided into three parts.

Chapters 1–7: Nehemiah returns to Jerusalem. He inspires his people to rebuild the walls of the city against fierce opposition. He introduces much-needed religious reforms.

Chapters 8–10: Ezra reads the law of God to the people. They are deeply moved, confess their wrongdoing and turn afresh to God.

Chapters 11–13: Nehemiah's work as governor of Judah, appointed by the Persian emperor.

New birth

Long before the time of Jesus, the prophet Jeremiah had seen that men and women need to be completely remade from within if they are to have a renewed relationship with God. In his discussion with the Jewish leader Nicodemus, Jesus made the same point. He said that only a complete 'new birth' would allow people to make this fresh start.

This fundamental change occurs when a person becomes a Christian. 'When anyone is joined to Christ, he is a new being; the old is gone, the new has come.' Baptism is the outward sign of this new life. The new life is given by the Holy Spirit, the eternal life of God's kingdom, shared with others in the family of the church.

See also *Baptism*.

Psalm 51:10; Jeremiah 31:31-34; John 3:1-21; 2 Corinthians 5:17

New Moon

See *Feasts and Festivals*.

New Testament text

In the case of the Old Testament we have barely enough evidence for the text. With the New Testament we have almost too much! Scholars are faced with many thousands of different ancient manuscripts of the New Testament. They have to decide which of these are most trustworthy and which have preserved the most accurate version of the original.

The New Testament was originally written down in Greek. Scholars have many thousands of Greek manuscripts to which they can refer. In addition they possess early translations of the New Testament–in Latin, Syriac, Egyptian (Coptic) and other languages. They can also refer to quotations which some early Christian writers and theologians made from the New Testament (though these are sometimes inaccurate).

Many of the Greek manuscripts contain a text of the New Testament which was standardized in the fifth century AD. The first printed edition of the Greek text came in 1516–in a form prepared by the Dutch scholar Erasmus. Up until then no-one had questioned the accuracy of this text.

The opening page of Mark's Gospel from the illuminated manuscript made on the island of Lindisfarne, England, in about AD 700.

During the next two centuries, some Bibles included notes to indicate where certain other manuscripts varied from the standard version of the New Testament. Particularly important examples include the text of Stephanus, used in translating the King James' Version in England (1611), and the edition of Elzevir (1633), which became the standard for New Testament translations in Europe (it came to be known as the Received Text, *Textus Receptus*).

But during the eighteenth and nineteenth centuries, scholars began to delve deeper into the history of the New Testament text. They discovered that many older manuscripts of the New Testament differed from the fifth-century standard text. They showed that it was more important to ask how old a manuscript was and how good it was, than how many copies survived. Other scholars found that manuscripts could be grouped together in 'families' which share a similar kind of text. Older 'families' of texts such as the 'Alexandrian' and the 'Western' texts are now known to preserve a more accurate version of the original writings than the standard fifth-century text.

How the manuscripts were copied
Before the invention of printing in the West, in the fifteenth century, all writing had to be hand-copied for circulation. This was usually done by a group of scribes, each of whom wrote out his copy of the manuscript as the head scribe dictated. If a scribe did not hear clearly, or failed to concentrate, mistakes would occur. Even a single copyist working from an original manuscript sometimes misread the writing, or accidentally introduced his own mistakes.

Very few private individuals could afford to own a handwritten manuscript. They were expensive to make, and Christian churches would usually own manuscripts which all their members could share. At first the New Testament books must have been written on scrolls made of papyrus, leather or parchment. But from about the second century Christians probably began to use the book form which we use today (the *Codex*). This was much easier to handle than an awkward scroll.

A reliable New Testament text Two of the most important groups of manuscripts for our New Testament are the Bodmer Papyri (one of which dates from the late second century) and the Chester Beatty Papyri (probably from the early third century). But these contain only parts of the New Testament. The *Codex Sinaiticus*, which dates from the fourth century, contains the complete New Testament; and the *Codex Vaticanus* has everything up to Hebrews 9:13. Both of these manuscripts were probably made by professional copyists in Alexandria, Egypt.

These two codex manuscripts were the main sources for the Greek text of the New Testament prepared in the nineteenth century by the scholars Westcott and Hort. Most scholars agree that they are more accurate than the standard fifth-century text which so many previous versions had used. The two papyrus collections were discovered after the time of Westcott and Hort. They in turn have been used with others to achieve an even more accurate version of the New Testament text. Since then, still more papyrus evidence has been discovered. No single manuscript is clearly the best. The evidence of each has to be weighed carefully.

Over the last 250 years many careful scholars have worked hard to make sure that we have a New Testament which is as close as possible to what its authors originally wrote. The few small areas of doubt which remain are over minor matters of wording. But none of these questions raises any doubt whatever about the basic meaning of the New Testament.

How the New Testament books were collected Although there is little direct evidence from the earliest years, we have a good idea of how the New Testament took on its present shape. The first gatherings of Christians probably followed the practice of the Jewish synagogues and had regular readings from the Old Testament during their meetings. Since they were worshipping Jesus Christ, it was natural for them to add an account of some part of his life and teaching.

At first this may have been in the form of a first-hand account from someone who had known Jesus during his lifetime. But then, as the churches grew in numbers, and as the eye-witnesses began to die, it became necessary to write these stories down. This was the way the four Gospels (Matthew, Mark, Luke and John) came into being, and they obviously had an important place in the worship and life of the early churches.

Then the apostles and other leaders had written a number of letters to various churches and individuals. Since these often gave general guidance on Christian life and beliefs, their usefulness for the whole church was soon recognized. Acts was accepted because it continued the story from Luke's Gospel. It preserved the only full account of the beginnings of Christianity.

We know that by the year AD 200 the church was officially using the four Gospels–and no others, although fictitious tales about Jesus and writings by other Christian leaders who came after the apostles were in circulation. But the mainstream church clearly accepted only the Gospels of Matthew, Mark, Luke and John as their authority for the life and teaching of Jesus. By this time, too, Paul's letters were generally accepted as of equal importance with the Gospels.

It was only later that the remaining books of the New Testament became generally accepted. Revelation, for example, was certainly read in the second century. But not until the third century was it circulating widely. Hebrews was read towards the end of the first century, but took longer to become accepted in the Western churches. It was not generally acknowledged by the church in the West until the fourth century, partly because of doubts as to whether Paul wrote it.

It took longer, too, for 2 Peter, 2 and 3 John, James and Jude to be accepted by the church as basic Scripture. Perhaps this was because of questions about the content of these books. The New Testament books were mainly used at first for public reading. If they were unsuitable for this purpose, their usefulness must have seemed limited.

It is clear that no church council arbitrarily decided that certain books composed the New Testament. Rather, over a period of time, the church discovered that certain writings had a clear and general authority, and were helpful and necessary for their growth. At the Council of Laodicea (AD 363) and the Council of Carthage (AD 397) the bishops agreed on a list of books identical to our New Testament, except that at Laodicea Revelation was left out.

Above all, the churches were concerned to make sure that the documents they included in the 'New Testament' truly represented the witness and experience of the apostles–the men who lived closest to Jesus.

New Year

See *Feasts and Festivals*.

Nicodemus

A Pharisee and a member of the supreme Jewish council (the Sanhedrin). He came to talk to Jesus secretly, at night. 'No one can see the Kingdom of God,' Jesus said, 'unless he is born again.' Nicodemus did not understand what he meant then, but later he spoke up for Jesus when the Pharisees wanted to arrest him. After Jesus' crucifixion Nicodemus brought spices to embalm his body.
John 3:1-20; 7:50ff.; 19:39-42

Nile

The great river of Egypt on which the country's whole economy depended. The Nile flows from Lake Victoria in the heart of Africa, about 3,500 miles/5,632km to the Mediterranean Sea. The fertile valley of the Nile (never more than about 12 miles/19km wide in Upper Egypt) is flanked on either side by desert. Every year the river flooded its banks in spring, leaving behind a layer of fertile mud. Crops would grow wherever the water reached. Too high a flood meant destruction; too low a flood, starvation. The river was also a useful means of transporting goods from one part of the country to another. About 12 miles/19km north of modern Cairo the Nile divides into a western and an eastern branch. Between them is the flat marshy land known as the Delta.

The Nile features in the dreams of Joseph's pharaoh. The pharaoh at the time of Moses' birth ordered his people to drown all Hebrew boy babies in the Nile. Moses himself was hidden in a basket in the reeds at the river's edge. The Nile also features in the sequence of plagues sent by God when the pharaoh refused to free the Israelites. It is often mentioned by the prophets.
Genesis 41:1-36; Exodus 1:22; 2:3-10; 7:17-25; 8:1-15, etc; Isaiah 18:2, etc.

Nineveh

An important city in Assyria, notably in King Sennacherib's reign. The Bible says that Nineveh was founded by Nimrod the hunter. The site certainly has a very long history, going back to about 4500 BC. From about 2300 BC the city had a temple to the goddess Ishtar.

Nineveh grew in importance from about 1250 BC, as Assyria's power increased. Several Assyrian kings had palaces there. Sennacherib undertook a great deal of rebuilding and other work.

Reliefs carved on the walls of his new palace show his victories, including the siege of Lachish in Judah. At Nineveh, too, archaeologists discovered a clay prism (the Taylor Prism) which describes how King Hezekiah was 'shut up like a bird' in Jerusalem.

Ashurbanipal, the next king but one, added to Nineveh's greatness. Whole libraries of inscribed tablets, including the *Epic of Gilgamesh* (containing a flood story) and the creation epic (*Enumaelish*), have been discovered at his palace and in the temple of Nabu. Nineveh fell to the Babylonians in 612 BC.

King Ashurbanipal and his queen feasting in their garden at Nineveh; from a seventh-century BC Assyrian relief.

In the Bible, Jonah was sent to save Nineveh; Nahum prophesied against it. See also *Assyria*.
Genesis 10:11; 2 Kings 19:36; Jonah 1:2; 3; Nahum 1:1; Luke 11:30

Noah

Noah was a good man at a time of great evil and violence. It was so bad, God could no longer tolerate it and sent a terrible flood. Only Noah and his family were saved. Noah followed the instructions God gave him and built a large boat about 430 feet/133 metres long. People saw what he was doing but refused to listen to his warning. When the rains came, Noah, his wife, his three sons and their wives, boarded the ark, with pairs of every kind of living creature. The ark floated until the flood went down. It came to rest on a mountain. After the flood God made a promise to Noah for all time: never again would he send a flood to destroy all living things. The rainbow was the sign of that promise. Noah lived to a great age and his sons became the ancestors of many nations.
Genesis 6–9; 1 Peter 3:20

Numbers

The book of Numbers tells the story of the Israelites during almost forty years of wandering in the Sinai Desert. It begins two years after their escape from Egypt and ends just before they entered Canaan, the land that God had promised to give them.

The name Numbers comes from the two 'numberings' (censuses) of the Israelites at Mt Sinai and on the plains of Moab, across the River Jordan from Jericho. Between the two censuses they settled for a time at the oasis of Kadesh Barnea, and then travelled to an area east of the River Jordan.

The Book of Numbers is one long, sad story of Israel's complaints and discontent. The Israelites were often afraid or disheartened when faced with difficulties. They rebelled against God and their leader Moses. Although they disobeyed him, God continued to care for his people. But only two men who escaped from Egypt, Caleb and Joshua, survived to enter the Promised Land.

O

Oak

There are many kinds of oaks in Israel, some of them evergreen. They are strong trees growing for many years. The wood was used for oars and for carving statues. Absalom was caught in an oak when he fled from King David.
2 Samuel 18:9-10; 1 Kings 13:14; Isaiah 2:13

Obadiah

1. The book of the prophet Obadiah is the shortest book in the Old Testament. It was written after the fall of Jerusalem in 587 BC.

The Edomites, Judah's old enemies from the mountains south-east of the Dead Sea, took the opportunity to invade Judah.

Obadiah attacked the pride of the Edomites. He prophesied their fall. In the fifth century BC the Arabs defeated them; in the third century BC the Nabataeans overran them. They finally disappeared from history.

In contrast, Obadiah prophesied the return of Israel to her homeland.
2. A steward in charge of King Ahab's household. When Queen Jezebel gave orders for all God's prophets to be killed, Obadiah hid 100 of them in caves and fed them until the danger was over. He risked his life again when Elijah asked him to arrange a meeting with Ahab.
1 Kings 18

Og

King of Bashan, a land east of the River Jordan. The Israelites, led by Moses, defeated Og and captured his sixty fortified cities. The land of Bashan was given to half the tribe of Manasseh.
Numbers 21:32ff; Deuteronomy 3; Joshua 22:7

Old Testament text

The Old Testament is made up of the first thirty-nine books of the Christian Bible. These books are the holy writings–or scriptures–of the Jewish people, and their religion, Judaism. They were first written down in Hebrew and Aramaic, the ancient languages of the Jews. Many of these writings are so old that little is now known of their origins. The Jewish scribes used to make new copies of the Hebrew sacred writings from time to time. But documents did not last long in the climate of the Bible lands, and so we rarely find very old copies of the writings.

Until 1947 the oldest known Hebrew manuscripts of the Old Testament dated from the ninth and tenth centuries AD. They were copies of the first five books of the Bible–the Pentateuch. Then in 1947 came the remarkable discovery of the Dead Sea Scrolls. These were early manuscripts from the library of a Jewish religious group who flourished at Qumran, near the Dead Sea, about the time of Jesus. These manuscripts are about a thousand years older than the ninth-century AD documents. Amongst the Dead Sea Scrolls are copies of all the Old Testament books except Esther.

These early manuscripts from Qumran are very important because they have essentially the same text as the ninth-century manuscripts. The text of the Old Testament had changed very little for a thousand years. The careful copyists had made few errors or alterations. Of course there are a few places where different words and expressions are used. And sometimes it is no longer possible to discover exactly what the Hebrew words meant. But we can be confident that the Old Testament as we now have it is substantially the same as its authors wrote many centuries ago.

The text of the Old Testament has also come down to us in other early translations. Some of these, too, confirm the accuracy of the Hebrew text of the Old Testament that we use today.

One of the most important translations is the Greek version of the Old Testament, the *Septuagint*. Greek-speaking Jews and many Christians used the *Septuagint* in the first Christian centuries. Another early document, *The Letter of Aristeas*, suggests that the *Septuagint* was compiled for Jews living in Egypt during the reign of Pharaoh Ptolemy Philadelphus (285–246 BC).

Greek was the main language of the Roman Empire, and several other Greek versions of the Old Testament were in use during the first Christian centuries. Sometimes the Greek translation helps to make clear obscure parts of the Hebrew text, but often it is not precise. The other translations can help occasionally in this way. For examples, study the notes in any modern translation. Later, as Christianity spread to people who spoke other languages, the Old Testament was translated into Latin (the Vulgate), Syriac (the Peshitta) and Egyptian (Coptic).

It is not possible to know for certain how the Old Testament came together in the collection of books we now know. But we do know which books made up the Old Testament in the period just before the birth of Jesus, and we can know which books Jesus and his apostles would have regarded as their 'Bible'.

The Jews have a strong tradition that the scribe Ezra (whose story is told in the Book of Ezra) arranged and collected the books of the Old Testament. But collections of the first five books ('the books of Moses', or the Pentateuch) and of some of the sermons of the prophets were in existence much earlier, as were the psalms and proverbs.

The Jews arranged their sacred books into three groupings: the Law, the Prophets and the Writings. 'The Law' consisted of the first five books of the Old Testament (Genesis-Deuteronomy). Although Genesis contains no 'law' as such, it was included because all five were thought to have been written by Moses. 'The Prophets' contained not only the messages of men like Amos, Jeremiah, Isaiah, and many others, but also the books of history–Joshua, Judges, 1 and 2 Samuel, and 1 and 2 Kings. These books were included in this section because they are concerned not only with the facts but also with the meaning of history as God sees it. The Writings included the books of Wisdom (wise sayings)–Proverbs, Ecclesiastes, Job–some books of history that were written later, such as Ezra, Nehemiah and Chronicles, and one book of prophecy, Daniel.

It is clear that by the time of Jesus the Hebrew Scriptures usually consisted of the thirty-nine books we know today as the Old Testament. Most of the books of our Old Testament are quoted somewhere in the New Testament. This makes it likely that Jesus and his followers were familiar with the Old Testament as we know it.

As well as the thirty-nine books of the Old Testament, the Jews had other sacred writings. In the Greek version, these were given the same respect as the other Old Testament books. But these additional books, known as the *Apocrypha*, were not given the same recognition as the other Old Testament books in the Hebrew version.

Olive

Olive tree.

One of the main tree-crops of ancient Israel. The berries were harvested in about November, by shaking or beating the branches with poles. Some olives were eaten pickled, but most were taken in baskets to the presses, where the valuable oil was crushed out. Olive oil was used for cooking, as fuel for lamps, and as a soothing lotion for the skin. In ancient Israel it was also used to anoint kings and priests. It was the way a person was set apart for special work. The trees themselves can live to an age of several hundred years. The wood can also be carved and polished for fine work, as in Solomon's temple.
Deuteronomy 24:20; Judges 9:8; 1 Kings 17:12-16; 1 Samuel 10:1; 1 Kings 6:23

Olives, Mount of

See *Mount of Olives*.

Omri

Commander of the army of King Elah of Israel. His fellow officers made him king when they heard that Zimri had murdered Elah. Omri was a strong and vigorous king. He reigned twelve years (885–874 BC). He chose Samaria as his new capital–well-sited at the top of a steep hill and easily defended. Omri lost some of his cities to Syria but conquered Moab. As a result Moab paid a heavy tax to Israel each year. Omri worshipped idols, and his son, Ahab, followed his example.
1 Kings 16:15-28; 20:34

On

An ancient city in Egypt, famous for its worship of the sun-god Ré. Joseph married the daughter of the priest of On, and they had two sons, Ephraim and Manasseh. On is mentioned later in the prophets, once by its Greek name 'Heliopolis' (city of the sun).
Genesis 41:45, 50; 46:20; Ezekiel 30:17; compare Isaiah 19:18; Jeremiah 43:13

Onesimus

A slave who belonged to Philemon, a Christian friend of Paul living at Colossae. Paul met Onesimus, probably in Rome, after he had run away from his master. While he was with Paul, Onesimus became a Christian. Paul wrote the letter to Philemon asking him to forgive Onesimus and accept him as a brother-Christian. Onesimus travelled back with Tychicus who was taking Paul's letter

to the Colossians.
Colossians 4:9; Philemon

Onesiphorus
A Christian who helped Paul when he was at Ephesus. He later encouraged Paul by visiting him when he was in prison at Rome.
2 Timothy 1:16ff.; 4:19

Ophir
A country famous for its gold. It may have been in South Arabia, or East Africa (Somalia), or even India.
1 Kings 9:28, etc.

Ornan
See *Araunah.*

Orpah
A Moabite girl who married one of Naomi's sons.
Ruth 1

Othniel
The first of the Judges in Israel. Othniel stopped the Israelites worshipping idols. As a result God gave him victory over Cushan-Rishathaim, king of Mesopotamia.
Joshua 15:16-17; Judges 3:7-11

Owl
Owls are night-time hunters, flying on almost silent wings to swoop down on the small creatures they eat. The Eagle Owl (the largest), Tawny Owl, Barn Owl and Scops Owl (the smallest) are all known in Israel. In the Bible the owl is pictured as the inhabitant of ruined and desolate places.
Leviticus 11:16; Isaiah 34:15

An Eagle Owl.

P

Paddan-aram
The area around Harran in north Mesopotamia. Abraham sent his servant to Paddan-aram to choose a wife for Isaac from the branch of the family which had settled there. Jacob later fled from Esau to his uncle Laban, who was living at Paddan-aram.
Genesis 25:20; 28:2

Palm (date)
A tall tree with a straight trunk topped by a tuft of huge 6ft (2m) leaves, amongst which the clusters of dates grow to provide valuable food. The palm became a national symbol of Israel, standing for victory. The people waved palm leaves when Jesus rode in triumph into Jerusalem. The shape of the palm was often copied for decoration in stone carving.
John 12:13

Pamphylia
A region on the south-west coast of modern Turkey. The town of Perga, visited by Paul, was in Pamphylia. Jews from this region were in Jerusalem and heard Peter and the apostles on the Day of Pentecost.
Acts 2:10; 13:13

Paphos
A town in the south-west of Cyprus. Paul visited Paphos on his first missionary journey. Here he met the magician Elymas; and the governor of the island, Sergius Paulus, believed God's message.
Acts 13:4-13

Papyrus
A sedge which grew in the marsh areas of the Nile Delta (and still grows in northern Israel), from which the paper of the ancient world was made. Its mop-like flower-heads are 10ft (3m) high or more. The three-cornered stems were cut into thin strips. Two layers, one at right-angles to the other, were laid out on a hard wooden surface and hammered together. These sheets of paper were then pasted end to end to form a roll. Much of the Bible would have been written on papyrus. It was also used to make boats and baskets (like the one in which Moses' mother put her baby son), ropes and sandals.

Papyrus.

Parable
A way of teaching spiritual truths by using a picture or short story. Much of Jesus' teaching was given in parables. See *Jesus' teaching.*

Paran
A desert area near Kadesh-barnea, where Hagar's son Ishmael grew up. The Israelites passed through it after the exodus. From here they sent spies into Canaan.
Genesis 21:20; Numbers 10:12; 12:16; 13:1-16, etc.

Parents
See *Family Life.*

Partridge
The name probably includes three kinds of partridge: the Rock Partridge, the Desert Partridge and the Black Partridge. All are game birds whose flesh and eggs can make a good meal. The Rock Partridge hides itself so well that it is more often heard than seen.
1 Samuel 26:20

A Rock Partridge.

Passover
See *Feasts and Festivals.*

Patmos
An island off the west coast of modern Turkey. The place where John had the visions written down in the book of Revelation.
Revelation 1:9

Paul (Saul)
The great apostle and missionary whose letters form a large part of the New Testament. Paul was a Jew, and a Roman citizen. He was born in Tarsus and educated by the Rabbi Gamaliel in Jerusalem. He was a Pharisee opposed to the Christians and present at the stoning of Stephen. Paul was on his way to Damascus to arrest the Christians when he saw a dazzling light and heard Jesus say to him, 'Why do you persecute me?' Blinded by the light, he was led to Damascus. Ananias was sent by God to visit him and restore his sight, and Paul was baptized. At once Paul started preaching about Jesus in Damascus. When the Jews plotted to kill him, he went to Jerusalem. The Christians there were afraid of Paul but Barnabas introduced him to the apostles. After a plot to kill him, Paul returned to Tarsus.

Some years later, Barnabas fetched him to help the church at Antioch in Syria. The two men were later sent to Cyprus and then to Asia Minor (Turkey) to take God's message to many peoples. After the Cyprus visit he was known as Paul, which is the Greek form of the Hebrew name Saul. Paul returned and reported back to the church in Antioch. He also helped the Jewish Christians in Jerusalem to accept the fact that Jesus Christ was the Saviour of all nations, not just the Jews.

On his second journey Paul took Silas as his helper. They visited the converts in Galatia. At Lystra, Timothy joined them as another helper. From Troas they sailed to Greece where Luke, the writer of the Gospel and Acts also joined them. A Christian church was started in Philippi, but Paul and Silas were beaten and thrown into prison. After their release, they travelled through Greece. Paul preached in Athens and then stayed in Corinth for eighteen months. Then he returned to Jerusalem with gifts for the poor from Christians in Greece and Asia Minor. For a while Paul stayed in

Syria. Then he set out again for Ephesus. For almost three years he preached to Jews and Greeks there. After visiting Corinth again, Paul returned through Greece and Asia Minor to Jerusalem. He was arrested and sent to Caesarea to be tried by Felix. For two years he was kept in prison, waiting for his case to be heard. By the time he was tried, Festus had replaced Felix as the Roman governor. Paul appealed to Caesar and was sent for trial in Rome. On the way Paul's ship was wrecked just off Malta, but no one drowned. When they reached Rome, Paul was kept under house arrest for more than two years. He was probably set free after his trial and may have preached in Spain. After a second arrest, Paul was executed in Rome by Nero, about AD 67. He had taken Christianity to Europe, left the priceless legacy of his writings to the church for all time, and kept his faith to the end.
Acts 7:58ff.; 9–28; the letters of Paul: Romans to Philemon

Peace
The Hebrew word for 'peace' has a very broad meaning. It really means 'wholeness' and describes fullness of life in every aspect. It can refer to bodily health, or a long life which ends in a natural death. It is also used to describe safety, and harmony for the individual and for the community. Peace is the most precious of all gifts, and it comes from God himself. 'The Lord is peace.' On the other hand, 'There is no (peace), says the Lord, for the sinners.'

Peace becomes the hallmark of the future age when God will establish his kingdom. God's Messiah, who was to bring in this new age, is called the 'Prince of Peace'. So the New Testament declares that Jesus, 'has brought us peace'. He 'came and preached the Good News of peace to all'–a peace bought by his death on the cross. His gift to every Christian is peace with God; and peace with our fellow men. It is also a deep peace of heart and mind unaffected by circumstances. 'Peace,' he told his disciples on his last evening with them, 'is what I leave with you; it is my own peace that I give you. I do not give it as the world does. Do not be worried and upset; do not be afraid.'

See also *Reconciliation.*
Genesis 15:15; Psalms 4:8; 85:8-10; Judges 6:24; Isaiah 48:22; 2:2-4; 9:6; Romans 5:1; Ephesians 2:14-18; John 14:27; 2 Thessalonians 3:16

Pekah
A captain in King Pekahiah's army who seized the throne of Israel (740–732 BC). He was an evil king who worshipped idols. Pekah made an alliance with King Rezin of Syria and both countries invaded Judah. King Ahaz of Judah appealed to Tiglath-pileser III of Assyria for help. As a result the Assyrians invaded Israel and captured several cities. Shortly after this Pekah was murdered by Hoshea.
2 Kings 15:25-16:5;
2 Chronicles 28:5-6

Pekahiah
King of Israel after Menahem, his father, 742–740 BC. Pekahiah allowed the Israelites to continue worshipping idols. He was assassinated in the second year of his reign by Pekah, a captain in his army.
2 Kings 15:22-26

Pentecost
See *Feasts and festivals.*

Penuel/Peniel
A place near the River Jabbok, east of the Jordan, where Jacob wrestled with the angel.
Genesis 32:22-32

Perga
A town just inland from Antalya (Attalia) on the south coast of modern Turkey. Paul visited Perga on arrival from Cyprus on the first missionary journey, and again when he returned to the coast.
Acts 13:13; 14:25

Pergamum
The administrative capital of the Roman province of Asia (west Turkey). The first temple to be dedicated to Rome and the Emperor Augustus was built at Pergamum in 29 BC. Pergamum was also the centre of the pagan cults of Zeus, Athena, and Dionysus. There was a centre of healing connected with the temple of Asclepius (a fourth great pagan cult).

Pergamum was one of the seven churches to which the letters in the Book of Revelation are addressed. The phrase 'where Satan has his throne' may refer to emperor worship.
Revelation 1:11; 2:12-16

Persia
The Persians were nomadic Indo-Europeans who entered Iran not long before 1000 BC. By the seventh century they had settled east of the Persian Gulf in an area still called Farsistan. They were ruled by the family of Achaemenes. The first we know of in history is Cyrus I, about 640 BC. Cyrus's grandson, Cyrus II (the Great), overthrew the Medes (550 BC), then defeated Lydia (547 BC) and Babylon (539 BC). He established Persian rule over most of the Old Testament world. Cyrus's son, Cambyses, added Egypt to the empire (525 BC), and his successor, Darius, parts of the Black Sea coast.

Cyrus's empire allowed subject peoples to follow their own customs and religion, as long as they remained loyal. Governors were often local princes. But the highest government jobs were kept in the hands of noble Persian and Median families. Persia outstripped Babylon in land and wealth. This can be seen in the magnificent buildings of Persepolis and Pasargadae and the quantities of gold plate and jewellery found in Persia (descriptions in the Book of Esther agree with this). Craftsmen from every province were employed on the great king's buildings.

A bearded sphinx which decorates the palace staircase at Persepolis, Persia (Iran).

Although the Persian language was written for display in a cuneiform script, Aramaic and Elamite were used for most of the administration.

Persians were nature worshippers at first but, probably in the reign of Darius I (522–486 BC), adopted the teachings of Zoroaster. He taught that there was one god, Ahuramazda, the Good–seen in purifying fire and water–and a dark power of evil, Angramainyu (Ahriman). Revolts and intrigues weakened Persia, so that the empire fell to the Greek, Alexander the Great, in 331 BC.

Peter
Leader of the apostles and of the early church. Like his father and brother Andrew, Simon Peter was a fisherman. When Jesus called him to be a disciple he changed Peter's name from Simon to Peter, which means 'rock'. Later, Jesus asked his disciples who people thought he was. Peter answered, 'You are the Christ, the Son of the Living God.' Jesus replied, 'You are Peter and on this rock I will build my church.' Peter was one of Jesus' closest disciples. He was with Jesus at his transfiguration and in the Garden of Gethsemane just before his death. After Jesus' arrest Peter was afraid and said three times that he did not know him. But at once he was bitterly sorry. Knowing this, Jesus appeared specially to Peter after his resurrection. At Lake Galilee he told Peter to care for the Christian 'flock' as a shepherd.

On the Day of Pentecost Peter preached boldly about Jesus to the crowds in Jerusalem. About three thousand people became Christians that day. At first Peter preached only to the Jews. But at Joppa God gave him a special dream to show him he must share the Good News with non-Jews, too. King Herod arrested Peter and put him in prison, but the Christians prayed and God set him free. Peter wrote two of the New Testament letters, probably while he was in Rome. Mark probably got some of the story of Jesus for his Gospel from Peter. Peter is said to have died in Rome during the persecution begun by the Emperor Nero–crucified, like Jesus, but upside down.
Matthew 4:18-19; 10:2; 14:28-33; 16:13-23; 17:1-9; 26:30ff.;
Mark 1:16-18, 29-31; 5:37; John 1:40-42; 18:10-11; 20:2-10; 21;
Acts 1-15; Galatians 1-2;
1 and 2 Peter

Peter's Letters
1 Peter A letter addressed to scattered groups of Christians in the five Roman provinces which covered much of what is now western and northern Turkey. It was probably written by Peter in Rome at the time

when the Emperor Nero was persecuting the Christians (AD 64). Peter's purpose was to encourage and strengthen Christians who were facing suffering.

Peter reminds his readers of the Good News about Jesus Christ. God the Father has given us 'new life by raising Jesus Christ from death. This fills us with a living hope'. He urges them to regard their suffering as a 'test' of their faith. The letter is full of comfort and encouragement to lead lives worthy of people who belong to Jesus Christ. No matter what trouble comes, God is in control: 'he cares for you' (5:7).

2 Peter A letter addressed to a wide circle of early Christians 'from Simon Peter'. It was written at a time when Christians were confused by false teaching–particularly about how they should behave, and about the return of Jesus Christ.

The writer emphasizes true knowledge–the first-hand account of Jesus which those who saw and heard him have passed on (chapter 1). False teachers who disrupt the church will be punished (chapter 2). The return of Jesus is certain. It could happen any day, and Christians must be ready (chapter 3).

Colossal statues of Pharaoh Ramesses II at the entrance to the rock-cut temple of Abu-Simbel, Egypt.

Petra

See *Sela*.

Pharaoh

Title of the kings of Egypt. Several 'pharaohs' are mentioned in the Old Testament including:

1. The pharaoh visited by Abraham. Genesis 12:10ff.
2. The pharaoh who made Joseph his prime minister.
Genesis 40ff.
3. The pharaoh who was forced to let Moses lead the Israelites out of Egypt, probably Ramesses II, who built great store cities.
Exodus 5ff.
4. The pharaoh who sheltered Hadad after David defeated the Edomites.
1 Kings 11
5. The pharaoh who gave Solomon his daughter in marriage.
1 Kings 9:16
6. Shishak. He encouraged Jeroboam to lead the ten tribes in revolt against King Solomon's unpopular son, Rehoboam. Later he raided Jerusalem and took away the temple treasure.
1 Kings 11:40; 14:25-26
7. So, who was asked by King Hoshea of Israel to form an alliance against Assyria.
2 Kings 17:4
8. Tirhakah led his army against Assyria during the reign of King Hezekiah. The Assyrian army had to abandon its attack on Jerusalem to meet the Egyptian forces.
2 Kings 19:9; Isaiah 37:9
9. Neco, 610–595 BC. He killed King Josiah of Judah at the Battle of Megiddo. For four years Neco made Judah pay tribute to him, but then he was defeated by Nebuchadnezzar of Babylon at the battle of Carchemish (605 BC). After that Judah was in Babylon's power. Neco spent his later years defending Egypt and trying to strengthen his country.
2 Kings 23:29ff.; 24:7;
2 Chronicles 35:20-36:4
10. Hophra, 587–570 BC. He supported King Zedekiah's rebellion against Nebuchadnezzar of Babylon.
Jeremiah 37:5; 44:30; Ezekiel 17:15ff.; 29:2

Pharisees

The name may mean the 'separated ones'. The Pharisees were a strict, religious sect, probably beginning in the second century BC. They were mostly ordinary Jews–not priests–who kept closely to the Jewish Law. They often extended the way the laws applied, so that they became very hard to keep. The forbidding of work on the sabbath is an extreme example. Pharisees counted as 'work': walking more than 3/5 miles (about 1 km) from one's town; carrying any kind of load; lighting a fire in the home. Strict rulings like this often led to people being so concerned to keep the law in every detail that they lost sight of the 'spirit' behind it. But the motive was good. Pharisees believed that their rules 'built a fence around the Law'. By keeping these other rules people would be in less danger of disobeying the actual Law of God.

Although the Pharisees were the largest Jewish sect in the time of Jesus, there were only about 6,000 of them. Many Pharisees were very godly men. But they tended to despise those who did not, or could not, keep their burdensome laws, and referred to them as 'sinners'. Jesus frequently argued with the Pharisees. He condemned their self-righteousness and legalism. And he identified himself with the common people whom the Pharisees, as religious leaders, had written off. Nicodemus, who became a secret follower of Jesus, was a Pharisee. So too was Paul.
Matthew 12:1-42; 22:34-23:36; Mark 7:1-23; Luke 18:9-14; John 18:3; Acts 23:6-10

Pharpar

See *Abana*.

Philadelphia

A town in the Roman province of Asia (modern Alashehir, in western Turkey). Philadelphia was one of the seven churches of Asia to which the letters in the book of Revelation are addressed.
Revelation 1:11; 3:7-13

Philemon

A private letter from Paul to Philemon, a Christian convert and friend at Colossae (western Turkey). Philemon owned a slave named Onesimus, who had run away. Onesimus eventually met Paul in prison and became a Christian. Paul wrote urging Philemon to forgive and welcome back his slave as a Christian brother. The letter was probably sent back to Colossae along with Onesimus, and the letter to the Colossian church.

Philip

1. One of the twelve apostles. He came from the lakeside town of Bethsaida in Galilee, the home town of Peter and Andrew. Philip went straight to Nathanael, told him he had found the Messiah, and introduced him to Jesus. Faced with a crowd of five thousand hungry people, Jesus tested Philip's faith. 'Where can we buy enough bread to feed all these people?' he asked. Philip was wondering where the money would come from. But Jesus fed them all from five small loaves and two fish. At the last supper, when Jesus said, 'No one goes to the Father except by me,' Philip asked Jesus to show them his father. 'Whoever has seen me,' Jesus answered, 'has seen the Father.'
Matthew 10:3; John 1:43-46; 6:5-7; 12:21-22; 14:8-9;
Acts 1:13
2. Son of Herod the Great. His wife, Herodias, left him to marry his half-brother, Herod Antipas. John the Baptist was beheaded because he condemned this marriage.
Mark 6:17
3. Another son of Herod the Great, brother of Antipas and Archelaus. He became ruler of Ituraea.
Luke 3:1

4. Philip the evangelist. One of seven men chosen to help the apostles in the work of the church at Jerusalem. He fled to Samaria when the Christians in Jerusalem were being persecuted by Paul. There he preached and healed many people. An angel sent Philip to meet the Ethiopian chancellor, travelling from Jerusalem to Gaza. This man became a Christian and was baptized. Philip then went and preached in every town along the coast from Ashdod to Caesarea. Philip's four daughters were also involved in making God's message known. About twenty years later Paul stayed at Philip's home in Caesarea.
Acts 6:1-6; 8; 21:8-9

Philippi

A town 8 miles/12km inland from Neapolis on the coast of Macedonia (northern Greece). It was named after Philip of Macedon. Philippi was annexed by the Romans in 168 BC. It was the site of a famous battle between Antony and Octavian (Augustus) against Brutus and Cassius in 42 BC. Some years later, Octavian made Philippi a Roman colony, which gave its people the same rights and privileges as any town on Italian soil.

Paul visited Philippi on his second missionary journey, after seeing a vision of a Macedonian man appealing to him for help. The first Christian church in Europe was established at Philippi. Paul and Silas were illegally imprisoned here but later released with an apology when they made it known that they were Roman citizens. The letter to the Philippians was written to the church at Philippi.
Acts 16:6-40; 20:6; Philippians 1:1, etc.; 1 Thessalonians 2:2

Prisoners taken captive by Ramesses III. They are, from left to right, Libyan, Syrian, Hittite, Philistine and Syrian.

Philippians

Paul founded the church at Philippi–the first in Europe–in about AD 50. He wrote this letter from prison, possibly in Rome about AD 61–63. Or it may have been from Ephesus, in about AD 54.

Paul explains his situation to the Christians at Philippi, and thanks them for gifts they had sent him. He encourages them in the faith. He urges them to forget pride, and follow the example of Jesus, 'who was humble, and walked the path of obedience'. He sets out the joy and peace which belong to those who trust Christ.

Although Paul was worried by false teachers in the church at Philippi, his affection for the Christians there shines through.

Despite the dark background of prison, his letter is full of the joy, confidence and hope of the Christian life.

Philistines

The Philistines lived in five cities to the south-west of the land of Israel: Ashdod, Ashkelon, Ekron, Gath, and Gaza. They controlled the coast road from Egypt. It was perhaps to avoid them that God did not take his people into the Promised Land 'by the road that goes up the coast to Philistia, although it was the shortest way' (Exodus 13:17).

War with the Israelites In the days of the Judges, and of Samuel, Saul, and David, the Philistines were a constant threat to the Israelites. Both peoples wanted control of the same land. Their military pressure was one factor in Israel's demand for a king. ('We want...our own king...to lead us out to war'–1 Samuel 8:20.)

Only after fierce struggles were their attacks finally ended by David, who drove them 'back from Geba all the way to Gezer' (2 Samuel 5:25). Yet the Philistines remained independent, and caused occasional disturbances in later times. They extended their rule northwards along the coast, and inland, whenever they could. Although they were never in control of much of the country for long, it was the Philistines who gave their name–as Palestine–to the whole of the land west of the Jordan.

Rulers Each Philistine city was ruled by a 'lord'. This title (*seren*) is a non-Semitic word, probably belonging to the Indo-European speech of the Aegean area. A word for helmet (*koba'*) found in stories about the Philistines (for example, Goliath in 1 Samuel 17:5) and the names Goliath and Achish may belong to the same family of languages. This evidence from two words and two names can be linked with information from Egypt. There, in the thirteenth and twelfth centuries BC, pharaohs recorded how they beat off invasions by the 'peoples of the sea'. One of these peoples was the Philistines. After defeating them, the Egyptians used some as soldiers to garrison provincial and frontier forts, and allowed others to settle along the coast of Canaan, an Egyptian province.

'Sea Peoples' While the Sea Peoples' warriors reached Egypt by ship, and fought the Egyptians on water, their families and household goods trekked down the coast of Syria and Canaan, according to an Egyptian text. These details, and some items in Egyptian pictures of Sea Peoples, point to them as intruders into the Near East. Amos 9:7 states that they came from Crete (Caphtor). Deuteronomy 2:23 says that this was where the men of Gaza came from. 'Philistine' pottery found in Israel is evidence of this link. The pottery belongs to the Mycenean type made in Greece, Crete, and Cyprus. It is found in levels of occupation dating from 1200–1100 BC, especially at sites on the coast. Nothing else has been found that can be called 'Philistine' as distinct from Canaanite or Israelite.

Religion and culture The Old Testament gives Philistine gods Semitic names: Dagon, with temples at Gaza and Ashdod; Baalzebub, worshipped at Ekron; and Ashtoreth (Astarte). We know too little about their cities as yet to be sure whether they had their own designs for houses or temples. Metal-working, especially in iron, was a Philistine skill. Goliath's armour was impressive, and the Israelites had to pay their neighbours to sharpen their iron tools.

Early Philistines Long before Israel entered the Promised Land, their ancestors met Philistines in southern Canaan. Many scholars consider that these stories were composed much later, after the Philistines had settled there in the thirteenth century BC. Or the name Philistine may have been used by a later editor to replace an out-of-date name in the story (as St Petersburg would be replaced by Leningrad). There are some objects from the Philistine area which show that there were connections with the Greek region as early as 1900 BC. But apart from the documents of the Old Testament, no others have yet been found which specifically mention the people of the district at that time.
Genesis 21:32, 34; 26; Judges 16:21ff.; 1 Samuel 5; 13:19-22; 17; 31:9, 10; 1 Kings 1:2

Phinehas

1. The son of Eleazar and grandson of Aaron. When the Israelites were mixing with Midianite women and worshipping their god, Phinehas executed two of the worst offenders. His action stopped an epidemic which had already killed 24,000 people. His faithfulness to God was rewarded with the promise that he and his descendants would always be priests.
Exodus 6:25; Numbers 25; 31:6; Joshua 22:13ff.; Judges 20:28
2. One of Eli's two sons. (See *Hophni and Phinehas*.)
1 Samuel 2:12ff.; 4

Phoenicians

The Israelites never occupied all of

Phoenician boats with horse-headed prows and high sterns transporting logs; from an eighth-century BC Assyrian relief.

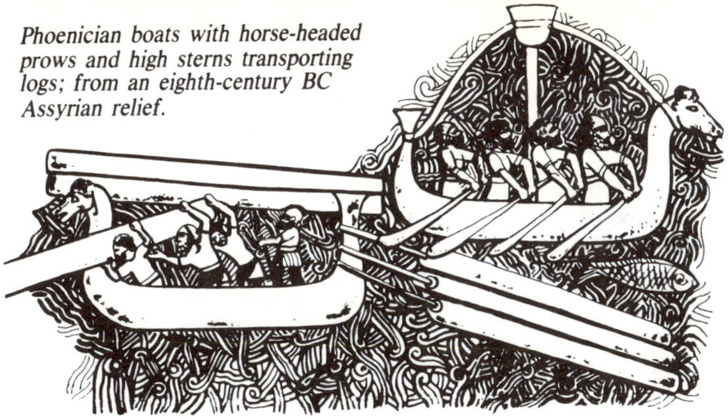

the land God originally promised to them. The Canaanites whose homeland it had been for centuries remained in some areas, particularly on the coast to the north-west–modern Lebanon. One of their towns was the ancient city of Byblos, possibly the place where the alphabet was invented. At any rate the Greeks, who borrowed the alphabet, also borrowed the name of the city as their word for book (*biblos*).

Trade Byblos had a flourishing merchant shipping trade from at least the eighteenth century BC. But it is two nearby ports that are most often mentioned in the Bible. The power of Tyre and Sidon increased and overtook Byblos after 1000 BC. It was about this time that David and Solomon formed trade alliances with King Hiram of Tyre. He supplied fine wood, and gold, and skilled craftsmen for building the temple and palaces at Jerusalem, in return for twenty towns in Galilee (1 Kings 9:10ff.). Hiram and Solomon also combined in operating a fleet on the Red Sea. The ships brought back gold and jewels.

The chief exports of Tyre and Sidon were cedarwood from the mountains of Lebanon and purple dye from cuttle-fish. But the people built their empire on trade. They were middlemen, dealing in linen from Egypt, silver, iron and tin from Spain, ivory and ebony from the coastlands (Ezekiel 27 gives a very full description). They spread their colonies across the Mediterranean, to North Africa, Italy, and Spain, where they were known as the Phoenicians. Their language was a form of Canaanite, similar to Hebrew, but their literature is known only at second-hand. Their religion, too, continued Canaanite ideas. (see *Canaanite Religion*). It was brought into Israel by the marriage of King Ahab to Jezebel, daughter of the king of Sidon. Ahab built a temple to Baal at his capital and Jezebel and the prophets of Baal threatened Elijah's life (1 Kings 18).

Phrygia

A land in the centre of Asia Minor (modern Turkey), the home of an Indo-European group. In Assyrian records and the Old Testament it is called Meshech. According to Ezekiel it was a warlike nation, trading in copper and slaves. Several of the rulers were named Midas (though this may be a title, like 'pharaoh') and were buried in richly furnished tombs around Gordium, the capital, which has recently been excavated. After the middle of the seventh century BC, Phrygia came under Lydian rule (an event reflected in Ezekiel 38 and 39). In 116 BC it became part of Roman Asia. From 25 BC the eastern part was counted as being in Galatia.
Ezekiel 32:26; 38:2, 3; 39:1; 27:13; 38; 39

Pilate

Roman governor in Judea AD 26–37. He was cruel and unpopular with the Jews. When Jesus was brought to him to be tried Pilate knew that Jesus was innocent. But he was afraid there would be a riot, and the Emperor would remove him as governor. So he condemned Jesus to death.
Matthew 27; Mark 15; Luke 3:1; 13:1; 23; John 18–19

Pisgah

One of the peaks of Mt Nebo.

Pisidia

A mountainous inland area inland from the south coast of modern Turkey. Paul passed through this remote and dangerous region on his first missionary journey, on his way from Perga to Antioch.
Acts 13:14; 14:24

Pithom

One of Pharaoh's two store-cities, built by Israelite slave labour. It lay east of the Nile Delta in Egypt. See also *Raamses*.
Exodus 11:1

Pomegranate

Scarlet flowers contrast with deep-green leaves on this large shrub. The yellowy-brown edible fruits are the size of an orange. Inside the hard rind is a juicy pulp, full of seeds. The shape was copied in embroidery round the edge of the high priest's robe, and carved on the pillars in Solomon's temple.
Exodus 28:33; 1 Kings 7:20

Pontus

The ancient name of the Black Sea, and so of the land along its south coast. This became a Roman province, stretching along most of the northern coast of Asia Minor (Turkey). This was one of the lands to which Peter sent his first letter. The Christian message may have reached Pontus very early, as Jews from there were in Jerusalem on the Day of Pentecost.
Acts 2:9; 18:2; 1 Peter 1:1

Poplar

Jacob peeled poplar shoots when he tricked Laban. The white poplar has fast-growing shoots and gives a dense shade. The 'willows' of Babylon, where the exiles mourned, were probably a kind of poplar.
Genesis 30:37; Psalm 137:2

Potiphar

Egyptian official who bought Joseph as a slave. (See *Joseph*.)
Genesis 37:36; 39

Pottery

By comparison with the products of her neighbours, Israel's pottery seems poor and not very artistic. There is an immense difference between the painted pottery of the Canaanites and Philistines and the limited designs of the Israelites when they eventually occupied the land. But this is because the Israelites were making their pots with a view to usefulness rather than decoration. The forms were good and they were carefully produced.

At the time of King David, craftsmanship improved. There were new shapes and there was some form of decoration. This progress went on and, during the time of the kings, the making of pottery developed into a minor industry with small 'factories', mass production, some standard shapes, and trade marks. Many more pots were made, but the standard was high.

In New Testament times it seems that a good deal of fine pottery was imported.

The potters It is possible, especially during the time of the later kings, that several potters worked together, with their apprentices (often their own sons). There is evidence that potters kept the temple worshippers supplied with pots fit to use for cooking a sacrificial meal in the temple courts.

There also seems to have been a royal guild of potters 'in the service of the king' (1 Chronicles 4:23). They probably produced large jars for storing produce from the king's private estates. Jars have been found (holding about 10 gallons/45 litres) with a stamp on the handles: 'Belonging to the king'. Underneath is the name of one of four cities: Hebron, Ziph, Socoh, or Memshath. These may have been the sites of royal vineyards, or centres where the people brought their taxes in the form of produce.

Israelite pottery.

The potter's workshop The whole process of producing pottery was probably carried out on one site. There had to be a handy water supply (a stream or cistern), wheels for shaping the clay, and kilns for firing it. The yard of the potter's house or workshop would be used for preparing the clay and no doubt also became the place where broken pottery or rejects from the kiln (potsherds) would pile up.

Jeremiah 19:2 speaks of the 'Potsherd Gate' near the Valley of Hinnom. Presumably there was a potter's house there. In Nehemiah 3:11 and 12:38 we read of the 'Tower of the Ovens' or 'Tower of the Furnaces' and these expressions may refer to pottery kilns in Jerusalem.

Preparing the clay Pottery was made from the local red clay. The potter did not alter the quality of the clay, except by mixing it occasionally with ground limestone, which was readily available. This enabled the finished pot to withstand heat (useful in the case of cooking-pots), but it meant that the potter had to fire the clay at a lower temperature, otherwise the limestone would decompose.

The raw clay was exposed to the sun, rain and frost to break it up and remove impurities. Then water was added and it was trampled into mud (see Isaiah 41:25). This needed skill. The water had to be measured and poured on evenly, and the air removed.

Working the clay When the clay had been prepared, three methods of working it were open to the potter.

1. The clay could be pressed down in a mould. Canaanite plaques were made this way, and so also were most of the lamps of New Testament times. Job 38:14 refers to the imprint of a seal on clay.
2. The clay could be modelled free-hand. In Israel the only things made in this way seem to have been toys, ovens and a few pots.
3. Or the clay could be shaped on a wheel–and this was the usual method of working.

The earliest type of potter's wheel known was a circular disc, rotating on a vertical shaft. But about the time of the exodus a different type came into use. This had a second, larger disc, mounted below the first. This speeded the turning and may have been kept moving by the potter's assistants. Potters' wheels were probably used everywhere, but the Bible only mentions one once (when Jeremiah visits the potter's house–Jeremiah 18:3), and wheels are rarely found. Perhaps they were usually made of wood or clay and so have not survived. Stone wheels have been found at Megiddo, Lachish and Hazor. There is no evidence of a foot-operated wheel before 200 BC, although it was widely used in New Testament times.

When the pot had been shaped, it was allowed to harden. Then it could go back on the wheel and be turned into more delicate forms. At the time of the later kings production was speeded up in various ways. Sometimes a very large lump of clay was put on the wheel and pots were shaped from the top of it, each one being 'pinched off' as it was completed. Sometimes unskilled workers shaped the clay roughly on the wheel. They used cheap clay and made thick pots, which were then turned into the desired shape and thickness by skilled potters.

Firing The firing of the clay objects in a kiln was the ultimate test of a potter's art. Different clays needed different treatment. But the methods of firing are not known. A number of kilns have been found. Some of them have a U shape, but it is not easy to tell whether they were used for pottery or for copper.

Decoration The Israelites did not glaze their pottery but they had three main ways of decorating it.

1. They could use a 'slip'. Fine clay with a rich iron content was thinned with water and then brushed over the parts which the potter wished to decorate.
2. Sometimes they painted a line of red or black around the shoulder or middle of the jar or jug.
3. They could 'burnish' pots either by hand or on the wheel. To do this, a tool of stone, bone or wood would be rubbed against the clay after drying but before firing. These areas would then shine after firing.

The 'slip' and 'burnish' were sometimes combined.

Some of the perfume jugs which have been found are black. It is not clear how these were made. They may have been dipped in milk or olive oil before firing and then lightly polished.

Glazing was used by the Greeks and Romans.

Articles made by the potter Pottery articles can be divided into two basic designs.

The bowl This could range from a large banquet bowl with four handles, to a small cup (which rarely had handles). Bowls were used for mixing wines, serving food, holding coal, cooking, and so on. The household oven was really an inverted bowl with the bottom missing. The clay would simply be moulded into shape. It hardened when used as an oven. Broken bits of pot were plastered round the outside to moderate the heat.

Lamps were thrown in the same way as a bowl, and the rims were pinched in while the clay was still soft. Their style changed considerably during the history of Israel, but the basic design was the same. The gradual changes, at different stages, enable the experts to use them as an indication of date.

The jar or pitcher There were jars for wine, for water and for oil. Jars were also used for storing documents. And small juglets were specially produced for perfume.

Other objects made of pottery included water bottles for a journey; articles for industry (crucibles, clay moulds, spindle whorls, loom-weights); toys (dolls, horses, camels), and clay objects connected with the Canaanite religion.

If pots were broken, they were sometimes mended with rivets or wires. Sometimes notes or letters were written on pieces of broken pottery. For example, we know of a series of letters (the 'Lachish Letters') written on pieces of pottery (ostraca), from the commander of a smaller garrison to his superior at Lachish during King Nebuchadnezzar's final attack on Judah.

Praise

The joy God's people have in him is expressed in 'praise'. They praise him as their Creator and as their Redeemer (Saviour).

One of the Old Testament words for praise comes from a Hebrew word which means 'to make a noise'. It appears in our word 'hallelujah'. Israelite worship included joyful shouting and singing and the sound of many musical instruments. We see this again and again in the psalms (the hymns sung in the temple).

This same note of praise characterizes the Christian church. Christians rejoice above all in the great act of salvation brought about through the life, death and resurrection of Jesus. Angels sang when Jesus was born. Praise is a constant part of Christian prayer–rejoicing, asking God with a thankful heart. Heaven itself continually rings with praise.

See also *Creeds and hymns.*

Psalms 136; 135; 150; 34:3; 35:18 and many other passages; Luke 2:13-14; Philippians 4:4-8; Revelation 4:6-11

Prayer

Men and women were made to live in fellowship with God. In this 'sharing', prayer was the normal relationship through which God fulfilled his purposes. It is because of the coming of sin and evil that this relationship is often broken now, and so prayer can seem unnatural or unreal.

But those who trust in God share their life with him in prayer. We pour out our hearts before him. We are open to God in confessing our sin. We ask things of God, confident that God answers prayer. And our prayers always include thanksgiving to God.

The faithful Israelite prayed three times each day. Samuel was so sure of his duty to pray that he considered it a sin if he failed to pray for those in his care. There is no particular pattern laid down for Christians to follow but Paul expects prayer to have a central place in the life of the Christian and the church. It will have a natural place in the restored relationship of God and his people.

Prayer is a Christian family activity. Jesus' model prayer begins 'Our Father...' It is the work of the Holy Spirit to help Christians to pray, tuning their minds more and more to the mind of God. 'The Spirit himself pleads with God for us in groans that words cannot express,' wrote Paul to the Romans.

As well as the private prayers of individuals, the New Testament often mentions groups of Christians praying together. From the very beginning Christians shared in 'the fellowship meals and... the prayers'. They prayed for courage when the Jewish Council banned Peter and John from preaching. They prayed for Peter when he was imprisoned. They prayed for the success of the missionary work of Barnabas and Paul. These prayers were spontaneous, but they are full of the spirit and language of the Old Testament.

Some of the actual words of early Christian prayer are still known. **Marana tha** (1 Corinthians 16:22). These are two Aramaic words, meaning 'Our Lord, come!' They were addressed to Jesus, calling him by the same name, 'Lord', that Jews had reserved for God alone. *Marana tha* comes again in the last prayer of the

Bible: 'So be it. Come, Lord Jesus!'

The word **abba** (Mark 14:36) was used by Jesus himself in addressing God. It is an Aramaic word meaning 'dear father' or 'dad'. A child would use it to speak to his own father. Jews would have thought it an irreverent way to speak to God. They used the word *abinu*, 'our father', instead. But Jesus' relationship with God was so close that he could use this family word, and encourage his disciples to do the same. The word comes twice in Paul's letters: 'when we cry out to God, "Abba, my Father!", God's Spirit...declare(s) that we are God's children.' And: 'To show that you are his sons, God sent the Spirit of his Son into our hearts, the Spirit who cries out, "Father, my Father".'

Amen This is a Hebrew word used in the temple and synagogue services at the end of prayers. It means, 'It is sure', or even, 'There is no doubt about that.' So, in the worship in heaven described in Revelation 5, when the cry goes up, 'The lamb who was killed is worthy to receive power, wealth, wisdom, and strength' the prayer is concluded with a great 'Amen'. 'Amen' ends a prayer in Romans 15:33, a blessing on God in Romans 9:5, an expression of praise in Galatians 1:5, and a blessing upon fellow Christians in Galatians 6:18.

Psalm 62:8; 1 John 1:9; Mark 11:24; Philippians 4:6; 1 Samuel 12:23; Colossians 4:2; James 1:5-6; Acts 12:12; Romans 8:26

Jesus' teaching on prayer:
Matthew 6:5-15; 7:7-11; 26:41; Mark 12:38-40; 13:33; 14:38; Luke 11:1-13; 18:1-14

Prayers of Jesus:
Matthew 6:9-13; 11:25-26; 26:36-44; Mark 14:32-39; Luke 10:21; 11:2-4; 22:46; 23:34, 46; John 11:41-42; 12:27-28; 17

Some other great Bible prayers:
Exodus 15; 32; 33; Deuteronomy 32-33; Joshua 17; 10; Judges 5; 6; 1 Samuel 1; 2; 2 Samuel 7; 22; 1 Kings 3; 8; 18; 19; 2 Kings 19; Ezra 9; Nehemiah 1; 9; Job 42; Psalms; Daniel 2; 9; Jonah 2; Habakkuk 3; Luke 1:46-55, 68-79; 2:29-35; Acts 4:24-30, and many prayers in the New Testament letters

A model of Levites offering sacrifices in front of the tabernacle.

Priests and Levites

The Levites were originally just one of the twelve tribes of Israel, descended from Levi, one of the sons of Jacob. But they were given a special position among God's people, because they defended his honour at the time when the rest of the people worshipped the golden calf. So they were dedicated to serve God. They became his own tribe in a special way.

They were set apart from the other tribes for religious duties. As they did not own any land, they had to be supported by the other tribes. To do this the people gave a 'tithe' (a tenth) of all their harvests and livestock to God. In Israel forty-eight towns were set aside for the use of the Levites.

Levi had three sons (Kohath, Gershon, and Merari) and their descendants formed the three clans of Levites. During the time in the desert the Kohathites were responsible for carrying the tabernacle furniture; the Gershonites carried its curtains and coverings; and the Merarites carried and set up the tabernacle itself.

One family, belonging to the Kohathite clan, was set apart for special service. This was the family of Aaron, the brother of Moses. He and his descendants were appointed priests. Only priests could offer sacrifices. The other Levite families did the more menial jobs, and were virtually servants of the priests. So the priests were the most 'holy' group within Israel. That does not mean, of course, that they were the most godly; many were not (for example, Eli's sons, who are described in 1 Samuel 2:22-25). 'Holy' is used in the special sense of 'belonging to God'. These men were the professional officials of the tabernacle and temple. Because of their special position they were subject to strict rules. A man of this family became a priest at the age of thirty.

The man in charge of the priests was the chief or 'high priest'. He had one privilege allowed to no one else. He could enter the 'holy of holies' once a year, on the Day of Atonement.

Levites: Exodus 32:25-29; Numbers 3:12-13; 18:21-24; 35:2-8

Priests: Exodus 28-29; Leviticus 8-10; 16; 21-22

The duties of the priests and Levites are mostly connected with the tabernacle and temple sacrifices and worship. But they also had a number of other duties. A group of men from each of the three Levite clans formed the temple choirs, and they may have composed several of the psalms (for example, Psalms 85 and 87).

The priests and Levites also had to give answers in God's name to questions that could not otherwise be decided (for example, whether it was the right time to go out to battle). For this purpose they used the sacred stones called Urim and Thummim, which were kept in a pouch worn on the high priest's chest. If the priest pulled out the Urim stone, the answer was 'no', but if it was the Thummim stone, the answer was 'yes'.

More important, they were also responsible for teaching the people the Law of God. When Moses blessed the tribes of Israel he said that the Levites will first 'teach your children to obey your Law'; and, secondly, 'offer sacrifices on your altar'. The Book of Nehemiah describes one occasion when Ezra and the Levites held a reading of the Law to all the people. The prophet Malachi sums up their role: 'It is the duty of the priests to teach the true knowledge of God. People should go to them to learn my will, because they are the messengers of the Lord Almighty.' Sadly, the prophets often had to call the priests and Levites to task for failing in these duties.

1 Chronicles 6:31-48; Leviticus 13; Deuteronomy 33:8-11; Nehemiah 8:1-12; Malachi 2:7; Jeremiah 23:11-32; Ezekiel 34

Priscilla

See *Aquila*.

Prophets

The great prophets whose messages we have in the Old Testament appeared on the scene at times of crisis in the nation's history. They were God's men for the moment and their messages were generally concerned with particular times and places. They remain valid and helpful because the same kind of situations have recurred again and again in history.

The early prophets The prophets first emerged as a group in the time of Samuel, who is often described as 'the last of the Judges and first of the prophets in Israel'. The Philistines were a great threat to Israel at the time. These early prophets, with their enthusiasm for Israel's God, strengthened the Israelites' determination to be free and independent. When the young Saul met them he was overcome by their sense of God's dynamic energy. He joined in excited prophesying as God's power took control of him.

Samuel himself does not seem to have been caught up in the ecstasies of these prophetic groups. He played an important role as a judge of the people. He also reproved them for worshipping foreign gods, and prayed to God on their behalf for forgiveness. (These were also important aspects of the work of later prophets.) Samuel obviously also had other, supernatural gifts. When Saul was out looking for his father's lost asses Samuel could tell him they were found–and also predict what would happen to him on his way. But these are comparatively trivial matters. Samuel is best remembered for the fact that he, like many of the prophets, was the one through whom God's choice of a king was made known. He anointed Saul, and later David, as God's chosen rulers.

While David was still king, the prophet Nathan was similarly involved in king-making. But it was not until the middle of the ninth century BC that prophecy came to the fore with work of Elijah and Elisha.

A crisis in the northern kingdom of Israel formed the backcloth to the work of these prophets. Foreign gods had been imported into the worship of Israel by Jezebel, wife of King Ahab. She had brought from her home city of Tyre 850 prophets of Baal and Asherah, a Canaanite god and goddess. Elijah realized that he must challenge this false religion and uphold faith in Israel's God.

So Elijah challenged the Canaanite prophets to a contest on Mt Carmel where God proved by fire that 'The Lord is God; the Lord alone is God!' Elisha continued Elijah's mission. He performed miracles of healing and later in his life had Jehu anointed king of Israel. He gathered a number of disciples–'sons of the prophets'– who preserved the memory of his deeds.

1 Samuel 7:3-17; 9-10; 2 Samuel 7; 1 Kings 1:11-40; 17-19;
2 Kings 1-9

Later prophets None of the 'older' prophets have left us any books of their prophecies, though we do know a little of what they said and did. But in the 'classical' period of prophecy, from the eighth to the fifth centuries BC, many of the prophets' messages were written down and compiled into the Old Testament books we now have: Isaiah, Jeremiah, Ezekiel, and the Book of the Twelve Prophets (the 'minor' prophets–Hosea to Malachi), plus the Book of Daniel.

The crisis behind this new period of prophecy was the changing political scene that led first to the exile of Israel (the northern kingdom) after its capital, Samaria, was captured in 721 BC, and then to the exile of Judah (the southern kingdom) after Jerusalem had been destroyed in 586 BC.

The message of these prophets centres on the exile. Some looked ahead to it. Others reflected on its meaning. And the later prophets encouraged the nation to rebuild itself out of the disaster.

Before the exile The prophets warned that judgement was inevitable. Amos and Hosea did so in the northern kingdom in the eighth century; Jeremiah in the southern kingdom in the late seventh century. They called on the people to repent. It was not yet too late for God to change his mind. But the prophets were forced to realize that the people were in no mood to repent. They had been given many chances, but they refused to take them. At this point Amos speaks for all the prophets. This is God's message: 'Get ready to face my judgement!'

What had Israel done to make God so angry? Different prophets exposed different aspects of Israel's sin. Amos attacks social injustice; Hosea Israel's unfaithfulness to God; Micah the sins of Israel's rulers; Jeremiah the false gods and the unchecked corruption in Judah. For these sins, the righteous God must punish his people, even though it pained him to the heart to do so.

Amos 9:1-4; Hosea 11:5-7;
Jeremiah 25:8-11; Amos 5:14-15;
14:6-12

The exile and after Once Judah as well as Israel had gone into exile, some, at least, began to realize that they had deserved this punishment. From this time on, the prophets were able to stir up hope. Ezekiel foresaw a day when the nation, lifeless as a heap of dead bones, would begin to live again as the Spirit of God breathed new life into the people. He looked forward to the rebuilding of the temple and a new settlement of the land. The prophecies of Isaiah 40–55 also brought a message of assurance to the people. God was about to bring the exiles back from Babylonia to Jerusalem.

Then, after the first exiles had returned, and the excitement of the beginning of temple rebuilding had worn off, a new generation of prophets was needed to meet the crisis of disillusionment and despair. If Haggai and Zechariah had not encouraged the people to work on the temple, it would never have been completed. The return from exile would have been a failure if the worship of God had not been properly restored.

Ezekiel 37; 40–48;
Isaiah 40:1, 9-10

The role of the prophets The prophets are best understood as messengers. Their speeches (or 'oracles') often begin with the words 'God says' or 'God spoke'. This is the way a messenger in the ancient world would begin a message he was bringing by word of mouth. The prophets were called by God to hear his plans and his messages. Then they were sent by him to bring this message to Israel and the nations. Sometimes they saw visions; sometimes they preached sermons; sometimes they used parable or poetry or drama to speak to the people. They tell us little about how they actually received their messages. But they were completely convinced that what they said came from God.

The prophets were usually against the mainstream of opinion. When all seemed well, they attacked the evils of their society and predicted its doom. When their people were pessimistic, they prophesied hope. They brought these disturbing, challenging words from God because God's call had broken into their own lives and changed them drastically.

The prophets were also teachers calling Israel back to obey God's laws. They were not preaching a new religion, but applying the word of God to their own day.

The Old Testament owes a great deal to the prophets. Not just the books of the prophets, but many of the history-books, especially those from Joshua to 2 Kings, were written either by prophets or by men who had learned much from the prophets' teaching. They wrote history as God sees it.

Jeremiah 23:18, 21-22; Amos
7:1-2; Zechariah 1:7-21;
Jeremiah 7; 18; 19; Isaiah 1;
Ezekiel 5:17; 1 Kings 18:19; Amos
7:14-16; Isaiah 6; Jeremiah 1

False prophets All through Israel's history there were false prophets who claimed that their messages came from God, when in fact they did not. A prophet might begin his preaching with 'God says', but that was no guarantee at all that it really was a word from God. It needed spiritual insight to decide, in a particular case, what actually came from God. The Law in Deuteronomy recognized the problem and gave two helpful rules. If a prophet predicted something and it did not happen, he was a false prophet. And if his message led people away from God and his laws, it was false.

1 Kings 22; Jeremiah 28; Micah
3:5-7; Jeremiah 23:13-32;
Deuteronomy 13; 18:21-22

The message of the prophets Jeremiah saw that the exile meant the end of God's covenant with Israel: 'Both Israel and Judah have broken the covenant that I made with their ancestors.'

Yet the prophets believed that God would not desert Israel even though they no longer had any claim upon God. That is why even those prophets who pictured a dreadful future for the people could still look beyond the tragedy to a time of hope. In Amos it is promised that the family of David will be restored to the throne; in Hosea that God will heal Israel's faithlessness; in Jeremiah that God will re-make the covenant.

So the prophets' message looked to the past, recalling Israel to obedience; to the present, dealing with the crisis of faith in which the people found themselves; and to the future, because they believed that God had committed himself to Israel. The commitment might mean the destruction of Israel for a time but it would end in rebuilding. The time when Israel would be destroyed and rebuilt was sometimes called the 'Day of the Lord'. The hope of a Messiah who would bring about a restoration has its roots in the Old Testament, but it became important only in the last centuries before Christ. For the prophets, it was God who would step in to restore Israel.

Jeremiah 11:10; Amos 9:11-12;
Hosea 14:4; Jeremiah 31:31-34;
Amos 9:9; Zechariah 13:8-9;
Isaiah 2:12-17; Zephaniah

Prophecy in the New Testament With the outpouring of God's Holy Spirit on all believers, everyone, men and women, can proclaim God's message. But there is still a gift of 'prophecy' mentioned in the New Testament. This is one of God's special gifts given to various members of the church in order to build it up.

The prophecies of the Book of Revelation, like those in the Old Testament Book of Daniel belong to a type of literature called 'apocalyptic'. This contains a special kind of imagery and symbolism which can be understood only if it is applied first to the time in which these books were written.

Acts 2:17; 1 Corinthians 11:5;
14:24, 29; 1 Corinthians 12:10, 29

Proverbs
Proverbs is a book of wise sayings and proverbs intended to guide a young man in a good and godly life. Much of it is blunt day-to-day advice, set down in forms which were popular at the time of writing, not just in Israel but also in neighbouring countries.

Much of the book probably dates from the time of the first kings of Israel, although the final editing was much later. King Solomon–famous for his wisdom–is named in the title of the book, but it is not clear what part he played in the collection.

The book sets out what is right and wrong. Its basis is the principle that 'to have knowledge you must first have reverence for the Lord'. It then applies this wisdom to every area of life: marriage, home, justice, decision making, attitudes; everything a person does, says or thinks.

The short sayings in the book reveal the views of Israelite teachers about how people should behave in various situations. Proverbs underlines the need for such qualities as humility, patience, concern for the poor, hard work, loyalty to friends and respect within the family.

The book begins with a section in praise of wisdom (chapters 1–9). The rest of the book contains six collections of sayings (10:1-31:9) and a poem on the ideal wife (31:10-31).

Psalms
The Book of Psalms is a collection of hymns, prayers and poems. They were composed over a long period by different writers. They were read, sung and chanted by the people of Israel in their worship. It is difficult to give an accurate date to particular psalms, but they were collected from the time of David–or earlier–through to the time after the exile.

The Psalms include poems of contrasting types. There are prayers for help, for God to rescue and protect; songs of praise and worship to God; calls for forgiveness; outpoured thanks for God's goodness. There are also requests that God will punish enemies. Some psalms are concerned with the feelings of individuals; others deal with national needs. A frequent theme is the greatness of God in creation, and his loving care for the nation of Israel.

The Psalms express every type of human emotion and experience. This has helped make them favourite reading all down the ages. Above all they express a deep faith in the living God.

The Psalms often use picture language, like poetry from many other countries. A characteristic feature of the poetry of the Bible is the way in which the thought expressed in one line is echoed in the following line ('parallelism'). There are many examples of this in the Psalms.

The Book of Psalms is made up of five separate sections: Psalms 1–41; Psalms 42–72; Psalms 73–89; Psalms 90–106; Psalms 107–150.

Ptolemais
The Greek name of an ancient city on the coast of northern Israel; Old Testament Acco. Paul sailed here from Tyre on his last visit to Jerusalem, and spent a day with the Christians here. The city is now again known by its early name Akko (Acre), but has lost much of its importance since the growth of modern Haifa near-by.
Judges 1:31; Acts 21:7

Pul
See *Tiglath-pileser.*

Purim
See *Feasts and Festivals.*

Put
An African country, probably part of Libya (as in some modern Bible versions).
Genesis 10:6; Jeremiah 46:9; Ezekiel 27:10, etc.

Puteoli
The port near Naples in Italy where Paul landed on his way to Rome as a prisoner. The town is now called Pozzuoli.
Acts 28:13

Q

Quail
Quails provided the Israelites with meat as they journeyed from Egypt at the time of the exodus. Twice a year vast numbers of quails fly across this region, migrating north in summer, south in winter. Exhausted by the long flight, they fly low above the ground and are easily caught.
Exodus 16:13; Numbers 11:31-35

Quails.

Quirinius (Cyrenius)
Roman governor of Syria at the time of the census which brought Mary and Joseph to Bethlehem.
Luke 2:2

R

Raamses/Rameses
Egyptian city near the coast on the east side of the Nile Delta. Pharaoh Ramesses II had a palace here. Earlier this was the Hyksos pharaohs' northern capital, Avaris. Exodus records that the Israelites built the cities of Pithom and Raamses as supply centres for the king. It was from Raamses that they set out on their escape from Egypt.
Exodus 1:11

Rabbah
The capital city of the Ammonites (see *Ammon*), sometimes also called Rabbath-Ammon. The Israelites defeated Og, king of Bashan, whose 'iron bed' (or coffin) was preserved in Rabbah. This territory east of the Jordan was given to the tribe of Gad. But it was still occupied by the Ammonites until David's general Joab captured Rabbah. When David fled from his rebellious son Absalom he received help from Rabbah. After Solomon's death Ammon seems to have become independent again, and to have been once more a cruel enemy. The prophets denounce the wickedness of Rabbah and prophesy its destruction.

The city later took the Greek name Philadelphia, and became one of the ten cities of the Decapolis (see *Decapolis*). The name of the ancient people, the Ammonites, is preserved in the modern name, Amman. It is now the capital of Jordan.
Deuteronomy 3:11; Joshua 13:25; 2 Samuel 11:1; 12:26-31; 17:27; 1 Chronicles 20:1-3; Jeremiah 49:2; Ezekiel 21:20; 25:5; Amos :14

Rabsaris, Rabshakeh, Tartan
Titles given to Assyrian officials sent by King Sennacherib to bully King Hezekiah and his subjects into surrendering when Jerusalem was besieged.
2 Kings 18–19; Isaiah 36–37

Rachel
Beautiful daughter of Laban. Jacob worked seven years without pay for Laban because of his love for Rachel: then a further seven, after Laban tricked him into marrying Leah first. For many years Rachel was childless: then Joseph was born. When Jacob left for home, Rachel secretly stole her father's household gods. In Canaan Rachel died giving birth to a second son, Benjamin.
Genesis 29–30; 35:18-20

Rahab
A prostitute who lived in a house on the wall of Jericho. She hid Joshua's two spies because she believed God would give Canaan to the Israelites. In return the spies promised to save Rahab and her family when they captured Jericho. Rahab's name is given as the mother of Boaz in Matthew's list of Jesus' ancestors.
Joshua 2; 6; Matthew 1:5; James 2:25

Ramah
A Hebrew name meaning 'height', and used of several towns on hills. Two of these are important in the Old Testament story.

One was at er-Râm, 5 miles/8 km north of Jerusalem. Near here the prophetess Deborah lived. This Ramah was later close to the border between Judah and Israel. It was captured and fortified by Baasha, king of Israel, and recaptured by Asa of Judah. Isaiah pictures the Assyrians approaching Jerusalem by way of Ramah. Later, when Jerusalem actually fell to the Babylonians, Jeremiah was set free at Ramah. The place was resettled after the exile in Babylon. Rachel's tomb was said to have been near Ramah, and Jeremiah spoke of her weeping for her chil-

dren. Matthew refers to this prophecy about Ramah in his account of what happened after Jesus' birth.
Judges 4:5; 19:13; 1 Kings 15:17, 22; 2 Chronicles 16:1, 6; Jeremiah 31:15; 40:1; Isaiah 10:29; Ezra 2:26; Nehemiah 11:33; Matthew 2:18

The second Ramah was about 12 miles/19km further north-west. It was probably the birth-place and home of the prophet Samuel, and may have been the same as New Testament Arimathea. It was also called Ramathaim-Zophim.
1 Samuel 1:1; 2:11, etc.

Ramoth-gilead
A city of refuge east of the Jordan which changed hands several times in the wars between Israel and Syria. It may be the same as Mizpah in Gilead, and so the home of Jephthah at the time of the Judges. One of Solomon's twelve district governors was stationed at Ramoth. King Ahab of Israel was killed in battle here. And Jehu was anointed king.
Joshua 20:8; Judges 11; 1 Kings 4:13; 22; 2 Kings 9:1-10

Raven
The name probably includes crows and rooks as well as ravens. All are large, black, flesh-eating birds. After the flood, Noah sent out a raven to see if the land was dry. Ravens are also said to have fed Elijah in a time of famine.
Genesis 8:7; 1 Kings 17:4

Raven.

Rebekah
The wife of Isaac and mother of Esau and Jacob. Rebekah grew up in Harran, the city where Abraham lived on his way to Canaan. Her father was Abraham's nephew. When Abraham decided it was time for Isaac to marry he sent Eliezer, his chief steward, back to Harran to find a suitable wife. The first person who came to the well where he was resting his camels was Rebekah. With her family's blessing Rebekah set off for Canaan. Isaac loved her on sight. For twenty years Isaac and Rebekah prayed for a son. Then twin boys–Esau and Jacob–were born. Home-loving Jacob was Rebekah's favourite; Isaac preferred Esau. When Isaac was old and nearly blind Rebekah helped Jacob to trick his father into giving him the blessing which belonged to Esau, the elder twin. To save him from Isaac's anger, Rebekah sent Jacob to her brother Laban in Harran.
Genesis 24; 25:19-26:16; 27

Reconciliation
To 'reconcile' two people is to bring them together when they have been enemies. The story of man in the Bible begins with the break in relationships between him and God. It is followed immediately by man's hostility to his fellow man (Cain murders Abel). It is only when the relationship with God is restored that relations between people can be truly healed. This is the effect of the 'reconciliation' which God offers to all.

So it is not surprising that people are often described in the Bible as enemies of God. They are opposed to all that God is and all that he stands for. Mankind is cut off because of sin. It is impossible to reconcile ourselves to God. But, as Paul explained, 'God was making all mankind his friends through Christ.'

This was done in the life, death and resurrection of Jesus himself. It is possible now for people to be friends, in fact children of God, rather than enemies. Sin, the reason for the original estrangement, has been dealt with by Jesus. Yet we are not automatically reconciled to God. It is a gift he offers and which we must accept. But it is a gift that is available for all, and so Christians are expected to explain the 'way of reconciliation' to others.

Reconciliation not only brings peace with God but also peace between one man, or woman, and another. Those who once were enemies find themselves members of the same family when they are reconciled to God. The things that divided them are unimportant compared to the relationship with God which now unites them. This is the solution the New Testament offers to the most bitter racial conflict of Bible times–the split between Jews and non-Jews.

See also *Atonement, Cross, Peace.*
Genesis 3; Romans 5:10-11; 11:15; 2 Corinthians 5:18-20; Ephesians 2:11-18; Colossians 1:19-22

Red Sea
The meaning of the Hebrew word translated Red Sea is 'sea of reeds'. In the story of the exodus it refers to the area of lakes and marshes between the head of the Gulf of Suez and the Mediterranean Sea (the Suez Canal area). It is also used for the Gulf of Suez, the Gulf of Aqaba (the northern arms of the Red Sea proper) as some modern Bible versions make plain.
Exodus 13, etc.; Numbers 33:10; Deuteronomy 1:40

Redemption
To 'redeem' something is to buy it back. Jesus said that he came to 'give his life to redeem many people'.

The picture is that of a slave being 'ransomed'. Man is said to be a 'slave to sin'. Even if we want to give up sinning we cannot do so. But by his life, death and resurrection Jesus paid the price that would set us free.

Christians are therefore 'the redeemed', just as the Israelites who had been brought out of slavery in Egypt were 'the redeemed' in the Old Testament. They now belong to God. Paul urges his readers to consider the price that was paid for their redemption and give themselves wholeheartedly in the service of God. A redeemed person is also a free person, so Paul urges his readers not to fall back into the old ways but to allow God to rid them of the marks left by their former slavery to sin. But even the Christian will not experience full freedom immediately. That must wait until the end of the age, when Jesus returns and his people will know the perfect freedom of living in the presence of God himself.

See *Cross, Freedom, Sons of God.*
Mark 10:45; John 8:34; 1 Peter 1:18-19; Exodus 13:11-16; 1 Corinthians 6:20; Romans 6:12-14; 8:19-23

Regeneration
See *New birth.*

Rehoboam
Son of King Solomon. Rehoboam became king after his father's death but was so unwise a leader that the people rebelled. As the prophet Ahijah had predicted, the ten northern tribes made Jeroboam their king. Only Judah and Benjamin stayed loyal to Rehoboam. From this time on, the northern kingdom was known as Israel, and the southern kingdom Judah. Rehoboam was defeated by Egypt and for much of his reign was at war with Jeroboam.
1 Kings 11:43–14:31; 2 Chronicles 9:31–12:16

Religion of Israel
Abraham The starting-point of Israel's religion is the day when God spoke to Abraham, telling him to leave his land and his family home and go to a new country. On that day God promised to make Abraham the founder of a great nation. Abraham took God at his word. 'He put his trust in the Lord, and because of this the Lord was pleased with him and accepted him.'

So the very first and most basic belief of the Jewish and Christian religions is the certainty that God is a real person, and that human beings–individually or as a group–can know him. Abraham, we are told, did as God said. He moved to Canaan, and in various places where he set up camp he built an altar and worshipped God.

Abraham's faith in God was at times shaky. But he knew that God had committed himself to him and to his family, that was to grow into the nation of Israel.
Genesis 15:6

Jacob The history of Israel as a nation begins with Abraham's grandson Jacob (renamed Israel) and his twelve sons, from whom the twelve tribes were descended. 'I am the Lord, the God of Abraham and Isaac,' God said to Jacob. 'I will give to you and to your descendants this land...I will be with you and protect you wherever you go, and I will bring you back to this land. I will not leave you until I have done all that I have promised to you.' Famine came. Jacob and his sons followed Joseph into Egypt. Their descendants remained there for centuries. But God's promise still held. This family and nation were his people. When the Egyptians made slaves of them and they cried out for help, God heard.

Moses One day, in the desert, God spoke to Moses. 'I am sending you to the king of Egypt,' he said, 'so that you can lead my people out of his country.' Moses needed to know how he could describe God to the people, and so God explained more about the kind of God he was. He revealed his own personal name, Yahweh ('the Lord'), and also his mysterious name

'I am', or 'I will be who I will be'. That name showed two things. God was unchanging: he was completely reliable. But also he was always alive, active, creative. It was the knowledge of this God that Moses brought to his people.

But God did not just give information about himself. He proved by what he did that he was that kind of God.

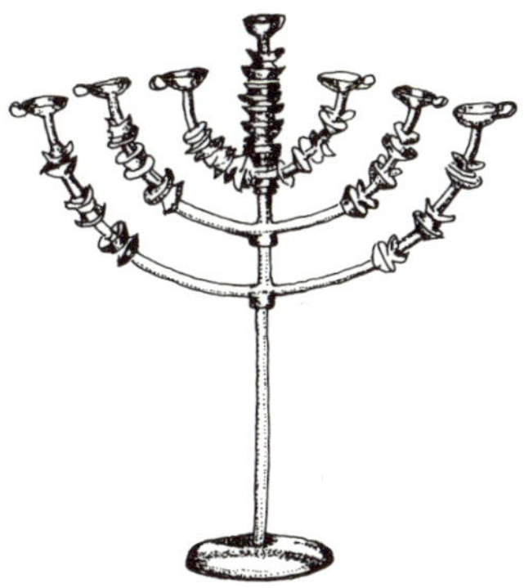

A model of the seven-branched candlestick first made for the tabernacle. This candlestick came to symbolize religious freedom.

When he rescued the Israelites from Egypt to keep the promises he had made to their ancestors, he showed his reliability. But also, when he led them through the unknown wilderness, he met their need for food and water and cared for them in spite of their rebellions. Here was the living God in action.

The Exodus and Mt Sinai In Moses' time, God made himself known as a God who acts and speaks. At the exodus from Egypt he proved that he was the defender of oppressed people and the enemy of the unjust. That in itself was a revelation of his character. At Mt Sinai he revealed himself still further. He told Moses that he was 'a God who is full of compassion and pity, who is not easily angered and who shows great love and faithfulness'. He also revealed his will for his people in the commandments. The Israelites could see from them what he required of them and what his own character was like. The law was to become the pattern of their life–moral, social, religious. The feasts and festivals and sacrifices were to be a constant reminder of their relationship to God. (See separate entries.)

The time of David and Solomon In this age, Israel became an independent state for the first time. The Israelites were impressed by the pomp and splendour of kingship, but they recognized that the dignity of their earthly kings was only a shadow of the greatness of the Lord, the King of kings. A new sense of the grandeur of God can be seen in the temple and its worship and in the psalms sung in the temple, hailing God as a 'mighty God, a mighty king over all the gods'. Along with the solemnity of the temple worship went a strong sense of joy: 'The Lord is king! Earth, be glad! Rejoice, you islands of the seas!' Gladness and reverence went hand in hand, as many of the psalms show.

In the age of David and Solomon God also made a new promise: he would make David's kingdom a lasting one; his dynasty would never end. This kept Israel loyal to the kings of David's family line even when they did not deserve it. And it developed in the end into the hope that God would send a new David, a son of David who would rule justly. So in that promise to David lay the seeds of an expectation of a Messiah.
Psalm 95:3; 97:1; 2 Samuel 7

The prophets The greatest contribution the prophets made to Israel's faith was not a new revelation from God, but a new challenge to be faithful to what God had already made known of himself, and to return to God in repentance. The prophets never tired of hammering home the fact that true religion is not just a matter of ritual, or even of belief, but also of behaviour. They mercilessly attacked the religion of their day, not because it did not follow the patterns laid down in the law-books like Leviticus, but because it was not matched by right behaviour. The prophets spoke to the conscience of Israel. They gave warning of the approaching disaster of the exile. And when God's punishment had come upon Israel, they offered hope and God's promise for a new future.
Amos 5:21-24

The exile The exile was not a gap in the history of Israel, an unhappy experience best forgotten as quickly as possible. Though it was a time of misery for many thousands of Jews, it was one of the most creative periods in Israel's history. For in it the people of Israel found again both themselves and their God. In the exile they came to recognize, in a way they had never needed to before, how much the two things were connected. Israel had no reason for existing apart from the treasure it possessed in knowing God. Unless they saw themselves as the people of God, Israel was no different from any other nation on earth. It could be wiped off the map as easily as many nations have been in the course of history. Many Israelites saw the exile only as a disaster. But those who saw in it God's discipline of his people could also see the exile as a time of purification.

The Jews who returned to the land, 'whose heart God had moved, got ready to go up and rebuild the Lord's Temple in Jerusalem'. They realized that they would only survive by keeping themselves separate from other nations and by insisting on obedience to the letter of God's Law. This was the only realistic attitude; and although, eventually, it led some of them into legalism, it produced a piety that is very praiseworthy.
Ezra 1:5

After the exile The Jews who returned to Israel had no king, but the high priest became their natural leader, assisted by a new class of 'scribes' who were able to explain the Bible's laws. The lesson had been learnt so well that after the exile the prophets never had to rebuke the Jews for worshipping foreign gods, though they did protest at their laziness in rebuilding the temple and their reluctance to pay their tithes.

The Jewish community of returned exiles was a small one, probably less than 75,000 people. It was very aware of being different from the surrounding nations. Three things which stressed this 'difference' were specially emphasized at this time: strict observance of the sabbath, of the rite of circumcision, and of the Jewish food laws.

The focus of religious life was to be not so much the temple but the synagogue, the local place of meeting and teaching, that had been developed in the years of exile.
Haggai 1; Malachi 3:7-11; Nehemiah 13:15-27; Isaiah 56:6-7; Genesis 17; Leviticus 11 (see also Daniel 1)

Between the Testaments Hopes for the future were very much alive in the time of Christ. Several centuries before, the prophets had predicted the end of Israel as a nation-state, and those prophecies had been fulfilled by the exile. Some of their prophecies seemed, though, to reach beyond the near future into a distant future when God would, as Haggai put it, 'shake heaven and earth' and a totally new age would dawn.

From the second century BC on, a new type of writing called apocalyptic (meaning 'revelation') was produced. The writers of these apocalyptic books were sure that the end of the world was close. God was about to step in, destroy the foreign rulers, whether Greeks or Romans, and begin a new era in history. One apocalyptic group was the community of the Dead Sea Scrolls (see *Essenes*).

The Messiah Many of the hopes for the new age centred on the Messiah. In the Old Testament the Hebrew word 'Messiah' meant simply 'someone who has been anointed' and could be applied to kings, priests, or prophets. Some prophets, such as Isaiah, spoke of a future king descended from David who would 'reign in righteousness' and upon whom God's Spirit would rest.

In the century and a half before the coming of Christ, many people began to look forward eagerly for such a ruler. The men of the Dead Sea sect looked for two 'Messiahs', one would be a priest, the other a king. The collection of hymns from the first century BC called the *Psalms of Solomon* was one of the first writings to use the phrase 'the Lord Christ (that is, Messiah)' (or, 'the Lord's Christ') for this coming ruler (compare Luke 2:11).

Most often the Messiah was expected to be a warrior who would rid the Jews of hated foreign rulers. It is not surprising that Jesus, whose kingdom 'does not belong to this world' was reluctant to let himself be called 'Messiah'. It created the wrong impression. But the disciples, who in the end understood what kind of a king he was, often used this title for him: 'Jesus the Christ'.
Isaiah 9:1-7; 11:1-9; John 18:36; Mark 8:29-30; Luke 22:67

Resurrection Another hope had also developed: for personal resurrection. In Old Testament times the Israelites generally believed that after death good and bad people alike entered the land of *Sheol*. This was a kind of underworld existence which was only a shadow of real life, and from which no one could return. Occasionally the prophets expressed hope for the resurrection of the nation–as in Ezekiel's vision of skeletons which became men again. But the nearest the Old Testament comes to a hope of resurrection of individuals is in Daniel 12:2, 'many of those who have already died will live again'.

But by the time of Jesus, most Jews (except the *Sadducees*) probably believed in a resurrection for everyone. The righteous would 'rise again into life eternal' (*Psalms of Solomon* 3:16) in 'the garden of life' (1 *Enoch* 61:12), or 'Abraham's bosom' The wicked would be thown into Gehenna, the underworld equivalent of the Valley of Hinnom, the rubbish dump of Jerusalem, where fires always burnt.
Job 7:9-10; Ezekiel 37; Daniel 12:2; Luke 16:22

Belief in angels and demons Israelites had always pictured God as a king surrounded by his courtiers, the angels. God's decisions were made in his council-room, and the prophets thought of themselves as listening in. Not much attention was paid to 'bad' angels. But when they are mentioned, they are clearly under God's control.

In the time between the Old and New Testaments there was great debate about the names and duties of the angels and demons.

The evil angels were sometimes identified with the 'sons of God' or 'supernatural beings' mentioned in Genesis 6:1-4. They and their assistants, the demons or unclean spirits, were held responsible for evil in the world. In the Old Testament Satan was 'the tester', trying to find grounds to accuse man before God. But now he was regarded as a demon prince opposed to God. He was also called Belial and Beelzebub.
Job 1-2; Jeremiah 23:18, 21-22; 1 Samuel 16:14; Daniel 10:13; 8:16; Matthew 12:24; 1 Peter 5:8

Other developments As well as these changes in belief, there were two other important developments in the last centuries before Christ. It was a time when the Law was studied, and extended, as never before (see *Pharisees*). And during this time various religious and political groups sprang up. We meet some of them–Pharisees, Sadducees, scribes–in the New Testament. But even those not named had an effect on the Jewish religious 'climate' of New Testament times.
See also *Feasts and Festivals, Law, Priests and Levites, Sacrifices, Synagogue, Tabernacle, Temple, Worship.*

Repentance

'Repent sincerely and return to me', God said through Joel, 'with fasting and weeping and mourning. Let your broken heart show your sorrow; tearing your clothes is not enough.'

Jesus called for the same inward change of heart. Repentance means more than saying sorry, or even being sorry, for sin. It involves a decision to leave it behind. Jesus' parable of the Pharisee and the tax collector shows the importance he placed on an inward change of heart.

Jesus' message links repentance and faith. 'Turn away from your sins and believe the Good News.' Repentance is not something which comes naturally to people. It is the gift of God. But when men and women meet Jesus for themselves, they repent. There is no other way into the kingdom of God. God 'commands all (people) everywhere to turn away from their evil ways'.

See also *Forgiveness.*
Joel 2:12-13; Luke 18:9-14; Mark 1:15; Acts 11:18; Luke 19:1-10 (and other examples); Acts 17:30

Resurrection

The claim that Jesus rose from the dead is the key fact of the Christian faith. 'If Christ has not been raised, then your faith is a delusion and you are still lost in your sins,' wrote Paul. There was no doubt, however, in the apostles' minds that Jesus had risen from the dead, as he had said he would. They had seen him on various occasions, and this to them was evidence enough. Paul lists the people who had seen Jesus alive. The disciples were transformed overnight, from being a weak and cowardly bunch into being a fearless group of people who preached and performed miracles in the power of their risen Lord. The grave was empty, and the Jewish authorities could not produce a body to disprove the claim that Jesus was alive.

Paul teaches that Jesus' followers will share in his resurrection. When a person becomes a Christian he already experiences the life of the risen Jesus working in his own life. And in the future, Christians can look forward with confident expectation to their own resurrection at the end of the age. Believers must face physical death, like everyone else, but they are assured of a future with Christ in a new spiritual existence. Christianity does not look for the immortality of a soul (a Greek idea), but the resurrection of the complete person in a new and more wonderful body.

See also *Heaven.*
Matthew 28; Mark 16; Luke 24; John 20; 1 Corinthians 15; Acts 1:3; 4:10; Romans 1:4; 6:4-13

Reuben

Eldest son of Jacob and Leah. He tried to save Joseph's life when his brothers plotted to kill him. Years later he offered his own two sons as hostages to guarantee Benjamin's safety. Reuben was founder of the tribe named after him.
Genesis 29:32; 37:21-22; 42; 49:3
Also land belonging to the tribe of Reuben, east of the Dead Sea.
Joshua 13:15-23

Reuel

Another name for Jethro.

Revelation

Human beings can never know God unless God chooses to 'reveal' himself. In his purity and majesty, he 'lives in the light that no one can approach'. We can know something of God's character through the world he has created (even *this* is revelation) and our own experience of it. But otherwise we can know nothing unless he shows it to us. Moses' encounter with God in the burning bush is a clear example of God revealing to a person what he could never have found out for himself.

In the history of Israel God most often revealed himself through what he did, particularly in delivering his people from slavery in Egypt. But time and again they failed to see God at work in their history. So God sent prophets through whom he spoke directly to his people to explain to them what he was doing.

'In the past God spoke to our ancestors many times and in many ways through the prophets, but in these last days he has spoken to us through his Son,' wrote the author of the New Testament letter to the Hebrews. Jesus Christ himself is the final and complete revelation of God. He is God shown to us in a form we can understand, living as a person on earth.

The Bible itself is 'revelation'. It is the written record of what God did and said in history and through Christ–of his message to his people, from the call of Abraham to the time of the New Testament apostles. Its books were written by people under the guidance of God himself.
Ecclesiastes 5:2; Isaiah 58:8-9; 1 Timothy 6:16; Exodus 3; 6:7; Isaiah 1:3; Amos 3:7; Hebrews 1:1-2; John 1:14; 2 Peter 1:21; 2 Timothy 3:16; John 14:26; 16:13

Revelation, Book of

Revelation was written to Christians who were being persecuted for their faith. Its author is named as John, and it may have been written about AD 90–95, when the Emperor Domitian was persecuting Christians and John was an exile on the island of Patmos (off the west coast of modern Turkey).

The writer wanted to encourage his readers in their time of suffering. He wrote down a series of visions or 'revelations' in vivid picture-language (a special style of writing known as 'apocalyptic' and found in the Old Testament Book of Daniel). Christian readers would understand their meaning, but not outsiders.

The great message of the book is that God is in control. Jesus is the master of history. At the end of time God will totally defeat all his enemies, through Christ. His faithful people will be rewarded in a new heaven and a new earth.

Chapters 1–3: the book opens with a vision of Christ, and a series of letters with special messages for the seven churches of Asia Minor.

In chapter 4 the scene changes to heaven and a great vision of God.

John begins to see the things that 'must happen after this' (4:1). He sees a scroll with seven seals which the Lamb breaks open; a vision of seven angels with seven trumpets; a woman, the dragon and the two beasts; the seven bowls of God's anger; the destruction of 'Babylon'; the wedding-feast of the Lamb; and the final defeat of the Devil, followed by the great judgement (chapters 4–20).

The book closes with a dazzling picture of the new heaven, the new earth, the new Jerusalem (chapters 21–22), where God is with his people, and sin, death and suffering are gone for ever.

Rezin

The last king of Syria. Rezin made an alliance with King Pekah of Israel. When Rezin and Pekah attacked Judah, King Ahaz appealed to the Assyrian King Tiglath-pileser III for

help. Tiglath-pileser captured Damascus, the capital of Syria, and killed Rezin.
2 Kings 15:37–16:9; Isaiah 7:1ff.

Rhegium
A port on the toe of Italy, on the Strait of Messina opposite Sicily; the modern city of Reggio di Calabria. Paul's ship called here on his voyage to Rome.
Acts 28:13

Riblah
A town in Syria on the River Orontes. King Jehoahaz of Judah was taken prisoner at Riblah by Pharaoh Neco of Egypt. Later, King Nebuchadnezzar of Babylon had his headquarters here. And King Zedekiah, the last king of Judah, was taken to him at Riblah for sentence following rebellion.
2 Kings 23:33; 25:6-7

Roads
There were few paved roads until the Romans began to build a system of fine roads, connecting the provinces of the Empire to Rome, but not with each other. This is why 'all roads led to Rome'.

Before the Romans, conquest, rather than trade, was the usual incentive for road-building. The Romans built roads to keep their Empire together, to make it possible to move troops, goods and send Imperial despatches long distances at speed. A courier on the Roman roads could cover about 75 miles/120 km a day.

Roman roads were superbly constructed, and many sections remain intact, even today. They were paved with flat stones or with specially-cut blocks of stone on top of two or three layers of foundation material. The road-builders overcame every obstacle. They built bridges over rivers, causeways through marshes, and tunnelled through rock. Altogether the Romans built more than 50,000 miles/80,000 km of roads.

Even so, the roads only went where the Romans wanted them to go. There were still many journeys that had to be made on the old 'roads', unsurfaced and worn by travellers over the centuries.

In towns the streets were not very clean, so the Romans provided pedestrians with raised pavements and stepping-stones to allow them to avoid the dirt and mud.

Rock hyrax
(In the Authorized Version, 'coney', Revised Standard Version, 'badger'.) A small, shy animal about the size of a rabbit, with neat ears and no tail. The hyrax lives in colonies in rocky places.
Proverbs 30:26

Romans
Paul wrote his letter to Christians in Rome in about AD 57, after his three major missionary journeys. He had not yet been to Rome, but intended to go there. He was writing to prepare the Christian group, some of whom he knew (see chapter 16), for his visit.

The letter sets out at length Paul's understanding of the Christian message. It was written after his letters to the Thessalonians, Galatians and Corinthians. It might be called Paul's manifesto. It gives us his fullest and most clearly reasoned statement of basic Christian beliefs.

Paul opens the letter by greeting the Christians in Rome. He explains the basis of his letter: 'the gospel reveals how God puts people right with himself: it is through faith from beginning to end' (1:17).

Paul then shows how all people need God's remedy for sin, both Jews and non-Jews. We can be put right with God through faith in Jesus Christ (chapters 3–4).

Paul describes the free pardon and new life God gives us through Christ. He explains the relevance of God's laws and the work of God's Spirit in the life of every Christian (chapters 5–8).

In chapters 9–11 Paul tries to see what place Israel now has in the plan of God. He believes that the Jews will not always reject Jesus.

Paul continues (chapters 12–15) with some plain words about how Christians should behave. He talks about Christians and the government. He talks about our duties to one another, and how to live in a non-Christian world. He also deals with some tricky questions of conscience.

The letter ends, characteristically, with personal messages to friends and praise to God (chapter 16).

Rome
The beginnings of the city of Rome are lost in legend. The story was that it had been named after its founder, Romulus, whose ancestors had escaped from the Greek destruction of Troy. The date was said to be 753 BC. That was the year from which the later Romans counted the beginning of their history.

Early history For centuries Rome was a small and struggling city-state. But it was well placed at a crossing of the River Tiber in the centre of Italy. At first it had kings, and some of them probably belonged to a mysterious and almost forgotten nation, the Etruscans. These kings were at last driven out, and Rome became a 'Republic', headed by two 'consuls' elected for a year and a council called the 'Senate'. After times of strife, poverty and war, Rome slowly won ground, and by 275 BC controlled all Italy.

Rome grew partly by war, but also by a policy of alliances in which Roman citizenship and other rights were freely granted to allies. Right from the start the Romans were good organizers. They built fine roads and unified the whole of Italy. They were very different in character from the Greeks. They were not very original. But they were practical men, loyal to the state, hard-working and disciplined.

The forum, the political and business centre of ancient Rome.

Wars It was not long before Rome faced a new enemy, Carthage. Carthage was on the coast of modern Tunisia, and controlled the sea-routes and trade of the western Mediterranean. The struggle was to last for over a century. The Carthaginians had a leader of genius, Hannibal. He is best remembered for his bold crossing of the Alps with elephants. He invaded Italy and defeated Rome on her own soil, but he got no support and finally had to retreat. The Romans destroyed Carthage in 146 BC.

By this time Rome had also been drawn into the affairs of the East, where Hannibal had joined Rome's enemies. The Romans defeated Antiochus III of Syria and gave his lands in Asia Minor to their ally Eumenes II of Pergamum. They destroyed Corinth in 146, and began direct rule over Greece. In 133 the last king of Pergamum left his lands to the Romans. Out of them they made the province of 'Asia'.

World power So Rome became a world power. But there were great changes. The Greeks had a remarkable influence on their conquerors. Romans studied Greek language and thought and copied Greek styles of art and writing. But there were also other changes, for the worse. Asia, in particular, was very rich, and Roman officials began to use their new position to enrich themselves by robbing their subjects. The Senate in Rome was not able to control them. And this was only part of a larger problem. It was not possible to govern a world empire in the same way as a small city. Large armies and regular organization were needed. Ambitious men began to struggle for power. As a result, there were several civil wars in the first century BC.

In 63 BC the Roman general, Pompey, occupied Jerusalem. From that time Rome had a controlling influence on Palestine. Later, Pompey became the Republican champion, against the ambitious Julius Caesar. But Caesar defeated him and took the title 'dictator', a position which gave him special emergency powers. Caesar was a brilliantly able and vigorous ruler. But he was murdered in 44 by the Republicans Brutus and Cassius. Caesar's friend Antony and his heir Octavian defeated the Republicans in 42 at Philippi in Macedonia, a city well known in the New Testament. Then the two victors quarrelled. Octavian defeated Antony and his ally Cleopatra, queen of Egypt.

The Empire and the emperors People were weary of so many years of war. Octavian gave them peace. In 27 BC he received the title 'Augustus'. He claimed to have brought back the Republic and was careful to disguise his real power. He kept control of the army and became, in fact, the first ruler of what we call the 'Empire', though he never used the word. He united the whole Mediterranean world under one peaceful government. It became possible to travel safely by land or sea to every part. There was great thankfulness everywhere for Augustus. He died in AD 14.

Jesus was born in the time of Augustus (Luke 2:1). His teaching, death and resurrection took place in the reign of the next emperor, Tiberius (AD 14–37). Paul travelled during the reigns of Claudius (AD 41–54) and Nero (AD 54–68), the 'Caesar' to whom he appealed at his trial (Acts 25:11).

The Romans and the Jews Palestine was occupied by the Romans in the time of Jesus. They tried at first to rule there through kings of the Herod family. When this failed in Judea, they sent a Roman governor called a 'procurator'. Although the first emperors were usually careful to respect the feelings of their subjects, they found it difficult to cope with the religion and nationalism of the Jews. Pontius Pilate (AD 26–36) and his successors angered them by their harsh misrule, and in AD 66 there was a desperate rebellion against Rome. When Nero died, rival generals fought for power in Rome. Vespasian, commander of the Syrian frontier army, finally won and became emperor (AD 69–79). It was his son Titus who ended the Jewish rebellion. He destroyed Jerusalem and its temple in AD 70.

Rome had often favoured and protected the Jews in the past. Paul was both a Jew and a Roman citizen. He naturally looked to Rome for justice and protection. Rome had provided the peace and freedom to travel and spread the gospel. When Paul was treated unjustly he used his right as a Roman to appeal to the Emperor. He may not then have known what an evil man Nero was becoming.

Life in Rome Rome was now the centre of the world, a city of well over a million people. We have vivid pictures of its life: the tall buildings and narrow, congested streets where people lived in fear of fire, and the constant noise of carts kept them awake all night. The emperors and nobles lived in great luxury, but also in fear. There were free men and slaves of many races thronging the streets. The emperors tried to keep the peace by organizing corn from Egypt and bloodthirsty public shows where men or beasts fought to the death. When a great fire broke out in Rome in AD 64, Nero blamed the Christians, and tortured many of them to death.

The good and the bad For all its achievements there was clearly a bad side to Roman civilization. We can understand how Rome was hated in the occupied country of Palestine. Governors like Pilate, Felix and Festus had no interest in the matters of faith which Jews and Christians debated. Yet Jesus commended a Roman's faith (Luke 7:1ff.) and Peter found another Roman officer, Cornelius, to be a man who sincerely sought God (Acts 10:11).

After the fall of Jerusalem Christians faced new problems. The Emperor Domitian (81–96) insisted on being worshipped as a god. A faithful Christian could not obey. Rome became an enemy. The Book of Revelation was written when Christians needed strength to meet Roman persecution. Rome on its seven hills (Revelation 17:9) was pictured as a luxury-loving prostitute, like ancient Babylon.

See also *Greek and Roman Religion*.

'Rose'

Two plants may be called 'rose' in the Bible: a mountain tulip and narcissus.

The word often translated 'rose' in the Bible is not the rose as we know it: but probably the narcissus in Isaiah 35:1, and a mountain tulip in the Song of Solomon 2:1

Ruth

The peaceful story of Ruth contrasts with the violent times of the Book of Judges, in which it is set.

Ruth, a Moabite woman, married an Israelite. When he died, Ruth showed unexpected loyalty to her Israelite mother-in-law, and trust in the God of Israel. Finally she found a new husband among the relatives of her dead husband. By this marriage she became the great-grandmother of King David, and an ancestor of Jesus himself.

Although religion generally was weak in these times, the Book of Ruth shows the faith of an ordinary person–a foreigner who turned to the God of Israel.

S

Sabbath

See *Feasts and Festivals*.

Sacrifices

The practice of animal sacrifice goes back to very early times. Genesis 4 tells how Abel killed one of his lambs and gave the best parts as an offering to God. Noah made a sacrifice of animals and birds after his escape from the flood. The agreement between God and Abraham was sealed with a sacrifice.

The details of the sacrifices are described in the Book of Leviticus. There we learn certain basic facts about their meaning.

1. Sacrifice is always made to God himself. So only the best is good enough. Sacrifice was also a way of setting apart for God something belonging to a man.
2. Sacrifice is a way of approach given by God. He gave the rules for sacrifice. It is not simply man's own attempt to earn favour with God, it is God's way for men to make their peace with him. All the same, a person must freely wish to make use of the ritual which God has laid down.
3. Sacrifices are for everyone. In most religions, rituals like these are the secret of the priests. The fact that they alone know how to approach the god helps them to keep their special position in the community. But in Israel, the laws of sacrifice (that is, the Book of Leviticus) are part of the Scriptures that belong to everyone. And in fact in Israel most sacrifices were actually carried out by the worshipper, and not by the priest.
4. There are limits to the effectiveness of sacrifice. In most cases, the sacrifices could only compensate for accidental or 'unwitting' sins. For deliberate disobedience sacrifice could only express repentance. If a sinner is to be pardoned, he must seek pardon directly from God. The New Testament also makes it clear that the blood of bulls and goats could not take away sin.
5. Sacrifice is a substitution. Sometimes, the death of the sacrificed animal was seen as taking the place of the person who brought the sacrifice. Sin that deserved death could not be atoned for by sacrifice, but a person who had repented of his sin and had been forgiven by God, would often bring a sacrifice as a sign of his sorrow for sin. In the New Testament, the death of Jesus is understood as a sacrifice which *did* take the place of the sinner.

Genesis 4; 8:20; 15; Leviticus 1–7; 16–17; 4:2, 13, 22, 27; Psalm 51:16–17; Hebrews 10:4; 9:11–12; 10:12

There were several types of sacrifice:

Burnt-offering The whole animal, except for the skin, which went to the priests, was sacrificed to God. The worshipper placed his hands on the animal to show that it was a sacrifice for his own shortcomings. The animal had to be in perfect condition (only the best is good enough for God). The blood of the animal was sprinkled on the altar as a further sign that the life of the animal given in death had been dedicated to God.
Leviticus 1

Grain-offering This was an offering of flour, baked cakes, or raw grain, together with oil and frankincense. It was a good-will offering to God. Part of it–a 'memorial portion'–was burnt on the altar. So it was a way of asking God to 'remember' the worshipper for good. It was also a contribution to the upkeep of the priests. Again, it was a sacrifice of the best

the worshipper could give.
Leviticus 2

Peace (fellowship)–offering The ritual was similar to that for the burnt-offering, except that here only the fat–which the Israelites considered the best portion–was burnt on the altar, and the meat was shared by the worshipper and his family. Since God also shared in the sacrifice, it was thought of as a friendship meal with God too.
Leviticus 3

Sin-offerings These sacrifices were offered when a person had sinned against someone else or against God. This sin 'defiled' (contaminated) the holy place of tabernacle or temple, and so it needed to be cleansed. The blood of the sacrifice was sprinkled as a sign that the defilement had been removed through the death that had taken place. Some of the sacrifice was taken as food for the priest. When the worshipper saw the priest eat the meat without being harmed he knew that God had accepted his act of repentance.
Leviticus 4; 5; 7

The ritual of sacrifice on the Day of Atonement (Leviticus 16) is somewhat different. Here, as well as other sacrifices, two goats were used. One was killed as in the usual sin-offering, but the other was sent into the wilderness as a symbol that the sins were being removed. (See *Atonement.*)

Sadducees

This group was smaller than the Pharisees, but more influential. Most Sadducees were members of the families of priests. They supported the Hasmonean high-priest kings and later the Roman rulers. We have little reliable information about the Sadducees, since most of it comes from their opponents. But we do know that they did not accept the Pharisees' extensions of the Law (the oral law, as distinct from the Old Testament written law). That is why they could not believe in resurrection, for it is not clearly taught in the Old Testament Law (Genesis to Deuteronomy).
Matthew 16:1-12; Mark 12:18-27; Acts 4:1-2; 5:17-19; 23:6-10

Saint

See *Holiness.*

Salamis

A commercial centre on the east coast of Cyprus. A number of Jews lived here, and when Paul visited the town he preached in synagogues.
Acts 13:5

Salem

See *Jerusalem.*

Salome

One of the women who looked after Jesus and his disciples while they were in Galilee. Salome was present at the crucifixion. On the resurrection morning she was one of the women who took spices to the tomb to embalm the body. Many believe that Salome was the wife of Zebedee and mother of James and John.
(Matthew 27:56) Mark 15:40; 16:1

Salt Sea

The Old Testament name for the Dead Sea, given because the water contains very heavy deposits of salt. See *Arabah.*

Salvation

God's act of rescue. People are helpless to escape from the situation in which sin has ensnared them. Only God can bring deliverance.

There is a past, present and future tense in the use of 'salvation' in the New Testament. God sent Jesus into the world to 'save his people from their sins'. Sin was dealt with by Jesus in his death and resurrection. By faith in him we can now be 'saved'. This free gift is offered to all, no matter what their religious, racial or social background. 'Everyone who calls out to the Lord for help will be saved.' Christians are already 'saved', because they already have forgiveness and new life. But they will not experience the full meaning of salvation until the end of the age and the return of Jesus Christ. In the meantime they are 'being saved'.

In the Old Testament, salvation is more than just spiritual deliverance. The major act of salvation was when God freed the Israelites from actual slavery to the Egyptians. The New Testament also teaches that God's salvation affects far more than a person's 'spiritual' life. It concerns the whole person. Nearly a third of the references to salvation in the New Testament are concerned with being set free from specific ills such as imprisonment, disease and demon possession. When a person becomes a Christian, Christ's salvation affects the whole of life, physical as well as spiritual. But no part of him will be completely whole until he is finally 'saved' at the return of Christ.

See also *Atonement, Freedom, Redemption.*
Matthew 1:21; Ephesians 2:8-9; Romans 10:13; 13:11; 1 Corinthians 1:18; Philippians 2:12; Matthew 9:21-22; Luke 8:36 (where 'saved' is translated 'cured')

Samaria

Capital of the northern kingdom of Israel. The city was on the main north/south trade-route through Israel and was built on top of a hill so that it could easily be defended. The work of building the city was started about 875 BC by King Omri. It was continued by his son Ahab, who added a new palace. So much carved ivory was used to decorate the palace that it became known as the 'ivory house'. Over 500 pieces of ivory, some covered with gold leaf, have been discovered by archaeologists in the ruins of the palace.

One of the beautiful ivory carvings which once adorned King Ahab's palace at Samaria.

From the start, the people of Samaria followed pagan religions. Several Old Testament prophets condemned their idol-worship and warned that the city would be destroyed.

The Syrians attacked and besieged Samaria many times, but it was the Assyrians who finally captured the city in 722/1 BC. The people were exiled to Syria, Assyria and Babylonia. They were replaced by colonists from different parts of the Assyrian Empire. When Samaria fell, the kingdom of Israel ceased to exist. The whole area, not just the city, became known as Samaria.

By New Testament times the city of Samaria had been rebuilt by Herod the Great and renamed Sebaste (Greek for Augustus). A few half-caste Jews still remained in Samaria and claimed to worship God there, but these 'Samaritans' were despised and hated by the Jews in Judea. Jesus showed his concern for them by travelling through their land and staying with them. After Jesus' death and resurrection Philip went to Samaria to preach the gospel, and his work was followed up by Peter and John.

A small group of Samaritans still live in Nablus and Jaffa and worship on Mt Gerizim.
1 Kings 16:24, 32; Isaiah 8:4; Amos 3:8; 2 Kings 6:8–7:17; Luke 17:11; John 4:1-43; Acts 8:5-25

Samson

A Judge in Israel famous for his great strength. Before Samson was born, an angel told his mother he was to be specially dedicated to God as a Nazirite and destined to save Israel from the Philistines. As a sign of this his hair was never to be cut. When Samson grew up he harassed the Philistines singlehanded, although he never fully freed his people. His weakness for women was his undoing. In the end he told a Philistine girl, Delilah, the secret of his strength. Samson was captured. His hair was cut. He was blinded and put in prison. As his hair grew long again his strength began to return. At a festival Samson was taken to a Philistine temple to amuse the crowd. He grasped the two pillars which supported the temple, prayed and heaved with all his might. The building crashed to the ground, and Samson died with the Philistine leaders and people.
Judges 13–16

Samuel

The son of Elkanah and Hannah who grew up to be the last great Judge in Israel and one of the first prophets. When Samuel was born, Hannah's heartfelt prayer for a son was answered. In return she kept her promise to God and took Samuel to the shrine at Shiloh to be trained by Eli, the priest. One night Samuel received a message from God that Eli's family would be punished because of his sons' wickedness. When Eli died, Samuel faced a difficult situation. Israel had been defeated by the Philistines and the people felt God no longer cared

about them. Samuel told them to destroy their idols and obey God. Samuel ruled Israel all his life and under his leadership there was peace. When Samuel was old he made his sons judges and handed his work over to them. But the people were not happy and asked for a king. At first Samuel was against this, but he was guided by God to anoint Saul. After Saul had disobeyed God, Samuel anointed David as the next king. Everyone in Israel mourned when Samuel died.
1 Samuel 1–4; 7–16; 19:18ff; 25:1

Books of Samuel

The two books of Samuel give a history of Israel from the last of the Judges to the final years of King David. They are named after Samuel, the last great Judge, not because he wrote them, but because he towers over the early chapters. They were originally one book in the Hebrew Bible.

Samuel anointed Israel's first two kings, Saul and David, as God's chosen rulers. The books cover roughly the period 1075–975 BC. The author/historian several times refers to the separate kingdom of Judah. This means that the books must have been compiled in their final edition after 900 BC. But they contain much material that is contemporary with the events they describe–especially the story of intrigue at the court of David in 2 Samuel 9–20, which many scholars believe to be the work of professional court secretaries who actually witnessed what they wrote about.

The books of Samuel are mostly concerned with the story of God's dealings with the nation of Israel.

1 Samuel tells how Israel changed from rule by the Judges to rule by kings.

Chapters 1–8: Samuel's years as Judge of Israel.

Chapters 9–15: the story of Saul, first king of Israel.

Chapters 16–30: the relationship between David and Saul. The book ends (chapter 31) with the death of Saul and his sons. Although the people now had a king, both he and they were seen as living under the rule and judgement of God.

2 Samuel tells the history of David's reign as king, first of Judah in the south (chapters 1–4) and then of the entire nation, including what later became the kingdom of Israel in the north. We read how King David enlarged his kingdom and became a powerful ruler. He was a man of deep faith in God, and very popular. But he was sometimes ruthless in his efforts to gain his own ends–for example in his determination to have Bathsheba, wife of one of his generals, for himself. The book contains David's famous lament over the death of his close friend, Saul's son, Jonathan.

Sanballat

A Samaritan governor who tried to stop Nehemiah rebuilding the walls of Jerusalem.
Nehemiah 2:10, 19; 4; 6; 13:28

Sapphira

See *Ananias.*

Sarah

Abraham's wife; the mother of Isaac. Abraham married Sarah while he still lived in Ur. Because she was beautiful Abraham twice passed her off as his sister instead of his wife, to protect his own life. When it seemed she would never have any children to inherit the blessing God had promised, Sarah gave her maid Hagar to Abraham, and Ishmael was born. Abraham and Sarah were both old when an angel told Abraham that Sarah would have a son. At first she laughed at the idea, but in due course Isaac was born. He was Abraham's heir. Sarah sent Hagar and her son Ishmael away after Isaac's birth. When Sarah died Abraham bought a cave near Hebron as her burial-place.
Genesis 11–12; 16–18:15; 20-21

Sardis

A city in the Roman province of Asia (in modern Turkey) situated at the point where two main trade-routes met. In Roman times there were thriving dyeing and woollen industries here. One of the seven letters to churches in Asia, in the Book of Revelation, was addressed to the Christians at Sardis. The church had become apathetic. They relied on the past instead of concentrating on the present–an attitude typical of the city as a whole. It had been the capital of the kingdom of Lydia and at one time ruled by Croesus. His wealth was legendary; gold was easily obtained from a river which flowed close to the city. The first gold and silver coins were minted at Sardis.
Revelation 1:11; 3:1-6

Satan

Satan is the Hebrew name and Devil the Greek name for the being who personifies all that is evil and opposed to God. Both names mean 'accuser', showing that Satan is the one who tries to tempt people to do wrong so that he can accuse them before God.

The battle between good and evil is not an equally balanced contest. God is all-powerful and eternal; Satan often appears to be in control, but his work is limited by God. He destroys and undermines by tricks and cunning, rather than power. But within the world he holds such power that he can be called its ruler.

Jesus came 'to destroy what the Devil had done', and through his victory over evil in his death and resurrection Satan has been defeated. Although he is still active within the world his defeat will be total at the end of the age.

We can see clearly how Satan set himself against God's work in the life of Jesus. Jesus was tempted by the Devil in the desert. Peter was used as a tool of Satan and had to be rebuked by Jesus. The betrayal by Judas Iscariot was another part of Satan's work. Jesus had many clashes with evil spirits under Satan's control, but his many exorcisms showed that his power was far greater than that of Satan and the forces of evil.
2 Corinthians 11:14; Ephesians 6:11; John 14:30; 1 John 3:8; John 12:31; 1 Peter 5:8; Revelation 20:10; Matthew 4:1-11; 16:23; Luke 22:3; Matthew 12:22-28

Saul

First king of Israel. Saul was the son of Kish, a man from the tribe of Benjamin. The Israelites asked their leader, the prophet Samuel, for a king, like other nations. God was their real king but he allowed Samue to do as they asked. Samuel was guided by God to anoint Saul, the tallest and most handsome man in Israel. Saul was acclaimed as king after he had proved himself in battle.

To begin with he was humble, bui he soon became proud and deliberately disobeyed God. Samuel was sent to tell Saul that God had choser another man to be king. Saul began to suffer from fits of madness. David was known for his skill on the harp and was sent for to soothe the king with his music.

At first Saul treated David kindly, but soon grew jealous of his popularity and tried to kill him. David was forced to escape to the mountains. Saul's power as a leader failed and he was unable to overcome the Philistines. When the Philistine army was preparing to attack Israel again, Saul turned to a medium for help. In the battle which followed, Saul and Jonathan his son were both killed.
1 Samuel 8–31; 2 Samuel 1ff.

Scribes

The scribes were the experts in the Law and are also called lawyers or teachers (rabbis). They interpreted the Law and applied it to everyday life. Jesus had not been to one of the schools for rabbis, but his own disciples called him 'teacher' (rabbi). So too did many of the professional rabbis. They were greatly impressed by his understanding of the Law. Later, Paul came to Jerusalem as a student of Rabbi Gamaliel.
Mark 7:28-29, Luke 2:41-47; Acts 4:5-7, 18-21; 6:12-14; 22:3

Scythians

The horse-riding Scythians ('Ashkenaz') came from central Asia in the seventh century BC. Some groups of Scythians burst into the Near East. They destroyed Urartu, and joined with the Medes, in alliance with Babylon, to overthrow Assyria. In due course they provided men for the Persian army. One Scythian troop marched through Syria to raid Egypt, reaching Ashkelon about 630 BC.
Jeremiah 51:17

Bronze models of Scythian archers on their horses: from about 500 BC.

Second coming of Jesus
In his first coming to this world Jesus came quietly, lived the life of the humble servant of God and died on the cross. But during his life he promised that he would return at the end of the world, this time with power and glory for all to see. Many people ignored Jesus when he first came, but when he returns no one will be able to ignore him, and for many it will be a time of grief because it will be the day of judgement. For those who believe, both dead and living, it will be the moment of their final salvation, when Jesus will take them to be with him for ever in a totally re-created world order.

There is no way of finding out when the great day will be. Jesus said that before he comes, the gospel will be preached to all nations. Before he comes, sin will increase and worship be offered to one who falsely claims to be God. But no one can calculate when he will come, for it will be 'at an hour when you are not expecting him'. The Christian must always be ready, so that he is not caught out and ashamed when Jesus returns.
Matthew 24; 26:64; Mark 13:26; John 14; Acts 1:11; 3:19-21; Philippians 3:20; Colossians 3:4; 1 Thessalonians 1:10; 4:13-5:11; 2 Thessalonians 1:5–2:12; 2 Peter 3:8-13; Revelation 19–22

Seir
Another name for Edom.

Sela
Capital of Edom. The name means 'rock' or 'cliff' and was given to this fortress-city because it was built on a rocky plateau high up in the mountains of Edom. About 300 BC the Nabataeans took Sela and carved the city of Petra (the Greek word for rock) out of the rocky valley at the foot of the original settlement.
2 Kings 14:7; Isaiah 16:1; 42:11

Seleucia (Seleucia Pieria)
The port of Antioch in Syria. It was built by, and named after, the first Seleucid king. Paul and Barnabas set sail from here for Cyprus on their first missionary journey.
Acts 13:4

Senir
Another name for Mt Hermon. It is also used to describe a nearby peak and the whole range of mountains.

Sennacherib
King of Assyria, 705–681 BC. He strengthened the Assyrian Empire, sending armies to put down rebel subject nations. After Hezekiah refused to pay tax, Sennacherib attacked Jerusalem. Although he had captured several cities in Judah, Isaiah encouraged Hezekiah not to surrender. Jerusalem was saved. The Egyptian army threatened from the south and death struck the Assyrian army. Sennacherib returned to Nineveh, where he was murdered by two of his sons.
2 Kings 18–19; 2 Chronicles 32; Isaiah 36–37

A relief of Sennacherib praying to the god Assur.

Sepharvaim
A town as yet unidentified, captured by the Assyrians. People from here were brought to Samaria after the Jews had been sent into exile.
2 Kings 17:24, 31; 18:34

Sergius Paulus
Roman governor of Cyprus. He was interested in religion and came under the influence of a magician named Elymas. (See *Elymas.*)
Acts 13:7ff.

Seth
Third son of Adam and Eve, born after Cain had murdered Abel.
Genesis 4:25ff.

Shadrach
See *Abednego.*

Shallum
1. The son of Jabesh; he murdered King Zechariah and made himself king of Israel, 752 BC. Shallum reigned for only one month. He was assassinated by Menahem.
2 Kings 15:10-15
2. A son of King Josiah, usually known as Jehoahaz. (See *Jehoahaz.*)
1 Chronicles 3:15; Jeremiah 22:11

Shalmaneser
Name of several kings of Assyria. Shalmaneser V (727–722 BC) defeated King Hoshea of Israel and made him pay tax to Assyria every year. When Hoshea rebelled, Shalmaneser besieged Samaria, capital of Israel. After three years Samaria fell and the Israelites were exiled to Assyria.
2 Kings 17

Shamgar
One of the Judges in Israel. Shamgar fought off the Philistines.
Judges 3:31; 5:6

Shaphan
Best-known of several men of this name is one of King Josiah's important officials. He helped supervise the temple repairs and reported to Josiah the finding of a scroll of God's laws.
2 Kings 22; 2 Chronicles 34

Sharon
The coastal plain of Israel. It extends from Joppa to Caesarea–about 50 miles/80 km and is about 10 miles/16 km wide. Today the plain is one of the richest agricultural areas in Israel. In Bible times few people lived here. The land was used as pasture for sheep, but much of it was left in its natural state of thick scrub. The writer of the Song of Solomon (Songs) refers to the 'rose of Sharon', one of the many beautiful wild flowers which grew on the plain.
1 Chronicles 27:29; Song of Solomon (Songs) 2:1

Sheba
A country in south-west Arabia, now the Yemen. Sheba became a wealthy land by trading spices, gold and jewels with the Mediterranean world. In the tenth century BC a queen of Sheba travelled over 1,000 miles/1,600 km by camel caravan to visit King Solomon and test his wisdom. She possibly also wished to arrange a trade agreement. The remains of a great dam and a temple to the moon-god Ilumquh have been discovered at Marib, once the capital of Sheba.
Psalm 72:15; Isaiah 60:6; 1 Kings 10:1-10, 13

Shebna(h)
One of King Hezekiah's most important officials, sent to negotiate with King Sennacherib's spokesmen.
2 Kings 18–19; Isaiah 22:15-25; 36–37

Shechem
1. The son of King Hamor, a Hivite king. Shechem raped Dinah, Jacob's daughter.
Genesis 34
2. An ancient Canaanite town which became an important religious and political centre for the Israelites; in the hill-country of Ephraim, near Mt Gerizim.

Abraham stopped at Shechem on his journey from Harran to Canaan. While he was here God told him, 'This is the country that I am going to give to your descendants.' Jacob also visited Shechem and set up camp outside the town.

When the Israelites had conquered Canaan Joshua gathered all the tribes together at Shechem. Here they renewed their promise to worship the God who had rescued them from Egypt, and to have nothing to do with foreign gods. But in the time of the Judges Canaanite worship was practised in Shechem. The inhabitants of the town gave Gideon's son Abimelech money from the temple of Baal-berith so that he could pay to have his seventy brothers killed. Abimelech made himself king of Shechem but the people soon turned against him. In revenge he destroyed the town.

After the death of King Solomon ten of the Israelite tribes rejected Solomon's son Rehoboam at Shechem. Jeroboam, the first king of the new northern kingdom, started to rebuild Shechem, and for a short time made it his capital.

Shechem survived the fall of Israel. It became the Samaritans' most important city and they built a temple here. A few Samaritans still live in Nablus, the modern town north-west of the site of Shechem.
Genesis 12:6-7; 33:18–35:4; 37:12-18; Joshua 24; Judges 9; 1 Kings 12

Sheep and goats
From very early times, before there

was settled farming, nomads depended on their flocks of sheep and goats for milk, cheese, meat and clothes. Goatskins were the standard water-bottle. Black goat-hair was woven into strong cloth for tents. Wool from the sheep was spun and woven into warm cloaks and tunics. Both sheep and goats were killed in the tabernacle and temple sacrifices. They were well suited to rough hill pasture. Shepherds often looked after mixed flocks of sheep and goats, protecting them from wild animals and leading them to fresh grazing and watering-places.
Genesis 27:9; 4:2; Exodus 26:7; Leviticus 1:10; Matthew 25:32; John 10:1-12

Much of Israel's wealth depended on sheep and goats.

Shem
Noah's eldest son. He survived the flood and became the ancestor of several 'Semitic' nations, the group of people to which the Hebrews belonged.
Genesis 6–10

Sheshbazzar
Sheshbazzar led the Jewish exiles back to Jerusalem when King Cyrus of Persia allowed them to return to rebuild the temple. Cyrus handed over to him the treasures Nebuchadnezzar had taken from the temple in Jerusalem before he destroyed it. Sheshbazzar laid the foundations of the new temple.
Ezra 1:8ff.; 5:14ff.

Shiloh
The town where the worship tent (tabernacle) was set up after the conquest of Canaan. Shiloh became the centre of Israel's worship, and the tent was replaced by a more permanent building. Each year a special festival was held here. Hannah and Elkanah travelled to Shiloh to worship God. On one of these visits Hannah, praying for a son, promised that she would give him back to serve God. When Samuel was born Hannah kept her promise. She brought him back to Shiloh and he grew up in the temple, under the care of Eli the priest.

Archaeological evidence shows that Shiloh was destroyed about 1050 BC, probably by the Philistines. Jeremiah the prophet warned that the temple in Jerusalem would be destroyed just as the place of worship at Shiloh had been. But it seems that some people lived on the site of Shiloh, at least until the time of the exile.
Joshua 18:1; Judges 21:19; 1 Samuel 1-4; Jeremiah 7:12; 41:5

Shinar
Another name for Babylonia. See *Babylon.*

Ships
In Bible times travel by sea was even more difficult than land travel. The Mediterranean was safe for sailing only in the summer. Between November and March, ships set sail only in an emergency.

The great seafaring nations of the Old Testament period were the Egyptians and the Phoenicians. They built warships and trading vessels, powered by sails and oars. Israel's only successful attempt to develop a navy came during the golden age of Solomon's reign, at a time when the Phoenicians ruled the waves of the Mediterranean Sea.

Israel's border had been extended south to the Red Sea, and Solomon's alliance with Hiram, king of Tyre in Phoenicia, provided him with expert help in constructing a merchant fleet based on the town of Ezion-geber, at the head of the Gulf of Aqaba. Ezion-geber became an important trading-post. From here Solomon's ships carried copper and iron to 'Ophir' (probably southern Arabia, at the other end of the Red Sea) and returned with luxury goods. The round-trip–about 1,250 miles/2,000 km each way–took three years.

A century later, in about 850 BC, King Jehoshaphat attempted to revive the trade but his fleet was wrecked by a violent storm, and Israel's brief seafaring history was over.

In the New Testament the Gospel writers record several occasions when Jesus crossed the Sea of Galilee by boat. These journeys were probably made in the fishing boats used on this inland lake, 7½ miles/12km wide. The wind funnelling through the surrounding hills can whip the lake into sudden violent storms.

Paul's missionary travels included sea journeys as well as long treks overland. The account of his voyage to Rome given in the Book of Acts reads like a ship's log, with details about weather conditions, seamanship, and even a passenger list. It is one of the most vivid descriptions of a voyage in the whole of ancient literature.

Rome controlled the Mediterranean Sea at the time of Jesus. Corn grown in Egypt and exported from Alexandria on the Nile Delta was vital to the economic stability of the Empire. State-run grain-ships, some as much as 200 ft/60 metres long, carried the corn to Italy. During the summer the winds took the ships straight across the sea from Egypt to Italy, but out of season the safer course was by shorter stages, or round the coast.

A Roman merchant ship built to carry large cargoes of grain.

Paul sailed in a corn-ship taking the safer route in late September or early October. When the ship was wrecked, the rest of the cargo and even the ship's tackle were thrown overboard before the valuable grain. It was another ship from Alexandria that took Paul on from Malta to Italy after the shipwreck.

Puteoli, on the Bay of Naples, was the main port of Rome until New Testament times when the harbour at Ostia, nearer to Rome, was improved and eventually became the principal port for the capital city of the Empire.
1 Kings 9:26-28; 10:11-12, 22; 22:48; Mark 4:35-39; Acts 27–28:15

Shittim
A place on the plains of Moab, across the Jordan from Jericho, also known as Abel-shittim, 'field of acacias'. The Israelites camped here just before they crossed the River Jordan into Canaan. They were probably at Shittim when the king of Moab tried to persuade Balaam to curse them. Preparations were made here for the conquest of Canaan. A census was taken of men able to fight; Joshua was chosen as Moses' successor; and two men were sent to spy out Jericho.
Numbers 25:1; 22–24; 26; 27:12-23; Joshua 2; 3:1; Joel 3:18

Shunem
A place in the Valley of Jezreel, in northern Israel, modern Sôlem. The Philistines camped here before the battle on Mt Gilboa when Saul and Jonathan were killed. Elisha was the guest of a woman of Shunem, and he restored her child to life. The girl Abishag, who served David in his old age, was also a Shunnamite. The young woman called a 'Shulammite' in the Song of Solomon (Songs) may have come from the same place.
Joshua 19:18; 1 Samuel 28:4; 1 Kings 1–2; 2 Kings 4:8-37; Song of Solomon (Songs) 6:13

Shur
A desert area in the north-west part of the Sinai peninsula. Traders followed the 'Way of Shur' across the desert towards Egypt. Hagar fled this way after Sarah had treated her unkindly. When the Israelites had crossed the Sea of Reeds after escaping from Egypt they had to travel through this desert, and complained bitterly about the lack of water.
Genesis 16; Exodus 15:22-25

Sidon
A Phoenician (Canaanite) port on the coast of modern Lebanon. Many skilled craftsmen worked in Sidon. Carved ivory, gold and silver jewellery and beautiful glassware were among its exports. Each Phoenician city was virtually self-governing.

When the Israelites conquered Canaan they failed to take Sidon. In the time of the Judges the people of Sidon attacked and harassed the Israelites. The cultures began to merge and the Israelites were accused of worshipping the gods of Sidon–Baal and Ashtoreth. Jezebel, who promoted Baal worship in Israel, was the daughter of a king of Sidon. Because Sidon was opposed to Israel and the worship of God, the Old Testament prophets predicted the town's downfall. Sidon was captured, in

The harbour at present-day Sidon.

turn, by Assyrians, the Babylonians and the Persians. Later it came under Greek and Roman control.

In the time of Jesus most of the inhabitants of Sidon were Greek. Many travelled to Galilee to hear him preach. Jesus also visited Sidon and the neighbouring city of Tyre. He compared Chorazin and Bethsaida, two towns in Galilee, with Tyre and Sidon, saying how much more readily the non-Jewish cities would have responded to him. Paul stopped at Sidon on his journey to Rome and stayed with friends in the city.
Judges 1:31; 10:12, 6; 1 Kings 16:31; Isaiah 23:1-12; Ezekiel 28:20-24; Luke 6:17; Mark 7:24-31; Matthew 11:20-22; Acts 27:3, etc.

Silas
A leader of the church at Jerusalem who travelled with Paul on his second missionary journey, in place of Barnabas. At Philippi (in northern Greece) both Paul and Silas were beaten and thrown into prison. After an earthquake shattered the prison they talked to the jailor about Jesus and he became a Christian. Silas stayed in the nearby town of Beroea while Paul went south to Athens, but joined him again in Corinth. He is almost certainly the Christian called Silvanus in some of the New Testament letters. Silvanus helped Peter write his first letter and may well also have helped Paul with his letter-writing. Paul sends greetings from Silvanus in his two letters to the Thessalonians.
Acts 15:22–17:15; 18:5;
2 Corinthians 1:19;
1 Thessalonians 1:1;
2 Thessalonians 1:1; Peter 5:12

Siloam
A pool, originally underground, which was one of Jerusalem's main sources of water. The water in the pool came through a tunnel from the Gihon Spring outside Jerusalem. When the Assyrians threatened to besiege Jerusalem Hezekiah knew that in order to survive the city must have its own water supply, and gave orders for work on the tunnel. It is 1,750ft/538m long, cut through solid rock.

When Jesus healed a man who had been blind all his life he first put clay on his eyes and then told him to wash in the Pool of Siloam. The tower of Siloam which collapsed, killing eighteen people, probably stood on the slope of Mt Zion, above the pool.
2 Kings 20:20; John 9:1-12: Luke 13:4

Simeon
1. Second son of Jacob and Leah. When Simeon and his brothers went to Egypt to buy corn, he was left behind as a hostage to make sure they brought Benjamin with them next time. Simeon was the ancestor of one of the twelve tribes of Israel.
Genesis 29:33; 34:25ff.; 42:24ff.; 49:5
2. An old man who had been told by God that he would not die until he had seen the Messiah. In the temple he took the baby Jesus in his arms and praised God. His prayer is known as the *Nunc Dimittis*.
Luke 2:22-35
3. A teacher at the church in Antioch. He was probably an African and may well be the Simon of Cyrene who carried Jesus' cross.
Acts 13:1-2
4. The land given to the tribe of Simeon, in the Negev, the southernmost part of Israel. It seems that the area was considered an extension of Judah's territory.
Joshua 19:1-9; compare Joshua 15:20-32

Simon
1. Simon Peter. (See *Peter*.)
2. One of the twelve apostles. He had been a member of the Zealots, an extreme Jewish nationalist group pledged to drive out the Romans.
Matthew 10:4; Acts 1:13
3. A brother of Jesus.
Matthew 13:55
4. A leper who invited Jesus to his house in Bethany. While Jesus was there, a woman anointed his head with expensive perfume.
Matthew 26:6; Mark 14:3
5. A Pharisee who invited Jesus to his house. At dinner a woman wept at the feet of Jesus, dried them with her hair and poured perfume on them.
Luke 7:40ff.
6. Simon of Cyrene, who was ordered to carry Jesus' cross.
Matthew 27:32
7. Simon Magus, a magician at Samaria who tried to buy the apostles' God-given power.
Acts 8:14-24
8. A tanner with whom Peter stayed in Joppa.
Acts 9:43ff.

Sin
The Bible uses many words to describe sin. It is rebellion against God, as the story of Adam and Eve shows. Men and women are therefore enemies of God. Sin is also often described as 'missing the mark' or falling below the standard required by God. A person can be held guilty for *failing* to do what God requires, as much as for deliberately disobeying God's commands. But the essence of all sin is that it is an offence against God. Because of this, men and women are cut off from God and face his anger and judgement. Because of sin, suffering and death came into the world.

The Bible does not concern itself with the thorny problem of where evil comes from. It accepts it as a fact. Satan is its source, but men and women are not allowed to blame Satan for their own downfall, although Adam and Eve tried hard to do so. They are responsible and held guilty for their own sin. In Jesus Christ God has dealt with the problem of sin, and there will come a day when sin and evil are no more.

See also *Death, Fall, Forgiveness, Hell, Judgement, Suffering.*
Genesis 3; Psalm 51; Isaiah 1:18-20; 59; Romans 1:18–2:11; 3:9-26; 5–8; Revelation 20–21

Sinai
A mountain in the Sinai peninsula and the area of desert around it. Three months after leaving Egypt the Israelites reached the mountain and set up camp. Here, at Mt Sinai, God gave Moses the Ten Commandments and other laws. The exact identification of Mt Sinai is not known. It was probably one of two peaks–Gebel Musa or Ras es-Safsafeh–in the south of the peninsula.
Exodus 19–32

Sisera
Captain of the army of Jabin, king of Hazor. He had under his command 900 iron chariots and for twenty years made life unbearable for the Israelites. Sisera was defeated by Deborah and Barak. He escaped on foot, but was killed by Jael when he hid in her tent.
Judges 4–5

Slaves
Some projects–for example, the building and mining works of the Old Testament kings, and the building works of Herod the Great and his successors–needed enormous numbers of workmen. In Old Testament times slavery was accepted in Israel, but it was not widespread. Men and their families became slaves to better-off households when they were unable to meet their debts. Prisoners-of-war were also made slaves. The Old Testament laws about slaves are remarkably liberal for their time, although people may not always have lived up to these ideals. The Israelites were never allowed to forget that they, too, had once been slaves in Egypt. So they were to free their slaves after six years' service.

King David, however, forced prisoners-of-war to work on his projects. And Solomon organized a system of forced labour using Israelites as well. They were expected to work for the king one month in three. These men, with the slaves, built the roads, fortresses and temples that made Solomon famous. They looked after the king's farms and worked in his factories and mines. Long before, the prophet Samuel had warned the people that having a king would mean compulsory armed service and forced labour. State slavery, if not conscription, probably continued all through the time of the kings of Judah.

In New Testament times there were both Jewish and non-Jewish slaves in Palestine. But they were not forced to do heavy work. For the most part they were servants in the houses of the wealthy and of the court. There do not seem to have been many of them. Workmen for the building projects were more usually hired by the day (as in Jesus' parable of the workers in the vineyard–Matthew 20:1-16). When the temple begun by Herod the Great was completed–AD 62-64–more than 18,000 men were thrown out of work.

Paul and Peter gave advice to Christian slaves in their letters to various church groups. These men and women lived in the wider Roman Empire, and probably had a much harsher life than that in Palestine.
Deuteronomy 15:12-18;
2 Samuel 12:31; 1 Kings 5:13-18;
1 Samuel 8:11-18; Ephesians 6:5-9;
Colossians 3:22-25; 1 Timothy 6:1-2;
Philemon; 1 Peter 2:18-25

A Roman slave badge which reads 'Seize me if I should try to escape and send me back to my master'.

Smyrna
A port serving one of the main trade-routes across Asia. It is now the city of Izmir in modern Turkey. In New Testament times it was a beautiful city with many splendid public buildings. One of them was the temple built in honour of the Emperor Tiberius, where emperor-worship was practised. One of the letters to the seven churches in the Book of Revelation is addressed to the Christians at Smyrna.
Revelation 1:11; 2:8-11

Sodom
The town where Lot settled and which became notorious for its immorality. Sodom was suddenly destroyed, along with Gomorrah. Lot was warned of the impending disaster and escaped. Sodom probably now lies submerged at the southern end of the Dead Sea.
Genesis 13:8-13; 14; 19

Solomon
The son of King David and Bathsheba. Israel's most famous king. David had fought many wars to create a strong kingdom; Solomon inherited peace. He protected his country by keeping up a strong army and building fortresses. He also made marriage-alliances with the kings of surrounding countries. Israel became a rich country under Solomon's rule. He traded copper and horses for precious cargoes of gold and jewels. Solomon's God-given wisdom made him famous. The Queen of Sheba (southwest Arabia) visited him to test his wisdom.

Solomon built the first temple for God in Jerusalem. The building materials and skilled workmen were provided by Hiram, king of Tyre, in exchange for wheat and oil. It was a magnificent building and stood for 400 years until Nebuchadnezzar destroyed it in 586 BC. He also built palaces for himself and Pharaoh's daughter, one of his wives. Solomon's reign was spoilt by his ill-treatment of his subjects and by his many marriages. He made his subjects angry by demanding free labour and high taxes from them to carry out his building programmes. In the end, Solomon's foreign wives made him turn away from the true God to worship their own gods. When Solomon died, the ten northern tribes rebelled against Rehoboam, his son, and made the rebel leader, Jeroboam, their king.
2 Samuel 12:24; 1 Kings 1-11;
1 Chronicles 22:5–23:1;
28–2 Chronicles 9

Song of Songs
The Song of Songs is a collection of love poems between a man and woman. It is sometimes called the Song of Solomon because it is probably credited to Solomon in the Hebrew text.

The poems are set in the countryside in springtime. They are full of the passion and joy of human love. They express frankly the delights of physical attraction.

Both Jews and Christians have seen the love expressed in the Song as a picture–of God's love for Israel, or of Jesus' love for the church. There is no backing for this either in the book itself, or anywhere else in the Bible.

Sosthenes
1. Appointed chief official of the synagogue at Corinth when Crispus, the previous ruler, became a Christian. Sosthenes was beaten up after a group of Jews had failed to persuade Gallio, the Roman governor of Achaia, to condemn Paul. If he was later converted, this Sosthenes may be the same as 2 below.
Acts 18:17
2. A Christian known to members of the church at Corinth. The first letter to the Corinthians was sent from Paul and Sosthenes.
1 Corinthians 1:1

Soul
The Bible sees human beings as a unity. It does not speak of an immortal 'soul' locked up in a decaying, sinful body. This was a Greek idea, though it has been held by many Christians through the centuries.

When we read the word 'soul' in the Old Testament it means the whole of a person's being. When the psalmist says, 'Praise the Lord, my soul', he is calling on himself to respond as a whole person to God.

The New Testament uses the word 'soul' in a similar way, meaning 'people'. It is the word used to show that people are more than physical flesh and bone; they have a mind and will and personality. For instance, Jesus said, 'Do not be afraid of those who kill the body but cannot kill the soul; rather be afraid of God, who can destroy both body and soul in hell.'

See also *Body, Flesh.*
Psalm 103:1; Matthew 10:28,
and so on

Sparrow
The word is often used to mean any small bird suitable for eating, but in some places refers specifically to the Hedge Sparrow. Larks and finches as well as sparrows have often been trapped or shot to be cooked and eaten. Jesus used the sparrow to emphasize how much God loves his creatures. If he cares, even for the smallest birds, how much more will he care for people.
Matthew 10:29-31; Luke 12:6-7

Spikenard (nard)
A sweet-smelling ointment was made from this plant which grows in India. It was imported to Israel in sealed alabaster jars to preserve the perfume. This was the costly gift that Mary lavished on Jesus.
Song of Solomon 4:13; Mark 14:3;
John 12:3

The fragrant spikenard plant.

Spinning
See *Clothes-making.*

Spiritual gifts
When Christ left this earth to go back to his Father, he gave 'gifts' to his followers. These gifts are given by the Holy Spirit to individuals within every local Christian church so that they can continue Christ's work. They show the supernatural nature of the church. As a community of God's people, its work is not limited to its members' natural abilities. The Spirit of God gives those gifts which are needed to build up the church. He gives as he thinks fit.

In Ephesians 4 Paul lists some of the gifts which marked people out as having a special work as leaders of the church–apostles, prophets, evangelists, pastors and teachers. In 1 Corinthians 12 Paul takes other examples, this time emphasizing those which would be found among the members–wisdom, knowledge, faith, healing, miracles, speaking and explaining God's message, speaking in strange tongues and explaining what is said. At the end of the chapter he adds to the list those who have the power to help or direct others. Romans 12 lists some other gifts: service, encouragement, sharing with others and acts of kindness. None of these lists claims to be complete.

Paul believed that in every local church each member should be free to use his God-given gift of ministry. Gifts of the Spirit are not given for private enjoyment but for the good of all, and for this reason Paul deals at some length with the question of speaking in tongues. Paul himself spoke in tongues and was keen for others to have the same gift, but he insisted that there must be someone to interpret. Otherwise no one would understand it, and no one would be helped.
Romans 12; 1 Corinthians 12 and 14; Ephesians 4

Sport
See *Games and Sport.*

Stephanas
Stephanas and his family were the first people to become Christians in Achaia (southern Greece). They were amongst the few Christians whom Paul baptized personally at Corinth.
1 Corinthians 1:16; 16:15ff.

Stephen
A Greek-speaking Jew who was the first Christian to die for his faith. Stephen was one of seven men chosen by the apostles to arrange care for poor widows in the church at Jerusalem. He had great faith in God. As well as looking after practical matters Stephen preached and worked miracles. He was arrested and brought before the supreme Jewish council (the Sanhedrin). At the end of a brave speech he accused the Jews of killing God's Son. He was stoned to death, but as he died asked God to forgive his murderers. Paul who was at that time still persecuting the Christians, saw Stephen die.
Acts 6 and 7

Stork
Both White and Black Storks pass through Israel every year, flying north from their wintering-places in Arabia and Africa. The larger and more numerous White Stork is seen most often. Storks live mostly on small animal life-snakes, fish, mice, worms and insects.
Jeremiah 8:7

Succoth
1. An Egyptian town. The Israelites made their first camp here on their journey out of the country.
Exodus 12:37; 13:20;
Numbers 33:5-6
2. A town in the Jordan Valley which became part of the territory of Gad. Jacob stayed for a while in Succoth after he and his brother Esau agreed to go their separate ways. In the time of the Judges the people of Succoth refused to provide Gideon and his army with food while he was fighting the Midianites. When Gideon was victorious he returned and punished the town officials.
Joshua 13:24, 27; Genesis 33:12-17; Judges 8:4-16

Suffering
Suffering is seen in the Bible as a *misfortune.* It entered the world because of sin; it is a result of the continuing activity of Satan. Jesus came into the world to free men and women from suffering and death. In his life on earth he showed his love and care by healing many people. And in the new heaven and earth there will be no suffering.

Suffering is also a *problem* in the Bible. As God has total control, suffering must ultimately come from him. Yet how can a God of love allow the innocent to suffer? It is easy to see that sin brings suffering, and not just to the individual but to his whole family. And it is possible to accept that God allows suffering in order to discipline his children. But the Book of Job is an honest attempt to discuss the problem of the suffering of innocent people. Job discards all the theories that are offered him, and in the end accepts his suffering. He does not find a rational explanation, but he sees in God a certainty which can overcome all his doubts and fears.

In the life and work of Jesus we are shown suffering as a way of life. He lives out the life of the suffering servant outlined in Isaiah 53. He is innocent. He is not suffering for his own sin, but he is suffering because of the hatred of sinful people, and in order to save them from their sin. The Bible does not give us a rational answer to the problem of suffering, but it does give us a practical answer. God took responsibility for it in the death of his son.
Genesis 3:15-19; 2 Corinthians 12:7; Romans 8:21; Revelation 21:4; Amos 3:6; Psalm 39:11; Hebrews 12:3-11; Job; Isaiah 53

A winged bull from the palace of Darius I at Susa, built in the sixth century BC.

Susa
Capital of the Elamite Empire until King Ashurbanipal of Assyria destroyed the city in 645 BC and exiled its inhabitants to Samaria. Under the Medes and Persians it once again became an important city. Darius I built a splendid palace here. The ruins, in modern Iran, can still be seen.

The story of Esther, the Jewish girl who became queen of Persia, took place at the royal court in Susa. It was here, too, that Nehemiah acted as royal cupbearer. The city was later captured by Alexander the Great.
Ezra 4:9-10; Esther 1:2, etc.;
Nehemiah 1:1

Sychar
A Samaritan town close to Jacob's well, where Jesus met and talked to a Samaritan woman who had come to draw water. Many people from Sychar believed Jesus was the Messiah when they heard what the woman said about him. The exact site is unknown.
John 4:1-42

Syene
A place on the southern border of Egypt; modern Aswan. Isaiah pictures dispersed Jews returning to Jerusalem from as far away as Syene. Papyrus deeds found here record activities of Jewish settlers about 450 BC (the Elephantine Papyri).
Isaiah 49:12; Ezekiel 29:10; 30:6

Synagogue
Synagogues probably first began during the exile, when there was no temple and the people were far away from Jerusalem. By the time of Jesus, most Jews outside Jerusalem normally met together on the sabbath at the local synagogue. The service at the synagogue was mainly for readings from the Bible (usually a passage from the Law and one from the Prophets) and prayers.

The service began with the *Shema*: 'Hear, O Israel, the Lord our God is one Lord; and you shall love the Lord your God with all your heart, and with all your soul, and with all your might.' The Bible passages were read in Hebrew. But since most Jews in Palestine at the time of Christ spoke Aramaic, an interpreter gave a verse-by-verse translation and explanation (a *targum*). Sometimes there was also a sermon.

Every synagogue had a chest ('ark') in which the scrolls of the

A reconstruction of a synagogue based on plans of the third-century AD synagogue at Capernaum.

Law were kept. The leaders sat in front of the ark, facing the people. Men and women sat separately.

Jesus went regularly to the synagogue, and read and taught there. Paul, on his missionary journeys, went first to the synagogue in each town, and spoke there.

The synagogue served as the local school and as the centre for local government as well as worship.
Deuteronomy 6:4-5; Luke 4:16-30; 6:6; Acts 13: 14-18; 14:1, and other references in Acts

Syracuse
An ancient city in Sicily, where Paul spent three days on the last stage of his voyage to Rome after shipwreck on Malta.
Acts 28:12

Syria
In the Old Testament, Syria is the land occupied by the Aramaeans to the north and north-east of Israel. The capital of Syria was Damascus. See *Aramaeans.*

T

Tabernacle
The tabernacle was a large tent made by the Israelites to a design given to Moses at Mt Sinai. It was the place where they worshipped God on their journey from Egypt to Canaan. Each time they camped (see Numbers 1:50–2:31), the Levites set up the tabernacle. It stood at the centre of the camp, with the Levites' tents around it on all four sides. Behind them were the tents of the twelve tribes of Israel, three tribes on each side. The tabernacle was the centre of Israel's religious life. It was a sign that God was always with them. Even though they had been kept out of the Promised Land for forty years because of their disobedience, still God was willing to protect and go with them. So the tabernacle is often called the 'tent of meeting' (between God and man) and 'the dwelling place' (of God).

The tabernacle and its furniture The tent was supported by a frame of acacia wood. It was about 45ft/14m long, 13$\frac{1}{2}$ft/4m wide, and 15ft/5m high. Four types of coverings were draped over this frame. First came linen curtains, decorated with blue, purple and scarlet tapestry which could be seen inside Next came a set of curtains made of goats' hair. These were a little longer than the linen ones, and one of them formed the door of the tent.

On top of these curtains went a weatherproof covering, made of rams' skins, dyed red.

Finally, there was another waterproof covering made from the skin of some other animal (translated 'badger', 'porpoise' or simply 'fine leather').

Inside, the tent was divided into two rooms. The smaller one, furthest from the door, was called the 'holy of holies' or 'the most holy place'. Only the high priest, once a year, was allowed to enter the 'holy of holies'. A linen curtain separated this from the larger room, which was called 'the holy place'. The entrance to it was covered by another embroidered linen curtain.
Exodus 25–27; 30:1-10, 17-21

The Covenant Box/Ark of the Covenant This was a rectangular box (about 4x2$\frac{1}{2}$x2$\frac{1}{2}$ft/ 115x70x70cm). Like the framework of the tabernacle, it was made of acacia wood, a very durable timber which grows in the Sinai Desert. The wood of the box was overlaid with gold. The box was carried by poles pushed through rings at the four lower corners. It contained the two tablets of the Ten Commandments, a golden pot of manna, and Aaron's rod that blossomed overnight. The lid was of solid gold and at both ends were the figures of two creatures (cherubim) with wings spread out as a sign of God's protection.

The Covenant Box stood in the 'holy of holies'. It was thought of as the place where God was invisibly enthroned because he said, 'I will meet you there, and from above the lid between the two winged creatures I will give you all my laws for the people of Israel.' It was sometimes carried into battle, as a symbol of God's protection. The fact that on one occasion it was captured by the Philistines showed it had no power of its own.
Exodus 25:10-22; Deuteronomy 10:1-5; Hebrews 9:4-5; Joshua 6:6, 8; 1 Samuel 4:3

The incense altar In the holy place, in

A reconstruction of the tabernacle based on the description given in the Bible.

front of the curtain which screened the holy of holies, stood a small altar on which incense was burnt each morning and evening. It was made out of acacia wood, overlaid with gold. It had a horn at each corner, and rings were attached to two of the sides to make it easy to carry.
Exodus 30:1-10

The golden lampstand The seven-branched lampstand was hammered out of one piece of gold, weighing 66lbs/30kg or more and decorated with flowers and buds like almond blossom. It was the only source of light in the tabernacle.
Exodus 25:31-39

Table of showbread/Bread of Presence Each sabbath, twelve new loaves, one for each tribe, were placed as an offering on the gold-overlaid table that stood in the holy place.
Exodus 25:23-30

Courtyard The tabernacle itself stood in the western part of a courtyard about 150x75ft/50x 25m. The courtyard itself was enclosed by a screen of linen curtains. There was an entrance on one side, with a curtain of embroidered linen drawn across it.
Exodus 27:9-19

Laver The laver was a huge bronze basin on a bronze base. It was used by the priests for washing their hands and feet each time they were about to enter the tabernacle or offer a sacrifice.
Exodus 30:17-21

Altar of burnt offering Here sacrifices of lambs, bulls, and goats, and other animals were made. (See *Priests, Levites and Sacrifices.*) This altar, like several objects in the tabernacle, was made of wood overlaid with bronze. It was about 7$\frac{1}{2}$ft/2.5m square and 4$\frac{1}{2}$ft/1.5m high. Halfway up the altar was a ledge on which it seems the priests stood to make their sacrifices. The altar may have been filled with earth, or empty and used like an incinerator.
Exodus 27:1-8.

Tabernacles
See *Feasts and Festivals.*

Tabitha
See *Dorcas.*

Tabor
An 1800ft/550m steep-sided mountain rising from the Plain of Jezreel. The place where Barak gathered his army at the time of the Judges.
Judges 4; Psalm 89:12; Hosea 5:1

Tahpanhes
An Egyptian town in the east part of the Nile Delta. The prophet Jeremiah was taken to Tahpanhes after the fall of Jerusalem and probably died there.
Jeremiah 43:5-10; Ezekiel 30:18

Tamar
1. The daughter-in-law of Judah and mother of his twin sons.
Genesis 38
2. David's daughter, raped by Amnon, her half-brother.
2 Samuel 13

Tarshish
The distant place for which Jonah set sail when he disobeyed God's command to go to Nineveh. A source of silver, tin, iron and lead. It may be Tartessus in Spain. (Some modern Bible versions translate it as Spain.)
Jonah 1:3; Isaiah 23:6; Jeremiah 10:9; Ezekiel 27:12

Tarsus
A town on the Cilician plain 10 miles/16km inland from the south coast of modern Turkey. An important university city in New Testament times, housing 500,000 people. Tarsus was a meeting-place of East and West, of

Greek and Oriental. Paul was born at Tarsus and proud of it. He returned there not long after becoming a Christian. But Barnabas brought him to Antioch to help teach the new Christians.
Acts 9:11; 21:39; 22:3; 9:30; 11:25-26

Tartan
See *Rabsaris*.

Tekoa
A town in the Judean hills about 6 miles/10km south of Bethlehem. A wise woman from Tekoa pleaded with King David to allow his son Absalom to come back to Jerusalem. Tekoa was also the home of the prophet Amos.
2 Samuel 14:2, etc.; Amos 1:1

Teman
Part of Edom. The people of Teman were famous for their wisdom. It was the home area of Job's friend Eliphaz. Jeremiah 49:7; Job 2:11

Temple
Solomon's temple When the Israelites conquered Canaan the tabernacle was no longer carried about with them. For a long time it remained at Shiloh. The Covenant Box was taken into battle and captured by the Philistines. But it brought them trouble and they sent it back.

Eventually King David brought it to Jerusalem. He had bought a piece of land just north of the city, and planned to build a permanent temple there for God. But although he longed to do this he was unable to do so. As he explained to his people, it was because 'I am a soldier and have shed too much blood'. So he had to be content with getting materials together. Solomon, his son, became the builder of the first temple in Jerusalem.

This temple was not large by today's standards, but it must have been the largest building the Israelites had constructed up to this time. It measured about 30x87ft/9x27m, and was 43ft/13.5m high. No other temple quite like it in plan has been found, though a Canaanite one recently excavated at Hazor, and a ninth-century BC shrine found in Syria have the same basic three-room design. The temple was very similar in layout to the pattern of the tabernacle.

The priests entered the temple through a large porch. Then came the main room, the 'holy place'. In it stood the incense altar, the table for showbread, and five pairs of lampstands.

The inner room, as in the tabernacle, was the 'holy of holies' (the most sacred part of all). It was probably approached by steps from the holy place. It contained two cherubim made of olive-wood and covered with gold. They were the symbols of God's protection of the most important object in the holy of holies: the Covenant Box (ark; see *Tabernacle*).

The walls of each room were panelled with cedar, carved with flowers, palm-trees and cherubim, and overlaid with gold. No stonework could be seen from inside the building. The holy place was dimly lit by high windows and by the lampstands. But the holy of holies–the place of God's presence–had no windows and so was completely dark.

Incense was burnt in the temple itself, but the sacrifices took place in the courtyard outside. Only priests and Levites were allowed inside the temple building.

A full account of how the temple was built and furnished is given in 1 Kings 5–7. All the skill and resource King Solomon could muster went into the construction and decoration of the temple. It was God's temple. Even the stones were prepared at the quarry 'so that there was no noise made by hammers, axes or any other iron tools as the temple was being built'.

When it was finished, Solomon held a great dedication service. The cloud of God's presence filled the temple and King Solomon himself led the worship:

> 'You, Lord, have placed the sun in the sky,
> yet you have chosen to live in clouds and darkness.
> Now I have built a majestic temple for you,
> a place for you to live in for ever.'

From this time on the centre of worship was the temple at Jerusalem, though the ten tribes who later broke away to form the northern kingdom of Israel set up their own temples in other places.

King Solomon's temple was finally destroyed by King Nebuchadnezzar of Babylon when he captured the city of Jerusalem in 587 BC. Its remaining bronze and gold and silver furnishings were taken to Babylon.
2 Samuel 6; 7; 24:18-25;
1 Chronicles 28:2-3; 1 Kings 5-8; 12;
2 Kings 16:5-9; 24:10-13; 25:8-17

Zerubbabel's temple (the second temple) When Cyrus allowed the Jews to return from Babylon to Jerusalem in 538 BC, he commanded them to rebuild the temple. He also gave them back all the gold and silver objects which Nebuchadnezzar had taken from Solomon's temple. They began work straight away, but soon became discouraged. Only after the prophets Haggai and Zechariah had spurred them on was the temple completed in 515 BC.

Although it stood for 500 years we know very little about this temple. It almost certainly followed the plan of Solomon's temple, but was not nearly so splendid.

When the Syrian ruler Antiochus IV banned sacrifices in the temple in 168 BC and defiled it by offering a pagan sacrifice, a revolt broke out (the Maccabean revolt). Three years later the temple was re-dedicated–the event still remembered at the Jewish festival of *Hanukkah*. (See *Feasts and festivals*.) It was destroyed by the Roman general Pompey in 63 BC.
2 Chronicles 36:22-23; Ezra 1; 3–6

Herod's temple In 19 BC King Herod the Great began work on a new temple at Jerusalem. He wanted to win favour with his subjects and to impress the Roman world with his splendid building. The main building was finished by about 9 BC, but work continued for many years afterwards. Built on the same plan as Solomon's temple, this temple was by far the grandest. It was twice as high as Solomon's temple, and covered with so much gold that it was a dazzling sight in the bright sun.

The most impressive feature was the great temple 'platform', still in existence today, where pilgrims gathered and sacrifices were offered. The walls of this platform extended beyond the summit of the hill to enclose an area of 35 acres. At its southern end, it stood 100-150ft/30-45m above ground level. One of the southern corners of the platform is probably the 'pinnacle' from which the devil tempted Jesus to throw himself down.

A covered cloister (where Peter and John taught the people) ran right round the outer courtyards. The main entrance was from the south, and led to the Court of the Gentiles. Anyone could enter this part of the temple. But notices in Greek and Latin forbade non-Jews to enter the inner court of the temple. The result of breaking this rule was likely to be death. Acts 21, describing Paul's arrest, gives an idea of the intense feelings aroused by the suggestion that a non-Jew had 'defiled the holy place'. The next court was the Court of the Women. This was as far as women were allowed to go into the temple itself. Men could go further, into the Court of Israel, and they could even enter the Priests' Court for a procession round the altar at the Festival of Tabernacles.

The temple was destroyed by the Romans at the time of the Jewish rebellion in AD 70, and its treasures taken back to Rome.
Matthew 4:5-6; Mark 13:1; Acts 3:11

Jewish worship in the temple In New Testament times the temple was still at the heart of Israel's religious life. Crowds of pilgrims went there for the great annual festivals. It was also a centre for religious teaching. And, as in Old Testament times, the priests serving in the temple carried out the

Herod's temple, surrounded by the Court of the Gentiles. The Fort of Antonia, in the north-west corner, was garrisoned by Roman soldiers.

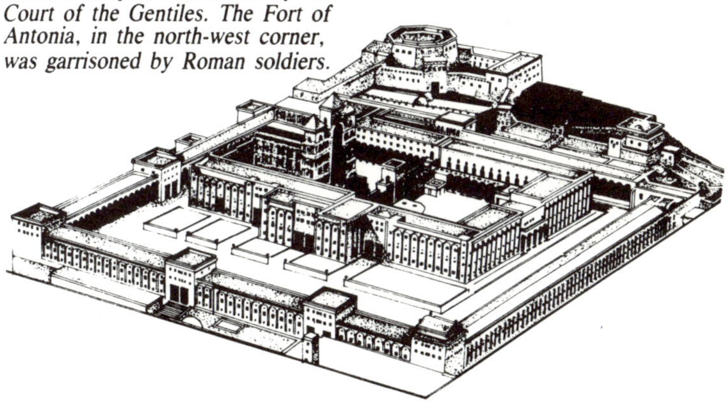

rites and sacrifices of the law.

Each day began with the recitation of Bible passages and prayers. The chief rituals were the morning and evening sacrifices. Then the priests would address the worshippers with the words of the ancient blessing:

'May the Lord bless you and take care of you;
May the Lord be kind and gracious to you;
May the Lord look on you with favour and give you peace.'

Hymns were sung by the temple choirs of Levites, but sometimes the people joined in, especially in the torchlight procession at the Festival of Tabernacles.

The Gospel of Luke describes Jesus' first visit as a boy to the temple, for the Passover Festival. John's Gospel records that when he grew up, Jesus often went to Jerusalem for the festivals, and much of the teaching in that Gospel was given in Jerusalem, in the temple courtyards. After Jesus' ascension his followers met and taught there, too.

Luke 2:41-49; John 2:13-25; 5:7-8; 10:22-38; 12:12 and following; Acts 2:46; 3; Mark 14:58

Temptation

God allows his people to be tempted, or tested. Such testing reveals the worth of their love for him. And every test that is overcome strengthens and leads them forward.

The word 'temptation' is more commonly used to refer to the activity of Satan in trying to lead men into sin, as in the temptation of Jesus. The other classic example of temptation is in the story of Adam and Eve. The serpent gradually leads the woman into doubt and confusion about the will of God; she then sees the fruit, recognizes what it is worth, desires it, realizes what it could do for her, and finally takes it.

Christians are told to be on their guard against temptation. They also have God's promise that he will not allow the testing to become too great to bear. He will provide the power to endure it.

See also *Satan, Sin.*

Genesis 3; Exodus 20:20; Deuteronomy 8:1-6; Matthew 4; 6:13; 1 Corinthians 10:12-13; Ephesians 6:10-18; Hebrews 2:18; James 1:12-16; 1 Peter 1:6-9; 4:12-16

Ten Commandments

See *Law.*

Tent

See *Tabernacle.*

Terah

Father of Abraham. He set off from Ur with Abraham, intending to go to Canaan. Instead he settled at Harran and died there.

Genesis 11:27-32

Terebinth

A spreading tree, less than 25ft (7m) high, common in warm, dry hilly places in and around Israel.

Thebes

The ancient capital city of upper Egypt, on the River Nile, about 330 miles/531km south of modern Cairo. Two great temples of the god Amun (Karnak and Luxor) mark the site. From about 1500–1000 BC, when Amun was the official god of the Egyptian Empire, wealth and treasures poured into Thebes. But despite the city's remoteness it fell to the Assyrian King Ashurbanipal in 663 BC. The prophets Jeremiah and Ezekiel pronounced judgement on Thebes (No-Amon) and other Egyptian cities.

Nahum 3:8-10; Jeremiah 46:25; Ezekiel 30:14-19

Theophilus

The person to whom Luke addressed his Gospel and the Acts of the Apostles. He knew something about Christianity but Luke wanted him to have a much fuller explanation. The name 'Theophilus' means 'friend of God'.

Luke 1:3; Acts 1:1

Thessalonians

1 Thessalonians Thessalonica, a free city, was capital of the Roman province of Macedonia (in northern Greece). Paul started a church there during his second missionary journey. When he reached Corinth, Paul heard from his fellow-worker, Timothy, that the Jews at Thessalonica were still making trouble because the non-Jews were so interested in Paul's message.

Paul wrote 1 Thessalonians in response. It is one of his earliest surviving letters, and dates from about AD 50, only twenty years after Jesus' death.

In the letter Paul encourages and reassures the Christians at Thessalonica. He thanks God for the good news from them and recalls his visit (chapters 1-3). He urges them to lead lives that will please God (4:1-12). And he answers some problems about Jesus' expected return (4:13–5:11). When will he come again? What will happen to Christians who die before he returns? He ends with practical instructions, a prayer and greetings (5:12-28).

2 Thessalonians Despite Paul's letter (see 1 Thessalonians, above) the Christians at Thessalonica remained puzzled about Jesus' return. Some thought the day of his return had already come. In this second letter, written a few months after the first, Paul warns that before Jesus comes again, there will be a time of great wickedness (chapter 2). He finishes his letter by urging the Christians to keep the faith, and keep at their work (chapter 3).

Thessalonica

The chief city of Macedonia (northern Greece), on the Egnatian Way, the main Roman road to the East. Thessalonica (now Thessaloniki) is still a major city. Paul visited Thessalonica on his second missionary journey. But the anger of the Jews forced him to move on to Beroea. His two letters to the Thessalonian Christians were written soon after he left.

Acts 17:1-15; 20:4; 27:2; Philippians 4:16; 1 Thessalonians 1:1; 2 Thessalonians 1:1, etc.; 2 Timothy 4:10

Theudas

Leader of a band of 400 rebels. When he was killed, his men scattered and the movement died out. Gamaliel quoted this example when the apostles were on trial. The movement Jesus had started would similarly come to nothing, unless God was behind it.

Acts 5:34ff.

Thistles, thorns and tares

Thistles and thorns abound in dry lands like Israel–over 120 kinds, some growing to over 6ft/2m. Some, such as the milk-thistle, have beautiful flowers, but can quickly suffocate young plants at the edges of fields (as in Jesus' story of the sower and the soils). Thorns were plaited into a mock-crown for Jesus at his trial. The 'tares' in the story of the wheat and the weeds are darnel, which looks exactly like wheat in its early stages.

Genesis 3:18; Matthew 13:7; Mark 15:15, 17-18; Matthew 13:24-30

A thistle (on the left), the weed called darnel or 'tares', and thorns.

Thomas

One of the twelve apostles. His name means 'twin'. Jesus decided to go to Judea when he heard that Lazarus was ill. Thomas knew that the Jewish leaders there might again try to kill Jesus, but was willing to go and die with him. Thomas's question at the last supper led Jesus to declare, 'I am the way, the truth and the life.' Thomas was not with the disciples when Jesus appeared to them on the first Easter day. He said he would not believe Jesus was alive again unless he saw and touched the scars. A week later, Thomas saw Jesus for himself. 'My Lord and my God,' he said. There is a later tradition that Thomas went as a missionary to India.

John 11:16; 14:5-7; 20:24ff; 21:1-14; Acts 1:12-14

Thyatira

A town in the Roman province of Asia (now Akhisar in west Turkey). Thyatira was a manufacturing centre for dyeing, clothes-making, pottery and brasswork. Lydia, the business woman from Thyatira who became a Christian when she met Paul at Philippi, was a 'dealer in purple cloth'. One of the seven letters in the Book of Revelation was addressed to the church at Thyatira.

Acts 16:14-15; Revelation 1:11; 2:18-29

Tiberias

A spa town on the west shore of Lake Galilee. It was founded by King Herod Antipas and named after the

Roman Emperor Tiberius. It was a non-Jewish town, and there is no record that Jesus ever went there. Tiberias is still a sizeable town today, unlike all the other lakeside places mentioned in the Gospels.
John 6:23

Tiberius
Emperor of Rome in Jesus' lifetime. He ruled AD 14–37. In the Gospels he is simply referred to as 'Caesar'.
Luke 3:1

Tiglath-pileser
Tiglath-pileser III (Pul) was king of Assyria, 745–727 BC. He increased Assyrian power by going to war against smaller nations. Israel was one of the countries he invaded. King Menahem paid Tiglath-pileser a large sum of money so that he could remain king of Israel. After King Pekah of Israel and King Rezin of Syria had attacked Jerusalem, Tiglath-pileser responded to King Ahaz's appeal for help by capturing Damascus and several cities in northern Israel. Ahaz became subject to Tiglath-pileser.
2 Kings 15:29; 16:7ff.
2 Chronicles 28:16ff.

Tiglath-pileser III standing in his state chariot, shielded from the sun by a parasol.

Tigris
The second great river of Mesopotamia. The Tigris rises in the mountains of eastern Turkey and flows for more than 1,400 miles/2250km, joining the River Euphrates 40 miles/64km from its mouth on the Persian Gulf. The Tigris floods in spring and autumn. The great Assyrian cities of Nineveh, Calah and Assur were all built on the banks of the Tigris. The Bible mentions it as one of the four rivers of Eden.
Genesis 2:14; Daniel 10:4

Time
Time was not rushed in the Jewish home. Before the Greeks and Romans used candle clocks and water clocks, the usual way of measuring time in small units was by the movement of a shadow (although the Egyptians were using hour glasses much earlier than this). Three different systems seem to have been used in Bible times.

Early in the Old Testament period, when Canaan was under Egypt's influence, the day started at sunrise. There was a twelve-month calendar of thirty days with five extra days at the end of the year. The days of the month were marked by putting a peg into a bone plate which had three rows of ten holes.

Later, perhaps under Babylonian influence, the calendar seems to have changed. The day began at moonrise (1800 hrs) and a whole day became 'an evening and a morning'. The evening was divided into three four-hour watches.

The Romans changed this into four three-hour watches. A new month also began with the moon. The first sign of the new moon was signalled by lighting bonfires on the hills. Months were then only 28/29 days long, so there had to be an extra month at the end of some years to keep the calendar right with the sun. The priests decided when to add this month.

Timnath-serah, Timnath-heres
The town which Joshua received as his own. He was later buried here. The place was in the hill-country of Ephraim, north-west of Jerusalem.
Joshua 19:50; 24:30; Judges 2:9

Timothy
A Christian from Lystra who was a friend and helper of Paul. His mother was a Jewish Christian; his father Greek. Paul chose Timothy to help him while he was on his second missionary journey. After Paul had left Thessalonica Timothy went back to encourage the persecuted Christians there. Later Paul sent him from Ephesus to Corinth to teach the Corinthian Christians. Timothy became leader of the church at Ephesus. He often lacked confidence and needed Paul's encouragement. But he was always loyal and faithful. The two letters which Paul wrote to the younger man are full of wise advice on the leadership of the church.
Acts 16:1-3; 17:13-15;
1 Corinthians 4:17;
1 Thessalonians 1:1; 3:1-6;
1 and 2 Timothy

Timothy, Letters to
1 Timothy Timothy was a young Christian, son of a Greek father and a Jewish mother. He came from Lystra in the Roman province of Galatia (central Turkey). He travelled with Paul and helped him on his later missionary journeys. He was a rather shy man, and not strong physically. He needed encouragement and support.

When Paul wrote to him, Timothy was looking after the church in Ephesus. The letter offers much advice and help in church affairs. It warns against false teaching in the church, particularly about a mixture of Jewish and Gnostic ideas about salvation and the nature of the physical world. Timothy is given instructions about how the church should be organized and led (chapters 1–3), and the letter closes with more personal advice to Timothy about his service to the church (chapters 4–6).

Because it is difficult to fit this letter, along with 2 Timothy and Titus, into what we know of Paul's life, and also because it is so different in character from the other letters of Paul, many scholars believe that it came not from Paul himself but from one of his followers. He may have written all three of these letters after Paul was dead, but using material that Paul himself had left behind.

2 Timothy Much of this letter is taken up with Paul's personal advice to Timothy. He urges Timothy to stay faithful to the Good News of Jesus Christ. He encourages him to stand fast as a teacher and evangelist, despite opposition and persecution. Paul warns against pointless arguments, and encourages Timothy with the example of his own faith, which is still strong after a lifetime of suffering. 'I have run the full distance,' Paul writes, 'and I have kept the faith. And now there is...the prize' (4:7-8).

Tirhakah
See *Pharaoh.*

Tirzah
A town in northern Israel, noted for its beauty. It was one of the places captured by Joshua. Later it was the home of Jeroboam I, and the first capital of the northern kingdom of Israel. King Omri later moved the centre of government to his new city of Samaria. The site of Tirzah is Tell el-Far'ah about 7 miles/11km north-east of Shechem (Nablus).
Joshua 12:24; 1 Kings 14–16;
2 Kings 15:14, 16; Song of Solomon (Songs) 6:4

Tishbe
The place from which Elijah, 'the Tishbite', presumably came. It was in Gilead, east of the Jordan, but the actual site is unknown.
1 Kings 17:1, etc.

Tithing
Each year a 'tithe' (a tenth of one's produce) was given to God for the upkeep of the priests. A second tax was used for a sacrificial meal, in which the worshipper and his family shared at one of the festivals. A third tax was used to help the poor.
Leviticus 27:30-33; Numbers 18:21;
Deuteronomy 14:22-29;
Matthew 23:23

Titus
A non-Jewish (Gentile) Christian who was a friend and helper of Paul. Titus was with Paul on one of his visits to Jerusalem and probably travelled with him quite often. For some time Titus worked with the Christians at Corinth. He smoothed over the bad feeling between the Corinthian church and Paul. When Titus rejoined Paul and told him how much better things were, Paul wrote the second letter to the Corinthians. Titus went back to Corinth with this letter and helped organize a collection there for needy Christians in Judea. He was working in Crete when Paul sent his letter to Titus.

The church there had problems similar to those Timothy faced in Ephesus: problems of false teaching and pointless arguments.

The letter reminds Titus that Christian leaders should be of good character (chapter 1). It explains his duties to the different age-groups in the church (chapter 2) and closes with general warnings and advice about behaviour and attitudes among Christians.
1 Corinthians 16:10; 2 Corinthians 2:13; 7:13ff.; 8; 12:18;
Galatians 2; 2 Timothy 4:10; Titus

Tob
A region south of Damascus. At the time of the Judges Jephthah lived there as an outlaw. The people of Tob helped the Ammonites against David.
Judges 11:3; 2 Samuel 10:6

Tobiah
An Ammonite who tried to force Nehemiah to stop rebuilding the walls of Jerusalem.
Nehemiah 2:10ff.; 4; 6; 13

Topheth
The place in the Valley of Hinnom where children were sacrificed. The shrine was destroyed by King Josiah.
2 Kings 23:10; Jeremiah 7:31; 19:6, 11-14

Towns
The difference between a town or city and a village in Bible times was not its size but its defences. Villages were unwalled settlements. Towns had walls around them. They were built on top of a hill (or a mound formed by the ruins of earlier towns) for defence. They also needed a good water supply close by. At Megiddo a tunnel was dug from the city to its spring, to bring water inside in case of siege. Towns were usually built in fertile parts of the country, where crops were good and people needed to get together to protect themselves against invaders. They were also often sited at a cross-roads or junction of trade routes.

Towns in early Israel Towns were very small–often only about 6-10 acres–the size of a modern city square (640 acres make a square mile). There would be about 150-250 houses inside the walls, with 1,000 people living there. From a distance the towns in Canaan looked rather like castles. When the tent-dwelling Israelites first entered the country their spies reported seeing 'cities with walls that reached the sky' (Deuteronomy 1:28). These fortresses first began when nomadic clans decided to settle permanently. The clan chief became a 'king' over his own territory. There was no central government, and the kings of different towns often squabbled and fought.

To begin with the Israelites simply patched up the houses and buildings in the cities they captured from the Canaanites. They had to learn building skills from their neighbours. In times of peace there was a large 'overspill' from the towns, and people camped outside the walls, grazing their cattle and working the land.

Life in the towns was very cramped. Houses were poorly built and joined on house to house. Where the ground sloped, houses were built one above the other. There were no real streets–just spaces between houses –narrow alleys leading to nowhere in particular. There was no paving. Drains were open channels. Mud and rubbish–garbage, broken pots, old mud-bricks–piled up outside, so that the level of the alleys was often higher than the ground-floor of the houses. Rain turned the whole mess into a swamp. In winter, people were cooped up in the damp and filth. The summer sun helped, though the smells remained. But by then most of the people had moved away, to live and work in the fields. In peacetime they were country-dwellers for two-thirds of the year, townsmen for one-third.

The fortified gateway was the main open space in each town. In daytime the gates were noisy and crowded, bustling with life–merchants arriving; people buying and selling; elders meeting in council; others settling disputes and hearing cases. Beggars, pedlars, workmen, scribes, visitors, traders and shoppers–with their asses, camels and even cattle–all gathered at the city gate.

In the bigger towns there was more space for the shopkeepers. Sometimes each trade had its own area, but there were no specially-built shops. Each tradesman set out his goods on a stall at the side of the street. At night they were packed away. The city gates were closed and barred.

A reconstruction of the town of Lachish, surrounded by double walls built by Rehoboam in the tenth century BC. The large building in the centre is the Israelite palace.

Important buildings Most towns had one or two larger buildings, as well as houses. From King Solomon's time, when government became more centralized, the town grew more important as an administrative centre for the district. At his capital, Jerusalem, Solomon had his 'cabinet'–including a head of administration, secretary of state, keeper of the palace, chancellor of the exchequer and minister of forced labour. He organized twelve tax districts from which he collected food. This involved putting up buildings in which the food could be stored, and providing lodgings for his royal servants and officials in the main towns of each district.

Some of the most important buildings in Israel were connected with religion. There were important religious centres not only at Jerusalem, but also at Dan and Bethel. Most towns had their own small shrine with an altar, very like the Canaanite shrines (the 'high places') which were supposed to have been destroyed.

Solomon introduced slave and forced labour to carry out a great building plan. At Jerusalem he built the temple, palaces for himself and his queen, and other large halls (one probably to store arms; one as a court of justice). They were impressive stone buildings with cedar beams and panelling. The temple was beautiful, with olive-wood doors decorated with carved figures, all covered in gold. The Israelites, taught by skilled craftsmen from Tyre, had come a long way since their nomadic life in the desert (though even then they were able to produce beautiful work, as the making of the tabernacle shows).

Solomon also rebuilt and fortified a number of cities, to strengthen his country's defences. The three most important were Gezer, Megiddo and Hazor. The double walls and massive gateways in all three were built to the same plan. There were also warehouses, and stables for horses and chariots.

When the Jews were in exile in Babylon they could no longer go to the temple at Jerusalem. Instead they met together on the sabbath (Saturday) to listen to the law and hear it explained. When they returned, they built local meeting-houses for this purpose. These were the first 'synagogues' (the Greek word *synagein* means 'to meet together').

New Testament times With the coming of the Greeks and Romans, towns were planned more carefully. The great cities of New Testament times were very different from the fortress towns of early Israel. Antioch in Syria (the city which was Paul's base) had wide streets, some paved with marble, baths, theatres, temples and market-places. It even had lights at night. Many towns now had tall buildings, several storeys high, set in narrow streets.

King Herod the Great rebuilt Samaria (renamed Sebaste) and Caesarea in the Roman style, with a main street through the centre of the city, lined with shops, baths and theatres, and crossed at right angles by smaller streets. Houses were built in blocks of four. The Romans built aqueducts to bring piped water into the cities. They built public baths and introduced more efficient drainage works to take away waste water and sewage. Life in the cities, for the rich at least, was now much pleasanter than in earlier times. The poor, and those in more remote places, were less affected by these changes.

In Jesus' day, the most dazzling sight in Jerusalem was the great temple being built by the Herods out of white marble, with parts of the walls covered in gold. The temple drew pilgrims from all over the Mediterranean world, especially for the great religious festivals. There may have been as many as a quarter of a million people living in the city. Its streets were crowded with people buying and selling. The shops and stalls sold everything, from necessities like sandals and cloth, meat, fruit and vegetables, to the luxury goods offered by goldsmiths, jewellers, silk, linen and perfume merchants. There were seven different markets, and two market days each week. Jerusalem had its restaurants and wine shops for ordinary people as well as its grander buildings–the palaces, Roman amphitheatre, and the fortress of Antonia.

Trachonitis

A district linked with Ituraea (see *Ituraea*). Together they made up the territory ruled by Herod Philip at the time when John the Baptist began his preaching. Trachonitis was a rocky volcanic area, the haunt of outlaws, east of Galilee and south of Damascus.
Luke 3:1

Trade and commerce

Sale of land One of the earliest business deals recorded in the Bible is Abraham's purchase of a field and cave from Ephron the Hittite. From the time when the Israelites settled in Canaan the buying and selling of land was disapproved of. Men held their land in trust from God. They were not the owners. Each family had received a plot of land as its own inheritance. It should therefore remain as part of that family's property.

So there were laws of 'redemption', which provided that, if a man became so poor he had to sell land, a member of his own family must buy it. There were also the laws concerning the 'Jubilee' years, which laid down that every fiftieth year, all land must be returned to its original owner. How far, and at what times in history, these laws actually operated is not known. The system certainly did not operate successfully under the kings. King Ahab of Israel engineered the death of his subject, Naboth, in order to take his property. And rich men bought up the land of those who were unable to pay their debts.

There were ancient customs connected with acquiring land. In the Book of Ruth the seller takes off his shoe and hands it to the buyer. This may have symbolized taking possession by placing one's foot on the land. When Jeremiah bought a field there was a deed of contract and a copy was stored in a clay jar (the Old Testament equivalent of a safe deposit).
Genesis 23; Leviticus 25:8-34; 1 Kings 21:1-16; Isaiah 5:8; Ruth 4:7-8; Psalm 60:8; Jeremiah 32:6-15

Local trade Israelite farmers were poor. They generally only produced enough for their family's needs, and there were few things they needed that they could not make themselves–apart from pottery, and metal tools and weapons. Travel and transport were difficult. The ass carried most of their loads, as a pack animal, and carts were small. So, for a long time, local trade was probably very simple. But market-places gradually developed around the gates of towns and cities. Farm produce, sheep and goats were sold there. Potters and smiths made and sold their goods, and visiting foreign merchants set up their stalls.

International trade Three factors led to Israel's involvement in international trade, especially at the time of the kings.

The first was the growth of 'industries' which needed imported raw materials. Metal-working and clothes-making were the most important of these.

The second was Israel's conquest of new territories which were on the international trade routes.

Thirdly, the kings themselves had an interest in creating wealth and buying luxury goods.

The fact that traders were popularly called 'Canaanites' probably reflects the fact that for a long time the Israelites were confined to the hills and so were not involved in foreign trade. The prophet Isaiah talks of Tyre 'whose merchant princes were the most honoured men on earth' (23:8). But Hosea declares: 'The people of Israel are as dishonest as the Canaanites; they love to cheat their customers with false scales' (12:8).

Trade routes by land Israel stood at the junction between Asia Minor (Turkey and Syria), Egypt and Arabia. The Israelites made good use of this fact, although it was nomadic desert tribesmen who actually carried the goods by camel caravan.

From Asia Minor they travelled over the Taurus mountains, west of the Syrian desert, through Aleppo, Hamath, and Damascus to Israel.

From Mesopotamia they went north of the Syrian desert via Harran and Aleppo, then south into Israel.

From Arabia their route was by the Red Sea shore and at Aqaba, either north to Damascus, via Moab and Gilead, north-west to Jerusalem, or west to the port of Gaza.

Trade routes by sea Right up to Roman times sea transport was controlled by the Phoenicians. They travelled to the west Mediterranean, perhaps as far as Britain, and operated a coastal route from Lebanon to Egypt, calling at such places as Ugarit, Byblos, Sidon, Tyre, Acco, Caesarea, Jaffa and ports serving the Philistine plain. As time went on, wharves and warehouses were built and extended. There was also a route down the Red Sea and the east coast of Africa, but trade with this area fluctuated.

Royal projects Some of the kings of Israel formed alliances with neighbouring lands, especially Tyre. This may have been done deliberately to help foster trade, as well as to ensure peace. Tyre at this time became the largest sea power in the Mediterranean, with colonies and ports all around the coast.

Solomon also seems to have acted as a middleman between various countries. It seems he imported horses from Cilicia and chariots from Egypt, and then exported them both to Syria.

When the Queen of Sheba visited Solomon, she may have been part of a trade delegation from South Arabia (where incense was produced). And when Solomon fortified Tadmor (Palmyra), it may have been to make it easier for traders to cross over the Syrian desert.

Solomon enlisted the help of the Phoenicians to build ships at Ezion-geber, at the head of the Gulf of Aqaba. They manned them and sailed to 'Ophir' (probably on the north-east coast of Africa). Later Jehoshaphat, king of Judah, had a joint venture with the kings of Israel and Tyre to renew this trade, but the ships were wrecked in a storm.

It seems to have been a practice for kings to try to secure the right to open markets in foreign cities to sell their own produce. King Ahab of Israel had this right in Damascus.

Under some of the kings the nation grew prosperous, and wealth poured into the country. But the prophets viewed this situation with strong disapproval. Prosperity bred pride, corruption, debt and slavery. There was more for the rich, but less and less for the poor. What was worse, imports included not only material goods but also foreign religions.
Ezekiel 27; 1 Kings 5; 9:11; 10:28-29; 2 Chronicles 9:28; 1 Kings 10:1-13; 2 Chronicles 20:35-37; 1 Kings 22:48-49; 20:34

New Testament times The 'Roman peace', especially when Pompey had cleared the seas of pirates, provided ample opportunities for trade. In Palestine the profession of merchant was held in great respect, and even the priests engaged in commerce. The range of exports and imports increased.

Trade routes by land had come under the control of the Nabataeans, whose capital was at Petra (in modern Jordan). Camel caravans were often long and there was always danger from robbers. This seems to be particularly true around the area of Jerusalem, although King Herod took measures to suppress it.

Jewish records show that, in spite of Jerusalem's remote highland position, no fewer than 118 different kinds of foreign luxury goods were being sold there. There were seven different markets. Those who brought goods to market paid heavy taxes, and prices were high. There was a busy trade in goods required for worship at the temple, especially animals for sacrifice. Jesus objected to the fact that this trade went on in the temple court, the only place where non-Jews could worship. The temple was probably the most important factor in Jerusalem's commerce. Every Jew had to make payments to the temple treasury, and this no doubt helped Jerusalem to pay for imports.

The Jewish rabbis had strict rules for business deals, and there were market inspectors to see that they were carried out. Scales and weights had to be cleaned regularly. Buyers had the right to complain. And no interest was to be charged to fellow-Jews. Personal belongings could be handed over as security against a loan. But essentials such as cloaks, ploughs and millstones were not to be sold in the event of non-payment. These rules clearly have their roots in the Old Testament law, but they were especially emphasized at the time of Jesus.
Luke 10:30-37; Leviticus 19:35-36; Deuteronomy 25:13-16

Payment In the earliest times trade was by bartering. In Genesis 33:19 and Joshua 24:32 the word used for 'money' means literally 'cattle', which originally no doubt fixed the price of the goods. Gold and silver were soon introduced, but coins were not used until the seventh century BC and after. A shekel was not a coin, but a weight of gold or silver.

So trading involved carrying about large amounts of metal, and merchants were needed to weigh and test the ingots. There is no evidence of any banking systems in Israel before the exile, though these did exist in Mesopotamia.

By New Testament times there were local currencies and a regular system for banking. Trade between countries with different currencies called for the services of money-changers.

Transfiguration

The transfiguration of Jesus came at a turning-point in his life. Peter had just recognized Jesus as the Messiah, and Jesus went on to teach his disciples about his coming death and resurrection. Then he went up a mountain (traditionally thought to be Mt Hermon) with Peter, James and John. There they saw Jesus transformed by a heavenly glory, and Elijah and Moses talking with him. The experience ended with a voice from heaven, similar to that at the time of Jesus' baptism, which said, 'This is my Son, whom I have chosen–listen to him.'

Moses and Elijah represented the two major parts of the Old Testament, the Law and the Prophets. By their presence they showed that all was fulfilled in Jesus. Peter wanted tents to be put up, to make the experience last. But that was not the point. The transfiguration confirmed the rightness of the way Jesus had chosen. It pointed to the glory that would one day be his. But before that time he had to die on the cross. This was the topic of conversation with Moses and Elijah–Jesus' 'exodus'. But the disciples did not understand this until after the resurrection.
Matthew 17:1-8; Mark 9:2-8; Luke 8:28-36

Travel and transport

The Bible describes many journeys: Abraham moving home from Ur to Canaan; Jacob going down into Egypt; the Israelites journeying through the desert; the Queen of Sheba visiting King Solomon. These are just a few of the journeys recorded in the Old Testament. In the New Testament the travels of Paul and other Christian leaders are recorded in some detail in the Book of Acts, and Jesus himself must have covered very considerable distances during his public ministry.

Pedestrians In Bible times most journeys were made on foot. Not everybody could afford to keep a pack-animal and, even if a family owned an ass, on a family journey someone would have to walk.

This terra-cotta model of a covered wagon was made in about 2500 BC.

Animals Although the nomads of the desert kept camels, the main beast of burden throughout Bible times was the ass. The ass was domesticated long before either the horse or the camel, and was always the most popular means of general transport.

Abraham possessed camels, though he probably acquired them after he left Harran. When Jacob settled in Canaan, he seems to have had no further use for them, for they are not mentioned among his property when he went down to Egypt. His son Joseph sent him provisions for the journey on asses. With the development of international trade, particularly the Arabian spice trade, camels were used more and more in Israel from about 1000 BC.

Horses were usually kept for war. They were expensive to feed compared with camels and asses and could not carry as much. But by New Testament times they were often used for civilian purposes, when chariots for transport developed from the basic war-chariot.

'Caravan' convoys Traders travelled together as a 'caravan'–a convoy of asses and camels–for company, safety and as a protection against thieves. Joseph was sold to one such group of travelling merchants.

The caravan routes crossed Israel in all directions. With the Mediterranean Sea to the west and the Syrian desert to the east, all traffic between Mesopotamia and Arabia, Egypt and the rest of Africa had to pass through a narrow corridor about 75 miles/120 km wide.

Great cities grew up at strategic points on these routes. One of these was Palmyra ('Tadmor in the wilderness'), a desert city fortified by King Solomon.

Vehicles In Old Testament times the use of wheeled transport was limited. Horse-drawn chariots were used by armies and by noblemen–chariots may even have been an indication of rank. (Joseph, for instance, was given a royal chariot to ride in; his family travelled to Egypt in wagons or carts; and the goods were carried by asses.) But without properly made up roads, the condition of the ground restricted the use of chariots. The Egyptian chariots pursuing Moses and the Israelites stuck in the mud of the sea bed and, many centuries later, King Ahab had to race back to Jezreel before the rain came.

Carts drawn by asses or cattle were used on farms. On two occasions it seems that the sacred Covenant Box (ark) was carried in an ordinary farm cart. And the prophet Amos describes the people of Israel groaning 'like a cart loaded with corn'.

By New Testament times the Romans had built first-class roads, and chariots of various types were used–from the light chariots raced in the games, to more substantial carriages with room to seat at least two people.

Most streets in towns were very narrow, and those who could afford it travelled in litters. These litters were couches with a framework so that curtains could conceal the traveller. They rested on poles which were carried by men or sometimes by horses.
Genesis 41:43; 45:19; Exodus 14:23-25; 1 Kings 18:44-45; 1 Samuel 6:7-8; 2 Samuel 6:3; Amos 2:13; Acts 8:29-31

Inland waterways Apart from the Nile, the Tigris and the Euphrates, not many rivers in Bible lands were navigable. Barges (with sails) were used on the Nile, bringing corn to the seaport, but there was no other important river traffic. Although canals were often planned by Roman emperors (Nero, for example, wanted to join the Adriatic and the Aegean Seas by a Corinth canal), few were actually constructed.
See also *Roads, Ships.*

Trinity

This word is not used in the Bible. It is the name given to the statements about God in the creeds drawn up in the early centuries of the church to explain what is meant by saying that God is Father, Son and Holy Spirit. This is the teaching of Jesus and the New Testament as a whole. From earliest times it was stated at every Christian baptism.

The Jewish teaching was that there is only one God. Nothing and no one must compromise that belief. Yet the New Testament writers clearly show God as the Father who created and sustained everything in his love and power, as the Son who came into this world, and as the Spirit who worked in their own lives.

After the end of the New Testament period the church found it necessary to work out carefully-worded statements about three persons in one God, in order to uphold the truth of the New Testament against false beliefs.

See also *God, Holy Spirit, Jesus Christ.*
Matthew 28:19; John 5:19-29; 8:23-29, 58; 14-17; Acts 2:32-33; 2 Corinthians 13:14 and so on; Exodus 20:2-6; Deuteronomy 6:4; Isaiah 45:5

Troas

A port about 10 miles/16km from Troy, in what is now north-west Turkey. Paul used the port a number of times on his travels. It was at Troas that he had his vision of a Macedonian man calling for help, and he sailed from there on his first mission to Europe. On a later visit to Troas he restored Eutychus to life after he had fallen from an upstairs window while Paul was preaching.
Acts 16:8-12; 20:5-12; 2 Corinthians 2:12; 2 Timothy 4:13

Trophimus

A Christian from Ephesus who travelled with Paul to Europe and Jerusalem.
Acts 20:4; 21:29; 2 Timothy 4:20

Tychicus

A friend and helper of Paul, probably from Ephesus. It is almost certain he travelled with Paul to Jerusalem because he had been chosen by the churches of Asia Minor (Turkey) to take the money they had collected for needy Christians in Judea. Tychicus was with Paul while he was in prison. Paul trusted him and sent him to Colossae and later to Ephesus

with the letters he had written. During his last imprisonment in Rome, Paul sent Tychicus to Ephesus to help the Christians there.
Acts 20:4; Ephesians 6:21-22; Colossians 4:7-9; 2 Timothy 4:12; Titus 3:12

Tyre
An important port and city-state on the coast of Lebanon. Tyre had two harbours, one on the mainland, the other on an off-shore island. In about 1200 BC the Philistines plundered Sidon, the other important Phoenician port 20 miles/32km or so to the north. From that time on Tyre became the leading city.

Tyre's 'golden age' was the time of David and Solomon. King Hiram of Tyre supplied wood and skilled men to build the temple at Jerusalem. Trade flourished. Tyre's own specialities were glassware and fine-quality purple dye made from local sea-snails.

King Ahab of Israel married the daughter of the king of Tyre. The city is often mentioned in the Psalms and by the prophets, who condemned Tyre's pride and luxury. In the ninth century BC Tyre came under pressure from the Assyrians. The city paid heavy tribute in return for a measure of freedom. In the same year as the fall of Samaria, Sargon II of Assyria captured Tyre. When Assyria lost power Tyre became free and prosperous again. For thirteen years (587–574 BC), King Nebuchadnezzar of Babylon besieged the city. In 332 BC Alexander the Great managed to take the island port by building a causeway from the mainland.

In New Testament times Jesus himself visited the area around Tyre and Sidon and spoke to the people.
See also *Phoenicia*.
2 Samuel 5:11; 1 Kings 5; 9:10-14; 16:31; Psalm 45:12; Isaiah 23; Ezekiel 26; Matthew 15:21; Luke 6:17; Acts 21:3

Drawing of a partial reconstruction of the great ziggurat at Ur, built about 2100 BC as a temple to the moon-god Nannar.

U

Ur
A famous city on the River Euphrates in south Babylonia (modern Iraq); the home of Abraham's family before they moved north to Harran. The site of Ur had been occupied for several thousand years before it was finally abandoned about 300 BC. Excavations have uncovered thousands of inscribed clay tablets describing the city's history and life. The Royal Graves (about 2600 BC) contained many treasures, examples of beautiful craftsmanship: gold weapons, an inlaid mosaic gaming-board, the famous mosaic standard showing scenes of peace and war, and many other things. Ruins of a great stepped temple tower (ziggurat) still remain.
Genesis 11:28-31, etc.

Urartians
The Urartians lived in the east of Turkey, around Lake Van. They may have been related to the Hurrians and Armenians. The mountains in the land were named after the kingdom. The highest of all is now called Mount Ararat. It was on one of the mountains of the Ararat range that Noah's ark came to rest. About 750–650 BC strong Urartian kings tried to dominate northern Syria and check the Assyrians. They gave sanctuary to the sons who murdered King Sennacherib. Their temples and palaces show distinctive designs and decoration. But they used the cuneiform script to write their language. The Urartians worshipped a god called Haldi, and called themselves the children of Haldi.
Genesis 8:4; 2 Kings 19:37

Uriah
1. A Hittite soldier in King David's army, and husband of Bathsheba. Because David was in love with Bathsheba, he had Uriah sent to the front line, to get him killed.
2 Samuel 11
2. A priest in Jerusalem. He obeyed King Ahaz's instructions and redesigned the temple to a pattern approved by the Assyrians.
2 Kings 16:10ff.
3. A prophet at the time of Jeremiah; killed by King Jehoiakim because he spoke out against the people of Judah.
Jeremiah 26:20ff.

Uz
The home country of Job, probably in the region of Edom.
Job 1:1

Uzzah
One of the men who helped King David take the Covenant Box (the ark) from Kiriath-jearim to Jerusalem. He drove the cart on which it was placed. When the oxen stumbled, Uzzah put out his hand to steady the ark and died.
2 Samuel 6:3-7

Uzziah
See *Azariah*.

V

Vashti
The queen King Ahasuerus divorced when she refused to obey him.
Esther 1

Villages
The 'village' of Old Testament times was simply an unwalled farming settlement. Villages grew up near a stream or spring that would provide water all the year round. As soon as animals were domesticated and people began to grow crops for food, they tended to settle in one place rather than move about. People were farming at Jericho, using picks, axes and digging sticks, as long ago as 6000 BC. At this stage there were only villages and no towns.

The possibility of towns (large settlements) came with the invention of the bronze ploughshare (some time after 4000 BC), when food production increased. Towns (fortified villages) were needed because of the struggle between the settled people and the nomadic people who wanted the same water supplies. Towns were therefore built up as larger, protected centres of civilization (see *Towns*). In peacetime, people lived out in the villages, but when invasion threatened they gathered to the safety of the town. During the summer months, too, the population left the towns for the villages, to work in the fields.

Ownership of land Abraham and his family lived a partly nomadic, partly settled life. They moved about with their flocks but they also cultivated crops. In Mesopotamia, where Abraham had come from, there had been a 'feudal' system of allocating land. The king provided gifts of land ('fiefs') in return for a promise of personal service, and the land was passed on from father to son. When the Israelites entered Canaan the idea stayed in a new form. God was their king, and he gave them their land. Each family received their land by lot (Joshua 15), just as the fiefs had been given by lot in Mesopotamia.

Because it was God's land, he told them how to make proper use of it and how the produce was to be shared. One plot of land was given to each family, and it seems to have become the family burial-ground as well as the place to grow food. Each person's land was the gift of God (Isaiah 34:17), not to be casually bought and sold. (This was why Naboth would not sell his plot to King Ahab–1 Kings 21:1-16.) If a family fell on hard times, it was the duty of their nearest relative to buy the land and keep it in the family. As far as we know, the family property went to the eldest son, so it was very important to have a son to carry on the family name and property. Every fiftieth year was a year of Jubilee, when any land which had been mortgaged to pay off a debt, was to be returned to the family. This helped keep everyone on the same level and avoided a sharp division between rich landowners and poor labourers. It also emphasized the importance of the family holding.

The land immediately around the village was therefore private property. The land further outside the villages was looked upon as common land. It was divided into plots, which were distributed by lot to families each year. Under the kings, beginning with David and Solomon, the old equality began to break down. A new wealthy class of rulers and officials grew up. They oppressed the poor and bought up land. Big estates took the place of small family farms. The people who had lost their land had to hire themselves out as farm labourers. The poor were very poor, and suffered great hardship. The prophets spoke out against all this (Isaiah 5:8; Micah 2:2).

The change in the ownership of land led to a change in housing. In the tenth century BC, all the houses in a town or village were the same size, but by the eighth century BC, some houses were bigger and better and were grouped in a particular part of the town.

Daily work In early Old Testament times almost everyone in the village was a farmer, growing what was needed for food (see *Farming*). They kept sheep, goats and cattle. These provided food for the family–and also manure for the ground.

The seasons set the pattern of work for the year. The wet season, from October to April, was used for ploughing, sowing (by hand from an open basket), harrowing and weeding. Then the harvesting began–first flax, then barley (April/May), then wheat. Work on the vines began in the spring, when the plants had to be pruned. As they grew, trailing branches had to be propped up clear of the ground. Grapes were ready for picking from July to October. Most people also had fig and olive trees. The main crop of figs came in August/September. The olive harvest was last, in October/ November, when the grape gathering was over.

Every day the women baked bread. First came the back-breaking effort of grinding the grain into a coarse flour. This was mixed with salt and water to make dough. Usually some of the fermented dough from the day before was mixed in and the bread left to rise before baking. Another vital job each day was to fetch water from the local spring or well. Only a few houses had their own well or water-storage cistern underground. The women carried the heavy waterpots home on their head or shoulder. There was always plenty to do, from dawn to dark. There might be milk to make into cheese and yoghurt. There was also wool to be spun and woven. The work in the fields was not all left to the men. Everyone helped with the harvest and with crushing the grapes and olives in the presses. The working day ended at sunset, when the whole family gathered together for the main meal of the day.

Progress and problems Country life changed very little down the centuries. The plough and other implements improved. But even in New Testament times they were still primitive, the plough cutting one furrow at a time. As time went by there was more specialization on large estates. There were skilled professionals to prune the vines, to drive the teams of oxen and to plough. 'Unskilled' workers weeded the fields, spread manure, and did countless other tasks.

The main problems also remained the same. Water was the first concern in a hot country with no rainfall at all for three or four months in the summer. The village well had to provide drinking water for the family and their animals, and water for the land. Sometimes an endless chain of leather buckets was used to bring the water to the surface and run it along irrigation ditches to the roots of the crops.

Locusts were another problem. Without warning they could arrive in swarms to eat every bit of living greenery. Wild animals–wolves, jackals, lions–could kill the livestock, too.

A third problem, completely disrupting village life, was a human one. Time and again invading armies attacked or passed through the country, taking prisoners or conscripting young men. If they came at the end of the wet season, the new growing crops were destroyed. If they came at harvest, the crops were taken away as booty or used to feed the army. Either way the villagers were likely to starve.

A trailing shrub producing grapes, one of the most important of all fruit-crops. Moses' spies brought back huge clusters of grapes as a sign of the richness of the Promised Land. Vines were planted in rows in carefully prepared vineyards on the sunny hill slopes. Each spring the vines were pruned, and as the grapes ripened the owner kept a sharp look-out for intruders–animal or human–from a special watch-tower. At harvest time the grapes were picked and taken to be trodden out at the winepress. Some were also made into raisin-cakes. The fermenting wine was stored in new skins or pottery jars to mature. The vine was a national emblem in Israel, a symbol of peace and prosperity. Jesus used it in five of his parables, and described himself as the true vine on which the branches (his followers) depend.
Numbers 13:20, 24; Matthew 9:17; 20:1-6; 21:28-32, 33; Luke 13:6-9; John 15:1

W

War

War is a dominant theme in the Old Testament, despite the fact that God's law protected life and stood firm against murder. The reason is that God himself was vitally involved with a single nation, Israel. They lived in troubled times. 'The Lord is a warrior,' sang Moses, after the escape from Egypt. Then, when the people of Israel set out to enter Canaan God told them that the battle was his: 'The Lord your God is going with you, and he will give you victory.' The former inhabitants of the land must all be destroyed ('devoted' to God). It was a 'holy war'. But its ultimate goal was peace and well-being. Israel should trust and obey God, otherwise their enemies would win. This is the message of the Book of Judges.

The prophets often continued this theme. When the kings went to war for political reasons and put their trust in horses, chariots and cavalry, defeat was often seen as God's way of punishing his people for their lack of faith.

But after the exile, when the people came back to their homeland, things changed. The Jews had experienced many defeats and so the idea grew that war was more the work of Satan than of God. They hoped that God would send his own warrior-king to fight a final battle and bring victory and peace to his people, either in this world or in the next. This was the Jewish hope, centred on the coming Messiah.

Jesus himself rejected this view of the Messiah. He came to bring God's peace. There would be division between those who believed and those who did not, but men were not to be regarded as enemies. Only in the visions in the Book of Revelation is Jesus seen as a warrior. But Christians are pictured as soldiers engaged in a spiritual war against evil. Victory in this war is certain, for Jesus by his death and resurrection defeated Satan. Physical, historical wars are among the signs that the end of the age is near.
Exodus 15:3; Deuteronomy 20:4; Isaiah 31:1; 5:25-30 and many other passages; Revelation 19:11; Ephesians 6:10-17; John 12:31

The army From the early days of Israel's history every man was called to be a soldier. He could be summoned by a tribal leader, as Abraham, led men out to rescue Lot from his captors. Each of the tribes was responsible for occupying the land assigned to them. They sometimes helped one another in the task, as they rallied under one leader to resist the Canaanites and Philistines, and to defeat the desert tribes who were constantly raiding Israel. Any tribe which did not respond to a call for help was treated with scorn.

There was no standing army until Saul became king. He appointed 3,000 men as a permanent army, under his direct command but with Abner in charge. King David was a military genius. Joab, his commander-in-chief, captured Jerusalem and taught the Israelites new methods of warfare. David was the first king to have a personal bodyguard of great warriors. These men had been with him when he was an outlaw and had proved their loyalty to him.

The Bible speaks of 'fifties' and 'hundreds', with their commanders, but very little is known of the detailed organization of the army. For a long time the army was composed almost entirely of foot-soldiers, some equipped as archers or slingers, others for hand-to-hand combat. The cavalry and chariots used by the Egyptians, Philistines and Canaanites, were introduced in Israel under Solomon but the Israelites fought mainly in the hills where these methods were impractical. 'The gods of Israel,' say the officials of King Benhadad of Syria, 'are mountain gods.' The later kings of Judah still sent to Egypt for chariots and horsemen. King Ahab of Israel, however, kept a huge force of chariots, and his stables have been discovered at Megiddo.

Assyrian soldiers sack the city of Hamaan.

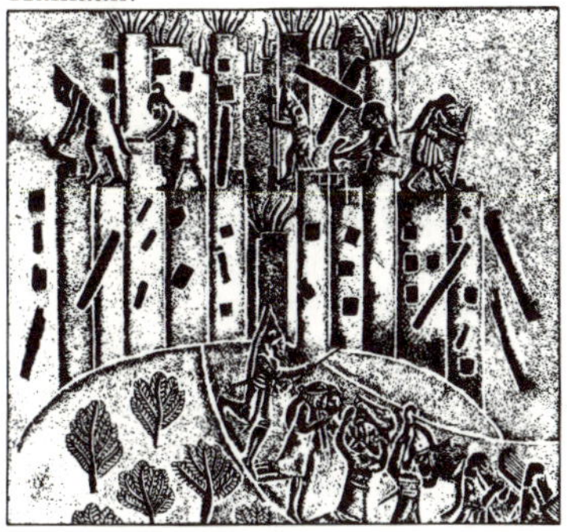

After the exile there was no Jewish army except for one short period, when non-Jewish as well as Jewish soldiers were employed and paid a wage. Herod the Great had his own forces. They, too, included foreign mercenaries, and were under Roman command.
Genesis 14; Judges 1; 5:15-17;
1 Samuel 23:1-5; 25; 13:1-2; 17:55;
2 Samuel 23:8-39; 1 Kings 10:26;
20:23-25; 2 Kings 18:24

War in the Old Testament There were three kinds of weapons used in fighting. In hand-to-hand fighting, clubs, axes, short and long swords were used. There were darts, spears and javelins for throwing. And there were many missiles, from stones and boulders to bows and arrows.

The soldier wore armour to protect himself and carried a shield for defence. The Israelites seem to have used two types of shield. A small round one was carried by the light armed infantry, and a large rectangular one was used by the men at the front, so that the battle line presented a solid front. The shields were made of a wicker or wooden frame covered with leather, which needed regular oiling. Inside the shield was a handle for holding it. There is little information about the soldiers' armour. Before David's battle with Goliath, King Saul tried to dress him in a helmet and a 'coat of mail' (breastplate). But it was so heavy that he could not walk! There may also have been 'greaves' to protect the legs, and a lower skirt of mail.

The kings built fortresses to protect their land. Saul fortified his capital, Gibeah. David, in addition to work on Jerusalem, built the fortresses of Libnah, Lachish, Gezer and Beth-horon in the foothills as a defence against the Philistines. Solomon strengthened many cities, especially Gezer, Hazor and Megiddo, guarding the strategic pass through the Carmel hills. When the kingdom was divided, border fortresses were established at Geba and Mizpah. (See also *Building*.)
1 Samuel 17:4-7, 37-40

Fighting methods Israel suffered a great deal from raiding bands of desert tribes, especially before the time of the kings. Their attacks were swift and unpredictable. Often they rode in on camels. They plundered the villages, destroyed crops, and took cattle and captives.

Where there was open combat a trumpet gave the signal for attack. And sometimes there was an arranged war-cry, like Gideon's 'a sword for the Lord and for Gideon'. A line of men carrying rectangular shields and long lances would advance, and the archers let fly a volley of arrows to cover them. When the lines met, fighting was hand to hand. Sometimes the issue was decided by contest between two or more champions. Often the army was divided into two companies, to close in on the side and the rear of the enemy. Under King David the general strategy and tactics of open warfare began to be more skilfully planned.

An attack on a city often took place just before dawn to take the defenders completely by surprise. A favourite ruse was to advance with only half the army and then retreat. When the inhabitants joyfully pursued, the other half of the army would enter the city. In David's time the Israelites began to adopt the practice of laying siege to a city. Usually, though, they were the victims, rather than the initiators of this kind of warfare.

The experts in this were the Assyrians. Spies would be sent to discover a city's weaknesses, and, if a succession of towns had already fallen, a delegation was sent to try to frighten the town into submission. All lines of communication were cut off, and they took control of all the water supplies in the neighbourhood. It was to prevent this that King Hezekiah of Judah diverted water into the city by digging a tunnel. The enemy then prepared for a long stay, while conditions in the city grew gradually more horrible. To hasten defeat the Assyrians would construct causeways up to the walls, and wooden machines on wheels. These served as platforms from which arrows could be shot at the defenders, and as battering-rams to weaken the walls. Sometimes they would try to tunnel under the wall. Finally an all-out attack was made. The archers kept up heavy fire, while the rest of the army, protected by shields, scaled the walls with ladders. The defenders meantimes hurled down burning arrows, boiling oil and stones in an attempt to keep them off.
Judges 6:1-6, 11; 2 Chronicles
13:12; Judges 7:20; 20:29-36;
2 Samuel 12:27; 2 Kings 18-19;
6:24–7:20

The aftermath of battle When a city was taken, it was the usual practice to kill, mutilate or enslave all male inhabitants. Women and children were taken captive. The walls were broken down and buildings burnt, and the soldiers were usually free to take whatever plunder they could find, though the more valuable items were claimed by the king. If a city submitted, hostages were taken and a heavy tribute demanded.

The Roman army In New Testament times the Mediterranean world was at peace under Roman government. No book of the New Testament is written against a background of war, though occasionally the Roman army is present. From time to time Jews rebelled and these rebellions were fiercely crushed by the Romans. The province of Syria, of which Palestine formed a part, being on the border of the Empire, was a potential source of danger. It was therefore under the direct command of the emperor, with detachments of soldiers permanently stationed there.

Roman soldiers often behaved as if the Jews were their servants. But some, especially the officers, won respect from the people. A company of Roman soldiers, detailed to keep the peace in Jerusalem at the time of the Passover Festival, took part in the arrest of Jesus and enjoyed some rough horse-play at the prisoner's expense. In general, however, the Romans had a reputation for justice. Roman soldiers prevented Paul being lynched in Jerusalem, and brought him safely under armed escort to their headquarters at Caesarea, when there were threats against his life.

The emperor had a personal bodyguard, the Praetorian guard, stationed in Rome and some other provincial centres (including Ephesus). When Paul was in prison the 'whole palace guard' knew that he was there because he was 'a servant of Christ'.
Luke 13:1; Matthew 5:41;
Luke 7:1-10; Acts 10; John 18:3;
Mark 15:16-20; Acts 21:30-36;
23:16-24; Epesians 6:14-17;
Philippians 1:13

Water

Israel has the desert at its door and the rain comes only in winter. It is a land where it has always been important to save and store water. The Jordan is the only river of any size, and that empties uselessly (from the point of view of conserving water) into the Dead Sea–where water evaporates from the surface at a rate of 60in/1,500mm a year. The Jordan flows all the year round, fed by snow from Mt Hermon. But this is exceptional. Most streams flow in sudden spates, followed by months when their beds are dry. So, from earliest times, the towns and villages of Israel have relied on wells and springs for their water supply. The right of access to a well was a valuable privilege. If the wells in an area were blocked up, the inhabitants were left to die of thirst. As cities grew bigger, the problem of keeping them supplied with water became acute. Jerusalem, high in the porous limestone hills, needed a whole system of waterworks. King Hezekiah 'built a reservoir and dug a tunnel to bring water into the city' to safeguard the supply of water if the city was besieged (2 Kings 20:20).

The Romans built aqueducts and irrigation canals to cope with the problem. But after they left, the works fell into disrepair. Only in the twentieth century have they been restored or replaced. However, the modern state of Israel was not content to watch its main water resource–the Jordan–run untapped into the Dead Sea. A project has been developed in recent years for diverting Galilee water to other uses. Part of the problem is, of course, that both the Sea of Galilee and the Jordan are far below sea level and, if their waters are to be used anywhere outside the rift valley, it is necessary to pump water up over the 'spine' of

Israel. This has now been done, and the water is taken south down the coastal plain in a series of canals and tunnels. These go as far as the Tekuma reservoir, near Gaza. They have made town supply schemes and irrigation possible as far south as the fringe of the desert.

Weaving

See *Clothes-making.*

Weddings

See *Marriage.*

Weights and measures

There were standard weights and measurements of length, dry and liquid capacity, but there was little *exact* measurement. Standard length measurements based on the relative sizes of the human arm and hand arose out of general use. Measurement of distances in Old Testament times were based on a day's journey or even a bowshot.

Foodstuffs were measured by volume rather than by weight. The terms used are often the names of the containers which held the food. A *homer* was an 'ass-load' (perhaps 200 litres) and was the largest measure for cereals. The *ephah* was a container, closed with a lid, holding about one tenth of a *homer.* The *bath* is the same as the *ephah,* but is used for liquids. The *omer* (meaning 'sheaf') was the amount of manna gathered each day. Other measurements were also in use in the market. A *letek* is half a homer. A *hin* was six times the amount a man needs to drink in a day. The *log* was another small unit for liquids.

Precious materials and metals were measured by weight. Small things were weighed on a beam balance with scale pans. The weights were kept in a purse. Merchants sometimes used the fact that they had two sets of weights–one when they were buying, the other when they were selling–to cheat their customers. But the law of God insisted on strict honesty. 'Do not cheat when you use weights and measures. Use true and honest weights and measures, so that you may live a long time in the land' (Deuteronomy 25:13). 'The Lord hates people who use dishonest scales and weights' (Proverbs 20:23) The verb 'to weigh' is *shaqal* in Hebrew and the name has been given to the basic unit of weight–the *shekel.*

Measurements of length
Cubit 17.5in/445mm Measured from elbow to finger-tip; the long cubit was a handbreadth longer 20.4in/520mm New Testament cubit 21.6in/550mm
6 cubits = 1 reed
Finger or digit ¾ in/19mm Measured from the forefinger; ¼ handbreadth
Palm 3in/76mm Width of the hand at the base of the finger
Span 9in/230mm The outstretched hand from thumb to little finger: three handbreadths, or half a cubit
Weights
Table of Old Testament weights
1 gerah = approx. 0.5gm
10 gerahs = 1 bekah (approx. 6gm)
2 bekahs = 1 shekel (approx. 11gm)
50 shekels = 1 mina (approx. 500gm)
60 minas = 1 talent (approx. 30kg)
The heavy royal shekel weighed 13gm.
The heavy, double standard talent weighed 60kg.
New Testament weights
The litra (pound) = approx. 327gm
The talent = 20 to 40kg
Old Testament liquid measures
Kab = 1.2 litres
Hin = 3.66 litres
Bath = 22 litres (10 baths = 1 homer = a 'donkey load')
Old Testament dry measures
Log = 0.3 litre
Kab = 1.2 litres
Omer = 2.2 litres
Seah = 7.3 litres
Ephah = 22 litres
10 ephahs = 1 homer = 220 litres

Willow

The willows of Israel are shrubs or small trees, often found in thickets beside streams. See also *Poplar.*

Wolf

Fierce and dangerous hunters which usually feed on smaller animals, but will also attack and kill deer, sheep and even cattle. The Bible speaks of cruel and evil leaders as 'wolves' and Jesus described his followers as 'sheep among wolves'.
Matthew 7:15; Luke 10:3

Word

The 'word of God' is a phrase the Bible often uses when it speaks of God revealing himself to men. Just as we can only know one another well through speech, so God made himself known by his words as well as his acts.

The 'word of the Lord' is God's spoken word. The phrase often occurs in the books of the prophets. This word was not always heard; sometimes it was seen. Jesus, the final and full revelation of God, is also described as the Word. This time God's word could be seen, touched and heard. It is this word or message that the Christian church must make known.

The word of God–his whole 'revelation' of himself–'endures for ever'. It is powerful and does all that God plans for it to do. And no one is to add anything to it or take anything away from it.

See also *Revelation.*
Jeremiah 1:4; Ezekiel 1:3-28; John 1:1-14; 1 John 1:1-3; 2 Timothy 4:2; Isaiah 40:8; Revelation 22:18-19

World

The Greek word *kosmos,* 'world', normally means 'the physical created world'. It is used in this way in the New Testament to describe the world God made.

. It is also used to speak of the 'state of the world'. 'The world' is in rebellion against God. So Satan can be called the prince or ruler of 'this world', and the whole world is said to lie in his power. 'World' (represented sometimes by another Greek word, *aion,* meaning 'age' or 'spirit of the age') describes all that is in opposition to God.

The 'world' hated Christ and shows similar hatred to his followers. And yet God loved the world. Christians do not belong to the world but they live in it. They must not share the world's attitudes or conform to its self-centred materialist standards. But they must live with those who are in rebellion, because God loves them and Jesus died for them.
John 1:10; 14:30; 1 John 5:19; John 15:18-19; John 17:16-17; Romans 12:2; John 3:16-21

Wormwood and gall

Wormwood is the bitter-tasting absinthe, used in the Bible as a symbol of sorrow and bitterness. Gall may be the juice of the opium poppy.

Worship

'I am the Lord your God,' says the first Commandment, 'Worship no god but me.' To worship is to give God the honour due to him. In the psalms God's people worship him for who he is; for what he has done in creation; for what he has done in redemption, rescuing and freeing his people; and for all his good gifts and blessings to individuals.

In the New Testament when Christians met together, they expressed their gladness by 'praising God'. Filled with the Spirit they were to speak to 'one another with the words of psalms, hymns, and sacred songs,' to 'sing hymns and psalms to the Lord' with praise in their hearts. Everyone could take part. 'When you meet for worship one person has a hymn, another a teaching, another a revelation from God, another a message in strange tongues, and still another the explanation of what is said.'

'God is Spirit, and only by the power of his Spirit can people worship him as he really is,' said Jesus. Worship must be real. It must come from the heart. In the Old Testament God spoke sternly against the kind of worship which is only an outward show. True worship is a genuine response to God which shows itself in a life lived to please him. Worship centres on God. His message fills it with content and meaning. As Paul wrote: 'Christ's message in all its richness must live in your hearts. Teach and instruct each other with all wisdom. Sing psalms, hymns, and sacred songs; sing to God with thanksgiving in your hearts.'

The earliest Christians were Jewish, so it is not at all surprising that they drew very much on their Jewish background for their forms of worship. Acts 2:46 tells us: 'Day after day they met as a group in the Temple, and they had their meals together in their homes, eating with glad and humble hearts.' They continued to worship at the Jewish temple, and added a special Christian meal.

But Christians came to see that the temple sacrifices were no longer necessary, since Jesus' death had been the final, once-for-all sacrifice for sin. So Christians tended to break away from temple worship, especially when there began to be conflict between Jews and Christians. But for several decades many Jewish Christians continued to attend the synagogues. Paul usually began his preaching in any town in the synagogue, and continued worshipping there until he was forced out.

Two aspects of Jewish worship

especially influenced Christian worship. The Passover ritual is reflected in the Lord's Supper. And the synagogue service, with its Bible reading, prayer and sermon, formed a model for early Christian services.

Worship is not simply a human activity on earth. In heaven, God's whole creation–humans and angels–praise and worship him.

See also *Creeds and Hymns, Lord's Supper, Praise, Prayer, Priests and Levites, Sacrifices, Synagogue, Temple.*
Exodus 20:1-3; Psalms 29; 136:4-9, 10-36; 116; Acts 2:43-47; Ephesians 5:18-19; 1 Corinthians 14:26-40; John 4:21-24; Micah 6:6-8; Colossians 3:16; Revelation 4; 5; 7; 15

Writing

Archaeologists working in the Near East have discovered many written documents. These give names of places, kings and other people. They tell of invasions and wars, of famine and inflation. They may describe social customs and behaviour, or disclose them incidentally. Some may be hymns and prayers, reflecting religious beliefs; or they may be spells, relating to magic. There may also be stories of gods and heroes of the past. In fact, once writing had been invented, any aspect of life could be recorded.

Cuneiform Writing was invented in Babylonia between 3500 and 3000 BC (see *Babylonians*). The first language to be written down seems to have been Sumerian. This language used picture symbols to represent words. The Semitic Akkadian language (a name used for Assyrian and Babylonian) quickly followed. That was different from Sumerian, and the Sumerian word-signs were more often used as syllable-signs to reproduce Akkadian.

Other Semitic languages in the west (Syria and Palestine) were written in cuneiform. So too were the Indo-European dialects spoken in the area of modern Turkey (generally called Hittite), and another different language, Elamite, which was spoken in Persia. Cuneiform writing continued to be used in Babylonia until as late as the first century AD.

Egyptian The idea of writing was carried from Babylonia to Egypt soon after it was invented. Egyptian clerks made up their own system of picture word-signs, which we call hieroglyphs. Some of these were very often written for their sounds only (syllables), as in Babylonia. But they were not used without the word-signs to the extent that they were in cuneiform, and so the system was less easily adapted for other languages.

The Egyptian script kept its picture form for inscriptions on buildings and other monuments until the fifth century AD, when people stopped using hieroglyphs. For ordinary records, letters, accounts and books, a simpler handwriting, called hieratic, was developed. A sort of shorthand, now called demotic, grew out of that after 1000 BC.

Books and everyday documents in Egypt were written on paper made from the papyrus reed. Long thin strips of its pith were laid side by side, with another layer of strips pressed onto them at right angles, to produce a page of writing material. It was rather rougher than modern paper, but just as strong and flexible. Papyrus documents buried in tombs or ruined buildings in the dry sands of Egypt have survived until the present day. But papyrus cost money, and unimportant matters–such as short notes or school exercises–were written on flakes of stone or pieces of broken pottery (called *ostraca*). People usually wrote with reed brushes using black ink made from soot.

Wherever Egypt ruled or traded, the Egyptian writing system followed. Examples of Egyptian writing are found in Palestine and Syria, and far south into the Sudan.

The earliest picture writing: on a stone from Sumer, about 3500 BC.

Other systems Between 2000 and 1000 BC other scripts were used in different parts of the Near East. In Turkey the Hittites had their own form of hieroglyphs. About seventy signs stood for simple syllables (*ta, ki,* etc.), with a hundred or more word-signs. A similar system was used in Crete, where three related forms have been discovered. The last of these, known as Linear B, had about eighty-five syllable-signs and some word-signs. These were scratched on clay tablets to record government affairs in an early Greek dialect. Another branch of that group of written languages was used in Cyprus, and a few examples have been found in Syria.

All these methods of writing were difficult to learn, so that only a few people, the professional scribes, could read and write. Most people who wanted to send a letter, to write a will, or to keep accounts, had to call on a trained man. The scribes' services were also needed to read a letter or a legal deed, or to check accounts. Naturally, some scribes rose to high positions in the royal courts, while others sat at street corners waiting for customers.

The alphabet The scribes' monopoly was broken when the alphabet became widely known. Archaeology has enabled us to recover quite a lot of examples of the alphabet in its early stages. But there are many aspects of its development which are not yet known. It seems that a scribe in Canaan realized that it was possible to write a language without the many signs which the Egyptians and Babylonians had. He studied his language and drew one sign for each consonant. He apparently chose the signs on the scheme 'door stands for d'. But they were used only for sounds, never as word-signs. There were no separate signs for vowels, and this creates problems in reading Hebrew and Arabic writing even now.

Examples of the early alphabet have been found in Israel. These are very short, probably men's names, written on pottery, stone and metal. Canaanites working in the Egyptian turquoise mines in south-western Sinai scratched prayers on rocks and stones. They used the letters of the alphabet, and have left us the best specimens we have of the alphabet at an early stage (about 1500 BC).

How it developed over the next five hundred years can be seen from more scattered examples. (Unfortunately for us the scribes usually wrote on papyrus, which rots when buried in damp soil.) During that time the letters took standard shapes. Scribes trained in Babylonian traditions at Ugarit in Syria saw the advantages of an alphabet over the other scripts. There they composed an alphabet of thirty letters in cuneiform and wrote their own language with it.

By 1000 BC the alphabet was firmly established. In Syria and Canaan the newly settled Aramaeans, Israelites, Moabites and Edomites adopted it. Soon afterwards the Greeks learned it from the Phoenicians. They made some adjustments to suit their own language, especially the use of distinguishing signs for vowels.

The Aramaean tribes of Syria spread into Assyria and Babylonia, and many were carried off captive by Assyrian kings. They took with them their form of the alphabet. Jewish exiles adopted it and popularized it in Jerusalem in preference to the older Phoenician-Hebrew form. Arab tribesmen (the Nabataeans) borrowed it too, and the modern Arabic script is descended from the letters they developed.

The alphabet brought reading and writing within the reach of everyone. The scribes did not go out of business, nor did everyone become literate, but far more people learned their letters in areas where the alphabet was used. This is made clear by the fact that in seventh-century BC Judah many people had seals with their names on them but no distinctive designs. These would have had no value if their owners and others could not read them.

The scribes in Assyria and Babylonia, and in Egypt, usually worked with great care. There were several checks to make sure that books were copied accurately. The number of lines was counted and compared with the original; and damage to the original was noted; and sometimes a second scribe checked the whole copy. The Israelite scribes no doubt followed the same conventions when they copied the books of the Old Testament.

Z

Zacchaeus
A tax collector who lived in Jericho. Because he was a little man, Zacchaeus climbed a tree in order to see Jesus when he came. Jesus looked up and asked if he could visit his house. Zacchaeus was a changed man as a result of his meeting with Jesus.
Luke 19: 1-10

Zadok
In King David's reign Zadok and Abiathar were the most important priests. At the end of David's reign Abiathar supported Adonijah's claim to the throne. Zadok crowned Solomon as the new king and was rewarded by being made high priest.
2 Samuel 15:24ff.; 17:15; 19:11;
1 Kings 1:7, 32ff.; 2:35

Zarephat/Sarepta
A small town that belonged to Sidon, later to Tyre. The prophet Elijah stayed with a widow there during a time of drought. Later he restored the widow's son to life.
1 Kings 17:8-24; Luke 4:26

Zealots
This group of nationalists kept alive the spirit of Judas Maccabaeus–the guerrilla leader who had succeeded in regaining the temple from the Syrians in the second century BC. They refused to pay taxes to the Romans and held themselves ready for the war that would bring in God's kingdom. They engineered several revolts. One of these was ended only by the Roman destruction of Jerusalem in AD 70. At least one of Jesus' disciples, Simon (not Simon Peter), had been a Zealot.
Luke 6:15

Zebedee
A fisherman; the father of James and John, the apostles.
Matthew 4:21-22

Zeboiim
One of a group of five early cities, of which the most famous are Sodom and Gomorrah. See *Admah, Sodom, Gomorrah.*

Zeboiim was also the name of a valley near Michmash, in the desert north-east of Jerusalem, the site of a Philistine raid in the days of Saul.
Genesis 14:2, 8; Deuteronomy 29:23;
1 Samuel 13:18

Zebulun
A son of Jacob and Leah. Father of one of the twelve tribes of Israel.

Also the land belonging to the tribe of Zebulun, in Galilee.
Genesis 30:19-20; 49:13;
Joshua 19:10-16

Zechariah
1. Zechariah, king of Israel, who reigned for only six months and was murdered by Shallum (752 BC).
2 Kings 14:29; 15:8-12
2. A prophet and priest born during the Jewish exile in Babylon. His first message was given in 520 BC and is recorded in the Book of Zechariah. By that time the Jews who had returned from exile in Babylon had lost heart and given up rebuilding the temple. Zechariah encouraged them to carry on with this work and promised a bright future.
Ezra 5:1-2; Nehemiah 12:16;
Zechariah
3. A priest: the husband of Elizabeth and father of John the Baptist. He was on duty in the temple at Jerusalem when an angel told him he would have a son who would prepare people for the Messiah. Zechariah and Elizabeth were both old. Because he did not believe the angel, Zechariah remained dumb until John was born.
Luke 1

Book of Zechariah
The prophet Zechariah came from a family of priests. Like Haggai, he was involved in getting the temple rebuilt. The temple was finally completed in 516 BC.

Chapters 1–8 of his book are prophecies delivered between 520 and 518 BC. They come in the form of visions and deal with restoring Jerusalem, rebuilding the temple, purifying God's people, and the promise of a coming Messiah.

Chapters 9–14 are a distinct collection of spoken messages, possibly by a different author. They tell of the expected Messiah and the last judgement.

Zedekiah
1. Last king of Judah, 597–586 BC. He was placed on the throne by King Nebuchadnezzar as his subject. When Zedekiah rebelled, Nebuchadnezzar besieged Jerusalem. After several months the Babylonians captured and destroyed the city. Zedekiah was blinded and taken prisoner to the city of Babylon.
2 Kings 24–25; 2 Chronicles
36:10ff.; Jeremiah 21, 32, 34; 37–39
2. A false prophet who lived in the reign of King Ahab.
1 Kings 22; 2 Chronicles 18

Zephaniah
A prophet who lived in Judah in the reign of King Josiah; probably great-great-grandson of King Hezekiah. Zephaniah's message is recorded in the Old Testament book named after him. He warned people in Judah of God's coming judgement if they continued to worship idols and disobey his laws. He also warned of destruction coming to Israel's neighbours. Injustice would be punished. But for those who returned to God, there would be a bright future.
Zephaniah

Zerubbabel
Grandson of King Jehoiachin and a leader of the exiles who returned from Babylon to Judah in 537 BC. He became governor of Judea and worked alongside Joshua, the high priest. Under their leadership the foundations of the temple were laid. The work ground to a halt until the prophets Haggai and Zechariah encouraged them to spur the people on and finish the task.
Ezra 2:2; 3–5; Haggai; Zechariah 4

Ziklag
A town in the south of Judah taken by the Philistine city of Gath. King Achish of Gath gave it to David when he was an outlaw from King Saul. David recovered the captives after Amalekites had raided the town.
Joshua 15:31; 1 Samuel 27:6; 30

Zilpah
Leah's servant and one of Jacob's wives. She was mother of Gad and Asher, two of his twelve sons.
Genesis 29:24; 30:9-13

Zimri
Commander in the Israelite army. Zimri killed King Elah and reigned as king of Israel for seven days (885 BC). He was overthrown by Omri.
1 Kings 16

Zin
An area of desert near Kadesh-barnea where the Israelites camped after the exodus.
Numbers 13:21; 20:1; 27:14, etc.

Zion
The fortified hill which David captured from the Jebusites to make it his capital, Jerusalem. The name is often used in the Psalms and by the prophets.

Ziph
A town belonging to the tribe of Judah, in the hills south-east of Hebron. David hid from Saul in the desert near Ziph, and Jonathan came to encourage him here. But the men of Ziph betrayed him to Saul, and he moved to Maon and Engedi. Later, Ziph was one of the places fortified by King Rehoboam. The site is still called Tell Zif.
Joshua 15:55; 1 Samuel 23:14-29;
2 Chronicles 11:9

Zipporah
Wife of Moses and daughter of Jethro, the man who gave Moses a home when he escaped from Egypt. She was the mother of Moses' two sons.
Exodus 2:16-22; 4:24-26; 18:2-4

Zoan/Tanis
An ancient Egyptian town in the north-east of the Nile Delta. From about 1100 to 660 BC Zoan was used as the capital of Egypt.
Numbers 13:22; Isaiah 19:11, etc.

Zoar
One of five cities probably at the southern end of the Dead Sea. Lot fled to Zoar at the time when Sodom was destroyed.
Genesis 13:10; 14:2, 8; 19:18-30

Zobah
An Aramaean kingdom defeated by David; it was between Damascus and Hamath.
2 Samuel 8:3; 10:6; 1 Kings 11:23

Zophar
One of Job's three friends who talked to him in his suffering.
Job 2:11